"This is one of the most useful tools I've found to work with schools that want to become arts infused or integrated. I use it every summer in institutes including Spoleto Creative Teaching Institute. It is simply fabulous."

**—Christine Fisher,**
State Project Director, Arts in the
Basic Curriculum, South Carolina

"This book has helped me so much. It made so much sense. I had to get a new copy because my first one was so tabbed and folded over."

**—Hollie Steele,**
Fourth Grade, Battle Academy,
Chattanooga, TN

"This inspiring book is a must-have for every classroom teacher."

**—Carolyn Roberts Attaway,**
Catoosa County Schools
Catoosa County, Georgia

"This is truly the bible of arts integration. I can't tell you how beneficial it has been to me— both with my undergraduates and my second graders. Every time I read it I find new ideas, but mostly, it reinforces to me, time and again, that "with, about, in, and through" the arts is the best, most meaningful way to approach teaching and learning."

**—Bernadette Chilcote,**
Ashley River Creative Arts Elementary,
Charleston, SC

"Claudia Cornett has done all the legwork. The book's thorough research-base makes it suitable for our pre-service education program; yet, the practical aspects ensure that teachers will continue to use it year after year. Arts advocates appreciate the powerful case she makes for integrating arts processes and strategies throughout the curriculum. I personally love the book."

**—Wrenn Cook,**
Director, SC Center for Dance Education,
Columbia College

"We have used *Creating Meaning Through Literature and the Arts* as our textbook for three semesters. We love it. And our students love it. Thank you for providing such an exquisitely valuable text."

**—Donna Farrell,**
The University of Texas at Dallas

"Claudia Cornett's approach to arts and literacy really resonates with teachers. Even the most seasoned classroom teachers have rated her book and workshops as one of the most useful and effective resources and experiences in their careers."

**—Rodney Van Valkenburg,**
Director of Communications/Arts Education
Allied Arts of Greater Chattanooga

# Creating Meaning Through Literature and the Arts

## Arts Integration for Classroom Teachers

### Fourth Edition

**Claudia E. Cornett**
*Professor Emerita, Wittenberg University*

Boston   Columbus   Indianapolis   New York   San Francisco   Upper Saddle River
Amsterdam   Cape Town   Dubai   London   Madrid   Milan   Munich   Paris   Montreal   Toronto
Delhi   Mexico City   Sao Paulo   Sydney   Hong Kong   Seoul   Singapore   Taipei   Tokyo

**Senior Acquisitions Editor:** Kelly Villella Canton
**Editorial Assistant:** Annalea Manalili
**Vice President, Director of Marketing:** Quinn Perkson
**Senior Marketing Manager:** Darcy Betts
**Production Editor:** Gregory Erb
**Editorial Production Service:** S4Carlisle Publishing Services
**Manufacturing Buyer:** Megan Cochran
**Electronic Composition:** S4Carlisle Publishing Services
**Interior Design:** S4Carlisle Publishing Services
**Cover Designer:** Linda Knowles

Credits and acknowledgments borrowed from other sources and reproduced, with permission, in this textbook appear on appropriate page within text. All uncredited photos were taken by Susan Rudeen Jarrett.

Library of Congress Cataloging-in-Publication Data

Cornett, Claudia E.
  Creating meaning through literature and the arts : arts integration for classroom teachers / Claudia E. Cornett. — 4th ed.
    p. cm.
  ISBN 978-0-13-704832-8
  1. Arts—Study and teaching. 2. Literature—Study and teaching. 3. Interdisciplinary approach in education.
  LB1591.C67 2011
  372.64—dc22

                                    2010006277

10 9 8 7 6 5 4 3 2 1 EDW 14 13 12 11 10

www.pearsonhighered.com

ISBN-10: 0-13-704832-7
ISBN-13: 978-0-13-704832-8

*To Charles, my Pygmalion*

# Brief Contents

# Contents

# Part I
## An Introduction to Arts Integration

# Chapter 1
## Creating Meaning Through the Arts: *Why? What? How?*   1

# Chapter 2
## Philosophy, Research, and Theories That Support Arts Integration   28

## Chapter 5
### Seed Strategies for Literature and Poetry   124

## Chapter 6
### Integrating Visual Art Throughout the Curriculum   141

# Chapter 7
## Visual Art Seed Strategies 178

# Chapter 8
## Integrating Drama Throughout the Curriculum 201

# Chapter 9
## Drama and Storytelling Seed Strategies 229

# Chapter 10
## Integrating Dance and Creative Movement 255

## Chapter 11
## Dance and Movement Seed Strategies 286

## Chapter 12
## Integrating Music Throughout the Curriculum 303

## Chapter 13
### Music Seed Strategies    337

## Epilogue    357

## Bibliography    358

## Bibliography: Children's Literature References    368

## Appendix A
### Developmental Stages and the Arts    371

## Appendix B
### Differentiating for Students with Diverse Needs    373

## Appendix C
### Checklist for Planning with Artists    375

## Appendix D
### Assessment Tools and Resources    376

## Appendix E
### Discipline Prevention and Intervention    381

# Special Features

# Foreword

There is a quiet but determined movement throughout K–12 education in this country led by teachers who have discovered the power of integrating the arts into their teaching. Each year more teachers are incorporating the arts into their classrooms, often in partnership with arts specialists. These educators are using a variety of teaching strategies that lead to active student participation. This, in turn, leads to livelier classrooms.

Because our lives do not naturally fall into 50-minute segments during which we focus on one subject at a time, many educators are also taking a second look at integrating multiple disciplines in their instruction, with an eye on making learning more meaningful for students. These ideas—teaching by integrating subjects and using the arts to teach other curriculum areas—are not new to education; indeed, they have been advocated by arts groups and many educational institutions for years.

In the 1960s, arts education began to enjoy the spotlight through the work of such organizations as the National Endowment for the Arts and the John D. Rockefeller III Fund. Since then, educators and arts organizations have worked together more closely to provide arts education experiences for students. Over the intervening years, hundreds of arts organizations have made it part of their mission to support the classroom teacher in efforts to teach in, through, and about the arts.

Practitioners in the arts education field have begun to realize that professional development in the arts is valued not only by experienced teachers, but also by university students learning to become teachers. Indeed, professional development in the arts for practicing teachers is such a growing field precisely because course work in the arts is limited or nonexistent for preservice teachers. It is time to provide more resources and information about the arts and integration at the undergraduate level. With this book, Claudia Cornett has provided such a resource.

*Creating Meaning through Literature and the Arts* will be a valuable resource to preservice teachers and veteran teachers who are new to the concept of arts integration. Educators will find basic information about the four arts disciplines of dance, drama, visual art, and music; diverse applications of literature; strategies and lesson plans for interdisciplinary teaching; resource lists; and an extensive bibliography. Readers will enjoy Dr. Cornett's incorporation of many practical examples and appreciate the Research Updates, which highlight arts and education research and facts. Additionally, readers can witness integration through classroom vignettes placed throughout the chapters. In these "snapshots" and "spotlights," actual lessons are described in which the arts are integrated into teaching and learning. As teachers continue to hear the cry for education reform, school change, and school improvement with ever-increasing frequency, many have turned to the arts. With her book, Dr. Cornett has provided a tool to guide teachers on the path toward making the arts a meaningful part of the classroom experience.

**Barbara Shepherd**
*Director, National Partnerships*
*The Kennedy Center*
*Washington, DC*

# Preface

*Come to the edge, he said.*
*They said, we are afraid.*
*Come to the edge, he said.*
*They came.*
*He pushed them and they flew.*

French poet and art critic Guillaume Apollinaire, 1880–1918

Since the first edition of this book, arts integration has blossomed in schools across the United States, and now in Canada, the United Kingdom, and Australia. Thousands of teachers have felt compelled to "come to the edge." Their courage to make the arts the "fourth R" has produced impressive learning results. Mounting research now supports substantial links between the arts and academic achievement. Underlying gains show the ways the arts engage students in phenomenal ways. Students become intrinsically motivated to develop important cognitive, social, and emotional skills. Arts-based learning restructures how students think and feel by changing them from information recipients into active meaning makers. This deep change often eludes measures used in standardized testing. Most importantly, students, teachers, and parents involved in arts integration say they are just plain happier.

## Fueling Arts Integration

*I have a real heartburn for those who somehow believe that there is a disconnect between arts and education and, quote, "real education," because I would contend that arts education is—real education, and it's a critical part of the other disciplines.* (Mike Huckabee, Governor of Arkansas)

The engine of arts integration is being fueled by many sources. Most prominent are the following:

- Growing dissatisfaction with the test-driven school culture that has not narrowed achievement gaps
- Research that confirms the arts "level the playing field" for disadvantaged students
- Federal legislation that designates the arts as core disciplines
- Philanthropic organizations such as Annenberg, Ford, and other foundations that have given millions of dollars to support arts-based education
- National organizations like the Kennedy Center's Partners in Education and Arts Education Partnership that support school efforts to put arts-based research into practice
- Government-sponsored support for numerous model arts integration projects across the country
- Standards for teacher preparation that now specify what classroom teachers need to know and be able to do in the arts

Unlike other educational reforms, the foundation for arts integration has been built by a broad-based coalition. Educators, arts and cultural organizations, government agencies, and hundreds of businesses and corporations have joined forces. They are united by one goal: to improve education and thereby improve everyone's lives. Collaboration among such diverse groups has caused integration to be honed into a powerful tool. *Meaningful* arts integration creates the conditions for transfer of learning from the arts to traditional academic areas and vice versa. What's more, arts-based learning transfers to life in the 21st century where demands for creative problem solving have escalated.

## Literacy IS the Arts

This book tells the story of how arts integration has grown so much so fast. It is the story of hundreds of arts-based schools. Some are brand new, such as Hilton Head School for the Creative Arts. Others have been at it for a decade or more. The featured school for this edition is Ashley River Creative Arts, now celebrating more than 25 years of arts integration. Old and new, public, magnet, and charter, these schools are combining research, standards, and constructivist beliefs to transform education. In particular, they view literacy as greater than competency with the language arts. They embrace the concept that all communication forms are vehicles to understand and express thoughts and feelings with the arts in both leading and supporting roles. From an arts-based perspective, literacy *is* the arts.

The traditional stars of the curriculum, reading and math, are means to understand and express meaning. But the arts are equally and uniquely needed to accomplish these same communication purposes, and more than ever in our multimedia, technologically driven world. Calls for innovative thinkers and thinking come from every corner of our society. Arts integration is answering that call to develop the creative problem-solving capacities students need to survive and thrive in the third millennium.

As our first communication tools, the arts have long been valued for their power to uplift and elevate. They are now part of the inner circle of learning, an essential piece of the educational puzzle. Integration is the opposite of isolation. Arts integration unites, combines, and orchestrates learning, raising the act of teaching to an art. The arts expand the message with visual images, give emotional context through music, and bring words to life through dance and drama. The arts give voice to those whose words may never be heard. The arts give life to learning; the arts give life to life!

## Book Organization

The fourth edition describes *why* arts integration is now an important school reform and *how* arts integration can be implemented. Although there is no one right way, common building blocks are presented to make the arts integral, not curricular add-ons. In this edition, 10 arts integration building blocks are used to organize use of the arts as learning tools in a manner that is consistent with "arts for art's sake." Center stage is the classroom teacher. In the pages that follow I have synthesized *what* teachers new to arts integration need to know and be able to do.

This edition has two parts. Part I is an overview of arts integration in three chapters. Chapter 1 introduces the concept of *creating meaning through the arts* using updated research. Chapter 2 describes the beliefs, research, and theories that support arts integration, including new brain research and a description of the creative problem-solving process. Chapter 3 is an overview of the *arts integration building blocks*, a set of 10 implementation principles addressed in schools using diverse arts integration frameworks.

Part II begins an in-depth look at the integration of each of five arts with two chapters each for literature, visual art, drama, dance, and music. Even-numbered chapters explain practical ideas for using the building blocks (e.g., planning units and lesson plans, arts literacy, best practices, differentiating instruction, assessment *for* learning). Odd-numbered chapters with thumb tabs are compendia of seed strategies—brief idea starters in the categories of energizers, teaching arts elements and concepts, and curricular areas.

## Features New to This Edition

Other features include:

- New **MyEducationLab** boxes in every chapter direct readers to video assignments showing arts strategies in action; demonstration lessons using music, visual art, drama, and dance; and interviews with arts specialists in addition to chapter-specific Questions to Guide Reading and Response Questions.
- Revised **Research Updates** summarize arts-based studies and research in newer fields such as visual imagery.
- Updated **Ready References** outline sources and information teachers often need. Included is the basic arts knowledge base recommended for classroom teachers in the standards created by Interstate New Teachers Assessment and Support Consortium (INTASC).
- Revised **Planning Pages** show examples of actual arts-integrated lesson and unit plans in each chapter.
- Updated **Arts-Based Children's Literature** selections are used in every curricular area.
- New **Seed Strategies** prompt creative thinking about integrating each arts area.
- **Teacher as Leader: Arts Integration Advocacy Boxes** invite teachers to make a difference in novel ways outside the classroom.
- Revised **Appendixes** identify important tools that support arts integration including key websites, a dozen assessment tools, an arts-based bibliography of children's books, strategies for differentiating for students with special needs (including English language learners), and guidelines for arts-based field trips.
- Encore presentations of favorite **Snapshots and Spotlights** of actual teachers, classrooms, students, and artists

help paint the big picture of how arts strategies are orchestrated in lessons. Bolded strategies help focus on how teachers make meaningful integration happen.

Note: Most of the teachers in this book have given me permission to use their real names. A few names are pseudonyms.

### myeducationlab

## The Power of Classroom Practice

"Teacher educators who are developing pedagogies for the analysis of teaching and learning contend that analyzing teaching artifacts has three advantages: it enables new teachers time for reflection while still using the real materials of practice; it provides new teachers with experience thinking about and approaching the complexity of the classroom; and in some cases, it can help new teachers and teacher educators develop a shared understanding and common language about teaching. . . ."[1]

As Linda Darling-Hammond and her colleagues point out, grounding teacher education in real classrooms—among real teachers and students and among actual examples of students' and teachers' work—is an important, and perhaps even an essential, part of training teachers for the complexities of teaching in today's classrooms. For this reason, we have created a valuable, time-saving website—MyEducationLab—that provides you with the context of real classrooms and artifacts that research on teacher education tells us is so important. The authentic in-class video footage, interactive skill-building exercises and other resources available on MyEducationLab offer you a uniquely valuable teacher education tool.

MyEducationLab is easy to use and integrate into both your assignments and your courses. Wherever you see the MyEducationLab logo in the text, follow the simple instructions to access the videos, strategies, cases, and artifacts associated with Activities and Applications on MyEducationLab. MyEducationLab is organized topically to enhance the coverage of the core concepts discussed in the chapters of your book. For each topic on the course you will find most or all of the following resources:

**Activities and Applications.** Designed to save instructors preparation time, these assignable exercises show concepts in action (through video, cases, or student and teacher artifacts) and then offer thought-provoking questions that probe your understanding of theses concepts or strategies.

**Building Teaching Skills and Dispositions.** These learning units help you practice and strengthen skills that are essential to quality teaching.

**Video Examples.** These short clips demonstrate specific strategies or offer interviews with school professionals that expand on concepts in the text.

---

[1] Darling-Hammond, L., & Bransford, J., Eds. (2005). *Preparing Teachers for a Changing World*. San Francisco: John Wiley & Sons.

**General Resources on Your MyEducationLab Course.** The *Resources* section on your MyEducationLab course is designed to help you pass your licensure exam, put together an effective portfolio and lesson plan, prepare for and navigate the first year of your teaching career, and understand key educational standards, policies, and laws. This section includes:

- *Licensure Exams:* Access guidelines for passing the Praxis exam. The *Practice Test Exam* includes practice questions, *Case Histories*, and *Video Case Studies*.
- *Portfolio Builder and Lesson Plan Builder:* Create, update, and share portfolios and lesson plans.
- *Preparing a Portfolio:* Access guidelines for creating a high-quality teaching portfolio that will allow you to practice effective lesson planning.
- *Licensure and Standards:* Link to state licensure standards and national standards.
- *Beginning Your Career:* Educate yourself – access tips, advice, and valuable information on: Resume Writing and Interviewing: Expert advice on how to write impressive resumes and prepare for job interviews; Your First Year of Teaching: Practical tips to set up your classroom, manage student behavior, and learn to more easily organize for instruction and assessment; Law and Public Policies: Specific directives and requirements you need to understand under the No Child Left Behind Act and the Individuals with Disabilities Education Improvement Act of 2004.

**Book-Specific Resources.** **Questions to Guide Reading** documents may be downloaded for each chapter; these are designed to focus readers on the overarching points.

**Response Options** documents provided for each chapter offer ideas for individuals to extend what they learned from reading and projects for teachers to complete and reflect on as a group.

**Bibliographies of Arts Based Children's Literature** documents for each of the five arts (literature, visual arts, drama, dance, and music) provide readers with a rich resource of arts based books that 1) are about the art form (e.g. history), 2) are about making or creating in the art form, 3) are about artists (people), 4) have the arts as part of the theme or 5) are artworks, themselves, such as picture books or scripts. These books enhance the list of children's literature Websites listed at the end of Chapter 4. For more books with artistic protagonists, go to the Children's Literature Web: www.ucalgary.ca/~dkbrown/ or www.carolhurst.com.

**FAQs about Arts Integration** is one document within the Chapter 3 resources that readers may download and keep with handy responses to the most frequently asked questions by teachers who are working to integrate the arts.

*Visit www.myeducationlab.com for a demonstration of this exciting new online teaching resource.*

## Acknowledgments

This book reflects the dedication of many educators to arts integration. In particular, I want to thank Jayne Ellicott, Principal, Ashley River Creative Arts Elementary, and Cathie Middleton, Assistant Principal, for being true collaborators. I especially want to thank Bill Langston for his expert work on the videos that support this edition. The teachers of Ashley River were a delight to work with and give this book life. I want to acknowledge those I've worked with in the past and those who were involved in this edition:

Elizabeth Allen, Judi Beaudrot, Susan Brandon, Ann Cheek, Bernadette Chilcote, Carol Cope, Chris Crawford, Natascha Ferguson, Robin Fountain, Janelle Fredrich, Alison Graham, Jennifer Hanson, Cindy Hines, Sylvia Horres, Kelly James, Ismaker Kadrie, Marty Kearney, Jeannie Laban, Michelle Lowe, Barbara Lunsford, Mary Mac Jennings, Jeff Jordan, Cheryl Leonard, Deborah Menick, Dianne O'Neill, Susan Peebles, Fannie Petros, Carole Rathbun, Jill Roberts, Linda Roberts, C. J. Rozzi, Ashley Sires, Cherrie Sneed, Jill Sneed, Kathryn Stonaker, Stacey Sturgell, Lisa Trott, Judy Trotter, Amy Walker, Joyce Wiggins.

Over the years I have been fortunate to work with so many others who have contributed to this book in some measure, including Charlotte Smelser, Director of ArtsSmart in Texarkana; Kay Thomas and Jennifer Unger, teaching artists at ArtsSmart; Laurel Shastri, teaching artist and Associate Director of Ballet Tennessee; Hollie Steele and Carolyn Attaway at Battle Academy in Chattanooga, Tennessee; Rodney Van Valkenburg, Allied Arts of Greater Chattanooga; Kristy Smith, Beaufort County Schools; Wrenn Cook, Columbia College; Ava Hughes, Arts Partnership of Greater Spartanburg; Mary Lou Hightower, University of South Carolina; Christine Fisher and Ray Doughty, South Carolina ABC Schools; Gretchen Keefner, Principal, and teachers at Hilton Head School for the Creative Arts (Colleen Skibo, Tara Caron, Erin Duffy, Tennille Kasper, Karen Cauller, and Marcia Underwood); Terry Bennett, Principal, and teachers at Lady's Island Elementary; Amy Goldin, New York University Steinhardt School and Progressive School of Long Island; Debbie Fahmie, Tallahassee, Florida; the Executive Board of the South Carolina Alliance for Arts Education; and the Beaufort Art Association.

I also wish to thank the reviewers of my manuscript for their comments and insights; this is a better book for their efforts: Nancy Hauck, Dixie State College; Jacob Langerak, Nazareth College; Patricia Lust, Longwood University.

Thanks to all the folks at Allyn & Bacon/Pearson and at S4Carlisle who work so artfully to turn typed pages into beautiful books. In particular, I want to acknowledge Kelli Jauron, Mary Kriener, Greg Erb, and Annalea Manalili. I want to thank my editor, Kelly Villlella Canton, for her openness to new ideas, good humor and use of the creative problem solving process I describe in the book. It was wonderful to work with someone who understood how to use the process so central to the book's theme to actually create the book.

On a more personal level I want to thank the many friends and family members who have been so supportive during the writing process. In particular, thanks to Kat Shehata, Andrew Shehata, and Jo Ellen McElwee for sharing their talents and their artistic spirits.

Of course, first and last, time present and time past, there is my husband, Charles, to whom this book is dedicated. Without his superb research skills, insightful suggestions, and unwavering support I could not write books. And he still makes me laugh every day.

*Claudia Cornett*

# About the Author

Claudia Cornett is Professor Emerita, Education Department, Wittenberg University. During her tenure at Wittenberg, she directed the Reading Center and taught graduate and undergraduate courses in all aspects of literacy, children's literature, and arts integration. Wittenberg's Alumni Association honored her with the Distinguished Teaching Award. Before moving to the college level, she taught grades 1–8, was a reading specialist, and earned a PhD in Curriculum and Instruction from Miami University.

Claudia has written numerous books and articles about literacy, bibliotherapy, the strategic use of humor, and using the arts as teaching tools. *Comprehension First: Inquiry into Big Ideas and Important Questions* was published by Holcomb Hathaway in 2010. She has also been involved as a writer and on camera in various educational television productions including *Sounds Abound*, a series on early literacy, and *Art Chat,* a series of interviews with artists in their studios. She also does costumed interpretation in the role of Harriet Beecher Stowe for various events.

Claudia regularly does keynote speeches and conducts professional development for educators throughout the United States, Europe, and Canada. Her current research focuses on addressing literacy issues using an arts-based teaching model. She lives with her husband, a retired school superintendent, in historic Lebanon, Ohio. She can be reached at ccornett@wittenberg.edu.

# Creating Meaning Through the Arts:
## Why? What? How?

*We have an achievement gap partly because we have an arts gap among the haves and the have not children.* (Annenberg Institute for School Reform, 2003)

## Overview

This chapter introduces the idea that the arts are "remarkable meaning makers" that have become the centerpiece of a curricular reform called "arts integration (AI)." Included are reasons why arts-based teaching is an important strategy for addressing low test scores and for preparing students for 21st-century life and work. Of special importance are the unique contributions the arts make to learning that are rarely captured by traditional tests.

Building blocks for *meaningful* AI are introduced and examples of different AI models are presented with links to their websites. This chapter also introduces educators from Ashley River Creative Arts Elementary (ARCA), which is the focus AI school for this edition. ARCA is an example of what can happen when AI practices are thoughtfully introduced, expanded, and institutionalized by innovative educators.

## Introduction

You may have seen the clip of Susan Boyle who first stunned British audiences with her rendition of "I Dreamed a Dream" from *Les Miserables*. This plain, 47-year-old Scot courageously endured the anticipatory snickers of the judges as she declared she had never dated and never been kissed. Yet after singing just a few bars, eyebrows raised, jaws dropped, and by the end of the song the entire audience was on its feet and in love with Susan. YouTube made it possible for the whole world to experience the power of the arts to provoke emotion and change perspective. Millions teared up and got goose bumps at her performance, made even more touching by a back story of the self-sacrifice of an unsung hero.

Such arts power is now being unleashed every day in hundreds of ordinary classrooms made extraordinary through arts-based teaching. Unresponsive students begin to engage and become motivated to learn. Former "discipline problems" focus as the arts work their magic of attracting attention, promoting

concentration, and causing students to want to do hard thinking to solve problems at the core of arts-based investigations. The transformation is not limited to students. Teachers claim they are professionally reinvigorated by arts integration, an educational reform strategy that taps the unique qualities of the arts to increase learning in all curricular areas—to cause students to create meaning.

AI is now in full bloom after well over a decade of work in large-scale projects in urban schools like those in Chicago and Minneapolis. AI is a seedling in small programs in rural schools in Tennessee, South Carolina, Arkansas, and many other states (Burnaford, 2007; Weiss & Lichtenstein, 2008). The AI sprouts show a vigor that is uncommon in the history of educational reforms. Imagine shy students becoming confident and articulate during drama responses to literature. Imagine formerly passive students now motivated and engaged as they collaborate in planning and constructing a group mural to show social studies learning. Picture students with attention difficulties in deep concentration as music is made integral to science lessons. These images are a reality in hundreds of schools across this country.

Literature invites us into hearts and minds of others. Visual art gives new perspectives while satisfying our need for beauty. Drama welcomes us to suspend disbelief, to pretend and consider "what if." Dance extends communication of thoughts and feelings through use of the body. Music "soothes the soul" while giving insights into ideas and emotions beyond words. The arts engender concentrated work punctuated with play. Curiosity is aroused and interest is piqued as we consider the possibilities arts materials, tools, techniques, and products present to express thoughts and feelings.

Arts-based learning is all about creative thinking, which is all about coordinating higher order thinking processes to solve problems. Creative thinking proceeds with a sense of wonder and mystery that motivates students to learn new ways to understand and express themselves. Educators are particularly excited about the achievement gains among low performing students in high poverty schools that have implemented principles of AI. Indeed, low performing students and English learners have proven to be the greatest beneficiaries of this educational reform strategy that embraces the arts as essential learning vehicles. Research Update 1.1 describes example results.

# Research Update *1.1*   Arts Integration and Learning

- **Chicago, IL** Twenty-three arts-integrated CAPE schools showed test scores rising up to two times faster than in demographically comparable schools without arts integration (Deasy, 2002).

- **Dallas, TX** A 3-year study of *ArtsPartners* schools found that disadvantaged and struggling students performed better in reading comprehension than a matched control and low achieving students improved their quality of writing. Achievement gaps reported between white, Asian, Hispanic, and African American students narrowed dramatically for writing. Students appeared more engaged in learning (e.g., asking questions, revising work, studying another child's work). These effects were most pronounced in low achieving students. www.bigthought.org/Portals/BT/AP2ndYr_Assessment.pdf

- **Minneapolis, MN** Arts-integrated schools reported substantial academic gains for all students. For example, students in grades 3 through 5 made significant year over year gains in reading. The greatest beneficiaries were English learners and low performing students whose higher order thinking and motivation to learn increased (Ingram & Riedel, 2003; Rabkin & Redmond, 2005).

- **North Carolina** Students at A+ schools achieved gains over a 3-year period equal to gains statewide in both mathematics and reading. However, A+ served larger proportions of minority students. In addition, improvement was found in student and teacher attendance, discipline, and parental involvement (Corbett, McKenney, Noblit, & Wilson; 2001; Marron, 2003).

- **Mississippi** All but one Whole Schools Initiative (WSI) school met their AYP in reading and all but two did so in math. By comparison, more WSI sites attained their growth targets than did matched comparison schools and fewer failed to achieve AYP in reading and math. This meant that WSI students experienced added values of arts-based learning *and* performed similarly to peers in nearby schools and throughout the state. This was not an inconsequential achievement in the face of the narrowed instructional programs in other schools. This finding is an important support for arts integration: "the arts and the acquisition of basic skills in a high-stakes environment did not necessarily conflict with one another" (Corbett, Wilson, & Morse, 2005).

- **New York City, NY** A multiyear study of ArtsConnection schools found a strong link between English/language arts and drama. Speaking and listening showed particular improvement. Researchers concluded that arts-based lessons enhanced thinking, especially higher order processes used in creative problem solving. Increases were also shown in confidence, positive risk taking, cooperation, expression of ideas and feelings, and ownership of learning. Teachers became more comfortable with the arts and exhibited more collaboration. Teacher ability to view students from new perspectives was positively correlated with the project (Hefferen, 2005).

- **New York** A 5-year evaluation of Empire State Partnerships schools showed increased student engagement in learning and collaborative work. Test scores were mixed, but low achieving students performed better than expected. The most positive result was considered to be students' expectations of success (Baker et al., 2004, p. 43).

- **South Carolina** Arts in Basic Curriculum (ABC) evaluators analyzed 3 years of state tests in English/language arts and math. They found a steady increase in the percent of students identified as proficient or advanced in ABC schools, as compared with schools with similar student profiles (Horowitz, 2004).

- **Texarkana, TX** Based upon 2 years of program evaluation, a team concluded that ArtsSmart positively impacted students' academic learning, artistic development, expression, creativity, imagination, self-confidence, engagement, and motivation (ArtsSmart, 2006). Website: www.trahc.org. One school, Trice Elementary, nearly tripled the number of third graders at the advanced level of literacy and doubled the number of fourth graders at the advanced level. In math, numbers of third graders doubled and in fourth grade there was more than triple the number at the advanced level (Blaine Sapaugh, assistant principal, 2009).

- **Tucson, AZ** Students at Opening Minds through the Arts (OMA) schools have significantly higher scores in math, reading, and writing than non-OMA students. The arts have closed the gap between minority and white students (*Arts Education: Improving Students' Academic Performance,* March 2005 broadcast: www.ed.gov).

- **Coast to coast** A study of 10 "high-poverty" schools in the continental United States found that arts integration and arts education contributed significantly to higher test scores, and closing the achievement gap, especially in reading and math (Deasy & Stevenson, 2005). Students in the 130 arts-based Waldorf schools outperformed national averages on the SAT (Oppenheimer, 1999).

- **Canada** A 3-year study of 6,000+ elementary students in Learning to Read Through the Arts showed an 11-point increase in math in the 170 schools. Literacy scores remained the same, but students reported being happier about school and researchers saw them as more engaged (Upitis & Smithrim 2003). Website: www.ltta.ca.

Pantomiming escaping slaves

## Classroom Snapshot
### Multiarts Integration with Social Studies

The opening Classroom Snapshot invites you to see arts power at work in a first grade. The school was one of the first in America to implement the tenets of AI. It is Ashley River Creative Arts Elementary in Charleston, South Carolina. The teacher is Judy Trotter. Key arts-based teaching strategies are bolded to draw attention to how she uses music, drama, and literature to help students make sense of important concepts in social studies. In particular, notice how Judy presents a series of open-ended problems to students, which ignites creative thinking.

**The background music** is barely audible. The lights are off. Judy sits on the arm of a wingback chair. There is complete silence as she closes the picture book she has just finished reading to her first graders. The book is *Barefoot* (Edwards, 1997). It is about slaves running from their captors.

"Find your **personal space**," Judy tells them, almost in a whisper. Students slowly stand up. They begin to spread out and adjust so no one is within reach of another.

Judy waits for students to look at her and then says, "Okay, **show me** walking in place—barefoot. Begin."

In their personal "space bubbles," 17 children begin to drag, shuffle, slide, and tiptoe to a slow steady beat. **Background percussion** sets the tempo. Judy **side coaches** to increase engagement.

"**I see** faces full of effort. Good job of concentrating. I see everyone thinking about walking with bare feet in mud, on rocks, through water. Careful, don't let them hear you," she warns.

"Stop!" Judy calls. Students relax and become first graders again. Judy stops the CD.

"Who were the other people in the story?" she asks. Students talk about the slave hunters, what they were like, what they wanted, and how they felt.

"Now let's **pantomime their feelings**," Judy tells them. "Places!"

Once again in their personal spaces the children are at the ready.

"Action!" Judy cues and a contrasting mime of "boots" begins. This time, students use a very different array of actions and facial expressions. They slash, stomp, squat, peer, and glare.

"**Freeze**," Judy directs. This follow-up to the read-aloud continues with a *narrative pantomime* (Heinig, 1993). Judy retells the plot as students mime the major events in this story set during the Civil War. No props are used, except a flashlight to suggest stars that mapped the path for escaping slaves.

## Teacher Spotlight
### Judy Trotter

*The mind should "act as a waffle iron on batter." (I. Kant)*

Judy Trotter has been teaching fourth and first grade off and on at Ashley River Creative Arts for more than 15 years. She is uncompromising when she declares, "Teaching through the arts is the best way to teach."

"Teachers get in a testing panic and think they don't have time for the arts. They get worried about our state PACT test. But if students truly learn, they will do well on the tests," Judy states confidently. "Teaching should not be about teaching to the test. Teaching should be structured so students learn for the pure joy of it."

### Integral Connections

After teaching at this renowned school for so long, Judy says she is "always thinking about arts connections."

Currently she is also doing another arts-based read-aloud (Cornett, 2006) of the chapter book *Because of Winn Dixie* (DiCamillo, 2000). She is animated as she describes how you can take any story and "go off in any arts direction."

"It just flows," she says. "The arts are a natural connection." That *natural* connection has to do with her concern about *meaningful* arts integration. She talks passionately about teaching issues of social justice, big ideas, and compassion. A main focus is developing her students' capacity to take new perspectives, and "a respect for the unknown."

It is clear Judy believes that school life should prepare students for life outside of school. "I believe in teaching the whole child," she explains. "Art is everywhere. It is totally integrated into our daily lives. We live in the arts and should be able to learn through arts. They enrich life and learning."

## Assessment

Judy talks just as passionately about assessment. "We must work with the standards," she insists, "but I use many ways to gauge student progress—journals, for example, for poetry, math, writing, science, and social studies." She laughs, "They know they have to prove they have learned it!" The journals, she explains, are simple black and white composition books.

Like all the Ashley River teachers, Judy plans standards-based units that use the arts as central tools to cause students to make sense. "We were immersed in Asian culture at the time of the tsunami," she recalls. Students learned to use paintbrushes to write in black paint. They studied the picture book art of Soerpiet, a Korean illustrator known for watercolors. Students listened to Chinese CDs and made costumes to celebrate Chinese New Year. She describes how she read poems to Chinese music and asked the children to take an imaginary trip to China, drawing upon images from a previously viewed CD-ROM of China. It is a routine to end each unit with exhibits

and performances that tap the motivational power of using audiences. Most importantly, these arts-based curricular responses show what the students have learned. "Of course, there was a Chinese celebration," Judy adds excitedly.

## Management Issues

Judy is equally committed to preparing new teachers to integrate the arts meaningfully and is on the faculty at the College of Charleston. She also does workshops for practicing teachers on using music and movement strategies. How does she respond to concerns about students dancing? "I do it with them!" she explains. "I teach my students how to control their voices and bodies and we take movement breaks daily."

What's next? Judy is excited about the current African culture unit using *Follow the Drinking Gourd* (Winter, 1997) and folk tales. "We will compare the art of the Chinese with African art. I want students to value how other people sound and look—deep down all people are so much the same. This is one of the big ideas behind the arts."

## Meaningful AI

Judy Trotter's lessons are examples of *meaningful* arts integration. At Ashley River, AI is made meaningful beginning with collaborative planning by grade-level teams who plan using resources such as science, social studies, literacy, math, and arts standards. Arts specialists consult with teams to ensure arts standards are given equity with core academic areas.

To prepare students to use the arts to create meaning during units, Ashley River teachers teach and assess specific arts concepts and tools. Visual art is used to stir children's senses, but that means teaching them how to "read" art. Drawing is prominent in the writing process because students have been taught how to create art compositions *before* they write, which has increased the quality and quantity of writing. Students have also been taught how to write songs and different types of poetry to summarize important units. Background music is routinely used to engage emotions, but teachers take the response further by coaching students to think about the composer's messages and the musical tools used to send those messages. In the same vein, drama is used to bring life to areas, such as history, making it vivid and real through use of specific drama tools, such as pantomime. Similarly, dance basics are taught so students not only experience the joy of movement, but also have the know-how to create meaning kinesthetically.

Teachers at Ashley River use multiple forms of assessment, including observation checklists and rubrics, to track student progress in traditional academic areas *and* in the arts. Arts-based lessons taught during the literacy block are also frequently connected to science and social studies units. Students are engaged throughout lessons, cognitively, physically, emotionally, and socially using best practices for teaching reading and writing *and* for teaching about arts products and processes. Teachers explicitly teach students how to understand and express their thoughts and feelings using the arts key communication tools. Teachers

Arts-based read-aloud to prepare for pantomime

not only pose problems, but also teach students *how to* use a full set of creative problem-solving strategies. In particular, they ask many open-ended questions and expect a range of "right" answers.

Ashley River teachers draw upon the arts as they are used outside of school, as forms of literacy to understand, respond to, and express ideas and emotions. The arts are integrated as powerful communication tools to *create* meaning and instead of reducing content to fit the world of the classroom, classrooms become laboratories to "make sense of the content of the world" (Grumet, 2004, p. 54). The teachers act on the maxim, "A mind should be well made rather than well filled" (Immanuel Kant), which is a common belief at AI schools. ✴

# The Push for Arts Integration

> *You know, I often say that I might not have been president if it hadn't been for school music.* (Bill Clinton, *Good Morning America*, June 16, 2000)

The impetus for AI has come from *inside* schools where principals and teachers lead the charge to align learning with both research and life. Educators like those at Ashley River also reach out to forge collaborations with those in the arts community, including artists, who share the goal of transforming how teaching and learning happens during literacy and math lessons, and science and social studies units. Bringing the outside in goes further: Economic, political, social, and technological changes have accelerated the need for an educational revolution (Deasy, 2008). The push is now on for learning to become embedded with artistic ways of thinking and working essential to contemporary life.

## Outside Forces

President Clinton translated his school experiences into a theory of education that connects the arts with the motivation and self-discipline needed for achievement in any field. He is not alone among American civic and business leaders who credit their success to an upbringing rich in arts experiences.

The National Governors Association concluded that the arts provide a competitive advantage. Its report, *The Impact of Arts Education on Workforce Preparation* (2002) describes how 21st-century workplaces demand such assets as flexibility, interpersonal skills, and problem solving, common to work in the arts. Schools cannot remain lodged in the last century where memorizing facts and applying rigid formulas paved the way to lucrative careers. Jobs that require formulaic decisions are rapidly being lost to outsourcing and automation (Hetland, 2008). According to the Partnership for 21st Century Skills, "many of the fastest growing jobs and emerging industries rely on workers' creative capacity—the ability to think unconventionally, question the herd, imagine new scenarios, and produce astonishing work" (www.21stcenturyskills. org). Nonroutine creative thinking is a basic competency needed for job categories predicted to increase in the next decade, 80 percent of which haven't even been conceptualized (Chairman, Cisco Systems, in speech at Wake Forest University).

Innovative problem solutions have never been more needed than in this second decade of the 21st century (Duncan, 2009). CEOs lament that there is a "crisis of creativity" (Boston, 1996, p. 2; Pink, 2006). Business leaders point out that American business survives and thrives on new ideas. A strong economy depends on individuals who can imagine and design products for a global market. Such creative problem solving needs an environment where leaders believe questions and problems seldom have one answer. A powerful argument for arts-based education is that the arts engage students in creative problem solving and use of new technologies that prepare them for a world guaranteed to change in unimaginable ways (Deasy, 2008; Duncan, 2009; Pink, 2006). In 2010 an "Arts Skill Map" was developed by the Partnership for 21st Century Skills and leading arts professional organizations to show how the arts engage these and other essential skills. View the map through the Arts Education Partnership website (www.aep-arts.org).

**Big Money and Many Jobs.** *In Ohio alone the creative industries bring more than $25 BILLION in revenue, and support 231,200 jobs* (www.oac.state.oh.us/). The arts not only prepare students for workplaces that demand creative problem solving and collaboration, but also serve as important career destinations. Arts-related professions are wide ranging—from architect to dance teacher, set designer to car designer. A rigid and constricted education that does not promote the arts as career options limits the personal futures of our youth and the creative arts industry. And that industry is enormous. Often an unacknowledged part of daily life, the arts industry is a multibillion-dollar business. The economic impact is staggering (Florida, 2004). One Cezanne exhibit in Philadelphia generated more than $100 million in revenue. A Bruce Springsteen concert series grossed $40 million for 39 concerts and almost $200 million just for Nashville's economy. The nonprofit arts industry alone employs some 5.7 million jobs and generates $166.2 billion in economic activity. Every $1 billion in spending by nonprofit arts and culture organizations and their audiences results in almost 70,000 full-time jobs. Nonprofits also return nearly $30 million in government revenue each year (Americans for the Arts, www.artsusa.org/).

With more than 578,000 arts-centric businesses employing nearly 3 million people, arts education becomes a critical tool in fueling the creative industries of the future with arts-trained workers (Richmond-Cullen, 2005; U.S. Bureau of Labor Statistics, www.bis.gov). It is estimated that at least one third of today's students will become employed in arts-related occupations (Education Commission of the States, www.ecs.org/).

**Arts Education and Arts in Education.** Quality comprehensive and sequential arts education, provided in special classes taught by arts specialists, is one avenue to prepare students for specific arts careers and the greater world of work. Research confirms the long-term benefits of arts education for working in the new economy (Richmond-Cullen, 2005). The arts deliver precisely the kinds of thinking and working skills needed in the workplace of the new millennium:

- Higher order thinking such as analysis, synthesis, evaluation, including critical judgment

- Imagination and creativity focused deliberately on content and quality end products
- Prudent risk taking and experimentation
- Teamwork that relies on collaborative problem solving
- Technological competencies
- Flexible thinking and an appreciation for diversity
- Self-discipline, persistence, and taking initiative

The use of the arts *in* general education classes adds another dimension to education that can leverage learning. Arts-based teaching or AI is now acknowledged as a key approach to teaching other subjects, which acknowledges the need for specialized arts classes (Burnaford, 2007). Education integrated with the arts is credited with boosting the kinds of creative thinking and working skills produced by traditional arts education, plus AI has been shown to have positive effects on school attendance, recidivism rates, communication skills, self-esteem, and the acquisition of job skills, especially for at-risk populations. Arts-based education is correlated with both increased academic performance and reduced juvenile crime rate.

The world of work needs and wants artistic thinkers and creative problem solvers and puts a premium on employees who can use diverse thinking—people who readily combine intuition with analysis, synthesis, and evaluation to solve problems and make judgments (Boston, 1996). Arts-based learning gives students an understanding of the skill, discipline, perseverance, and sacrifice necessary for achievement at school, in the workplace, and in personal life (Psilos, 2002). Why? Arts-based learning engenders high motivation to create quality products because it taps into innate propensities to pursue unique solutions to problems and view mistakes as opportunities. As Aristotle observed, "Art loves chance. He who errs willingly is the artist." Trying new ideas and finding multiple solutions capitalizes on natural human inclinations. These are orientations both needed and valued in the 21st-century workplace. What's more, "If you look into the faces of children who are involved in a creative activity, you will see their enthusiasm for learning and their pride in being part of a creative experience," says Alabama Governor Don Siegelman, and chair of NGA's Economic Development and Commerce Committee (www.nga.org).

## The Push from Inside Education.

> *Students will not learn to think for themselves if their school expects them to stay in line and keep quiet.* (Rabkin & Redmond, 2005, p. 46)

The 2008 National Assessment of Educational Progress, a congressionally mandated standardized test, released new findings that show the average performance of high school students in reading and math has not budged since the early 1970s. Scores are flat. Two-thirds of American adolescents read at or below basic level. They can do literal thinking, but not inference, analysis, or critique. The same goes for writing. Students can create simple narratives and informational paragraphs but not extended text or persuasive arguments. Students achieving in some aspects of reading at grade 3 may not be reading at all by grade 8. It seems that "the longer American children stay in school, the worse they perform compared to their international peers (McKinsey and Company, 2009). It is also disappointing that little progress has been made in closing the achievement gaps that separate black and Hispanic students from white peers. This

gap "imposes the economic equivalent of a permanent nation recession" on our country (McKinsey, 2009).

**Schools as Don't Places.**  Many schools, especially in low-income areas, dwell on basic skills, testing, and rigid discipline (Rabkin & Redmond, 2005). It's all about don'ts. Don't talk, don't move, don't touch, don't laugh, don't color outside the lines, don't work together. Schools must become DO Places. The 21st century requires creative problem solving and teamwork. These are not developed by educational approaches that create "student boredom and academic failure that follow prompt calls for more testing and discipline" (p. 46).

Legislative mandates that threaten teachers and schools with punitive measures for low scores have not motivated educators to create the kind of innovative curriculum and instruction needed to close the achievement gaps. Teachers from coast to coast bemoan learning time lost to testing; life has been squeezed out of the curriculum with the loss of the arts and whittled down time for social studies and science. A narrowed focus has not paid off, even for reading. In Reading First schools where the teaching of reading was reduced to phonics, vocabulary, and fluency skills, there were no real gains in reading comprehension despite billions invested in professional development and materials (Whitehurst, 2008). Not surprisingly, adding up low level pieces of reading did not cause students to acquire the problem-solving skills needed to comprehend texts. Comprehension should have been first, but it wasn't, so it came in last (Cornett, 2010).

**Achievement Gap.**  Sprinkled throughout the somber educational landscape are compelling images of success, particularly for disadvantaged populations involved in arts-based learning (Deasy, 2008). At-risk youth are experiencing striking successes in arts integration programs thoughtfully implemented in both urban cities and rural communities. Research Update 1.1 samples some of the results. As Richard Riley, former U.S. secretary of education, put it, "The arts teach young people how to learn by giving them the first step: the desire to learn." Student testimonials also point to how the arts can be a feel-good alternative to drugs and other destructive means to "get high." As one college student explained, "While other kids were getting high on drugs, I got high playing my flute." In addition, the arts contribute to increased self-esteem and the development of creative problem-solving skills that build independence (Deasy, 2002; Fiske, 1999).

**Arts and Academic Achievement.**  The problems of education cannot be solved with slogans and acronyms that pander to those who want simple solutions. Arts integration is much more than another label. It is based on a thoughtful and well-reasoned look at a substantial body of research that shows strong positive relationships between arts involvement and academic gain. Several summaries explain positive findings from dozens of studies of AI projects, most notably *Champions of Change* (Fiske, 1999), *Critical Links* (Deasy, 2002), *Third Space* (Deasy & Stevenson, 2005), and *Arts Integration Frameworks, Research & Practice: A Literature Review* (Burnaford, 2007).

**Integral Connections.**  Rodney Van Valkenburg, director of Arts Education, Allied Arts of Greater Chattanooga, believes that the reason the arts work is that "the skills necessary to be a good artist are the same skills that are needed to be a good student: self-control of your body, voice, and mind" (2005). The arts go further to engage the same kinds of cognitive processes used in reading, writing, and math, making the potential for learning in the arts to leverage learning in those areas. Structural analogies between arts and other disciplines can be exploited to activate transfer.

When the arts are integrated, subject area boundaries become blurred, making learning more like real life. Works of art and artistic thinking link social studies, mathematics, science, and geography, "opening lines of inquiry, revealing that art, like life, is lived in a complex world not easily defined in discrete subjects" (p. 2, J. Paul Getty Trust, 1993). The arts provide unique ways to perceive new relationships, to notice details and patterns and connect ideas across disciplines. Ready Reference 1.2 summarizes some of the integral connections.

## Ready Reference 1.2 — Integral Connections: Reading, Writing, Math, and the Arts

CPS refers to creative problem solving process, the following are examples from the countless overlapping relationships between reading, writing, mathematics, and the arts. When teachers make these kinds of connections explicit, students gain an understanding of how integrally related all things are in learning and life.

### READING:
*Decoding symbols in order to comprehend a text (print or nonprint).*

**Visual Arts:** Artwork is "read" in a way similar to reading word-based print text. The reader/viewer must first perceive the work as a whole and then relate subordinate parts to discover relationships and connections, along with important emphases. Making sense of any painting, sculpture, or artwork requires coordinated use of higher order thinking skills (CPS), in the same way CPS is used to understand traditional texts.

**Drama/Theatre Arts:** Comprehension of dramatic texts closely parallels thinking to understand any written work and performance is largely about interpretation of words using CPS. Actors usually do a first read to derive big ideas in a script, which entails visualizing the setting. They also zero in other literary elements to create meaning, especially the conflict or problem, which sets the plot in motion (rising and falling action, crisis, and climax). Actors read to analyze their characters' motives and relationships to other characters and the plot.

**Dance:** Viewing a dance involves nearly the same comprehension strategies to those used in reading traditional texts, that is, coordinated CPS thinking. Dance compositions are created about the same themes and big ideas that are at the core of the literary arts, again using CPS.

**Music:** Reading a piece of music is virtually identical to reading print text and includes decoding symbols for the purpose of making sense. Reading music notation requires reading ahead, determining phrases and the overall structure, locating accents, interpreting symbols and verbal indicators, and discriminating between the main and subordinate ideas. Listening to music requires thinking, albeit aesthetic-oriented thinking to comprehend or understand.

### WRITING:
*Encoding thoughts and feelings using symbols.*

**Visual Arts:** The composition process used to create a piece of art is virtually the same as that for creating written compositions (e.g., preparing, data gathering, visualizing, experimenting, revising).

**Drama/Theatre Arts:** The process used to write scripts and plays involves the same thinking skills as creating any other form of writing. The difference is the writing form (e.g., script). The process includes prewriting, drafting, revising, editing, and publishing, which parallels CPS.

**Dance:** Choreography uses the same thinking and processes as writing, such as brainstorming, improvisation, selecting and organizing, revision, rehearsal, evaluation, and publishing/performance.

**Music:** Writing music phrases, sections, and compositions using notation symbols involves many of the same processes used in English language arts.

### MATHEMATICS:
*Using symbols to solve math problems.*

**Visual Arts:** The geometric shapes, proportions, and relationships used in visual arts are used in mathematics. During the process of creating a painting or sculpture, spatial relationships are explored including proportion, shapes, patterns, measurement, estimation of space and distance, making plane and solid figures, and description and creation of three-dimensional objects using different perspectives.

**Drama/Theatre Arts:** Mathematics principles used to stage and to design and construct scenery are the same as those used in geometry, algebra, and physics. For example, to design and construct a simple flat, one would need to measure and use measurement tools, add, subtract, multiply, divide, create angles, use geometric principles and geometry tools, write down numbers to communicate, use proportion, and use mathematical problem-solving skills.

**Dance:** In the creation and execution of dance, a variety of math concepts are used including sequencing, symmetrical and asymmetrical shapes, geometric forms and designs, relationships between metered time and fractions, organizing skills, patterns (rhythm, movement, and body shape), and measurement (e.g., movements and space).

**Music:** Composing and performing music involves thinking about mathematical concepts such as proportion (e.g., fractions) and skills such as counting. Like, unlike, and empty sets in mathematics are the same as music measures with similar or dissimilar rhythm or melody patterns or measures with no notes in them. Greater than, less than, or equal to correlates with comparing music intervals, dynamics, and rhythm values (e.g., fractions: rhythm and meter). Proportions in mathematics equate to relationships between music intervals and rhythm values. Reciprocals in mathematics relate directly to inversions of music intervals (perfect fourth to perfect fifth, major third to minor sixth, etc.).

## Research Update *1.3* Arts and Young Children, Graduation Rates, and School Safety

**Young children.** Studies confirm that arts-involved children are better prepared to start school (Welch, 1995). Arts experiences can create a "reverential spell" (Lewis, 2002) that deeply affects young children and invites them into learning. Children who hear and sing nursery rhymes (literature and music) build a language foundation for reading and writing. They dance, sing, laugh, and learn to love language and school. As they explore meaning making through chalk, paint, clay, and collage, they learn to take risks, experiment, and problem solve. They see how they can make an individual mark with materials that respond to their will and delight in manipulating color, line, shape, and texture. This delight can last a lifetime, be the start of an art avocation, or lead to one of hundreds of arts-related careers.

**Graduation rate.** Signs of being at risk for academic troubles develop early. Children who start school expecting success and continue to enjoy learning are more likely to stay in school. According to Welch (1995), arts programs are important to dropout prevention. In particular, schools may lose students who are especially creative thinkers and those who dismiss science and math if they are taught as dismal piles of facts, dates, and graphs. Unconventional

"creative spirits" such as Einstein, Freud, Steve Jobs (Apple), and Bill Gates (Microsoft) are typical of those who make the breakthroughs in science and math (Gardner, 1993a). Students need to use the connections among math, science, visual intelligence, kinesthetic knowing (dance/drama), and musical thinking. Meaningful connections give students more means to enjoy learning and achieve understanding, and reasons to return to the arts in the future. Programs such as the Duke Ellington School in Washington, D.C., use the arts for these purposes. Ninety percent of the participants in the Boys Choir of Harlem go on to college (Gregorian, 1997).

**Safe schools.** Research links arts-based learning to more positive school environments (Deasy, 2002; Welch, 1995). The mood and culture change as classrooms are transformed into places of discovery. Collaboration is emphasized among students and teachers as integration is sought. As teachers focus on uncovering hidden strengths, the dynamics between teachers and students change. The physical nature of school buildings and classrooms is altered as walls become sites for murals, room is made for movement, and director's chairs, plants, and easels add to the decor.

The case for arts-based learning is convincing enough that Secretary of Education Rod Paige wrote a letter to all school superintendents emphasizing the significance of the arts in achievement. He reminded the nation's educational leaders that "the arts are a core academic subject under President Bush's *No Child Left Behind Act*" and lamented the "disturbing and just plain wrong" misinterpretation of NCLB used to shrink the role of the arts in schools. He referred to the National Longitudinal Study of 25,000 students that found a strong correlation between the arts and better test scores. What's more, high arts students "performed more community service, watched fewer hours of television, reported less boredom in school, and were less likely to drop out." Paige points out that the findings held for students from the lowest socioeconomic quartile "belying the assumption that socioeconomic status, rather than arts engagement, contributes to such gains in academic achievement and social involvement" (letter available at: www.ed.gov/policy/elsec/guid/secletter/040701.html).

**Whole School Reform.** The arts are now leading contenders among interventions to differentiate instruction for diverse student needs. The value of AI is supported by a growing number of studies (Burnaford, 2007; Deasy & Stevenson, 2005; Ruppert, 2006). Students who are involved in the arts enjoy the benefits of increased motivation, problem-solving skills, creative capacities, plus broader multicultural understanding—which account for higher test scores. In addition, school attendance increases. For example, after the arts were integrated at Guggenheim Elementary in Chicago, attendance rose to 94 percent; 83 percent of students are now at or above national

norms in reading and math. Being in school is of significant value. The annual cost of truancy to the nation is $228 billion, with 85 percent of daytime crime committed by truant youth. In addition, there is the cost to train unskilled youth who drop out—about $30 billion annually (Boston, 1996). Research Update 1.3 gives examples of how the arts contribute to preparing children for school, retention in school, and safe supportive learning environments.

The positive effects of AI extend beyond students, as faculties report being revitalized by it. In particular they report more teacher collaboration and transformation of instructional practice. Communities also become more involved and supportive (Deasy, 2002; Deasy & Stevenson, 2005; Fiske, 1999; Jack, 2005).

**What Matters Most?** At a recent AI workshop, teachers brainstormed characteristics of an "ideal student." Although not a scientific study, this was an informative exercise. They readily listed traits such as alert, engaged, open, cooperative, thinking, respectful, polite, responsible, disciplined, self-motivated, positive, hardworking, curious, confident, energetic, independent, problem solver, and persistent. It took about 5 minutes to completely fill a piece of chart paper. There was not one mention of test scores or grades.

The ensuing discussion showed that teachers simply expect good grades to result from "ideal" cognitive, social, and personal behaviors and dispositions. To paraphrase Einstein, everything that *counts* isn't countable and what we can count may not count. What does count? Many well-rounded successful people were not straight-A students. Author Thomas Friedman contends that CQ + PQ > IQ, or curiosity plus passion is greater than the intelligence quotient when it comes to life success. Friedman asks, "What does it tell you when two of our greatest innovators (Steve Jobs and Bill Gates) are both college dropouts?" What matters most in a broader view of success? Ferrero (2005) reminds us "schooling is always and inevitably about cultivating persons" (p. 26).

According to Dick Allington (2005), past president of International Reading Association, our fund of professional wisdom (teaching experience) is a valid source in designing curricula and instruction that can produce both high scores and other more important results. In the Chattanooga workshop, we estimated 800 years' teaching experience. The next step was to examine if and how AI might contribute to developing ideal student attributes. This book documents many discoveries that were found.

**More than Test Scores.**  In the past decade many educators have made a strong commitment to school restructuring, site-based decision making, and standards-based reform. They have worked to make curricular decisions that acknowledge that American education goals have "never been simply to raise test scores" (Deasy & Stevenson, p. xiv). Teachers and administrators who choose AI reform believe the future favors students who will routinely apply creative problem solving, which activates higher order thinking and assumes flexible perspectives. They understand that motivating students to do excellent work is a high priority and that arts-based learning is perceived by students to be more meaningful and relevant. They see the importance of students learning to take prudent risks and to experiment with alternative ways to show understanding. Educators involved in diverse AI projects observe how students persist when confronted with obstacles when they learn in an aesthetic environment. Students develop resilience that will serve them well in life. AI educators realize "we cannot teach participatory democracy in authoritarian classroom" nor can we develop "deep thinking in classrooms drenched in routine and cynicism" (Grumet, 2004, p. 64).

Real hope lies in "re-visioning" learning and teaching. Hope is bolstered by a belief in the innate potential of all students to make sense, including creating meaning from the diverse print, digital, and multimedia texts that typify 21st-century living. Incidentally, these texts themselves are often arts based, ranging from the iPod with its visual images and stunning capacity to interact with websites that feature music from every genre and by any artist.

**Back to the Future.**  There actually is a longstanding relationship between education and the arts grounded in beliefs that the arts make unique contributions to our lives. Efforts to put the two together for the sake of learning date back to the 16th century. Johann Comenius argued that school life should change from being like a prison to a *scholae ludus* (play site), where "curiosity is aroused and satisfied." He urged teachers to reduce rote learning and "engage the child's interest through music and games and through handling objects, through posing problems (project learning) and stirring imagination by dramatic accounts of the big world." The mixing of the arts and traditional academic disciplines may seem like a surprising strategy to address 21st-century challenges but, as previously discussed, the third

millennium demands exactly the kind of creative problem-solving skills the arts nurture.

Bringing the capacity and expertise of the arts community to bear on academic achievement problems has created educational partnership possibilities that are just beginning to be tapped. Promising examples of narrowing achievement gaps through the arts have emerged in schools from Cleveland to Los Angeles. Now numbering well over a thousand, these "arts-based" schools are popping up in every state and in Canada, Australia, Finland, and the United Kingdom.

AI offers an innovative way to address the needs of the whole child and differentiate instruction to meet the needs of a student population increasing in diversity. At AI schools, Comenius's ideas are made into reality, and then some. Teachers collaborate with artists to plan inquiry-based lessons in which the arts are central to literacy, math, science, and social studies lessons. Comenius's great ideas have been rediscovered, reworked, and now boast a research base that goes much beyond the narrow gauge of standardized tests. AI is part of a broad-based revival of interest in whole child learning, translating into long-term differences in children's personal, emotional, and cognitive growth (Ruppert, 2006).

## The Arts as Meaning Makers

Americans are beginning to realize "the breadth and depth of the contribution the arts can make, both to education reform and to the quality of the workforce" (Boston, 1996, p. 3; Deasy, 2008; Rose & Gallup, 2005). The arts are proving to be powerful instructional tools essential to close achievement gaps and meet the goals of standards-based educational reform (e.g., see Burnaford, April, & Weiss, 2001. Key is how arts-based approaches raise the learning bar by creating a culture of excellence that expects more than high grades. This kind of excellence has long been associated with the arts as is evidenced in our world arts treasury—a resource that stands ready to reignite in students the imagination and passion inherent in its creators. An understanding of how the arts can become "the sense and soul" of the curriculum grows from a careful look at how the arts are remarkable communication tools used to create meaning.

## The Fundamental Nature of the Arts

*Ars Longa, Vita Brevis.* (Art is long. Life is short.)

The arts are time-honored ways of communicating that predate both literacy and numeracy. From their earliest beginnings our human ancestors seemed compelled to make art. Theologian Karen Armstrong (2004, p. xix) even traces the source of art and religion to identical human needs. She makes the case that both appeared at the same time as people tried to make sense of their existence. Stunning cave paintings in southern France and Spain depict stories of hunts and handprints and date back more than 30,000 years (Chauvet, Deschamps, & Hilliare, 1996). A continent away, Alaskan petroglyphs with similar images are estimated to be as much as 12,000 years old. The world's oldest musical instrument was recently found in a cavern near Ulm, Germany; the

35,000-year-old ice age flute was carved from a bird wing bone (Hotz, 2009). Paintings and ancient drums were not just decorations in the lives of early people, although there was also art for that purpose: 100,000-year-old bling bling has been unearthed from deep inside the Skhul Cave on Mount Carmel in Israel.

These works of art were the latest technology of the time used to record what people saw and felt. They were vital forms of communication that connected humans through "space and time to other minds" (Hotz, 2009, p. A9). It would not be until thousands of years later that the first writing system would not be invented: cuneiform (circa 3,000 BC).

Words used by early humans displayed practical roots, but like painting and drumming, verbal language also evolved into art forms. Storytelling emerged and timeless folktales survive to proclaim the power of early word art. Every culture still uses stories to pass on core beliefs and values about persistent human concerns. Stories also show commonalities among people, regardless of ethnicity. For example, themes about hopes for "fairy tale endings" transcend cultural differences and time periods, as demonstrated by the more than 300 versions of the Cinderella story. Interest in this one particular story form persists into the 21st century with new versions every year, including *Adelita* (dePaola, 2002), a Mexican version called *Chickerella* (Auch & Auch, 2005), and even a jazz age version, *Ella's Big Chance* (Hughes, 2004). Early verbal arts also record curious customs and troublesome rituals. For example, the Mother Goose rhyme "Eeny meeny miny mo" has been traced to an epoch when human sacrifices were "counted out."

**Meaning Making.** Why are humans driven to use the arts to explain themselves, answer questions, and console one another? Why is it common for art to emerge from those involved in traumas such as the twin Trade Tower bombings and Hurricane Katrina? It seems to be about the human drive to make sense of the incomprehensible. Reflected in Mozart's symphony, written at age 16, is his struggle to come of age (Lockwood, 2005); and in Picasso's *Guernica* is found deep thoughts about the desperation and horrors of war. Jazz pieces, plays, paintings, collages, songs, sculpture, and dances act as means of releasing painful thoughts and feelings. Indeed, the arts are able to bring us together in a "third space" of new understanding (Deasy & Stevenson, 2005).

Of course, a full and definitive explanation of art is impossible. In fact, trying to use words to explain communication that exists because words are inadequate is a conundrum. It is possible, however, to consider unique aspects of the arts and their special contributions that give spark and substance to life and learning. Foremost in a long list of special contributions of literature, music, art, drama, and dance is their unique potential to allow us to make sense of ourselves and the world. The arts open vital communication channels in unmatched ways.

Consider, for example, how meaning is altered when the art form of poetry is used instead of ordinary prose to convey a message. For example, I recently read on a Hilton Head Island restaurant menu, "Our feature is blackened swordfish with grilled vegetables." This simple informational prose offers customers important facts. The writer probably spent very little time selecting each word for its emotional impact, although it did make me salivate. For contrast, read aloud this short poem with an aabb rhyme scheme.

> Mahi mahi, swordfish steak
>
> Shrimp scampi, crab cakes
>
> Blackened broiled, potato-breaded
>
> I love fish, except with heads-on.

This poem gives information, but now poetic devices such as rhyme, rhythm, and assonance (repetition of vowel sounds) direct attention to the sound as well as the message. The poem is meant to be *heard*, not just read silently. A first reading might bring the urge to read it again—just for the sound of it. The poet wrote with an ear to musical elements of language as well as to the sense she wanted to share. Language choices are creative, and a new perspective is offered on the topic of seafood. We feel something about the words—delight, perhaps, at the poet's inventiveness. In sum, poetry uses words, as does prose, but it is different in the kind and degree of intended *emotional and sensory impact*. This is one significant piece of the "what is art" puzzle that has attracted the attention of educators.

Like poetry, visual art is made to communicate ideas and feelings, but the communication transcends words. Visual images, left open to interpretation, cause fine art, and even decorative art, to engage us cognitively and emotionally and may even stimulate a physical response. Visualize Leonardo da Vinci's *Mona Lisa* and, for contrast, the red and white label of a Campbell's soup can. Both pieces were made using the art elements of color, shape, size, and texture and composition principles such as unity and balance. An artist for Campbell's Soup Company undoubtedly worked hard to create a design that would catch attention and raise associations with "m-m-m good" feelings. Red is a warm color, set off with white, and is faintly patriotic. The touch of gold adds a classy feel.

Now imagine Andy Warhol's *paintings* of soup cans. Warhol's art and da Vinci's paintings are both classified as fine art. They provoke a different kind and degree of cognitive and affective involvement than advertisement or decorative art. The intensity of engagement derives from art's power to cause us to question, and wonder. Of course, the potential of art to arouse curiosity and trigger interest is not lost on educators bent on harnessing these forces in the name of learning.

Some complain that fine art is hard to understand, but artists may intentionally disconcert to create cognitive dissonance that elicits an emotional reaction. One artistic goal is to jar viewers or listeners out of complacency—to change perspective. Art can awe us with its beauty and it can also gag us with disgust. I'm thinking here about an art exhibit in Cincinnati, in which a cross was suspended in a jar of urine and the "dung" art made during the late 1990s.

It is likely that da Vinci intended to leave us with more questions than answers about Mona Lisa. Like all good art, this work engages us in questions that support meaning making: "Why is she smiling?" "Who is she?" "Why did he use those colors?" "How did he get that expression on her face?" "How did he do that?" Dan Brown's *The Da Vinci Code* has even further heightened interest in possible meanings of da Vinci's art. People look and look, moving closer and closer to discern its essence. The Louvre long ago had to protect the Mona Lisa with a glass box.

# Unique Contributions of the Arts: Processes and Content

Sir Ken Robinson, an internationally known expert on creativity, points out, "If the human mind was restricted to academic intelligence, most of human culture would not have happened" (2000, p. 5). Imagine a world without stories, music, theatre, paintings, architecture, or dance. Robinson suggests these fruits of our creative nature "are rather large factors to leave out of a model of human intelligence" (p. 5).

My husband just finished our taxes. He is not an accountant, but he doesn't need to be. Software does the math. We can also download forms for making a will or contract blanks to sell our own houses. It's no longer just about the disappearance of factory jobs. Daniel Pink, author of *A Whole New Mind: Why*

*Right Brainers Will Rule the Future* (2006) explains that any job is vulnerable, if it can be replaced by a computer. How do we prepare students for a future where many "good" jobs no longer exist? Certainly not by making our students into "armies of test takers" who are little more than "vending machines for the correct answers" (Taboh, 2009). Pink joins millions who realize personal and professional success is more about having empathy, taking risks, and doing innovative thinking than high test scores. He points out, "[T]he idea that you can succeed as an engineer today by simply being good at math problems is wrong" (2006). Creative thinking made America, and there is no better way to engage creative thinking than through artistic approaches to problem solving. AI puts creative problem solving at the core of education.

The American public now overwhelmingly believes the arts are vital to a well-rounded education (Deasy, 2008; Ruppert, 2006). Chapter 2 goes into more detail about research that connects arts-based education to traditional measures of achievement. In this section the focus is on contributions the arts make that go beyond what standardized test scores can reveal. Ready Reference 1.4 summarizes these special contributions. The following discussion elaborates on why the arts are considered the "fourth R."

---

**Ready Reference 1.4** Fourteen Unique Contributions of the Arts

1. **Communication.** Literacy includes language and arts-based communication used to understand, respond to, and express thoughts and feelings. In particular, the arts are unparalleled symbolic languages that exist because all thoughts cannot be captured with words. Arts communication is integral to the cognitive, social, and personal effects of the arts.

2. **Content of the arts.** The arts are not just a process. A vast worldwide arts treasury stands ready to change hearts and minds.

**INTELLECTUAL CONTRIBUTIONS.**
It takes high level thinking to understand and create through the arts.

3. **Creative problem solving (CPS)** is the process used to construct meaning and is at the core of the arts. CPS is used to seek connections and synthesize diverse solutions.

4. **Critical thinking** is a part of CPS. It is a focus of the arts where quality is highly valued. In particular, critique is used to analyze details and patterns, compile evidence, and apply criteria to make judgments.

5. **Comprehension** is understanding. Across disciplines comprehension is the result of actively finding and creating big ideas using problem-solving processes including data gathering, imaging, taking divergent perspectives, and synthesizing original connections. The arts also provide diverse texts from which comprehension can be derived.

6. **Composition** is the process of expressing meaning. The arts contribute special principles, techniques, and materials to the composition process. The arts offer a range of composition forms as options to express thoughts and feelings.

**SOCIAL CONTRIBUTIONS.**
Meaning is altered by social circumstances.

7. **Culture.** The arts uniquely record ways people have lived throughout history. They also provide rich contexts for growth, including positive classroom climates.

8. **Cooperation/collaboration.** The arts involve students in group problem solving (e.g., ensembles, choirs, troupes, skits).

9. **Community.** The arts create a sense of belonging based on respect for the distinctive contributions of each person.

10. **Compassion.** The arts build empathy by providing experiences that create new perspectives.

**PERSONAL/EMOTIONAL CONTRIBUTIONS.**
The arts engage the emotions and reflect personal values.

11. **Commitment/interest.** The arts develop intrinsic motivation because they are inherently engaging. Persistence, based on curiosity and choice, gives satisfaction, and people feel the rewards of commitment.

12. **Concentration.** The arts capture attention and develop concentration because they are emotionally compelling.

13. **Confidence.** The arts develop the courage to take risks and develop pride in one's unique contributions to solving problems.

14. **Competence/control.** The arts develop skills to work with tools and materials and develop control over mind, voice, and body. They build special strategies to plan, think, work, and produce. Artists feel free to break rules after they have mastered them.

# Communication

Ernest Boyer, former U.S commissioner of education, explains, "The arts are, above all, the special language of children, who, even before they learn to speak, respond intuitively to dance, music, and color" (1993). The arts speak to us directly in old languages that transcend words, so we say things like "a picture is worth a thousand words."

The arts are widely acknowledged as unmatched communication vehicles, without which, many ideas and feelings remain trapped. Through the arts we are given special tools to look inward to understand ourselves and outward to understand others. As Eisner (2000) explains, the limits of language do not determine the limits of our thinking. Thoughts cannot be reduced to words. An overarching justification for AI is to extend communication possibilities by no longer sequestering the arts in special classes.

Arts integration balances the current literacy curriculum that gives inordinate weight to reading and writing word-based texts. Curricula is realigned with a model of communication that reflects 21st-century life (e.g., digital and media literacy). Literacy is redefined to include *all* means people use to understand, respond to, and express thoughts and feelings.

Communication through the arts is interrelated with the cognitive, social, and personal/emotional effects of the arts. Arts contributions in these areas further justify the integration of the arts into daily learning and are discussed subsequently.

# Content of the Arts

The arts are not only processes, but also content. A vast worldwide treasury of art products is readily available for classroom use through virtual tours of museums like the Louvre. There is now a website on nearly every artist, art form, art style, and art period and every genre of music from any conceivable culture can be downloaded (e.g., www.songs-of-the-century.com). The work of local poets, playwrights, composers, and artists are other important "texts" that can serve as key learning tools.

Artworks including prints, cultural artifacts, songs, music, and poetry are key ways to introduce and develop lessons and units in AI classes. These engaging art forms invite students to form new perspectives on the myriad topics about which art is made. In addition, texts can be studied as models of skill and technique by asking questions, such as "How do you think the artist created that mood?" Thus, students learn to work backwards from a finished product to understand the kinds of thinking, skills, and values it represents.

# Intellectual Capacities

Of course the arts are deeply cognitive. No art is created or understood without higher level thinking informed by careful observation, pattern finding, taking new perspectives, making qualitative judgments, visualizing and use of metaphors and symbols. Artists use such thinking to transform and represent what is noticed and imagined, just as similar inquiry-based thinking is central to work in the fields of science, math, and history (Eisner, 2005).

The arts compel us to consider diverse views with artists, actors, musicians, and poets. Their provocative nature charges us to respond by using higher order thinking to make sense. It can happen with a song like John Lennon's "Imagine" or a dance performance such as "River Dance." We listen or sing along and feel our pulse entrain to the tempo. We do indeed begin to imagine different worlds in which we are Celtic dancers or where worldwide peace is possible. Similarly, powerful films like *Hotel Rwanda* alter perspective by stimulating empathy for innocent victims of ignorance.

Students who use paint or a slab of marble to communicate and solve problems are, according to Howard Gardner (1993), using intelligences central to life. The arts link cognition to emotion in a myriad of aspects of our lives ranging from advertising jingles to comic strips. As students learn to think through the arts they discover new capacities and experience pride that motivates them to be more diligent. Center stage in cognitive contributions of the arts are four processes: creative problem solving, critical thinking, comprehension, and composition.

**Creative Problem Solving (CPS).** The set of higher order thinking skills that make up CPS is at the heart of how artists think and work. CPS is also parallel with how expert readers comprehend and how writers compose. Indeed, CPS summarizes how intelligent people problem solve in all fields. For example, science is all about solving problems by using evidence and creative insight (Subramaniam, 2006).

The CPS process is how meaning is constructed. It is grounded in seeking and synthesizing diverse problem solutions, purposefully capitalizing on mistakes, making paradoxical connections, and embracing surprises. The novel, different, and abnormal are valued. Key processes include data gathering (e.g., brainstorming, observation, and research), experimenting, incubating ideas, and connecting and transforming ideas. Synthesis produces new compositions that are critiqued and tweaked before a final solution is accepted. CPS is discussed in detail in Chapter 2.

Business leaders consider creative problem solving to be one of the most important skill sets for the 21st century. Why? CPS produced plasma television, hybrid cars, the iPod Nano, and humble Velcro. CPS is also central to achieving the main goal of literacy: to create personal meaning, depth of comprehension, and effective expression of thoughts and emotions.

**Critical Thinking.** A particular focus of the arts is doing quality work. Critical thinking occurs during CPS and takes a heightened focus on thoughtful and skilled use of ideas, techniques, and materials. For example, arts critique entails closely analyzing details and patterns, compiling evidence, and using evaluation criteria to make judgments (Soep, 2005).

Students need to learn to use critical thinking to judge their own work and that of others. In doing so they learn that opinions matter but need to be supported with evidence. Even young children can be prompted to discover details in paintings, interpret messages in music, and draw conclusions supported by "text" evidence.

Critical thinking is hard work, but students will persist at the hard brainwork if it is self-rewarding—arts-based work is that (DeMoss & Morris, 2002). Students become enamored of details and patterns that occur in interesting contexts and provide clues to meaning making, just as artists like Claude Monet got hooked on haystacks. Monet persisted because he was intrigued by questions about the effects of light, realizing that details matter and "the subtle is significant" (Elliot Eisner). In a parallel manner writers also dwell on "few seminal issues" and do intellectual tinkering, but use the written word (Lucy Calkins). Our children are blessed with so many things, they can easily miss the lesson that small things can make large differences. The arts help refocus on the potential of a single word, a small sound, or a slight gesture to speak volumes—as Mr. Spock's raised eyebrow demonstrates.

**Comprehension.** Comprehension has long been considered the sine qua non of reading (Beck & McKeown, 2002). A 21st-century view of comprehension places emphasis on deep understanding, not on the number of books read or words written. Comprehension is not about memorizing facts and being literal. Across disciplines understanding must be actively created. Students must learn to seek to make sense and have the creative problem-solving skills to do so. The comprehension product is big ideas that are found and constructed from texts ranging from a song to a painting to a social studies textbook (Cornett, 2010). The arts stress such personal meaning making with special attention to visualizing, taking new perspectives, and making original connections among ideas.

The National Reading Panel report, used to draft the No Child Left Behind Act, singled out comprehension as a top priority and reiterated the importance of giving teaching priority to deep understanding. Unfortunately, this message sometimes got lost in the frenzy over standards and testing. When instructional time has been weighted in the direction of phonological and phonemic awareness, phonics, and vocabulary to the neglect of comprehension, students suffer (Whitehurst, 2008). Early positive effects of dwelling on lower level pieces of reading eventually fade; by fourth grade many students slip into a decline. Without being taught a full set of problem-solving tools to create meaning, many students don't develop comprehension capabilities (Kamil, 2004; Williams, 2002). They remain at the bottom in the race to the top.

Calls for "comprehension first" now come from literacy experts (Cambourne, 2009; Cornett, 2010). Important is using explicit instruction to teach how to use CPS to create artworks and interpret arts "texts," that is, to do coordinated thinking to make sense. Young children can be engaged in using CPS with songs and visual art long before they have the decoding fluency to do so with word-based texts. Teacher questions such as "What do you see? How does it make you feel? What is this about?" invite use of higher order processes that result in comprehension.

**Composition.** This is the process of *expressing* meaning using both word-based and arts forms, including multimedia such as PowerPoint. The composition process begins with seeking solutions to problems. Whereas the main problem for a reader is to make sense or comprehend printed text, which starts with *receiving* thoughts and feelings from texts, composition is the reverse. Writers construct meaning, which they express in texts that show their thoughts and feelings. The same kinds of thinking used to comprehend word-based print text or to create written compositions are used to understand and create arts-based compositions; however, the arts add unique principles, techniques, and materials that extend possibilities for compositions, including technology-based ones that rely on the arts to produce texts such as the stunning videos on YouTube.

Students who grow up creating, responding, and performing in the arts have a history of using the higher order thinking embodied in CPS. In fact, arts such as pantomime, dancing, and drawing are often are the only ways young children can express feelings and ideas; higher order cognitive work in the arts is possible long before students have the skills to do such thinking using printed word-based texts (Cunningham & Shagoury, 2005).

Teachers can use students' arts backgrounds as foundations for teaching reading comprehension and written composition. As an example, at a Connecticut elementary school, students are taught how to combine the complementary composition processes of visual art with the writing process. Students keep sketch journals and make drawings to plan writing. Olhansky's (2008) research on involving students in art making to increase writing performance confirms how painting and making collage compositions give students a writing advantage.

## Social Capacities

People are group animals. Meaning is made and altered by social circumstances and a measure of a satisfying life rests on relationships with other people. The arts make significant contributions to our social development as individuals and group relationships.

**Culture.** Eisner (2002a) explains how the two meanings of culture relate to arts-based education. First, culture has to do with shared ways of living. The arts are culture vaults that house records of ways humans have lived throughout history. Pots, paintings, and plays show what we value, what we worry about, and what is important to us. The arts are a kind of museum of collective memories (Paige & Huckabee, 2005). Second, a culture is a rich medium for growing things. The arts provide stimulating contexts for growth when they are used to alter school and classroom ecologies. The arts are a medium for growing children's brains.

Demographic projections predict that minorities, with distinct cultures, will become the majority in the United States in 40 years. Currently, some 400 languages are now spoken in schools nationwide. To live in harmony in such diversity requires appreciation of the contributions each culture can make. One source for such understanding is the arts. The arts are naturally interdisciplinary and provide a neutral ground to experience varied languages, content, values, and beliefs. The arts help us better understand the joys and sorrows of others. For example, musical theatre, like *Les Miserables,* has engaged millions in vicarious suffering caused by poverty and loss.

AI advocates see the arts as windows that allow us to view culture and history from the different perspectives of diverse peoples. The arts mirror individual and group values and are indeed remarkable ways people construct and express thoughts and feelings.

**Cooperation/Collaboration.** Collaborative work is integral to 21st-century living and working where "understanding is rarely, if ever, a solo enterprise" (Balick, 1999, p. 153). The arts build cooperation by involving students in collaborative problem solving in the contexts of ensembles, choirs, troupes, and skits. Through arts experiences, they learn to work as a team, to respect diverse points of view, and to see that relationships among people and ideas matter.

**Community.**   An artful view of learning sets in motion a cascade of physical and psychological changes. In Jayne Ellicott's words, "Arts integration makes school a happier place." The arts create a sense of belonging based on delight and respect for each person's distinctive contributions. Experiences as audience members and as performers connect students in reciprocal relationships. As concertgoers and museum visitors they are bound together in listening and viewing experiences that create shared background. They experience the dependent relationship of arts consumers and producers that builds a sense of community on which the arts make an indelible mark.

**Compassion.**   Compassion means to be in passion with another. The arts develop concern for, sensitivity to, and "response ability." The arts intentionally invite empathy by their emphasis on and respect for the unusual, different, and extraordinary. Empathy is created through experiences that cause students to grasp another's understanding. Like respect, empathy comes from acknowledging the circumstances of another person and leads to compassion when a person fully imagines oneself in those circumstances. Such deep understanding allows students to experience the power of arts materials and processes to allow them to communicate ideas that have previously eluded expression.

## Personal/Emotional Capacities

*Emotion drives attention, and attention drives learning.* (Robert Sylwester)

No longer can educators divorce emotion from cognition. Brain and psychological research confirms what experience has long told us: Students are whole beings. Full brain and body engagement is a key to academic success. Engagement is more than entertainment, however. Engagement seeks understanding, not fleeting amusement. Thinking, feeling, and using somatic perception (body) are the vehicles for engagement.

Arts integration, unlike conventional schooling models, does not compartmentalize the intellectual and emotional aspects of being human. The arts are tapped for their unique capacity to integrate the personal and emotional into any learning. In particular, the arts turn on emotional areas of the brain to uplift spirits and give hope in the form of a good laugh, a beautiful song, or a satisfying painting. Enthusiasm for learning is sparked when students experience the joys of playing with ideas and the pride of creative discovery. Research Update 1.5 summarizes research that gives new meaning to the idea that fun is fundamental to learning.

**Commitment/Interest.**   The arts engage people in uncommon ways. It isn't unusual to hear an artist admit to being "addicted" to making art or music or dance. The arts are inherently interesting as evidenced by artists who work with intense involvement, joy, and delight—as surprising results emerge. Artists report they rarely feel their work is finished, which causes them to return to the same themes and topics over and over. Artists persist because they are curious and interested and see alternative possibilities.

Arts integration gives students opportunities to experience all these dimensions of intrinsic motivation experienced by artists plus a sense of satisfaction that comes from a commitment to complete what they begin, and the feeling of a job well done. Students also feel ownership of artwork in ways that never happen with textbooks, worksheets, or computer work. For example, a special educator recently described a textile art project she taught during a family folklore unit. Her 11 students gathered fabric from family members and eventually created a quilt to honor important events and people. The products were so striking that the teacher offered to buy them. The students were from poor families, and she thought her offer would both help them out and could be used to create a permanent school display. The students, however, would not give up their art. One irate grandmother came to school to protest. Tearfully she objected to her granddaughter selling something so beautiful and personal.

Just as sports encourage some students to stay in school, the arts can cause students to commit to learn. A sculpture project in social studies or learning to play the recorder in music class can become central reasons for students to come to school. Great

---

**Research Update *1.5*   AI for the FUN of It: From Entertainment to Engagement**

Students in grades 1 through 8 were studied to parse out what they meant by "fun." Probes of learning experiences were conducted before and after non-arts and arts-based units.

Arts-Based Lessons *Versus* Traditional Lessons: Students . . .

- saw learning as more fun *versus* boring.
- equated fun with working in groups to solve problems that often resulted in a performance or exhibit *versus* not fun to work alone or in competition with peers.

- thought many arts tasks were hard, but perceived hard as something they could deal with *versus* believing tasks were hard because of the teacher or materials or blaming themselves.
- pursued learning outside of school: 42 percent in the arts based *versus* 27 percent in traditional.
- thought the goal of learning was to understand; to figure things out *versus* take tests and complete worksheets.

*Source:* DeMoss & Morris (2002).

teachers from children's literature come to mind: Jesse's music teacher, Miss Edmunds, in *Bridge to Terabithia* (Paterson, 1979), who helped him find beauty in his dismal life; and Mr. Isobe, in *Crow Boy* (Yashima, 1965), who tacked up an outcast child's art and changed Chibi's life with a stage performance.

**Concentration/Attention.**    The arts are compelling. They capture attention and sustain concentration because they provoke interest. There is a print literacy connection here. Unlike the details in a work of art or the nuances of sounds in a musical piece, letters can seem unattractive. Letters can seem to be mindless details until they are set within words that are set within phrases and sentences that make up paragraphs and eventually full texts. Unfortunately, many children lack the persistence to wade through years of skill drill, never knowing the intrinsic rewards that await them if they achieve print fluency. The arts can give such children hope. In the arts, details are not presented out of context, but within a song, dance, or painting. Details have meaning and can be discovered and enjoyed with minimal background since we are born with the capacity to communicate through the arts. Reading and writing, on the other hand, are accrued skills.

Children who learn to "read" art then experience the good feeling that comes from creating their own story about a picture. The arts make learning concrete, especially for young and struggling learners and motivate them to attend and concentrate. This bears fruit when students experience the inherent joys of creating meaning. With artful teaching, these positive associations can be transferred to cause students to concentrate on print, which is just another symbol system.

**Confidence/Courage.**    Tom Stang, a teacher in an arts-based program for troubled youth in Phoenix, believes "the arts are the soul of the education program" (Larson, 1997, p. 94). It isn't unusual for problem students to become the high achievers when learning is arts based. Success in the arts can be a bridge to other areas of learning. For example, in case studies of disadvantaged students in New York City involved in ArtsConnection, these students used more self-regulatory behaviors and had a sense of identity that made them more confident and resilient (Oreck, Baum, & McCartney, 1999). One elementary student explained, "It's like I became addicted to dance" (p. 70).

The arts develop the confidence and courage to take risks and experiment. Pride in one's unique contributions develops as teachers and peers positively respond to efforts. The arts create confidence in one's ability to do original problem solving. Confidence increases willingness to take more risks and be more flexible.

**Competence/Control.**    The arts develop self-control and skill with special tools and materials and reinforce special strategies to plan, think, work, and produce. Anyone who ever learned to play an instrument knows that thousands of hours of practice are necessary to become good. Adults who recall forced lessons by parents are often thankful. Self-chosen practice and rehearsal is motivated by the desire to produce quality work. One college student's journal entry speaks for so many: "At first I just wanted to make my parents proud and I loved the applause at recitals. Eventually I found out I could get so much out of just playing—for

myself. I could relax, escape, and really just change from a negative mood to a positive frame of mind by sitting down and playing for an hour or so. Other kids got high or zoned out with drugs or booze. I guess I just got high on music!"

It is simplistic to advise students to "just say no." Students have to be shown healthy ways to feel good—alternatives to sticking a destructive substance up their noses, down their throats, or in their veins. The arts provide these alternatives, giving students control over minds, bodies, and emotions.

# What Is Integration?

> . . . *more than ever, the ability to integrate art, science, music and literature with the hard sciences is what produces movements like the iPod revolution or Google. This means educators need to go beyond the "frog-march" of kids from math to science to English . . . education should focus on "mashing" subjects together, something kids do naturally. He who mashes best will mash most and be wealthiest.* (Thomas Friedman)

Integration is not a 21st-century notion. Earlier in this chapter I mentioned that Comenius was making integrated proposals in the 1500s. Hundreds of years later in the United States, the "Committee of Ten" (1892) recommended "one hour per week be given over to nature study? . . . and that all work be conducted without the aid of a textbook. In addition, every attempt should be made to correlate the science observations with work in language, drawing, and literature." In 1935, the National Council of Teachers of English defined *integration* as the unification of all subjects and experiences. Today most professional associations support integration designs. Examples include:

National Council for the Teachers of English (NCTE) and the International Reading Association (IRA) standards focus on the need for students to "participate as knowledgeable, reflective, creative, and critical members of a variety of literacy communities" ( www.ncte.org).

National Science Teachers Associations (NSTA) Standard B directs educators to emphasize understanding through inquiry and make connections among science and other curricular areas (www.nsta.org).

National Council for the Teaching of Mathematics (NCTM) Standard 4 addresses the need to make connections among math and other curricular areas (www.nctm.org).

National Council for the Social Studies (NCSS) standards include a culture and cultural diversity strand that recommends study that integrates "language, stories, folktales, music and artistic creations" (www.social_studies.org).

## Definition

Integration is derived from the Latin word *integrare,* which means "to make whole" (Grumet, 2004). Throughout its history the concept of integration has operated under many labels: interdisciplinary instruction, unit teaching, the project approach, inquiry method, and whole language. By any name it is combining diverse elements into harmonious wholes with a synergistic result. Synergisms are valued because, while individual elements maintain their integrity, the "sum is more than all the parts." What is a buckle without its belt or a sleeve without a shirt? The part is not usable, nor understandable, without the whole. In art terms, it is putting figures against a background or giving particulars a context. In life terms, integration is how we live.

## The Case for Integration

A practical argument for integration is that there is just too much to know. It is impossible to teach it all. The Harvard University's library acquired more volumes in the last 5 years than in the previous 100 years, and the Internet testifies to the immense store of information on millions of websites. Instead of continuing to cram in and cover more, AI connects big ideas found and created through inquiry directed by important questions. Isolated facts and outdated information are dropped from the curriculum as priorities are reset and time allocated to what is most important in our profoundly integrated world.

Curriculum 2.0 acknowledges that success in the real world demands integration. From small personal problems to problem solving in the workplace, subject area delineations are disregarded as we draw upon all background knowledge and apply diverse thinking skills to solve problems. Of particular value is the use of knowledge in new ways or for different purposes such as melting shower curtains together to create the now ubiquitous bubble wrap.

Integrated instruction creates an economy of time and materials. More is achieved with whatever is at hand. Time is blocked for science and social studies units to which literacy instruction is linked. Informational science and social studies texts are used to teach reading as readily as narrative fiction. Teachers and arts specialists collaboratively plan integrated units, which involves ferreting out goals and standards that are redundant. They create ways to combine instruction in meaningful ways.

Making school more life like is key to motivating students to learn, and a school day organized around isolated skill teaching and fragmented into subjects is poorly matched with life. Integration is about using information and meaning-making skills to solve important and interesting problems, which adds purpose and relevancy to learning. AI brings a creative problem-solving orientation to bear on the entire curriculum by causing students to seek diverse connections and build new relationships among ideas. It's not surprising that a meta-analysis of 30 studies showed students in integrated programs consistently outperformed those in traditional classrooms on national and state tests (Hartzler, 2000). Traditionally segmented areas of the curriculum are connected and problem solving is used to tap a unified knowledge base for creative purposes. The result is an educational approach that is more consistent with 21st-century living and working conditions that demand multitasking and group problem solving to create innovative solutions.

**Holistic Learning.** Gestalt psychologists explain that humans are predisposed to bring pieces and parts together into comprehensible wholes. The integration process results in a sense of completeness because disconnected ideas are meaningfully linked.

Integrated units are developed around significant life questions and major themes—important "truths" that pull together disparate facts. Meaningful connections are sought, not superficial ones like counting beans in *Jack and the Beanstalk* and calling that integration of math and literature.

Of course, students of any age and stage need to attend to parts, details, and facts as they study subjects and learn skills. In reading, students need to notice the differences among similar letters like *b* and *d*. A key to student motivation, however, is for them to see purpose. Isolated concepts and skills are hard to perceive as worthy. Letters are pretty meaningless until they are ordered in patterns to make whole words. Words have minimal meaning until they are placed or integrated into the context of a phrase, sentence, paragraph, or story. What does *run* mean? Is it a verb, as in "to run away," or is it a noun, as in "a run in my hose"? I could have a "run of bad luck" or "run into" another car or have a "dog run" in my backyard. Meaning changes based on context.

**Wholes and Parts.** Even adults who are novices at a task tend to proceed from whole to part, from the gross to the particular, dwelling first on the most obvious, such as large shapes and intuited feelings. Anyone who has first used computer-drawing tools has experienced the compulsion to play around with the mouse. Psychologist Daniel Goleman (1995) explains the evolutionary significance of reacting first to the holistic experience and then to details by describing a jogger who spies a long slender dark curved something coming along his path. "Snake!" screams the ancient emotional impulse and the jogger stops dead in his tracks. Saved from a poisonous bite by primitive instincts, she now uses newer (in evolutionary time) powers of logic to see the details of the something. This time it's just a stick. Think of the consequences if we routinely stopped to analyze the pieces before responding to the whole.

The arts play an important role in integrating wholes and parts. Literature, visual art, drama, dance, and music can interact with science, social studies, math, and literacy to multiply learning about life skills, key concepts, themes, and big ideas. Traditional lines between curricular areas become muddied. "Is it art or science as a child mixes colors and discovers that blue and yellow make green? The child notices curves and angles in letters and then makes them with his or her own body or draws them in the air; is this language arts or dance?" (Stinson, 1988, p. 95).

Authentic learning does not happen when artificial boundaries are used that do not reflect life. Professional organizations like the National Middle School Association (NMSA) agree. Their "Position Statement on Curriculum, Instruction, and Assessment" describes quality curriculum as relevant, challenging, integrative, and exploratory. According to the NMSA website, an excellent curriculum focuses on "coherent ideas and concepts irrespective of arbitrary subject boundaries" and enables students to "see connections and real-world applications." Integrative teaching can and should do the following:

- Engage students in rigorous, in-depth study.
- Address reading, writing, and other fundamental skills within all subject areas.
- Enhance critical thinking, decision making, and creativity.
- Require students to reflect on their learning experiences.

- Enable students to apply content and skills to their daily lives.
- Cultivate multiple intelligences and students' individual learning styles.

Outdated pigeon holing of study into isolated areas impedes learning. The public, parents, and certainly professional educators are tired of temporary, piecemeal, and simplistic school fixes. Children are whole, integrated persons when they arrive at school and should be fully engaged in experiences planned with connectedness in mind, which makes transfer of learning more likely.

# What Is Meaningful Arts Integration?

*The arts are not an educational option; they are basic.* (John Goodlad)

Booth (2003) traces the role of arts in American schools beginning with "arts for art's sake," moving to "arts for the sake of the workplace," and now a current emphasis on "arts for learning sake." He sees the third focus dominating the 21st century. Arts for learning is embodied in the arts integration visitors see at Ashley River Creative Arts and hundreds of other schools nationwide (Richmond-Cullen, 2005). Large-scale arts-based reform projects have now been implemented in urban schools in such cities as New York, Minneapolis, Washington, D.C., and Chicago. Like Ashley River, these schools have chosen AI because of theoretical, philosophical, and research support for the kinds of learning engagement that the arts make possible. In particular, AI has earned a special reputation for success with low performing students, especially those who are economically disadvantaged and from minority groups (Deasy & Stevenson, 2005). Ready Reference 1.6 lists example AI projects.

The National Endowment for the Arts has taken the position that it is impossible to make schools more effective centers of learning without the arts (Welch, 1995). From Charleston, South Carolina, to Oklahoma City, Oklahoma, schools have gotten the message and are using the arts as essential teaching tools—not just in the occasional art class or interdisciplinary unit but as pedagogical pillars. These schools share a common belief: Literature, visual art, drama, dance, and music have the power to energize and humanize the curriculum. Integrated arts schools are acting on research that confirms how arts experiences help "level the educational playing field" for disadvantaged students and "close the achievement gap" (Deasy & Stevenson, 2005; Fiske, 1999; Rabkin & Redmond, 2005). The arts are no longer on the curricular fringe of public education. They are an acknowledged part of national strategies to transform schools (Barton, 2005; Boston, 1996; Huckabee, 2005).

## AI Definition

*Interdisciplinary learning is learning to know something by its relation to something else.* (Leonard Bernstein)

Arts integration now goes by many aliases: arts infusion, arts immersion, arts based, and interdisciplinary learning, to name a few.

The terms *arts integration* and *interdisciplinary* both appear in the content standards for the each of the national arts standards (dance #7, music #8, theatre #6, visual art #6). Arts integration may also be subsumed under interdisciplinary and inquiry learning (*Authentic Connections,* 2002). Schools implementing multiple intelligences research quickly find themselves involved in AI as well, as three of the intelligences are arts: music, visual/spatial, and kinesthetic (dance and drama). Gardner's other five are also arts linked. For example, verbal intelligence is used with literary arts and in drama and music.

Mello (2004) and others draw distinctions among some terms, suggesting that arts based involves teaching arts content while arts infusion does not. In this book *arts based* and *arts infused* are used interchangeably with arts integration; both arts content and arts processes are embedded in traditional academic areas resulting in mutual benefits to student learning of all areas involved.

From a broad research and experience base, a general definition of quality arts integration has emerged. *Arts integration is the meaningful use of arts processes and content to introduce, develop, or bring closure to lessons in any academic area.* The goal is to transform learning by using the arts to actively engage learners in problem solving that creates understanding and expands expressive communication abilities.

## Ten Building Blocks for *Meaningful* Arts Integration

Important to the definition of AI is the provision that the arts can be powerful teaching and learning tools if used *meaningfully*. Just as literacy educators have fought to maintain the integrity of literature as an art form in literature-based programs, so the arts community has rightly insisted that music, visual art, drama/theatre, and dance/movement be *used*, but not abused. Meaningful arts integration entails more than cosmetic changes to schools and classrooms.

Although there is no one right way to integrate the arts, there are shared features among the many projects implemented nationwide. Ten building blocks common to successful AI designs follow, with most supported by the Consortium of National Arts Education Associations (*Authentic Connections,* 2002). The building blocks are "general operating principles" necessary for full implementation and form the skeleton of all subsequent arts-specific chapters. Meaningful use of the arts in education is facilitated by the following:

**1.** *Philosophy of education.* Arts-based learning is built on strong beliefs about and value for diversity, creative inquiry, engaged learning, and student independence. Of particular importance is a belief in the capacity of all individuals to construct personal meaning using a variety of communication tools (language arts and arts) and materials.

**2.** *Arts literacy: content and skills.* Basic arts concepts and processes need to be explicitly taught by classroom teachers and arts specialists to increase students' capacities to communicate and problem solve across disciplines. The arts are integral to the literacy curriculum because they are fundamentally communication vehicles.

## Ready Reference 1.6  Examples of Arts Integration Projects

In addition to the following projects, there are more than 500 arts-based magnet schools and scores of charter schools now affiliated with arts organizations (Fineberg, 2002).

### A+Schools

This North Carolina effort involves more than 35 participating schools. Douglas A+ Creative Elementary Arts and Science Magnet School in Raleigh is considered a model school. The A+ network is nationally recognized as a top education reform effort and has spread to Oklahoma, South Dakota, and Arkansas. Website: http://aplus-schools.uncg.edu.

### Alabama Institute for Education in the Arts

Comprehensive AI professional development is provided to schools throughout the state including a weeklong summer institute. Website: www.artseducation.org.

### Arts in the Basic Curriculum Project (ABC)

This statewide initiative by the South Carolina Department of Education, the South Carolina Arts Commission, and Winthrop University has a grants program to support implementation of arts-based education. ABC schools have high levels of support for arts immersion and classes are provided weekly in all four arts disciplines. Arts teachers participate in team planning with classroom teachers. More than 40 schools statewide have been coached through the planning and implementation of ABC. Website: www.winthrop.edu/abc/.

### Arts for Academic Achievement

The Minneapolis Annenberg Challenge for Arts Education is a partnership between the Minneapolis Public Schools and the Minnesota Center for Arts Education. Schools are categorized at three levels of integration: (1) minimal arts with one arts specialist, (2) actively working toward arts integration with two or more arts specialists, and (3) more than two arts specialists and long-term partnerships with local arts organizations. Research findings are available at the website: www.annenberginstitute.org/Challenge/sites/minneapolis.html.

### ArtsBridge

This California University collaboration involves 22 programs in 13 states and one in Northern Ireland. College students and fine art faculty are partnered with host schools. ArtsBridge programs claim to create learning environments that promote creative thinking and significant interdisciplinary connections. *The Journal for Learning through the Arts: A Research Journal on Arts Integration in Schools and Communities* is an online repository the documents the project. Website: artsbridge.ucdavis.edu/.

### ArtsConnection

Over 120 New York City public schools are involved in this AI project that features teaching artists who instruct students and plan with classroom teachers. Website: www.artsconnection.org.

### ArtsSmart

This is a collaborative partnership between Texarkana Regional Arts and Humanities Council and 34 schools. Based on their level of commitment, schools partner with ArtsSmart for professional development, AI planning, artist residencies, and community arts projects. Website: trahc.org/artssmart.shtml.

### The Annenberg Challenge for Arts Education

In New York City, schools are partnered with colleges, community organizations, and cultural institutions such as museums and arts groups. *Promising Practices: The Arts and School Improvement* (2005) profiles 9 of the 81 public schools whose students frequently work with artists. Arts organizations conduct family days and workshops facilitate co-planning with teachers. Website: www.cae-nyc.org.

### Changing Education Through the Arts (CETA)

The Kennedy Center partners with schools in districts in the Washington, D.C., metropolitan area (including Virginia and Maryland) to effect arts-based school reform through professional development. Despite high populations of English learners, there is an upward trend in test scores in CETA schools. A coaching component involves artists in co-planning, conducting class demonstrations, and co-teaching with teachers. Teachers and principals must make a multiyear commitment (Duma, 2005). Website: www.kennedycenter.org.

### Chicago Arts Partnerships in Education (CAPE)

There are 19 partnerships in 30 Chicago public schools matched with artists and artistic resources to integrate the arts. Curricula are developed and delivered through collaboratively planned instruction. Research is available in *Champions of Change: The Impact of Arts on Learning* (Fiske, 1999). Website: www.capeweb.org.

### Dallas ArtsPartners

Collaborative partnership between the Dallas Independent School District and 62 arts organizations. Website: www.dallasartspartners.org/.

### Empire State Partnerships (ESP)

This statewide large-scale project is sponsored by the New York State Council on the Arts. It involves 113 schools and is founded on these beliefs: The arts are key ways to differentiate instruction for diverse learners, the arts provide "redundancy" that enhances academic learning, and teaching artists are able to further engage students in learning.

### Transforming Education Through the Arts Challenge

Thirty-five schools in eight states were supported by the J. Paul Getty Trust and the Annenberg Challenge for Arts Education in this 5-year period. Teachers developed integrated units with the arts at the core with the goal of increasing student achievement (Hutchens & Pankratz, 2000).

### Value Plus Schools

Six Tennessee schools participate in this program under the direction of the Tennessee Arts Commission. It is supported by a grant from the U.S. Department of Education's Arts Education Model Development and Dissemination program. Value Plus emphasizes learning through the arts by integrating performing, visual, literary, and traditional art forms into non-arts subjects. Dance, visual art, theatre, and music are also taught as stand-alone subjects. Website: www.arts.state.tn.us/value_plus_schools.htm.

## Whole Schools Initiative (WSI)

The Mississippi Arts Commission (MAC) has funded schools since 1991 to embed the arts into regular classroom instruction. The WSI label underlined the intention that the arts should be more than a set of add-on activities. According to the state's accountability program, 88 percent of the WSI school sites were "successful" or better. Website: www.mswholeschools.org.

---

3. *Collaborative planning.* Classroom teachers and arts specialists need to co-plan standards-based lessons and units that focus on relationships among big ideas, key concepts, and skills—especially those that transcend individual disciplines. When a natural fit is found among arts content and processes and other curricular areas, lessons can be planned that facilitate a mutual transfer of learning.

4. *Aesthetic learning environments.* Physical and psychological conditions create classroom ecologies that should support positive attitudes toward learning, celebrate diversity (including cultural and ethnic differences), and promote respect, risk taking, and understanding.

5. *Literature as a core art form.* Over the past three decades, high-quality literature has become the primary material to deliver literacy instruction. Every literary genre, from poetry to science fiction, is now integrated into every academic area. Because the literary arts are the most readily available arts material and literature is the most frequently integrated art form, literature is a core aspect of arts integration.

6. *Best practices.* Research and professional wisdom have yielded conclusions about what constitutes "best instructional practice" at this time. These practices include explicit teaching (what-why-how) about authentic arts concepts and processes, especially the creative problem-solving process, and use of high-quality materials and arts examples. Transfer of learning is sought through explicit attention to making connections that produce "big ideas." Co-teaching with artists and arts specialists is an important vehicle for student learning and allows classroom teachers to build an arts knowledge and skill base.

7. *Instructional design: structure and routines.* A thorough and predictable focus on arts-based learning is assured through pronged lessons and use of specific arts routines in the classroom and school schedule. Pronged lessons feature a clear introduction, development, and conclusion that lead students to clear objectives for both academic and arts learning. Routines range from using energizers, to introducing lessons, to creating morning rituals such as arts-based literacy openers, to forming school arts clubs. Time for students to pursue special interests and engage in long-term projects needs to be built into the schedule.

8. *Differentiation.* Instruction needs to be made different in response to learner strengths and to meet diverse needs. Arts communication processes and materials, including multiple intelligences interventions and multisensory methods, expand options for learners to comprehend and express ideas and feelings.

9. *Assessment FOR learning.* Assessment needs to be used as a motivational tool to increase learning. This happens when learning expectations are made clear at the outset and continuous feedback on progress is provided which makes it more likely that they will meet criteria. Multiple forms of assessment are needed with focus on students having alternative ways to "show they know" especially through long-term projects that result in performances, and exhibits.

10. *Arts partnerships.* Co-planning and co-teaching with arts specialists from within and outside the school is necessary. Teaching artists may be brought in to plan, coach teachers, and do residencies with students. Partnerships with community arts agencies need to be sought as sources of expertise and other forms of support, including financial.

Chapter 2 addresses the first building block about the philosophy on which AI is founded. A comprehensive discussion of Building Blocks II through X forms the bulk of Chapter 3. Use of the building blocks and principles related to each art form are explained as they relate to each of the art forms in separate chapters of this book. In the following Spotlight, the principal of Ashley River Creative Arts explains how arts integration has evolved at her school. Notice how the administration and faculty have addressed the 10 building blocks.

Entry to Ashley River Creative Arts Elementary

# School Spotlight

## Arts Integration in Action

*The kids love to be here. They can't wait to start each day.*
(Jayne Ellicott, principal)

Teachers at Ashley River Creative Arts Elementary integrate the arts throughout the curriculum all day, every day. In over two and a half decades this small K–5 school in Charleston, South Carolina, has become one of the most well-known arts-based schools in the United States. It is also a National Blue Ribbon School and was honored as a Kennedy Center's "Creative Ticket School of Excellence." It's fitting that the mascot is a unicorn, a fanciful creature associated with hope and creativity.

Unlike large-scale AI projects in Minneapolis and Chicago, Ashley River Creative Arts is a small-scale effort that began at the grass roots level. The story of ARCA's journey is both informative and inspirational and serves as a real-life example of the importance of strong leadership and community involvement in AI implementation.

## Philosophy

"This is a school born of the imagination of the first principal," explains Jayne Ellicott, principal since 1994. She should know. Ellicott was Rose Maree Myers's assistant when the school opened in 1984. "Rose Maree was a visual art teacher with a theatre background. She had a very musical son who was not academically inclined. Her vision was to use the power of the arts to give all children a love of learning."

Ms. Ellicott witnessed the transformation of a condemned building with broken windows and weeds above the roof into what began as a magnet school. At first, half the students were "zoned in," and the other half were chosen by lottery. By the third year, all students were chosen from a waiting list. Now, all students are chosen by lottery each January.

Ms. Ellicott is convinced Ashley River started with an advantage because they didn't try to force an arts-based program on an existing school. The first faculty was handpicked for their commitment to using the arts as core instructional methods. From the get-go, teachers knew they were being hired to *create* an integrated arts school. Ms. Ellicott remembers, "It was hard to gel that personality force, but Rose Maree inspired the faculty to trust her and she was very goal centered."

## Growing Teachers' Arts Literacy

Over 25 years ago, the combination of excitement and focus motivated the administrators and teachers to do evening and Saturday professional development. Jayne Ellicott smiles as she reminisces about weekly meetings during which Rose Maree would demonstrate integrated arts lessons. As with most teachers new to arts integration, some were intimidated by dance and movement, others by the prospect of visual art. Some found music to be the challenge. "We didn't have any special supplies. We didn't even have ceiling tiles and very few electric plugs that first year," she laughs. But she believes that those limitations were the catalyst that caused the faculty to bond.

## Collaboration

According to Ms. Ellicott, AI requires hard work, especially collaboration among teachers within grade levels and with arts specialists. This is achieved in many ways, including monthly meetings with specialists at each grade level. The focus is on the basics, but the arts are the "delivery path." Ongoing informal interactions among specialists and teachers also happen at lunch, in the halls, and after school. She insists "doors to classrooms need to be open so anyone can walk by, enjoy, and even come in and participate."

## Assessment

All of Ashley River's students now do well on PACT (South Carolina's state academic test), but Ms. Ellicott points to what she considers more important indicators of the school's success. "Our students show they know and understand in many ways. They know what to do with free time and they all think they can become 'expert' at something—painting, dancing, playing an instrument."

Ms. Ellicott cites other results she attributes to their arts-based approach by contrasting students who enter as kindergarteners and remain versus latecomers. "Late arrivals have trouble because our students all learn early on to cooperate, communicate, and process information on a higher scale. They quickly learn to plan and work together when they are engaged in the arts. They learn to achieve consensus and are more confident. For example, in drama class I've seen even the most shy student just bellow out!"

## Arts Partnerships

Ms. Ellicott credits most of the school's success to the arts-based curriculum, but points out that parents decide their children will be at Ashley River. That choice makes a difference. Ms. Ellicott emphasizes that the school does not select academically gifted kids over other children, nor do they have more money than other schools. ARCA does have a strings teacher, a drama specialist, and an extra music teacher, which is three more teachers than "normal." Parents furnish the instruments for the strings program. The extra teachers, along with special equipment such as musical Orff instruments and a photography lab, are funded by aggressive pursuit of grants like those from ABC (Arts in the Basic Curriculum) provided by the State Arts Commission. "We have used start-up grant monies, Wachovia Bank matching grants, Sam's Club, Project Artistic (U.S. Department of Education), and individual donors. We continue to invite private benefactors to be a part of Ashley River's mission," she explains.

## Differentiation for Diverse Students

Is Ashley River without problems? "No," admits Ms. Ellicott. "We have all the same issues as any school." Nineteen percent of the students are on free or reduced lunch. Forty percent of the students have learning disabilities. Thirty-eight percent are from a minority group. Parents think that kids who couldn't make it somewhere else can make it at ARCA, she says. "We are able to work through our problems using artistic thinking that focuses on cooperation, persistence, more risk taking and experimentation, and respect for diverse ideas."

Over the years Ashley River has added many choice arts opportunities for students, such as the Drama Troupe (fourth and fifth grade), a chorus, a strings/violin club, a ballet club, and a clay club. These have proven to be important curricular adjuncts and powerful public relations tools. Ms. Ellicott recalls the reaction when she took the strings group to a local Rotary meeting. "Community leaders were shocked to see kindergartners play the violin. I saw tears in the audience."

### The AI Mission

Jayne Ellicott sits in her office papered with children's art and writing. She reflects on the years past and yet to come. "There is so much about the adult world that has nothing to do with standards and measurement, so much that is more important that we don't and can't measure. I watch the kindergartners bowing away on the violin or the little ballet dancers (boys and girls) with their underpants hanging out. I wish that every teacher would be a believer. Not all do. You have to have the passion that the arts are making this difference. Of course, I think all it takes is walking through a classroom to see how the arts transform learning. I just happen to work with teachers who are believers."

Postscript: In 2010, Jayne Ellicott moved her entire staff into a brand new building. Charleston County has made a bricks and mortar commitment to arts integration. For more information, visit http://ashleyriver.ccsdschools.com/home.aspx.

Assistant Cathie Middleton and Principal Jayne Ellicott, Ashley River Creative Arts Elementary

## Levels and Models of Arts Integration

> *We had a few minutes left in class today. It was too late to start something but we needed to fill the gap. I dug out my Claude Monet book and had students guess the focus of the painting* Winterscapes *(without looking at the title). I couldn't believe it—middle schoolers who were joking with me one minute turned serious, intently looking at the painting. Someone commented, "I like the way he did that in the back." I responded by saying, "You mean the horizon in the background?" and a boy said, "Yeah, that!"*
>
> *They were different people. When I first asked if they had heard of Claude Monet, they said they knew of "Jean Claude van Damme." Anyway, it was such a fleeting but intense experience. Also, they now beg me every day to do drama from the novel we are reading. I feel I'm depriving them if I don't do it. I believe integrating the arts, even if it's just 5 minutes a day, is so incredible—especially to see it at the middle school.* (Bethany Gray, education major, Wittenberg University).

### Quantity Matters

Bethany Gray is an example of a teacher who is just starting out. Like other novices, she is gradually increasing the amount and intensity of AI as she builds her arts knowledge and skill base. Teachers in schools undergoing whole school reform may be involved in a year of professional development and collaborative planning with arts specialists before beginning. Individual teachers who begin on their own may be like Bethany; they have taken undergraduate integrated arts courses or enroll in graduate classes.

There are many different designs for arranging the building blocks into meaningful AI. Not to be dismissed is the amount of arts learning. This is underscored by a pattern of academic superiority of students in schools that devote 25 percent or more of the curriculum to arts courses (Horowitz, 2004; Perrin, 1994). Teachers who integrated the arts into their mathematics lessons "a lot," had students with greater gains than those who integrated "very little" (Ingram & Seashore, 2003, pp. 4–5). When it comes to learning, the more arts integration the better. Exposure to the arts is not enough.

### Quality Matters: Levels of Arts Integration

It isn't just the amount of AI, but the quality that makes a difference (Burnaford, 2007; Corbett, Wilson, & Morse, 2005). Teachers typically spend 2 to 5 years in study before they reach *meaningful* status with all 10 building blocks in place and well developed.

There is support for a continuum of increasingly meaningful AI from Music-in-Education National Consortium (MIENC), a national network of universities, arts organizations, school reform foundations, and schools (Scripp & Subotnik, 2003). For MIENC, meaningfulness entails addressing the issue of maintaining the integrity of the art form as a separate discipline while also affirming the value of teaching for transfer with regard for concepts and processes shared by the arts and academic disciplines. The ideal is for AI to involve both synthesis and differentiation with the latter, including defined learning within an arts discipline as taught by qualified and trained arts professionals (Myers & Scripp, 2007).

Several AI projects have worked on describing qualitative stages of implementation. South Carolina ABC schools have continuum of "arts infusion" that is useful in thinking about progress points. It is available at http://edpsych.ed.sc.edu/ope/projects/artseducation/. Ingram and Seashore (2003) observed 31 Minneapolis schools and found five distinct activities that reflect a progression that they call "Varieties of Arts Integration (VAI)."

1. Early on, artists were brought in for residencies, with little or no preplanning with teachers.
2. In "elaborated residencies" collaborative planning between classroom teachers and artists created arts-based lessons that addressed the strengths and needs of particular students.
3. When teachers observed teaching artists present arts-based lessons and began to study AI, they built their "capacity" to engage in meaningful AI.
4. Co-teaching (team teaching) with an artist after collaborative planning demonstrated how teachers were increasing their confidence in using the arts.
5. The most mature AI approach occurred when classroom teachers and arts specialist did collaborative planning that focused on finding common concepts and standards across curricular areas (p. 3). The full VAI grid can be examined at www.education.umn.edu/CAREI/Reports/Annenberg/VAI-Intro.htm.

**AI Ladder.**    In 1997, Jane Remer, from Americans for the Arts, spoke at the Kennedy Center's Partners in Education conference on arts integration. She presented the concept of teaching *with* and *about* the arts. In this book that idea is expanded to teaching *with*, *about*, *in*, and *through* the arts to conceptualize levels or degrees of meaningful integration. These levels can be thought of as a ladder of increasing instructional depth and arts sophistication.

Any AI effort begins with teachers individually, or as a faculty, examining their beliefs about learning and teaching for the purpose of gauging the match with the tenets of AI. Simply making connections between learning in the arts and academic areas is a frequent beginning orientation. Snyder (2001) cautions, however, that making connections is not a meaningful way of linking disciplines if the arts are just used in the service of another discipline; arts concepts and skills must be explicitly taught for integration to be meaningful (p. 34).

Top-level integration occurs when big ideas, supported by themes and key concepts, guide instructional planning. Relevant disciplines, including the arts, are used as tools for creating meaning, which involves both finding and constructing key concepts and themes using the inquiry-based creative problem-solving processes common to all disciplines. The following section outlines a progressive professional development ladder set in motion by an initial commitment to AI.

**Level One: WITH.**    Teachers usually begin at a modest level and teach *with* the arts. They experiment with a few arts strategies in an arts area of most comfort and interest. Bethany was using the Close Looking strategy along with open questions to promote student inquiry. She also is experimenting with drama, which has a strong research connection to comprehension (Deasy, 2002). Daily arts routines like Art Print Discussions or Poem a Day (see Chapter 3 Classroom Snapshot) are easy to put in place and have natural connections to the literacy curriculum. Another starting place is to set up arts-based centers and stations for independent follow-up work by students (see Chapter 3, Building Block VII).

**Level Two: ABOUT and IN.**    More meaningful integration happens when teachers have opportunities to observe artists (e.g., during residencies) and co-plan with arts specialists. The goal is to plan lessons that include teaching *about* arts content and skills that naturally connect to established units, often related to science and social studies. Songs, dances, music, and art from historical periods and different cultures are frequently the first kinds of arts content classroom teachers use. At first, arts works may be used to introduce or conclude lessons. Eventually, as in Judy Trotter's room, art forms become integral to literacy and social studies, science, and math instruction. Teachers begin to involve students *in* using the ways of thinking, creating, and responding that are the province of the arts. This happens through explicit teaching, such as use of think-alouds to model different aspects of the higher order thinking that make up creative problem solving (CPS).

Here again, teachers usually work with an arts area that is personally comfortable. Each of us has natural inclinations and competencies and teachers should pursue their strengths. Modest creative challenges provide a success orientation for students and for teachers. For example, a teacher who plays a musical instrument may accompany students on the guitar or flute as they sing curriculum-related songs. Students see a whole new dimension of a teacher who takes this risk and is willing to discuss the act of music making. What's more, the class is bonded through the unique power of music to bring groups together. Of course, depth of teaching *about* and *in* depends on the arts knowledge base of teachers and the quality of planning done with arts specialists to ensure authentic use of the arts.

**Level Three: THROUGH.**    The fullest AI is teaching *through* the arts. This involves creating an aesthetic school and classroom environment in which substantial content units are taught using the arts as both learning tools and unit centers. Both academic and arts standards are targeted, along with attention to big ideas, as teachers co-plan units with arts specialists. Lessons are taught using best practices that are congruent with arts-based learning. In particular, the inquiry-based creative problem-solving process is explicitly taught. The 10 AI building blocks are in place, including assessment of arts learning and assessment through the arts.

**Professional Development.**    At any level, arts-based instruction is only as good as a teacher's knowledge base about learning theories, research, and the teaching practices judged to currently be the "best" given the evidence available. Developing increasing expertise in AI requires commitment to long-term study. Lesley College in Boston and the Center for

Community Arts Partnerships at Columbia College are two of a growing number of institutions offering degree programs related to AI; certification programs are under consideration in several states, such as Maryland (http://www.aems-edu.org/). Other teachers strike out on their own with self-study using books, articles, websites, and professional development videos (see Bibliography and Appendices). The Annenberg Foundation's video series for teachers can be viewed online (www.learner.org). To locate an arts-based school near you, consult websites sponsored by organizations such as Arts Education Partnership and the Kennedy Center's Arts Edge site. Ready Reference 1.6 lists example school sites.

Chapter 2 provides an overview of the philosophical, theoretical, and research underpinnings of AI about which teachers and teaching artists need to be well acquainted. Central to success is creating schools where all teachers and learners embrace collaborative work and problem solving (Scripp, 2003). A particular focus of this book, explained in Chapter 2, is how AI engages teachers in using and teaching the creative problem-solving process (CPS) at the heart of artistic thinking and integral to making sense of any text, be it print or nonprint, word based or multimedia. Theories, such as CPS, accompanied by a clear vision and knowledge of research, create conditions for educators to devise unique and appropriate variations on the innovative practice of AI.

**Center Stage: Teacher Changes.** Findings from diverse arts integration school projects emphasize the role of teachers and document characteristics of those who reach high levels of meaningful integration (Deasy & Stevenson, 2005; Freeman, Seashore, & Werner, 2003; Horowitz, 2004; Ingram & Seashore, 2003; Weissman, 2004). Characteristics include:

*Changed beliefs.* Teachers realize struggling readers and writers can become successful when given arts options. Teachers come to believe that all students can succeed when they see unmotivated students become motivated to learn. Teachers become coaches and facilitators rather than knowledge dispensers and witness the power of teaching students *how to* problem solve and use exploration and experimentation to arrive at personally meaningful connections. Teachers also find unknown strengths in themselves and begin to take more leadership. For example, in North Carolina A+ schools teachers became more resilient to problems like funding cuts or loss of their principal which sustained arts integration in their schools (Horowitz, 2004).

*Application of research and theory.* Teachers design hands-on, heads-on, hearts-on multisensory instruction informed by theories such as multiple intelligences, creative problem solving, and brain research. They engage students more directly in inquiry and students learn to give original interpretations and create novel solutions reflected in diverse arts products.

*Reaching diverse learners.* Arts experiences reveal different aspects of students so teachers deepen their understanding of abilities and potential. Overlooked students become significant players in the learning game as teachers learn alternative ways to assess and employ strategies that tap learner strengths.

*Increased culture of excellence.* Schools and classrooms become aesthetic places as teachers make physical and psychological changes that create stimulating environments and embrace high expectations for all students.

*Increased strategy repertoire.* Teachers expand their toolkits through collaborative planning and co-teaching with arts specialists. They acquire arts strategies that are new ways to engage students that often parallel best practices for teaching reading and writing. Students are motivated by the "power of the audience" and chose to revise work through arts-based processes such as expert use of critique.

*More arts instruction and two-way transfer.* The arts are placed on an equal footing with other subjects. The arts become key teaching tools in core subjects when they are viewed as forms of literacy central to learning; but it doesn't stop there. Core academic content and skills are just as likely to be used to teach arts content. For example, units may focus on an artist or artform, such as picture book artist Eric Carle or a study of historical ballads.

*Big ideas and important questions.* Grade-level integrated units and schoolwide curricular themes become organizing features. Teachers and students learn how to ask important questions that lead to big ideas and use creative problem-solving thinking processes to reach the meaning destination.

*Networking.* Teachers seek partnerships with artists, arts agencies, and the community to make arts integration work. For example, at Normal Park Museum Magnet in Chattanooga, Tennessee, teachers created family nights to involve parents in the arts. The "openings" of student exhibits draw others into the excitement of arts integration.

# Arts-Based Reform: National, Regional, and State Efforts

In a recent study, three-fourths of schools undergoing restructuring were using interdisciplinary designs like arts AI as reform options (Grossman, Wineburg, & Beers, 2000). In the past dozen or so years various national and regional models have emerged, many using startup money from private philanthropies such as the Ford Foundation and the Annenberg Foundation. Early projects include the Minneapolis Arts for Academic Achievement (AAA), Chicago Arts Partners in Education (CAPE) model, and the North Carolina A+ model. The U.S. Department of Education also made grants to multiple sites to develop arts-integrated curricula. One highly successful example is Tucson's "Opening Minds Through the Arts," a consortium of the Tucson Symphony Opera, the University of Arizona, and the Tucson Arts Connection (Deasy & Stevenson, 2005). The focus is music integration. Other recipients of grants, from $500,000 to $1,000,000, include Rockford, Illinois, schools; the Mississippi Arts Commission (state arts agency); and Arts Connection in New York City for an arts/literacy project (Corbett, Wilson, & Morse, 2005; Fineberg, 2002).

Schools at all grade levels in all 50 states and in Canada, Australia, and the United Kingdom are now undergoing arts-based school reform. Comprehensive research reports document how learning can be transformed through thoughtful implementation AI principles (Burnaford, 2007; Deasy, 2002; Deasy & Stevenson, 2005; Fiske, 1999; Longley, 1999).

A single model for arts integration does not—and should not—exist. Frameworks have evolved to suit individual school sites, with the quality of implementation looming large in student growth (Burnaford, 2007; Corbett, Wilson, & Morse, 2005; Rabkin & Redmond, 2005). The Southeast Center for Education in the Arts lists 50 program models across the country at their website (http://handbook.laartsed.org/models/search.ashx).

As Marron (2003) points out, active teacher involvement in developing and implementing AI is a key factor in changing the school culture (p. 95). Teachers must feel empowered to make change. As teachers acquire more and more arts knowledge, their teaching repertoire is enlarged so they are able to differentiate instruction more readily and more effectively. Teachers observe how students respond positively to arts-based strategies and raise their expectations for all students with more focus on identifying and teaching to strengths and needs.

# National Initiatives and Legislation

*Very little that has come down through the ages has not in some way filtered through something that we can all identify as the arts.* (Sherri Geldin, Wexner Art Center, Columbus, Ohio)

Several important national initiatives support arts integration. First is the creation of national standards.

**National Standards.**    Members of major professional organizations for each discipline (e.g., National Council of Teachers of Math) consulted current research and used professional wisdom to outline what students should *know* and be able to *do* in every academic area and the arts. The standards provide impetus for integrating the arts by supporting education of the "whole child" that acknowledges the interconnectedness among body, mind, and emotions (e.g., see the September 2005 issue of *Educational Leadership*). Academic and arts standards call for students to meet goals that will be impossible to achieve without the concerted efforts of classroom teachers and arts specialists.

National and state standards documents now drive curriculum development, instruction, and assessment strategies in American classrooms. Both teachers and artists need to be mindful of publications that articulate content and performance standards in curricular areas, including each of the arts disciplines. Nearly every state department of education includes downloadable standards for each subject area at their respective website. Another recommended source is *Standards for Excellence* (1998), available from the Council for Basic Education. The Association for Supervision and Curriculum Development (ASCD) also has a fully developed library of standards for each subject in public school curricula that includes a CD-ROM, charts, and a handbook, available through its website (www.ascd.org).

**Arts Standards.**    *The National Standards for the Arts* (1994) were developed by the Consortium of National Arts Education Associations and calls for comprehensive and sequential arts education for all children. The *Standards* represent agreement on what U.S. students should know and be able to do in each of the arts by the time they complete high school. Also addressed is the importance of using the arts in education in the form of interdisciplinary learning exemplified in AI.

The *Standards* address four arts disciplines: dance, music, theatre, and the visual arts. Grouped by grade levels K through 12, they suggest a basic body of knowledge and skills required to make sense and to make use of the arts. Standards specify desired results. Teachers design the actual instruction and choose materials to meet them. They are organized as follows: (1) communication in each art form, (2) ability to think critically about art forms, (3) acquaintance with exemplary works of art from a variety of cultures and periods, and (4) ability to relate types of arts knowledge and skills within and across arts disciplines. A full copy of the *Standards* is available from the Music Educators National Conference (www.menc.org).

Beginning in the 1990s, state and federal budgets made it possible for local school districts and state departments of education to develop and implement arts standards. To date, every state except for Iowa has adopted arts standards. Twenty-seven states have mandated arts standards and 20 states have set voluntary standards. Seven states explicitly address the importance of interdisciplinary connections among the arts and other disciplines, that is, arts integration: Arizona, Idaho, Illinois, Indiana, Kentucky, Louisiana, and New Mexico. Arizona offers examples of integration options (Arizona State University & the Arizona Board of Education, 2007. Available at www.mpsaz.org/arts/perf_arts/performing_arts. htm). Kansas, Nevada, and Washington, D.C., have standards for limited AI (in two or three of the arts). For other examples go the departments of education for most states.

The main K–8 arts standards are shown in Ready References in the even-numbered chapters of this book, beginning with Chapter 4. Recommended teaching strategies meet one or more of the *Standards,* if they are developed and implemented appropriately. Chapter 4 on the literary arts includes separate standards prepared by the National Council of the Teachers of English and the International Reading Association.

**What's Missing in the Standards.**    Teachers soon note that standards fall far short of specifying all that is important for students to know and do. In particular, standards do not address what students are to *be*. For example, persistence, self-discipline, creativity, responsibility, and resilience are just a few from a long list of desirable traits that many teachers and parents would place ahead of many standards. Teachers involved in AI and other "whole child" educational projects consider standards as one source for curriculum development, but go further to plan for students to reach important goals not specified in standards documents.

**Standards for Teachers.**    Standards aren't just for kids. Working under the auspices of the Council of Chief State School Officers, representatives of professional organizations collaborated to create model standards for licensing new teachers. The 10 Interstate New Teacher Assessment and Support Consortium (INTASC) principles are currently used by universities to organize undergraduate and graduate teacher preparation and are consistent with the advanced certification standards of the National Board for Professional Teaching Standards. Standards have also been created for classroom teachers with regards to what they should know and be able to do in the arts (INTASC, 2002). The standards can be downloaded at www.ccsso.org/intasc.

**National Assessment.** With goals and standards comes assessment, the process of collecting evidence. That evidence can be used for many purposes, one of which is to make a determination about the extent to which standards are being met. Fiske (1999) warns that in a "society that values measurements and uses data-driven analysis to inform decisions about allocation of scarce resources, photographs of smiling faces are not enough to gain or even retain support. Such images alone will not convince skeptics."

Educators can feel threatened by assessment, but a clear destination makes the success of the learning journey more likely. It is important to remember that a test is just a sample of what a student can do and is limited in predicting what a person may become. There currently is a firestorm over what constitutes appropriate assessment of important real-life skill sets such as cross-disciplinary problem solving and higher order thinking, which are difficult to assess out of context and with paper-and-pencil tests. What's more, traits increased by arts involvement, such as persistence, responsibility, taking initiative, and creativity so important for success in 21st-century life, are nearly impossible to assess with standardized tests.

Schools currently use many state and local assessments, and one national assessment. For more than 20 years, the National Assessment of Educational Progress (NAEP), or the Nation's Report Card, has been the barometer for American students for achievement in reading, writing, math, and science. Samples of students in grades 4, 8, and 12 are tested. In 2008, two of four arts areas were tested with lackluster results. The results show that a gap persists: White and Asian students scored higher, on average, than African American and Hispanic students in both music and visual arts. Girls outscored boys, and private schools outperformed public (http://nces.ed.gov/nationsreportcard/arts/). In response one blogger wrote, "Who cares? We should concentrate on higher math and science." Another blogger responded, "I would like to know when this guy last used either his knowledge of calculus or high school chemistry in his daily life, versus how often he enjoys magazines (graphic design), listens to the radio (music), or watches a movie (theater/drama)."

**Legislation: No Child Left Behind.** The controversial NCLB Act of 2002 promised to eliminate the achievement gap, improve teacher quality, empower parents, and promote school safety. Although opinions are still mixed on its success in those areas, arts education and AI projects did benefit when NCLB's continued the designation of the arts as "core academic skills," which was first written into law in Goals 2000 legislation. That legislation suggested the place of the arts in schools should be comparable to that of the language arts, math, and science.

Unfortunately, NCLB mandated expectations that caused some schools to unjustly cut or curb arts programs and teach to standardized tests for reading and math. Curriculum constriction continues despite a body of evidence that the best schools teach for understanding. In fact, directing students to focus on test performance, instead of understanding, has been found to decrease motivation and depth of learning (Allington, 2005; Guthrie, 2004). Mandatory high-stakes tests put a premium on instructional time, and narrowing the curriculum has led to decreases rather than increases in test scores (Yen & Ferrara, 1997). Assistant Secretary of Education Susan Scalafani did try to right the tipping ship. She called learning in and through the arts "central" to fulfilling the NCLB's goal of improved student achievement. Department of Education support of the arts remains confounded, however, by accountability and research policies, such as an emphasis on "scientific" research that places almost all the weight on quantitative data. Of course, qualitative studies more clearly reveal the broad-based and more long-term effects of the arts, as well the effects of other complex school reform strategies.

So, NCLB proved to be a challenge, but it also provided opportunities since it made demands that would be unachievable without the arts, such as expecting students with special needs to meet the same standards as other students. This was an opportunity for educators whose work is grounded in using the arts to shine. The success of at-risk students in arts-based learning is now well documented. Disadvantaged students, who are under the greatest pressure, have made the greatest academic gains using arts-based strategies (Burnaford, 2007; Deasy, 2002; Deasy & Stevenson, 2005; Weiss & Lichtenstein, 2008). Teachers concerned about curriculum constriction and teaching to the test, both of which also create low morale, can be bolstered by real evidence that quality arts integration is connected to academic achievement. Teachers need no longer feel they are pitting the arts against academics (Gunzenhauser & Gerstl-Pepin, 2002).

Dissatisfaction with many of the provisions of NCLB provides impetus for the new administration to make changes (Rose & Gallup, 2005). However, it is unlikely that the Race to the Top initiative will move us any closer to universal proficiency in reading any more than NCLB did unless the focus is elevated beyond basic decoding skills and comprehension becomes the literacy priority. Aggressive arts integration builds a strong bridge between low-level thinking and the higher order skills needed for comprehension.

For more information on the arts and NCLB, check out *No Subject Left Behind: A Guide to Arts Education Opportunities in the 2001 NCLB Act* (2004) at www.symphoy.org/govaff/what/042502education.shtml.

## Government-Affiliated Organizations

Notable organizations exist for the express purpose of reforming education using arts-based models. These include the Arts Education Partnership and the Kennedy Center's Partners in Education.

**Arts Education Partnership (AEP).** First created under Goals 2000, AEP is a national coalition of arts, education, business, philanthropic, and government organizations. The primary focus is helping states and local school districts integrate the arts into their educational improvement plans. The partnership was formed through a cooperative agreement among the National Endowment for the Arts, the U.S. Department of Education, the National Assembly of State Arts Agencies, and the Council of Chief State School Officers. AEP sponsors nationwide forums and publishes a quarterly newsletter featuring articles and resources related to promising practices. Its website (www.aep-arts.org) is a recommended starting place.

**The Partners in Education of the John F. Kennedy Center for the Performing Arts.** This nationwide program based in Washington, D.C., fosters partnerships among arts agencies and schools. There are now Kennedy Center teams in 43 states, Washington, D.C., and Mexico, with Ohio and South Carolina boasting the most sites. Schools and arts agencies partner to provide professional development to classroom teachers interested in using the arts as teaching tools. Teams use local artists and the Kennedy Center's teaching artists for workshops. The program also has a grants program for arts-based research and offers workshops to train artists for classroom teaching. Barbara Shepherd, director of the Kennedy Center National Partnerships, puts high priority on "institutionalizing" arts in education through total education reform, including changing concepts about teaching, beginning at the preservice level. Her greatest wish is for "every student and classroom to have access to a teacher who can integrate the arts plus arts specialists and visiting professional artists" (May 2005 phone interview). The annual conference of Partners in Education brings teams together to plan. ArtsEdge is a premiere arts education website that grew out of the program and is a must visit for all educators. To find out about memberships, visit the Kennedy Center's website, www.kennedy-center.org/education/partners/.

# Teacher Spotlight
## First-Year Teacher

This book is for teachers, so this chapter began with a vignette about Judy Trotter, a veteran teacher. It is appropriate to end with another real teacher. This time it is a first- year teacher, also on the faculty at Ashley River Creative Arts. Fannie Petros believes arts-based learning causes students and teachers to "think of the whole picture of learning, not just one aspect." She speaks as a teacher and as a student. She graduated from the Chattanooga School for the Arts and Sciences, a K-12 arts-based school.

Fannie first visited Ashley River during a practicum when she was an undergraduate at the College of Charleston. She recalls a teacher showing students how to draw math story problems. "This wasn't a typical school. The doors were open, there was art everywhere and so much active participation."

Fannie says her fellow teachers became her most valuable resources for arts integration when she was hired. "Their strongest message is to use your imagination to create what you need," she says. She adopted their concept of arts integration that focuses on active hands-on learning. "Kids have to create their own meanings, and they do this through exploration."

Fannie notes that it takes time to plan for the core curriculum and be true to the school's arts-based mission statement. "But it is worth it. When you see how much the kids love to be here and they are really getting it, you know. Even with the lowest kids it is clicking. It's why I became a teacher."

Fannie believes the arts give students learning advantages. "I see that ah-ha moment when kids learn through the arts—especially ones who weren't succeeding otherwise. I tell them when they accept their Oscars, they better remember their first-grade teacher!"

Fannie especially loves to dovetail the arts with literacy. Every day the kids sing and "act out" words—even high-frequency words. She emphasizes spelling patterns using musical elements like rhythm. If they are learning the word *low*, they spell it in a low voice. "As a student I hated vocabulary. My students love it." Like the other AR teachers, Fannie connects literacy to science and social studies. During a recent unit, students studied Chinese culture through reading, writing, and origami. They also learned and performed the Chinese dragon dance. "Students learn to be in an audience and in front of an audience. It builds so much confidence when you are in the spotlight," she explains. "Right now, we're so excited because we are learning about Grandma Moses!"

# Conclusion

*A child who has not pretended, doodled, danced, and hummed will not only have trouble reading and writing, he will have trouble BEING.*

As schools shift focus to adjust to the realities of the 21st century, the arts become more important than ever before. As historical sources of creative and imaginative thinking, the arts can lead the way to a revolution in teaching and learning. With their inquiry-based problem-solving nature, the arts involve us in looking at contemporary problems, including resource shortages, from new perspectives. Grounded in "what if" thinking, the arts liberate risk taking while drawing upon every person's repertoire of knowledge and strategies to imagine new solutions.

Students who have an expanded communication repertoire that includes the arts have an advantage in the 21st century. In particular, the arts are the center of new technologies. Without artful thinking, PowerPoints, blogs, YouTube, and other digital and multimedia technologies would not exist. Artful thinking creates these innovations, and the arts are at the core of how they function as they rely on music, visual art, drama, storytelling, music, and dance. Internet-based social networking now goes beyond chitchat to launch political revolutions, such as Twitter-inspired demonstrations in 2009 in Russia and Iran.

Arts integration draws upon unique contributions the arts make to life and learning. When the "arts for learning" relationship is cultivated a different classroom ethos is created that transforms how teachers think about their students. Much instruction takes place in unit designs that emphasize hands-on projects developed through creative problem solving. Students find and construct big ideas in science and social studies texts using both arts strategies and arts texts that are intellectually challenging and emotionally engaging. Risk taking is encouraged as teachers consistently support thinking about possibilities from arts perspectives.

To ensure that arts integration is more than a curricular veneer, educators strive to plan *meaningful* use of the arts. Diverse models have developed to meet the needs of individual schools, but shared building blocks exist and 10 were introduced in this chapter. Teachers are eased into an artistic view of education by first teaching *with* the arts and moving more deeply into teaching *about* and *in* the arts. The goal is teaching *through* the arts, using the arts as primary learning and communication vehicles. The success of arts integration depends on increasing the degree or quality of arts-based work by growing the classroom teacher's arts literacy, usually through collaborative work with teaching artists.

Subsequent chapters build on ideas introduced in this chapter, especially the "with, about, in, through" progression and the 10 building blocks. In the next chapter the philosophies (beliefs) that support arts integration are discussed, along with more specific research and educational theories that connect to arts integration. In particular, the creative problem-solving (CPS) process is described to help teachers teach higher order thinking process to construct meaning from diverse texts.

---

### Teachers as Leaders: AI Advocacy

Create a 5- to 10-minute arts integration advocacy talk (e.g., "Top Five Reasons") to present to a faculty meeting, PTO, school board, or community group. Use Twitter to get the word out or consider videoing your talk and posting it on YouTube.

---

### PEARSON myeducationlab

Go to the Activities and Applications section for Topic *Arts Education Foundation* at MyEducationLab for your course and complete the video activities entitled "Reforming Literacy Instruction Using Arts Integration Principles" and "Arts Integration as Whole School Reform." Also go to the Activities and Applications section for Topic *Strategies for Teaching* and complete the video activities entitled "Using Pass and Pretend Warm-Up" and "Using Side Coaching for Detail." Finally, go to the Activities and Applications section for Topic *Safety and Classroom Management* and complete the video activities entitled "Dealing with Nonparticipation."

Go to the Book Specific Resources section in the MyEducationLab for your course, select your book and Chapter 1 to view the Questions to Guide Reading and Response Options for this chapter.

## Resources

Also see the Appendix.

### Audio/Video

Free, on demand 14 video library on how to do arts integration: www.learner.org

Podcasts about artists and the arts at pbs.org and comprehensive websites below.

*Arts for life.* (1990). The Getty Center for Education in the Arts (15 min.; arts integration rationale and classroom examples).

*Teaching in and through the arts.* (1995). The Getty Center for Education in the Arts (25 min.; classroom examples).

*The arts: Tools for teaching.* (1994). Washington, DC: John F. Kennedy Center for the Performing Arts.

*The arts and children: A success story.* Arts Education Partnership (15 min.; why integrate the arts).

### Websites: Also see Appendix J

Arts Edge: http://artsedge.kennedy-center.org (comprehensive site with many lesson plans)

Arts Education Partnership: http://aep-arts.org (comprehensive site)

Arts for Learning: www.arts4learning.org (interactive site to help plan, create, and conduct arts-based lessons)

Young Audiences: www.youngaudiences.org (videos and a booklet of success stories)

# 2

# Philosophy, Research, and Theories That Support Arts Integration

*I dropped out of Reed College and had nothing to do so I took a course in calligraphy. And it all went into the Mac keyboard.* (Steve Jobs, Stanford University commencement, 2005)

## Overview

This chapter addresses the first building block for meaningful arts integration: philosophy. Arts integration (AI) is rooted in the progressive philosophical beliefs of John Dewey and traditions of constructivist education. In this chapter beliefs are organized into five Ps: people, places, principles of learning, programs, and pedagogy. Research that supports AI follows, including an update on brain research. The last section summarizes key learning theories with example implications for AI. The final theory addresses creativity and describes the creative problem-solving (CPS) process in detail.

## Introduction

Arts integration (AI) is not about using the arts casually, but Steve Jobs's experiences are a reminder of the potential effect on innovative thinking when the arts are put in the mix. Imagine the impact when students are immersed in arts experiences *designed* to expand their inclinations and abilities to do creative problem solving. That is what AI is about.

We have a renewed imperative to deliver high-quality education to all students. AI is an innovative response that promises a permanent place for the arts in the curriculum as well as more substantial learning in well-established curricular areas. More than using the arts as free time diversions, or solely as culminating projects to demonstrate understanding, AI succeeds by putting the arts on an equal footing with other curricular areas. Arts processes and content are respected as coherent disciplines alongside being tools to introduce, develop, and conclude lessons. Arts integration is analogous to reading in the content areas or writing across the curriculum, because they all focus on meaningful use of alternative communication forms for reciprocal learning. Classroom teachers explicitly teach about arts content and processes and assess student learning in the arts, which

can yield arts products that rival or exceed those created in specialized arts classes (Rabkin & Redmond, 2005 b).

AI projects are initiated with teachers examining beliefs about how students learn best and how curriculum should be developed and structured to meet student needs. AI educators seek answers to the question, "WHY integrate the arts?" That question is central to this chapter. Beliefs about how learning happens and what constitutes the best teaching practices are at the core of any educational philosophy. AI philosophy is based on a growing body of research findings and theoretical models of learning that support constructivist views. Of course, teachers need to know *how* to put all this into practice and so teaching implications are included for each area.

In the opening School Spotlight, notice how beliefs, research, and theories play significant roles in arts-based school reform and sustainability of efforts at one elementary school.

## School Spotlight
### Schoolwide Reform

A flamboyant mural across the front of Lady's Island Elementary School (LIES) is one sign that this is no ordinary school. LIES is the first of its kind in the district, a site-based, deregulated school of choice in which arts infusion is the guiding philosophy.

Inside the front doors dozens of American flags, painted on ceiling tiles, greet visitors. A primary class sits on a colorful rug next to a piano with a sign that reads "Sing Your Way to Reading." A huge shrimp sculpture comically gazes down the center hall, and children's mobiles dance overhead. The halls are covered with every sort of student art, from cartoons to portraits to abstracts. Much of it is framed. On each classroom door is a teacher's name on a large artist's palette. All this before you even reach the office.

This is Terry Bennett's school. It is obvious how he feels about his job as principal—he smiles all the time. It is a place full of energy created by happy teachers and students. But just a few years ago this little school on an island in South Carolina was in turmoil. Changes in racial makeup, caused by a new elementary school built in a bedroom community, left LIES with just over 200 students, 75 percent of them on free or reduced lunch. A massive faculty exodus left only 50 percent of the teachers. It was a school without a focus. How did Mr. Bennett lead the transition to arts integration? He outlined the step-by-step process.

**1.** *Identify Strengths.* "When I came here, I knew we needed a focus. I had many conversations with teachers, parents, and school leaders. I didn't ask about problems. I already knew those. I wanted to identify strengths. I didn't begin with the idea to infuse the arts. The arts just emerged as areas of expertise and interest. Also, I noticed there weren't any discipline problems coming from the art and music classes. That told me something."

**2.** *Gather Research.* Mr. Bennett went looking for connections between the arts and academics. "I was surprised to find so much. The National Assessment of Educational Progress in Arts Education showed that students who received arts instruction outperformed other students. Another study by the Wolf Trap Institute for Early Learning Through the Arts explained how the arts prepare children for their first years of school. Brain research is showing that stimuli provided by pictures, songs, movement, and drama are essential for children to develop to full potential. These activities are the languages of the child, the multiple ways in which kids understand and interpret the world. The arts pave the way for the child to use [written] language to read and write."

Because of the nature of the LIES school population, Mr. Bennett was most interested in research on at-risk students. Findings show that active engagement in the arts improves self-esteem, confidence, leadership skills, and overall academic performance (Deasy, 2002; Rabkin & Redmond, 2004).

"I shared all this with teachers and parents. I even wrote a letter to the local newspaper outlining Catterall's analysis of 25,000 students as they moved from grade 8 to grade 10, illustrating the significant correlations between the arts and higher grades, higher scores on standardized tests, better attendance rates, and participation in community affairs." Bennett also publicized how students from poorer families improved more rapidly than other students when there were arts involved.

"Of course, everyone is impressed by College Board reports that show students who study the arts more than 4 years score 59 points higher on the verbal and 44 points higher on the math portions of the SAT than nonarts students. That is 103 points higher on the SAT!"

**3.** *Mission Statement.* Early on, South Carolina's Arts in the Basic Curriculum (ABC) Program Director Christine Fisher presented an overview of arts integration to the LIES faculty. She explained how they could address problems with attendance, achievement, and teacher turnover by using the arts.

Mural outside Lady's Island Elementary School

Mr. Bennett and the music teacher then attended an ABC workshop to develop a mission statement. "That was our first year together as a school team." Note: The LIES mission statement and beliefs can be viewed online at http://web.beaufort.k12.sc.us/education/school/school.php?sectionid=21.

**4.** *Plan of Action.* "I'm not an artist. What I am is a leader. My staff needed someone to suggest and to push them—to support them," Mr. Bennett explains. It took a year for the school staff to develop a schoolwide plan to bring in artists in residence and to integrate the arts throughout the curriculum.

**5.** *Professional Development.* Mr. Bennett believes in "in-house" professional development. "Our arts specialists took on leadership roles from the beginning. They have a regular place on every faculty meeting agenda." They also worked with the district arts coordinator to bring in outside consultants to kick off the school year. "Our focus was to give classroom teachers arts integration strategies," he says. In addition, teams began to visit other arts-based schools such as nearby Ashley River Creative Arts in Charleston.

**6.** *Implementation.* "During the first year we jumped in. We're not 'there' yet, but teachers are going toward more and more integrated units, and there is an increasing tie-in between what goes on between arts classrooms and regular classrooms." Like every school, a common planning time for classroom teachers to collaborate with arts specialists is the goal.

"We've got kindergartners studying Warhol and Rodin. Classroom teachers do units on local artists, too, like Jonathan Green. Projects and performances are emphasized because they encourage students to apply complex knowledge and skills from several areas simultaneously." Mr. Bennett adds that LIES also partners with local arts agencies and has started after-school arts clubs like one for strings. "One child was in my office whining about something the other day and I said, jokingly, 'Let me play my fiddle.' She said, 'You're not holding it right!'"

In addition to art and music, students now dance once a week in place of PE. The certified dance teacher uses PE standards.

**7.** *Maturation and Evaluation.* Enrollment continues to rise with over half choosing to attend because of the arts focus. The gifted and talented program also identifies artistic abilities. "Students are happier. Every child likes some art form, and they touch all four every day. With happiness comes better attendance. I hear kids say things like, 'I don't want to be absent on Monday because my class has art on Monday.'"

Test scores started up right away. "I attribute this to arts infusion. Teachers are teaching a new way, but emphasizing state standards. We're teaching the same things by teaching differently," Mr. Bennett says. "We believe what Richard Riley, U.S. secretary of education, said: 'The creativity of the arts and the joy of music should be central to the education of every American child.'"

## LIES Update

The LIES cafeteria has now been remodeled into three arts spaces: (1) a music and strings classroom with extra storage for instruments, (2) a dance classroom with dance floor, and (3) a drama classroom. The arts spaces are the center of the building. Teachers completed a yearlong curriculum map project to ensure the arts-integrated curriculum meets state standards. Test scores keep going up. Students exceeded all 17 areas required for NCLB. Last year, the third-grade state PACT scores were excellent: 97 percent scored at the basic level or above in mathematics, and 93 percent scored at basic or above in English language arts.

"The local phone book features artwork from students at LIES. Businesses display framed work throughout the community," Mr. Bennett says proudly. For the fifth year LIES students were in the South Carolina Honors choir. Teacher Deborah Smith was one of the Milken Foundation National Educator Award winners. She believes an integrated arts approach was a key.

Terry Bennett thinks these changes show the arts are "not only the heart of the building but also its soul." He is both reflective and indomitable when he adds, "We continue to struggle with scheduling, funding, state and national requirements—just like every school. However, our focus on student achievement with arts integration has not diminished. We continue to be Beaufort's best kept secret!" ✷

# Why Arts Integration?

*If you believe in great things, other people will too.* (O. W. Holmes)

All of us possess a framework of beliefs that shape our perceptions and determine our behavior, including professional teaching behavior. Philosophy matters. Beliefs and values "create our

sense of what makes life worth living, and therefore what is worth teaching" (Ferrero, 2005, p. 21). Respected beliefs are informed by both research and professional wisdom and judged by how well they support student growth and happiness (Noddings, 2005, p. 10). Ferrero reminds us, however, that beliefs and values have to do with normative questions "not easily settled by empirical means" (p. 22). In other words, experimental research conclusions are not the only source for the "should and ought to" beliefs held by teachers, parents, and students.

## Arts Integration Philosophy: Five Ps

The following are shared beliefs among educators involved in AI. They form interlocking conditions for learning and are in no order. They are organized around five Ps: people, principles, places, programs, and pedagogy.

**People.** Teachers and students have both common and diverse physical, emotional, cognitive/communication, social, and moral dimensions. In particular, all people have creative capacities that have caused the human species to both survive and thrive.

**Creativity.** Arts integration rests on a strong belief that people are innately creative and can learn to intentionally use inherent creative abilities to solve problems, especially the problem of making sense. The arts provide a fertile environment for developing the cognitive skills that are hallmarks of creativity: brainstorming, data gathering from diverse sources, experimentation, imaging, questioning, critiquing, synthesizing, and evaluation using evidence and aesthetic criteria. In addition, the arts develop creative dispositions essential to school success and adult life such as persistence, resilience, collaboration, empathy, and openness to divergent perspectives.

Creativity blooms in an environment where students feel safe taking risks and asking questions. Humor, which has its roots in grappling with problems using a playful approach, is essential to creative thinking. Rigidity, unyielding time restraints and close surveillance can be inhibitors. AI teachers create classroom environments that encourage students to experiment without fear that their initial predictions will be ridiculed. Teachers model creative problem-solving thinking and exhibit creative traits when they ask open questions and encourage out-of-the-box thinking. They use flexible time blocks to permit students to work on long-term projects that result in performances, and exhibits. These learning "products" synthesize understanding and make visible the big ideas that emerge from the creative problem-solving process.

**Teacher Characteristics.** "Research confirms that teachers are the single most important factor in raising student achievement" (PEN, 2004). According to Booth (2003), "Eighty percent of what you teach is who you are" (p. 24). The "artistic teacher" factor looms large in AI because meaningful implementation depends on deeply committed creative teachers who radiate possibilities. Such teachers invite students into a "magic circle" of learning that "awakens the dormant need to participate" (Keppel, 2003, p. 29). These teachers talk passionately about their belief in heads-on, hearts-on, hands-on learning, and readily do extra work because they believe the cause is great. Teachers involved in AI personally use creative problem solving and grow their own arts

## Ready Reference 2.1  Characteristics of Artful Teachers

- **Enthusiasm** for engaging and stretching all students through the arts
- **Desire to learn** new research, theories, and methods related to the arts
- **Passion** about the power of the arts to transform student learning
- **Flexibility** to change schedules and materials and take advantage of teachable moments
- **Openness** to experiment with creative variations on strategies
- **Collaborative** planners willing to co-teach with artists
- **Creative problem solvers** who seek diverse solutions to learning problems
- **Optimism** about teaching and reaching *all* children through instruction that is differentiated using arts-based strategies

- **Humor** to create a positive learning climate and to deal with problems
- **Artistry** in which one-of-a-kind imprints are made on each child by the teacher's unique personality and style
- **Mentorship** of students by sharing personal abilities and interests (e.g., teachers who play instruments, write poetry, paint, or dance), which causes students to choose to apprentice themselves to these "masters"
- **Relationships** with students that form the core of classroom discipline
- **Courage/confidence** to make mistakes and not be threatened by the opinions of nay sayers

---

experiences, which increases their capabilities to take an artful view of teaching and learning. Ready Reference 2.1 lists teacher characteristics that elevate the act of teaching to an art.

**Learner Characteristics: Development and Differences.** AI embraces a developmental view of learning in which students are thought to mature through predictable physical, cognitive, emotional, social, and moral stages. Piaget and others have described such broad stages of development; however, every brain has its own genetic blueprint. Rarely, do any two people, even twins, develop in exactly the same way or at the same rate. Stages are thus perceived as guides, not rigid benchmarks. Learning is a result of experiences, which differ for every person, in either actuality or in the perception of the experience. Indeed, learning is believed to be a consequence of thinking as reflected in each person's brain structure.

AI assumes that genuine efforts to reach educational excellence require educators to consider commonalities of learners while addressing their diverse natures and backgrounds. Teachers focus on differentiating instruction to align with student strengths, needs, and differences to make full development possible. To do so, arts-based instruction and materials are matched to general developmental needs, as well as individual needs, for optimum growth. For example, different visual art materials and tools are provided for less mature students.

At AI schools, teachers also pay considerable attention to teaching in a culturally responsive manner (Cambourne, 2002). The degree of respect for diversity is a significant measure of the effectiveness of arts integration, as is the degree of increase in diverse thinking of teachers and students. Conformity, uniformity, and other marks of standardization are not marks of quality arts-based programs.

As our students' bodies and brains grow more diverse, it behooves us to adjust. Arts integration offers increased possibilities for differentiated instruction because it adds communication options. Teachers have a greater repertoire of strategies to structure lessons so students are provided with appropriate challenges

and they are taught how to create and express meanings in unique ways. Chapter 3 includes a discussion of developmental and individual differences, and specific ways to differentiate by using the arts. There are also suggestions for diversifying lessons in subsequent arts chapters. A flexible developmental continuum of arts development is included in the Appendix.

**Principles of Learning.**  Learning principles are beliefs about how students learn best. They should be rooted in informed perspective. Prominent in AI is a constructivist view of learning.

**Constructivism.**  *Constructivist* proposals align well with central goals of AI that focus on causing students to be active meaning makers individually and in collaboration with others. Constructivist philosophy is supported by 30 years of psychological theory and research that has dissuaded educators from thinking of learning as rote memorization of discrete facts. Instead we are persuaded to focus on the brain's capacity to construct meaning by connecting new information to existing understandings (Bruner, 1960; Dewey, 1899; Gardner, 1990; Levi-Strauss, 1967; Piaget, 1977). The premise is that all knowledge, including that derived from the arts, exists in an interconnected and interdependent web used to interpret and order our experiences (Grumet, 2004).

A growing body of research supports the effectiveness of constructivist approaches in promoting the achievement of diverse students (Au, 2002). Important constructivist tenets embodied in AI follow here.

**Communication.**  Humans are distinct among animals in our intense need and ability to understand and express our thoughts and feelings. The arts are evidence that communication existed before words and the arts persist because words are not up to the task of capturing the wide range of human thinking. Effective communication depends on possessing multiple ways to understand, respond to, and express thoughts and feelings. This includes the language arts (listening, speaking, reading, writing) and the arts (literature, visual art, music, dance, and drama).

At the heart of AI is teaching students how to be fully literate, which entails attaining proficiency in using the arts as basic communication tools. Thus, the arts become integral to the literacy curriculum and expand students' options for comprehension and expression of ideas and feelings throughout all curricular areas and life.

**Personal Meaning-Making.**    A key point in constructivism is that meaning-making is personal. Meaning is "imposed" on texts and events by individuals, not "just uncovered" by them (Au, 2002, p. 29). Meaning is not just found or located, as in "finding the main idea." Meaning is *created* by each person based on his or her background experiences. This need to make sense appears in infancy and the "explanatory drive" persists throughout life (Gopnik, Kuhl, & Meltzoff, 1999).

Arts-based lessons tap into individual interests and backgrounds, which motivates students. Arts-based lessons employ creative problem solving which provides students with the thinking repertoire to act on the human predisposition to create sense. The inquiry-based creative problem-solving (CPS) process is used to construct meaning across disciplines and assumes there are many right answers to problems so students feel encouraged to seek solutions that are distinctive in nature. Arts-based lessons culminate in externalized understandings that students show through mime, sculpture, and other arts media, including technology that uses visuals, music, role-taking (drama), and movement (dance).

**Meaning at the Core.**    John Dewey believed school should not be seen as preparation for life but a part of life. So do teachers at AI schools. Learners are involved in important and purposeful work that contributes to their own happiness and the happiness of others. Relevance is increased by tapping student interests, connecting to their background experiences, and engaging them in hands-on, heads-on, hearts-on inquiry (Maxim, 2010).

Arts integration extends meaningfulness by focusing on teaching students to use problem-solving skills needed in real life, along with how to use diverse materials, tools, and techniques connected to the real world. Meaningfulness is extended further when learning is structured around projects that provide authentic contexts for problem solving and products that will be shared with audiences.

**Ways of Knowing.**    Given (2002) explains that students have cognitive needs (e.g., need to know and self-monitor), emotional needs (e.g., to feel pride in one's efforts), social needs (e.g., need to belong), and physical needs (e.g., need to move). At AI schools learning is all about the integration of these multiple mind and body systems. Teachers orchestrate experiences that are thought provoking, aesthetic, concrete, and physically engaging. Teachers employ the power of emotion to boost learning by acknowledging that every thought, decision, and response are accompanied and often determined by emotion.

Arts-based teaching activates all the perceptual senses. As a result, making and doing the arts changes how we think and how we feel because they use alternative channels for perception and expression, including moving and touching. Image-based thinking, rather than word-based, allows thinking without words. Visual, sound, emotional, and physical images move through our minds and bodies and are projected using dance, drama, music, and art. Teaching strategies such as arts-based warm-ups, open questions, and descriptive feedback invite cognitive, affective, and physical engagement.

**Processing of Wholes and Parts.**    The brain makes sense by sorting and connecting. This requires attention to the big picture and small details and is the kind of problem solving evident even when the task is simply to rearrange the furniture in a room. Students must learn how isolated skills and individual concepts add up to big understandings. They can do so when taught how to listen to a whole song or view a whole painting and be open to cognitive and emotional responses. The whole experience comes into focus as they notice details. The details, in turn, have meaning because they are part of the whole, just as letters are meaningless until they are put into words, which also need greater context to actually make sense.

Whole with part teaching causes students to stand back and move in close to create meaning. Arts-based teaching combines zoom out and zoom in with a focus on aesthetic knowing through all senses. Students are explicitly taught pieces, parts, and elements of the arts as means to understand, respond to, and express meaning—not as ends in and of themselves.

**Response and Transformation.**    The root of the word *responsibility* is response. Children become responsible when they are taught appropriate ways to respond using myriad arts tools, materials, and techniques. Indeed meaning construction depends upon acting on, representing, and changing ideas. This transformation connects new ideas to those already known.

Andrew miming his caterpillar art
*Source:* Jo Ellen McElwee

Active student engagement that targets making sense of diverse texts and events is believed to result in a higher level of motivation because it promotes feelings of student ownership and involvement in learning (Maxim, 2010). Active engagement is also thought to create deeper understanding because it focuses on transforming ideas (e.g., from written to visual) through thinking, doing, and feeling. In the arts this translates into a broad array of actions, such as making, molding, moving, creating, doing, acting, and singing.

Arts integration seeks to teach students to make novel links among disparate ideas. Hooking to previous experience is vital, so teachers often begin lessons with brainstorming what students already know about a topic. During lessons students are drawn to significant details by prompting them to take time to zoom in and then zoom out to find patterns. Asking and coaching is valued over telling. Specific arts elements and concepts (details) are explicitly taught as anchors so students have specific tools to transform their ideas. Students are taught to use creative problem solving, which includes synthesizing patterns to arrive at new perspectives and products. This kind of transformation yields deep understanding.

Meaningful work with artists and arts content and materials also causes students to *be* transformed. Over time they build a reservoir of knowledge and skills to work in new ways. Many AI projects are yoked to multiple intelligences theory for this purpose.

**Drive for Independence.** From toddlerhood on, it is obvious that children want to do it themselves and in their own way. Learners feel more confident when they gain the competence to solve their own problems. The arts are about expanding ways to understand, respond, and express meaning independently. Arts-based teaching focuses on explicit teaching of arts concepts and skills that provide students expanded communication options. Teachers move students toward independence by explicitly teaching problem-solving strategies, scaffolding practice, and providing time to work independently, with feedback. Students also need to understand that independence is gained through hard work. Artists provide significant role models of hardworking people who persist at overcoming obstacles to independence.

Constructivist views of learning assume a developmental perspective, which guides lesson planning, and instruction that embraces learner diversity. A main goal is to expand each student's capacity to independently problem solve, enabling them to create new meanings throughout their lives. Teachers emphasize the development of arts knowledge and creative problem-solving skills so learners can increasingly create meaning with more independence.

**Conscious and Unconscious Learning.** Attention, concentration, and focus are necessary for learning. Attention is critical to memory, but human beings have both conscious and unconscious attentive capabilities. Children learn language, behavior, values, and beliefs by both direct and indirect attention (Schacter, 2002).

Concentration involves sustained attention and is best achieved through deep engagement in creative problem solving ("flow" is the most engaged state). Arts-based learning occurs in contexts set up to maximize attention through aesthetic stimulation. Teachers also use arts-based strategies to capture students' focus, sustain concentration, and give time for incubation, which allows unconscious integration of ideas. At AI schools lessons routinely include conscious reflection on work and self-evaluation against specific criteria, often set out in rubrics.

**Intrinsic Motivation and Depth of Learning.** The arts develop internal motivation because they purposefully focus on inside-out meaning construction. The motivational character of the arts stems from curiosity, wonder, and yearning. Fun is taken seriously and tapped for its *fun*damental role in engaging through movement, novelty, challenge, surprise, and group work (DeMoss & Morris, 2002). A focus on time to pursue interests and having choices are particularly key to intrinsic motivation (Guthrie, 2004) and account for large effect sizes in comprehension.

Arts integration minimizes extrinsic reinforcers such as stickers and praise, because they decrease interest in learning for its own sake. These external controls are not needed when students are motivated by arts engagement. However, learners must believe they are capable of creative problem solving and be competent in using it. If problems are too difficult or students lack knowledge or skill to participate, they can become overly frustrated or bored.

Arts integration relies on noncompetitive social interaction in which groups work to solve problems and share ideas, which may result in individual products. Competitive practices are minimized because they can threaten and cause students to lose hope or give up. Arts integration motivates individuals by tapping the unique contributions each can make. This also increases the likelihood of more complex understanding for all students.

**Social Influences.** Humans are group animals who have evolved to take advantage of the specialized talents of members of the group. We are very sensitive to those around us and the meanings we make are heavily influenced by both the context of learning and its social circumstances, that is, where and with whom you learn. Social interactions among peers and with the teacher are thought to change the quantity and quality of meaning-making (Vygotsky, 1986; Au, 2002). Social relationships fill needs to belong and be heard, recognized, and respected (Gopnik et al., 1999; Maslow, 1970). Learning to learn from and work with others is essential to success in the classroom and the workplace, where cooperation is needed to solve problems and create new products. Healthy personal relationships are built on cooperation and respect.

The arts provide multiple opportunities for students to learn important social skills through choirs, ensembles, and clubs. In each of these arenas, students must tackle inevitable problems that arise when two or more people assemble. Audiences are a social force that can cause shy and reluctant students to blossom. Students learn how to take on the role of an audience member, too, which increases their social adeptness and capacity to enjoy, appreciate, and gain aesthetic satisfaction.

**Places.** Learning cannot be separated from its context. The teacher must create an environment that convinces learners they need to engage as deeply as possible (Cambourne, 2002). It is impossible to imagine deep engagement in sterile or unpleasant classrooms.

Arts integration emphasizes creating an aesthetic learning ecology in which sights, sounds, and smells are used to stimulate the senses. The psychological feel of a classroom also affects student success. Students will not take risks if they do not feel that it is physically and psychologically safe to make mistakes. The teacher's personality, beliefs, and teaching approach are the greatest determiners of climate. Caine and Caine (2005) recommend that the classroom be low threat and high challenge, which creates a "relaxed alertness"—an optimal state in which fear and pleasure centers of the brain are moderated.

Albert Einstein once commented that it was nothing short of a miracle that the modern methods of instruction have not yet entirely strangled the holy curiosity of inquiry. He called curiosity a "delicate little plant" that needs freedom as much as stimulation to thrive. As we consider the reasons behind the growing momentum for arts integration, it is important to consider the role of freedom in schooling. Worldwide, America is nearly synonymous with freedom and yet school structures and classroom practices don't always mirror the principles of our democracy. Classrooms cannot be dictatorships if we want our students to learn how to participate in the democratic process for solving problems. The concept of arts integration is rooted in core values that find coercion and conformity repellent. Like Einstein, thoughtful educators and arts advocates worry about the potential for "rank and ruin" if educational practices don't promote "engagement of seeing and searching," possible only in a climate that celebrates risk taking, freedom of expression, and individual differences that give strength to a society. Students learn democratic values by living them as citizens of the school. Children at arts-based schools learn to make thoughtful decisions and manage their own behavior because they are given the reins to experiment and then expected to become informed decision makers. Mistakes are viewed as opportunities. Self-reflection and critique are emphasized to increase quality of work and depth of learning.

**Programs.** Local educators and arts specialists, based on the unique needs and resources of their schools, shape meaningful AI curriculum and instruction. There is not one model. Some programs are district wide, others are schoolwide. Some use grants to fund artist residencies and provide collaborative planning time for teachers and specialists. Others involve individual teachers that plan together with in-house arts specialists using limited budgets. All successful programs are the result of addressing the 10 building blocks introduced in Chapter 1, including intentional curricular design that addresses standards, use of research to ground instruction, and teacher development through ongoing professional development related to increased best practices in the arts, collaborative planning, and co-teaching skills.

Most AI programs share the goal of integrating multiple art forms throughout the curriculum. Overlapping concepts and skills are found among arts and academic areas. At first, just one art may be used and perhaps one or two integrated units per year. Some schools dedicate a specific amount of school time to integration (e.g., arts-based literacy block). The speed and quality of integration is determined by the arts knowledge depth and the pedagogical base of teachers and arts specialists.

Most programs start small, with emphasis on teacher comfort and arts predispositions. Some schools, such as Hilton Head Creative Arts, spend a year or more studying research and visiting schools (Keefner, 2005). All schools must eventually construct a philosophy that guides the program design. This includes a mission statement and consensus operating principles to make clear how teachers agree to put beliefs into action.

**Pedagogy.** Quality arts integration rests on good teaching. Research confirms that the effects of AI on learning depend on the length and specific nature of arts integration (Corbett, Wilson, & Morse, 2005). The pedagogy of quality arts integration is flexible, but draws on three basic sources: (1) general, research-based, best teaching practices (Allington, 2005; Zemelman, Daniels, & Hyde, 1998), (2) general practices that relate to the arts, and (3) practices peculiar to each art form. Teachers grow their repertoire of best practices over time when they have opportunities to collaborate with other teachers and arts specialists.

**Teacher Roles.** AI envisions teachers in the following roles to meet cognitive, emotional, and physical needs of students (Given, 2002).

- Specialists and generalists
- Mentors and models
- Collaborators in co-planning and co-teaching
- Facilitators and coaches
- Managers, directors, and guides
- Talent scouts
- Co-learners with students
- Motivators
- Assessors and evaluators

**Instruction.** Specific best teaching practices integral to arts integration are discussed in Chapter 3. Specific arts practices are addressed in separate arts chapters. Basic beliefs about pedagogy are summarized here using six Ts of effective teaching (adapted from Allington, 2002).

*Talk.* Allington (2005) suggests that "even small amounts of conversation produce huge comprehension benefits." Focused conversation among students increases learning. Arts integrated classrooms are not dominated by teacher talk. Instead, teachers use mini-lessons to introduce and demonstrate, and students are quickly set to work to solve problems. They learn to take turns, share ideas, and actively listen to others as they brainstorm solutions. Students learn to question, clarify, and reflect. Through drama, students learn to be comfortable improvising and controlling their voices and bodies. They learn to subdue their own volume as background music is played. Most of all, students learn that voicing their own ideas is valued.

*Tasks.* The major task is to actively engage students in constructing meaning from diverse texts relevant in today's world. This communication task has three parts: creating understanding (comprehension), responding, and expressing ideas and feelings. Meaning construction is accomplished using the creative problem-solving process, associated with the arts, and aligned with the reading-writing processes and inquiry used in science and social studies. The goal is to engage students in sustained inquiry and for them to learn self-monitoring. Specific arts content, skills, and materials are taught for use during creative problem solving. These expand the communication possibilities and enable students to transform ideas and feel a sense of ownership about the products they create.

*Texts.* Texts are no longer conceived as traditional printed material, such as textbooks. A 21st-century concept of "text" includes paintings, sculpture, architecture, songs, musical pieces, and dances that are heard and seen on everything from an iPod to television programs. Texts can also reflect any genre ranging from informational to poetic. Students need to be taught to make sense of all types and forms of texts in today's world that record ideas, values, and emotions. Classroom teachers and arts specialists can work in concert to teach students the arts literacy needed to "read" arts texts, including how to decode each art's symbol system (e.g., how pitch, tempo, and dynamics are used to make music).

*Time.* Differentiation to meet diverse student needs requires that time be flexible. In general, different students need different amounts of time to learn the same thing. Time is an important variable. For example, the creative problem-solving process is central to arts integration, but teachers must vary instructional time to accommodate this process. Incubation time is needed for students to take a recess from a piece of writing or visual art project so they can return with a fresh perspective. One prominent feature of AI is long-term projects that deepen understanding through higher order thinking used in creative problem solving. These take time, but the result is stunning exhibits and performances that show how students can synthesize learning, when time is made available for meaningful work.

*Transfer.* The promise of transfer of learning from arts experiences to academic areas has intensified research efforts and increased hope, especially for disadvantaged students. Significant arts involvement appears to narrow the gap between students from low-income families and those from more affluent backgrounds (Catterall, 2003; Deasy & Stevenson, 2005).

There is no debate that arts engagement requires higher order thinking, problem-solving skills, and motivational dispositions common to success in school and life. The arts promote curiosity, inquiry, persistence, experimentation, synthesis, and flexible thinking—all of which are important beyond the school walls and critical to 21st-century job success (*Arts Skills Map*, 2010). Pedagogical issues related to the potential of transfer of arts learning depend on how explicit the teacher is about common links between learning in the arts and other subjects (Winner & Cooper, 2000). For example, transfer is more likely when teachers demonstrate parallels between CPS and the reading and writing processes. Ideally, transfer goes back and forth. Students who understand that written composition shares much with the composition process in visual art are likely to use skills from each to enrich both (Olhansky, 2008). This is two-way transfer. Three-way transfer is the ultimate goal—arts to academics, academics to arts, and both to life.

*Tests.* The arts have a long history of using nontraditional ways to show achievement—primarily portfolios, performances, and exhibitions. In arts integration these assessment tools are fully employed. Instead of relying on paper tests, students "show they know." They externalize learning by creating dance, drama, visual art, music, and poetry responses that synthesize ideas. Portfolios of work, rubrics, and self-evaluation are common and combine with performances and exhibits to do more than gauge what was learned. These "tests" motivate students to want to learn. When assessment is used *for* learning and not just *of* learning, it is viewed as less threatening and more valuable (Stiggins, 2002). "How am I doing?" is a question students ask because they earnestly want to improve, not just get a higher grade. Hope is sustained through a belief that there is a strong chance of success.

## Mission Statement

Schools embarking on arts integration usually begin by creating a philosophical statement of beliefs that embraces the power of arts to facilitate learning. The five Ps discussed previously can be an organizer for this work. When individual teachers or groups integrate the arts on their own, they too must begin with clarity about what they believe is right and good for students. Increasingly beliefs are coalescing around arts integration. More and more the word *arts* is becoming a part of school names, as with Hilton Head Creative Arts (renamed 2006), formerly the Island Academy.

At Hand Middle School in Columbia, South Carolina, the staff developed a 5-year plan based on the mounting evidence linking cognition to the arts. According to their new mission statement, "All students should be enriched by exposure to the fine arts through high quality, comprehensive fine arts courses and the integration of the fine arts into every subject." Principal Marissa Vickers calls the arts an "integral component" and an "anchor" for students' daily learning. Examples of arts integration at Hand include use of familiar melodies to learn the order of the planets and the muscular system, focus on using descriptive adjectives first in art and then in writing, setting original poetry to music, drawing editorial cartoons in social studies, and dance and drama performances of science content such as the laws of motion and rain forest destruction. To view the mission statement and other information about Hand Middle School, visit http://hand.rcsd1.org/home.aspx.

# What Research Supports Arts Integration?

*The best arts integration programs demonstrate a strategy that can help close the achievement gap and make schools happier places. It is a strategy within reach of most schools and districts, even those in the poorest communities.* (Rabkin & Redmond, 2005)

The track record for arts integration as a tool for academic gain continues to strengthen. As more teachers use the motivation and communication powers of the arts, reports of increased concentration, more cooperation, better comprehension, and greater self-discipline among students are on the rise (Deasy, 2002; Deasy & Stevenson, 2005; Corbett, Wilson, & Morse, 2005). Studies of successful adults show that effort and persistence pays off; the arts increase persistence (Thompson & Barniskis, 2005). Persistence derives from motivation; in arts-based schools it becomes apparent that it wasn't that students couldn't learn—it was that they wouldn't. The arts make students want to learn. What's more, students become more resilient to setbacks when they have the opportunity to learn through arts-based inquiry lessons that emphasize experimentation and learning from mistakes.

## Controllables

Teachers can feel helpless when faced with evidence that the most powerful correlates of academic achievement (IQ, parent's income, and education) are beyond their control. Fortunately, several controllable factors correlate with high scores and with important attributes not measured by tests. Arts integration is one of those "controllables." A solid body of evidence correlates meaningful teaching through the arts with higher academic achievement and desirable personal and social behaviors (Deasy, 2002; Corbett, Wilson, & Morse, 2005; Ruppert, 2006).

Researchers will probably never be able to identify all the particulars of AI that cause the strong correlations. Consider how just one factor, the teacher, plays a major role. A charismatic, highly skilled teacher can make the most boring worksheet into a significant learning event, while a dull, rigid teacher can corrupt the most wonderful piece of literature. Arts integration intentionally dwells on "live performers," leaving it highly vulnerable to the influence of specific personalities.

Arts integration is also defined in numerous ways and implemented to different degrees. It is difficult to create a research design that deals with such complexities. In whole school reform it is particularly hard to use the classic experimental design that yields cause–effect findings with random sampling and control groups. Who would want their children to be in a control that uses less than the best of what is known about good instruction? Furthermore, the standard for success of educational programs is often an unrealistic expectation of 100 percent. Scientific research is held up as a model, despite the acceptance of much lower effectiveness levels in scientific fields. For example, pharmaceuticals are offered as research models even though 90 percent of drugs only work with 30 to 50 percent of the population (Allen Roses, geneticist and vice president of GlaxoSmithKline, quoted in Connor, 2003). Imagine proposing an educational approach that only works with one third to one half of kids. The consequences of overreliance on "scientific research" have become apparent as more and more "proven" treatments, such as silicone implants and Vioxx, have been shown to have life-threatening side effects.

## Testing Inadequacies

A compelling argument is made that measuring complex thinking in the arts is beyond the capabilities of current tests. Hetland and Winner (2000) call the research on the arts–academics connection "inconclusive," but make the case that the arts should not be justified by their ability to increase test scores. The arts have inherent merits such as an unquestioned ability to compel interest, induce empathy, and give new perspectives. These and many of the other important influences of the arts are not easily measured in standardized testing formats (Efland, 2002). Artistic processes resist standardization. As Eisner (2002a) is quick to point out, that which is easily measured may not matter and what matters is not easy to measure.

Scripp (2003) argues further that "one-way cause and effect" models of research are appropriate when it is only possible that the treatment affects the outcome. He points out, for example, that smoking causes cancer, but cancer does not cause smoking. Arts-based learning is not a one-way street. Learning in music enhances math, but math undoubtedly enriches music achievement. One-way transfer is unlikely and is a constricted view of learning. That said, most available research looks at what the arts might do for academics, not the other way around.

## Meta-analysis

A relatively new methodology, meta-analysis, allows researchers to examine a wide range of research and draw conclusions by averaging effect sizes across studies. One controversial study can no longer be used to "discredit the general trends of a diverse collection of research over time" (Scripp, 2003, p. 127). Meta-analysis has added a degree of stability to interpretation of results. Of special importance is "triangulation" that uses "multiple ways of assessing learning outcomes which may corroborate each other and lend credence to inferences about what leads to what" (Catterall, 2003, p. 114). A growing body of work compares results across multiple studies, and dozens of studies are finding the same thing: Significant arts involvement changes how children think and how they feel about learning. That fact is reflected in test scores and in vast quantities of survey, interview, observation, and anecdotal evidence.

## Research Findings

The following findings are organized according to the diverse relationships found between arts engagement and (1) academic achievement, (2) cognitive/higher order thinking, (3) literacy/math, (4) affective/motivational changes, (5) social growth, (6) learning environment, and (7) diverse learners. In general, the literature reports data to support an array of positive influences. The subsequent summary describes important research findings. Many studies cited were descriptive in nature and yielded correlational findings from which potential causal relationships between the arts and other areas are inferred. Most of the conclusions were drawn from syntheses of large numbers of studies. The quantity of studies that produce similar findings is important and alleviates, to some extent, concerns about the ability to conclusively discern cause–effect relationships.

There have been several important digests of research on the effects on students and teachers involved in arts-based teaching and learning. The information that follows comes from several sources (Burnaford, 2007; Catterall, 1998; Catterall,

Chapleau, & Iwanaga, 1999b; Darby & Catterall, 1994; Deasy, 2002; Deasy & Stevenson, 2005; Fiske, 1999; Horowitz, 2004; Keirstead & Graham, 2004; Project Zero, 2000; Rooney, 2004; Upitis & Smithrim, 2003). Additional references are included where needed to help locate particular studies.

# Academic Achievement

## (as Measured by Test Scores)

1. *Arts-involved students score higher than other students.* Differences range significantly from 16 to 18 percentage points (test scores). Students whose parents had lower incomes scored lower, but their scores were still significant. Researchers include Darby and Catterall (1994), a meta-analysis of 188 reports; Catterall (1998), a survey of more than 25,000 students over 10 years; and Catterall et al. (1999), Deasy (2002), Fiske (1999), Harvard's Project Zero (2000), and Upitis and Smithrin (2003).

2. *Greater arts involvement yields higher test scores.* Longer and more intense work in the arts had more impact. This effect was particularly strong for low-income and ESL students (Fiske, 1999; Ingram & Riedel, 2003; Stronge, 2002).

3. *Academic achievement builds over time.* "Gain scores" (year-over-year comparisons) were significantly higher for third, fourth, and fifth graders in arts integrated classrooms (Ingram & Riedel, 2003).

4. *Arts experiences especially benefit "undereducated" students.* Researchers include Corbett, Wilson, and Morse (2005), Deasy (2002), Deasy and Stevenson (2005), and Upitis and Smithrim (2003). See additional findings under "Diverse Learners."

# Cognitive Effects

Schools that integrate the arts develop essential thinking such as "careful observation of the world; mental representation of what is observed or imagined; abstraction from complexity; pattern recognition and development; qualitative judgment; symbolic, metaphoric, and allegorical representation" (Rabkin & Redmond, 2005, pp. 46–47). These are the same kinds of thinking used in science, math, social studies, reading, and writing. Basically this is thought to be why students in arts-based schools reach higher academic standards. Teaching students to use complex thinking beyond literal or memory levels is difficult, and there has been only limited success using traditional methods (Kamil, 2004; Cornett, 2010). No one debates that the arts engage higher order thinking. The problem is that these effects may not show up in test results or on traditional measures of academic achievement (Efland, 2002). Here are the findings to date.

*Arts experiences engage and strengthen higher order thinking.* These include increases in comprehension/meaning construction, spatial reasoning (the capacity for organizing and sequencing ideas), conditional reasoning (theorizing about outcomes and consequences), problem solving/decision making, and the components of creative thinking (originality, elaboration, and flexibility) (Deasy, 2002; Efland, 2002; Eisner, 2002a; Horowitz, 2004; Mardirosian & Fox, 2003; Psilos, 2002; Winner & Hetland, 2000a, 2000b).

*Critical thinking is developed through the arts.* For example, students used more "evidentiary reasoning" and broadened their understanding of interpretation itself from discussing paintings (Horowitz, 2004; Project Zero, 2000).

*Creativity as a "capacity for learning" is expanded.* High arts students are more fluent, flexible, original, elaborative, and willing to resist closure (A+ Schools, 2001; Burton, Horowitz, & Abeles, 1999; New American Schools, 2003).

*Spatial reasoning, organization, planning, self-direction, and self-assessment improve.* Music, in particular, has been found to enhance spatial thinking (Burton et al., 1999; Darby & Catterall, 1994; Deasy, 2002; Fiske, 1999; Psilos, 2002).

# Literacy and Math Effects

*Arts instruction complements basic reading instruction.* Arts lessons have been found to enhance the learning of letter names and sounds, spelling, and decoding processes including phonics (Deasy, 2002; Myers & Scripp, 2007).

*The arts offer additional ways to understand and represent ideas and feelings.* This includes improved language and literacy skills related to use of drama and music. For example, dramatic enactments of stories and text improve writing, reading comprehension, and ability to read materials not seen before. The effects are even more significant for children from economically disadvantaged circumstances and those with reading difficulties. Planning and organizing skills inherent in music are parallel with planning and producing writing (Deasy, 2002).

*Increased communication leads to other effects.* Students are more cooperative, have greater rapport with teachers, show more sustained focus, and are more willing to perform and exhibit learning (Burton et al., 1999; Darby & Catterall, 1994; Deasy, 2002; Rooney, 2004).

*Music instruction develops math-related skills.* Spatial reasoning and spatial temporal reasoning skills used in music are fundamental to understanding and using mathematical ideas and concepts (Deasy, 2002).

# Motivational/Affective Effects

Motivation to pursue and sustain learning is essential to achievement. Learning in the arts nurtures motivation through active engagement, boosting self-confidence and self-efficacy. These increase attendance, educational aspirations, and ownership of learning. Arts-based teaching makes learning more equitable by broadening access to understanding and ways to express meaning (Annenberg Institute for School Reform, 2002; Darby & Catterall, 1994; Fogg & Smith, 2001; Morrow, 2001; Rooney, 2004).

*Self-esteem, flexibility, and willingness to take risks, experiment, and tolerate uncertainty increases* (A+ Schools, 2001; Catterall et al., 1999a and b; Eisner, 2002a; Jensen, 2001; Ritter, 1999; Rooney, 2004; Stronge, 2002).

*Fewer at-risk behaviors were found.* In particular, students involved in music showed this pattern (New American Schools, 2003).

*Empathy for others increased.* Drama, in particular, was found to show this effect. Stereotypical views toward minority cultures decreased when arts instruction focused on Native American music and culture (Catterall et al., 1999; Edwards, 1994).

*Students stay in school longer and have more positive attitudes* (Catterall et al., 1999a and b).

## Social Effects

Studies of arts-based learning experiences in drama, music, dance, and multiple arts activities show student growth in self-control, conflict resolution, collaboration, empathy, and social tolerance.

*Quality of classroom participation increased.* Students involved as makers and doers in the arts showed the greatest ability to collaborate, reflect, and make choices (Deasy, 2002; Fiske, 1999).

*Self-discipline/regulation increased.* Students were more cooperative, paid attention, persevered, did more problem solving, took initiative, asked questions, took positive risks, used feedback, and prepared. Greater communication skills developed through the arts enhanced ability to achieve consensus (Burton et al., 1999; Deasy, 2002).

*The arts make education more equitable.* The arts are "instruments of cognitive growth and agents of motivation," so unfair access to the arts "brings consequences of major importance to our society" (Catterall et al., 1999, p. 17). The National Assessment of Educational Progress (NAEP) data demonstrates how the arts can level the educational playing field. For example, among all areas in which students were tested, music scores reflected the narrowest gap between varying races and minorities.

*Arts-based instruction can increase family and community support* (Annenberg Institute, 1998). Dramatic increases were found in "syntactic complexity, hypothetical reasoning, and questioning approaches" that enable planning and give youth "language with which to collaborate productively and respectfully," allowing them to participate in social enterprises to improve their communities (Heath & Roach, 1999, p. 27).

## Learning Environment

It is critical that students learn in a positive context. The arts help create the kind of learning environment that boosts success by "fostering teacher innovation, a positive professional culture, community engagement, increased student attendance and retention, effective instructional practice, and school identity" (Deasy, 2002, pp. iii–iv).

*The arts enhance learning by creating "strong school ecologies."* A "complex web of stimulation and influence creates an enhanced learning environment [which is] key to academic achievement" (Rooney, 2004). Arts-infused environments increase opportunities for engaged, active, interdisciplinary teaching and learning (A+ Schools, 2001; Burton et al., 1999; Fiske, 1999; Fogg & Smith, 2001; Seaman, 1999).

*The arts promote a greater spirit of cooperation and participation.* Teachers work more collaboratively and are more creative, artistic, and enthusiastic. They think more deeply and are more open and flexible. Teachers involved in AI are more likely to participate in professional development and acquire a broader repertoire of teaching strategies (A+ Schools, 2001; Burton et al., 1999; Rooney, 2004).

## Diverse Learners

Imagine Leonardo da Vinci in an average American school. "This illegitimate son of a poor woman, a left-handed writer who loved to draw and challenge conventional thought, would be labeled an at-risk special education candidate" (Murfee, 1995, p. 8). The arts engage and offer challenges for all students—at risk, disadvantaged, delayed, and gifted from every cultural background. AI presents a menu of learning opportunities that widens success possibilities by increasing participation by all students. The open-ended problem-solving nature of AI encourages individual inquiry. In addition, arts teachers tend to be more diverse so students interact with role models from various backgrounds. Findings from large-scale projects such as South Carolina's ABC schools show that AI offers hope for increasing the capacities of all children, especially diverse learners. For more in-depth information about research programs for diverse learners, visit the Very Special Arts website, www.vsarts.org.

*Arts-based teaching engages a wide range of learners.* By introducing flexibility, teachers can better promote individuality and diversity. All arts-involved students showed higher levels of learning, especially at-risk and underachieving students (Deasy, 2002; Eisner, 2002a, 2000b; Fiske, 1999; Goldberg & Phillips, 2000; Ingram & Riedel, 2003; Mason, Thormann, & Steedly, 2004; New American Schools, 2003; Stronge, 2002; Upitis & Smithrim, 2003). Students who have struggled with traditional modes of instruction find success in inclusive environments that build on commonalities, while respecting differences.

*Arts-based teaching and learning "opens avenues."* Students who are not part of the dominant culture benefit from expanded opportunities for learning that the arts provide (Annenberg Institute, 2003; Darby & Catterall, 1994; Mason et al., 2004).

*Significant relationships and improvements in reading, writing, and math were found.* This research focused on disadvantaged low-scoring students involved in the arts experiences such as using multimedia from photographs, objects, and videos to advanced computer software (Ingram & Riedel 2003; National Center to Improve Practice [www2.edc.org/NCIP/]).

## Brain Research

*Good teachers know that lecturing on the American Revolution is far less effective than acting out a battle.* (Robert Sylwester, University of Oregon)

Since the early Greeks, we have known that the brain is the locus of cognition. Beyond that, the brain was a mystery—until now. Tools such as positron emission tomography (PET) and magnetic resonance imaging (MRI) allow neuroscientists to see brain growth and development. They see a "tight correlation" between arts engagement and improved cognitive skills, including ability to attend (Dana Foundation, 2008).

Unfortunately, brain science is not far enough along to give much direction to educators, but this hasn't stopped some from drawing unfounded instructional connections. Oversimplified "neuromyths" continue to circulate. At present there is no "grand scheme of brain-based education that will instantly transform learning" (Hall, 2005, pp. 27–28). We know relatively little about "how the brain thinks, remembers, and learns" (Bruer, 1999, p. 648). A cautious approach is recommended that acknowledges incomplete knowledge but also the reality of children waiting to be taught every day.

## Misconceptions

There are three basic areas of misunderstanding.

1. *Constructivism.* The constructivist view of learning at the foundation of arts integration is based on more than three decades of *psychological* research (Bruer, 1999). It is psychological, not brain, research that has yielded findings about memory and the effects of prior knowledge on learning. Bruer says "to claim that these are 'brain-based' findings is misleading" (p. 649).

2. *Left–right brain dichotomy.* There is no evidence that people do anything but use their whole brains, unless the corpus collosum is severed. Split-brain models are now considered crude. Such is the conclusion of Christopher Chabris and Stephen Kosslyn, leading researchers who call it "folk theory" to lump "conglomerations of complex mental abilities, such as spatial reasoning, to one hemisphere or the other" (Bruer, 1999, p. 650). Different brain areas are specialized for different tasks, but the specialization occurs at a finer level than being able to say something like visual imagery occurs in the right brain (p. 651). Mental picturing is not isolated to one hemisphere and neither are speech, writing, and reading (Shaywitz, 2004). Both hemispheres are used to hear phonemes in words, decode the pronunciation of written words, give meaning to words, construct the gist of a written text, and infer as we read. Simply stated, "both hemispheres are involved in all activities" (Bruer, 1999, p. 648).

3. *Windows of development.* It has not been established that there is a "sensitive period between the ages of 4 and 10 during which children learn more quickly, easily, and meaningfully" (Bruer, 1999, p. 648). Some neuroscientists contend that there is a biological window when learning is easy, efficient, and durable. It is accepted that there are critical periods for "species-wide skills, such as seeing, hearing, and acquiring a first language; but these seem to be the exception rather than the rule in human development" (p. 655). The debate continues about whether the time of excess brain connectivity gives children greater opportunity to retain and increase efficiency of connections. It is a fact that much, if not most learning takes place after age 10 when pruning is complete. We may actually be more efficient learners after puberty when the brain is growing less.

## Brain Facts and Educational Implications

The following are implications from brain research that have bearing on arts integration.

**Environmental Effects.** At birth, the brain has 100 billion neurons, which in turn make more than 50 trillion synapses. In early childhood, neurons begin to hook up according to sensory input. This process is known as "synaptogenesis" (Hall, 2005, p. 28); the growth happens "like a budding and branching tree," depending on which areas are stimulated. By age 3, trillions of connections will have been created, more than the brain can possibly use. Over time, unused, seldom used, and redundant connections are eliminated. As early as age 10, a "draconian pruning" occurs and some neurons die (Hall, 2005, p. 28; Nash, 1997, p. 50). The elimination of connections is not genetically predetermined (Simmons & Sheehan, 1997). While synapse pruning is scientific fact, it is not known whether adults with greater synaptic density are more intelligent and developed. By adulthood the number of neurons in the brain reaches 100 trillion (Hall, 2005). The brain continues to grow much longer than previously thought (Bruer, 1999; Hansen & Monk, 2002). It is well established that we don't lose brain cells as we age—we are always capable of growing.

So, the human brain has infinite potential, but the environment has a great influence on whether a child "grows up intelligent or dull, fearful or self assured, articulate or tongue-tied" (Begley, 1996, p. 56). A child's environment alters both the number and complexity of brain synapses; there is no preprogrammed unfolding (Bransford, 1999). Even animal studies demonstrate that those raised with playmates and toys grew 25 percent more synapses than deprived ones. Experiments also have shown that kittens remain blind in one eye when the eye, sewn shut at birth, is reopened. Other kittens raised in an environment with only horizontal lines grew to be cats that did not see vertical lines. The horizontal cats ran right into vertical bars as if they didn't exist (Hubel, 1988). In humans there seems to be a window for visual acuity development that lasts until about age 8. If the brain does not receive the right information, results can be devastating. For example, children born with cataracts became permanently blind in affected eyes if the clouded lens was not removed by age 2. Studies also show brain development is inhibited by restricted physical activity (Begley, 1996). For example, a child in a body cast until age 4 never learns to walk smoothly.

**Implications.** Arts integration creates a highly stimulating learning environment featuring arts materials, tools, and strategies to increase the possibilities for sensory input. In AI classrooms it is common for students to work in groups and to be out of their seats. Drama and dance allow students to move and learn kinesthetically. Student passivity is replaced with hands-on problem solving.

Because the brain is constantly changing during childhood, it is important to be responsive to individual maturational strengths and needs as well (Hansen & Monk, 2002). Arts integration focuses on the "power of one," in which each child is valued for his or her uniqueness, while being sensitive to general developmental patterns. Strengths and needs are assessed and teaching focuses on developing, not suppressing, differences.

**Stress.** Research confirms the negative impact of early stress on brain function (Lindsey, 1998–99). Stress causes the amygdala to flood the brain with chemicals potentially harmful to development of the cortex, which causes problems with understanding. The result is that "children who don't play much or are rarely touched develop brains 20% to 30% smaller than normal" (Nash, 1997, p. 51).

**Implications.** Arts integration happens in a "synapse-stimulating" aesthetic environment. AI philosophy is grounded in beliefs about encouraging students to experiment and feel free to make mistakes. Teachers attempt to create safe conditions of low threat and high challenge so students will take risks in an environment rich in multisensory stimulation. The arts are used to relax and calm in the forms of background music, and even the use of color on classroom walls.

**Repeated Experiences.** Pioneering brain research implies links between types of brain activity and how the brain comes to be structured (Bransford, 1999; Hansen & Monk, 2002). How a child is raised affects how the brain chooses to wire itself for life (Simmons & Sheehan, 1997). Each child's brain can form quadrillions of connections, but the number and strength depend on the transformative power of repeated experience. As Nash (1997) points out, "[T]he potential for greatness may be encoded in the genes, but whether that potential is realized . . . is etched by experience in those critical early years" (p. 56).

**Implications.** The potential of substantial arts experiences, such as learning to play keyboards, has gotten significant attention in recent years. Music is heard and a link is made, beautiful colors and shapes surround a child and connections are forged, a baby is rocked or cuddled and another circuit is wired. The key is not simple exposure. A pattern of repeated stimuli sculpts the brain. We learn from the experiences in which we engage the most. Students seek experiences connected to interests, and the arts are inherently interesting. Engaged students enjoy the arts and repeat and extend these activities by choice. This intensity of effort and concentrated focus changes the brain (Zull, 2005).

**Empathy.** It is also now clear that children at younger ages than previously thought are capable of complex deductive thinking and empathy (Lindsey, 1998–99; Wingert & Brant, 2005).

**Implications.** Babies are now taught to use sign language long before they use words. The arts expand communication in the same way. AI embraces the concept that the limits of language are not the limits of thinking (Eisner, 2002a). AI diversifies and intensifies children's experiences including providing opportunities to use innate capacities to empathize. The hope is if they use it, they won't lose it during synapse pruning.

**Emotion.** Brain changes are most extensive and powerful when emotion is part of learning. The chemicals of emotion,

such as adrenalin, serotonin, and dopamine modify synapses. Modification of synapses is the very root of learning. Connections may not occur at all if the emotion chemicals and structures in the brain are not engaged (Zull, 2005).

**Implications.** The arts are arguably the most important tool a teacher has to engage the emotions. Artists intentionally create things to engage others emotionally, which makes arts products compelling instructional materials. Creating art is emotionally engaging as well. Arts-based lessons employ emotions to release memory proteins as students are engaged in experiences that call for feelings to be felt and expressed. Thus, consuming and producing art changes the brain (Zull, 2005).

Arts-based learning is strongly associated with motivation and interest. Students are given freedom and ownership that are "part and parcel of the neurochemistry of the arts" (Zull, 2005). Creativity is based on the decisions made by the creator, which causes the brain's reward system to kick in (Zull, 2005). Chemicals, such as dopamine, are released in the region of cortex used to create ideas, problem solve and make decisions, and plan actions. Students feel satisfaction and pride when they create original ideas and objects.

Arts integration includes dramatic play, movement exploration, and experimentation with art materials. These all have the potential to alter brain chemistry by creating a feeling of optimism and well-being. Play taps into brain chemicals involved in pleasure: Dopamine causes elation and excitement, and endorphin and norepinephrine heighten attention (Brownlee, 1997).

**Shared Networks.** According to Posner and Rothbart (2005), "MRI studies have revealed common (neural) networks underlying many important tasks, such as reading and number skills" (p. 99).

**Implications.** Several studies in the past decade link music and cognitive development (Rauscher, et. al., 1993; 1995; 1997). In particular, significant relationships have been found between math achievement and music performance in elementary students (Deasy, 2002). Analysis of music reveals obvious connections to counting and proportions. One theory is that brain networks are shared by tasks such as music and math (Scripp, 2003). Close associations between music and math seem almost impossible to understand except with neurological explanations. There may be "underlying deep principles and rich learning processes that can be made explicit" through arts integration (p. 130). This suggests two-way transfer potential between the arts and other areas.

## New Brain Research

The Dana Foundation is responsible for bringing together cognitive neuroscientists to grapple with the question of why arts education has been associated with higher academic performance. Initial findings "allow for a deeper understanding of how to define and evaluate the possible causal relationships between arts training and the ability of the brain to learn in other cognitive domains" (Gazzaniga, 2008, p. v). Conclusions are as follows:

- An interest in a performing art leads to a high state of motivation that improves attention and thus other domains of cognition.

- Links exist between high levels of music training and the ability to manipulate information in both working and long-term memory; these links extend beyond the domain of music.
- In children, there appear to be specific links between the practice of music and skills in geometrical representation, though not in other forms of numerical representation.
- Correlations exist between music training and both reading acquisition and sequence learning. One central predictor of early literacy, phonological awareness, is correlated with both music training and the development of a specific brain pathway.
- Training in acting appears to lead to memory improvement through the learning of skills for manipulating semantic information.
- Adult self-reported interest in aesthetics is related to a temperamental factor of openness, which in turn is influenced by dopamine-related genes.
- Dance learning that employs effective observation is closely related to physical learning in the level of achievement and also reflected in the neural substrates for complex actions. Effective observational learning may transfer to other cognitive skills.

Gazzaniga (2008) calls it "remarkable and challenging to find that learning in the arts changes the brain" (p. vi). He goes further to note that sometimes it is not structural brain changes but changes in cognitive strategy that are key to how the arts make a difference. View the full report at the Dana Foundation website, www.dana.org/.

# Arts Integration and Learning Theories

Theories are more than hunches. They are sets of well-founded assumptions that explain phenomena. The "well founded" part means conclusions are drawn from a wide range of research, not just one study and not solely experimental designs. Research is an investigative process to make discoveries. The theories in this chapter were mostly constructed from systematic observations of children and adults.

## Multiple Intelligences Theory

Today there are new theories about what constitutes intelligence and intelligent behavior (Bransford, Brown, Cocking, Donovan, & Pellegrino, 2000; Eisner, 1998a and b; Gardner, 1983; Perkins, 1998). Most prominent is that of Harvard researcher Howard Gardner who became an educational celebrity because of his multiple intelligences (MI) theory (1983, 1993). Decades of work with normal and gifted children, as well as brain-injured adults, led him to reject a narrow concept of intelligence as a single general capacity (Armstrong, 2000; Blythe & Gardner, 1990). Gardner pluralized intelligence and reconceptualized it to include multiple capacities humans use to solve problems and create products that are valued in cultural settings.

Multiple intelligences theory presents the arts as distinct modes of thinking that fall under the umbrella of intelligence. Originally Gardner described seven "ways of knowing," but an eighth intelligence, naturalistic, was added later, and there is a list of more possibilities (See Ready Reference 2.2). Four of the eight intelligences are arts domains: verbal (literary arts), visual/spatial (visual art), musical, and body/kinesthetic (dance/drama). The other four are linked. Logical, interpersonal, and intrapersonal intelligences are used during creative problem solving in the arts, including emphasis on self-reflection and critiquing. The arts also involve high-level cooperative work with others (e.g., choirs, plays).

Gardner explains that intelligences seldom operate "in isolation" and believes that everyone has capacities in all eight areas (Blythe & Gardner, 1990, p. 33). If this is so, it behooves educators to try to develop all modes of understanding and expression. Gardner implies that this broadened focus increases student performance. Gardner argues, further, that everyone has strengths in particular intelligences, and those strengths are instructional guideposts. Arts-based intelligences are a large chunk of developing breadth in students' ways of knowing. Unfortunately, American education has historically privileged the teaching of verbal and logical intelligences. Students with proclivities in other domains have been misunderstood and neglected.

Gardner thinks it is educational malpractice to continue to serve education in the same way to all students and urges teachers to use stronger intelligences to reach less dominant areas. For example, musically inclined students can learn fractions by using eighth, quarter, and whole notes as examples. By listening to and comparing varying note values, they grasp the concept of fractions—sometimes for the first time. Musically smart students can be invited to compose melodies or rhythms to express understanding and use the mnemonic power of music to boost memory. For example, a group of students stuck on prepositions wrote "preposition lyrics" set to "Yankee Doodle": "Out, from, under, in between, over, of, into, through" (first line). Another class used the "Turkey in the Straw" melody to summarize bodily processes: "Oh, the bile from the liver it emulsifies the fats (3X), and it does it in the small intestine." Music adds new viewpoints, too. For example, students studying real people or literary characters can do music "imaging" to force deeper understanding (e.g., thinking of melodies the spider Charlotte in *Charlotte's Web* might have hummed or sung as she spun her web).

**MI Practice.** Gardner thinks deep understanding only happens when ideas and skills are transformed from one domain to another. The arts offer diverse means of transformation. Thinking and learning is made visible, and the arts become important assessment pieces that both delight and inform audiences and participants. Arts-based schools across America now use MI theory. Following are a dozen example strategies.

1. *Informal intelligences assessment.* Teachers profile students' strengths and preferences to differentiate instruction and guide students in making choices. The information in Ready Reference 2.2 can be used to construct a self-assessment checklist. An informal assessment can also be done using the following MI-based questions. Ask students to step (or

## Ready Reference 2.2 Gardner's Eight Intelligences

*Verbal:"Word lovers"* (Barak Obama, Paul Lawrence Dunbar) GOOD AT and LIKE TO: See and hear words, talk and discuss, tell stories, read and write (poetry, literature), memorize (names, facts), use or appreciate humor, use word play, and do word puzzles.

*Visual: "Imagers"* (Mary Cassatt, Pablo Picasso*) GOOD AT and LIKE TO: Think in pictures and see spatial relationships, draw, build, design and create, daydream and imagine, look at pictures, watch movies, read maps and charts, and do mazes and puzzles.

*Musical: "Music lovers"* (Igor Stravinsky,* Wynton Marsalis) GOOD AT and LIKE TO: Sing, hum, and listen to music, play instruments, respond to music (tap rhythms), compose, pick up sounds, remember melodies, and notice pitches and rhythms.

*Interpersonal: "People–people"* (Oprah Winfrey, Mother Teresa) GOOD AT and LIKE TO: Have lots of friends, join groups, talk out or mediate and resolve conflicts, empathize and understand, share, compare, relate, cooperate, interview others, and lead and organize.

*Intrapersonal: "Loners"* (Sigmund Freud,* James Baldwin) GOOD AT and LIKE TO: Reflect on feelings, intentions, dreams, and goals; work alone; have own space; self-pace work; pursue own interests; and do original thinking.

*Logical: "Reasoners"* (Albert Einstein,* Stephen Hawkins) GOOD AT and LIKE TO: Experiment, ask questions, problem solve, figure out how things work, explore abstract relationships, discover patterns, classify, reason and use logic (inductive and deductive), do math, and play logic games.

*Kinesthetic: "Movers"* (Martha Graham,* Tiger Woods) GOOD AT and LIKE TO: Dance and use body to communicate; touch and use hands, face, gestures; do hands-on learning; prefer kinesthetic–tactile activities, sports, and drama.

*Naturalistic: "Nature lovers"* (Jacques Cousteau, Jane Goodall) GOOD AT and LIKE TO: Have and raise pets, visit zoos and parks, study animals and nature, garden, be out of doors.

---

*Exemplars in *Creating Minds* (Gardner, 1993) who expressed extreme "intelligence" in at least one area, but used all intelligences. None were very successful in school settings.

---

dance) forward from a circle or line to respond. Check off students on an MI list. Ask, "How many of you like to . . ."

- Draw? Make mental pictures? Enjoy television or movies, look at pictures, make art? (visual)
- Read? Write? Listen to stories? (verbal/word smart)
- Play sports? Dance? Make things with your hands? (body/kinesthetic)
- Do math or science experiments? (logical/math)
- Listen to music, sing, or play an instrument? (musical)
- Be with groups of people? (interpersonal/people–person)
- Work alone? Think about your own ideas and dreams? (intrapersonal)
- Be outside? Be around animals and nature? (naturalistic)

2. *MI planning.* Teachers can code lesson plans to track intelligences used to provide a balance of learning activities. Use a spreadsheet to graph the days of the week along one axis and the eight intelligences along the other. Map out the music, art, dance or movement, drama, and literature (linguistic intelligence) addressed each day to make sure no area is neglected. Use the ideas in the following arts chapters to present academic content in alternative ways and to give arts response options to students. Teachers also can design centers or stations that offer students eight ways to transform ideas and "show they know."

3. *Eight-minute energizer.* This routine (Armstrong, 1994) budgets 1 minute on each intelligence:
   - *Visual:* Make pictures in your head (e.g., places you'd like to visit, colors and shapes that are happy). Take students on a fantasy journey by describing an imaginary trip to a place. Relate this to a unit under study (e.g., planets).
   - *Verbal:* Write down all the words you can think of (e.g., that start with a letter or rhyme—pick any category). Make up quick poems or riddles. Write a class motto or chant.
   - *Musical:* Hum or sing together. Play a piece of music and move to it. Choose a song for a class anthem and sing it regularly (e.g., "High Hopes," "When You Wish upon a Star").
   - *Intrapersonal:* Think about a goal. What would you like to do or be, and how could you do it? How could you be a better person or student? Drop it in the Tomorrow Box.
   - *Interpersonal:* Get a partner and give each other honest compliments or share about an interest.
   - *Logical:* Do quick math (e.g., add, subtract, or multiply in your head). Do logic puzzles (e.g., Plexers or Mind-bogglers) or quick categories (e.g., table, chair, sofa _____).
   - *Kinesthetic:* Do physical warm-ups such as toe touches, waist stretches, sky reaches, and jumping jacks (see Drama and Dance Seed Strategies in Chapters 9 and 11).
   - *Naturalistic:* Use a magnifying glass to study a plant or animal for 30 seconds and then share all the things you noticed. Look out the window at nature and share observations.

4. *Assessment criteria.* Make clear criteria for quality work before students begin so they are free to explore multiple ways to meet the criteria and to critique their work against the criteria. Optimally, teacher and students co-develop criteria. The key is to decide what competencies are to be achieved, not just to describe what students will experience. The emphasis on clear criteria gives focus to the problem-solving process and prepares students to deal with the limitations of time, materials, and money typical of any workplace.

5. *Inform parents.* Invite parents to evaluate their intelligences. Do a short MI overview for a PTO meeting and include short MI ideas in class newsletters.

6. *Explicit teaching and goal setting.* Plan lessons on MI so students expand their concept of ways of knowing. Invite students to goal set for each intelligence as it is studied. Ellison (1992) recommends creating a goals form that include a sentence description for each intelligence. Ask students to think of how to achieve their goals in different ways. Encourage the use of all intelligences by taking time each week to discuss what they tried. (Sources for MI posters include Illinois Renewal Institute, 800-348-4474; or Zephyr Press, Tucson, Arizona.)

7. *MI people resources.* Match the intelligences with authors, artists, athletes, or fictional characters (e.g., Charlotte in *Charlotte's Web* is verbal and kinesthetic) or use Gardner's eight exemplars from *Creating Minds* (1993a) to study different intelligences. Students can also find peer examples using a Bingo game format. Make cards with intelligence characteristics in each box. Students circulate and find names of peers that fit in each. A "Career Day" can be organized around invited guests from each of the eight intelligences to round out the search for diversity.

8. *Apprenticeships.* Invite local artists, musicians, dancers, and actors to mentor students who have propensities in these intelligences. A combination of shadowing a mentor, discussing, and being coached on projects can profoundly influence learning.

9. *Choice and interest.* Learners are more motivated when given choices and when work connects to interests. Students also need to have the choice, at times, to work alone. Invite students to think of alternate ways to express understanding using different intelligences. Offer options other than traditional reports to synthesize content (e.g., write stories, poems, songs; construct games; make charts, drawings, sculptures, tableau; or create dances).

10. *Co-planning.* If teachers share their MI profiles with one another, they can intentionally draw on one another's strengths as they plan. Collaborative planning with arts specialists is an important way to discover alternatives to instructional goals.

11. *Field-based learning.* Class trips to places that focus on a particular intelligence can be powerful (e.g., symphony for music, art museum for art, library for verbal, dance concert for body). Discuss the MI focus of each.

12. *MI schools.* Visits to schools using MI theory are the best way to understand how the arts are integral to implementing this theory. Two examples are the Key School in Indianapolis and Arts PROPEL schools in Pittsburgh. To find AI schools to visit, check the websites listed in Ready Reference 1.6 and the Appendix.

## Piaget's Stages of Cognitive Development

Jean Piaget, a Swiss biologist and epistemologist, is famous for a four-stage theory based on observing children. He reasoned that the key stimulus for development was interaction with the environment. Piaget thought that, along with genetically programmed biological changes, touching, seeing, hearing, tasting, smelling, moving, and interacting with people cause children to make discoveries that alter their worldview. He observed that children develop intellectually by experimenting; what adults see as play is serious work.

Piaget believed children organize reality into mental structures used to understand. He called these cognitive structures *schema*s (or schemata). A person either *assimilates* new information into a schema or creates new or modifies old schemas through the process of *accommodation*—thinking is adjusted based on new information. For example, a child may not recognize a beanbag chair as a chair and call it a "ball" because he is trying to understand using an old schema. Once the child is shown how to sit in the chair, this new information is assimilated. Accommodation occurs if new information is added to the category of "furniture." Most learning involves both assimilation and accommodation. Piaget thought these stages were natural and sequential, building on one another in a progression toward more complex thinking (See Ready Reference 2.3). He believed in a genetic predisposition toward increasingly complex cognitive development that involves continually trying to achieve equilibrium when something is not understandable. In other words, we are innately programmed to want to make sense. Piaget cautioned against trying to hurry development. He believed it took too long to teach something to a child who was not ready. His flexible age guidelines show a developmental progression and suggest learning expectations be appropriately matched (Piaget, 1980).

Piaget believed a child's thinking is consistent with his or her stage across situations, but more recent research shows that children show characteristics of one stage in certain situations and can think at a higher or lower stage in other situations. For example, Gelman (1979) reported incidences of 4-year olds speaking in simpler sentences when they talked to 2-year-olds, indicating they considered the needs of the younger child. This behavior was thought by Piaget to not develop until around age 7. More recently, studies of baby brains show that young children are much more intellectually sophisticated than their communication capabilities can show. Wingert and Brant (2005) report research that babies have "startling powers of deduction and ability to notice details and patterns." Infants can discern small differences, especially in faces, that adults and older children no longer notice. Until 3 months, babies can recognize a scrambled photograph of mom just as quickly as a normal photo—a kind of "Picasso think" (Wingert & Brant, 2005).

**Piaget and Arts Integration.** The following are educational implications connected to arts integration for primary and intermediate students.

**Concrete Experiences.** Arts integration increases hands-on learning options. Drama and dance are literally hands on. Both use the whole body to transform concepts. For example, a tableau (frozen body picture) can be used to show understanding of critical moments in a plot or show relationships among parts of a cell.

**Engagement First.** Artists are always seeking ways to engage creative thinking. It is not surprising that there are dozens of arts

## Ready Reference 2.3 Piaget's Stages of Development

**Sensorimotor Thinking: Birth to 2 Years**

- Explores using senses. Relies on nonverbal communication.
- Realizes objects exist when not seen.
- Gains control of body actions.

**Preoperational: 2 to 7 Years**

- Starts to think with images and symbols. Likes fantasy, imaginative play, and pretend.
- Rapid language and concept growth.
- Cannot understand how objects can change shape but remain the same object.
- Difficulty seeing other points of view because of egocentrism.

**Concrete Operations (Hands-on Thinking): 7 to 11 Years**

- Basic concepts of objects, numbers, time, space, and cause–effect links develop.
- Needs concrete objects to draw conclusions.

**Formal Operations (Abstract Reasoning): 11 to 15 Years**

- Makes logical predictions, thinks hypothetically, and can do meta-cognition (self-questions; thinks about own thinking).

*Sources:* Ginsberg & Opper, 1969; Piaget, 1950, 1980.

---

warm-ups, which ease students into creative problem solving. Engagement strategies hook students so they willingly participate in longer, more complex work. Strategies include open questions such as "What do you think of when I say *dance*?" and activities that involve solving problems using imagination, intellect, voice and body, and diverse art materials. Students can be engaged before arts performance by using previews to cue them for what is to be experienced. For example, give "listen fors" (a character's line or song), so students are more likely to stay actively engaged.

**Short Explanations.** The arts focus on "doing" problem solving. A 5-minute lesson on pantomime can give enough options to use the face, body, and in-place movements to "become" a character. Students can then mime "frozen statues" to convey character knowledge.

**Rich Experiences.** Field trips to museums, concerts, and plays are all examples of rich experiences that extend learning. Guest artists, storytellers, and musicians give students direct experiences.

**Exploration and Variety.** Literature, art, drama, dance, and music are distinct ways of thinking, with special languages and symbol systems. Each permits different ways of expressing and receiving ideas and feelings. The arts add ways to explore; teaching basic arts concepts expands thinking by adding new categories. For example, once students know that dance includes locomotor and nonlocomotor movements, they can brainstorm some of each and experiment with a range of movement. In the area of language arts, verbs and adverbs might then be danced, both in place and from point to point. For example, the verb *lean* can be shown with different body parts, in place, and in motion across space. Adverbs can be added for interest and to elaborate meaning: We can lean quickly, slowly, casually, lazily, rigidly, and hungrily.

**Higher Order Thinking.** Piaget believed there is a natural inclination for higher order thinking to develop, but it depends on experiences. Complex thinking is a major goal of education, but it is difficult to teach. The arts provide a rich context for cognitive development because they thrive on changing points of view and mental experimentation. Mistakes are not seen as failures so children feel safe using paint or clay to think through problems. Art materials allow primary children to edge into this type of thinking before they have the verbal language to do things like "explain perspective."

**Coaching.** Children need help thinking. The arts have long used the concept of coaching to support problem solving. There is a tradition and a wealth of readily available strategies. Coaching is discussed in all the arts chapters but, for now, suffice it to say that it involves questioning, prompting, and encouraging students before and during work. Descriptive feedback is used more than praise.

**Life-centered Learning.** A study of 91 schools showed the arts significantly contribute to developing the kind of flexible and adaptable knowledge businesses seek in today's workers (Longley, 1999). Real-life success comes from hard work, self-control and discipline, cooperation, problem solving, flexibility, humor, responsibility, motivation, productivity, risk taking, and passion. These are all developed through the arts, and arts-based learning focuses on explicitly teaching how to solve problems in a creative manner.

## Maslow's Hierarchy of Needs

In the 1970s, Abraham Maslow proposed a theory of motivation that has become widely used in psychology, business, and education. The theory gives teachers a tool for understanding why children do what they do—or don't do. Maslow's research caused him to conclude that people were motivated by specific needs. He categorized these needs and organized them into a hierarchy, with the basic needs for surviving, such as food, clothes, and a place to live, on the bottom (See Ready Reference 2.4). He posited that once lower-level survival needs and safety needs were met, people moved up the ladder. He thought the three top levels, including the need for beauty, represented needs that were never filled, so people continued to always seek more in these areas, in contrast to low-level needs.

**Maslow and AI.** Maslow's theory of needs-based motivation summarized in Ready Reference 2.4 suggests that children who are hungry, thirsty, too hot, or worried won't see purpose in aesthetically focused arts activities. Arts integration will not feed and clothe children, but the arts are communication vehicles that allow children significant ways to release fears and concerns. In arts integrated schools, the psychological safety of children is in the forefront. Risk taking is squelched in threatening environments, and creativity withers without risk taking. Comfort and safety needs (second level) are routinely met using strategies that derive from an arts-based philosophy—teaching how mistakes are normal and instructive, giving second chances after genuine effort, and offering choices of art materials and writing forms. Humor and creative thinking are parallel in nature and both are problem based, so it isn't surprising that much laughing occurs when the arts are integrated. Humor is a tension reliever and can be used intentionally to relax students. Riddles can activate problem solving and cause children to release stress. Teachers who poke fun at their own mistakes show students how to deal with embarrassing moments and bond class members together in laughter.

American culture places high value on diverse thinking. The popularity of blogging is a recent manifestation of this value. The human need for group approval, however, is very powerful (third level). It is common at the start of arts integration for students to doubt that they have unique and different ideas. They may feel compelled to copy or imitate peers. Some students are actually afraid of being different and worry about being laughed at and ostracized. Teachers need to be sensitive to the belonging needs of students. Teachers can share stories about artists who have taken risks to be different (e.g., cubism was thought ridiculous by Picasso's contemporaries) and celebrate novel student responses with clear descriptive feedback: "Joe painted his sky with orange and red in it." The need for group approval can also be met by forming learning circles for students to work on projects, such as writing songs and poems. Dance and drama naturally demand group work and can fulfill belonging needs while encouraging experimentation with different ways of thinking in the safety of pretend context.

Children are not easily pigeonholed and may have needs operating simultaneously at several of Maslow's levels. Stories about people who deny themselves survival and safety needs to pursue artistic works, aesthetic needs, and self-fulfillment can help students think about the motivational force of higher order needs. For example, students might find out why Monet and other Impressionists made paintings others thought looked unfinished so they wouldn't buy them (see *Lives of the Musicians,* 1993, by Kathleen Krull).

Maslow helps us understand that while we are motivated to get some things, many activities are self-motivating. Teachers involved in AI find they can design lessons around arts experiences that require no extrinsic rewards such as food or stickers. Work in the arts is intrinsically motivating. Just being in a beautiful room or listening to music can be emotionally and cognitively satisfying. With the help of students, teachers can fill the classroom with plants, artwork, background music, and even potpourri. Another powerful intrinsic motivator is interest, which can be developed through regular times to work on interest-based projects. Choice also satisfies the basic need for control over one's circumstances. Achievement needs can be addressed by allowing time and other opportunities to pursue independent projects involving the arts. For example, students might study a person or topic in the arts that connects to a unit. Teachers can encourage being curious with a "Wonder Box" to drop questions and topics that students would like to learn about or information they would like to share. Idiosyncrasies about artists or artworks can cause otherwise apathetic students to become excited about learning.

## Vygotsky's Social Development

Russian psychologist Lev Vygotsky (1978, 1986) is another researcher who has given educators a theory that supports many aspects of arts integration. Unlike Piaget, Vygotsky thought teachers should intervene in children's learning. He called this intervention *scaffolding*. The idea is to use techniques to bridge the gap between where a child is functioning and a stage just out of reach, but attainable. He called this developmental position the *zone of proximal development* (ZPD) and demonstrated how students can often solve problems with help (cues, suggestions, steps, encouragement) when they cannot do so independently.

**Vygotsky and AI.** Using ZPD theory begins with observing students. Teachers must determine when students can proceed independently, when they can succeed with some assistance, and

---

**Ready Reference 2.4** Maslow's Hierarchy of Needs

**Highest level:** Self-fulfillment
Aesthetic need for beauty and order
Knowledge and intellectual needs
Approval and recognition from others
Belonging, love, acceptance by others
Physical and psychological safety
**Lowest level:** Survival needs, including food, clothes, water, shelter

*Source:* Maslow, 1970.

Social studies learning synthesized into an exhibit at Hilton Head Creative Arts

# Creativity and Creative Problem Solving

*Creative children look twice, listen for smells, dig deeper, build dream castles, get from behind locked doors, have a ball, plug in the sun, get into and out of deep water, sing in their own key.* (Paul Torrance, 1973)

Economic collapse, terrorist attacks, horrific genocides, pandemics—the kinds and quantities of 21st-century problems are mind-boggling. What's more, many are new, at least in their degree. New problems call for new solutions. It is not possible to Google any one of these plagues and get *the* answer. Solutions have to be created, and much of that task will eventually fall on the shoulders of today's children. Teaching children to memorize facts and do rote skill application—too often the focus of schooling—doesn't prepare children for their future.

It is common to associate creative thinking with artists, but creative thinking is also a vital daily survival skill set. Those who strive to stretch a personal budget, go green in their homes, or invent affordable quality health must all use innate creative thinking abilities.

## Predispositions

Fortunately, children come to school inclined to problem solve creatively, and more so when they have been involved in the arts. Even before birth, fetuses respond to musical rhythms, pitches, and volumes. Young children are compelled to pretend, make up songs, experiment with art tools, and explore ways to move their bodies. When we tap this natural excitement, we engage the intrinsic motivation to do difficult higher order thinking. Arts integration is founded on the premise that the arts are central to learning. At the core of thinking through the arts is creative problem solving. In other words, creativity is the source of the arts, but it is also the source of discoveries in science, math, and history.

The need to encourage creativity has become a pressing societal issue. Diverse theories and research provide information about the sources of creativity, its nature, and how it can be developed. It seems that Plato's concept of a muse that can spark creative work can actually be summoned. Educators now have access to the same strategies used in high-powered think tanks around the world. We no longer need to wait for the muse's visit. Each teacher can be a muse.

## Problem-Based Thinking

It is clear that creative thinking has its origins in problems. Using poetry as an example, Robert Frost explained, "A poem . . . begins as a lump in the throat, a sense of wrong, a homesickness, a lovesickness. It finds the thought, and the thought finds the words." The personal struggle to make sense—perhaps the most ancient human problem—has honed human practices that have ensured the survival of the species. Those practices favor creative

when the problem or activity is not appropriate at all. Determining this match involves instructional creative problem solving to find appropriate scaffolds. Scaffolds can be as simple as giving more examples or feedback that a student is on the right track.

Vygotsky also believed social interactions were key to cognitive development. He and other social learning theorists advise educators to increase student success by involving them in applying or practicing new learning in a group situation, before going it alone. Telling students to "write a song" or "make a play" or "make up a dance" is overwhelming—even many teachers would need scaffolding through the creative problem-solving process for each of these tasks.

Problem solving during drama and dance almost always is done in groups, and learners can both view and do visual art (e.g., murals) in pairs, trios, quads, or whole groups. By listening to each other tell what they see in a piece of art or hear in a piece of music, everyone has the chance to get another perspective and make new connections (peer scaffolding).

## Child Development and the Arts

Gardner, Maslow, Piaget, Vygotsky, and others each give us a piece of the whole picture of child development. Teachers draw on these and other theories to create arts-based lessons.

Choosing and creating developmentally appropriate experiences for students is like a doctor writing a prescription for a patient. Teachers need information about developmental patterns as guideposts to think about specific children and adapt daily instruction. The Appendix includes a developmental chart to help teachers think about what's appropriate for primary, intermediate, and middle school students. Classroom teachers should also consult with school arts specialists about appropriate materials, tools, and processes for specific students.

thinking that relies on careful observation of details, noticing patterns, and summoning mental images.

## Creativity Defined

The most important things in life are hard to define: love, happiness, art. Creativity is no exception. Consider Perkins's (1987–88) definition that implies everyday people have what it takes. He proposes that creativity is simply "using ordinary resources of the mind in extraordinary ways" (p. 38). To use one's experiences, knowledge, and thinking capacities in a clever way to produce something somewhat new seems doable. What's more, original products needed or wanted by specific groups become highly valued, such as the iPod. But, what is deemed creative in one culture or time period is not in another. For example, restickable mini-notes probably wouldn't have been hot among 12th-century European peasants. Small modern conveniences, such as the paper clip and roll toilet paper, are no longer considered creative, but they must have delighted first users.

## Creativity Theories

Researchers have tried to make sense out of the concept of creativity using four angles.

1. *Observing creative people, especially adults.* This has been the focus of researchers such as MacKinnon (1978), Torrance (1962,1973), and Tardif and Sternberg (1988).
2. *Studying the stages or process.* Study of the development of creativity and the problem-solving process goes back to Plato, who thought creativity was a divinely inspired, mystical process manifested in bursts of insight. Aristotle explained creativity with natural laws used to understand any thinking. His work was later used by many theorists including Perkins, Guilford, and Weisberg. Other notable theorists using the stages and process approach are Wallace (1926), Csikszentmihalyi (1990), Maslow, and Vygotsky.
3. *Identifying influences.* B. F. Skinner concluded creativity was a function of behavioral influences: It occurs naturally and, if reinforced, will be repeated.
4. *Developing an interactive theory.* In this view creativity is a manifestation and interaction among cognitive processes (e.g., divergent thinking), functioning in particular domains (e.g., math or science), and environment (culture and time period). Sternberg, Gardner, Csikszentmihalyi, and Amabile (1996) have all proposed variations on this theory.

The following sections draw on each of the four lines of inquiry, beginning with the studies of highly creative people.

## Creativity Profile

Traits of creativity emerge during childhood, and highly creative people show heightened traits earlier on (Csikszentmihalyi, 1990; Dacey, 1989; Gardner, 1993a; Getzels & Jackson, 1962; Tardif & Sternberg, 1988). Example traits are shown in Ready Reference 2.5. The list can help teachers understand the diversity of traits that are included in the concept of creativity. Such a body of traits can be used to observe students, to set goals, and to plan an environment that encourages creative thinking. Of course, no two people have the same profile of traits and there is no "right" profile; we all possess degrees of the characteristics. Notice that some traits are even undesirable under certain circumstances. Teachers can encourage desirable behaviors for which students have particular tendencies, and should try to develop positive traits in themselves as well.

## Creativity in Action

An understanding of the stages or process of creative thinking has emerged from the work of researchers such as Csikszentmihalyi (1990) and Wallace (1926). Here is a glimpse into the process at work.

**National Public Radio Interview (August 27, 1995).** "It takes an enlightened stubbornness to produce anything," declared a man with a British accent. Trevor Baylis was talking about the fruits of his own stubbornness. It all started when he was watching a TV program on the AIDS problem in Africa. Baylis became aware of ballooning disease statistics and efforts to educate the African population by radio. The part of the problem that intrigued Baylis was the inability of people to afford or obtain batteries. It cost a month's salary to buy batteries, and some people actually gave up precious rice to buy them. Baylis began to visually imagine being in Africa in a pith helmet with a monocle and glass of gin. This input triggered the image of a windup radio.

"It just popped into my head," he laughed.

He said it seemed so simple he was sure someone else must have already thought of it. But he investigated and his inquiries showed no one had. "Everyone has a good original idea, but most don't come to fruition because we worry about humiliation—people laughing, or that our idea is not new," Baylis said. He wasn't worried. He experimented with different springs and was able to make a radio that would play for 40 minutes with 20 seconds of winding. Now the Third World has a cheap way to use mass communication. Today wind up radios are available worldwide and are indispensable in disasters such as the Haitian earthquake. Baylis's story illustrates the stages people go through when they do creative problem solving. These are not just chance. We can manage the processes by knowing the conditions necessary to "prime the pump" of imaginative (image-based) thinking.

## The Creative Problem-Solving Process

*I never do a painting as a work of art. All of them are researches. I search constantly and there is a logical sequence in all this search.* (Pablo Picasso, in Gardner, 1973).

Many researchers have studied how people go about solving problems creatively (Csikszentmihalyi, 1990; Dewey, 1997; Eberle, 1971; Osborne, 1963; Wallace, 1926). CPS contrasts with linear problem solving in which one answer is sought and may even be known (e.g., solving multiplication problems). During CPS,

## Ready Reference 2.5 Creativity Profile

Rate yourself on these creative traits, using the scale: 0 = not evident to 5 = very evident. Follow with goal setting to increase the trait.

### Cognitive Characteristics

1. Approaches problems playfully; likes to experiment
2. Inclination to explore possibilities versus saying "It won't work" right off
3. Likes open-endedness and freedom to try new ways
4. Is a problem finder
5. Uses mistakes to solve problems
6. Fluent; likes to brainstorm and generate ideas
7. Flexible; shifts perspectives and thinks in categories quickly
8. Original; creates unique ideas and likes to transform
9. Elaborates; can flesh out ideas with details
10. Observant; notices details; senses are acute
11. Intelligent, but understands that intellect does not guarantee high creativity; threshold level is necessary
12. Logical; uses details and evidence to support ideas
13. Imaginative and resourceful; combines ideas in new ways with vivid detail
14. Uses hunches and guesses; intuitive
15. Seeks possibilities; likes variety, divergence, and novelty
16. Visualizes; uses metaphoric thinking to problem solve
17. Organizer; likes to create order from chaos
18. Prefers complexity and asymmetry
19. Goal and task oriented; focused
20. Sets own standards to judge

### Personality Characteristics

1. Curious and questioning
2. Likes to explore; seeks adventure
3. Spontaneous, impulsive, uninhibited
4. Emotionally secure
5. Risk taker, but not reckless; courageous
6. Nonconforming; opinions of others not a priority
7. Confident in own worth and work
8. Loses track of time; dislikes deadlines
9. Strong sense of destiny
10. Independent; unlikely to follow the crowd
11. Likes original ideas
12. Skeptical of authority; resists "right" answers
13. Easily bored with routine
14. Heightened sense of humor
15. Critical of self
16. Not often satisfied, but not easily discouraged
17. Likes to work alone; may appear aloof; may not fit in or seek out groups
18. Motivated, hardworking, and persistent; not easily frustrated; willing to struggle and sustain effort
19. Playful, almost childlike, in sense of wonder and delight
20. Tolerant of ambiguity; doesn't need a right answer
21. Broad interests and hobbies

*Sources:* Barron, 1969; Dacey, 1989; Isaksen & Treffinger, 1985; MacKinnon, 1978; Tardif & Sternberg, 1988; Torrance, 1962.

---

divergent perspectives are actively pursued, surprises embraced, and uncommon tools and materials tried. For example, visual artist Gay Torrey paints her thoughts about people and places using lace and bubble wrap. She says she thrives on finding bizarre ways to express her ideas, including printing from a dead fish coated in tempera.

**Parallel Processes.** It shouldn't be surprising to find there is a common set of thinking process used by people in the vast of array of circumstances that require creative solutions to problems. CPS is used to construct new environmental policies as well as choreograph a dance. Scientists use CPS when they employ the *scientific method* to make discoveries, which requires creative leaps of imagination. Readers achieve comprehension by using the *comprehension problem-solving process,* which parallels the CPS process, to make sense from print (Cornett, 2010). Writers routinely use prewriting, drafting, and postwriting—thinking and working processes congruent with CPS. Diverse labels are used across disciplines that are near synonyms including "inquiry," but students need to understand that the thinking processes used to construct meaning are more alike than different. In this book, CPS is featured to summarize the complex way people coordinate higher order thinking to make sense of the constellation of problems encountered in life and learning. Of course, CPS is the process used by artists to create art forms.

**Description.** The CPS process begins with the expectations that there are many solutions to any problem or diverse ways to make sense of events and texts. Freethinking is valued, time has to be flexible, and risk taking needs to be supported. There is a general order, but the steps are recursive and flexible. People go back and forth among questioning, data gathering, experimenting, prioritizing, synthesizing, and evaluating. Readers, writers, painters, dancers, and musicians move in and out of these kinds of thinking during CPS, continually referring to the problem under investigation and redefining the problem as they proceed. Brain hemispheres collaborate to work options that make sense so CPS is a whole brain experience. Creativity does not reside in the right hemisphere. Think about Mr. Baylis and your own experiences related to this description of the CPS process summarized in Ready Reference 2.6.

### Before (Get Ready)

**Set Purpose:** A problem is presented or found and then pinned down as much as possible. There is conscious awareness that a problem exists or a desire to do problem finding—a

## Ready Reference 2.6 Creative Problem-Solving (CPS) Process

*Knowing how to shift intellectual gears beats rigid thinking every time.* (Bruce Boston, 1996)

**Before: Get Ready**

1. Set purpose: Problem is presented or found.
2. Motivate: Display "can do, will do, want to do" attitude.
3. Propose solutions: Preview, predict, brainstorm.

**During/Drafting: Make Sense by Connecting**

1. Gather data/find facts: Read, research, observe, interview.
2. Explore and experiment: Visualize, empathize, SCAMPER (substitute, combine, adapt, modify, put to use, eliminate, reverse/rearrange).

3. Question/clarify: Utilize meta-comprehension/fix-ups.
4. Focus: Zoom in to critique details. Zoom out for patterns.
5. Time-out: Realize incubation period.
6. Insight: Infer Ah ha! conclusions.
7. Connect and transform: Summarize, synthesize, and organize using FFOE and metaphorical thinking.

**After: Responses and Solutions**

1. Reflect and evaluate: What works? (preset criteria)
2. Revise: Edit, reorganize, elaborate.
3. Publish: Make public or visible with performance, exhibits, etc.

*Sources:* Csikszentmihalyi, 1990; Dewey, 1920; Root-Bernstein & Root-Bernstein, 1999; Wallace, 1926.

---

personal decision to look for new uses, products, and the like. Problem seekers capture fleeting idea sparks through sketch journals, idea notebooks, or photographs. Musical artists record bits of sound or patterns and, like the composer in the TV advertisment, can be inspired by the arrangement of birds on a set of telephone wires that seem to depict a musical score. In school, problems are often presented to students. For example, "Figure out how to summarize the story's themes through tableau." Of course, the central problem in reading any text is to make sense by finding and creating "big ideas" (Cornett, 2010).

**Motivate:** A "can do, will do, want to do" attitude is needed. The perception of important goals, freedom of choice, interest, and emotion cause motion or movement toward goals. Many students can do, but won't. Arts integration can cause them to "want to."

**Propose Solutions:** Possibilities or hypotheses are generated by previewing available sources to get an overview (e.g., do a text walk-through), predicting possible solutions, and brainstorming solutions. The goal is to generate *lots* of ideas from which "good" ideas can eventually be selected. Judgment of ideas is withheld for later. NOTE: The classic "brainstorming" rules are: Quantity first! Generate many ideas. Cluster to organize ideas (Osborne, 1963).

**Question:** Questions are generated. Basic ones are: What do I know already? What do I need to know? How can I get to know what I need to know? (i.e., plan, resources, information).

**During/Drafting.** Sense is created and problems solved by finding ideas and making new connections.

**Gather Data.** As John Dewey explained, "We can have facts without thinking, but we cannot have thinking without facts." Cultivation of creative thinking depends on commitment to growing a depth of knowledge in the areas where work is to be done (e.g., arts literacy). No one creates in a vacuum or without

building on foundations laid by others. Ideas must be gathered for solving the problem by reading, listening, and observing (facts, details, and patterns). This includes any kind of research, including work on the internet. Much of creativity is attributed to taking an observant mental stance to notice more. This feeds the engine of the brain, as does collaboration with others. Artistic thinkers are known to seek out unusual perspectives from other people and use novel sources.

**Explore and Experiment.** This stage is about divergent thinking versus convergent thinking. The search is for many diverse possibilities. As with all higher order cognition, creative problem solving seems messy and disorganized as problem solvers collect data and play with materials and ideas. The following are common ways to explore.

*Visualize:* The root of imagination is image. Visualization is creating mental images or picturing inside the brain. Einstein claimed that this was how he did most of his thinking that led to his greatest discoveries. Expert readers usually visualize as they read.

*Empathize:* German scholar Theodore Lipps coined the term *empathy* at the turn of the 20th century to explain what audiences had to do to understand art. Empathy is more than sympathy. It is deliberately trying to make meaning by taking the point of view of others. It is also more than "critical distance," because imagination is used to see and feel as others do.

*Scamper:* Playing with ideas gives depth to understanding and can lead to surprising connections. SCAMPER (Eberle, 1971) is a set of verbs to cause mental play with ideas. They are: substitute, combine, adapt, modify, put to other use, eliminate, reverse/rearrange. SCAMPER time can be scheduled as a warm-up to use "what if" thinking to stretch the imagination. For example, if students complain about a short recess, ask, "What if school time and recess time amounts were reversed?" or "How can we combine school and recess?" Ask students to generate "what ifs" for 1 minute on each SCAMPER verb.

**Question/clarify:** Continual self-questioning is used with focus on the five Ws and H (who, what, when, where, why, and how). The question "Is this making sense?" is asked to gauge meaning construction success. If the answer is "no," fix-ups are used to redirect meaning-making. For example, reread, read aloud, read ahead, and visualize text material. Artists often look at past work or even turn artwork upside down to get a new perspective.

**Focus:** According to Jean Piaget (1950), "The second goal of education is to form minds which can be critical, can verify, and not accept everything they are offered." This step zooms in. Ideas are analyzed and critiqued. Important details/evidence is the focus.

**Time-out:** Creative solutions need time. The brain has to combine its assets in a way that isn't completely conscious. Incubation is an unconscious or idle period. Sleep, rest, and time away from the work allow the subconscious to take charge.

**Connect:** This is the insight or "ah-ha" stage. A light goes on and there is a conscious focus on newfound ways to organize and summarize to make sense. Thinking is nearly impossible without connections, especially visual ones key to meaning making. Gestalt psychology explains the human tendency to bring together disparate pieces, to connect the dots and create a coherent whole. In essence, we seek to understand by relating the new to known ideas. Sometimes organizational frames are used to help summarize. For example, the following categories can be used to prompt connective thinking: Learned-Wonder-Like (LWL), Interesting, Questions, Useful (IQU), and Exciting, Puzzling, Connecting (EPC).

Another tool, FFOE, causes more connections and fleshes out ideas: Fluent: generate many possibilities, Flexible: change point of view (POV) and organize differently, Original: make unique connections and don't take the first idea, and Elaborate: add details and examples/nonexamples.

**Transform:** At this stage best ideas are synthesized and ranked. This goes beyond summarizing. Questions such as "What do I now know/feel? How can I best communicate it?" provoke thinking about altering the ways ideas might be represented. Artists intentionally strive for audiences to experience a cognitive and emotional reaction so they ask questions such as "How can I cause them to want them to stop and say 'How did she do that?'" (Gay Torrey, visual artist). Metaphors and analogies are examples of creative connections that transform thinking. For example, a "bridge" is a metaphor for teacher. The image pulls together important relationships like supporting and transporting students.

### After (Responses and Solutions).

**Evaluate:** Reflection on "what works" is done using preset criteria to judge (e.g., quality, time, money, values). This includes self-evaluation using checklists and rubrics.

**Revise:** The solution is edited, reorganized, and reworked as needed. It's like Regis saying, "Is that your *final* answer?"

**Publish:** Publish means "to make public." This happens through any sharing that makes learning visible. Examples are performances, exhibits, and use of author/artist chair. All efforts are celebrated at this point.

## Creative Planning and Teaching

Development of creativity should be a high-placed criterion for sorting out what goes in and should come out of today's jam-packed curricula (Starko, 1995). Teachers who fill children's days with dull worksheets and maintain silence with glares are not keeping up on current research. Time is limited. Children spend about a third of their childhood in school. The future depends on focusing classroom assets on essential skills and critical concepts. The CPS process is an essential skill set at the heart of artistic thinking and working and should be at the core of any AI implementation. Appendix D, example 1 shows an assessment tool to engage students in growing their artistic thinking, with emphasis on developing the higher order thinking embodied in CPS.

This ability to produce creative solutions is valued in careers from advertising to fashion design. Not to be overlooked is the role CPS plays in teaching, including both planning and teaching arts-based lessons. Creative instructional planning starts with the belief that there are infinite means of achieving targets such as standards and goals. Celebrated teachers are known for creative instruction. Film depictions dramatize the power of CPS in teaching. In *Dead Poets' Society*, for example, Robin Williams portrays a teacher who uses the power of literature and drama to move students. *Fame* (1980) tells the story of a New York City high school specializing in the performing arts, and *Mr. Holland's Opus* (1996) portrays an inspirational music teacher. In *Music of the Heart* (1999), an inner-city teacher challenges her students to learn the violin well enough to perform at Carnegie Hall.

### Valuing Creativity.

*To engender creativity, first we must value it.* (Sternberg & Lubar, 1991).

Teachers don't go around saying, "I can't do math" or "I can't read." If they did, we would think they should be fired. Some teachers, however, seem to feel no shame in saying, "I am not creative." Such a view limits teachers, personally, and limits students by denying the importance of a key feature of being fully human. Development of innate creative abilities depends on belief that everyone possesses them and a deep value for the unique problem solving that creativity makes possible. It is unacceptable for a teacher to claim that she or he cannot do important life-linked creative thinking that students need to be taught.

### Practice the CPS Process.
Here are facts about CPS, followed by an "if–then" frame. Consider the proposition (if) and think of ways a teacher may put the information into practice (then).

- When people have blocks of time to become deeply involved in a creative problem, they can enter a mental state called *flow*

(Csikszentmihalyi, 1990). Decades of cross-cultural research on happiness from Tokyo teens to Italian farmers found people who recalled being so engaged they lost track of time. Flow is an optimal active experience that is highly motivating. You feel focused, exhilarated, and satisfied. People freely spend large amounts of time and energy during flow. They report a sense of discovery from connecting ideas that feel like a "new reality." The whole world seems closed out. *If this is true, then teachers should . . .*

- Creativity involves a leap that transcends logic but is built on a base of knowledge and skills. Expertise is absolutely necessary. You cannot create without a reservoir of ideas or skills. *If this is true, then teachers should . . .*
- The creative process is facilitated by (1) knowing strategies, such as SCAMPER, to manipulate ideas in content areas, (2) finding new problems, and (3) working with content in new ways. *If this is true, then teachers should . . .*
- Motivation and positive attitude play a prominent role. These mental states keep individuals committed to a task long enough for exploration, problem finding, and creative thinking to happen at all. *If this is true, then teachers should . . .*
- There is no creation without frustration. Creative problem solving is bringing order to chaos, relating the unrelated, discovering patterns, and raising and answering questions. These higher order thinking processes are a struggle and messy. Teachers who substitute activities requiring that students follow directions may think they are helping students by making it easy. They actually rob students of opportunities to become resilient and independent—the products of overcoming obstacles. Feelings of accomplishment and pride stem from successful struggles. *If this is true, then teachers should . . .*
- Producing and consuming humor use thinking processes similar to creative thinking. Humor is rooted not in happiness, but in conflict and problems, just like creative thinking. Even a riddle is a problem to be solved creatively. *If this is true, then teachers should . . .*
- We can accumulate important data to fuel the fire of creativity by looking and listening carefully, observing details, and noticing patterns. *If this is true, then teachers should . . .*
- We stand on the shoulders of our ancestors in our creative efforts, building bit by bit in a long, constantly evolving effort. We must know the past to envision the future. *If this is true, then teachers should . . .*
- The CPS process is goal oriented and focused. It demands concentration. *If this is true, then teachers should . . .*
- There is a difference between problem solving and problem finding. The latter is as much needed as the former. Consider these problem types: (1) ones given to us with known solutions (most school problems), (2) ones given with solutions unknown, and (3) problems sought and found, and without known solutions. Example: Advertisers try to create markets for products we don't even know we need or want. *If this is true, then teachers should . . .*
- Creative problem solving includes many types of thinking, including metaphoric (comparisons), divergent (open ended), and combining opposites (e.g., jumbo shrimp). *If this is true, then teachers should . . .*
- The CPS process is parallel to the scientific method, the writing process, and the reading process. *If this is true, then teachers should . . .*
- Teachers can intentionally boost creativity, and they unintentionally inhibit it. *If this is true, then teachers should . . .*

**Creativity Deprivation.** Struggling learners may actually be harmed if engagement in CPS is postponed until such skills as decoding and spelling are mastered. Young children who are denied opportunities to use problem solving may not develop internal motivation to create meaning. Left to low-level memory or following direction tasks, they can develop distaste for learning. What is to sustain attention to the squirrelly details of our alphabet? Letters like *d, b, p,* and *q* are all just circles with sticks, devoid of meaning. They do not conform to a child's world where a shoe or crayon is still a shoe and a crayon, no matter what direction you turn them. Parents and teachers may not always look favorably on creative behaviors such as wanting to "do their own thing" and resisting conforming to adult expectations. Just like Lionni's main character in *Frederick,* creative behaviors may cause children to be seen as troublemakers. Studies document the decline in children's creative thinking as they move through school. Some conclude that fourth grade is the peak of creativity for many learners. Ready Reference 2.7 lists common creativity inhibitors. More are available at www.goshen.edu/art/ed/creativitykillers.html.

**Creativity Boosters.**

*I have no special gift. I am only passionately curious.* (Albert Einstein)

Enhancing creativity rests on developing habits that include celebrating differences of mind, spirit, and body. Students need to be taught to make choices within moral limits and follow personal interests. I think here of the boy, Philo Farnsworth, reading old science magazines in the attic of his family's Iowa farmhouse. Time to pursue a teenage fascination with electrons led him to visualize the rows of his plowed field as a metaphor that created the cathode ray tube. Philo Farnsworth thus gave us television.

CPS can be embedded in the teaching of any subject, and if taught systematically, becomes a substantial vehicle for understanding. Playing creative games and puzzles is not enough. Learners must have a knowledge base and be taught to question, change, elaborate, and transform ideas. Such teaching must also forecast the consequences of human creation. As the Jewish folktale about the golem reminds us, creativity, mindless of morality, is a destroyer (see *Golem,* by David Wisniewski, Caldecott Medal in 1997). Ready Reference 2.8 lists creativity boosters. Also, visit http://creativeeducationfoundation.org/.

**Final Suggestions.** This entire book is about how to teach using CPS in the framework of AI. Of special importance is using CPS personally to plan lessons and learning experiences and in other life pursuits.

## Ready Reference 2.7 Creativity Inhibitors

Common inhibitors to creative thinking follow:

1. Tests: too often, too soon, or too long
2. Positive evaluations and successes: can inhibit risk taking
3. Hovering: students feel overly monitored as they work
4. Extrinsic reinforcers: focus on "getting things" rather than learning for its own sake (grades, points, stamps, praise)
5. Worry and fear: not feeling safe enough to take risks
6. Competition: especially if there is great hope for success
7. Products: overemphasis on final product versus learning
8. Choice: little or no choice about assignments
9. Overemphasis on order, neatness, and following directions
10. Preponderance of questions that are literal or have "right" answers
11. Time: lack of incubation or wait time to think
12. Data: insufficient information, skills, or materials
13. Rush to judgment: "That won't work" right off the bat
14. Learned helplessness: doing things *for* children that they could do themselves
15. Lack of time to pursue interests
16. Solemnity: taking things too seriously (e.g., teachers that rarely laugh, play, or use humor)
17. "One-way" thinking: stereotyped or dictated art that emphasizes "staying in the lines" and one right answer
18. Predigested activities: focus on following directions or copying models

*Source:* Lowenfeld & Brittain, 1975, pp. 22–25.

## Ready Reference 2.8 Creative Thinking Boosters

1. Brainstorming steps: Go for quantity. List all ideas, even way-out ones. Keep driving, don't brake! Piggyback on ideas. Set a time limit. Group ideas and evaluate (Osborne, 1963). Notes: Individual before group brainstorming can produce more ideas. Giving evaluation criteria before brainstorming reduces the number of ideas, but may increase quality.
2. Reverse brainstorm. Squeeze out nonexamples—opposites instead of examples.
3. Word association (like brainstorming): List or web ideas connected to a word. Use to introduce any lesson. Example: Associate ideas for *foundations* for "The Three Little Pigs."
4. Question frames: Prompt with stems: "How might we _____?" "What if _____?" "What are all the ways _____?" "An idea nobody would think of is _____." Focus on a problem under study: How might we move if it were winter and we were marching from Valley Forge?
5. Stumped or stymied? Take a time-out. Listen to music or do something physical: stretch, bend, or dance.
6. Turn mistakes into opportunities. Make lemonade! Be open to surprises. See *The Big Orange Splot* by D. M. Pinkwater (1993) and the Itzhak Perlman story about playing a concert without a full set of violin strings at the end of Chapter 13.
7. Gather data. Read, observe, discuss, use the internet to get ideas and different perspectives. Look at past work, reread, examine others' ideas.
8. Don't take the first idea. Sleep on it. Generate lots of possibilities. The best idea may come right after you think you've run out.
9. Mind meld. Open an encyclopedia, dictionary, or magazine and pick an idea (noun, verb). Combine it with the one you are trying to develop. Don't worry about weird ideas. Example: I spotted scissors by my computer. I can force a relationship between the scissors and this chapter: I want to *cut out* drab teaching and can make *points* for why teachers should use arts-based teaching. Scissors and the arts can be *tools or weapons*. There are *different kinds* of scissors (pinking, pruning, etc.), just as there are various ways to integrate the arts.
10. Thinking hats (adapted from deBono, 1991): Get with four people. Each person "wears a hat" or takes a perspective:
    - Hat 1 describes what is known.
    - Hat 2 gives feelings about the problem.
    - Hat 3 tells what is not known.
    - Hat 4 thinks of associations or images.
    - Hat 5 lists ideas not at all related—opposites or nonexamples.

    This is similar to "cubing" (Neeld, 1986) in which a topic is explored in six ways: (1) Describe it. List its parts. (2) Tell how it feels. (3) What do you associate with it? (4) Use or apply it. (5) Compare or tell what it is like. (6) Argue for or against it. This can be timed (e.g., spend 2 minutes on each "side" of the cube, or do one or two sides a day).
11. SCAMPER. See Ready Reference 2.6 on CPS.
    - Explictly teach CPS using mini-lessons on each aspect.
    - Demonstrate relationships between (1) arts problem solving and CPS and (2) making meaning during reading, writing, science, and math and CPS.
    - Look for teachable moments to connect CPS to daily life.
    - When kids get stuck, refer them to CPS processes such as data gathering, brainstorming, and SCAMPER.
    - Plan regular time for students to do choice CPS.

## Conclusion

*Research now substantiates what some teachers and parents already knew intuitively—that the arts are critical to learning.* (Murfee, 1995)

This chapter has concentrated on the philosophical beliefs, research, and theories that suggest arts integration is a moral imperative. It is the right thing to do. The role of philosophy, theory, and research cannot be underestimated in both initiating and sustaining arts integration. A focal point of the chapter was the description of creative problem solving (CPS) which is at the heart of artistic thinking and creating meaning. CPS orchestrates higher order thinking needed to construct sense across disciplines and is the central process students must strategically use to create meaning.

### Teachers as Leaders: AI Advocacy

AI doesn't become meaningful without a focus on creative problem solving. Contribute to enlarging the education profession's thinking about CPS. Here are options: Create a blog about using creative problem solving in your daily life. Participate in a discussion about creative problem solving using www.skype.com/. Create a Wikipedia entry on creative problem solving. Offer to do a short presentation on CPS for a group of teachers (e.g., try at least the creativity boosters and share the results).

### myeducationlab

Go to the Activities and Applications section for Topic *Strategies for Teaching* at MyEducationLab for your course and complete the video activities entitled "Using Riddles for Creative Problem Solving."

Go to the Book Specific Resources section in the MyEducationLab for your course, select your book and Chapter 2 to view the Questions to Guide Reading and Response Options for this chapter.

## Resources

Also see the Appendix.

### Recommended Videos

*Journey within.* (1990). Renascence Films (uses of art and importance of play). Website: www.touchstonecenter.net/publications.html.

*The beginning. A wiggleman's tale* (an oldie but a goodie short about creative thinking).

# Teacher Spotlight
## Risk, Creativity, and Children

A common justification for arts integration is that the arts encourage students to take more risks. Fifth-grade teacher Carol Rathbun has had the opportunity to judge the importance of "risk" during her 20 years at Ashley River. "Most children were 'at risk' in my first classes," she explains. "I was 'at risk' myself. I had to take risks to help my at-risk students." The arts proved to be an avenue of success.

"I believe every child is creative—especially the one who painted Paul Revere green," Carol says. She includes all the arts, but particularly likes movement and drama. For example, during an immigration unit students recently moved along timelines as they assumed roles of people on Ellis Island. Each had prepared a monologue about the immigration experience. "I think impromptu is the best use of drama," she explains. Carol draws this conclusion from comments of students who return to visit her. "It is drama they recall, especially creating the Plantation House!" She becomes more serious as she points out they "vividly remember how it felt for brother to be against brother on the battlefield."

# Student Spotlight
## Day's End

A boy who had been miming plant parts stopped by where I was taking notes. "Write down that I like learning through the arts," he says. "I like that my teacher wants us to be different and not just be good test takers." He points to a quote above the door. They are words from Dr. Seuss, "Say what you think and be who you are. Those that mind don't matter, and those that matter won't mind" (Ashley River Creative Arts, February 2005).

# 3

# Arts Integration Building Blocks

*What is now proved was once only imagined.* (William Blake)

## Overview

Picking up from the arts integration (AI) Building Block I of philosophy, discussed in Chapter 2, this chapter goes into detail about the remaining nine AI building blocks. The building blocks are key operating principles that interlock. Teachers gradually weave them together as they move through increasingly sophisticated levels of integration. Although there are a variety of AI designs in any model, all 10 building blocks must be addressed to ensure meaningful implementation of arts integration philosophy.

## Introduction

Arts integration is embedded in the larger context of school reform that embraces whole child views, constructivist beliefs, curriculum integration, use of multiple intelligences theory and inquiry-based approaches that target teaching higher order creative problem-solving processes. AI is also related to curricular reforms that focus on increasing learning engagement, differentiating instruction, and developing multiple literacies, which include quickly evolving technology-based communication formats.

This chapter moves ahead to a closer examination of these ideas and other key concepts that teachers need to know to implement AI. The chapter goes beyond the question of *what is* AI to address *how-to* questions. The arts integration building blocks are presented as enabling conditions, not as a definitive model. Faculties must tailor any framework to the strengths and needs of their particular school, which results in a unique AI design. The building blocks will be similar, but the emphases will differ. For example, schools vary in their use of artist residencies, innovative assessment, kinds of professional development, nature of collaborative planning, multidisciplinary units, and in their amount of focus on the creative problem-solving process (CPS).

The opening School Spotlight features a middle school that uses extensive collaboratively planned units—a key building block of AI. This school's story continues the emphasis on reform driven by research, and serves as a reminder that many important effects of AI are not assessed by traditional tests.

At Tanglewood Middle School the motto is, "I can create art. I am an artist. There is art in me," explains Karen Kapp, principal of Tanglewood, which is located in an impoverished area of Greenville, South Carolina. The school adopted an AI approach using inquiry-based units to turn their motto into an educational reality.

"The arts captured the children internally from the start by awakening their emotions and physical self. We now have kids with fire on the inside," Kapp says proudly (April 28, 2005, interview).

Tanglewood adapted the Chicago Teacher's Center model. Teacher comfort with an art form was an important criterion for getting started. The goal was for teachers to learn to use the art form by working with artists. The first arts-based units were designed around "essential questions" and were approximately 3 weeks in length. The units consisted of two planning sessions with an artist followed by eight sessions with students.

Ms. Kapp cites the school's 2005 Arts Project progress report as evidence of the power of arts integration. Findings are as follows:

- Students scoring *below basic* improved 12 percent in English/language arts on South Carolina's state test. Similarly, students scoring *basic* improved 16 percent and students scoring *proficient* and *advanced* increased 9 percent during the first year of arts integration at Tanglewood.
- Students scoring *below basic* in math improved 8 percent in a single year; those scoring *basic* increased 4 percent and *proficient* and *advanced* scores improved 6 percent in a single year.
- Tanglewood made dramatic adequate yearly progress (AYP). In 2 years of arts infusion, the school met 20 of 23 AYP targets.

Kapp thinks the effects of arts infusion are especially visible in special education classes. "Students examined the *Mona Lisa* and discussed da Vinci. Students who were off the charts are completely engaged and making their own pieces."

The school climate has also changed significantly. "There is just more spirit and engagement," she says, using words like "passionate," "energized," and "missionary zeal" to describe the teachers. "Teacher attendance is the highest in the district—a complete reversal."

Tanglewood's implementation plan is unique but the results are similar to other middle schools where achievement in reading and writing rises into the double digits (Bolak, Bialach, & Dunphy, 2005). Underlying these gains are consistent reports of more engaged students and greater teacher enthusiasm. ✸

Me, Myself, and I: Self portraits painted by Ashley River students

# How to Plan and Implement Arts Integration

In schools across America, AI has developed along a continuum from using one or two art forms to a small degree to complete arts infusion. The latter includes a deep respect for the arts as separate disciplines, and a focus on using the arts as investigative tools. For example, in social studies, themes such as "courage" are examined from the viewpoint of a poet, painter, musician, and dancer. Students are led to understanding through the arts as they examine August Rodin's immense sculpture, *The Burghers of Calais*. Six town leaders stand frozen about to give their lives to save their small French town from an English army. The message of courage comes through mass and shape. This kind of art gives a richness of perspective that changes what students *know,* what they can and will *do*, and perhaps most importantly, what they might *be* (Drake & Burns, 2004).

## Levels of Arts Integration

In a fully integrated arts design, teachers present skills and information about and from the arts *and* use the arts as teaching and learning vehicles. Booth (2003) calls this using the arts for art's sake *and* for learning's sake. Teachers mature through levels of implementation to reach full AI: teaching *with, about, in,* and *through* (WAIT), as introduced in Chapter 1. Starting at a beginning level they are as follows:

*Teaching* **With.** Teachers experiment by using the arts casually for enjoyment and give students chances to work creatively. Usually these are isolated arts experiences and students explore art materials or ideas with minimal teacher guidance. Students may sing holiday or patriotic songs or be given drawing time after reading a story. These activities are not normally keyed to standards, and may only be loosely related to academic units and lessons.

*Teaching* **About and In.** Gradually teachers build an arts knowledge base that allows them to plan lessons for students to learn *about* and do work *in* the arts. The goal is to have students do creative problem solving through the arts and develop personal artistry. Teachers begin to co-plan with arts specialists and artists to construct lessons that connect arts content and skills to other curricular areas. Often music and art teachers help classroom teachers locate artwork and music from historical periods or particular cultures to introduce social studies units. Classroom teachers teach rudimentary arts content and skills to give students the means to problem solve using the arts. For example, an investigation of van Gogh's struggles and triumphs may be paired with studying a period in social studies. The events of van Gogh's life become a historical lens to view the times. Map and globe skills may be used to pinpoint his life journey. Literacy is developed around reading biographies and writing about van Gogh in forms that range from informational reports to poems.

Teachers begin to give substance to casual routines, such as opening songs. They do mini-lessons about composers, display musical elements charts, and ask students to do close listening to details to make sense of the music and lyrics. When teaching *about* and *in* the arts, there is a conscious effort to develop aesthetic thinking. Students are engaged in exploration, creation, response, performance, reflection, and evaluation. Lessons are tied to district standards, and there is an effort to assess arts literacy, along with growth in linked curricular areas.

*Teaching* **Through.** At this level the arts are prominent through daily arts routines, an aesthetic classroom environment, and as both content and means of learning in co-planned, standards-based units. The creative problem-solving process is explicitly taught and applied in science and social studies units engaging students in seeking big ideas through asking important questions (Cornett, 2010). The arts, language arts, and math become tools to explore unit questions.

Teaching through the arts seeks high aesthetic standards and involves students in significant arts experiences connected to units. Lessons producing "25 identical Kachina dolls from a pattern or slopping paint thoughtlessly on brown kraft paper to represent ancient cave drawings" are questionable teaching practices (Remer, 1996, p. 339). Teachers become more selective and choose to not integrate some lessons. Indeed, "dancing in geometric patterns does not substitute for learning to calculate area and perimeter" (p. 339). Artifacts are studied to make sense of cultural history and values from particular times and places. The emphasis in teaching *through* the arts is creating meaning *using* the arts.

## Beyond Entertainment

Teachers actually move in and out of phases of teaching *with, about, in,* and *through* the arts. Each level offers entry points to fit student needs, curricular structures, materials, and time constraints. In particular, teachers need to feel comfortable gradually developing arts literacy and pedagogy. The type and pace depends on the people involved. Too much, too soon can overwhelm even the best. Teachers choose at various times to integrate multiple arts or just one and when to plan alone or plan collaboratively.

The goals are the same for all these models—to make natural and meaningful arts connections that add depth to learning.

Most of the study about and collaborative planning for AI comes to fruition in individual classrooms. While an artist residency can be a unit centerpiece and co-teaching with arts specialists is desirable, the sustainability of AI rests with the classroom teacher.

# Arts Integration Building Blocks

Research Update 3.1 describes results from AI in schools across the United States. Successful projects share common building blocks. Ten AI building blocks form a flexible blueprint to plan, teach, and assess. The building blocks are grounded in research, and theories discussed in Chapter 2, along with professional wisdom honed in the "crucible of the classroom." AI building blocks go beyond the *why* to answer *what* and *how* questions. The central goal is to create meaning through artistic thinking that features the coordinated use of thinking skills summarized in the CPS process. The 10 AI building blocks appear in Ready References 3.2 and 3.3. Each is discussed next. Subsequent chapters address the building blocks related to each arts area.

---

## Research Update 3.1    Arts Integration and Academic Achievement

**Chicago, Illinois** Thirty-seven arts-based CAPE schools outscored non-arts schools in reading and math on two standardized tests. By sixth grade, more than 60 percent of CAPE students were performing at grade level and by ninth grade, CAPE students were a full grade level higher than non-CAPE students in reading (Fiske, 1999). CAPE students also reported enjoying learning more, playing closer attention, and remembering more (DeMoss & Morris, 2002).

**Columbus, Ohio** At Arts IMPACT schools students receive specialist arts classes and arts integrated lessons in the regular classroom. Test scores are significantly higher on math, science, and citizenship. Significant differences were not found between participating and nonparticipating students on other subtests (Kinney & Forsythe, 2005).

**San Marcos, California** Multilingual K–5 students in AI lessons made significant gains in English and comprehension. The SUAVE program received a development and dissemination grant in 2003 (Goldberg, 2004).

**New York City, New York; Hartford, Connecticut; Philadelphia, Pennsylvania; Baltimore, Maryland** A 3-year study of 2,000 students found a significant relationship between rich arts programs and competencies needed for school success. Authors suggest arts learning transfers

because students use "certain habits of mind which have salience across subject areas." Arts-based lessons invite traveling "back-and-forth across subject boundaries" (Burton et al, 1999, p. 36).

**Rhode Island** SmART Schools' students showed a 13 percent improvement in mathematics as compared to 2.8 percent in comparison schools. In writing, on average the AI group scored 26.9 percent higher in writing as compared to control schools (Preble & Knowles, 2005).

**Wilmington, North Carolina** Disciplinary actions dropped from 130 to 50 and suspensions from 32 to 3 during the first year of A+ arts integration. In addition, state writing test scores for fourth graders improved 30 percentile points (Corbett et al., 2001; Marron, 2003).

**Multiple Sites** In a 3-year investigation of 41 schools using multiple intelligences, which integrates all arts forms, 20 schools had improved standardized test scores and 22 had improvements in discipline (Harvard Project Zero, 2000).

**Edmonton, Canada** A longitudinal study of K–9 ArtsSmart schools found that 73 percent of teachers reported positive changes in practice, and parent and community attendance improved at arts-based school activities (Stack, 2007).

**AI Building Blocks Questions**

Ask the following questions when planning and implementing AI.

1. ***Philosophy of arts integration.*** What and how do students need to learn to be happy and successful in the 21st century? How does arts integration address these needs?
2. ***Arts literacy: Content and skills.*** What arts literacy do students need in order to effectively use each art form for communication?
3. ***Collaborative planning.*** What are the important overarching understandings (big ideas) and processes (e.g., thinking skills) students need? What concepts and processes are shared among disciplines? What unusual contributions do the arts make to learning/teaching?
4. ***Aesthetic learning environments.*** How can learning ecologies be created that (1) are low threat and high challenge, and (2) facilitate aesthetic attitudes toward learning?
5. ***Literature as a core art form.*** How can literature integration be used as a model for arts integration? How can the vast store of arts-based literature be used throughout the curriculum?
6. ***Best teaching practices.*** What teaching methods align with beliefs about AI? What pedagogy, both general and arts specific, is supported by research and professional wisdom?
7. ***Instructional design: Routines and structures.*** What organizational ideas support systematic implementation of AI? What lesson sequence works best? How is time organized? What are common routines and structures?
8. ***Differentiation.*** How can the arts be used to motivate and help meet the wide range of student needs? How can arts teaching be differentiated for strengths and needs?
9. ***Assessment for learning.*** How can arts-based assessments enhance learning and teaching?
10. ***Arts partnerships.*** Who are potential arts partners with teachers? What special knowledge and skills do artists bring to planning, teaching, and assessment? How can collaboration for AI be made to happen?

---

# Building Block I: Philosophy of Arts Integration

The first building block lays the foundation for the rest. It is philosophy or beliefs about the goals of education, teaching, and learning that are informed by research and professional wisdom which directs AI implementation. Central AI beliefs include strong values for diversity, creative inquiry, active learning (heads-on, hearts-on, hands-on learning), and student independence. Of particular importance is a belief in the capacity of all students to construct personal meanings using a variety of communication tools (language arts and arts) and materials. Chapter 2 described five Ps to organize beliefs: people, principles, places, programs, and pedagogy.

# Building Block II: Arts Literacy

I'm listening to a local radio station in Brevard, North Carolina, home of the well-known summer music series. A group of girls is singing a country song about redneck women who live in trailers and keep Christmas lights up all year. The song celebrates the freedom to live as you like, with a toe-tapping rhythm and a catchy refrain. After two verses, I sing along. Art takes many forms.

It is well within the classroom teacher's capabilities to engage students in the many forms of arts, but the meaningfulness depends on the teacher's continual personal growth in arts literacy (Burnaford, 2007). Arnheim (1989) explains how a teacher might begin by taking time to talk with children about messages in real art. For example, when students are invited to look closely at Australian

Aborigine bark paintings they can discover details that reveal much about the people who created them. Looking closely allows investigation into a culture that can inform art making during which students can be coached to discover the kinship between the "beautiful paintings of a distant race and their own artwork" (p. 48). In this manner, art is treated as a "text" to be understood and a form that is created to share thoughts and feelings, that is, communication.

## Teacher Standards

National educational and arts organizations have collaborated to produce a document outlining the arts knowledge and skills needed by classroom teachers. The *Model Standards for Licensing Classroom Teachers and Specialists in the Arts* (INTASC, 2002) acknowledge that even in nonintegrated schools, much arts instruction is provided by generalist teachers. These standards are organized around principles of good teaching used in the Interstate New Teacher Assessment and Support Consortium (INTASC) document that guides many teacher preparation programs. Principle 1 addresses art subject matter that is included in this book. Standards can be retrieved at www.ccsso.org/Projects/interstate_new_teacher_assessment_and_support_consortium/

In AI the classroom teacher creates the context for the arts to be made integral to the entire curriculum, especially literacy, while arts specialists continue to provide comprehensive and systematic in-depth arts instruction. The role of classroom teachers is to co-teach the following aspects of arts literacy as they relate to integration efforts.

- Purposes of the arts (*why*)
- Processes of the arts (*how*)
- People (*who*)
- Arts products as texts (*what*)
- Arts elements, skills, and concepts (*what*)

# Ready Reference 3.3 Ten AI Building Blocks Chart

| | **1** Arts Integration Philosophy | **2** Arts Literacy | **3** Collaborative Planning | **4** Aesthetic Learning Environment | **5** Literature as a Core Art |
|---|---|---|---|---|---|
| **W H A T** | Stated beliefs about five Ps including principles of learning and literacy<br>• Focus on constructing meaning through "head, hands, heart" creative problem solving. | Literature, art, drama, dance, music (LADDM)<br>• Knowledge base: content, products, skills, people, artistic thinking, techniques, tools, materials | Systematic planning among teachers and arts specialists used standards and other goals<br>• Assessment<br>• Pronged lesson plans<br>• Key materials<br>• Unit types<br>• Schoolwide themes<br>• Field-based learning | Climate or culture created in classroom and school by psychological and physical factors<br>• Spaces/Places<br>• Arrangement<br>• Movement<br>• Performances<br>• Displays<br>• Storage | Arts-based literature: all genres from biography to picture books connecting to the arts including multimedia versions of books |
| **W H Y** | Guide: planning, teaching, assessment, and evaluation | Arts for learning's sake *and* arts for art's sake | Increases ownership, higher quality results | Social contexts that promote creative problem solving/ meaning-making | Literature is the most used art form in the elementary curriculum<br>Natural fit |
| **H O W** | Create school mission statement and consensus operating principles | Teachers and arts specialists do explicit teaching with visuals and demonstrations<br>• Literacy connection emphasized | During school day, summer, weekly, monthly, written, and casual conversations<br>Professional development, teacher reference library, text studies, websites | Teacher philosophy and personality: alter physical and psychological environment<br>Question: Is it anesthetic or aesthetic? | Selection Sources<br>Arts-based class library<br>Coding collections |

**Purposes of the Arts.** Literacy is the ability to both understand and express thoughts and feelings effectively. In the 21st century, literacy includes all means of communication—the language arts plus dance, music, drama, poetry, and visual art. Language arts (verbal), visual arts, and performing arts share the same purpose: to communicate ideas, emotions, and values; but each art form has its own language. Arts symbol systems are like alphabets and range from musical notation to the visual art elements of color, shape, and line. Messages are created and sent using the language chosen by artists. How messages are understood depends on the receiver's ability to "read" texts ranging from book illustrations to body language.

Hands-on arts experiences are important means of helping students understand how the arts are basic ways people solve problems—specifically, communication problems. Because the arts are so personal, they can uniquely help students grasp the concept that it is not what they "take" from a text, but what they "make" of it (Eisner, 2002a). Ready Reference 3.4 lists topics for arts mini-lessons (discussion and writing).

**Processes of the Arts.** Specific artistic skills range from learning to focus so you don't get dizzy while dancing (e.g., find a spot on the wall) to painting techniques like dry brush. While the main purpose of the arts is to communicate, creative problem solving is the process that drives artistic decisions about *what* to communicate and *how*. In the arts, the problem is often self-chosen and has to do with how to develop a new meaning. Artists are quick to point out that acquiring new ways to view and do the arts is a self-motivating journey.

Of course, not all problem solving is creative and not all cognition is artistic, but the 21st century skills calls for a heightened need for creative thinking that seeks innovative solutions. Artistic thinking, feeling, being, and doing are born of imaginings. "What if?" and "Why not?" are key questions that seek divergent answers. Thinking without words is common, especially in using visual images. Writers, for example, often begin with mental images of places and characters.

Artistic processes are not confined to arts; they are used across academic disciplines. Think about how these verbs, which

| 6 Best Teaching Practices | 7 Instructional Design | 8 Differentiation | 9 Assessment for Learning | 10 Arts Partnerships |
|---|---|---|---|---|
| 1. Teacher as person<br>2. Inside-out motivation<br>3. Engagement/active learning<br>4. Creative problem solving (CPS)<br>5. Explicit teaching<br>6. Apply, practice, rehearse<br>7. Aesthetic orienting<br>8. Process or product<br>9. Managing behavior, time, and materials<br>10. Independence and self-discipline | Scheduling time, events, spaces. Schoolwide and classroom structures, predictable routines:<br>• IDC design<br>• Energizers/warm-ups<br>• Opening/wrap-up routines<br>• Performances and exhibits<br>• Centers<br>• Groupings<br>• Clubs/Projects | Adapting for strengths and needs:<br>• Place<br>• Amount<br>• Rate<br>• Time<br>• Instruction<br>• Curriculum<br>• Utensils (including technology)<br>• Level<br>• Assistance<br>• Response | Data gathered to ascertain strengths Clear expectations used to motivate<br>• Ongoing and multifactored<br>• Focus on observations, performances, displays, long-term projects<br>• Program evaluation | Collaboration among general educators, artists, arts teachers, teaching artists, arts agencies, universities, community groups, parents |
| Research and professional wisdom in arts and education should direct instruction | Make sure the arts are integral<br><br>Institutionalize routines, rituals, and structures | Diverse students have different strengths and needs | Motivate learning and gauge progress<br><br>Standards and goals-based: know-do-be | It takes a village . . .<br><br>Funding issues<br><br>Share resources and expertise |
| Informed by: research updates, PD, professional journals, websites: ArtsEdge, Arts Education Partnership, ASCD | Set up ongoing structures and routines with emphasis on student-led activities | Assess, with focus on observation and consultation with students and parents<br><br>Differentiate for success | Tell, show, develop criteria in collaboration Arts portfolios, rubrics, and checklists for teacher, peer and self-evaluation | Joint planning: lessons, grants, and fund raising<br><br>Features: parent nights (display openings), school arts directory |

exemplify artistic work, also relate to science and math: *wonder, seek, discover, notice, perceive, visualize, empathize, experiment, connect, capture, transform, compose, create, synthesize, reflect, criticize,* and *judge.* AI involves explicit instruction of these processes across disciplines using CPS as a unifying structure.

**People.**    Artists themselves are rich content for study. CPS dons a face when students learn about artists through residencies, websites, books, and videos. Students may like to develop an ongoing chart of "found" artist characteristics as a resource for problem-solving strategies. Consider the following suggestions.

* "You can't break the rules until you've mastered them," explains Joan Templar, an accomplished visual artist and art professor. She creates dramatic abstract works from joint compound and collage materials. Like most artists, from Picasso to Michelangelo, she studied the masters before striking out on original paths. A solid knowledge and skill base is needed to open up choices for how to use materials and tools in innovative ways.

* Artists are highly observant. They notice details and patterns—and not just in formal art. Anything can be aesthetically perceived, as in the "not what they take from a 'text' but what they make of it" point suggested earlier. An artist looks at an old tire and sees a unique tread pattern. The wear makes a kind of thumbprint. Artists take delight in the individuality of people, nature, and objects.

* Artists study other artists and adapt ideas to create original works. Each artist has unique ways of working—style, techniques, and materials. Any or all of these can ignite a fire in students. I think here of the popular video of Eric Carle painting his collage papers. He has inspired students from first grade through college to try the technique that gave us *The Very Hungry Caterpillar* and many other vibrant picture books.

* Artists use strategies to start up and get unstuck. For example, they often rework one piece or continue to work with one idea for a long time (e.g., Monet repeatedly painted haystacks). This suggests that students reread books, write on the same topics, and study a subject for an extended

## Ready Reference 3.4 Topics for Arts Mini-Lessons

Use these questions to prompt writing and discussion.

### Literacy and Communication

- How do people communicate ideas and feelings (understand, respond, express)? How are the arts ways to communicate?
- What is literacy? Communication? How are the arts languages or forms of literacy?
- How are the arts different from and like the language arts?
- What does it mean to read? What "texts" do we read? How is reading art or music different from reading books?
- What arts words and processes are common across disciplines (line, play, shape, composition)?

### Nature of the Arts

- How are the arts a part of daily life (e.g., work, business, social, clothes, Internet)?
- What is art?
- Why does art exist? What is the function or purpose of the arts now? Originally?
- How does something become art?
- What is good art?
- What makes something music, visual art, drama/theatre, dance, or poetry?
- When are arts practical? What art forms used to be functional and now exist just for aesthetic purposes (e.g., horse training/dancing)?
- What is beauty? Why is it an important idea?
- What does "arts for art's sake" mean? What disciplines exist for their own sake?
- How would life be different if the arts disappeared? (Lowry's *The Giver* uses this theme.)

### Cognition, Emotion, and Motivation

- What makes us want to learn? How do the arts connect to motivation?

- What role does problem solving play in the arts? How do we solve daily problems?
- How do people think/feel differently when they are engaged in the arts?
- What is the role of "transforming ideas" in understanding? What do the arts have to do with transformation?
- How is the process of making art like problem-solving processes in reading, writing, and scientific method?
- How does thinking use images? How can you think without visual images?
- What do the senses have to do with the learning? The arts?

### Creativity and Imagination

- What is creativity?
- How are problem solving and creativity related?
- Why and when do people have to be creative?
- How is creativity related to survival?
- What do the arts have to do with creativity?
- Why do artists practice/redo/rework/rehearse so much?
- What is imagination? How is imagination used in problem solving? Life? Reading? Writing? Arts?

### Artistic Thinking

- How does making, viewing, or listening to the arts feel?
- How do artists think? What does it mean to think artistically?
- What do artists value?
- How do materials change how we think?

### Other

- What do these clichés mean, and why have they become cliché (e.g., a picture is worth a thousand words; arts for art's sake)?
- Why do people say they cannot sing, dance, or draw when they so readily deny ability to read or write? What does "artistic denial" do to the possibility of singing, dancing, or making art?
- Why do we applaud? (Note: Chimps and seals do, too.)

---

time—ideas that heretofore were considered problematic or even cheating.

- Artists routinely start where they last worked, but tweak ideas. They also take the work of others and give it a new twist. In the picture book field, this popular idea produced an assortment of new fairy tale versions, such as *Sleeping Ugly* (Yolen).
- "Go away and come back" is a way to get fresh perspective. Artists say they find new insights after putting the work aside for a day or so. This aligns with research on creativity that shows incubation is needed to achieve critical distance and to forge new connections and discover new perspective. This strategy can increase satisfaction with products because work is more likely to be of higher quality and greater complexity.
- Successful artists are known for their persistence and resilience. Dr. Seuss is an example. Theodore Geisel persisted in trying to publish his first book, *And to Think I Saw It on*

*Mulberry Street,* after getting 43 rejections. Students need to have models that delight in hard work and show that effort is the key to success—not just talent or luck. Students need to know that the path to success is interesting, long, and rocky. Artist studies are rich sources for students to see that they are not alone in their struggles.

**Arts Products as Texts.** The arts take diverse forms from watercolors to contra dances. These products are "texts" that preserve culture and history. Although arts products may look pretty and entertain, the focus of integration lies deep below the surface. Students learn to "read" nonword art forms alongside learning to read word-based literary art forms. Arts products are used as lesson anchors to probe for deep understanding.

Directed hands-on examination of cultural artifacts is one stepping-stone to understanding the values and lifestyles of any group. Students learn to dig for cultural information from arts products about and from historical periods and use the arts as windows to see how people think, feel, and live. Students can be coached to hypothesize about what is expressed in any dance, painting, sculpture, or song. Through questioning they can realize that people have used the arts to say what is most important to them for thousands of years.

Each of the arts chapters of this book features example arts products that can be used as texts to develop literacy aspects, especially vocabulary and comprehension. Arts products are also suggested to introduce, develop, and conclude lessons in math, science, and social studies. Arts specialists can suggest additional resources. Numerous arts-based websites are suggested in each chapter. The ArtsEdge site is a recommended starting place.

**Arts Elements, Skills, and Concepts.**   All of us can enjoy the arts without instruction. Enjoyment, however, can end at entertainment, which evaporates quickly. AI targets deep engagement. This does not happen without explicit teaching of arts concepts (elements and symbols) and skills that form the language of each art. Basic arts literacy enables us to talk about, respond to, and create with the arts. Lockwood (2005) explains, "Without a basic symbolic vocabulary art remains impenetrable. We need to teach how to look at the 'thing.' How an oak in a painting suggests strength and longevity, or olive as peace." Students lacking arts literacy become frustrated, along with the teacher, when they try to "read" art, even in picture books. Picture book art is a readily available "text" to teach students to decode visual symbols, but success depends on learning art elements and how to investigate meanings in the composition. For example, picture book artists often orient figures to direct the eye to move to the next page. Short lessons on a few arts words and concepts free students to notice more and create meaning from what they see.

Meaningful AI depends on teaching about key arts concepts, which informs higher order problem solving. Students need to learn how arts concepts can be combined in an infinite number of ways to create art. Students who know basic visual arts elements ask questions such as "Why would Eric Carle use primary colors that are much brighter than in nature?" and "How would it change the feel and meaning if he used more pastels?" Making pastel collage art about nature would be one way to answer that question, which would show how art making involves use of the thinking skills within the problem-solving process.

Classroom teachers do not need a vast arts background. They can learn alongside students and gradually add arts knowledge. To do so, many teachers sit in on lessons of school arts specialists, which also models for children an openness to learn and take risks—essential teacher dispositions for successful AI. This initiative also lays the groundwork for planning with arts specialists to integrate the arts.

## Visual Mnemonics

Art element charts, word walls, banners, and big books are important aids for teachers and students alike, because the brain is constructed to attend to visual images. Amazingly, visuals can increase learning 400 percent (3M Corporation, 2001). Arts visuals are useful tools to help generate questions and serve as useful references to guide reflection on performances and other arts

products. Teachers who are tight on space are urged to be creative (e.g., use ceiling tiles or install a write on inexpensive roll-up shades). The Ready References in the chapters that follow summarize basic arts concepts, elements, media, tools, processes, styles, genre, and forms. Teachers may also consult local arts curricula, the INTASC website, and the MENC *National Standards for the Arts* (www.menc.org), which includes an arts glossary.

# Building Block III: Collaborative AI Planning

Deep learning depends on accessing and forging brain connections. AI planning seeks meaningful connections across grade levels and among disciplines to make instruction more brain friendly and more lifelike. In particular, the arts are connected to literacy and expand the number and kinds of communication pathways for students. AI teachers plan with this arts communication focus and seek out overlapping ideas, concepts, and skills found in separate disciplines by planning with arts specialists. The search is for mutually supportive relationships. The search is motivated by the potential of multidirectional transfer of learning especially needed since instructional time is shrinking in proportion to growing demands upon it. For example, parallel composition thinking processes in writing and visual arts can be explicitly taught by classroom teachers and visual arts specialists with a compounding effect on student learning. The same is true for teaching proportion concepts in both math and music. Separate disciplines even share some of the same terminology. Ready Reference 1.2 shows examples integral connections and Ready Reference 3.5 lists shared vocabulary.

## Planning Overview

National and state documents provide a framework for curricular planning; however, standards should not imply that conformity is the goal. No child is helped by narrowed curriculum, rigid criteria, and teaching only to tests. More consistent with the moral principles of our democracy is using creative means to achieve important ends. The arts provide diverse paths by which diverse students can reach important educational destinations. For example, AI engages students with motivation and literacy difficulties by taking new tacks. Achievement disparities shrink between high- and low-income students as they experience innovative ways to expand thinking and communication.

The most common paradigm is for arts-based units to be collaboratively planned by teachers, with arts specialists and artists. Units can be planned around many focal points, including artworks, artists, and arts processes, but frequently they center on science and social studies concepts and involve long-term inquiry projects. This sequence is logical, as science and social studies are the other two major content areas; math, reading, and the language arts are primarily skills used to process content. While particular processes are used in social studies and science, the content, or conceptual underpinnings, mostly have to do with understanding relationships among people and the natural world, respectively. Even literature, at its core, is fundamentally

## Ready Reference 3.5  Shared Vocabulary: Multiple Meaning Arts Words

The following are examples of arts vocabulary. Teach the multiple meanings to increase understanding and to show links between the arts and other curricular areas.

| | | | | |
|---|---|---|---|---|
| act | energy | make | plot | space |
| action | focus | middle | prop | stage |
| back | frame | mind | rate | step |
| bend | freeze | mold | read | stretch |
| block | front | mood | role | theme |
| body | hard | motion | round | time |
| bright | high | move | rhythm | turn |
| circle | level | opening | set | voice |
| cold | light | pattern | setting | volume |
| color | line | pitch | shade | walk |
| curtain | loud | place | shape | warm |
| direction | low | play | soft | write |
| draw | | | | |

an exploration of science and social studies issues, that is, finding truths about people and the world.

## Pronged Focus

After a unit is roughed out, the teacher creates sequenced daily lesson plans. Lesson plans feature objectives that specify what students will know and be able to do in the arts, as well as in the connected academic area, by the end of the unit. Among the possible integration prongs, there has to be at least one significant arts teaching point that complements a focus in the other discipline. From the pronged focus, student objectives are written that explain what students should know and be able to do by the lesson conclusion. To make it easier to assess, objectives are written using observable verbs that describe learning evidence (see Planning Page 3.10, later in chapter). To keep AI meaningful, planning must also focus on how to teach important concepts and skills *about* the arts that connect to content learning in other curricular areas. The goal is to use the arts, not abuse them.

## Planning Questions

AI involves students in living, working, and learning through the arts. To make this a reality, curriculum planners recommend that units be structured around important concepts, developed into big ideas, and explored through the use of important questions (Burnaford, 2007; Cornett, 2010; Drake & Burns, 2004; Wiggins & McTighe, 2005). The goal is to engage students in arts-based CPS work to find and create meaning. The result is deeper understanding, that is,

which is also called comprehension. Ready Reference 3.6 provides questions to facilitate AI planning.

## Standards and Benchmarks

As discussed in Chapter 1, national standards list what students should know and be able to do in each curricular area. Nearly every state has used national standards to create state documents. Local districts go further to designate "benchmark" behaviors that describe learning progress by grade level and/or by developmental stage. These documents are important planning tools. Many states now align testing with standards so that teachers will no longer have to be stretched between what is on the test and what is in the standards.

Teachers need to consult standards documents, realizing that all standards are not equally important and it is impossible to

Collaborative planning at Ashley River Creative Arts

## Planning Page 3.6
### Questions for AI Unit Planning

- What do we want students to *know, do,* and *be* by the end of the unit (Drake & Burns, 2004)?
- How can we target important understandings that are "secrets of the universe" (e.g., patterns, questions, themes) so students will be motivated to investigate?
- What are overlapping standards in different disciplines that apply to this unit?
- How can lessons be introduced to pique student interest?
- How could the unit be made more appropriate for particular students? How can the concept of diversity be advanced?
- How will the unit create new perspectives, that is, cause students to make meaning? How would an artist view the problems/questions? A scientist? A mathematician?
- How will the integrity of each discipline be maintained during integration? In what meaningful ways might the arts contribute to unit foci?
- What authentic arts materials and methods would be appropriate for this unit?
- How can student learning best be assessed and evaluated in both the arts area and nonarts area?

address each standard in individual lessons. Integration is an efficient way to deal with duplication across disciplines and many arts standards dovetail with standards in every curricular area, especially when it comes to goals related to the development of thinking and communication. Integrated programs have proved to have significantly more positive effects on achievement, teacher practice, and school culture than standards-based programs alone (Rabkin & Redmond, 2004, p. 12).

Standards represent important goals, but they do not comprise all that we want children to know, do, and be. Drake and Burns (2004) point out that teachers actually give priority to character traits (e.g., what students should *be*), which is uncommon in standards. Teachers explicitly or implicitly add value-based end goals as they plan (e.g., students will work cooperatively, have empathy, be honest). AI uniquely develops cognitive abilities, social skills, and emotional dispositions that are assumed but not always written into academic standards. See Ready Reference 1.4 for a summary of the unique contributions of the arts.

Many school districts now follow the recommendations of professional organizations when it comes to designing units. Most advocate life-centered unit and project approaches that focus on 21st-century skills such as creative problem solving and collaboration. The websites of state departments of education are good places to search for initiatives and partnerships within the state that may be using arts-based units. North Carolina has created a kind of Cliffs Notes of useful standards. *Reference Guides for Integrating the Curriculum* can be purchased at www.ncpublicschools.org. Also check the Arts Education Partnership site (www.aep.org).

## National Standards for the Arts

The *National Standards for the Arts* is an important planning tool for classroom teachers and arts specialists. It specifies the knowledge base, skills, and some affective achievements expected of students in each of the arts in grade groupings of K–4, 5–8, and 9–12. Teachers with minimal background in arts disciplines will find many questions clarified. For example, the K–4 dance standards call for students to "accurately demonstrate non-locomotor/axial movements (such as bend, twist, stretch, and swing)," and "create a sequence with a beginning, middle and end" (Consortium of National Arts Education Associations [CNAEA], 1994, pp. 23–25). Once teachers understand concepts such as nonlocomotor and three-part sequence, they can better envision how movement can be meaningfully used in math, literature, social studies, and science. The arts standards also include a glossary of arts terms. View the standards at the MENC website (www.menc.org). Each arts chapter of this book includes a summary of general standards for that arts area.

## Unit Planning and Organizing

Integration goes by aliases such as interdisciplinary, multidisciplinary, and transdisciplinary but in any design, there is a unifying center (Drake & Burns, 2004; Jacobs, 1997). Generally, academic disciplines, along with arts areas, are examined for possible connections to a unit center, which can be done in creative ways (Freeman et al., 2003; Horowitz, 2004). For example, at A+ Schools, unit planning included cutting the state curriculum into sections, laying them out across the room, and then discussing how to cluster and fit pieces to specific themes. Drake and Burns (2004) recommend using different colored highlighters to code. For example, both arts and academic standards address communication and research skills that need to be taught in almost every unit. Code those red!

The following planning models use a unit structure. Most culminate in student performances and exhibits that occur daily and weekly, and serve to wrap up units of any length. For example, Normal Park Museum Magnet in Chattanooga, Tennessee, works with museum professionals to plan school exhibits that "open" every 9 weeks. Joyce Tatum, the museum liaison, points out that "as a museum school, we are a museum."

**Big Ideas and Important Questions.** One of the joys of 21st-century teaching is that we have edged beyond simply "covering material." Increasingly, educators co-plan based around important big ideas and processes that cause lessons to fly. They reject a focus on tallies of facts, dates, and isolated skills that cause lessons to flounder. How so? Every human being wants to know secrets and truths about people and the world—how to succeed and be happy. Research confirms that directing students' attention to learning for understanding, rather than grades, is superior (DeMoss & Morris, 2002; Guthrie, 2004).

Key themes, concepts, and topics from literature, social studies, and science are the building blocks to big ideas. For example, *Charlotte's Web* is more than the tale of a pig and a spider. It plumbs the theme of friendship at a deep level to reveal big ideas: "Good friends stick by you during tough times" and "True friends see good in you that you don't see." "Friends live in our hearts because they positively alter our existence." Literature and the other arts offer tools to grapple with big ideas, especially how struggle hones the spirit, how wisdom is achieved, and where beauty is found.

Teachers access innate inclinations to learn when units are planned around big ideas that are explored using an inquiry approach. Jacobs (1989, 1997) offers a practical way to organize units across grade level, namely, curriculum mapping. First, a big calendar is made of topics each teacher presently teaches, month by month and by grade level. Next comes vertical and horizontal analysis to examine where integration is possible. Units are then developed around important questions that lead students to do creative problem solving to find and construct big ideas (Cornett, 2010). Planning Page 3.7 summarizes a unit development process that begins with standards and topics and moves to targeting big ideas and important questions.

**Big Ideas versus Topics.**    In the past, teachers worked hard to develop units around topics such as plants, quilts, and dinosaurs. Such units can produce dramatic arts products like giant papier mâché dinosaur sculptures, elaborate plant dances, and class quilts. As AI has evolved, however, there has been increasing emphasis on depth rather than flash (Burnaford, 2007). Units that are a simple string of activities, loosely associated with a topic, have questionable meaningfulness. Edelsky, Altwerger, and Flores recommend using a line of inquiry—a chain of tasks that grow out of important questions connected to big ideas (e.g., "How might we help others in our lives have a better life and in doing so help ourselves?"). Units are not "loaded with activities" and resources are not used to "rev up lagging interests but to satisfy already heightened curiosity" (1991, pp. 64–66).

Big idea units and lessons take themes and topics further (Cornett, 2010). For example, in literature, patterns and cycles that repeat in the lives of people—dead and alive, real and fictional—reveal big ideas (e.g., "If you keep trying, you will succeed" and "Evil beings lose in the end"). Teachers first study the material and then generate full-sentence big idea statements using themes. Next comes writing starter questions. This does not mean students are only led to preidentified big ideas drawn from themes or that the teacher is the sole question creator. The larger goal is for students to discover their own "truths," to wrestle with problems and think deeply because they are motivated to find out why. The arts contribute to this process by actively engaging students and providing a problem-solving process to search for "big thoughts."

Drawing upon unique prior experiences and interpretations, even young children can synthesize personally relevant big ideas (Block, 2004; Block & Pressley, 2007). They do so when teachers ask the right questions: What did you learn? What was this mostly about? What did this tell you about people or the world? What will you remember forever from this book or song?

Meaningful AI lessons cause students to *create* understanding and develop skills connected, but not limited, to standards. For more examples of big ideas, consult the National Standards for Social Studies and the websites of both the Virginia Department of Education (www.pen.k12.va.us) and the Michigan Department of Education (www.michigan.gov/mde).

**Common Unit Centers.**    AI units usually have a center supported by cluster concepts and skills that have relevance across disciplines (e.g., shapes and forms in art and math, patterns and cycles in dance and science, change and constancy in social studies and literature). The center may also be a person such as

# Planning Page 3.7
## Unit Development Sources and Process

This process is recursive as teachers consult back and forth during the planning steps.

1. Consult academic and arts standards. Add other goals (e.g., develop character traits).
2. Choose from five unit centers or bodies:
   - *Concept, topic, theme, or problem.* Examples are courage, family, Africa, Civil War, often science/social studies-based.
   - *Core work:* A single book, poem, painting, or play
   - *Genre:* Study of a form (e.g., fairy tales, landscapes)
   - *Person:* Real or fictional person (e.g., life and works of an author, artist, scientist)
   - *Event or experience* (e.g., field trip, residency)
3. Generate big ideas: By the end of the unit, students should know/understand . . .
   - Write three to five big idea statements to form a complete thought. Example for topic unit on families: *Families can be structured in different ways with each member taking important roles to contribute to its success.*
   - List three to five important questions: *What family roles are necessary? Who determines what each person does? How and why?*
   - **NOTE:** Solicit from students additional big ideas and questions as the unit develops to increase ownership of learning.
4. List key concepts that support understanding/problem solving
   - *Examples:* family, roles, needs, power
5. List skills and processes: By the end of the unit students should be able to:
   - *Examples:* generate questions, visualize, give alternative perspectives, summarize/synthesize, prioritize/evaluate
6. Determine arts connections (co-planned with arts specialists)
   - What arts content, skills, and processes overlap or connect?
   - How will the art form(s) contribute to the understandings, concepts, and skills?
   - What arts materials and tools are needed?
   - How will the arts be a part of assessment?
7. Plan for multifactored assessment: What assessments? By whom? How? When? (connect to standards, goals, and objectives)
   - Portfolios, performances, and exhibits
   - Rubrics, checklists, self-assessment
8. Create a timeline
9. Write lesson plans: Two-pronged with objectives for academics and art(s). Where will arts be involved and how? Introduction/development/conclusion? (See plans in each arts chapter.)

an artist or author. A genre or form can be the center of study, as can a core work. For example, a core unit using the book *Sarah, Plain and Tall* (McLachlan, 1985) offers plentiful opportunities to examine big idea theme statements, such as "Families can be structured in a variety of ways" or "The role of mother in a family is central," using the arts to create understanding. Arts-specific ideas can be the center as well, and the arts are often integrated with other arts, as happens in real life. For example, Beethoven used the poem "Ode to Joy" to create his Ninth Symphony.

In sum, there are five common unit centers: (1) author, artist, or person; (2) genre or form; (3) problem or topic; (4) single book, poem, or song; and (5) event or trip. As the unit planning web depicted in Planning Page 3.8 shows, whatever unit center a teacher selects, the nine "legs" of the planning web—the content areas and disciplines—remain the same: science,

social studies, mathematics, reading and language arts, literature, music, dance, drama, and art.

**Inquiry Orientation.** In full-fledged *inquiry-based integration*, student interests and questions form the center of study and have the benefit of naturally engaging students (Short et al., 1996); but any well-planned AI unit can actively engage inquiry. Instead of a cute teddy bear unit, a more meaningful unit can be structured around a big idea, such as "Inventions and discoveries result from happy accidents," with students researching examples of this conclusion as well as the conditions under which this happens. Units on core thinking about problem-solving processes, such as CPS, are also common and result in interdisciplinary learning across science, social studies, math, and literacy. Processes and skills, however, need content—texts about which

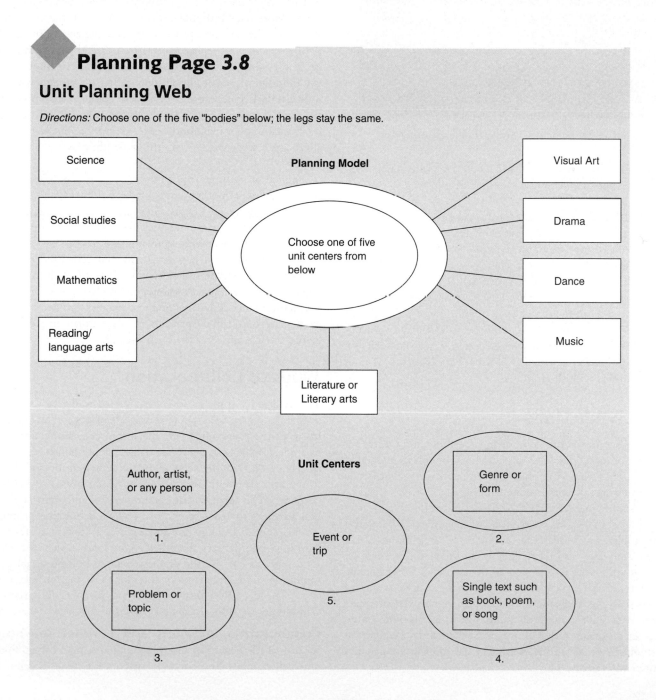

## Planning Page 3.8
### Unit Planning Web

*Directions:* Choose one of the five "bodies" below; the legs stay the same.

**Planning Model**

Science

Social studies

Mathematics

Reading/language arts

Choose one of five unit centers from below

Visual Art

Drama

Dance

Music

Literature or Literary arts

**Unit Centers**

Author, artist, or any person
1.

Event or trip
5.

Genre or form
2.

Problem or topic
3.

Single text such as book, poem, or song
4.

Curriculum quilt at Hilton Head School for the Creative Arts

to read, write, and make art. That's where literature, science, social studies, and arts content texts come into play.

**Unit Length.**    A unit may be part of a day or form an entire integrated day. The unit may last a few days or a month, or may be a schoolwide focal point for an entire year (e.g., "celebration" or "diversity"). Ashley River teachers post current unit titles on their doors. At Hilton Head Creative Arts, a "curriculum quilt" shows all the AI units for the whole school. Some units are project based, and most arts-integrated units involve long-term work over several weeks that culminates in a display or performance. Field-based units may connect to a single site, such as a museum, or several sites such as Normal Park Museum Magnet which partners with seven museums.

## Schoolwide Units

Discoveries, patterns, problem solving, creativity, and dreams are examples of topics that have united whole schools in integrated studies that last from a month to an entire year. One school studied a core work, a George Seurat painting, for 5 weeks as part of a social studies project (Short, 2001). A multicultural focus may also serve as a selection criterion for the big idea, "All cultures solve problems in similar, but unique ways." A schoolwide extended study may also focus directly on the arts. For example, the topic of communication could be expanded to the theme, "The arts are vital ways all human cultures try to understand and express thoughts and emotions." To plan these units, arts specialists meet with grade-level teams, just as in any unit. Often topics are recycled every 2 or 3 years. See "Birthday Buddies" in Appendix G for a yearlong integrated arts project that matches children with artists.

## Arts with Arts Integration

Aspects of arts disciplines can serve as the focal point of study with other arts areas pulled in. For example, a visual art unit on the "nature and effects of color" would be well served by children's literature that explores color in books such as Baylor's (1992) *Guess Who My Favorite Person Is,* the poetry in O'Neill's (1989) *Hailstones and Halibut Bones,* creative movement in response to colors, and music that stimulates color imagery.

## Field-Based Arts Integration

School trips to an art museum or to hear a concert are not unusual. What is unusual is meaningful integration of field events. In Dallas, Texas, 4,500 teachers integrate field trips and arts residencies into literacy, science, and social studies (Ford Foundation, 2005). More than 150 public schools work with museums, theatres, and other arts groups to boost academic achievement. The ArtsPartners project replaces "drive-by art" field trips with learning tied to the state curriculum. Standardized tests show bigger strides in literacy, especially writing. Scores of students with the most arts involvement rose 10 points—as compared to 3 points for the control group. Hogg Elementary students—mostly English learners from poor neighborhoods—are turning out writing like advantaged students. By fourth grade they write like sixth graders.

Single or multiple trips can serve as unit centers or be important adjuncts. In other words, field experiences can be the focus or a tool to reach a focus. Their meaningfulness depends on planning (before, during, and after the trip) that ties the experience to arts and academic standards and goals. Trips are then timed and aligned with appropriate unit content. Pretrip lessons are needed to prepare students, and follow-ups help make the most of the experience. Assessment is needed, too. Without the preparation and follow-up, field experiences can become little more than social time. Appendix H offers a planning tool with before, during, and after field trip strategies.

## Types of Collaboration

The goal is for students to learn targeted understandings and skills in academic areas *and* in the arts. Teachers and arts specialists work together to find genuine, not forced, connections. For example, teachers and drama specialists might brainstorm or create a Venn diagram between reading comprehension and drama to discover that both areas focus on taking points of view of characters. This suggests that comprehension and drama are natural partners to teach point of view. Collaborative planning would proceed to align the processes and content of the arts with important literary themes. If a core work such as the *Three Little Pigs* was chosen, the drama would go beyond literal pantomiming of pig behaviors or the plot to drama related to the story's big ideas. The following are ways teachers and arts specialists work together during planning and subsequent teaching.

**Collaborative Planning and Parallel Teaching.** Individual teachers or groups plan with arts specialists to find a unit center. They find overlapping concepts (e.g., "cycles" or "balance") or processes that are shared and create big idea statements. In this model, instruction happens separately; classroom teachers use arts ideas from the planning, and arts teachers address "nonarts" material—all focusing on the common connection. For example, the music teacher may develop first graders' phonological awareness by teaching the song "Down by the Bay," followed by having students substitute beginning sounds of words to make new rhyming lyrics. During the same unit, the classroom teacher would work with phonological awareness using songs and other resources suggested by the music teacher. The big idea would be for students to understand, "Hearing the small units of sound in words (phonemes) is important to creating and understanding the meaning of language."

This type of arts integration is only meaningful when teachers show students that arts experiences are connected to key unit ideas. Being explicit about connections is essential to transfer and creates a sense of cohesion that is a goal of integration.

**Co-planning and Co-teaching.** Classroom teachers and arts specialists plan together and then co-teach lessons. Specialists include arts teachers within the school and artists brought in from outside. One advantage of this model is classroom teachers directly observe artists using strategies so it becomes part of professional development.

**Grade-Level Planning and Arts Consultants.** Classroom teachers receive professional development in arts content and processes from arts consultants. They then plan arts-based units or lessons with grade-level teams. Teachers teach their own arts-based lessons but can consult with others undergoing the same effort. School-based arts specialists are available for consultation during planning and teaching (e.g., questions, materials, and strategies).

**Artist Residencies.** Artist residencies are used to give students arts experiences the faculty cannot provide. Residencies should be collaboratively planned so that work directly supports academic and arts curricular goals. Teachers need to be present during arts experiences to expand their arts teaching repertoire and extend student experiences after the residency (see Building Block X).

# Building Block IV: Aesthetic Learning Environment

The "place" of learning deeply affects learners. John Dewey pointed out that if classrooms are not "aesthetic," they are "anesthetic." Picture anesthetic classrooms with stark, dirty walls—students slumped in their seats with sullen glares. Teacher talk dominates, especially giving directions and orders. Silence and control hold sway over the messy, noisy work of problem solving. Such circumstances are mind numbing (Rabkin & Redmond, 2006).

Arts integration seeks to do the opposite—to energize learners by using the physical and psychological climate as major teaching tools. Aesthetically stimulating schools and classrooms provide settings that provoke curiosity, surprise, and a sense of mystery.

The design of a classroom and the mood, reflecting each teacher's personality, combine to create a positive context. The décor includes wall murals, clouds painted on ceiling tiles, numerous plants, bright carpeted areas, background music, couches, pillows, grouped desks, and displays of children's art (at their eye level). The room displays minimal teacher-made and store-bought decoration. Boxes of children's books, organized by units, genres, and levels, dot the room. Most importantly, intensity emanates from the joy of discovery. Classrooms buzz with activity as students move about. Teachers laugh, sing, and express delight as students take risks.

## Stendhal Effect

Computer artist David Addington explained his reaction to a dramatic presentation this way: "I sat in the theatre paralyzed after the play *Boom Boom Room*." His physical response to beauty is called the Stendhal effect, after 18th-century novelist Henri Beyle who used the pseudonym Stendhal. Stendhal observed that the arts have the power to stun—to raise the hair on the back of the neck, to elicit sighs and profound sobs. Like Addington, I have had a few Stendhal effect experiences. Once in Florence's Academie Museum, I was caught off guard by Michelangelo's towering *David*. I audibly gasped.

The arts are forms of beauty that intrigue, refresh, and excite passion. They give hope by reminding us that within everyone there is lovely potential. When students are surrounded by art, "their eyes drift across the paintings and sculptures"; behavior changes as they are calmed by music (Lockwood, 2005). They listen more actively and notice more details. Just being in the presence of art gives a sense of history and social context. The result is a deep love and appreciation of art and an understanding of how beauty can affect the senses (Lockwood, 2005). To explain more about how and why to immerse students in an aesthetic environment, the following Snapshot describes a special "museum magnet" in Chattanooga, Tennessee.

# School Snapshot
## Normal Park Museum Magnet

Normal Park is not a normal elementary school. First, there is a museum-quality gallery on the school's main floor with student exhibits changing quarterly. Then there are the sculptures and woodcarvings by noted local artists displayed throughout the campus, along with large colorful murals and three-dimensional sculptural arches. This "museum magnet" has been named one of the top magnet schools in the nation. The school was recognized for its efforts to increase diversity and academic achievement and involve parents and the community through its special form of arts integration.

Working with seven local museums, Normal Park's curriculum connects museum study visits with science and social studies standards-based units. Favorite past units have centered on the human body, healthy choices, the rain forest, and Egypt.

Museum professionals act as consultants to design high-quality exhibits that grow out of the curriculum. A strong indicator of the program's success is the jump in standardized test scores since becoming a museum magnet in 2001. The fifth grade boasts 100 percent proficiency—the highest level on the state test. What's more, teacher Jenifer Zeigler claims that 100 percent of parents say their children want to come to school. "Attendance problems just don't exist."

Grade-level teams plan the units, and arts specialists collaborate to teach the unit's big ideas, key concepts, and skills using arts strategies. Every 9 weeks the students work to visually show what they have learned in units. Principal Jill Levine says students are motivated to have real audiences. On opening night visitors are greeted with punch and cookies, and students from the P–5 school act as docents. They are trained to conduct informative tours of the student work.

Ms. Zeigler says, "Using the school environment as a learning tool is a plus because it allows students to take ownership." ✴

## Aesthetic or Anesthetic?

In school after school, a frequent comment among parents and teachers is that children look forward to the joys arts-based inquiry brings. Kids don't want to be absent because they don't want to miss a chance to docent in the school gallery or the Friday reader's theatre, for example. It is not only the opportunities the arts bring, but also the invitational climate that flows from teachers' personalities and philosophies. Artful teachers celebrate differences, embrace cultural and ethnic uniqueness, and immerse students in a relationship of respect. Respect builds trust. Trust creates the comfort necessary for risk taking and experimentation—essentials for CPS. When aesthetic values set the stage for learning, students are more engaged.

## Small Changes

Teachers can take a cue from Eisner (1997) who advises that the "subtle is significant." Spaces can be arranged with attention to order, balance, harmony, and color. Even small changes have large effects. Grouping desks implies that collaboration is expected. Open spaces indicate movement is part of the plan. Centers with buckets of brushes, baskets of arts-based books, and worktables give a sense that hands-on learning is valued. Classrooms look more like living rooms—comfortable sanctuaries and pleasant places filled with plants, fresh flowers, bright curtains, and framed student artwork. Imagine beautiful background music and pools of light from small lamps that illuminate reading areas. Image the wonderful smell of potpourri. These environmental changes are more stimulating to the senses—more aesthetic.

## Start with the "Known"

Disney's many parks are examples of arts-based places that assume everyone loves the arts and can participate, regardless of age or ability. Teachers in arts-based schools understand this concept. An aesthetic classroom climate is founded on the belief that all students have untapped arts capabilities. Even young children know how to modify their voices, facial expressions, and body posture to assume roles as sister, brother, friend, and student. They know how to "read" musical elements in their mothers' voices. These expressive elements say more than the words themselves. They know colors for sad, shapes that symbolize happiness, and lines that are scary. Every student arrives at school equipped to think through the arts.

## Displaying Art

Interesting art does the same thing for the classroom as it does for homes and offices. In particular, framed student art enriches the classroom and gives honor and respect to the artists, especially if they are taught to make "museum labels" for their work. Students are also challenged by artwork of peers, and such aesthetic displays can activate interest in further learning, such as visiting local museums and virtual visits to museum collections on the Internet.

## Background Music

At Hymera Elementary School (Hymera, Indiana), a CD player sits directly inside the front door. As at many other schools, background music plays in classrooms, halls, and the cafeteria to craft a positive atmosphere. Teachers are implementing the multiple intelligences theory that includes music as a unique way to think and feel. Current brain research also supports using music to stimulate brain activity. Since distinct regions uniquely respond, it is hypothesized that elevated brain activity generated by music can boost learning.

## Student Contributions

When students are invited to make the classroom a place that celebrates the arts, they feel a sense of ownership and become enthusiastic about the transformative power of aesthetic places. Get ready for fresh flowers, air freshener, and lots of music. In my own classroom one student brought in a CD of pianist George Winston, which started a run on instrumentals. Next came Wynton Marsalis (trumpet) and then classical guitar (Andrea Sergovia). The finale was a visit by a father who is a classical guitarist. The third graders were enthralled with guitar music so different from what they had heard before. "It's like an angel's harp," said one girl. "Except he has long fingernails," a boy pointed out. Student-contributed artifacts often become springboards to additional study that develops pride and expertise.

Children learn what they live (Nolte, 1959). As the well-known poem by this title explains, if we want children to be curious, joyful, sensitive, courageous, and hopeful, then we structure environments that encourage those characteristics. Teachers who operate from an aesthetic frame of reference make heightening the senses a priority.

# Building Block V: Literature as a Core Art Form

Literature is the most readily available arts material in our schools. It is also the most frequently integrated art form with an integration history decades long. Unfortunately, literature is not always treated as an art form. In recent decades, high-quality literature has become the primary material to deliver literacy instruction, sometimes at the expense of aesthetic understanding. In this book, literature is included as one of five major arts and is treated as a full-fledged art with the power to engage deep thinking and emotional understanding beyond that of any worksheet.

The next two chapters focus on how to integrate literature as an art form. Since the literary arts span every curricular topic and every literary genre, from poetry to science fiction, it is easy to integrate literature with almost any lesson in any other academic or other arts area. Literature is also a significant source for integrating the other arts of music, dance, drama, and visual art because of the availability of "arts-based" literature.

## Arts-Based Literature

A special body of literature is *about* the arts. This includes fiction and nonfiction books, narratives and informational books about artists, music, visual art, drama, and dance. Of course, all picture books are automatically arts based, regardless of their content, because the visual art is equal to the text in presenting the message.

Arts-based literature is a key material to integrate the arts into any curricular area. For example, biographies of artists and musicians enrich the study of every historical time period, because their work gives unique insight into values, ways of life, and issues of the time.

Every classroom needs a collection of arts-based books students can choose from during independent reading times and as references for work during units. Teachers often organize the books using crates for each arts area, or they code them with color dots. Arts-based read-alouds are now a fixture in many schools, including Ashley River Creative Arts.

Subsequent chapters offer arts-based literature recommendations. Appendix J provides a bibliography, and additional arts-based books are available at MyEducationLab.

# Building Block VI: Ten Best Teaching Practices

Meaningful AI ultimately rests on *how* lessons are taught. General "best teaching practices" are the means by which good instruction is delivered. Shelves of books have been written on the subject, but there is no single set of best practices. There are, however, "legitimate practices" within the bounds of research-based principles, professional wisdom, and shared values (Ferrero, 2005, p. 23). Arts-based lessons rely on these practices. In general, they take an inquiry approach that puts problem solving at the center (see Ready Reference 3.9). While teachers may co-teach lessons with artists or school arts specialists, most often they work solo on the classroom stage. This section highlights best practices that serve as pedagogical guideposts for AI.

## What You Teach Is WHO You Are

AI teachers readily assume multiple roles as directors, coaches, performers, and audience members in their own classrooms. To do so they need personally uplifting and provocative arts experiences to stay fresh. Teachers like Judy Trotter at Ashley River

---

**Ready Reference 3.9** Best Teaching Practices for Arts Integration

1. *What you teach is who you are.* Teachers show "arts confidence" and display enthusiasm for the arts.
2. *Inside-out motivation.* Intrinsic motivation is activated by focus on understanding, interests, choices, clear goals, and group work.
3. *Engagement and active learning.* Arts strategies are used to engage the head, heart, and hands in problem solving that transforms ideas.
4. *Creative problem solving.* The arts are given equity in the literacy curriculum with the CPS process center stage in teaching how to use the arts as communication tools to make meaning.
5. *Explicit teaching.* Mini-lessons directly teach the why-what-how-when-where of arts concepts and skills. Transfer is explicitly addressed by teachers and specialists.
6. *Apply-practice-rehearse.* Teachers coach students as they practice using specific feedback that produces higher quality work.
7. *Aesthetic orienting.* Teachers slow it down and teach students to use all their senses to understand, especially observing carefully to find evidence to ground interpretations.
8. *Process and product.* Arts processes are emphasized over products. Examples are used more often than models. Dictated art is avoided.
9. *Management: behavior, time, and materials.* Expectations and limits are clear. Flexible time blocks and predictable routines structure learning, but there is time for personal interest and to explore using authentic arts materials that unlock thinking.
10. *Independence and self-discipline.* Students become independent as they gain control of body, voice, and mind and learn persistence. They learn important work habits including self-help fix-ups.

Creative Arts say they cannot turn creative problem solving off. The unique architecture of local buildings and the beauty of backyard nature are mined for arts-based lesson ideas. Teachers end up writing down teaching ideas in the dark at films, plays, and concerts.

**Enthusiasm and Passion.** Enthusiasm is one of the most desirable teacher attributes. Students of every age rank it above subject matter knowledge. AI demands both. The etymology of *enthusiasm* explains that it originally meant "to be in god" (*theo*) or "to be in spirit." Teachers who are possessed of a creative spirit exhibit a passion that draws students. They share their own arts experiences and tell personal stories of creative efforts, including how obstacles are overcome through persistence. Such examples help dispel the myth that artistic and creative individuals are innately talented and do not have to work hard.

**Arts Confidence.** Children adopt the attitudes and dispositions of the people around them, especially those they care about. A teacher who says, "I can't sing" or "I'm not good at drawing" is writing the arts off. A commitment to weaving the arts throughout the curriculum brings many benefits and the obligation for teachers to approach the arts respectfully, with a can-do, will-do, want-to-do attitude. Sometimes that can be scary, but it is done in the belief that meaningful AI is worth it. So, no put-downs, please, especially arts self-deprecation.

## Inside-Out Motivation

In real life, people choose to engage in creative work because it is inherently motivating. A survey at a statewide conference found that the use of the motivational power of the arts was the number-one reason for AI (www.lander.edu/scaae). Points and sticker bribes are not needed. The arts are their own reward (Booth, 2003).

Certain conditions trigger intrinsic (internal) motivation (Guthrie, 2004). The arts align beautifully with these. Students *choose* to do arts problem solving when they resist similar thinking during reading and writing (DeMoss & Morris, 2002). The arts get students from "won't" to "want to." Six key factors behind internal motivation are (1) understanding, (2) interest, (3) choice, (4) meaning and purpose, (5) goals and expectations, and (6) the group effect.

**Understanding.** AI works because the arts add ways to understand/comprehend and express. Research confirms that students persist, produce higher quality work, and enjoy learning more when teachers focus on understanding, instead of grades or points (DeMoss & Morris, 2002; Guthrie, 2004). Teachers undermine intrinsic motivation when they orient toward extrinsic rewards such as higher test scores. Teachers need to stress "learning for understanding" in conferences with uptight students and nervous parents.

**Interest.** The arts draw attention and sustain interest. They make us ask, "How did she do that?" AI uses this power by teaching *to* interests and developing new interests. Because interest accounts for some 25 times the variance in comprehension, it seems reasonable to first find out what students are interested in

(assessment). Next comes connecting to interests and creating new interests. Appendix D includes an interest inventory.

**Choice.** The power of choice has been made clear in many experiments. For example, when children were given puzzles to assemble or collage materials *and* were given the choice about *how* to do so, they had more intrinsic motivation to repeat the task. Students in the choice group were significantly more intrinsically motivated even after 2 weeks, and they stuck with the task longer, as compared to no-choice students (Amabile, 1996). In addition, choice groups produced more creative products. Choice plays a "crucial role in intrinsic motivation" (p. 169). The arts offer a multitude of communication choices, but the quality of choices is key. The urge to investigate is not activated if selections are low level (e.g., choosing which planet to write a report) (Starko, 1995).

**Meaning and Purpose.** Even young children have a strong desire to know *why*. Having a purpose creates motivation. A classic study conducted by Langer (1989, 1997) drives this point home. Confederates in the study approached people at a copy machine and asked to "cut in." People let cutters in 60 percent of the time; but when confederates added a reason, such as "I'm in a hurry," percentages increased to 95 percent. People were willing to step aside even when confederates gave a nonsensical reason, such as "because I need to make copies." We respond to reasons because we respect purposes and understand the need to reach goals.

Purposes give relevance and meaning to learning, especially if they connect to life. For example, students need to know why they are using strategies such as SCAMPER (Ready Reference 2.6) in math. Teachers should take time to explain why and make real-life connections, and empower students even more by asking them to generate purposes.

**Goals and Expectations.** Goals are destinations for which there are multiple paths. The arts expand the number of paths to academic goals, but students need to know the expectations up front if they are to be motivated. It makes sense to discuss what will be assessed and how (e.g., rubric criteria). Good teachers make goals clear and involve students in personal goal setting.

**The Group Effect.** Constructivism and social interaction theory propose that the social effect of group work is significant. Successful groups believe they need each other, think each person can make a contribution, and share leadership during creative problem solving. Successful groups reflect on what worked, or is working, and how they can work together better (Daniels & Bizar, 2005). Group social power yields a greater quantity and quality of ideas with students gaining perspectives not possible in solo work.

The arts have a long tradition of group work, for example, choirs, dance ensembles, and drama troupes. In AI, problem solving is almost always done in groups. Partners plan pantomimes, small groups create murals, and students switch off as audience members, performers, and exhibitors. Teachers help by giving time limits, focus, cues, frames, and by teaching CPS.

Groups who take risks together are more confident about sharing efforts. Audiences raise the stakes. The motivational power of the audience is well established. When students think others will hear their songs and watch their dances, they become more concerned about quality, so they prepare and perform with greater intensity. AI taps into this effect, making performances and exhibits key features. This does not mean arts problem solving should be done exclusively for audiences. It does mean students benefit from performing, even for classmates. Students also benefit from learning how to be a part of an audience, especially how to be active listeners and show appreciation.

## Engagement and Active Learning

Eisner (2002a) reminds us that parents send their children to schools to have their "minds made" (p. 9). Most everyone can recall a change of mind or change of heart experience in response to an arts event, such as Susan Boyle's 2009 mind-altering "I Dreamed a Dream" singing performance. The arts engage us intellectually, emotionally, and physically, which is a major reason why educators are drawn to arts-based education. Learning never gets off the starting line without engagement. It's a simple idea that has been difficult to implement, until now.

**Arts-Added Education.** Booth (2003) explains "bringing artistic experiences into the learning equation does something exciting to learning" (p. 15). The "something" he refers to is a "kind of alertness" or "awakeness" that changes any learning connected to the arts. He could have used the word *engagement*.

Intrator (2004–2005) calls engagement the "grail of teaching." His long-term pupil observations revealed students were most vibrant when creating—especially when they were encouraged to generate original ideas (p. 4). Didactic teaching that relies on "telling" and "assigning" lacks the potential to engage students in meaning-making. Worksheets rarely captivate, and answering end-of-chapter questions is perceived as busywork (De Moss & Morris, 2002). AI rejects such practices and substitutes genuine cognitive, emotional, and physical engagement that produces diverse thoughtful arts products ranging from pantomimes to collages.

Engagement is more than a buzzword in education. It means *concentrated focus for the purpose of understanding*. Getting attention is not enough. Even concentrated focus, devoid of understanding, is not engagement. It may be entertainment, but not engagement. AI seeks deep engagement, which ignites intrinsic motivation for difficult tasks such as long-term projects that produce exhibits and performances.

Students persist when there are bumps in the road because the arts charge learning with a kind of energy and intensity that can last a lifetime. For example, a reporter sent to interview Pablo Casals arrived to find the 95-year-old great cellist practicing. Asked why he possibly would need to practice, Casals replied, "I think I'm getting better" (Marron, 2003, p. 15). That's engagement.

**Head-Heart-Hands.** The arts are teaching tools without equal in potential to cause mental, physical, emotional, and spiritual response. AI unites head, heart, and hands to discern and create meaning. An arts-based science plants unit can involve serious learning about photosynthesis using singing and dancing. Students can show understanding by performing monologues in the role of a bean sprout and moving to show the concept of the "rootedness" of plants. This kind of mental and physical problem solving transforms how kids think. The experiences are memorable because they integrate mind, body, and emotions. Imagine fourth graders showing what they know about converting sunshine and water into energy through pantomime and dance. Imagine students eager to come to school and begging to stay in from recess to prepare for performances. Imagine a teacher who knows how to assess standards using rubric criteria to observe these kinds of artistic student presentations. Imagine this and you've glimpsed engaged learning through AI.

**Engage, Then Inform.** In artful lessons teachers use the arts to get attention and spark interest before they delve into information. Arts strategies stress purposeful activity that causes students to want to information, not resist it. Arts strategies often are used in lesson introductions to create intellectual unrest, which sets CPS in motion. Teachers pose problems, provoke curiosity, and ask open questions related to an artwork, even a cartoon connected to the upcoming lesson. Surprise, novelty, riddles, and physical warm-ups are used to challenge students to use logic and leaps of imagination to "get it." See odd-numbered seed strategy chapters that follow for energizers and warm-ups.

Humor is also a common engagement tool and dovetails with the arts because humor is naturally motivating and has problems at its core. To "get it," you have to make novel connections. Of course producing and understanding humor is an art itself. Students readily engage in use of humorous "texts." Creating cartoons and riddles is all about CPS and these art forms can be used to synthesize ideas from any subject (Cornett, 2001). For example, students can create cartoon strips to show understanding of sentence types (declarative, exclamatory, or interrogative) using speech bubbles.

Generic engagement strategies, such as think-pair-share (TPS), can also be used alongside arts strategies. For example, after asking a question, give think time. After a minute or so, partner for sharing. Or use the every pupil response (EPR) strategy; for example, ask for "thumbs up" to show students have a response. If the response is important, then wait for most students to signal.

**Transformation.** Passive listening to a lecture or watching a video is not a likely road to understanding. AI professes that if you don't think, feel, and act, you don't learn. The arts are not about sponging up. Subject matter is transformed as topics or questions are problem solved and "re-presented" through visual art, drama, music, dance, and poetry. It is each student's job to use head, heart, and hands to create meaning using the arts as transformation tools.

## Creative Problem Solving

Arts-based lessons naturally engage all or part of CPS (Ready Reference 2.6). This problem-solving process is central to life. It is how we construct meaning from texts and how we create new texts ranging from PowerPoints to paintings. It is used any time we undertake inquiry, realizing we cannot predict all possible answers. Even adults are usually not aware they are using CPS and all of us can learn to use it more effectively. Sadly the potential for creative thinking can be stultified by years in schooling marked by learner passivity, and focus on rote responses and "right" answers.

The goal is teach all students to use CPS intentionally and skillfully, with increasing independence and sophistication. CPS teaching throughout curricular areas can begin in the primary grades when children are both capable and eager to do creative thinking (Cornett, 2010). CPS processes must be taught daily within science, social studies, math, and literacy if students are to become adept at creating meaning using the full range of 21st-century texts: visual arts texts, digital, multimedia, and Internet hypertext. Ideas for teaching CPS components follow in this and every chapter. To begin, post the full CPS process as a visual reference.

**Setting the Stage.**   The classroom is an ideal haven for students to experiment and make mistakes. CPS does not occur if the classroom environment is threatening. Risk taking should be celebrated, even when the results don't work: "I'm glad you tried to write a poem without rhyme. You say you don't like the poem. Is there a part you do like? How could you use that part?" These questions acknowledge the courage it takes to experiment. Creative risk taking can also be studied through stories about real people who endured ridicule. For example, the avant-garde work of both Monet and Stravinsky was publically disdained. The daily newspaper is a good source of other examples. Consider creating an add-on bulletin board to honor risk takers.

**Connections.**   The brain works by making and accessing connections to create meaning. CPS is all about connecting, especially through metaphor and analogy. When we ask, "What is this like?" we ask students to call up known images to understand new ideas. Artful teaching stretches students to make unusual comparisons and not just use "hard as rock" clichés.

Teachers can teach problem solving by asking for connection at simple levels: "What letters do you know in the word?" or "What chunks?" helps students figure out unknown words. Arts-based lessons include questions such as "What do you know about shapes? Colors? Jazz? Charlie Chaplin?" Students are asked to brainstorm what they know about key concepts (e.g., "balance") in visual art, dance, math, and writing. The KWL strategy is beneficial: Students list what they *know*, what they *want* to know, and after the lesson is finished, what they *learned* (Ogle, 1989).

**Visual Imaging.**   It is nearly impossible to think about the past or plan for the future without mental images. This is our internal art. Best teaching practice is informed by this fact. Explicit teaching about why and how to picture in your head or use *imagination* (root is *image*) is basic to CPS. Teaching students how to apply this one thinking strategy to texts can double comprehension (Gambrell & Koskinen, 2002). Here's how: Ask students to visualize a concept such as *dog*. Prompt with the arts elements: Add color, shape, and texture. Next, interview students about what they see. What *dog* means will be unique to each student because everyone visualizes using different background. Demonstrate your own visualizing by thinking aloud for students. Finally, cue students to make mental images when they read or listen.

**Empathy.**   The word *empathy* is commonly used to mean "taking alternative points of view." Empathy was originally coined to label a distinct response to an arts experience. Empathy is more cognitive than sympathy and more emotional than critical distance.

Arts-based lessons provide a rich context for developing this high-level thinking in which we stand in the shoes of others, see as they must, feel as they might. Empathy, alone, solves many problems. Classroom teachers develop empathic thinking by giving students experiences with diverse art forms and asking questions such as "How did the artist who made this think and feel? What would you say/do if you were _____?" Drama strategies focus on assuming roles so they are powerful ways to develop empathy.

**Inquiry and Questioning.**   CPS encourages children to be "explorers and questioners, rather than passive acceptors" (Starko, 1995, p. 114). Good teachers "propose problems to think about that are currently being grappled with . . . in the world beyond the classroom" (Hetland, Winner, Veenema, & Sheridan, 2007, p. 7). Real problems rarely have one right solution. Indeed students are made to "feel dumb" when teachers concentrate on "right answer" questions and this practice can damage the relationship between teachers and students (Booth, 2003, p. 23).

Inquiry approaches such as AI engage students in investigations that involve fat questions: "What makes you think that? How do you know that? What do you see? What have you discovered? Why?" These questions provoke more thinking than closed ones that call for yes or no answers. Open questions also call for personal meaning-making and signal an invitation to collaborate in inquiry. Closed questions have a single right answer—no meaning-making, just recall—a door slammed in your face if you're wrong.

A dull, closed question such as "Who was the first president of the United States?" can be upgraded to "What do you know about the first president?" More CPS is engaged with "Show me what you know about the first president," which can produce pantomimes of tree chopping, horse riding, posturing, and even lying in a funeral pose. Fat questions stimulate integrated thinking because they ask for ideas to be retrieved, synthesized, and transformed. A good habit is to use questions that begin with *what if, why* or *how*. Avoid yes-no queries that start with *who, could, would, should,* or *when*. Couple questions with a wait time of at least 5 seconds to get more responses of better quality.

Teachers further activate inquiry when they teach students to pose questions. "What questions do you have about this song?" invites students to inquire. Such routines as "Question of the Day" and "Answer of the Day" encourage additional inquiry. For example, one student wanted to know how much trash the school threw away. Students interviewed custodians and cafeteria workers and surveyed kids about how much they left on their plates. Students provided a PowerPoint presentation with colorful graphs as they assumed roles as reporters (drama) to present findings.

## Explicit Teaching

Howard Gardner, architect of multiple intelligences, believes students need more than "opportunities" to paint, to pot, or to dance. They "crave arts knowledge and skills that expand their understanding and expression capabilities" (1989, p. 141). Without instruction, student work can become "either derivative from the mass media, or show a vestige of a good idea but lack the technical means to express it properly" (p. 141). Students with a creative inclination may not have the basic skills to take the idea further. Opportunity without tools is not opportunity at all. Explicit teaching provides clear instruction, modeling of the thinking and working needed for genuine opportunity to learn.

**I Do, We Do, You Do, Re-Do.** Explicit teaching makes visible our invisible thought processes such as imagination. Teachers talk aloud to demonstrate so students clearly grasp concepts and thinking skills embodied in CPS.

Explicit teaching lets students in on the purposes and lesson agenda at the outset. Short 5- to 10-minute mini-lessons are used to teach why (purposes), what (actual content or skills, including labels), and how (demonstration, with examples). Special educator professor Chuck Novak teaches the mnemonic I DO (teacher sets purpose, shows, and explains), WE DO (scaffolded practice with coaching), and YOU DO (independent practice, rehearsal, reflection) to explain explicit teaching. RE-DO enables students to revise based on feedback.

Clear teaching about arts concepts and skills is necessary for meaningful AI. It is the responsibility of both classroom teachers and arts specialists. For example, if students are expected to use movement to understand and express themes of *The Three Bears,* they need explicit instruction in dance elements (known by the acronym "BEST": body, energy, space and time). Teachers begin with questions about how we communicate through our bodies—to say hello and goodbye. Next, students are coached to explore body, energy, space, and time. Teachers demonstrate examples to clarify ways to show thoughts and feelings through movement. Emotions can be danced, such as showing *surprise* using just fingers or toes. Students can be stretched to show *surprise* with different body shapes and moves. During group practice, teachers describe BEST elements students use appropriately. Questions such as "What's another body part you could use?" can be used to coach students, along with suggestions to try different levels and speeds to discover the effects. Finally, students can be grouped to select key movements to capture key concepts from the story's beginning, middle, and end (BME) to create a dance. Dance criteria, such as using variety and ability to sustain focus, are discussed to help students plan with quality in mind.

**Transfer.** How do teachers cause thinking learned in one context, such as the arts, to transfer to other academic contexts? At the onset, there should be a reciprocal and respectful relationship between the arts and other academic areas in which transfer is not seen as a "one-way" street. Instead "one subject challenges the other" (Rooney, 2004, p. 11). Explicit teaching for transfer (e.g., telling and showing how dance composition ideas can be used in writing) is a commonsense idea. Classroom teachers and arts specialists must be direct about connections between learning in the arts and how that learning can be used in other curricular contexts and in life. At the Conservatory Lab Charter School in Boston, this process boils down to five shared processes that crosscut disciplines (Scripp, 2003). They are listen/describe, question/investigate, create/transform, perform/demonstrate, and reflect/connect/self-assess (Davidson, Claar, & Stampf, 2003). The processes, similar to CPS, are taught and applied in every subject. Clearly these are ways to think and learn that have high transfer potential because they are integral to any deep learning.

**Two-Way Transfer.** A bus transfer allows a rider to use one ticket to get to more than one place. It is a great idea because you get more for your money. Transfer of learning is similar. Students can get to multiple destinations from integrated lessons. Students make substantial gains in "basics," but also become better overall thinkers using arts-based academic lessons that engage inquiry-based problem solving (Rabkin & Redmond, 2004, p. 8). For example, the concept *proportion* is just as important in music and visual art as it is in math, but standards are not cross-referenced using important concepts and skills shared by disciplines. AI teachers seek out these connections and plan instruction that targets shared concepts, big ideas, and processes, thus maximizing the level of instruction. If a subject such as math is taught well, then it seems logical that music be integrated and vice versa. Learning about the role of counting and fractions in each area should amplify learning in both areas. Fractions can be taught in a math-only manner, but learning has more depth and breadth if students use the multiple lenses of the arts.

When teachers are explicit about why and how CPS is used across curricular areas, transfer of CPS use is more probable. Teachers point out how strategies, such as SCAMPER, can be used to extend understanding in math, science, social studies, reading, and writing. They use think-aloud to demonstrate how to substitute, combine, adapt, minimize, or maximize ideas in prewriting as well as to solve science problems by experimenting. A CPS chart is an important visual reference for both teachers and students moving into making inquiry central to learning. It allows students to see how problem solving is about the flexible use of thinking skills to make meaning across disciplines (Ready Reference 2.6).

It is antiquated to think about teaching and learning using no-way or one-way transfer models. Integration is about connections and advocates that any concept or discipline can be understood from the perspective of another, which is how real-life problem solving occurs. Ultimately, math is not about scores on math tests, any more than visual art instruction is about creating an exhibit. American schooling should prepare students for productive lives in a democratic country faced with a constellation of 21st-century challenges. Teachers need to know how to align schooling with life. This book focuses on that kind of know-how.

## Apply–Practice–Rehearse

A serious problem in schooling is inappropriate and inadequate amounts and kinds of practices. Without practice, it is almost impossible to achieve competence. Competence puts us in control of our lives by giving us a range of ways to solve problems, that is, savoir faire. Rehearsal or repeated practice of introduced content and skills boosts student confidence about learning so they feel more empowered to succeed. AI goes beyond low-level fact and skill practices to engage students in purposeful application of new knowledge and skills. Application solidifies learning.

**Coaching.** Coaching has long been used in the arts to scaffold work in dance, drama, music, among others. Coaching supports learners during practice and challenges them to solve their own problems. Coaching is about cuing and suggesting, not giving answers. Thought-provoking and leading ("what if") questions are key: "What if Cinderella had a swollen bunion when the prince put on her shoe. How would she feel and how can you show that with your face, body, and voice?" Students enjoy exploring the "what ifs" while they apply the kind of thinking used in our world that is rife with such strategies. Coaching is used as students practice alone or in groups. During drama, teachers coach students to stay focused, to stay in character by saying, "Make me believe" or "Make it real." Signals remind students to concentrate on using the face, body shape, and movements to show understanding.

**Descriptive Feedback.**    Of particular importance is coaching with descriptive feedback, which goes beyond praise. "Good! Great! Awesome!" are vague, overused, value-laden compliments whose genuineness can be doubted. We tend to believe specifics. Specific truthful comments give guidance and cause students to feel the giver thought them important enough to notice details. Descriptive feedback takes time, thought, and attention, but it provides a mirror for students to examine reflections of their behavior. Consider the difference between "Super job!" and "Rudy, you used a variety of facial expressions. That showed me you understood the range of emotions George Washington must have felt when asked to be president."

Imagine how you'd feel if your teacher said you'd get a certificate on Friday—if you were *good* all week. I'd want to know exactly what was meant by "good" so I could decide whether I wanted to "be good" and whether I wanted to be good just to "be good" or be corrupted by a focus on what I'd get for being good. The point is that it is important to be specific. When we describe what we see and hear, we liberate and empower students to think, which can set them on a path to creating higher quality work. Basic arts elements, outlined in the subsequent arts chapters, can be used to describe what students make, do, and say. In addition, using the child's name and emphasizing positive progress connects feedback to goals. For example, "Colette, I see that you used unusual colors in your portrait of George Washington which shows you are experimenting more with showing emotions in new ways, which was one of your goals."

## Aesthetic Orienting

The aesthetic dimension of learning is difficult to grasp, but it is too big to leave out. Aesthetic orientation is something like the engine of learning or a chemical that creates the fizz (Weissman, 2004). Either metaphor acknowledges that aesthetic understanding is a force.

The arts have tremendous potential to engage emotions, develop sensitivity, and promote empathy, thereby increasing comprehension. Teachers activate emotional intelligence and give it direction by orienting students toward aesthetic features of instructional materials and experiences. Students are given aesthetic orientation when we ask for sensory and emotional responses before cognitive ones. For example, instead of first using picture book art to predict problems and events, students can be oriented to look closely at the cover to describe emotions it provokes. Asking "What did the artist do that causes these feelings?" goes further to scaffold thinking about using evidence for conclusions.

**Observe, Interpret, and Reflect.**    Integrating the arts requires habits of the heart and mind that help remove "get it covered quickly" guilt. At the heart of AI is CPS, which depends on careful observation, basic to data gathering. This takes time, as does coming to a sense of what makes quality work in the final stages of CPS.

The observe-interpret-reflect sequence is about taking time to slow students down; they learn to listen closely, look for telling details, and notice patterns. Teachers ask students to pause and examine a spider web glistening with dew outside the window and to listen to the principal whistle as she walks down the hall. Taking time to gather such data gives specifics on which to base interpretation and draw aesthetic conclusions.

Teaching students to create meaning using the prism of the arts has the potential to increase aesthetic understanding—comprehension in the fullest sense. But the artist in us will not be hurried. It takes time for students to explore body shapes to deepen understandings, such as showing understanding of verbs such as *hunker down* or *slink*. It takes time to coach students to become aware of their own movements as they interpret word meanings, but such descriptive feedback and piggybacking on students' ideas cause students to reflect on performances and stretch their thinking about possible interpretations. Teachers must relax, step back, watch, and listen. Eventually students learn to control instant judgments that occur when they react superficially with "unexamined prejudices" (Booth, 2003, p. 22).

**Delight in Diversity.**    Students cannot assume an aesthetic orientation to learning unless their teachers show that they believe each person works and learns differently. These teachers show students how to transform ideas and demonstrate understanding in new ways that feature the arts. For example, meanings of words can be shown through body actions, art materials, sounds, and musical instruments. Artful teachers show delight when students surprise with performances of meaning no one else imagined. They affirm diverse ideas by saying, "I never thought of that," and "What an unusual idea!" They speak the truth: "Marla has an idea no one else has mentioned" and "Joe's idea is different from everyone else's." Questions can affirm, too. "What are some other answers? What's another way we could do this?" convey strong messages. Of course, it isn't just what is said, but how it is said; it is helpful to periodically tape lessons to evaluate how your voice sounds (i.e., musical elements used to express thoughts and feelings).

**Integrated versus Isolated.**    The National Assessment of Educational Progress (NAEP, 2008) reports that students do well with literal comprehension that relies on low-level memory. Unfortunately, in high school students continue to have difficulty with implicit messages (i.e., actually making sense), rather than just finding stated ideas. Isolated teaching of comprehension strategies and bits of reading is thought to be a culprit (Pressley, 2002; Whitehurst, 2008). The conclusion is that students lack the content and/or thinking to get beyond the obvious, and getting beyond the obvious is a requirement in today's world.

Schools that establish "learning dichotomies, isolating content, employing traditional pedagogies of drill and repetition" make learning hard by draining relevance and interest from the curriculum (Grumet, 2004, p. 54). Meaningful blending of core disciplines with the arts allows students to discover links between concepts and processes nested in different subject areas, especially when they are coached to find them (p. 63).

The ways artists think are the ways students need to think: how to hone in on problems, ask questions, pursue interests, gather evidence, examine options, make interpretations and choices, form alternative solutions, express ideas in different ways, and judge worthiness. During arts work, these mental operations are set within contexts where working well with others is a necessity, taking responsibility is assumed, and persisting to overcome obstacles is common. These processes are not special provinces of the arts but integral to working in the arts. AI, at its most meaningful, involves students in using artistic processes in an integrated manner for the purpose of increased learning in nonarts areas.

AI balances wholes and parts by teaching students to zoom in on details and zoom out to see the big picture. Eisner (1997) explains the balancing issue using map reading. A map has to be seen as a whole design, not a collection of discrete pieces. The reader must understand that each nation is situated within a continent. Where a continent is situated on the globe is as important in understanding geographical space as where a city is within a nation. This descends to the house level. Pieces are meaningless without such context. The brainstorming process can also be used to illustrate this same point. It is ineffective to practice a type of thinking apart from actual problems. Brainstorming is not a gimmick; it is a tool to be used purposefully. Thinking taught in isolation simply does not stick (Pressley, 2002).

Attention to the whole, while noticing component parts, is key to creative thinking and motivation. When teachers fragment learning into piecemeal skill or concept lessons, students can be left feeling dissatisfied. For example, students with reading difficulties are often frustrated with repeated zooming in on letters and sounds. They are unable to see the parts as relevant. When we teach students to zoom out and see relationships among words and sentences, they discover interesting ideas, making aesthetic understanding possible and providing a highly motivating type of learning (Guthrie, 2004).

## Process and Product

The arts are fundamentally processes used to solve communication problems (Larson, 1997). Both teachers and students grasp this big idea over time as they use CPS processes, questions, and activities that are arts based. When teachers ask questions such as "How can you use your body to communicate confusion? What lines and shapes communicate confusion? How can confusion be expressed using music?" they are emphasizing that the arts are about understanding and expressing meaning. When students and parents see how modern communication is embedded with music, visual art, dance, and drama, they give AI increased respect. Ready Reference 3.4 lists arts topics to discuss and write about.

It follows that teachers need to emphasize artistic thinking and working over producing "perfect" end products. Dance, drama, and music performances and visual art exhibits are important features of AI, but these products are mainly learning vehicles. Interestingly, a focus on quality thinking (e.g., CPS) does

produce better products, ones that reflect a range of diverse meanings students can make.

A process emphasis is demonstrated when student artwork is exhibited in school galleries that change monthly, while discussing and making art happens *every day*. Visual art making becomes integral to prewriting as well, not only postwriting or as a postreading response. Sketching is used as an alternative to journaling. Creative movement and dance, singing, and close listening to music become daily routines. In AI, art making is not about making something cute to decorate the walls or give to mom, nor is the goal perfect dance technique or expertly executed lines in yearly plays. The arts are used to make sense and express meaning, not to entertain and impress. Children learn to please the inner audience as they work for deep understanding. The bottom line is, the thinking that goes into the work is what is most important. Quality work reflects quality thinking.

**Dictated Art.** Tracing patterns is not art. Neither is work done in coloring books or with black outlines. Art educator Peggy Jenkins (1986) calls this work "dictated art." Making look-alike products such as hand turkeys does not engage genuine art problem solving. Thinking is stalled at following directions. Copying offers little emotional outlet and emphasis on these kinds of literal thinking can diminish students' beliefs about their own creativity. Students get the wrong idea that there is a "right" way. They can become confused and rigid as they struggle to "stay in the lines" and become reluctant to use independent thinking. Stereotypes emerge about colors of people and shapes of animal. Images of suns, birds, and emotions are reduced to iconic symbols, which indicate the philosophy of AI is shallow and the arts knowledge base is inadequate.

**Examples versus Models.** Mimetic work deprives students of the opportunity to engage thinking to create meaning. This happens when well-meaning teachers direct students to memorize and imitate. If teachers show one piece of artwork, and display it, students will proceed to copy it. Education is not about copy work. Copying is imitation and may be a compliment to the originator, but the children should be the originators.

Instead of presenting a "model," use examples. As Albert Schweitzer explained, examples are not the important thing—they are everything to understanding. Instead of demonstrating dance steps to imitate or showing a collage and giving step-by-step directions, teachers should show several examples that present options for creative problem solving. Over time, specific arts concepts and skills can be taught to expand children's toolkit in each arts area. Students can be coached to create products using processes such as data gathering to glean ideas from a variety of sources. In this way the creative impulse to make meaning is scaffolded, not squashed.

## Management: Behavior, Time, and Materials

Meaningful AI requires a combination of clear expectations, flexible time blocks, and predictable routines. Students need to learn to work responsibly and skillfully with arts techniques, tools, and materials and with each other. They need to be taught how to concentrate and focus, how to control their bodies, minds, and voices.

**Structure and Limits.** In the world outside of school, work is defined by expectations, and so it is with AI. Arts-based learning is not loosey-goosey, do-your-own-thing work. Teachers and students learn to work within the boundaries of time and materials and limits can increase creative thinking. For example, it has been during some of the most difficult economic times that the most innovative ideas and products have emerged. Creativity thrives when open-ended problem solving is needed to survive. To understand this point, try this short experiment: First, take 1 minute and be creative. At the end of 60 seconds note how you thought about this open-ended directive. Now try this. Take 1 minute to think of ways to use a pencil to make an annoying fan stop rattling. Compare how increased limits focused your problem solving.

CPS is further ratcheted up by discussing what constitutes quality work and providing opportunities to work on authentic problems. This means students need criteria for "creative work" up front so they focus on qualitative possibilities. For example, a "good" dance needs a beginning, middle, and end and use of various levels in order to be interesting and effectively communicate. Such factors should be discussed and presented in a rubric or checklist to direct student work. Students also need to be taught that use of arts materials is contingent upon following rules. Flexible boundaries imply self-discipline, and respect is expected. Higher quality work results, and students take more pride in their efforts.

**Personal Projects.** It is easy to set aside time, at least once a week, for interest work, which drives motivation to learn. Short- and long-term projects provide important opportunities for students to extend their independence by conducting in-depth investigations. Students should be encouraged to develop collections (e.g., rocks, cards, pictures, words) that can spur independent study and be arts-making resources (e.g., poems about rocks). Personal investigations cause students to take pride in growing their expertise and individuality.

**Time to Explore.** Creative ideas do not pop out of nothingness. You have to mess around to be creative, and that makes a mess. Students need time to explore whenever new skills, techniques, tools, and materials are introduced. After a brief introduction about ground rules and simple techniques, students should be encouraged to play with art media, observe the work of others, brainstorm, read, or listen to music to release possible ideas. Exploration time is not "doing nothing." Exploring and experimenting are key artistic start-up strategies that include seeing where the materials can take you. Exploration builds motivation so it provides a foundation on which teachers add more specific directions and discussions about expectations. It is recommended that teachers show students how to set up a "Great Ideas" folder to save sketches, notes, pictures, and words to use as sources for experimenting.

**Real-World Stuff.** We were looking for a new house recently. We found one on the Internet. My brother-in-law, Bob, emailed us 60 pictures and a four-page property report. It looked great, but it was not enough. Being there was necessary. Twelve hundred miles later, we were there and we knew in 5 minutes the house was not for us. So it is with the arts. Live concerts, theatre performances, real art (not reproductions), and authentic materials and tools are not equal when it comes to understanding.

Although teaching relies on simulations, AI seeks to expand the use of primary sources. Reliance on workbooks and thick texts can create a disconnect for students who want to play significant roles inside and outside of school. Primary source materials such as diaries, autobiographies, and actual paintings make learning more interesting because they are real-life objects. Problem-solving processes used by real artists and researchers (e.g., data gathering through surveys) trump reading about the findings of others when it comes to understanding. Hands-on and face time give life to learning.

**Unlocking.** Students can never have enough arts. Each new tool, technique, and medium contributes to expression and may be the spark for learning. For example, at a local art museum exhibit I met a man who began painting at the age of 70. He had cerebral palsy, was wheelchair bound, and for most of his life was not able to express himself because he could not talk. One day, an art therapist attached a paintbrush to a headband. Ralph Bell proceeded to paint every day for the rest of his life—more than 1,000 paintings. These kinds of stories help students realize that much is locked inside each of us waiting to be released through the arts. The point about how the arts unlock potential to communicate is brought home by thinking about the importance of the guitar in the life of Elvis Pressley or moonwalk dancing for Michael Jackson.

## Independence and Self-Discipline

It is time consuming, frustrating, even painful to watch students struggle to do what we could do for them. It is easier to just draw a horse for the child who cannot draw one. The question is, What is the goal of instruction? If the goal is to end up with a great horse portrait, perhaps the teacher should do it. AI is not usually about ending up with great representations of horses or anything else. It is about students experiencing the pride that comes when they persist and do the work themselves. If work is done for students, they may be grateful, but they cannot be proud. Pride derives from effort. That's the "tri" in *triumph*.

**Controls.** A frequent mantra in AI schools is "control your mind, body, and voice." This does not mean shut up, sit still, and follow directions. Students need to be taught how to manage their own thinking, imagination, body parts, and voices so they can become adept at using diverse options to communicate their thoughts and feelings.

**Persistence.** Well-intentioned teachers and parents may shield children from frustration, which can create a "learned helplessness" syndrome that can seriously handicap progress. Personal struggle is essential for independence to be achieved (Erikson, 1950). That does not mean students should not be supported. Coaching and other forms of scaffolding are keys to increased self-efficacy.

In particular, students need examples of how others have struggled with tasks and used diverse thinking and media to solve problems. We need to reject the false notion that great ideas emerge without the work of data gathering, experimentation, and practice. A balloon must be filled before it pops. So it is with people and CPS. Creative thinking rests on pumping in knowledge and skills, and then great ideas seem to literally pop out. Few artists hit the jackpot on the first or second try, so most can serve as biographical examples of how not giving up pays off. They repeatedly experience rejection, but they persist in painting, dancing, acting, singing, writing. I'm thinking here about a kid who was dismissed by a music teacher because he was thought to possess little music potential. He kept plucking away at his guitar, inventing new sounds that would eventually be used to share his visions around the world. His name is Paul McCartney.

**Fix-Ups.**   Of special importance is teaching self-help "fix-ups." Posting problem-solving steps, arts elements charts, and book response choices (see Appendix F) gives students independent resources. We can also teach such strategies as set work aside and come back later, stop and get input from another source, use music to relax, examine past work for ideas, and make use of mistakes, brainstorm, or web. A general expectation is that students should "try something" before asking for help. Teachers can then attend to help signals (e.g., a red flag stuck in a ball of clay) by asking, "What have you tried? What do you know? What could you try? What has worked before?" It is pitiful when children to have no way to cope except to passively wait for someone to do it for them.

**Work Habits.**   Independence is built through clear expectations. General expectations and responsibilities should be outlined and practiced beginning the first day. These include classroom rules (see Appendix E for examples), cues for attending (e.g., teacher claps a rhythm), process for making space for drama and dance, materials use and cleanup, cooperative group behaviors, and peer critique procedures. It's all about teaching students to control their bodies, minds, and voices so they can use these tools to learn.

# Building Block VII: Instructional Design

Both research and learning theories support predictable but flexible instructional design using time structures, regular routines, and rituals that reflect AI philosophy. Routines and structures can be established and used in the classroom and school schedules to ensure that the arts are permanent curricular members, not drop in visitors. Structures include how lessons are introduced, developed, and concluded. Routines range from energizers to start lessons to wrap-up rituals. Time for long-term projects and pursuit of arts interests is built into the schedule as well (e.g., through clubs and centers).

In the following Classroom Snapshot, a teacher organizes the day around arts-based literacy routines and science and social studies units. Key teaching strategies are bolded.

# Classroom Snapshot
## Arts Routines and Inquiry-Based Units

A long wall outside the classroom displays a **timeline of artists' birthdays.** It is at a level so primary students can write and read comments about artists. These appear in "speech bubbles" along the timeline. To the left of the door is a large framed **watercolor mural** painted by students—the culmination of a study of Monet's water lilies. An invitation to walk through "Monet's Garden" refers to an actual garden outside that the children tend daily.

Inside wooden easels display framed prints by Monet, van Gogh, da Vinci, and Rembrandt. A van Gogh **learning center** is in one corner along with baskets of art materials. On display are his portraits and landscapes. A stack of **"Arts for Life" journals** is on the bookshelf. A crate holds arts-based books, including biographies and informational books including *Painting with Children* and *Crayons.* In one corner a sign says **"Book Nook."** Pillows and a beanbag chair make it look inviting. A recipe box holds student recommendation cards and a "smiley face" rating for books. A ficus tree fills another corner, and philodendron tentacles crawl along the windowsill.

The bell rings and Ms. Lucas turns up a CD. The room fills with Vivaldi. Smiling children burst in. One boy shouts "The Four Seasons!" A debate ensues about which season is playing as kids hang up coats and greet Ms. Lucas with "bonjour" and "goedemorgan." Ms. Lucas says she teaches a bit of the language of each focus artist. So far they know greetings in German, Italian, Russian, French, and now, Dutch, for van Gogh. Students scurry to get their journals. They settle at their desks or at centers. Some use materials at the art center, which offers many tools and media. Ms. Lucas hands me a **blank book** with "Arts for Life" on the front. We are the only two not on task, so I find a spot to write, and so does she. Inside the wallpaper cover there is a note that says, "The arts are what give heart to our lives. Imagine a day without literature, music, art, dance, or drama. Write or sketch about how the arts are a part of your life." I count 27 engaged second graders as Vivaldi plays on.

After about 10 minutes, Ms. Lucas says, "Find a place to pause." Students put away the journals. An agenda on the board lists the order of events. The children seem well rehearsed in the **arts-based literacy routines.** A few examples are as follows:

*Composer of the Day.*   Rae Lyn and Jake give a 1-minute report on Vivaldi, telling interesting facts from his life.
*Art Docent.*   Tony sits in a red chair and talks about a self-portrait made on wet cloth with chalk. He says his inspiration was van Gogh's poses, lines, and colors. The audience comments and asks questions, such as "How did you do that?"
*Poem a Day (PAD).*   Two children put up a transparency of Lillian Moore's poem of questions, "Yellow Weed." Missy points at the poem poster while Douglas reviews the directions for "echoic" reading. Missy and Douglas take turns reading lines, with the class echoing the music of their voices: dynamics, tempo, pitch, pauses, and stress. The class

applauds and Ms. Lucas asks what they want to say about the poem. They talk about their feelings and particular words.

*Sing In.* Ms. Lucas asks for song nominations, and there is agreement on "Oats, Peas, and Beans" and "The Green Grass Grew All Around." Song posters on a clothesline feature lyrics in large letters. Julian chooses a pointer and takes charge: "We'll start with the oats song. Everyone stand up and take a deep breath. Now, ready, 1–2–3–begin!" When they sing "The Green Grass Grew All Around," another student hands out word cards (e.g., *ground, hole, root, tree, branch*) and corresponding pictures. Students put them in a pocket chart as they sing the song.

## Unit Questions

The arts routines take about 15 minutes. Ms. Lucas uses each to reinforce literacy skills by asking about phonic patterns in poems and songs. The rest of the morning is organized around **a science unit that addresses key questions:** "How do plants affect people? What causes these effects? What affects plants?" The central concern is exploring causes and effects. Students work in centers, learning circles, independent inquiry work, and guided groups with Ms. Lucas. She explains that most literacy skills are connected to science and social studies units. For example, in this unit students are reading informational books, such as Sylvia Johnson's *Why Flowers Have Colors* and Barbara Cooney's *Miss Rumphius*, and writing observation reports, poetry, and reader's theatre scripts using books they've read. Every unit uses the literary arts, visual art, drama, dance, and music to introduce and offer response options to unit content.

## People Focus

Every unit also has a focus on scientists, composers, and poets who have wrestled with the questions the unit addresses. The artist van Gogh is part of the plant unit because of his expressive plant paintings. The goal is to find meaningful connections and go further to explore why he painted the *way* he did (causes). Science is treated as the study of people who discover relationships among living and nonliving things, not as a study of isolated things and processes. Vivaldi's compositions on seasons connect to the effects of the seasons on plants. Students also investigate the effects of his music on people. Vivaldi's messages about the seasons are different from that in informational books on the cycle of seasons and plant life, and yet there is overlap. Ms. Lucas explains students need to both know and feel when learning. Much thought has gone into the role of emotional intelligence in structuring these integrated units.

## Assessment

Each unit culminates in a portfolio of work. Unit questions are followed by a table of contents:

I. Music and plants: songs and pieces
II. Art and plants: artists and their artwork
III. Drama and plants: scripts and drama workshops
IV. Dance/movement and plants
V. Literature and plants: fiction and nonfiction
VI. Writing about plants: informational and creative writing

Bulges indicate audio and videotapes. Ms. Lucas explains that boxes are used for portfolios when art projects are three dimensional. Highlights are presented at the unit culmination when relatives and friends come to **"Portfolio Performances."**

After lunch Ms. Lucas uses arts strategies with a social studies unit. Sometimes the units are combined, but combinations are not forced. For the same reason, math is integrated only as there is a fit; counting bricks in *The Three Little Pigs* is not an authentic math/literature link. Students get isolated lessons in math and language arts, as needed, and some lessons are not connected to the unit directly. However, Ms. Lucas tries to tie skill-based lessons to units to increase relevance in the eyes of her students.

## Day's End

Another set of **student-led routines** wraps up the day. Students sing and tell what they liked learning. There are "book ads" to advertise "must-reads." A grand finale is a pantomime in which students assume roles as seeds and grow into tall irises. The silent drama is interrupted by the bell. Out the door they go with calls of "arrivederci" and "bonsoir!"

"You know so much about the arts. Are you an artist?" I ask.

"I am learning a lot, just like my students. Am I an artist? Of course, aren't you?" Ms. Lucas cocks her head. "Would any teacher say she isn't a reader or can't do math or write?"

"Some say being an artist is different," I suggest.

"Being an artist is a part of being human. To say you aren't an artist—not a creative being with unique ways to understand and express yourself—is to say you're less than human. Teachers must be artists. Anything less than an artist–teacher is just not good enough for my children or anyone's children." Ms. Lucas has the wise face of a veteran teacher who is confident that the arts have changed the lives of her students. ✸

## Instructional Design

Effective lessons share a general organization that is used in arts-based instruction: introduction, development, and conclusion (IDC). Just as a good meal or a well-written paper has a beginning, middle, and end, so does an effective lesson. A short introduction prepares students for learning and allows teachers to assess students' background. The mood of the lesson is set, and the purposes or focus of the lesson is made clear so students feel the lesson is meaningful. Teachers may begin with a provocative question or introduce vocabulary through a riddle or "mystery bag" containing items related to key lesson concepts. The introduction should be brief but, if skipped, students may never tune in and remain uninvolved in subsequent lesson segments.

In the development stage, the teacher presents or demonstrates. A sense of the whole is developed, perhaps through storytelling, sharing artwork, or listening to a piece of music. A skill or strategy may be presented to use with a problem or question previously introduced. Students explore and discuss, practice, and apply skills, strategies, or media use in this stage.

In the lesson conclusion, students are expected to go beyond mere imitation of demonstrated skills and pull together problem solutions, showing they have learned and used personal creativity, artistry, and higher order thinking. The conclusion provides the satisfaction of completion and is an important part of continuing learner motivation.

Introduction, development, and concluding strategies are the backbone of instruction (see the integrated lesson plan in Planning Page 3.10). The arts are natural motivators, attention getters, and interest generators so they fit naturally in introductions. For example, Picasso's *Guernica* might be displayed to generate questions or reactions to prepare for a social studies unit that examines "war." Drama activities could be used to introduce a unit dealing with "cycles or patterns" by involving students in mime of everyday activities done in the morning, afternoon, and evening. "The Star Spangled Banner" could be examined as a source of feelings and messages to start a unit on American history. The arts are equally valuable as responses to learning in a lesson conclusion. By writing songs and poems, making art, and performing skits and dances, students show what they know. Fourth graders wrote the following song after studying the chemical effects of humor on the body (to the tune of "Ghost Busters").

> When you're all alone and your smiles are gone, who ya' gonna' call? GRIMBUSTERS! When you're feelin' blue and you don't know what to do, who ya' gonna' call? GRIMBUSTERS! They'll make you laugh 'til you cry. Give you a natural high. So, who ya' gonna' call? GRIMBUSTERS!

In general, most lessons proceed in a whole–part–whole manner, giving opportunities to experience the arts aesthetically before examining the parts and pieces. This is accomplished when artful teachers create their own variations on the previous lesson framework. Planning Page 3.10 is a framework for integrated planning. More plan examples appear in subsequent arts chapters.

## Energizers and Warm-Ups

It would be unimaginable to go to a fine restaurant and start the meal with filet mignon. Arts-based lessons need starters, too. Divergent thinking needs to be unlocked, muscles need to be warmed up, and voices need to be prepared. Energizers and warm-ups (E/WUs) are available for these purposes plus they give focus, attract attention, boost concentration, relax, and stimulate CPS. E/WUs are common in AI lesson introductions. They are not lengthy and include use of questions, movement, games, chants, poems, songs, and word play.

Each of the arts seed strategy chapters describes activities to warm up for creative work. Many collections are also available, such as *Playfair* (Weinstein) and books by Viola Spolin and David Booth. Of course, the Internet is a rich source: Use the searchword "warm ups." *Focus Ball* is one example. It is a mirroring activity for concentration. A leader holds her hands together, as if

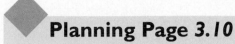

### Planning Page 3.10
#### Two-Pronged Lesson Plan

*Two-Pronged Focus:* What specific skills and concepts are to be taught? Prongs include (1) arts content and (2) core academic content.
*Student Objectives:* What important student behaviors will be developed and assessed/evaluated? (tied to focus prongs)
*Teaching Procedure:* How will the arts and other strategies be used to help students problem solve? (I–D–C organization)

**Introduction:**
1. *Attention/focus:* Eliminate distractions and use signals.
2. *Interest:* Present questions, riddle, mystery, or problem.
3. *Set mood:* Vary voice, music, and lighting.
4. *Set purpose:* Focus on understanding. Connect to life.
5. *Review and relate:* Activate background with prediction activities, fat questions, brainstorming, or webbing (also yields assessment data).
6. *Make ground rules and expectations clear.*
7. *Energizers and warm-ups:* Engage head-heart-hands.
8. *Vocabulary:* Elements and important concepts are introduced using visuals, movement, and context.

**Development:**
1. Teacher presents, shows, and provides an experience to engage students in problem solving.
2. A story may be told or piece of artwork displayed.
3. A skill or strategy may be presented to use with a problem or question previously introduced.
4. Students explore, discuss, experiment, practice, and apply.
5. Students plan and rehearse as the teacher circulates and coaches/scaffolds.

**Conclusion:**
1. Students "show they know." Students go beyond mere imitation of a demonstrated skill or idea. They pull together a problem solution, apply new knowledge and skills, and show they have learned using personal creativity and artistry. This often involves a performance for peers.
2. Self- and peer-assessment, as well as teacher assessment occurs, including debriefing.
3. End with a calming activity (e.g., fantasy journey, journal entry).

**Assessment:**
Return to the objectives to gauge student progress. Items may be added to a portfolio to connect work to stated goals/standards.

there is an invisible ball. Students mirror as the ball is slowly raised, lowered, made larger, and made smaller.

## Opening/Closing Routines

We all know the best way to diet and exercise is to set up an ongoing schedule. One of the most effective ways to ensure that the arts are a living part of learning is to establish daily arts routines.

Ms. Lucas used such routines in the Classroom Snapshot. Opening arts routines include everything from artist of the day to arts journaling. Any of these may be part of a circle meeting. Closing routines can include variations on morning routines or ones suited to wrap up (e.g., singing an ending song together during cleanup). After-lunch rituals are common, especially arts-based read-alouds and journaling to music. Generally, each takes a few minutes. Students can sign up or be selected to lead routines as they do for class jobs. Other routines include the following:

*Word of the Day (WAD).* Students or the teacher chooses an interesting word (e.g., *baroque*, *scumbling*, *onomatopoeia*) and displays it. A 1-minute lesson is presented. The "word expert" can sing or say the word, use it in context, mime or show pictures, use objects, explain or show examples, and give nonexamples. The class is asked to use the word in different contexts throughout the day. In "Beat the Teacher" the class tallies the times WAD words are used.

*Pattern Finds.* Patterns give clues to meaning so helping students discover patterns can be a learning breakthrough. Any text can be used to engage students in finding high-frequency symbol patterns, both graphic (visual) and aural/oral. Once they realize that artists, authors, musicians, dancers, and actors use many of the same ideas over and over, students feel it is acceptable for them to follow suit. As an example, in the riddle, "What is the name of the boy who hangs on the wall?" (*Answer:* Art), students can find phonic patterns such as the diphthong "-oy" in *boy*. Others might notice the word pattern "hangs on the wall" that evokes visual imagery. Students see how words can be spelled the same, but have different meanings and pronunciations determined by context (see Ready Reference 3.5). Repeated elements can be found in music (refrains), art (geometric shapes), dance (locomotor moves), and drama (facial expressions). Patterns even occur at note and letter levels and make up the large structures called genres (e.g., science fiction and jazz).

## Performances and Exhibits

When students expect learning to be synthesized into a culminating event, motivation increases. The force of the audience stokes the fire of learning further as a level of anxiety energizes performers and exhibitors in hopes of a positive reception. Performances and exhibits are also experiences that bond students and give a sense of belonging.

The most powerful performances grow out of student ideas. Students take leadership with minimal teacher direction. Weekly performances include "poetree presentations" and a reader's theatre. Students regularly adapt poems and other reading material to create theatre scripts that summarize learning in units. On a given day, students know they are responsible for poetry performances (Ready Reference 5.4). Many AI schools schedule grade-level and schoolwide events at the ends of units that include everything from art exhibits to PowerPoint presentations. At the Conservatory Lab Charter School they have an assembly every Friday (visit www.conservatorylab.org/). Performances and exhibits are memorable events that heighten students' learning, satisfaction, and pride for work well done.

## Grouping

AI draws upon grouping practices to meet student needs. Large group work happens each day, but a great deal of time is also scheduled for small group work. Classrooms are organized with tables and grouped desks to encourage collaboration. There is generally space for the teacher to do guided instruction with small groups as other groups work together, sometimes at centers and stations. Groups are sometimes pulled together for common needs, but common interest is also high-placed criterion. The goal is for students to learn to work in diverse groups. Younger children need to work in pairs and smaller groups at first. Most students benefit from working in groups of four to six, whether it is for a book discussion or to plan a drama. See ideas for facilitating groups under Building Block VI.

## Centers and Stations

Centers allow students to work independently with materials. *Station* refers to a narrowly focused area (e.g., a computer station might have software to explore unit topics). A center is a space that has independent learning options from several sources (e.g., art materials, CDs, props, game boards, and other activities related to a unit).

All arts-based learning is problem centered and often results in making invisible learning visible. "How can you show _____?" through drama, dance, music, or visual art is a central question. Arts-based centers offer opportunities to independently explore possibilities with drama props (e.g., hats and scarves, pictures of dance steps and shapes, a variety of CDs, rhythm instruments, and art materials). Most items are not expensive or hard to come by. They invite alternative ways to express ideas and feelings.

A general arts-for-life center can include inspirational quotes about arts and artists collected by students and displayed in a special area. Definitions of art can be found and created by students as they explore the idea of using the arts as learning tools. An arts timeline with birthdays of artists and other significant arts events is important. For example, alongside the 1839 invention of the camera, students post pictures and notes they collected. A world map makes a good display with pins to mark the homes of artists. The center may house arts-based books organized by genres, art forms, or artists/authors.

## Clubs and Projects

Regular formats for students to pursue arts-based interests are crucial. Time may be set aside within the school day to do art making or listening to music. Many schools allow daily or weekly time within the school day or after school for arts clubs. Ashley River Creative Arts holds a breakout time every day. Students may join an art guild, chorus, clay club, photography club, or study Suzuki violin or ballet. Fourth and fifth graders can join the drama troupe. Recently they performed "Goldilocks" in Spanish and in English. "It is like an after-school program, but within the school day," explains Assistant Principal Cathy Middleton. Students learn choice and responsibility.

Children also feel a sense of belonging in a club that represents their interests. Under the direction of an interested teacher

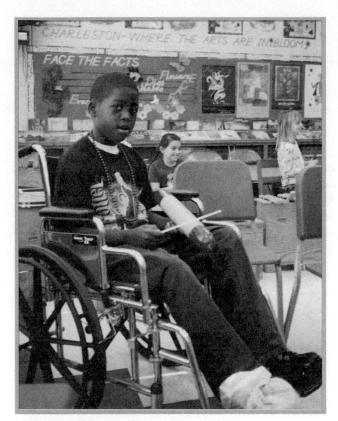

Anthony playing a rhythm instrument

they learn ideas, skills, and tools that allow club interests to grow artistically. Students learn how to use puppets, music, and other props in storytelling and develop oral dramatic skills so important in life in and outside of school.

# Building Block VIII: Differentiation for Diverse Needs

*This is the saddest part of the current fetish with test scores. Life is about being good at what you are and need to be. Art helps you find it and do it. Almost all other school learning is about learning other people's ideas—imitating their voices. Learning important "content" is not the goal of school. Learning to use content to accomplish great things is the goal of school (Wiggins, 2007)*

Meaningful AI is about finding arts connections that are appropriate to student needs. The theories and stages described in Chapter 2 are resources to help decide whether certain arts content or processes are right for individuals and groups. In addition, teachers must accommodate for special needs of students and work with arts specialists to make adaptations. Developmentally appropriate ideas are presented in each chapter, and in Appendix A.

## Differentiated Instruction

Arts advocate Jane Remer has a motto: "All the arts, of all cultures, for all the children and youth, of all cultures." It's a beautiful dream. To make the dream a reality, educators use the power of arts integration to "differentiate" instruction. Differentiation is about responding to students' differences in a manner that honors, not suppresses, differences. The concept of individualization is key; the meaning of its components are: *in* = not, *di* = two, *vid* = see, *ual* = one, *tion* = process. This translates into "the process of not seeing or treating two people as if they are one."

Differentiation and standards-based teaching have to coexist if the goal is success for all students, but Tomlinson (2002) proposes educators step back and ask if standards are reflected in the curriculum, or whether they have *become* the curriculum. The goal is to teach students to make sense of ideas and master skills, not race through material to meet benchmarks. Standards are but one source for curriculum development. They offer guidance about *what* to teach. Differentiation, on the other hand, is process oriented and focuses on *how* to teach (Tomlinson, 2002).

Differentiation is not a recipe; and it is not as simple as changing the amount of learning material. Struggling learners do not need "less of what they don't understand, and advanced learners don't need more of what they already know" (Tomlinson Brimijoin, & Narvaez, 2008). On the contrary, it is part of instructional problem solving initiated by assessment. Assessment data informs instructional planning that responds to student difference and makes student success more likely.

Differentiation is necessary for all students to reach goals and standards about what they should know, be, and do. In current practice, differentiation results in instruction that varies in delivery, materials use, and activities. Teachers differentiate by using creative thinking processes in instructional planning. Example questions used to initiate such creative problem solving are as follows:

- What do I know about the student's strengths and needs?
- What content (ideas/concepts) and processes (skills/strategies) are to be learned?
- Why is the lesson important to the learner?
- How might the learning product or process be adjusted for student strengths and needs (e.g., pretest and then compact the content)?
- When would the student be most successful? Is the student ready for this lesson?
- Where would the student learn best? With whom?
- What materials are best suited to this student's needs?
- What options can be offered for students to show comprehension (i.e., express meaning)?

Differentiation is about treating individuals differently. Painting all students with the same brush does not create masterpiece lessons. The following are overlapping strategies to differentiate curriculum and instruction. The strategies are based on the belief that every child needs "particular" accommodations to ensure progress toward independence. Often the changes are minor. Chances for student success increase when teachers adjust the PARTICULAR: place, amount, rate, target

## Ready Reference 3.11  Differentiation for Students' Strengths and Needs

Use these 10 PARTICULAR categories to differentiate instruction for diverse students. See Appendix B for more ways to adapt for students with special needs, including English learners.

**Place:** (learning setting)
**Amount:** (time and materials)
**Rate:** (frequency)
**Targets:** (lesson objectives)
**Instruction:** (teaching strategies)

**Curriculum:** (scope and sequence of experiences and materials)
**Utensils:** (technology and tools)
**Level of difficulty:** (complexity)
**Assistance:** (scaffolding)
**Response:** (ways to show learning)

---

objective, instruction, curriculum, utensils, levels of difficulty, assistance, and response (Ready Reference 3.11).

*Place (Learning Setting).* Change the learning space. Rearrange desks, add carpet and cushions, create centers, play background music, adjust lighting.

*Amount (Time and Materials).* Give more or less time (e.g., to explore materials). Use more repetition, examples, and feedback. Give additional practice. Break into smaller steps. Reduce or increase the number of things to be learned.

*Rate (Frequency).* Slow or quicken the pace. Give more breaks. Create more or less structure by changing the intensity of teacher direction during lessons.

*Targets (Lesson Objectives).* Make objectives clear. Use graphing and check-off sheets for goal attainment. Alter goals and the means for a student to reach targets. Connect to students' interests and lives. Decide what a child can realistically achieve (know and be able to do).

*Instruction (Teaching Strategies).* Use appropriate kinds and amounts of explicit instruction (model, demonstrate, examples, coaching, feedback, scaffold). Engage students cognitively, emotionally, and physically (heads-on, hearts-on, hands-on learning). Use open questions, every pupil response, and projects. Organize lessons from whole to part. Use inductive and deductive teaching. Set up routines to provide security, but encourage student choices. Use multiple intelligences, arts-based, and multisensory approaches that cause students to be active in processing through visual, auditory, kinesthetic, and tactile modes.

*Curriculum (Scope and Sequence of Experiences and Materials).* Use easier reading materials or adapt by highlighting key concepts, tape recording, or rewriting. Change order. Give choices within limits. Use all the arts throughout the curriculum.

*Utensils (Media and Tools).* Use visual and auditory aids. Use hands-on materials such as games, computers, and art media Teach problem-solving tools and strategies, such as ways to figure out unknown words or what to do when you don't understand. Teach shortcuts and mnemonics. Use cue sheets and cards. Focus attention on details and patterns to help make meaning. Teach why and when to use strategies and how.

*Level of Difficulty (Complexity).* Make the lesson easier or harder to challenge appropriately. Highlight text essentials. Allow notes during tests. Alter structure or supervision.

*Assistance (Scaffolding).* Use peer tutoring, one on one, and small groups. Make the lesson agenda clear, and use prompts and cues. Coach toward independence by teaching fix-ups and directing attention to connecting known to the unknown, finding patterns, and using mnemonics.

*Response (Evidence).* Allow students to show they know in a variety of ways. Use projects that call for a product or piece to perform, especially for audiences. Give exemptions (e.g., from oral reading). Distinguish among assessment, evaluation, and grading.

## Detrimental Differentiation

Differentiation is not always a positive instructional tool. The following examples of instructional practices are detrimental to learning:

- Lower quality activities that focus more on skills and less on making sense
- Placement in the lowest groups and instructional tracks where isolated-skill instruction dominates
- More teacher-dominated instruction that expects passive student response
- More assignments to read and write single words and short texts rather than lengthy texts
- Less computer access and focus on low-level practice-oriented software

**Low Expectations.**  Of particular concern is abundant research that shows teachers often get what they expect when it comes to student achievement. Children live up to high or low expectations communicated in verbal and nonverbal ways. For example, teachers tend to touch and stand closer to students who are successful; they also smile at them more, give them more chances, and affirm their efforts. More disturbing is how teachers tend to focus on higher order thinking to create understanding with high achievers and create a "culture of low expectations" for low achievers (McDermott & Varenne, 1995; Tauber, 1997). This is especially true for children disadvantaged by poverty or background. These low status students receive unwarranted amounts of drill, practice, and rote learning activities, such as filling in worksheets and literal level questions. In the absence of challenging work marked by "what if and I wonder why" questions, children suffer (Gambrell, Morrow, & Pressley, 2007, p. 35; Villegas & Lucas, 2007, p. 32).

**Diverse Populations.** The subject of the arts is the subject of life. The arts provide avenues to self-understanding, making meaning of the world, expression of talents in unique ways, and creating empathy for those different from us. Through the arts, children discover common bonds with people. This understanding and awareness are the essence of the arts and can build a feeling of kinship. In a world where quality of life depends on the quality of our relationships with others, the arts can lessen feelings of alienation and be great levelers. No one is considered greater or lesser than another in his or her creative expressions and aesthetic tastes. With this in mind, we can think about similarities among diverse populations of students and stress commonalities, not just differences. We are all human with basics needs: to be respected, to belong, to achieve, and to communicate. Suggestions are given in Appendix B for additional adaptations for students categorized as having diverse needs, including English learners.

**English Learners.** There are now nearly 5 million English learners (ELLs) in the United States, or nearly 20 percent of the school population. That is an increase of 95 percent since 1991 (NCELA, 2006). Sixteen states have an ELL population that exceeds a 200 percent increase.

ELLs are not homogeneous. The ELL population displays the range of differences found in students whose first language is English (e.g., age and development stage) plus they differ in a multitude of other factors such as country of origin, mother tongue, socioeconomic status, and previous access to formal schooling (Carlo, 2007; Gersten & Baker, 2000; RAND, 2002). Almost 80 percent are Spanish speakers and less than 2 percent are Vietnamese, Hmong, and Cantonese. The rest represent 380 different language groups.

Compared with monolingual English speakers, English learners typically have the following characteristics.

- They have less background for topics in English texts or tests.
- They know less English vocabulary.
- They have difficulty with questions that rely on background (e.g., García, 1991).

Successful English learners use strategies that can be taught to all ELLs. For example, successful ELLs often use strategies and knowledge acquired in a first language to approach learning in the second language. They also used bilingual strategies, such as drawing upon cognates, paraphrased translating, code mixing, and switching (RAND, 2002, p. 80). Less-successful ELLs tend to not transfer strategies across languages and some think they have to keep languages separate to prevent confusion (p. 80). See Appendix B for more specific differentiation ideas.

## Response to Intervention

Response to intervention (RTI) is a federal initiative that created a multitiered process to provide services to struggling learners at increasing levels of intensity. RTI requires teachers to engage in creative problem solving to differentiate instruction at the first signs of difficulty. There is no "one size fits all" model for RTI. The federal government purposely provided few details for the development and implementation of procedures, stating specifically that states and districts should be given the flexibility to establish models. AI expands options as teachers design instruction that fits their particular students by allowing students to learn through diverse arts processes and materials, including use of multiple intelligences strategies and multisensory methods. Websites with reliable RTI information include the following:

http://idea.ed.gov/download/statute.html
www.handsandvoices.org/articles/docs/RtI.pdf
http://www.reading.org/

# Building Block IX: Assessment for Learning

*Isn't it ironic, the state doesn't test what really makes us special. They don't even know how.* (Roberts, 2004)

At a recent conference, a speaker quipped, "If the government has its way, there will be no child's behind left." Indeed, the *No Child Left Behind Act* mandated expectations that caused some schools to fixate on standardized tests, which has demoralized many students and teachers. Intimidated schools began to constrict the curriculum to teach *to* tests, even though 61 percent of the public disapproves of this tactic, and research shows early gains are not sustained (Herman & Baker, 2005; Rose & Gallup, 2005). Furthermore, overly directing students to test performance has been shown to decrease motivation, reduce achievement, increase dropout numbers, and reduce the graduation rate (Allington, 2002; DeMoss & Morris, 2002; Guthrie, 2004; Stiggins, 2002).

Popular metaphors about overbearing assessment procedures crop up regularly: "Just weighing a pig doesn't fatten it up," and "Opening the oven too soon causes a cake to fall." The high-stakes environment can lead to hopelessness. Assessment methods used in AI add hope. Arts-based schools follow research that shows it is more fruitful to teach for understanding than to spend much time on test preparation (Allington, 2002, 2005; Guthrie, 2004).

Assessment is as necessary in the arts as it is in any other curricular area, but arts assessment has traditionally been interwoven with the processes of creating art with focus on increasing the quality of work. Unlike widespread heavy-handed testing in reading and math, the arts have historically relied more on self-assessment and peer critique during work, as well as finished products. Evaluation criteria continually evolves, and is collaboratively created by artists, not solely imposed by onlookers. As a result, we have grown to expect a degree of excellence in the arts that is comparable only to perfectionist expectations about products such as airbags.

## Definition and Purposes

Assessment is part of the instructional problem-solving process. It is about gathering information. Assessment is distinct from evaluation and grading which focus on making value judgments and assigning labels. The main purposes for assessment are to: (1) motivate students to learn, (2) plan and differentiate instruction, (3) track student progress toward standards and goals, including in the arts, and (4) obtain information for program evaluation.

Educators use selected purposes to determine *what* is assessed and *how*. The first three purposes are addressed in this book. Program assessment is beyond the scope of this text, but a recommended resource is the South Carolina ABC schools website that features *Opportunity to Learn Standards* converted into clear evaluation tools (www.winthrop.edu/ABC/). In Kentucky a pilot project is underway for schools to self-evaluate arts instruction against a rubric based on program standards, indicators of quality, and ratings of performance. Full implementation is set for the 2011–2012 school year. For information visit the Kentucky Department of Education Preliminary Information about Program Reviews (www.kde.state.ky.us/KDE/).

Most 21st-century assessment is correlated with standards and goals about what students should know, do, and be (Drake & Burns, 2004). Good assessment gives students multiple ways to show what they know and can do, and who they are *becoming*. Information is gathered about where students are in a learning progression; experiences are then designed to move them forward. Thus, assessment is used to plan "what next?".

## Issues

Teachers who fail to understand the purposes of assessment or the multiple ways to assess may dismiss assessment as a waste of time. It is tempting to focus on student arts products more than the quality of the learning that produced them. They may dwell on "formal or technical understanding or easily tested outcomes" (Baker, Boughton, Freedman, Horowitz, & Ingram, 2004, p. 32); arts integration is more about process. Then there is the myth that assessing artistic work somehow crushes creativity. Teachers may misconceive arts assessment as "subjective and therefore problematic" (p. 32). Artists generally do not see it this way. With clear arts vocabulary anyone can talk with students in constructive ways and help them understand criteria to increase quality of work. Examples of "high-placed criteria" are included subsequently.

Of course there is the issue of what is most important to assess. We cannot create and use rubrics and checklists for everything. Standards help prioritize, but teachers need to judge their relative value; all standards are not equal. Many important goals are left out of standards. Decisions need to be made about weight given to different criteria within rubrics as well. There is no one right way to resolve these issues. It is clear that teachers and artists are the point people in the debate about what makes quality.

## *For* Learning versus *Of* Learning

Arts integration gives priority to assessment *for* learning, not just *of* learning (purpose 1). The focus is on how assessment can alter learning, not just measure it. Assessment *for* learning is formative and ongoing (e.g., giving feedback on a paper so a student can rewrite it). In contrast, assessment *of* learning is summative—it describes the final result. Summative assessment happens after work is complete so assessment data is not intended to change the work.

Assessment for learning rivals one-on-one tutoring in effectiveness, especially with low-performing students. It is a strong motivational tool that increases quality of work because relationships between effort, feedback, and achievement are emphasized (Stiggins, 2002). Criteria for good work are made clear using work samples, rubrics, and checklists. Students track their own progress and make changes, based on feedback, to increase quality. At AI schools these kinds of formative assessment are embedded in lessons and student self-reflection is emphasized. The following are features of assessment for learning.

*Criteria for quality work is frontloaded.* Students need to know from the outset what criteria will be used to judge their work. Frontloading sets up motivation to learn and unites students and teachers to work for excellence. Students see that feedback about progress is intended to better their performance, not just grade it. Criteria should be developed *with* students by discussing what "good work" might look like. Several exemplars of work, as well as examples of weak work, should be used to give a picture of possibilities—not of work to be copied. Artwork and videos of dance, music, and drama performances can be analyzed against criteria for good work. These boundaries give focus and increase problem solving so students create more thoughtful solutions.

*Assessment criteria are fluid.* While criteria should be specific, room is needed for discoveries made during learning. When these are found, criteria are modified.

*Continuous specific, doable feedback is given during and after learning.* Feedback helps sustain student motivation and makes it more likely they will meet criteria. Questions such as "What is working?" and "What do you need to do?" ensure that students understand feedback. Peers should give feedback as well.

## Assessing Assessment

Four characteristics of effective assessment stand out.

1. *Focus on strengths and needs.* Identifying weaknesses (what students do not know or cannot do) is less effective than identifying strengths and using them to address needs. To do so teachers use diagnostic tools such as an interest inventory early in the year.

2. *Is authentic.* Information should be gathered in a context and manner that shows what students really know and can do. Paper-and-pencil tests can be inauthentic because they are unable to capture complex thinking, such as CPS. Valid assessments must also be humane and doable. They should uplift, not defeat. In AI the challenge is to create assessment tools and processes as creative and diverse as the arts themselves.

3. *Multifactored.* No single observational checklist, nor one anecdotal note, can create a portrait of a child's growth. Multiple and varied assessments can give insight into student thinking during work and document growth over time. Culminating projects and portfolios can combine with traditional tests. The opportunity to have multiple means to show learning motivates students, especially those who have a track record of failure on traditional tests. The arts add ways to assess and arts-based assessments can enhance learning.

4. *Continuous.* Data are collected in many ways and from a variety of sources, especially observation, in an ongoing manner. Self-reflection and peer feedback are integral to lessons. For example, in dance, teachers punctuate lessons with debriefings to discuss what is working, what is not working, and how to make it work. Drafts and work samples are collected that lay out concrete evidence of progress. Teachers use sticky notes on a clipboard to jot down observations so they can be easily transferred to student folders.

## Assessment Tools

A veritable cornucopia of formal and informal assessment tools is now available, but not all are congruent with arts-based philosophy. Multiple-choice tests cannot show how a student uses CPS with artistic materials in the same way as a long-term project. Formal tools, such as standardized tests, are mostly appropriate to obtain summative data on students and for program evaluation. The most useful tools for teachers are informal ones because they yield specifics, not just percentiles or grades. Students can also use informal tools to reflect and set goals. Informal tools focus on assessment for learning, which changes what is taught and how in response to needs. Appendix D includes additional examples of the following assessment tools.

**Checklists.**   This assessment tool is used to track concepts and skills to be learned during activities. A checklist of tasks allows students to independently track their progress.

**Rubrics.**   A 2-year study on assessing the progress of special needs students showed a consensus that rubrics improved speed of learning and cognitive development. However, some teachers remain confused about how to create and use rubrics (Mason & Steedly, 2006). While there are a variety of types of rubrics, put simply, rubrics make a gradient of performance clear, using a rating scale (e.g., rating on a scale from 1 to 4). Some districts create grade rubrics to make criteria for each letter grade more understandable. Internet resources include the following:

http://school.discovery.com/schrockguide/assess.html
www.eduscapes.com/tap/topic53.htm
http://rubistar.4teachers.org/index.php

## High-Placed Criteria

Rubrics and checklists should focus on key concepts and processes shared by arts and academic areas. Examples include the following:

- Using the arts to effectively communicate ideas and feelings
- Using and articulating CPS thinking to create meaning
- Showing ownership of work with original ideas that reflect personal style and voice
- Attending to details and patterns that support important meanings
- Using arts vocabulary to describe and give evidence
- Engaging in active participation (e.g., concentration/focus, staying in role, listening)
- Persisting in problem solving, especially when encountering difficulties

- Making connections, especially unusual ones
- Showing appropriate and creative use of artistic tools and techniques
- Explaining artistic choices
- Working collaboratively, including listening, and giving suggestions

**Benchmarks.**   When using a rubric, it is helpful to create benchmarks. This involves "attaching quality to a small, rank-ordered body of student work" (Baker et al., 2004, pp. 28–30). Once student work is collected and ranked, these works can then be used to make comparisons for the purpose of improving work. Students can do this as well. A study of AI lessons found that collaborative discussions using benchmarks of learning dramatically changed how teachers and artists viewed and used assessment (Baker et al., 2004).

**Performance-Based.**   Some argue that understanding can only truly be assessed, and for that matter, even achieved, through performance; students must do something that puts understanding to work (Perkins, 1998; Wiske, 1997). Quality and quantity of progress in the arts has long been demonstrated through performances, exhibitions, and portfolios. Learning is made visible through the arts as work is assessed using criteria for excellence connected to academic areas. In arts integration, the arts are both assessment tools and areas that are assessed. Arts-based assessment yields clearer indicators of the kind and degree of learning and is a more comprehensive means of documenting growth.

**Projects.**   Long-term projects often culminate in exhibits and performances that synthesize learning and involve audiences. Project-based units focus on struggling with authentic problems. Project criteria are developed with students in advance. The process to create the product is CPS.

**Exhibits.**   Class museums and displays are a visual means for students to show learning. A school or class museum may just be a special wall. Mounting and framing student art shows it is valued. Museum information plaques should accompany work and contain the artist's name and birth date, title of the work, media used and surface, and date the work was completed. Students can also prepare catalogs to go with exhibits for visitors to learn about the art and artists. These artifacts of learning are judged against prespecified criteria.

**Portfolios.**   Showing capabilities with collected work has long been used in the arts. Work samples give evidence of progress toward criteria. For example, dated entries on audiotapes of oral reading show fluency growth. Drama responses and dances can be photographed and videoed so students can view, reflect, and set improvement goals. Students learn to self-evaluate using much the same criteria the teacher uses.

Not every piece of work should be kept; work that shows something important is the focus. Keeping just the good work does not allow students to see progress over time. Date work and connect items to specific goals. Revisit the work to celebrate progress and past successes. Some schools now use digital portfolios, especially in the upper grades. A set of guidelines for creating arts folios is in Appendix D.

**Anecdotal Records.**  Teachers can easily make informal notes, against preset criteria, as students engage in activities and as they observe products. See an example for dance in Appendix D.

**Self-Assessment.**  Student reflection on learning criteria gives a sense of how the real world operates. From the mechanic to the doctor, there are expectations that each worker will continually reflect on performance and make necessary adjustments. Students should examine successive drafts of work to monitor change. Ready Reference 3.12 lists questions to prompt reflection about the CPS process. There are more in Appendix D.

**Peer Feedback.**  Students need to be taught *why* and *how* to respond to performances and exhibits of classmates. The art of noticing has to be practiced so students can make evidence-based comments about what they see and hear. Direct them to describe using specific arts concepts and their feelings: "It made me feel ____. I wonder ____." The learn-wonder-like (LWL) strategy can be used to jot down responses. Students should be taught that asking questions is a form of feedback, too. Role-play giving and receiving feedback for practice and to develop empathy as students feel the effects of thoughtless remarks.

**Individual Conferences.**  Personal conferences give valuable insight into children's thinking and convey the message you care about working toward goals. Short conferences of 3 to 5 minutes allow students to discuss goals and show progress. Students may be asked to bring a piece of artwork and explain how CPS was used or to read aloud to check fluency. Checklists, notes, rubrics, and work samples in the child's folio can be reviewed.

**Interest Inventories.**  Interest has astounding effects on learning, but in interviews about memorable school experiences, Starko (1995) did not find a single student who remembered being allowed to study a personal interest. We cannot base all lessons on students' interests, but we can shift the balance in that direction and make achievement based on motivation more likely.

Teachers can inventory interests in many ways. One is to ask students to divide a piece of paper and list "Interests and Talents" and "Problems and Questions" (also used by writers and artists to find topics). Inventories can be done orally: Write questions on cards and draw them out for discussions. To use movement, make a circle and ask students to step in (twist or slide) in response to interest categories. Use the inventory in Appendix D for ideas.

# Building Block X: Arts Partnerships

Arts partnerships form a web of mutual support based on common needs and goals. Important partners are school arts specialists, teaching artists, community arts organizations (local and state), arts councils, museums, community orchestras, colleges and universities (arts and education departments), national arts organizations and alliances, businesses, and governmental organizations such as the National Endowment for the Arts (NEA) and the National Endowment for the Humanities (NEH). Some community agencies provide "in kind" support, such as space. In Chattanooga, Tennessee, museum professionals help design school exhibit spaces. Many schools partner with businesses and arts organizations to pursue funding for professional development and artist residencies. Numerous foundations (e.g., Ford, Rockefeller, Getty, Annenberg) have been funding arts integration programs since the 1960s (Fineberg, 2004). The Council for School Corporate Partnerships (http://corpschoolpartners.org) has guidelines for partnerships. The International Network of Performing and Visual Arts Schools (http://artsschoolsnetwork.org) is a source for partnership models. Local universities are potential partners, especially as more offer courses on arts integration and want to place students in schools for practicum experiences (Rabkin & Redmond, 2005 a and b). The California-based ArtsBridge project is an example (www.artsbridge.ucdavis.edu/).

## Arts Specialists

Licensed arts teachers, professional artists, teaching artists, and professionals in community arts organizations are potential arts partners. Teachers should personally seek out these people to provide direct service to students and/or serve as planning consultants.

**Arts Teachers.**  School-based arts specialists are the closest sources to plumb curricular connections. Most are extremely supportive of AI, if they understand it is not intended to replace specialized arts classes. Teachers often begin by sitting in on arts classes to learn more about the arts and about students' arts intelligences. This may mean giving up a planning period. Some schools have reorganized so planning time is before or after school to make this happen, which also makes planning with arts specialists more workable. At most schools much planning happens during lunch

---

**Ready Reference 3.12**  Questions to Prompt Reflection

Use the following questions to start discussions or prompt writing about work in arts.

- What were you trying to do?
- Where and how did you get your ideas?
- Why did you do what you did (decisions)?
- What did you try that you've never tried before?
- How is this connected to other learning? Arts?
- What was most difficult?

- What worked? What will you do next?
- What did you learn most? What did you like best?
- What three to five words describe your work?
- How did this compare with other work you've done?
- What advice would you give to someone else working on this problem?

conversations and impromptu meetings. Committed teachers find ways using phone calls, e-mails, and other means. Of course, it is ideal when the schedule facilitates planning time. Some schools use paraprofessionals for duties or negotiate early release for students as often as once a week. Progressive schools have redefined the role of arts teachers to include "arts coaching." Arts teachers have a reduced teaching schedule so they have time to plan with teachers, observe, and co-teach integrated arts lessons.

Some schools are fortunate enough to have drama specialists as well as music and art. However, physical educators often embrace creative movement and can direct teachers to natural connections, (e.g., math and dance). Arts teachers often are willing to synchronize with lessons and units in the regular classroom if teachers prepare a curriculum map or calendar—a month-by-month list of units in science, social studies, reading, language arts, and math. Arts teachers especially like to co-plan with teachers if the goal is two-way integration. Arts teacher should be able to expect classroom teachers to support their units as well. An example is Duxberry Elementary in Columbus, Ohio, where teachers supply specialists with lesson topics, units, and goals for the coming grade period. Specialists do the same for teachers, and teachers solicit ways to follow up on arts classes to extend learning.

### Artist Residencies.

*"I used to be the cream on the cake and all of a sudden, I'm the cake! I am part of the actual work, not as much a flash in the pan, but part of a long-term partnership."* (Artist quoted in Freeman et al., 2003)

The arts can be popular and enjoyable, but may add little to academic understanding if performances are perceived as entertainment and the emphases are left up to the artists. Ineffective AI happens when artists come in without planning and/or students are not prepared. There are horror stories about artists who come late, cannot control the class, fail to connect to the curriculum, act inappropriately, and focus on being center stage, instead of involving students. Artists complain that teachers are sometimes not ready, have dirty classrooms, fail to understand the arts/learning connection, talk negatively about kids in front of the class, and may leave or sit in the back of the classroom, not participating (Fineberg, 2004).

Artists feel they can make important contributions to student thinking and communication skills and are usually receptive to overtures to plan around academic standards. They are grateful for assessment insights and there is much that needs to be discussed about classroom management before any residency. According to Waldorf (2002) artists have four goals for getting involved in partnerships.

1. *Artistic.* Instill a passion for the arts, and help students learn new ways to think
2. *Educational.* Develop students' learning skills and confidence; expand teacher's instructional strategies
3. *Social.* Promote equity, diversity, and community
4. *Personal.* Develop their own teaching skills and further their careers

At Ashley River Creative Arts teachers plan five to six artist residencies a year. Residencies are funded through sources such as the PTA and the South Carolina Arts Commission. Each is 1 to 2 weeks in duration. Recently, a textile artist did a residency in fifth grade on molas to go with a social studies unit. In K–2 classes, artist Laura Rich told African folktales that connected to animal units (kindergarten), emotions (first grade), and weather (second grade). With fifth graders, she added script writing and performances using drumming and songs.

How are these residencies made integral? Everyone has to be clear about roles, goals, procedures, materials, schedule, and room preparation. A written agreement needs to be negotiated that addresses these questions and establishes what the artist will be paid, how, and when. Appendix C includes topics to be addressed in a planning discussion with artists. It is appropriate to ask for and contact references.

### Teaching Artists.

While many artists have little or no background in teaching or in child development, *teaching* artists do. Like the teaching artist in the following Spotlight they have special training that focuses on pedagogy. A new journal, *Teaching Artist Journal,* is dedicated to helping artists make the transition to teaching artists. Teaching artists bring invaluable knowledge and skills to planning, teaching, and assessment. In particular they are accustomed to doing CPS. However, teaching creative problem solving is another matter. They need to understand that the bulk of a residency should be about causing students to problem solve using the arts, not for the artists to demonstrate personal artistry. It is important to have an upfront discussion about explicit teaching of CPS. Offer a copy of the CPS process (Ready Reference 2.6) to establish a common language and discuss the focus on learning arts processes versus creating impressive arts products/performances. Resist capitulating to the "hysterical demand for polished performance" and emphasis on representational artwork (Fineberg, 2004, p. 59).

Some teaching artists also work with teachers in a coaching relationship that provides professional development through reciprocal classroom demonstrations and consultations. In the Kennedy Center's Changing Education through the Arts (CETA) model, artists serve as coaches, teach classes, observe teachers doing arts-based lessons, and provide feedback (Dumas, 2005). Kennedy Center's publication, *Creating Capacity,* also offers ideas for preparing artists for teaching (www.kennedy-center.org). If your district is affiliated with the Kennedy Center Partners in Education, you can check with administrators about workshops. More information can be found at www.teachingartist.com/. This site includes links to videos of teaching artists working with students and their blogs.

## Teacher Spotlight
### Teaching Artist

Kim Keats is a Hilton Head Island teaching artist who says she started as a "guest artist" who just demonstrated artwork. Her role evolved as she began to help teachers learn to create art, especially fiber art. She now does staff development for teachers and team planning, and she recently completed a yearlong residency connecting quilt making and ecology. She co-planned with an English/language arts teacher around an ecology theme and taught monthly lessons with kids on thinking through symbols. The teacher continued the work in between Kim's lessons. She coached the middle school students through the CPS process, and the result was a magnificent quilt that narrates the natural history of South Carolina, entitled "From the Mountains to the Sea." The quilt now hangs in the Coastal Discovery Museum. Students wrote throughout the project, which gave them a deep understanding of how visual art expands communication. Their writing became more "detailed and vivid" as they went back and forth between words and art (Interview, September 2005). Why did Keats become a teaching artist? She says it goes hand in hand with doing your own work. "As a teacher you are always learning. This is conducive to producing art yourself. I teach what I love."

## Arts Agencies/Organizations

There is no substitute for teachers and administrators taking initiative to find partnership possibilities in the community. Local and state arts councils are good clearinghouses and all have websites. Check sources such AAA, travel agents, and real estate brokers, who often have packets that detail cultural opportunities. Once you locate a potential partner about school outreach, make an appointment to discuss the kinds of arts expertise you are seeking. Take along a copy of the school standards and a curriculum map to show the calendar of units. Be ready to explain the concept of teaching and learning through the arts at the heart of AI.

## Arts Directory

Specialized arts knowledge and skill may be close at hand. A school/community survey can locate people who may be willing to do single visits or may be capable of an arts residency. The PTA may be willing to undertake construction of a directory using member email lists. All it takes is the circulation of a short form to adults requesting names and contact information for arts resources. Encourage people to list themselves. The teacher next door may own every piece of big band music ever written, or the principal may play the African slit drum. Students can be surveyed, too. At Normal Park Museum Magnet all parents agree to 18 hours of work at the school; volunteers can be tapped for artist talents, too.

## Conclusion

*The spirit of Creative America has spurred us to say and write and draw what we think, feel and dream . . . to celebrate through dance, in songs, in paint and on paper, the story of America: of who we are, where we have been, and what we hope to be.* (Hillary Rodham Clinton)

This chapter describes the 10 building blocks that form a flexible blueprint to plan and implement arts integration. The building blocks are interlocking and create scaffolding for specific arts strategies described in subsequent chapters.

---

### Teachers as Leaders: AI Advocacy

Work with a group to do one the following: (1) Submit a proposal for a presentation about AI building blocks at a local, state, or national professional meeting. Conference schedules are available at professional education websites (e.g., International Reading Association, www.reading.org; National Council for the Teaching of English, www.ncte.org). (2) Write a short article on the AI building blocks for a school newsletter, local newspaper, or professional journal.

---

### myeducationlab

Go to the Activities and Applications section for Topic *Strategies for Teaching* at MyEducationLab for your course and complete the video activities entitled "Preparing for Creative Problem Solving", "Concluding Lessons Using Debriefing", "Using Debriefing to Solidify and Extend Thinking", and "Using the Tell One Thing Strategy to Increase Participation."

Go to the Book Specific Resources section in the MyEducationLab for your course, select your book and Chapter 3 to view the Questions to Guide Reading, Response Options, and FAQs about Arts Integration documents.

---

## Resources

Also see the Appendix, including websites.

### Videos, DVDs, and CDs

Professional Development Series: www.learner.org/resources. Click on "discipline" and "arts."

Jacobs, H. (1993). *Integrating the curriculum* (series). Alexandria, VA: Association for Supervision and Curriculum Development (ASCD).

Jacobs, H. (1999). *Curriculum mapping: Charting the course for content.* Alexandria, VA: ASCD.

Erickson, H. (2002). *Creating concept-based curriculum for deeper understanding.* Thousand Oaks, CA: Corwin Press.

# Integrating the Literary Arts

*I now enjoy Tolstoy and Jane Austen and Trollope as well as fairy tales and I call that growth; if I had had to lose the fairy tales in order to acquire the novelists, I would not say that I had grown but only that I had changed. A tree grows because it adds rings; a train doesn't grow by leaving one station behind and puffing on to the next.*
(C. S. Lewis, 1980)

## Overview

This chapter is the first dedicated to one art form. Integration of the literary arts is examined using the 10 arts integration building blocks and a three pronged focus: *why* literature should be integrated, *what* teachers need to know about literature to integrate it meaningfully, and *how* to plan and implement literature integration.

## Introduction: Literature at the Core

*It's not what we read, but what we remember that makes us readers.*
*(Inez Tennenbaum, South Carolina State Superintendent)*

Arts integration is a heads-on, hearts-on, hands-on learning approach that takes an inquiry-based orientation key to successful comprehension instruction (Cornett, 2010; Kamil, 2004; Moats, 2004). The literary arts are center stage. Daily read-alouds to students, independent reading by students, and guided small group instruction for students are main events. Literature is used to enliven historical eras and give faces to the facts of science. With the availability of wonderful award-winning nonfiction on nearly any topic, science and social studies units no longer revolve around a textbook. Math is not exempt. Authors have discovered that math makes for a great storyline.

In the opening Classroom Snapshot, Amy Weiss uses arts-based read-alouds to "hook and hold" students with literature (McTighe & Wiggins, 2004). Her artful teaching causes students to transform the content of a chapter book using creative problem solving (CPS). The book was selected because of its fit with a social studies unit on families. Ms. Weiss uses at least a half dozen literacy/arts strategies. Count for yourself.

## Classroom Snapshot
### Social Studies/Arts-Based Read-Alouds

Students are seated in learning circles on a worn oriental carpet. There are stacks of red and blue cushions in the center.

"Diamond people, come and pick up four wallpaper books," Amy Weiss announces.

Six students rush to the cushions and rummage through blank books with wallpaper covers. There's momentary commotion as "diamonds" return to their groups.

"Do we get to keep these?" asks one girl.

"Yes! What do you think they're for?" Ms. Weiss asks mischievously. Hands go up. "Phil?"

"To write or draw in?" Phil asks.

"You are right on. These are **Lit Logs** for a core book unit. There's at least a page for each chapter I'm going to read to you, starting right now."

Ms. Weiss flips the overhead on. **"Write Right Away" (WRA)** is written on a transparency.

"We've done this kind of writing before. What do you remember?" Hands go up. "Rich?"

"WRA means just write whatever you think about."

"Exactly. What else do you remember?"

"It gets your brain going," says a tiny girl.

"It's just like a quick write," another girl adds.

"It helps you think because you start with what you know and then think about more as you write. We did it in social studies when we started states and capitals."

"You are right, Shaena, we did," Ms. Weiss says. "Our WRA today is to prepare your brains for the first chapter." Ms. Weiss pulls down the transparency. "Read this title with me." They chorally read, "The Day I Was Born."

"Think about anything your parents or grandparents have told you. Two people in here were adopted, so you might write about when you were first brought home," Ms. Weiss explains. "Open your Lit Logs and write today's date and the title—like I'm doing on the overhead. We'll write about 5 minutes. Questions?"

"Do we need to write in a paragraph?" a girl asks.

"Remember, with WRA, it doesn't matter. This is process writing to get ideas out. Write in any form, even a list. Other questions?"

Seeing none, Ms. Weiss uses **public writing** on the over-head to show how to experiment during writing. She crosses out words, circles others, and uses a caret to insert. Some students watch at first and then start writing. Most look up periodically.

After 5 minutes, she says, "Find a place to stop." She waits and adds, "Let's use **Pairs Share.** With your partner, either read what you wrote or pick out ideas to tell."

Kids hook up in twos. One boy explains how he was a preemie and stayed in the hospital a month. Some read aloud. Ms. Weiss circulates listening, smiling, questioning, and commenting.

"OK, let's come together. Who heard a story that should be shared with everyone?" she asks. Students **volunteer their partners.** One girl tells about the surprise of twins. A boy explains that his partner was born in Korea, but his adopted parents were at the hospital. After a few minutes, Ms. Weiss makes a transition.

"Think about what the **core book** I'll be reading might be about. Remember, literature usually has problems at its core." After a wait time period, she nods and hands go up. She moves to chart paper and picks up a marker. "Arman?"

"It could be about getting born and the problem of no one wanting you." Ms. Weiss writes his idea on the chart. "Tim?"

"Maybe it's about a new baby, and the other kids are jealous."

Several more problems are **predicted and listed.** She then shows the cover of the book *Sarah, Plain and Tall* (MacLachlan). A few children make "oo-oo" sounds.

"How many have read this book or seen the movie?" Two children raise their hands.

"Sandy and Mechelle know the plot, so they already know some connections to our Write Right Away. Get in a comfortable spot, and I'll read Chapter 1. **Try to make different connections.** Afterward we'll discuss what is important in the chapter."

Kids scurry to spots on the rug. Some stretch out. Others grab cushions. Ms. Weiss sits in a rocking chair. She begins to read. She uses **expressive reading.** Her voice is soft at first, and she changes pitch to distinguish characters. Sometimes she reads slowly and pauses. Other times she reads fast. It is almost like she is singing. When she gets to the point where the father says he has received a letter, she stops, lays the book down, and walks over to a board.

"And I have received a response," Ms. Weiss says in a deep voice. She is using **Teacher in Role** to pretend she is Jacob, the father. She takes an envelope from the class message board. It is a stamped letter. She opens it and reads it aloud, still in the character of Jacob. It is a letter from Sarah Elizabeth Wheaton. When she finishes, she puts it in the envelope and walks back to her chair. The class is silent with expectation. Ms. Weiss picks up the book and finishes the chapter. She reads the last line, "Ask her if she (pause)." The class chimes in "sings!"

Ms. Weiss returns to the **"Best Guess"** prediction chart, and students do thumbs up or down about whether each prediction was confirmed or rejected. They then brainstorm important ideas in the chapter as Ms. Weiss scribes ideas on a web: "Missing someone." "Grief." "Wanting to remember." "Being a family." "Loving each other." "Hope." Next, she asks them to do a **Quick Mime** to pretend they are "missing someone." At their places they use facial expressions and body shapes. She **reminds them** that drama and dance require concentration. She points to a chart that lists **Dance Elements** in the categories of body, energy, space, and time (BEST).

"Get a **personal space**. Reach out and make sure you have room. Let's explore some more. I'll count and on three, **freeze in a shape** that shows 'missing someone.'" She counts. The room fills with statues. Many are bent over. Some are curled in a ball on the floor. **Ms. Weiss describes** body shapes and levels they are using. "When I touch you, come alive, look around, and describe shapes and levels you see." She touches five children. They describe curves, angles, and levels of peers. They explore **Frozen Shapes** three more times and then **debrief.**

"You showed unusual thinking. How did the shapes feel?"

"I felt the memory of losing somebody in my arms and my whole body!" a girl says.

"What else?" Ms. Weiss asks.

"I saw lots of us ball up, almost like you have a stomach ache," a boy adds.

"Yeah! I felt like that," another boy piggybacks.

Ms. Weiss uses Frozen Shapes with other ideas from the web. She then leads the class to create a **Dance Machine** around the big idea "Family members each have a different role." Students reflect on Chapter 1, focusing on character actions. One comes up and rolls dough. Another sweeps. A third sits and writes. Eventually, all join the Machine.

"When I say *family*, **add a sound**, and when I say *stop*, just freeze," Ms. Weiss announces. "Ready, *family*." There is a cacophony of giggles and noises.

"I see people really concentrating on body shape and moves," she comments. Giggles subside. The class focuses on being a family machine. Ms. Weiss calls, "stop."

Students return to their Lit Logs to write about an idea in Chapter 1 that means something to them personally. Ms. Weiss writes, too, but this time in her own wallpaper log.

By the end of this unit, the Lit Logs are full of chapter responses and include artwork. Examples of Ms. Weiss's chapter strategies appear in Ready Reference 4.1. See the seed strategy index for more information on strategies. ✺

# What Are the Literary Arts?

*At one point, J. K. Rowling's first three Harry Potter novels occupied the top three spots on the* New York Times *hardback fiction best-seller list. This caused such heartburn among the literati that a best-seller list of children's books was created so that Rowling's books could be banished to it.* (George Will, November 11, 2001)

When the sixth book in the Harry Potter series was released, it broke publishing records. The initial run in the United States was 10.8 million copies. Nearly three out of four kids ages 11 to 13 have read at least one of the books (Hallett, 2005). Harry Potter is a literary phenomenon. What is it about Rowling's books that has turned many nonreaders into readers and causes youngsters to carry them around before they can even read them?

Art is both process and product. The process used to make any art form is creative problem solving. It is the process Rowling used,

## Ready Reference 4.1  Chapter-by-Chapter AI Strategies

The following are AI strategies for the book *Sarah, Plain and Tall* (McLachlan).

1. ***Before.*** Write Right Away (WRA) "Day You Were Born." ***After reading:*** Quick Mime and Frozen Shapes to explore concepts related to theme. Dance Machine on "family" (big idea for social studies unit).
2. ***Before.*** Pretend and Write to Sarah as a character (point of view drama). ***After:*** Compare lists and letters with Sarah's and write back to Sarah. Start Class Museum.
3. ***Before.*** Chain 7 poem about a theme. ***After:*** Hot Sock drama game with key concepts.
4. ***Before.*** Character map Anna. ***After:*** Listen to "Sumer Is Icumen In" and teach song by rote.
5. ***Before.*** Character One Liners (drama). ***After:*** Somebody-Wanted-But-So plot map (Schmidt, in Macon, 1991).
6. ***Before.*** Mini-lesson on poetry elements. ***After:*** Web examples/effects of assonance, consonance, imagery, rhyme, repetition, hyperbole, metaphor, and simile.
7. ***Before.*** Acrostic poem about a character. ***After:*** Revise poem. Make poem posters with colored pencil art. Exhibit in Class Museum.
8. ***Before.*** CAP prediction using key words: *overalls, argument, strange clouds, tears, barn, wait, eerie, hail, drive, glass.* ***After:*** Rainstorm (music energizer).
9. ***Before.*** Colored pencil sketches of key book moment for Class Museum. ***After:*** Tableau of important book scene. View video and Venn diagram literary elements.

---

as did Shakespeare. It is set in motion by the desire to combine ideas and feelings in imaginative ways. The process yields many products: paintings, songs, dances, and, when words are used, literary art. Literature is literary art. It is made, like all art, to convey thoughts and emotions. The intent is to use words artfully.

Literature is structured into different forms or *genre* that range from fables to science fiction, play scripts to alphabet books. The subject matter can literally be anything. A controversial aspect of any art form is its role as a vehicle for truth. Authors are artists who share their truths through the word arts of story and poem.

multiple intelligences, and creativity. The research and theory focus continues in this section, accompanied by beliefs connected to AI philosophy. All are used to justify literature's privileged place in literacy, and a growing presence in math lessons and science and social studies units.

Russell (1994) writes that children's literature should be studied to "bring the advantages and the joys of reading to all children, for without reading the ideas of the past would be lost forever, and we would be forced naked into the world" (p. 16). The following are more reasons to "clothe" students in quality literature.

# Arts Integration Building Blocks

Chapter 3 introduced the arts integration building blocks (see Ready Reference 3.3). The first building block has to do with *why* arts integration should be implemented—philosophy based on research and theory. Next comes *what* teachers should know (art literacy) and *how* to plan, create an aesthetic environment, use literature and best practices, design instructional routines, differentiate instruction for diverse learners, assess, and partner with arts specialists. These building blocks are applied to integrating the literary arts in this chapter.

# Building Block I: Philosophy: WHY Integrate Literature?

In Part I support for arts integration was presented in the forms of research on and theories about learning, cognition, motivation, developmental stages,

Reading the art of a picture book

## Adds Arts Power to Literacy

The search for why some never get the reading habit has been long and intense. Findings suggest that when interesting literature is integral to instruction, students read more and comprehend at higher levels (Guthrie, 2004; also see Research Update 4.2). But, good books do more than teach the skill of reading. The Harry Potter phenomenon gives testimony to the effects of literary artistry on children's reading behaviors. For many this series has been the singular motivation to read above grade level and persist in the face of an intimidating number of pages—not about racking up points or getting stickers. Harry affects readers aesthetically. He has made many into book lovers or "bibliophiles." Thank you, Ms. Rowling.

## Causes Active Meaning Construction

Before I read *Black Beauty* in second grade, it had never occurred to me that someone would intentionally hurt an animal. For months the book's images haunted me, but they also helped me form a value for living things. Like all art, good literature offers the opportunity to construct personal meaning.

"Only connect," was writer E. M. Forster's famous injunction. It applies to AI in general and literature integration in particular. Literature is all about inviting students to use higher order thinking to inquire into possible relationships and connections among the arts, other disciplines, and their own lives. Literature offers the prospect of new and deeper understanding of self, society, and life's themes. Think of great books you've read. Did they not teach something—facts and ideas that connected to your life? Did the authors not use words to build visual and emotional bridges between you and the book?

**Visual Imagery.** Reading provocative literature triggers greater brain activity than television viewing. The mental activity centers around personally relevant visual images that are both satisfying and important to comprehension success (Jensen, 2001; Norton & Norton, 2005; Sadoski & Paivio, 2004). Excessive television may even cause brain atrophy and impair the ability to visualize. The National Center for Educational Statistics

---

### Research Update 4.2  Literature-Based Instruction

- A 7-year study demonstrated the effects of interest on reading achievement. Sixteen low-income K–6 students were tracked. Kids started carrying around Harry Potter books by second grade. By fifth or sixth grade they had read them all. Fourteen of the 16 students achieved or surpassed benchmarks for reading level (Hallett citing Barone, 2005, p. 47).
- Urban second graders taught with literature gained phonics skills equal to those taught with scripted phonics materials. However, the literature-based groups made greater comprehension gains (Wilson, Martens, Arya, & Altwerger, 2004).
- When teachers frequently used literature, third graders developed reading and writing skills at higher levels than when the focus was on isolated instruction in skills such as decoding (Cantrell, 1999).
- Literature approaches, supplemented by decoding lessons, were favored over other approaches in a study of 50 classrooms and 1,000 second graders. Literature groups were superior to controls in achievement gains and reading attitudes (Eldredge & Butterfield, 1986).
- Fifth graders who were taught history using literature showed increased interest in history and significantly enhanced retention of information (VanSledright & Kelley, 1998).
- Third graders who received literature-based reading and science lessons scored higher than controls in reading and science (Morrow, Pressley, Smith, & Smith, 1997).
- Second graders in a literature group had superior performance to those in a basal control group on measures of retelling, story rewriting, and original writing (Morrow, 1992).
- Sixty-three first graders matched with 2,000+ books scored 93 percent on Utah proficiency test (13 points higher than the state standard and 4 months earlier than

"normal"). Reading scores were in the 99th percentile, and most were above grade level (Reutzel & Cooter, 1992).
- A yearlong study of second graders in a literature-based program showed they became highly engaged with books and grew in overall reading, including decoding skills, fluency, and comprehension. They also made gains in written composition (Baumann & Ivey, 1997).
- In New Zealand, a literature-based program for first graders had such impressive results that a nationwide staff development was instituted to prepare all teachers to use the program. Since then the program has been widely used in the United States under the title Reading Recovery (Holdaway, 1982; Pinnell, 1986).
- Boys given hundreds of paperbacks to read and released from making book reports showed significant gains over a control group on measures of self-esteem, attitudes toward reading, comprehension, verbal proficiency, and anxiety (Fader & McNeil, 1976).
- Children in literature-based programs read up to 100 books in a year. In no literature programs students read an average of 7 minutes during reading class and only one or two reading textbooks a year (Anderson, Hiebert, Scott, & Wilkinson, 1985; Hepler, 1982).
- New York City second graders from low socioeconomic backgrounds and a history of academic difficulties were studied during a year of literature integration using read-alouds, independent reading, and book response options. They significantly outscored a control, taught with traditional reading materials, in both vocabulary and comprehension. The study was replicated with the same results (Cohen, 1968).
- Students involved with multicultural literature showed less negative attitudes toward those different from themselves (Pate, 1988; also see *Social Education*, April/May, 1988).

reports that students who watch 1 hour of television per day have an average score of 224 on the National Assessment of Educational progress. Scores fall to 196 with 6 or more hours (1992–2000). That's a 30-point difference. This data suggests students need to be engaged in activities that cause them to generate meaning, not just be passive consumers. Art making, reading, writing, drama, dance, and singing qualify.

## Builds Empathy and Respect for Others

*The world changes according to the way people see it and if you alter, even by a millimeter, the way a person looks at reality, then you can change it.* (James Baldwin).

For decades we've had success stories about using literature to broaden cultural attitudes (Hansen-Krening, 1992). Literature is proving to be indispensable in the fight against xenophobia. Books bring us close to characters of every race, religion, and creed, lessening our fear of the unknown. Given the chance to "walk a mile in the moccasins of others," learners develop empathy. Beyond sympathy, empathy taps aesthetic senses to perceive and understand viewpoints of others. Empathy unites emotion and intellect and is much needed in this time when "getting along" is among our greatest concerns.

Respect for diversity begins with respect for self. Through literature, students discover both differences and commonalities with others. For example, hard work is valued in all cultures and is a character trait that pays off in most literature. It isn't surprising in African trickster stories about Anansi, the lazy spider, we find that laziness gets him nothing but a bad reputation.

## Deepens Understanding

Children's author Katherine Paterson and psychiatrist Robert Coles believe we are on a quest for the "secrets of the universe." From the early myths that explain life's mysteries with gods and goddesses, to new genres, such as science fiction, we have a literary treasure trove to help us consider what we are and imagine what we might become.

Good literature deals with universal concerns and questions about life's obstacles. Literary problems probe human relationships; other times they grow out of conflict between nature and humans. Thus, appealing literature parallels life. When children see literature as "meaningful and complex, they sense its capacity to inform their lives" (Grumet, 2004, p. 67).

Quality literature reveals truths, often beautifully, and in so doing satisfies our need to know. We are persuaded to think about large life questions: "What is good? Right? Wrong? What is my place in the world? What contribution can I make?" Themes emerge from engagement with this thought-provoking, emotional art form. Stories and poems provide readers with tools to both pleasurably gain information and practice use of moral and ethical standards to vicariously solve problems they may likely confront in life.

Who has read *Charlotte's Web* and not felt wrapped in the warm coziness of the barn, or imagined sitting on a stool, watching Charlotte and listening to the sounds E. B. White evokes through his imagery? We can travel back in time or forward to the future through literature that takes us places we may never physically go. As Emily Dickinson explained, "there is no frigate like a book to take us lands away."

## Gives Comfort and Insight (Bibliotherapy)

Just as the disciples asked Jesus why he spoke in parables, so it is reasonable to ask why teachers should use story and poem to teach. From the words of the master teacher comes the answer. Stories give us a palatable way to understand—to realize we are not unique, nor alone, in our suffering. Such insight gives solace. The process of using books to promote insight and give comfort is called bibliotherapy. Stories are believed to "heal the soul" if a person encounters the right one at the right time (Allen, 1999; Cornett & Cornett, 1980). As we vicariously experience a character's joys and struggles, we can empathize or "become" the character and distance ourselves from stressful issues.

Perhaps you had an experience like I had reading Paterson's *Bridge to Terabithia*. I found the characters believable, the premise engaging, and the plot forceful, but it was the use of language that left me envious; I caught my breath and grieved with Jess when Leslie died. When I closed the book, I felt changed, cognitively and emotionally altered, as if a mirror would reflect an altered visage. This was a bibliotherapeutic experience.

While teachers are cautioned not to begin bibliotherapy without careful study, anytime literature is used to give comfort, a degree of bibliotherapy naturally takes place. This is particularly true when teachers use approaches, such as Rosenblatt's (1985) "reader response," which calls for personal connections to stories and poems. Teachers interested in appropriate books and strategies for bibliotherapy can consult references such as *The Bookfinder*. In the meantime, most fine literature will automatically have bibliotherapeutic effects.

## Fulfills Aesthetic Needs

Literature provides for the basic human need for beauty, pleasure, awe, and joy—needs as basic as those for food and shelter, just higher up Maslow's pyramid (1970). When literature is treated as an art form, first and foremost, aesthetic responses go further to motivate through the force of art. Indeed, motivation is cognitive commitment to "extending one's aesthetic experience" (Guthrie, 2004, p. 382). Motivation extends from a sense of engagement in an important task, and it gives energy and direction.

Like other art forms, literature can produce the Stendhal effect. However, children do not automatically gain aesthetic joy from literary experiences. For example, learners who have reading difficulties may not be able to suspend belief, which inhibits imagination (Purcell-Gates, 1988); and imagination is central to comprehension (Cornett, 2010). Children who start school lacking read-aloud experiences may see only a troublesome decoding task ahead as they confront a page of text; halting word identification is no fun. A level of fluency is needed to savor books, and even fluent readers benefit from learning strategies that help them visualize, make connections, and draw conclusions.

## Provokes Higher Order Thinking Used in Problem Solving

Good literature moves us from an egocentric, single perspective into complex abstract thinking. At its core is conflict, which drives the plot. In simple nursery rhymes, conflict may be introduced and resolved quickly, as in "Little Miss Muffet." In three short lines she encounters a problem and solves it. Children use higher order thinking skills or HOTS to make sense of such literary problems. Techniques such as "put your thumb up when you find the problem" engage analytic thinking and help students understand that CPS is called for. Children can be guided further to hypothesize/predict, gather data, and brainstorm solutions as they read and hear stories.

Literature allows students to practice use of higher order thinking within the context of problem solving used in successful family living and in the workplace. Other HOT processes triggered by literary problems include empathizing to take new perspectives, evaluating character actions, and making personal connections to themes. For example, *Charlotte's Web* offers the opportunity to take the role of farmers who raise pigs and must kill them to make money to feed and clothe their families. Primary children are thus able to gain facility at seeing alternative points of views using literary problems that connect to life. Teachers scaffold such life-literature connections by (1) using think-alouds to demonstrate higher order processes (Lehr, 1991), (2) participating as inquirers, not experts, during discussions, and (3) offering choices of how to respond to literature (Tompkins & McGee, 1993, p. 15).

## Stimulates Moral Thinking

Teaching values is a sensitive issue for schools. However, no one denies that children must learn right from wrong and come to understand and behave using shared values for honesty, initiative, responsibility, and so forth. Actually, value-free lessons are virtually impossible. In particular, the content of the arts, including literature, is personal perspectives, which are by nature value laden. Authors intentionally and unintentionally weave personal beliefs into words.

Literature integration offers a chance for students to use personal values to think about and respond to conflicts inherent in stories. From Aesop's fables to *Goosebumps*, authors create characters that act in ways that reveal the author's take on right and wrong. Literary discussions inevitably give rise to moral dilemmas, which provide opportunities to discuss alternative viewpoints. Literary texts offer a chance to sort out thoughts and feelings under safe circumstances. In this chapter and the next, discussion and response strategies are described that target discussions that stretch thinking using a variety of strategies. Students can learn to question and comment using evidence in text-based discussions, connect to experiences others may not share, and do creative extrapolations of "what if?" *Note:* Provocative literature produces questions about censorship issues. Teachers should prepare by using the resources of the American Library Association (www.ala.org).

## Reveals Cultural Heritage

History and culture have long been passed on through story. Storytelling is an ancient art that grew from the need to make sense of the world. Our rich literary treasury is the product of a continuous search for truth and a celebration of the human need to create and consume art. For example, on the surface, Lewis Carroll's "Jabberwocky" is wonderfully alliterative nonsense. We smile and enjoy the pure sound of it. Then we wonder at Carroll's creativity as he causes sense and nonsense to collide. His feelings for words are illuminated, his command of his craft revealed, and we think differently about what makes sense.

Through poems and stories, children become privy to bittersweet lessons and can view a landscape of previously unimagined possibilities in literary themes. Students come to understand how good can drive evil underground through the courage of a single individual like Rosa Parks, the subject of numerous biographies. No history text will ever make us feel the pain of war as acutely as Crane's *The Red Badge of Courage*. No science book will ever reveal the poetry of the universe the way Seymour Simon's picture books do. No lecture or character-building activity can bring home moral lessons more effectively than the world's collection of folktales. And who has read Jules Verne's *Twenty Thousand Leagues Under the Sea* and not marveled at how his imagined inventions became reality these many decades hence?

## Increases Literacy

High correlations link amount of literary experience with linguistic development. Good readers emerge. For example, literary read-alouds increase vocabulary and give opportunities to assimilate complex sentence patterns into speech and writing (Chomsky, 1972; Purcell-Gates, 1988). Children who start school with hundreds of read-alouds under their belts (up to 5,000 hours) know that "book language" is different from regular talk. People just don't normally go around saying things like "hickory dickory dock." The rhyme, rhythm, and repetition of Mother Goose attune the ear to language sounds. Dr. Seuss's creative distortions of rimes and onsets, vowels and consonants present phonological concepts necessary to successful reading development. Children immersed in literary experiences simply grow to value reading more and are fortunate to have a found a pleasure that can last a lifetime (Sostarich, 1974; Trelease, 1995).

**Story Structure.** Through "lap reading" children hear the musical elements of language and allow the expression of meaning. They also come to understand how stories are made with the building blocks of plot, character, and theme. This concept forms the bedrock for understanding any story and doing original writing. Even preschoolers can discover motifs, such as the recurring patterns of "threes" in fairy tales (e.g., three pigs and three tries) and the presence of very bad and very good characters. Children who have had a wide range of literary experiences come to expect good to triumph and can get annoyed with modern fairy tale versions that spare evildoers. Read-alouds also help children develop the "concept of reading," which poor readers often lack. How invisible people speak through print is pretty strange, but those who do not achieve this concept remain foggy about why they should learn to read. No clear concept equals no real motivation to become a reader.

**Writing.** Artists are quick to admit they "ape the greats" they have read. Indeed, the kinds of books we read can dramatically affect how we write. Children need to see themselves as artists who create word art as they write. They do so when they try on for size strategies employed by adept authors and artists who represent ideas in innovative ways. Exposure to works with well-developed literary elements allows children to assimilate writing techniques; students write with higher quality and use more complex sentences, variety of literary forms, and poetic devices such as rhythm, rhyme, and repetition (Dressel, 1990; Tompkins, 2003). For example, my 5-year-old niece, Sarah, heard Wanda Gag's *Millions of Cats* and was moved to write her own book about her sister going in search of a dog. Mimicking, but modifying, Sarah's character returned with "billions and zillions and pavilions of dogs."

## Is a Learning Vehicle for Social Studies, Math, and Science?

It is no coincidence that within the word *history* is the word *story*. The most exciting history teacher I know now lives in the mountains of North Carolina. In retirement he continues to do what he did his whole teaching career—tell compelling stories about men and women who changed the world. Bob contends that history is but a jumble of lifeless facts without its stories, as is science, math, art, theatre, and dance. Integrating literature throughout the curriculum literally means bringing in the stories that give life to numbers, verbs, dates, and names. Fiction and nonfiction allow teachers to engage students in study of important academic content with compelling results. For example, sixth graders who read historical fiction recalled more history than those who used the social studies text (Levstik, 1986).

How can quality literature be found to serve as a vehicle for content learning? Available source books and websites categorize picture books on nearly every topic or skill. Other sources match fiction and informational books to social studies and science. Ready Reference 4.9, later in the chapter, lists example sources. Additional sources and examples of high-quality literature categorized by science, social studies, and math are described in Chapter 5.

## Combats Illiteracy and Aliteracy

Illiteracy afflicts about one-fifth of American adults, rendering them incapable of reading newspapers, job applications, and food labels. Millions more *can* read, but do not. These "aliterates" never developed a love of stories, poetry, or plays—what David Russell calls "belletristic reading." Bookless individuals suffer a poverty of mind and spirit; they miss reading experiences that

can change a life. Hyperbole? Consider actor Walter Matthau who claims that the book *The Secret in the Daisy* by Carol Grace caused him to change from "a miserable, unhappy wretch to a joyful, glad-to-be-alive human." He says he fell so in love with the book he "searched out and married the girl who wrote it" (Sabine & Sabine, 1983, p. 136).

### Materials Matter.

> *I lik reding, but not workshits.* (Doug, second grader)

Educational researcher Marilyn Adams likes to say in her talks, "If they can do the worksheet, they don't need it. If they can't, it won't help them." Boring, unnatural texts are not part of the solution to the literacy problems that now afflict one in five children. Standardized tests are currently the hot ticket to gauge literacy progress. What do they show? Vocabulary and comprehension are learned well when good literature is plentiful and opportunities to write imaginatively are frequent. Students gain up to 4 years in reading in 1 year when literature is the core of the reading program. In addition, attitudes toward reading are more positive when trade books replace basals and workbooks (Five, 1986; Reutzel & Cooter, 1992; Tunnell & Jacobs, 1989). The results of using literature-based approaches in special education are also encouraging (Allen, Michalove, & Shockley, 1991; Roser, Hofman, & Farest, 1990). This is significant because the bulk of learning disabilities involve literacy difficulties.

**Matthew Effect.** Literacy expert John Guthrie (2004) explains that one of the most well-established findings in reading research is that comprehension is an outgrowth of a wide range of purposeful, motivated reading activities. His fellow literacy expert, Dick Allington, puts it this way: Students who read the most read the best (2005). Good readers read 10 times more than poor readers. In one first-grade study, low readers averaged 16 or fewer words per week versus high readers who read 1,933 words (Samuels, 2002).

The label for this phenomenon is the Matthew effect, which is a biblical allusion to the "rich get richer" verse. Alarmingly, less than 1 percent of children now read in their spare time. The National Center for Educational Statistics reported that the number of 17-year-olds who say they hardly ever read a book rose over 100 percent in the last 20 years (2005). Another grim statistic is from the American Library Association which reports that only 5 percent of the population checks out library books. While many people now do considerable reading on the Internet, the previous statistics serve to remind us to not assume that because we teach students *to* read, they will automatically enjoy it.

Good literature can create a taste for particular genres and authors and students can be taught to relish literature. Literature integration, within an AI context, gets at the roots of illiteracy and aliteracy. The arts, including the literary arts, can stimulate the senses, challenge the intellect, and touch the heart. A childhood spent in experiences with Pooh, Max, and Harry makes it likely that literature will be a lifelong close companion.

Rockin' with Harry Potter

# Building Block II: Arts Literacy: Literary Content and Skills

> *When I was ten, I read fairy tales in secret and would have been ashamed if I had been found doing so. Now that I am fifty I read them openly. When I became a man I put away childish things, including the fear of childishness and the desire to be very grown up.*
> (C. S. Lewis, 1980)

Much of what we call civilization and culture is preserved in art created by past generations. Ancient human history recorded in shadowy cave drawings and haunting stone sculptures are prized. These telling artifacts have extraordinary beauty, but they also allow us to glimpse our past. Unfortunately, huge quantities of music and dance have been permanently lost because they could not be recorded. Much literature, which began as oral art, had the same fate. We can imagine early ancestors huddled around flickering campfires telling stories of heroes on noble quests, adventures of clever animals, acts of foolish peasants, and the search for perfect love. Mixed with dance, mime, and song, the literary arts are believed to have their origins in these tales. Stories that have survived do so because of retelling. Primitive societies used these stories to both entertain and instruct, just as we do today. Remnants of a vast oral tradition are preserved today in written versions of fables, rhymes, proverbs, and parables.

## What Teachers Need to Know

Literary knowledge is necessary for meaningful integration. It includes background in the following:

- History and definitions of children's literature
- Literary elements
- Literary genres, forms, or types
- Selection sources for good literature
- Authors and artists of children's literature
- *National Standards for the English Language Arts*
- Literary meaning-making strategies, especially how to read and write literature
- Approaches to teaching literature as content

## History of Children's Literature

Today, high-quality literature is widely available. Thousands of books are published in the United States each year, with more than 5,000 considered children's literature. How did we come to have such a surfeit of this specialized literature? All art reflects the milieu in which it was created, and so it is with children's literature. Attitudes toward children and schooling evolved in response to political, social, religious, and economic forces. Between Aesop's fables and Harry Potter lie centuries of changing beliefs about childhood and education, mirrored in stories and poems. Until "childhood" was recognized, there was no literature specifically for children (Darigan, Tunnell, & Jacobs, 2002).

Imagine children eavesdropping by ancient hearths to hear tales meant for adult ears—journeys plagued with horrific beasts with magical powers. Even Aesop's fables were not originally meant for the young. Children appropriated stories that appealed to them, ones with animal characters, fast action, and swift justice. Early adult books were also assimilated. For example, *Robinson Crusoe* (1719), with its captivating characters and high adventure, could not be passed up. Today it is included in children's literature. Nineteenth-century children also gobbled up Stevenson's *Treasure Island*, which created a voracious appetite for more realistic fiction. We continue to delight in new genres divined by creative authors. It is odd to imagine that ones such as science fiction did not always exist.

Like most art, children's literature has evolved a dual purpose: to offer aesthetic enjoyment and to instruct. At times the didactic purpose has overshadowed the aesthetic. Authors and publishers still struggle to maintain balance for an audience made up of children who are particularly vulnerable to the power of art.

## Definitions and Characteristics

Two features distinguish children's literature from other literature: (1) It is intended for a young audience, and (2) unlike adult literature, it nearly always holds out a degree of hope. Hope is offered even in death: When Charlotte dies we know she will live on in her spider children. While much of art offers some hope, even if it's the hope born of expanded perspective, children's literature seems to have a greater degree. The following definitions may help clarify children's literature.

". . . an art form, as are painting, sculpture, architecture, and music. . ." (Russell, 1994, p. 212)

". . . all instances in which language is used imaginatively. . . Literature speaks of the mysteries of the human condition, although in books for children, treatment of these themes is adjusted according to the age-related interests and capacities of the audience. . ." (Cullinan, 1989, p. 8)

". . . the main characters themselves are often children, and often more emphasis is placed on the actions than on the thoughts of the characters. . . The book becomes a child's book when children read, enjoy, and understand it. . ." (Glazer, 1997, pp. 5–7)

**Literary Elements.**   The elements of plot, theme, character, point of view, and style (Ready Reference 4.3) are used to both write and understand literature. Decisions by authors can create memorable literary writings as well as forgettable works. How so? These elements are merely tools in the creative process. It is the artistry that makes the magic. By giving students tools, techniques, and materials to work with, we provide them with the means to read and write creatively. Literary elements are also indispensable tools when it comes to understanding the unique features of genre and subgenre. Teachers need a thorough grounding in literacy elements in order to teach students how to comprehend, respond to, and create good writing.

**Theme.**   Theme *is* the unifying truth in literature. When we read and write stories and poems, we construct private meanings. These messages form literary themes, which are value-laden conclusions that tie a story together. To find them, ask, "What is the story really about?" Go beyond theme topics. For example, *Charlotte's Web* is about friendship. To pull a theme statement together, ask, "What about friendship?" One answer is "Good friends stick by you during tough times." This is an important big idea. Writers reveal themes in two ways, explicit and implicit themes.

*Explicit themes* are directly stated. These are present as morals in fables. An explicit theme statement from *Charlotte's Web* is: "Life is always a rich and steady time when you are waiting for something to happen or to hatch" (White, 1952, p. 176).

*Implicit themes* are not directly stated; they are implied truths that can be inferred by reading closely and considering the characters' actions and outcomes. The previous theme statement about the topic of friendship is implied in *Charlotte's Web*.

Themes can also be uncovered by asking, "What does the author seem to believe?" If the writer implies, "We only show courage when we are afraid," then characters, plot, and other elements should unite to support this big idea. Note that themes are not story retellings. They are value-based conclusions about life and the world.

**Plot.**   Plot is the order of events. The question "What happened?" gets at the plot. Plot action is usually set in motion by a

---

**Ready Reference 4.3**   Literary Elements

*Theme:* the unifying truth or universal message in literature
  *Key question:* What is the story or poem really about? (Go beyond a topic to a complete truth statement—a big idea.)

- Explicit theme statements: messages directly or literally stated
- Implicit theme statements: indirectly stated truth statements

*Plot:* the order of events set in motion by a problem or conflict
  *Key question:* What happened?

- Four types of conflict: between (1) character and nature, (2) character and society, (3) character and another character, or (4) within a character
- Types of plot patterns: (1) linear three-part series: introduction-development-conclusion (includes climax and denouement); (2) cumulative: events build on one another; and (3) episodic: mini-stories tied together
- Plot variations: cliffhangers, flashbacks, foreshadowing

*Character:* person, animal, or object taking on a role
  *Key questions:* Who is it about? Who wants something? Who has a problem? Who changes the most?

- Ways characters revealed: (1) descriptions, (2) their actions, (3) their speech and thoughts, and (4) what others think and say
- Types: protagonist/antagonist, round or flat/stock, dynamic or static, foil, stereotype

*Setting:* the time and place
  Key questions: When and where does the story take place?

- Types of settings: scenery backdrop or integral
- Aspects: place or location, time or time period, weather
- Primary world: real world
- Secondary world: a created world used in fantasy

*Point of view:* the vantage point from which a story is written
  *Key questions:* Who is telling the story? How?

- First person point of view: uses "I" to tell the story
- Omniscient or third person: all-knowing, using third person
- Limited omniscient: omniscient but only a few characters
- Objective: events reported with no interpretation

*Stylistic or poetic elements:* words for artistic effect
  *Key question:* How are words used in special ways?

- Figurative language is the use of words to stand for other things: imagery, personification, metaphors, connotation and denotation, motifs, archetypes, symbols, and allusions.
- Mood is the feeling created. Mood is related to the tone.
- Irony is saying or doing the opposite of what is meant.
- Humor is the simultaneous juxtaposition of sense and nonsense to produce a surprising result.
- Sound and musical features of style include rhyme, rhythm, repetition, alliteration, consonance, assonance, and onomatopoeia.

*Assonance:* repetition of vowel sounds any place in a series (e.g., note the vowel sounds in "soul" and "hole" in "Concentrated is my soul in my molar hole when I have a toothache" [Sigmund Freud])

*Onomatopoeia:* use of words that sound like their meanings such as *zip* and *clap*

## Genre: Literary Forms

In human history, millions of pieces of visual art and music have been created and millions more stories and poems. To fathom this immense creative storehouse, it is necessary to group it. Literature can be classified by *age* of intended audience (baby books), *topic* (humor, travel), *problems* (disease, aging), and *length* (novella, short story). Each is useful in planning lessons. Going further, however, we find divisions of a different sort. Poetry and prose represent distinct bodies of writing, with poetry among the oldest valued writing and a genre all its own. Prose also covers a wide range of forms, subject matter, and style; it can be narrative or expository, fiction or nonfiction. Fiction can be subdivided into traditional literature, realistic, fantastic, historical, and contemporary. What is left is nonfiction, which includes informational books from alphabet books to biography. Of course, literature is created by humans, who defy classification. The reality is much literature fits into more than one area. For example, there are picture books in every genre that are enjoyed by adults, as well as children.

Literature integration focuses on providing rich aesthetic literary experiences to children and teaching students to create meaning use word art. Genre knowledge (Ready Reference 4.4) makes the following contributions to these goals.

1. It helps plan for diverse experiences so students develop flexible literary "tastes."

2. It provides categories to teach students how to think about texts. Genre knowledge enables us to make better predictions before reading and help comprehension during reading by providing story structure scaffolds that explain how characters act, how the plot will unravel, and so forth.

3. It increases options for forms of writing students can choose. Knowledge of genre patterns is a tool that allows writers to create within accepted structures and invent new genres, such as ones that combine characteristics of several genre.

**Poetry.**   Poetry is a genre very different from prose. In particular is features (1) compact and emotional language; (2) rhythm, rhyme, and other sound patterns created by alliteration and repetition; and (3) metaphor and other figurative language. Children respond to these characteristics of poetry long before they are conscious of their impact. Through nursery rhymes, Dr. Seuss, and other word play, babies learn to enjoy language. Poetry attracts attention, makes us want to move, and gives comfort. The joyous language play of preschoolers is sustained when teachers know quality poetry to use and have strategies to meaningfully integrate it throughout the day. Of special importance is knowing kinds of poems children enjoy and how to broaden interests.

*Poetry elements* are used in every genre and are included in the literary element of style (Ready Reference 4.3). Poets use these elements and the following structures to give life to words.

*Verse* is a line of poetry or a stanza, particularly one with a refrain. Verse also refers to light-hearted poems.

*Stanza* is a grouping of several lines together.

*Meter* relates to repeated patterns such as beat and accent.

*Rhyme scheme* is usually coded. For example, abab is a four-line poem with lines 1 and 3 rhyming and lines 2 and 4 rhyming.

*Blank verse* is unrhymed iambic pentameter (Shakespeare uses it). An iamb is the accent pattern "dah DAH," as in "Do what?" Iambic pentameter is 5 iambs.

*Free verse* does not use traditional meter or stanza patterns.

*Lyrical* poetry is flowing, descriptive, and personal; it follows no pattern and can be set to music—hence the word *lyric* in both music and poetry.

*Narrative* poetry tells a story. It usually has no refrain. Hiawatha is an example. *Ballads* are narrative poems with short stanzas, with or without music.

*Sonnets* are 14 lines long, often in iambic pentameter, and with the rhyme scheme abab cdcd efef gg.

---

## Ready Reference 4.4   Nine Genres and Example Subgenres

**Poetry:** Couplet, limerick, concrete or shape, diamante, haiku, free verse

**Traditional:** Folktales, Mother Goose rhymes, proverbs and parables, fables, myths and legends, tall tales

**Fantasy:** Animal, toy and tiny-being tales, modern folk and fairy tales, science fiction, high fantasy, time fantasies, horror

**Realistic fiction:** Contemporary stories about sports, animals, survival, school, and family; also includes historical fiction, mystery; often occur in a series

**Informational:** Factual writing about art, music, dance, theater, ecology, psychology, sexuality, and technology; also includes alphabet books, counting books, concept books, biography, and autobiography

**Picture books:** Combine visual art and text, but can be wordless stories (all art); available in all genres

**Humor:** Combines sense and nonsense using structures such as jokes, riddles, tongue twisters, spoonerisms, hink-pinks, Tom Swifties, palindromes, and chants

**Predictable:** Can be in any genre; follows a highly repetitive pattern that appeals to young children

**Multicultural:** Can be any genre, but presently is dominated by folktales from diverse worldwide and international groups, with emphasis on Native Americans and those groups who have immigrated (by choice or force) in large numbers to the United States (Asians, Mexicans, Africans)

**Interest.** Children's interest in poetry usually declines without teacher intervention (Kutiper & Wilson, 1993). Teachers can maintain and expand interest with narrative poetry that uses rhyme, rhythm, and humor. Light verse can be used as a bridge to more diverse poetry that extends perception of "good" poetry beyond rhyming and cute. Through aesthetic experiences children can learn how poets express strong ideas and feelings using many word tools and many forms that may or may not use rhyme.

**Writing Poetry.** Poetry patterns are scaffolds anyone can use to experiment. Ready Reference 5.2 lists ones appropriate for children. By using CPS strategies, such as data gathering and brainstorming, students can learn to generate ideas before writing, and then experiment with word images. It is helpful to begin with writing poems collaboratively, showing students how to try topics other poets use. Teacher-directed discussions can lead students to see how poem patterns vary and sound patterns can be created without rhyme (e.g., assonance). Ready Reference 4.5 lists well-known poets.

**Traditional Literature.** Folktales reveal truths that endure over time and across cultures. The names of the creators of most are now lost; they are anonymous rhymes, fairy stories, myths, legends, and tall tales that predate the printing press. But the "old stuff" remains popular, along with modern versions, such as "feminist" tales like Yolen's *Sleeping Ugly*.

*Folktales* are passed down orally. (*Note:* Folk*lore* is the beliefs and customs of a society.) This subgenre includes fairy tales, cumulative stories, and talking beast, noodle head, and fool stories. Point of view is omniscient and characterization is flat and static and often includes archetypes: a wicked stepmother or cunning animal (Frye, 1957). Settings are vague, with time and place referred to as "long ago" or "in a land before time."

*Fairy tales* include magical objects, spells, wishes, and transformations. Characters are either ordinary humans or humanlike animals transformed because of kindness or sacrifice. The plots involve unfortunate heroines rescued by true love, and characters are often flat and static. They contain stock characters such as witches and giants. Themes involve good overcoming evil, perseverance, and hard work. The style uses conventional openings and closings, repetition, and archetypes like the colors red, white, and black, dark forests, and water.

*Cumulative tales* have a unique plot structure; characters or objects are added in a chain. Animals occur often and sometimes rescue humans. These tales frequently include food, such as large vegetables, as in *The Enormous Turnip* (Tolstoy).

*Talking beast stories* have anthropomorphized animals. There is usually a lesson at the end, much like a fable. The conflict involves a confrontation between characters who are flat—good or bad, stupid or clever. An example is the *Three Little Pigs*.

*Trickster tales* have a character who outsmarts others. Tricksters often take animal forms, such as B'rer Rabbit in the Uncle Remus stories or Anansi in African tales.

*Noodlehead or fool tales* involve characters who are stupid or clever, good or bad. Foolish decisions result in silly consequences. These tales are full of absurdity and can be like a roller-coaster ride, but by the end everyone is happy.

Examples of folk and fairy tales are as follows:

Aardema, V. (2008). *Why mosquitoes buzz in people's ears.* Dial.
Climo, S. (1992). *The Egyptian Cinderella.* HarperCollins.
Trivizas, E. (1997). *The three little wolves and the big bad pig.* Aladin.

*Fables* are brief stories with stated morals or themes. The most well-known are Aesop's fables from Greece. Main characters are one-dimensional personified animals that are strong or weak, wise or foolish. The plot centers on one event and the setting is a barely sketched backdrop. Conflict is between characters. Lobel's *Fables* is a contemporary example.

*Nursery rhymes* include Mother Goose rhymes and other light verse, chants, and songs. They are usually short and full of action and memorable characters, such as Old King Cole and pencil-thin Jack

## Ready Reference 4.5 Well-Known Poets

### Excellence in Poetry Award
Every 3 years, the National Council of Teachers of English recognizes a poet. Recent recipients are Lee Bennett Hopkins (2009), Nikki Grimes (2006), and Mary Ann Hoberman (2003). Other recipients are X. J. Kennedy, Eloise Greenfield, David McCord, Aileen Fisher, Karla Kuskin, Myra Cohn Livingston, Eve Merriam, John Ciardi, Lilian Moore, Arnold Adoff, Valerie Worth, and Barbara Juster Esbensen.

The Newbery Medal has gone to two poetry books: *A Visit to William Blake's Inn* (Willard) and *Joyful Noise: Poems for Two Voices* (Fleischman).

*Horn Book Magazine* and the *Bulletin of the Center for Children's Books* regularly review poetry.

### Websites
Academy of Poets (www.poets.org): information about poets, poems, lesson plans, and additional links

Children's Choices (http://reading.org/): also available yearly in October issue of *Reading Teacher*
Scholastic (http://teacher.scholastic.com/)

### Children's Favorites: Examples
*Humor:* Edward Lear, Lewis Carroll, Shel Silverstein, William Jay Smith, and John Ciardi (all at http://poets.org/)
*People, Place, and Problems:* David McCord: http://factmonster.com/ipka/A0760972.html
*Animals:* T. S. Eliot: http://poets.org/; William Blake: http://poets.org/; Jack Prelutsky
*Nature:* Robert Frost: http://poets.org/; Byrd Baylor; Paul Fleischman: www.indiana.edu/~reading/ieo/bibs/fleisp.html
*Emotions:* Langston Hughes: http://poets.org/; Cynthia Rylan; Alfred Noyes: http://poets.org/

Sprat. Themes have to do with everyday worries and struggles such as single parents with children to feed. Like much original traditional literature, they are full of violence and death, from drowning to decapitation. Beautiful lines are also found, such as "Over the hills and far away" and "One misty moisty morning when cloudy was the weather." Classic collections include:

> De Angeli, M. (1979). *Marguerite De Angeli's book of Mother Goose and nursery rhymes.* Penguin.
> dePaola, T. (1985). *Tomie dePaola's Mother Goose.* Putnam.

**Myths** feature gods and heroes with supernatural and magical powers. Myths explain natural phenomena, such as the origin of the world and seasons. Pourquoi (French for "why") tales explain how the tiger got its tail or how Native Americans got horses (e.g., Yolen's *Sky Dogs*). Settings are barely sketched.

**Legends** are usually based in facts about a person who did something important. Over time the character achieves hero status and the great deed is embellished. DePaola's *The Legend of the Indian Paintbrush* is an example.

**Epics** are long narratives or poems about legendary figures. "The Iliad" and "The Odyssey" are Greek epics, and "Beowulf" is a Norse epic.

**Tall tales** are based on actual people. Exaggeration is the distinguishing feature. Tall tales are relative newcomers to traditional literature, with the most well known from North America, including Paul Bunyan, Pecos Bill, Johnny Appleseed, and John Henry.

**Fantasy.**   This modern genre features the impossible. Its timeless quality has provided us with classics such as *Alice in Wonderland* and *Harry Potter*. In fantasy, imaginary worlds come to life. The setting is integral—time and place significantly affect plot action. Readers have to suspend belief and feel that strange worlds can exist. For example, in Anderson's classic *Three Hearts and Three Lions* characters live in a world where magic rules. Themes are lofty, dealing with truth and goodness. Good destroys evil, usually through struggle and suspense. Sometimes characters have supernatural traits. A few are round and dynamic, like Anderson's hero, Holger, but most are flat and static, firmly on one side or the other of the "dark." Point of view is often omniscient to give needed background. All this is especially true of high fantasy and science fiction. The plot is usually linear and features impossible events and magical objects. Usually the hero is forced into a quest (e.g., find a magic sword) and pulled into some threatening world. Trials forge the hero's character, but a protector often helps out. When the hero's spirit is finally honed, she or he goes home. Campbell's (2008) *Hero with a Thousand Faces* is a classic book about these common traits. The subgenres of fantasy overlap.

**Animal fantasy** uses personified animals such as Charlotte who protects the hero pig. Old and new classics include:

> Camillo, K. (2006). *The tale of Desperaux.* Scholastic.
> Grahame, K. (1966). *The wind in the willows.* Companion Library.
> Selden, G. (2008). *The cricket in Times Square.* Square Fish.

**Toy or tiny beings** are the peculiarity of this subgenre. Pinocchio comes to life to grow a long nose. Inch-high borrowers live under the floor and snatch things in Norton's *The Borrowers*. Other favorites include:

> Banks, L. (2010). *The Indian in the cupboard.* Yearling.
> Van Allsburg, C. (1981). *Jumanji.* Houghton Mifflin.

**Modern folk and fairy tales** use the elements of oral tales, but are written works with identifiable authors. Examples include:

> Calmenson, S. (1991). *The principal's new clothes.* Scholastic.
> Thurber, J. (1998). *Many moons.* Fitzgerald.

**Fantastic events, situations, or imaginary worlds** use exaggeration, the ridiculous, and imagined settings. In Dahl's *James and the Giant Peach*, an unhappy child travels inside a huge peach, and in the Never Land of Barrie's *Peter Pan*, one never grows up. Other classics include:

> Carroll, L. (2010). *Alice's adventures in Wonderland.* Collins Design.
> Sendak, M. (2010). *Where the wild things are.* Scholastic.
> Van Allsburg, C. (2005). *The polar express.* Houghton Mifflin.

**Time warp** fantasy distorts time, so Tom can enter a special garden from the past in Pearce's *Tom's Midnight Garden*, and a Connecticut man is carried back to Camelot in Twain's *Connecticut Yankee in King Arthur's Court*. Others not to be missed include:

> Babbitt, N. (2007). *Tuck everlasting.* Square Fish.
> Rohmann, E. (1997). *Times flies.* Dragonfly.
> Yolen, J. (2004). *The devil's arithmetic.* Puffin.

**Science-fiction** fantasy is set in the future and relies on science fact and fictional inventions, often extensions of modern technology. A classic is L'Engle's *A Wrinkle in Time*. Classics include:

> Norton, A. (1984). *Cat's eye.* Del Ray.
> O'Brien, R. C. (1986). *Mrs. Frisby and the rats of NIMH.* Aladin.

**High fantasy** is a subgenre with characteristics of romance. The forces of good and evil collide in ultimate confrontations. And old and an new classic include:

> Lewis, C. S. (2000). *The lion, the witch, and the wardrobe.* Collins. (Narnia series).
> Rowling, J. K. (2009). *Harry Potter and the deathly hallows* (last in series). Scholastic.

**Horror** stories speak to our urge to be a little afraid—under safe circumstances. The *Goosebumps* series is a popular example, as is Schwartz's *Scary Stories*.

**Realistic Fiction.**   These stories mirror reality and are popular among children. The content can be controversial. Some books deal with death, drugs, AIDS, homosexuality, and gangs. However, tame series such as the Hardy Boys are still popular.

Realism uses a variety of plot patterns, including flashbacks, which stretch out problem resolution. First-person child-narrator point of view is common, especially in young adult books, which gives immediacy and helps with reader identification. Other points of view are found, however. Themes usually relate to modern life with the real-world settings. Characters are lifelike and fully developed with conflicting emotions and motives.

**Contemporary realism** is set in current time. The settings resemble places in the lives of children. DiCamillo's Newbery award book, *Because of Winn-Dixie*, is an example, as are Bunting's *Smoky Nights* and Jukes's *Like Jake and Me*.

**Historical fiction** is a subgenre of realism with a setting in the past and in specific regions of a country (the South, Appalachia). These stories allow readers to vicariously live history and appreciate others different from themselves. For example, Polacco's *Pink and Say*, set in the Civil War, gives historical information, but uses invented dialogue to forge emotional connections to real people and events. Historical fiction should only be used to teach history if (1) it has an authentic setting and accurate details and (2) makes clear it is fiction (i.e., aspects are invented). Historical fiction often reflects as much about the time in which it was written as about the time written about. This means readers need to keep the viewpoints at the time of the publication in mind. A good example of this is Twain's *Huckleberry Finn* in which language is used that was acceptable at the time. The 2000 Pura Belpre award winner, *Esperanza Rising* (Ryan) is a fine example.

**Informational Books.** These are factual stories about people and natural phenomena that allow readers to learn about life literally and aesthetically. The story is important, but so is accuracy of information and illustration. A picture book example is *Seabiscuit* (Shehata & McElwee, 2006).

General informational books are how-to and "all about it" stories about a process or topic in the sciences, social studies, arts, and so forth. This genre is the place to look for resources on authors and artists. For example, *Talking to Faith Ringgold* is a picture book that shows how to think about and make art.

*Concept books* give information in simple form by showing relationships between objects and actions. Basic facts about colors, shapes, and letters are presented, often with striking art and humor. Many are art-based, such as *Mouse Paint* (Walsh, 1989) and *So Many Circles, So Many Squares* (Hoban, 1998).

*Biography* is a factual account of someone's life written by another person. *Autobiography* results when someone writes about his or her own life. For a biography to be authentic, facts must be documented and characters, dialogue, or scenes are actual, not invented. Biographies may deal with a part of a life, and some attempt a complete recounting. Either way, a good biography gives a sense of wholeness within a certain time and place. Famous actors, inventors, artists, composers, dancers, and sports icons are the focus, usually with the plot centering on overcoming obstacles. The best brings the person to life by presenting a balanced picture, rather than an unrealistic, one-dimensional character. Texts are often extended by illustrations, as in Freedman's *Lincoln, a Photobiography*.

Real-life characters are role models who give opportunities to "try on" occupations and lifestyles so children need honest representations of both genders and faces and races of the world. The potential for solid information giving about different people makes biography an important way to increase tolerance in our youth. A recommended website for information on over 25,000 great people is Biography (*www.biography.com/*).

*Biographical fiction* is both realistic and fanciful. Based on fact, it includes invented dialogue or events. Some degree of fictionalizing occurs in most children's biography, but should be pointed out to children. Many videos, DVDs, and audiotapes of authors and artists are available with biographical books (e.g., Nichol's *Beethoven Lives Upstairs*).

**Picture Books.** Art and text each play an integral role in conveying meaning in these books. In some cases, the artwork tells the whole story (wordless books). Picture books are written in diverse genre, from poetry to biography, but in contrast to other genre, they are classified by appearance. For today's children bombarded with visual images, picture books are an important fine art experience. More flexible viewpoints emerge when children learn to examine diverse picture book art that uses a range of styles and media.

**Book Parts.** Picture books are good tools to teach "book parts" such as title and half title pages, borders that may be used to tell a side story, and gutters that connect two pages and are important in double-page spreads. Endpapers are immediately inside the front and back covers of a book and may be used to set mood with art. Of course, art styles and media used by the picture book artists are key teaching points. Chapter 6 has ideas for teaching art concepts using picture books. A website that explains the anatomy of picture books, gives a time line, and has a glossary is Picturing Books (*www.picturingbooks.com/*).

Tremendous change has occurred in picture book art during the past 50 years. Illustrations now portray positive multicultural images and make art integral to the story rather than a decoration. Baby board books, pop-up, and other toy books continue to be popular. An important award is the Caldecott Award (*www.ala.org*), created in 1936 to recognize the picture book genre. Picture books are available for all ages. Even wordless picture books exist for all levels; for example, *The Silver Pony* (Ward) is a wordless chapter book. Other examples of popular wordless books are Day's *Good Dog, Carl* and the *Anno* series.

Illustrations should be examined to see if they date otherwise timely content. Note how the art interfaces with the mood and tone of the story. Question the degree to which the art does the following:

1. Elaborates on the setting, plot, characterization, and theme (What do art elements such as color, line, shape, and texture contribute to meaning?)
2. Foreshadows events and shows action
3. Shows detail (Are the details accurate and nonstereotypical?)
4. Uses media (collage, photography, etc.) to develop setting, plot, characterization, and theme
5. Creates a mood appropriate to the art's style
6. Interacts with the actual print on the page
7. Plays an integral role in the book (Norton, 2003)

**Humorous Literature.** Humorous books and poems top the lists of children's favorites so this category is not to be laughed at. Laughter is an important safety value and blasts us with new perspectives. When used to uplift and elevate, not denigrate or devastate, humor can enrich and energize (Cornett, 2001). See Ready Reference 4.11 later in the chapter for bibliographic sources. Examples of books of pure humor, such as word play, jokes, riddles, and tongue twisters, include:

Agee, J. (2006). *Why did the chicken cross the road?* Dial.
Mauterer, E. (2005). *Laugh out loud: Jokes and riddles from Highlights.* Boyds Mills.
Rosenbloom, J. (1986). *Silly school jokes and riddles.* Sterling.
Schwartz, A. (1974). *A twister of twists, a tangler of tongues.* Deutsch.

**Predictable Books.** With release of research showing children more easily read with materials using a repetitive structure, teachers have clamored for such literature. These books also provide patterns for writing and unique features.

**Repeated Phrase, Sentence, or Refrain.** These stories often have a musical or poetic quality. In Martin's *Brown Bear, Brown Bear,* a rhythmic question is repeated, "Brown Bear

Brown Bear, What do you see?" In Barrett's *Animals Should Definitely Not Wear Clothing,* the title repeats.

**Word Play and Rhyme.** These books have predictable word patterns or poetry elements (e.g., couplets or internal rhymes) as in Cameron's *I Can't Said the Ant* and Gwynne's *The King Who Rained* (idiomatic expressions).

**Predictable Plots.** In Charlip's *Fortunately,* a boy has both fortunate and unfortunate events in his life.

**Cumulative.** These stories have a series of words or events that repeat and build to a climax. The process is then usually reversed, as in Wood's *The Napping House.*

**Concept Books.** These informational books on the alphabet, numbers, colors, shapes, and days often are predictable (e.g., Anno's *Counting Book* and Elting's *Q is for Duck*).

### Multicultural and International Literature.
I recently saw a photo of a fourth-grade class in Los Angeles, California. The names and faces reinforced how the United States is a nation of multiple cultures.

The term *multicultural* is used to refer to minorities outside the sociopolitical mainstream, including African Americans, Asian Americans, Native Americans, and Hispanics (Bishop, 1992). Multicultural literature and art also include works from regional and religious groups (e.g., Appalachian, Moslem). Multicultural and international books (first published in other countries) exist in every genre and are increasingly well represented by picture books, such as the 1997 Caldecott winner *Golem,* a Jewish folktale. As a symbol of our growing respect for the culture of minority groups, this area is set apart as a separate literary category (Faltis, Hudelson, & Hudelson, 1997).

Of course, all children need to read and see images of diverse types of people. Children's cultural differences need to be acknowledged, and multicultural literature offers validation. Multicultural literature is now available about most centers of civilization, but concerns persist about stereotypical language and images, inappropriate retellings, and the small number of books published on some cultures. Key to quality is how well characters and culture are portrayed and the accuracy, amount of detail, and extent to which language or text perpetuates stereotypes (Norton & Norton, 2005). The International Board on Books for Young People (*www.ibby.org/*) publishes a quarterly journal, *Bookbird: World of Children's Books,* to help teachers find appropriate literature. A website that includes advice and criteria for choosing multicultural books is *http://teacher .scholastic.com/products/instructor/multicultural.htm.* For more bibliographies and reviews, go to the Multicultural Children's Literature site (*www.ncrel.org/sdrs/areas/issues/educatrs/presrvce/pe3lk28.htm*).

The National Council of Social Studies website provides bibliographies of recommended books in the following categories.

**African American.** Traditional African American literature has its roots in cultures, such as Swahili, Mali, Zulu, and Ashanti. Many stories were brought by slaves to America and retold, some mixed with Caribbean stories. These tales flourished and evolved; for example, Anansi, the trickster spider from the Ashanti, became "Aunt Nancy" in some tellings. Brer Rabbit stories, collected by Joel Chandler Harris in the 19th century, were traced to the African tradition of cunning animal characters. This literature is rich in themes about perseverance, beauty, and generosity and has

engaging language. For example, Bryan uses chanted verse in *Beat the Story Drum, Pum-Pum,* a collection of pourquoi tales. Set in Zimbabwe, *Mufaro's Beautiful Daughters: An African Tale* (Steptoe) is a Cinderella tale and a Caldecott honor book. Noteworthy traditional and contemporary books include:

> Hoffman, M. (2007). *Amazing grace.* Frances Lincoln. (realistic fiction)
> McKissack, P. (1997). *Mirandy and Brother Wind.* Dragonfly Books. (fantasy)
> Medearis, A. (1994). *The singing man.* (fiction, CSK Honor Book)
> Myers, W. D. (1997). *Harlem.* Scholastic. (poetry)

**Native American.** There are more than 300 tribes in North America from the plains and eastern woodlands, to the southwestern deserts. Together with Canadian cultures, these groups have a vast store of art and ritual, and a nearly 30,000-year history of storytelling (Norton, 2005). Despite distinct differences, there are common patterns: (1) creation myths (how the world arose from chaos), as in Bruchac and London's *Thirteen Moons on a Turtle's Back;* (2) family myths about kinship; (3) hero myths (young hero is a trickster until he gains virtue, usually through a quest), such as *Anpao: An American Indian* Odyssey (Highwater), which is an award-winning collection of myths; and (4) rites of passage myths (involve crossing in and out of a dream state) (Bierhorst, 1976). Contemporary and traditional examples include:

> Endrich, L. (1999). *The birchbark house.* Hyperion. (Ojibwa/ historical fiction)
> Goble, P. (1990). *Iktomi and the ducks: A Plains Indian tale.* Orchard.
> Pollock, P. (1996). *The turkey girl: A Zuni Cinderella story.* Little Brown.
> Rafe, M. (1998). *Rough-faced girl.* Putnam. (Cinderella tale)
> Seattle, C. (2002). *Brother Eagle, Sister Sky: A message from Chief Seattle.* Puffin. (Suquamish)

**Hispanic American/Latino.** Spanish-speaking children are the largest and fastest-growing second-language learners in the United States (Faltis et al., 1997). Unfortunately, Hispanic literature can be hard to find. This stems from confusion over the many settings to which the term alludes: islands of the Caribbean and Puerto Rico, South America, and Mexico. Some prefer the term *Latino* (Norton, 2005). Noteworthy books include:

> Bernier-Grand, C. (2005). *César: Sí, se puede! (Yes, We Can!).* Marshall Cavendish. (poetry about Cesar Chavez)
> Farmer, N. (2002). *The house of the scorpion.* Simon & Schuster.
> Ircon, F. (2005). *Poems to dream together. Poems para sonar juntos.* Lee & Low. (poems written in both Spanish and English)
> Reich, S. (2005). *Jose! Born to dance.* Simon & Schuster. (biography)
> San Souci, R. (1998). *Cendrillion: A Caribbean Cinderella.* Simon & Schuster.

**Asian American.** This literature includes stories and poems from Japan, Vietnam, China, India, the Philippines, and Pacific Rim countries. Examples are scarce and books may stereotype characters devoid of individual traits (e.g., *Five Chinese Brothers*). Positive examples are *Yeh-Shen: A Cinderella Story from China* (Louie, 1982) and Yep's *The Rainbow People,* a collection of folktales from Chinatown. Fine examples include:

> Demi, T.-S. H. (trans.). (1994). *In the eyes of the cat: Japanese poetry for all seasons.* Holt.
> Huffman, J. (trans.). (1999). *The cat who lived a million lives.* University of Hawaii Press. (Japan)
> Park, L. (2001). *A single shard.* Houghton Mifflin. (Korea)

Say, A. (2004). *Music for Alice.* Houghton Mifflin/Walter Lorraine. (Japan)
Staples, S. (2000). *Shiva's fire.* Farrar, Straus & Giroux.
Whelan, G. (2000). *Homeless bird.* HarperCollins. (India)

**Other Areas of Diversity.** Many religious cultures are increasingly represented in children's books. Examples include:

Bell, H. (2003). *Flame.* Simon & Schuster. (Persian legend)
Highwater, J. (1994). *Rama: A legend.* Holt. (Hindu)
Macaulay, D. (2003). *Mosque.* Houghton Mifflin. (Islamic)
Rylant, C. (2007). *A fine white dust.* Aladin. (Protestant)
Wisniewski, D. (1997). *Golem.* Clarion. (Jewish)

*International books* are from or about other countries. An example is Fox's *Possum Magic* (Australia). A growing group of fine books is being translated. Classics not to miss include:

Bjork, C. (1987). *Linnea in Monet's garden.* R & S. (Sweden)
Gallaz, C. (1985). *Rose Blanche.* Creative Education. (France)
Maruki, T. (1982). *Hiroshima no Pika.* Lothrop, Lee & Shepard. (Japan)

# Building Block III: Collaborative Planning

In Chapters 1 through 3, the concept of levels of integration was introduced using the concept of teaching *with, about, in,* and *through* the arts. This idea should guide literature integration. The goal is to co-plan to get beyond using books primarily for entertainment, literacy skill development, or as prompts for artificial copycat writing. To do this, teachers need to teach students how to *use* literary knowledge to increase reading comprehension and to inform the written composition process in a genuine manner. Beyond the *about* and *in* is teaching *through* literature. This involves using literature and literary writing as tools to make sense of science, social studies, math, and the other arts. Unit structures and planning models described in Chapter 3 are important for meaningful literature integration.

## National Standards: Literary Arts

The National Council for the Teachers of English Language Arts (NCTE) and the International Reading Association (IRA) collaborated to develop literacy goals that embrace the literary arts. The result is a set of broad standards statements of what students should know and be able to do. The standards are used at both state and local levels to develop curriculum and construct assessments. Ready Reference 4.6 lists the National Standards for the English/Language Arts.

The standards are starting points that make clearer literature integration possibilities for units and lessons. Note that actual pieces of literature are not listed. State and local standards and courses of study give additional information about key concepts and skills expected of students, often divided into grade groupings.

---

**Ready Reference 4.6** ## Standards for the English/Language Arts*

*Overall focus:* Literacy growth through experience and experimenting with the language arts and other communication forms, with focus on diverse texts, especially literary works.
  Goals: Students will do the following:

1. **Read a wide range of print and nonprint texts** (fiction and nonfiction, classic and contemporary works, including digital texts)
2. **Read a wide range of literature from many periods in many genres** (understand the human experience through literary works from all genre and time periods)
3. **Apply a wide range of strategies to comprehend, interpret, evaluate, and appreciate texts** (coordinate higher order thinking strategies to make sense of texts, including visual imagining, text feature cues, and responding to literature in diverse ways)
4. **Adjust use of spoken, written, and visual language: vocabulary development, variety of audiences for a variety of purposes**
5. **Employ a wide range of strategies as they write:** writing process, patterns from books read, different audiences and purposes
6. **Apply knowledge of language structure, language conventions, media techniques, figurative language, and genre to create, critique, discuss print and nonprint texts** (creating meaning through use of literary and visual art elements and patterns of writing)
7. **Conduct research on issues and interests by generating ideas and questions and by posing problems: gather, evaluate, and synthesize data from a variety of sources; use literary experiences to solve problems; seeks out books for personal information**
8. **Use a variety of technological and informational resources: libraries, databases, computer networks, and video**
9. **Develop an understanding of and respect for diversity in language use, patterns, and dialects** (multicultural literature, including poetry sharing)
10. **Participate as knowledgeable, reflective, creative, and critical members of a variety of literacy communities** (discussions and conversations, oral sharing of poetry, evaluating literary and artistic merits of books, books clubs)
11. **Use spoken, written, and visual language to accomplish their own purposes** (oral interpretation of poetry, writing in different genre, book making, arts responses, reading for enjoyment, storytelling, developing literary preferences)

---

*Copyright 1996 by the International Reading Association and the National Council of Teachers of English. Adapted from 12 Standards, as applicable to AI. Ideas in parenthesis following standards represent the author's interpretation.

## Integrated Units

AI units focus on life-centered themes and questions, are adapted for student interests and needs, and make arts processes (e.g., CPS) and concepts integral to making sense. Literary methods and content are used to enable students to construct conclusions (big ideas) about concepts ranging from justice, to power, and human rights. Whereas science and social texts offer explanations, literature offers the lives of people. For example, in a core book study using a fine biography such as Russell Freedman's *The Voice that Challenged a Nation: Marion Anderson and the Struggle for Equal Rights* (2004) students are emotionally engaged as biography puts face and feelings to facts and allows readers to vicariously experience life as a black person in the early 20th century. Readers become detectives, mining for clues about how African Americans struggled for equal rights, and can relive the pivotal moment in 1939 when Anderson gave her landmark performance on the steps of the Lincoln Memorial.

**Unit Structures.** Literature-based units can be planned for time blocks ranging from several days a month, or a year-long study in a schoolwide unit. Common unit centers are (1) core or single literary work such as a poem or story, (2) a literary genre, (3) a person, usually an author or poet, (4) a topic/issue, and (5) an event. For example, *Sarah, Plain and Tall* (MacLachlan) was the core work for the opening Classroom Snapshot. Any genre can be a focus, with works studied to discover shared genre traits. An author and artist of a picture book are frequently the organizers for a unit on a person. A topic or real-life issue, usually connected to science or social studies, is often used as an organizing center (Chapter 3 has examples). Finally, event-based units may start or culminate with an author visit, attending a play based on children's literature, or seeing a film version of the book (e.g., *Because of Winn-Dixie).* An author–artist unit planning web appears in Planning Page 6.14. Information sources and guidelines for artist–author studies appear in Planning Page 4.7.

All unit centers are developed using the process outlined in Chapter 3 with focus on writing big idea theme statements and important questions to guide study. Ready Reference 3.7 shows the unit planning process and Planning Page 3.8 depicts nine-legged planning to integrate curricular areas. Planning Page 4.8 shows how one teacher planned a core book study on *Millions of Cats* starting with themes about making choices.

**Field Trip or Literary Event.** The most common literature event used to organize a unit is a visit by a children's author or book illustrator. Scheduling and preparing for author visits is discussed under Building Block X. Literary field trips can also include visits to art museums to compare artworks with picture book art, public libraries to hear storytellers or talks about special collections, newspaper offices to understand publishing, or studios of artists and writers. Of course, field trips can be an event that connects to any unit, from fairy tales (e.g., a play based on *Cinderella*) to death rituals (e.g., cemetery field trip). The field trip guidelines in Appendix H can help ensure trips are meaningful and integral to learning.

## Planning Page 4.7
### Author–Artist Study Sources

**Websites**
See websites at the end of this chapter.
Link to popular author and illustrator sites through the following:

Kid Space: www.ipl.org/div/kidspace/ (author information, including FAQs and photos)
KidsReads.com: http://kidsreads.com (information about favorite books and authors)
Reference librarians can give access to Thompson Gale's research site: www.gale.com

**Popular Author–Artists: Example Websites**
Barbara Cooney: www.carolhurst.com/authors/bcooney.html
Tomie dePaola: http://tomie.com
Susan Jeffers: www.susanjeffers.com/home/index.cfm
Ezra Jack Keats: http://lib.usm.edu/~degrum/keats/main.html
Robert McCloskey: http://falcon.jmu.edu/~ramseyil/mccloskey.htm
Chris Van Allsburg: www.chrisvanallsburg.com/redirect.html
David Wiesner: www.houghtonmifflinbooks.com/authors/wiesner/home.html

**Book Sources**
Estes, G. (1987). *Dictionary of literary biography, American writers for children.* Gaci.
Hopkins, L. (1995). *Pauses: Autobiographical reflections of 101 creators of children's books.* HarperCollins.
McElmeel, S. (1992). *Bookpeople: A multicultural album.* Libraries Unlimited.
McElmeel, S. (1993). *An author a month (for dimes).* Teacher Ideas Press.
McElmeel, S. (2004). *Children's authors and illustrators too good to miss.* Libraries Unlimited.
McElmeel, S. (2006). *Authors in the pantry.* Libraries Unlimited.
Rockman, C. (ed). (2008). *Tenth book of junior authors and illustrators.* Wilson.
Roginski, J. (1989). *Behind the covers: Interviews with authors and illustrators of books for children and young adults.* Libraries Unlimited.
*Something about the author: Facts and pictures about contemporary authors and illustrators of books for young people.* (1971–2006). Gale Research. Online at: www.gale.com/ebooks.
*A state-by-state guide to children's and young adult authors and illustrators.* (1991). Libraries Unlimited.

## Special Connections

What's a hornbook? Ever heard of a battledore? Both are early forms of children's books and provide child view entrees into early American history. Of course there is science in bookmaking, including how inks, paper, the printing press, and other machinery were invented. Then there is math. For example, Poe used mathematical formulas in his poem *The Raven.* Do not

## Planning Page *4.8*

### Core Book: CPS for Comprehension

The following problems require students to "think through the arts" to make meaning from the story *Millions of Cats* (Gag). The focus is using CPS to find and create themes/ big ideas.

#### Music Problems

1. *Fluency:* Change pitch, tempo, and dynamics for the refrain to match the mood. Try crescendo and decrescendo, solo, and group voices.
2. *Word choirs:* Each group chooses an important emotion or word from the story and decides how to say it. One student is the conductor and indicates how the group is to respond (e.g., piano, forte, repeated, choral).
3. *Put to music:* Create a melody for the refrain. Decide how to sing it (1) when the Old Man first sees all the cats, (2) when the cats eat and drink up everything, and (3) when the Old Woman sees them coming. Change musical elements to show emotions.

#### Visual Art Problems

1. Emotion Art: List key emotions under beginning, middle, and end. Choose an important emotion and think of several colors, shapes, and lines associated with it. Make abstract art that shows your thinking. *Variation:* Choose an important moment in the story.
2. Select one page from the book to study closely. Talk or write about the details you observe: What do you see (types of lines, shapes, lack of color)? How does the art make you feel? How did Gag make the art (techniques, media)? Why did she organize it the way she did (composition)? What is communicated in the art that was not in the words?

#### Drama Problems
**(OW = Old Woman; OM = Old Man)**

1. Use pantomime (body shapes and moves, facial expressions, gestures) to show . . . three things OW did while OM was away or things the cats did before he arrived.
2. Use pantomime to show how OM and OW felt at the beginning, when OM saw all the cats, when OM was trying to decide, and how the cats felt when OW said they should decide.
3. One liner: Take a character role (change voice using musical elements) and say a sentence to show thinking and feeling at an important moment. Use body shape to show the character. Do not say who you are or be obvious with what you say.
4. Tableau: Work with a group to create a frozen picture about a theme. In other words, create a "composition" using only your bodies and faces. *Variation:* Take turns "coming alive" to say a one liner, in character.

#### Dance Problems

1. List ways characters moved in the BME. Examples: trudge, climb, wait, work. Explore each using *BEST* elements (e.g., trudge fast, slow, high, low, lead with different body parts).
2. Transformation: Create a dance that shows a how a character changed from the beginning to end of the story (e.g., lonely to not lonely). Start in a frozen shape to show the emotion. Plan dance movements to an 8 count. End the dance (frozen) to show contrast from the beginning.

#### Poetry Problems

Write a poem about important ideas or emotions in the story. Adapt a poem pattern (lune, syllable, bio, haiku, etc.). Example: CLERIHEW (abab): Old Woman and Old Man/Were very lonely/The solution they planned/Left one cat only.

---

ignore the economic influence of children's books from book selling, to publishing and advertising, to a career in writing.

## Two-Pronged Lesson Plan

The concept of the AI lesson framework, with at least a two-pronged focus (an art form and another curricular area) was introduced in Chapter 3. This framework includes a predictable teaching sequence: introduction, development, and conclusion (IDC). The structure is used to plan and teach lessons that integrate literature with other curricular areas. Planning Page 4.9 shows an example.

## Building Block IV: Aesthetic Literary Environment

Teachers who love literature show it. Their classrooms are stocked with books from every genre and reading level. Book nooks are lined with pillows. Sofas, rockers, and reading lamps make the classroom feel like a "living room." Teachers add claw-foot bathtubs, telephone booths, Conestoga wagons, and lofts as intriguing places to read. The chalk tray becomes a display for "books of the week" with enticing advertising slogans, such as "A dog with an attitude. Read: *Officer Buckles and Gloria*" (Rathman). Special pages can be tabbed for "sneak peaks." Other book displays, connected to units, promote choices for independent reading. Poem charts are pinned on clotheslines, ready for poetry routines. Poetry walls are posted with student favorites. Poem pockets, made from library pockets and shoe bags, invite students to add one or take one for a personal anthology collection.

## Print-Rich Environment

We tend to "own" what we help create, so it is important for kids to participate in the design of the classroom. Invite students to bring in their own posters and quotes that celebrate reading. I start every year with a student-made collage of images they find of people reading and writing torn from magazines and newspapers. A routine that allows them to share well-loved poems and family stories extends ownership. Students can root out

## Planning Page 4.9

### Literature and Social Studies (Third Grade)

**Two-Pronged Focus**
1. Literary elements/concepts: point of view (POV), informational genre (authentic versus fictionalized biography)
2. Social studies big idea: historical record depends on who is "telling the story"

*Standards:* 3, 6, and 11 (Ready Reference 4.6)
*Student Objectives:* Students will be able to do the following:
1. Give the POV of books using examples.
2. Give reasons why an informational book is authentic or fictionalized and tell why knowing this is important.
3. Explain how POV is important in life.
4. Use POV to write about an event from two perspectives.

*Materials:*
- Four copies of three books:
  Yolen's *Encounter* (Columbus's landing in 1492 from the point of view of a native islander)
  Columbus's diary entries in *The Log of Christopher Columbus*
  Dyson's *Westward with Columbus* (third-person informational)
- Ocean music (any CD of waves) and one copy of Hoban's *Look Again*

**Teaching Procedure (S = Student(s))**
**Introduction**
1. Thumbs up if you know a Cinderella story. Group and give each a role: mice, stepsister, stepmother, father, neighbor, king. Use teacher in role to interview. Ask, "What happened?" Ask about the answers. Why were they different?
2. Show visual: "POV is point of view." Show pictures in *Look Again* and ask S to guess what they are (close-ups of ordinary objects). Ask S to relate this to POV. Ask volunteers to describe the classroom from the POV of a bug on the ceiling, a kindergartner, the principal, an eighth grader.
3. Ask how POV and perspective make a difference in real life.

4. Tell S they will be using POV and perspective to think about the social studies unit on "exploration and discovery" and that writing workshop will be about this next week.

**Development**
1. Ask what S knows about Columbus. Record comments on chart.
2. Show covers and a few pictures from the three books. Use predict–prove strategy. Focus on POV each might take. Show rest of POV chart with the different types and examples.
3. Explain that the books are fact based, but authors sometimes make up dialogue or characters to add interest. Show "Informational genre: Authentic biography and fictionalized" transparency and explain. Tell S they will buddy-read during independent reading using a choice of the Columbus books. The goal is to find out the POV and clues about whether the book is authentic or fictionalized. Number off in pairs. Number 1 picks book and gets with partner to read for 15 minutes. Give evidence chart to pairs to record findings.
4. Pull together three groups based on three books. Share evidence charts. Circulate to give feedback and coach to find more evidence from books (actual details).
5. Assemble all and ask one from each group to report findings on POV and subgenre decisions. Compare with predictions on chart. Add new information about Columbus.

**Conclusion and Informal Assessment**
1. Ask S to tell one thing (TOT) they learned about POV and authentic versus fictionalized biography. Ask S to write down something they predict will happen in the book (buddy reading will continue) and a question they have about Columbus. Collect questions.
2. Tell S to think about a real event, at school, home, in the news, to write about using a different POV. Ideas will be webbed at the start of writing workshop. Point out displayed books written from different perspectives (e.g., *The True Story of Three Little Pigs* by A. Wolf).

---

writers and readers in their families to "make public" how the literary arts are alive outside of school. Children are proud to find uncles and aunts and dads who are bibliophiles—voracious readers who make wonderful classroom guests to interview.

Even if the school has a wonderful library, the classroom is closer. When literature collections exist in classrooms, students read 50 percent more than those in classrooms without collections (Morrow, 2003). A classroom needs several hundred trade books. If the school does not provide these, teachers can collect books in inexpensive ways, for example, send home a letter asking for used books (list criteria), go to tag sales, buy from book clubs such as Scholastic and Trumpet (teachers get bonus books), or ask the PTA to conduct a book drive (set limits on what can

be contributed). Of particular importance is obtaining multiple copies of books for core book studies. This means enough copies for small groups to read the same book (six to eight copies) or class sets. In addition, teachers need to accumulate class "text sets" of literature around yearly units. For example, text sets of 15 to 25 books, stories, and poems are created for topics such as weather and for genre studies of fairy tales. No teacher starts off with such book wealth, but by targeting one or two units a year, the collection grows.

Books are commonly stored in colorful crates labeled by genre or topic: informational, realistic, plants, animals, and so forth. Readability levels can be indicated with color-dot on book covers, but keep in mind book levels are flexible. Interest, happily, can overthrow any leveling system and enable children to exceed assessed expectations.

# Building Block V: Literature as a Core Art Form

The nature of children's literature, its ready availability, and its decades-old history of integration, especially in the literacy program, make it a core art form. The goal of literature integration is to infuse *artful* literary products into literacy, science, math, social studies, and arts lessons—to immerse students in aesthetic experiences with words. So many books, genre, and elements mean many decisions about teaching reading and writing. Decisions should not hinge on finding just any books that connect to units in superficial ways. Planning for literature integration has to involve considerations of what makes quality.

## What Makes Literature Art?

As with any art, literary evaluation can be difficult and is to some extent personal. It begins with considering criteria for judging quality. School media specialists and children's librarians at the public library are specialists who can help cull artful books that can be meaningfully connected to units from the thousands now available. Equally important is for students to be taught to think in terms of literary quality. Anchor concepts help. Three important interlocking criteria are creativity, unity and balance, and taste.

**Creativity.**   A key question is, Are literary elements used in original ways? Remember from Chapter 2 how a creative idea is not "entirely new," but a twist or substitution. The author needs to use the ordinary literary elements of characters, setting, plot, and style in *extraordinary* ways. Are they varied to create a story or poem that seems to be both a new invention and a close friend? Or are the characters dull, the plot tired, or the style cliché?

Quality literary works have an imaginative energy that makes them seem alive. In the final analysis there is the question of the degree to which new insights are provoked, that is, meaning made. So we must ask, Are there strong universal themes, motifs, and archetypes embedded within the work? Creative literature provides us with a sense of rejuvenation and hope born of a capacity to surprise and delight with insights into themes and big ideas.

**Unity and Balance.**   In quality literature, literary elements work in concert to make an integrated whole. Characters may be believable and fascinating, but they need a plot that intrigues and an appropriate setting. Beautiful words that go nowhere soon frustrate even the most poetic soul, and a well-drawn setting without compelling characters to act in it seems a frill. As with all fine art, good literature is provocative; it is creative invention that disturbs our cognitive universe. Enduring truths about people and the world are subtly unveiled, not rammed down our throats. We must feel that the author has unified the elements to allow readers to make discoveries rather than be victimized by didacticism.

**Taste.**   Adults risk alienating children by forcing classics and award-winning books on them without considering taste. A book

can be high in creativity, unified, and balanced, but still not be beloved. Judging art always includes personal taste, which has to do with what we like, feel comfortable with, and suits us at this moment in our lives. Judging literary quality must include thinking about a right fit for individuals. We cannot expect everyone to want a house designed by Frank Lloyd Wright just because his is considered great architecture. Literary critics consider series books such as the *Bobsey Twins* to be mediocre and formulaic, but they are as popular now as they were in the 1950s and are joined by *The Babysitter's Club* and *Goosebumps* books. A taste for series books satisfies comfort needs we all possess and many children need some escapist reading. That doesn't mean we shouldn't ease them into more interesting books through read-alouds, book talks, book displays, and more. Interest is piqued by exposure so literary tastes can be expanded through teacher interventions.

Ready Reference 4.10 has additional criteria that can be simplified for use with children. In particular, it is worthwhile to have students contribute to an ongoing list of what they think makes particular books, stories, and poems good and great.

## Selection Sources

Ready Reference 4.11 and 4.12 list selection sources teachers can use to locate appropriate literature. The following are also important tools to find good literature for units (core book, author or genre study, topic or event based); connected to student interests, including bibliotherapy aids; and to match reading levels.

**Award-Winning Literature.**   The American Library Association (*www.ala.org*) gives two well-known children's book awards: the Newbery and the Caldecott. The ALA site lists the most recent winners. Carol Hurst's Children's Literature website (*www.carolhurst.com*) is also excellent. Access lists of all awards at her site plus book reviews, author/artist links, lesson plans, and bibliographies of books by grade levels and curricular areas.

**Newbery Medal Award (1922+).**   This award is presented by the ALA to the U.S. author of the most distinguished contribution to children's literature published during the preceding year. An award winner and runner-up honor books are chosen. The 2009 winner was *The Graveyard Book* by Neil Gaiman, illustrated by Dave McKean (HarperCollins). In 2008, the award went to *Good Masters! Sweet Ladies! Voices from a Medieval Village* by Laura Amy Schlitz (Candlewick), and in 2007, to *The Higher Power of Lucky* by Susan Patron, illustrated by Matt Phelan (Simon & Schuster).

**Caldecott Medal Award (1936+).**   The ALA awards this medal to the artist of the most distinguished picture book published in the United States in the preceding year. Only U.S. residents or citizens are eligible. The 2009 winner was *The House in the Night* illustrated by Beth Krommes, written by Susan Marie Swanson (Houghton Mifflin). In 2008, the award went to *The Invention of Hugo Cabret* by Brian Selznick (Scholastic), and in 2007, to *Flotsam* by David Wiesner (Clarion).

**Coretta Scott King Awards (1969+).**   These awards (sponsored by the ALA) commemorate Martin Luther King Jr. and his wife, Coretta, for promoting peace and brotherhood. They are restricted to African American authors' and illustrators' contributions.

## Ready Reference 4.10  What Makes Good Literature?

*Directions: Evaluate a piece of literature using these criteria. Rate from 1 = very evident to 5 = not evident. Indicate 2, 3, or 4 for ratings in between. NA = not applicable.*

### Plot

_____ 1. Conflict is clear and believable.

_____ 2. Gains momentum from the conflict.

_____ 3. Does not depend on coincidence.

_____ 4. Is original versus dully predictable.

_____ 5. Raises suspense by withholding problem solutions.

_____ 6. Uses subplots and/or flashbacks to enhance, not just complicate.

_____ 7. Uses climax to hint at conflict resolution.

### Theme

_____ 1. Possesses universal truths that can be understood on more than one level.

_____ 2. Contains subthemes that support main theme/big idea.

_____ 3. Causes reader to confront a problem, that is, see life as it might be.

_____ 4. Avoids imposing values, prejudices, and opinions.

### Characters

_____ 1. Reveals characters' nature through:
   _____ a. Physical description
   _____ b. Actions
   _____ c. Speech and thoughts
   _____ d. Others' thoughts and words

_____ 2. Develops more through action than description.

_____ 3. Are believable, original, and consistent (age, background, ethnicity).

_____ 4. Causes protagonist to change or grow.

_____ 5. Uses foils and flat characters in novel ways.

_____ 6. Avoids stereotypes.

### Setting

_____ 1. Sets stage for action with key details and background.

_____ 2. Develops time and place with references to well-known sites and language use.

_____ 3. Uses details that are appropriate to the time and place.

### Point of View (POV)

_____ 1. Reveals characters using appropriate POV.

_____ 2. Contains objectivity appropriate to the reader's maturity.

### Style

_____ 1. Matches language to characters and intended reader audience.

_____ 2. Uses artistic and creative language.

_____ 3. Creates mood effectively.

### Conclusions

What are your overall reactions?
How do the literary elements work together (unity/balance)?
How creative is the work?
How well written is the work?
Did you like it? Why or why not?

---

Recognized in 2009 was the arts-based book *Bird* written Zetta Elliott and illustrated by Shadra Strickland (Lee & Low); in 2008, *Elijah of Buxton* by Christopher Curtis (Scholastic), and in 2007, *Copper Sun* by Sharon Draper (Simon & Schuster).

**Carnegie Medal (1937+).** The British Library Association gives this award to the author of the most outstanding children's book first published in English in the United Kingdom.

**Hans Christian Andersen Award.** This international award is given every 2 years and is sponsored by the International Board on Books for Young People. A living author is honored along with a living illustrator.

**Mildred Batchelder Award (1968+).** This ALA award goes to the most outstanding books originally published outside the United States in a language other than English and then translated.

*Orbis Pictus Award* **(named for the world's first picture book).** The National Council for the Teachers of English gives this award to an author for excellence in children's nonfiction published in the United States.

**Awards Bibliographies.** *Children's Books: Awards and Prizes* from the Children's Book Council (CBC) summarizes most awards, even ones given by other countries and states in the United States. For example, Ohio gives the Buckeye Book Award each year.

**Authors and Artists.** Sources for biographical and other information, especially for units that focus on these special people, are listed in Planning Page 4.7.

**Children's Favorites.** Children's Choices are lists of "best books" selected by children. The list is published annually in the October *Reading Teacher* (International Reading Association, *www.ira.org*).

**Literary Canon.** Classic literature is "news that stays news" (Ezra Pound) and includes books that have endured the test of time. The significance of the theme, credibility of the characters, reality of the conflict, and an engaging style explain why some books remain in circulation. These books fill human needs to know, belong, and experience beauty. Horn Book (*www.hbook.com*)

## Ready Reference 4.11   Selection Sources for Literature

Use to find bibliographies for genre and topic studies, author and artists units, read-alouds, bibliotherapy, and age groups. Check Teacher Resources at the end of the chapter.

### Websites

American Library Association: www.ala.org/ala/alsc

Best Children's Books: www.best-childrens-books.com/childrens-books-about-handicaps.html (books featuring handicapped characters)

Children's Book Council: www.cbcbooks.org

The Center for Children's Books: ccb.lis.uiuc.edu/collection

### Books

*A to zoo: Subject access to children's picture books,* 4th ed. (2001). Bowker.

*Accept me as I am: Best books of juvenile nonfiction on impairments and disabilities.* (1985). Bowker.

*Adventuring with books: A book list for pre-K and grade 6.* (2002). NCTE.

*Award-winning books for children and young adults.* Scarecrow. (annual publication)

*Best books for children: Preschool through 6.* (2005). Libraries Unlimited.

*Beyond picture books: A guide to first readers.* (2007). Libraries Unlimited.

*Books kids will sit still for: The complete read-aloud guide,* 2nd ed. (2006). Libraries Unlimited.

*The bookfinder: A guide to children's literature about the needs and problems of youth aged 2–15.* (1993). American Guidance.

*Books to help a child cope with separation and loss.* (1994). Bowker.

*Children's books: Awards and prizes.* (2005). Children's Book Council.

*Children's books in print.* Bowker. (annual edition)

*Choosing books for children, a common sense guide.* (2000). University of Illinois.

*The elementary school library collection: A guide to books and other media.* (1998). Brodart.

*More exciting, funny, scary, short, different, and sad books kids like about animals, science, sports, families, songs, and other things.* (1992). American Library Association.

*Hear no evil, see no evil, speak no evil: An annotated bibliography for the handicapped.* (1990). Libraries Unlimited.

*A Hispanic heritage: A guide to juvenile books about Hispanic people and cultures.* (1991). Scarecrow.

*The literature of delight: A critical guide to humorous books for children.* (1993). Bowker.

*More notes from a different drummer: A guide to juvenile fiction portraying the disabled.* (1984). Bowker.

*Pass the poetry please.* (1998). HarperCollins.

*Science and technology in fact and fiction: A guide to children's books.* (1980). Bowker.

---

## Ready Reference 4.12   Poetry Book Examples

### Single Poet Collections

Adoff, A. (1992). *Eats: Poems.* HarperCollins.

Fleischman, P. (2004). *Joyful noise: Poems for two voices.* HarperCollins.

Greenfield, E. (1991). *Under the Sunday tree.* HarperCollins.

Koontz, D. (2001). *The paper doorway: Funny verse and nothing worse.* HarperCollins.

Livingston, M. C. (1991). *Earth songs.* Scholastic.

Moss, J. (1989). *The butterfly jar.* Bantam.

Pomerantz, C. (1993). *If I had a paka: Poems in 11 languages.* HarperCollins.

Prelutsky, J. (1994). *The new kid on the block.* Random House.

Siebert, D. (2006). *Tour America: A journey through poems and art.* Chronicle.

Silverstein, S. (2004). *Where the sidewalk ends.* HarperCollins.

Silverstein, S. (2005). *Runny babbit: A billy sook.* HarperCollins.

### Anthologies (many poets under one cover)

*Another jar of tiny stars: Poems by NCTE award-winning poets.* (2009). Wordsong.

Bryan, A. (2001). *Ashley Bryan's ABC of African American poetry.* Atheneum.

Carlson, L. (ed.). (2008). *Cool salsa: Bilingual poems on growing up Latino in the US.* Holt.

de Regniers, B., Moore, E., White, M., & Carr, J. (1988). *Sing a song of popcorn: Every child's book of poems.* Scholastic.

Kennedy, C. (2005). *A family of poems: My favorite poetry for children.* Hyperion.

Kennedy, X. J., & Kennedy, D. (1999). *Knock at a star: A child's introduction to poetry.* Little, Brown.

Marsalis, W. (2005). *An A–Z collection of jazz portraits.* Candlewick.

Orozco, J. (2005). *Rin Rin Rin Do Re Mi.* Orchard.

Prelutsky, J. (2000). *The Random House book of poetry for children.* Random House.

Prelutsky, J. (1999). *The 20th century children's poetry treasury.* Knopf.

Worth, V. (1999). *All the small poems and fourteen more.* Farrar, Straus, & Giroux.

### Poems as Picture Books

Adoff, A. (2004). *Black is brown is tan.* Amistad.

Atwood, A. (1977). *Haiku vision.* Scribner's.

Baylor, B. (1995). *Guess who my favorite person is.* Aladin.

Hopkins, L. (1993). *Ragged shadows: Poems of Halloween night.* Little, Brown.

Johnson, J. (2007). *Lift every voice and sing.* Amistad.

Lobel, A. (1993). *The rose in my garden.* HarperCollins.

Longfellow, H. W. (2009). *Paul Revere's ride.* Picture Window Books.

Noyes, A. (1999). *The highwayman.* Oxford University Press.

publishes a list of children's classics, as does the Children's Literature Association (*http://chla.wikispaces.org/*). On nearly every list are works such as Aesop's fables, Andersen's fairy tales, Mother Goose rhymes, Perrault's fairy tales, *Charlotte's Web, Little Women, Winnie the Pooh, The Wizard of Oz,* and *The Adventures of Huckleberry Finn.*

**Poetry Sources.** Ready Reference 4.12 lists poetry selection sources for units. Included are lists of children's favorite poems and poets, collections of poets and anthologies, and poetry awards. Examples of enduring favorites to use with children include:

Eleanor Farjeon's "Cat"
Ogden Nash's "Adventures of Isabel"
John Ciardi's "Mummy Slept Late and Daddy Fixed Breakfast"
Ann Hoberman's "A Bookworm of Curious Breed"
Karla Kuskin's "Hughbert and the Glue"
Irene McLeod's "Lone Dog"
Laura E. Richards's "Eletelephony"
Judith Viorst's "Mother Doesn't Want a Dog"
Shel Silverstein's "The Unicorn" and "Sick"
Jane Yolen's "Homework"
Langston Hughes's "Dreams"
Jack Prelutsky's "Willie Ate a Worm Today" and "The Lurpp Is on the Loose"

**Popular Poets.** The humorous poetry of Shel Silverstein and Jack Prelutsky dominates children's choices (Kutiper & Wilson, 1993). Other popular poets are David McCord, Aileen Fisher, Myra C. Livingston, Eve Merriam, Lilian Moore, Arnold Adoff, Valerie Worth, John Ciardi, Eleanor Farjeon, Ann Hoberman, Langston Hughes, Edward Lear, Vachel Lindsay, Ogden Nash, Karla Kuskin, Irene Rutherford McLeod, Laura E. Richards, Judith Viorst, Paul Janeczko, and Jane Yolen (Kutiper & Wilson, 1993; Norton, 2003).

**Arts-Based Literature.** Literature is an art form generated by the same creative process as any other art. Literature is also a storehouse of information about music, visual art, drama, and dance and the artists who create these arts. Arts-based literature comes in all genres: biographies of artists, information and how-to books, and fictional stories with artist characters and/or arts-related themes. Picture books are automatically arts based with a winning combination of visual art and literary art. Together, books, stories, and poems related to arts, in any way, are deemed *arts based.* Each of the subsequent arts chapters includes examples of arts-based books for that particular art. There is also an arts-based bibliography in Appendix J.

There is also literature about literature. Stories and biographies about writers, the writing process, and actual books make up "literature-based" literature. These books can grow students' understanding of how the literary arts are made and the people who make them. Examples include Julius Lester's *On Writing for Children and Other People* (2004) and *If You Were a Writer.* Many books feature protagonists who read and write, such as Duvoisin's *Petunia.* Carol Hurst lists more at www.carolhurst.com.

# Building Block VI: Best Teaching Practices

Examples of AI best teaching practices are described next as they relate to literature integration. Ready Reference 3.9 shows all 10 practices.

## What You Teach Is Who You Are

There is no substitute for a teacher who personally loves books. A literary arts knowledge base is essential, but enthusiastic teachers wrap knowledge in a compelling package. Teachers who know the power of books to uplift and inform have a passion to pass on a legacy. Charlie Brown reminds us that it is never too late to learn, but sometimes it is too early. Some teachers do not become bibliophiles until they take college courses in children's literature. Also, hanging around teachers who have the passion is really contagious.

## Teachers as Role Models

Fresh ideas do not flow from a mind fixed on right answers. If children are to interpret literature aesthetically, they must learn how to make heartfelt connections and create meaningful responses. Those with teachers who demonstrate these behaviors are fortunate. In the same vein, students learn to write with artistry and passion, when their teachers write with them. Together teachers and students can collaborate to create a myriad of compositions from senryu poetry to digital stories (see Chapter 9). The source of these literary compositions is the same source used by "real" writers: topics that reflect problems they care about investigating (e.g., peace, love, misfortune, disease). Such topics naturally relate to curricular areas.

## Mighty Motivators

Literature integration motivates students through the inherent power of the arts. Central factors are interest, choice, active engagement, and the group effect.

**Interest.** No amount of points or pizza coupons will ever match the force of interest in increasing the appetite for reading and writing with interest accounting for more than 25 times the variance in reading comprehension (Barr, Kamil, & Mosenthal, 1996; Guthrie, 2004). People simply read more and better when materials are interesting. Abundant fiction and nonfiction is now available on any subject, from sports to fantasy to cooking, in both hard copy and digital forms. Appendix D has a sample interest inventory to help match readers with interests using selection sources like those in Ready Reference 4.11. AI also seeks to expand interests. One way is to deeply engage students with good books using strategies such as arts-based read-alouds (Cornett, 2006). We can capitalize on the familiar and make the unfamiliar familiar by actively engaging students in making meaning of literary gems by adding the force of visual art, dramas, music, and dance to the word power of good books. Routines such as "book ads" introduce new books using a 30-second commercial format. Informed by contemporary media that is totally integrated with art, music, dance, and drama, book ads can be created by both teachers and students.

**Choice.**  When we force students to travel lockstep through the same reading material we work against the motivational power of choice. The same goes for assigning all students to write the same way at the same time. For example, why must everyone write a letter to a character when there are dozens of writing choices (see Ready Reference 5.1 ). Convenience is unsatisfactory justification. The power of choice is so mighty it cannot be ignored. Teachers need a repertoire of authentic choices to offer to students. The arts are a bottomless well of options.

No single assignment is more in need of revision than the despised book report. Even "good readers" think these dull assignments are responsible for many "readicides." Appendix F has over 100 arts-based response options. Ready Reference 5.2 gives choices for writing poetry. Of course the CPS process itself is a series of choices. Brainstorming, data gathering, and SCAMPER verbs generate choices, including the most basic literary choice: the freedom to create personal meaning from a text.

The theme of this text is reflected in its title. Creating meaning through literature and the arts only happens when students are motivated. Teaching students how to use the arts as alternative ways to understand and express thoughts and feelings opens up a world of choice. Clearly, teachers need to make choice a priority. Students need to be taught how to make good choices about what and how to read and know how to respond meaningfully through writing and other communication arts.

**Active Engagement.**  The literary arts are naturally heads-on, hearts-on learning. At their core is conflict. Writers artfully introduce thinking problems that soon engage emotionally, as well. We empathize with the protagonist, disdain the antagonist, visualize the setting, and anticipate the plot. Literary engagement is compounded when other arts are added to the experience. Drama, music, and dance used before, during, and/or after reading increase thinking and emphasize hands-on learning. Book-related artworks can be focal points for prereading discussions or follow-up reading. Literature activities are now mainstays in science and social studies units where students take the roles of literary characters to show comprehension and write songs that summarize themes and big ideas.

Of course all-purpose engagement strategies such as brainstorming can be used with any literature. Such tools jump-start CPS. Ogle's KWL (1989) is another example that motivates the search for information. It can be done collaboratively or independently. Here's how: Make a three-column chart: K for *know*, W for *want to know*, and L for *learned*. The first two columns are used before reading or writing. Students list what they already know about a topic or problem. Then they list what they want to learn. Students then gather data and list ideas in the third column about what is learned, which becomes the basis for writing or any arts making. *Variation:* The acronym AQUA can also be used and stands for: Already know, QUestions to answer, and Answers found.

**The Group Effect.**  It is unimaginable that arts-oriented literature strategies would not be integrated into main literacy events that often have the added motivational potential of the group effect, such as daily read-alouds, independent reading, and routines, such as discussions, described under Building Block VII. Ready Reference 4.13 lists questions to create more engaging discussions.

## Creative Problem Solving

Most literacy instruction is now literature based. A major portion of instruction is devoted to discussing, creating, sharing, and performing the meaning students make from literary works. An uninterrupted daily block of about 2 hours is dedicated to reading, writing, listening, and talking about good stories and poems. Students are involved in the concentrated search for big ideas found in implicit and explicit literary themes. They learn that reading and writing are complementary forms of literacy, and along with the arts are about creating meaning. Of particular importance is teaching the strategy set used by skilled readers and writers to create meaning. These higher order processes fall into before, during, and after reading stages (Pressley, 2002). Writers call the stages prewriting, drafting, and revising/editing, but the same thinking is used. The set of strategies also parallels how lessons are planned to meet student needs. The countless labels for this process can be confusing to teachers and students. More important than any label is explicitly teaching the common set of thinking strategies along with when, where, how, and why to use them. In this book the creating meaning process is called creative problems solving (CPS) and is summarized in Ready Reference 2.6. An example CPS applied to reading follows.

Good readers start with the general problem of how to make sense, which sets purpose and motivates through interest. Perhaps a reader is worried about a friend who has lung cancer. The reader generates specific questions she wants answered and begins searching for information. She may surf the Internet or leaf through books to hypothesize and predict if the material might be of use. Before in-depth reading she will gather bits and pieces from overviews and previews of materials. She may skim small sections to get a sense of the writing style. At first any material may be accepted, but the reader becomes more selective as she reads on. The reader chooses texts with the most potential and scans to find the relevant sections. Then the reader studies these sections carefully or skims to get the gist.

The reader continually returns to her initial problem and begins to prioritize ideas that make the most sense. The reader sifts and sorts, visualizes and organizes. She shifts in and out of perspectives using empathy for her friend or the views of doctors and survivors. Periodically she pauses and tries to make connections, asking, "What does this mean?" and "Does this make sense?" The reader may reread to clarify. Some general categories begin to emerge—possible causes, symptoms, and treatments. The reader may stop and call the friend to get more details about the diagnosis or go back and forth between websites and books. This problem solving may go on for an hour or days. At some point the reader decides that she has made as much sense as she can, and synthesizes conclusions. The reader may then share her results in any form from a letter to a poem or simply be satisfied with a greater understanding of the problem.

## Ready Reference 4.13 Questions to Prompt Literary Meaning-Making

Also see Ready Reference 4.14 on page 117.

*Before: Look at the title and a few pictures; then ask:*
- What do you think this is about? Why?
- Who? When? Where? (characters/setting)
- What might be the problems in a book with this title? (theme)
- How does this make you feel? Why? (aesthetic response)

*Read a bit, then ask:*
- What did you notice so far?
- What's the big question? How do you know? (theme)
- What's the problem? How might it get solved? (conflict/plot)
- What kind of person is this character? How do you know?
- What should the character do (critical thinking)? Why?
- What are the important things that have happened? Why? (plot)
- Whose story is this? (point of view)
- What do you notice in the pictures (color, texture, shape, line, perspective)? How does this affect/add to the story?
- What will happen? Why? What would you like to find out? (predict)

*Read more, then repeat from above or ask:*
- What do you now know/feel that you didn't know before? (POV/empathy)
- What questions got answered? (confirm/reject predictions)
- What is confusing? (clarification)
- What events are important? How do you know? (critical thinking)

- What words or language stands out? Why? (style)
- How does this story make you feel? (illustrations, mood)
- What does the dialogue tell about the main character?
- What pictures are you making in your head? (visual imagery)

*After the entire reading ask:*
- What happened? Why? What were the problems? How were they solved? (plot, cause/effect, conclusions)
- What did you like? What were your favorite parts? Why? (critical/aesthetic thinking)
- What was this story really about? (themes/key concepts/big ideas)
- How is this story like something in your life? (connections)
- Was it right that . . . ? Why or why not? (critical thinking)
- Was . . . believable (seem real) character? Why? (evaluation)
- What was special or important about . . . ? (inference)
- What did . . . believe/value? (inference)
- What will you remember about this story next week? Next year? (big ideas)
- How is this story like others you've read? (connections)
- What was special about the illustrations? (aesthetics)
- What is special about how the author writes? How did the author make the story interesting? (style)
- Why did the characters do what they did? What does the story tell you about people and behavior? (conclusions/big ideas)
- Did the story end the way you predicted? Why or why not?
- How did the characters change in the story? Why? (conclusions)
- Why did the author write this story? (conclusions)

---

This example was about reading nonfiction. There are some variations for fiction. For example, reader stance is weighted more in the direction of enjoyment, with meaning-making focused on deriving themes from characterization, plot events, and setting.

**Personal Meaning.** Students who expect to create their own meaning are more likely to be actively engaged since owning a problem has motivational effect, as does the opportunity to find innovative solutions. Notice that the solution to the previous reader's problem might be similar to other readers, but not identical. A specific purpose achieved through use of CPS is likely to result in personally constructed understanding. How a reader visualizes and connects, organizes and concludes creates a one-of-a-kind transformation.

Comprehension that results from CPS can take diverse forms: writings, collages, and musical compositions. The chosen art form also alters the nature of the meaning. Writing an essay brings a dimension to understanding different from making a sculpture. If the reader worrying about her friend's cancer uses her synthesis of information to create an artistic product, she will be restarting the CPS process. One creative solution becomes the impetus for another cycle. This kind of connecting and transforming is common in the arts. Think of films like *Philadelphia*

*Story* (transformation of HIV-AIDS information into a story/drama) or *My Darling Clementine* (transformation of a song about a drowned lover). Poems have been composed to try to make sense of every known human emotion from terrible loss ("On Flanders Field" from World War I) to courage ("Charge of the Light Brigade"). What compels poets, musicians, and dancers to make this kind of art? The answer is complex, but the initial motivation has to do with sensing a problem and a deep need to construct personal meaning.

**Limits Liberate.** A creative effort can be overwhelming since any problem has countless solutions. This holds for the many meanings hidden in literature and the possible ways to express ideas in writing. One way to channel creative stress is to use strategies such as timed writings—unstructured free writes to release what is already known. Even list writing works. For example, most children can be asked to list ways people write in real life. Another list can be made of important moments or ideas in a book. These lists can be combined to give focus to choices. A student might pick the letter form and the moment when Jack chose to go up the beanstalk the third time, which will cause different meaning making than if the choice is to write a news article.

**Risk Taking.** Our words have the power to give hope and encourage student risk taking. FFOE thinking (Ready Reference 2.6) during CPS can be encouraged with comments such as "You showed *fluency* with so many ideas," "It shows *flexibility* to use the fable structure to write about Columbus's voyage," "That's an *original* idea that no one else used," or "The details you added made me really see your point" *(elaboration)*. This kind of feedback is a joy to give because it uplifts students. Students also develop the courage to risk from encouraging messages such as "I think you're on the right track with writing a haiku about *Charlotte's Web*. It is about nature so you made a meaningful connection."

## Explicit Teaching

In Chapter 3, the idea of explicitly teaching basic elements of art forms was explained. Clear, specific teaching about why, what, how, when, and where to use arts concepts and skills happens through demonstrations. Teachers think aloud and provide scaffolded practice, with feedback. In the area of literature, explicit instruction can focus on specific CPS processes used for reading and writing, literary elements, and genre traits, which give students the tools to read at more depth and write with greater variety.

In particular, struggling learners often fail to understand that reading and writing are about creating meaning by using problem-solving strategies. I saw this repeatedly in our reading center during interviews. Children routinely declared they were not good readers because they did not know how to "pronounce all the words" or "read fast." Rarely did these students with reading difficulties key in on making sense. They did not understand that comprehension is the goal of reading. Reading and writing cannot be reduced to literal acts of sounding out and spelling correctly. Children need clear goals that give context to practicing decoding (e.g., phonics). They need to be shown how successful readers and writers in real life orchestrate thinking strategies for the purpose of making sense.

**Wholes and Parts.** Teaching nitty-gritty literary elements and genre traits can be dull and irrelevant if students do not understand why and how they can be used to create personal meaning. Literary arts components have little value as isolated bits of knowledge. Memorizing them and picking them out of texts is not meaning oriented. Explicit teaching targets explaining why to learn such elements and showing students how to use them to expand comprehension.

In general, the process of teaching literary concepts begins with experiencing literature. This means reading aloud stories and poetry, as well as daily time for independent student reading. Once students have enjoyed poems, fables, and mysteries, they are ready to learn their inner workings. This whole-part-whole instruction starts with reading and oral sharing of literature, moves to explicit teaching about elements and traits, and returns to the whole again to generate new works or reread with broader perspective.

**Arts Aids.** Literary elements and genre traits cannot be easily learned without visuals. Students can collaborate to make bookmarks, banners, or big books (e.g., one page on characters, another on theme). Pages can include examples from literature, definitions, and artwork. Genre charts can be made using large roll paper to grid: traits of a genre down the left side and actual literature titles across the top. The chart is filled in as students discover trait examples as they read, view, and listen to works.

Songs and other mnemonics can also be written by students to transform literary concepts elements. Second graders wrote this song to the tune of "Frère Jacques": "Plots and themes (2X). Make a story (2X). Add in characters (2X). Play with words. That makes style."

**Mini-Lessons.** Five to 10 minutes of explicit instruction is enough to target specific information or skills needed to read and write literature with more artistry. The following seed strategy chapter (Chapter 5) offers ideas for literary elements, genre characteristics, and authors and illustrators.

## Aesthetic Orienting

High engagement of the senses happens when teachers slow the pace, so literature can be savored. Students should be taught to observe carefully, notice how words make them feel, respond to images, and ground interpretations in evidence. Zoom in/zoom out teaching orchestrates and balances wholes and parts.

**Reader Response Theory.** Literature grew out of a storytelling tradition that thrives because of the power of artful words. Children who are taught to enjoy the music of poetry and vicariously experience the thrill of book journeys are primed for a literary life. Unfortunately, in an effort to boost skills, the literary arts have been milked, sometimes by trampling on their aesthetic richness.

Response to literature has become an important subject in reading instruction, in large part because of Louise Rosenblatt's (1985) work. She theorized that readers take different stances as they read. An efferent stance dwells on getting information—just the facts. Unfortunately this focus has dominated much instruction, including the study of literature. Fortunately, the power of good literature can neutralize insistence on facts. For example, Sadoski and Quast (1990) found that students who were assigned to read to find typographical errors intentionally inserted in a literary work reported as much imagery and affect as students assigned to read a story for pleasure. It seems stance may be less consequential than proposed; a good story captivates even when we are directed to read efferently.

Rosenblatt proposed that readers and writers are involved *aesthetically* when they attend and respond to sounds and images associated with words—to experience emotional, as well as denotational, word properties. Teachers stimulate this response when they direct students to listen to and read aloud chosen words and phrases for the purpose of enjoying language. Students are asked to notice the music of words. "Why would the author use such words?" and "How do these words make you feel?" are questions that invite aesthetic response. Students learn to use literary language to prompt mental images; not just literal ones, either, but richly embellished pictures drawn from background experiences.

Rosenblatt's work has helped give instructional parity to aesthetic reading, which promises to increase comprehension, without diminishing the possibility of gaining key information from texts (Sadoski & Paivio, 2004; Sadoski & Quast, 1990). A balanced instructional focus promises broader based reader engagement, including triggering visual imagery essential to literary understanding. The practice of engaging aesthetic responses prior to focusing on information can enliven literary discussions and change the tenor of student sharing of personal writing. Putting aesthetic understanding first demonstrates respect for literature as an art form and encourages students to express feelings and attitudes based in emotional intelligence. Student integrity is developed when they learn they need to support aesthetic responses with evidence or reasons grounded in facts.

**Critical Approach.** Knowledge of literary elements and genre characteristics can help students notice more, which is important to the artistic habit of careful observation. Noticing details and patterns increases aesthetic experience and helps in data gathering for CPS. A critical approach to teaching literature focuses on teaching literary concepts and language so students are better able to voice ideas and opinions and to structure their own writing.

The goal is to teach students to understand, respond to, and express themselves through the literary arts using both aesthetic and efferent stances. Balanced questions include: "How did the story or poem make you feel? Why? What was the mood of the story? How did the author create the mood? What struck you about how the story was written? How were words and pictures used to create a feeling in the book? How would the story be different if the author had chosen to write in another genre?"

**Visual Literacy.** Children need time to experience the capacity of books to stir the imagination with "what if" questions, thus giving fresh perspectives on problems. Picture books add a concrete visual art dimension to the aesthetic experience. Art appreciation is extended when attention is drawn to the many art styles used by picture book artists. What's more, visual literacy is developed.

We are most fortunate to have readily available art in the form of picture books that can be used to build visual literacy. Picture books have a story, but they are called *picture* books. Teaching children how to "decode" art increases both understanding and enjoyment. For example, the Look Closely art strategy directs students to take time to discover as they are coached with visual art elements (Chapter 6) to stretch observation. Students are asked to share how the art makes them feel and speculate about how the artist causes emotional reactions. Questions such as "How does this picture make you feel?" and "What do you see?" are starters. Even primary students can see how color is used to balance a composition. They are delighted to learn that artists intentionally use line to lead the eye and make the reader turn each page. They enjoy noticing repeated shapes that move the eye around and give a sense of rhythm. With a bit of Internet research on book illustrators (see publishers' websites), teachers can collect useful information about how these artists work. Selection sources to help locate picture books with specific visual art features are included in Building Block V and Ready Reference 4.11. Chapters 6 and 7 add more detail. Ready Reference 6.12 and 8.11 list questioning strategies. Ready Reference 7.6 has picture book ideas.

**Stretching Time.** Discussions that go beyond plot retellings take lots of time. Arts-based responses to literature mean time to plan, rehearse, and perform. Where does it come from? When teachers meaningfully integrate the arts, school time is not expanded; time use is changed. Two important changes involve discipline and motivation. Students who are aesthetically engaged are more interested. They savor words and linger over pictures, which leads to the intrinsic rewards of literature. Poignant moments happen in arts-based literature lessons. Students "re-member," or become members again of the human family, held together by common beliefs and history, both of which are revealed in literature. Engaged students are motivated learners, not discipline problems. Motivation based on stickers and points may seem fast, but the effect does not last.

## Independence and Self-Discipline

It is relatively easy to teach students a variety of arts-based ways to respond to and write literature. More challenging is ensuring that new tools be used meaningfully. The teacher who asks, "What have you tried?" when a student complains, "I don't know what to write" or "I can't figure out this word" is setting an expectation for independence. Independence is not acquired easily, but it is a high-placed AI goal. The following are scaffolds teachers can use to move students to independence.

- Discuss with students that you are not going to think for them, but you will help them problem solve.
- Teach self-help strategies such as word fix-ups (e.g., spell aloud, chunk, and use synonyms), spelling fix-ups (e.g., use a synonym, circle and go on, write down a few letters you know), and comprehension fix-ups (e.g., make pictures in your head, reread, think about what's most important [big ideas]).
- Teach students how to select books at appropriate reading levels. Use the rule of thumb or five-finger method: Open to one page in the middle and read. For each unknown word, raise one finger. If you get to the thumb, the book may be too hard. Ohlhausen and Jepsen (1992) explain book selection by likening it to Goldilocks's decisions. Students decide if a book is too hard, easy, or just right, keeping in mind that a book may be too difficult, but a child's interest can compensate.
- Teach how to prepare for discussions. See Ready Reference 4.14.

# Building Block VII: Instructional Design: Routines and Structures

Daily rituals and routines institutionalize literature integration. When teachers get in the habit of using arts-based literature strategies to introduce, develop, and/or conclude lessons, they guarantee head-heart-hands engagement. It becomes routine to intentionally teach students to concentrate, focus, and engage CPS. In particular, the lesson introduction sets the stage with energizers and warm-ups.

## Energizers and Warm-Ups

Just as in any arts area, we need to help students get ready to read and write about literature. Chapter 5 describes a dozen energizers

**Ready Reference 4.14**  Preparing for and Starting Literary Discussions

**Teacher**

*Ask . . .*
1. About the meaning of the title
2. One or two *important* questions with many possible answers (ones that related to big ideas)
3. Open or fat questions (e.g., *why* or *how*) for which there is text evidence
4. Questions you don't have answers for
5. Students to "quick write" or "take a think" (1 to 2 minutes) about a question before discussing it
6. For evidence to support answers (i.e., *why* questions)

*Scaffold for student independence . . .*
1. Post questions for students to choose from (see Ready Reference 4.13).
2. Demonstrate how to take notes using categories such as learn-wonder-like (LWL), interesting-questions-useful (IQU), and exciting-puzzling-connecting (EPC).

3. Demonstrate how to find themes and convert them to big ideas (e.g., Ask, "What was it *really* about?" and coach for complete thoughts).
4. Teach how to do visual imagining during reading.

**Students**
1. Focus first on enjoying the story, including the word artistry. Reread to find evidence to support conclusions.
2. Make visual images or pictures in your head during reading
3. Read to find and create themes and big ideas
4. Plan to read aloud sections to support conclusions (note page numbers).
5. Note connections to other texts, yourself, and the world (TSW).
6. Use frames with categories to take notes (e.g., LWL, IQU, EPC).

---

and warm-ups to engage the CPS. Check all seed strategy arts chapters, as other arts energizers work for literature. Following is one example.

**Riddle of the Day.**  Riddles trigger higher-order thinking, especially CPS, and contain attractive language for quick lessons on patterns (e.g., spelling/phonics). Riddles are basically a question and an answer, and students can easily write their own about any content. Here is a sequence: (1) Write the riddle in a special place. (2) Put blanks for the answer. Fill in a few letters, especially consonants, to guarantee success. For example, "What do you call a boy that hangs on the wall?" ＿＿ ＿＿ ＿＿ (3) Chorally read the riddle, pointing to the words. (4) Students guess letters, *not* the answer! Letters are written as guessed. (5) When most are guessed, students signal if they know. If so, the answer is said chorally; if not, add more letters until everyone is "in the know." (6) Students find patterns and interesting words (e.g., silent ee, double vowels, verbs, homographs). Oh, by the way, the answer is ART.

## Opening and Closing Routines

Most teachers use predictable routines to start and end the school day. Energizers can also be used at these times. Chapter 3 featured some of Ms. Lucas's many arts-based routines. Here are other favorites.

**Spotlights.**  An author/artist spotlight is a mini-unit on a children's author or book illustrator using the "few minutes a day" plan. A special easel or chair can actually be lit with a flashlight. If the spotlight were on Ezra Jack Keats, a student might share a fact about him, talk about a picture from *The Snowy Day*, or read a passage. Variations: with "Laugh a Day," students share

humor such as a joke, riddle, poem, cartoon, or hink pink. Humor uses both creative language and art, so it can be squeezed for insights about sounds, images, multiple meanings, and unusual connections. "Poem a Day" is daily arts-based poem sharing. Ready Reference 5.4 lists ways to do poem performances.

**Writer's Chair.**  Students share original writing in this routine. The class gathers around a special chair in which the writer sits. The writer reads aloud from his manuscript, and students practice good audience etiquette: active listening, giving descriptive feedback, and asking open questions. This strategy helps children feel that writing is more than an assignment; it becomes a way to share emotions, ideas, and their CPS. For example, students may write a fantasy using learned genre traits. *Variation:* Use a reader's chair to share favorite books or poems and an artist's chair for artwork.

**Book Ads.**  These are like ads done on *Reading Rainbow* or *Cover to Cover*. The purpose is to interest classmates in a book. First, teachers demonstrate and then invite students to sign up. Children see so many TV ads that they readily have good ideas. Ads are usually only 2 or 3 minutes and typically include (1) a short introduction (attention getter, tell title/author, display a few pictures, read chapter titles or book blurb, or share author facts), (2) a short excerpt, perhaps of some dialog, and (3) a conclusion (ask for predictions about the book and invite the audience to read to find out if they are right). Students may choose to make an audiotape or video or write a jingle or slogan. Ads are more interesting if props and music are used. For example, I like to play the beginning of Beethoven's Fifth Symphony and read the first couple of pages from Rylant's *All I See* as a book ad. Ads can also be as book responses to show student comprehension.

Principal's weekly discussion group

## Reading and Writing Workshop

Reading and writing workshop is a block of time during which students mostly read and write. Usually the workshop begins with explicit teaching using a mini-lesson that targets something students need. Mini-lessons last 5 minutes or so. For example, a teacher may demonstrate spelling fix-ups or how to generate metaphors to make writing interesting. Students then read and write independently for 30 to 45 minutes. Students may be at any of the three writing and reading stages in their work (e.g., before-during-after) with some doing responses to books and other brainstorming to generate ideas to get started. During workshop times, students may read with a partner, write in Lit Logs, and work at learning centers. Teachers circulate to coach as students work, schedule groups for guided reading and writing, and do individual conferences. Throughout the workshop students are guided by the expectation they are to document their progress with work evidence. In arts integration that work is usually connected to upcoming performances or exhibits.

## Arts-Based Read-Alouds

According to the National Reading Panel (2000), "instructional methods that generate high levels of student involvement and engagement during reading can have positive effects on reading comprehension" (pp. 4, 124–125). Daily read-alouds have that kind of engagement potential. When this powerful teaching strategy is made artful by coupling it with arts-based strategies, the result is *arts-based read-alouds*.

Teacher read-alouds are standard events in most literacy blocks these days. Arts-based read-alouds are a variation during which the teacher reads aloud *to* and *with* children, with focus on providing an aesthetic experience. Like independent reading, arts-based read-alouds may include arts-based children's books. Any literature, however, may be introduced, developed, or concluded with arts strategies that involve problem solving. Planning Page 4.8 shows arts responses to *Millions of Cats*.

From picture books to chapter books, arts-based read-alouds are an important platform to teach the most difficult and

most important kind of comprehension—higher order thinking, which includes critical thinking and synthesis of ideas (Cornett, 2006; Kamil, 2004). Struggling readers, in particular, have great difficulty understanding exactly what reading is. Some teachers skip teaching this and assume children understand that reading is meaning-making using clues from the abstract "art" of letters. That's unfortunate. Read-alouds seem to fill the gap. Reading aloud makes the invisible visible.

**EAR: Fluency.** A important purpose of arts-based read-alouds is for students to hear expressive reading—making music from print. Interpreted meaning of printed text is vividly portrayed using variations in pitch, dynamics, tempo, stress, and pause. In literacy circles this is called *fluency,* which boils down to expression, accuracy, and rate (EAR). In a book like *Tuck Everlasting,* literary language, unlike normal talk, is heard that may very well be above students' reading levels, but at their interest levels. "She was a great potato of a woman" is just one metaphor Babbitt uses to paint mind pictures. Read-alouds also bond groups like singing does. Read-alouds are a daily routine that should include pre-, during, and post arts-based responses, such as those Amy Weiss used for *Sarah, Plain and Tall* in the Classroom Snapshot earlier in this chapter. In addition, pausing to discuss words and inviting students to chime in with predictions increases involvement. Predictions can be mimed and sketched as well as verbalized.

## Independent Reading

Research confirms that the amount of time spent reading is the main determinant of reading achievement (Guthrie, 2004). Research supports budgeting time each day for student independent reading (Krashen, 2005). Common names for this routine involving reading choice books are SSR (sustained silent reading), SQUIRT (silent quiet independent reading time), and DEAR (drop everything and read). Whatever it is called, students need to just plain read (JPR) and not just have lessons about reading (Allington, 2005; Trelease, 2005). Full participation of everyone is important; the teacher acts as a role model, using the following guidelines.

1. Plan for 10 to 20 minutes (shorter with primary children).
2. Students need to be ready and have an extra book in case they finish. Students can repeat readings of books for fluency.
3. Everyone should be comfortable and stay put. Buddy reading can be used, especially with young children who need the support of a partner (or books on tape).
4. Soft background music may be played to set mood.
5. After reading, plan time for writing and arts-based responses. Generic questions can be used: "What was the most exciting or interesting part? What were special words? How did the pictures make you feel and why?" Ready Reference 4.13 lists examples.

A variation involves giving a choice related to units. For example, students all read a biography to prepare for writing a biography. Despite the importance of having "free reading" every day, some days can be designated to promote arts-based reading.

This, too, is made more relevant by offering choices that connect to units. For example, set out several books about musicians who lived during a period the class is studying.

## Literature Discussions

Longitudinal research on the amount of talk heard by children shows children raised by parents with professions start school having heard 30 million more words (Hart & Risely, 2003). Allington (2005) insists that teachers can close this gap with conversation. Even a little makes a huge difference in students' language development and motivation. Scheduling extended literature conversations promises more. One form is discussions.

Discussions are socially and intellectually engaging ways for students to do group meaning-making. Well-structured discussions have unmatched potential to increase comprehension because talking out thoughts and listening to others generates a web of meanings. But, high-level discussing is an art to be learned. Discussion that seeks meaning-making is not about ping-pong question-and-answer sessions between teacher and students. Nor are they about dull plot retellings (Cornett, 1997). High-level discussions are "grand conversations" among participants who all know the plot and realize greater understanding is possible when more heads are involved (Eeds & Wells, 1989). The leadership shifts away from the teacher (see Ready Reference 4.14).

As an integral part of the daily schedule, discussions may connect to read-alouds or any unit work. The following ideas help to prepare students to artfully participate in and lead discussions.

**Discussion Guidelines.** The goal is to eventually have discussions in which everyone comes away with new perspectives. To begin, discuss the following rules.

1. Come prepared. Read the book to participate. (Give note-taking frames for during reading such as LWL: learn, wonder, like.)
2. Aim for the goal of creating meaning by sharing different ideas.
3. Support interpretations and opinions with evidence.
4. Restate others' ideas before you present an opposite idea.
5. Try to learn something never considered before.
6. Show active listening with "body talk." Respond to others with positive comments.

**Preparation.** Even adults are reluctant to speak up if they feel either unprepared or their point of view will not be respected. Consider the following options to help students prepare.

*Discussion cards.* Give students an index card to jot down ideas to discuss. Suggest categories such as important events, most interesting, emotional parts, things characters say, special words, questions, and useful ideas.

*EPC charts.* Give a frame with three columns or circles: exciting part, puzzling part, and connecting part (Cornett, 1997). Put these in three large circles or three columns. During reading, students note pages that fit these categories. They star one or two to discuss. *Note:* Connections can relate to personal experiences, another book, or the world.

*Read-alouds.* Students choose a part to read aloud to start the discussion and tell why they chose it (e.g., important event, use of language, connected to their lives). Students should rehearse so reading is fluent. Suggest that the section contain a whole idea and give time limits to prevent monopolizing.

**Organizing Discussions.** Here are start-ups for teacher-led discussions, adaptable later in the year for student-led discussions.

*Use role-play rules.* Practice giving feedback, paraphrasing, and asking clarification questions (e.g., "Show me being an active listener," "Use your face and body to make me believe," or "Now show me a poor listener").

*Sit in a circle so everyone can see.* Try the fishbowl technique: Volunteers come into an inner circle to discuss while an outer circle listens in. At stop points, the outer circle follows up on comments heard and asks questions. For example, "I liked what Mimi said because I did not think that the boy might have died" (Lowry's *The Giver*) or "I would like to ask Tom why he thought the mother committed suicide" (Creech's *Walk Two Moons*). Next, circles exchange positions. This teaches listening as well as speaking.

*Use write right away/quick writes.* Give students 3 to 5 minutes to write about a question before discussing it. Choose a question for which there are clues in the story, but no one answer.

**During the Discussion.** Encourage all to participate. Start with volunteers or call on any student—the first rule of coming to the circle is "be prepared." Use "no hands up" to make it more conversational. Weave a more complex web of meaning with questions such as "What do the rest of you think about Bobby's idea?" "Who had a similar idea?" "Is this a new idea for anyone?" "Who has an opposite idea?" and "What in the story supports Bobby's idea?" Periodically stop and recap important ideas that have been shared so far.

**Concluding the Discussion.** To wrap up, ask students to share (1) the most important points made, (2) what made sense, (3) what someone said that was a new idea, and (4) how people had similar ideas. The "tell one thing" strategy can be used, with a pass option to allow face saving. Usually this is "pass and come back," since by the full go around many ideas have been expressed and it is acceptable to repeat ideas.

Ready Reference 4.14 lists discussion questions. Post examples to give students choices and use as examples to create questions. Emphasize that good questions are ones they care about and want answers.

## Performances and Exhibits

Chapter 3 introduced the idea of using performances and exhibits to drive learning. Literature-based performances include reader's theatre, in which students present expressive oral reading of original literature-based scripts or those of others (see Chapter 9). Weekly poetry performances are another common routine. For example, every Friday is "Poetree Day" in Rebecca Hofmeister's fifth grade. Students write or find poems, rehearse

schedule causes students to anticipate a portfolio review. This is what assessment *for* learning is about. Students know you will be asking for evidence of progress toward goals, such as "reading a variety of genre" which sets up motivation, including the anticipation of being proud of progress. New goal setting is important, too, for example, trying alternative arts responses and listing new books each child wants to read. Collaborative goal setting also generates more student ownership of learning. Conference time can also be designated to discuss aspects of books and listen to a child orally read, with focus on *expressive* reading, not just accuracy and rate. Try using a conference notebook, with a page for each child, to note goals and progress made toward each goal, in addition to portfolio notes.

# Building Block X: Literary Arts Partnerships

Many teachers and librarians share goals that can be accomplished through literature integration. A good librarian knows sources for excellent trade books for any unit or a genre study. Our local library offers a phone-order service. Call up with a unit request, and they pull 30 books to keep a month. To find literary arts specialists, create a directory by surveying teachers, students, and parents about favorite books and writing experiences. There are poets, novelists, and genre experts hidden among the faculty, staff, and parents. These specialists may be available to co-plan or act as "teaching artists" in classrooms. In addition to the information on partnering with arts specialists in Chapter 3, the following suggestions help to optimize school visits by children's book authors and illustrators.

## Author/Artist Visits

Today, the writers and illustrators of children's literature are celebrities who draw admiring audiences at conferences. There are even picture books about visits such as Pinkwater's *Author's Day* and Fitch's *The Other Author Arthur*. Authors travel to schools for residencies lasting a day, or longer for local authors. Visits can be the basis for an "event" unit that culminates with the author/artist visit.

As with any arts event, planning is everything. Here are tips for working with children's writers and artists for an in-school residency. Two recommended references are McElmeel's (1994) *ABCs of an Author/Illustrator Visit* and Saunders's (1999) *The Author Visit Handbook*.

1. Check *www.smartwriters.com* for a list of speakers.
2. Search the Internet for background information, including the publisher's website.
3. Plan early (a year ahead). Contact the publisher through the website to arrange with an appearance coordinator. Do not hesitate to ask for references.
4. Investigate fund raising possibilities with the PTA. The publisher may sell quantity amounts of books at a discount so they can be resold at a profit.

5. Plan objectives. Use the ELA standards in Ready Reference 4.6 and in your local district's curriculum guides. Set it up so students expect to have an aesthetic experience and learn information/skills.
6. Spell out everything in a contract: date, time, schedule, equipment, and expectations. Plan a budget to cover expenses. (Budget at least $500 a day plus expenses. Even local authors rarely are free and should be offered some honorarium.)
7. Confirm the agenda. In writing, describe the number of presentations and length, room arrangement, group sizes, types of presentation, request for autographs, and advance book orders.
8. Request publicity materials from the publisher. Ask for biographies in quantity, black and white pictures, book lists, posters, bookmarks, and jackets. Ask if there is a DVD or any material showing the author working or an interview. Nationally known author/illustrators may have been filmed, or there are CDs/tapes available of them. Teacher guides for books may be printed free from some websites. Send a press release to the local newspaper. Ask the publisher for a generic one you can adapt.
9. Prepare the students: Do an author–artist core unit. Check out the author's website. Read lots of books and generate class and individual lists of questions for the artist. Have students do a variety of arts-based responses such as those in Appendix F. Arts transformations deeply connect students to the books and make personal meaning-making richer.
10. Rehearse what the students are to do and how they are to interact with the author/artist. Role play audience etiquette. Assign roles such as host, guide, logistics, and introducer.
11. Follow up the visit with "what did you learn" response activities. This includes thank-you notes from students, and arts responses such as poems, artwork, songs, or videos of dances or dramas. Send these to the artist/author.
12. Note that phone interviews are rarely free. Generally, $50 to $75 for a half-hour is expected. You need a speakerphone for the whole class to benefit.

The following websites have more information.

Scholastic: *http://teacher.scholastic.com/products/tradebooks/authorvisits/*
*Teacher Librarian* magazine: *http://teacherlibrarian.com*

## Conclusion

Social, religious, and economic forces continue to influence the evolution of children's literature. Children are now expected to be independent earlier and, some say, are hurried into adolescence. With many overscheduled and overstressed, it is increasingly important that we tap the power of literature to slow them down and give joy. We must continue to guard against potential abuses of literature, as we implement research on its power to motivate children to read, write, and learn in curricular areas. Literature, like all art, needs to be primarily regarded for its aesthetic contributions, and not simply as a tool to achieve literacy.

This chapter offered ideas for meaningful literature integration that balances aesthetic enjoyment with information gain. Specific literature integration examples were offered for the 10 AI building blocks. The next chapter is the first of five strategy seed chapters with idea starters to plan more specific literary arts integration.

## Teachers as Leaders: AI Advocacy

Start an adult book club to discuss children's literature using the discussion guidelines recommended in the chapter. Be sure to discuss some arts-based books. Stretch further to try a few arts responses to literature. Go to www.skype.com to check out how to do a discussion via the internet.

**PEARSON**
## myeducationlab)

Go to the Activities and Applications section for Topic *Strategies for Teaching* at MyEducationLab for your course and complete the video activities entitled "Teaching Literary Character Traits Using Drama (TV Reporting)", "Teaching How to Find Big Ideas and Themes in Literature", and "Using the 5 W and H Questions to Understand Visual Art."

Go to the Book Specific Resources section in the MyEducationLab for your course, select your book and Chapter 4 to view the Questions to Guide Reading and Response Options for this chapter.

## Resources

See Chapter 5 and the Appendix for additional materials and websites.

### Websites

Carol Hurst's Children's Literature Website: www.carolhurst.com
Kathy Schrock's Guide: http://school.discovery.com/schrockguide
The Reading Zone: http://ipl.org (part of the Internet Public Library)
International Children's Digital Library: http://en.childrenslibrary.org/
Nancy Keane's Children's Literature webpage: http://nancykeane.com
LibrarySpot: www.libraryspot.com
Vandergrift's Children's Literature Page: http://comminfo.rutgers.edu/
professional-development/childlit/ChildrenLit/index.html

### Professional Organizations

American Library Association (ALA): www.ala.org/
Children's Book Council (CBC): www./cbcbooks.org
International Reading Association (IRA): www.ira.org
National Council of Teachers of English (NCTE): www.ncte.org

### AV Source

Weston Woods: http://teacher.scholastic.com/products/westonwoods/
(videos about authors, artists, and children's books)

### Journals (Research, Articles, Reviews, Author profiles)

*Bookbird* (International Board on Books for Young People)
*Booklist* and *Book Links* (ALA)
Bulletin of the Center for Children's Books
*Children's Literature in Education* (APS Publications)
*Horn Book Magazine* (Horn Book, Inc.)
*Language Arts* (NCTE)
*Reading Teacher* (IRA)
*School Library Journal* (Bowker)

# Seed Strategies for Literature and Poetry

*You think your pain and your heartache are unprecedented in the history of the world, but then you read. It was books that taught me that the things that tormented me most were the very things that connected me with all the people who were alive, or had ever been alive.* (James Baldwin)

## Overview

This chapter includes starter or "seed" ideas to integrate the literary arts throughout the curriculum. The first three sections are energizers and warm-ups, literary elements and genre traits, and curricular areas. The first two sections give tips on how to build students' literary knowledge and skill base so they meaningfully participate in arts integration (AI). This chapter also features a fourth special section on poetry.

## Introduction

The seed strategies in the chapter assume knowledge about literary elements and principles for teaching literature—the focus of the previous chapter. The strategies are undeveloped and intentionally not grade leveled. They are intended as prompts for creative thinking during the planning of literature-based lessons. Seed Strategies should be selected as they fit curriculum standards and they need to be differentiated for student needs. Most seeds are adaptable for grades K–6 using the PARTICULAR differentiation ideas in Ready Reference 3.11.

## Classroom Snapshot
### Verbs, Literature, and Pantomime

This chapter opens with a look at how one teacher integrates two art forms: nonfiction literature and drama—to teach about parts of speech. Look for evidence of AI building blocks, such as aesthetic classroom climate and best teaching practices such as coaching. Bolded strategies can be further investigated by checking the index.

The desks in Stacey Sturgell's room are arranged in a U shape. A couch with a red pillow is along one wall. "Interesting Words" hang from a clothesline. A collage of nouns covers one wall and words cover the windows. On the chalk tray is a display of books for daily DEAR time. Overhead a sign reads, "Control your voice, body and mind."

Stacey sits in a director's chair. Her second graders are seated on a colorful rug. She smiles, "Eyes up here," she says and points to a sign that reads, "A verb shows action."

"Today's read-aloud is about verbs. Listen and be ready to plug in actions from *To Root to Toot to Parachute* (Cleary). She reads using **oral cloze** to increase engagement; she stops before words and waits for students to supply verbs. She also uses **inserted questions,** such as "What do you notice about verbs?"

Stacey **reads expressively** using a variety of pitches, volumes, stress, and tempos. Her vocal dynamics make the reading sound musical, which is an essential for fluency. She also accurately pronounces and adjusts rate to purpose.

After the read-aloud, Stacey asks what they know about **charades.** Some have played this drama game with Mr. Jordan, the drama teacher. They say charades requires no talking. It's pantomime. They seem ready to show what they know about verbs.

Stacey holds up a basket with blue cards and gives one to each child. "Put on your creativity hats!" she says. "I want each person to think of an action word or _____ (students say 'verb') and write it on the card." Stacey pulls out a purple card.

"Here is my **example.** Get ready to be **close observers.** Put your thumb up if you know the verb." Stacey mimes rubbing her fists in her eyes and stretches her mouth downward. She counts to three for all to say, "cry." She laughs and gives another example. This time she stands up, then sits down and reaches to her right. With her thumb and forefinger she quickly pushes down. Only one child puts his hand up. His other hand is over his mouth suppressing a giggle. Stacey winks.

"Watch again. Notice what I do from the very beginning." This time she pretends to pull down her pants and does the quick action with her hand. Most hands immediately go up. The whole class no laughs.

"One, two, three," she counts. They yell, "Flush!"

"So, verbs are words that show _____?" Stacey waits. Hands go up. She holds up one, two, then three fingers as a signal.

"Action! Action! Action!" is the choral chant.

"Right. Now, I want you to think of interesting verbs to pantomime. Remember that **creative thinkers** don't use their first idea. **Brainstorm** in your groups. Put your verb on one side and your name on the other. You have 3 minutes." Stacey groups students in fours. She cues them when there are 30 seconds left.

"**Criss-cross applesauce.** Eyes up here" Stacey says. Students scurry to pretzel sit on the carpet. She draws out a card.

"Okay, John, **remember to show** with your face and body. Audience, remember to look closely and notice details. John, when you are ready, say **'begin.'**"

John stands still and focuses on a spot above his classmates' heads. He says, "begin" and starts to raise and lower both arms. He slowly spreads his fingers and tilts from side to side. Thumbs go up. **"Curtain,"** he says. John looks around and chooses a boy.

"Flying?" John nods and smiles. The class applauds.

"Oops, remember soft," Stacey says, and she demonstrates clapping with two fingers.

**"What did John do that helped?"** she asks. Students mention the flapping and his "concentration like an eagle."

"**What are other ways to show** flying?" she asks, and a girl shows with one hand a plane-like movement. Stacey smiles, **"That was really different.** That's what we want, people who think of unusual ways to show ideas." She draws more cards and students take turns miming. Throughout, she **coaches** them to "control body and mind" and show meanings in different ways.

After about 10 minutes the kids become distracted: a large roach is crawling up the wall. Stacey announces, "This is South Carolina and there are bugs. Let's name him!"

Someone calls out "Charley!" so Stacey says, "So Charley is crawling up the wall. What is the verb?" "Crawling!" they respond. Stacey whispers, "If you can hear me, tiptoe to your desks. The verb is *tiptoe.*"

When students are seated, Stacey explains she will leave the **verb basket** up front. They can add to it from today's reading.

"Even from science or social studies?" one boy asks.

"Especially science or social studies!" she responds.

"Can we do this again, then?" a girl asks.

"Of course, how about this afternoon?" Stacey asks.

"Yeah!" is the class response. A boy adds, "Let's skip recess!"

Note: More books by Brian Cleary include *A Mink, a Fink, a Skating Rink* (nouns); *Hairy, Scary, Ordinary* (adjectives); and *I and You and Don't Forget Who* (pronouns).

The classroom as a living room—sofas and rocking chair for free reading

# Organization

Seed strategies are organized into four sections, even though many can cross over. The order is (1) energizers and warm-ups; (2) literary elements and genre traits; (3) curricular areas: science, social studies, literacy, and math; and (4) a special section on poetry.

# I. Energizers and Warm-Ups

Energizers and warm-ups prepare students for creative problem solving by promoting concentration and focus and activating higher order thinking. There are energizers and warm-ups at the start of each seed strategy chapter. In this chapter, the focus is on provoking artful word integral to the literary arts.

**Tongue Twisters and Lip Blisters.** In addition to favorites such as "Bugs Black Blood" and "Swiss Wrist Watch," there are new ones in books such as *Six Sick Sheep* (Cole, 1990). "Aluminum Linoleum" and "Rubber Baby Buggy Bumpers" gets everyone puckered and giggling, relaxed, and ready to do creative work. The Internet also has tongue twisters on any topic.

**Chants and Action Poems.** Many collections are available, such as Cole's *Miss Mary Mack* and Booth's *Dr. Knickerbocker.* Ask students to echo line by line. Display words on a transparency or chart and add actions. For example, with Dr. Knickerbocker the chant suggests actions: "Let's put the rhythm in our hands" (clap clap). Encourage variations.

**Word Association.** Form a circle. Leader says a word connected to upcoming lesson. Person to right says the first thing that comes to mind. Connect quickly! Example: spider

**Minister's Cat.** Do this memory/category game to a rhythm. Form a circle. Go around with each student plugging in an adjective, in alphabetical order: "The minister's cat is an *active* cat. The minister's cat is a big cat. The minister's cat is a c_____ cat." Adapt for characters (e.g., Charlotte was an *artistic* spider, *brave* spider).

**Who Stole the Cookies?** Leader asks, "Who stole the cookies from the cookie jar?" The group names the person to the leader's right and says, "_____ stole the cookies from the cookie jar." That student responds, "Not I," and the group chants, "Then who?" Leader names a student, who becomes IT saying, "_____ stole the cookies . . ." IT repeats first question and play continues.

**Uncle Charlie.** Leader thinks of a category and gives clues by saying, "Uncle Charlie likes _____ but not _____." For example, "Uncle Charlie likes pepper but not salt." Guessers reply, "Uncle Charlie likes _____" and gives an example that fits. The leader then says, "Yes, you can come in," meaning they are right or "No, you can't come in," if they are wrong. Here's another clue: "Uncle Charlie likes butter but not bread." (If you said, "hammers but not saws," you can come in: the category is "words with double consonants." *Suggestion:* Brainstorm possible categories before starting.

**Rhyme Change.** Nursery rhymes and other chants and poems are great verbal warm-ups for creative thinking. For example: "Hickory Dickery Dock, A mouse ran up the . . ." (students supply rhymes). Change vowel sounds for phonemic development: Dack, Deck, and so forth.

**SCAMPER Journey.** Use SCAMPER verbs (Ready Reference 2.6) to stretch thinking about a character. Take students on a visualization journey: *Think about Wilbur. Imagine him turning into a little dog looking up at Charlotte's web. Now change him into a big dog. Now think of Wilbur as a pig with a dog body. Make this new Wilbur really small. He is trying to talk to Charlotte, but he gets littler and littler. Oops, now he's growing, growing, growing. He is getting giant. Look at Charlotte's expression. Now he shrinks back and Charlotte starts to grow.*

**Eight Count Character Intro.** First brainstorm a list of characters and then form a circle. The group claps and counts to 8 in unison twice. Leader creatively moves to the center to the eight count on the second round. When she arrives on the eighth count, everyone stops clapping. The leader then says, "My name is (character) and I like _____." As she says this, she pantomimes. She then starts the eight count clapping. The group joins in as she exits back to her place. The person to her left dances into the circle and when he arrives on the eighth count, everyone stops clapping. He introduces himself by saying, "My name is (character) and I like _____," and so forth. *Variation:* Instead of "I like," say "I can" (action).

**Webbing.** This is brainstorming on paper. Put a topic in the center and draw out three to five legs. Write down connected ideas on the legs. Generate lots of ideas or more legs. Next, group ideas by circling or coding similar ones. For example,

before reading *Jack and the Beanstalk,* web "greed." *Variation:* Web any literary element, genre, or person.

**Word Pairs.** Select an even number of important words from an upcoming book or poem. For example, choose eight words that could make four pairs. Ask students to work in groups to pair words any way that makes sense. Ask groups to explain reasons. Celebrate unique connections. *Variation:* Students make up a short story using all the words and tell them in small groups.

**Chain 7.** Choose a topic. Write a first word below it that connects to the topic, a second word connected to the first, and so on. Connect the seventh word to the sixth *and* to the topic. For example, for greed: (1) hog, (2) fat, (3) greasy, (4) slimey, (5) green, (6) puce, and (7) ugly. *Note:* This can sound like poetry when read aloud.

**Cubing (Neeld, 1986).** Examine a literary theme, topic, or character six ways. For example, Cube greed: (1) describe it, (2) analyze it (what are its parts), (3) associate feelings, (4) apply it (what it can be used for), (5) argue for it (pro), and (6) argue against it (con). *Variations:* Write six ways on a cube. Roll it and do 1 minute on each side.

**Squiggle Compositions.** Ask students to draw a squiggly line on paper and then use their imaginations to turn the squiggle into something that makes sense. Show how to emphasize the original line with color by making it darker or thicker so it stands out. Invite students to share drawings and compare processes to written composition and CPS. To wrap up, share *The Squiggle* by Carole Lexa Schaefer. *Variation:* Give everyone the same shape from an upcoming book. Invite imaginative meaning-making. Compare with actual shape in book.

**Mystery Bag.** Make a bag of objects connected to an upcoming book. Reveal one at a time and ask students to find the common connection. For example, sticks, red items, and a basket. For suspense, take out the easiest last. Tell students to not "call out" so everyone sees everything before any guesses. *Variation:* Students make book-related collections and present mystery bags in small groups. Pictures can be used instead of objects.

**Write Right Away/Quickwrite.** Students do timed free writes to activate prior knowledge or synthesize ideas (e.g., before or after a discussion). Set a time limit (e.g., 3 to 5 minutes). *Example:* Do a 5-minute freewrite on "beauty is on the inside" to introduce *Beauty and the Beast.*

**CAP Prediction.** Prepare a list of words from an upcoming book that relate to characters, actions, and problems (CAP). Students then sort the words into the three categories by predicting how they might connect with C, A, or P. Word cards can be put in a pocket chart or coded with the letters.

**NEWS Corners.** The leader prepares a list of theme statements. Label the room corners NEWS. Students are each given a number. The leader reads each statement and makes corner assignments for groups to form and discuss the theme. Example: North corner = students 1–12 odd; East = 1–12 even; West = 13–24 odd; and South = 13–24 even. Theme statement example: "Good friends stick by you in hard times."

**Silly Riddles.** Students write and share riddles with three clues, arranged general to specific. Use these steps: (1) Choose any subject such as *cats.* (2) Use a book title or character and brainstorm words that sound like the syllables: Wil=bur=chill, hill, still, fill, sill; bur=stir, her, purr, sir. (3) Combine syllables to fit the subject: Wil-purr. (4) Make up a question: What did a fan of *Charlotte's Web* name his cat? (Wilpurr)

**Imagination Journey (Concentration/visual Imagery).** Tell a story, based on a piece of literature, using concrete words. Ask students to make mental pictures. This example is based on *The Red Balloon* (Lamorisse) or *The Blue Balloon* (Little). Students can also respond physically. *Example:* Stand in personal spaces. Teacher narrates as students follow. *You are an empty balloon. Feel how limp you are. Someone is now blowing you up. You are getting fuller and fuller. Now you are completely filled with air. You are tied to a string and you float back and forth. You bob up and down. When I say "pop" you quickly deflate and sit in your seats. Ready: POP!*

# II. Teaching About Literary Elements and Genre Traits

*If you want your children to be brilliant, tell them fairy tales. If you want them to be very brilliant, tell them even more fairy tales.* (Albert Einstein)

This section offers starter ideas to teach about literary elements and different literary structures or forms (genres).

**Analogy Go Round (adapted from Starko, 1995).** Use this to review literary elements. The goal is to stretch and twist thinking. Set up a verbal frame to fill in as you go around a circle:

*Opposites:* Force opposite characters together: *Wilbur* is like *Templeton* because _____. Use other literary elements, such as setting: The *farm* is like the *fair* because _____.
*Random combinations:* Combine any idea with a literary element: Wilbur is like a *pencil* because _____. Plug in ideas in the first blank and give reasons in the second.
*Personal analogies:* I am like *Charlotte* because _____.

**Venn Diagrams.** Venn diagrams are used to compare and contrast different aspects of two books or stories: literary or art elements, genre traits, versions of the same story, or books by the same author. Two overlapping circles are drawn. Separate circles are for the individual characteristics of the two things being compared. The overlap area is for commonalities. Example: Compare the main character in the Harry Potter series and Frodo in *Lord of the Rings.*

**Big Bingo (Literary Elements).** Use bulletin board paper cut into 4-foot lengths and folded four times to make a giant bingo board. Display elements. Group students and give time to write the elements randomly in the blanks on the giant card. Play by giving a definition and students cover elements with index cards. When a group wins, they read back the labels, paraphrase a definition, and give an example from a specific literary work.

**Character Wheel.** Write a character's name in the center. Draw and label spokes on the wheel to represent character aspects: speech, thoughts, actions, and appearance and what others think or say about the character. Students work in groups to fill in the wheel. Other categories include character's feelings, worries, hobbies, talents, skills, personality. *Adaptations:* For biographies, change the spokes to include fitting categories: obstacles faced, significant achievements, special life events.

**Character Graph.** Make a graph with boxes at least 1 inch square and with enough spaces on the X and Y axes to write the names of important characters. List the names twice: on the left side in a vertical column and then at the top across the row of squares. Where two names intersect, students write in how the characters interacted or related.

**Sociowheel.** Put the name of a character in the hub of a wheel. Write the names of three or four characters on the rim. Spokes should connect the hub character to each of the rim characters. On each spoke, write how the hub character is connected to each rim character. *Suggestion:* Do on the overhead as a class. *Variation:* Students draw and cut two circles, one as big as a coffee can lid and the other 1 inch diameter bigger. Fasten the circles in the center. Students then write the names of characters around the edges of both circles. Line up names and discuss the ways the characters relate. Turn the wheel and a new character pair lines up and discussion proceeds. *Adaptation:* Make one large wheel for the class. Laminate it so character names can be changed.

**Character Inventories.** Students fill out a personality inventory on a character. Possible items: Favorite foods? Likes? Dislikes? Favorite books? Films? Hobbies? Encourage students to think beyond literal information in the book. *Variation:* Describe clothes, hands, eyes, or body.

**Character Poems.** Use any poem pattern such as diamante, couplet, cinquain or clerihew in to write about characters.

**Character Report Card.** After reading, students complete a report card to grade characters on talent, tact, poise, appearance, honesty, and so forth. With younger students, do this collaboratively. Ask students to justify the grades.

**Somebody–Wanted–But–So (Character, Motive, Problem, Plot).** Make a chart with the four words across the top (Macon, 1991). Students draw or write about the main character (somebody) in the first section, what the character wanted (second section), roadblocks or conflict (but), and the resolution in the "so" section.

**Plot Lines.** Linear, mountainlike, circular, and episodic patterns of events in stories can be drawn using a plot line with events written along it (Tomlinson & Brown, 1996). Roadblocks or obstacles are indicated by bumps in the line. For example:

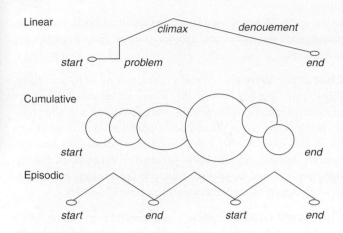

Linear

Cumulative

Episodic

**Episode Cards.** Key plot events are brainstormed and written on small cards. Cards are placed in plot order on the floor or using a pocket chart or clothesline.

**BME Map (Plot Structure).** Show students how to map plot events into BME (beginning, middle, end) or IDC (introduction, development, conclusion) by listing key events under each category (Tompkins & McGee, 1993). Students can then draw or write about a beginning event (problem) that sets the plot in motion, a key middle event, and an end event that resolves the problem. Students can also use the map to plan original stories. BME maps can be used to plan drama responses and prepare for student-led discussions. Ask students to star items they wish to discuss.

**Circle Maps or Pie Story.** These are similar to the BME plot map, but are drawn on a large circle divided into pie pieces. At the top of the circle, a house is drawn to show how stories often begin in a calm homey place. Explain how characters have an adventure, but return home at the end. Events are written or drawn, one at a time, while moving clockwise around the circle. The pie slice below the house is where students begin. When the circle is complete, the story ends in the same place it began. *Adaptations:* Make a large pie map on the board or chart paper and do an example together using, for example, Little Miss Muffett. Note that completed maps are useful props for retelling. *Variation:* Use a baseball diamond instead of the pie image.

**Life Ladder.** Ladders are especially good for biography and similar to a lifeline (Tompkins & McGee, 1993). Students list important events in a character's life on the rungs. Rungs lead up to a climatic event. Earlier events (chronologically) are closer to the bottom.

**Setting Sense Web.** Write or draw the setting in the center. Label five extending legs: see, taste, smell, hear, and touch. Students brainstorm using the web. For example: "What would you see, hear, taste, smell, and touch in the setting of *Peter Rabbit?*"

**Theme Stretch.** Brainstorm themes from a story by asking, "What was it *really* about!?" As an example, choose one from the list and stretch it by asking, "What about _____?" until you have a complete sentence. Example: S = *Charlotte's Web* is about death. T = What about death? S = That everything dies, but you live on through your children or in memories. Work in pairs to have each stretch another theme. *Extension:* Explore the big idea

statements further by creating or finding art work, drama, dance, or music about the statement.

**Take a Stand (Themes).** Themes derived from a story (see Ready Reference 4.3) are written on the board and numbered. Students stand on a "strongly agree to strongly disagree" imaginary line to show their feelings about the theme as each theme number is called. Students can be interviewed about reasons for where they stand.

**Genre Traits Chart.** Write several story titles, from the same genre, in boxes across the top of large paper. The characteristics of the genre are then written down the left-hand side. Story examples are sought during reading to go with each trait. Example traits: folktale (1) opening or closing special language, such as "Once upon a time," (2) vague setting—could be anywhere, (3) plot is a simple chronological order, (4) flat or one-dimensional characters (good or evil, foolish or genius), (5) problem involves a journey from home to perform tasks and confront obstacles, and (6) miraculous events.

**House of Genre.** Read several works from the same genre and make a list of how they are alike. Draw a floor plan of a house and place common traits in the same rooms. *Note:* Get example plans from websites such as HGTV. Example: Write examples of how fairy tales begin in the foyer or on the front porch.

**Genre Web.** Write the story title in the center. Draw legs out to show the traits of the genre to which the story belongs. Brainstorm story examples. See previous folktale genre characteristics. *Variation:* Do as a class.

**Biography Website.** Find guidelines for writing biographies at Biography Maker (www.bham.wednet.edu/bio/biomaker.htm).

**Biography Webs.** Write a person's name in the center. Legs are labeled with important events in the person's life. Smaller legs are webbed off main events. *Extension:* Use webs to write biographical summaries.

# III. Connecting Literature to Curricular Areas

This section offers prompts to plan lessons that integrate literature with science, social studies, literacy, and math. For ideas on how to use literature with drama, music, visual art, and dance, consult the literacy sections of each of the seed strategy chapters. Also see "Book Response Options" in Appendix F.

## Science Focus

**Science Standards.** Curricular standards can be accessed at the National Science Teachers Association (NSTA) website (www.nsta.org).

**Good Literature.** NSTA and the Children's Book Council identify *Outstanding Science Trade Books for Students K–12* each year. Access extensive lists from 1973 forward at www.nsta.org/publications/ostb/. The list of recommended books by subject and grade level is provided.

Camp, C. (2004). *American women inventors*. Enslow. (super book about women who created inventions such as the square-bottom paper bag)

Hopping, L. (2006). *Bone detective: The story of forensic anthropologist Diane France*. Joseph Henry. (comprehensive book on this topic)

Pasachoff, N. (2004). *Linus Pauling: Advancing science, advocating peace*. Enslow. (inspirational story of Pauling's interest in science from childhood to his Nobel Prizes)

Steele, P. (2008). *American women inventors*. National Geographic Society. (illustrated with prints and photographs)

### Earth and Space Science.

Malone, P. (2008). *Close to the wind: The Beaufort scale*. Putnam. (illustrates the Beaufort scale for measuring wind force at sea using fictional voyage)

Platt, R. (2009). *Moon landing*. Candlewick.

Skurzynsk, G. (2004). *Are we alone? Scientists search for life in space*. National Geographic Society. (explains the search for extraterrestrial intelligence)

### Environment and Ecology.

Collier, M. (2008). *Over the mountains: An aerial view of geology*. Mikaya. (photographs by Michael Collier)

Harris, J. (2005). *The least of these: Wild baby bird rescue stories*. Westwind. (beautiful book about bird rehabilitation and identification)

Morrison, G. (2008). *Nature in the neighborhood*. Sandpiper. (valuable beautiful book about urban animals and plants)

Nivola, C. (2009). *Planting the trees of Kenya*. Farrar, Straus, and Giroux. (Nobel Peace Prize winner, Wangari Maathai changed the world one seed at a time.)

### Archaeology, Anthropology, and Paleontology.

Holtz, T. (2008). *Dinosaurs: The most complete, up-to-date encyclopedia for dinosaur lovers of all ages*. Random House. (comprehensive guide)

Turner, P. (2009). *A life in the wild: George Schaller's struggle to save the last great beasts*. Farrar, Straus, & Giroux. (illustrated with photographs of "the great beasts")

Wenzel, G. (2004). *Feathered dinosaurs of China*. Charlesbridge. (describes astonishing fossils of feathered dinosaurs found in China)

### Life Science.

Arnold, C. (2009). *A platypus' world*. Picture Window Books.

Montgomery, C. (2007). *The tarantula scientist*. Sandpiper. (stunning close-up photos and discoveries about the biggest and hairiest spiders)

**Genre Studies.** Certain genres have a special connection to science. Informational books are important resources, but biographies of scientists and inventors are also key literature. For example, Fox's *Women Astronauts: Aboard the Shuttle* (1987) tells the stories of eight women, including Sally Ride. In addition, a science fiction genre study can focus on verifying which science information is "real." Poetry is available that contains accurate science information in a literary format. For example, the books *Monarch Butterfly* (Gibbons, 1989) and the poem "Chrysalis Diary" in Fleischman's *Joyful Noise* are recommended for an insect unit.

**Meaning Prompts: Informational Books (Adapted from Brozo, 1998).** Provide generic prompts for students to respond as they read informational books. For example: *What is . . .*

1. The MOST INTERESTING OR EXCITING word, phrase, sentence, or picture? Why?
2. Something you feel STRONGLY ABOUT? (e.g., an idea, detail, issue, or concept ). Why?
3. An EMOTION OR FEELING connected to the idea, detail, issue, or concept?
4. A CONNECTION between your own experiences and the ideas, details, issues, and concepts?
5. The MOST IMPORTANT idea in the book? Why?

**Things to Write and Say.** Ready Reference 5.1 lists writing forms that can be used in science. For example, write a letter to a favorite character about big ideas you are learning in science.

**Poem Patterns.** Ready Reference 5.2 lists patterns that can be used to write about science topics or processes. For example, write an abab four-line poem about the circulatory system.

**Color Poems.** Students select their favorite color and write the title as a question: What Is Yellow?

Each of the six lines tell how the color connects to the following:

1. *World or nature:* Yellow is the sun and yolks of eggs.
2. *Emotions:* Yellow is happy.
3. *Smells:* Yellow is lemony.
4. *Touch:* Yellow is warm.
5. *Taste:* Yellow is buttery.
6. *Sounds:* Yellow is the ice cream truck's song on a summer day.

*Three-line option:*

Line one: Describe something you associate with it: Yellow is summer.
Line two: Compare it to something: Yellow is like waking up well after being sick.
Line three: Use a verb to describe or show what it does: Yellow lights up my life.

*Four-line option:*

Line one: How the color makes you feel: Yellow cheers me up.
Line two: Three verbs ending in *-ing*: sparkling, shining, streaming.
Line three: A place where this happens: On the beach.
Line four: Repeat color name: Yellow.

## Ready Reference 5.1 Writing Choices A–Z

*Directions: Use this list of writing forms to write about any work of art (literature, song, dance, drama). Any writing can also be done "in character" for drama. Ready Reference 5.2 lists poetry writing forms. The following websites are also useful.*

*ePals.com:* http://epals.com/
Find email partners all over the world
*Blogger.com:* www.blogger.com
Kids can publish their own blogs
*Blogging:* How-to ideas:
www.education-world.com/a_tech/
tech/tech217.shtml
www.edtechpost.ca/gems/
matrix2.gif
http://www.microsoft.com/en/us/
default.aspx (search "blog")

Acceptance speech
Advertisement
Advice column (Dear Abby)
Announcement
Apology
Award presentation
Blog
Brief biography
Bumper sticker
Call or holler
Campaign speech
Certificate
Chant
Cheer
Command
Commercial
Complaint

Compliment
Contract
Curse
Definitions (of unusual words)
Editorial
Email
Epilogue
Excuse
Fable
Funny word list
Greeting card
Headline
Holler (see call or yell)
Horoscopes
Insult
Introduction
Invitation
Irony
Jingle
Journal, log, or diary
Jump-rope rhyme
Letter (business or friendly)
Lie
Limerick
List (to-do, grocery)
Love note
Magic spell
Marquee notice
Menu
Mixed metaphor

Nominating speech
Note
Obituary
Ode
Paradox
Poem (Ready Reference 5.2)
Postcard
Poster
Propaganda (card stacking, etc.)
Ransom note
Remedy
Report
Résumé
Slogan
Stinky pinky
Telegram
Thank-you note
Title (book, TV program)
Tongue twister
Tribute
Tweet
Understatement
Wanted poster
Warning
Weather forecast or report
Wikipedia entry
Will
Wish
Yell (see call or holler)

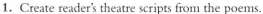

*Variations:*

1. Create reader's theatre scripts from the poems.
2. Create visual art to go with poems or incorporate art into poems themselves (collage, watercolor, paper making, framing, etc.).
3. Write poems about other concepts: trees, flowers, animals, fish, etc.

**Five Ws and H Webs.** After reading an informational book or story, students web the five Ws and H questions: who, what, when, where, how, and why to summarize. Add details to support.

**Acronyms and Acrostics.** *Mnemonics* are memory devices that work because the brain seeks patterns and associations. Invite students to play with acronyms, in which letters in a word stand for a concept. For example, *McHale* is a mnemonic for the forms of energy (mechanical, chemical, heat, atomic, light, electric). Acrostics are mnemonic sentences. Students

remember more when they create their own for science, but here are examples: Nine planets from the sun: "My very eager mother just served us nine pies." (This acrostic includes demoted Pluto.) Stages of the cell: "In Paris, men are tall" (interphase, prophase, metaphase, anaphase, telephase). Soil components, "All pretty hairy men want big sharp razors" (air, particles, humus, minerals, water, bacteria, salts, and rock. Zoological groups in descending order: "Keep pretty cats off fat gorilla stomachs" (kingdom, phylum, class, order, family, genus, species).

## Social Studies Focus

**Social Studies Standards.** You can access standards at the National Council for the Social Studies (NCSS): www.socialstudies.org.

**Good Children's Literature.** NCSS and the Children's Book Council produce *Notable Social Studies Books for Young*

# Ready Reference 5.2  Poem Patterns

*Suggestions: Share poems orally first, asking students to notice details, patterns, and feelings. Then brainstorm personal and important ideas, images, and feelings found. When writing poetry, encourage varying repetition in lines and words and use of alliteration, rhyme, imagery, onomatopoeia, and metaphor. See "IV. Special Focus: Poetry Sharing and Writing" later in the chapter.*

**Repeated lines:** Write repeated lines that start with a stem:

  **I wish:** I wish the sky would stay red all day. I wish I could touch a cloud.

  **Is:** Thunder is grumpy. Happiness is yellow and fizzy.

  **Color:** Red is red hot pepper. (See *Hailstones and Halibut Bones* by O'Neill.)

  **I used to (think or feel), but now I (think or feel):** I used to think poetry had to rhyme, but now I think I can just write all my feelings and the images in my head.

  **If/So or If/Then:** If I were a light bulb/I would glow hot and bright/So people could read in bed at night.

**Five senses:** Greed sounds like whining / Looks like a pile of brown glue / Tastes acidy / Smells like an old sock / Feels slimy.

**Five-line:** Each line has a focus: (1) a thing, (2) a person, (3) a special place, (4) a feeling, (5) a sound. Geraniums/Grandma/Along the driveway/ Hot summer day/Crunching cinders

**Riddle poems:** Give three clues, with the first most general and the third most specific. Example: 1. Easy to carry. 2. Full of words inside. 3. Rhymes with cook.

**Lie poem:** Each line is something not true (do collaboratively). I can write with my feet. I love anchovies. Tuesday is before Monday. Bologna is a vegetable.

**Preposition poem:** <u>Within</u> the drawer / <u>In</u> a desk / <u>Inside</u> the metal tray / <u>With</u> a row of teeth (stapler).

**Concrete or shape:** Words are placed on the page to look like the poem's topic (e.g., a swing, tree, a kiss shape for love).

**Couplet:** Two lines end in rhyme. Sometimes trees / Have knobby knees.

**Triplet:** Three lines that rhyme. Add to couplet: Which gives climbing ease.

**Quartet:** Four lines with a different rhyme patterns: aabb, abab, abcb, abca.

**Clerihew or bio poem:** Quartet about a person: Barak Obama/Created much drama/By being elected/the first president African American

**Limerick:** Humorous five-lined verse with aabba rhyme pattern. The rhythm pattern is important:

    There once was a cat on a porch
    He sat in the sun 'til he scorched
    His paws and backside
    Were both nearly fried
    So his friends starting calling him "Torch."

**Syllable and word count:**

  **Haiku:** Japanese nature verse using three unrhymed lines. There are 17 syllables in the poem distributed by line as 5-7-5.

  **Lune:** Three lines with 3-5-3 words in each line: My funny husband/Tells silly stories/About 4H Camp.

  **Tanka:** Five lines with these syllables per line: 5-7-5-7-7.

  **Cinquain:** Five-line poem that does not rhyme. Number of words per line: 2-4-6-8-2 (subject, adjectives, action, feeling or observation, adjective/synonym).

  **Diamante:** Seven-line poem, shaped like a diamond. Line pattern: 1 noun, 2 adjectives, 3 -*ing* words, 4 word phrases or nouns, 3 -*ing* words, 2 adjectives, 1 antonym. *Note:* The topic can be changed in the middle to relate to the antonym. For example:

    Halloween
    Spooky Fun
    Running Screaming Eating
    Costumes Candy Bunny Baskets
    Hunting Coloring Singing
    Happy Pastel
    Easter

**Found poems:** Cut random phrases from magazines, newspapers, or cards. Phrases are arranged until a poem is created (need not rhyme).

**Other pattern possibilities:** Tongue twisters, jump-rope rhymes, and advertising jingles.

---

People each year. Access the extensive annotated bibliography at www.socialstudies.org/resources/notable/.

## Biography.

Denenberg, D., & Roscoe, L. (2006). *50 American Heroes Every Kid Should Meet.* Millbrook Press.

Harness, C. (2007). *The adventurous life of Myles Standish and the amazing-but-true survival story of Plymouth Colony.* National Geographic Children's Books.

Lekuton, J. (2005). *Facing the lion: Growing up Maasai on the African savanna.* National Geographic. (journey of a young Kenyan man)

Lasky, K. (2003). *The man who made time travel.* Farrar, Straus & Giroux. (timepiece for longitude; revolutionizes sea travel)

## Contemporary Concerns.

Christelow, E. (2008). *Vote!* Sandpiper. (electoral politics for youth)

Hampton, W. (2007). *September 11, 2001: Attack on New York City.* Candlewick.

Lewis, J. (2006). *Heroes and she-roes: Poems of amazing and everyday heroes.* Dial.

Pin, I. (2007). *When I grow up, I will win the Nobel Peace Prize.* Farrar, Straus & Giroux. (introduction to the Nobel Peace Prize)

Literary Elements

### Geography/People/Places.

Lester, A. (2006). *Are we there yet?* Miller. (journey around Australia from a child's perspective)

Foreman, M. (2007). *Mia's story: A sketchbook of hopes and dreams.* Candlewick. (Mia and her family harvest scrap from a dump in Chile)

Ancona, G. (2003). *Murals: Walls that sing.* Marshall Cavendish. (history of murals)

### History, Life, and Culture in the Americas.

Bates, K. (2003). *America the beautiful.* Putman. (line of poetry match places in the United States)

Hansen, J., & McGowan, G. (2003). *Freedom roads: Searching for the Underground Railroad.* Cricket. (a must-have book on how historians use primary documents)

Lefkowitz, A. (2007). *Bushnell's submarine: The best kept secret of the American Revolution.* Scholastic Nonfiction. (submarine mission during the American Revolution)

Uhlberg, M. (2009). *The printer.* Scholastic. (deaf printer in the 1940s warns about a fire)

Weatherford, C. (2007). *Freedom on the menu: The Greensboro sit-ins.* Puffin. (child and civil rights in 1960s)

### World Culture and History.

Matthews, J. (2007). *Pirates.* Atheneum. (pirate lore)

Deem, J. (2006). *Bodies from the ash: Life and death in Ancient Pompeii.* Houghton Mifflin. (illustrated with prints and photographs)

Patz, N. (2003). *Who was the woman who wore the hat?* Dutton. (experiences of interned Jews)

### Environment/Energy/Ecology.

Revkin, A. (2007). *The North Pole was here: Puzzles and perils at the top of the world.* Kingfisher/Houghton Mifflin. (stories of North Pole expeditions)

Levey, R. (2006). *Dust Bowl! The 1930s black blizzards.* Bearport.

### Economics.

Smothers, E. (2003). *The hard-times jar.* Farrar, Straus & Giroux. (migrant family saves money in a jar)

**Multiple Genre Investigations.** Although any genre has potential connections to social studies, informational books, biography, and historical fiction have particular links; each can present unit content from a different angle. With historical fiction, students can use informational books to verify accurate versus fictional details. Poetry can be connected with informational books. For example, the narrative poem "The Midnight Ride of Paul Revere" by Longfellow can be paired with a Revolutionary War study. It is also available as a picture book.

**Culture Unit Maps and Webs.** To structure a culture unit, have students use multiple fiction and nonfiction source books to "map" or organize information they find using categories such as the following. Example categories are (1) language, the dialect or actual words used in a book; (2) values, as they contrast with mainstream America; (3) art, music, drama, or dance in the book and what each art reveals about values, customs, and the like; (4) historical facts; (5) customs and traditions; (6) significant contributions the culture has made; (7) special events and issues associated with the culture; and (8) foods, clothing, and housing uniqueness.

**Folktale Detectives.** Students study a culture by (1) reading folktales to find out what is valued or (2) exploring how the literature of the world's cultures has common motifs. For example, use a Venn diagram to compare Snow White and the Queen: young versus old; happy versus bitter; inner strength versus focus on magic and spells. *Suggestions:* Contrast characters and settings in folktales—high versus low place, young versus old, bad versus good (Levi-Straus, 1967).

**What-If Writing.** In *Jokes to Tell Your Worst Enemy* (Corbett, 1984), there is a section on "History Rewritten Mother's Way" (e.g., Paul Revere's mother will not let him go out). Use this as a prompt for "what-if" writing about historical events. Discuss the humor and possible serious side effects. *Arts Extension:* Create drama scenes to show what ifs.

**Joke Books.** There is now a collection of jokes and riddles about most important places, events, and people, including nearly every president. Start a "Joke of the Day" routine for social studies to provoke critical creative thinking. For example, *The Abraham Lincoln Joke Book* (DeRegniers, 1978) is a gem because most are stories and jokes he actually told.

**Mystery Person.** After reading a piece of historical fiction or a biography, students choose a character and find three objects that represent him or her. Objects are then revealed to the class one at a time, with the most obvious one (in its connection to the character) coming last. Students guess who the person is by connecting the three items.

**Biography Boxes.** Students fill boxes with objects, pictures, and poems that may have been important to a person. Boxes are shared. Students learn that things used or seen each day are also things famous individuals used. *Variation:* Use with any book character or an artist or author.

**Book Maps.** Use a biography or piece of historical fiction and draw the setting or a portion of it to show where and what story events take place (Johnson & Louis, 1987). Use the following steps.

1. Demonstrate map making. Read aloud a story with simple events and setting, and keep track of characters on a setting drawing.
2. Guide map making. Read aloud another story with simple events and settings with the students tracking where the characters are and the events of the story. Each decides what he or she would like to include in the map and how.
3. Encourage or assign map making for independent reading.

**Timelines.** Timelines are visual representations of historical events and can be used to summarize an informational book or historical fiction. Use a horizontal line and make hash marks vertically to record chronologically important dates and events.

**Point-of-View Guide.** *Before* reading a historical or informational book, pairs interview one another about characters that will appear in the book (e.g., settlers, explorers, or any persons). Interviewers ask five Ws and H questions and write down responses. *After* reading, students review interviews and compare and contrast with book information. To develop comparisons, students can role-play a press conference or TV talk show.

**Lifelines.** The goal is to record significant events in a person's life by rereading biographies and recording events on long shelf paper (Tompkins, 1990). A line is drawn down the middle. Dates of important events are put chronologically on the line, marked by hash marks. Beside, above, or under each date a title, description, and/or picture of each event is shown. Photocopied pictures can be used or students may create illustrations.

**Story Cloths.** Adinkra are African story cloths that are both worn and read. Story themes (e.g., peace) that reflect a country or culture (e.g., West Africa) are derived and painted or drawn on plain fabric such as split pillowcases. Students display or model finished textile art and explain the concepts it contains (Wright & Kowalczyk, 2000).

## Literacy: Reading and Language Arts Focus

**Literacy/Literature Standards.** Standards can be accessed at the websites of the National Council of Teachers of English (www.ncte.org) and the International Reading Association (www.ira.org).

**Predict–Prove (Stauffer, 1969).** This strategy sets problem solving in motion before reading. Evidence-based guesses are solicited using a book cover or page art. Students then read to confirm or reject predictions so there is active meaning-making. The basic steps are as follows:

1. Read the title, show the cover, and selected illustrations.
2. Ask for predictions about characters (Who will it be about?), setting (When and where?), and plot (What problems might be in the story?).
3. Record predictions on a chart.
4. Students read independently or teacher reads aloud.
5. Students give evidence during think stops to confirm or reject predictions. *Suggestion:* Celebrate both rejection and confirmation.

**Lit Logs.** Literature Logs (wallpaper bound books or composition books) increase focus for independent reading. Students date entries, note stories read (titles and pages), and write reactions or questions about the plot, characters, and style. They may retell plot events, make predictions, write a poem, and/or free write about feelings. *Variation:* Logs may be exchanged to write peer responses, or the teacher may write comments. *Note:* Teachers need to demonstrate how to write entries and responses on the overhead, especially how to respond constructively.

**Prequels and Sequels.** After reading a story, students write what may have happened before the book was written or after the end. Encourage students to attend to details and literary elements so they can write in a similar style, use appropriate characters, and add fitting plot events. Emphasize consistency as well as plausibility in the plot. *Arts Extension:* Create prequel or sequel art.

**Class Newspaper.** News articles, weather forecasts, advertisements, interviews, comics, classifieds, and obituaries can be created about any literature. For example, a Charlotte's Web Newspaper might involve students in writing forms used in different parts of a newspaper including the five Ws and H structure of articles. The newspaper could be a culmination of a core book unit or developed chapter by chapter (e.g., do cartoons for one chapter, classifieds for another, and obituaries at the end).

**Real-Life Writing.** Ready Reference 5.1 shows many forms in which people write. Students can use these to write about any topic or book they have read. *Example:* Blog about the behavior of the Big Bad Wolf.

**Word Walls.** Word walls make visible a critical element of literature—words. Student-generated word walls boost interest in seeking out words to post (use cards or sticky notes). A word wall can be a source for new writing ideas and an aid for unknown words. Words can be webbed, individually or as a class, and expanded using common affixes (*-ed, ing, -s, -er*). For example, the word *range* can be webbed or expanded into: *ranger, arrange, arrangement, arranging, deranged,* and *rearrange*.

**Word Sorts.** Students list interesting words found *during* reading on cards. Afterward, pairs categorize the words. Possible categories are characters or people, setting, time, problems or conflict, main idea or themes, and plot or actions. *Adaptations:* (1) Present a list of words from the story or poem *before* reading. Students group words as a prediction activity. (2) Post a chart listing literary elements. Students jot down a key word for each element as they read.

**Vocabutoons.** Students create cartoons to show the meanings of words. See the book by this title by Sam Burchers (1996). *Variation:* Cartoon scenes where characters use types of sentences such as declarative, exclamatory, and so forth.

**Buddy Reading.** Use this variation for independent reading. Partners share a book in these ways: take turns reading aloud, read chorally, or read silently. They agree to stop at points to discuss (1) exciting or puzzling parts, (2) connections to their lives, the world, or other books, and (3) most important ideas. They can use the five Ws and H questions to question each other and strategies such as fat questions, explicit (right there) questions, or implicit (between the lines) questions. See Ready Reference 4.13 for questions to post as choices. For older students, pair to discuss parts read silently using strategies such as EPC (see Chapter 4, Block VII).

**Partner Writing.** Students read a story and then write to a friend about it. Possible entries are a letter, a note about what they liked or didn't like and why, or a mini book review

Literary Elements

(appropriate for students who've read book reviews; consult *Book Review Digest* in a library or get reviews from journals such as *Horn Book* or *School Library Journal* as examples). For example:

Dear Jenny,

    I want to recommend *Walk Two Moon* to you. The book really makes you think because there are lots of flashbacks. It is sort of like a mystery because you only get clues to what is going on and then you find out the truth at the very end.

    The author makes you love the characters—especially the grandparents. This book made me cry, but I felt like it made sense at the end. It also made me treasure my parents and grandparents.

                             Your buddy, Lou

**Bridges (Berthoff, 1981).** Draw a vertical line down the middle of a page; this is the bridge. The left-hand side is used to write down words, phrases, sentences, or passages students find interesting or important *during* reading. On the right side, students bridge the ideas from the left column to their own experiences by writing connections. *Variation:* Use to prepare for discussion by asking students to write questions in the right column. These can be prioritized by starring important ones. Follow with time to write about how the discussion changed their thinking.

**Picture Book Art Criticism.** Teach students how to see and discuss art, thereby increasing comprehension of a picture book. The steps are shown in Ready Reference 5.3.

**Heads-Up Guides.** Display three to five theme-based statements for a book students will read. They rate their agreement on a continuum or mark each as true or false and discuss reasons for ratings. Next, students read to confirm or change ratings. *Adaptation:* Do rating as a follow-up to stimulate discussion of a book or ask students to generate statements. Example from *Like Jake and Me*: Directions: Rate from 1 = Strongly agree to 5 = Strongly disagree.

1. Everyone is afraid of something.
2. It is important for people to feel needed by other people.
3. Boys should not dance because that is a girl thing.
4. When people talk about something, they are sure to understand each other.

**Story-Map Yourself.** Teach story structure by having students map their own lives. Map sections are: Who? (main character is the student), When and where? (setting), Problems? Goals? Plot (key events to reach goals), Plot resolution (what the student hopes will happen). A variety of maps can be used: (1) web with three legs labeled beginning, middle, and end; (2) bubbles for each literary element; (3) E-shaped charts with the theme along the vertical line, key events on the beginning, middle, and end on the horizontal lines, and characters in the open spaces.

**Sentence Frames.** Frames are response prompts used to jump-start thinking. Frames can be used *after* any book or lesson. Use them for writing or as an oral response. Repeat the frame as many times as desired (e.g., three times for each). The following are mostly based on children's books.

1. Fortunately _____ Unfortunately _____
2. Someday _____
3. Why _____? Because _____
4. _____ is the hardest when _____ and is the easiest when _____
5. I used to (think or feel) _____, but now I (think or feel) _____
6. When I _____ I look or feel like _____ because _____
7. I seem to be _____, but really I am _____
8. The important thing about _____ is that _____. It's _____, it's _____, and it's _____. But the most important thing about is it's _____
9. I am _____ I saw _____ I heard _____ I smelled _____ I tasted _____ I felt _____
10. When I was young _____
11. If _____ then _____ because.

## Ready Reference 5.3   Picture Book Art Criticism

1. List and describe everything you see.
   - Subject matter: anything that can be identified
   - Shapes, lines, texture, light/value, colors, and use of space
   - Techniques: how the materials, tools, and techniques are used
2. Analyze and connect the things you see.
   - Tell about relationships among the parts, how the art is organized or composed (balance, movement, pattern, overlapping, proportion, unity and variety).
3. Describe the mood.
   - List emotional reactions or feelings and how the art seems to cause them.

4. Draw conclusions about the meaning.
   - Explain what you think the art is about and give evidence for conclusions.
   - Explain what you think the artist was trying to show.
5. Evaluate the "goodness" of the art.
   - Give your opinion supported by evidence from the artwork.
   - Tell what you like and do not like and why.
6. Speculate.
   - Give ideas about "what if" the art was bigger, a different color, made of other materials, and more.

**Letter Books (Tierney, Soter, & O'Flahavan, 1989).** Use Cleary's *Dear Mr. Henshaw* or *Dear Mr. Blueberry* (James) to introduce writing letters to an author or artist. Ask students to note what the characters included (e.g., questions about creating characters, ideas or feelings about books, and why the artist chose a certain art media or style). Students then write to an author. *Note:* A creative book in which actual letters are delivered to characters is *The Jolly Postman's or Other People's Letters* (Ahlberg, 1986). The letters can form the basis for drama or writing (e.g., writing other letters in roles). *Variation:* Students may also write a letter to the editor based on issues in a book. Students take a stance and give reasons to defend it. This could also be done as a *before* reading activity.

**Take-Offs.** This type of writing involves adapting a story pattern to make a new story. Predictable books such as Williams and Chorao's *Kevin's Grandma* provide a take-off framework. For example, Zolotow's *Someday* is a series of episodes that all begin with the word *someday*. Books can be illustrated and bound.

**Word Collections.** Students list interesting words found *during* reading. Words can be used to structure book discussions: Students discuss how each word describes or relates to the themes and main character. For example, use words from *Lindbergh's View from the Air*: nature, season, pasture, nestled, transformed, perspective.

**Twenty Questions.** A student or panel assumes the role of a character (e.g., fairy tales). The audience then asks "yes or no" questions, but questions cannot be "Is your name _____ ?" The goal is to guess the identity in 20 or less questions. *Variation:* Form teams to guess and alternate. Periodically ask students to put thumbs up if they know the identity. Coach for better questions by asking, "What would be a question you could ask to find out an important detail?"

**Found Object Story Boxes.** Students find objects related to a book or poem and arrange them in any box as a container. Items can be glued to the exterior and interior of the box. Students present boxes by discussing the connections to the book. *Resources:* Found objects are natural or man-made items used by artists, such as Picasso, to make collage or assemblage art. See the Tate Gallery Online Glossary (www.tate.org.uk/collections/glossary/definition.jsp?entryId=112).

Websites of artists creating found object and assemblage art include the following:

www.johndahlsen.com/enviro_art.html

www.artofpeace.com/home.htm

www.fowldwellings.com/whatwedo.html

www.bonniemeltzer.com/

## Math Focus

**Math Standards.** All standards can be accessed at the National Council of Teachers of Mathematics (www.nctm.org).

**Good Literature.** Teachers often feel that math is harder to integrate with literature and writing than other areas, but there are now many math-based pieces of literature. In addition to the Anno books, the following are two favorites.

Lionni, L. (1960). *Inch by inch.* Astor-Honor. (length, capacity, area, and volume)

Scieszka, J., & Smith, L. (1995). *Math curse.* Viking. (many math concepts)

NCTM has reviews of more than 550 titles with analyses of books' content and accuracy, illustrations, style, and any included activities. Order: *The Wonderful World of Mathematics: A Critically Annotated List of Children's Books in Mathematics, Second Edition* (www.nctm.org).

Following are examples of math-based children's literature.

Anno, M. (2004). *Anno's mysterious multiplying jar.* Putnam.

Burns, N. (2008). *Greedy triangle.* Scholastic.

Caple, K. (1988). *The biggest nose.* Houghton Mifflin. (length, area, volume)

Ellis, J. (2004). *What's your angle Pythagoras?* Charlesbridge.

Ellis, J. (2010). *Pythagoras and the ratios*: A math adventure. Charlesbridge.

Evans, E., et al. (2002). *Mathlinks: Teaching to the NCTM 2000 standards through children's literature.* Libraries Unlimited.

Hopkinson, D. (1995). *Sweet Clara and the freedom quilt.* Knopf.

Levy, J. (2004). *Journey along the Erie Canal.* Powerkids Press.

Schwartz, D. (2006). *How much is a million?* Harper Collins.

Schwartz, D. (2006). *Millions to measure.* Harper Collins.

Tang, G. (2003). *Math-terpieces.* Scholastic.

Tompert, A. (1997). *Grandfather Tang's story.* Crown. (tangrams)

Various authors. (2004). *Math literature series.* Math Publication Solutions.

**Math/Literature Websites and Resources.** Elaine Young's website (http://sci.tamucc.edu/%7Eeyoung/literature.html) is a comprehensive, sorted by math topic, and extensive list of children's literature around a mathematical theme.

**NCTM Lesson Plans.** For examples of lesson plans that involve children's literature go to the NCTM website (www.nctm.org) and search "lesson plans."

**Math Poetry.** Many types of poetry depend on math concepts for their construction (e.g., counting syllables, words, and lines in haiku, diamante, and limericks). Show students different poem patterns (Ready Reference 5.3) to use to write math poems (e.g., a haiku about numbers in nature: A two-eyed giraffe/Uses four legs to reach high/And eat with one mouth).

**Story Problems.** Use math-based literature to create story problems. For example, in Carle's *The Very Hungry Caterpillar,* the caterpillar eats a certain number of things each day. How many total items did he eat?

**Chapter Books.** Students create a math character and write a story with several chapters. In each chapter the character solves another math problem. The problems can be related to math skills and concepts previously taught (D. Smith, Lady's Island Elementary School).

**Plot Line Graphs.** Graphing can be used to display a variety of student responses such as the excitement level of events or whether they are "good news" or "bad news" (Johnson & Louis, 1987). Here's how:

1. Label the vertical axis, for example: the top line "very exciting," and the bottom labeled "not exciting" (or use "good news/bad news"). The horizontal axis is labeled with numbers that will represent key story events. Present the graph on the overhead or Smart Board to show how it works.
2. Brainstorm story events. Number these in chronological order, which is represented by numbers along the horizontal axis.
3. Rate each plot event according to its excitement level or whatever the graph topic is. Place a dot at the intersection and then connect the dots. Ask students for conclusions.
4. Students create their own graphs for another story. *Variation:* List favorite stories and graph how much students like them.

**Math Shape or Concept Books.** Students choose a geometric shape or a concept (addition, fractions, etc.) and write stories using shapes or concepts as characters. Informational books can also be created with pages that explain the math concept. Books can be illustrated and bound. *Variation:* Show the video *Dot and the Line,* a romance between these two art elements.

**Math Copycat Books.** Use math-based children's books as frames to write copycat books. For example, McMillan's *Counting Wildflowers,* Carle's *The Very Hungry Caterpillar,* or Sendak's *Chicken Soup with Rice* can be used as frames.

**Picture Book Math.** Give groups stacks of picture books and ask student to find the math necessary to make a book. For example, find number of pages (often 32), size of pages, words per page (or in whole book), and so forth.

**Math POV.** Students can be asked to read any book from a mathematics perspective. List math concepts such as measurement, counting, proportion, and discuss the book's theme, plot, characters, setting using those concepts. Sort into important and unimportant connections. *Example:* number of times Charlotte wrote in web.

**Sequence Story.** Write or tell a story with each line beginning with a number, in consecutive order. For example, "*One* day Mary was sleeping when the doorbell rang. *Two* men were at the door. *Three* fingers were missing on one man's hand. *Four* minutes passed before Mary decided what to do." Teams can work to try to get as far as possible.

# IV. Special Focus: Poetry Sharing and Writing

*It is hard work to write science poems. But it is good hard, not the bad hard where you don't want to do it and don't know how. I get my ideas out when I write poems.* (Carlos, age 10)

Poetry is sound and sense. Words seem to sing when rhyme, rhythm, and repeated sounds combine. Thinking through poetry is a sensory experience that, like Carlos says, "gets ideas out" in ways no other art form does. Read aloud, "Easy Pickin'?" What do you notice about the sound patterns? What is the sense or meaning?

Cobbler pie cereal toppin'
There's no stoppin', easy pickin'
Blackberries

In the thicket
Stickers prickin'
Splinters stickin'
Blackberries

Tricky pickin'
Fingers prickin'
Sticky pickin'
Blackberries

Finger lickin'
It's addictin'
Oh so wicked
Blackberries

Time's a tickin'
Neck's a crickin'
Gettin' sickened
Blackberries

Cobbler pie cereal toppin'
There's no stopping, easy pickin'
Blackberries

Poetry is particularly important to literacy development because it gives most children their introduction to the intoxicating music of words (e.g., Mother Goose rhymes, Dr. Seuss). This section is a brief overview of how to make poetry integral to daily literacy, math, science, and social studies instruction, including how to use the abundance of poetry *about* math science and social studies. Poetry performances (Ready Reference 5.4) are one way to bring poetry to life. Poetry writing strategies (Ready Reference 5.2) are important ways for students to "create meaning" of key curricular concepts. Poetry also naturally connects with other art forms using strategies such as poem prints (visual art strategy) or setting poetry to music. To get started, recommended poets and poems are listed in Ready References 4.5 and 4.12. Building Block II (in Chapter 4) describes poetic elements that are important to teach.

## General Principles for Poetry Integration

As with any arts area, the emphasis in poetry integration is on the process of sharing, responding to, and creating poetry to engage students in making meaning. The focus is not on perfect poetry recitations or writing poetry that conforms to rigid rules. The following are general poetry integration principles.

- Poetry is sound. Nothing is as important as sharing poems orally, using a variety of strategies that focus on enjoying the aesthetic experience of hearing interesting word sounds.

## Ready Reference 5.4 Poetry Performance Strategies

*Directions: Following are ways to perform poetry.*

**Choral or unison.** Do all together.

**Cumulative.** One or two start and gradually more voices come in. Everyone reads the last line.

**Antiphonal.** Two opposing group (e.g., high and low, loud and soft).

**Line-a-child.** Each student reads one line.

**Refrain with groups.** Repeated lines are done by a chorus.

**Character voices.** Assume a character and use appropriate voice.

**Narrative pantomime.** Do actions the poem suggests as narrator reads or recites.

**Sign language.** Use finger spelling or American Sign Language to perform.

**Background music or art.** Play music or show art as poem is read.

**Cloze.** Use sticky notes and cover predictable words. Students then guess.

**Reader-responder.** Reader reads one line and responder orally improvises (e.g., *Mary had a little lamb.* Responder: *I bet her husband was surprised*).

**Reader's theatre.** Set poem up like a script with names and parts.

**Use props.** Add musical instruments, puppets, objects.

**Sound effects.** Assign sounds to be made when certain words are read.

**Question and answer.** Find poems in question and answer form (e.g., Q = Who has seen the wind? A = Neither I nor you) (Christina Rossetti). Everyone gets a Q or A and reads when it makes sense. *Note:* Students can then write their own Q & A poems.

**Actions.** Children dance or mime certain words or phrases.

**Memorize and recite.** Change volume, pitch, tone, rate, pause, and stress to do oral interpretation.

**Q-U (cue you).** Sequence reading in which you read your line on a cue card after a cue line. For example:

**Q:** *Mary had a little lamb.*
**U:** *Its fleece was white as snow.*
**Q:** *Its fleece was white as snow.*
**U:** *And everywhere that Mary went . . .*

**Call and response (echoic).** Students echo leader's oral interpretation line by line.

**Canon or round.** Read like a round. Different groups start at different times.

**Ostinatoes.** Repeat a word or phrase that is important (e.g., "Who has seen the wind?" then repeat *Wind-Wind* or chant throughout reading).

---

- Poetry is sense. Students need to hear poetry read well to make sense of it. No one knows all that a poem means, so students should be encouraged to use the poem and their reactions as data to experiment with possible meanings. Teachers should go light on interpreting *for* students.

- Creating and sharing poems gives a sense of control over language, which gives students confidence and leads to reading and writing growth.

- Risk taking should be encouraged. Poets freely explore the strange, the silly, and the far-fetched; so should children. Rules about grammar, punctuation, and capitalization simply do not apply.

- Students need to be guided to discover what makes poetry. Ask questions that allow them to figure out that poetry is often more compact, emotionally intense, full of sound patterns (rhythm and rhyme, onomatopoeia, alliteration), and figurative language (metaphor, imagery).

- Teach the sound qualities. Rhyme, rhythm, repetition, onomatopoeia, and alliteration are what make poetry seem musical.

## Ongoing Poetry Routines

- "Poem a Day" (PAD) is about actively *doing* poems using performance strategies (Ready Reference 5.4). Poem charts are useful props that allow everyone to see the words.

- For "PoeTree," place a small branch in a pot filled with plaster of Paris. From the limbs, students hang copies of poems

they find, adapt, or write (Hopkins, 1987). Poems can be shared during PAD performances.

- Poetry anthologies occur when students collect favorite poetry and write their own to create a private collection. Trading is encouraged. Personal anthologies can be made into books or organized in recipe boxes under categories such as animals, humor, weather, people, places, holidays, and feelings.

## Poetry Sharing and Performance

- Warm up the face and voice. See energizers and warm-ups in Chapters 9 (drama), 11 (dance), and 13 (music). For example, use tongue twisters.

- Encourage repeated sharing of the same poems to increase enjoyment and attune the ear to special use of words.

- Organize choral reading to add the power and support of the group. Teach lessons on musical dynamics: sing together; do rounds; group the class into twos, threes, or fours and give each a musical phrase, ostinato, or refrain.

- Use musical signals for start, stop, slow, fast, loud, and soft. Conduct poems in the style of an orchestra maestro (see Chapter 13).

- Teach rhythm and beat by encouraging clapping, snapping, and tapping. Divide the class in half, with one group chanting a phrase or refrain while the other claps the beat. Challenge by giving the second group a different, syncopated refrain to the same simple beat.

- Coach students out of shyness. Focus on images in the poem, ask students to add simple gestures and movements, try different voices, or read louder and slower.
- Ask students to give each other feedback with focus on what worked.

## Memorizing Poetry

- Memorizing is a valuable, ongoing activity *if* students are allowed to choose poems and given options for performance (e.g., partners, tape recordings, use of visual aids, props, or puppets).
- Warm up memory and imaging skills with daily activities such as "The Minister's Cat" or "I'm Going on a Trip" which require remembering and repeating ideas. Another warm-up is to do a 1-minute category of the day. For example, list all the red things in your house.
- Start simple with one line for each student. The class can then recite with each one doing his or her line. A longer poem with a refrain can be used with students learning just the refrain while the teacher reads or recites the rest.
- Use the build-it-up method: Teach the first line of a poem, then recite it and add the second line, then add the third, and so on until the whole poem is memorized.

## Composing Poetry: Written and Oral

- Start with oral sharing: Children learn to listen and speak before they learn to read and write. See poet Jack Prelutsky conduct a workshop on writing poetry at http://teacher. scholastic.com/writewit/poetry/jack_home.htm
- Set up a station with examples of different poem patterns like those in Ready Reference 5.2. Janeczko's award-winning anthology, *A Kick in the Head: An Everyday Guide to Poetic Form* (Candlewick) is a recommended source.
- Coach students to write about concrete things and feelings using specific details. Show students how to think about any topic using the five senses.
- Sharpen observation skills. For example, ask students to describe an object in the room, then one not in the room. Ask for details. Ask students to describe an object in the room using only three words or offer nouns, such as *cat, tree,* and *sky* and ask for possible adjectives to describe each.
- Provide a line and challenge students to expand with details. For example, "The man walked down the street." (Expand and elaborate by inserting words and adding phrases.)
- Teach imagery: Use think–aloud to demonstrate how to make pictures in your head. Tell about what *you* see when you think of a cat, tree, and so forth. Create idea charts and lists using categories, such as places, feelings, animals, colors, flowers, noises, smells, vehicles, and weather.
- Teach metaphor: (1) Ask students to look at a familiar object or the sky. (2) Ask what it looks like—what it *is* like, what it reminds them of. Use cubing to stretch thinking (see energizers). (3) Make two lists of nouns and compare something from one list to something on another. (4) Offer a choice of objects; then ask students to write a detailed objective description of it. Then have students write a poem made up of one-line comparisons to something. For example, A _____ is like a _____ because _____.
- Use poem patterns (Ready Reference 5.2) to provide structures to adapt. For example, for the "I wish …" pattern, ask each student to write a line that includes a color. The class shares the poem using line-a-child. Another example: Select an object or person. Each student says one line about the subject. Encourage students to use senses (e.g., I see, I hear, It feels).
- Teach the concepts of line, syllable, and counting syllables: Cut up a poem into lines. Have students reassemble it. Put separate lines in a pocket chart or have students each hold a sentence strip with a line as the class reads it. Count lines in poems. Count syllables by feeling the Adam's apple as words are said. Exaggerate and stretch syllables for emphasis.
- Teach about rhyme: Read a poem, leaving out rhyming words. Pause for students to provide (cloze strategy). Use contests: Groups try to recite the longest list of rhymes. Use challenges: (1) Write a silly poem using as many rhyming words as possible. Start by picking a word and ask for three to five rhymes. Next, write a poem using those as end words. Repeat with three pairs of different rhymes. (2) Try orally composing poems in rhymed couplets. Give the first line, and the students supply the second, back and forth. (3) Memorize four-line nursery rhymes. Take out the familiar rhyme words and ask for new ones. Explore combinations and discuss what happens. (4) Write original quatrains using different rhyme patterns: aabb, abab, abcb, abca.
- Teach rhythm and beat: Start with songs, keeping time with hands, feet, or rhythm instruments. Overemphasize the beat in choral recitations. Replace the words with numbers or scat phrases such as "doo-wop."

**Literacy Poetry.** Acclaimed poet, Lee Bennett Hopkins put together a glorious anthology of poems about literacy written by—well-known poets such as Emily Dickinson, Eve Merriam, and Nikki Grimes. Share these to inspire students to write about similar topics. The 2004 book is *Wonderful Words: Poems about Reading, Writing, Speaking, and Listening* (Simon & Schuster).

**Poetry Art.** Ask students to examine a piece of art and note the mood/feel, use of media, style, and art elements (Ready References 6.7 through 6.10). Give students examples of poetry patterns (cinquain, haiku, limerick; see Ready Reference 5.2). Write collaborative pattern poems and then individual ones based on art. *Alternative*: Students write poems and then create art to go with poems. For example they can print or stomp over the top of the poem, create collages around poem edges, or do watercolors with poems written across the bottom.

**Poem Match.** Students find or write a poem that connects to a work of art (see poem patterns in Ready Reference 5.2). Art and poetry can be shared during docent talks and displayed together in a class museum.

**Visual Poetry.** Create concrete poetry written in the shape of the subject. For an example of a whole book with this type of poetry, see Froman's *Seeing Things: A Book of Poems.*

**Onomatopoeia Poems.** Create sound poems by using objects or rhythm instruments. Begin by exploring sounds using different objects. Work in groups to plan a five-line poem that builds from one sound up to five sounds. Decide which sound will be line 1, which two sounds will be line 2, and so on. Encourage thinking about rhythm patterns, accent, tempo, and dynamics. Students can rehearse their sound poems, present them, and then write them down. For example, note the onomatopoetic words in this poem:

> Ding
> Bang Bang
> Shush Shush Shush
> Rattle Rattle, Clap Clap
> Ding Bang Shush Rattle Donk

**Collections.** Collect poems about music (e.g., Shel Silverstein's "Ourchestra") for individual and class anthologies. Display special poems on posters and perform with rhythm instruments. Myra Cohen Livingston's *Call Down the Moon* is recommended.

**Poem Pantomimes.** Pantomime possibilities exist in many poems. For example, de Regniers's, "Keep a Poem in Your Pocket" is about what a poem can do for you. Students mime as the poem is read (narrative pantomime). Beyer's "Jump or Jiggle" poem describes the ways different animals walk; Crane's "Snow Toward Evening" describes a calm, peaceful snowy night; and Hillyer's "Lullaby" is about a rowboat drifting along. In Miller's "Cat," movements are described in detail. *Note:* Select poems for narrative pantomime carefully because poetry is hard to edit.

**Reader-Responder.** Do in partners. Reader reads one line and responder orally improvises by saying whatever comes to mind. Continue throughout the poem. For example, reader: "Jack and Jill went up the hill." Responder: "I wonder how high the hill was."

**Choral Reading.** Choral reading invites experimentation with the musical elements of words (volume, tempo, pitch, pause, and stress) that build fluency. Options include the following: (1) Leader reads a line and the class echoes; (2) leader reads a section and the class reads a refrain or creates an original refrain; (3) solo readers read sections and the whole group reads the rest; or (4) two groups take turns reading. (See poetry performance ideas in Ready Reference 5.4.) Do repeated readings to increase fluency.

# Classroom Snapshot
## Arts-Based Read-Alouds

Literature integration was introduced in Chapter 4 using an arts-based read-aloud. This Classroom Snapshot brings us back to this literature integration strategy and leads into the next chapter on integrating visual art. Notice how the teacher uses inserted questions to keep attention and cause students to think about deep meanings. Afterward, she **coaches** students through the **problem-solving process** with more **open questions** to create a composition. The thinking process includes the same pre-during-post steps as written composition, but arts materials are used. In particular, notice how Fannie Petros directs attention to **details** and focuses on **experimentation** and diverse products.

"Today I'm going to read *Sweet Clara and the Freedom Quilt* (Hopkinson)," Fannie Petros says. "I want you to look and listen closely so you can make your own quilts."

Fannie begins to read in a soft southern dialect that is her own. She uses **inserted questions** to keep attention and engage. They are all fat questions with multiple answers, such as "Why was she away from her mama?" She takes time to show each picture and asks **what they notice**. She weaves information about the artist into the story.

An inclusion teacher periodically offers extended explanations about key concepts such as "big house." She also asks open questions such as "What is she going to do?" "Why would she make a map?" "What would she do with a quilt?" and "Why are they trying to get to Canada?" The inclusion teacher is there for an autistic girl, a boy with learning disabilities, and another student with language delays. To this last question a red-haired girl answers, "To be free." A girl with braids says, "To escape slavery." And a boy with glasses answers, "For happiness."

Fannie reads with lots of **vocal dynamics**—she pauses, stretches words, and changes pitches. All of these musical elements of fluency make the story come alive.

"What does it mean to 'get big with listening'?" she asks at one point.

A boy in a sweatshirt says he thinks it is "listening hard."

A girl responds, "It helps you get somewhere."

Fannie reads on and asks, "What was the underground railroad?"

"A secret place," says a boy with large blue eyes.

A boy elaborates, "It was going from house to house and to boats and houses to get away."

After the read-aloud, students choose partners.

"Choose wisely," Fannie advises. "Work with your 3D pattern blocks to experiment. Think of how many ways you can make a North Star."

"It can be anyways," pipes up a small boy.

"That's right. Let's look at examples of the many ways. See these. Some repeat so they have a _____." Fannie waits and students fill in with "pattern."

"What else do you notice?"

"Different colors."

"Kinds of shapes."

"I see patterns," says a girl,

"So, why are we doing the North Star?" Fannie asks.

"For the Freedom Train Riders—to point the direction to freedom," exclaims a boy.

"OK, choose where you will sit and start to experiment with your 3D pieces," Fannie says.

Students begin to partner and work with the soft rubber shapes of all sizes and forms. Fannie circulates and responds to inquiries with comments, such as "You choose. Make them your own way. Yes, repeat the pattern, but make yours different. Nobody should be copying. Use your own imagination."

Students confer about possible arrangements and periodically call out shape names.

"Hexagon, cool!" says one boy.

After about 10 minutes Fannie shows students how to use construction paper to transfer their rubber shapes "draft" into final draft form. ✴

## Conclusion

*In the long history of man, countless empires and nations have come and gone. Those which created no lasting works of art are reduced today to short footnotes in history's catalog. Art is a nation's most precious heritage, for it is in our works of art that we reveal to ourselves, and to others, the inner vision which guides us as a Nation. And where there is no vision, the people perish.* (Lyndon B. Johnson, signing ceremony for the National Foundation on the Arts and Humanities Act of 1965)

This chapter is a compendium of seed strategies to jump-start planning for literature integration throughout the curriculum. The ideas are intended to prime the pump for creative thinking as teachers plan literature-based lessons and integrated units.

---

### Teachers as Leaders: AI Advocacy

Prepare a short talk for other teachers or the PTA on reasons to integrate poetry into science, social studies, math, and literacy instruction. Share specific poetry examples and involve the audience as much as possible. See Ready Reference 5.4 on poetry performance ideas.

---

**PEARSON**
**myeducationlab**

Go to the Activities and Applications section for Topic *Strategies for Teaching* at MyEducationLab for your course and complete the video activities entitled "Using Tableau to Build Comprehension" and "Debriefing about Thoughts and Feelings After Tableau."

Go to the Book Specific Resources section in the MyEducationLab for your course, select your book and Chapter 5 to respond to the Questions to Guide Reading and Response Options for this chapter.

## Resources

See the Appendix for more resources, including websites.

### Websites

Lesson Plans, articles, and Internet resources:
ReadWriteThink: www.readwritethink.org
TeachersFirst: www.teachersfirst.com
Scholastic Teachers: http://teacher.scholastic.com/
Reading Online: www.readingonline.org/

# 6

# Integrating Visual Art Throughout the Curriculum

*The arts expand the message with visual images, give emotional context through music, and bring words to life through dance and drama.* (Claudia Cornett)

## Overview

This chapter is an introduction to meaningful integration of visual art into other curricular areas. There is a brief synopsis of *why* visual art provides a unique tool to create meaning and *what* visual art knowledge classroom teachers need. Most of the chapter deals with the 10 AI building blocks, which are general principles for *how* to integrate visual art.

## Introduction: Visual Learning

*A painter takes the sun and makes it into a yellow spot. An artist takes a yellow spot and makes it into a sun.* (Pablo Picasso)

Humans are profoundly visual beings so it is not surprising that we have created a world that is flooded with visual images. The digital revolution has made imagery ubiquitous. The combination of human inclination, availability of images, and image-making technology "creates an extremely promising environment for increasing the influence of the visual arts on society, culture and the individual" (Deborah Reeve, executive director, National Art Association, March 6, 2007). Arts integration allows classroom teachers and visual arts specialists to join forces in using the power of visual art to enhance learning.

Technology now provides ready access to every kind of visual art from the most common to the most refined in world-class museums. Behind the profusion of digital images aren't just computer skills. Creative thinking and visual art know-how have never been in more demand. Most countries cannot produce enough workers to meet the need. For example, in the United States, the Alliance of Motion Picture and Television Producers asked the governor of California to declare a state of emergency because Hollywood cannot find digital artists. It seems there are plenty of folks who are computer literate, but they all lack drawing skills (Eger, 2004).

## Visual Literacy

The idea that we use visual images to communicate is not new. Historically, religious frescoes and paintings in churches throughout the world have educated the print illiterate. According to stained glass artist Dee Mayes, the word *story* came to be applied to levels of buildings because stained glass windows that told stories were built up and up as generations added more to the tale. Today visual communication is touted as one of the "new literacies."

Visual literacy is about understanding and knowing how to create visual images to express thoughts and feelings. Visual literacy has incredible potential to elevate school achievement, as it promises increased lifelong enjoyment and gives students a leg up in today's job market. AI educators develop students' visual literacy by working alongside visual art specialists to meet standards in this area.

The power of the visual arts to transform learning has much to do with our visually biased brains. It is astounding that visual brain receptors outnumber auditory receptors 30 to 1. Many argue that it is nearly impossible to think without visual images and cite case studies such as Albert Einstein's claim, "I rarely think in words at all." Einstein explained he only used words to express thoughts after they had been formed visually. His brain weighed less than most men's, and he solved physics problems through imagination. He would imagine himself riding alongside a light beam or falling in an elevator. "The way I do it is I visualize a structure in my imagination, maybe it's complex, maybe it's simple. And I rotate it, and I put different combinations together. And I can sit all day doing this" (Shaw, 2000, p. 210). When he was told that many folks only thought in words, Einstein simply laughed.

It isn't surprising that learning through images is superior. Learning is about thinking and thinking relies on images. Try to think about what happened yesterday or what you're going to do tomorrow. As I write this nonfiction text I find myself constantly making mental images of real and imagined teachers, students, and school contexts. Research Update 6.1 shows examples of important research on visual imagery.

Educators are awakening to how visual learning is central to communication (Gambrell & Koskinen, 2002; Sadoski & Paivio, 2001; Tompkins, 2003. Sanders Bustle (2004) calls visual communication the most "powerful meaning-making device[s] in young peoples lives" (p. 417). In particular, literacy specialists tap plentiful and accessible visual art resources, such as picture books, to boost motivation and extend comprehension. Cutting-edge teaching of visual imaging strategies is now used to improve both comprehension and written composition (Alejandro, 2005; Chu, 2005; Greenberg, 2005; Kiefer, 2005; Cornett, 2010). Although this work has not generally fallen under "arts integration," the pedagogy is consistent with AI beliefs. We can construct meaning using the visual images inside our minds that have the same features as visual art outside.

Visual imaging is integral to creative thinking (see CPS in Ready Reference 2.6) so teachers are behooved to demonstrate how to imagine. To do so they coach students to "make pictures in their heads" and demonstrate how to do so by describing the colors, shapes, textures, and so forth, of their own interior brain art (Gambrell & Koskinen, 2002). Teachers readily use materials such as picture books to coach students to create meaning from visual messages, including inviting deeper understanding by delving into choices artists make about use of art elements, techniques, and media.

The teacher in the opening Classroom Snapshot joins others who teach students to develop the artist's eye (Starnes & Siegesmund, 2004). Notice how Mr. Novak causes his students to use CPS to "read art." He coaches them to gather detailed data and connect experiences, which are tried and true ways to increase comprehension (Pressley, 2002). He uses descriptive feedback and pushes them to draw conclusions about big ideas. Mr. Novak's inquiry orientation contrasts with an outdated focus on "covering" content, but it is in concert with the kind of teaching that has become a springboard for teachers and artists involved in AI (Burnaford, 2007). Today best teaching practices are about in-depth study of texts—artwork in this case with focus on student-meaning construction. For information on bolded strategies in the Snapshot, consult the index.

---

## Research Update 6.1    Visual Imagery

- We have 30 times more visual nerve fibers than auditory; 30 percent of the brain's cortex is devoted to visual processing, only 3 percent for hearing (Lindstrom, 1999).
- There is strong evidence for the influence of visual images on comprehension (Alejandro, 2005; Chu, 2005; Greenberg, 2005; Kiefer, 2005; RAND, 2002).
- Comprehension involves forming a "mental model" of a text, and along with emotional response, is vital to aesthetic understanding (Sadoski & Paivio, 2004, p. 31).
- Imaginative response is central to comprehension of literary works and is related to more objective response such as evaluation of plot importance (Sadoski & Paivio, 2004, p. 31).
- Readers comprehend by making perceptual and motor representations of story events and update mental simulations as information changes. Research on real-time reading shows brain regions activating that closely mirror those used when people actually perform or observe real-world activities. For example, when a character "pulled a light cord," activity increases in a frontal lobes region associated with grasping motions. When a character "went through the front door into the kitchen," activity increased in the temporal lobes (Speer, Reynolds, Swallow, & Zacks, 2009).
- Decades of empirical studies show that mental imagery, concreteness, and verbal association play major roles in representing and comprehending knowledge, learning and memory of school material, effective instruction, individual differences, and motivation (Clark & Paivio, 1991).
- Texts of all lengths with high "imageability" were more than twice as comprehensible and memorable than abstract language (Sadoski & Paivio, 2001).
- Word imageability is one of the best predictors of oral reading performance. Beginning readers read concrete, imageable words more accurately than abstract words with effects more prominent for poor readers (Coltheart, Laxon, & Keating, 1988; Jorm, 1977; Juel & Holmes, 1981).
- What is most imaged and felt during reading is what is most retained. Recall was overwhelmingly associated with emotions and imagery during the reading, not what was rated as important. In sum, what was comprehended most was the subjective, aesthetic experience (Sadoski & Quast, 1990).

### Instruction

- Influential teachers of reading use concrete (visual) examples and help students analyze abstract concepts in concrete terms (Ruddell, 1997).
- Instruction to form mental images significantly enhances reading comprehension and memory. Numerous studies show that elementary students can create mental images. With only brief training and scaffolding, most can effectively use imagery to increase comprehension (Gambrell & Koskinen, 2002; Sadoski & Paivio, 2001).
- Third graders told to *make pictures in their heads* to remember what they were to read remembered twice as many facts and made twice as many accurate predictions as a control group told to just think about what they read to remember. Even with minimal inducement, children can use mental imagery to increase comprehension (Gambrell, 1982; Pressley, 2002).
- Teachers can teach visual arts elements and these five mental actions to increase visualization: (1) transfer long-term memories into temporary visual memory, (2) zoom in on details, (3) embellish images, (4) rotate image, and (5) scan visually with your mind's eye (Bruer, 1999).
- The questioning protocol used in the Visual Thinking Strategies Imagery Training has successfully increased an array of student thinking capacities (Housen & Yenawine, 2000; website: www.vue.org).

# Classroom Snapshot

## Fantasy Unit with Chagall

*Every child is an artist. The problem is how to remain an artist once he grows up.* (Pablo Picasso)

The artist easel is draped with a black cloth. Mr. Novak sits on a low chair. This morning 2-hour literacy block takes a workshop approach. Students are actively involved in using comprehension and composition strategies that parallel CPS. The fourth and fifth graders read and write in a variety of genres, including nonprint multimedia forms.

"What is this?" Mr. Novak asks.

"The **mystery bag,**" the class responds.

"Right. You know the routine. First item." Mr. Novak pulls a yellow rubber duckie from the bag. Students giggle.

"**Look closely.** Think about the colors, what it means, how it makes you feel." He pauses. "Next item." Out comes a yellow ball.

"Oh, oh," one boy raises his hand, "I know."

"Keep looking. We have two more items. Charles, glad you are making **connections**" Mr. Novak gives this **descriptive feedback** while he struggles to reveal a floppy teddy bear. Charles looks puzzled.

"Last item. Think about how the items are related." He pulls out a child's tutu. More giggles.

"I see several **thumbs up.** Take a few more seconds. Look closely. Make connections. Okay, Michael."

"Things from our past."

"Why do you say that?" Mr. Novak asks to **coach** for evidence.

"Because they are little kids' stuff—soft and man-made."

"Yes. You're right. Who else? Sonya?"

"They are happy things. They remind me of having fun when I don't have to go to school." The class laughs.

"What do you think of Sonya's idea? Aspen?" Mr. Novak asks to cause students to respond to one another's comments.

"I agree they make you feel happy and I agree with Michael about the past. I think it goes together. Soft toys and pleasant memories." Several shake their heads to agree.

"Charles, you had an idea early on. What were you thinking?"

"I thought you were just doing 'yellow' or 'plastic.' Then you brought out the teddy bear. The yellow part fits because, um, it is an uplifting color."

After a few more minutes, Mr. Novak unveils the bottom half of the **shrouded print.**

"Cool," one boy says.

"What is it?" someone else says.

"**Look closely. What do you see?**" asks Mr. Novak.

"Really weird stuff. Is that a tree?"

"I see two people and one is green with white lips."

"Look, a cross. He has on a ring, too."

"The nuts or flowers are exploding. See the splattered paint!"

"Wow, those are strange shapes, like a moon eclipse. But it's red. Look there's a ring with an apple on it. Maybe this artist

didn't have a lot of toys and had to play with this stuff," concludes one boy.

"It's not a person on the right. Look. It's more the shape of a snout or something. Maybe he played with a pig!" The class laughs at this creative interpretation.

"You are really noticing colors, shapes, and images," Mr. Novak gives descriptive feedback and then coaches further, "What else? How does this make you feel?"

"It has bright yellow so it's happy. There is the cross. Maybe he's religious."

"But the guy is green. Of course, when you're a kid, colors don't matter. Maybe a kid painted this?" Kristen asks.

The class continues with many more discoveries until Mr. Novak asks them to get ready to see the rest. The class is still. Many lean forward. Slowly he pulls up the cloth. Little by little the print is revealed. The kids gasp.

"Make connections," Mr. Novak urges them.

"This is crazy. The people and houses are upside down. The woman is milking a cow in the head of a horse! That can't happen."

"But the colors are really interesting. It's like a dream. Things can be anything in your dreams," concludes a girl who hasn't spoken before.

The discussion is animated as students make more discoveries. Comments converge on themes about dreams, toys, happy memories, and childhood. One child uses the term "abstract" and another mentions "collage." About 15 minutes into the lesson, Mr. Novak explains that a Russian Jew named Marc Chagall painted it in 1911. He was inspired by pleasant childhood memories and folktales. Mr. Novak asks about their memories of stories from childhood. They list fairy tale titles and Disney films.

## Lesson Development

Mr. Novak asks what makes fantasy. Students list characteristics, such as "something not real" and "dreamlike places and events," and he writes them on the overhead. He then explains they are starting a **genre unit** on fantasy. He asks them why Chagall might have painted fantastic images in *I and the Village*. The students return to the "good feelings and freedom" ideas from earlier. He then asks about *Charlotte's Web* (White) and how it relates. Students comment on the elements of fantasy in the story (e.g., animals talking) and also how most heard it read aloud in second grade. It was a good memory from their childhood.

## Lesson Conclusion

Mr. Novak asks why people might write, read, or paint fantasy. There are many responses: for entertainment, relaxation, to make money, to be creative, to get ideas out, to feel good. He brings out a **text set** of fantasy books: *Tuck Everlasting* (Babbitt), *Able's Island* (Steig), *The Borrowers* (Norton), *Bunnicula* (Howe & Howe), and *The Indian in the Cupboard* (Banks). He says they'll be able to choose one book for the fantasy study and a goal is to find more specific characteristics. He puts books on the chalk tray for browsing. Students will rate their choices by the end of the day. Five **book circles** will form for discussion and students will eventually create their own fantasy pieces using both writing and visual art.

## Postscript

The fantasy unit lasted a month. Students met daily to discuss books. Mr. Novak held "**What do you see?**" discussions of other fantasy paintings, such as Henri Rousseau's *The Dream*, and students explored the artists' motives and ways for creating these works. The unit culminated in a **museum display** of student paintings. All were framed. At an **"exhibit opening,"** students acted as **docent guides** for students and adults who came to tour the museum (part of the hall).

# Arts Integration Building Blocks

Chapter 3 includes a plan for arts integration (AI) based on progressive implementation (teaching *with*, *about*, *in*, and *through* the arts) of 10 building blocks (Ready Reference 3.3). Teachers gain increasing competence at customizing curricular goals and standards to meet student needs. This works because, by nature, the arts are about celebrating, accommodating, and promoting differences, that is, differentiation.

The 10 AI building blocks attempt to balance the use of art as a teaching and learning tool (arts for learning sake) with respect for visual art as a discipline itself (arts for art's sake) (Booth, 2003). Curriculum integration involves more than a reorganization of subject areas. It evolves because of a "change in philosophy" (Coufal & Coufal, 2002, p. 113). The foundation stone (Building Block I) of AI is an educational philosophy informed by research and learning theories. This is the *why* of AI. In this chapter it is followed by the visual arts that literacy teachers need to know for meaningful implementation. This is the *what*, which is followed by the *how* blocks: how to plan collaboratively, create an aesthetic environment, use visual art–based literature, adapt best teaching practices, design instructional routines, differentiate instruction for diverse learners, assess, and partner with visual art specialists.

# Building Block I: Philosophy: Why Integrate Visual Art?

*Every genuine work of art has as much reason for being as the earth and the sun.* (Ralph Waldo Emerson)

Examples of research studies that support visual art integration appear in Research Update 6.2. Such findings combine with educational theories and professional wisdom to inform AI

---

## Research Update 6.2    Visual Art and Achievement

- Teaching students how to use visual thinking strategies to understand visual art produced growth in cognitive skills including observing, hypothesizing, and evidence-based reasoning, which were transferred to reading and writing (Housen & Yenawine, 2000; website: www.vtshome.org).
- Research conducted in New Hampshire, Texas, and 36 other states on the visual art-based literacy models "Image-Making" and "Picture Writing" shows students made significant gains in reading and writing on standardized tests. At-risk learners made the greatest gains. Both models focus on students making art during the writing process (Olshansky, 2006). Reports, including scores, are available at www.picturingwriting.org/effectiveness.html.
- Hundreds of third graders in the Guggenheim Museum program performed better in six categories of literacy and critical thinking, including description, hypothesizing, and reasoning (website: www.learningthroughart.org/research_findings.php).
- Seventh-grade "reluctant readers" were more active readers and showed improved skills when visual art was integrated. Strategies included drawing pictures of images during reading, illustrating, and visually representing key details in nonfiction (Deasy, 2002).
- Children who drew pictures and then wrote about the art had improved writing. Students used more elaborative thinking, as well as stronger descriptive and more concrete language (Andrzejczak, Trainin, & Poldberg, 2005).

- Although no causal links were found between using visual art and increasing attention to detail, there was a positive impact on reading when visual art was used to introduce lessons (Burger & Winner, 2000).
- Nine- and 10-year-olds in a New York City "visual thinking" curriculum developed reasoning skills when taught to use visual evidence to "read" art. This translated into better "reading" of evidence in science (Deasy, 2002).
- When sixth graders' understanding of history was assessed through drawing as well as writing, they were able to show comprehension. This was true for both language proficient and English limited students (Deasy, 2002).
- Students with learning disabilities gained 1 to 2 years in developmental levels after 8 weeks of special drawing instruction. The program was found to increase reading, writing, math, and language skills up to 20 percent (Brookes, 1996).
- Visual thinking using color tools increases the cognitive processes of problem solving, organizing, and memory (Longo, 1999).
- Reading and math scores were significantly higher for 96 students in eight visual-art-enriched first grades. Students scored an average of 77 percent at grade level, compared to 55 percent for the control group (Gardiner, 1996).
- Visual arts students scored an average of 47 points higher in math and 31 points higher on the verbal section of the SAT. For more information, visit http://professionals.collegeboard.com/gateway; click the "search" button and enter "national report."

beliefs, that is, philosophy. Teachers should integrate visual art because art:

Is a basic communication vehicle
Engages emotions and motivates
Develops aesthetic understanding
Promotes attention to detail
Develops higher order thinking
Gives confidence to be unique
Promotes respect for diversity
Develops concentration, responsibility, and self-discipline
Is a natural partner with other curricular areas
Is a way to assess

## Art Is a Basic Communication Vehicle

There is a story about Picasso doing a portrait of a man's wife. When the man saw the painting, he complained it did not look like her. "Do you have something that does?" Picasso asked. The man opened his wallet and pulled out a photo of his wife. "Awfully small, isn't she?" Picasso remarked.

Word and nonword communication relies on *representing* ideas, not being literal. Neither words nor images can ever show everything we mean. Think of drawings in the dictionary, photographs in history texts, and plastic models in science. None of these images are "real." Maps, charts, and diagrams are abstractions that show "significant properties" (Arnheim, 1989, p. 30). "A human figure carved in wood is never just a human figure, a painted apple is never just an apple" (p. 29). Words and images are tools to help us make sense of the world; they hold aspects of the truth, not the whole truth.

As discussed previously, our brains are prewired to think visually. Visual thinking is apparent even in early childhood. The child who sees a "fingernail" in the night sky is using metaphor to make sense. She compares a known image with something inexplicable. Unfortunately, the visual capacity can wither if not stimulated (see brain research in Chapter 2). What's more, children need more than visual exposure; they need to be taught how to understand and express themselves through visual communication. For example, students can be asked to discuss what an image like a single tree, against a desolate background, conveys. Such an image can communicate a sense of loneliness that would take paragraphs to describe. Even with paragraphs, words cannot entirely capture the range of emotional and cognitive messages that can be created from image.

Unfortunately, art is often confined to the aesthetic realm and not respected for its profound communication potential. For example, the Schuster Center, in the Wright Brothers hometown of Dayton, Ohio, is known for its stunning architecture. In particular, the theatre ceiling gives a beautiful illusion of twinkling stars enjoyed by patrons. Few know that it is a scientifically accurate replica of the night sky as it would have appeared when Orville and Wilbur Wright made their first flight. The cultural bias for *verbal* communication is particularly persistent in schools. Visual images are pervasive in instructional materials, but teachers give minimal attention to decoding art messages, even in picture books, which are center stage in literacy programs. Scarce instruction in visual literacy crops up in children's art: stereotyped use of colors, shapes, and symbols.

Even middle schoolers still depict the sun as a circle with sticks coming off or draw birds as joined commas. Children are capable of more complex perception.

Classroom teachers who act on a broadened definition of literacy teach students to decode visual symbols and use them to express understandings; the result is expanded communication capacity—visual literacy. Mr. Novak was working in this vein when he taught students to look closely at details, to observe how artists use color, shapes, and line in nonliteral ways. Such lessons tap innate abilities to think symbolically.

Long before children can read words in print fluently enough for high-level comprehension, they can do high-level thinking about artworks and achieve insight. When taught how to peel away layers and unwind bits of any visual message, students experience "ah-ha" moments. They can further learn to decode meanings in visual patterns, and acquire new tools and techniques to *express* ideas and feelings. It's all about using CPS.

## Art Engages Emotions and Motivates

At the start of the 21st century we are gaining new respect for the role of intuition in understanding. *Emotional Intelligence* author Daniel Goleman (2005) claims, "A view of human nature that ignores the power of emotions is sadly shortsighted . . . intelligence can come to nothing when the emotions hold sway" (p. 4). Arts-based teaching taps the power of emotion to motivate.

The roots of both the words *emotion* and *motivate* have to do with motion. Emotions cause us to take action that can result in positive or negative consequences. While art involves the intellect, it activates affective ways of knowing, too. It is an outlet for ideas and feelings. It is a safety valve that can allow emotional catharsis. Jenkins (1986) calls this "externalizing" what we feel and know (p. 15). Both viewing and doing art can give emotional release. This is evident in art therapy sessions when clients report feeling relaxed and joyous. Delight can arise from something as simple as making a line curve in a special way or as complex as the emotions stirred by the famous *National Geographic* cover photo of a stunning green-eyed Afghani girl.

## Art Develops Aesthetic Understanding

*I come here every day on my coffee break because it is some kinda purdy.* (Landscaper, Sapphire Valley Golf Course, North Carolina)

Aesthetic responses lie at the heart of living. Aromas, sounds, colors, tastes, and textures fill our environment and stimulate responses. Brain research shows that smell, for example, is directly processed by the brain with effects so long-lasting we almost never forget them. Aesthetic knowing results when senses are sharpened, which heightens the awareness of experiences (Feeney & Moravcik, 1987). This perceptual process feels stimulating and satisfying, which accounts for why so many enjoy visual arts experiences (Lowenfeld & Brittain, 1975).

Broudy (1979) argues all thinking and action depend on aesthetic thinking, especially image making, which gives the imagination "the raw material for concepts and ideals" (p. 63).

Moore (1998) uses the old-fashioned word *beauty* to describe a common aesthetic conclusion. He argues that beauty is a source of imagination "that never dries up." He explains that a thing can be absorbing, without being pretty. It can even be ugly "yet seize the soul as beautiful" (p. 278). Some artworks are so arresting that they "lure the heart into profound imagination" (p. 278). Aesthetic experiences are thus primary sources of understanding vital to every child's education.

Art is hands on and tangible. We touch materials to make art using color, line, and shape. When we view art, both kinesthetic and tactile senses are activated by brushstrokes that go up or down or are heavy or light. What we see is a function of sensory perception—a painting can evoke the sounds and smells of a summer boat ride or a raucous party. As the senses are stimulated, we respond mentally, physically, and emotionally. Thus, the symbols used in art are sensory rich and form a language that beckons us to consider new perspectives and use prior knowledge to make personal meaning.

Even though children may not have verbal language to express aesthetic understanding, they often are at a higher level of aesthetic development than we deem possible. Think of expressions of wonder and delight at flowers, butterflies, or pictures—gasps and sighs that show heightened sensitivity. Parsons's research (1987) on stages of aesthetic development is summarized in Ready Reference 6.3. It describes a progression that is not intended to be prescriptive, but can give teachers an expanded vision of developmental possibilities.

## Art Promotes Attention to Details

Grumet (2004) explains that, "art does not communicate its messages in generalities" (p. 64). Think of the way we know people by their particular features. Now consider the results of an amazing study where subjects were shown 10,000 images, each for 5 seconds over 5 days. On the last day they were shown a random sample of 160 images. Subjects identified images from pairs previously show with 73 percent accuracy (Standing, 1973). The impossibility of these results is explained by the size of the brain's visual cortex and the fact that our eyes contain nearly 70 percent of the body's sensory receptors. Millions of signals are sent every second along the optic nerves to the brain's visual processing centers (Wolfe, 2001, p. 153). The capacity for long-term memory of images and the capacity to notice details appears unlimited.

Even infants are capable of high-level thought using visual details, as shown in their reactions to human faces (Wingert & Brant, 2005). Young children also use higher order problem solving during art *making*. Their drawings of people and trees show how they shrewdly analyze and translate observations using basic shape patterns. These are more than mechanical imitations of what is seen; they are expressions of what children *know*. For example, preschoolers make stick drawings of people with huge heads. This is not what children see; they are showing that they have concluded that the head is the most important feature of humans.

Eisner (2005) urges a greater focus on teaching details. Most teachers would agree that there seems to be a cause–effect relationship between acute visual perception (detail orientation) and the ability to read and write well. Visual art thrives on particulars with artists striving to make each work unique, sometimes with just a slight change in color or line. Students can be drawn into understanding the importance of details by inviting them to react to a changed smile on *Mona Lisa*, digitally altered with a slight upturning of the line. Even young children "read" meanings into minor details and can be coached to transfer this skill to other learning. As one teacher involved in visual art integration explained, "I think that concentrating on the details in artwork gave them the eye and the patience to go back into their writing again . . . the art helps the writing and the writing helps the art" (Baker et al., 2004, p. 7).

## Art Develops Higher Order Thinking

*A room hung with pictures is a room hung with thoughts.* (Sir Joshua Reynolds)

The headline is "Cops Study Vermeer," and it's no joke. New York City police officers are now trained to solve crimes by looking at art. It's all in the details. Art educator Amy Herman instructs the

---

## Ready Reference 6.3 Aesthetic Development Stages

*Stage 1: Favorites.* Children delight in virtually all paintings, especially the colors. They like to pick favorites and talk about personal connections.

*Stage 2: Subject matter.* Focus on representational art; the more realistic, the better. The artist's skill is admired.

*Stage 3: Emotions.* Concern is for emotional stimulation, the more intense the better. Now the person has more than a personal preference and has developed an appreciation for how an artist causes the viewer to respond with emotion.

*Stage 4: Style and form.* The viewer now understands that art is socially and culturally influenced and is important because of its meaning-making capabilities. Art is viewed as an important communication vehicle. Color, texture, space, and form are analyzed as the person judges the competence of the artist to create new perspectives.

*Stage 5: Autonomy.* Judgments are made on a personal and social basis. Art is now viewed as an important tool to consider the human condition and life itself through the questions it raises and the ideas and feelings it evokes. Artworks are used to seek truth and share meaning with others in a kind of "conversation about life."

*Source:* Adapted from Parsons, Michael, J. (1987). Talk about a painting: A cognitive developmental analysis. *Journal of Aesthetic Education, 21*(1), 37–55.

NYPD to notice the who, what, where, why, and when of art from Rembrandt to Renoir—and do it quickly. She teaches them to systematically look from foreground to background to get a sense of the whole scene. Officers practice drawing inferences and conclusions based on what they see. One captain found grand larceny and felony assault in El Greco's *The Purification of the Temple*. A detective explained that crime and art are both solved by noticing little things (Bryon, 2005). The same classes are also taught to medical students to help in diagnostic work.

There is a growing respect for how art involves more than use of the hands. Visual perception is a cognitive event—understanding is indivisible from seeing. Through guided CPS, students make this discovery. They learn to think beyond the literal when they are taught to examine details and make sense of symbols and patterns. For example, students can learn that cubism expresses thoughts and feelings without *literally representing* anything. Through art *making,* students go further to experience the joy of creating their own meanings using hands-on materials. Students who expect to generate rather than imitate, think deeper. In contrast, teachers distort art when they give black line pages to color or directions that mimic painting by number. Art pedagogy abandoned these practices long ago, but a few still lag behind. We see the results in look-alike artworks pasted on school windows. This work shows kids can follow directions; it is not evidence of higher order thinking. Furthermore, it is not authentic art.

Higher order thinking develops through confrontation with problems. The arts provide the opportunity to do qualitative inquiry using our senses, imagination, and craft and appraisal skills (Eisner, 2002a and b). Whereas artists give us clues to create meaning, children must be taught how to arrive at their own conclusions. Teachers either advance or thwart this development. When students are given distorted ideas about what art is and how it comes to be, the latter occurs. For example, if they are taught art must always look like something, they can lose faith in their abilities to create art. Some eventually refuse to try. Arnheim (1989) explains that making realistic artworks is not the end all and is even rejected by some cultures. For example, a realistic depiction of pharaoh would suggest he was a mere human. At one time that could get you killed.

CPS orchestrates higher order thinking for a specific purpose—to solve problems. Ready Reference 2.6 shows how skills are coordinated. Some teachers also use a taxonomy to construct higher order thinking questions, such as Benjamin Bloom's (1956) well-known taxonomy. He divided cognition into levels. Recently, one of Bloom's students reordered his taxonomy and placed "creative thinking" (synthesis) at the top. I like the idea of creativity being at a high level, but what is more important is teaching students *how* and *when* to synthesize ideas and feelings. Following are the original Bloom levels with example questions and prompts.

1. *Memory:* just the facts (literal) (What are the primary colors?)
2. *Interpretation:* read between the lines and add your own experiences to infer (Explain *in your own words* how to create shades and tints.)
3. *Application:* put a skill to use (Use what we've been learning about mixing colors to make different skin tones.)
4. *Analysis:* examine pieces to develop understanding (Look closely to discover the repeated elements in this art.)
5. *Synthesis:* put pieces together to make a creative whole; requires invention and imagination (How can you use collage materials to show what you learned about the environment?)
6. *Evaluation:* make a judgment based on the goodness or badness, rightness or wrongness using certain criteria (What do you think about this piece of art? Why do you think as you do?)

Students can also use Bloom's taxonomy to generate their own questions and to respond in any art form. For example, a synthesis-level art project could be planned to demonstrate key learning from an ecology unit. The goal is cause students to think beyond the memory or literal level and coordinate higher order thinking skills to solve problems.

## Art Gives Confidence to Be Unique

*Art is an extension of a person, an expression of who I am and what I am.* (Sabe & Harrison)

In a 2-year study of teachers who integrated visual art, McDermott (2004) found that children who struggled in regular classrooms were often successful using art. He concluded art did not "make them feel vulnerable." Instead it provided them with countless ways to think about and express ideas (p. 13). Expression is a primary goal of education and is linked to understanding. Students gain confidence as they learn to use art concepts and skills to express themselves. They feel free to use knowledge about science, culture, and narrative in artwork without "one answer" looming over them (Olhansky, 2006)

Art doing and viewing adds another way for children to communicate. In particular, it stretches perspectives. Creativity is more openly valued so students are more willing to experiment. The focus on novel thinking in a noncompetitive context allows them to vie with internal standards of what makes sense. Through imaginative problem solving, students make personal discoveries. As art offers new ways for students to manage emotions, images, and their environment, they gain a sense of confidence. Visual art integration seeks to transfer such positive feelings to other curricular areas.

## Art Promotes Respect for Diversity

The aphorism "God is in the details" reminds us how much small things matter. Any artwork is a window into an artist's experiences in a particular time and culture. Art is thus ideal for studying the details of values and customs of the world's peoples using visual images and objects that grab attention. Students are motivated to find out more about people and places when they see portraits, landscapes, still lifes, sculptures, and architecture from outside their world. Students' interest piques further when teachers ask them to examine the art to uncover particulars about the people who created it. A cultural print or artifact can reveal how diverse peoples address common human problems in multiple ways. For example, art often shows the uniqueness of cultural dress, while illuminating the common need for protective clothing.

AI supports "culturally responsive teaching" which expands opportunities and means for diverse students to express themselves.

Meaningful visual art integration gives teachers concrete ways to teach students that knowledge is flexible and changeable. Children can be taught to use visual art materials and tools to enhance "their own cultural lenses" and to visually "construct and share their knowledge of the world" (McDermott, 2004, p. 13). For example, when students learn to share artworks by serving as docents for class museums and discussing works shared in an "artist chair," they realize no one's work is the same. Difference is interesting and exciting. Students become more collaborative, and teachers learn to celebrate innovative efforts, regardless of the performance level.

## Art Develops Concentration, Responsibility, and Self-Discipline

No teacher wants to spend much time managing behavior. Visual art integration can cause children who resist learning to want to try. The learning culture shifts from the "right answers" focus in math and spelling to a more invitational climate (McDermott, 2004).

Children choose to use materials that are self-motivating. Art materials fill the bill, ranging from paint, to clay, to innovative computer drawing software. With AI, students also learn that using art materials is contingent upon disciplining oneself to use them appropriately. Teachers who decry the inability of children to stay on task and complete work with pride find that art also offers a viable means of developing responsibility, concentration, and focus. Students learn sticking with work to completion is a path to feeling proud. As peers admire the work of those who are self-disciplined, they gain insight into what it takes to be successful. Students see that those who take risks, handle materials appropriately, and complete work are responsible, which earns them status and additional privileges.

## Art Is a Natural Partner with Other Curricular Areas

Look around to see the art of life—furniture, clothes, cars, dishes. Chair designs, from the throne to the beanbag, show how sitting signals relationships and status. Chair materials also reflect advances in science and technology. Art shows how we create to survive and thrive. Art reflects the life for which students are being prepared in school; thus, should not school be rich in the arts?

Visual art connects to every area of the curriculum. Art making and written composition are good partners since both have to do with exploring, experimenting, and organizing ideas using tools and materials (Weissman, 2004; Olhansky, 2008). Both writers and artists do rough drafts and refine products through revision and editing. For example, da Vinci's "cartoons" were drafts for paintings. Teachers now use art to prompt writing and show how students keep sketchbooks to record ideas for writing. Sketchbooks are also used to record science observations, which is a common use of art in the science world. Through art making, students are helped to explore topics before writing, which is a useful strategy to break writer's block.

Art simply offers an alternative way of knowing. It is an intelligence that can be used in social studies, math, and science. For example, it is impossible to think about plants in the same way after seeing Georgia O'Keeffe's paintings. Looking through the aesthetic lens of visual art develops new viewpoints. Examining art about historical events or people yields insights not available otherwise. Art pieces can also be used to introduce or elaborate on information knowledge gained from print texts. It is dreary to imagine learning without art—books without illustrations or maps, no globes, nor models of the human body. Heart, head, and hands-on learning are combined to create, evaluate, understand, and respond to visual art. The aesthetic frame of reference of visual art experiences goes further to unveil beauty embedded in all disciplines.

## Art Is a Way to Assess

*Art is a private feeling made into a public form.* (Judith Rubin)

Assessment is about gathering information to make decisions about how to increase student learning. However, the most important thing we want students to learn is to think, which is invisible. Visual art makes the invisible visible. Student-made visual arts allows us to look inside their private world of thoughts and feelings, but not without a caveat. We need to be cautious about inferring too much. Excessive use of black may just mean the black crayon was the one nearby. Given that warning, teachers should examine artwork for signs of cognitive, emotional, and physical development. For example, circle, vertical, horizontal, and diagonal lines used in drawings are evidence that children are ready for handwriting instruction.

A child's artwork can provide important progress evidence, particularly about those who lack verbal fluency. A child may be able to express ideas with paint or clay not possible through words. Art can also stimulate passionate tales of events that surprise and delight. Think about what is shown in regard to language development of 5-year-old Liza in her story based on her drawing of an erupting volcano.

> The town was afraid. They could hear the insides making growling sounds. Then it happened. The lava broke out and ran all over the people. It was blood red because it was hot rock. Hot hot rock. So hot it burned up the people. But see here. This is a people bird. The people were burned to ashes but the ashes molded into lava birds that could fly so high no volcano could ever touch them again. The end.

## Building Block II: Visual Art Literacy: Content and Skills

*Every artist dips his brush into his own soul.* (Henry Ward Beecher)

Integration occurs when two or more ideas are combined for mutual benefit. All parts retain their worth, but a synergism is created in which the sum is greater than the parts. Classroom time is maximized. In the case of visual art integration, teachers must have a knowledge base *about* visual art if they are to meaningfully teach *through* it. Sources for the visual art literacy needed by classroom teachers include state and local student standards, along with teacher standards produced by the Interstate New Teacher Assessment and Support Consortium (INTASC, www.ccsso.org/Projects). These standards are consistent with those of the National Board for Professional Teaching Standards. Teachers can consult the full text of *National Standards for the Arts* (for K–12 students) available at http://menc.org.

## What Do Teachers Need to Know to Integrate Art?

In K–6, the basic visual art content and skills include studying (1) the historical, social, and cultural role of each art in our lives; (2) communication through art forms by creating, exhibiting, and responding to art; and (3) valuing art and developing aesthetic sensitivity (the roles of beauty and emotion in life). What classroom teachers need to know to integrate art at the *about* and *in* levels is organized into the following seven categories: Purposes: Defining Art; Processes; People: Artists; Art Media: Materials and Techniques; Products: Actual Artworks; Visual Art Elements and Concepts; and Discipline-Based Art Education. Two websites for definitions of art concepts are http://artlex.com and www.artcyclopedia.com.

### Purposes: Defining Art.

> *Art is the imposing of a pattern on experience, and our aesthetic enjoyment in recognition of the patterns.* (Alfred North Whitehead)

Art is visual communication: using art elements, tools, techniques, and materials to create and express ideas and feelings. It was one of the earliest ways humans expressed and understood each other and still serves this basic purpose. The concept of what art *is* can be difficult to grasp, however, primarily because of quality issues. The word *art* implies something "good" and gets into aesthetic tastes. Discussions aimed at defining art can be lively, but should not be avoided just because there are no right answers. Start by guiding students to list characteristics of what makes something art; perhaps present three items, such as a toy, a shell, and a painting (use a reproduction, if necessary). Ask students to describe characteristics and decide which items are art. From there, probe for characteristics of art that can be revisited repeatedly. Make this a weekly routine to create depth of understanding by discussing additional art examples that call for editing the list of traits.

### Processes.    Visual art can be created, *made,* or *viewed* using cognitive and emotional processes.

### Art Making.    The overall art-making process involves creative problem solving. Artists decide about subject matter, style, media, and materials to create a composition. The composition is made using art elements in varying ways by applying principles of design. The elements and processes teachers need to know are described in this chapter, mostly in the Ready References.

### Art Viewing.

> *I shut my eyes in order to see.* (Paul Gauguin)

Visual "decoding" (viewing art) and expression skills are now embodied in most literacy standards. In particular, visual imagery plays an invaluable role in adding concrete sensory substance to thinking; taken literally, this is what "making sense" is all about (Sadoski & Paivio, 2004, p. 13). The richer the elaboration of mental representations and the more interconnected, the more meaningful our response (p. 20). Our mental pictures actually reconstruct the neural pathways originally formed during the actual experience (Siegel, 1999), which is why we say things such as, "I see what you are saying."

To become visually literate, students need to be taught how to read visual images and use art tools, including digital technology, to make meaning. Teachers also need to teach basic art concepts to ensure that art is more than an amusement. Students are motivated to learn elements, media, or styles if they have had positive art-making and viewing experiences.

As with the other arts, visual art must be experienced as a whole before teachers address component parts. Elements can also be introduced informally as teachable moments arise. Teachers can point out lines, shapes, textures, and colors in children's clothes, school architecture, nature, and in picture book art. Charts of visual arts elements are important references.

*Art Appreciation.*    People look at art to try to understand and to enjoy it. The later is often called *appreciation*, but appreciation actually rests on understanding. Teaching art viewing involves showing students how to read clues to the artist's message. Students can grow to enjoy art they didn't "like" as a result of learning to decode visual information. Understanding ("I get it") increases enjoyment. This is especially true for art abstracted from reality and nonrepresentational art not intended to depict "things."

There is art about any topic in the curriculum. Learning is enriched by its presence when teachers meaningfully use this vast reservoir, such as in the following teaching ideas.

*Social, economic, cultural, and historical factors.* Meaningful visual art integration is facilitated when artworks are put in context. Time period, culture, and social norms affect both art making and understanding. Create a web of understanding by discussing clues in art that reveal factors that influenced its creation. This can be a highly motivating discovery process that engages students in analysis of details to support their conclusions.

Nothing is ever made in a vacuum, which explains why art so naturally integrates with social studies. Artworks about a time in history or art created during particular eras illuminate social studies concepts. Teaching about an artist's background gives a context for when and where the art was created as well. Example teaching strategies follow:

- Ask students to predict the place and time based on close examination of the art's subject matter.

- Give groups a variety of art postcards to arrange chronologically according to predictions based on close examination of details.

*Art criticism.* Criticism is close analysis. It involves examining the art (elements, style, media, and composition) to construct meaning. The focus should be on how the art is "portrayed," not on dissecting art the way critics do with films (Clements & Wachowiak, 2010). Students can learn to problem solve art by coaching them with questions such as: "What do you see? What is it about (subject matter)? How did the artist make this (media/techniques)? What arts elements and design ideas were used? Where might the artist have gotten ideas?"

*Aesthetics.* Aesthetic understanding involves response to ideas and feelings that are often hidden in artworks. Aesthetic development also has to do with the acquisition of individual tastes and preferences. For example, recently my community had an aesthetic discussion about whether the sculpture for a new waterfront park should be realistic (dolphins) or fanciful (mermaids). The debate was heated. Students can be drawn into these kinds of stimulating discussions with focus on questions such as, "Why do you think _____?" and "How do you know _____?"

**People: Artists.** Over time, teachers can come to know many artists, from Mary Cassatt to Frida Kahlo; these people can be the focus of a unit, or their work can be integrated into other units. There are other reasons for teachers to build their knowledge base about artists. First, our most robust role models are real people. Students can gain courage to take risks from the personal struggles of real artists and see that being creative does not mean starting cold. For example, Picasso copied African masks and Degas worked from photographs. Both then twisted, combined, reshaped, and stretched the ideas gathered from these sources. Second, children find the childhoods of famous artists compelling, and studying the lives of artists is a natural connection to the literary genre of biography. Timelines about artists' lives emerge when teachers provoke student interests about the era when the person lived. Third, maps and globes become important art forms to locate places where men and women created the world's art treasury. Fourth, styles of art reflect the society in which artists lived, so studying their lives also gives a more personal entrée into understanding effects of economic and social circumstances. For example, the chaotic turn into the 20th century was the context for the birth of abstract art, cubism, and dada.

Art-related careers should be included in any career education study. Artists take many roles, including painter, sculptor, architect, animator, curator, critic, historian, and teacher. A list of names and sources for artist information is listed in Ready References 6.4 and 6.5. Check Chapter 4 for sources for picture book artist-author studies. Presented later in this chapter, Planning Page 6.14 shows a planning web for a unit on Chris Van Allsburg.

**Art Media: Materials and Techniques.** Architect Frank Lloyd Wright said that he "could feel in the palms of his hands the Froebel blocks." It was in early childhood when these shapes "had become instinctive to him, giving him his first strong perception of the meanings of volume and form" (Bill, 1988, p. 29). No teacher's words or any book can ever substitute for work with actual art tools and materials. The kinesthetic–tactile intelligence activated in these encounters may indeed trigger a life devotion.

Teachers with a repertoire of strategies beyond "draw a picture" can offer students options, which increase and change their responses. Indeed media use alters the message of art. For example, "violence" in a cartoon comes across differently than when it is expressed in a marble sculpture. Students learn a broad range of communication tools from knowledgeable teachers. Materials and tools open doors. For example, Robinson (2000) points out that Paul McCartney probably wouldn't have been become much without the guitar. Alternative materials motivate and increased choices pique interest. Ready

---

## Ready Reference 6.4    Picture Book Artists

Planning Page 4.7 lists other sources for artist studies.

### Artists Commonly Studied

| | |
|---|---|
| Brown, Marcia | Macaulay, David |
| Carle, Eric | McDermott, Gerald |
| dePaola, Tomie | Peet, Bill |
| Dillon, Leo and Diane | Polacco, Patricia |
| Dr. Seuss | Potter, Beatrix |
| Fox, Mem | Ringgold, Faith |
| Keats, Ezra Jack | Sendak, Maurice |
| Kellogg, Steven | Van Allsburg, Chris |
| Lobel, Arnold | Yolen, Jane |

**The Caldecott Award** is given yearly by the American Library Association for picture book art. All Caldecott artists are listed at www.ala.org. **Horn Book** publishes interviews with all winners (www.hbook.com)

**Example Picture Book Artist Video:** *Eric Carle, Picturewriter* (making collage)

**Artist/Author Videos:** http://teacher.scholastic.com/products/westonwoods/

# Ready Reference 6.5  Well-Known Artists

Use these as starter sources to plan studies of artists and works.

## Websites with Artist/Works Information

www.artcyclopedia.com/
http://school.discovery.com/schrockguide/
http://educationindex.com/art/
http://famousPainter.com
http://gardenofpraise.com/art.htm
http://loggia.com/index.html (comprehensive site)
http://nwrel.org/comm/topics/arts.html
http://princetonol.com/groups/iad/lessons/middle/
    index.htm (comprehensive site)

## Artists and Example Artwork

Albert Bierstadt, *The Rocky Mountains Landers' Peak*
Pieter Bruegel the Elder, *Children's Games*
Sandro Botticelli, *The Birth of Venus*
Michelangelo Buonarroti, *The Creation of Adam* (Sistine Chapel ceiling)
*Mary Cassatt, *The Boating Party*
Paul Cezanne, *Apples and Oranges*
Marc Chagall, *I and the Village*
John Singleton Copley, *Paul Revere*
Salvador Dali, *The Persistence of Memory*
Edgar Degas, *Little Fourteen-Year-Old Dancer*
Albrecht Durer, *Young Hare*
*Vincent van Gogh, *Starry Night*
Paul Gauguin, *Vision After the Sermon, Hail Mary*
Francisco de Goya, *Don Manuel Osorio Manrique de Zuniga*
El Greco, *View of Toledo*
*Winslow Homer, *Snap the Whip*
Pieter de Hooch, *Woman Peeling Apples*
Edward Hopper, *Nighthawks*
Vassily Kandinsky, *Improvisation 31* (Sea Battle)
Paul Klee, *Senecio* (Head of a Man)

*Frida Kahlo, *Self Portrait with Cropped Hair*
*Jacob Lawrence, *Parade*
Roy Lichtenstein, *Wham*
René Magritte, *The Eye*
Henri Matisse, *The Swan*
Joan Miro, *People and Dog in the Sun*
Piet Mondrian, *Broadway Boogie Woogie*
Claude Oscar Monet, *Impression: Sunrise, Bridge Over a Pool of Lilies*
Grandma Moses, *Through the Old Covered Bridge*
Edvard Munch, *The Scream*
*Georgia O'Keeffe, *Red Hills and Bones*
*Pablo Picasso, *Mother and Child*
Jackson Pollock, *Painting, 1948*
Raphael, *St. George and the Dragon*
Rembrandt van Rijn, *Self Portrait*
*Remington, *The Smoke Signal*
Renoir, *A Girl With a Watering Can*
Diego Rivera, *Pinata*
Norman Rockwell, *Marbles Champion*
Henri Rousseau, *Woman Walking in an Exotic Forest*
*Georges Seurat, *La Grande Jatte*
Gilbert Stuart, *George Washington*
*Henry Tanner, *The Banjo Lesson*
Henri Toulouse-Lautrec, *At Moulin Rouge*
Jan Vermeer, *The Love Letter*
Leonardo da Vinci, *Mona Lisa*
Andy Warhol, *Campbell's Soup Can*
James McNeill Whistler, *Arrangement in Black and Gray*
*Grant Wood, *American Gothic*
*Andrew Wyeth, *Christina's World*
N. C. Wyeth, *The Giant*
Wang Yani, *Baboons*

*Recommended ones to get started.

---

References 6.6 and 6.7 list materials, tools, and ideas. Another recommended resource is *The Art Teacher's Book of Lists* (Hume, 2005). Here are basics:

- Assorted brushes, chalk, pencils, water-based markers, crayons, and paints (tempera, watercolors, and paint crayons)
- Different kinds, sizes, and colors of paper, including brown kraft paper, sketchpads, and construction paper
- Clays for sculpting and modeling (e.g., Crayola's Model Magic)
- Glues and pastes, especially white glue
- Scissors appropriate for children
- Collage materials such as shells, buttons, pebbles, and lace
- Boxes and tubes for construction and papier mâché bases
- Cleanup supplies
- Workspace (easels and tables covered with shower curtains)

**Products: Actual Artworks.** Efland (2002) explains that artworks can serve as cognitive landmarks to provoke learners to think deeply, to go behind images, ideas, and processes and make a web of connections between what they find and other disciplines. This is more likely to happen when children have real art to observe, including reproductions/prints, art postcards, arts-based books, cartoons, photographs, 3-D examples, and cultural artifacts such as masks, pottery, and fiber art. Ready References 6.7, 6.10, and 6.11 give examples of picture book art categorized by art concepts.

Other useful teaching materials are art quotes, facts about artists, and art–related songs and music to be used in daily routines. Many materials are available for little cost. Give friends, other teachers, school staff, and parents a list of items to save (e.g., paper towel tubes to use for "looking closely"). Stores that sell wallpaper may donate sample books. These make quick book binders for writing and can be used in collage. Paper and photography companies often give away paper products.

*Picture files* are valuable tools and practically free. Collect magazines, calendars, postcards, greeting cards, old photos, and

## Ready Reference 6.6 Art Materials and Media Techniques

*Directions: Use these ideas to integrate art making throughout the curriculum.*

***Bookmaking:*** pop-up, accordion, big books, mini-books

***Calligraphy and block lettering:*** embellished lettering or letters simply cut from standard-sized blocks (e.g., construction paper)

***Collage:*** design made by pasting or gluing assembled materials on a surface

***Craft:*** handcrafted item such as pottery or quilt

***Diorama:*** shadow box made with shoebox to create a scene

***Display:*** arrangements around a concept or theme

***Drawing:*** linear art made with pencil, charcoal, pen, crayon

***Enlargement:*** use overhead projector to make images larger

***Fiber art:*** fabrics, yarn, string, and so forth

***Fresco:*** paint on wet plaster

***Intaglio:*** process of engraving

***Lithography:*** printing method in which pictures are first drawn with chalk or paint on a plate, which is submerged in water. Ink adheres to chalk or paint. Heavy pressure prints the design.

***Mask:*** paper bag, tag board, balloon with papier mâché

***Mixed media:*** paper, wire, paint, fabric are used in one artwork

***Mobile:*** three-dimensional art that moves, usually suspended

***Montage:*** combination of several distinct pictures to make a composite picture

***Mural:*** large wall art

***Painting:*** use of tempera (pigment in egg base), acrylic (made from polymer), watercolor, oil (pigment in oil base)

***Pastel:*** chalk, usually with oil mixed in

***Print:*** pull an image from something coated in paint or "stamp" using textured objects

***Puppet:*** made from bag, hand, finger, stick, sock, or box

***Rubbing:*** paper is placed over objects and crayons or markers are used to bring up images

***Scratchboard:*** black crayon or ink is placed over another color such as silver or multiple colors; sharp tool is used to scratch surface and reveal color

***Sculpture:*** three-dimensional art made from wood, clay, metal, found objects, plaster, or papier mâché

***Wash:*** translucent watercolor used over another medium

---

restaurant place mats to use for art making and study. Also useful are collections of interesting words and phrases that provoke images, such as headlines and advertisements.

Sort pictures into labeled folders (words and phrases, styles, subject matter, cultures, people, holidays, emotions, places, dance, and movement). Mount or use plastic sleeves. Write drama/oral expression and writing strategies on each folder. Make a table of contents to keep the folders organized for the following projects.

- Students can sort pictures into categories such as subject matter, media, style, artist, or art elements. In doing so they use vocabulary and thinking skills such as comparing, contrasting, and classification.
- Pictures can prompt both art and writing or be actual art-making materials (e.g., for collage).
- Picture files can be used as prompts for drama and storytelling (see Chapters 8 and 9).
- Poems, quotes, and cartoons about art and artists can also be collected and used in routines or on bulletin boards, or as inspiration to make poem or quote books.
- Ready References 6.12, 7.1, and 7.6 list ideas for art-based discussions using pictures.

### Visual Art Elements and Concepts.

*A line is a dot that went for a walk.* (Paul Klee)

Art specialists think art viewing and making is teachable and dispute that instruction about art elements endangers creative thinking. Arts integration rests on the belief that all people have the capacity to understand and use visual language. Neither children nor accomplished artists can state all they want to say unless they have acquired the visual literacy to do so (Arnheim, 1989).

In AI, visual art knowledge is taught on a "need-to-know" basis considering developmental levels and task demands. Visual concepts are taught in a meaningful context, such as a unit, so students understand that visual art is a communication tool used to make sense of important content. Isolated concept and skill lessons are avoided. Ready Reference 6.8 lists visual art elements teachers need to know and teach.

**Design Principles.** Artists have to decide how to arrange and organize their work to create a coherent whole that says what they want to say. This is parallel to what writers do. Ready Reference 6.9 summarizes the principles and concepts teachers need to know to do mini-lessons, question, and coach students. Ready Reference 6.10 lists children's books to support elements and design lessons.

**Artistic Styles.** The unique styles artists create are important concepts in visual arts integration. Higher order thinking skills are honed as students learn to analyze and evaluate style traits. Discriminating and appreciating diverse styles also enlarges understanding and tolerance. Ready Reference 6.11 lists examples from picture books. There are additional arts-books about artists and styles in Appendix J. For example, see *Talking with Artists* (Cummings, 1992) with interviews of children's book illustrators. Check out sources for author/artist studies in Planning Page 4.7.

## Ready Reference 6.7 Art Media in Children's Books

Use these books to teach about a media. Most are well-regarded "classics" that should be easy to find. A good reference is Bang's *Picture This: How Pictures Work* (2004).

### Collage

Bunting, E. (1999). *Smoky night.* Sandpiper. (illustrated by D. Diaz)

Young, E. (2005). *Beyond the great mountains: A visual poem about China.* Chronicle.

Hughes, L. (1995). *The block.* Metropolitan Museum of Art.

### Crayons and Colored Pencils

Brown, M. (1982). *The bun. A tale from Russia.* Harcourt Brace Jovanovich.

Lionni, L. (2005). *Fish is fish.* Knopf.

Van Allsburg, C. (1986). *The stranger.* Houghton Mifflin.

### Drawing

Barrett, P., & Barrett, S. (1972). *The line Sophie drew.* Schroll.

dePaola, T. (1999). *The art lesson.* San Val.

Johnson, C. (2009). *Harold and the purple crayon.* Library Binding.

McCloskey, R. (2004). *Make way for ducklings.* Live Oak Media.

### Fiber Art

Hall, D. (2004). *The ox-cart man.* Viking. Live Oak Media.

Kroll, V. (1995). *Wood-Hoopoe Willie.* Charles Bridge.

Paul, A. W. (1991). *Eight hands round.* HarperCollins. (American quilt patterns)

*Ringgold, F. (1991). *Tar beach.* Random House.

Roessel, M. (1995). *Songs from the loom.* Lerner.

### Mixed Media

Alarcon, F. (2005). *Poems to dream together.* Lee.

Bang, M. (1987). *The paper crane.* HarperCollins.

Young, E. (1989). *Lon po po. A Red Riding Hood story from China.* Philomel.

### Mural

Ancona, G. (2003). *Murals: Walls that sing.* Cavendish.

Winters, J. (1994). *Diego.* Dragonfly.

### Painting

Agee, J. (2004). *The incredible painting of Felix Clousseau.* Farrar.

Cooney, B. (1985). *Miss Rumphius.* Puffin. (acrylics)

dePaola, T. (1996). *The legend of the Indian paintbrush.* Putnam.

Dunrea, O. (1998). *The painter who loved chickens.* Farrar, Straus & Giroux.

Locker, T. (2001). *Where the river begins.* Lutterworth. (oil)

Pastels/Chalk

Howe, J. (1994). *I wish I were a butterfly.* Voyager. (illustrated by E. Young)

Lach, W. (2002). *Baby loves.* Atheneum.

Van Allsburg, C. (2005). *The polar express.* Houghton Mifflin.

### Pen and Pencil/Ink

Testa, F. (1993). *If you take a pencil.* Puffin.

Gag, W. (1956). *Millions of cats.* Coward, McCean & Geoghegan.

Macaulay, D. (1982). *Castle.* Sandpiper.

Mayer, M. (2003). *Frog goes to dinner.* Dial.

Viorst, J. (2009). *Alexander and the terrible, horrible, no good, very bad day.* Atheneum. (illustrated by R. Cruz)

### Photography

Angelou, M. (2003). *My painted house, my friendly chicken.* Crown Books.

Brown, L., & Brown, M. (1996). *Visiting the art museum.* Dutton.

Desalvo, J., Stanley, C., & Olive, J. (photographers). (2001). *CowParade Houston.* Workman.

Freedman, R. (1989). *Lincoln. A photobiography.* Houghton Mifflin.

Sandler, M. (2005). *America through the lens: Photographers who changed the nation.* Holt.

Kissinger, K. (2002). *All the colors we are.* Redleaf.

### Printmaking

Carle, E. (2009). *The tiny seed.* Little Simon.

Haley, G. (1988). *A story, a story.* Aladin.

Lionni, L. (1973). *Swimmy.* Knopf.

Waber, B. (1996). *"You look ridiculous," said the rhinoceros to the hippopotamus.* Houghton Mifflin.

### Sculpture (Three-Dimensional Art)

dePaola, T. (1982). *Giorgio's village.* Putnam. (paper sculpture)

Haskins, J. (1989). *Count your way through Mexico.* Carolrhoda. (papier mâché)

Hoyt-Goldsmith, D. (1990). *Totem pole.* Scholastic. (wood carving)

Prokofiev, S. (1986). *Peter and the wolf.* Viking. (paper sculpture; illustrated by B. Cooney)

### Watercolor

Bunting, E. (1992). *The wall.* Sandpiper. (illustrated by R. Himler)

Le Ford, B. (1995). *A blue butterfly. A story about Claude Monet.* Doubleday.

Potter, B. (1902). *The tale of Peter Rabbit.* Warne.

Wheeler, L. (2006). *Mammoths on the move.* Harcourt.

Yolen, J. (2007). *Owl moon.* Philomel. (illustrated by J. Schoenherr)

### Weaving

Castaneda, O. S. (1995). *Abuela's weave.* Lee & Low.

Govenar, A. (2006). *Extraordinary ordinary people: Five American masters of traditional arts.* Candlewick.

Miles, M. (1985). *Annie and the Old One.* Little Brown.

## Ready Reference 6.8 Visual Art Elements

**Line:** a horizontal, vertical, angled, or curved mark, across a surface (e.g., long, short, dotted)

**Shape:** the two dimensions of height and width arranged geometrically (e.g., circles, triangles), organically (natural shapes), symbolically (e.g., letters)

**Color:** (hue = color names), primary, secondary, and complementary; warm (red/yellow) and cool (blue/green)
  **Value:** lightness (tints) or darkness (shades) of colors
  **Saturation:** vibrancy/purity vs. dullness of color

**Space:** the two-dimensional area that objects take up (positive space) and that surround shapes and forms (negative space); in-depth illusions are created by techniques such as perspective and overlapping

**Texture:** way something feels or looks as it would feel (e.g., slick, rough)

**Form:** three dimensions (height, width, and depth) shown by contours (e.g., sphere, pyramid, cube)

## Ready Reference 6.9 Art Concepts and Design Principles

**Composition:** arrangement of the masses and spaces
  **Foreground, middle, and background:** the areas in a piece of art that appear closest to the viewer, next closest, and farthest away

**Structures and forms:** two dimensions—art with length and width, such as paintings or photography; three dimensions—art also has height/depth, such as sculpture

**Balance:** weight of elements distributed symmetrically or asymmetrically

**Emphasis:** areas that are stressed and attract the eye

**Variety:** no two elements used are the same

**Repetition:** elements used more than once (e.g., shapes, lines) create pattern and texture

**Contrast:** opposition or differences of elements (e.g., created by light colors next to dark)

**Rhythm/motion:** sense that there are paths through the work

**Unity:** the sense there is a whole working together

**Light:** illusion created with lighter colors

## Ready Reference 6.10 Art Elements and Children's Books

These visual art-based children's books can fit under more than one category.

Adoff, A. (2004). *Black is brown is tan.* Amistad. (skin tones)

Crews, D. (2000). *Sail away.* HarperCollins. (air-brushed shapes show pattern through repeated images of objects)

Crosbie, M., & Rosenthal, S. (1993). *Architecture colors.* Wiley. (colors are photos of architectural features. Series includes *Architecture Shapes* and *Architecture Counts*)

Ehlert, L. (1994). *Color zoo.* HarperCollins. (wordless book with holes that form shape-changing abstract animals)

Heller, R. (1995). *Color! Color! Color!* Grosset & Dunlap. (rhythmic language; acetates that overlap to show mixing)

Jonas, A. (1989). *Color dance.* Greenwillow. (children dance with overlapping cloth to create new colors)

Polacco, P. (1996). *Rechenka's eggs.* Putnam. (patterns abound in Ukrainian story about Pysanky eggs)

*Sendak, M. (1964). *Where the wild things are.* Harper & Row. (expressive lines used in this story about a naughty boy)

Shalom, V. (1995). *The color of things.* Rizzoli International. (colors are drained from a town, and children paint them back)

Shaw, C. G. (1992). *It looked like spilt milk.* HarperFestival. (free-form shapes turn into ordinary objects)

Yenawine, P., & the Museum of Modern Art. (1991). *Colors.* Delacorte. (MOMA artwork illustrates this concept book; series includes *Lines, Shapes,* and *Stories*)

*Yolen, J. (1988). *Owl moon.* Philomel. (a snowy night depicted with contrast and perspective)

*Caldecott Award books.

### Subject Matter: What Art Is About.

*The source of art is not visual reality, but the dreams, hopes, and aspirations which lie deep in every human.* (Arthur Zaidenberg)

Subject matter groupings help students understand art and give options for original art making. For example, a response to characterization in a piece of literature might be a portrait.

Following are common visual art classifications with book examples.

- Portrait: person(s)
  Locker, T. (1994). *Miranda's smile.* Dial. (an artist tries to paint his daughter)
- Cityscape: city view
  Ringgold, F. (1991). *Tar beach.* Random House.

- Landscape: outdoor scene
  Blizzard, G. S. (1992). *Come look with me: Exploring landscape art with children.* Thomason-Grant.
- Seascape: view of a body of water
  Lionni, L. (1973). *Swimmy.* Knopf.
- Interior: inside view of a room or building
  Wood, A. (1984). *The napping house.* Harcourt.
- Still life: arrangement of nonliving objects
  Lacey, S. (2000). *Still life.* Copper Beach.
- Abstract: focus on color, shape, line, and texture
  Spilsbury, R. (2009). *Abstract expressionism.* Heineman.

Art elements, design principles, styles, media, and subject matter need to be taught explicitly using mini-lessons. Art concepts should also be used to generate questions. Chapter 7 describes seed strategies for visual art concepts using word sorts, games, and questioning. This does not mean students shouldn't have free time to make art. Children are regularly given free time to read, but they are also taught *how* to read. Children need to be taught *how* to read art and express through visual language, too.

Cityscape mural at Ashley River Creative Arts

## Ready Reference 6.11 Art Styles in Children's Books

### Cartoon Style: Simple Lines and Use of Primary Colors

Schulz, C. (2001). *Peanuts: The art of Charles M. Schulz.* Pantheon.
Schwartz, D. (2004). *How much is a million?* HarperCollins. (illustrated by S. Kellogg)
Seuss, Dr. (1957). *Cat in the hat.* Random House.
Spier, P. (1988). *People.* Doubleday.

### Expressionism: Leans toward Abstract, Focuses Emotions

Bemelmans, L. (1992). *Madeline.* Viking.
Carle, E. (1995). *The very busy spider.* Penguin.
Le Tord, B. (1999). *A bird or two: A story about Henri Matisse.* William B. Eerdmans.
Livingston, M. C. (1988). *A circle of seasons.* Holiday House. (illustrated by L. Fisher)
Martin, B., & Archambault, J. (1989). *Chicka chicka boom boom.* Simon & Schuster. (illustrated by L. Ehlert)
Raimondo, J. (2005). *Express yourself! Activities and adventures in expressionism.* Watson-Guptill.
Williams, V. (1984). *A chair for my mother.* HarperCollins.

### Folk Art/Naive: Nontraditional Media/ Untrained Artists

Aardema, V. (2008). *Why mosquitoes buzz in people's ears.* Dial. (illustrated by L. & D. Dillon)
Hall, D. (2004). *The ox-cart man.* Viking. Live Oak Media.
Polacco, P. (1988). *Rechenka's eggs.* Philomel.
Provenson, A. (1997). *The buck stops here: The presidents of the United States.* Brown Deer.

Xiong, B. (2001). *Nine-in-one Grr! Grr!* Minnesota Humanities Commission. (illustrated by N. Hom)

### Impressionism: Dreamlike Quality, Relies on Light

Bjork, C. (1987). *Linnea in Monet's garden.* R&S. (illustrated by L. Anderson)
Howe, J. (1994). *I wish I were a butterfly.* Voyager. (illustrated by E. Young)
McCully, E. (2000). *Mirette and Bellini cross Niagara Falls.* Putnam.
Mayhew, J. (2001). *Katie and the sunflowers.* Orchard.
Zolotow, C. (1962). *Mr. Rabbit and the lovely present.* Harper & Row. (illustrated by M. Sendak)

### Realism: Represents Reality in Shape, Color, and Proportion

Holling, H. C. (2000). *Paddle-to-the-sea.* Houghton Mifflin.
McCloskey, R. (2004). *Make way for ducklings.* Live Oak Media.
Turkle, B. (1992). *Deep in the forest.* Puffin.
Viorst, J. (2009) *Alexander and the terrible, horrible, no good, very bad day.* Atheneum. (illustrated by R. Cruz)
Zelinsky, P. (2002). *Rapunzel.* Puffin.

### Surrealism: Distorts Images; Fantastic Quality

Bang, M. (1996). *The grey lady and the strawberry snatcher.* Aladin.
Brown, A. (2000). *Willy's pictures.* Candlewick.
Brown, A. (1998). *Willy the dreamer.* Candlewick.
Say, A. (2000). *The sign painter.* Houghton. (Edward Hopper style)
Sciezka, J. (1996). *The true story of the three little pigs by A. Wolf.* Puffin. (illustrated by L. Smith)
Van Allsburg, C. (1981). *Jumanji.* Houghton Mifflin.
Winter, J. (2008). *Follow the drinking gourd.* Knopf.

**Discipline-Based Art Education (DBAE).** Walling (2001) writes, "For much of the 20th century visual art education centered on one overriding goal, helping students realize 'creative' self-expression." He calls this a "self-limiting philosophy" (p. 626). In the 1980s, the Getty Center created an influential curricular model that recommended decreased emphasis on art making and an increased focus on teaching art history, aesthetics, and art criticism. The model retained hands-on art but stressed art inquiry. The rationale was grounded in the belief that art education, based entirely on creating art, does not give a sense of the place of art in life and the world.

The Getty curriculum raised questions about the lack of visual and artistic literacy among students who could complete 13 years of school with little opportunity to reflect on the immense bank of world art. Today it is accepted that a balanced program of art experiences is needed. Ready Reference 6.12 offers questions and strategies to guide visual art discussions. While children's cognitive growth (e.g., language and conceptual development) is greatly facilitated by exploration through drawing and other art making, even young children benefit from opportunities to examine and discuss their art and that of others (Alexander & Michael, 1991; Gardner, 1990; McWinnie, 1992). Curriculum ideas are presented at the Getty website (*www.getty.edu/education/for_teachers/curricula/*).

# Building Block III: Collaborative Planning for Visual Art Integration

Visual art integration planning is about finding connections with other academic areas. Meaningful connections can leverage learning in science, social studies, literacy, and math by using the power of the visual arts to engage and promote the higher order thinking, especially problem solving. Teachers and arts specialists

---

## Ready Reference 6.12 Art Discussion Questions and Strategies

*Directions: Use these guidelines to help students decode artwork, make personal connections, and extend comprehension. Phillip Yenawine is shown using such strategies in the video What Do You See? (Chicago Art Institute).*

1. **Concrete to abstract.** Young children have difficulty with questions such as, "Why might the artist have painted this?"(motives /intentions) and understanding how symbols like colors represent seasons. Try such questions, but if kids have trouble, use concrete ones that begin: "What is?" *Note:* Give time to examine abstract art, which many prefer to detailed realism.

2. **Plan ahead.** Create a *line of questioning* that leads to a main point. Help students see something they would not have seen otherwise. Go for the "Ahhh" or aesthetic response.

3. **Ask open questions.** "What do you see? What's this about? What does this tell us about people? What story does this tell?" These activate CPS higher order thinking and teach that there is no one interpretation of art. The goal is honest response supported by evidence from the artwork.

4. **Give time to look.** Encourage curiosity and engagement by guiding students to look carefully. Set an amount of time to observe details and not talk.

5. **Speak at children's level, but do not patronize.** Connect to their experiences and try to include each child, at least with eye contact. Vary your voice. Smile and make eye contact to sustain attention.

6. **Use wait time and signals.** More students respond with longer and more thoughtful answers if a question is followed by a pause of 3 to 5 seconds. Next, ask for a signal, such as thumbs up. For important questions, wait for most to signal, then call on a few.

7. **If the question does not work, then rephrase.** Keep trying!

8. **Be sensitive to interests.** Take advantage of teachable moments to follow through on curiosity (e.g., examine art elements in raindrops).

9. **Respond to children's answers.** Use active listening. Do not rush or interrupt. Give students time to speak.

10. **Compliment honest and appropriate answers.** Use descriptive feedback, not just praise.

11. **If a wrong response is given, do not embarrass.** Say something like "That's an interesting idea. Who has a different idea?" Use dignifying techniques: If a student says Monet painted "The Four Freedoms" you might say, "This was done by a man, but he was American, not French. Do you know an American artist who may have painted it?" Other ideas: Ask the student to explain why he thinks so; ask for others' ideas; cue toward accurate answers with hints, especially charts.

12. **When an answer is partly correct, rephrase the question using the correct information.** You create another question in the process: "Yes it is true that _____, but let's look again and see if we can find _____."

13. **Follow up the responses.** Ask for evidence. Use this sequence: *Question:* What season of the year is it? *Answer:* Winter. *Follow-up:* How does the artist show this? OR: Ask students to tell more about their thinking. Paraphrase responses and ask if you have done so accurately. Ask others to respond: "What do the rest of you think about Joan's point?").

14. **Encourage student questions.** Ask: "What questions do you have?" or invite students to write questions. Put them in a hat and draw them to help students feel safe.

15. **Plan small-group discussion.** Start with pairs or trios and work up to groups of four to six students. Give a few minutes to discuss, such as "Partner to talk about choices the artist made to create this work." This allows shy students to participate and prepares all for large-group discussion.

16. **End the discussion.** Ask students to tell something they learned, what someone said that made sense, something that was surprising, or what interesting ideas they heard.

collaborate to plan lessons *about* aspects of visual art and involve students *in* using art knowledge and skills to think differently about science, social studies, math, and more. Teachers work with visual art specialists to identify the basic art knowledge and skills students will need to be taught, including specific visual art language and examples of art-making options.

Meaningful visual art integration causes students to grow their visual literacy while using it to think about other subjects in ways not possible otherwise. Visual art literacy is not developed by simply telling students to draw pictures after reading something or having them look at pictures without guidance. Opportunity, without instruction, demeans art as a discipline and cripples children's use of visual communication. A critical planning question is, "What will my students learn *about* each discipline being integrated?" rather than "What subjects are to be used in the lesson?"

## Unit Planning

Chapter 3 summarized the ways specialists and classroom teachers collaborate to plan arts-based integrated units. Planning Page 3.7 shows the unit development process. Important points related to visual art integration are as follows:

- Academic and visual art standards are used, along with other goals.
- Assessment and instruction are aligned to standards and goals with focus on how visual art can increase understanding and expression, and how student art products can be used to show learning.
- Connections are sought between visual art and the nonarts area as both relate to specific unit goals. Overlapping concepts and skills are found.
- Unit centers are further developed into big idea statements and important questions are posed.
- Flexibility is addressed so student interests and questions can be accommodated.

- Project work is planned including culminating exhibits that will be central assessment pieces.
- Field-based units are considered that focus on visits to special sites, such as museums, and involve work with visual arts professionals.
- Sequenced, two-pronged lesson plans are made with visual art as one prong.

**Standards.** The National Standards for the Arts includes a visual art section that is an important planning tool for lessons and units. Visual Art Standards help teachers incorporate learning *about* and *in* visual art into lessons in other subjects. Ready Reference 6.13 shows the main standards. View the full document at http://menc.org. See examples of state versions of standards, with lesson examples and assessment ideas, at state departments of education websites, such as that of Connecticut.

**Finding Visual Art Connections.** What does art have to do with science, social studies, or math? During the search for meaningful connections, go deep into the heart of the discipline. Ready Reference 1.2 shows examples, in addition to the following ones.

**Social Studies.** The focus of social studies is relationships among people and includes history, geography, economics, politics, and sociology. A unit that employs visual art might include or center on the lives of artists, period artworks, art styles that reflect periods, societal influences, cultural art, the economic impact of visual art, or visual art careers. Any culture can be studied through visual art since art has been produced by every culture and reflects the lifestyle, geography, and values of the people who produced it. Economics might be studied through the phenomenon of blockbuster museum exhibits or the multibillion dollar art auction business. Remember, kids are intrigued by big numbers!

**Science.** Art and science were interchangeable in Leonardo da Vinci's world. He wrote about art and drew about science. He

---

## Ready Reference 6.13 National Standards for Visual Arts

*Overall focus: Create, express, and respond through visual media; express feelings and emotions; use new ways of communicating and thinking; apply knowledge to world problems, historical and cultural investigation; and evaluate and interpret the visual world.*

1. ***Understanding and applying media, techniques, and processes.*** Example: Communicate ideas and experiences through visual art. Use materials safely.
2. ***Using knowledge of structures and functions.*** Example: Explain art messages and what an artist does to convey meaning.
3. ***Choosing and evaluating a range of subject matter, symbols, and ideas.*** Example: Explain possible content for artwork and ways to show meaning in different ways.

4. ***Understanding the visual arts in relation to history and cultures.*** Example: Examine how aspects of culture and history are expressed in works of art.
5. ***Reflecting upon and assessing the characteristics and merits of their work and the work of others.*** Example: Explain purposes for art and how people's experiences influence their art.
6. ***Making connections between visual arts and other disciplines.*** Example: Find similarities and differences between making visual art and writing. Make art to show understanding in all curricular areas.

*Source:* Content Standards (material in bold type) excerpted from the *National Standards for Arts Education*, published by Music Educators National Conference (MENC). Copyright © 1994 by MENC. Reprinted with permission. The complete standards are available from MENC, 1806 Robert Fulton Drive, Reston, VA 20191 (telephone 800-336-3768).

applied the science of color, explored anatomy, and invented machines (Walling, 2001, p. 631). Art and science have much in common. In particular both disciplines require "careful observation, contemplation, record keeping, attention to detail and, in the 21st century, use of advanced technology" (Bopegedera, 2005, p. 55). Scientific problem solving is called the scientific method, but teachers involved in AI soon discover that this is the same problem solving as that used by artists, that is, CPS (Chessin & Zander, 2006).

Eisenkraft, Heltzel, Johnson, and Radcliffe (2006) explain that "all artists are chemists" (p. 33). Both science and art include the study of pigments, the science behind color, the chemistry of art materials, the physics of art forms (e.g., sculpture and mobiles), the creation of optical illusions, and the photographic process. Many artists integrate science and visual art. For example, artist Thomas Locker integrates science and art in picture books, including *Cloud Dance* and *Water Dance,* which contain exquisite paintings of nature with activities that promote scientific inquiry.

**Literacy.**    The basic processes for decoding meaning and encoding/expressing understanding in visual art and the language arts are the same. The difference lies mainly in the symbol systems (Cowan & Albers, 2006). The language arts uses letters and words while the arts communicate through color, line, shape, texture, and so forth. Visual literacy is now accepted as a requirement for effective communication. There is mutual benefit when visual art and the language arts are integrated. For example, art vocabulary (e.g., labels for art elements) adds to general vocabulary for reading, writing, speaking, and listening. Students also develop all levels of thinking needed for comprehension when they are engaged in art criticism (Housen & Yenawine, 2000). These are all natural and meaningful art/literacy connections. (See Planning Page 7.5 for a guided literacy/art lesson.)

**Math.**    Art and math are integrally related. For example, linear perspective is math based, and both art and math focus on geometric shapes. Planning Page 6.14 is an example of a math and visual art integrated lesson using the two-pronged plan format.

**Arts.**    Art and music share many elements, including line, rhythm, and pattern. Think of looking at art and imagining what you hear. Music can inspire art, and vice versa. Art is used in theatre sets and actors' costumes. Art and dance share elements such as lines that move and shapes that are positioned to create a composition. Dancers remain an inspiration for art (e.g., Degas's ballerinas).

**Literature.**    Perspective and framing are analogous to point of view in writing (Weissman, 2004). Art and literature are natural partners in picture books. Art strategies can also be used before reading a book, during reading, or in response to a book. For example, directing students to think about the actual words of an author can trigger visual images rich in color, line, and texture. Babbitt's description that "Mrs. Tuck was a great potato of a woman" can be mined for color, texture, shape, and line (*Tuck Everlasting*). Students can create their versions of images with diverse media and techniques including collage, drawing, or soft sculpture materials.

Arnheim (1989) points out that good work in biology or mathematics is done when the student's natural curiosity is awakened, when the desire to solve problems and to explain mysterious facts is enlisted, and when the imagination is challenged to develop new possibilities. In this sense, scientific work, the probing of history, or the handling of a language is every bit as "artistic" as drawing and painting.

**Unit Types.**    Any of the five unit types can be used to integrate visual art: (1) author or artist, (2) genre or form, (3) problem or topic, (4) book, poem, or song, or (5) event or trip (Planning Page 3.1). Visual art can be the body/center of a unit or one of the legs of the planning web. When planning any unit, remember to web ideas, align activities with art and other academic standards, plan initiating or starting events, sequence lessons to develop the unit, and create a culminating event to wrap it up (Planning Page 3.8).

**Artist Studies.**    A common classroom unit that integrates visual art is the artist/author study. The focus is usually creators of picture books. Students engage in art criticism of illustrations, research biographical information, and learn how the artist does creative problem solving to create a unique style. Other arts and subject areas are used to explore the person being studied. Sources for information on artists and authors appear in Planning Page 4.7. Planning Page 6.14 depicts a planning web for an author-artist study. Following are guidelines to plan an artist-author unit. Ready References 6.4 and 6.5 list artists that may be the focus.

*Guidelines and ideas.* Involve students in the following research, as much as possible.

1. Collect materials about artists. Check publisher's websites and sources in Planning Page 4.7. Books such as *Something about the Author* (Hedblad, 1998) have biographical information, audio and videotape sources, quotes, and interesting facts.
2. Make an artist "map" with categories such as name and vital statistics, books illustrated or main artworks awards, art information, childhood, hobbies, interests, how and why the person creates, quirks, and quotes about or from the person.
3. Read a biography or autobiography. Aliki's *How a Book Is Made* is helpful to learn about artists and bookmaking.
4. Locate on a map where an artist lives.
5. Use art criticism questions to discuss the book art.
6. Experiment with the artist's media and styles. Invite a local artist to demonstrate or visit an artist's studio.
7. Find other art and books in the same media and style.
8. Arrange a conference call. Make contact through the publisher's website (expect a fee).
9. Write or email the artist.
10. Do a presentation on the artist and artwork. Become the artist and present in first person.
11. Make a display, posters, or brochure on the artist.
12. Write and bind a book about the author or artist.
13. Interview a local author/artist about the art process.
14. Create artist/author blurbs for class books.
15. Visit a local printing or publishing company.

**Field Trips with a Visual Art Focus.**    Opportunities for art-related field trips abound with virtual trips on the Internet to the Louvre or Museum of Modern Art in New York City.

# Planning Page 6.14
## Artist-Author Study Web

**Center:**
Chris Van Allsburg
12 + picture books

Sculptor – likes to build things
No art classes in high school.
Took college art "on a lark."
Wife is an elem. tchr. Detail oriented. Pictures → Stories.

**Science**
- "What if" in scientific investigation
- Experimenting
- Problem-solving
- Wreck of the Zephir
- Polar Express – time as a variable
- environmental issues
- Just a Dream
- The Stranger
- Seasons – Polar Express
- "What are mysteries in science?"
- Determining truth or fact
- Fact vs. fantasy
- What could happen? – Polar Express – Stranger
- Animals – wild vs domesticated
- insects

**Art**
- Symbols – dog (pay homage) – cat (Cecil)
- What do you see? (discussions)
- Strategies – make-board game – alph. bk. – cartoon pics w. captions
- Compare with – Balthus – Magritte – Hopper – use of borders – cartooned as a child – lots of detail
- Style – surrealism – pointillism – chiaroscuro – mood
- Materials – pastels – pen + ink – charcoal
- Art elements – perspective – odd scale/size – color b+w – texture especially in landscape
- imitate style & use his materials – studio field trip

**Soc. St.**
- artist training
- Career – book illustrator – financial
- Geography – Ben's Dream
- History – Ben's Dream
- Social Values – what's important?
- Economics – book pub.
- text – art
- bookmaking – math

**Drama**
- Storytelling – from pictures – before / after
- Z was Zapped – convert to RT
- What if...
- Pantomime – What if...
- Verbal – interview – universal – time
- what if dances "Detail" dances – Non-loco/frozen sculptures

**Math**
- details
- measurement – In stories – patterns
- shapes
- geometry in art
- angles / perspective
- VA int "homage"
- Themes?
- Patterns?
- Vocabulary – words in stories – odd names – 8 art terms

**Dance**
- what if dances

**Music**
- "Ants Go Marching" – Dreams – sea chanties (Wreck of the Zephyr)
- Songs – Music (mood mysterious)
- Instruments – VA plays recorder – violins (Wretched Stone) – bell
- Compose – find bkground music for books – Sounds to go w. rdgs.

**Rdg./LA**
- Comprehension – Lit. response options – student led – Discussion
- Storymap – Retelling etc – websites
- Write poetry – poem – patterns – What if...
- Write – diary or log – fantasy – book/film review – time variation
- Read – Reviews & Interviews – 12+ books – Books that are ch. lit – related
- Imaginary place

**Literature**
- Genre – Folktales – fable – Fantasy – fairy tale – picture bk – tall tale
- used in film "Jumanji" – What if songs
- Archetypes & Motifs – water / dreams – sleep – journey → quest – cycles – magical objects
- Poetry Alive strategies
- Poetry – Dreams – Silverstein's "What if..." – Mysteries – Puzzles – Animals
- Book Connections – Flat stories – Imagine's Antlers – The Big Orange Slit – The shrinking of Treehorn
- setting – landscape – "Imaginary as real"
- Lit. elements – Mood-text thru' art – Characters – Flat – Plot – cliffhangers – Ants – journey structure
- Info on author – Something About the Author – "Devil or God is in the details."
- Themes – Art allows us to express feelings & ideas words cannot. – There are things that are unexplainable – Imagination + dreams give us insight.

---

Most museum sites have extensive resources for teachers. Websites are listed at the end of this chapter. Examples are as follows:

The Smithsonian Institution is the world's largest museum complex. Find activities and information at www.si.edu.

Hirshhorn Museum and Sculpture Garden's site includes an education section with interactive features (create a sculpture): http://hirshhorn.si.edu/

Kidsart's website lists top museum sites for students: www.kidsart.com/tt0101.html. On the list are the National Gallery of Art in Washington, D.C., and the Minneapolis Institute of Arts. The Museum of Fine Art (Boston) and Children's Museum of Indianapolis have wonderful sites, too.

Art connections can be made to most field trips; for example, art such as Picasso's *Paul as Harlequin* or Chagall's *The Blue Circus* can be examined before a circus field trip and serve to inform art making afterwards. Walking trips to examine local architecture of churches, monuments, or cemeteries are chances to build art vocabulary, gather data for an art project, and develop community pride. A simple trip around the block can provide rich images to categorize by colors, lines, shapes, and textures. Appendix H offers field trip guidelines for pretrip, during trip, and posttrip planning.

***Museum trips.*** Here are guidelines to make sure students get the most out of a museum visit.

- Before the visit: Use Ready Reference 6.15 as a guide to activities. Ask if the museum provides materials to prepare and if there will be a docent to guide. Try to get postcards of art children will see. Do sorts, matching, and discussions of elements with the cards.
- Study art elements, practice looking at paintings, study artists and forms you'll see, and list what you want to find out together. Plan curriculum connections. For example:

math (shapes/size), social studies (portraits/landscapes/events), and science (landscapes/nature/animals). Recommended books are Brown's *Visiting the Art Museum* and the following:

Browne, A. (2003). *The shape game.* Farrar, Straus & Giroux.
Hooper, M. (2000). *Dogs' night in the art museum.* Millbrook.
Micklethwait, L. (1993). *I spy two eyes: Numbers in art.* Greenwillow.
Weitzman, J., & Glasser, R. (1998). *You can't take a balloon into the Metropolitan Museum.* Dial.

- During the visit: Give students specific things to look for and do. Have students take roles and do close looking, storytelling, and sketching. Students may want to buy postcards to start a personal collection.
- After the visit: Follow up with activities to find out what students learned. Ask them to write about favorite paintings or do art response projects (media, styles, forms) and drama. Continue with postcard activities (see Chapter 7).

## Ready Reference 6.15 Museum Scavenger Hunt

Use before the trip and during the visit.

### Ask Students to Find Examples of Art with the Following:

- Striking colors (e.g., complementary)
- Strong use of line
- Interesting ways artists create texture
- Obvious use of light (white?)
- Different moods
- Shapes and masses (e.g., geometric, organic)
- Different subject matter: still life, landscape, portrait, abstract, seascape, cityscape, interior
- Examples of perspective: atmospheric, linear, overlapping
- Lots of detail and ones without
- Unity, as sense of wholeness
- Patterns, motifs, or repeated elements
- Unusual arrangements or compositions
- Media examples: sculpture (materials), watercolor, acrylic, oil, tempera, collage, fabric art
- Different time periods
- Different frames (e.g., oval, fancy gold frame) and the effect

### Things to Identify

- What's in the background?
- Eyes: Where do they look? Do they follow you?
- Hands: details? where, why, and how placed? folded?
- Brushstrokes (e.g., scumbling is dry brush painting)
- Edges: lost and found, contours, and shadows

### Things to Say to Students

- Take a few minutes to look. I'll meet you in the next gallery.
- Look up close, middle, and far away. Find the magic view spot.
- Look closely at details. Go beyond the obvious.

### Example Questions

- What is going on in the art?
- What is the mood? How does it make you feel?
- What do you see? Colors? Shapes? Images?
- Where does the artist want you to enter the work? What is the focal point?
- Where does your eye go first? Why? Next?
- Decode or read the painting. Squint. See the shapes and colors. What stands or pops out?
- Use your senses. What do you see? Feel? Smell? Hear? Music? Taste?
- What do you notice about the brush strokes? Why did the artist do this? What is the effect?
- What story did the artist want to tell?
- Find examples of "beauty of the masses."
- What is the subject matter: Landscape? Seascape? Still life?
- Portraits: What about the background? How does it affect the composition? What is the essence of the person? What do you notice about hair? Hands? Eyes?
- What adjectives or nouns can you connect to the art?
- What is the time of day? How do you know?
- Nudity: Why is it used? (e.g., shows timelessness because clothes date; symbol of superiority or nothing to hide; beauty of human curves)
- What about edges? Hard? Lost?
- What did the artist choose to do? What arrangement? What purposes?
- What does the title have to do with the work?
- How does the artist use color to move your eyes?
- What did the artist want you to think or feel?
- How are _____ and _____ alike and different?
- What if _____ was changed? (e.g., size, color, materials)

**Projects.** Art-making projects are highly motivational and are a common part of unit study. Projects offer concrete assessment information about learning, as well. They are usually interest and discovery based and may be done in small groups (e.g., murals). Projects are easy formats to teach CPS, which begins with exploration of a problem. A project can involve any media and subject matter and take any of the forms described under "art literacy." The anticipation of a culminating exhibit can drive a unit or an entire school program, such as Normal Park's in Chattanooga, Tennessee.

The Italian Reggio Emilia schools shape the entire curriculum around hands-on projects that are shared and displayed. Work at these schools has informed U.S. educational theorists and teachers involved in creating AI frameworks. At Reggio Emilia schools children learn through inquiry. They investigate and document their explorations in an environment structured like a studio or atelier. Learning is made visible through the arts (Gandini, Hill, Cadwell, & Schwall, 2005; Project Zero and Reggio Children, 2001). Teachers in the atelier also take an inquiry stance observing, documenting, researching, and theorizing about students' learning. The atelier concept elevates the place of expressive education, in general, not just with and in the arts (Gandini et al., 2005).

**Two-Pronged Lesson Planning.** Meaningful integration entails the use of lessons with two or more prongs: art and math focus, art and language arts focus, art and dance, and so forth. Planning Page 6.16 shows an art/math example.

## Planning Page 6.16

### Art/Math Lesson Plan Grade 4

*Two-Pronged Focus:* (1) Art elements of shape, pattern and repetition, abstract, and asymmetrical. (2) Math concepts of pattern and geometric shapes.
*Art Standards:* 1, 2, 3, and 5 (Ready Reference 6.11)
*Student Objectives:* Students will know and be able to:

1. Use five elements of shape and repetition to create a pattern.
2. Orally label geometric shapes (rectangle, circle, triangle, square).
3. Write examples of how shapes are a part of life and why pattern is important.

*Teaching Procedure:* The teacher will . . . (S = students)

#### Introduction
Post discussion rules: looking closely, use of art materials. Tell S we'll do two silent activities. They are to figure out how they are related.

1. Mystery bag: draw out fabrics in different patterns (dots, plaid, stripes) and tell them to look closely to find what they have in common.
2. Without talking, put five elements of shape word cards in pocket chart (Brookes, 1996): circle, dot, straight line, curved line, and angled line. Gesture for S to draw these. Circulate, smile, and nod as S follow directions. Repeat with eight word cards that have a series of elements to make a pattern (dot, dot, horizontal line, horizontal line, curved down line, curved up line, triangle, triangle).

#### Development
1. Ask: "How were the mystery bag and the drawing activities related?" If necessary, scaffold by holding fabric up to cards. "What did both have?"
2. Tell S the goal is to learn the five elements and use them to create an abstract work of art.

Show two prints: Kadinsky's *The White Dot* and Wyeth's *Due North*. Explain the difference between a reproduction print and an original work of art.

3. Ask: "How are these two artworks alike and different?" Probe for five elements. When they are named, write them on the board.
4. Tell S that Wyeth's work is called realistic because we recognize what it is and Kadinsky's work is called abstract because the focus is on color and elements of shape, not on representing things in a real way—the feel is more important. Label each work.
5. Divide into small groups to find examples of elements of shape, geometric shapes, and patterns (repeated elements). Give each group a clipboard to record.
6. Reassemble and take reports by randomly calling on S. Ask: "Why did you find so many examples? Where are there shapes outside of school? Why are patterns made? Used? How do patterns affect people?"
7. Tell about making abstract art: Important to experiment, fill up the space with elements, shapes, patterns. Give paper, markers, and 10 minutes to explore. Play tranquil New Age background music.
8. Reassemble and ask S to tell one thing they discovered about materials, elements, and patterns. Ask if these drawings are realistic or abstract, and why.
9. Do directed abstract activity: Say (1) draw two lines that go to the edges of the paper, (2) draw three dots, (3) draw four curved lines, and (4) draw a circle that touches another line. Fill in all the spaces with colors or collage materials.

#### Conclusion/Assessment

1. Circulate and give descriptive feedback about elements and concepts as S work.
2. Do art docent talks in fishbowl arrangement, with docents telling elements, shapes, pattern, and how they got ideas. Audience members ask one question or give a comment. Use a writing frame to wrap up: The five elements of shape are _____. Five geometric shapes are _____. When elements are repeated, they form _____. Patterns in my life are (1) _____ and (2) _____.
3. Frame art and put up in class gallery.

# Building Block IV: Aesthetic Learning Environment

*Though we travel the world over to find the beautiful, we must carry it with us or we find it not.* (Ralph Waldo Emerson)

Visually enriched contexts surround students with art and invite them to look closely. Whole schools now strive to create an aesthetic classroom environment for learning (Deasy & Stevenson, 2005). The school campus can become the site for outdoor and indoor sculpture gardens and flower gardens inspired by Monet's own. These create opportunities to respond to color, texture, line, and shape. As the accompanying Teacher Spotlight shows, however, the individual classroom remains the site of most learning; each teacher creates a unique classroom canvas.

# Teacher Spotlight

## Sylvia Horres's Classroom

A banner proclaims, "Painting the Past: Style of Grandma Moses." Displayed are 15 watercolors by first graders. Not one has a simple band of sky at the top or a mere ribbon of green grass along the bottom. There are no "joined comma" birds. The space on the paper is completely filled with rolling hills that meet skies of pink, purple, orange, and green—defying any notion that primary children are limited to thinking the sky is blue. There are foregrounds, midgrounds, and backgrounds in each painting, created by roads that narrow in the distance.

Student desks are arranged in sixes, indicating group work is the norm. A set of addition problems, depicted with Picasso-like eyes, bears the title, "Picasso Math." The windows are covered with poetry. Abundant books fill crates, arranged by levels and topics. There are also manipulatives, calendars, plants, and word webs for Chinese New Year. A large Venn diagram contrasts words for "apple" versus "pumpkin" with shared concepts in the center. Phases of the moon are displayed with black and yellow shapes.

# Immersion

Walt Whitman knew little about the brain compared to what we know today. Yet, when he wrote about a child who went forth each day and became the object he looked upon, he poetically expressed what research now confirms: The images that enter the brain become the basis for the images we create and the people we become. Children need to see beautiful images. The same consideration needs to be given to classroom design as is put into our homes. Broken blinds, dirty floors, mismatched furniture, and peeling paint indicate apathy. They imply a low priority for aesthetic understanding and do not invoke a sense of pleasure.

Children feel and behave better in places that please the senses. Cleanliness is a given. Color schemes need to complement one another. Light should be soft, not glaring white, to relax and make learning pleasant. Storage areas are needed to organize tools and materials. Framed art, live plants, music, pleasant smells, fresh air, and art displays all heighten aesthetic response. Positive attitudes are created and spirits uplifted. Although there is no one best aesthetic environment, consider the following questions (Jensen 2001; Koster, 1997).

- Is there plenty of soft, natural light?
- Are there carpeted and uncarpeted areas that are visually pleasing, inviting, and functional?
- Are learning centers balanced with open areas?
- Are walls and furniture neutral so there is an illusion of space? (Bold primary colors negatively affect some children.)
- Are walls a neutral backdrop to display art?
- Is student art displayed respectfully?
- Do displays seem planned or hurriedly put together?
- Is artwork displayed on easels? Is it changed regularly?
- Are art displays at students' eye level?
- Are displays focused with a few select items at a time?
- Is there organization and order for supplies and books?

The next questions should be answered with "no":

- Are holiday decorations stereotypical?
- Is cultural art trivialized by displaying it only for holidays?
- Are bulletin boards teacher made, with cutesy art and cutouts that limit aesthetic response and reinforce stereotypes?

**Color.** Most people have color preferences, perhaps because the body needs what color gives. We see color by absorbing light through our eyes, where it is converted to energy. Even people without sight feel it. The light energy stimulates the pituitary and pineal glands, which regulate hormones. Red stimulates, warms, and increases the heart rate, brain activity, and respiration. Pink soothes and relaxes. Orange makes us hungry and reduces fatigue. Yellow jars memory and boosts blood pressure and pulse rate. Green calms and makes us feel hopeful. We associate it with spring and new beginnings. Blue relaxes by lowering the blood pressure, heart rate, and respiration. It makes us feel cooler (Friedmann, 2004, p. 2). Paint colors matter. Pink is currently used in prisons (and University of Iowa's opposing team's locker room) and hospitals. Classrooms are painted blue for calming purposes. Shades and values matter as well, requiring additional research at the onset.

**Exhibit Space.** An aesthetic classroom needs a place to display artwork. A bulletin board or cork strip can be used for quick displays. A clothesline or drying rack with clothespins or clips can also serve to exhibit completed projects, if art is arranged with some plan. Not all kids want their work up and this should be respected. Some prefer to keep art in a portfolio or scrapbook for personal use rather than public consumption.

**Respectful Art.** Children enjoy what is familiar and may shrink from the strange; but if they are to become accepting of dimensions of beauty, they need immersion in all its variations. Classrooms should contain art in many styles showing people of different ages, races, ethnicity, genders, and skin colors. Art should reflect different places and time periods—images of people going about life in ways that may seem foreign and yet show how basic needs for food, clothing, shelter, knowledge, love, and beauty are universal. Respect for diverse peoples is encouraged when art shows people in dignified, contemporary situations, not just historical garb. Overuse of art showing half-naked Native Americans wearing feathers is inaccurate, to say the least.

**Stultifying Art.**    Commercial cutouts, cute cardboard pinups, and coloring book art should be avoided because they blunt thinking. Just as damaging are traceable patterns and punchouts of ethnic groups and races dressed in historical costumes, suggesting they are less advanced and still live this way. Think how absurd it would be to show Americans in Pilgrim outfits as if they were "typical" Americans. Images of Japanese people in kimonos and Eskimos in igloos are limiting if not balanced with contemporary images. Original art sculptures, fine art prints, postcard prints, and coffee table–type art books are sources of the full range of authentic cultural art.

**Art Sources.**    Students see art and artifacts brought from home (pottery, quilts, photographs) as intriguing sources of aesthetic stimulation and family heritage. Aesthetic sensibilities can be cultivated by planning quiet times to pass around personal objects for close examination. A "beauty center" stocked with student finds can include shells, leaves, and rocks and serve as discussion starters about the special "magic" feelings possible when you see a field of sunflowers or touch a new baby's velvety hand (Koster, 1997).

# Building Block V: Literature as a Core Art Form

In our homes we proudly display pricey coffee table tomes. These are visual art–based books that contain beautiful art or are about artists or art topics. School libraries have thousands of such books, making literature the most available art in schools. Literature also has the longest history of curricular integration, providing a model for the integration of other art forms.

## Planning Pointers

When the goal is meaningful visual art integration, teachers should not think literally about literature. Many powerful visual art–based books do not contain art and are not literally *about* art. Important book themes may be developed through the role visual art plays in the narrative. For example, the Newbery book *Abel's Island* (Steig, 2007) is about a mouse that gets stranded on an island. His psychological survival depends on art making—giant sculptures he makes of loved ones. Teachers are urged to think about significant visual art connections that may have previously been ignored in familiar classics. Is Charlotte's web not a magnificent work of art that results from expert creative problem solving? Isn't the *Snowy Day* (Keats) about the delight in discovering the art that is a part of any day, if you zero in on shapes, patterns, and textures?

School libraries and classrooms now house magnificent picture books. These books make powerful statements about art's central place in learning. Prominent in collections are Caldecott winners.

## Caldecott Medal Award

The Caldecott Medal Award (1936+) is presented yearly to the artist of the most distinguished picture book published in the United States in the preceding year. The 2009 winner was *The House in the Night* illustrated by Beth Krommes, written by Susan Marie Swanson (Houghton Mifflin). In 2008, the award went to *The Invention of Hugo Cabret* by Brian Selznick (Scholastic), and in 2007, to *Flotsam* by David Wiesner (Clarion). Access the full list of Caldecotts at www.ala.org.

The art in Caldecott winners goes beyond literal illustration of ideas in the printed text. The art makes an aesthetic statement, thus making these books gold mines for integration. There are books in most art media and styles and about nearly every kind of artist.

## Other Sources

The Ready References in this chapter list numerous examples of art-based children's book examples on a variety of visual art topics. More can be found in Appendix J and in Planning Pages and Ready References in Chapter 4. Websites devoted to children's literature are good sources (see the end of Chapter 4).

## Picture Book Integration

Picture books are available on nearly any curricular topic. In their short history (about 75 years), they have become a mainstay of the literacy curriculum and are often used as core material in science, social studies, and math lessons with students in all grade levels. During a Civil War unit, a picture book such as Polacco's *Pink and Say* can give both an aesthetic experience and historical information. *Mirandy and Brother Wind* (McKissack) is a lovely book about a special dance in the African American culture and uses authentic dialect. Seymour Simon's books are a stunning blend of photography and science, which makes them popular with all grades.

Any fine picture book can serve as material to develop language and visual literacy skills by using the "What do you see?" strategy described in Ready Reference 6.12. Art strategies to explore picture book art are given in Ready Reference 7.6. The reference book, *A to Zoo: Subject Access to Children's Picture Books* (Lima, 2005) is a bibliography of picture books, categorized by author, title, and subject or topic. Ready Reference 4.11 lists other print and web-based sources.

**Visual Literacy: Picture Book Guidelines.**    Use the following strategies to teach students to read picture book art.

1. Teach the names and ideas behind art elements and concepts so students have words to think with and talk about the art.
2. Use "think-alouds" to demonstrate how to decode art. Describe what you think and how the art makes you feel. Hone in on messages that go beyond the print text.
3. Give students magnifying glasses or paper tubes to isolate and examine line, color, and other elements as well as the media, style, and mood. Discuss how the book would be

different if it has no art or the art was in a different style (e.g., cartoon versus impressionistic).

4. Compare the art in versions of the same story. Many folktales, such as Little Red Riding Hood, are available in picture books. Do Venn diagrams on chart paper or the overhead.

5. Ape the greats. Use the CPS process (Ready Reference 2.6) to experiment with various media and styles used by artists. Try out book formats such as pop-ups and shape books.

6. Plan artist-centered units. Involve students in examining the body of artwork produced by artists such as Maurice Sendak, Tomie dePaola, or Patricia Polacco so they can view the creative process up close and in depth. Students can become versed in the concept of style, and grow to understand various styles. Aesthetic development occurs as preferences form, but students cannot like what they do not know.

Two recommended references on using pictures books for visual literacy are *The Potential of Picture Books: From Visual Literacy to Aesthetic Understanding* (Kiefer, 1994) and *Picture Books for Looking and Learning: Awakening Visual Perceptions Through the Art of Children's Books* (Marantz, 1992).

### Picture Book Detectives.
Children are often more attuned to details than adults and enjoy doing "look closely" to find small, surprising aspects of art. For example, artists may insert repeated "side notes" (Chris Van Allsburg puts his dog in most books). Ask students to examine book art to find what the art tells about the following:

- Setting: where and when
- Characters: especially body shapes and parts such as hands and faces; look for how characters change from the beginning
- Plot: pictures show events not in the text, even subplots or asides (as in Gilman's *Something from Nothing),* or foreshadow events and create tension with hints and clues)
- Style: use of exaggeration, humor; how mood is created
- Point of view: where the viewer enters the picture

In addition, books should be examined to find whether the story is extended through art or the art merely literally illustrates the text. Ask about how book parts contribute to the message (endpapers, gutters, borders, double-page spreads, where the story begins in the art).

Questions such as "What does the artist do that surprises you?" and "How does the book make you feel and why?" help children discern aesthetic differences. Ask them to compare two books to find details artists use and the amount of action or movement in the art. Teach students that subtle changes make significant differences: A well-placed line or a small shadow can say so much.

### Book Responses.
Making art is an important way for students to respond to any book. Art can also accompany any writing. It is important, however, for students to learn diverse ways to respond through art. Ready References 6.6 and 6.7 list media and forms that can be used to respond to picture books. Also see Appendix F.

Students can also respond to important ideas in any literary text by creating art using subject matter that connects a landscape (outdoor scene in the story), portrait (a character in the story),

cityscape (view of a city in the story), interior (inside a room or building in the story), seascape (a view of a body of water in the story), still life (nonliving objects in the story arranged on a surface), or abstract (color, shape, line, and texture to express feelings).

# Building Block VI: Best Teaching Practices

*Elementary art was not motivating for me because of lack of choice.* (Gloria Dalvini, professional watercolorist, Beaufort, South Carolina)

Arts integration takes a discovery orientation that captivates students who may ordinarily find schooling uninviting. A focus on seeking the unusual increases engagement; the "uncommon" is at the core of creating, understanding, and responding. The questions "what if" and "why not" become forces to propel teachers and students to break out of rigid thinking that can stall or stop learning. Teachers pose questions for which they do not know answers. Students are prompted to "try it" and learn from mistakes. Mistakes are "re-viewed" as avenues to new understandings in the way watercolorists say they let paint direct them. Materials exploration become sparks to "see what happens" and make something of it. Inspiration is oblivious to the perspiration that forms when students are deeply involved in the genuine work of creativity. They lose track of time and groan when recess is announced. It's all about good teaching.

AI educators have enthusiastically embraced the many research syntheses on best teaching practices, including that by Marzano, Pickering, and Pollock (2001) which drew upon psychological research regarding learning through imagery. Ready Reference 3.9 lists general best AI practices. The following are elaborations that particularly apply to visual art.

## Center Stage: Teachers

Classroom teachers often lack confidence in their art abilities and/or have limited personal art experiences. Lack of confidence manifests itself in rigidity—using tasks that involve precut assemblages, painting by number, coloring in the lines, and tracing. This is not art making. The goal of visual art integration is not to keep students busy with hands-on work, nor is the focus on getting kids to make art that always "looks like something."

This book is intended to give enough philosophy, research, and knowledge for readers to become emboldened to pursue better practices. This often means rejecting destructive practices that focus on convenience and outdated traditions ("That's the way it's always done."). Teachers lay the foundation for learning. That foundation must be strong. Teachers should NOT . . .

- Model step-by-step directions for students to copy rather than have them create actual art.
- Display "cute and convenient" commercial materials purchased at teacher stores.

- Rely on stencils/cutters to trace or punch out letters and shapes. (Instead, teach students how to cut block letters and create fonts using a variety of tools.)
- Make the bulletin boards, rather than involve students in planning and construction.
- Exhort students to "stay in the lines" and use stereotypes, such as blue sky, pink skin, and icons that halt thinking (e.g., hearts, birds, ball and stick suns, rainbows).
- Do art *for* students or have "artistic" students do it.

**Danger Signs.** One red flag is students saying, "I can't do it" or "I can't draw" when art activities are introduced. These comments show students have little confidence in their own creativity. Teachers need to address danger signs directly: Explain that the focus of visual art is using creative thinking with art materials. When children know few ways to express themselves (e.g., stick drawing), it is clear they need to be taught options for techniques, materials, and tools. If students say that they hate certain styles, such as abstract art, it is clear they do not know that the goal is to understand, not like or dislike. Preferences naturally emerge, but they should be based on broad deep experiences with art, not quick judgments.

## Creative Problem Solving and Authentic Art

Teachers who are committed to AI have a "what-if" orientation. They invite students to pose problems, experiment, gather ideas, suggest solutions, reflect, and feel the joy of discovery. Teachers accept that CPS creates dissonance. Initially students who are used to being told what to do and think can become exasperated. Creative thinking can even exasperate master artists, including Georgia O'Keeffe. There is a story about one day when she was teaching college in Texas. She became frustrated as she tried to get her students to think for themselves. She went to the board and wrote, "Would all the fools in this class please leave!" One student immediately asked, "Then who will teach us?" To her credit, Ms. O'Keeffe laughed.

Children's author Katherine Paterson reminds us in *Sign of the Chrysanthemum* that "it is only through fire that the spirit is forged." We should not back away from engaging students in higher order thinking that fires CPS and sets them on the road to independence. Ready Reference 2.8 gives boosters to massage the process so as to free student ideas.

**Visual Imagery.** Key to CPS is activating mental art or visualizing. In addition to teaching students to imagine art elements such as color and shape, five mental actions can be taught: how to (1) transfer background memories into temporary visual memory, (2) zoom in on details, (3) embellish images, (4) rotate images, and (5) scan with your mind's eye (Bruer, 1999). These kinds of visualizations used during reading can dramatically increase comprehension (Ready Reference 6.1). This makes sense since we mostly remember in images, not words; our mental pictures are reconstructions of neural pathways originally formed during the experience (Siegel, 1999).

Another strategy is called *guided visualization*. Students are asked to make mental pictures as a story is read or told. Before a plant unit, teachers might describe a trip through a plant. The five previous mental actions could be evoked with vivid and accurate adjectives. Students can be directed to zoom in on details and elaborate by changing colors, shapes, and textures. The images may be turned upside down or sideways. Such personally created mental art can motivate students to read and learn more.

**Explicit Teaching.** Visual art scholar, Rudolf Arnheim (1989) urges teachers not to "foist upon the learner technical tricks that go beyond his or her stage of conception." He advises that art knowledge be left to emerge naturally with an emphasis on discovery rather than telling or showing students what to do (p. 42). Those involved in AI have a deep respect for discovery learning, but they acknowledge the benefits of explicit instruction. Effective instruction nurtures natural response, but respects that learning depends on disciplining one's mind and body. Deep learning is more than "a flight of the imagination or an exercise in the affective fallacy" (Sadoski & Paivio, 2004, p. 50). Visual art integration is about finding the appropriate balance for individual students.

When given materials and tools to create art, children will experiment and use imagination. When explicitly taught how to use materials and tools, they work with greater satisfaction and depth of problem solving. This can be as simple as showing how to paint using different strokes and amounts or using effects like dripping and splattering. Short demonstrations can preface student exploration that leads to a product, or experimentation, period. Explicit instruction in art basics can prevent tendencies of students to abandon art expression in upper grades.

Mona Brookes (1996), founder of Monart, goes further to make a convincing argument that "natural" symbolic art development is entirely different from learning to create representational or realistic art. She has shown that explicit teaching of realistic drawing need not hinder symbolic expression. Without instruction, however, she says most children do not automatically discover how to draw realistically, which may be why many abandon drawing by their teens. Going further, when adults say they cannot draw, they mean they do not know how to represent an image realistically and expertly. Interestingly the same level of quality is not demanded to claim one can read or write as is applied to "artist" status. We are shocked by print illiteracy and should be equally shocked by arts illiteracy that shudders understanding and limits aesthetic fulfillment.

Of course, children can be distracted when teachers make them aware of what they have been doing unconsciously when they make or look at art. Consciousness is necessary, however, if they are to grow. In particular, students need to be conscious and able to deploy CPS processes in strategic ways.

**Art-Making Guidelines.** Most students will not discover the range of arts communication possibilities just by exploring. Most need explicit instruction in how to use a variety of media, tools, and techniques. Check Ready References 6.6 through 6.9 for ideas and add experimentation with different surfaces (e.g., fabric, wood). Chapter 7 has more art-making specifics. Following are general guidelines.

- Provide several examples as references, not models to copy. Too frequently even young learners are encouraged to imitate adult models. This can have a detrimental impact on motivation as children realize they cannot produce what is modeled. More worrisome is copy work, which deprives children the opportunity to use creative problem solving. Imitation does not use high order thinking. Instead, several "examples" should be shown that present options to meet the goals of the assignment. The work of previous students can be used and it is helpful to show work depicting several levels of success.

- Use an "explore–practice–express" sequence. Exploration piques interest in learning to use tools and materials. Consider a sequence of (a) time to explore, (b) time for practice with feedback, and (c) actual use of materials.

- Limit direction giving, which creates impatience, but demonstrate basic ways to use materials and tools before exploration, especially in regard to safety issues. Materials and tools can be put out with brief introductions, leaving students to discover possibilities. We want doers, not just listeners and viewers.

- Repeat use of the same materials and subject matter to allow depth of experimentation. This leads to more confidence and skill. The focus remains on involving students in making art.

- Give clear feedback: "You have used four shapes" is more effective than "Good shapes!" Describe what students are doing. Use art vocabulary. Focus on what is being learned. "Good job!" and "Great!" teach nothing. Also, do not interrupt with comments when students are concentrated and involved.

- Do not insult by asking, "What is it?" Instead, offer comments and ask about art elements or the process: "How did you do this? I see you are trying to put the wash over the candle drawing." Ask about artistic decisions: "Why did you do it this way?" Challenge them to predict: "What do you think will happen if _____?" or "How could you _____?"

- Expect appropriate behavior. Art making should be a time for concentration. Play music without lyrics (see Chapter 12) and make rules about quiet. Brookes (1996) believes children must be taught the pleasures of silence because they rarely experience it. She says it takes time for children to be comfortable with quiet, but stresses that it is necessary for concentration.

- After students finish, invite them to give docent talks about their work to explain their use of the CPS process.

- Invite students to write or tell stories about their art, find music to accompany it, or create musical compositions.

- Have students sign their own art, like artists (who usually don't write anything except their signatures *on* the art). Students can then title or write about the art on separate paper at their developmental spelling levels.

- Connect art to students' lives. Instead of isolated art activities or art used as a reward for finishing work, integrate art using the *with, about, in,* and *through* model. Use art in routines and content units in science and social studies.

**Ban the Deadly Dozen.**   According to teaching artist Kay Thomas, one way to help children break out of thinking in visual stereotypes is to post the most common symbols used to represent emotions and ideas (see Ready Reference 6.17) and then ban them in student art. Students have to think more deeply about love, happiness, and nature when they cannot represent them with hearts, smiley faces, "m" birds, and circle and stick suns. Be sure to discuss the purpose of the ban and brainstorm options with students that include innovative uses of colors, lines, shapes, and textures (2009).

**Teach How to "Read" Art.**   Just as the language art of reading is not just "caught" and has to be "taught," so it is with visual art. Students need to be taught art language and concepts so they can understand and discuss their work or that of others. The elements of art are its alphabet or "code." Students learn to decode art through explicit and incidental teaching of basic art elements and concepts. Explicit teaching is described in Chapter 3 and includes teaching what, how, when, and why through demonstration and coached practice. Explicit teaching should be accompanied by charts, class word walls, and other visuals that can dramatically increase retention. Post memory aids to help with concepts such as the spectrum—ROY G. BIV is an acronym for "red–orange–yellow–green–blue–indigo–violet."

**Personal Words.**   Students also need personal arts vocabulary references and records. Art "word walls" made with file folders, arts dictionaries using blank books, and word rings (cards punched and hooked on metal shower curtain rings) reinforce vocabulary and build feelings of pride and ownership. These tools help students gain independence with reading art products that function as "texts." Children are particularly proud when they learn to read book art and use art terms to discuss illustrations in science and social studies books, often better than their parents.

**Evaluative Judgments/Higher Order Thinking.**   Students do not automatically know how to make good judgments, especially when looking at art. Without instruction, they tend to want to stop at loving or hating a work. These reactions halt thinking. Children need to be taught to take time and describe what they see and the feelings the art evokes. They can be coached to create stories (interpretations) from art. Art criticism is teachable, even to primary students. "Think-alouds" can be used to model critique that rests on giving evidence for opinions. Ratings of judgments (on a scale of 1 to 5) of "goodness," or how much a work is liked, can be used, too, and then discussed. These practices create an expectation for reflection, first. Respect for considered thinking can be taught so breezy conclusions are soon seen as just that. Ultimately, students need to grasp that to appreciate art means to understand it, not that you have to like it.

## Aesthetic Orienting

*A first-rate soup is more creative than a second-rate painting.* (Abraham Maslow, quoting a client, 1968)

Teachers do not need to be able to draw realistically or sculpt well to help children do so. Artistic teachers are those who set up an aesthetic classroom, ask provocative questions, respond with descriptive comments, and model how to listen, look, and feel the world's beauty. Consider the following strategies.

**Aesthetic Scanning.**   Norton (2003) describes "aesthetic scanning" as a scaffolded sequence in which students look closely at picture book art to describe the emotions, meanings,

**Ready Reference 6.17**  Kay's Deadly Dozen

Visual art specialist, Kay Thomas, recommends that children be told to not use these stereotypes in their artwork. Banning these "icons" encourages them to create more thoughtful work. She advises teachers to post and discuss these and other images that may stunt artistic growth.

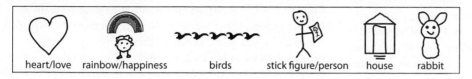

heart/love   rainbow/happiness   birds   stick figure/person   house   rabbit

cloud   cross/religion   sun   smiley face/happiness   star   peace sign

---

organization, and method by which the art was created (pp. 140–141). Teach that taking time to notice details can lead to new discoveries about everyday things. Use cardboard tubes or magnifying glasses to zero in on fabrics and art for details. Colored transparencies and transparency frames make interesting "windows" to focus attention. Books such as Hoban's *Look Again* can be inspirations to analyze the visual world by looking at parts of plants, animals, and clothes. Hoban overlays frames over photographs to cause viewers to see only a tiny piece of a whole, such as a seed or a tail. A similar effect can be achieved using note cards or sticky notes to mask part of a picture (e.g., mask half of a print and predict images, colors, and shapes). Model use of descriptive language such as "I see rounded shapes or a muddy brown color" and ask students to describe using the "I see _____ and _____ structure."

**Aesthetic Aromas.**  The perfume industry knows well the power of smell to affect behavior. We avoid nasty smells and seek out attractive aromas. A classroom with fresh flowers, potpourri, and fresh air sets the stage for creative work. Encourage students to share discoveries about good smells through discussions, journals, and collaborative charts. Give feedback to stretch language and encourage use of descriptive words (e.g., "You smell as fresh as laundry on a line!").

**Aesthetic Sounds.**  Easy rhythm instruments can be made to explore the differences in sounds. For example, put beans in a butter tub or make sand blocks by gluing sandpaper to old cassette tape cases. Record environmental sounds and create art to go with the sounds. At times, play music as students make art. Discuss art in terms of the sounds associated with it (e.g., a seascape or landscape). Write sound poems about art, like this onomatopoeia poem about a schoolday: "Ring/ha ha ha/patter patter/slam/creak/ring ring/achoo/gobble crunch slurp/scribble/sigh/whew/ring/trip-trap, trip-trap/honk toot roar."

**Texture/Touch Aesthetics.**  Develop tactile perception in the following ways, so students grasp the concept of texture in artwork.

1. Ask students to describe feelings as they finger paint, use collage, and try chalk using different pressures. Model this, saying, "When I press hard, the line is darker and thicker."
2. Make feely bags. Put them at a station or use for circle times; students reach in and either describe the item's nature or use it in an add-on story. For example: "There was once a thin bendy creature who wore paper clothes" (stick of gum).
3. Ask students to bring items for topical displays on rough, soft, silky, cold, or hard.
4. Go on texture walks to find thin, thick, and heavy items. Use items for "found things" collages or table displays.
5. Make texture books (e.g., fabrics, foils, papers) by gluing items to card stock and fastening with brads or make big books with text from students.

## Process and Product

*Dictated art is not art but a contradiction of it.* (Blanche Jefferson)

Visual art integration has two main focuses: looking at art to understand it and creating art. A balance is needed between appreciation and creation, impression and expression, viewing and doing. Draw on mental and physical processes to result in "products." Students can learn to look at art using seeing and thinking processes that result in conclusions, mental products that may take the form of visual images. In making art, thinking processes and hands-on techniques are used to work with media and tools to create tangible products.

Balance is needed, with a tilt toward process for P–6 children. When it comes to art making, an inquiry or studio attitude is recommended which gives children ample time to explore.

This parallels a writing workshop that budgets time to "mess around" with new materials and ideas. Students need time to do what most of us did when we first used computer-drawing tools—scribble and experiment. This sets the stage for explicit teaching to give students specific ways to stretch work with tools and materials to create original art. Criteria for quality products can be introduced to motivate work toward excellence.

Process and product need to be similarly balanced when the focus is on understanding artwork of others during close looking investigations. Memorizing names and dates of artworks is not useful. The hub of artwork discussions should be about working together to create new meanings. Of course, students need to be taught language to describe aesthetic qualities (e.g., color, texture). This knowledge is a valued product. Like adults, children will want to borrow ideas from the work of others gained from close looking. Key is encouraging them to adapt ideas and not do wholesale copying.

**Dictated Art.**  Black outlines intended for coloring are not art and really have no place in AI. If teachers feel compelled to use them, at minimum they should encourage students to apply CPS: add lines, use unconventional colors, tear off sections, paste materials on, add captions or titles, or scrunch the paper to give it texture. The question is: Why use the outlines to begin with? Giving out blank paper for free drawing is not great teaching, but it is preferable because children have to make more decisions. Instructional choices have to be measured by their ability to move students toward independent problem solving. Dictated art does little to prepare students to live in a democratic society whose citizenry values individuality and freedom.

# Building Block VII: Instructional Design: Routines and Structures

Visual art integration becomes a way of life when it is institutionalized through predictable routines. Teachers can make it a habit to use visual art strategies to introduce, develop, and/or conclude lessons (see IDC in the teaching procedure, Planning Pages 3.10 and 6.16). Here are other ways to make visual art integral.

## Energizers and Warm-Ups

Art energizers and warm-ups can be used in almost any lesson introduction to activate visual thinking needed to understand. These activities focus on stimulating the senses and preparing students to concentrate and focus. Students learn to think like artists, which includes using strategies to spark ideas and overcome blocks. Mr. Novak used the mystery bag energizer in the opening Classroom Snapshot to jump-start the wondering process. Chapter 7 has more ideas.

## Daily Routines and Rituals

ASAP students should take responsibility for visual art routines that start and wrap up the day. To involve shy students, use a puppet (named "Art" with a smock and beret) to speak to the group and share riddles, poems, and songs about art and artists. Barbara Streisand's song "Putting It Together" is an example about making art. Examples of routines to start or end the day include Docent Talks, Print of the Day, and I Spy.

**Docent Talks.**  The word *docent* simply means "teacher" and has long been used in the art world. Art docents give museum tours that teach about art and artists. When students do docent talks, they present a piece of art (original or that of an artist), tell about the media used, aspects of the creative process tried, what they learned by experimenting and making mistakes, and other pertinent information. Classmates can respond with descriptive feedback about what they see or how the piece makes them feel, or they may ask questions. A special artist's chair can be used for docents to sit and share information. *Note:* Post the CPS process to help guide students.

**Print of the Day.**  In this routine a piece of art is displayed along with question(s) for students to think or write about: "What title would you give this art (main idea)? What words describe how it makes you feel (adjectives)? How did the artist cause the feeling (cause-effect)? What catches your eye first (priorities)? What can you find that no one else will (details)? How would a mathematician describe this art? What would a scientist see (point of view)?" These questions cause students to do both critical and creative thinking. After a few minutes, discuss in pairs or small groups or as a class.

Teachers may use the same art all week with a different question each day. Another option is to give the title, before showing the art, and ask for predictions about art elements such as colors, lines, shapes, and media (categorical and hypothetical thinking). Ask for evidence for student ideas to emphasize that conclusions must be justified. The "full reveal" follows and close looking confirms or disproves predictions.

**I Spy.**  During I Spy, the teacher asks students to notice details and patterns. A large magnifying glass adds interest. Start by saying, "I spy four geometric shapes or three primary colors" as a challenge to look closely. Students examine details of the composition and volunteers "show they know" with the magnifier. A student is then chosen to lead the I Spy challenge.

## Art Discussions

Art-based discussions can focus on both criticism and aesthetics. They can take place daily, connected to read-alouds, guided reading groups, or social studies and science. The goal is to engage students in making sense of art using CPS processes. Any art material can be used, including student art and art in textbooks. Art prints are available from companies such as Shorewood and the National Gallery. Many cost only $1. Calendar art goes on sale for up to 75 percent off in January. Invite students to bring in prints, sculptures, and paintings to use as well.

The first step is to "look closely." Students must learn to take time to look at the whole and then zoom in on details. (Most people average less than 10 seconds looking at museum art.) Next, ask students to describe: "What do you see?" and "How does it makes you feel?" are key questions that call for response to subject matter and art elements. Then ask the following:

1. How did the artist make this? (media/techniques)
2. What arts elements and design principles were used?
3. Where/how might the artist have gotten ideas?

Next, ask for interpretations: "What does this mean? Why do you think the artist did that?" Finally, ask students to interpret the art, which can include creating stories. The interpretive and creative part of the discussion tends to be the most engaging, but the quality of interpretation is based in the data gathering done in previous steps (Housen & Yenawine, 2000).

In the partial picture preview variation (or shrouded print), the teacher shows a section of the art and asks students to predict about the covered portion. In another effective strategy, the teacher asks groups to choose a section on which to focus (e.g., background). Groups can then serve as "experts" on their sections. Teachers can also ask students to imagine what happened 1 minute after the art piece was finished, which can initiate a writing or drama response. Students can use magnifying glasses to zoom in on brush strokes, shapes, and colors, or a flashlight or laser pointer to highlight areas during discussions.

Eventually, students see how the artwork of others expresses diverse messages. Group discussions move into more meaningful areas. Students become comfortable expressing their ideas under safe, structured circumstances where unique perspectives are valued; they also learn to lead discussions. Ready Reference 6.12 has how-to ideas for discussions and there are more guidelines in Chapter 4.

## Stations and Centers

Stations (a place with a single focused activity) and centers provide opportunities for independent work that extends a lesson or a personal interest. They do not have to be elaborate and many can be set up on a permanent basis. Examples follow:

*Book-making station:* with wallpaper, fabric, and other materials to bind student-made books

*Puppet-making station:* with examples of different types of puppets and materials to make them (see the types in Ready Reference 7.4)

*Books about art and artists:* in a book nook center with shelves or areas with children's literature related to other arts areas

*Art-making corner:* with art opportunities changing every few weeks (One month the corner can be a collage center with small containers of feathers, buttons, and a variety of papers. Then transform the space into a sculptor's studio with modeling clay, play-dough, and simple tools such as popsicle sticks or plastic knives. Watercolors, pastels, markers, watercolor crayons, and a posted list of ideas to try should be available. See possibilities in Ready Reference 6.6. Include a few books that show how artists use different media and styles, such as in Ready References 6.7 and 10.11.)

*Multicultural arts center:* with examples of different kinds of art and actual artifacts (This is a place to include a picture file of art to examine for different styles or media.)

*Masterpiece corner:* with arts prints displayed at children's eye level on easels, adding a feeling of importance with such special furniture (Find cheap easels at flea markets. Use the ideas previously given for a discussion routine. For example, display a question and a print as a journal stimulus: "Why do you think the artist chose to paint this?" Postcards, matching the large print, can be used to make comparisons or to set up as a matching station. Or buy two copies of the same print and cut one up so students can attend to art details by matching pieces with the whole. Provide information about artists and share books about artists when displaying a work of art. Krull's *Lives of Artists* is a source, and others are given in Appendix J.)

Note: Be sure to tell students that prints and posters are not original art so they understand the real thing may be much larger and look different. Students are usually interested in the dimensions of original art and locations where they might travel to see it in a gallery.

*Beauty center:* with a small table for students to display items they consider beautiful (This simple area can send students on a yearlong search and invite endless discussions. Students can also be shown how to make personal beauty boxes with collections of pictures and objects that evoke pleasant responses. Box items can prompt writing and start discussions about individual concepts of beauty.)

# Building Block VIII: Differentiating for Diverse Needs

*Children who are encouraged to draw and scribble stories at an early age will later learn to compose more easily, more effectively, and with greater confidence.* (U.S. Department of Education, *What Works: Research about Teaching and Learning,* 1986)

# Visual Art and Child Development

Children's early drawings are no longer seen as poor attempts at art, anymore than babbling is considered bad speech. It is clear that art reflects cognitive, affective, and physical development. Children's drawings reveal how they think, their emotional state, and fine and gross motor development. Symbolic drawing development grows in stages, similar to growth in verbal communication. Beginning with the basic art element of line, art development can be seen in toddlers who use art tools to extend fingers to make marks. Small steps lead to giant leaps as general abilities become increasingly refined. Artistic developmental signs show the cognitive and physical growth necessary to write; drawing tools are writing tools, too. Art lines and shapes are the same as those used in handwriting—circles, horizontal, vertical, slant, and curved lines.

## Meaningful Scribbles

Kellogg (1969) broke the ground in recording children's art development. She spent 20 years collecting more than 1 million samples of children's drawings that unveiled a universal artistic journey. The early developmental sequence moves from random scribbles to more controlled scribbling and then to formation of enclosed shapes that show increased understanding of spatial relationships. Shapes evolve into symbols, such as mandalas and suns, used to create people shapes. Ready Reference 6.17 shows the stages. Lowenfeld and Brittain (1987) extended Kellogg's work through the adolescent years and theorized that children make advances naturally, without being taught to draw. However, by age 9, baselines and skylines appear, and "x-ray drawings" show understandings about the unseen. But by age 12, many begin to abandon spontaneous drawing.

## Developmental Stages or Waves

Gardner (1990) postulates that development occurs in waves rather than stages. Waves of knowledge rise and then spill over into other intelligences. For example, children draw animals and make the sounds of the animals as they draw, which pulls musical intelligence into the visual-spatial realm. More commonly, general stages are used to *describe* children's development; they should not *prescribe* what they can or cannot do (Clements & Wachowiak, 2010). It is impossible to categorize a child using age or grade characteristics; even identical twins are different because of their experiences. Children are products of genetics and their experiences—nature and nurture. This must be remembered as descriptors are used to plan for strengths and accommodate needs. It also is important to understand that later is not better. The artists Pablo Picasso and Henry Miller, for example, worked to recapture art thinking from childhood, producing masterful art. See Ready Reference 6.18 and Appendix A for more about developmental stages.

Human development is more spiral than sequential, with a gradual building during which children may skip or reverse stages depending on, for example, their familiarity with materials (Clements and Wachowiak, 2010, p. 33). We all tend to regress to "messing around" when we try a new tool, just to see how it works. Patterns of development are more obvious in early years before culture and education do major sculpting of children's minds. Education matters. Different cultures emphasize different aspects as well (e.g., realism is not as important in some). As in all development, interests play a powerful role and further individuate development. In general the stages begin to become

---

**Ready Reference 6.18** From Scribbles to Pictures

| Ages | Benchmarks |
| --- | --- |
| 1–2 years | *Random scribbling.* Exploration of tools and materials, showing increasing fine and gross motor control. Single and multiple dots and lines (vertical, horizontal, diagonal, and wavy) produce some 20 basic scribbles that eventually include loops, spirals, and circles. Examples: |

| Ages | Benchmarks |
| --- | --- |
| 2–7 years | *Shape making.* Scribbles begin to be intentionally used to make basic shapes or diagrams. Children combine shapes and use overlapping. Eventually, the shapes form aggregates (three or more diagrams together). Examples: |

| Ages | Benchmarks |
| --- | --- |
| 3–5 years | *Symbol making.* Lopsided geometric shapes are made. Mandalas and suns are drawn and evolve into human figures. At first, arms and legs stretch from the head. Eventually, torsos emerge and human figures are drawn with more and more completeness. Examples: |

Based on Kellogg (1969) and Lowenfield and Brittain (1987).

Note: Children's drawings reflect growth in thinking (cognition) and in physical control (gross and fine motor) over materials and art tools.

muddied as diversity increases. Predicting becomes increasingly more difficult.

In visual art "observed knowledge" is a big player in development. Instruction alters the quality of the development of the ability to see and to do art. As more detail emerges, we can infer the child has keenly observed art elements in the world. Each piece of art is tangible evidence of connections forged in the child's brain. Instruction is everything. Without teaching, students can stall in their development, lose interest, and get frustrated. Finding your medium is one of life's mysteries, but some never find it. Imagine Michelangelo without marble or Alexander Calder without mobiles. It is hard to predict how specific children will respond to media/tools (e.g., clay versus drawing). Diverse experiences are vital.

### General Patterns of Artistic Growth.

Artistic development parallels cognitive, physical, and socioemotional growth outlined by theorists such as Piaget, Erikson, Maslow, and Gardner (see Chapter 2). In general it proceeds in the following directions.

*General to specific.* It proceeds from general to specific, wholes to parts, with increasing attention to detail. For example, drawing starts with tadpole-like and stick figures using geometric shapes and moves to bending limbs, curved and sausage limbs, joints, and use of overlapping and foreshortening. At first, figures float with no base. Young children use proportion/size to show what is most important (e.g., big head). Stereotyped colors for grass and sky are still common in primary grades, but color is used expressively, too, to show emotions.

*Uncontrolled to controlled.* This direction is from exploration of media and tools to skilled use of lines, shapes, and colors to represent ideas.

*Known to seen.* At first people are drawn with general traits children "know," not what they really look like (Clements & Wachowiak, 2010). As children develop, they notice more. What they see changes what they know. While older children are more conscious of "feelings," younger children use color, lines, and shapes expressively.

*Me to others.* Children become increasingly group/peer oriented, with steady growth of interest in the community and the world.

*Single to multiple perspectives.* This direction involves increasing use of evidence to draw conclusions. As children become more logical and more systematic, they gain ability to self-evaluate.

*"Abstract" to realistic.* This begins with images that represent the "known" and show feelings. These evolve into realistic images, which peaks about age 11. *Note:* Paul Klee and others try to recapture early "naïve" perceptions.

*Gender awareness.* Children increasingly show more boy/girl details, such as hair and clothes, in their art.

Art preferences grow from art that connects to personal interests, to preference for realism, and finally to diverse understandings and tastes that reflect experiences (i.e., understand expressive art and use art in more expressive ways). See Ready Reference 6.3.

### The Brick Wall.

Art educator Mona Brookes (1996) offers an explanation for why some youngsters stop drawing. Children naturally produce symbolic drawing, based on what they "know," not what they "see." It develops in a predictable way like all communication. Young children create symbols for animals, people, and trees and talk to themselves as they draw, often telling a story. For example, "Here is my cat, Tigger. Charles taught her to sit up and dance like a bear." Symbolic drawing usually culminates in abstract stick-figure images.

About age 8 or 9, children give up symbolic drawing and want to draw realistically so others recognize the images. Brookes and others argue that this realistic drawing skill does not usually happen without instruction (Brookes, 1996; Clements & Wachowiak, 2010). To show the importance of instruction, Brookes gave children prompts to "draw a person," which produced stick-figure images. After one lesson on analyzing shapes and attending to detail, the drawings showed dramatic differences. Brookes teaches a drawing alphabet with five elements of shape to "analyze and break down what is seen" so they can "see with an educated eye" (p. xxx). While children can be taught to do realistic work, she emphasizes that they should be free to do symbolic drawing (1996).

### Literacy Parallels.

One clear example of the close relationship between visual art and the language arts is how beginning writers readily interchange drawings and words, integrating the two symbols to make meaning (Coufal & Coufal, 2002). Drawing is actually the "first language of all children." Children proceed to separate the two because we teach them to narrow their view of literacy. We can just as well teach them to become literate in both areas. The stages of development are parallel (Yenawine, 2005). Progress moves in steps that show increasingly complex thinking and detailed seeing. This is especially clear in spelling/handwriting that begin with scribbles and "pretend writing." Spelling proceeds from gross approximations, representing just beginning and ending sounds to representing words, with increasing accuracy. Details of words, especially the middles or the spellings of sounds like the schwa, are the last to develop. For example, the spelling of the word *bird* evolves from B to BD to BRD to BerD to bird. It is obvious that noticing details and visual patterns is as basic to becoming a good speller as it is for growth in visual art literacy.

## Early Primary K–2 Suggestions

### Art Discussions.

Younger children are more concrete and less product oriented. They like bright colors and may prefer abstract or simplified representational art. Students can describe the subject matter but have trouble with style and composition. They like to pretend and take roles in art and do "what-if" discussions. Teach concepts such as cool/warm colors using matching (paint chips) and mixing. They can usually connect personal experiences to art and learn arts vocabulary.

### Art Making.

Students are interested in topics such as animals, games, toys, and weather as art subjects, and they can tell stories about their art. Keep directions short and supervise work by coaching. Let students repeat subjects and try new tools (e.g., sticks to engrave). Use big paper and coach them to fill the page. Show them how contrast is created with light/dark shapes. Involve students in cooperative murals, printing with erasers, clay, found objects, hands, and feet. Use clean foam trays for incised relief prints. Show students how to pinch, poke, stretch, coil, and ball clay. Use the subtract versus add method for stable sculptures.

## Primary/Intermediate Grades 3–4 Suggestions

Students are being drawn toward realism but abstract art coexists, so art does not have to "look right" to them. This is a transition period during which students rely on what they know, but this is now being informed by what they see. They are able to focus more and are interested in other cultures, life processes, plants, and animals.

**Art Discussions.**   Students can look at art longer and use more arts vocabulary. They can compare and contrast art and recognize style, media, and forms.

**Art Making.**   Children now are more deliberate and like to plan their art. Shapes are more in proportion, and they like to use action. They can be taught color mixing for tints and shades and use of the color wheel. Students can be shown how to use diminishing size and overlap and how to create a horizon. Sketch trips help students see distance, overlap, pattern, and texture in the world. Contour drawing with fat soft pencils is recommended. Use everyday objects and direct attention to the environment for radiating lines, colors, patterns, and emphasis in nature. Teach how to make collages by tearing, pleating, and curling for texture and use tissue paper for topics such as dreams, moods, and sounds. Use collages to teach positive/negative shapes. Continue with prints made with vegetables, clay, and found objects, and work with clay pinch pots.

They now can do some self-evaluation of their work so help them consider criteria such as variety and filling page.

## Upper Grades 5–6 Suggestions

"Identity versus role confusion" is the main crisis (Erikson, 1950) at this stage, and students have self-doubts that can carry over into art. Making art may decline if they believe they are no good at it. Students become self-critical, but this can be put to good use to engage them in identifying strengths and needs in their own work. They tend to conform and want to "do it right," so teachers need to show diverse examples of "good art" and ask students what they notice. They will experiment with tools, techniques, and media in a supportive environment.

Students need to be taught more art vocabulary, tools, and skills, or they remain static or even regress. Aesthetic discussions help to stretch the concept of good art so they do not overly focus on realism. Students need freedom to use their more developed individual interests. Students are gender and group focused. They are interested in heroes, history, community, and environment. They need personal time to reflect and concentrate using sketch journals.

**Art Discussions.**   Students can discuss compositional features, style, mood, and symbols and compare and contrast works by form and meaning. They like to learn tricks of the trade like the speech bubbles and stars to show violence in comics. They need more arts vocabulary to see more for discussions. They are impressed by size and cost of art, and the artists' motives in creating art. Interest in the surreal (macabre/bloody) emerges. Metaphoric images are understood (e.g., isolation represented by a single flower). The preference for super realism peaks near age 11, so stretch them by asking for evidence for preferences to expand thinking.

**Making Art.**   Students can use perspective, shadows, movement, and overlap. Challenge them to create unity. Continue contour drawing. They have more advanced color awareness so direct attention to the environment and show more mixing. Collages can be used to teach positive and negative space in three dimension. Students can be taught to score, to indent paper for tearing. Printing remains important and students can do linoleum prints.

## General Preferences

Children prefer realistic works, especially in upper elementary. Use single subjects with young children and more complex compositions with older students. Subject matter is the primary factor in children's preferences, and there is a strong difference between boys and girls. They may react negatively to abstract art or works showing objects they do not like, such as dead animals. Alternatively, if a primary child likes dogs, he will probably like dog art. The second most important factor is color. Primary children prefer lots of contrast and color. Older students prefer more tints and shades (Clements & Wachowiak, 2010).

## Differentiating Instruction

At all stages children have certain common needs; they are more alike than different. For example, all children benefit from learning in an aesthetic environment from a teacher who uses best practices. All students need to be stretched to make visual discoveries and, in general, achieve more when there is an inquiry stance to learning and teaching.

Children also have differences. Chapter 3 presents a set of 10 strategies to differentiate instruction, called PARTICULAR. Following are ways to meet developmental and special needs of students.

*Place:* Set up work areas with fewer distractions.
*Amount:* Use projects that require a few simple steps so success is more likely.
*Rate:* Go more slowly with directions and allow more time to finish.
*Target objectives:* Make the goals clearer by showing more examples.
*Instruction:* Give more explicit instruction with clear art language; build in more repetition through questioning and choral responses.
*Curriculum materials:* Use more visual aids (e.g., color wheel, elements chart with symbols, and personal elements charts for each desk for prompting).

*Utensils.* Use a children's rotary cutter for those who cannot handle scissors. Tape paper in place. Use scented paint and markers for those who have limited sight. (Scents such as lemon can be added.) Attach drawing and painting tools to head gear or tape to a hand to improve control. Thicken paint and use shorter and larger brushes. Use collage materials that can be rearranged. Start with larger pieces or objects that are easy to grasp. Wrap crayons and markers with masking tape or foam curlers to provide better grips.

*Level of difficulty:* Build in more time to explore materials so that students feel more in control.

*Assistance:* Use the "guided hand technique" to help students get the feel of drawing or painting (put your hand over theirs or theirs over yours); allow students to work with a partner.

*Response:* Consider different ways students can respond other than the project selected. For example, give materials choices, rather than all make a paper bag puppet from collage materials. Consider stages, interests, background, and unique needs when designing art-making or art-looking lessons.

Appendix B offers additional suggestions for working with students who have special needs.

## Websites

The Federal Citizen Information Center (http://kids.gov/k_arts.htm) offers links and clear information about developmentally appropriate art lessons.

This University of Florida site details developmental stages: www.arts.ufl.edu/art/rt_room/teach/young_in_art/intro.html

The Arts Education Partnership (http://aep-arts.org/publications/info.htm?publication_id=10) offers a downloadable publication on developmental stages called *Young Children and the Arts: Making Creative Connections* (1998).

# Building Block IX: Assessment for Learning

Chapter 3 describes four purposes of assessment that are congruent with arts integration philosophy. The most important is using assessment to motivate and modify learning and teaching. The guiding principles and characteristics of good assessment apply to visual art integration (i.e., continuous, multifactored, authentic, and focused on strengths and needs). Because visual art has obvious "products," it is important to keep in mind that the thinking and working processes are still the focus of assessment.

## Exhibits

Display of student art should be much more than eye candy. New thinking about goals and methods focus on thoughtful and respectful exhibits that are planned by students and structured to engage viewers in meaning-making (Zuk & Dalton, 2001). Displays of artwork are important for their motivational power and the degree to which they show evidence of learning. In addition to art exhibited on walls, designated tables or cases for completed projects are ideal ways to make learning public. By expecting students to have 3-D work others will want to see, we change how they think and plan. That's the assessment *for* learning idea.

Meaningful displays include titles with works "tagged" so that others understand their significance, much like a museum plaque. Criteria for art displays needs to direct the process for creating work. Focus attention on what makes quality work. Such criteria are needed for the visual environment of the whole school. Refer to the building blocks section on aesthetic environment for ideas and consider asking a museum professional to collaborate on designing exhibit space for schoolwide displays. Appendix D offers examples of assessment tools, and a rubric is included at the end of the final Classroom Snapshot in this chapter. Two points specific to visual art, task completion and student portfolios, are discussed next.

## Task Completion

While the emphasis of visual art integration is on process, it is important that students finish work, which demonstrates persistence and commitment. It is difficult for teachers and students to judge artwork unless it is completed. The satisfaction of success is withheld, too, if effort is not made to reach closure. Self-discipline is developed by working through problems and frustrations with support. Therefore, it is important to insist an art project, once undertaken, be carried as far as possible, especially if it is self-chosen. This is not an unwarranted imposition. Anybody who has watched children "spend long periods of time on some challenging piece of construction or deconstruction knows that there is no end to patience, once the goal is sufficiently attractive" (Arnheim, 1989, p. 34). Task completion is expected in other curricular areas to show evidence of learning and should be a goal that is assessed in visual art.

## Student Portfolios

Student growth, both artistic and otherwise, can be documented by setting up a portfolio for each student. Most are organized around a few goals, attached to the front of a container, that are aligned with visual art standards (national/state/local). Clear goals serve to motivate students to want to reach them. Two basic goal categories are (1) knowledge and skills to make art and (2) knowledge and skills to read/understand art. These parallel "comprehension" and "composition" goals in reading and writing.

Progress in using art vocabulary, media, and tools should be tracked. Arts teachers with hundreds of students cannot do this kind of assessment. At integrated arts schools, classroom teachers are increasingly taking this on because they realize the power of assessment to motivate learning. For example, several schools in Chattanooga have designated visual art goals for each grade level by working with arts specialists. Teachers set up student arts folios that are mostly maintained by students. For large art samples, a container is made using packing tape to bind together two large pieces of cardboard and connecting strings to tie it shut. Items placed in the collection are dated and titled. A note is attached about the media and the assignment to explain how it is connected to one or more of the goals. Teachers conference with students using these portfolios, and provide regular times for students to share folios with peers and others. See details on arts folios in Appendix D.

**Program Evaluation.** For checklists to assess the visual arts component of arts integration, go to *www.winthrop.edu/ABC/*. South Carolina ABC Schools have converted the Opportunity to Learn Standards into a useful format for this purpose.

# Building Block X: Visual Art Partnerships

> *Life is a great big canvas and you should throw all the paint you can on it!* (Danny Kaye)

Potential visual arts partners with classroom teachers include the school art teacher, local artists, teaching artists, museum professionals, and gallery owners. There are a wide range of artists in any community, from sculptors and jewelry makers to quilters, potters, and newspaper photographers. Videographers/camera people from the local television station may be available for at least a guest spot.

Collaborations between classroom teachers and art specialists are only fruitful if all participants feel there is a common need and each person plays an important role. While the classroom teacher will know the students better, the specialist knows more about art, which brings expertise and depth to visual art integration efforts. Meaningful integration rests on the knowledge and commitment of the teachers and arts specialists and the ways in which available resources are connected and then sequenced.

A successful collaboration begins with planning together. Chapter 3 outlines guidelines for collaborative planning in the arts building block and in Block X about arts partnerships. Appendix C provides a checklist for planning with artists. The unit development process (Planning Page 3.7) is also a helpful guide.

The focus of any planning should be on standards and goals and finding meaningful connections between visual art and other curricular areas. Clusters of standards that overlap between visual art and other curricular areas can be found by "scanning" for common processes and content. This should happen, to some degree, even for a guest artist appearance.

If specialists are from outside the school, they may not be aware of safety concerns such as toxicity of materials and fumes from markers and sprays before they work with students. This needs to be discussed. Also discuss the appropriateness of art subject matter. Nudity in art may be a problem for a particular school context.

Teachers should remember that some artists may not have a wide range of teaching strategies and need to understand that children need active involvement through questions, visual aids, and demonstrations rather than a lecture. Discuss a lesson introduction that begins with questions or a demonstration. Planning Page 6.19 shows a unit planned by a stained glass artist and a fourth-grade teacher around shared concepts about communication.

Check out community-based programs that may offer trained volunteers to teach lessons about artists and subject matter or to do art projects. Arts Go to School is often based in a museum, and volunteers are trained as docents to go into classrooms. An example in operation is at the Ella Sharp Museum (*www.ellasharp.org*) in Jackson, Michigan. The Springfield (Ohio) Museum of Art has a similar program (*www.spfld-museum-of-art.org*). Contact museums nearby about school programs or discuss starting one of the above with education curators.

# Classroom Snapshot
## Problem Solving Through Visual Art

In this chapter many strategies have been introduced to achieve meaningful visual arts integration. All of the pieces are best understood when they are put together in a lesson. Each art-based lesson is unique, but here is another example to expand the image of possibilities. It is from the classroom of Robin Fountain at Ashley River Creative Arts in Charleston, South Carolina.

A large print of *Starry Night* hangs on the wall of the first room. Students are using imaginary paintbrushes to get the feel of the strokes van Gogh may have used. On the chalk tray are two books: *Under the Quilt of the Night* (Hopkinson) and *Follow the Drinking Gourd* (Winter).

Don McClain's "*Starry Night*" **song is playing**. Robin holds up the picture book, *The Starry Night* (Waldman), which has end papers of a child's version of the painting. She reminds the students that they have talked about the lines and colors van Gogh used. Now she asks them to **look closely** at the lines.

"He changed the positions," notices one boy.

"But they go together," adds another.

"Those are good observations. I want you to keep thinking and looking, like we've been doing for two weeks."

"I see short curvy lines and dashes," says a blond girl.

"Show me with your imaginary brushes," Robin says.

The class begins to dab in the air with small strokes and quick comma-like movements. Robin takes time to look at each student and give **descriptive feedback**.

"Our focus has been the night sky. Today you will be able to create your own night sky with oil pastels. You will be working on your background—not the foreground. This is not a cityscape. Think about what you want in your night sky using your own ideas about color. Later you'll be able to do a foreground."

"Any colors?" asks one student.

"Yes! **Everybody's needs to look different.**"

Robin asks the students what they remember about how to use oil **pastels** as she passes out large blue paper. The boxes of pastels are in the center of desks pushed together.

Robin changes to a CD from World Playground. It is **"international music"** with a steady beat and a fast tempo. The song "Tqure Kunda" is from Senegal.

Students begin to dab and circle, using long and short strokes. Robin circulates giving more feedback, encouraging students to fill up the space and noticing the use of a wide

# Planning Page 6.19

## Hollie's Stained Glass 9-Day Plan

Hollie Steele, Grade 4, Battle Academy; Dee Mayes, Stained Glass Artist, Chattanooga, Tennessee

**Big Ideas:**
1. The more ways we have to communicate, the better we can express our thoughts/feelings and understand others. We use more than words to communicate.
2. Art, reading, and writing share the same CPS process and many of the same words and concepts.
3. You can read thoughts and feelings in art.
4. People affect each other's lives.

**Essential Questions:**
1. How is the visual art process like/different from the language arts? Why are both called *arts*?
2. Why are all the arts important to communication?
3. What makes a good reader/writer/artist?
4. How do other people's stories help us to plan our lives?

*Shared vocabulary/concepts:* BDA (before, during, after)/BME (beginning, middle, end) reading sequence/plot, "stories" (in stained glass and reading), symbols, compare-contrast, line, strategy, biography
*Reading vocabulary:* almanac, indentured servant
*Art vocabulary:* mosaic, tile, grout, shape, texture
*Materials:* Books: *Molly Bannacky* by Alice McGill, *Dear President Jefferson.* Materials: glass, white paper, grout, Elmer's All Glue

**Timeline (9 days) Teaching Procedure (S = Students):**
*Day 1:* Art Preview of *Dear President Jefferson* (first African American almanac writer and mathematician, Benjamin Bannacker). Ask S to tell what they see. Ask how art elements make them feel. Ask what the message of the art is and how it is we can read it without words. Read aloud, stopping to ask about art messages. Explain biography. Ask about why we need to know about people who made an *impact* (a word on TN test) in our lives. Brainstorm people who have made an impact on their lives.
*Day 2:* Focus on the book's sequence/plot. Ask S to make mental pictures of something that happened in the beginning, then middle, and then the end (BME). Partner to share, then ask for volunteers to describe one of each. Prompt: What colors, shapes, lines, and textures do you

image? Post an arts vocabulary chart for reference. Ask about (1) importance of images in reading and art and (2) sequence the writer must have used to write the book: pre, during, post. Choose one person from the brainstorm. Begin interview and writing biographies about a person in their lives. (Homework: Interview person)
*Day 3:* Do an art preview and read aloud *Molly Bannacky.* Synopsis: *English milkmaid tips her pail, which is considered stealing. She is saved from death because she can READ, but is banished to the American colonies. She earns her freedom, starts a farm, and buys a slave whom she teaches to read. They fall in love and marry. One of her grandsons is Benjamin Bannacker, whom she taught to read.* Ask why reading is important. Discuss what good readers do before, during, and after (BDA) reading. Compare with the writing process. Continue writing biographies.
*Day 4:* Ask S what they know about stained glass. Relate to picture book art. Give examples of symbols (heart, cross) and ask for examples. Explain that letters and numbers are symbols. Ask what letters symbolize. Explain the sequence to make stained glass. Brainstorm and design, on a large paper, images and symbols from the BME of *Molly Bannacky.* Continue biography writing.
*Day 5:* Revise designs and create larger symbols to show the sequence. Prompt S to think about art concepts, and design principles of balance and unity. Groups color-code the design for colored glass placement. Focus on juicy descriptive images in biographies. Use books for examples: *Maniac McGee, George Washington Socks, Molly Banacky.*
*Day 6:* Stained glass artist, Dee Mayes, will tell the background of stained glass: glass in churches told stories, and they were built on top of one another (origin of "stories" for building). She will help S glue paper to a clear glass window. S will begin gluing pieces of colored glass to the other side of glass.
*Days 7, 8, and 9:* S will finish gluing. Finish the biographies and share in author's chair. Ask S to compare and contrast the processes for writing, reading, and making the stained glass. Ask: "What happened BDA?" Ask: "How do each deal with images? Ideas? Feelings?"

---

range of colors. The song "Three Little Birds" (Jamaica) comes on and the children sing along as they make their art.

"If you can't hear the music, you are too loud," she reminds them and then begins to sing along herself. She is standing under a poster that reads, "Control your voice, body, and mind."

Robin explains that the next step will be for the students to tear black construction paper to create the foreground. Just as with previous Grandma Moses artwork, these pieces will be evaluated using a **rubric**. The students know in advance what

they need to include. It is that balance of freedom with boundaries that structures a problem-solving context in which children are motivated to strive for excellent work.

## Robin's Art/Social Studies Rubric.

Grandma Moses painted her past so the paintings were student images of their pasts. Students self-evaluated using these criteria: perspective, horizon, and three things from the past: games, animals, and clothes. ✺

Artist Dee Mayes works on stained glass project.

# Student Spotlight

## What Kids Think

A group of Libba Allen's fifth graders are in the hall working on a pictogram. They explain how arts integration has changed them.

"You get more of a perspective on what you want to be when you grow up," says one boy.

Another chimes in, "We get exposed to more things and different things."

"Thanks to drama I got into the School of the Arts," a third adds.

"My mind is more at ease," offers a fourth boy.

"Yeah, it stretches you, especially your mind. I love all the arts," says a tall girl.

They return to the pictogram. It is to be a collage of favorite football teams. The lone girl reminds them they need symbols that everyone can understand and "not just the Georgia Bulldogs." The boy accepted at School of the Arts insists that they use lots of detail. Each listens and responds with comments such as, "That's a good idea," and "We could try that."

"We need to include everyone," a short boy explains. "Let's get pencils so we can sketch and talk out ideas." ✳

# Conclusion

*Art is the lie that enables us to realize the truth.* (Pablo Picasso)

This chapter discussed visual art integration using the 10 AI building blocks. A rationale for art integration (*why*) was presented in Building Block I. In particular, visual art was presented as much more than an act of the hand. It is an unmatched communication vehicle central to the most innovative digital technology. Visual literacy is no longer just an option. AI teachers collaborate with art

specialists to meet the challenge. Children learn that returning to artwork to revise it or use art as a source for ideas involves the same thinking skills used in written composition. Children learn to draw and talk about artwork created in response to science and social studies units, and realize their cognition is restructured. Visual art is restored to its rightful place as a primary means of understanding and expressing thoughts and feelings.

Building Block II outlined *what* visual art literacy teachers need to know, have and teach to accomplish meaningful art integration. Building Blocks II through X focused on the *how* of art integration—general principles for planning, teaching, and assessment. Finally, partnerships with visual art specialists were discussed as an essential AI component. The next chapter is a categorized collection of starter "seed" ideas for integrating visual art that extend the *how* to a more specific level.

---

### Teachers as Leaders: AI Advocacy

Choose a visual art-based strategy, such as explicit teaching of visual imagery to improve comprehension. Set up an action research project in a classroom to investigate effects. Report results at a faculty meeting, in a district newsletter, or on the school website.

---

**myeducationlab**
PEARSON

Go to the Activities and Applications section for Topic *Strategies for Teaching* at MyEducationLab for your course and complete the video activities entitled "Teaching Chromotography through Visual Art", "Introducing Visual Imagery for Comprehension", "*What Do You See*? Questioning to Increase Comprehension of Visual Art", and "Teaching Visual Imaging."

Go to the Video Examples section for Topic *Strategies for Teaching* to view the video "Using the Docent Chair to Debrief about Creative Problem Solving." Also go to the Activities and Applications section for Topic *Attaining Arts Literacy* and complete the video activity entitled "A Visual Art Consultant Discusses the Art Basics."

Go to the Book Specific Resources section in the MyEducationLab for your course, select your book and Chapter 6 to view the Questions to Guide Reading, Response Options, and Bibliography of Visual Arts Based Children's Literature.

---

# Resources

The Appendix lists additional resources, including websites. Chapter 7 lists resources, including sources for prints and multicultural art. An indispensable reference is Hume's *The Art Teacher's Book of Lists* (2005. A visual arts handbook for teachers is available from the North Carolina Department of Public Instruction (www.ncpublicschools.org).

## Websites: General (Also See Appendix I)

National Art Education Association: www.naea-reston.org/

Crayola Home Page: www.crayola.com (searchable resource for art projects)

ArtsEdNet (Getty Museum): www.getty.edu/education/

## Websites: Museums and Exhibitions

Metropolitan Museum of Art: www.metmuseum.org/

WebLouvre: www.louvre.fr/llv/commun/home.jsp?bmLocale=en (virtual exhibit of this famous French museum)

World Art Treasures: www.epfl.ch/BERGER/index.html

National Museum of American Art: www.nmai.si.edu

KIDART: www.naturalchild.org/gallery/ (children's artwork from many nations)

The Art Institute of Chicago: www.artic.edu/artaccess/ (ideas for visual art responses to literature)

Education World: www.educationworld.com/a_tech/sites/ sites052.shtml (links to worldwide sites)

World Wide Arts Resource (Metropolitan Museum of Art): wwar.com/ default.html

Indianapolis Museum of Art: www.imamuseum.org/

Tate Online: www.tate.org.uk/ (over 65,000 works of art are available)

The Smithsonian: www.si.edu/

## Websites: Funding (See Appendix I)

## Websites: Resources

3D Artist: www.3dartist.co

Internet Art Resources: www.ftgi.com, www.kinderart.com

## DVDs/Videos

*Art's place.* (1994). Princeton, NJ: Films for the Humanities.

*Lively art of picture books.* Weston, CT: Weston Woods.

*Picture thoughts.* (1994). Columbia, MD: Hamilton Associates. (critical thinking and art)

*Traditional expressions.* Santa Cruz, CA: Multi-Cultural Communications. (multicultural art projects)

*What do you see?* Art Institute of Chicago. (how to discuss art)

*What is visual literacy?* (1996). Portland, ME: Stenhouse. (video by Steve Moline)

# Visual Art Seed Strategies

*I found that I could say things with color and shapes that I had no words for.* (Georgia O'Keeffe)

## Overview

This chapter is a compendium of starter ideas to help plan visual arts integration. Seed strategies are presented in these categories: Energizers and Warm-Ups, Arts Elements and Concepts, Using Different Media, and Curricular Areas: Science, Social Studies, Literacy, and Math.

## Introduction

The chapter opens with a Classroom Snapshot of a teacher using visual art and math to develop creative problem-solving skills. Notice how she questions to cause students to data gather to draw conclusions and motivates them to do creative math work. Information on many bolded strategies is available through the index.

## Classroom Snapshot
### Problem Solving Using Art and Math

*Creation begins with a vision.* (Henry Matisse)
*The arts escalate consciousness.* (Elliot Eisner)

Painted ceiling tiles in Ashley Sires's room feature children's books, including *Ramona Quimby, Age 8* (Cleary). On an easel is *Math-terpieces* and *The Grapes of Math* (Tang), along with Picasso prints. Students are writing in composition books when the morning television newscast comes on. The principal, Jayne Ellicott, interviews students and forecasts daily events. The opening routine continues with a calendar activity for patterns and predicting. Then student teacher, Deana, takes over. She uses the overhead to do a **warm-up** that links math and haiku.

"Haiku is 5 plus 7 plus 5 syllables for a total of _____? Thumbs up when you know." Most students put thumbs up. On her signal they call out "17."

"Today we are doing more work with shapes," Deana explains. "What ones do you remember?"

Students call out pyramid, cone, and cube.

"How many sides on a cube?" she asks.

"Six!"

"And what are they called?"

"Faces."

"Right. I'm going to show you some art by famous artists," Deana holds up *Math-terpieces*.

"Oh, Vincent van Gogh," a boy says.

"What shapes do you see?"

The students list many, including circles.

"How did he create the circles?"

"Swirling and curving," a girl suggests.

Deana turns to an abstract with red squares and lines. It is by Mondrian. She repeats the **"What do you see? What do you feel? How did he do that?"** sequence of **open questions** and then connects it to a previous field trip to Cyprus Gardens.

"Let's make a **web.**" She creates a drawing with **spokes for the five senses** and extends the "What did you see?" to smell, hear, feel, and taste. Students list a dozen ideas—lots of animals such as alligators and butterflies. One boy connects to Monet's bridge painting.

"Today we are going to **look closely** at a Picasso painting. Scoot up to see more." She calls teams to the rug.

"This is *The Three Musicians*. Why would I show it to you today?"

"Just to make us happy."

"You are right that art makes us feel things," Deana says. **"What do you see that causes that?"**

"Lots of shapes," says a boy in a T-shirt.

"Tell me exactly. Look closely."

Students inch forward and **brainstorm.**

"Why is it called *The Three Musicians?*" Deana asks. They say the obvious: There are three people and they have instruments.

"**Look closely.** What are the instruments?"

"A guitar!"

"Oboe?"

"Piano."

"OK, now look at the people. How are they different?"

"I see trapezoids!"

"Look at the quadrilaterals."

"I see a dog, now."

The students begin to point. An inclusion teacher interjects, "Many people are counting sides."

"Show us a hexagon," Deana invites and a boy jumps up to run his finger around the six sides.

"How about five sides?"

"Pentagon!" several say.

Deana next reads from a biography of Picasso that makes the point that artists paint according to their moods. She asks, "What does this make you think?" and a boy immediately says, "Blue period!"

"Yes, when Picasso's friend died, he painted lots of blue pictures. Then he fell in love so what do you think he painted?"

"Pink."

"Red."

**"Why do you think that?"**

"Because they are happy colors."

"They make you feel warm inside."

"They do. He went on to a stage using lots of cubes. This is his cubist period." Deana shows an abstract of Picasso's friend.

"Look at this!" says a girl. "It's a broke-up face."

"Exactly. He broke up the cube. Now look at a different painting of three musicians."

"It feels countryish."

"It is so brown. There aren't many geometric shapes."

"Picasso's is more like a jazz musician," comments a boy.

"Why do you think that?" Deana asks.

"Because it is more adventuresome. It is more alive."

"Great connections. Now, I'm going to **give you a problem.**"

"Good!" says a boy. Deana smiles.

"I want you to use the pattern blocks differently than ever before. Look on the five senses web. Your challenge is to **create cubist art** that shows Cyprus Gardens."

She passes out black paper and asks, "Where will you start?"

"Experimenting with shapes," a girl responds.

"What else can you do to problem solve?"

"Gather other ideas. We can look in *Math-terpieces.*"

"We can add more to the web."

"Yes. Try lots of patterns. Don't take your first idea."

Deana puts a crate of rubber shapes in the center of each group. There is already a toolbox of glue and scissors in the center. Students eagerly begin to experiment.

Later, students will write haiku to go with their cubist art, all related to Cyprus Gardens. ✸

Making pattern snakes

# Organization

*Art is not what you see, but what you make others see.* (Edgar Degas)

Deana is beginning her teaching career under the tutelage of a teacher who is an arts integration (AI) veteran. She has already learned how to flesh out many art seed ideas to create lessons appropriate for these students. This chapter includes such undeveloped seed strategies to ignite creative thinking about ways to meaningfully and purposefully integrate visual art. These seed strategies cannot stand alone. Successful use depends on having a background in the basic principles for visual arts integration (10 building blocks) described in the previous chapter.

The seed strategies are intentionally ungraded. Most can be differentiated for grades K–6 using the 10 PARTICULAR ideas in Ready Reference 3.11. Seeds are organized into sections, but many fit in more than one section. The first three sections, Energizers/Warm-Ups, Elements/Concepts, and Media, are provided to help teach students to do meaning construction using visual art.

# I. Energizers and Warm-Ups

Energizers and warm-ups are used to ready students mentally and physically for creative problem solving. These activities help students to relax, focus, gather, and release ideas. Many can be used to introduce any lesson that intends for students to be engaged in CPS—in other words, nearly every lesson.

**Art Walks.** Take walks to find art and beauty in nature. Use clipboards to note colors, textures, and shapes. Return to the same spots to find differences during the year. Stop to sit in special places to listen to sounds. Tell students to close their eyes and picture what they hear. Prompt with visual art vocabulary. After walks, sketch or paint the experience.

**Scribble and Doodle.** Tell students to draw lines, dots, and circles of all shapes and sizes to fill up the entire paper. Encourage overlapping and working both rapidly and freely.

**Eyes Warm-Up.** Tell students to warm hands by rubbing them together. Lightly place warm hands over eyes for a minute. *Variation:* Close eyes and imagine colors and shapes mentioned by the teacher.

**Visual Gym.** Teacher describes a series of images to sketch or imagine. Stretch and shrink angles, curves, dots, circles, triangles, ovals, colors, and textures. See *Put Your Mother on the Ceiling* (Mille).

**SCAMPER (Eberle, 1971).** This acronym represents verbs for brainstorming. Display the verbs and practice with a piece of art or any problem: Substitute, Combine, Adapt (change), Modify (minify or magnify), Put to other uses, Eliminate, and Rearrange or reverse. *Example:* What surfaces can be painted on? What if you made the image upside down? What if you took a part of the picture and made it huge? Tiny? *Variation:* Show how artists use SCAMPER (e.g., Picasso's bull's head made from a bicycle seat and handle bars).

**See–Feel–Think–Wonder (SFTW).** This develops observation and higher order thinking. Show art related to a lesson. Students write or tell what they *see* (focus on art elements and subject matter), *feel* (ask what causes the feelings), *think* (make connections to their lives or other art or topics), and *wonder* (ask questions the art brings up). An oral or written frame can be used: I see . . . I feel . . . and so on.

**Mirror Image (Concentration).** Give any line drawing and ask students to draw the mirror image. Try an abstract scribble (e.g., a jagged line).

**Shape Blitz.** Give teams 1 minute to find and list these shape elements: circles, dots, and straight, angled, and curved lines in the room. Count and graph. *Variation:* Search for one shape element for 1 minute.

**Shape Match.** Give each group a set of word or picture cards with the five shape elements: circle, dot, and curved, straight, and angled line. Display any art and ask groups to turn over one card and find an example in the art. Share and continue.

**Doodle Log.** Instead of free writing to release ideas, students can doodle about favorite words, their day, and so on. Doodle logs can also be used when students finish projects (contributed by Ohio art teacher, Misty Kaplafka).

**Art Poems.** Collect poems about art or poems that inspire art making. A classic collection on color is O'Neill's *Hailstones and Halibut Bones*. Designate a color of the day and perform using the poetry performance ideas in Ready Reference 5.4.

**Riddles.** Find or create riddles about art, artists, styles, and particular works. Start with an answer such as "Picasso." Take each syllable in the word and think of sound-alikes. Then, make up a question: "What pig artist liked to make abstract paintings?" Answer: Pigasso.

**Make a Mess.** Give time to explore new materials and techniques before creating a product. The goal is to make discoveries and gain confidence and control. Take time to debrief.

**Brain Squeeze.** Before making art or doing interpretations, take time to squeeze ideas. For example, "What are things we can look for in art?" Recorded in web form or in a list.

**Mystery Bag.** Introduce a piece of art or an art project by finding three to five objects that connect to it in some way. Pull each out of a bag and ask students to solve the mystery for how they relate. Mr. Novak used this in the Chapter 6 Classroom Snapshot.

**Twenty Questions.** Use an art concept or an object in a bag that represents an idea (e.g., texture). Students ask yes-no questions to discover it. For example, "Is it something about landscape?" "Is it something you mix?" Students cannot guess the item until all 20 questions are asked.

**Senses Stations.** Stimulate the senses before making or viewing art by setting up areas for students to perform the following:

*Taste:* Close eyes and try salt, sugar, lemon (use sticks)
*Touch:* Feely boxes with sandpaper, silk, foil
*Sight:* Magnifying glasses, tubes, kaleidoscopes
*Smell:* Perfumes, potpourri, oils, candles
*Hear:* Environment sounds, seashells, bags to shake

**Look Back.** When students have trouble coming up with ideas, suggest they look through past art for an idea to redo differently. A part can become a whole piece; a tree or shape in the background can be the subject of a new work.

**Browsing.** Keep files of magazine pictures, cards, photos, and book covers for students to look through to trigger art making.

**Picture Book Starters.** Use book art for ideas about how to use different media, styles, and subject matter. For example, in Bunting's *Smoky Night* collage, materials are used and many Eric Carle books are made from his "painted papers."

**Collections.** Use scrapbooks, photo wallets, albums, or clear shoe bags to organize items that grab aesthetic attention. Beans, sand, and pebbles can be layered in jars to study the effects of pattern. Student collections serve as conversation starters and for art making or as writing prompts.

**Postcard Categories.** Art postcards are great for sorts and finds. For example, groups can sort by subject matter (e.g., portraits, landscapes), styles, and art elements (e.g., color, texture). Connect sorts to units: sort by cultures, animals, and plants.

**Open Sorts.** Students are given random postcards and they create categories to group them.

**Postcard Collections.** Postcards are indispensable and inexpensive collections. When a teacher is enthusiastic about collecting, students often catch the spirit. Students can collect and make art postcards using index cards and original art or magazine art (e.g., ads for fine art appear in magazines such as *Architectural Digest*). Art postcards are also wonderful to remember birthdays or as cards to send notes to parents.

# II. Teaching Art Concepts and Elements

*Color in a picture is like enthusiasm in life.* (Vincent van Gogh)

This section includes ideas for teaching specific art knowledge for viewing and doing art. Pair these ideas with best practices from Chapter 6.

**Concentration.** Play this memory game using 10 pairs of art cards that can be matched (e.g., two pieces by Renoir). Small groups lay out cards face down. Use a pocket chart for large-group play. Each person gets a turn to flip two cards and make a match. If successful, the player keeps the cards and plays again. If not, she must replace the cards face down. The play passes to the next person, who tries to remember where cards are located. To reinforce art learning, students must name the artist or style or "say something true" about each card turned over.

**Art Elements Mnemonics.** Use a grid (paper divided into eight to ten sections). Label each box with an art element: color, line, shape, and so forth. Students then do a drawing that serves as a mnemonic for each element. *Variation:* Do on large paper with groups collaborating.

**One-Minute Find.** Call out an art element and give groups 1 minute to find examples (e.g., kinds of lines in the classroom). Ask them to count ones found and/or write answers. *Variation:* Graph results.

**Big Book or Poster Elements.** Displays of art elements and concepts are useful references during art viewing and making. The class can make big books, posters, or individual books with titles such as *The Facts about Color.* Use poster board for the covers of big books; roll bulletin board paper can be folded and stapled with a long-arm stapler for pages.

**Word Charts.** The goal is to find unusual and descriptive words to expand concepts behind art elements and add words to charts. For example, for textures, words such as *rough, smooth, silky,* and *bumpy* may be added to the chart. For patterns, words like *checked, striped, borders,* and *dotted* are likely.

**Songs and Chants.** Compose art songs with students to remember art concepts and elements. For example, for primary colors and mixing, "There was an artist who had some paints—red and yellow and blue. And with the paints he made his art—red and yellow and blue. Here a red, there a blue, now it's purple—what a hue!"

**Hot Sock.** Make a set of cards with art elements or concepts. Tie a sock in a knot. Sit in a circle with IT in the center. IT closes his eyes and throws the sock, which is a "hot potato" no one wants. IT calls "stop" at any time. The person caught passes the sock to the right, and that person holds the sock while IT reads one card. The caught person must name a set number of items in the category (four to six) while the sock is passed from person to person around the circle. The goal is for IT to finish before the sock gets back around; otherwise a new IT goes to the center. *Variation:* Use with any categories or alphabet cards.

**Elements Exploration.** Start with lots of newsprint and one paint color and ask students to bring in a brush like a sponge, baster, or bottle washer. Slowly direct exploration: *Paint different lines:* angled, curved, lying down, angry, calm, excited, thick. *Create different shapes:* dots, circles, triangles, uneven, loose, happy. *Take one shape and paint it different sizes. Group the same shapes. Paint a group of shapes that are the same size. Change colors and color code "same" shapes or same sizes. Outline shapes in a lighter or darker color. Try painting slowly. Try using very little paint to dab. Smear a lot on.* Give feedback as students work. Afterward, ask what they discovered about art elements. *Adaptation:* Ask students for exploration ideas.

**Game Boards.** Make all-purpose game boards using file folders or pizza cardboard. Laminate and print information needed on a board. Make separate cards for different concepts. For example, create art question or concept cards (colors, shapes, lines, styles). Students play by naming as many ideas in a category and move the number of spaces designated by a spinner or dice.

**Bubbles.** Explore shape and color with bubbles: Mix 1 tablespoon of dish detergent, 5 tablespoons of water, and 1 tablespoon of glycerine. Blow bubbles and catch on paper painted with wet tempera. Explore organic and geometric shapes with bubbles made through straws, pipe cleaner wands, plastic berry baskets, funnels, and plastic from soda six packs.

**Be the Sculpture.** Look at famous statues and discuss their emotions and why statues exist. Look closely to see how different body parts are arranged. Have students assume a statue pose and when tapped, say a one liner about what he or she is thinking or feeling.

**Art Questions.** Post open questions to stimulate close looking and deep thinking: *What is special about _____ ? What is happening? What does this make you think about? How did the artist make this? How do you think the artist felt when she created this? Why?* Find–trace–point to elements or concepts, (e.g., biggest, brightest). Ready Reference 7.1 has more questions and activities about art elements.

**Compare and Contrast.** Create a large Venn diagram to record likenesses and differences between paintings. For example, compare and contrast the elements, media, style, and subject matter of two paintings called *First Steps,* one by van Gogh and one by Picasso.

**Expert Predictions.** Cover half of a painting or ask small groups to choose a focus section (e.g., foreground, background). Groups serve as "experts" on their section and report to the whole group.

**People Compositions (Tableau).** Students pose for a group photograph that might happen or happened in literature, history, or science (e.g., family watching shuttle launch). Students decide about the composition, background, and so forth. Pose-freeze-photograph and discuss results.

**Food Alternatives.** Food items, such as potatoes for printing, are commonly used to make art. However, children need to distinguish art materials from food—for safety reasons and for aesthetic purposes. Instead of pasta, consider using buttons, shells, or

**Visual Art**

## Ready Reference 7.1    Art Elements: Questions and Activities

### Line

- What kinds of lines do you see? Straight, curved?
- How do the lines make you feel? Tired, busy, relaxed?
- Which are repeated? Why do you think?
- Which lines are strong? Which are faster?

*Activities:* Students pick a line and follow its movement with their hands or draw in the air. Use a flashlight to "trace" a line or students can make light chalk lines on the floor to get the feel of lines. Use lines as a stimulus for dance or movement: Shape your body in angles, move in a zigzag, make curves with different body parts.

### Shape

- What kind of shapes do you see in the painting?
- How do the shapes create a pattern?
- Which are organic? Geometric?

*Activities:* Students make a shape with their arms, fingers, or bodies. Ask them to look for a shape in the room and find that shape in the art. Paint or draw all kinds of lines (e.g., wavy, zigzag). Go on a shape walk to find shapes within shapes (e.g., windows, roofs, cars).

### Texture

- If you could touch the objects in the art, how would they feel?
- How has the artist made the textures appear real?

*Activities:* Ask students to touch the floor, face, and chairs and describe how each feels. Tell them to cup their hands to make a fist telescope to isolate an area of a painting. Ask about the kinds of brush strokes the artist used.

### Color

- How has the artist used color? How does it make you feel? Why?
- How would the painting be different if _____ was changed to _____?
- Name all the colors. What colors are used the most?
- What are some unusual uses of color?
- What happens when white is used?
- What happens when colors are put next to each other, for example, red and green?

*Activities:* Close your eyes and think of a color in the painting. Imagine yourself turning into that color. How do you feel?

Find complementary colors, primary colors, and examples of hues, tints, and shades. Get paint chips from paint stores to show hues. Brainstorm color names using paint chip titles as idea starters.

### Space and Composition

- Why and how has the artist created a foreground, mid-ground, and background?
- Introduce perspective. How is the space broken up? Where do you think the artist was standing? Why?
- Where does your eye go next in the painting? Why?
- Squint and look at a picture. What masses stand out?
- Why are some things smaller, blurrier, overlapped? How did the artist do that?

*Activities:* Choose a small part of a picture and magnify it by drawing just that part much larger. Use paint or markers. Create a tableau (frozen picture) of a painting by asking students to assume the same positions as figures or become a tree, pond, or hills.

### Light and Shadow

- What is the possible light source? From what direction is it coming? How has the artist created volume (modeling gradations of light and dark)?

*Activities:* Imagine the painting in a different light. Ask how the feel of the painting would change. Use a flashlight to shine light in different directions on an object and ask what they notice.

### Perspective

- How does the artist show that some things are closer and others are far away?

*Activities:* Look at objects from different angles and distances: stand on a chair, use microscopes or a magnifying glass.

### Emotion and Mood

- How does the painting make you feel? Why? How do you think the artist felt about his or her subject?
- What do you hear? Taste? Smell?

*Activities:* Show with face and body shape how the art feels. Make a list of feelings and how to create them, such as sad shapes and colors.

---

pebbles in collages or cut up straws to string pieces. Sponges or foam can be cut in creative shapes for printing (precut sponges are not recommended because this is dictated art).

**Subject Matter: Questions and Activities.**    Ready Reference 7.2 lists ways to involve students with art subject matter.

**Square Foot Display.**    Students can learn to organize and compose by arranging flowers, furniture, or collected nature items. Give each a square foot of space for a choice display. Cause summary and synthesis thinking by labeling displays.

**Sing Art.**    Display a landscape, seascape, or cityscape and brainstorm sounds associated with different parts. Encourage creative thinking about what "might be." Come to agreement about sounds for five or six parts of the art. Discuss the pitch, dynamics, and how many times the sound will be repeated. As a conductor points to an area students make the sounds, sustaining them or repeating them, as directed. Try harmonizing, changing pitches, dynamics, tempo, or using the round form. *Variation:* Asking groups to find or create songs for people depicted in artwork in which they are singing. Come back together to perform.

**Parent MiniPage.** Parents often do not know how to respond to children's art. They may not know why or how to encourage art making. Following are suggestions to share.

1. Don't ask "What is it?" because that's insulting. Instead, do the following:
   - List what you see in your child's art (e.g., colors, shapes, lines).
   - Explain how the art makes you feel or think.
   - Ask your child to "tell about the art."
   - Ask how the art was made. Emphasize process and the effort.
2. Make art projects alongside your child.

3. Keep a folder of your child's art and date the pieces.
4. Set up a special place or table to do art.
5. Visit museums and other special art displays. Stop to talk about what you see and feel.
6. Regularly share what you think is beautiful and tell why. Invite your child to talk about what is beautiful to him or her.

**Art Bags.** Use large zip-lock bags to send home a piece of art, a book related to it, and a related artifact or object. Invite students to check these out to share with their families. For example, a spring bag can have prints or postcards of Monet's garden art, the book *Linnea in Monet's Garden* (Bjork), and flower seeds to plant.

## Ready Reference 7.2 — Reading Art Subject Matter

Meaningful experience depends on learning to look longer, notice details, respond personally, ask questions, and think about possible messages from the art. Guide students to look at art for at least 30 seconds, to make discoveries such as how art reflects the time and culture that produced it. For example, 20th-century art reflects values for originality and individuality in a world of mass production and imitation.

**Landscapes** *are about the land.*

- What is the mood? Season? How do you know? If you were there, how would you feel?
- Where do you enter the work of art? Why did the artist create this position for you to take?
- What did the artist do to make you feel a part of the scene?
- Do you feel like an onlooker? If so, how did the artist keep you at a distance?
- Look closely to see if there are people. If so, how are they related to the landscape?
- Does the landscape seem real or imaginary? Why? Does it describe or capture an actual look of a place, or does it give more of the feeling of a place (expressive)? Why?
- What title would you give this work? Why?
- Walk into the painting. What do you see, hear, feel? What could you do there?
- Think of a special place you have been. What made it memorable? If you could artistically re-create this setting, what medium would you use (oil paint, watercolor, pastels, charcoal, pencil, collage)? What would you emphasize? Why?

**Portraits** *are of people but show more than what a person looks like.* Artists use a "visual vocabulary" to communicate this. Consider this special artistic vocabulary as you look at a portrait (see Ready Reference 6.8).

- ***Subject:*** What does the artist tell about this person? How does this person feel?
- ***Clothing:*** What clues does the person's dress give?
- ***Facial expression, posture, and gestures:*** What does the person's body language say? What do the eyes, eyebrows, mouth, throat, forehead, and angle of head tell? Where is the person looking? How does this affect you? How is the person positioned? Why? What is he or she doing with his or her hands? Take the position yourself. How do you feel? Would you want to meet the person? Why or why not?

- ***Background and accessories:*** Where is the person? What clues does the environment provide about the person? What might the specific objects in the setting mean?
- ***Size and medium:*** Is the portrait life size, or smaller? How does the size change the way you feel? What media and materials do you think the artist used? What if the materials were different? How would marble give a different feeling than paint?
- ***Details:*** Start at the head and slowly observe. Pretend you are the person and walk, sit, and stand. Be the person and say one thing in role.
- ***Variation:*** Look at real people through a tube or frame to see shapes of eyes, lips, and head. Observe groups of people: How close are they? How are they grouped (line, circle, random)?

**Still lifes** *are paintings of inanimate (nonliving) objects.*

- What attracts your eye? What do you discover that you did not notice at first glance?
- What is the most important part of the painting?
- How does the artist make it seem that there is light on surfaces?
- What kind of lifestyle do the objects represent? Why might the artist have chosen these objects? What might the objects represent (symbols)?
- What objects could you use to make a still life (e.g., toys, fruit, school items)? Why? How would you arrange them? What would you want to say in a still life?

**Abstract art** *goes beyond showing the visible world to allow expression through color, line, and shape. Images are "abstracted" from what they represent.*

- What is your first reaction? How did the artist cause you to react like this?
- What are you curious about? Why do you think the artist chose to create an abstract work?
- How does the work's abstractness change how it makes you feel?
- How would you describe the personality of the art? What contributes to it? How does it cause you to stop and think?
- What meaning or feelings do you think the artist intended? What does it mean to you?

# III. Using Different Media

This section begins with ideas to prevent problems by planning ahead for art making.

## General Tips

Before doing art projects, be sure to prepare for contingencies, and consider the following tips.

- Make student cleanup a routine part of projects. Make this expectation clear in advance.
- Collect a variety of paint tools. Use Q-tips to make "dot art" similar to Seurat's style. Students can also paint with rolled newspaper "brushes."
- Collect egg cartons or ice cube trays. Use half for different paint colors and the other half for mixing. *Alternative:* Use washed juice cans, cut in half, and set in student milk cartons for stability. *Note:* Do not give out all possible colors. Students need to explore mixing.
- Use baseball-size clay balls to store markers. Poke holes so each looks like a multiholed bowling ball. Let clay harden.
- Use clear plastic shoeboxes and bags to store materials.
- String a clothesline to hang art. Hang straw beach mats and use drapery hooks to hang anything that you can punch a hole in and put over the hook. Use plastic drying racks that have clothespins on each arm as a way to display or as mobiles.
- Use old shirts to cover clothes. Cut off long sleeves and button backwards. Garbage bags can also be used: slit and then cut arm and neck holes. Warn children about putting bags over their heads.
- Trim paintbrushes with scissors to keep them fresh.
- Use warm iron to flatten curled art.
- Mount or frame student art to give it a finished look. Transparency frames make quick frames. Save the tabs off soda cans to tape hangers on the back of pictures.
- Stain removal: Try toothpaste to get crayon from clothing.
- Students should do most of the work (e.g., let them cut out shapes). If there is too much preparation, it is probably not an appropriate art activity for children.

## Mixing Colors: Color Triangles

To show primary colors and the secondary colors made from them, draw a large triangle with the three points: red (top point), yellow (next point moving clockwise), and blue. Draw an upside down triangle over the first triangle to create a star. Label these points (moving clockwise from top right) orange, green, and purple (the last is also called indigo-violet). By combining two adjacent points on the star you get the color in between (e.g., red and yellow make orange). Students can make color triangles for their desks.

**Mixing Hints.** Always start with the lighter color and add the darker. (1) White paint tints or makes lighter and creates pastels. White is used a lot, so buy double. To tint, start with white and add color to it, a bit at a time. (2) Black shades or makes darker or

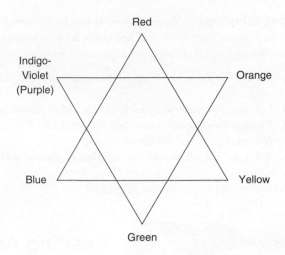

duller. Add a small amount of black to a color (e.g., black to white makes gray and black to red makes brown). (3) Skin colors can be made with black, brown, yellow, red, and white. Start with lighter and add darker colors to create shades (e.g., blend white chalk with orange crayon). Remember that skin can be almost any color and most artists use many colors, even in a single face. (4) Use a clear pie pan on an overhead to drop food coloring to show mixing. Turn out the lights and let the colors fill the room. (5) Color sugar with food coloring and layer in jars. (6) Show how to mix colors on a color wheel. (These can be purchased at art supply stores.) (7) See children's book in Ready Reference 6.10 about mixing colors (e.g., *Color! Color! Color!* by Heller and *Colors* by Felix).

## Drawing and Rubbing

*To draw you must close your eyes and sing.* (Pablo Picasso)

Drawing is linear art made with any tool that can make a mark; it is also a precursor to writing. Human beings seem born to draw.

Rubbings are made by placing paper over objects such as coins, shells, wire, or any texture and then using crayon, marker, and so forth to bring up the lines from the textured surfaces underneath. Scratch art or etching is scraping away a surface to reveal a lighter color. Resist consists of using a wash of paint over something that resists it (e.g., crayon).

**Tools and Media.** Fingers, sticks, toothpicks, and straws can be used, along with pencil, charcoal, marker, pen, crayon, pastels or chalk, and shaving cream. Children can draw on a blank surface, in paint or any medium, such as glass wax sprayed on windows. (Color glass wax with tempera paint, or add food coloring to hand lotion or toothpaste, for a drawing medium. Note: Food color stains.)

**Computer Technology.** Computers have revolutionized the making of both commercial and fine art. Computers are used in two ways. First, teachers and students can create and manipulate images (art making, including planning and producing two-dimensional virtual objects). A sketch can be scanned and then, using a program such as Adobe Photoshop, the image is manipulated. The Internet is invaluable to investigate visual art

(art history criticism, aesthetics), even virtual tours of museums—often with sound and video clips that elaborate on the historical period with music and interviews. Interactive CD-ROMs offer searchable text and images. See websites at the end of Chapter 6 (e.g., www.virtualfreesites.com/museums.museums.html).

**Surfaces.** Experiment with a variety of papers, cloth, sandpaper, bags, towels, wrapping paper, paper doilies, graph paper, or chalkboard. Draw on T-shirts with fabric markers or crayons (cover with a paper bag and iron on warm to fix crayon). Scratchboard can be made by first using light crayons, and then covering with heavy black or dark crayon. Scratchboard can also be purchased with silver on top and black underneath. Use a nail or stick to etch.

**Drawing Ideas.** Buy or make sketchbooks to capture ideas. Encourage "looking closely" and sectioning off an area (e.g., with a portrait, try looking at the face in fourths). A squiggle on a paper, traced hands and feet, or thumbprints can be starters to create animals, objects, people, or abstract art. Draw to music or draw without looking down while a "model" is studied. Some artists have success drawing upside down.

**Crosshatching.** To add texture artists draw fine black lines parallel to one another and then cross them. Crosshatching can be light or heavy, adding depth and texture.

**Shape Elements.** These elements can be taught directly and used to analyze any image and produce a realistic drawing of most anything.

1. Dots (oval, round, elliptical, and kidney shapes)
2. Circles in different shapes (oval, round, elliptical, and kidney) and that are "empty" rather than "colored in" like dots
3. Straight lines
4. Curved lines
5. Angled lines (Brookes, 1996, p. 59)

**Drawing Figures.** Start with a focal point: eye, hole, or center. Look closely and analyze. Notice dots, circles, straight lines, angled lines, and curved lines. For *overlapping,* draw things in the front, first, and then draw things farther away. If a mistake happens, make something out of it by repeating it, adding to it, or transforming it. Break people down into circles and tube shapes—the head is an egg shape and the neck is a tube. Grid off face to position eyes, nose, and so on.

**Creative Crayon Ideas.** Peel and break crayons, use them on their sides, or tape several together. Encourage mixing of colors and creation of hues of one color by changing amounts of pressure. Blend white chalk with orange or brown crayon for skin tones. Rub crayon drawings with a cloth to give them a gloss. For *crayon resist,* try painting over crayon drawings with tempera, watercolor, or food color. Use black construction paper for the background and paint over crayon drawing with white paint. An alternative is to use white crayon or a candle to draw on white paper and then wash over with paint to reveal the image. This seems like magic!

**Chalk Ideas.** Encourage children to break chalk, use it on its side, or dip it in water (once dipped, it is ruined for regular use).

Try wetting the paper with a little sugar water and then using chalk. The chalkboard and sidewalks have great surfaces because of their size and texture. Tape the end of chalk to keep hands clean.

**Cartooning.** Examine books like Hoff's *Sammy the Seal,* Stevenson's *Could Be Worse,* Griffith's *Grandaddy's Place,* and Steig's *Caleb* and *Kate.* List what is noticed about shapes and lines. Start with simple shapes in classroom. *Emphasize* no copying.

# Painting and Painting Tools

*You paint what you are.* (Andrew Wyeth)

**Types of Paint.** Acrylic, oils, tempera (comes in liquid, powder, and blocks), watercolors, watercolor crayons, and even melted crayons can be used to paint. (Turpentine melts crayons. Consider safety issues before using this. Always ventilate.) Refillable paint markers with felt tips can be an alternative way to use tempera. Paints can be made by combining food color and egg, or adding food color to shaving cream, liquid starch, hair gel, or even Vaseline. Explore stains and paints made from tea, mustard, berries, bleach, shoe polish, or just water.

**Tools.** Use a variety of brushes: toothbrushes, hairbrushes, combs, and brush curlers. Fingers, feet, hands, feathers, rags, old deodorant rollers, sponges, squeeze bottles, sticks, Q-tips, cotton balls, and straws can be used as paint tools. Newspaper can be rolled into tubes and used as a throwaway brush. Chalk can be dipped into tempera to create interesting effects.

**Painting Surfaces.** Paint can be applied to wood, canvas, fabric, paper plates, windows, doilies, transparencies, plastic sheets, cookie sheets, or wallpaper. (Many stores will donate old wallpaper books to schools.) Rocks can be painted, too; just add liquid white glue to the paint to help it stick. Frescoes are created by using paint on wet plaster. Ceiling tiles in the school can be painted with tempera or acrylic plants using a theme (e.g., celebration). The class may collaborate on a theme or topics, as well. *Note:* Students should sketch out ideas. Use masking tape to divide off sections for group work. In some classrooms, tiles are painted based on children's books or are painted to look like clouds.

**Techniques.** Have a brush for each color, and encourage experimentation with mixing: add white to tint and black to shade, and use the color wheel to mix secondary and tertiary colors from the primary colors of red, yellow, and blue. Introduce *scumbling* by showing how to use thick paint over dried paint (i.e., dry brush). Explore dabbing, spatter painting (use a ruler to flip a brush), blob painting (place blob on paper and fold), and straw painting (blow blobs by using a straw). Add salt, Epsom salts, flour, oatmeal, sand, sawdust, or soap flakes to give texture or thicken (salt gives a bubbly effect). Liquid starch, corn syrup, or detergent can be added to change how paint spreads. Soap helps tempera adhere to glossy surfaces.

Hand painting includes pounding and dabbing with the fingers, fist, or side of hand. When sponge painting, clip a clothespin to the sponge for a handle. Bleach can be applied to construction paper or bright cotton fabric, but do not let children work with bleach. To tie-dye, fold cloth or knot and then dip in bleach or dye. For marbling, mix linseed oil and tempera drops to a thick cream. Put a half-inch of water on a cookie sheet and drop the mixture onto it. Carefully lay a sheet of paper on top and lift up, dry. The teacher can flatten with warm iron.

**Painting Tips.** Watercolors can stain clothing. Keep a bucket of soapy water and towels handy for cleanup. Never have children mix dry tempera powder because it is easily inhaled.

## Printmaking

Prints are made using techniques to produce many copies (e.g., woodcut, linoleum, silk screen). Monoprints produce only one print. Prints can be pulled from a surface (e.g., a table on which students have fingerpainted) or stamped with found objects: erasers, vegetables (carrots, potatoes), woodcuts, linoleum cuts, or any form that is raised. Real flowers can be pounded into paper to make a monoprint.

**Tools.** Collect objects for printing: pieces of carpet, wire, mesh, bubble wrap, corrugated cardboard, fingers (use watercolors), feet, hands, sponges, erasers, corks, wood block, and nature (leaf prints). Cut print shapes from clean foam trays, rubber-tire inner tubes, or shoe insoles, and glue to blocks for a handle. Vegetables and fruits can be used, but take care that kids do not confuse food and art materials. *Note:* Soles of feet can be painted and used to print animal bodies. Knuckles can be used to print rows and patterns, for example, a border of small pumpkins (idea from teacher A. Wirz, Lady's Island Elementary School).

**Surfaces.** Print on paper, fabric, wood, clay, or even paper towels.

**Techniques.** Place folded newspaper under the printing surface to cushion. Put paint in shallow tray (e.g., cookie sheet or paper plates). Have a separate container for each color. Use a brayer (roller) to paint onto the item with which you will print. Too much paint will smear image. Make repeated patterns with vertical or horizontal prints. Overlap, twirl, and swirl to create designs. A print can also be made by outlining an image in white glue. Let it dry. The raised glue can be rolled with paint to print. Alternatively, roll paint over glued-raised items or yarn on paper towel tubes. Any carved item (see three-dimensional art) can be used for printmaking.

Children can make giftwrap, greeting cards, T-shirts, and stationery using printing or stenciling. Stencils can be cut from plastic or paper (e.g., fold paper in half, cut out a shape, open and use as a paint stencil—not much paint is needed). When stenciling, use a sponge or round brush to dab on paint. Use various thicknesses to create a more interesting image.

## Collage

The word *collage* derives from the French word *coller*, which simply means "to paste on." Collage consists of assembling materials and then ordering them. Pablo Picasso and George Braque invented collage and used it in their abstract cubist works in the early 1900s. Children enjoy the tactile nature of collage, and this medium invites an experimentation attitude—realism is not the goal. Collage can be stimulated by any topic or theme (e.g., seasons, plants, school). Encourage a variety of shapes and sizes, both torn and cut. Protect desks with newspapers.

**Materials.** Just about anything can be used, from stones, sticks, and other found nature objects to string, yarn, ribbon, or buttons to make a collage. Collage can be made from paper including sandpaper, foil, construction, cardboard, newspaper, tissue, wallpaper, greeting cards, and magazines. Wetting crepe paper and colored paper can produce interesting effects, but the bleeding can stain clothes. Children's own old paintings can be torn or cut up. Paper doilies offer possibilities for texture. Broken and shaved crayon pieces create a mosaic effect, as can small squares of other construction paper shapes. Sprinkle shavings on paper, fabric, T-shirts, or old sheets; then cover with newsprint and press with a warm iron. Consult references for pictures of mosaics before beginning. Bits of fabric can be used, as well. Colored rice, sawdust, or sand can be made by using tempera paint; do not let students use dry paint. Teachers should do the mixing. Collages can be sprinkled with sugar or salt to create sparkle and increase texture. Be sure to sprinkle over wet glue.

**Backgrounds.** Use roof shingles, cardboard, poster board, plastic lids, foam, and sandpaper as surfaces on which to arrange and glue. Leaves, crayons, and colored tissue can be pressed between wax paper using a warm iron (cover with newsprint so iron does not get sticky). For a thicker base and more texture, make a dough by combining half salt and half flour and adding water. Objects can then be pressed into the dough and coated with thinned white glue. Use a shoebox or egg carton lid, or foam tray to hold the pressed-out dough. Plaster of Paris can also be used. Just mix according to the directions and press objects such as shells or buttons into it. Food coloring can be added to the plaster. It sets up fast, in about 15 minutes.

**Collage Glue.** White glue is usually best. It can be thinned with water when working with colored tissue or used as an overall coating for finished work, as in decoupage. See "Pastes" in Ready Reference 7.3. Have popsicle sticks or Q-tips available for students who do not want to use fingers. Wet sponges or towels are needed to wipe off glue.

## Artistic Techniques: Enlarge, Simplify, Crop

Many artists make small things very large or simplify a subject down to basic geometric forms (e.g., triangle or circle). Georgia O'Keeffe is an example. She also cropped pictures (cut them off so only part of a flower showed). Show examples of these techniques and allow students to experiment with enlarging, simplifying, or cropping objects, plants, animals, and so forth. To enlarge, make a transparency of anything and display on an overhead projector. Pull the projector back to make the image bigger. For example, basic fairy tale character shapes can be traced on transparencies. Next, tape large paper to the wall and project each transparency to use as sketch bases. Sketch outlines should be used in original ways—do not turn this into a big coloring book activity! Students can also trace each other's bodies to get outlines for large-people paintings.

# Displays and Bulletin Boards

Bulletin board space should be primarily for displaying student work, and students should be involved in planning the design. Interactive displays can be made by adding question cards or flip cards to lift for answers. Teach basic calligraphy techniques and how to cut block letters to create labels (versus using commercial cutters). See Appendix J and bibliography at MyEducationLab for books on calligraphy. Block lettering uses the idea that any letter can be made from a block of paper—just cut straight lines. Begin by cutting as many blocks as letters needed. Blocks can be any size. Then imagine the letter and make straight cuts. Do not worry about "hole" letters like *B* and *R*. Cut through joining areas because they will be glued or stapled down.

To frame or finish off a bulletin board, make a border with ribbons or leaves. Here's how to cut a border the old-fashioned way, like paper-doll strips: First, pull off about 3 feet of large paper from a roll of bulletin board paper. Roll into a tube and cut slices about 2 to 3 inches long using a paper cutter. Creatively cut a pattern along one of the longer edges (zigzag or scallops). Open the strip and staple onto the bulletin board.

Posters and signs can be made to advertise any content. Take time to examine ads for ideas students can adapt through CPS like that used in SCAMPER (Ready Reference 2.6).

# Murals

Murals are large wall paintings that have become popular public art created by groups. In school, murals can be any big composition on a wall space, such as collaborative work based on an environmental unit (Chilman, 2004). Murals help children learn to cooperate and take pride in group work. Group planning and sharing are essential aspects of mural making.

Murals are made from a variety of media, from crayons to collage. The easiest are ones where students each add an item (e.g., a nature collage mural or a print of a foot or hand). Students can learn how to plan full scenes relevant for science, social studies, or literature. Check out community murals online at www.tcom.ohiou.edu/community/murals/.

# Mixed Media

Use paper, wire, paint, fabric, and any other materials in one artwork. Banners, murals, and even portraits, landscapes, or abstracts can be made with any imaginable combinations. Children's books such as Bunting's *Smoky Nights* and Ringgold's *Tar Beach* show examples.

**Fiber Art.** Cloths and yarns can be used to create art with texture and pattern. Fabric art connects well with social studies: clothing of cultures and time periods and careers (knitter, weaver, quilter, tailor, seamstress). There are wonderful pieces of children's literature that deal with fiber art; for example, weaving is central to *Annie and the Old One* (Miles). For a science connection, explore natural dyes, such as carrot tops for a green–yellow, onion skins for an orange dye, and tea for brown or orange. Colored drink mixes can serve as dyes, too. An adult can use an ordinary crockpot to heat. Be sure to wear rubber gloves and rinse with cold water to set the dye. *Note:* See Judy Chicago's dramatic fiber art, *The Dinner Party,* at her website (www.judychicago.com/).

**Crafts.** Crafts include handcrafted traditional art such as pottery, weaving, and quilt making.

**Color Window Quilt or Banner.** Give each child a ziplock bag, colored tissue paper, and cellophane. Children cut, tear, and arrange their piece and then the bags are taped together with clear, wide tape. Make into window banners or quilts.

**Class Quilt.** Everyone's quilt background should be the same size to start off. Origami paper works and other media can be added. (See examples of random patterns used by quilters like the ladies at Gee's Bend: www.quiltsofgeesbend.com/quilts/. Be sure to click on "sales.") Subject matter can vary. For example, each student can make a personal quilt piece about herself. In math, quilts can be used to explore geometric shapes (squares, triangles) and for counting. Experiment with printing, lettering, and collage. Encourage students to avoid the obvious: This need not be representational art; it can be abstract. Use chalk to mark placement on large bulletin board roll paper. (I tape two long pieces together side by side.) Glue finished quilt pieces. Wipe off chalk. Create a border using steps explained previously under displays and bulletin boards. Students can make cartoon-type "speech bubbles" telling about their creation process to post with the finished quilt.

**Literature Quilts.** Quilts are particularly adaptable as literature responses. Each student can make a square for a class book quilt. Encourage use of diverse art materials and styles. The subject matter could be a book everyone has read, a favorite book, an author-artist study, or a genre.

**Self-Portrait Banner.** Materials: white paper, white fabric (12 × 12 inches), pencil, chalk, water, mirror, permanent black marker, and masking tape. Directions: (1) Look in a mirror and examine your face closely. Sketch each half, really thinking of shapes and line. Outline in black marker. Add whatever you want to represent you (e.g., hat or symbols). (2) Put fabric over paper and tape down. Trace black outline with marker. Wet fabric—do not soak. (3) Use chalk to put in color. When dry, spray with nonaerosol hair spray. (4) Sew or glue all portraits into banners or a quilt.

# Photography

*Good art is not what it looks like, but what it does to us.* (Roy Adjak)

Now that disposable and digital cameras are readily available, classroom photography is easy. Cecil and Lauritzen (1994) recommend teaching a few important aspects of composition, using a series of tasks and discussing results: (1) Take the same person or object close up and far away. (2) Take a person or object with a lot of light and then with shadows or less light. (3) Take pictures of different subject matters: people, places (land, water, interiors of houses), animals, and action shots. (4) Create a still-life arrangement and photograph it. (5) Photograph the same person or object in the center of the picture and then off center (more to the left, right, top, or bottom).

Students can sort pictures depending on what they judge works best. Display with captions created by students on poster board. *Variation:* Students take a series of pictures of people, places, and events and then write a story that pulls the photographs together. Story and pictures can be made into a book.

**Great Tips: Photographing and Filming.** Get 10 great how-to tips at www.kodak.com/eknec/PageQuerier.jhtml?pq-path=38/13915/39/317/10032&pq-locale=en_AU.

## Three-Dimensional Art

Three-dimensional art can be made from assorted materials, including found objects, papier mâché, paraffin, and soap using the add or subtract methods. Three-dimensional art projects give tactile stimulation and an emotional outlet through touch because of the versatility of the materials.

**Materials.** Clays and doughs (see recipes in Ready Reference 7.3) and firing clay (from earth used for pottery) can be used. See Baylor's *When Clay Sings* for clay examples. Wood, paraffin, and soap can be used for carving, as well as materials from recipes. Papier mâché is also inexpensive and versatile (recipe follows).

**Tools.** Fingers, spoons, nails, sticks, cutouts (not cookie cutters), rolling pins, and things to press in to give textures (e.g., potato masher) are all possibilities.

**Techniques.** Use each of these methods to sculpt: add, subtract, punch, slap, pound, pinch, and stack. Children will naturally use clays and doughs to make cylinders and then balls and then pancake shapes. Modeling and plasticine clays hold their shape well but need to be warmed to make them pliable. Let children know they must knead the clay to warm it, which develops finger strength.

**Paper Mâché.** This is molding and sculpting material that is cheap and yields delightful shapes to paint or collage. Cut or tear up newspaper into 2-inch-long strips. Use thinned white glue or wheat (wallpaper) paste and dip strips. Run strips between fingers to remove excess. Let dry. Start with bases such as a foam tray and boxes. Move to more difficult curved and rounded shapes such as balloons and cardboard tubes.

It is easier to have one group at a time work on paper mâché because of the mess. Begin with a project in mind, rather than explore as you would in other media. Be sure to clean up immediately, because the mix hardens and makes floors slippery. Shower curtains are useful to cover work surfaces.

Puppet heads can be made by starting with a base as simple as a wad of newspaper on top of a paper tube reinforced with masking tape. Spaghetti or candy boxes can be covered with papier mâché, painted, and used for puppets (make sure children can get fingers or hands inside). Papier mâché can be bought from sources such as Dick Blick (800-447-8192, www.dick-blick.com) or at www.proteacher.com/080005.shtml.

**Mobiles.** These 3-D artworks move. Show Alexander Calder's mobiles for ideas. Use sticks, hangers, or picture frames to suspend items from wire, yarn, cord, or ribbon. Mobiles can be made from found objects or by attaching created items. Encourage experimentation with balancing the weights of objects.

**Other Sculptures.** Make stick sculptures using a clay ball as a base and pushing in toothpicks, buttons, shells, and other similar objects. Make sand molds by pressing objects into damp sand (lids, pencils, buttons, shells). Pour a thin mix of plaster of Paris (like salad dressing) about 1/2-inch deep into the depression. Put a pop-can tab or paper clip in the mixture to make a hanger.

**Soap.** To make soap clay for carving, mix 3/4 cup soap powder and 1 tablespoon of water. Whip until stiff. This can be used to coat projects to create a snow effect or molded (with wet hands). It dries hard and can be painted.

**Paper.** Crepe paper sculptures can be made by tearing paper, soaking 1 to 2 hours, pouring off the water, and adding wheat paste. It dries hard and can be sanded.

**Yarn.** Soak yarn in white glue and then wrap it around a balloon, as sparsely or densely as desired. When dry, break the balloon.

**Vermiculite.** Combine vermiculite (available from plant stores) and plaster. Add water and stir until thick. Pour into a mold or small box. Tear the box away when dry and carve with a table knife, nail, or blunt scissors. *Note:* Check with visual art professional about safety issues.

**Diorama or Shadow Boxes.** These are scenes made by using a shoe box or other container to create a stagelike setting with 3-D objects that are made or found.

**Architecture.** Teach basic shapes such as the cube, arch, sphere, cone cylinder, pyramid, rectangular solid, and triangular solid. Then take a neighborhood walk to find examples in buildings. Books like McLerran's *Roxaboxen* can be used to motivate students to think about construction as art making. Arches can be made with boxes and blocks, and cardboard tubes make a base to construct columns that can become corinthian, doric, or ionic with some papier mâché, glue, and paint. This is a particularly relevant art connection to studies of communities and countries. There's a post office or government building with Greek columns in nearly every American city. Terms that relate to architecture, such as *arch, beam, column, post,* and *lintel* can be taught to give students conceptual anchors. The Pittsburgh History and Landmarks Foundation's *Introduction Architecture* is available online at www.phlf.org. It includes excellent drama, dance, and field-based sketching, mask, and mural activities for teaching basic architectural concepts.

**Puppets and Masks.** Ready Reference 7.4 describes ways to make puppets and masks with readily available materials.

## Bookmaking

Pop-up, accordion, big books, minibooks, sewn books, and shape books can be made to bind up student writing and artwork. Many books are available on making and binding (e.g., use wallpaper to cover or "sew" with yarn through hole punches). Example resources are *The Elements of Pop-up* (Carter) and *Read a Book, Make a Book* (Norris).

**Animal Flip Books.** This book type combines animal parts to create new creatures. Students draw or find magazine pictures of animals and insects that have distinct heads, bodies,

## Ready Reference 7.3  Recipes for Clays, Doughs, and Pastes

**Note:** These should be prepared by teachers who carefully monitor students for safety purposes. None should be tasted by students.

### Clays and Doughs

#### Soft Dough
*Ingredients:* 1 cup water, 1/4 cup salt, 1 tbsp vegetable oil, 1 tbsp alum, 1 cup flour (nonrising), food coloring (optional—stains skin and clothing!)

Bring water to a boil. Add salt and food coloring. Remove from heat and add oil, alum, and flour. While it is hot, mix and knead for 5 minutes. *Note:* If you add food coloring, it is best to do so at the beginning or add to dough after mixing using a few drops at a time and folding dough over color to mix. To change the texture, add cornmeal, sawdust, coffee grounds, sand, or other grainy items. Store in plastic bag.

#### Goop
Mix one part cornstarch and one part cold water.

#### Baker's Clay
*Ingredients:* To make 1 cup for ornaments or jewelry: 4 cups flour, 1 cup salt, 1/2 cup warm water, food coloring (optional—STAINS skin and clothing!)

Mix ingredients, kneading until smooth (5 minutes). Add more flour as needed. *Note:* If you add food coloring, do so a few drops at a time and fold dough over color to mix. Dough should be used the day it is made. Add 1 tsp alum and put in plastic bag to keep longer. The dough can be baked at 300°F until hard, approximately 20 to 60 minutes depending on the thickness. For Christmas ornaments, make holes for hanging before baking. Clay can be painted with felt tips on enamel or use half tempera and half white glue. Spray with fixative when done.

#### Soda-Starch Clay
*Ingredients:* To make 1 cup: 1 cup baking soda, 1/2 cup cornstarch, 2/3 cup warm water, food coloring or tempera paint (optional—will stain!)

Mix ingredients in pan until like mashed potatoes. Stir to boiling. Pour on a cool surface and knead when cool. Add coloring during kneading. Store in plastic bag until ready to use. Shape beads by using a drinking straw to make holes. To speed dry, bake 10 minutes at lowest oven setting or 30 seconds on medium in microwave. *Note:* Make a day or two ahead. Make batches in different colors. You can use crayons, paint, or marker to paint clay. Set with clear nail polish or shellac.

#### Salt-Starch Clay
*Ingredients:* 1 cup cornstarch, 1/2 cup salt, 1/2 cup water

Mix and cook over low heat until it hardens. Salad oil delays drying.

#### Sawdust Clay
*Ingredients:* 2 cups fine sawdust, 1 cup wheat paste (wallpaper), 1/2 to 1 cup water, 1 tsp alum to keep from spoiling

Mix to bread dough consistency. Let dry slowly. Keeps in plastic bag or refrigerator. *Note:* Good for making puppet heads and relief maps. Can be painted with tempera.

### Pastes

#### Cornstarch Paste
*Ingredients:* To make 1/2 pint: 1/4 cup corn starch, 3/4 cup water, 2 tbsp sugar, 1 tbsp vinegar

Mix cornstarch and cold water in pan. Add sugar and vinegar. Stir constantly and slowly heat until it clears and thickens. Cool before using. Saves in refrigerator up to several weeks if sealed. *Note:* Cornstarch paste has a pleasant smell and texture. It is not too sticky; and it is safe, almost colorless, and dries clear. It forms a stronger bond than flour paste and can be used for lightweight items such as fabric, yarn, rice, and cardboard. It is a stronger homemade paste, but it must be cooked ahead of time. It is hard to remove when dry; requires soaking and scrubbing.

#### Flour Paste
Add water to flour until it is thick but spreadable. *Note:* It can be used on most paper, it is safe, and does not stain. The texture is different from school paste, so it makes an interesting change. It wrinkles thinner papers and makes a relatively weak bond, so it is not recommended for collage. Washes off easily when wet, but requires soaking and scrubbing if dry. Cannot be stored. Use when first made. Add oil of wintergreen or peppermint to resist spoiling.

---

and legs. Pictures should be similar in size. Each animal is a page in the book that needs to be fastened together so that body parts are in approximately the same place on each page. Each page is then cut into thirds: head, body, legs. By turning the different page parts, new animals are created and can be named. This can evolve into creative writing by setting up categories for students to use to invent a description of their new creature: habitat, food, habits, and movements. For younger students, body parts can be placed on cards and assembled on a table. *Variation:* For older students, use a grid, listing or depicting animal or insect heads across the top of a page, and bodies down the left side. By finding the intersection of the X and Y axes, students create new visual combinations (e.g., X [heads] for goat, cow, llama, cat, and Y [bodies/legs] for dolphin, turtle, snake, duck).

**Big Books.** Big books are enlarged copies of favorite books, poems, or chants about the size of poster board. To construct a big book as a response to a book, lesson, or unit of study:

1. *Paper:* You will need 18 × 30 inch white chart paper and 12 × 18 inch white construction paper, plus two pieces of

**Visual Art**

## Ready Reference 7.4  Puppet and Mask-Making Ideas

**Finger puppets:** Cut off fingers of cheap work gloves to make individual puppets. Students can glue on materials or use fabric paints. *Alternatives:* Use small candy boxes (e.g., Milk Duds boxes) as a base. Students can also create figures from paper or cardboard and attach "finger rings" to slip the puppets on.

**Glove puppets:** Each child needs one glove. Each finger becomes one character to be created from a story. Five characters are possible or some fingers can be objects in the story.

**Stick puppets:** Attach a popsicle stick, tongue depressor, ruler, or wooden dowel to a character made of paper, paper mâché, or cloth. *Variation:* Find sticks from trees to use as a base.

**Shadow puppets:** Cut character body parts from construction paper and hinge arms, legs, and so forth together with brads. Lay on overhead projector and move body parts to tell story.

**Paper bag puppets and masks:** Use small paper bags to create a character's face or body using paint, collage, markers, and so on. The puppet's mouth can be placed at the fold so that it looks as if it is talking. Yarn, grass, and twigs can be added for hair and paper or cloth for clothes. Use grocery bags to make puppet masks that students wear on their heads—cut eyes, mouth, and nose holes.

**Sock puppets:** Students sew or glue scraps of fabric, yarn, and pipe cleaners on socks. The sock can also be cut at the toe to create a mouth or held so that a mouth is created by a fold.

**Paper plate puppets:** Paper plates can be used for puppets and for masks. Students add materials to create a character and then tape sticks or rulers to the back for handles. *Variation:* Use plastic coffee can lids instead of paper plates as the base.

**Paper mâché heads and masks:** Use a recipe for paper mâché. Apply to a ball of newspaper, attached to a toilet paper tube with masking tape. When dry, paint and attach other materials to create a character. A fabric body can be glued or sewn using a generic body pattern made from two pieces of cloth or paper. To make a mask, paper mâché over a balloon. When dry, paint, trim, and cut holes for eyes, nose, and mouth. Can be a full head or cover just the face.

**Object puppets:** Find and adapt objects that relate to a story and lay them on top of a box (used as a stage) or table as the story is told, for example, a covered thread spool (tuffet), a plastic spider, a tiny doll (Miss Muffet), or a toy spoon. Check craft stores for a variety of tiny objects, often in packages with multiples. *Variation:* Painted rock puppets: Collect rocks and paint to represent characters. Display and manipulate as story is told.

**Clothespin puppets:** Use old-fashioned clothespins as the base to create characters. Clip to a ruler to give extra height.

**Envelope puppets:** Use large or small envelopes as the character base. Combine several envelopes for a different effect.

**Pipe cleaner puppets:** Bend, cut, and combine pipe cleaners to form puppets. Create a handle from one pipe cleaner.

**Paper cup puppets:** Use foam or paper cups as the creation base. Use cups of different sizes and combine cups for creative effects (e.g., create taller puppets with several cups).

**Card puppets:** Use index cards as bases. Attach to sticks or use on a flannel board by gluing coarse sand paper or felt to the back. Card puppets can be placed in a pocket chart as a story is told.

**Tagboard masks:** Cut tag board into ovals big enough to cover a face. Make four 1-inch slits, one on each "corner," to give the mask contour. Use masking tape to secure. Draw ovals for the eyes and a space to cut out a mouth. Paint and use collage materials to decorate according to a variety of cultures (display books with pictures of masks for data gathering).

**Plaster gauze masks:** The face is covered with Vaseline and then gauze, soaked in plaster, is applied, and allowed to set up. (Keep nose, mouth, and eye areas clear.) Mask is removed and painted with acrylics or tempera. (Make sure students are not claustrophobic.)

---

poster board at least 18 × 30 inches, and clips, metal rings, or cord to secure the cover.

2. *Art materials:* Glue, markers, crayons, wallpaper sample, and other collage materials

3. *Type of book:* Replica or new version? To make this decision, select a predictable story or poem with obvious patterns or rhyme (see predictable books in Chapter 4 under "Genre"). Reading the book or poem several times invites children to chime in. Prepare for writing by brainstorming ideas. Students can dictate a rough draft to the teacher on a large chart or older students write independently. Then the story or poem is reread and revised.

4. *Text:* Words are printed on white construction paper and glued on the larger sheets of paper. The text should be divided evenly across the pages of the book so that there is room left for artwork.

5. *Illustrations:* Students can use materials, styles, and techniques. Encourage experimentation with the styles of various artists.

6. *Title page with the copyright year and the names of authors and artists:* Design a title page and, if the book is a replica, a statement such as "Retold and illustrated by Mr. Walker's class." If the big book is an adapted version, use a statement such as "Based on Charlotte Zolotow's book, *Someday.*" Make a dedication page for the beginning of the book, a page about the authors, and a reader comment page at the back.

7. *Cover:* Students design a front and back cover, and it is glued to the poster board.

8. *Page sequence:* Have students order the pages, and put the book together with front cover, title page, copyright page, dedication page, story, page about the authors, comment page, and back cover. Use rings, cord, or metal clips to bind.

# IV. Connecting Visual Art to Curricular Areas

This section gives seed ideas to connect visual art and science, social studies, math, and literacy.

## Science Focus

The full science standards document can be accessed at the National Science Teachers Association (NSTA) website (www.nsta.org).

**Art News.**   John Mieyal, professor of pharmacology at Case Western Reserve in Cleveland, says the arts are important communication tools. He shows his students how to doodle, cartoon, and diagram to explain how substances affect human biology and might be used for medicinal purposes (Jack, 2005).

**Art and Nature.**   First, students examine how an animal, plant, or natural object is shown in different ways by artists. Present three to five pieces of art that contain an image. For example, use dog images and ask what dog information is shown in each, how each picture feels different, and why the artists showed the dogs as they did. Picture book art can be used. Compare art with science facts gathered. Example: Compare Gag's *Millions of Cats* and Pinkwater's cat in *The Wuggie Norple Story*.

**Nature Collage.**   Plan art walks to collect natural items to display or use in collages. Examples: twigs, leaves, stones, bark, and feathers. Add museum tags to displays.

**Nature Displays.**   Students create displays from "found" nature, including seasonal collections like a fall display of leaves, twigs, stones, and dried flowers. Label each using museum tags with common and Latin names (make up for creative thinking). *Note:* Killing insects for displays is inappropriate.

**Camouflage Drawings.**   After examining pictures of animals in their environment, students choose an animal for a camouflage drawing. Students sketch it and then use oil pastels to add color and pattern to the animal. Finally, students add a background that reflects the patterns and colors of the animal. Art can be displayed and critiqued for its ability to camouflage animals. Note: The word *camouflage* is from the French word *camoufler*, meaning "to blind or veil." Review the history of camouflage at www.arts.ufl.edu/art/rt_room/sparkers/camouflage/history.html.

**Fish and Bird Art.**   Students choose a fish or bird and research where it lives, what it eats, and how it moves. This information is then connected to how the fish or bird looks (color, shape, size of body parts). Students then create a new fish or bird by thinking of answers to the three questions and using a variety of art media. New animals are named. Students can do oral presentations and display work in the class museum.

**Food Mural.**   Students work in teams to research a food's origin. Use paint and collage materials to construct a mural to show how food ends up on the dinner table. For example, show how wheat is planted, harvested, processed, baked, wrapped, and delivered to stores.

**Scientific Drawings.**   Examine the drawings of Beatrix Potter and Robert McCloskey, both of whom studied animals and plants carefully to render their images. Students can then choose to do a careful scientific drawing, focusing on important details. Use photos or actual plants for close looking. *Variation:* Examine the drawings of Audubon at www.nytstore.com (go to "fine art," "Audubon").

**Invisible Animals.**   Examine water under a microscope or with hand lenses and sketch living organisms. Show students how to do quick sketches with pencils to capture important details. Do close looking to draw specifics. Sketches can be enlarged into full drawings or paintings. *Note:* In the video *The Lively Art of Picture Books* (Schindel, Weston Woods), Robert McCloskey sketches ducks. *Variation:* Invite a local artist to demonstrate sketching.

**Habitat 3-D.**   Use boxes to create dioramas of animal habitats (land or water). Add clay sculptures, tempera paint, found objects, and papier mâché in construction. Emphasize the importance of showing how the habitat would enable the animal to survive (food, shelter, etc.). *Variation:* Create habitat mobiles—one per animal.

**Assemblage Sculptures.**   Assemblage is combining pieces of "this and that" to create a three-dimensional artwork. Invite students to bring in scraps of wood, cloth, metal, and interesting bits of paper and string. Show them how to experiment with arranging the objects in boxes and lids until they have a composition to glue down. Finally, paint everything one color. Resource: American sculptor Louise Nevelson is known for her assemblages of wood, found objects, metal, and other materials arranged as collections in boxes of various sizes and then painted with a single color, usually black, white, or gold. Images can be found at http:www.artprojectsforkids.org/2009/02/louise-nevelson-found-sculpture.html.

**Habitat Hat.**   Students research different habitats to discover unique characteristics. See www.fi.edu/tifi/units/life/habitat/habitat/html for ideas. Students then bring in magazine pictures (wildlife magazines are a good source) and "found" objects (shells, sticks, etc.) to affix to hats. Use old hats or paper hats as a base. Provide raffia, construction paper, tempera paint, and glue (idea provided by teacher C. Kotarsky, Lady's Island Elementary School).

**Museum Scavenger Hunt.**   During a museum visit, give pairs or teams a scavenger hunt form on which to record "finds" in these categories: animals, plants, and other images related to space and land forms. Make spaces to note title, artist, date, media, and a place to comment about subject matter (facts/feelings) for each piece of art.

**Pounded Flowers.**   Do this project in the spring. Collect a variety of fresh flowers. Discuss their names and how they look similar and different. Students then place the flowers on light-colored construction paper and cover them with clear plastic wrap. Pound each flower with a hammer until the color is embedded in the paper. Frame and display.

**Moon Journals.**   Students observe, draw/sketch, and write to document learning about the phases of the moon, time, changes of seasons, and other natural phenomena (Chancer & Rester-Zodrow, 1997). Journal entries should be dated.

**Nature Sculptures.** Use types of clouds (e.g., stratus, cumulus) to inspire soft sculptures. Use clay or recipes in Ready Reference 7.3.

**Science of Color.** Groups each need a prism to investigate color. Paint or use crayons to record observations and discover the pattern (ROY G. BIV: Red, Orange, Yellow, Green, Blue, Indigo, Violet). Follow up with data gathering regarding the how and why of the spectrum.

**Light and Shadows.** Set up stations for students to investigate using the following:

- *Flashlight:* What materials are transparent, translucent, or opaque? What causes light to change colors? What makes shadows? What affects the size and shape of a shadow?
- *Laser light:* What can block or interrupt this light? How far can it go? Can it bend? How can you draw with it?

**Rock Paintings.** Students select fist-sized rocks. Add white glue to tempera paint or use acrylics to make paint that will stick. The paintings can be abstract or students can carefully study the rock shape to see what images are suggested (e.g., mouse, cat). Display abstract and representational works for ideas. *Examples:* Show Matisse, Miro, and van Gogh prints for ideas about colors and lines. Be sure to tell students that Michelangelo believed the image was in the stone waiting to be freed; he did not impose his image on the stone.

**Step into the Painting.** Invite students to think like scientists. Display and discuss the scientific process. Focus on observing details and asking questions. As a group brainstorm observations from a piece of art (e.g., a landscape). Look closely with magnifying glasses. Focus on the content and how the painting might have been made. Give five Ws and H questions as a frame for student questions.

**Grow a Head.** Use knee-high hose to make living heads sculptures. Fill hose with a teaspoon of grass seed and then a mixture of soil and sawdust. Tie snugly with a string. Paint on face with fabric paint. Put head in a shallow dish and pour water over it. Place in a sunny area and watch the grass "hair" grow. Ask students to record daily observations in a science journal (e.g., measurements, colors, textures).

**Garbage Art.** Use clean trash to make collages that promote looking at throwaways differently. Emphasize experimenting with how to group items on cardboard and use patterns. Encourage tearing, scrunching, and even using pieces of plastic and glass for mosaic effects (take care about sharp edges). *Variation:* Combine with painting, fabrics, and nature materials.

**Foot Painting.** Put on music and ask students to listen to its rhythm and mood. Spread out large paper. Use shallow trays of tempera. Tell students to roll up pant legs. Start with a choice of a few colors. Students create art by painting with their feet—to the music. Ask students to label foot parts and note details caused by different feet (e.g., ridges on footprints). *Variation:* Do finger and handprints in study of body parts, including skin and bone studies.

**Everyday Objects.** Check out an unusual book that uses ordinary things as unit centers: *Inquiry-Based Learning Using Everyday Objects: Hands-on Instructional Strategies that Promote Active Learning in Grades 3–8* (Alvardo & Herr, 2003).

## Social Studies Focus

*Pyramids, cathedrals and rockets exist not because of geometry, theories of structures, or thermodynamics, but because they were first a picture—literally a vision—in the minds of those who built them.* (Eugene Ferguson, historian)

The full social studies standards document is available from the National Council for the Social Studies (NCSS) website (www.socialstudies.org).

**Global Firsts.** Explain that without the creative thinking of individual artists the world would be completely different. Show examples of art works from different cultures and time periods, including contemporary contributions such as Graciela Rodo-Boulanger of Bolivia, Lim Kok Boon of Indonesia, Raúl López García of Mexico, Nikos Chatzikyriakos-Ghikas of Greece, and Vladlena Gromova of Russia. Students then research artists who created "firsts" such as collage, wood block print, oil painting, and porcelain and share aspects of their CPS. *Variation:* Create a timeline about artists and their firsts.

**Art for Peace.** Check out the Global Art Project whose mission is "to spread world peace by promoting tolerance and nonviolence through art." Their website is www.globalartproject.org/index.html.

**Make Me a World.** Paper mâché, used over a balloon base to create personal globes, can accompany individual research projects related to countries, continents, and oceans. Paint with tempera and label major areas. (See previous papier mâché directions.) Hang with string from the ceiling. *Variations:* (1) Study history of globes and students choose to make a globe in a style from a time period; (2) use in science to make planets.

**Signature Art.** Part of social studies involves coming to respect individual differences. Show a facsimile of signatures (e.g., on the Declaration of Independence). Give students paper and choices of tools and media. Allow time to write signatures many different ways. Display products and discuss differences in size, color, lines, and shapes. Focus on what makes each name so different and the effect on a viewer.

**Paraphs.** These are special designs John Hancock and Queen Elizabeth I added to their signatures to prevent forgery. Download examples of paraphs at http://art.lex.com. Discuss how art often has its roots in functional needs of people (e.g., antique tools are displayed for decorative purposes; show horse trainers teach horses to "dance" using steps originally needed in ranching). Give students large paper to experiment with creating personal paraphs.

**Group Composition.** Learning cooperative behavior is a key goal of social studies so any art project that expects students to take individual responsibility and come together to create a whole work is appropriate. For example, all these are collaborative art: murals, class topic quilts (state, city, transportation, etc.), group sculptures such as totem poles, or constructing with cardboard boxes, tubes, or papier mâché around a topic such as inventions. *Note:* Art need not be representational to convey important messages.

**Multicultural Art.**   Any country or culture can be studied through its art forms. Assemble prints, pictures, and artifacts. Ask students to observe the art element details and patterns. Ask about what the figures are doing and why. Ask about the emotions conveyed by the art and why the artists showed what they did. Students can research pieces of art (media, techniques) and then experiment with these. Emphasize the values portrayed in each art form by asking, "What does this show about the people?" *Note:* Skin tone mixing was described earlier. *Variation:* Each child begins a personal collection of art from a culture or ethnic groups using magazines, advertisements, and postcards. Display in a class museum.

**Artifacts.**   Artifacts are tools or ornaments made by humans using design principles and art elements. Many were originally for functional purposes. Artifacts can be coordinated with units and used for art interpretation, art making, writing, and drama. Invite students to contribute to a display of artifacts from their own lives. Discuss the five Ws and H about family artifacts. Label each with a museum tag. Compare with historical artifacts that reveal aspects of everyday life of a people. Baskets, carvings, quilts, pots, and jewelry give us hints about the values and needs of cultures and the artists.

**Holidays.**   Many are concerned that the "holiday curriculum" trivializes social studies. The problem lies in superficial ways holidays are studied and the lack of connections to standards. Stereotypical and dictated art abound and need to be avoided. Instead of tracing hand turkeys and coloring Pilgrim and Indian heads at Thanksgiving, it is more meaningful to have students use a variety of media to create art about big ideas such as: (1) meals are rituals used to celebrate events in many cultures, (2) people offer food gifts to show appreciation and love, and (3) we give thanks in diverse ways. Teach use of diverse art forms, media, tools, and techniques to cause students to better express understandings. Personal construction of meaning that has fealty to basic facts is the goal.

**Mandalas.**   The mandala is an ancient circular shape used in all cultures. Mandalas come in all sizes. Motivate students to find many examples of circles in life and art, including advertisements such as the Coke sign. Brainstorm circles in nature, such as the sun and moon or the cycle of seasons. Discuss why the circle is so common. After this data gathering, students are ready to create original mandalas. This broad idea can be interpreted in any way, from round abstract artworks to poster-sized realistic works containing multiple circular-shaped images. Any material may be used. Young children especially enjoy collage mandalas. Discuss final products by asking students to become "art docents" to tell about why they made their choices of media and how they arranged their compositions. Focus on how each mandala feels and causes for the emotional effect.

**Update Art.**   Do a modern-day version of an artist's work to make it reflect the current time rather than an historical time.

For example, change the background or dress in portraits (e.g., *Mona Lisa*). *Note:* This has become a popular idea using Grant Wood's *American Gothic.*

**Class Flag.**   Examine the flags and symbols of countries. Discuss how and why they use the colors, shapes, designs, materials, and lines they do. Divide into groups to create a class flag to represent what's important about the class. Make fabric, paper, paint, and collage materials available for design.

**Famous People Sculptures.**   Students choose a person who has made a significant contribution (e.g., explorer, president, artist, activist). Brainstorm what students would like to know focusing on the five Ws and H questions. Charge students to find details about favorite foods and how the person looked, moved, talked, and dressed, what was valued, and achieved. Students then construct sculptures from paper mâché or make puppets (see Ready Reference 7.4). Crayola's Model Magic is a bit pricey, but works well. Use sculptures for "expert presentations" or panels done in role.

**Peer Sculptures.**   Partners take turns sculpting each other using famous poses from historical paintings or sculptures (e.g., *Washington Crossing the Delaware, The Thinker*). *Variation:* Half of the class assumes a famous pose while the other half pretends to be museum visitors who tour in pairs and use dialogue to show what they see, how they feel, and who they are.

**Draw to Music.**   Listen to music about a relevant place, person, or topic (e.g., "Grand Canyon Suite" or "American in Paris"). Write or draw to the music and then share what and how the music communicated important messages.

**Sound and Show Compositions.**   Students prepare a sound and art presentation around a choice social studies topic, such as a culture or country. They may work in groups or pairs to find a piece of music to play as they present art on transparencies, PowerPoint, or an easel as the song is played. Art can be student made or "found art."

Integrating math, art, and literature

# Literacy: Reading and Language Arts Focus

*My favorite thing is to draw words.* (Andrew, age 6)

The full standards literary/literature standards document is available from the National Council of the Teachers of English (NCTE) and the International Reading Association (IRA) at their respective websites (www.ncte.org or www.ira.org).

## Planning Page 7.5
### Guided Art and Literacy Lesson (GALL)

**Introduction:**

*See and feel.* Students closely examine a work of art for a period of time (e.g., 2 minutes). Ask: "What do you see? Look closely for details. How does it make you feel? Why?" Do not allow talking at this stage. Display: "Art Concepts and Elements" to prompt thinking. *Example art: I and the Village* (Chagall).

*Predict.* Students hypothesize/predict possible messages the artist intended. Ask students to tell (1) what they saw/felt and (2) what it might mean. The teacher can scribe for young children using chart paper or overhead. *Example:* The artist has everything going in different directions, so he may be trying to say he is confused.

**Development:**

*Data gather.* Read about the artist and/or the work of art. Teachers may read to the students or show a video. *Example:* Read Greenfield's *Marc Chagall*.

*Evidence.* Students give evidence to confirm or reject predictions. Emphasize that "being right" is not the goal. Do in pairs, small groups, or whole group. *Example:* Prediction about confusion is rejected because Chagall was being playful and childlike. He focused on dream qualities.

**Conclusion:**

*Write.* Students respond in writing (Ready Reference 5.1). *Example:* Write a letter to Chagall or a story about his dream. The story could start at the top of the picture and move to the bottom.

*Art making.* Students do an art response connected to the original art (Ready References 6.5 and 6.11). *Example:* Watercolor paintings of dreams or a class mural of good memories done in Chagall's style.

*Publish.* Students' responses are made public through displays, oral sharing, and bookmaking (e.g., class big book).

*Variations:* Any piece of art can be used for tableau and can be danced. Students can take the role of an artist and explain thoughts and feelings about making the art. Music can be found that "fits" the art and played during a close viewing.

**Guided Art and Literacy Lesson.** In this generic lesson structure, visual art is the literacy material used to develop listening, speaking, reading, and writing. Thinking in the CPS process is the framework. The teacher-directed lesson has an introduction, development, and conclusion. Students can also learn to direct guided art and literacy lessons (GALL) if steps are posted and practiced (see Planning Page 7.5). "Imaginative and affective processes are how a text is 'lived through' or 'brought to life'" (Sadoski & Paivio, 2004, p. 31).

**Main Lesson Book.** This strategy is used at all Waldorf schools. It consists of two phases: First students listen and observe a presentation of new material (e.g., stories, drawings, hands-on experiences). Next students construct images that summarize key points in the main lesson book. These art representations of comprehension provide assessment of student understanding (Nordlund, 2006).

**Picture Books.** Ready Reference 7.6 lists many ways to teach arts and language arts with picture books.

**Cinco Parts of Speech.** Look closely at a piece of art. Number your paper 1 to 5 and list: (1) nouns you see, (2) verbs and actions, (3) adjectives, (4) adverbs, and (5) a sentence using the ideas you've generated. *Note:* Abstract art works well.

**Listen and Draw.** Partner students and give one a secret object. They sit back to back as one describes the object while the other tries to draw it. Encourage students to tell size, shape, and color and focus on use of visual details. *Variations:* Do by arranging sets of objects or with one partner describing a drawing while the other draws (e.g., a geometric or organic shape).

**Note-Taking Sketches.** Imagery facilitates memory and is a powerful way to learn words and concepts. For example, students can draw or make mental pictures of words versus memorizing dictionary definitions (Wolfe, 2001). Show students how to take notes using a split-page format: Make a vertical line to separate paper into one third and two thirds. Take notes on the two-thirds section. Stop periodically and sketch out important ideas on the one third.

**Artist Birth Mates.** See Appendix G for a complete description of the yearlong research project that matches each student with an artist born on his or her birthday.

**Artists Like Me.** After studying an artist, have students write about all the ways the artist was like them. Suggest categories such as feelings, family, physical characteristics, interests, places lived (idea courtesy of Misty Kaplafka, Ohio art teacher).

**Art Stories.** Choose any art print(s) as a prompt for group or individual stories. Use portraits for characters, a landscape for the setting, and an abstract or nonfigurative work for problem/conflict ideas. Teach students to establish the problem quickly and be descriptive about the setting and characters. *Variation:* Use for circle storytelling followed by individual writing.

## Ready Reference 7.6   Picture Books Art Strategies

1. *Ape the greats.* Explore picture book styles and media using Ready References 6.7, 6.10, and 6.11. Experiment with an artist's media and styles. Adapt using SCAMPER (Ready Reference 2.6).

2. *Predict from art.* Before reading, show one or two pictures. Prompt to look closely. Ask for predictions, using only the pictures, about (1) Who? *characters,* (2) When and where? *setting/time,* and (3) What might the problems be? Ask for evidence from the art. Record ideas in a three-column chart so students can confirm or reject.

3. *Clothesline prediction.* Use two copies of the same book. Take one apart and cut off the text. Display the pictures before reading. Coach students to come to an agreement about an order they think will happen. Use a clothesline to pin pictures up in order. Next, read the book and check picture order. Rearrange as necessary. *Variation:* Partner students to write or tell a story to go with the pictures before reading.

4. *Experts.* Each child or group selects a picture. The goal is to notice everything by looking closely. Small magnifying glasses make this fun, or use toilet paper tubes. Give categories to observe: art elements, media, style, decisions the artist made, composition (arrangement). Expert panels report.

5. *Blow-up art.* Many books are available as big books so the art is easy to see. Use the *art discussion strategies* in Ready Reference 6.12 with any picture. Another option is to make color transparencies of selected pages. Stewig's (1988) series, *Reading Pictures,* has lesson plans and poster-sized art from picture books.

6. *Partial picture preview.* Cover part of one picture and ask students to examine the remaining part. Ask "What do you see?" and other open questions. Ask students to predict the covered portion. *Variation:* Look at pictures in a mirror (reverse image), upside down, or from far away to discover new colors and shapes. Composition can be studied by squinting to see masses, instead of details. Ask for hypotheses about why the artist made certain choices.

7. *Style match.* Compare art done in the same style as the book (e.g., impressionistic, folkart (see Ready Reference 6.11). Example: compare and/or create a Venn diagram using Monet's work and Emily McCully's art in *Mirette on the High Wire* (light, color, shapes, and edges).

8. *Scavenger hunts.* Students search pictures for specifics: media, style, borders, perspective (within and among books). Set up a bingo-type format. *Note:* Students need access to many books and must know the art elements for this activity that can become an ongoing routine.

9. *Wordless books and LEA.* Language experience approach is a classic strategy to teach reading and writing. To use it with wordless books: Ask students to dictate a story that goes with the pictures (or write their own). Finished stories become the reading material for lessons (e.g., play I Spy to locate high-frequency phonic patterns) and for independent

reading. *Suggestion:* To build independence and keep attention, ask students to spell aloud when you take dictation from them.

10. *Book parts.* Teach about book parts: end papers, set the mood, and gutters should not break up pictures across double pages. Examine the effects of borders. Teach title page, half-title page, and credits to increase visual literacy. See Chapter 4 for websites.

11. *Compare–contrast books.* Use a Venn diagram to record likenesses and differences between the same story written and illustrated by two different picture book artists. This provides an opportunity to work on the higher order thinking skills of analysis.

12. *Create characters.* Combine the body, head, and legs from different characters in picture books to make new characters. Either cut up picture books or use the art as an inspiration for drawing (not copying). Write a story to go with the new creatures.

13. *Make a picture book.* Students can write/illustrate picture books in any genre: alphabet, concept, predictable, or fairy tales. Encourage use of a variety of media and styles.

14. *Frame favorites.* Treat picture book art as art. Cut apart or make color copies to frame, write to publishers for posters or prints, or use publishers' catalog pictures to create framed art. Create a picture book arts gallery.

15. *Concentration/memory game.* Make pairs of cards—a photo of an artist on one and example art on the other. Turn upside down to play. The goal is to remember the location and pick up matched pairs. E-mail publishers to request photos and examples of book art or use publishers' catalogs or book covers.

16. *Set the scene.* Recreate a book scene with tableau (freeze-frame drama). Simple props and costumes can be used. *Example:* Make classroom into a water scene from *Swimmy* (Lionni).

17. *Puzzles.* Cut up pictures and give each child a piece. Each child studies the piece to try to find as much as possible about it. Assemble to see the whole picture. Do before or after reading a book.

18. *Special days.* Everyone picks a book with a special trait (e.g., pop-up, alphabet, special endpapers, borders). Each child studies the book, then presents the focus in 1 minute.

19. *Storytelling.* Cut up several picture books. Students mix up art to make a new story. Make sure there are pictures of characters and settings. *Variations:* Do storytelling in a circle with each student picking a picture and adding. Groups can take picture packs to write or tape their stories. An alternative recording idea is to story map the stories students told or will tell.

20. *Collages.* Use old picture books as source material for collages (e.g., by media such as cartoons and watercolor, subject matter such as portraits and landscape, or topics such as plants and animals).

Visual Art

**Talking Art.** Each student writes something a person in a piece of art might be saying. Give each student a blank piece of paper and show how to cut cartoon-type speech bubbles. Bubbles are displayed around the art.

**Learn–Wonder–Like.** Students pretend they are going to meet the artist of a particular work. In preparation they generate a list of comments and questions about what they *learned*, *wondered*, and *liked* about the art. *Variation:* Do in a talk show format.

**Fine Art Storytelling.** Review the literary elements (Ready Reference 4.3). Use an art print as a stimulus to tell a story. Pass the print around a circle with each student adding to the tale. *Variation:* Use several portraits and a landscape (or seascape or cityscape) to set up the characters and setting.

**Parts of Speech.** Display parts of speech categories. Under each category, ask students to find verbs, adjectives, and the like related to a piece of art. This can be done in small groups, with each group taking a part of speech.

**Word Squeeze.** Look closely at a piece of art to find all the colors, shapes, places, textures, lines, feelings, actions, things, and so forth. Make columns on a piece of paper and brainstorm words for each. Tell the students to squeeze the art like a sponge to find things no one else sees.

**Seeing Systematically.** Give each student a magnifying glass or cardboard tube (or use fist) to examine a piece of art. Slowly guide them to look at the art systematically: foreground–background, top–bottom, left side–right side, edge–center using at least 10 seconds on each. Afterward, students free-write and then prioritize important observations. *Variations:* Create titles for the artwork that capture the big ideas/feelings.

**Name a Color.** List all the color names students know. Divide into groups to find new words for the colors (e.g., cerise for red) using the dictionary, thesaurus, and other references. Follow with doing a piece of art to experiment with making new colors through mixing. Student can also create new names.

**Long Paper Poems.** Show Henri Matisse's "Red Room," "Yellow Curtain," "Purple Robe," "Lady with the Green Stripe," or other color-inspired art. Students choose a color and poetry form (Ready Reference 5.2). Use colored markers to write final draft on long narrow paper strips or on paper that is the color of the poem. *Variations:* Use other topics such as emotions and/or create small paper poems.

**Walk into a Painting.** Students pretend to physically enter a landscape, seascape, or cityscape. Take them on a guided journey through the work. Afterward, students write or tell how they felt and what they saw, using all five senses.

**Art Ads.** Teach the most common propaganda devices: bandwagon, glittering generalities, celebrity endorsement, common folks, and everybody's doing it. Break students into groups to create a 1-minute ad to sell a piece of art using the techniques. These can be written or presented orally.

**Artist Interview.** Ask students to brainstorm questions to ask an artist about a piece of art (sculpture, collage, painting). Example starters: "I was wondering why _____, I am wondering how _____, I am puzzled about _____." Set up pairs to interview each other by alternating roles as artist and interviewer. *Variation:* Use student-made art for the interviews.

**Mini-Museum.** Students need a sturdy box to create a display of collected items that relate to a book, story, or poem. Items may be made or found that connect to characters, setting, and theme. Museum tags are added to items with a title, approximate date, and material for each. Set up museums as stations to be visited by groups, with creators serving as docent guides to talk about the items.

**Wanted Posters.** Show examples of wanted posters and portraits. Student then select a character or important person. To draw the portrait they must examine the shape of the face and measure the distances between eyes, nose, mouth, and so forth. At the bottom of the poster, students write a description of the character, the place and time last seen, and a contact person. Rewards or other notifications may be added. Suggest rereading for accurate details.

**Stretch-to-Sketch.** Students interpret what happened to characters and the roles each played by making sketches—quick rough drawings (Harste, Short, & Burke, 1988). Each character or person can be sketched in several actions to summarize events. Students present drawings by explaining interpretations and comparing how others saw the same events differently and why.

**Tear Apart Predictions.** A picture book (or a photocopy) is taken apart and pictures displayed in "bookological" order. Students look closely (2 to 3 minutes), without talking, to get clues about the upcoming story from the art. Then students use literary and art elements language to discuss findings. Ask, "What can you tell about the setting? Characters? Plot? Mood? How do you know?" Next, read the story. Reuse pictures for partner retelling. *Variations:* (1) Students write captions for pictures. (2) Before reading, present pictures out of order and ask students to agree on a predicted order; read the story and then rearrange.

**Quickdraws.** Before reading, activate visual imagery by giving time to sketch about a topic related to upcoming reading (Tompkins, 1997). Students then use their sketches while reading to confirm, reject, and modify ideas to make clearer meaning.

**Sketchbooks.** Each child has a sketchbook to draw in before, during, or after reading or listening to literature. Sketchbooks can be used during discussions. Sketching prompts include characters, setting, most exciting points, special objects or symbols, plot, theme, and style. Special words can be sketched, such as "sliding egg yolk" in *Tuck Everlasting* (Babbit). Sketches can also be used as writing prompts for poems, paragraphs, and so forth.

**I Spy (observation/vocabulary).** Set this up using any book art (including textbooks) and the format of the *Where's Waldo* books. Say "I spy" to start. Ask students to find special elements to finish the phrase. Encourage them to look closely for big shapes, little shapes, curvy lines, light, and dark and to try to find action and details. Use with abstract art to stretch thinking. See the *I Spy* art series (Marzollo) which focuses on finding something in masterpieces, such as letters, animals, and toys.

**Art Match Vocabulary Stretch.**   Show a variety of shapes and colors on separate cards (e.g., construction paper shapes and colors). Display an art print and ask students to list the names of shapes and colors they see. Prompt to notice patterns made by repeating, just as in writing.

**Visual Memory Challenge.**   Tell students to study a piece of art for 1 to 2 minutes. Then cover it up. Ask them to list everything they remember. Do individually or in groups, orally or in writing. Uncover and check for observation accuracy. *Note:* Repeat and extend the time to stretch observation and memory.

**Art-Based Word Wall.**   Designate a space for students to put up interesting words using artistic shapes that show meanings. Use sticky notes or make any card sticky with removable glue sticks so words can be alphabetized or grouped by color, shape, media, and style.

**Art Word Web.**   Put an art category in the center of large paper. Attach radiating lines or yarn. Students add to the web by finding examples in artwork (draw or write the idea). Students can underline and write their initials beneath personal contributions. For example, a "line" web category would include zagged, straight, curved, or thin.

**Artist Chair.**   Teach the CPS process (Ready Reference 2.6). After making art, ask students to write or tell about the CPS

used. Scaffold writing with a form divided into CPS sections: attitude, problem definition, data gathering, experimenting, and so forth. Students sit in a special artist chair to share and be interviewed.

**Dialogue Journals and Logs.**   Students write individually, in dialogue with a partner, or create team journals. Topics to write back and forth about include "What do you think about the painting? How does it make you feel? What does it make you think about? What mood do you think the artist was in when he or she created this work of art? Why did the artist entitle the work of art as he or she did?"

**Compare and Contrast.**   Different messages are conveyed using different media (e.g., sculpture, poetry, dance). Compare and contrast two pieces of art that evoke similar feelings and messages. "How does each artist create the response? What do both artists do that is similar?" For example, look at art about courage, love, family, war, suffering, or nature.

**Storyboard.**   Picture book artists often begin with a storyboard—brief sketches or mockups of how the finished book might look. To make a storyboard, create a series of drawings (in order) that tell a story and glue them on a poster board.

**Art Prewrite.**   Students create art or collect art (postcards, pictures, pottery) to use as topics for writing. The art is "squeezed" for writing ideas by brainstorming. For example, web the five Ws and H questions related to a piece of art. Any of the writing choices in Ready Reference 5.1 can be used (caption, letter, list).

**Artist Experts.**   Ready References 7.7 and 7.8 offer reading/writing ideas for becoming an expert on any artist.

## Ready Reference 7.7   Artist Experts

To become an expert on any artist . . .

Read about . . .

1. The artist's life and collect biographical information: birth, death, marriage, children, friends
2. Who and what most influenced the artist
3. Time period in which the artist lived
4. Country or countries where the artist lived
5. Style in which the artist worked or school of art to which the artist belonged
6. Influence the artist had on the world of art (for what the artist is known)
7. Other artists of that period
8. Media the artist used
9. A particular artwork the artist made, especially the most famous or controversial
10. Criticism about the artist and his or her work

Write . . .

1. Letters: to artists or someone in art, such as a museum curator to request information

2. Biographical sketch of artist
3. Fiction or nonfiction story about a great artwork (see *Girl in Hyacinth Blue*—adult example, Vreeland, 1999)
4. Story about how the work of art came to be
5. Menu that might be served during the time the art was created
6. Report on the customs of the time of the artist
7. Report on the clothing styles of the artist's time
8. Description or criticism of a piece of art
9. Report about the period of art
10. First-person monologue about what the artist would do if alive today
11. Script for play or scene about the artist's life
12. Comparison of the work of two artists; Venn diagram
13. Timeline of the artist's work
14. Book for children about the artist, medium, or style (see bookmaking ideas in this chapter)

## Ready Reference 7.8   Artists Alive!

Students pick an artist and do the following to bring the artist to life.

- **Collection:** Find and save works of art by the artist (e.g., prints, calendar art, postcards).
- **Ape the greats:** Use the artist's colors, mood, style, and techniques to create adapted artwork.
- **Update:** Make a modern-day version of the artist's work (e.g., change the costumes).
- **Vary it:** Do another version of the art: instead of van Gogh's *Starry Night*—do Sunny Day, Rainy Day, Stormy Night, Foggy Night, and so forth.
- **Guests and experts:** Invite a local artist, curator, or college professor to speak about the artist or interview the person.

- **Art gallery:** Visit a museum and see the real thing.
- **Artist's studio:** Visit the place where an artist works; ask to shadow the person for a day.
- **Video:** Watch a video of the artist's life (e.g., *Lust for Life* about van Gogh).
- **Art show:** Have an event to exhibit the artist's work and students' together.
- **Mini art gallery:** In the hall, classroom, or a special place in the school, include works by famous artists and students' works of art.
- **Painting of the week:** Students select a favorite from among several artworks and display using cut-out "speech bubbles" to tell things they know, think, or feel about it.

## Math Focus

Access the full math standards at the National Council of Teachers of Mathematics (NCTM) website (www.nctm.org).

**Quilts.** Create class geometric quilts using traditional patterns found in folk art or by observing patterns in the environment (dots, checkerboard, and stripes). Give each student a square of paper (about 10 × 10 inches) to plan. Patterns can be painted or made from cut paper, fabric, newspaper, and the like. Glue squares onto a large piece of bulletin board roll paper (black makes a good background). A border can then be added. *Variations:* Set limits to stretch thinking (e.g., use one shape, such as a triangle, and experiment with variations using SCAMPER).

**Origami Art.** Japanese paper folding involves the study of shape, line, symmetry, and angle. Special origami paper in a package with variety of colors works well and is available from any art supply store. There are many resource books (LaFosse, 2003) on simple origami shapes, such as bird shapes, and the children's book *Sadako and the Thousand Paper Cranes* (Coerr) would be a wonderful story addition to this art–math project.

**Word Problems.** Use the format of a math problem but cast in terms of art thinking. Give an example and then have students write their own and exchange. *Example:*

You have five different colors of paint. How many different ways can you paint a box if you make each side a different color?

**Color Recipes (Measurement).** Pair students and give each pair an eyedropper and three small cups of tempera (red, yellow, and blue; use ice cube trays cut in half). Students then experiment to create colors. They record the number of drops to create each color. Ask pairs to name their new colors. *Variation:* Give students one primary color and a cup of white and black. Experiment with recipes for shapes and tints (numbers of drops).

**Art Auction.** Students prepare information about pieces of art to "sell" the works. Each student takes a turn at selling and auctioning. Give each a sum to spend at the auction.

**Story Problem Art.** Students create art to go with story problems that they are given or they can write and illustrate original ones. Problems can be exchanged for solving. *Suggestions:* Teach basic drawing shapes. See previous drawing and sketching ideas.

**SCAMPER.** Collaboratively brainstorm shape manipulations using Eberle's SCAMPER steps: substitute, combine, adapt, minify or magnify, put to other uses, eliminate, and reverse or re-arrange. Students then create a piece of art to show the things they did with geometric shapes (triangle, square, or circle). Use any media.

**Count Me In.** Groups are given a piece of art to examine for numbers of things. Give a time limit and then share as a group (e.g., 11 curved lines, 8 right angles, 14 red flowers).

**I Spy Math.** Find the math in any piece of art (print, collage, sculpture) or picture book. List geometric shapes, patterns (anything repeated), types of lines, and use of symmetry. Discuss any parts that give a feeling of infinity and how it is accomplished. Use a large magnifying glass.

**Symmetry.** Each student gets half of a picture from a magazine or print. By carefully studying the half, the student tries to duplicate it on the opposite side.

**GeoMath Art.** Use geometric art, such as that of Mondrian or Escher, and ask students to discuss how the artist might have made it and why. Have students try their own geometric math art by repeating shape patterns.

**Step into the Painting.** Students become mathematicians and tell or write observations based on a math point of view. Encourage thinking about how the painting might have been made and the content of the work. Before beginning, list specific math vocabulary/concepts students may use. *Example:* "I see a four-sided work that has a triangular composition. There are five figures with the male figures being greater than the female in size."

**Infinity Art.** Show examples of Seurat's dot art (pointillism) and ask students to look closely to discover how the images are made. Discuss how the dots make up sets to create a whole image. Students can make their own dot art using Q-tips to paint.

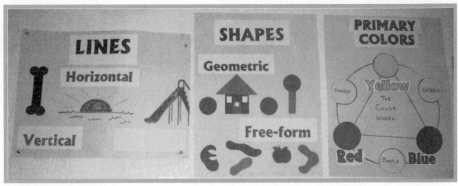

Art elements display

## Teacher Spotlight

### My First Year in Arts Integration

How do teachers phase into AI? Here is a first-person account from a first-year teacher (at Lady's Island Elementary).

"I have conscientiously worked to tie art and the other curricular standards together. I am seeing a huge difference in my fifth graders' retention of information and interest level.

"In science we classified animals as vertebrates and invertebrates using the art form of collage. We also made camouflaged butterflies and hid them in the classroom. The ones with the best camouflage were not found at all. This was a wonderful demonstration of understanding. The students also invented animals and drew special adaptations for survival.

"In social studies students researched Indian tribes and used authentic techniques to make crafts. We've done a lot with drawing of historical events, too. Recently, we studied cartooning, and the students drew political cartoons. Some were better than the newspaper! One was a Pilgrim shooting airplane-shaped bullets at a turkey who had the head of Osama bin Laden.

"In math, students made drawings about square numbers. They had to internalize the concept to depict their number. They also created 'measurement monsters' to learn measurement equivalencies, such as 2 cups equal 1 pint. Students wrote number sentences that described themselves and included self-portraits.

"In English/language arts, students wrote and illustrated four framed comic strips, each with a different type of sentence: declarative, interrogative, exclamatory, and imperative. The process was amazing. Not only did they have to write each type of sentence, but it had to be creative and funny! We've also illustrated poems (me, too, actually) and made simple masks to act out stories for the kindergarten children.

"It has been an amazing year, and it is just October!"

## Conclusion

*Art is either plagiarism or revolution.* (Paul Gauguin)

I think Gauguin's idea has great relevance for teachers. We are constantly borrowing ideas from anywhere we can get them. The seed strategies in this chapter are the result of years of collecting. This particular cache of

nuggets can initiate planning visual art connections with other curricular areas. When these are used within the context of the AI building blocks and transformed by individual teachers to fit their students, these ideas can become revolutionary.

### Teachers as Leaders: AI Advocacy

Nothing advocates for the power of visual art more than a public exhibit. Locate an empty public space—any blank wall or empty display window. Libraries, malls, and businesses are possibilities. Work with an art specialist to obtain art and plan the display. Mount and create tags for each artwork. Wall text should state the goals of the art so it is clear how it represents thinking and learning. I was able to create a permanent exhibit space by carpeting a hall wall in a college academic building. My AI classes (education majors) created art about every 2 weeks to show what they were learning about AI. Art was exhibited, sometimes with "speech bubbles" to make visible the artist's thinking. A comment box was available for faculty and students to leave notes. Several students were actually asked to sell their artwork!

### myeducationlab

Go to the Activities and Applications section for Topic *Strategies for Teaching* at MyEducationLab for your course and complete the video activities entitled "Using Visual Art and Literature to Teach Science", "Using Cut Paper/Finger Painting to Teach Science", and "Using a BME Chart to Prepare for Response to Literature."

Now, go to the Activities and Applications section for the Topic *Art Production* and complete the video activity entitled "Making Emotion Arts to Increase Literature Comprehension." Under this topic you will also see videos that give pointers on teaching a variety of visual art media, tools, and techniques.

Go to the Book Specific Resources section in the MyEducationLab for your course, select your book and Chapter 7 to view the Questions to Guide Reading and Response Options for this chapter.

## Resources

See Appendix I for further study, including more websites. For a list of websites to access online resources on multicultural art and art history, museum collections, lesson plans, and additional information on various cultures, see the journal *Kappan* 87(8) (2006) inside the back cover.

The authors also list sites to display and view artwork created by students from around the world (Bloom & Hanny, 2006).

## Multicultural Art Sources: Artifacts

### *Example Books*

Braman, A. (1999). *Kids around the world create! The best crafts and activities from many lands.* New York: Wiley.

Cavanaugh, B. (1997). *Multicultural art activities.* Teacher Created Resources.

Edwards, L. (2009). *The creative arts: A process approach for teachers and children.* Prentice Hall.

Kohl, M., & Potter, J. (1998). *Global art: Activities, projects, and inventions from around the world.* Beltsville, MD: Gryphon House.

Schuman, J. (2003). *Art from many hands: Multicultural art projects.* Davis.

Terzian, A. (1993). *The kids' multicultural art book: Art & craft experiences from around the world.* Charlotte, VT: Williamson.

## Websites

Art Institute of Chicago: www.artic.edu/ (e.g., beadwork, weaving)

Christian Children's Fund: www.christianchildrensfund.org/

Museum of Modern Art: www.moma.org/ (Chinese brush paintings)

Oxfam America: www.oxfamamerica.org (worldwide handmade items)

Save the Children: http://savethechildren.org (Africa and Asia)

Southwest Indian Foundation: www.southwestindian.com

## Sources of Prints and Posters

Art Institute of Chicago, The Museum Shop: www.artinstituteshop.org/

National Gallery of Art: www.nga.gov

Print Finders: http://printfinders.com

Sax Visual Arts Resources: www.saxarts.com

Crystal: www.crystalpublications.net

Shorewood Prints: www.artforschools.com

UNICEF: http://art.cafepress.com/unicefUNICEF

## Software

Software is continuously being released. Visit a rating site such as www.epinions.com/ to find current recommended products.

# 8

# Integrating Drama Throughout the Curriculum

*Drama is life with the dull bits cut out.* (Alfred Hitchcock)

## Overview

This chapter introduces classroom or creative drama as an art that has one of the strongest research records for having an impact on academic learning. Drama is discussed within the 10 AI building blocks that promote meaningful integration. In Building Block X there is a snapshot of drama specialist, Jeff Jordan, teaching a drama-based writing lesson.

## Introduction: Arts in Education

Hobart Elementary is the second largest elementary school in the nation. Ninety percent of its 2,000 students come from households with incomes below the poverty level. All are from immigrant families, primarily Hispanic and Asian. None speak English as a first language, but Rafe Esquith's fifth graders read far above grade level. Their test scores are in the top 5 to 10 percent of the country. How does he do it? It's all about drama. Mr. Esquith immerses them in Shakespeare—his plays, life, and times. The year-long study ends in April with a full production. One year, it was *Hamlet*, the next *The Taming of the Shrew* (Trudeau, 2005).

Drama expert Rodney Van Valkenburg explains, the effectiveness of arts-based methods like those of Rafe Esquith lies in their ability to "put students' knowledge to work. You can't act, paint, or dance unless you know something about your subject" (2005). The arts uniquely value risk taking and experimentation with the proviso that learners reflect on the consequences of their actions. These options balance freedom with responsibility.

The arts have the potential to transform parts of each individual's worldview. Music not only connects students with their past and present condition, but also uplifts emotional moods. The literature and visual realms connect students to worlds they never knew existed. Dance brings learning to its feet. Drama brings new insights about life and stretches students to feel the joy and pain of others. This exceedingly rich array of experiences has the potential to transform how students see themselves within the larger context of humanity.

## Drama in Education

Theatre and drama have a long history of relationships with human behavior and education. Primitive peoples pantomimed rituals to cast out demons; Aristotle thought theatre gave audiences a catharsis to release emotions. Medieval priests used theatre to explain Christianity to the masses. Drama in schools, however, did not come on the scene until the early 20th century. Progressive educators emphasized students *doing* rather than just reading and memorizing. Like Hitchcock, they wanted the dull bits cut out. John Dewey and others looked to the arts as tools to make learning active. Drama proved a natural.

Now 21st-century research suggests that the problems of many students could be prevented with high-quality dramatic work (Arts Education Partnership, 1998). Findings that connect reading, writing, and drama are particularly strong. Drama also stimulates motivation to learn by engaging students in real-life problem solving (Deasy, 2002). Research Update 8.1 summarizes research examples.

In the opening Classroom Snapshot, Sarah Lane puts this research into practice. She has been teaching sixth grade for 7 years and she is a vivacious teacher. She began integrating drama after a staff development project 2 years ago. Now she uses drama daily to engage students in creative problem solving to increase comprehension. This lesson showcases performance as well—which taps drama's potential to expand expressive communication. She combines several drama strategies, such as one-liners and teacher in role, to teach toward standards in social studies and theatre/drama.

## Classroom Snapshot
### Social Studies through Drama

*Good teaching is one-fourth preparation and three-fourths theatre.* (Gail Godwin, *The Old Woman*, 1937)

Sarah Lane's class is in the middle of an environmental issues unit on how humans have changed the environment. They have been reading about problems with the coral reef in the Bahamas.

Sarah holds up a yellowish-red piece of coral. "I'm going to pass this around and you can each say a **one-liner** about it. You can **pass** and we'll come back, if you want."

## Research Update 8.1  Drama and Academic Achievement

- Nineteen studies found positive effects of drama on language development, including written and oral story recall, reading comprehension, reading readiness, oral language, and writing (Deasy, 2002).
- Drama caused the lowest-scoring children to use comprehension strategies used by proficient readers because they became immersed in stories. By the end of the year, nine of ten students scored in the proficient or grade-level range (Adomat, 2009).
- A meta-analysis of studies from 1950 to 1999 testing the claim that arts-based study leads to academic improvement found three areas of reliable causal links. The strongest was between use of drama and verbal skills. Drama-based lessons improved verbal skills with respect to texts being used as well as new texts (Winner & Hetland, 2000 a).
- A drama-based method for teaching primary students to use reading strategies was found to be more effective than traditional methods. In addition, students in the experimental group gained positive perceptions of drama (Güngör, 2009).
- A multiyear study of ArtsConnection schools found a strong link between English/language arts and drama (Hefferen, 2005).
- Students from families with low incomes who were involved in drama outscored noninvolved students in reading by 9 percent by eighth grade. The difference favoring drama/theatre students grew steadily. By 12th grade, nearly 20 percent more students were reading at high proficiency (Fiske, 1999).
- Seven meta-analyses of 80 studies conducted in the United Kingdom, United States, and Holland from 1965 to 2000 showed drama instruction had a positive impact on oral and written story understanding, reading achievement, reading readiness, oral language, vocabulary development, and writing. The author theorized that since students are asked to process text more actively in drama settings, they develop literacy skills in a more rigorous, active manner (Podlozny, 2000).
- When drama was used as a rehearsal for writing, letter and narrative writing were significantly improved (Moore & Caldwell, 1993; Wagner, 1988).
- First and second graders who participated in drama to recreate a story previously read aloud had better story comprehension than a control (Deasy, 2002).
- Ten weeks of in-class drama coaching in a remedial third–fourth grade transformed reading instruction which improved students' attitudes and success in reading. Dramatic training and expression allowed students to see themselves as active readers and experience a sense of achievement (Deasy, 2002).
- Fifth-grade remedial readers who used drama as a learning tool consistently scored higher on the Metropolitan Reading Comprehension Test and outperformed a control (Dupont, 1992).
- Fifth and sixth graders who participated in a yearlong improvisational drama program had greater expressive and interactional language. Expressive language showed higher order thinking such as speculating, predicting, and evaluating. Interactional language was found in peer exchanges and brought up moral issues. "Drama puts back the human content into what is predominantly a materialistic curriculum" (Deasy, 2002).
- Students with learning disabilities involved in drama show improved behavior and oral expression. They acquired social skills such as courtesy, self-control, focus on classroom work, and ability to follow directions. These benefits were sustained when tested 2 months after the project ended (Deasy, 2002).
- Drama activities, including role playing, improvisation, and writing stories, enabled elementary students to achieve significant gains in vocabulary and reading comprehension. Students also reported improved attitudes relating to self-expression, trust, self-acceptance, and acceptance of others (Gourgey, Bousseau, & Delgado, 1985).
- Use of creative drama positively affected student achievement in a variety of areas, such as reading and oral and written communication. Sixteen studies of students K–12 showed that drama positively affected the ability to take on the roles or perspectives of others—that is, to increase empathy (Kardash & Wright, 1987).
- Sixty Head Start students who received regular and frequent drama and sign language instruction had higher language scores than a control group (Arts Education Partnership, 1998).
- Positive relationships were found between oral language growth (speaking) and use of creative drama in fourth, fifth, and seventh graders (Stewig & McKee, 1980).
- ESL (English as a second language) students who were involved in drama exhibited significantly greater verbal improvement than a control group (Vitz, 1983).
- Economically disadvantaged African American and Hispanic students in grades 4–6 who participated in drama showed improved reading achievement and more positive self-concepts (Gourgey et al., 1985).
- Drama increased interaction among fifth graders with and without mental handicaps (Miller, Rynders, & Schleien, 1993).
- About 12 percent of students involved in theatre thought making a racist remark would be acceptable, whereas 40 percent of "no drama" students thought so. The advantage for students involved in theatre is statistically significant (Fiske, 1999).

They form a circle and she starts with a boy on her left. He takes it and grins as he explores the surface.

"I'm hard and I'm dead," he says and passes it on.

"They're killing us by polluting our home," the next boy says.

A small girl takes the coral and says, "I pass."

It takes about 5 minutes to go around the circle. The last boy says, "I could make a lot of money if I could just find a way to get around the authorities." Sarah then nods to the girl who passed earlier. The girl reaches for the coral.

"Without the coral reef, our country will not survive. When we kill it, we kill ourselves," she says softly.

The class observes a moment of silent reflection on her comment before Sarah speaks.

"It was interesting how you took on so many different roles. Shana, you seemed like a very concerned Bahamian. **What did the rest of you notice?**" Hands go up.

"The sadness in her voice," says a boy.

"She looked sincere," another boy comments.

"Some people spoke as the coral. That was really cool. I'd never have thought of doing that," a girl says.

Others comment about how classmates showed feelings with words and how the coral was held.

Sarah moves on and summarizes recent social studies topics they've been studying: the Bahamian economy, lifestyle, and its people's relationship to the reef. She asks what she has left out, and several comment about the destruction of the reef and the tourist trade. Sarah then forecasts what will come next.

"We now need to really go into detail about the interaction between people and the environment. Last night's reading assignment will help you use drama to become characters. She points to a sign with "Drama Elements" listing: Imagination, Face, Body and Voice. "Remember the goal is to use all these to make us all believe in your ideas."

Sarah picks up a **Mr. Mike** from the table. "Imagine you are a Bahamian citizen who has a specific interest in the reef. Think of all the points of view you have read about. We are just getting ready for a live **telecast** to inform everyone in the Bahamas about the issues."

She explains that **half** will be the **audience** and half the **panel.** All will have a chance to speak.

"Let's set up. **Five minutes to show time.** Panel members take these chairs. Audience, get into two rows." Sarah gives directions rapidly. It seems chaotic as students make decisions, but in a minute all but two chairs on the 10-seat panel are taken.

"Great work. Okay, only 2 minutes to show time. I'll be asking **panelists** to introduce themselves and make a short statement about their position. **Audience members**, you can respond with remarks and questions."

Sarah pushes a button on a CD player. She flips the lights out. Bahamian rhythms fill the room and the **lights** go on. She holds up the mike.

Drama specialist, Jeff Jordan, directs an emotion pantomime.

"Welcome to *Bahama Today*. I'm Sarah Lane and I'd like to welcome our guest panelists and audience members who are here to discuss issues surrounding the coral reef. We'll begin with our panel members. Please introduce yourselves and tell us why you have come."

Sarah hands the mike to the panel member nearest her. The panel proves to be a diverse group ranging from fishermen to a politician. Some show they are vehemently opposed to government interference. Others use their voices to show they are passionate about saving the reef. Sarah next opens it up to the audience.

"Please stand, give your name, and tell why you have come," she tells them.

Audience members direct comments to specific panelists and ask questions. All but two participate. After about 10 minutes, **Sarah sums up remarks** and ends with, "I'd like to thank our guests for coming and remind viewers to watch every day at this time to learn more about current issues on *Bahama Today*."

She starts the music and flips out the lights. The music plays a bit longer before she turns on the lights.

"Let's talk about what just happened," she says. After a half-minute of no response Sarah backs up.

"I think you are still processing all this. Let's do a **Write Right Away** to **debrief.** Use the next page in your journal and let's go for 2 minutes."

Students get pencils and journals. Sarah moves to an overhead and begins to jot down her observations. At first a few watch her. She **writes publicly** but uses only sentence fragments and key words. Eventually, everyone begins to write. She gives them nearly 5 minutes and then asks them to find a place to stop.

"Please **form groups** of three or four with people nearest to you and take a few minutes to share what you wrote. Read or just tell it."

Sarah waits until everyone is in a group and **circulates** as students talk.

"You think that you made the politician too stereotyped? **Why do you say that?**" she asks a boy who has critiqued his own performance.

She comments and asks **clarification questions** such as "What do you mean by _____?" and "Are you saying _____?"

The room is full of discussion. After about 5 minutes, Sarah brings them back together.

"I could tell you understood the importance of using **details** and **examples** to create believable characters. It sounds like many of you are planning to find out more specifics before I spring another drama on you!" The students laugh.

"Let's do more group work to think about the issues and what just happened on the TV program. We'll use groups of family, friends, or neighbors that viewed the telecast. Assume a role in your group to discuss the show. Count off in fives."

Sarah directs each group number to a certain area. The room is carpeted, so most sit on the floor. There is a general commotion. She dings a **push bell** and says, "When I ring again, begin to talk in your group. Ready," she dings. Ten minutes pass before she rings and says "Freeze." She moves to a group and knocks on a desk. She is back **in role,** this time as a **"newcomer."**

"Hi everybody. Sorry I'm late. I just watched the TV show on the reef. What are you doing?"

A boy summarizes the gist of their discussion. It turns out they are fishermen sitting on a wharf. Sarah becomes a fisherman, too. They commiserate about the hardships placed on them by the government. A girl in the group brings up concerns about the long-term survival of the reef. This takes about 2 minutes. Then Sarah steps out of role and compliments them on the diversity of roles they chose.

She concludes the lesson by making an assignment, due at the end of the week. Students are to **write, in a role,** to show different perspectives on the reef issue. It can be a letter, newspaper article, editorial, diary entry, or even a song. The students seem excited and ask questions about whether they will get to share what they write. Sarah seems genuinely delighted with this idea.

"Especially if it is a song," she grins. ✺

# Arts Integration Building Blocks

I enjoy watching old episodes of _Whose Line Is It Anyway?_ It's total improvisation, and there are always great laughs from the theatre games they play: Weird Newscasters, Party Quirks, Scenes from a Hat. I'm always amazed at the creativity with which Colin Mochrie and Ryan Stiles use props in as many ways as they can think of in a minute. My favorites are the "Do it as if" challenges Drew Carey gives them to sell CDs or narrate a silent movie segment. I'm entertained, but it goes beyond that. It's all about the kind of creative problem solving we do every day as we take different roles and figure out how to make our lives work. That's drama.

Drama is now in the lead among the arts in showing potential to increase students' learning, especially literacy (Deasy, 2002). Why is drama so influential? Some answers are in the philosophy section of the AI building blocks previously introduced and summarized in Ready References 3.2 and 3.3.

The building blocks scaffold meaningful arts integration around these questions: _Why_ should the arts be integrated?, _What_ should teachers know (arts literacy)? _How_ can teachers carry it to success? They plan lessons, create an aesthetic environment, use arts-based literature and best teaching practices, design instructional routines, differentiate instruction, assess, and partner with specialists. The place of drama in the building blocks is the subject of this chapter.

Drama integration usually begins as teaching _with_ drama—doing simple activities here and there. As teachers gain more drama and theatre literacy they can move into teaching _about_ and _in_ drama. Using drama as a teaching and learning vehicle _throughout_ the curriculum is the goal. Each level builds on the other, but quality integration depends on attention to each of 10 major aspects summarized in the building blocks.

# Building Block I: Philosophy: Why Integrate Drama?

> _The best drama uses as much truth as possible._ (Dorothy Heathcote)

Teachers who incorporate drama into daily learning say they are giving students safe havens to try different roles on for size. They report increased motivation and substantial effects on learning in science, social studies, math, and language arts. It does not stop there, however. Research Update 8.1 shows drama results in schools across the country. The following summary further explains the reasons that underlie increased test scores.

## Increases Motivation, Concentration, and Focus

Drama grabs attention with its novelty. There is a sense of occasion when performance is anticipated even it is only one half of the class presenting to the other half. The topics of drama derive from real-life problems so they have inherent interest. When used to introduce a lesson, drama causes students to tap into feelings, speculate, and want to learn more. For example, a problem from an upcoming lesson can be explored through pantomime or verbal improvisation, causing interest to be piqued and prediction thinking to be activated. All this is highly motivating.

Taking roles using pantomime and verbal drama also fills a basic need for both mental and physical activity. In particular, it activates aesthetic imagining as an additional motivator. Drama integration includes explicitly teaching students to concentrate, focus, and control their bodies, minds, and voices. These tools help students to "make others believe." Drama invites us to escape into imaginative worlds as we use all our intelligences, including verbal and bodily kinesthetic, and engage the senses and emotions. Drama integration is set in the social context of a classroom of peers; it would be surprising if students were not motivated.

## Stretches Perspective Through "In-Role" Practice

*Art is the only way to run away without leaving home.* (Twyla Tharp)

Dorothy Heathcote explains the difference between the real world and the "as-if" world of drama. In the latter, "we can exist at will. Brecht calls this 'visiting another room'" (Robinson, 1990, p. 8). According to Heathcote, our actions are controlled in these rooms by how free we feel to experiment. "If we needed a reasonable reason for including the arts in schools, surely it is here in these two rooms" (p. 8).

Drama capitalizes on children's natural desire to pretend and take roles during play. Drama expands the number of roles students can assume, which enlarges perspective. Students rehearse life roles in which they will make future decisions as parent, friend, or boss. These dramas often center on universal questions related to important themes like those in great literature: How do humans respond when they are given success, rather than earning it? Why do people feel so strongly about freedom? How must we deal with evil? During drama, children examine different viewpoints and try them out to answer such questions. In an accepting atmosphere they feel free to sort out beliefs and values. In this way, drama shapes ideas and feelings, allowing students to make sense. Students may assume the role of experts in debates like Sarah's students did or take on creative problem solving for the answers to other science issues, such as the growing resistance of certain bacteria to antibiotics. During a career education unit, students might pantomime significant aspects of careers they have investigated, all the while creating interior visual images that are forever altering their brains.

**Enhances Reading Comprehension and Writing Fluency.** Preservice teacher education and professional development for practicing teachers now routinely include an examination of drama strategies. Drama integration has earned a solid place in literacy by demonstrating power to increase reading, writing, and general language skills. Studies clearly show that children who dramatize stories have higher comprehension scores than those who only read the story (Deasy, 2002; Henderson & Shanker, 1978). Students who dislike reading decide to put forth effort to comprehend when they find out drama participation depends on getting information from reading. Students who know they will be pantomiming significant actions of a character from a text are also given a point of concentration. They are reading so they will be able to **do.** Textbooks are given life when teachers involve students in dramatizing important ideas in science and social studies.

Vocabulary increases as students read, write, speak, and listen to interesting words related to drama activities. Writing becomes more descriptive. Students write greater amounts and with greater proficiency, which shows clearer thinking about how to organize and develop ideas (Deasy, 2002). Most exciting is the transfer potential. For example, one research finding is that students who use drama to understand one text transfer those thinking skills to unfamiliar texts (Catterall, 2002).

## Develops Speaking, Listening, and Nonverbal Communication

*After three months, desperate to reach him, she asked him to play a character in a story and he began to speak in role. At the end of the year the class was asked to complete the sentence, "Drama is a gift to me because . . ." The formerly silent boy wrote: "Because it makes me brave enough to say what I want to say."* (Lushington, 2003)

Drama gives voice because it engages a different kind of thinking. We feel free to say things in role that we wouldn't normally say. In life we alter what we say, and how, according to the situation and the roles we play therein. Drama prepares us for life. It unties tongues that can get tangled if not made supple through practice. Teachers set up scenes with questions, such as "What should the father and the boys do to get the mother to come home?" when the problem is introduced in *The Piggybook* (Brown). Possible solutions are explored as students assume roles as the slob-like father and kids. It seems like play, but serious thinking is produced.

In the real world, the rule is "I hear what you say but I believe what you do." Research on muggers shows how they pick out victims by "reading" their body language. A limp or stagger nonverbally communicates vulnerability. Drama permits students to extend the ways they send messages and the ability to understand nuances. Students learn how a small gesture, body posture, or a person's gait can communicate hesitancy, excitement, or fear.

Drama involvement increases fluency in verbal language and nonverbal communication—use of body and face "language." They learn to match words with actions as they do focused work in pantomime and scenes requiring speaking in different roles.

## Increases Agility with Creative Problem Solving

*You can't depend on your judgment when your imagination is out of focus.* (Mark Twain)

Studies show drama can boost verbal and visual creative thinking in diverse groups from the young to the disadvantaged (Deasy, 2002; Karioth, 1967). How? Drama changes the classroom from a place where students are told what to do, to a place where thinking for yourself is a high priority. AI teachers learn to coach students to move from dull literal pantomimes into exciting dramas. Key is introducing problems for students to solve creatively. Instead of directing children to pantomime a squirrel gathering nuts, teachers ask students to mime a squirrel gathering nuts with something sticky on its paws. The conflict transforms an entertaining activity into a full problem-solving experience.

It is not surprising that students involved in provocative drama work increase their CPS skills. Students are coached to imagine, make hypotheses, test out solutions, evaluate ideas, and redefine problems using questions: "What are all the ways to show how Jack felt as he climbed the beanstalk each time?" "How can we show the meanings of the word *contrite*, using body, face, or one line spoken in a role?" "What if Cinderella didn't want to marry the prince because she fell in love with the doorman?" These are invitations to think about "what if" and experiment with possibilities. The seeds are sown for children to grow into adults who look at problems more flexibly—from alternative viewpoints and with respect for diverse solutions.

## Enhances Feelings of Well-Being

*Improvisation is a way of achieving identity.* (Alfred Nieman)

Drama allows students to express feelings under the protection of pretend. This safety permits therapeutic release of pent-up emotions. It is liberating for a child to realize she is not the first person to dislike another and that negative feelings can be channeled in positive ways. Students learn that all people feel a range of emotions they can express appropriately. Positive self-image emerges from repeated successes in drama problem-solving situations that call for control of body and words to express ideas and feelings effectively. This effect is pronounced for special populations (Deasy, 2002).

## Develops Empathy

Multiple studies confirm that drama causes students to understand character motivations and come to identify with characters at a deep level (Deasy, 2002; Lushington, 2003). This happens as students get deeply involved in assuming character roles drawing upon the senses (smell, taste, touch, vision, hearing, movement, and even sense of humor). When these combine with emotions and imagery, the result is greater perspective and total empathy. The meaning of empathy goes beyond sympathy. It involves "becoming" another person by feeling what another feels and thinking what another thinks.

For example, during a Civil War study, students demonstrated deep involvement with in-role "I statements" from different perspectives: "I saw smoke puff out of cannons so thick it looked like they were belching dragons." "I heard the nurse crying and I knew the man in the cot next to me had died of his gut wound." "I smelled burning grass as we torched the town." "I felt the stiffness in my good leg as I hobbled the final mile on a stick." "I couldn't stop laughing when I saw my wife come out on the porch as I walked up the dirt road of our farm." This kind of lived-through experience results in new viewpoints not possible through logic alone. By walking a mile in another's shoes, students develop tolerance and respect. They are less likely to hate or destroy those who behave, think, or feel differently.

## Promotes Reflection on Moral Issues and Values

As in life, the core of drama is conflict. Schaffner explains that drama "puts back the human content into what is predominantly a materialistic curriculum" (quoted in Deasy, 2002, p. 50). Drama permits students to become conscious of their values as during work through curricular and social problems. New values and beliefs become the end products as they work out problems using role taking.

A rule of thumb is to not impose values during drama. Instead, exploration and discussion is encouraged as students confront issues about rightness, wrongness, goodness, and badness in literature, math, science, and social studies. Dissonance is to be expected as students sort out their thoughts and feelings.

This is not to imply that teachers are to be value neutral. On the contrary, all teachers should clearly support universal values for honesty, truth, hard work, courage, integrity, and respect for others. Few lessons are valueless, making it nearly impossible to teach anything without addressing values. Drama places this sensitive and important area in a workable context. Even religious issues and religion itself become focal points, which is essential in coming to understand cultures; imagine trying to comprehend the Middle East without studying its many religious values.

## Builds Social Skills

Success in the world of work and family life demands extensive social skill, which makes this area a curricular priority. Teachers may complain that students cannot work in groups, as if this is a good reason to avoid group work. However, no teacher would argue that students who cannot read should not be taught to read. Cooperation can be taught as well. But teaching has to go beyond telling.

Drama is a key teaching tool with a track record of increasing peer interaction, social relationships, and conflict resolution skills (Deasy, 2002), because drama is a group art. Actors depend on one another and work together. Drama sets up ideal circumstances for team building—misfits and loners, along with the popular and the gregarious, must collaborate. Students develop active listening skills as they seek diverse problem solutions.

Drama integration eases students into group work by starting with pairs and trios. At first drama is more teacher directed with greater controls present. For example, students are confined to the desk space. As students gain experience they see the value of give and take. They gain respect for the unique ideas of classmates. They learn when and how to listen, and how to speak up without offending.

As students research hunger, poverty, and homelessness in preparation for roles, their awareness of social problems grows, too. As audience members for performances, students gain social knowledge as actors invite them into a staged world where they can vicariously live through plays dealing with social issues of every sort. Students are thus able to participate in the real world more fully because they have "played in the imagined" (Heathcote & Bolton, 1995).

## Contributes to Aesthetic Development

*Reason can answer questions but imagination has to ask them.* (Albert Einstein)

Drama and theatre provide rich opportunities for the Stendhal effect, the "ah" experience of being touched or moved (Lushington, 2003). Maslow calls these experiences "aesthetic" and places the need for them at the top of his motivation pyramid. Aesthetic needs for beauty and deep understanding are never completely filled, so they are perpetual motivators for learning. Since "drama integrates everything" (Chuck Tuttle, Chattanooga Theatre), its beauty-making is amplified many fold. The power of music, art, dance, and literature are brought together in theatre and drama, making them invaluable teaching tools.

The *National Standards for the Arts* set goals for students to understand the art of theatre and to learn about dramatic structure involving conflict and characters. Standards-based lessons cause students to deepen aesthetic sensory awareness and learn to express themselves through the artistic use of pantomime, dialogue, and improvisation.

## Is an Avenue to Understanding in All Curricular Areas

Drama is a learning tool grounded in informed exploration and discovery. It draws on innate abilities, especially the desire to try out different roles, that is, to pretend. We associate actors and acting with drama; it is *action* that makes drama captivating. Children want to do. We should welcome student action since we certainly do not need more passive citizens, but we also do not want children to grow up taking action without information and reflection. Drama creates a safety net to catch students when decisions are unwise. This net is made by a conscientious planful teacher who is knowledgeable about drama strategies and willing to adapt them for specific student needs.

Drama motivates students to learn any content from the bones of the body to levels of government. It is a powerful meaning-making tool to steer through a sea of curricular skills and facts. Dull information gains relevance as students take roles as nurse, mayor, parent, and scientist, and solve problems. Fascinating details of history, such as the use school dunce caps, no longer distract as they are treated as clues to understanding important life messages (Mantione & Smead, 2003). During drama, students explore character motives and actions in literature that define their relationships to one another (social studies) and to the world (science).

## Makes the Invisible Visible for Assessment

Concepts such as the structure of a cell or the movement of electrons are abstract. Understanding hinges on making them concrete or "image-able." Drama does this. It brings ideas and feelings to life in observable and audible ways using the body, face, and voice to "externalize" what is hidden in the mind. Drama offers an alternative way for students to show what they know and can do. It can also be used to preview or review a lesson allowing teachers to observe student performances and obtain assessment information to direct subsequent instruction.

Assessment needs to give accurate information about how students think. Pantomime and verbal improvisation are valuable means for students to demonstrate concepts and skills learned in any subject area. Once externalized through drama, the teacher and students can scrutinize the work together for evidence of meeting curricular goals. For example, students might be asked to write to a friend, in the role of Charles Drew, to explain scientific work. This kind of written role taking promotes depth of understanding through personal involvement. It also yields a document that shows how much was learned about scientific concepts.

## Drama Is Fun-damental

Over the door of a school in Richmond, Virginia, is a stone carving that reads, "Thou Shalt Have Fun." While many educators feel uncomfortable justifying inclusion of anything in curricula just because it is fun, it cannot be denied that fun is fundamental to happiness. One goal of education has to be to help students be happy (Noddings, 2005). Fun and entertainment help us forget, enable us to cope by giving respite from problems, and provide enjoyment—a state of elation, upliftedness, or joy that gives energy and hope.

We should not dismiss the importance of fun in learning, and drama is definitely fun. The word *play* is linked to theatre and drama. We go to plays and in theatre "the play is the thing." In drama, *play* is also a verb. Drama harnesses our natural motivations to play and shows students how to shape experiences (Lushington, 2003). Students have fun taking roles, solving problems, doing interesting things, learning new skills, working with people, meeting challenges, moving around, and making discoveries. Compare these aspects of fun with what we want to happen each day at school. Back to basics sounds pretty good if it means a return to fundamentals: *fun* plus *mental* work that is engaging, like that of drama.

# Building Block II: Arts Literacy: Drama Content and Skills

*I believe that every child I meet understands deep, basic matters worthy of exploration but they may as yet have no language for them. One of the languages they may develop is through dramatic work.* (Dorothy Heathcote)

## What Do Teachers Need to Know?

Successful arts integration depends on teacher knowledge and skill. Even if a drama specialist is on staff, classroom teachers need basic drama/theatre literacy and a repertoire of strategies to teach students how to create and express meaning through drama. INTASC (2002) is one source of what teachers need to know and be able to do in the arts. Those standards can be accessed at www.ccsso.org/Projects/interstate_new_teacher_assessment_and_ support_consortium/. Of course, the necessary level of teacher knowledge is governed by what students are expected to know and do. That falls under the *National Standards for the Arts* (see Ready Reference 8.4 later in this chapter).

These two standards documents are sources for drama/theatre arts knowledge base addressed in this section and include the following:

- Definitions of and background on drama and theatre
- Drama elements
- Drama processes/skills
- People: roles and careers
- Styles, forms, and genres (kinds) of drama and theatre (e.g., tragedy, comedy, musicals)
- Source of noteworthy works
- General approaches and specific teaching strategies
- Curricular connections, including overlapping standards with those in the *National Standards for the Arts*

**Classroom Drama: History and Pioneers.**   In recent decades, drama has become increasingly integral to the curriculum. In particular, drama has been embraced by those who teach the communication arts, but it has gained wide acceptance in science and social studies instruction, as well (Maxim, 2010). The following is a brief look at some of the people who made it happen. What they created, decades ago, is now called "classroom drama" which balances performance and process.

**Winifred Ward: Performance Focus.**   During the early 20th century, Winifred Ward started a program in Illinois schools that combined children's literature with drama. She used movement, pantomime, dialogue, and characterization activities. She believed performance was vital to child development and could be supported by simple to complex drama work. Her work is so respected that she is called the "mother of creative drama." In the decades after Ward's successes, other teachers and researchers in the United States and the United Kingdom were drawn to drama's educational potential to influence learning.

**Brian Way: Process Focus.**   Not everyone agreed with Ward about the importance of performance. Brian Way and others focused on the drama *process*. Way uses students' personal experiences to lead them to self-discovery and encourages teachers to "sneak" drama into the classroom, even for 5 minutes each day. His approach opposes teacher demonstration because he argues that acting skills are unnecessary for drama participation. Life events are used as the stimulus, with few performances and little focus on evaluation.

**Dorothy Heathcote: Problem-Solving Approach.**   It took a British woman to unite process and performance. Heathcote is now respected as the world's "preeminent classroom drama expert" (Catterall in Deasy, 2002, p. 58). In her approach, students are engaged in problem solving about life experiences. They reflect, analyze, and test out conclusions in the safe circumstances of an imagined, but authentic, context. Students are thrust into a sink-or-swim situation, with the support of teacher–leader, who is also a significant participant. Students learn theatre craft, history, and place of theatre in our lives, given "as if it were" drama to motivate study. They create plays, and perform for audiences. Heathcote's approach has taken center stage in designing classroom drama that connects to curricular areas (Wagner, 1999).

**Cecily O'Neill: Real-World Reflection.**   O'Neill shares Heathcote's philosophy and has extended it for American educators. O'Neill discourages reliance on drama games and exercises. She focuses on causing students to create dramatic roles in different contexts, which she considers the essentials of drama (O'Neill, 1995). Her goal is to not have students escape from the real world, but to reflect on it.

**Viola Spolin: Focus on Seeing and Doing.**   Spolin (1999, 2001) has the distinction of authoring two popular books among drama educators and teachers. She emphasizes getting participants to see and do, not just imagine or feel. Her goals are to have students lose all inhibition and learn intuitively. Her books of theatre games, also used in actor training, remain favorites.

**Geraldine Siks: Embedded in Language Arts.**   Siks (1983) placed drama in the categories of both art and the language arts, where it is found today in most curricula. Her major focus is on students' creative and expressive skills. Students learn to be audience members, players, and playmakers. Most importantly, students learn to problem solve through taking different roles.

**Defining Classroom Drama.**   Putting on rehearsed plays a few times a year is product oriented. The focus of this book, and most drama integration, is process drama—the use of drama concepts and skills to cause students to restructure content information, in other words, to transform it. On occasion, scripts are memorized, but process drama is used on a daily basis as a mainstay teaching tool, like writing is used. This chapter concentrates on creative or classroom process drama because of its successful track record to reform teaching and learning.

According to drama educator Ruth Heinig (1993), *creative drama* is the term most widely used in the United States to describe the kind of drama used in AI. Creative drama is more structured than the dramatic play in which children naturally engage. Other terms such as *improvisation, role playing, informal drama, drama in education (DIE), process drama,* and *educational drama* are used in Great Britain and other countries, some of which have a particular emphasis. For example, DIE invites students to project themselves into a "moment in time"; they learn more about a topic after first exploring it through drama (Heinig, 1993, p. 4).

The American Alliance for Theatre and Education (AATE) defines creative drama as "an improvisational, non-exhibitional, process-centered form of drama in which participants are guided by a leader to imagine, enact, and reflect upon human experiences" (*www.aate.com*). In contrast, theatre is performance: The emphasis is on a spectacle for an audience. Drama and theatre share basic structures, but "theatre is concerned with communication between actors and audience; drama is concerned with the experience of the participants, irrespective of the audience" (Way in Rosenberg, 1987, p. 31). Brian Way worries that the creativity of young children may actually be undermined by emphasis on viewing formal theatre.

Creative classroom drama is participant and process centered, with a teacher or leader guiding students though explorations of personal experiences, social issues, pieces of literature, and other curricular materials and topics. Children improvise action and dialogue and use drama elements during the process.

They are directed to imaginatively use voice, body, and space to make others believe in a mood, idea, or message. Creative problem solutions are sought from the perspective of "pretend" roles. Unlike role-playing for therapeutic reasons, classroom drama's purposes are artistic, emotional, social, and academic.

## Drama Elements

*Imagination is more important than knowledge.* (Albert Einstein)

Drama is a slice of every person's struggle to deal with conflict. As with every art, it has its own special "language" used to create and express/perform ideas and feelings. Drama shares much with literature. Characters (1) encounter problems, (2) in a specific setting, and (3) take action to resolve the problems. The main difference is that drama brings characters to life through actors and acting. A real or imagined stage is the setting or the space where the characters play out the action for an audience. Students study character motives and explore how to show them in ways that make characters seem real. Vocabulary and conceptual knowledge is increased as students figure out how to take roles and convince, convert, coax, sell, feud, or bargain.

**Characters.** Actors portray human and nonhuman roles and initiate and carry out the plot (action). The main character must be believable and care about what happens. This is the hero or protagonist who must face life, make decisions, and accept consequences. In drama, characters are created through actions, words, and what others say or how they react. When characters talk with each other, they use *dialogue*. Pantomime is free, creative, and mindful movement with no talking. It is used to express ideas and feelings through actions using the face and body.

**Conflict.** As with literature, there must be a conflict or problem that motivates characters to make decisions and take action. Conflict sets plot in motion and should create suspense and tension. There are four types of conflict: (1) between a character and natural forces, like the weather, (2) between a character and societal rules or institutions (the farm rule that runt pigs are slaughtered in *Charlotte's Web*), (3) between a character and another character, such as the other girls against a poor Polish girl in *The Hundred Dresses* (Estes), and (4) within a character as with Ramona who constantly struggles against her proclivity for misunderstanding situations. A fifth type of conflict may also occur, especially in science fiction, between a character and technology, such as in *The Wretched Stone* (Van Allsburg), a tale about problems created by a mesmerizing rock that glows blue like a TV screen.

**Plot.** The sequence of events set in motion by a problem or conflict creates the plot. The simplest plot structure has a beginning, middle, and end in a linear pattern. Action rises to a climax and falls as problems are resolved.

**Setting.** Time and place provide a context for action, which make up the setting. In drama this is a space with both imagined and real objects.

**Mood.** The feel of a piece is called the mood. It is created by the setting (time, lighting, music, description of the place), pace, and characters' use of word and body.

Ready Reference 8.2 summarizes the elements of drama.

**Drama Skills and Processes.** Drama is used to create and express meaning, just like visual art, music and dance, and reading and writing. The primary media, however, are the body, mind, and voices of people. The processes used to create drama come from the inside of a person and are brought to the outside or the reverse. For example, pounding on a table can produce anger and cause the emotion to "seep" into a person. What is shown during drama with the body, face, gestures, and words reflects thoughts and feelings taken in through the senses. To make drama, a person must concentrate, sense, perceive, imagine, and think; the physical body and speech communicate these inner processes.

Students need certain skills to create and understand drama. What's more, creative and artistic work depends on being in an

## Ready Reference 8.2  Drama Elements

Also see Ready Reference 4.3 on literary elements.

***Actors*** assume roles of characters.
***Space*** is where the action happens.
***Audience*** views the action and sometimes interacts with the actors.
***Conflict*** sets the plot/action in motion and creates suspense and tension. Five types:

1. Between a character/nature
2. Between a character/societal rules or institutions
3. Between a character and another character
4. Within a character (internal conflict)
5. Between a character and technology

***Characters/actors*** initiate and carry out the plot (action). Must be believable and care about what happens.

***Created through:*** actions, words, and what others say or how they react. When characters talk with each other, they use dialogue. When no words are used, drama takes the form of pantomime.
***Protagonist:*** main character or hero, who must face life, make decisions, and accept consequences.
***Plot*** is the sequence of events set in motion by a problem or conflict. The structure is beginning, middle, and end.
***Setting*** consists of the "created" time and place for action in a specific space.
***Mood*** is the feel created by the setting (time, lighting, music, place), pace, characters' use of words and body, among others.

environment that offers freedom with limits. In such a context students need practice with the building blocks of the art form—drama in this case. Drama elements are tools, as are skills and processes. All serve to assist in creative problem solving that seeks new personal meanings.

Ready Reference 8.3 summarizes basic drama skills and processes that focus on learning to control mind, body, and voice when taking roles during acting, although drama is certainly not confined to a narrow view of acting. Students can be involved in reading scripts (e.g., reader's theatre) and writing scripts based on real and imagined experiences. The script form is also an option for transforming any curricular material. Drama involves students in designing spaces (backdrops, sets) and simple costumes (e.g., scarves, hats), directing, and researching to gather information. Because drama is mostly a group endeavor, students learn collaborative problem solving, including how to give and receive feedback. Of particular importance is learning to change one's behavior based on self-evaluation.

Finally, while drama is process oriented, performance happens often in the form of peer audiences. Pairs perform for pairs or small groups perform for other groups. Sometimes groups perform for the rest of the class, and occasionally performances happen for outside audiences, especially other classes. This means students need to learn audience etiquette—how to attend, listen, and respond appropriately to performances.

**Styles, Forms, and Genre.** Theatre uses drama but drama doesn't always result in theatre. Theatre is about creating spectacle for an audience. Classroom drama engages student in the creative problem-solving process in a special way. The results of the process may or may not become a spectacle.

The kinds or forms of drama and theatre addressed in this book are: (1) improvisation using body, mind, and voice; (2) pantomime—nonverbal, creative, mindful movement to express ideas and feelings with the face and body; (3) reader's theatre; (4) storytelling; and (5) limited use of plays and scripts.

As with literature, theatre and drama can be tragic or comic, fiction or nonfiction. Any genre of literature can be transformed

through drama. The pinnacle of theatre is live performances and while not everyone can regularly take in a Broadway play, most communities have available live theatre. Teachers who integrate the arts owe it to themselves to see live theatre including special genres, such as musical theatre, which was born in America. Next best are the spectacular films we've all become accustomed to, in every genre from film noir to westerns. Of course, television also offers some excellent drama—and a lot that falls far short.

**People.**   People can take a vast range of roles in drama and theatre beyond acting. Career opportunities that can be integrated into many units include playwright, director, set and costume designer, sound and light technician, critic, historian, filmmaker, and teacher. Noteworthy people in the field can be foci of study as well. Of course, William Shakespeare appears on every list.

**Noteworthy Works.**   Books by Dorothy Heathcote, Viola Spolin, and Ruth Heinig are "must-have" practical resources for works and teaching ideas. Consult a children's drama specialist at your school or a local college for sources of scripts. The following are good for starters.

Aaron Shephard's website (*www.aaronshep.com/storytelling/*) offers free scripts. His newest book is *Stories on Stage* (2005). He also published *Folktales on Stage: Children's Plays for Reader's Theatre,* which includes 16 scripts from many cultures.

Wolfman's *Stories for Reader's Theatre* (2004) includes multicultural scripts with favorite tales like *Millions of Cats.*

Jenning's *Theatre for Young Audiences: Twenty Great Plays for Children* (2005) is an example of an anthology based on books such as *Charlotte's Web.* One website to order play scripts is (*http://childrenstheatre.easystorecreator.com/welcome.htm.*

**Approaches and Teaching Strategies.**   The approaches of Dorothy Heathcote and others each represent diverse goals for drama, teacher roles, stimuli for drama, and activities in which students are engaged. In this book, ideas from all the approaches previously described have been chosen for their appropriateness to meaningful AI. On the process/performance

---

**Ready Reference 8.3**   Dramatic Skills and Processes

*Acting skills:* taking roles, pretending, improvising using:
  *Body:* controlling and using the body to respond and express ideas and feeling. Includes use of appropriate energy, displaying sensory awareness, gestures, and facial expressions.
  *Mind:* using different kinds of thinking and feeling, especially:
    *Imagination:* creative problem solving that results in unique ideas, elaboration on ideas, and spontaneous thinking
    *Focus:* concentration, staying involved, making others believe in the realness of the character, following directions
  *Voice:* speaking clearly and fluently using appropriate variety in volume, rate, tone and pitch, pause, stress; ability to improvise dialogue

*Script writing:* transformation of personal experiences or curricular material into specific written forms
*Designing spaces and costumes:* basic sets and costumes
*Directing:* organizing performances
*Researching:* data gathering for background
*Evaluation:* giving feedback, using suggestions, self-evaluating, and adapting own behavior
*Social skills:* cooperation, conflict resolution, active listening, and responding
*Audience etiquette:* attending, listening, and responding appropriately to performances

teeter-totter, process is the heavier party in AI. Performance is used primarily, like any assessment product, to motivate, as well as demonstrate understanding.

Basically, in classroom drama the teacher's role is to guide students, using questioning and coaching, to define problems, improvise solutions, try out ideas, reflect, and evaluate. Drama knowledge is directly taught when students need tools to transform science, social studies, math, and literacy material into dramatic forms. While classroom drama does not dwell on student performances, teachers plan time for regular group sharing, at times, especially within the class. Classroom drama can be simple or complex; Spolin's theatre games and simple pantomimes are accepted as valuable drama work, as is Ward's story drama and Heathcote's in-depth explorations for personal meaning and perspective.

Successful drama integration usually begins with a few minutes a day. Eventually drama can be meaningfully integrated in science, social studies, language arts, and math. Gradual, thoughtful implementation ensures that justice is done to both drama/theatre (as an art) and as a teaching tool for learning content and skills in other academic areas. At times, teachers may have the luxury of being able to do drama lessons for an hour or longer, connected to units, like Sarah Lane did in the opening snapshot. Eventually drama can be used in the same way reading and writing are used—as vehicles for communicating ideas and feelings about learning. Even at its most humble level, the goal is to design drama-based lessons that are more than a series of isolated activities.

# Building Block III: Collaborative Planning

*Drama ... can be a mirror, a magnifying glass, a microscope or a searchlight.* (Cecily O'Neill)

## Meaningful Connections

Some insist drama can be used to teach any subject more effectively (McCaslin, 1990). Early in unit and lesson planning, the search for natural ways to engage students in CPS is bound to find drama as a partner. The goal, however, is *two-way* transfer: using drama for its learning potential, but also ensuring that students gain specific drama knowledge and skills. Next are examples of common links that are inevitably uncovered (also see Ready Reference 1.1).

**Literacy.** Drama and the language arts (speaking, listening, reading, and writing) share many goals. These include becoming skilled at verbal and nonverbal communication. Educators now consider drama and theatre to be central to the English language arts curriculum, because evidence shows that significant involvement in drama/theatre improves literacy skills (Deasy, 2002; Deasy & Stevenson, 2005; Palmarini, 2005). Drama can increase writing prolixity and reading comprehension, and improve oral expression. It seems likely that dramatic knowledge and skill is also increased by pairing it with literacy instruction; certain areas (e.g., playwriting) cannot disconnect drama and language arts literacy.

**Literature.** Literature and drama share most of the same elements from a focus on using tension or conflict to propel the plot to characters and setting. Their natural compatibility and both drama and literature understanding can be increased through integration.

**Science and Social Studies.** Since the progressive education movement began, integration of drama with other curricular areas has been popular. Dorothy Heathcote clearly demonstrates how learning can be given depth and breadth through drama integration, especially in science and social studies in the videos, "Dorothy Heathcote Talks to Teachers–Parts I and II," each about 30 minutes. In lieu of putting on plays with memorized lines, Heathcote helps children make sense of their relationships with each other (social studies) and the natural world (science) by causing them to reflect on life experiences.

**Other Potential Connections.** Some connections seem obvious—history of theatre and drama, science and math of theatre (e.g., stage construction, makeup), economics of theatre productions, and psychology (e.g., drama therapy). Not to be ignored are the vast connections to multicultural understanding gained from the works of playwrights and filmmakers. Then there is the concept that all of life demands skill at shifting in and out of roles, and varying use of body, thinking/imagination, and voice to suit specific circumstances. It could be argued that drama and life are inseparable, with success hinging on mindful and artful role taking.

# The National Standards for the Arts: American Goals

When a teacher signs a contract in a school district, he agrees to teach to standards and goals adopted by the board of education. Standards and goals in curriculum frameworks help teachers know *what* to teach, but do not explain *how* to teach. Teachers are hired with the expectation that they know current instructional methodology for planning, teaching, managing/disciplining, and assessing. Teachers are also expected to be able to select materials and adapt lessons for diverse student needs. For arts-based schools, that means teachers need a level of arts literacy and knowledge of best practices in each art form to teach through the arts.

Standards, and benchmarks that lead up to them, are desired goals, not material to be "covered" (McTighe & O'Connor, 2005). This implies teachers should plan with standards in hand but be selective. Meaningful integrated units and sequenced lesson plans are ones customized for specific students, and usually go far beyond the standards. Districts now expect teachers to specify connections between lessons and standards, so they are specified in Planning Pages in this book. In addition, it is just good teaching to make goals and objectives clear to students at the lesson outset; it is wise to communicate goals/standards to parents as well.

The *National Standards for the Theatre* (Ready Reference 8.4) can be viewed at *http://artsedge.kennedy-center.org/teach/standards/*. For permissions, go to *http://menc.org*. For examples of state-level arts standards, go to state departments of education websites. Many have useful documents, including Ohio, Kentucky, South

## Ready Reference 8.4 National Standards for Theater (K–8)

*Overall focus:* Learn about life, pretend and assume roles, develop socially, interact with peers, bring stories to life, direct one another, improvise, write, act, design, compare forms, analyze, evaluate, understand the world (history, cultures).

1. *Script writing by planning and recording improvisations based on personal experience and heritage, imagination, literature and history (K–4), and by creation of improvisations and scripted scenes based on personal experience and heritage, imagination, literature, and history (grades 5–8).* Example activities: Create classroom dramatizations; improvise dialogues to tell a story.

2. *Acting by assuming roles and interacting in improvisations (K–4) and by developing basic acting skills to portray characters who interact in improvised and scripted scenes (grades 5–8).* Example activities: Clearly show characters; use concentration and body and vocal elements to express characters; dramatize personal stories.

3. *Designing by visualizing and arranging environments for classroom dramatizations (K–4) and by developing environments for improvised and scripted scenes (grades 5–8).* Example activities: Use art media and techniques to make settings; organize materials for dramatic play.

4. *Directing by planning classroom dramatizations (K–4) and by organizing rehearsals for improvised and scripted scenes (grades 5–8).* Example activities: Plan a class play; use drama elements and skills; play the roles of director, writer, designer, and actor.

5. *Researching by finding information to support classroom dramatizations (K–4) and by using cultural and historical information to support improvised and scripted scenes (grades 5–8).* Example activities: Find literature to adapt for classroom drama (books, poems, songs, any material usable for plays); research time periods and cultures for dramatic material.

6. *Comparing and connecting art forms by describing theater, dramatic media (such as film, television, and electronic media), and other art forms (K–4). Comparing and incorporating art forms by analyzing methods of presentation and audience response for theater, dramatic media (such as film, television, and electronic media), and other art forms (grades 5–8).* Example activities: Compare how the different arts communicate ideas; describe visual, aural, oral, and kinetic elements of theater.

7. *Analyzing and explaining personal preferences and constructing meanings from classroom dramatizations and from theater, film, television, and electronic media productions (K–4). Analyzing, evaluating, and constructing meanings from improvised and scripted scenes and from theater, film, television, and electronic media productions (grades 5–8).* Example activities: Evaluate performances using specific criteria; explain characters' wants and needs.

8. *Understanding context by recognizing the role of theater, film, television, and electronic media in daily life (K–4). Understanding context by analyzing the role of theater, film, television, and electronic media in the community and other cultures (grades 5–8).* Example activities: Web ideas for why theater is created; attend performances and discuss what is learned about culture, history, and life from theater.

---

*Source:* Content Standards (material printed in bold type) excerpted from the *National Standards for Arts Education*, published by Music Educators National Conference (MENC). Copyright © 1994 by MENC. Reprinted with permission. The complete National Standards and related materials are available from MENC: The National Association for Music Education, 1806 Robert Fulton Drive, Reston, VA 20191 (telephone: 800-336-3768).

Carolina, and North Carolina. Connecticut includes theatre/drama standards and gives sample lesson ideas and assessment alternatives (www.state.ct.us/sde/dtl/curriculum/currkey3.htm).

## Unit Planning

Ready References 3.6 and 3.7 outline how to plan AI units and lessons. The first phase is collecting documents that clarify what students should know and be able to do. That includes local, state, and national standards for drama and theatre. While drama and theatre are not the same, the national standards include drama concepts and skills under the category of theatre. Ready Reference 8.4 lists eight standards related to drama that students are expected to meet. All the drama strategies and activities in this book relate to one or more of these standards.

Standards documents and local courses of study provide sources for drama content and guide teachers in choosing drama skills that mesh with other units being planned. A goal is for students to grow in their drama knowledge and skill. Abuse occurs when students know no more about drama at the end of the lesson than they did at the beginning. "Peppering" lessons with role taking is not sufficient (Palmarini, 2005, p. 3).

**Unit Centers.** Any of the five integrated unit centers or bodies can be used to teach school district requirements in math, reading and language arts, science, and social studies, as well as in the arts of music, art, drama, dance, and literature. Drama-based lessons and units can focus on one or more traditional subject areas. For example, a literature-based study of an author/illustrator (e.g., Byrd Baylor) can use drama and the other arts, along with math, science, social studies, and reading/language arts, as "legs" to support the unit. Drama would be a learning tool in such a unit, just as any other leg. An adaptation of this idea is to envision a unit with drama as the body with focus on the following:

1. Person (actor, playwright, director, author, artist)
2. Particular genre or form (improvisation, reader's theatre, comedy)
3. Problem or topic (e.g., censorship)
4. Book, poem, song, or play (e.g., *Hamlet*)
5. Event, such as a trip to see a play at a local theatre

The major concepts and skills in math, science, social studies, literacy, and the other art forms are used as support legs. Planning Page 6.14 shows an example of a unit planning web. Later in the chapter, Planning Page 8.8 shows drama strategies planned during a literature-based unit on author/artist Patricia Polacco and her books.

**Accommodating Interests.** Well-planned units are designed to draw on interests. Drama adds many options for developing interests. For example, in Heathcote's approach, drama-based lessons begin with identifying a point of great interest, tension, or conflict in a unit under study. To get to this point, she begins with discussions to elicit students' ideas, which yields a lesson focus. She then recommends that the teacher take the role of a character and engage students who assume roles. Teachers can step out of role to clarify directions or redirect thinking. Current events, moral and ethical problems, universal themes and questions, and the cognitive and affective domains become grist for the drama mill.

**Theatre Events.** Going to see a play is the most common event at the center of a drama-based unit and can be initiating or culminating events. Live theatre experiences have countless values, not the least of which is the opportunity to introduce children to an aesthetic form of entertainment they can enjoy for the rest of their lives. Without school trips to see live performances, many children only experience in-house assemblies. There is also a sense of occasion in going to the theatre—ritual and ceremony that children need to grow aesthetically.

Field trips to see *children's* theatre have the potential to develop aesthetic sensibilities and promote educational aims, including development of social awareness. Just as with other field trips, theatre experiences should align with curricular goals and be integral to the unit's messages. Lessons are needed to prepare for the trip and to follow up. See Appendix H for before, during, and after guidelines for field trips. With regard to theatre and drama, students need to understand the following:

- Live performances are different from video or television dramas, largely because the audience shares in the event and there is a feeling of spontaneity. The more the audience gives to the actors, the more the actors can give back to the audience.
- Audience etiquette is expected at any theatre so everyone can enjoy the performance and to show respect for the actors. Discuss issues such as talking, rattling paper, kicking seat backs, and other problem behaviors. Teach students when to applaud, when to stand, what an ovation means, and what happens if you arrive late to a play.
- The play will have characters, plot, conflict, and setting. Introduce such special vocabulary along with *set, costume, stage left, stage right,* and so on.
- Theatres are set up in different ways. Discuss the seating sections (e.g., orchestra, balcony).
- The styles or forms of the production are important. Is it musical theatre? Comedy? Will there be monologues?
- *Note:* Cue sheets or "look-fors" help students know ahead what they will see and hear. Students are more likely to experience a sense of discovery about the set, costumes, and

characters when they are prepared. Ask the theatre for materials ahead of time that have this kind of information. If not, check the Internet for background on the play.

After the play, it is helpful to have a discussion and, just as in literature discussions, it is important to encourage a variety of viewpoints. Some useful questions include: "What did you see? How did it make you feel? What in the play made you feel that way? What was important in the play? What was it really about? What was missing? What was the playwright trying to say?" Of course, this is a perfect time for drama-related activities; for example, ask students to do tableaux of important scenes.

**Two-Pronged Lesson Format.** All units are delivered through a sequence of lessons. One way to ensure that drama is made integral is to use the two-pronged format. Planning Page 8.5 offers an example. Because lessons may integrate several art forms, two prongs is certainly a minimum. Teachers must decide, in the case of multiart integration, which arts will be the focus for teaching *about* and *in* the art. Everything cannot be taught and assessed in every lesson.

# Building Block IV: Aesthetic Learning Environment

Aesthetic classrooms and schools create a supportive learning environment through physical and psychological means. Some schools, such as Lady's Island in Beaufort, South Carolina, managed to remodel to accommodate drama and dance spaces, but in reality, a stage can be any open space. Classrooms can be arranged with desks in a U shape or grouped to create an open area. If these are not options, then the students can "push back the desks" or go outside. Asking local carpet stores to donate samples can create a free or inexpensive carpeted area. Double-sided carpet tape can be used to secure squares. However the space is set up, it needs to be there. Giving space for drama shows that it is a priority. Drama is too important to not make space.

In addition to space, basic materials are needed. Drama is actually quite cheap. Scarves, hats, paper, socks—these are all simple objects that can be used as props for improvisation. An old trunk filled with these kinds of objects makes a class treasure chest. A video camera and tape player are wonderful to capture drama so students can enjoy and do self-assessment. Cameras are often shared by groups of teachers in arts-based schools.

The teacher determines most of the ethos of a classroom, and whose mood "makes the weather." A teacher can crush or liberate creative thinking without a single word. The medium of drama is the person. It is risky to put yourself out there. In a classroom where the teacher creates an inviting climate and openly values creative thinking, students will take chances that make for good problem solving and great drama. The aesthetic environment discussed in Chapter 3 lays a foundation for dramatic work to emerge. Students who have a teacher who is always ready to think of "what if" and do "let's pretend" have the drama advantage. Ready Reference 2.6 summarizes CPS, and Ready References 2.7 and 2.8 list creative boosters and blockers.

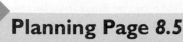

## Planning Page 8.5

### Drama and Science (Primary Grades)

*Two-Pronged Focus:* (1) Drama elements and skills: *pantomime* with focus on control, display of sensory awareness, use of gestures and face, and responding to nonverbal communications of others; focus and concentration; following directions. (2) Science concepts: components of habitat and effects on animals.

*Theatre Standards:* 2, 5, and 7 (see Ready Reference 8.4)

*Student Objectives:* Student will be able to:

1. Use body and face to show specific components of habitats (food, water, shelter, and space).
2. Concentrate and focus to control body and respond to others; follow oral directions (cues).
3. Predict responses of animals who are missing basic habitat components.

*Teaching Procedure:* The teacher will: (S = students)

**Introduction:**

1. Use Focus Ball to engage focus and concentration.
2. Ask S to list animals and places they live—from previous lessons. Record ideas on a chart (language experience strategy: ask them to spell chorally to help with phonics). Ask what *habitat* means and clarify, as needed.
3. Say today's lesson is about parts of habitats and what happens when a part is missing. Explain *narrative pantomime* (NP) will be used to show animals in their habitats. Ask what makes drama (drama elements/skills posted). Ask which drama uses no words (pantomime).
4. Do a series of Show Me pantomimes with focus on use of face: happy, thinking, worried, hungry. Repeat with whole body (at desk area). Divide class in half. Each half gives the other feedback on what they did that showed concentration and focus.

**Development:**

1. Put first habitat card in pocket chart: food. Read chorally and ask about foods in different habitats. Use a few S examples and stop and pantomime different animals eating those foods. Give descriptive feedback on body and face (shapes, movements, sizes) used to show the animal. Repeat with water, shelter, and space components.
2. Explain that NP is when someone tells a story while others use their faces, bodies, and imagination to show the

story. Review rules about start and stop signals. Tell everyone to find a personal space in the room.

3. Give each a card with an animal name. No one knows it but there are duplicates. Say "When I say 'start,' everyone is to explore ways to show their animal in a variety of ways, such as shape, moves, and size. Stay in your personal spot. At the 'freeze' signal, everyone should stop. Start." Give feedback on focus, concentration, unusual ideas. Repeat in *slow motion.*
4. Use signals for the NP (read slowly):
   You are hungry. You begin to look for *food* in your habitat. You find the kind of food you eat. Slowly you eat your meal. After a while you start to get full and begin to slow down. In an area nearby, you hear a sound and you become afraid. Your body shows you are scared. You look for *shelter* and move there. You watch carefully and you wait, being very still, until you know you are safe. The coast seems to be clear. You are feeling good because you are safe and full of food. You move around your habitat *space* showing you are satisfied. Because you ate so much, you are thirsty. You see *water* nearby and move there and begin to drink. The water is very cold. After a long cool drink, you begin to feel lonely, and you look for another animal like you. You move around noticing how other animals move to see if you can find another of your species. You greet your fellow animal when you find him or her. It has been a long day and you are getting tired. You move slowly to a place of shelter. You begin to get ready to rest. Slowly you drift off to sleep.

**Conclusion/Assessment:**

1. Ask S: What did you think about? What worked? What problems? How did you find another similar animal? Collect cards and repeat with new animals.
2. Brainstorm what might happen if a habitat part, like space, is limited. What if humans build a road through the habitat? Ask what information S needs to show the parts of habitat and animal behavior better. List ideas on the chart.
3. Let S choose an animal to read more about habitat needs (book display). Tell them the class will do a drama Tuesday using what they find; this time the animals will have inadequate habitat components, so there will be problems (conflict).

# Building Block V: Literature as a Core Art Form

Every genre of children's literature offers potential dramatic material. Biography can be particularly useful because the characters are real people in conflict-filled situations. In addition, drama and theatre-based books are available in every genre and on any topic imaginable. For example Allen Say's notable *Kamishibai Man* (2005) is about an elderly Japanese storyteller who relives the days when children flock to hear his stories.

Readers learn about the art of kamishibai, which is storytelling with illustrated cards, the precursor to manga and anime.

There are many drama-based informational books on acting, puppetry, storytelling, reader's theatre, and the history of theatre. There are also timeless pieces of fiction, such as the picture book *Crow Boy* (Yashima), in which a teacher puts a boy on stage and this event changes his life. Of course, there are dozens of books for children about Shakespeare and his plays. Other examples of drama/theatre-based children's books include the following:

Blackwood, G. (1998–2003). *Shakespeare . . .* (series). Dutton.

Blume, J. (1981). *The one in the middle is the green kangaroo.* Yearling.

dePaola, T. (2005). *Stagestruck.* Putnam.

Hoffman, M. (1991). *Amazing Grace.* Dial.

Park, B. (2004). *Junie B., First grader: shipwrecked.* Random House.

Robinson, B. (1972). *The best Christmas pageant ever.* Harper & Row.

Sendak, M. (1976). *Maurice Sendak's really Rosie; Starring the nutshell kids.* Harper & Row.

Suskin, S. (2004). *A must see: The art of broadway theatre.* Chronicle Books.

Van Allsburg, C. (1987). *The A was Zapped: A play in twenty-one acts.* Houghton Mifflin.

Appendix J includes an arts-based bibliography with more examples of drama/theatre-based books. An annotated sampling of literature that can be use *for* drama (pantomime and verbal improvisation) appears in Ready Reference 8.6.

## Ready Reference 8.6    Literature for Drama

See more at the end of Chapter 9, in Appendix J and at MyEducationLab.

### How-to Books

Caruso, S., & Kosoff, S. (1998). *The young actor's book of improvisation: Dramatic situations from Shakespeare to Spielberg, Vol. 1.* Heinemann.

Friedman, L. (2002). *Break a leg!: The kid's guide to acting and stagecraft.* Workman.

Kohl, M. (1999). *Making make-believe: Fun props, costumes and creative play ideas.* Gryphon House.

Stevens, C. (2009). *Magnificent monologues for kid 2.* Sandcastle.

### Literature for Pantomime

Adoff, A. (1995). *Outside/inside poems.* Lothrop, Lee & Shepard. (poems about feelings)

Berger, B. (1996). *Grandfather Twilight.* Putnam. (old man raises the moon)

Bunting, E. (1992). *The wall.* Sandpiper. (boy and father visit the Vietnam War Memorial)

Carle, E. (2008). *The very hungry caterpillar.* Philomel/Putnam. (caterpillar becomes a butterfly; challenge to use a variety of actions to eat; good for flannel board or puppet)

Carroll, L. (2007). *Jabberwocky.* Hyperion. (good for imagining ways to move, e.g., *gyre*)

Chaconas, D. (1970). *The way the tiger walked.* Simon & Schuster. (animals imitate tiger's walk)

Charlip, R. (1993). *Fortunately.* Aladdin. (narrative mime)

Cole, J. (1989). *The magic school bus inside the earth.* Scholastic. (field trips in a microscopic bus; series)

dePaola, T. (1997). *Strega Nona.* Little Simon. (Strega Nona has a magic pot; crowd scenes)

Emberley, B. (2007). *Drummer Hoff.* Library Binding. (cumulative story with mechanical movements)

Gerstein, M. (2008). *Roll over!* Clarion. (animals roll out)

Giff, P. R. (1999). *Today was a terrible day.* San Val. (mime school problems)

Johnson, C. (1998). *Harold and the purple crayon.* HarperCollins. (drawing adventures)

Kahl, V. (2002). *The duchess bakes a cake.* Purple House. (many characters to mime)

Keats, E. J. (2006). *The snowy day.* Weekly Reader. (mime boy's actions)

Kuskin, K. (2008). *The philharmonic gets dressed.* Library Binding. (mime getting ready; conducting)

McCully, E. (1997). *Mirette on the high wire.* Putnam. (girl walks the highwire)

Mendoza, G. (1989). The hairy toe. In G. Mendoza (Ed.), *Hairticklers.* Ten Speed. (choral refrain)

Parish, P. (2010). *Amelia Bedelia bakes off.* HarperCollins. (maid takes instructions literally)

Pinkwater, D. (1993). *The big orange splot.* Scholastic Trade. (interviews and pantomimes)

Ringgold, F. (1996). *Tar beach.* Crown. (girl imagines flying)

Rylant, C. (1994). *All I see.* Scholastic. (boy pretends to paint many things)

Seuss, Dr. (1961). *The Sneetches.* Random House. (machine mime)

Seuss, Dr. (2004). *Horton hatches the egg.* Random House. (choral chant)

Small, D. (1988). *Imogene's antlers.* Dragonfly. (girl grows antlers; family tries to cope)

Tolstoy, A. (2003). *The great big enormous turnip.* Sandpiper. (cumulative tale about pulling up a vegetable)

Van Allsburg, C. (1988). *Two bad ants.* Houghton Mifflin. (ants have adventures)

Wood, A. (1991). *The napping house.* Harcourt Brace. (cumulative)

Zemach, M. (1990). *It could always be worse.* Farrar, Straus & Giroux. (crowded family brings animals into their house)

### Literature for Verbal Activities

Aardema, V. (1992). *Bringing the rain to Kapiti Plain.* Dial. (African cumulative tale)

Aardema, V. (2004). *Why mosquitoes buzz in people's ears.* Dial. (African tale; domino effect of misunderstanding)

Bayer, J. (1992). *My name is Alice.* Puffin. (sequence drama)

Bemelmens, L. (2000). *Madeline.* Viking Penguin. (Madeline lives in a Paris convent)

Bennett, J. (Ed.). (2006). *Noisy poems.* Oxford University Press. (many sounds)

Bodecker, N. M. (1974). *"Let's marry," said the cherry.* Atheneum. (short, rhymed couplets)

Cameron, P. (1961). *"I can't," said the ant.* Coward-McCann. (broken teapot creates problems)

Chess, V. (1979). *Alfred's alphabet walk.* Greenwillow. (Alfred sees things like a "herd of hungry hogs hurrying")

Day, A. (1997). *Good dog, Carl.* Aladdin. (intelligent dog babysits squirmy child)

dePaola, T. (1996). *Legend of the bluebonnet.* Putnam. (Comanche tribe is saved by doll sacrifice)

*(continued)*

## Ready Reference 8.6  Literature for Drama (continued)

Galdone, P. (2007). *The Bremen town musicians.* Bell Pond. (animals encounter a band of robbers)

Haley, G. (1988). *A story—A story.* Aladdin. (African tale about spider who wants to own all stories)

Heide, F. P. (1992). *The shrinking of Treehorn.* Holiday House. (boy notices he is shrinking)

Isaacs, A. (2000). *Swamp angel.* Puffin. (tale about big girl)

Kellogg, S. (1992). *Can I keep him?* Puffin. (boy talks with his mother about a pet)

Marshall, J. (1972). *George and Martha.* Houghton Mifflin. (use for QU reading and interviews)

McDermott, B. (1976). *The Golem: A Jewish legend.* Lippincott. (Rabbi creates a clay figure; good for debates and interviews)

McGovern, A. (1992). *Too much noise.* Sandpiper. (old man tries to stop noises; use for expert panels)

Munsch, R. (2005). *The paper bag princess.* Annick. (princess rescues a prince; use for interviews)

Rathmann, P. (1995). *Officer Buckle and Gloria.* Putnam. (dog does tricks)

San Souci, R. (1989). *The talking eggs.* Dial. (girl gets riches; greedy sister punished)

Say, A. (2008). *Grandfather's journey.* Sandpiper. (good for interviews about home)

Scieszka, J. (1999). *The true story of the 3 little pigs by A. Wolf.* Viking. (use for POV storytelling)

Slepian, J., & Seidler, A. (2001). *The hungry thing.* Scholastic. (beast's sign reads, "Feed Me" tale)

Tresslet, A. (1989). *The mitten.* Houghton Mifflin. (mitten is a haven for animals)

Turkle, B. (1992). *Deep in the forest.* Puffin. (three bears story with a twist)

Van Allsburg, C. (1996). *The mysteries of Harris Burdick.* Houghton Mifflin. (great for storytelling)

Viorst, J. (1987). *Alexander and the terrible, horrible, no good, very bad day.* Aladdin. (everything goes wrong for boy in one day; repeated lines)

Winter, P. (1997). *The bear and the fly.* Knopf. (bear family has a nagging fly)

Wood, A. (2005). *King Bidgood's in the bathtub.* Harcourt. (king invites everyone to come in)

Young, E. (1996). *Lon Po Po: A Red-Riding Hood story from China.* Putman. (sisters outwit a wolf)

# Building Block VI: Best Teaching Practices

Drama educator Nellie McCaslin (1990) believes the attributes of any good teacher are the characteristics most needed to integrate drama: sense of humor, high standards, good discipline, imagination, respect for the ideas of others, sensitivity to individuals, ability to guide rather than direct, and a focus on sharing rather than showing. In the end, the imaginative teacher self-creates methods by adapting ideas like the seed strategies in the next chapter. Adventuresome teachers go further to readily combine drama with dance, music, and visual art. The following are general drama principles that elaborate on best practices introduced in Chapter 3.

## What You Teach Is Who You Are

Toronto teacher Matt Duggan says, "I used to think I wouldn't ask my students to do anything I was uncomfortable doing when I was a kid. Then I realized I was a very uncomfortable kid, so there was not a lot we'd be able to do" (as quoted in Lushington, 2003, p. 1). Duggan's sense of humor makes him a prime candidate for AI. He knows he has to stretch himself to stretch the kids. Teachers can show enthusiasm and commitment to drama as an art form in easy, but significant ways, especially through their own use of body, voice, and imagination. This includes intentionally using personal facial expressions, eye contact, gestures, and body postures as teaching tools. Daily read-alouds become designer lessons when teachers vary vocal dynamics, pitch, tempo, stress, and pause. Teachers can draw attention to the effects of voice and body by asking questions such as "How did I use my voice?" and invitations to compare the effect with reading in a monotone.

**Teacher in Role.** Teachers may assume a variety of roles, in any curricular area, to engage students in response. For example, become a bystander for a history or science moment and ask for clarification about what's happening. Students get used to spontaneously responding in role as the teacher becomes a next-door neighbor or a town official. If young children are confused by mixing pretend and reality, simply tell them you are in role or use a signal, for example, a hat or name tag.

Teacher in role allows the teacher to be in charge of the time and direction of the action. Questioning controls the amount of time and the depth of problem solving. Relationships are forged as the teacher is seen as a fellow risk taker, a "player" who is a part of the drama. A sense of mystery or urgency, belief, and commitment are engendered by the teacher's attitude and involvement.

Heinig (1993) explains that teachers who assume roles will extend belief, stimulate thinking, provoke discussion, direct problem solving, and break down barriers between themselves and students (pp. 265–280). The goal is to be low key and not overplay or stereotype a role. Other generic roles teachers can assume are helpless characters: "I don't know and need help," authority figures (challenger), messengers, one of the crowd, devil's advocates (boss, expert, chief), or antagonists (p. 277). Props may be used but are not necessary. My favorite is an on-the-scene TV reporter. A plastic mike is a must for this one.

**Motivation.**    Drama is naturally interesting and involves the students in every aspect of CPS. Group work and choices abound as students readily seek understanding in every curricular area—not for points, either. Drama captures the essence of play and play is self-motivating.

**Role of the Audience.**    When children are proud of their work, they want to share. The desire to perform is obvious evidence of motivation. The anticipation of performance increases the intensity of the learning experience. The presence of an audience during drama performance can also intensify empathy. Award-winning teacher Rafe Esquith tells the story of a fifth grader who was given the opportunity to a do a history recitation before the Supreme Court. The boy memorized a letter written by a Civil War soldier to his wife. He and other kids rehearsed together many times and the boy did fine. However, during the actual performance for the justices, he literally was transformed. The dramatic video of this child shows him slowly "becoming" the soldier as he reads further and further into the letter. His voice begins to crack, his breathing becomes labored, and a tear forms. As if on cue, it rolls down his left cheek—mesmerizing evidence of the power of an audience to heighten engagement. Never had this boy become so emotional or "gotten into it" to this degree in rehearsal (Esquith, 2008). See the Supreme Court video at www.hobartshakespeareans.org/.

The use of audience also deepens learning when students see how groups treat the same drama problem differently. One half performs while the other half views, interprets, and responds; then they reverse roles. Alternatively, small groups can take turns presenting with the rest of the class acting as audience. This is only made meaningful if the audience is clear about its role. Discuss audience etiquette: It is polite to listen attentively, remain quiet during the performance, be respectful and responsive, and applaud at the end. Audience engagement is heightened when students are aware they will be asked to give feedback to the actors. Of course, students need examples to prompt thinking. Stress feedback centered on what worked, such as ways students made the drama believable (i.e., set it up with focus on the positive).

Use role playing or narrative pantomime to firm up the concept of audience etiquette. For example, narrate as students pantomime:

> You take your seats. You show that you are excited to see the performance. The curtain opens and you carefully examine the set. The scene is a sad one. Then a character does something funny. Another character does something wonderful and you applaud. The scene ends and you applaud. The scene has been particularly good, so you stand and applaud. Now you take your seat and think about several things you'd like to tell the actors about their performance.

In addition to daily drama performance for classmates, a variety of audiences should be sought. Consider a standing invitation for parents to visit any time, not only for "special" events. Cooperate with fellow teachers to increase options. Seek out unconventional audiences—invite the custodians, cooks, and secretary. Take performances on the road to nearby nursing homes and senior service centers. The important idea is to not see the yearly play or concert as the only time an audience is in order.

## Creative Problem Solving

Drama relies heavily on CPS, so it is important for teachers to understand the process. Use ideas in Chapter 2 to boost creative thinking, and to learn what squelches it (see Ready References 2.6, 2.7, and 2.8). One specific strategy within CPS is visual imagery which can be stimulated by taking "pretend" or virtual field trips.

**Virtual Field Trips.**    Through the power of pretend, students can take vivid visual trips. These mental journeys work like radio and storytelling to trigger brain images of places, characters, and events. The tool is the teacher's voice. These mind journeys allow students to visit other countries, ecosystems, and even different time periods. Students' imaginations and creative thinking are stretched as they conjure up internal pictures. Simulated field trips can be used to introduce a unit or lesson or as a follow-up. Use the following guidelines to construct virtual field trips.

- Write, tell, or choose trip stories that provoke rich sensory imagery. Look to your science, social studies, or literature curriculum to obtain ideas for suitable topics.
- Have students clear away distractions from their desks, close their eyes, and be comfortable.
- Use your voice to calm students; speak slowly and softly and use pauses. Read or speak at a steady pace.
- Give students time to create the images in their heads using the senses of sight, hearing, smell, taste, and touch.
- Limit the trip to 5 or 10 minutes.
- After the trip, ask students to mentally review the high points. They can share what they experienced in small groups or do a Write Right Away, sketching, one-liner, or partner storytelling of a key moment.
- As a whole group synthesize what was learned (e.g., in social studies, science, or literature) from the trip.

**Examples versus Models.**    As in art or dance, students need to take a CPS orientation for drama. This means they understand that there are many ways to express feelings and ideas using body, voice, and imaginative thinking. For example, "Think of all the ways to use pantomime to show a feeling like greed or shyness. What body parts could be used and in what ways?" (Use BEST elements, Ready Reference 10.2, to stretch and twist thinking.) "What facial expressions can be used? How could these feelings be shown in pairs or trios?" Teachers should form a habit of asking for examples, rather than giving them, which helps students learn independent thinking.

**Discussions and Questioning Strategies.**    Nearly every chapter features Ready References on questioning, with example questions and general guidelines for discussions. Discussions are primary contexts for creative problem solving, but their effectiveness depends on questioning strategies. This is relevant to discussions held before, during, and after drama, in small- and whole-group circumstances. Discussions may take place to clarify key concepts or special language or words or to stretch thinking. While yes–no, "closed" questions have a place, open, or fat, questions generate more participation and a greater range of answers, which is the goal of CPS and meaning-making in general. Questions that get at universal themes are most likely to engage students. For example, before a drama ask, "Why do characters disobey their parents as in *Peter Rabbit* or *Little Red Riding Hood?*" The problem of understanding disobedience is then explored through drama. Frames can be used to extend thinking during and after drama as well. For example, ask students to complete these sentence stems related to the subject matter under study: "I wonder _____" or "What if _____." Later in the chapter, Ready Reference 8.10 lists more "all-purpose" fat questions.

## Explicit Teaching

Gustav Meyrink's (1994) fable "The Curse of the Toad" is about a millipede who loved to dance. It challenges us to consider the effect of bringing to a conscious level what we do unconsciously. An old toad who hates the millipede tests this effect. He asks the millipede,

> Tell me then, oh most honorable one, when you walk, how do you know which foot to lift first, which is the second, and the third, which comes next as fourth, fifth, sixth—whether the next is the tenth or the hundredth, what meanwhile the second is doing, and the seventh: is it standing, or moving; when you get to the 917th, whether you should lift the 700th, put down the 39th, bend the 1000th or stretch the fourth? . . . But the millipede was glued to the ground, paralyzed, unable to move one single joint. He had forgotten which leg to lift first, and the more he thought about it the less he could work it out. (p. 54)

It may be of concern that children's joy in pretending might be disturbed by instruction in specific elements and tools of drama. Might we not paralyze them as the toad did the millipede by imposing cognition on intuition? Children readily engage in "let's pretend," but drama integration involves more than spontaneous play. Just as we support a toddler's innate desire to walk, so we can and should extend the urge to pretend.

We can build on innate dispositions to role play using explicit instruction in the drama/theatre literacy base outlined previously. This involves direct instruction in what drama is and what is needed to make drama. In addition, children need time for discovery learning. Usually explicit instruction is done in short mini-lessons, followed right away by opportunities to use new knowledge. Explicit instruction includes demonstration, coaching, feedback, and teaching the elements and skills of theatre and drama. Of special importance is teaching ways to identify conflict (the core of drama) in literature, songs, and paintings and in life. For example, ask students to identify the problem and discuss what decisions must be made to solve it. From there students can learn to use pantomime and verbal improvisation to explore solutions.

Note: Most children understand the difference between pretend and reality, but it is useful to explicitly teach this and tell or ask about the difference. Students need to see drama as "pretend" time that allows practice of skills needed in real life. Ready References 8.2 and 8.3 list drama elements and skills.

**Organize and Structure.** As students explore the elements of drama, they need to be taught to use a three-part, beginning–middle–end (BME) format. This begins with teaching students to construct scenes that have these same three parts as stories have. Another structure for planning is: Who? Where? What problems, conflicts, or obstacles? What actions or feelings? A planning sheet with BME or the questions just listed can focus student work.

## Management of Time, Space, and Students

Drama activities are exciting. Students are often out of their seats, moving and talking as they solve problems in role. The stage needs to be set for classroom drama. Space needs to be organized, desks rearranged quickly. Teachers need ways to get attention, give directions, and move activities along. Here are basic pointers.

**Rules and Expectations.** We need to know and respect the rules and limits at home, at work, and in the stores where we shop. Ground rules and expectations for drama are needed, as well. Explain limits on space, time, and speed. For example, "Stay at your desk or in your personal spot. Walk in place. I'll count to five. Do this in slow motion." State expectations in straightforward language without sugar coating or paternalism. It is helpful to use cue words: *first, second, before, finally,* and *so forth.* After giving directions, ask "What questions do you have?" and then signal to begin work.

**Distractions.** Before beginning, desktops should be cleared, as should any area where the drama will happen. Keep props to a minimum or do not use them. If props are to be used, don't put them out until they are needed.

**Group Practice.** To make sure students understand what is to be done in a small group or individually, it is important to practice an example or two with the whole group. This goes for any teaching, not just drama.

**Signals.** Signals are valuable cues to help organize and get the action going—or to stop it. For example, say "places," "curtain," "lights," or "home" to start a drama. Lights, sounds, music, a drum, bell, or tambourine are effective signals, too. Every pupil response (EPR) signals after questions or directions teach students to control their own actions and learn to direct others. Ready Reference 8.7 lists attention-getting signals used by teachers for drama and other activities.

**Transitions.** Make transitions by calling groups or rows or by creative categories such as eye color, patterns of clothes, or birthdays. It is helpful to cue students that a transition is coming up by announcing the time left: "You have 1 minute to finish planning."

**Grouping.** Larger groups and larger spaces require more planning and controls. Start with smaller amounts of time and space. Have students work in pairs, before trying larger groups. Pantomiming in slow motion teaches self-control and calms students.

## Ready Reference 8.7  Attention Getters and Signals

1. Whisper directions.
2. Flick lights.
3. Play a favorite tape or CD.
4. Use tambourine, chimes, piano chord, or any pleasant sound.
5. Have children echo what you say. *Examples:* "Jambo Jambo" ("Hello Hello" in Swahili) or use a tongue twister (aluminum linoleum).
6. Ask children to echo a rhythm pattern, sign, or movement.
7. Start a chain reaction: Say to one student, "Would you tell the person next to you to _____."
8. Say, "I'm looking for someone who is _____." (fill in a behavior like "in a curved shape").
9. Write a message in large letters on the chalkboard.
10. Write directions on large cards. *Example:* "Look at me and smile."
11. Say, "Let's listen _____ to hear grass grow, clock tick."
12. Say, "I'd like to see _____ the color of everyone's eyes."
13. Have a secret code word (e.g., foreign language, special vocabulary, or phrases such as "chicka boom chicka rucka").
14. Tell students to close their eyes and make mind pictures.
15. Count aloud backward from 10 (invite students to join in).
16. Agree on a class signal to get attention if _____ (e.g., the ceiling was about to fall in, there was a fire, etc.).
17. Tell a joke or riddle. Knock knocks work well.
18. Call students' names who are ready to listen.
19. Have a nonverbal signal. *Examples:* touch pocket or ear, hold up two fingers, thumbs up.
20. Give a direction with universal appeal. *Example:* "Sit down if you ever wanted a 2-hour recess," "Freeze if you like money," or "Raise your hand if you'd like some ice cream."
21. Sit in a particular place or use a particular stance.
22. Do something different. Attire can attract attention (e.g., "Did you notice that _____ is wearing _____?").
23. Say, "If you can hear my voice, _____ (behavior)."
24. Call and response sequences: T = guaca guaca, S = guacamole; T = peanut, or S = butter; or T = bread, S = jam
25. Use a group reinforcer. *Example:* Use cloze blanks on the chalkboard and say, "I need to see people ready to earn another letter in '_____'" (letters spell out a goal such as *extra recess*).
26. Make up a class chant: "We're ready, we're ready as ready can be. In just 5 seconds, chicka rucka chicka bees."
27. Use sign language for directions such as sit down and line up. See *Joy of Signing* (Riekehof, 1987).
28. Ask students to close their eyes and imagine, for example, the sun setting or the ripples moving out from a stone thrown in a pond.

---

There is less teacher control when students work in small groups, but group work is crucial to dramatic problem solving and life outside school. Students learn to work in groups by working in groups. Create pairs, trios, and quads by counting off. At times, give a choice based on interests or ability to work together. Instead of "Find a partner," say "Find a partner who is your same height" or "Find two people you can cooperate with." This helps students learn to distinguish between friends and those with whom they work the best.

Avoid cliques by rotating groups. Learning circles can also be the basis for group work. Another option is to give each child a color or symbol (circle, square) and group by symbols. Group decision making is developed by asking students for their ideas. Once they understand the variety of choices in drama, ask them to set time and space limits. Suggest the amount of rehearsal needed and discuss whether to present to an audience or not.

**Participation.**   When drama is first introduced, invite volunteers instead of forcing participation; forcing can increase reluctance and be contagious. Students want to know what they are volunteering for, so explain the general idea. For example, "I need three people who know how to walk in place." The goal is to involve all students using the unison strategy. Unison means simultaneous "all-at-once" participation. No one is waiting for a turn, which creates boredom and prompts mischief. Students feel the comfort created by safety in numbers. Maximum involvement can be achieved through double casting (have two or more children perform the same role). For example, have three wolves in *The Three Little Pigs*.

## Discipline for Independence

The root of the word *discipline* is disciple. A disciple is not forced to follow a leader, but is present by choice. Drama-based lessons are intended to build this kind of relationship between teacher and students. Self-discipline and independence grow as students choose to follow such a teacher. They make more effort and persist because they are drawn into the magic circle of possibilities a teacher can create. They feel respected and give trust and respect in return. "She never believed I couldn't" was a tribute I once heard given to such a teacher.

Independence grows from learning how to control body, mind, and voice and ways to extend use of all three. Drama does this. It begins with clear expectations so students learn to focus, concentrate, and know the rewards of putting forth best efforts.

Control techniques used by drama specialists are now popular tools many classroom teachers use. They have been adopted wholesale in some schools. For example, Battle Academy in Chattanooga, Tennessee, uses teaching artist Sean Layne's controls for schoolwide discipline. Drama teacher Jeff Jordan has done the same for Ashley River in Charleston, South Carolina (e.g., "criss-cross applesauce" is used in every classroom as a signal).

Here are important guidelines. Appendix E also has a summary of discipline, prevention, and intervention strategies.

Chapter 10 includes additional discipline and management ideas, especially related to personal space and time limits.

- When a rule is broken, acknowledge the student's feelings to save face. For example, "I see that you want to be in Susan's group." Then restate the rule. Next, implement a logical consequence, not a punishment. "In this class we work in different groups. Work with this group or at your desk alone."
- Consequences should be clear from the lesson start, along with a review of rules. Chapter 10 has rule examples.
- Not everyone can be made happy. Try to ignore whiners. Small infractions are not worth attention, and some behaviors are to get attention.
- Watch for signs of need for attention, and give it frequently for *positive* behavior.
- Drama is fun and interesting. Do not cajole or beg. Start with those who want to participate; others will follow.
- Acknowledge failures and be honest, which models how to handle problems. Start over with a revised procedure. Students need to see drama as an experiment. It is not predictable.
- Veteran teachers know that "giving the eye" and being physically close are often enough to get students back on task. Circulate as students work and look them directly in the eye.
- Follow through with consequences. Neither threaten nor hesitate. Stop the activity if students are not on task. Wait until all are involved. Review consequences periodically, posting them if extra focus is needed.
- Use private conferences with repeat offenders and difficult children as soon after the lesson as possible. Public humiliation is unethical. If offenders must be removed, return them to the activity as soon as possible. Often a 2-minute time-out is as effective as total removal. Of course, readmission to class should be contingent upon agreeing to follow the rules.

**Drama to Teach Rules.** Drama is a tool to teach just about anything, including classroom rules. Students can create improvised scenes (Chapter 9) that show cooperation, active listening, compromise, respect for alternative opinions, and other desirable behaviors. Direct them to make sure scenes have a beginning, middle, and end. Scenes can be set up by first identifying characters, a setting, and a problem situation. Challenge students to think about "what-if" situations: What if some people didn't do their share of the work in a group project? Remind students to use CPS, which includes brainstorming ways to settle arguments. Students may choose pantomime or verbal drama. For example, students created a pledge based on the Golden Rule using a frame to structure thinking: "Because I like to _____, I will _____. Because I don't like _____, I will _____. Because I want _____, I will _____." Here is their final product:

> We, the sixth grade class of Overlook Elementary, want to have our opinions heard, so we promise to listen to others. We like to be treated with respect, so we will not disrespect others. We do not like to be touched in unfriendly ways, so we will not touch anyone with fighting on our minds. We want to work in groups, so we will cooperate and get work done together. We hereby so promise all the above on this day in September 2009.

# Building Block VII: Instructional Design: Routines and Structures

Classrooms run smoothly because of predictable routines and organizing structures. Within these frameworks lies great variability. One framework is the lesson itself, with a predictable introduction, development, and conclusion. What happens in each lesson segment is unpredictable.

## Lessons Structures

The two-pronged AI lesson framework introduced in Chapter 3 is a predictable structure. It can be used creatively to help students gain skills and learn concepts related to drama and other curricular areas. As discussed previously, integrated arts lessons need to include at least one arts concept—drama in this case—to ensure that the integrity of the art form is not lost when drama is integrated with another curricular area. When you teach a few concepts, students can go into some depth and become comfortable with the possibilities of each skill or element (e.g., pantomime). Direct or explicit instruction using the introduction, development, and conclusion structure is used in the example plan in Planning Page 8.5.

Note: After doing a drama, take time to comment on things you saw or heard during the lesson. No names are necessary, as the focus of drama is on the group working together. The conclusion should be a time for students to reflect and do self-evaluation: What worked? Didn't work? Why? What did you like? What did you learn? New ideas? What would you do differently? Teachers may also wish to invite students to repeat activities with a novel twist, even two or three times, if interest in this kind of exploration is shown during the discussion.

**Lesson Introductions.** The purpose of the introduction is to motivate and ready students for learning. Following are common introduction strategies.

- Remove visual or auditory distractions and get attention.
- Establish mood and set a climate for creative exploration (see Ready Reference 2.8 for creativity boosters).
- Build on prior knowledge and past experiences.
- Stimulate interest, which can account for 30 times the variance in understanding any subject. Interest building strategies include brainstorming, webbing, asking open questions, and doing warm ups.
- Coach students to concentrate and focus, to "make us believe," and not be hams.
- Ensure students know the content. If they are to do a drama about pollution, they need background from a variety of experiences. They need knowledge to inform the drama.

Lessons can sink or swim based on the introduction. This is the point in time where students need to perceive purpose. Take time to discuss the real-life connections of drama (e.g., roles we take every day) and develop the concept that the arts are forms of literacy. Use the mini-lesson topics in Ready Reference 3.4 to start. Students need to understand that drama is an enjoyable art form used for serious learning purposes. At first they may not understand why social studies time is used for drama; they may not see the arts as communication tools, parallel to reading and writing. Through discussions and reaching the point in drama where empathy and insight are experienced, students do begin to understand. For example, students unfamiliar with using drama acted silly when first pantomiming the Trail of Tears March of the Cherokees. In time, with coaching and more information about the dire circumstances of the migration, students were able to feel how hopeless, tired, and discouraged the Indians were after walking day after day through bad weather, starving and sick. See the generic lesson plan on Planning Page 3.10 for more ideas. Planning Page 8.8 gives examples of drama problem solving for comprehension.

**Energizers and Warm-Ups.** Students get used to the routine of starting lessons with short activities that can relax or rev up. Energizers are such brief activities that create a climate for risk taking, give focus, and facilitate concentration, imagination, cooperation, and self-control. Consider these samples for the body: (1) Make circle movements that slowly travel head to toe; (2) walk across the room in different ways, at different levels, or in a variety of "as-if" situations; and (3) direct students to pretend they are balloons blowing up and then collapsing (add sound effects, if you like). See the energizers and warms-ups in Chapter 9 and in all seed strategy chapters. In addition to the energizers and warm-ups in the next chapter, check out these websites: www.teachingonline.org/drama3.html and www.learnimprov.com.

**Routines and Rituals.** The routines and rituals used by schools and teachers establish habits of mind and body, and include the following:

- Create a morning school television show with students taking roles as newscasters, weather reporters, and interviewers.
- Use drama energizers and warm-ups to start/end lessons and the day.
- Use humor strategies to relax students so that they feel comfortable taking risks to be creative.
- Present reader's theatre scripts one day each week (Chapter 9).
- Make special times to discuss drama and theatre in real life, such as roles people play, actors on television, and why they are effective.
- Put up a marquee to announce noteworthy films or plays.
- Share theatre experiences. Have a "critic's corner" for students to post movie evaluations.
- Maintain an ongoing web of roles people play (e.g., pictures, words in collage form).
- Do morning drama (e.g., charades) to review yesterday's learning. Do drama (e.g., one-liners) to summarize at the end of the day.
- Sing action songs and do poems to start or end the day (see poetry performances in Ready Reference 5.4).

## Clubs

More and more arts-based schools have drama-based clubs like the drama troupe at Ashley River Creative Arts. Storytelling clubs, reader's theatre groups, and playwriting clubs are other interest-based groups students can choose, if the structures are

---

## Planning Page 8.8

### Drama Problems to Increase Comprehension

The following are examples of how drama can be used to deepen comprehension of Patricia Polacco books. They are divided into pantomime and verbal improvisation. These activities assume prior teaching about drama elements and skills.

**Pink and Say:**
*Pantomime: Key Scene Tableau:*
Prioritize the most "tension-filled" scenes. Group students to plan a frozen picture with their bodies that captures key emotions in the scene. Examples: a tableau of Pinkus helping Sheldon to safety or when the boys were being pulled apart after the Confederate soldiers discovered them. Frozen characters can be tapped to "come alive," and in character say a one-liner, such as "We are very scared and don't know if we will live or die." *Adaptation:* Have students freeze behind a white sheet with a light to emphasize body language.

*Verbal: Television Show:*
Students choose to become important book characters that form a discussion panel for a television show. The audience questions them about what happened and how they felt. For example, "How did it feel serving your country during the Civil War?"

*Verbal: Newsbreak:*
Students create 30-second factual news updates on what is going on in the Civil War related to the book. This involves social studies research to uncover facts. Character interviews can be included to get reactions to events.

**The Bee Tree:**
*Narrative Pantomime:*
Students mime as narrator reads: "You are a bee. Show how you fly to a flower and land. Show how you begin to gather pollen. Show how the pollen is sticky. Fly back to your beehive. Put down the pollen and go to sleep for the night."

*Verbal: Character Interviews:*
Students pair up. A is the interviewer and B is a story character.
Student A uses an Oprah style of interviewing and asks five Ws + H questions. Student B focuses on using a character's language and style of speaking. Switch roles and repeat.

**My Ol' Man:**
*Pantomime: BME Comic Strip:*
Break into four groups. Each group chooses a scene from the beginning, middle, or end. The comic strip will be four different frozen pictures or tableau. Give groups 5 minutes to plan. Group 1 poses for the first frame and holds 10 seconds. Next comes Group 2, and so forth. Debrief audience about what was most important in each frame and why.

*Verbal: Interview:*
Pair off with an A and a B. Student B becomes a newspaper reporter who just heard about this amazing man who is out of a job but keeps his hopes alive with the help of a magic rock. Student A is the extraordinary man. B interviews A to get facts to write a good news story (use five Ws and H questions). Switch roles. *Variation:* Students then actually write the news stories.

there. Some clubs meet within the school day, and others meet after school. All clubs need a sponsor. This may be a teacher, parent, or interested community member.

# Building Block VIII: Differentiating for Diverse Needs

Drama specialists are an invaluable source for differentiating instruction and should be consulted, if at all possible. General information about developmental stages is included in Chapter 2 and Appendix A. Teachers can use the basic principles for adapting instruction for at-risk students and those with special needs presented in Chapter 3. Ready Reference 8.9 gives examples of differentiation ideas. Drawing on students' abilities rather than focusing on disabilities is a key idea when considering any instructional modification.

Drama is unique in its ensemble focus: Partner and group work are emphasized. Group work can be particularly enjoyable for students with special needs. If reluctant or shy children are not forced to participate in uncomfortable ways, they grow to want to be involved because they see peers having fun. Puppets and props also help children feel safe.

A general rule of thumb is to order drama activities from easy to more difficult and from low content, such as personal experiences and interests, to more content-dense work such as drama using background in a particular subject area. In general, nonverbal (pantomime) activities are easier than verbal activities. The exception is older students who have body concerns that create discomfort with pantomime, which emphasizes body shapes and movements. Introduce pantomime by asking students to show ways it is used in daily life, such as common ways we greet different folks or how we show excitement. Space should be managed by beginning with limiting students to small areas, such as their desks. Explain to them that they will have larger spaces as they show the capacity to control their bodies, minds, and voices. Also consider that large areas such as cafeterias and gyms may have echoes, and the playground signals a recess attitude; the place of learning can facilitate or hamper success.

As with any creative problem solving, it is important to use energizers and warm-ups to relax students so they will feel comfortable experimenting and to jump-start the higher order thinking creativity requires. Humor can be used at the start of a lesson to activate creative processes and prepare students for the serious work of drama, which involves thinking about tension and conflict.

It is often helpful to start with whole-group, teacher-directed drama. Solo (individual) drama strategies done in unison under the teacher's direction prepare students for small-group work that requires more self-control and collaboration skills. Whole-group drama should be used to demonstrate and discuss the kinds of thinking and behaving expected in small groups, including how to use specific drama elements and skills. Finally, students often see ways to differentiate that teachers do not, so it is important to invite their ideas with questions, such as "What else would help?"

# Building Block IX: Assessment for Learning

Assessment should be integral to instruction. A combination of teacher, peer, and self-assessment are utilized in arts integration. Assessment methods depend on the purpose of the assessment. AI assessment is used to motivate learning, not measure it.

---

## Ready Reference 8.9  Particular Ways to Differentiate Drama

**Place:** Limit and define the space for drama. *Example:* Stay in desk area.

**Amount:** Do fewer activities or shorter ones. *Example:* Quick mime key character actions.

**Rate:** Go slower or faster to meet student needs. *Example:* Slow motion to increase control and focus.

**Targets:** Change the goals, make them clearer or more focused. *Example:* Repeat tableau but use body shape and different levels to show key thoughts and/or emotions.

**Instruction:** Give more direction, examples, or coaching. *Example:* side coach as students create a tableau with comments such as "make me feel the emotion" and "cheat your face toward the audience."

**Curriculum materials:** Use science and social studies texts, student experiences, and contemporary problems for drama.

**Utensils:** Use props such as nametags or headbands to help students understand the roles.

**Levels of difficulty:** Generally, pantomime is easier than verbal improvisation, and individual drama activities directed by the teacher are easier than group work. If students act silly, it may be they do not know what to do or feel they cannot do what is expected. Humor is often used to cover embarrassment. The material may be too conceptually difficult and should be altered or more examples may be needed. Use teacher think-alouds to help make thinking visible.

**Assistance:** Scaffold for success. *Examples:* (1) Children with hearing impairments need to see your face and mouth as you speak. (2) Forcing shy children to participate may increase reluctance so let them observe longer. (3) Coach students who have trouble ending a drama to plan an ending before presenting, ask the audience for ideas, or you take a role and end it.

**Response:** Alter what you expect as a demonstration of comprehension. For example, you may have planned for students to create a tableau, but they want to combine it with interviewing.

Assessment *for* learning, versus *of* learning, emphasizes formative feedback *during* lessons. Formative assessment boosts motivation and increases the quality of student work. It is particularly influential in boosting achievement of lower-performing students (Leahy, Lyon, Thompson, & William, 2005). In research in six countries, including the United States, students "achieved in 6–7 months what otherwise takes a year" (p. 19).

## Formative Assessment *for* Learning

The arts have a long history of using formative assessments. Drama and theatre specialists, in particular, rely on coaching—a form of formative feedback—during drama rehearsal. AI teachers learn to coach students to use drama elements and skills to more clearly and creatively show what they are learning in curricular areas. Summative assessment happens at the conclusion of units, too, in the form of culminating performances or products such as readers' scripts. Student progress in using drama as a learning medium can also be demonstrated and celebrated using portfolios, videotapes, and displays. The following examples of assessment introduced in Chapter 3 are appropriate for drama integration.

**Observation.** Arts educators have to be master observers because the arts involve "doing," which is the best evidence of learning. Drama growth is sometimes tricky to track because of so many teachable moments where important pieces of assessment information emerge. Keen observation of what students show they know is invaluable. A clipboard with sticky notes, each with a child's name, works well to jot down evidence of learning as it happens. These are called *anecdotal records*. Notes should be dated and given to students to put in their folios. Documentation of observations is also guided by rubrics and checklists.

**Written and Art Responses.** Written responses can be structured or informal. Writing can be promoted with open-ended questions or take the form of journals and learning logs, essays, research papers, reports, or reviews. Student drawings and other art responses are rich sources to see what students are thinking.

**Conversations and Conferences.** Conversations provide insight into student thinking and understanding. Examples that may be used for assessment include interviews, informal discussions, and oral questions posed to the class or to individuals. Brief individual student conferences to discuss progress and set goals are invaluable.

**Performances and Exhibits.** Performance assessment includes assessing oral presentations and demonstrations of projects, products, or any task, including a drama, dance, piece of music, or visual art display. Performances literally cause students to make learning visible and show learning externally.

**Portfolios.** Portfolios provide ongoing and varied types of documentation for what students know and are able to do. Written, audio, and visual examples of work should be included. Students should learn to create and maintain portfolios of items selected by both teacher and self. Portfolios allow students to monitor personal progress and thus increase motivation to learn. Additionally, portfolios may be used across grade levels or courses to show progress. See Appendix D for Arts Folio guidelines.

**Rubrics and Checklists.** Teachers and students alike can use rubrics and checklists that specify criteria to evaluate work. See the examples in Appendix D and more in the *Theatre Teachers Handbook* available from the North Carolina Department of Instruction (*www.publicschools.org*; click on "Curriculum," then "Arts Education," then "Resources"). Students should learn to help develop and use these tools for self-assessment and peer feedback, as well.

Rather than squelch motivation, deep thinking, and creativity with grades and traditional tests, rubrics and checklists can motivate students to work for excellence. This depends on setting criteria before work is begun, which provides clear focus and is simply being fair. A rubric for a drama performance would include criteria about general areas such as:

- Ability to inhabit a character (e.g., use of body posture and gestures, movement, facial expressions, eye contact)
- Variety in use of voice (volume, tempo, pitch, etc.)
- Use of imagination (details, connections)
- Cooperation with other actors

When drama is used as a teaching vehicle, additional criteria about *use of* drama are needed to show transformation of learning. For example, using historically accurate information about Clara Barton might be a criterion in a unit on individuals who made a big difference. Ready Reference 8.10 shows a drama skills checklist. Other high placed criteria are listed on page 85.

## Coaching: Formative Feedback

Formative assessment focuses on giving students the information to move forward. Written feedback can be given. In drama, however, offering specific oral comments as students work, a process called *side coaching,* is common. The line between assessment and instruction blurs as coaching is used to (1) remind about directions, goals, and assessment criteria; (2) scaffold students through an activity with suggestions and encouragement; and (3) maintain control. Coaching is also used to help the audience (usually peers) understand what actors are doing, and fill in awkward silences. Coaching is not about giving lots of directions—that's called *directing*. It strives to support and challenge students to use their imaginations, bodies, and voices in new ways. It is worth the extra time to cue carefully and coach. The effects increased student skills and confidence.

**Questions.** Coaching creates depth of understanding and high-quality expression of ideas and emotions. A common question is, "What else could you do to show the character's age or how the character feels?" Teachers ask many "what if" questions to stretch and direct: "What if the weather changed?" "What if someone got sick?" "What if the world stopped rotating?" "What if dinosaurs still lived?" To help students prepare, teachers ask or say the following:

- What does your character want? How can you show this?
- Tell me more about . . . (explore the emotion or thinking of the character).
- How can you show how the place affects how the character feels or acts?
- What else might you try?

## Ready Reference 8.10  Drama Skills Checklist

Name _____ Date _____

*Directions:* Evaluate using 1, 2, 3, 4, 5, with 1 indicating no evidence and 5 indicating very evident. Add notes and discuss.

_____ *Use of body:* ability to coordinate and control body, use of appropriate energy, display of sensory awareness and expression, use of gestures and facial expressions, communication through pantomime, interpretation of others' nonverbal communication

_____ *Verbal expression:* speaking clearly and using variety in volume, rate, tone and pitch, pause, emphasis, inflection, fluency, ability to improvise dialogue

_____ *Focus:* concentration and staying involved, making others believe in the realness of the character, following directions

_____ *Imagination:* creative thinking, unique ideas, elaboration on ideas, spontaneity

_____ *Evaluation:* giving constructive feedback, using others' suggestions, self-evaluation, adaptation of own behavior

_____ *Social skills:* working cooperatively in groups, listening and responding to others

_____ *Audience etiquette:* attending, listening, responding appropriately to others' performances

---

- What are other ways this problem could be solved?
- What do you want the audience to see and feel?
- How could props, lighting, and/or music be used?

**Descriptive Feedback.** It is especially important to note the unique and different ideas students devise. Do so by infusing "I statements" (e.g., "I see," "I notice," "I wonder"). Refrain from phony praise. Ask students to isolate part of a drama, such as a single movement in a pantomime, and solicit peer feedback. For example, ask a student to repeat the part where she was grasping the beanstalk before beginning to climb it. Ask peers what they see. This habit of doing (showing with hands, face, and posture) and then asking for observations uses a discovery or inductive method that promotes reflective thinking.

**Concentration and Focus.** Teachers and parents lament children's short attention spans. Concentration is a specific drama skill and a criterion that belongs in a rubric for most drama activities. Concentration can be taught. Here's how a lesson might go. Begin by asking students what helps them concentrate and what distracts them. Ask them to show concentrations with body and face. Give descriptive feedback and ask them what happened in their heads. Ask when concentration and focus is needed in the real world. Set goals to extend concentration and as students work on a drama problem, give feedback: "Fred is concentrating. He is remembering to keep his body bent like an old man." When children are totally involved in creative problem solving they will be in a concentrated "flow state." Giggling stops and students spontaneously add key details to drama. They claim time goes too quickly and ask to repeat activities. One class so enjoyed a narrative pantomime of *The Wretched Stone,* they asked to replay it instead of having recess. When students ham it up or show off, they are not genuinely involved. Discuss this before it happens. See the energizers and warm-ups in Chapters 9 through 11 for more ways to teach concentration and focus.

**Peer Feedback.** After drama presentations, students need to debrief. They need structures to facilitate expression of thoughts and feelings. Examples include the following:

- Tell what you saw and heard. Describe honestly, using drama elements and skills.
- Use frames for feelings supported with evidence: "I liked _____ because _____" or "It made me feel _____ because _____."
- Use writing frames: Make three columns to record what you liked, wonder, and learned. Use examples.

Teach students how to ask questions of others as a form of feedback and how to receive feedback using role play. This also shows students how rude or thoughtless remarks can make a person feel. Sensitivity and empathy are important to constructive feedback. To help teach students, discuss and reflect on their drama work, Ready Reference 8.11 has questions for students to use as guides.

**Arts Program Evaluation.** Review the checklists for theatre and drama in the *Opportunity to Learn Standards* at www.winthrop.edu/ABC/.

# Building Block X: Arts Partnerships

## Arts Agency Collaborations

There are now collaborations among a variety of arts organizations and schools across the country. See Ready Reference 1.6 for examples. One drama-based example is Shakespeare & Company, based in Lenox, Massachusetts, a theatre company that has partnered with public schools for 20 years (www.shakespeare.org/). The Kennedy Center Partners in Education lists partnerships in all states between arts organizations and schools. Check out their website to see if your school is a member and, if not, investigate joining.

Strong partnerships need two basic elements: shared goals and time to plan (Booth, 2005). Local college theatre departments and community theatre organizations are interested in

## Ready Reference 8.11 All-Purpose Fat Questions

Post questions so students learn to use different kinds to discuss and reflect on their work. Teachers should model use of open/fat questions and show how they cause more discussion. These questions help students think more deeply and facilitate oral expression.

- What worked?
- What did you enjoy?
- What would you change?
- How was the ending? What was the best moment? Why?
- How did you work with others?
- How did you show involvement?

- How did you get your idea? Where did you gather ideas?
- Why did you do what you did?
- What were you trying to do?
- What did you try that you've never tried before?
- What did you learn most?
- How is this connected to other things you are learning?
- What ideas did you use from what we've been learning about drama (elements, skills, concepts)?
- What did you learn? What was this mostly about? What did this tell you about people or the world? What will you remember forever?

---

growing audiences, making them potential partners for schools. They may not understand the concept of arts integration, however, so classroom teachers must become adult educators as they seek out partnerships. Teachers try to entice specialists into co-planning and perhaps working with students as well. Drama and theatre specialists can help teachers find connections with other disciplines and show how to make them without damaging the integrity of the art form.

Many arts organizations (e.g., ArtsSmart in Texarkana) provide drama workshops and consulting with teachers on a low- or no-charge basis. Contact university theatre departments and local arts councils to see if they are involved in partnership projects or interested in getting one started. Local workshops conducted by artists and classroom teachers engaged in arts integration are becoming more common at the state and national levels. Keep an eye out for advertisements related to conferences sponsored by professional organizations such as the International Reading Association, Association for Supervision and Curriculum Development, and arts professional organizations (see Appendix I for websites). Some states have arts integration conferences. South Carolina's Arts Alliance sponsors a conference each fall. Contact Executive Director Eve Wolford at Lander University for more information.

### Arts Education Partnership

A mission of the national Arts Education Partnership is to facilitate partnerships between schools and arts organization. Go to the site (http://aep-arts.org) to download publications, such as *Learning Partnerships: Improving Learning in Schools with Arts Partners in the Community.*

### Teaching Artists and Artist Residencies

Professional actors, playwrights, and other drama and theatre specialists may be available through a local arts council or college or by contacting artists in the community. Children's theatre groups may be willing to be involved in the classroom, and Theatre in Education projects are another dimension worth investigating. It is important to realize that artists often have little or no background in

teaching or child development. Before bringing an artist into a school or class, it is important to meet ahead of time to prepare. See the checklists in Chapters 3 and 4, under Building Block X. Appendix C has a checklist, too.

Of course, the best potential for partnership is with a drama teacher. More and more schools are fortunate to have a drama specialist. Specialists usually welcome invitations to plan with teachers, especially if integration is viewed as going both ways; at times the drama teacher should be able to ask for support for her unit focus (e.g., theme or topic). Classroom teachers can make it easy for a specialist to assist in integration by providing a month-by-month listing of units and lessons in science, social studies, reading, and language arts, so drama specialists can make suggestions. In addition, teachers can invite specialists to do the same with a list of topics and skills they plan to develop. Classroom teachers can also ask for ways to follow up on drama classes or extend drama work. It is highly recommended that generalists sit in on drama classes to learn more about drama and ways students can make meaning using drama. The drama teacher in the following spotlight will give you a sense of the possibilities.

## Teaching Artist Spotlight
### Poetry Making with the Drama King

Jeff Jordan has been the drama specialist at Ashley River Creative Arts elementary school for more than 10 years. He got the job by way of a drama residency. With a master's degree in speech/theatre from the University of South Carolina and experiencing teaching theatre, he was well prepared, but found he was "overwhelmed" by the school. "Jayne Ellicott (the principal) gives us the freedom to give students a true artistic experience," he passionately declares. "The arts expand the curriculum, while tests narrow it."

Jeff's schedule is: grade 1, once a week; grades 2 through 4, twice a week; grade 5, once a week. As a specialist, a key part of Jeff's role is to listen and offer suggestions to classroom teachers. He tries to mesh drama/theatre when it "fits meaningfully

Pantomiming emotions: Controlling body, face, and voice

into units." For example, in third grade there is a huge folk/fairy tale unit, so he teaches script writing and audition techniques.

What does it take to be a great drama teacher? I asked Jeff's students. "I like drama because Mr. Jordan is my teacher," explains a first grader. Second graders hone in on his "super warm-ups." They see him as a "great actor who loves to teach." Third graders say they know Mr. Jordan loves ARCA. They notice how he likes to write and read stories. The fourth graders point out that Mr. Jordan "makes us laugh" and helps them feel "it's okay to make mistakes." However, they add that he wants you to concentrate and try your best. They like it that he has taught them to "take risks." The fifth graders just call Mr. Jordan the "drama king."

## Drama Specialist in Action

*The essence of all art is to have pleasure in giving pleasure.* (Mikhail Baryshnikov)

The floor is brightly carpeted. There are no desks. A huge puppet stage takes up one corner. A folding chair and a desk are pushed into another corner. Pictures of students cover a bulletin board. Real kids are seated "criss-cross applesauce" in personal spaces on the floor.

"How many heard the storm last night?" Jeff Jordan asks. Most hands go up.

"Remember our school is Ashley River . . ."

Students chorally say, "Creative Arts!"

"What are all the arts, then?" he asks. Students call out the list.

"Okay, artists create! Right? So **we are going to create movable poetry**."

As if on cue, they begin to recite a poem they all know. Jeff coaches then to put in more voice, body, and facial expressions to show the feeling of the poem.

"Don't just say it like you are a choral robot," he teases. "**If you were** the director, what tips would you give to improve this?" Students immediately offer ideas:

"Bouncing voice!"

"Say it with feeling and energy."

"Don't be rigid and boring."

"Make your voice sound like your movement."

"Do your best."

"So, what if I said 'thunder'?" Jeff asks.

A boy stands right up and with a low pitch says, "Thunder," making his body large with a broad stance. A few students giggle.

"**Clap it back to me,**" Jeff demands, and the whole class claps his rhythm and is attentive once again.

He plugs an upcoming artist residency by Laura Rich and tells the class her focus will be on movement poetry and weather. Today is a warm-up for her work. He explains they will first write and then perform their poems.

They begin with the "**actor's warm-up.**" Jeff directs them to reach and stretch as if they are pushing up a bar.

"Shake out your hands. Put your imaginary bar at chest level and push and pull it back. Shake out. Shake. Now isolate. Shake one hand. Two hands. Both knees. Shake shoulders, stomach, face. Now do your whole body. Do not touch others. Do not fall down."

"OK, back to last night's storm. We are going to do **weather statues,** first. Think about being different. If you see low people, then you go high, etc. Action, and . . . freeze!"

Some students are spread out on the floor. Others pose on tiptoes with arms in jagged positions. No one looks the same. Mr. Jordan wanders among the statues **side coaching** to "Focus. Concentrate." He stops to describe facial expressions and body positions.

"On **3-second cue,** let's do *rainstorm*. 3-2-1." Students spring to life in new positions until Mr. Jordan calls, "Freeze." Again he **circulates and gives feedback.** This time he clicks his finger near a few faces and compliments those who keep concentration.

"Cut. Okay, 5-second cue for *lightning*. 5-4-3-2-1." This time students make large sweeping movements. Mr. Jordan repeats his coaching. Then they relax and he gives them a 4-second cue for *sunshiny day*. He reminds them that directors look for people who can hold their concentration. They then do snow and finally hurricane.

"**Criss-cross applesauce. Hands in lap. In your place,**" Jeff calls. Students return to seated positions on the floor. He explains they are going to do prewriting. He reads three poems written by students. After reading "Clouds" he asks, "**What did you notice?**"

"No rhyming," comments one boy.

Jeff responds, "Right, poems don't have to rhyme. What images?"

When there are no responses, he rereads "clouds like cotton candy" and asks them to **picture in their heads.** He repeats the line several times. "**What do you see and feel?**"

Students call out "sticky," "puffy," "pink," "fluffy," "sugary," and "towering." Next Jeff reads, "'When clouds cry'—that is personification!"

A boy says, "Once we saw a cloud that looked like a hammerhead shark!"

"You could do a poem on that image," Jeff says with a smile. He then reads a rainbow poem and asks more questions about images and feelings. There are many responses. Finally, he announces, "The Storm." He directs them to **listen closely** to the last line. He reads slowly, softly at first. His voice builds with the storm. Students are riveted.

At the conclusion Jeff asks for observations, feelings, and other **"noticings."** Words like *suspenseful, scary, dramatic, dark,* and *swirling* are suggested.

"These are pretty short," one boy observes.

**"Yes, good noticing.** Nobody said that before!" Jeff says with genuine delight.

"Now, you need to think about a weather moment and describe how the weather feels. Use your whole body to think of how the weather moment feels—like we did before. Then add words that describe the feelings and movements."

Students pass out clipboards and blank paper. **"Write first. Add the title later,"** Jeff advises. "Don't worry about spelling—sound it out, yeah, yeah, yeah," he sings Beatles-style and they giggle. One girl suggests they can use the dictionary, but Jeff suggests they do that after they get their ideas roughed out.

Jeff **circulates** as students work and gives feedback. "Arthur is starting with question. Mario has three lines already." He urges them to write fast and in 5 minutes most have filled a page.

The lesson has been fast paced and intense. One girl has written:

Balmy air surrounds me.
Full of heavy wet wind.
I try to breathe
I feel like I'm suffocating.
The hot humid weather
Is summer in South Carolina.

## When There Is No Drama Specialist

By starting a school directory of persons with drama background and skills, teachers have found drama expertise in nearby places. The teacher next door may have had courses in children's drama or may act in community theatre. A parent may have skills to do a workshop on nonverbal communication. Circulate a form to all adults in the school requesting names and contact information for people who could be used as drama or theatre resources. Encourage people to list themselves. Students, parents, and community groups can also be tapped for potential skills. Use the Internet to locate home pages of drama and theatre organizations at the local and state levels. Selected websites are listed in Appendix I for starters. Remember to contact the theatre departments of nearby colleges to find out about student internships or other ways college students might serve as drama resources.

# Classroom Snapshot
## Science Through Drama

This chapter ends with the day's ending activity in Amy Walker's third grade at Ashley River Creative Arts. A four-person group stands at the ready with props: paper plate sun, tambourine, and green crepe paper.

"Remember to present your skits like your audience is first graders who know nothing about photosynthesis. **Audience**—watch and listen so you can give feedback and ask questions. Action!"

On cue the narrator reads and a paper plate becomes a rising sun. Crepe paper transforms into plant leaves slowly emerging from a striped T-shirt. The tambourine player accompanies in the background, and is featured in solos during several dramatic moments in photosynthesis. The actors freeze, the audience claps, and the actors bow.

**"What did they do that worked?"** Ms. Walker asks.

"The narrator was loud."

"They worked as a team."

"Jerry—uh—I mean, the accompanist, was into it!"

"How do you mean?"

"Well, he showed the feel of it—like when he got faster or just stopped and then was slow and in the background. It created a mystery, sort of."

**"What questions do you have?"** Ms. Walker then asks.

"What type of food does a plant make?" asks a girl.

The narrator answers, "Sugar."

Other groups present their photosynthesis mini-dramas. One uses sound effects for water. Another uses a rain stick. Each performance adds new images to target science concepts. As both audience and performers, students listen closely to each other, observe, wonder, question, and learn. When applause erupts, there are smiles all around.

Out of nowhere come flags made with paper, fabric, paints, collage materials—each one on a twig stick. The flags bear symbols like masks, palettes, violins, and unicorns. Many have seven stripes. Why seven?

"Because there are seven specials at Ashley River," explains a tall girl. "The unicorn is our mascot."

"Remember our American Revolution test is on Friday. Let's chant the 13 colonies."

On the board is written the **mnemonic,** "Granny Smith never vacuums cats, dogs, people, newts, nannies or navigators, maybe rude monkeys." Ms. Walker points to each word as students **chant,** "Georgia, South Carolina, North Carolina, Pennsylvania, Virginia, Connecticut, Delaware, New York, New Hampshire, New Jersey, Massachusetts, Rhone Island, and Maryland."

"And who loved his flag?"

"Jasper," students shout chorally.

"How do we know?"

"Because he saved the flag at Fort Moultrie."

"Why do you think he did that?" Ms. Walker asks.

This time only three hands go up. She calls on each.

"For the group, the other soldiers."

"To get everyone to keep trying."

"To give them hope."

"Hurray! Let's wave our flags to say we want everyone in our class to have hope," Ms. Walker joins in the flapping frenzy as students hurry out to head home. ✳

## Conclusion

*Our doubts are traitors, and make us lose the good we oft might win, by fearing to attempt.* (William Shakespeare)

This chapter is about *why* and *how* to integrate drama throughout the curriculum. The goal is to provide teachers with enough information to have the courage to "give it a go." Solid research, clear theories, and a fund of professional wisdom justify the use of this powerful teaching and learning tool. To make drama integration meaningful, however, classroom teachers need drama and theatre literacy, and this chapter outlined the nature of this knowledge. The 10 AI building blocks were used as an organizer for thinking about planning, teaching, and assessing. Essential to bringing drama to life is collaborative work drama specialists to customize lessons for specific students. They also know good Shakespeare quotes.

---

### Teachers as Leaders: AI Advocacy

Create short (5-minute) before and after dramas about arts integration (e.g., use tableau variations). Share them in a public forum such as another college class or faculty meeting. Think out of the box: Email video of the dramas to Oprah or Arne Duncan, U.S. secretary of education. Become famous worldwide by posting on YouTube.

---

### PEARSON myeducationlab

Go to the Activities and Applications section for Topic *Strategies for Teaching* at MyEducationLab for your course and complete the video activities entitled "Using Drama as Literary Response", "Using Side Coaching to Increase Use of Details", and "Using Split Audience to Increase Participation."

Go to the Activities and Applications section for Topic *Attaining Arts Literacy* and complete the video activity entitled "Drama Specialist Interview about Setting Up."

Go to the Book Specific Resources section in the MyEducationLab for your course, select your book and Chapter 8 to view the Questions to Guide Reading, Response Options, and Bibliography of Drama Based Children's Literature.

---

## Resources

See Appendix I for additional materials, including websites.

The *North Carolina Theatre Arts Teacher Handbook* includes a bank of lesson plans and assessment items. Access at www.ncpublic-schools.org (click "Curriculum," then "Arts Education," then "Resources").

### Software and Games

Play Write, IBM Educational Systems (software)
Puppet Maker, IBM Educational Systems (software)
*Kid on Stage,* Music for Little People (games)

### DVDs and Videos

*Creative dramatics: The first steps.* Northwestern Film Library, 614 Davis St., Evanston, IL 60201.

*Max makes mischief* (30 min.). University Park: Pennsylvania State University (unit on *Where the Wild Things Are*). Available from the Instructional Media Center, National–Louis University, Evanston, IL 60201:
- *Dorothy Heathcote Talks to Teachers—Part I and Part II.*
- *Dorothy Heathcote Building Belief, Part I and II.*

*More Heathcote videos:* AV Centre, University of Newcastle, Framlington Place, Newcastle upon Tyne NE2 4HH, England.

# Drama and Storytelling Seed Strategies

9

*I would suggest that the future of our economy is more based in creating a creative class and creating a generation of people who can think artistically than people who can think mathematically.*
(Arkansas Governor, Mike Huckabee)

## Overview

This chapter is a compendium of ideas to prompt brainstorming for meaningful drama integration. First up are energizers and warm-ups to stimulate creative problem solving and provide practice with concentration and focus. Next are seed strategies for teaching pantomime and verbal improvisation followed by drama integration ideas for curricular areas. A special focus section on storytelling gives an overview of purposes, procedures, and seed strategies.

## Introduction: Drama Reminders

The goal is to find drama strategies that have a "meaningful fit" with student needs, lesson objectives, and curricular standards. The ideas in the chapter are in seed or kernel form, which means they are undeveloped. Seed strategies also are not "leveled," but most can be customized for primary and intermediate grades. No teaching strategy should be used, even by next-door teachers at the same grade level, without differentiation.

As you consider the seed strategies that follow, keep in mind that drama strategies are made more effective when teachers do the following:

- Focus on meaningful integration which has to include teaching about the unique aspects of the art of drama, as well as how to use drama to think about another curricular area.
- Focus on student problem solving through drama, not just following the teacher's directions. Drama is not about imitation of a model. Students need to feel free to create surprising ideas.
- Do explicit teaching of drama content: Name the strategy, tell its purpose, ask open questions, and give examples. Follow with time to experiment, and coaching with descriptive feedback.

- Coach students to "make me believe"—to focus, concentrate, and stay in role by controlling mind/imagination, body, face, and voice.
- Teach start and stop signals such as open curtain, close curtain, begin, end.
- Ask students for new ways to repeat the drama to make it communicate more.
- Teach the basics of audience etiquette—how to be good audience members.

## Classroom Snapshot
### Vocabulary Meanings through Drama

In the opening Classroom Snapshot, a teacher, using a book connected to a Civil War unit, uses many drama seed strategies to develop vocabulary. In particular, notice her use of coaching to increase problem solving. Second-grade teacher Martha Kearney is using a **sock puppet.**

"Say that like the president would say it," orders the puppet.

"I'll declare war!" shout the students.

The sock puppet speaks in a soft southern dialect that is Martha's own. "Workers were brought over here from _____."

She uses the **oral cloze strategy.** Students immediately show they are making sense because they say "Africa" in unison.

"And sold as slaves when they arrived in _____."

Some say "America," others "the South" and "the United States."

The puppet is shaking its head. "There are many right answers."

"So, what is the North's point of view?" the puppet asks.

"No slaves," says one boy.

"What is the South's?" she continues.

A girl with freckles says, "The slaves got what they needed, and the masters got what they needed."

"So what was the problem?" the puppet asks.

"The slaves were sad," a boy comments.

"What are some better words than *sad*?" asks the puppet.

"Miserable!" says a blond boy.

"That is a descriptive word," says the puppet. "I have to leave now. Goodbye."

**229**

Ashley River students pantomiming emotions

Martha marches the puppet to the closet. The class waves and calls out, "Goodbye" and "See you tomorrow." When she turns back around, the teacher has a large card with *miserable* printed on it.

"Yesterday we learned about a slave who felt miserable. Why?"

Hands go up, but Martha waits. She finally calls on one student.

"His master was going to sell him," explains a boy.

"Show me *miserable*," Martha coaches them to use their bodies and faces to show through **pantomime.** She takes time to describe how students use their mouths, heads, and arms. This **descriptive feedback** causes them to increase concentration.

"OK, when he was running away, how did he feel?"

"Scared!"

"Give me a synonym for *scared* that begins with /f/."

"Frightened!"

"Yes! **Show me the meaning** of *frightened*."

Students curl up and cover their faces as Martha describes the range of use of body parts and facial expressions they create.

"If I was the director of a play, show me why I should choose you to be one of my actors." Students respond with more focus, and some try to exaggerate their facial expression to show more fear.

"You are all hired! Now, he was _____." She holds up a card with the word *exhausted*. "When I say 3, everyone read it, 1-2-3."

"Exhausted!"

Martha lowers her volume and seems to take on the meaning of the word herself. "Why was he so exhausted?"

"He was tired from running."

"All the fear was wearing him out."

"OK, on 3 again. Show me *exhausted* and freeze."

Students do **frozen pantomimes** to convey the word meaning.

"On 2, sit up," Martha directs. She counts and then continues, "Then he made it to the safe house, but he became _____." She holds up another vocabulary card, *confused*.

The students immediately read the card chorally.

Martha now looks confused with her eyebrows and eyes squinted together. "Why was Louis confused?"

A boy who hasn't said anything before raises his hand. "He thought he was free when he crossed the river. But, he wasn't."

"Show me *confused*," she says. Students scratch their heads and look around with eyebrows together. Again, Martha gives feedback.

"Then he had a time when he was _____." The card reads *embarrassed*.

The students chorally read. Then she asks why Louis was embarrassed. Students describe Louis's clothes, and a boy finally summarizes the nature of the clothes as "women's."

At this point Martha tells them to stand up. She selects one student and tells him that he is a "kind man," and she will take the role of Louis. **In role,** she asks, "Why would you want me to wear a woman's clothes?"

"This will help you get away," says the "kind man."

"OK, everyone, get a partner. If you are a one, raise your hand. You are the kind man. Twos, you are Louis. When I say 'begin,' I want you to talk to each other. Louis people, you start. Begin."

## Pair Dialogue

As pairs begin to interact, Martha **circulates and coaches,** "Say that with more feeling," she urges one girl. The girl does and her teacher smiles. After a few minutes they reverse roles.

"You are all now going to be Louis. Think of how you feel in your surroundings in the slave quarters. Use your whole body. Concentrate. Close your eyes and picture in your head. I'll read the next part."

Martha reads from the chapter book *Long Journey Home* (Lester). The book has six stories on freedom. The one she reads is about a slave named Louis who is deciding what to take with him. During the remainder of the reading she **inserts mimes** to get students to "show" how they feel. At one point she reads about Louis walking slowly to the door. She tells students to walk to their seats like Louis.

Martha coaches several students to "stay in character." She continues to read as she walks around the room. One boy points to a painting of the North Star at an appropriate moment in the story, others mime actions at their seats, as suggested by the text.

Martha's voice is soft as she asks, "How are you feeling?"

The students almost whisper as they call out, "frightened," "thankful," "relieved," and "confused."

"Everyone, show me *relieved*," she says. Students sigh and slump. She then reads on, but pauses and spontaneously converts the text into **narrative pantomime** material.

"You have been running and running, and your chest is burning in pain. Show me this pain," she coaches.

The second graders grimace, clutch their chests, and hold their heads.

"Hold that feeling. Captains, please pass out writing journals," she says. They will spend 10 minutes **writing in character** about what they have just experienced.

# Organization

The first four sections of this chapter concentrate on energizers and warm-ups, pantomime, verbal improvisation, and specific curricular areas (science, social studies, literacy, and math). The final section focuses specifically on storytelling.

# I. Energizers and Warm-Ups

Energizers and warm-ups are used to motivate, relax, and increase concentration and focus. They stimulate thinking that primes the brain for creative problem solving using the tools of body, face, and voice. Most energizers trigger higher order thinking and require self-control. Energizers from other chapters, especially dance, can also be used for drama integration.

**Greetings!** (Relax). Everyone mills around until the leader says, "Greet." Everyone starts to greet people in different ways. The leader can suggest roles or dispositions: Pretend you are long-lost friends or are from another culture (e.g., Japan, France).

**Wiggle Worms.** (Focus). Students find a personal space. The teacher mimes opening a jar of worms and tells students to get ready to grab them. Toss the worms and direct students to catch and eat and become the wiggle worms. On "freeze" cue, students stop. Repeat with half the class being the audience who gives feedback. Then reverse halves. (Source: Jeff Jordan, Ashley River)

**Hand Study.** (Focus/Observation). Partners take turns examining each other's hands. Tell them to see and feel everything that makes hands unique. *Variation:* Use as a "get to know you" introductions activity: "This is Joe and he has very thick hands with short fingernails. His hands are tan as if he works outside a lot."

**Play Ball.** (Focus/Concentration). Form a circle. Leader holds an imaginary ball (show size with hands) and calls someone's name before it is thrown, saying, "Sue, basketball." The receiver then says, "Thank you, basketball." Play continues, with receiver calling a name and throwing the pretend basketball. After a few rounds, the leader introduces a second ball, saying, "Joe, beach ball," and Joe responds, "Thank you, beach ball." Continue to add more balls. At the end, call "stop" and ask everyone with a ball to hold it. The audience guesses the kind of ball by its size and how it is held.

**Concentration.** (Visualizing). Make a tray of items. Direct students to study the items by picturing them in their heads. Cover the tray. Students list all they remember. *Variation:* Students close their eyes and an item is removed or rearranged. They figure out the change. Use small wipe-off boards so all can write the missing item and show boards.

**Line Up.** Leader calls out various ways to line up: alphabetically, by birthday, by height, and so forth. Periodically stop and have students interview those around them to find out three things about one another. *Variation*: Give directions to group in north, south, east, or west locations. *Example:* Redheads take the north wall.

**Tongue Twisters and Tanglers.** (Vocal Fluency). First say each twister slowly as a group. Next, practice individually and in pairs or go around a circle. Make into a game where play begins over if a person mispronounces. Examples: "A hot cup of coffee from a proper copper coffee pot." "Aluminum linoleum." "Bugs black blood." "Six sick sheep." "Unique New York." Find more in *Six Sick Sheep* (Cole) and on numerous websites. *Follow-up:* Students collect and create twisters. Organize alphabetically in a recipe box. Put up a Twister Master chart to keep track of ones they say three times without error. Challenge with longer twisters such as "Peter Piper." (Schwartz's *A Twister of Twists: A Tangler of Tongues* offers the history of this classic.)

**Finger Plays.** (Focus). Teach finger plays such as "The Itsy Bitsy Spider." There are many collections and Little Richard has a wild CD of them. Here is an untraditional one for focus. Seat everyone on the floor and say, "I relax and focus" (point to self with thumb and lay hands in lap). "I gather in the good" (gather with hands brought in). "I push out the bad" (push outward with both hands). "I celebrate the joy all around me" (raise hands, spread fingers, and do a silent cheer).

**One Word at a Time.** Sit in a circle. First person says one word to start a sentence. The next person says a word, and so on. The goal is to make as long a "sensical" sentence as possible.

**Sound and Action Stories.** (Close Listening). A narrator tells a story while children echo lines and do actions. "Going on a Bear Hunt" is an example, and is accompanied by a walking rhythm. Between sections give time to mime. When the bear is seen, actions are reversed—double time. Another example of a sound/action story appears later in the chapter, in Ready Reference 9.2.

**Scavenger Hunt.** (Cooperation/categories). Give groups a time limit. For example, "In 5 minutes find a silky item, a book with an r-controlled word, something that moves, and something that can be used to create." Items can be collected or written down. *Variation*: Use the five senses to organize searches: "Find something that looks like ________, sounds like ________, feels like ________."

**Word Change.** Sit in a circle. First person says a sentence, such as "Mary had a little lamb." Next person repeats the sentence, but changes one word: "Mary had a little goat." Keep going all the way around. Challenge: Reverse and return the sentence to its original form.

**Partner Search.** (Close listening). Make cards with sounds or song titles and pass them out. For example, do five different titles on five sets of cards for 25 students. The goal is to have groups form by finding those who are singing the same song or making the same sound.

**Two Facts and One Lie.** Students list three facts about themselves. One item should be false. Students read aloud items. The audience applauds to show which one they believe is the lie. *Note:* Discuss how to use creative ideas without being obvious.

**Animal-Car-Flower.** (Categories). This helps students get to know one another. Students write down the three categories and an example that applies to them. For example, "My name is _____ and I identify with a cat because _____, a Jeep because _____, and roses because _____." *Variation*: Change categories to water, land, buildings, music, furniture, fruit, for example.

**Reverse Web.** (Team builder). Students form small groups. Use large paper and have everyone write. *Directions:* Draw a circle in the center with a leg coming out for each person. Write a name on each leg. In the center, write/draw things the group has in common. The more unusual the better (e.g., all like broccoli).

**Pass and Pretend.** (CPS/Visual Imagery). Sit in a circle. Pass around an ordinary object (e.g., a scarf). Students use it in a creative way by imagining what it can become. For example, a scarf could be rocked like a baby. Encourage focus on details of action (see "Invisible Object Mime"). *Variation 1*: Do without a prop and ask students to imagine an object, such as a pin, and pantomime using it. First person passes it to the next, who must use the same object and then transform it into something else. *Variation 2*: Pass a straw and say, "This is not a straw, it's a _____," and then demonstrate how it has transformed.

**Character Voices.** (Fluency). Make various character cards. Then make a list of random sentences: "Hi, how are you?" "Can you tell me how to get to the nearest hospital?" "We've really been having bad weather lately." "I'm so tired." Students draw a card and say the sentence, in character. Others tell what message and feelings they heard and clues to who it is. For example, Santa might "ho-ho-ho" in between his words or phrases.

**Laugh Contest.** (Focus/Control). A panel tries to resist laughing as one classmate has a go at telling jokes, making faces, and the like. Discuss school-appropriate humor before doing this!

**Belly Laughs.** (Team Builder). Everyone lies on the floor with his head on someone else's belly. At a signal, someone says "ha" and the "ha" travels around the circle. When it gets around, someone else starts a different laugh (e.g., "he he").

**Noiseless Sounds.** (Focus). Brainstorm ways to pantomime sounds without making any noise: laugh, applause, choke, sneeze. *Variation*: Ask students to divide the sound into three consecutive pantomime actions (e.g., steps in a sneeze). Groups practice and present to the whole class.

**What's Different?** (Concentration). Pair students and label as A and B. A faces B and concentrates on details of B's appearance. Leader signals and pairs turn back to back. B makes a change. Pairs turn around, and A gets three guesses to figure out "what's different." Then B takes a turn.

**Bell Tolls.** (Category Game). This requires fast thinking and movement. Give each student a 1/2-inch piece of masking tape. Make a circle. The person who is "IT" goes in the center. Everyone else stands on the tape. IT begins by saying, "The bell tolls for all those who _____," and plugs in a category (play an instrument, know Picasso's first name). Anyone who fits the category must move and try to get a new spot while IT tries to get a spot. The person without a spot is the new IT. At any point in the game, IT can shout "tornado" and everyone must move to a new spot, not right next door. Adapt for any unit (e.g., knows the capital of Maine).

**Name Sock.** (Concentration/Focus). Make two balls by knotting up socks. Stand in a circle and explain the purpose is to learn names. Ask each student to say his name. The class echoes. The leader then models how the game works by saying her name and the name of another person to whom she then throws a ball. That person says her own name, another person's, and throws to that person, and so forth. When things are going well, the leader throws out a second sock ball. *Variation*: Students each take an alias (e.g., book character, famous person).

**Hot Sock.** (Categories). Make a set of alphabet or general category cards and use a knotted sock. Sit in a circle with IT in the center. IT closes eyes and throws the sock. At will, IT says stop. Person caught with the sock passes it the person to the right who holds it. IT draws a card and reads it. Sock is now passed person to person around the circle while the "caught" person names five items in the category. *Example*: Five things that start with B.

**Voice Stunts.** (Focus). Form groups of four. Give groups a phrase. For example, "To be or not to be," "Zig-zag-zog," or "Slip-slap-slop." Each person says one word in the phrase and play goes around the circle, or IT can pass using eye contact or pointing.

**Stunts and Tricks.** (Confidence). Students perform stunts. For example, rub stomach and pat head at same time, balance balloon or pencil on the end of the nose, stand with left shoulder and side of left foot snug against a wall and try to raise right leg. See Goodman's *Magic and the Educated Rabbit* and Randi's *The Magic World of the Amazing Randi* for more ideas.

**Boring Words.** (Fluency). Brainstorm a list of dull words (e.g., *cardboard, the, dust, box*). Practice saying them changing dynamics (volume), tempo (rate), pitch, pause, and stress to make them interesting. *Variation*: Collect boring phrases and sentences for this activity.

**Stage Directions.** This activity requires quick thinking and concentration. Do this in an open space to teach stage directions, which are from the actor's viewpoint: stage right, stage left, and center stage. Designate a stage area and use tape to make a line for the audience area. Explain that you will be calling directions quickly and sometimes there will be more than one group at a place. When you call "audience," students must sit down behind the line. Divide the class into four groups. Call out the following directions quickly.

- Groups 1 and 4: Stage Right
- Group 2: Stage Left
- Group 3: Stage Center
- Groups 1 and 3: Audience

**Ways to Celebrate.** Use a variety of ways to celebrate good ideas. *Examples:* standing ovation, pat on the back, firecracker mime, or mime and say together, "Pat, pat, pat, on the back, back, back, for a job well done. Altogether now . . . REPEAT."

# II. Pantomime Seed Strategies

Pantomime or "mime" is acting without words. It demands that students take roles and pretend using their bodies, faces, and imagination. Pantomime is a form of drama that young children naturally exhibit before they learn to speak so it is often a starting place for meaningful drama integration. Pantomime is an important tool for differentiating instruction because it is a communication alternative for shy students or children with limited oral expression skills, such as English language learners, to express ideas and feelings.

Simple or complex, pantomime triggers CPS and makes student thinking visible. Conscious change of body shapes, movement, and facial expression are used to show emotion, age, size, weight, temperature—or any other sensory area. Mime can be as simple as "becoming" a teapot and pretending to tip and pour, but it can also show more complex ideas, such as the process of transforming from a seed to a plant or can show a character becoming increasingly confident. Through pantomime, students learn to imagine (visualize) and simulate places, events, and emotions that may never be experienced firsthand (e.g., walking on the moon). Pantomime can also develop into complex performances such as a reenactment of Columbus's travails on his voyage to the New World.

The teacher's role is to set up problems that cause students to think through body and facial action. A good place to begin is real-life roles that call for movement. For example, pretending to cook would involve showing mixing, stirring, and pouring. Curricular content should be examined for natural opportunities for students to role play. Student success is facilitated by use of easy structures, such as narrative pantomime and short experiences confined to small spaces like the desk area. Coaching enhances concentration and focus, for example, saying "I see _____" or "How else might you show _____?" Equally important is asking students to describe in detail what they see peers doing. Common problems, such as students who want to make pantomimes into guessing games, should be anticipated. Redirect them to focus on describing pantomime details that give the best information. When guesses are made, ask for evidence to support conclusions

The following section includes types of pantomimes adaptable for most curricular areas. Ready Reference 9.1 lists suggested

 **Ready Reference 9.1** Pantomime Possibilities: A–Z

*Directions: Brainstorm things to mime. The following are examples across curricular areas, such as miming verbs (action words) in language arts to show word meanings.*

- Actions: clean, travel, eat, ignore, cough, nudge, videotape
- Animals: moving, eating, sleeping; different categories (e.g., insect, bird, mammal)
- Book chapters: key actions in each chapter
- Character actions: spider writes in web, Jack climbs beanstalk
- Emotions or feelings: happy, angry, disgusted, surprised, embarrassed
- Foods: being gathered, prepared, eaten
- Getting ready: for school, to go to the beach
- Hobbies or vacations: juggling, jumping rope, tennis
- Holidays or festivals: wedding dances, party decorating
- Jobs, occupations, careers: bricklayer, seamstress, carpenter
- Machine movements: computers, mixers, vacuum, mower
- Making objects: shoes, quilt; shapes (e.g., types of Greek columns); musical instruments: being played, carried, cleaned
- Objects: holding and placing objects (e.g., fruit, animals, food)
- Pairs: anything that takes two (e.g., fold a sheet, play tennis)
- People: poses or actions of celebrities, politicians, inventors, or common roles (mother, police officer)

- Pets: how to care for, play with, train
- Places: beach, cave, closet, rooftop, edge of cliff
- Plants: changing, growing, blooming, dying
- Processes: nesting, cooking, building, manufacturing
- Rituals and customs: greetings, farewells
- Sensory responses to items: what if . . .? (good smell, scary sound)
- Sports: how to dress for, play, waiting your turn
- Things you: like to do, do not like to do
- Tools: use of, cleaning, carrying
- Toys: using, storing
- Vehicles: scooter, inline skates, tricycle
- Walks: in character, under different circumstances (moods, destinations); change levels, pathways, speeds
- Weather: response to conditions or pretend to be a kind of weather
- Wise sayings: for example, "You can lead a horse to water but you can't make him drink."
- Word categories: antonyms, homophones, three syllable

actions that connect to concepts in science, social studies, or math. The goal is give students additional ways to use CPS and *show they know*—to make thinking visible. Because CPS is used, students must use higher order thinking, which transforms their understanding about key concepts. Many pantomime ideas are especially valuable for causing students to summarize, but thinking is extended beyond simple recall of information, to synthesis to create pantomime and then evaluation thinking to gauge effectiveness.

**Mime Basics: Invisible Objects.** Use a "mystery" bag or basket. Tell students to think of objects related to a unit (e.g., colonial times or fairy tales). Sit in circle. First volunteer pretends to pull out an item and shows: shape, size, weight, texture, temperature, and a way it can be used. Guessers put thumbs up. IT calls on peers who must describe aspects of the mime that were most "telling" and name the item. To make an object look real, coach students to take time for the following:

1. Slowly study it (size, shape, texture, temperature).
2. Reach out as if to touch it (move toward it to show how you will take hold).
3. Take hold (imagine your hands on it, then feel it).
4. Use it as you would if it were really there.
5. Stop and slowly replace it.
6. Let go slowly and move away.

Afterward, invite students to isolate a part they did well and demonstrate, or ask them to give each other feedback on which steps looked most real and why.

**Quick Mime/Show Me.** Brainstorm key events from a story or unit texts. Next to each, list emotions caused by events in units or stories. For example, "disappointed you can't go to the ball." Use the list to give a series of "Show me with your face and body" directions. For example, "Show me exhausted from marching through mud."

**Action Songs.** Many songs have characters and actions that can be mimed, such as boat rowing, stars twinkling, or ants marching. Examples: "Little Bunny Foo Foo," "Grand Old Duke of York," "My Hat It Has Three Corners," and "This Old Man, He Played One." The *Serendipity Encyclopedia* (Coleman, 1997) has many. Ask students to examine lyrics for actions and think of unusual ways to mime each. *Variations:* (1) Write your own song adaptation with actions (e.g., if you're happy and you know it laugh out loud, smile a while, show your teeth, grin a lot). More songs are listed in the music chapters and in books in Appendix J. (2) Sing or recite nursery rhymes. Divide into groups and have each group plan which rhyme to say and mime, or just mime, for audience to observe and give feedback.

**Mirrors.** (Concentration). Brainstorm people or characters. Students pair up and face each other. Partner A pretends to be a character or person and looks into the mirror. B becomes the mirror. The goal is to align actions so that an observer cannot tell the "real" from the "reflection." Start in slow motion. *Example:* Student A pretends to be a self-centered stepsister getting ready for the ball. Reverse roles and B chooses a character. *Variation:* Teacher calls out an emotion or condition related to a character or moment: anger, worry, relief, glee. Student A physically portrays that emotion and freezes. B mirrors A. Both remain frozen until the next emotion is called out and B then takes the lead. Discuss what was easy and difficult (e.g., staying frozen). What did they notice about facial expressions, gestures, body shape?

**Solo Mime.** Students work individually but with the whole group, each in a personal space (Heinig, 1993). The teacher controls the action by coaching and narrating. For example, "You are Little Miss Muffet looking for a place to sit and eat. Remember, you've seen spiders in this garden before." Give signals to start and end, such as flick lights or count down.

**Number Freeze.** Number off in fives. Give a setting or context (e.g., the farm in *Charlotte's Web*). Call a number. That group pantomimes an action from the designated setting. Audience members (other groups) tell specifics they observe, followed by "naming" the action. The next number is then called, and so on. *Note:* Group members can perform the action in unison or give individual interpretations of the same action.

**Count–Freeze.** Give students a category, such as "things you do at school" (Ready Reference 9.1). Explain you will count to 10 as they pantomime. They are to freeze on 10. *Variation:* Do in pairs or trios, and count at different speeds. Literature example: "The Mouse at the Seashore" (fable): things the mouse might have done on his journey in the morning, afternoon, and evening.

**1-2-3 Mime.** Students are asked to imagine actions for a given topic and told to number each. For example, "Think of three things Goldilocks might do while traveling through the woods. Number them, one, two, and three in your mind. When I say a number, you mime your action." Coach students to "make it real" by using details and slowing down.

**Time Mime.** (Control). Students mime at different speeds from slow to fast and back to slow. For example, count slowly and tell students to move "as if you are under water." Slow mood music or a piece such as "Clair de Lune" can also be used to set pace. For fast motion pantomime, tell students to move like a fast-forwarded video. Play Scott Joplin songs or a fast piece such as the "Spinning Song." Note: Any pantomime can be replayed at different speeds.

**Transformations.** Brainstorm characters or things that change (e.g., young to old, seasons, phases of the moon). Ask students to break down phases and do in slow motion. Add music. Example: Become a fairy tale character and change, on a slow count of 10, into another character (e.g., a beast into a prince).

**Pair Pantomime.** Brainstorm actions requiring two people (e.g., playing checkers). Partner students. At a count, or with a time limit, students mime as many as they can. Example: Prince putting the slipper on Cinderella. *Suggestion:* Do an action in slow, regular, and then in quick time to increase self-control. *Variations:* Mime famous pairs like the Wright brothers. Add conflict in repeat playing to increase CPS (e.g., Cinderella's feet smell).

**Break It Down.** (Analysis/Sequence). Students list a series of actions in an event or a place (e.g., sneeze). Break into three to five parts to pantomime in order. For example, wrinkle nose, suck in breath three times while throwing back the head, throw head forward, wipe nose. *Variation:* Add conflict (e.g., cannot get to the "choo").

**Think Back Pantomime.** Students recall actions of characters or actions from science, math, or social studies (e.g., sewing the first flag). Each chooses one. At start cue, students repeat it, in place, until stop cue. Ask students to use the BEST (dance) elements to make changes and replay. *Extension:* Students line up and replay in plot order or get into groups (beginning, middle, end of story, importance, and so forth, to replay).

**Emotion Pantomimes.** Start with an emotional situation, such as being home alone and hearing strange noises. Ask students to brainstorm emotional moments in literature or other areas of study, times when a character has strong feelings. At start cue, students use face and body to mime examples. Coach, using "I see . . . statements" with focus on use of details to show action/emotion. Split class into actors and audience to share. Reverse so all have a chance to observe and tell what works. *Variation:* Add conflict to increase interest and creative thinking.

**What If: Obstacle Pantomimes.** Brainstorm actions of characters or people from units. Write ideas on a web. Do a unison pantomime of the ideas. Next, divide into groups and ask each to add a problem or obstacle (conflict) to one action (e.g., Charlotte is very sleepy). Groups each then present with audience feedback on what works.

**Chain Pantomime.** One person starts in the center of the room. Others join as they guess the topic (guessers can whisper answers to the teacher). Example: For a weather unit, first student might mime towering cumulus clouds. Others join and mime other types of clouds.

**Kalamazoo.** (Adapted from Heinig, 1993). Divide into two groups and each half decides on a pantomime category (e.g., jobs, animals, toys). Line up facing each other. Group 1 says, "Here we come," and group 2 responds, "Where are you from?" Group 1, "Kalamazoo." Group 2, "What do you do?" Group 1, "Here's a clue." Group 1 then pantomimes while group 2 guesses.

**Five Senses Pantomimes.** Brainstorm actions for five senses or categorize ideas from a book or unit under five senses. Call a sense and students pantomime. *Variation:* Add a problem, such as you are eating a chicken sandwich, but you bite into something hard (taste).

**Verb Mime.** Brainstorm actions (verbs) or ways to move from current units. (See BEST dance elements in Ready Reference 10.2 and Action Bingo in Chapter 11). Put words in a basket. Each person picks one and "becomes the move," while others guess its name. This can be done in pairs (e.g., all in group A twist, while those in group B observe and switch).

**Safe Fights.** Drama, literature, and history are full of conflict. It is a good idea to prepare for one kind that students often want to pantomime—fights. Ask students to practice showing different moves in personal spaces *without touching anyone* (e.g., punch, stab, claw, slap). Do in slow motion or to a count. Get into pairs. In slow motion, practice with one person responding. Emphasize no touching or falling down. Use start and stop signals.

**Charades.** This favorite pantomime game involves two teams. Each takes a turn. Traditional categories are book, song, TV show, film, and famous person, but any category can be used: one-, two-, or three-syllable words, rhyme pairs (hink pinks such as "sad dad"), synonyms, antonyms, words beginning with a letter or sound, homophones (*sum–some, red–read*), quotes, proverbs, famous pairs (e.g., peanut butter and jelly), states, countries, and so forth. Create nonverbal cues, such as sounds like (pull ear), short word (show size with fingers), long word (show with two hands moving apart), syllable numbers (show with fingers), movie (pretend to roll film), and book (use hands to show open book).

**Imaginary Place.** (Heinig, 1993). Students visualize a setting from history, literature, or science. Mark off space with tape to establish the place or allow a volunteer to establish the place through mime (i.e., bring in an item and place it). Each will then pretend to stock place with appropriate items. Subsequent actors must observe and follow suit with an object that fits. Coach the audience to hone in on specific actions for key clues. Pairs can work together for big items, such as bringing a stove into a kitchen. The next actor might then bring in a refrigerator and add detail like getting ice. *Suggestion:* Periodically, review all items and their placement to increase visualization.

**QU Plot Pantomime.** (Adapted from Heinig, 1993). Ask students to list key events in a story and then put in order. Type the list using a YOU (U) = _____ (what to do) and a Cue (Q) = _____ (what to look for). Include a Q to start the pantomime. Make two copies of the list. Cut one into strips to pass out. Retain full copy of the QU to keep track of the action. Double or triple cast so everyone participates. Here is an example of a full copy based on *Charlotte's Web.*

Note: Cut so each strip has a Q and a U. Give each student one strip.

Q: The leader says, "A Day in the Barn"
U: Pretend to be Charlotte spinning her web
Q: When Charlotte spins her web
U: Mime Wilbur eating out of his trough
Q: Wilbur eating out of his trough
U: Pretend to be Fern and come in and sit on a stool to watch
Q: Fern comes in and sits on her stool
U: Pretend to be Templeton sneaking around
Q: Templeton sneaking around
U: Applaud

*Variation:* Use to review content under study (e.g., steps in a science experiment).

**Sound-Motion Machine.** Choose a category to pantomime (e.g., a chapter in MacLachlan's *Sarah, Plain and Tall* has these movements: rolling a marble, sweeping, riding a horse). Each student chooses a repeatable movement related to the category. One person starts the pantomime, and others join in until all are moving in a space. On signal, everyone adds a sound. *Variation:* All members of a machine must be touching to show they are a connected whole.

**Prediction Pantomime.** Technically, all pantomimes should be creative, but prediction pantomime offers more room for improvisation. Instead of interpreting actions, this pantomime idea involves more "what if" thinking. For example, stop reading a story at a poignant point and ask students to pantomime predictions of what might happen next. Emphasize thinking about possibilities. For example, "I want to see three things Cinderella might do after she gets home after the first night. I'll count to signal. Let's begin. One." *Variation*: Do half of a science experiment or stop partway through a video and ask students to mime an event they anticipate.

**Improvised BME Scene.** Pick a scene that has a beginning, middle, and end (BME) and at least two characters. Start with simple familiar plots, such as the scene when Miss Muffet gathers the things she needs to have a meal on her tuffet, finally sits down to eat, and so forth. Signal students to "begin" and coach, as needed (e.g., "And it is cool outside so she needs a bonnet and coat."). When students prepare small-group scenes, remind them to use signals (such as "green" and "red" to start and stop so audience understands). *Variation:* Give each group a B, M, or E scene to plan. Provide rehearsal time and then each presents. *Variation:* Add captions or dialogue.

**One Minute After Scene.** Students imagine what happened 1 minute after a piece of art was finished or after a historical moment, such as signing the Declaration of Independence. Divide into groups to plan. Groups then present to the whole class.

**Character Improvisation.** Read a story and stop after the conflict is introduced. Break into groups to discuss the following questions, which are the same categories contained in a story map.

- What does the character want or need (goals or motives)?
- What is the problem or conflict?
- What stands in the way of the character getting what is desired?
- What actions can the character take to deal with the problem (plot)? Where might the character be (place)?
- What might the character say (e.g., a one-liner about the problem)?

Note: It helps to give students a planning sheet with the questions. Permit work in groups to plan a scene with a beginning, middle, and end to deal with the questions. A good way to structure is to create a one-liner about the problem to end the scene.

**Character Meetings.** Each student chooses a character from a text everyone knows. Partners then have conversations, in character, about their lives, problems, and so forth. Invite pairs to share conversation highlights with the class. *Variations:* (1) Use in social studies with historical characters. (2) At a signal, characters freeze and audience suggests an emotion. When conversation begins again, characters must use the emotion.

**Narrative Pantomime (NP).** This pantomime is teacher directed, giving it a degree of security to students new to drama. A narrator reads or tells a story as students create individual pantomimes showing their own creative thinking. Here is an example:

**Apple NP.** Tell students to find personal space and use their imaginations and pantomime skills to go on a journey. Say: "Show me finding an apple. Show where you are. Show getting the apple.

Following the "Drinking Gourd" stars

Show the size, weight, smell. Take a bite and show how it tastes. Oops, there is a problem. Show me what it is. Now show how you solve the problem. Now finishing the whole thing using your imagination to add your own details. Show what you do with the core. Show how you feel now that you are finished." Throughout the mimes, comment on what you see students doing, especially gestures and facial expressions that are telling. Repeat using split audience. Have half perform while others observe and comment. Reverse. *Extension:* Partner and repeat mirroring or have each take a turn miming while others tell what they see. Invite volunteers to perform for the class. *Variation:* Change objects.

**Material.** Start with familiar material from previous units or stories. Select stories with lots of action, a clear climax, and quiet ending. Beware of too much description and literary devices such as flashback. Stories of journeys, trips, or cycles of events (e.g., caterpillar turning into a butterfly or "day in the life of . . ." structures) work well for narrative pantomime. Van Allsburg's *The Z Was Zapped*, Van Laan's *Possum Come a-Knockin'*, Berger's *Grandfather Twilight*, Keats's *A Snowy Day*, and Chaconas's *The Way the Tiger Walked* are stories that need only minor changes to become usable texts. Ready Reference 8.6 provides an annotated bibliography; also see Appendix J.

**Procedures.** It works best to recast any story in the second person, "you," to cause students to take the role of a character. Edit stories by eliminating dialogue and extraneous description. Action can be added by changing descriptions to actionable text (e.g., instead "It was a hot hazy day" change to "You wipe your brow and squint as you look across the hazy horizon"). If there is a repeated sound, word, or phrase, then invite choral response. For example, Robert Munsch's *Thomas' Snowsuit* offers the repetition, "No!" A pause for students to add the word increases engagement. For chapter books or long stories, isolate one event to mime. For example, choose one chapter from *Because of Winn-Dixie* (Dicamillo) or *Junie B. Jones and the Stupid Smelly Bus* (Park). Remember to convert to "you" while reading, rather than use first person.

To introduce narrative pantomime, read the story aloud first. Ask students to listen for actions as they enjoy the story. During the second reading, read expressively and give students time to mime. Props, costumes, and scenery are not necessary. Imagination supplies all that is needed. If students are excited about developing pantomimes further, music may be added. In addition, teachers and students can add characters or actions by imagining others who might enter the story. An example of a narrative pantomime written by a teacher is provided in Planning Page 8.5. Habitat concepts were taught in a previous lesson.

**Variations.** Narrative pantomime is useful for introducing basic story structure (beginning, middle, end) and literary elements (plot, setting, characters, conflict, resolution) because students must physically engage these concepts. NP can also be written or told by students, but they need to understand to plan a beginning, middle, and end and add conflict to create a plot. Order is critical because it is difficult to mime a nonsequential narrative, such as "You wake up. You get up and brush your teeth. First you turn on the water and then you put paste on your toothbrush." Use the BEST dance elements in Chapter 10 to add variety to actions of any pantomime.

**Narrative Pantomime: Music.** As students sing or listen to a story sung through a ballad, invite them to interpret actions with pantomime. Example: Davey Crocket.

**Narrative Pantomime: Visual Art.** Students imagine they have tiny paintbrushes and not much space to paint. Narrate a pantomime in which you tell them to keep painting, but the size of the brush and the space keeps getting bigger and bigger. Music can be used to accompany this (e.g., "The Blue Danube" waltz). *Variation:* Use an actual painting to narrate its construction and invite students to visualize the product as they paint. Afterwards, show actual painting and compare with their mental images.

**Narrative Pantomime: Group Stories.** *Strega Nona* (dePaola), *Clown of God* (dePaola), and *Lentil* (McCloskey) are examples of children's literature with crowds or group scenes. These stories can be used for narrative pantomime and to ease students into dialogue. Do this by freezing scenes and asking actors to say a one-liner about who they are or what they feel at the moment. From there students can move into writing dialogue for groups.

**Tableau/Frozen Picture.** (Tortello, 2004). Pairs or small groups summarize learning by using frozen body shapes and facial expressions. For example, the most tension-filled scene or a key emotion can be selected from a narrative fiction or nonfiction work related to science or social studies units. To emphasize the "frozen picture" idea, large old picture frames can be held up as students "pose" for tableau. Audience members actively participate. Examples include the following:

- Describe what they see, with focus on the most significant details, and draw conclusions about the overall message.

- Ask questions of members of the tableau, especially in regard to their feelings and motives.
- Suggest specific ways to make the tableau more interesting or more intense (e.g., use of facial expressions, focus, variety of levels, use of arm positions). The audience may act as "sculptors" to actually move actors into new positions.

Audience members can also be given a role to develop point of view. For example, if the scene is Wilbur winning the blue ribbon, then the audience can be farmers, other farm animals, or Charlotte; and they tell what they see. Tableau variations include the following:

*Fast freeze.* Divide into groups of five to seven, and give each a name or number. Call out scenes to one group at a time. Without talking, the group who is up must quickly create a tableau without talking. Other students act as an audience. *Ideas:* Use any emotion, or captions such as "A day at the beach" or "Winter sports." Select important scenes from history, science, and literature to summarize curricular concepts. *Variation*: Signal for a tableau to come to life and actors begin speaking and moving.

*Count freeze.* Students create three different tableau to a count. For example, "Remain the same character but move into three different positions as I (slowly) say 3-2-1."

*Moving tableau.* Students freeze, then move (e.g., three steps), and then freeze on cue. Coach students to use movements that reveal telling details about who they are (e.g., emotions).

*One-liner tableau.* Students create scenes from artwork, history, literature, and the like. After they are "set," the teacher taps them one by one and each says one line about what they are thinking or feeling. *Variation:* When tapped, students come to life, do an action, and then freeze.

*Series tableau.* Groups each plan a series of tableau (e.g., from beginning, middle, and end of a story, creating a kind of cartoon strip with their bodies. *Variation:* Create what came *before* or *after* a scene from a painting, photo, or key moment in history.

*Captions.* Use book titles, newspaper headlines, current events, advertisement slogans, famous quotes, or phrases from units as prompts for tableau. For example, "Why does she always get to sit up front?" or "Hubble Telescope Repaired." *Variation:* Take photographs of tableau poses and post for caption writing.

*Silhouettes.* Use a light behind a taut sheet to create silhouettes. Students need to stand close to the sheet to present a clear image and turn lights off. Colored gels on the lights can be used for interesting effects. Ask students to discuss how using silhouette changes the tableau.

**Improvised Plays.** Create a play from any story without a script to memorize. Start with quality stories with lots of action and believable characters.

1. Read or tell a story and direct students to listen for (1) dialogue, special words, and refrains; and (2) to get the gist of the story.
2. Review essential dialogue and plot. Proceed to cast, adding characters, and even crowds so that all can participate. Plan

sound effects, music, and the space to be used (e.g., at desks or "stage" in a classroom space).

3. Decide who will narrate and how to start and end the drama.
4. Rehearse with the teacher coaching. If there are problems (e.g., if students do not know how to end), assume a character role and facilitate, or be the narrator and tell a conclusion with students following your lead. Circle or cumulative stories work well to begin (e.g., Henny Penny), as do episodic plots, such as Marshall's *George and Martha* books (Heinig, 1993).

**Song Skits.** Play a piece of music connected to a unit (e.g., "The Star-Spangled Banner"). Students develop a scene with a beginning, middle, and end to show how the composer used CPS to create the music or song. Remind students to include conflict in the beginning, and have a resolution to the conflict at the end of the scene. Coach students to use start and stop signals and to make events seem real or believable through concentration and use of imaginative details.

# III. Verbal Improvisation Strategies

Improvisation involves creating ideas spontaneously by "thinking on your feet." It can be done using only pantomime or, as discussed in the next section, with the addition of words. Verbal improvisation engages all types of thinking in the CPS process. In particular it is frequently used to summarize or review material, cause in-depth analysis, and make predictions at a stop point. The following strategies are organized from easy to more difficult.

**Sound Effects Stories.** Students add simple sound effects using voices or musical instruments (e.g., rhythm instruments) as the teacher reads or tells a story such as *Too Much Noise* (McGovern) or *Night Noises* (Fox). First, read the story aloud and ask students for sounds they heard. Plan how and who will make the sounds. Specific groups can be responsible for certain parts with everyone involved at some point. *Suggestion:* Use an imaginary volume signal and practice controlling loudness. Example stories with refrains or repeated lines are Viorst's *Alexander and the Terrible, Horrible, No Good, Very Bad Day*, Peck's *Hamilton*, and Hutchins' *Don't Forget the Bacon*.

**Sound Stories.** Find or write a story or poem that contains repeated words (e.g., character names) (Heinig, 1993). Brainstorm sounds for repeated words and post. Each time repeated words are read, students respond with a sound. To prepare, rehearse for each cue word. For example, Jack: "oops" and sad face, Jill: giggle and play with curl. Example stories and poems set up to use sounds are: "Laughing Time" in Jay's book by the same title, which has animal names that elicit a variety of laughs. McGovern's *Too Much Noise* and Murphy's *Peace at Last* are other good ones. *Variation:* Add actions. See an example sound story in Ready Reference 9.2.

**Volume Control.** Brainstorm sound categories (e.g., short vowels, city sounds, kitchen sounds, sounds from any story or unit). IT stands in front, calls a category, and "turn ups" the volume or "turns it down" using an agreed-upon cue. For example, move hand to low or high position. *Variation:* Do in pairs or small group, instead of whole class.

**Don't Laugh.** (Fluency/Control). Form four to five groups who each make a circle. An IT points at someone and asks a funny question. Person to the right of person questioned must answer. Everyone tries not to laugh. Go fast. *Example:* "Would you eat blue food?"

**Pair Sound Effects.** Brainstorm sounds from a context or event (e.g., ocean, storm, grocery store). Partners choose to be A or B. Partner A makes sounds and B stands behind A and makes actions that coordinate. Reverse roles. Everyone participates simultaneously, but a few can volunteer to replay for the class.

**One-Liners with Pictures/Props.** Students change their voices (dynamics, tempo, pitch, pause, stress) appropriate to

---

**Ready Reference 9.2**   ## Sound Story Example: "Stolen Tarts"

*Directions: Brainstorm and then rehearse sounds and actions the audience uses. During reading, pause after underlined words for response. Examples:*

| | |
|---|---|
| **Heart:** | Thump thump on chest with fist |
| **Queen:** | Blow kisses |
| **King:** | "Find him!" and point finger |
| **Knave:** | "Tee hee!" while smiling and shaking head |
| **Tarts:** | "Yum" and rub tummy |
| **Soldiers:** | Stomp feet |

Long ago in the Land of *Hearts* there was a terrible theft. It was on St. Valentine's Day that the *Queen* of *Hearts* baked some *tarts* to celebrate the national holiday. She baked raspberry, lemon, and custard *tarts* as a gift for the man to whom she had given her *heart*—the *King* of *Hearts*. The *Queen* placed her *tarts* on the windowsill to cool. While the *Queen* straightened up the royal kitchen, the *Knave* of *Hearts* sneaked up to the window. The *Knave* grabbed all the raspberry *tarts*. When the *Queen* saw the *tarts* were gone, she cried, "What *heart* less fellow has taken my *tarts*?"

The *Queen* went to the *King* for help. Quickly he dispatched his *soldiers* to find the thief and the missing *tarts*, saying, "Find him!"

It wasn't any time before the *soldiers* returned with the *Knave* and what was left of the raspberry *tarts*. The *King* ordered that the *Knave* have no *tarts* to eat for a whole year. The *Knave* of *Hearts* knelt before the *Queen*, asked for forgiveness, and crossed his *heart* to promise he would never steal her *tarts* again. It was a *heart* warming ending.

a role related to a picture or object. If a picture is used, students can become characters or objects in it. If an object is used, students can be someone who might use the object. Each student says a one-liner. Others tell how the actor best showed his or her identity. For example, after reading "Little Red Riding Hood," pass around a red cape. Students use the cape in some way and say a line the character might say. *Suggestions:* Create picture collections using magazines, cards, Internet, and so forth. Invite contributions to a class prop box for units (e.g., weather items and pictures).

**Say It Your Way.** (Fluency/Expression). Students say a sentence in a role or in a mood. Audience tells key vocal clues and guesses identity. Give time for students to rehearse the sentence many ways (e.g., angry, sad, confident). Coach to emphasize different words to change meanings: "*Who* is my friend? Who *is* my friend? Who is *my* friend? Who is my *friend?*" Cards with roles (character or person) may be used to stretch thinking. Following are sentence examples.

- I don't like your attitude.
- Everyone just left.
- She has a terrible headache.
- We only have five left.
- Remember to check each answer.
- Where do you think you are going?
- Turn out the light.
- Close the door.

**Conflicting Messages.** (Fluency/Expression). Students say a one-liner differently from what the words seem to convey (e.g., "I am happy" spoken with great sadness). Discuss effects.

**Character Talk.** (Fluency/Expression). Use to review any material. Students write important sentences or phrases from stories or a unit on cards. Mix cards in a basket. Students draw cards and read aloud as the character who said it. Ask about the context of each line.

**Sentence Frames.** (Fluency/Expression). Each person orally completes this frame: "I am _____ and I want _____." The goal is to not give names, but suggest a role the person played and a goal. Coach to vary dynamics, tempo, pitch, pause, and stress so each response is different in content and expression. After each student says the frame, the group can echo, "She is _____ and she wants _____." *Suggestions:* Use book characters or famous persons. See more sentence frames under "Reading and Language Arts" in Chapter 4.

**QU Scripts.** (Attention/Fluency). Short scripts that summarize a story or key ideas in any unit are written with "cue" and "you" directions (see previous QU pantomime directions). Type the script and use the copy/paste function to repeat the U line as the Q for the next reader. Cut QU lines apart with one Q and U on each strip. Students rehearse their U (YOU say this) with meaningful expression, and note the Q (the CUE). For example, Q = Mary had a little lamb. U = It's fleece was white as snow. The teacher follows a master copy during the reading. *Suggestions:* Jokes and riddles are easy to adapt because of the reader–response or question–answer

format. Poetry written in the first person, such as Silverstein's "Sick," works well (see Ready Reference 9.3). Adapt stories such as *If You Give a Mouse a Cookie* (Numeroff), *Pierre: A Cautionary Tale* (Sendak), or *The True Story of the Three Little Pigs by A. Wolf* (Scieszka).

**Conflicting Motives.** Brainstorm motives or reasons for actions of characters or real people and examples of what they do. Put motives on cards. Ask for two volunteers—A and B. Student A draws a motive card (e.g., to get B to sit down) and leaves the room. B draws a different motive (e.g., to get A to say the word "no"). A and B are brought back and given a context (e.g., "You are in the grocery and you meet an unpleasant neighbor."). Neither partner can verbally give away his or her motive. Audience observes how A and B interact, who accomplishes the goal, and how.

**Dialogue Cards.** (Fluency). Collect words, phrases, sentences, and headlines from magazines, newspapers, ads, and cards. Paste each on a card. Give each student a card face down. Pair and tell students to choose to be partner A or B. Turn over cards. Partner A begins the dialogue using the card. Partner B must respond and incorporate his or her card. *Variations:* (1) Do a chain activity. Everyone lines up and either reads the card expressively or goes in order but improvises a verbal response that connects to a previous person by using the card. (2) Separate question and answer cards (you need an equal number). Distribute randomly. Number questioners, who read in order. Whoever thinks they can answer with a card has a go at it.

**Emotion Conversation.** Each student chooses a character or person from current study. Roles can be from the same book or different (e.g., a real person from current events and a fictional character). Pair as A and B, and start with a volunteer pair to come up. Leader calls A or B to start the conversation, in role. Say "freeze" and ask audience to tell the emotions observed. Say "action" to continue the conversation. *Variation:* Freeze and audience suggests a new emotion that characters must assume (e.g., angry, surprised, elated).

**Quick Monologues.** Sit in a circle. Students each become a character or person from recent study. Go around with each making an announcement, a wish, or a complaint (see Ready Reference 5.1). Audience puts thumbs up if they know the character and can give evidence.

**Car Wash.** Form two facing lines. Students assume characters or are given a topic. Two end people walk between the lines. As they slowly pass, students say one-liners to them. Then the next two go and so forth. For example, when reading aloud *Officer Buckles and Gloria* (Rathman), stop where Officer Buckles feels like a fool. Tell students to think of good things about the dog. Walkers become Officer Buckles and pass through the car wash hearing "voices" comment on his friend.

**Television Shows.** Adapt game and talk show formats such as *I've Got a Secret, Jeopardy, Wheel of Fortune, Concentration, Password,* or *Oprah*. Students take roles and prepare show materials. Adaptations work best after a unit of study (e.g., Oprah discussion/interview format on endangered species).

## Ready Reference 9.3  QU Script Example

*Directions: Write or cowrite a series of statements that summarize a lesson, chapter, book or even a field trip. Use the copy paste function to prepare a script using the format below. Cut apart QU (cue-you) statements. Distribute and rehearse. The leader reads the first Q and the person or group with U reads next. Reading continues according to cues (summary statements based on Mirette on the High Wire, McCully, 1992).*

**Q:** Bellini's story.
**U:** I was a man in hiding—hiding from myself.
**Q:** I was a man in hiding—hiding from myself.
**U:** I just needed to rest.
**Q:** I just needed to rest.
**U:** Gateau's boardinghouse on English Street seemed as good a place as any.
**Q:** Gateau's boardinghouse on English Street seemed as good a place as any.
**U:** I did worry about the other guests seeing me.
**Q:** I did worry about the other guests seeing me.
**U:** It never occurred to me that I was being watched by much brighter eyes.
**Q:** It never occurred to me that I was being watched by much brighter eyes.
**U:** Mirette! The spunky redheaded daughter of Madame! Mais oui!
**Q:** Mirette! The spunky redheaded daughter of Madame! Mais oui!
**U:** She was not to be denied once the enchantment of the wire overtook her.
**Q:** She was not to be denied once the enchantment of the wire overtook her.
**U:** I saw her take her falls. I thought she'd give up.
**Q:** I saw her take her falls. I thought she'd give up.
**U:** But Mirette had the courage a young heart and a new dream give.

**Q:** But Mirette had the courage a young heart and a new dream give.
**U:** I did not want to be her teacher because I did not want her to discover my secret.
**Q:** I did not want to be her teacher because I did not want her to discover my secret.
**U:** I recognized the agent when he checked in.
**Q:** I recognized the agent when he checked in.
**U:** It was inevitable Mirette would learn my hidden fear.
**Q:** It was inevitable Mirette would learn my hidden fear.
**U:** Mirette's belief in me was greater than my fear of myself.
**Q:** Mirette's belief in me was greater than my fear of myself.
**U:** I bought the length of hemp and went to work. I worked automatically preparing for the walk.
**Q:** I bought the length of hemp and went to work. I worked automatically preparing for the walk.
**U:** But I could not move when I felt the wire touch my feet.
**Q:** But I could not move when I felt the wire touch my feet.
**U:** That child's face shattered the cage around my heart. Dear Mirette.
**Q:** That child's face shattered the cage around my heart. Dear Mirette.
**U:** Bravo for the children! They make us remember what it means to be alive.

**Discussions.**  A discussion becomes a dramatic encounter when students take roles (e.g., characters, famous persons, objects). Use the questions in Ready References 4.13 and 8.11, as well as suggestions for discussions in Chapter 4. Students can also brainstorm in the role. Chapter 2 has brainstorming guidelines in the CPS section.

**Empathy Role Discussions.**  Each student takes the role of a character or person everyone knows. The teacher begins a discussion or interview with a question concerning a key moment, problem, topic, or theme. An important question (e.g., one that begins with "why") should used that suggests a moral dilemma. Each student participates in character throughout. The teacher can call on students or ask for volunteers to respond. Example based on *Sarah, Plain and Tall* (MacLachlan): "We're here to discuss the issue of advertising for a husband or a wife. I'd like to find out what each of you think. Please introduce yourself and give your opinion." *Variation*: Students prepare by writing down who they are, what they want, and how they act and feel. Name tags can be used.

**Panels.**  Everyone can be the same or different characters who present views on an issue. Panels begin with opening statements, and then the audience asks questions. *Variations:* (1) Students take roles of consultants, experts, or advisers on a topic and research to plan for their roles. (2) Set this up as a press conference.

**The Chair.**  Person A sits in a chair. Person B takes a role and begins a conversation. Person A must figure out who B is and respond accordingly. For example, B is Thomas Jefferson, and A is Hillary Clinton. Adapt for literature, social studies, and science, and use for current events. *Variation*: Partners sit back to back. Pairs each take the role of a book character, an occupation, or family role. On signal, they face and the first to talk sets the situation. The second person must figure out who his or her partner is and respond in role.

**Elevator.**  Form small groups. The place is a jammed elevator. Students think about who they are, problems they have, and how they feel. On signal, the group starts a conversation. *Variations*: Brainstorm contexts from stories, time periods, and locations under study. Any public place can work. Students can be characters, persons in paintings, scientists, or historical figures.

**Teacher-in-Role Interviews.**  Teacher assumes the role of interviewer with students as characters. Questioning proceeds in talk show style with focus on control of face, body, and voice. A good starter interview question is, "What happened?" *Example:* Teacher is a TV host interviewing (1) characters in *Charlotte's Web* right after the first word appears in the web, (2) animals from fables, such as Lobel's "The Mouse at the Seashore," or (3) unpopular characters, such as a wolf, who present a point of view. If a panel is used, the class can question members who take roles (e.g., news reporters). *Suggestions:* Interviewers should introduce themselves (e.g., "I am _____ and I want to know _____."). Use microphone prop. Be sure to coach students to stay in role. *Variation:* Do interviews in pairs with one student as interviewer.

**Show Time.** Use as a review for any material. Groups write and present commercials, news updates, songs, and the like that summarize important points. Remind students to include key information, not empty glitz. This provides a good opportunity to teach propaganda devices such as bandwagon or glittering generalities. Limit time to 3 minutes. Following are two examples.

*Newsbreak:* "We interrupt this program to let you know that animals have been found to have four components in their habitats. Without water, shelter, food, and adequate space, animals cannot survive. We learned today that habitats are shrinking and our world may soon lose valued animal populations. More on this breaking story on Live at Six."

*Commercial:* "High/bad cholesterol? Stressed? Tired? You need the Laughter Prescription! With only 15 laughs a day, you can get your minimum daily requirement and be on the road to an energetic, happy life. Learn to laugh your way through life. Call 1-800-JOKE."

Note: Inventions make great advertisements (e.g., cotton gin for social studies or a graphing calculator in math).

**Book Ads.** Individuals, pairs, or small groups set up a scene based on a problem from a book. The scene must end, however, before the problem is solved. End each commercial with "If you want to know what happened, you have to read this book." *Variation:* Create commercials using music, songs, slogans, and props. Limit time to 1 minute—TV time is expensive!

**Debate.** Divide class in half and assign each a side in an argument. Give time to plan. At signal, begin with a person from each side stating a position. Alternate back and forth until all viewpoints have been heard. Rebuttal time can then be given to each side. To encourage alternative viewpoints, ask opponents to summarize each side's points at the end. Teachers should (1) moderate and can assume a role (e.g., police officer called to a "crime scene" in "Little Red Riding Hood"), and (2) comment, question each side, and open it up for audience questions. Can be done in pairs. For example, one side says Little Red Riding Hood

should be taken away from her parents because of negligence; the other side takes the opposing position. *Variation:* Do as expert panels (e.g., experts on wolf behavior).

**Improvised Scenes.** (Also see improvisation discussion under "Pantomime"). Select short scenes from familiar stories. Students plan a beginning, middle, and end scene based on a problem that is resolved by the end. Examples: (1) Stepsisters and stepmother are in the coach, going to the ball worried about the mysterious girl who charmed the prince. (2) Animals who saw the transformations of other animals are talking after Cinderella leaves for the ball. They want to get transformed, too.

As soon as possible, prompt students to think of their own scenes. Suggest they choose important moments or key emotional moments in literature. In science or social studies, consider significant events (e.g., when Philo Farnsworth gets the first television picture). Sources for improvised scenes include current events, wordless picture books, and "famous last words." Events, processes, and procedures from science, social studies, and math are also good resources. Focus on "let's suppose" and "what if" (e.g., switch characters, settings, or circumstances of any story or historical event). Create card sets with different characters (who), settings (where and when), problems, and props for an endless number of combinations. Following are examples for who, where, and problem.

1. Hurried shoppers. Grocery. A robbery happens.
2. Hungry mosquitoes. On the beach when Columbus first lands.
3. Five children. Hot summer day on the porch. Dad brings out two double popsicles.

Scaffold student planning with discussions about characters, the setting, plan of action for the problem or conflict, and resolution. A planning frame can be used for students to write down ideas about who, where, what problems, what to do or actions, solutions, and conclusion. Remind students to (1) plan a beginning, middle, and end; (2) plan how to show what the characters want; (3) develop conflict (have characters persuade, argue, obstruct, or bargain); and (4) plan a reasonable resolution. Time limits help students focus and get to important ideas. Offer options to signal the start and end of each scene and possible use of music to create mood.

After scenes, discuss what worked in terms of making sense. Scenes may also be replayed with a twist (e.g., teacher may take a role or students may be engaged in a written response such as a 5-minute quickwrite). Ready Reference 9.4 lists ideas for scenes.

**Drama**

## Ready Reference 9.4  Improvised Scene Source Material

*Directions: Use these categories to think about possible scenes.*

- Characters: lizard, baker, potter, wise woman, fortune teller
- Places: island, beach, cave, treehouse, barn, boarding house, jungle
- Character conflicts/motives: argue, convince, persuade, defend, plot, debate, tease, deny, confess, accuse, beg

- Rituals: graduation, inauguration, parade, eulogy, pledge
- Actions: eat, clean, drink, work, bathe, run, cook, swim
- Conditions or problems: ill, dark, nervous, hot, embarrassed, odor, stress, wet, lost, lonely, noisy

**I Heard It First.** Brainstorm famous songs, such as the Hallelujah chorus and "The Star-Spangled Banner." Break into small groups for students to plan a scene about the first time the music or song was ever heard by an audience and their reactions. Scenes should have a beginning, middle, and end.

**Role Play.** Role playing is used in every drama. It involves considering a situation from another's viewpoint and showing it through body and voice. Participants experience problem situations and explore feelings, values, and viewpoints under safe circumstances. Added perspective increases understanding of any subject.

Problems or topics can be selected from any curricular area. A particular kind of role playing, called *sociodrama*, focuses on real-world problems of the present and future. Guidelines to create a role play follow:

1. Choose problems or topics about which students know something.
2. Define a specific situation that requires the characters to take action. Example: a factory owner whose factory is polluting a river and an EPA agent who must enforce regulations about river pollution. A meeting has been called by the governor or mayor.
3. Give the audience a role. For example, they may be citizens who ask questioners at a break point or a mediation panel to consider the different positions.
4. Plan an introduction to set up the scene.
5. Replay the same scene with different groups, to compare versions.
6. Ask what students noticed about the drama aspects as well as the content of the scenes.

**Staging Basics.** Following are simple staging devices to improve drama performances:

- Use energizers and warm-ups to cause students to focus, concentrate, and activate. Use CPS thinking.
- Encourage students to work together in an "ensemble spirit" of cooperation.
- Practice to develop actors' use of voice, especially articulation and volume.
- Create triangular compositions when placing actors.
- Place nonspeaking actors upstage to give depth and interest to the composition.
- Coach students to orient their bodies toward the audience when speaking.
- Move speaking actors downstage when possible.
- Teach actors how to focus so that the audience knows where to look.

# IV. Connecting Drama to Curricular Areas

This section offers examples of pantomime and verbal improvisation to kick start thinking about how drama can be used as a teaching tool in academic disciplines. These are undeveloped seed strategies to prompt creative thinking with the goal of meaningful arts integration in mind.

## Science Focus

Science standards can be accessed at the National Science Teachers Association website (www.nsta.org).

**Project Wild.** *Project Wild* has hands-on, activity-oriented lesson plans for science. Drama, music, art, literature, and creative writing activities are suggested. Information is available online (www.projectwild.org). *Project Wet* is also available.

**Animal Features.** IT makes the sound of an animal, and the group pantomimes shapes and actions of the animal. *Variation*: IT makes sounds from everyday world (e.g., clock ticking or phone ringing), and the group creates actions to pantomime that context.

**Nature One-Liners.** Use pictures of natural forms (e.g., mountain, tree, stream, animals). Each student says a sentence, in role, to show known facts and use new vocabulary. For example, "My stalactites are growing vertically a lot today" (cave).

**Environmental Debate.** Divide students into two teams to research an environmental issue. For example, "Should whales be hunted?" Students assume roles as either pro or con debaters. Each side presents an opening statement and then gives pros or cons in a time limit. After each side presents, give time for rebuttal and a summary statement from each side.

**Famous Science Scenes.** Break into groups to do tableau (frozen pictures) of special moments in science, such as Alexander G. Bell's first telephone call, the Wrights' flight at Kitty Hawk, or Armstrong walking on the moon.

**Close Observation.** Take time to purposefully watch mammals, insects, or fish on a video or in real life. Ask students to use specific verbs and adverbs to tell how they move and why (e.g., to get food, to avoid predators). If animals are in groups, ask how they are organized (e.g., bird flight patterns). Next, small groups plan to pantomime an animal based on observations. Give time to rehearse. Groups present to class audience which describes what they see, not just guess the animal.

**Animal Charades.** Brainstorm (before or after a unit) ways to classify animals (wild, domesticated, herbivores, carnivores, insects, mammals, aquatic, land based). Small groups list animals in each category. Each student then picks an animal and mimes how it sleeps, moves, eats, and where it lives. Suggest students start frozen, then do several moves, and then freeze. Teams can write the animal or category guess on a wipe-off board, show and then give details noticed to support conclusions. Actors confirm correct conclusions. Emphasize science content by asking for reasons why the animal belongs in a category. To stress the drama aspect, ask students to give feedback on what the mime did to make them believe. Other categories include land forms and states of water. *Differentiation*: Limit number of categories. Plan and present only in small groups.

**Point of View Props.** Challenge students to use simple props to feel as animals do. For example, try to eat rice with your mouth as birds do or try to drink like a cat or dog from a tub of water. Use props to get the feel of snakes shedding their skins or birds in a nest (e.g., use garbage bag with end cut open; use leaves or build nests).

**Animal Panels.** Groups choose an animal to research. Each group becomes an expert panel, in the role of their animal. Each tells facts, feelings, problems, pros, and cons of being a dog, cat, or fish. Audience members ask questions of the panel. *Variation:* Focus on a planet or plant.

## Social Studies Focus

Social studies standards are available from the National Council for the Social Studies (NCSS) website (www.socialstudies.org).

**Moral Dilemmas.** Use historical fiction or biography and ask students to stop reading at a point where a character has to make a decision. Small groups take the role of the character and discuss the dilemma in first person, saying "I felt" or "I think" statements. Information from the story is used to propose possible actions. Groups reassemble to summarize the discussion or to role play a course of action.

Note: The dilemma should not have one clear right answer so students are forced to consider several options. For example, Avi's *Night Journeys* has many points where a "stop and discuss in role" would be appropriate. *Suggestion*: Stop when a problem has been found and ask students to describe the following:

- What is it?
- Who has the problem?
- What are the general circumstances of the problem?
- What is the goal for solving the problem?

Small groups then brainstorm problem solutions, such as the following:

- What possibilities would be legal and safe for all?
- What is the best solution (consider cost, safety, length of time, and legal, moral, and practical issues)?

The groups then try out possible solutions.

- Role play whether the problem gets solved.
- What does this say to you for the future?

Read the rest of the story and compare solutions with the one in the book (based on the work of Lawrence Kohlberg; adapted from Johnson & Louis, 1987).

**Portrait Conversations.** Pair students to plan a conversation between two portraits of famous historical figures that might hang side by side in a gallery. Look closely to examine the works for clues about time period, values, cultural aspects, message, and the like that give ideas for dialogue. These can be written or oral. *Variation:* Ask students to plan dialogue for figures in an historically based painting (e.g., *Washington Crossing the Delaware* or *The Signing of the Declaration of Independence*).

**Famous Portrait Monologues** Use portraits of famous figures (e.g., U.S. presidents). Students research persons in the art and prepare 1-minute monologues about the times, problems, values, economics, and customs. Monologues are presented in character in the first person.

**What's My Line?** Based on a 1950s television show, this drama focuses on discovering the occupations of panelists. Panelists can all have the same occupation or role (e.g., all might be signers of the Declaration of Independence). The audience can only ask yes or no questions and is given a time limit on number of questions (e.g., 5 minutes or 20 questions). The teacher acts as moderator, calling on audience members. To deal with monopolizers, use the rule that when a panelist answers "no," someone else gets a turn.

**Teacher in Role Interview.** Motivate reading of the social studies text by telling students you will be interviewing them the next day about assigned reading. They must choose to be a person related to the reading and you will ask them five Ws and H questions, beginning with "What happened?" *Suggestion:* Teacher pretends to be from a local TV station. Debrief about how preparing for the interview changed how they read the assignment.

**Biography Drama.** Groups read biographies from an historical period and note actions to pantomime, special events, important scenes, and special lines of dialogue. Students plan with biography groups. For example, they might improvise dialogue for the scene leading up to Patrick Henry saying, "Give me liberty or give me death." *Suggestion*: Focus on actual words the person used and conflicting positions the person took (e.g., Jefferson owned slaves).

**Costumed Interpreters.** Many communities have folks who dress up as historical characters and do talks. Contact your local historical society. Invite one as a guest speaker. Ask students to do research to prepare questions using five Ws and H questions. Study costumes throughout history from all over the world at Costumes.Org (www.costumes.org/).

## Literacy: Reading and Language Arts Focus

In many schools primary classrooms are required to spend 3 hours a day in reading instruction. It seems reasonable, given the research, that "such long stretches" should be punctuated with "language-directed dramatic activities" that have been shown to inspire increased participation, especially among students learning English as a second language (Catterall, 2003, p. 105).

Literacy/literature standards are available from the National Council of the Teachers of English (NCTE) and the International Reading Association (IRA) websites (www.ncte.org or www.rdg.org).

**Literacy Parallels.** Theatre and drama are language rich and naturally engage students in verbal communication. The commonalities shared between drama and the language arts account for strong effects of drama in research studies (Deasy, 2002). Students involved in theatre and drama spend time researching characters and settings, writing scripts, and interpreting lines. Nearly all pantomime and verbal strategies can be adapted for literacy lessons. This section provides numerous examples.

**Emotional Vowels.**   Form a circle. IT goes in the center and chooses an emotion. IT then expresses the emotion, but can only make a vowel sound (/a/, /e/, /i/, /o/, or /u/). Designate short or long vowels, schwa sound, or diphthongs such as *oy* or *ow*). The class echoes. Students then signal to name both the emotion and the vowel sound. IT calls on peers until a correct answer is found and that person becomes IT. Ask students to describe nonverbal and verbal clues to emotion.

**Word Types.**   Brainstorm types of words and examples (e.g., homophones, antonyms, rhyming words, silent *e* words). Form groups of four. Call out a category. Leader in each group pantomimes original examples while the rest write what they think is mimed, in order. Call time. Groups check with leader and new leader is chosen. Call next category. *Variation*: Use any topic or unit, such as things that are vertical, high, twisted, fast. (Students might mime, in order: elevator, clouds, pretzel, and electric fan.)

**Antonym Pantomimes.**   Make a card set with two antonyms on each card. A student draws a card and pantomimes one word. The audience must guess the opposite. This can be done in small groups with a set of cards for each group. *Suggestion*: Ask students to wait until the pantomime is done, write out a guess, and, on signal, hold it up. *Variation*: Use synonyms, homonyms, and homophones.

**Antonyms Partners.**   Pairs pantomime opposite emotions, heights, sizes, weights, and so on. Pairs present and audience guesses antonyms and tells evidence for conclusions.

**Daffynitions.**   Teams find unusual words. Each team member writes a definition for the word, but only one member writes the correct definition (use the dictionary). Each team stands and members orally read definitions in turn, trying to convince the audience that each has the correct one. The audience can applaud, afterwards, to vote on which they believe is correct. *Variation*: Use unusual objects instead of words.

**Rhyme Change.**   Nursery rhymes, chants, and poems are adaptable for word play that serves as verbal warm-up and stimulates creative thinking. Here is an example: "Hickory Dickory Dock, A mouse ran up my _____ " (students supply rhyme). All vowel sounds can be practiced (phonemic awareness) with variations such as Hickory Dickory Dack, Hickory Dickory Deck, and so forth.

**Spelling Mime.**   Students mime each letter in a word or a thing that starts with each letter. *Example*: CAT = cup plus apple plus typing. Groups can present a word with each member doing a separate letter.

**Story Captions.**   Brainstorm important scenes or events in a story. Give each a caption. Put on slips and drop in a basket. Tell students to find personal spaces. Read one caption and on "begin," cue students to freeze using their faces and bodies to show the feelings and message of the caption. Examples: "Cozy in the Barn" (*Charlotte's Web*) and "Proud of My Twig House"

(*Three Little Pigs*). *Suggestion*: Also use with nonfiction from science and social studies. *Extension*: Captions can be used to prompt art making about story mood and events.

**7-Up Words.**   Brainstorm "up" combinations: stand up, sit up, get up, wake up. Put in a hat. Form groups. Team captains draw from a hat and mime for their group. Do as a relay with captains tagging next group member to get a slip from the hat.

**Pretend and Write.**   Either assign roles or let students choose a role from literature, song, or artwork. Next, each writes a letter, chant, note, or any form, in role (Ready Reference 5.1 has writing options). Example: Choose a family member from *Sarah, Plain and Tall* (Anna, Caleb, or Jacob) after Chapter 2. Write a letter to Sarah introducing yourself and asking her questions. Students switch letters and become Sarah to write a reply. *Variation*: Do as a guessing game. Discuss how to give clues, without coming right out and giving the person's name or family role.

Note: Students do not sign the letters.

**Pretend and Write: Dear Abby.**   Show examples of the column "Dear Abby." Students then write a "Dear Abby" letter using a problem from a book. Partners exchange and, in the role of Abby, write a reply. *Example* (after the first chapter of *Sarah, Plain and Tall*):

Dear Abby,
　　My father is a widower and I think he really needs a wife. My brother and I also need a mother. What should we do? Worried daughter

Dear Worried Daughter,
　　Why don't you talk to your dad about how you feel? Be honest. This will let him know you think it is okay to look around. Abby

**Pretend and Write: Journals.**   Students become real or fictional characters and keep a daily journal. The point is to write about what *could have* happened, or feelings caused by events, not just think literally. When using historical fiction or biography, students extend the journal's authenticity by doing research on characters. *Variation*: For chapter books, provide time for entries after each chapter to document changes in the main character's thoughts and emotions in reaction to events. Students can pair up and read each other's journals for different perspectives.

**Pretend and Write: Letters.**   Focus is on using conventional letter-writing form, the writing process, grammar, and spelling. Students take a role of a character and write a friendly or business letter to another character or real person. Contents and purposes will vary. Students can pair and write back to sender, taking the role of the receiver.

**Point of View Roles.**   Students choose a character in a story or are assigned roles. Students read or listen to the story and answer questions in role in writing or orally. For example, using *Mirette on the High Wire* (McCully), students can be asked to imagine they are a touring artist staying at the rooming house. Answer the following questions (before the high wire act at the end).

1. What have you noticed about the man? How does he make you feel?
2. What do you think about his friendship with Mirette?
3. Why do you think he stays to himself so much?

**Masks: Six Dramatic Roles.** According to Temple (1991), story characters fill one or more of six roles and may also change roles. Use the following roles to create masks and puppets for retellings and improvisations of stories (see Ready Reference 7.4 for puppet/mask ideas).

1. The Lion Force: main character
2. The Sun or Object: what the Lion Force wants
3. Mars, the Rival: tries to keep the Lion Force from getting what she or he wants
4. Moon, the Helper: helps Lion Force achieve desired goals
5. Earth, the Receiver: benefits from Lion Force's actions
6. Libra, the Judge: decides if Lion Force may have the Sun or Object

**Character Sculptors.** In pairs, one becomes the clay. The other then "sculpts" the person into a character with specific emotions and actions concentrating on body shape and levels.

**Theme Tableau.** After reading a story, brainstorm what it was really about. List themes on a chart. Divide into groups with each selecting one theme as the topic for a frozen picture. Coach to use different levels, body shape, facial expressions, and focal points to convey the message. After each group performs for the class audience, ask audience to tell what seems most important and predict the theme being shown. *Variation:* Perform in the order of the story plot.

**Showtime.** After reading a book, form groups to create a commercial, jingle, news update, or newsbreak about a theme/big idea in the book. Number groups for order of performance. Give 10 minutes to plan. The whole group comes back together and the show begins.

**Reader's Theatre or Radio Plays.** Like a radio broadcast, reader's theatre is "of the mind." It is widely acclaimed as a fluency tool in literacy (Hudson, Lane, & Pullen, 2005). Readers sit or stand while doing oral interpretive reading from a script. The focus is on using the voice expressively; props are usually not employed. Reader's theatre is particularly suitable for intermediate students, but can be adapted for younger children by choosing shorter scripts and reading to them as they follow along on the first go-through. Adapted short poems are a good place to begin. For example, see Wolf's *It's Show Time!: Poetry from the Page to the Stage* (poem scripts). Tips for using reader's theatre appear in Ready Reference 9.5. Ready Reference 9.6 has a sample reader's theatre script, converted from an Old English tale.

**Drama**

## Ready Reference 9.5 Reader's Theatre Tips

- Find or create scripts connected to curricular areas and students' interests and abilities. Several companies and Internet sites publish scripts, and literature anthologies often contain stories in script form. The Institute for Readers Theatre in California has a script service. A list of more than 40 reader's theatre titles is available from www.amazon.com and includes everything from holiday scripts to fractured folktale scripts.
- Scripts initially can be read to students, read silently by students, or orally read in small groups.
- Form groups according to characters outlined in the scripts. Groups can prepare different scripts or perform the same script and then discuss the different interpretations.
- Students must rehearse with focus on varying voice dynamics (volume), tempo (rate), pitch, pause, and stress to convey meaning. Students can highlight their parts and mark words they think should be stressed. Nonverbal communication with the face, some gestures, and even body posture can be added, but the focus remains on oral interpretation.
- Place scripts in folders or binders so students can hold them without distracting the audience with page turning. Students may sit on high stools or stand. Stools of varying heights can be used to suggest character relationships.
- Reader's theatre is not about creating a visual spectacle, but students may shift position on stage (e.g., to indicate joining a group). Readers may start with their backs to the audience and turn around as each is introduced. Characters with major roles might stand to the far left and right, if they do not interact with one another. Characters with similar ideas can be grouped. Readers may stand when they read and then sit, or spotlights might be used. Lights can be used to signal scenes. With younger students hatbands or nametags can help the audience keep track of characters.
- Props should not be used, unless essential, since it is awkward to handle a script and a prop. Sound effects and music can be added, since these are part of creating the "radio play" effect.
- Invite creative ideas by asking, "What else could you try?" and "What are other ways to have the audience get the message or feeling?"
- The narrator should make eye contact with the audience to draw them in. Other characters may look up when not reading or when they can during reading.
- Review audience etiquette before performances. After the readings, invite performers and audience members to discuss what worked, what they learned, what they noticed about use of voice to establish character, what the most important parts were, and so forth.
- Follow performances with invitations to write different script endings, trade scripts with other groups, videotape, or even perform for other groups (e.g., a touring troupe to visit other classes).

Reader's Theatre Script Example

**Cast:** Narrator, Girl, Old Man

**Narrator:** A GIRL once went to the fair to find a job as a maid. A funny-looking OLD MAN agreed to hire her. When they arrived there, he said he had to teach her new names for things in the house.

**Old Man:** What will you call me?

**Girl:** Why master, or mister, or whatever else you wish, sir.

**Old Man:** No, you must call me "master of all masters." And what would you call this?

**Narrator:** The OLD MAN pointed to his bed.

**Girl:** Why bed, or couch, or whatever you wish, sir.

**Old Man:** No, that's my "barnacle." And what do you call those?

**Narrator:** He pointed to his pantaloons.

**Girl:** Breeches, or trousers, or whatever else you wish, sir.

**Old Man:** No, you must call them "squibs and crackers." And what do you call her?

**Narrator:** The Old MAN pointed at his cat.

**Girl:** Cat or kit, or whatever you wish, sir.

**Old Man:** No, you must call her "white-faced simminy." And now this, what would you call this?

**Girl:** Fire or flame, or whatever you wish, sir.

**Old Man:** No, no. You must call it "hot cockalorum." And what is this?

**Narrator:** He went on, pointing to the water.

**Girl:** Water or wet, or whatever you wish, sir.

**Old Man:** No, "pondalorum" is its name. And what do you call this?

**Narrator:** Asked the MAN as he pointed to his house.

**Girl:** House or cottage, or whatever you wish, sir.

**Old Man:** You must call it "high topper mountain."

**Narrator:** That very night the GIRL woke her master up in a fright.

**Girl:** Master of all masters, get out of your barnacle and put on your squibs and crackers. For white-faced simminy has got a spark of hot cockalorum on his tail, and unless you get some pondalorum, high topper mountain will be all on hot cockalorum!

*Source:* Based on "Master of All Masters," Old English folktale (Jacobs, 1890).

Reader's theatre is an appropriate use of oral reading because it is audience oriented and students rehearse before the performance, as opposed to unrehearsed round-robin reading that can distort students' feelings and thinking about reading. Other values of reader's theatre include the following:

1. It integrates listening, speaking, and reading and can include writing when students create their own scripts. Literary works and biographical material such as letters, diaries, or speeches can be adapted by the teacher, and students can learn to write in script form.
2. The ensemble or group nature of reader's theatre encourages cooperation and other social skills.
3. When readers assume character roles, they learn to empathize with a variety of feelings and viewpoints, which yields insights about people and the world.
4. Self-confidence is increased as students share exciting stories that evoke positive audience responses.
5. No lines are memorized. The focus is on oral reading fluency which targets using EAR: expression, accuracy, and rate.

## Math Focus

Math standards can be accessed from the National Council of Teachers of Mathematics (NCTM) website (www.nctm.org).

**Story Problems.** Give small groups the same story problem. The goal is to plan how to role-play the problem and end the scene by showing the answer. Each group presents its version. The audience gives feedback on what worked for each scene; and after all the scenes, they compare and contrast.

**Daily Math.** Brainstorm a list of times people use math every day (e.g., cooking, giving change, sewing). Pairs plan a 1- to 2-minute pantomime of an example. Pairs perform and the audience describes what they see and tell the math idea. *Variation:* Allow players to each say one sentence in role.

**Math One-Liners.** Sit in a circle. Pass around a geometric shape or a visual of a math concept (e.g., symbol for "greater than"). As each student receives the shape or symbol, the goal is to say one line in that role. *Example:* "I'm always right." "Three is not a crowd for me." "I always have an angle" (triangular shape). *Variation:* Add pantomime (e.g., greater than symbol).

**Math Improvisation.** Make a set of cards with math-related situations. Give each group a card to plan a scene. Scenes should have a beginning, middle, and end and a problem. An example card might have (1) Who? three men, (2) What? a quart of milk, and (3) Where? a 10-story building on fire (problem).

**Fraction Mime.** After introducing fractions, use an open space to pantomime. Give these directions: "As a class, become a 'whole.' Now divide up to become two equal halves. Now become fourths, thirds, and so on." When numbers are uneven, ask students how to deal with the "extras."

**Break It Down.** Pairs become an "answer." They plan combinations to mime. *Example:* 27 = 20 wiggling fingers plus 4 blinking eyes plus 2 ears plus 1 wrinkled nose.

**Talking Math Panels.** Children choose to become a math concept. They form expert panels to present. The audience questions them using the five Ws and H questions (e.g., panel of squares or the number 1).

*Drama*

**Math Commercials.** Students prepare ads to sell particular math concepts or skills: fractions, time, division. The goal is to convince the audience they need this math form.

**Number Talk.** Give each student a number from 1 to 5. Pairs or groups have a conversation, but each can only use the number of words designated. *Variation:* Tell stories but set limit on number of words, (e.g., 50 words).

**Math Vocabulary.** List a set of math words such as *add, subtract, less than.* Pair to create a story with a beginning, middle, and end using as many as possible.

# V. Special Focus: Storytelling, an Integrated Art Form

*You are the vessel for the tale.* (Heather Forrest, storyteller)

Storytelling has much in common with drama and theatre. Both rely on conflict to develop characters, plot, and themes. Storytellers take on roles and imaginatively use voice and body to bring words to life. At its core, storytelling is a dramatic vehicle so it is not surprising that Winifred Ward's course in storytelling led to the development of *creative drama* (Collins, 1997).

Storytelling is an art form that naturally integrates the arts; and, like other arts, storytelling is now being tapped for its learning potential. Storytelling also frequently includes use of movement and dance to suggest characters, mood, and places and storytellers may invite movement responses from the audience as well. Many tellers also sing, play musical instruments to accompany stories, and invite the audience to sing along. The "visual art" of storytelling has much to do with the colorful mental pictures tellers paint for listeners using rich descriptive language. The following Community Snapshot shows how that is happening at the initiative of one arts organization.

## Community Snapshot
### Storytelling Collaboration

The first weekend in May each year more than 8,000 students descend on downtown Jackson, Michigan. It's Storyfest! Teachers bring students to storytelling sessions conducted by national tellers such as Donald Davis, Charlotte Blake-Alston, Heather Forest, Eth-No-Tec, and Jay O'Callahan. Stories range from personal/family to historical tales.

"It is a community event that brings children and adults together," explains Virginia Lucas, former Storyfest chair. In addition to the school schedule, adult performances on Friday and Saturday night bring hundreds of families to the 1930s vintage Michigan Theatre.

Dr. Lucas cannot say enough about the artistry of the storytellers, but her description of the response of families reveals why she believes storytelling is important. "It is just amazing to hear them tell their own family stories before they even leave the theatre! Storytellers give us words in context. It is this gift of learning how to use words in context that makes us literate." Saturday morning is "interactive storytelling" for young children and their parents. Teachers attend workshops to learn to use storytelling throughout the curriculum.

Storyfest has long focused on storytelling's role in literacy development. "Oral storytelling shows children how to think in 'frames,'" says Dr. Lucas. "We need concepts like beginning, middle, and end to understand stories—oral and written." During storytelling students learn to use thinking skills such as prediction, inference, and drawing conclusions. These higher order skills can be used during storytelling long before children have print decoding fluency.

Young children engaged in storytelling also hear patterns and the rhythms of language in an enjoyable context. Dr. Lucas says children "listen to sounds of words and learn to create their own images." She worries that too much television creates dependence on sources outside themselves for visual images.

Jackson Storyfest is an example of a community-school-arts collaboration. With its focus on literacy, one goal of Storyfest is to develop the listening and speaking skills that are the foundation for reading and writing. Students also learn how to be participating audience members during live performances.

Storyfest is funded through grants from corporations like Target and Sam's Club. Dr. Lucas works all year with local businesses and individuals to raise the approximately $20,000 the festival costs. "The festival could not operate without the dedication of volunteers," she says. To learn about Jackson Storyfest, visit www.jacksonstoryfest.org.

## Why Storytelling?

Storyteller Rives Collins believes human beings are "storytelling animals" and explains how storytelling is a natural, common, and ancient human activity. Written accounts of storytelling date back 4,000 years to Cheops, the Great Pyramid builder. In every culture, people love to tell and listen to stories. From the griots of Africa to Navajo shaman and French troubadours, storytellers have preserved history. They continue to educate, enlighten, and enliven our lives.

We tell stories to prepare and reassure ourselves. We invent fantasy stories to amuse others, to make sense of the world, and to build relationships. We ask others, "Remember the time . . . ? "How was your day?" "What did you do at school?" "What do you think will happen?" We intuitively put great store in the power of stories. From biblical parables to creation myths and tall tales, stories engage us as no other words can. For example, someone stating, "We learn from our mistakes" has a different impact than hearing the following story with a similar theme.

A young man who wished to be wise went to a sage high on the mountain.

"How can I become wise?" the young man asked respectfully.

The old man looked thoughtful and replied, "Have wisdom."

"But how do I get wisdom?" asked the young man.

"Develop good judgment," the sage answered.

"But how can I get good judgment?" the young man cried.

"Experience," said the sage wisely.

"And how do I get experience?" said the young man in frustration.

"Bad judgment," said the sage.

According to S. H. Clark in *How to Teach Reading in Public Schools* (1899):

> If teachers should succeed in developing the state of mind that would cause the pupils to go to the printed page as they would go to the feet of one who has a story to tell, we should be willing to ask nothing else of them as a result of all their teaching.

### Storytelling is valuable because it . . .

- *Is rich brain food.* It involves a balanced diet of cognitive and emotional knowing.

### Storytelling is social/emotional because it . . .

- *Builds community.* Listeners are brought together in cultural tales that include powerful symbols and traditions. We learn people are more alike than they are different.
- *Bonds people.* A unique relationship is created between listeners and tellers that differs from read-alouds using books. Storytelling is more intimate, as if the teller is sharing something personal.

### Storytelling is cognitive because it . . .

- *Increases knowledge.* Listeners learn, but do not feel "taught." Stories give information, opinions, and new perspectives in an invitational way.
- *Stimulates higher order thinking.* Children internalize the structure or grammar of story even before they can read. They predict, analyze, synthesize, and evaluate as they listen.
- *Teaches problem solving.* Listeners hear provocative ideas that show how others solve problems in creative ways and are drawn to think of other creative solutions.
- *Stimulates further creative response.* Students want to extend storytelling by writing, drama, art, and music activities that allow them to think imaginatively.

### Storytelling is literacy because it . . .

- *Triggers visual imagery.* Storytelling causes listeners to make their own mental images, which is the kind of visual imagining frequently by fluent readers.
- *Increases vocabulary.* Students hear diverse dialects and unusual language that sensitizes them to the power of words to create images and provoke emotions.
- *Improves comprehension.* Understanding is built on listening, which is thinking about what is heard. Listening comprehension comes before reading comprehension.
- *Increases oral skills.* When listeners become tellers, they use oral communication skills.

### Storytelling is motivation because it . . .

- *Whets the appetite.* Students become interested and want to hear more. They seek out similar stories to read and write.
- *Develops empathy and identity.* Listeners come to like specific characters, see their points of view, and realize they share values, tastes, and ways of living.
- *Helps us cope.* Listeners come to better understand life, to make sense of conflict, and see that there are patterns, such as in relationships between good and evil.
- *Is superb entertainment.* Storytelling engages listeners so that they feel uplifted and renewed.

## Storytelling Strategies and Resources

There once was a rabbi who was a gifted storyteller. Everyone felt he gave each story just to him or her. A man finally asked, "How is it we all hear the same story but you touch each of our individual hearts?" In response, the rabbi told about a girl who shot arrows. Wherever an arrow stuck, she pulled it out and painted a bright bull's eye around it. "It is you that paints the target," the rabbi said, "inviting the story into your heart" (Collins, 1994).

Where can you get good stories like this to tell? What are pointers from professional storytellers? The following ideas serve as good starters. Ready References 9.7, 9.8, and 9.9 summarize pointers, and Ready Reference 9.10 is an example story plot

---

## Ready Reference 9.7 Choosing Stories to Tell

*Like love, knowledge, and fairy dust, stories are best when shared.* (From: *The Woman Who Flummoxed the Fairies*)

### Choose stories that . . .

- *Fit your personality.* Select stories you care about, are important to you, and you feel compelled to tell. Remember, we are the stories we tell.
- *Appeal to our better nature.* Include ones about courage, love, laughter.
- *Reveal an aspect of the human condition* (e.g., impatient, restless).
- *Evoke emotions that leave the audience enriched.*
- *Have the force of language.* Powerful words evoke visual images. They are beautiful and specific.

- *Are culturally authentic and fair to the original sources.*
- *Are audience appropriate.* Consider who will hear them. Consider audience characteristics (e.g., age, stage, time, place, occasion, interests).
- *Start strong and end in a satisfying way.* Try to get attention to start and end with a punch.
- *Are short.* Work up to longer ones.

Note: Plan to read 10 before you find one that suits you!

## Ready Reference 9.8  Learning Stories to Tell

- Visualize each event and character in relation to the climax. Rerun the story in your mind's eye like a movie.
- Use a whole-to-part process: Read or listen to the whole story several times before beginning to learn the parts.
- Focus on plot (storyline) first. Map out the sequence of images and events. Do not memorize.

  Note: Stories have a general structure that answers the questions of *who, what, where, why,* and *how.* Think about the beginning, middle, and end. Some tellers make a plot skeleton (Ready Reference 9.10) or make a map, chart, or list of events. Notecards or an outline of events can help, too. Heather Forrest uses a series of connected circles she calls "steppingstones." Another option is a series of stick drawings of events to use as a rehearsal device.

- Get a powerful first sentence to capture attention.
- Memorize the opening and ending to give yourself a frame in which to work. Also memorize any special phrases or refrains. Rehearse, but do not memorize, the rest. Use improvisation—the kind we use in real life to give directions or excuses and in conversation.

- Practice aloud. Use a tape recorder to listen to yourself. Tell it to the mirror. Videotape and critique your facial expression and gestures. Tell to a friend and then to a group. Own it by repeated retellings.
- Exaggerate gestures and vocal dynamics during practice to extend yourself. For example, open your mouth wider and increase volume to reach the "back row." Go into extra detail, count to three during a pause, say some parts very fast. Later you can tone down and select what you want to keep.
- Develop the characters. Imagine what they would wear, what their hands look like, how they would stand and move, and how their voices would sound. Interesting characters are created through detail (words, gestures, facial expressions, body use).
- Select words that paint pictures, describe feelings, and elaborate on details. Add sound effects where appropriate.
- If you use puppets and props, keep them out of sight until needed.

## Ready Reference 9.9  Pointers for Telling a Story

**Staging:** Dress so your appearance complements and does not distract. Choose a location without distractions. A circle creates an intimate climate.

### Introduction:

- Keep it short.
- Establish mood with your demeanor (posture, face, dress, gestures, tone of voice).
- Invite the audience to imagine and participate—to be together in a "mind space."
- Relax the audience with a smile or humor. Example: Knock-knocks build rapport with young children.
- Use a ritual, for example, light a candle, close your eyes, touch fingers of both hands together as if you are holding a ball and bow your head. Use a call and response, such as "When I say CRICK, you say CRACK" (West Indies).
- Motivate the audience to listen. Use a hook.
- Use poems, rhymes, games, riddles, and tongue twisters to get attention.
- Pass around an object or picture and ask questions. Example: What does this make you think of or feel?
- Use eye contact with audience members in different locations so that everyone feels you are telling to them.
- Be as physically close to your audience as possible.
- Personalize the story to the audience and place.

### Throughout:

- Remember, there is elegance in simplicity. Use only what you need.
- Show enthusiasm with your voice, eyes, body, gestures, and tempo.

- Use gestures, facial expressions, and movement to help define characters, create the setting, and set mood.
- Mentally picture the story so that you can make it live.
- Make word pictures by using language that evokes all five senses. Help the audience savor language by using words unique to the story. For example, when telling *The Baker's Scent,* storyteller Heather Forrest says, "The smell rose up like a hand and went down the street collecting noses" (Jackson, MI, Storyfest, 1994).
- Share story power by involving the audience.
- Increase suspense. Pause is waiting with a purpose. Pause to allow listeners to imagine and predict, to savor a moment. "The pause is like the big space that makes the beauty in Japanese paintings" (Heather Forrest).
- Give a sense of the place and the mood using voice, body, and descriptive words.
- Make each telling different to keep it spontaneous.
- Imagine being your own audience to give new perspective.
- Vary your voice for interest. Change the volume, rate, pitch, and pause (e.g., whisper, yell). Each character should have an idiolect. Use dialects as appropriate.
- Articulate and enunciate clearly. Refrain from using fillers such as "uh" and "um."
- Ignore interruptions as much as possible.

### Ending the Story:

The last sentence should have finality, so listeners feel satisfied and understand the tale is completed. There needs to be a signal for applause. You may want to use a closing ritual, for example, "Snip, Snap, Snout, This tale is told out."

## Ready Reference 9.10   Plot Skeleton for "Fable of the Farmer and Mule"

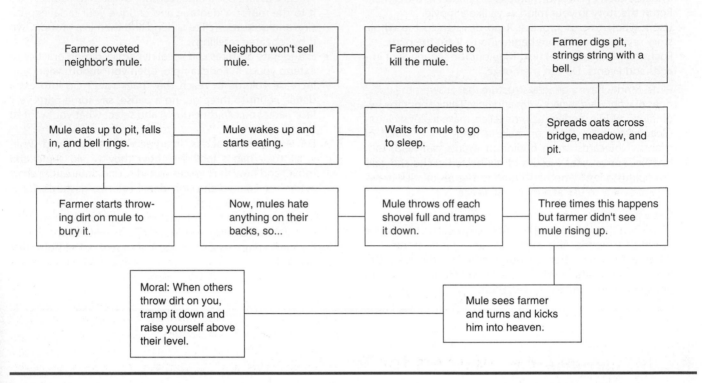

| | | | |
|---|---|---|---|
| Farmer coveted neighbor's mule. | Neighbor won't sell mule. | Farmer decides to kill the mule. | Farmer digs pit, strings string with a bell. |
| Mule eats up to pit, falls in, and bell rings. | Mule wakes up and starts eating. | Waits for mule to go to sleep. | Spreads oats across bridge, meadow, and pit. |
| Farmer starts throwing dirt on mule to bury it. | Now, mules hate anything on their backs, so... | Mule throws off each shovel full and tramps it down. | Three times this happens but farmer didn't see mule rising up. |

Moral: When others throw dirt on you, tramp it down and raise yourself above their level.

Mule sees farmer and turns and kicks him into heaven.

---

skeleton. Use these resources to find stories, learn to tell them, and involve students in storytelling. Here are seed strategies to get started.

**Opening Rituals.**   Collect and create opening rituals to get attention. For example (T = teller; A = audience):

- *Call and response:*
  T: Knock knock.
  A: Who's there?
  T: A story.
  A: A story who?
  T: A story for you.

  OR

  T: When I say hi, you say ho. Hi.
  A: Ho.
  T: Hi.
  A: Ho.
  T: When I say stop, you say go. Stop.
  A: Go.
  T: I will.

- *African ritual:*
  T: A story. A story.
  A: Let it come, let it go.

- *From the Sudan:*
  T: This story is the truth.
  A: Right.

  T: This story is a lie.
  A: Right.
  T: This story is both truth and lie.
  A: Right.

- *Candle lighting:*   Turn on a small battery-operated candle and say, "By the flame of the story candle we are freed to travel in our minds to other times and places."
- *Beginnings:*   A long time ago back before yesterday and use-to-bes. Long, long ago. In a time before time. Once upon a time.

**Audience Participation.**   Storytelling is always participatory, because the audience co-creates through imagination—especially visualization. Here are ideas to further increase audience engagement.

1. Stop and ask for ideas, for example, "What kind of fabric might the tailor use?"
2. Increase curiosity with a pause (e.g., "Nothing I'm going to tell you is true (pause) all the time.").
3. Use a cloze-pause for the audience to supply a refrain, phrase, or word (e.g., "...and the witch sang, 'Bubble bubble pasta pot, boil me some pasta nice and hot,'" from Tomie dePaola's *Strega Nona*). Or "Once upon a time there were three bears who got up one morning and made some _____."
4. Sound effects: audience supplies these creatively or "as rehearsed" before telling.

5. Add sign language to stories that an audience can mimic. *Joy of Signing* (Riekehof, 1987) is a clear reference.

6. Cumulative stories such as *This Is the House that Jack Built* (Taback) involve lists that repeat and build. Invite the unison response or have sections of the audience respond.

7. Story stops: Invite the audience to group mime or improvise dialogue with a partner. For example, from "Little Red Riding Hood": (1) Stop where Red first meets Wolf and ask audience to show how she felt using facial expression and body shapes/moves. (2) Pair so everyone is a Wolf with a Red and tell them to have a conversation at a signal. (3) Stop and ask audience to give Red advice about what she should do after meeting the wolf. (4) Stop and interview the audience as if they are story characters.

8. Questioning: Stop and ask the audience, "What do you know so far?" after the conflict has been introduced. After the story, ask, "What images do you have in your head?" that is less judgmental than, "What did you like best?"

9. Whisper a line to one person, who passes it on until it circulates around the room. This works for special surprises. For example, "And when he woke up on the end of his nose was a _____" (whisper "huge bologna").

**Vocal Expression.** Brainstorm the different ways to use voice in telling stories. For example, storytellers talk slowly, very fast, high pitch, scared, giggly, using regional accents and dialects. Choose a paragraph or sentence out of the newspaper or a book. Have each student read or say it aloud using three different voices.

**Talk with Your Body.** Practice ways to send a message using body gestures. *Examples:* "I'm tired. I'm bored. I'm afraid. It's freezing in here." Ask students to create original body sentences and pantomime. Do as pairs to get more participation. *Variation:* Try to show emotions without using the face (use mask).

**Follow the Leader.** This circle activity encourages using the body to communicate. IT mimes going on a walk (in place) and encountering a variety of obstacles (e.g., a crack in the sidewalk, a short wall, a fence with a gate, a puddle). The rest of the class imitates actions. Limit the obstacles to three, and then everyone guesses and a new IT can be chosen. *Variation:* Invite students to find actions in stories to mime. Start an ongoing chart (e.g., opening, reading, and closing a book; throwing types of balls; peeling and eating a banana).

**Painting Word Pictures.** This increases use of details. Sit in a circle. Give students a simple sentence. Go around, with each person repeating the sentence, adding description. For example: "The woman walked down the road. The bent old woman walked down the narrow road. The spry old woman walked frantically down the long hot road."

**Riddle Stories.** Riddles are a comfortable way to break into storytelling because they are short and they get an obvious audience response. Hundreds of joke and riddle books are available on nearly every topic from computers to insects. Here's a favorite: "Two legs was sitting on three legs with one leg in his lap. In comes four legs and snatches one leg. Up jumps two legs and picks up three legs and throws it at four legs and gets one leg back."

Note: Ask audience for guesses and then repeat more slowly so they "get it." (Answer: 1 leg = chicken, 2 legs = man, 3 legs = stool, 4 legs = dog.)

**Food Stories.** Food and stories go together. Ask each person or group to learn a story with a food connection. Stories are told and then everyone feasts. This works well with ethnic stories and folktales. *Examples: Stone Soup, Little Red Hen* (bread), *Three Wishes* (sausage).

**Circle Stories.** Sit in circle and use an opener, for example, "Once long ago when time was just getting started? . . ." Each person adds just one word or how ever many you want. The goal is to introduce a problem and resolve it after a designated number of rounds. *Suggestion:* Post a story structure chart to remind about setting, characters, problem, plot actions/events, resolution. *Variation:* Use to review, for example, "In science we've been studying about Mars and . . ."

**Key Word Storytelling.** Choose a list of up to 10 words that are important to an upcoming reading assignment. Pair students to tell a story that uses all the words. In one study, students remembered 90 percent of 120 words using this method versus 13 percent by the control (Wolfe, 2001).

**Story Challenge.** Give three words, phrases, objects, or pictures that must be used (do circle story, partner, individual, etc.). Example phrases include "a thorny rose," "lightning strikes," "one lost sneaker." Remind students that stories have a beginning, middle, and end and involve a problem. *Variations:* Use a phone book to get names for characters, spin a globe for a setting, and draw from a "problem box" (problems that children generate).

**Jigsaw Stories.** Tell a story to the group. Next, cut it up into parts so that each student has a section. Individuals rehearse their parts. Then the group assembles to tell the whole story. Number the sections the first time you try this.

**Alphabet Challenge.** Sit in a circle. Person 1 begins the retelling and must start with a word that begins with the letter *A*. The next person picks up the story, but must use the letter *B*, and so on. *Example:* A family of three bears lived in a dark wood. Bears need special furniture, and these three bears had chairs and beds to fit them. Chair Maximum was for Papa Bear, Chair Medium was for Mama Bear, and Chair Mini was for Baby Bear. (Thanks to second graders in Ohio, for this example.)

**Literature Frames.** Use a predictable book as a verbal frame, such as *When I Was Young in the Mountains* (Rylant). Partner and have students tell about when they were young, using the stem "When I was young _____." *Variation:* Do this in a ping-pong manner. Each student tells one line, and passes the turn by making eye contact with a student.

**Retell Favorites.** Students choose to paraphrase a family story. For shy students, invite them to use objects, props, or puppets. *Variation:* Each child makes a prop box of items to draw out as the story is told. This also helps students remember the story.

**Partner Retelling.** Students pair off and tell a favorite story. Partners must remember each other's stories. At a signal, all change partners and retell the story they just heard. This is excellent for listening skills. *Variation*: All students hear the same story and then partner to tell it to each other. Partner A begins and, at a signal, stops and B must pick up the story line.

**Personal Story Prompts.** Have students choose or draw randomly using a stem as a starter (e.g., "The funniest thing that ever happened to me was _____" or "The most embarrassing moment I've ever had was the time _____" or "The most memorable person in my family _____").

**I Am Stories.** Brainstorm with students roles they play, such as brother, sister, friend. In groups, ask students to use the stem "I am _____" and tell all the roles they play. They should feel free to add interesting details (e.g., "I am the shortest person in a family of six people, three of whom are my brothers.") (Collins, 1997).

**Rerun and Respond.** After a story has been told, invite students to rerun the story in their heads. They may use art, music, drama, dance, or creative writing responses to transform the rerun. *Example*: Rerun and think of three gestures and two sound effects to add. Students can also do a partner retelling (described previously).

**Round-Robin Retelling.** This is a kind of circle story. Students can retell picture books, fairy tales, and so forth. One person starts and passes on the story line. A ball of yarn with knots every yard can be passed and used as a cue. *Variation*: Retell from a different point of view than the original story, for example, Little Red Riding Hood from Grandmother's viewpoint. Use in science or social studies to retell events from different viewpoints.

**Backwards Stories.** This is a round-robin retelling, but the story is told from the ending to the beginning. This method demands concentration and thorough story understanding.

**Prop Stories.** Many stories have an object that can be used as a puppet or visual aid as the story is told. Young children especially love this, and older children are more comfortable telling stories if they can use a prop to focus the audience's attention. Here are example titles of stories/books with obvious props: Albert Lamorisse's *The Red Balloon,* Ruth Orbach's *Apple Pigs,* Robert Kraus's *The Tail Who Wagged the Dog,* Byrd Baylor's *Everybody Needs a Rock,* and Eric Carle's *The Very Hungry Caterpillar.*

**Art Story Map.** Provide students with portraits, landscapes, and nonrepresentational art (e.g., abstract), and ask them to choose one of each. Students create (write or tell) a story using portraits for characters, a landscape for the setting, and an abstract work for a story problem. Remind them to establish the problem quickly and be descriptive about the setting and characters. Share stories with art displayed. *Suggestion*: Arts postcards are inexpensive and great for this.

**Story Ballads.** Ballads tell tales through lyrics and music. First, share examples. Next, work with students to convert a familiar story to a ballad using rhythm instruments and singing parts. Action words can be used as the stimulus for mime or skits during the ballad. Rehearse. *Suggestion*: Videotape the end

product. *Variation*: After whole-group efforts, try small-group ballad writing.

**Puppet Shows.** Students plan a story adaptation, stage, and props to retell through puppets. For example, write a reader's theatre script (see Ready Reference 9.5). Help students map out the story using events in the beginning, middle, and end. Then decide who will make each character, scenery, and so forth. Chapter 7 describes 10 types of puppets. Stages can be made by using a push rod in a doorway to hang a curtain. Presentations can be made using the overhead projector (shadow puppets). Rather than memorize a script, encourage improvisation. As with all performances, rehearsal is needed to practice with puppet manipulation and oral expression. For tips on how to integrate puppetry into literacy lessons, go to Puppetry in Practice, http://puppetryinpractice.com/.

**Digital Storytelling.** Digital storytelling begins with writing a story then adding multimedia elements including images, music, and voice. The goal is a 2- to 3-minute product. For example, a personal narrative can be made into a short one-page script. Key scenes should be sketched on a storyboard, which is used to direct the search for images on the Internet. Students then use software such as *iMovieHD* (MacIntosh), *MovieMaker 2,* or *Photostory 3* (free downloads from Microsoft). See examples of student iMovies, photo stories, and book trailers created for science and literature units at Brigham Young University's Media Library (http://education.byu.edu/media/index.html?category=3).

### Example Websites

- Center for Digital Storytelling: www.storycenter.org
- DigitalStories.org: www.digitalstories.org
- Storytelling resources from Jakesonline.org: www.akesonline.org/storytelling.htm
- MovieMaker 2: www.microsoft.com/windowsxp/downloads/updates/moviemaker2.mspx
- Photostory 3: www.microsoft.com/windowsxp/using/digital photography/photostory/default.mspx
- iMovie HD: www.apple.com/ilife/imovie/

## Storytelling Sources and Resources

An excellent place to begin to search for stories and storytelling ideas is the National Storytelling Network (NSN), which offers workshops, periodicals, and a directory of storytellers. Check the website (*www.storynet.org/*) for details. Also see Story Arts Online (*www.storyarts.org/*) for lesson plans and tips on integrating storytelling. Be aware that most cultural stories are controversial because they focus on good overcoming evil (devils, witches, etc.), often employing violence. Western culture peculiarly emphasizes happy endings. Many traditional folktales have been sanitized to take out violent acts and dark characters. However, scholars feel this lessens the impact and denies children's need to cope with the "shadow" (see, e.g., Bruno Bettleheim's (1989) classic, *The Uses of Enchantment*).

Printed versions of multicultural folktales and fables can be found in the 398.2 section of the public library. Check both the children's and adult areas. Simplified versions are an excellent source for students to explore improvisation with storytelling. Other places to find stories to tell include the following:

- Children's literature, especially picture books
- Fables (Aesop, Lobel, Thurber) and folktales
- Personal ethnic or cultural traditions
- Family stories
- Retellings of stories you've heard others tell
- Bible or religious stories
- Historical events
- Contemporary news
- Childhood stories

### Anthology Examples

Chase, R. (2003). *Grandfather tales.* Boston: Houghton Mifflin.

Hamilton, V. (1993). *The people could fly: American black folktales.* New York: Knopf.

San Souci, R. (2001). *Short and shivery: Thirty chilling tales.* New York: Yearling.

Schram, P. (1993). *Jewish stories one generation tells another.* Dunmore, PA: Aronson.

Schwartz, A. (1986). *More scary stories to tell in the dark.* New York: Harper & Row.

Yolen, J. (1988). *Favorite folktales from around the world.* New York: Pantheon.

# Teacher Spotlight

## Science and Drama

This Teacher Spotlight returns to the focus of this chapter—using drama as a teaching tool.

The first graders are on the floor. Some are balled up. Others are on their sides. A few have their heads covered with their arms. The teacher, Liza Dean, **coaches** students to show being woodland animals in a hibernated state.

"Think of how you would feel if you had been asleep a long, long time—all winter. Think of how you will hold your head and move your arms and legs. When I say "begin," I want you to wake up. When I say **"freeze,"** you freeze. Ready, **BEGIN."**

Twenty-plus children begin to stretch limbs, rub their eyes, yawn, and wriggle. At first they move slowly. "I am going to count to 3 and then you will freeze. Ready. 1-2-3, " says Liza. On "3" the classroom grows silent and is filled with statues. Some are at the floor level. Some are at a medium level. A few are at a high level.

Why is Liza using **narrative pantomime** in a science unit? She thinks the drama strategies of moving and frozen pantomime, used after reading, cause students to become thoroughly engaged in **problem solving**, which is the foundation of comprehension. "It causes them to visualize and become a part of the action," she explains. "It is an important way to increase comprehension skills." She points out that it is hard to think without making pictures in your head. **"Visual imagery** is necessary to cognition, but it must be explicitly taught."

Liza explains the philosophy of her school. "We encourage each student to be different—to move in ways that make sense to them and to use their faces to show the emotions each of them thinks relate best to what we are studying. The arts are about difference, not sameness."

What about standards and tests? "Of course, we also look at the arts standards and expect students to learn techniques and concepts about the arts. We want to 'use' the arts, not 'abuse' them," she explains.

How are basics like vocabulary and phonics taught in arts-based lessons?

"Better!" Liza exclaims. "The arts are teaching and learning tools. The goal for using drama in this lesson was for students to show understanding of specific science concepts by thinking through body shapes, actions, and facial expressions. First graders can show more than they can say or write." ✺

## Conclusion

*Life beats down and crushes the soul and art reminds you that you have one.* (Stella Adler)

This chapter is a compendium of seed strategies to jump start planning for meaningful drama integration. Storytelling was a special focus. Both drama and storytelling are arts that give life to learning.

---

**Drama**

---

### Teachers as Leaders: AI Advocacy

Volunteer to demonstrate several drama strategies to a group of educators such as at a faculty meeting, staff development, or for a class. Distribute a list of 10 reasons to teach with drama that you have synthesized from this and the preceding chapter.

---

### PEARSON myeducationlab 🍎

Go to the Activities and Applications section for Topic *Strategies for Teaching* at MyEducationLab for your course and complete the video activities entitled "Using Storytelling to Teach Visual Imagery", "Preparing for a Pantomime Response to Literature", "Using Side Coaching to Increase Creative Problem Solving", "Using Big Idea Tableau to Show Comprehension", and "Setting Up for Tableau Creation."

Go to the Video Examples section for this topic to view the videos entitled: "Using Echo Reading to Prepare for Storytelling", "Coaching to Increase Thinking about Purposes of Pantomime", "Using Descriptive Feedback to Extend Pantomime", "Preparing for and Using Teacher in Role Interviews", and "Debriefing about Teacher-in-Role Strategy."

Go to the Activities and Applications section for Topic *Attaining Arts Literacy* and complete the video activity entitled "A Drama Specialist Discusses Basics."

Go to the Book Specific Resources section in the MyEducationLab for your course, select your book and Chapter 9 to view the Questions to Guide Reading and Response Options for this chapter.

# Resources

See the Appendix for more materials, including more websites.

## Website Sampling

Children's Theatre: http://faculty-web.at.northwestern.edu/theater/tya/

Educational Theatre Association/International Thespian Society: www.edta.org/

## Activity Books

Booth, D. (1994). *Story drama: Reading, writing, and role playing across the curriculum.* Marham, ON: Pembroke.

Erior, P. (2000). *Drama in the classroom: Creative activities for teachers, parents and friends.* Fort Bragg, CA: Lost Coast Press.

Heathcote, D., & Bolton, G. (1995). *Drama for learning: Dorothy Heathcote's mantle of the expert approach to education.* Portsmouth, NH: Heinemann.

Heinig, R. B. (1986). *Creative drama resource book for grades 4 through 6.* Upper Saddle River, NJ: Prentice Hall. (K–3 book also available)

Heinig, R. B. (1992). *Improvisation with favorite fairy tales.* Portsmouth, NH: Heinemann.

Heller, P. (1996). *Drama as a way of knowing.* York, ME: Stenhouse.

McClasin, N. (2006). *Creative drama in the classroom and beyond.* New York: Allyn & Bacon.

Mobley, J. (1992). *NTC's dictionary of theatre and drama terms.* Chicago: NTC Publishing Group.

O'Neill, C., & Lambert, A (1991). *Drama structures. A practical handbook for teachers.* Portsmouth, NH: Heinemann.

Pollock, J. (1998). *Side by side: Twelve multicultural puppet plays.* School Library Media No. 13. Lanham, MD: Scarecrow.

Rooyackers, P. (2002). *101 more drama games for children: Fun and learning with acting and make-believe.* Alameda, CA: Hunter House.

Rubin, J., & Merrion, M. (1996). *Creative drama and music methods: Introductory activities for children.* North Haven, CT: Linnet Professional.

Schafer, L. (1994). *Plays around the year.* New York: Scholastic.

Spolin, V. (1986). *Theatre games for the classroom: A teacher's handbook.* Evanston, IL: Northwestern University Press.

Walker, L. (1996). *Readers theatre strategies development through readers theatre, storytelling, writing and dramatizing!* Colorado Springs, CO: Meriwether.

Winters, L. (1997). *On stage: Theatre games and activities for kids.* Chicago: Review Press.

Zipes, J. (2004). *Speaking out: Storytelling and creative drama for children.* Oxford, UK: Routledge.

# 10

# Integrating Dance and Creative Movement

*If you can walk you can dance. If you can talk, you can sing.*
(Zimbabwean adage)

## Overview

This chapter is about the art that sets the curriculum in motion: dance. Thirteen reasons for dance integration are discussed under the first of 10 AI building blocks needed for meaningful integration. Block II is an overview of the basic dance knowledge classroom teachers need. Blocks III through X describe *how* to work toward complete curriculum integration using dance and movement as teaching tools.

## Introduction

### Curriculum in Motion

*Nobody cares if you can dance well. Just get up and dance.*
(Martha Graham)

Dance is very big in the world beyond school walls. TV shows like *So You Think You Can Dance* and *Dancing with the Stars*, along with films like *Take the Lead* and *Shall We Dance*, inspire Banderas, Gere, and Lopez fans to take lessons. Membership in the U.S. Amateur Ballroom Dancers Association has doubled. Dance studios are thriving. A recent documentary, "Mad Hot Ballroom," which portrays NYC fifth graders vying for a trophy, is the 10th highest grossing documentary ever. Even the Learning Channel debuted a dance program: *Ballroom Bootcamp*. Tango, waltz, samba, and salsa are all popular on college campuses from big Harvard to small Wittenberg University (Ohio).

Inside America schools arts integration is rescuing academic curricula from "dead ends . . . flat, dull routines of schooling that leave students intellectually unchallenged and emotionally disengaged" (Grumet, 2004, p. 50). Dance is the art that puts the curriculum in motion. Dance engages cognition within the context of compelling experiences that teach how to move one's body with intention. For example, in Waldorf schools, a math concept such as geometry is first experienced through movement. Students will walk or run a triangle, circle, square, pentagon, and so forth, using the entire body to come to understand aspects such as a right angle. With their bodies they learn to keep an equal distance from the center at every point to make a circle.

It is "the experience through the body that says 'circle' to his six-year old mind" (Barnes, 1978, p. 4).

Standards-free loosey-goosey "creative expression" is not the goal of AI, and dance integration is about much more than recreation and enrichment. Well-thought-out use of dance is the goal and seeks to cause heads-on, hearts-on, hands-on learning. *Hands on* was in the education lexicon before *heads on* and *hearts on*. Dance is hands on, feet on—*whole body on*. But dance is more than being physical. Like all the arts, dance is about creative problem solving—thinking on your feet. Students are challenged cognitively, emotionally, and physically.

As the saying goes, it is hard to keep your brain in gear once your bum goes numb. The more serious we get about standards, big ideas, and essential skills, the more we need the force of dance to motivate students. Serious studies show how students involved in quality AI programs deepen their motivation and engagement with learning and increase their use of higher order thinking, which account for substantial gains in basics, such as reading and math skills (Rabkin & Redmond, 2004, p. 8). The gains are most significant for low achieving students. The teaching challenge is to use dance *meaningfully* to teach science, social studies, math, and literacy. That's where the 10 AI building blocks come in.

In the opening Classroom Snapshot, teacher Wrenn Cook takes on the challenge. Wrenn is a dance education expert who believes integration should go two ways—using dance in the regular classroom and bringing traditional subject areas into dance lessons. She shows how important science content can be taught using an instructional sequence format that begins with a warm-up to engage physically and mentally. Kids say it is more fun to learn this way—emotion puts motivation in action (De Moss & Morris, 2002). Notice how Wrenn weaves problem solving throughout the lesson as students wrestle with how to transform skeletal information into choreographed dances. Also notice how she scaffolds them toward higher order original thinking by coaching, especially with descriptive feedback.

## Classroom Snapshot
### Science and Skeleton Dancing

The desks are pushed to the edges of the room. Twenty-four third graders stand in a circle. Music with a steady beat and moderate tempo plays just loudly enough to hear and feel

**255**

Lion dancers at Ashley River Creative Arts

the rhythm, but softly enough to hear directions. Ms. Wrenn Cook is guiding them through a "skull to phalanges" **warm-up** to cause students to isolate and move particular body parts.

"Let's tilt our skulls forward and return to center, forward and return to center," she says.

Students **chant,** "Skull-skull, skull-skull" to the beat.

After several **repetitions,** Ms. Cook proceeds to the jawbone. Students giggle as they try to say "mandible-mandible" while opening and closing their mouths.

"We look like my goldfish!" says one boy; they all start imitating gills. Ms. Cook **redirects focus** by moving on to clavicles and sternum until the warm-up has touched on every bone, head to toe.

## More than Imitation

"Now it's your turn. We'll go clockwise around the circle. **Create a new movement** for a bone. Corinne, show us a different way to move our skulls," Ms. Cook suggests.

Corinne tilts her skull side to side. The students and Ms. Cook follow suit, chanting, "skull-skull." For "ulna," a boy does a "karate chop" in which he strikes one forearm against the other in a downward motion.

"That's right, Kevin, ulna-ulna. See how he uses the pinky finger side of his lower arm? What lower arm bone is on the thumb side?" Ms. Cook asks. The students show her.

"That's right! The radius. Let's do Kevin's movement using the radius, instead of the ulna."

Students contort to touch their radius bones to opposite arms, until one **discovers** that upward chopping is easier.

"**Great solution!** Let's all do that together. Let's alternate arms. Radius right, radius left, radius right, radius left."

The warm-up lasts 10 minutes and has served as a review of content points from the previous day's lesson. By the time they reach the phalanges, students' eyes are bright and cheeks slightly flushed. They are fully alert.

"Everyone really stayed focused. Have a seat where you're standing." Ms. Cook gives out a skeleton dance handout. It lists seven "commands," beginning with "Touch some phalanges to a patella."

## Creative Problem Solving

"Here is your choreography problem," Ms. Cook pauses. "Each group is challenged to create a group dance about the skeletal system." She explains they are to come up with movements for all the commands. The goal is to create an interesting dance composition for an audience. She points out **"Choreography Tips"** on the handout that lists ideas for how to use dance elements to create visual interest.

"Try to find **unexpected ways** to dance the commands and to choreograph transitions from one segment to the next," she explains.

"Let's talk about the first command, 'Touch some phalanges to a patella.' Someone show me one way that a dancer could do that." Antonio jumps up and poses with the fingers of each hand touching each kneecap.

"That's one, Antonio! Now someone show us **a different way** to touch phalanges to a patella." A girl balances on one leg, touching her toes to the knee of the leg.

"Great balance, Danielle! What other ways can we touch phalanges to a patella? You don't have to make a still shape—you can move." Students have **multiple solutions,** and all show they understand phalanges and patella.

"I see you understand what to do. I can't wait to see your skeleton dances!"

At this point Ms. Cook shows them the evaluation **rubric** and invites questions to make sure they understand. She divides them into six preselected groups of four. They are **heterogeneous** and mix gender, race, and ability levels.

Ms. Cook circulates as the students start problem solving. She listens and **coaches** with questions and information.

"Hey, I know! While moving our pelvis right and left, we could jump up and down on the metatarsals, then we could switch," says one student.

"Okay. Then maybe we could each do a **solo**, and everyone else **freezes in a shape** until their turn," a boy responds.

Some immediately begin **inventing** and practicing movement. Others first talk through a plan from beginning to end. Ms. Cook mediates with a group who cannot agree. They work out a compromise. When one group asks if they can perform two commands simultaneously, Ms. Cook asks to see the movement they are considering. They perform a **complex sequence.** They accurately use the required bones, and she congratulates them for their originality. Another group adopts a narrative form. Ms. Cook responds with delight when they show a comedic section from their story dance.

After about 20 minutes, most are ready. Ms. Cook **cues them** that they have 5 more minutes to finish the choreography and rehearsal. She reminds them they need to memorize their dances since they cannot use handouts during the **performance.** As students refine their dances, Ms. Cook plays **two music selections** and asks groups to choose one to accompany their dance. She plays each again so students can rehearse with both and pick a best fit.

## Performance and Assessment

Finally they are ready. Students sit at the end of the room facing an area designated as the "stage." As they watch the dances, some exclaim, "Cool!" or "Awesome!" in response to the choreographers' creative choices. They laugh at some funny parts and nod knowingly as they recognize movements for specific commands. As each group performs, Ms. Cook watches closely, checking for accuracy and **making notations** on the rubric for the task. At the conclusion, students are asked to **comment**.

"I really liked how Tyler's group went down to the floor when they had to touch the lumbar vertebrae to the floor," a girl says.

"Jamica's group was really together when they did the part about waving their metacarpals," a boy says.

Ms. Cook notes use of **science vocabulary** and compliments them on observational skills. Students begin to push their desks back. A boy asks if they can perform the skeleton dances for a **"real" audience.**

"Yes, let us do it," they all begin to plead.

Ms. Cook promises to look into having the students perform at the upcoming school science fair.

"If you get to work right away on your science reading assignment," she explains.

With that, students smile and get out their science books to read more about the skeletal system. The lesson has lasted about 50 minutes. Dance has been the vehicle for science and acted as a motivational force.

Wrenn Cook's unit plan and rubric appear in Planning Pages 10.9 and 10.14. ✺

# Teaching *through* the Arts

> *Art engages the world. Artists make work about things, ideas, questions, relationships, emotions, problems, and solutions. Arts integration is modeled on the methods and purposes of real artists.* (Rabkin & Redmond, 2005a)

Most classroom teachers would agree that they could learn to do what Wrenn Cook did in the opening Classroom Snapshot. Although she had the advantage of knowing dance elements and ways to coach students through simple choreography (dance making), Wrenn had to study the science content to make a meaningful fit.

Classroom teachers just do the opposite when they integrate dance. That is what this chapter is about—how to go beyond a bit of creative movement here and there or teaching a folk dance during a culture study. To teach *through* dance demands a level of dance literacy. This chapter summarizes what to teach *about* and how to involve students *in* dance so that they can learn *through* it.

## Relax! You Need Not Be a Dancer

> *Nothing is more revealing than movement.* (Anonymous)

Our bodies and how we move them say a lot. So much, in fact, that muggers choose victims by watching how people move: They look for tentative, irregular, undirected walking. Movement is a powerful communicator that can fascinate or repel, delight or disgust.

Of course, our society is riveted on sports-based movement. The regular use of kinesthetic ways of knowing is less prominent in the classroom. Perhaps movement is so basic, we take for granted that students know how to use it skillfully to communicate thoughts and feelings. Some do, but most do not. Teenagers, in particular, are unaware of what exaggerated swaggers and awkward shuffles say. We suffer for those young people who lack confidence and the skill to manage their bodies.

AI is helping dance and the other arts regain their rightful foothold in the communication curriculum. For movement to become a full literacy partner, however, teachers need to acknowledge the primacy of this communication force—when words and actions compete, actions win out. Many times, dance and creative movement is the art form teachers feel least prepared to integrate.

Skeleton dance: waving metacarpals in the air

It is not surprising teachers may be uncomfortable using creative movement, especially if they are unsure exactly what that means. The look of one's body is overly important in our culture. Beautiful, intimidating body images bombard us daily through the media, and we have become very body sensitive. Teachers do not want to appear awkward or have their bodies targeted for student examination. Students often feel the same way, especially after the primary grades.

How can we move forward? Most important is to start with a foundational truth: We all love to move. It feels good to walk, run, stretch, wiggle, and shake. Equally important is putting life links at the forefront of introducing, such as how movement is integral to most careers—how you carry yourself certainly influences hiring decisions. The life link is vital to creating an openness to dance study. It is also pertinent to remember that *doing* trumps *telling* in the learning arena. These are just a few of the arguments for building a teaching strategy repertoire to put kinesthetic ways of knowing into action throughout the curriculum.

Teachers are center stage in the success of dance integration as they are in all AI. In particular, teachers have to be actively engaged in directing dance problem solving (Parrish, 2007). Be reassured that rarely has to do with demonstrating specific dances. When and if a decision is made to include structured dances (e.g., folk dancing in social studies), teachers can choose to demonstrate such dances or invite guests to do so, or perhaps work with the physical education teacher. If the school has an arts resource directory then it may well include folks who are willing to teach specific dances.

# Arts Integration Building Blocks

*There are shortcuts to happiness, and dancing is one of them.* (Vicki Baum)

The arts exist because they fill a niche. If people could express themselves solely in language, there would be no need to draw, paint, sing, and dance (Eisner, 1998b). The arts fulfill needs as basic as food and shelter, especially the need to make sense. Nothing delivers like the arts when it comes to liberating the flow of creative ideas to construct meaning, and dance holds its own in this respect. Dance changes how we feel and think (Rabkin & Redmond, 2005b).

In Chapter 3, the 10 AI building blocks were introduced as anchors to facilitate meaningful integration (see Ready Reference 3.3). First up in this section is a discussion of *why* dance should be integrated—the philosophical beliefs that have been synthesized from research, theories, and professional wisdom. The next block deals with *what* teachers need to know (dance literacy). The remaining building blocks describe *how* to plan dance-based lessons, create an aesthetic environment, use dance-based literature and best teaching practices, design instructional routines, differentiate for diverse learners, assess, and work cooperatively with dance specialists.

# Building Block I: Philosophy: Why Integrate Dance?

*I dance because it brings me closer to my creator.* (Morgan Grant, Saginaw dancer)

A philosophy is a set of beliefs. Educational beliefs grow from research, theories, and professional experience. What a teacher believes directs decisions about every aspect of instruction, making it essential that we continually examine and revise our beliefs in light of more current research. Research Update 10.1 summarizes research relevant to dance integration. Additional research and educational theories, such as those in Chapter 2, were used to synthesize the following 13 reasons to integrate dance.

## Dance Is a Primary Form of Communication

*If I could tell you what I mean, there would be no point in dancing.* (Isadora Duncan)

The importance of movement in communication cannot be minimized. If you saw *Meet the Fockers,* you know where this is going. Babies as young as 9 months have been taught to sign and can learn an average of 70 gestures, long before they have 70 words in their speaking vocabularies. Children can coordinate more behaviors in their hands before those in their throat and mouth. Researchers claim teaching baby sign frees kids to express feelings and desires and some eventually developed a 12-point IQ advantage and higher reading scores (Hochman, 2005).

Body language was the first language our ancient human ancestors probably used and retains first place as children develop. Even for adults, nonverbal language has primacy over verbal, especially when the two conflict: Imagine someone saying, "I'm delighted to be here" with a sneer on his face. It is fun and useful to ask students to generate examples of "when words and actions conflict" to make this point.

Movement is a universal language: the outstretched hand, a bowed greeting, and an up-raised shaking fist communicate similar thoughts and feelings across cultures. Yet, you can get into a lot of trouble assuming the OK sign means the same thing in Italy as it does in the United States. As Hanna points out, just like language "dance has many dialects" (1999, p.19).

Dance is a means of showing what we know and feel. It can enable children to express thoughts and feelings that are locked away. The kinesthetic mode is the one through which our earliest learning happens and it remains a force throughout life (Gardener, 1993b).

## Dance Develops Creative Problem Solving

*Great ideas originate in the muscles.* (Thomas Edison)

The ways artists think are the ways we all need to think in the 21st century: They seek alternative solutions to problems, think

## Research Update *10.1*   Dance and Achievement

- First graders who participated in 20 dance-based reading lessons scored higher in the area of phonetic knowledge and skills than nonparticipating students (MacMahon, Roe, & Parks, 2003).
- Achievement improved when boys were involved in dance lessons (Bloom, 2004).
- At-risk first graders who were taught basic letter and sounds through creative movement improved more than a control group. The conclusion is, "The development of linguistic abilities mirrors the development of dance phrase making . . . dance can help children discover the 'music' of language" (Deasy, 2002, p. 10).
- At Chicago's CAPE schools teachers link literacy skills with dance in the "Reading in Motion" program (www.reading inmotion.org). Students tend to improve significantly faster than those attending non-CAPE schools. For example, the number of sixth graders at CAPE schools with reading scores in the average to above average range grew six percentage points more than at comparable schools—that's twice as fast. Students with the greatest challenges have been the biggest beneficiaries (Catterall & Waldorf, 1999).
- Physical activity (e.g., walking) is linked to the ability to pay attention and seems to result in better academic performance according to University of Illinois researchers (Hillman, 2009).
- Teenagers serving time in detention facilities benefited from twice-weekly dance classes. "Patience, and sometimes even compassion, can be social by-products of aesthetic engagement" (Deasy, 2002, p. 13).
- Dance and music opportunities offered compelling social benefits for underprivileged students, including an emotional safe haven; making them feel special; acting as assimilation tools for recent immigrants and new kids; and bolstering friendships in new situations. The arts opportunities "helped most achieve success both in and outside of school" (Fiske, 1999, pp. 77–78).
- Students with disabilities who participated in a 12-week dance program showed significantly higher scores for creativity (fluency, originality, and imagination) than those in adaptive physical education programs (Jay, 1991).
- Third-grade science scores on tests about the water cycle were raised to 97 percent when dance was used as the vehicle. Previous year's students scored below average on the test (Baron, 1997).
- In Seattle, Washington, third graders who studied language arts through dance increased Metropolitan Achievement Test scores by 13 percent in 6 months (Gilbert-Greene, 1977).
- The College Board reports that for the 1999 school year, students with 4 or more years of dance background scored 27 points higher on average math and verbal scores. For more about SAT scores, go to www.collegeboard.org/prof/.

out of the box, take new perspectives, work collaboratively with others, critique work to elevate its quality, revise, share with others, and so on. This is authentic intellectual work that employs disciplined inquiry to find new ways to use knowledge and skills (Rabkin & Redmond, 2005b).

CPS begins with finding problems and then gathering information to solve them. Dance does this through its focus on exploring movement to unleash creative and artistic thinking. Teachers ask: "How many ways can you move across the room?" "What are all the body parts you can use to make circles?" "What are all the ways cats move? Leaves? Water?" "How can you show the idea of *addition* using dance?" "What are words that describe movements?" These kinds of fat questions engage creative thinking focused on problem solving.

In dance integration, students are taught basic tools to solve problems through dance. This includes achieving a command of basic dance elements and skills so they can communicate kinesthetically with artistry. Teachers go further to encourage risk taking and experimentation, coach students to visualize, show them how to research and draft dance compositions (choreograph), and scaffold students toward increasing independence. Time is provided to explore ways to use movement to communicate thoughts and feelings to free the unlimited powers of the imagination. That power is put to use to solve problems in every subject matter, including the subject of life (Parrish, 2007).

## Dance Is Integral to Real Life

*Consider how many times . . . you handled a basketball compared to the number of times you skipped to music.* (Ruth Murray)

John Dewey's idea that school should not be preparation for life, but actual life, fits here. Dance should be at least as prominent in school as it is outside of school—and our world is dance rich.

Dance has a valued place in religion and ethnic identity. It is integral to the rituals and ceremonies of our lives—weddings, inaugurations, proms, and holidays. Many states have designated state dances: North Carolina's is clogging and South Carolina's is shagging. Square dancing has been proposed as our national dance (Hanna, 1999).

It is intriguing to consider the response of audiences to entertainment phenomena such as "Lord of the Dance" and "Riverdance." Just as athletic games draw huge crowds, dance attracts entertainment dollars—another real-life connection. Certainly, part of the attraction of sports is the movement aspect. We enjoyed watching the light airy moves of Michael Jordan and marvel at the elegant golf swing of Tiger Woods. While sports are not the same as dance, there is a connection. In sports, as in dance, the body is used as a tool. Certain individuals go further to make their sport into an art form; they take their moves to a level of beauty that awes and inspires.

## Dance Develops Responsibility and Value for Hard Work

*In life as in the dance: Grace glides on blistered feet.* (Alice Abrams)

Dance often involves group work. Students develop responsibility when they are part of an ensemble in which their ideas and cooperation are needed. Responsibility is not just *caught;* it must be *taught.* Responsibility means, "having the ability to respond." Teachers need to teach students how to respond in a group and to specific group members. Dance integration provides rich opportunities to help students learn what it means to solve problems in a group and to teach specific behaviors such as active listening—paraphrasing another's ideas, asking for clarification, and using nonverbal responses such as nodding and eye contact.

All dance-based work demands focus and concentration to gain control over basic dance elements such as body, energy, space, and time. Students involved in dance integration get a taste of what it means to think kinesthetically. There is a pride that comes from conquering obstacles to body communication, then there is the thrill of performance, and the reinforcement given when an audience is present.

Students involved in formal dance study commit to rigorous work to develop skills in ballet, tap, and jazz. Students who choose such study must commit to a regimen of regular practice. They quickly see that struggle and hard work are needed to master new ideas. Why do they choose pain and hard work? One student put it this way: "It was mind over movement for me. I really liked the challenge to get my body to do what I wanted. Dancers who could do amazing moves inspired me. I wanted to stretch myself."

## Dance Increases Sensitivity, Respect, and Cooperation

Dance-based group problem solving gives students another context to discover that every person views a situation differently. Students learn to value the surprising ways peers express ideas through movement; no one body shape or locomotor movement is right or wrong. The emphasis is on finding original ways to think and feel about important concepts in science, social studies, and math. Students learn that working alone does not yield as many solutions, nor ones as diverse, as those generated by groups. Two bodies and heads are better than one.

Students come to delight in the artistry of fellow classmates as they witness the inventiveness of peers. Both teachers and students see that a "hyperactive" child may just need a kinesthetic medium to become engaged. A graceful slide or a humorous foot dab executed at the right moment provides a moment of insight—oohs and ahs, laughter, and even awe. Partner, small group, and circle dance work also require students to help each other to create a product that makes sense. The "we're in this together" situation mobilizes the motivation to cooperate.

## Dance Builds Focus and Concentration

Students involved in solving movement problems or exploring movement have to focus on making their bodies work. Dance is about developing control over body parts and movements using different amounts of energy given a defined space. To use dance as a learning tool requires self-regulation. Dance pedagogy gives teachers in AI specific tools to meet the challenge head on, since dance is all about learning to control the body, mind, and voice.

In particular, dozens of warm-ups develop focus and concentration. Teachers present small and easy movement problems and increase the difficulty over time. In very little time, students learn to create short meaningful dances with a beginning, middle, and end structure. As students work, teachers coach students with "I see statements," suggestions, and questions that relate to concentration and focus: "I see you were really focusing on holding that pose." "How might you show you are more involved?" and "Try to picture in your mind how you could do that."

Dance integration includes teaching students to appreciate pleasant feelings that come from being quiet and still. Students learn to enjoy the sensations of inner peace and pride in controlling body parts and shapes. Self-discipline develops as they learn to manage movement, gradually at first and then for increasing lengths of time and with more variety. Eventually they see that this control permits them to see things they missed before and express ideas and emotions in more original ways.

## Dance Develops Self-Control and Confidence

*Graceful movement is just the right amount of energy for what you're doing.* (Michael Ballard)

One of the first things strangers notice about a good friend of mine is her posture. She sits and stands very erect. She walks with fluidity and grace. The ways she holds and moves her body communicate that she is a leader—and she is. A former department chair at a college, she now heads up several community groups, including the Jackson, Michigan, Storyfest.

Famed dancer Jacques D'Amboise explains that by learning to take control of your body, "you discover that you can take control of your life" (quoted in Hanna, 1999, p. 29). He speaks from personal experience. His mother enrolled him in ballet school to get him off the streets of Harlem. Today he runs the National Dance Institute which partners with New York schools.

Dance integration seeks to extend each student's control over body parts and movements. Dance involvement builds endurance and strength, enabling participants to feel more poised. Students feel more confident because they have more ways to express ideas and feelings kinesthetically. Self-assurance is extended as teachers carefully scaffold dance problem solving so that students experience success. At a beginning level, teachers present short, simple problems, such as "How can you walk across the room in different ways?" or "What possible body shapes might George Washington have used as he was installed as the first president?" Students learn to gather data from observing real people and examining art, such as paintings of President Washington. They learn to use diverse resources to try body shapes and moves on for size, including attempting different poses they see in artwork. Students can be challenged to go further to try to walk as Mr. Washington would, right after the scene in the art.

# Dance Is Integrated Brain-Body-Soul Work

*I see the dance being used as a means of communication between soul and soul—to express what is too deep, too fine for word.* (Ruth St. Denis)

Gardner (1996) includes dance under body-kinesthetic intelligence, and neurologist Mark Hallett (1999) claims that using the body maximizes brain use. He explains that any athletic work at peak performance can use close to 100 percent of the brain, which dispels the myth that humans never use more than 10 percent. Dance is athleticism with artistry. The added dimension of the aesthetic permits creative and inner self-expression, crucial for happiness and satisfaction.

Dance is highly intellectual, with a mind-body connection that "activates far more brain areas than traditional seatwork" (Jensen, 2001, p. 72). The whole person is involved in dance construction. Students use multiple intelligences, not just kinesthetic intelligence. Examples are as follows:

- Patterns and counting are essential, so math and logic are used.
- Spatial intelligence is used to visualize floor patterns and choreograph.
- Dance and music are common partners because we naturally respond to rhythm and melody with movement.
- Dance has its own vocabulary, so it draws on verbal intelligence.
- Interpersonal intelligence is tapped when you dance with others or create dance for others (e.g., choreographers).
- Dance is intrapersonal in that it involves reflecting on personal development.
- Dance employs naturalistic knowing when movements are drawn from nature or have nature themes (Nelson, 1998).

Through dance we communicate what we think through our bodies. We also communicate what we feel and value, which involves emotional intelligence. Students who learn how to physically express important concepts in science, social studies, or math gain new views on subjects as more areas of the brain are engaged.

Dance is a special art form in that it is "a primary medium for expression involving the total self (not just a part, like the voice) or totally separated from the physical self (like painting or sculpture)" (Fleming, 1990, p. 5). Savvy teachers help children become "whole" people through the integration of the arts. Dance integration is particularly holistic.

# Dance Is Healthy

*My heart lifted my feet, and I danced.* (Nathan of Nemirov)

An ad from the American Heart Association features a silhouetted child in front of a television. The boldface caption reads, "Caution: Children Not At Play." Obesity levels of children have risen dramatically as youth mimic the passive television viewing habits of adults. On the average, they now spend about 4 hours a day viewing versus doing. Some spend more and the more they watch, the lower their test scores. Following are facts from the National Assessment of Educational Progress (http://nces.ed.gov/nationsreportcard). Children who watch:

- 1 hour of television per day scored 224
- 4 to 5 hours per day scored 213
- 6 or more hours per day scored 196 (13 percent of white students, 20 percent of Hispanic students, and 40 percent of black students)

What about during the school day? As the curriculum has been narrowed to "teach to the test," time spent using the body in active, physical ways has been squeezed. How much of the ballooning statistics about "hyperactive" kids has to do with children's bodies rejecting "sit still" classrooms?

Dance is exercise, and exercise makes us healthy. It increases blood circulation and muscle tone. Dance burns up calories. Like any exercise, dance triggers the brain to produce endorphins (natural painkillers) and catecholamine (an alertness hormone). No wonder children enjoy dance; they are out of pain and full of energy! Schools in states like West Virginia are taking advantage of the motivational power of dance to make children active. The popular video dance game "Dance Dance Revolution" is being provided to schools by the Public Employees Insurance Agency (Barker, 2005).

Dance is also a kind of therapy that provides emotional release, which alleviates stress. A University of Illinois study shows complex physical learning may even compensate for prenatal alcohol exposure (Smith, 2003). Dance used before, during, or after a lesson can increase physical readiness for cognitive learning by activating more brain areas.

# Dance Satisfies the Aesthetic Need for Beauty

There is hardly a sight more beautiful than a graceful human being. When students have opportunities to view dances and participate in dance creation, they increase their aesthetic sensitivity. Maslow (1970) placed the need for beauty near the top of his acclaimed motivation hierarchy. He argued that meeting this need was requisite to becoming fulfilled or "self-actualized." Beauty uplifts us and can give hope even in the form of a potted flower on a rotted window. It creates a sense that life is worth living.

Dance integration emphasizes releasing the expressive and imaginative potential of children. Such dance is creative and can add beauty to the lives of children. Captivating ethnic dances, such as the hora from Jewish culture, stretch children's concepts of beauty and offers information about how diverse groups celebrate. The spectacle of a cultural dance performance can be a powerful bridge. It is hard to hate those who are different when you have been touched by their gifts of beauty—their dance, stories, art, and music.

## Dance Is a Path to Cultural Understanding and Expression

*Sometimes dancing and music can describe a true image of the customs of a country better than words in a newspaper.* (Gene Kelly)

All art forms are vehicles for the ideas and values of their creators. Dance, like any art, reflects the time and place in which it is created. This makes dance an important means of coming to understand values and customs of other cultures (Hanna, 1999). For example, Batoto Yetu is a Harlem company that uses dance to pass on African cultural history to children. They believe this understanding builds respect and hope (*This Morning,* CBS, April 11, 1997).

Dances reflect changing values, tastes, economic conditions, and social trends making it a natural partner for social studies. Students can get a sense of the mood and values of a time by viewing and doing dance forms from different historical periods. The 400-year-old dance ballet reflects formal living at the Medici court life. Clogging gives clues to rugged mountain life in North Carolina. From the limbo to the lambada, there is rich material to study what groups think and feel.

Dance investigations can even yield surprising information that opens up thinking about historical events. One fourth-grade class discovered that Native American ghost dancers in the 19th century created dances to celebrate the return of the lands taken by the U.S. government. The dancers tried to conjure up the power of their ancestors and created such fervor among tribes that the government eventually forbade the dance. When ghost dancing continued, U.S. soldiers attacked and killed a camp of dancers, including many children. A children's book about the Ghost dancers is Morin's award winning book, *The Ghost Dance* (1995).

## Dance Can Be a Powerful Cross-Curricular Learning Tool

Students involved in dance learn effective ways to use their bodies as a language. Dance elements become conceptual anchors that can be creatively employed in any discipline to create meaning. In addition to the social studies examples previously discussed, dance is now used in schools across the country to both learn and demonstrate understanding of science processes such as making fossil fuels, planet rotation, life cycles, and decay. Students use their bodies to gain deep understanding of concepts such as dependence, interrelationships, and cause and effect.

Vocabulary is a key component of literacy and the meanings of many words can be extended and expressed through dance, especially verbs, adverbs, and emotion words such as

*contrite* and *ferocious.* As students learn dance elements they are analyzing and categorizing their own thinking. In an AI environment, students discover that there are many crossover concepts. Words such as *rhythm, space,* and *shape* are polysemous. They are the same word, with different meanings in the context of music, drama, and the visual arts. There is actually a great deal of crossover arts vocabulary and when students are helped to make these connections, depth of word meaning is developed. Dance concepts such as balance extend not only to other arts but also to science areas such as physics.

Dance choreography is parallel to written composition. There is potential two-way transfer as students learn to gather ideas, visualize ways to organize them, experiment with options, draft, revise, share, and evaluate results in both areas.

## Dance Gives Joy

*The place of the dance is within the heart.* (Tom Robbins)

Imagine a group of people dancing. Eyes sparkle. They smile and laugh as energy explodes in whirls and wiggles. Dancers surprise themselves as they discover ways bodies can be made to move to a musical beat or an internal rhythm.

Elizabeth Wall, a Richmond, Virginia, principal, explains that students changed when dance was integrated at her school. They expressed "a sense of humor and as attitudes and values changed, self-control developed. . . . They looked forward to school" (Fleming, 1990, p. 32). That's because dancing is just plain fun. It can give the feeling of being "high" or uplifted, just as any creative activity can.

Dance and creative movement are entertaining to do and view. Indeed, nothing is more interesting than people watching. It is so interesting to notice the unique ways people walk, how

Learning history through dance: minuet

they hold their head and body, how they get from one point to the next, how they move to music. These images captivate because they say so much about each person and can invite imitation. Think of the generations influenced by Elvis Presley's hip and leg moves or Michael Jackson's moon walking.

# Building Block II: Dance Literacy: Content and Skills

> *Dance is music made visible.* (George Balanchine)

Meaningful arts integration is largely defined by the quality and degree to which teachers teach dance concepts and skill so students can artfully use them to communicate—to create sense in any curricular area. Dance elements are taught in the same way we teach children reading and writing skills and for the same purposes: so they can understand and express ideas and feelings.

Children also need a command of basic dance vocabulary and the skill to construct basic dance phrases, sentences, and whole works. This composition process is called *choreography*, but it is essentially the same as written composition. Both processes use CPS thinking. In dance compositions within an AI context, students need to learn how to combine information with artistry.

## What Do Teachers Need to Know about Dance?

> *When one looks at the image of a rising arch or tower in architecture or at the yielding of a tree bent by the storm, one receives more than the information conveyed by the image. . . . The body of the viewer reproduces the tensions of swinging and rising and bending so that he himself matches internally the actions he sees being performed outside. And these actions . . . are ways of being alive, ways of being human.* (R. Arnheim, 1989)

The pursuit of dance literacy for integration purposes begins with teachers personally experiencing creative dance. This book cannot give that experience. There is no substitute for actual dancing. Hopefully the following information will give enough of a picture to motivate readers to seek out experiences to experiment with the language of dance.

The dance literacy level needed by teachers is contingent upon what their students are expected to know and do. Later in the chapter, Ready Reference 10.7 lists the *National Dance Standards* (K–8) for students. Standards for what classroom teachers should know and be able to do in dance were developed by the Interstate New Teacher Assessment and Support Consortium and can be downloaded at www.ccsso.org/Projects/ (see "All Projects" link).

In elementary and middle school, dance literacy basically involves studying (1) the historical, social, and cultural role of dance in our lives; (2) communication through dance by creating dance, understanding dance language, and performing; and (3) valuing dance for its aesthetic contributions. Classroom teachers need to know the following:

- Definitions of dance
- Purposes and roles of dance
- Dance elements
- Dance processes
- Genre, forms, and styles
- People of dance
- Sources for dance-related materials
- Teaching approaches

### Definitions of Dance.

> *Dance is not about something. Dance is something.* (Mary Joyce, 1994)

It does seem that animals dance. Dogs can be trained to twirl and jump, as can bears and cats. My nephew is a horse trainer and the range of moves he teaches the horses resembles dance, with steps, rhythms, even changing levels. There's even a cockatiel on YouTube that seems to dance—quite well. But are these animals really dancing?

In every art form the question is, "What makes it?" Dance is no exception and it follows the other art forms in emphasizing *intention*. Dance is movement aware of itself. It transcends just taking steps and is distinct from pantomime (drama). It is intentional communication using artful movement to express ideas and feelings, meaning aesthetic purpose is present.

Most parents expect children to master control of their bodies, but they may not understand how dance can make a significant contribution to this development. Dance adds creative purpose to control. This book has already presented many arguments for the importance of developing creative thinking. It should suffice to reinforce those arguments by noting that the same innovative thinking that produced hip-hop is used to invent in the worlds of science and business. This point is exemplified in the many dancers who have become successful in other fields.

Note: The word *dance* remains a touchy term in some communities, so some schools call it *creative movement*.

**Dance versus Movement.** As I type this sentence, I am moving. This is not dance. Yet, I can take my hands from the keys and begin to play with "typing movement." Now I experience the feel of my fingers moving and the shape of my hands on an abstract level. I can use other body parts to create the lightness of touch and the irregular rhythms of typing. I can do this with my toes, torso, and hips. The movement is no longer done to accomplish a task but to explore how kinesthetics is a way of knowing and feeling.

Movement becomes dance when the purpose goes beyond using physical means to get a practical task done. Dance is an art, and art is not created nor understood for just function. Even a sequence of skilled gymnastic movements performed to music does not make a dance. Murray explains, "There must be something present that pertains to the spirit of the performer, and the movement must communicate that spirit" (1975, p. 18).

**Creative Movement and Dance.** Dance involves becoming conscious of movement and being willing to play with it. Dance consciousness starts with awareness of body parts: close your eyes and focus on body parts, starting with your head and moving slowly down to your toes—exploring a bit of movement with each as you progress south.

Born of modern dance, "creative moment" had a heyday in the middle part of the 20th century. Its genesis was in use of natural movements, rather than a specific dance genre such as ballet. Creative movement still retains popularity in physical education classes across the country. This makes sense since dance is movement. Like dance, physical education uses movement to solve problems. The difference is that dance uses kinesthetics to solve problems creatively and the expression of feelings is integral to the process.

In the political angst over low test scores, dance is being reconsidered as a necessary cog in the wheel of education. Research, like that summarized in Research Update 10.1 has done much to cause a reawakening, as has Gardner's theory of multiple intelligences, which parceled out "kinesthetic intelligence" as one of the original magnificent seven. Educators have been brought back to the future as Gardner and others show how bodily kinesthetic intelligence is essential to learning—something common sense tells us and human history testifies to. Neuroscientists now suggest that the arts are the most productive ways to stimulate high achievement over the long haul of schooling (Jensen, 2001).

**Purposes and Roles.** The purpose of dance, like all art forms, is fundamentally to communicate. However, the intention of communication in the arts is not only to share information. Dance focuses on expression of feelings and values and intends to cause aesthetic response. Even early ballets, such as *Swan Lake* and *The Sleeping Beauty*, were performed with the dual purposes of providing ethical instruction in court behavior, but in a beautiful form (Hanna, 1999).

When the United States was but a young country, dance was commonly used as a vehicle to acquire social grace and get some exercise. Then the 20th century brought new educational philosophies, like that of John Dewey. Dance in education was given a boost by progressive educators who emphasized moving and doing. A new focus on self-expression triggered an evolution in emphasis that moved from ballet to folk to modern dance (Hanna, 1999). Martha Graham forever altered the concept of what dance could be. Isadora Duncan and others took creative expression through dance further, influencing how creative movement became creative dance that uses everyday movements. People began to see that dance could be much more than learning to execute the five codified ballet positions.

Today we still enjoy the beauty and messages of ballet, but our tastes are much more eclectic. We also enjoy and learn about cultures from world dances and are amazed at the athleticism of dancers like Pilobolus. Social dances from salsa to street dancing are hot because they permit a wide range of creative expression. The diversity of tastes and preferences and inventiveness of Americans is apparent in our large national dance menu. That menu should be a resource for the classroom.

**Dance Literacy.** William Safire (1991) points out that we have certain words that bridge the gulf between spoken and unspoken language. These mega-words overarch our thinking. Words such as *expression, understanding, communicating,* and *knowing* go beyond the limitations of normal words. We use these mega-words to describe the most important things we want to happen in learning, and they absolutely describe what happens in the arts.

The study of dance is a rich form of nonverbal expression, but it is not devoid of words. Martha Graham, the single greatest figure in modern dance, was hailed in her obituary for "creating a language" with movement (Hanna, 1999, p. 52). She used a special vocabulary that included "percussive contractions and releases and dramatic stories" (p. 15).

Dance has its own "vocabulary" in the literal sense and in the sense that there are units of understanding used to create dance phrases and sentences. Just as in written language, dance can use these units to create a full composition of meaning.

## Dance Elements.

*Technique—bodily control—must be mastered only because the body must not stand in the way of a soul's expression.* (La Meri)

Several systems are used for categorizing dance concepts. The goal is to be able to use dance symbols to understand and create movement for specific purposes and contexts. The following is a simple system of remembering dance elements that is useful for classroom teachers and students. (Thanks to Randy Barron, dance educator affiliated with the John F. Kennedy Center for the Performing Arts, for permission to use this concept.) It is easy to remember because it is organized around the acronym BEST: body, energy, space, and time. Ready Reference 10.2 summarizes BEST.

**Body Parts, Shapes, Actions.** We use all body parts to communicate, both those outside and inside. Think of the ways to move just your little finger or the effect on the body when you tighten inner core muscles. Body shape includes ways to form body parts to create everything from pleasant round and curved shapes to sharp angry angles and pointed shapes. Then there are all the ways to move in place or through a space. Stationary actions are called *nonlocomotor* and include stretch, bend, twist, rise, fall, circle, shake, suspend, sway, swing, and collapse. Movement through space is called *locomotor,* and includes actions such as walk, run, leap, hop, jump, gallop, skip, and slide.

*Energy* is the force a person uses and signals the mood the dancer intends. It includes the person's attack (smooth or sharp), weight (heavy or light), strength or tension (tight or loose), and flow (sudden or sustained).

*Space* is the personal or shared area where the body is used. Space is filled up by changing levels (low, middle, and high), directions, size, place or destination, and pathways (how to get to a destination—directly or in an indirect way). Focus or concentration, or where a person is looking, is used to signal importance.

*Time* is another element used during movement. It includes rhythm (pulse, beat), speed or tempo, accent or emphasis (light or strong), duration (length), and phrases (dance "sentences," or patterns and combinations of all different kinds of movements). For example, "three different middle-level slow, wringing shapes" is a phrase that may create a message about discomfort or struggle.

**Dance Processes.**

> *The activity is the art.* (Mary Joyce)

Choreography is dance making—creating, composing, and improvising movement to make meaning. Choreography involves planning and performing—or getting others to perform your designs. When students learn to make dances about concepts in science and social studies, they are involved in intense CPS using choreographic artistic principles, including repetition, contrast, unity, variety, balance, and pattern. Students learn to organize and structure their thinking using BEST elements to create dance phrases and sentences and organize them into themes with variations. For example, like in music, dance can use "call and response" or take a narrative structure and tell a story. It is even possible to learn to write the plan for any dance using a special notation system invented by Hungarian dancer Rudolf Laban. Ready Reference 10.3 shows his "qualities of movement" that teachers can use to direct creative movement exploration.

## Ready Reference *10.2*   BEST Dance Elements and Concepts

B = Body, E = Energy, S = Space, T = Time

### Body
**Parts:** head, neck, torso (hips, abdomen, shoulders, back), arms and elbows, hands and wrists, fingers, legs, knees, and feet (ankles and toes)
**Shapes:** curved, twisted, angular, small-large, flat-rounded
**Actions or Moves:**
- **Nonlocomotor:** stretch, bend, twist, rise, fall, circle, shake, suspend, sway, swing, collapse
- **Locomotor:** walk, leap, hop, jump, gallop, skip, slide

### Energy
- **Attack:** smooth or sharp
- **Weight:** strong or light
- **Strength or tension:** tight or loose and relaxed
- **Flow:** sudden or sustained, bound or free

### Space
**Level:** low, middle, and high
**Direction:** forward, backward, sideways, up, down
**Size:** large and small
**Place or destination:** where we move to
**Pathways:** patterns on the floor or air (e.g., circular)
**Focus:** where the dancer looks

### Time
**Rhythm:** pulse or beat
**Speed:** time or tempo
**Accent:** light or strong emphasis
**Duration:** length
**Phrases:** dance sentences, patterns, and combinations (e.g., twist, twist, twirl, and freeze)

### Choreographic Principles
Repetition, contrast, unity, variety, balance, patterns, and transitions used to make dance.

## Ready Reference *10.3*  Laban Qualities of Movement

Rudolf von Laban (1879–1958) was a dancer and a movement scientist. He studied the elements that create "qualities of movement." He discovered how different moods could be created by combining eight actions, with different degrees of effort and amounts of space. The eight actions are charted here against "sustained or sudden, strong or light, direct or indirect."

Post this chart to coach students to use different amounts of effort and space with the eight actions. This kind of exploration expands thinking through dance/movement. For example, wringing is a twisting and turning movement that can be sustained or sudden. It can be strong or light and involves several body parts going in different directions (versus direct movement toward a target).

| Three Choices: | Sudden/Sustained? | Strong/Light? | Direct/Indirect? |
| --- | --- | --- | --- |
| **Eight Actions:** | | | |
| Wring | | | |
| Thrust | | | |
| Slash | | | |
| Float | | | |
| Glide | | | |
| Press | | | |
| Flick | | | |
| Dab | | | |

Of course dance can also be viewed live or on video or film. The process to understand and appreciate what the dance is saying (i.e., to comprehend it) requires knowing how to "read" the language of dance. This involves noticing how the dance elements are used and responding to the effects created by dancers' bodies. When understanding is increased, it is likely that appreciation also increases and there is a more pronounced aesthetic response.

**People of Dance.**    Teachers need to know some key people who have made dance what it is today. A unit might focus on a particular dancer or dance as a door into an historical time period or culture (see Ready Reference 10.4). Dances and dancers have changed how people think during a time or for a culture. We see that kind of influence today on youth who have embraced hip-hop music and dance. The influence can be positive or negative. Either way, it needs to be acknowledged that it happens before educators and parents can decide what to do about it, if anything. It is well accepted that suppressing a form of communication makes it more seductive.

Dance offers a range of career opportunities from dancer to choreographer, dance critic, dance historian, and dance teacher. All of these options belong in career education studies. Ready Reference 10.5 lists examples of dances and dancers that can be integrated. Ross and Stangl's *The Music Teacher's Book of Lists* is a source for more choreographers.

**Genre, Forms, and Styles.**    Throughout history people have loved to invent dances. Today we are blessed with a gourmet menu to choose from as we seek personal enjoyment or plan innovative ways to teach. From ballet, tap, and jazz, we can find values,

beliefs, and lifestyles recorded. In folk dances we find cultural insight, as we can with fad dances. As the Macarena and electric slide slipped off the radar, in came hot hot salsa, which challenges us to draw conclusions about the changing times. Ready Reference 10.5 lists dances that can be integrated into social studies, understood through health science and math, and read for their messages.

## Sources for Materials

Once you have some space, dance is fairly cheap to integrate. It is helpful, over time, to accumulate music CDs, DVDs/videos, pictures of dances and dancers, books, and other material to use as references and in lessons. For example, jazz as a reflection of the time in which it was invented cannot be fully understood without seeing it danced. Check the websites at the end of the chapter for places to start on the Internet and some video sources.

**Music for Dance.**    Although there is a close association between music and dance, music is not always necessary for dance integration. It is useful for warm-ups, movement exploration, or free dance (Joyce, 1994). Beware of children's songs that consist of movement directions to follow. These are akin to a coloring book and can stifle creative thinking (Stinson, 1988). When music is used, choose music for dance that promotes creative, not stereotyped, movement and is rhythmic but not too complicated.

Shorter selections of simple classical music (Brahm's Fourth Symphony, Debussy's "Clouds," Wagner's "Forest Murmurs," and Copeland's "Billy the Kid") work well, as do children's songs that suggest, but do not dictate, movement, such as those by Ella Jenkins. Electronic and loud music promotes bump and grind movements

---

**Ready Reference 10.4**  Well-Known Dancers

| | |
|---|---|
| Martha Graham (modern dance) | Natalia Makarova (ballet) |
| Jacques D' Amboise (ballet) | Isadora Duncan (modern dance) |
| Mikhail Baryshnikov (ballet) | Ben Vereen (many styles) |
| Gene Kelly (modern) | Gregory Hines (many styles) |
| Fred Astaire (ballroom) | Alvin Ailey (modern dance) |
| Jillian Lynn (choreographer) | Rudolf von Laban (modern dance) |
| Rudolf Nureyev (ballet) | Michael Jackson (moon dancing) |

---

**Ready Reference 10.5**  Dance Forms and Styles

| | | | |
|---|---|---|---|
| African | Country/Western (contradanse) | Irish | Social |
| Asian | Courtship | Jazz | Square |
| Ballet | Creative | Jitterbug/swing | Street |
| Ballroom | Electric slide | Minuet | Tap |
| Belly | Flamenco | Polka | Theatrical |
| Caribbean | Folk and national | Reels | Turkey trot |
| Charleston | Fox trot | Religious/liturgical | Twist |
| Circle | Hip hop | Salsa | Waltz |
| Clogging | Indian | Shag | Warrior |

inappropriate to school. Go through your personal collections of tapes and CDs and look for music that does the following:

- Makes you feel like moving or dancing
- Has a predictable structure; it feels like it goes somewhere
- Has a clear quality (could invite marching or delicate movements).
- Has no lyrics, is instrumental (no words), or has words that are not important to the quality (e.g., Enya)
- Has different tempos and moods ranging from a nondiscernible beat to strong complex rhythms
- Uses a variety of instruments (saxophone, piano, violins, drum, etc.)
- Includes folk music from different countries, ethnic groups, or time periods (e.g., Putamayo's "A World Instrumental Collection")
- Is classical sounding, especially soloists and chamber ensembles (e.g., Chopin), and does not overwhelm

Categories of music especially helpful for classroom teachers are listed in Chapter 12. One resource is *Music for Creative Dance* (volumes 1–4) available at www.ravennaventures.com.

Music recommendations for dance appear in Ready Reference 10.6.

**Dancing Songs.** Many songs are naturally connected to movement (e.g., "The Grand Ole Duke of York") and many are action or movement songs, singing games, and song dances. Hap Palmer, Little Richard, Ella Fitzgerald, and Steve and Greg all have produced movement-oriented collections on tape and CD. Special songs with dances include "The Twist," "The Hokey Pokey," "Chicken Dance," "Macarena," "Monkey," and "Ponytime." Richard Simmons's workout tapes have examples as well. While teaching specific dance steps or moves is not the main goal of AI, these are good for warm-ups, especially if students are encouraged to create, not just imitate. To really stretch the imagination, ask students to move in ways that contrast with the song (e.g., What would not fit with a lullaby?).

## Teaching Approach

At times dance integration includes students learning structured folk or social dances, but the instructional mainstay is not demonstrating combinations of memorized steps. Dance integration is mostly about directing creative movement explorations that cause students to learn to create whole compositions ordered into a beginning, middle, and end.

The classroom teacher's purposes are best served by a focus on using dance for problem solving. This begins with guided discovery about the nature of movement. This open-ended approach embraces a variety of acceptable solutions. Creating dances and learning about dance aspects should be planned times for students to feel the joy that results from trying out their own ideas to solve dance puzzles.

If dance is to be a useful and joyful meaning maker, the focus needs to be on using dance language in creative ways to express thoughts and feelings. The dance symbol system, like those of all communication forms such as verbal language, math, art, and music, consists of teachable elements—tools for meaning making. See Ready Reference 10.2 for dance elements.

**Dance Differs from Pantomime.** Pantomime is often confused with creative dance. Pantomime does use movement without words, but it is a form of drama in which people take roles and pretend to be something or someone. Pantomime has more to do with taking roles and imitation than creative movement.

Pantomime and dance each make important contributions to learning, but teachers need to be clear about their different purposes and processes. In dance, movement is more abstract. The focus is on the movement itself, not on pretending to move *like* an animal or plant. Here's the essence of the problem. When teachers direct students to do something, such as "move like a cat," students usually *pantomime* stereotyped paw and claw movements. Pantomime is about taking a role and moving in ways consistent with that role. Dance uses a different frame of thinking. Consider

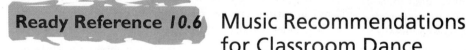

**Ready Reference 10.6** ## Music Recommendations for Classroom Dance

**Musical Artists and Groups**

Penguin Café (orchestra)
Keith Terry and Crosspulse
Chuck Mangione
Wynton Marsalis
Gotan Project
Tomita
Paul Winter
George Winston
Yanni

**CDs: Individual Artists with Sample CD**

Mickey Hart - "Planet Drum"
Peter Jones - "Gradual Movement" and "The Fifth Movement"
Ladysmith Black Mambazo - "Long Walk to Freedom"
Bobby McFerrin - "Circlesongs"
Gabrielle Roth and the Mirrors - "Initiation"
Glen Velez - "Rhythms of the Chakras"

**CDs: Various Artists**

"I Am Walking; New Native Music"
Putamayo presents "A World Instrumental Collection"?
"Colors of the World: Latin"?
"Spiritual Life Music"

the same direction using a dance/movement focus: "Show me the shape of a cat's body using just your arm. With your fingers show me a cat walking slowly. With your whole body show me stalking at a low level. Now at a high level." These directions cause students to do something that is different from "becoming a cat." Dance is about kinesthetic exploration—finding options for thinking about concepts (such as "cat") using movement.

When dance is used for problem solving, students are urged to consider the movement *possibilities of* an idea. For this reason, dance exploration is useful when teaching new concepts in science or social studies. Students can be challenged to explore different ways to develop a concept such as "cumulus clouds" by moving different body parts in many ways.

Contrasting pantomime and creative dance may seem like splitting hairs, but the teacher who makes the distinction can better harness the distinct forces of both art forms. Dance can add another dimension to making meaning of songs, poems, or children's literature. Miming Max's wild rumpus in *Where the Wild Things Are* is not dance. It is a way for students to become part of the story and think about characterization. Instead, children can learn to think beyond the literal and use dance to work on ways to express anger (the emotion that got Max sent to his room) using a full range of body parts and moves. Thus a concept important to the book's theme (anger) is explored through movement. The teacher needs to decide if the goal is to "become" or "be" the character—to take a particular role (drama) or probe the movement extensions of important ideas and feelings in a lesson (dance).

# Building Block III: Collaborative Planning

Meaningful dance integration does not seek to create a "program of little dances once a year for an audience taught under pressure and presented in the school auditorium" (Murray, 1975, p. 19). The words *integral, integrity*, and *integration* come from the same root that has to do with "essentialness." For integration to have integrity, the arts must be integral to curricular learning that targets important big ideas. This implies that classroom teachers and specialists have dual responsibility for planning, teaching, and assessing both arts and academic content and skills.

Co-planning is where dance integration should start. Planning with specialists helps set the stage for dance to be more than exercise or entertainment. Dance specialists can put dance in historical and cultural contexts and keep the focus on artistic ways of thinking and doing. Specialists are also good resources for dance-specific "best practices."

Planning Page 3.7 summarizes the unit development process. It begins with examining standards and goals.

## National Standards for Dance

The *National Standards for the Arts* is a national consensus document that includes dance standards. These standards have been used across the country to frame state and local standards. The *Standards* address the question, What should be taught in dance? They are structured around movement-centered and audience-centered goals that suggest sequenced, developmentally appropriate competences for students. The goal is for students to learn basic movements and dance vocabulary so they can understand and create dance composition. Dance Standards are grouped by grades 4, 8, and 12 and were used in the construction of the arts section of the National Assessment for Educational Progress (NAEP).

Standards, goals, objectives, and outcomes in curriculum frameworks only help teachers know *what* to teach. They do not explain *how*. They are meant to serve as a "template without stifling local creativity" (Hanna, 1999, p. 62). The seven dance standards students are expected to meet are summarized in Ready Reference 10.7. A full copy of the *Standards* is available from Music Educator's National Conference (http://menc.org). All the strategies and activities in this section of the book and the next chapter relate to one or more of these standards.

For examples of arts standards developed at the state level, go to the website of the department of education in your state. Other states you can use as resources are Kentucky, Ohio, Wisconsin, South Carolina, North Carolina, and Connecticut.

## Standards and Integration

Notice in Wrenn Cook's Unit Plan (later in the chapter, in Planning Page 10.9) how she listed both dance standards and science standards. As teachers work to increase the relevance and depth of learning through the process of arts integration, it is necessary to examine standards in each separate discipline and try to find those that overlap. Collaborative planning between specialists and classroom teachers makes this easier.

Standards can be scanned and clustered to find connections, but teachers are encouraged to think broadly. In the case of dance, there are certain standards that overlap with nearly every other curricular area. For example, Standard 3: "The learner will understand that dance can create and communicate meaning" obviously overlaps with literacy standards, but it also can relate to showing understanding in math, science, and social studies.

Standard 5: "The learner will demonstrate and understand dance in various cultures and historical periods" overlaps with social studies standards. Standard 6: "The learner will make connections between dance and healthful living" has a clear connection to science; and Standard 7: "The learner will make connections between dance and other content areas" is an explicit statement of the necessity to integrate.

## Complementary Connections

During co-planning it is helpful to look to life for dance connections as a strategy to help understand dance's curricular importance. The goal is authentic connections. Ready Reference 1.2 outlines examples of natural connections between dance and other curricular areas.

Wrenn's Classroom Snapshot, which opened this chapter, gives an example of one of many science/dance connections, but weather is full of movement, as are pulleys and levers (weight and balance). Imagine studying gravity by exploring strength,

## Ready Reference 10.7  Seven National Standards for Dance

Overall focus: Develop self-image, self-expression, and discipline, body awareness, movement exploration, and creative problem solving, appreciation of self and others, cooperation and collaboration, use of musical rhythms, performing for an audience, respect for diversity, and celebration of cultures.

1. ***Identifying and demonstrating movement elements and skills in performing dance.*** Example: Perform locomotor movements, create shapes, personal space, pathways, move to beat and tempo, show concentration, describe actions and dance elements.
2. ***Understanding choreographic principles, processes, and structures.*** Example: Create dances with a beginning, middle, and end structure. Improvise and create new movements. Use partner skills such as leading and copying. Create dance phrases.
3. ***Understanding dance as a way to create and communicate meaning.*** Example: Explain how dance is different from sports and everyday gestures. Discuss what a dance is communicating. Present original dances and explain their meanings.
4. ***Applying and demonstrating critical and creative thinking skills in dance.*** Example: Find multiple solutions to movement problems. Observe two different dances and discuss differences and similarities. Apply aesthetic criteria to observed dances. Demonstrate appropriate audience etiquette.
5. ***Demonstrating and understanding dance in various cultures and historical periods.*** Example: Perform folk dances. Share dances from own heritage. Put dance into historical periods based on style and elements. Analyze for values conveyed.
6. ***Making connections between dance and healthful living.*** Example: Set personal goals for a dancer. Discuss healthy practices. Create and use dance warm-ups.
7. ***Making connections between dance and other disciplines.*** Example: Create a dance to explain a concept from another discipline. Respond to dance by making a painting, song, or writing about messages it conveys.

*Source:* Content Standards (material printed in bold type) excerpted from *National Standards for Arts Education,* published by Music Educators National Conference (MENC). Copyright © 1994 by MENC. Reprinted with permission. The complete National Standards are available at http://menc.org.

energy, and force using the body. There is much to be understood through exploring the actions that created fossil fuels: time, heat, pressure, no air, and *no* movement.

**Science.** When students choreograph and perform a dance about photosynthesis they must use CPS to create understanding and use CPS again to create a performance of their understanding. This work of translating ideas from a science text to the code of dance anchors comprehension and extends it through providing a nonverbal vehicle to express understanding (Grumet, 2004, p. 60). The dance provides a "cultural object" that unites thoughts and feelings so everyone can consider each other's thinking (p. 60). Later in the chapter, Planning Page 10.9 shows examples of using dance to teach health/science concepts.

**Social Studies.** There are obvious connections between history, cultures, and dance, but there are sociology, economic, and psychology links as well (e.g., dance therapy).

**Math.** Dance and math of dance share many natural links such as counting and patterns.

**Reading.** Of course there is much to read *about* dance, but dances themselves can also be "read." Dances are built using elements comparable to the alphabet that are organized into phrases and sentences. When dance is presented as an alternative "text" to be read, students can see the parallels, laying the groundwork for two-way transfer. Dance also has a word-based vocabulary, and learning dance vocabulary adds to one's general vocabulary. Dance words are also interesting words that can invigorate less interesting words in areas such as spelling and phonics.

**Writing.** Dance is a communication system, so students can learn how to "speak" its language and use dance elements to compose. Writing and dance share the following processes.

- Brainstorming ideas
- Research
- Trying out words or phrases (trying out movements)
- Sequencing into first draft (beginning, middle, end)
- Revising (rehearsing)
- Editing (clean-up rehearsal)
- Final draft/publication (performance)
- Evaluation

Teachers who collaborate with dance specialists to point out the overlaps are leveraging knowledge gain in both areas.

Planning Page 10.8 shows a plan created by teaching artist Laurel Shastri, to cause students to use CPS thinking to both create a dance and come to understand the parallels between dance and reading and writing. Her use of open-ended questions and scaffolding show how students can be thoughtfully engaged in problem solving and create interesting dance products. There is also a dance writing symbol system, called Laban Notation, that students can use to record original dances.

**Arts with Arts Integration.** Not to be ignored is integrating dance with the other arts. The arts share a common core of ideas that should be integrated with one another, not just with traditional academic areas. For example, much of visual art involves movement (e.g., draw). Music, art, drama, and dance possess parallel elements such as line and shape. Dance can put sounds and feelings into motion. Students can dance a painting or paint the dances they create. When teachers show how the arts are interwoven, students develop more complex webs of knowing about the world. For example, shape can be explored by painting to music on big paper. Ready Reference 1.2 lists a few of the concepts shared across disciplines.

# Planning Page *10.8*

## Dance-Based Literacy Lesson*

**Title: Greetings Through Movement**
*Teaching Artist (TA):* Laurel Shastri, Associate Director of Ballet Tennessee

**Objectives:** Students(s) will. . .
1. Use creative problem solving to create a group dance in the form of a greeting card.
2. Give examples of how dance is like reading and writing.
3. Tell different kinds of thinking used during problem solving.
4. Compare performance and with audience participation.

**Materials and Setup:**
Open space
*Music:* "Bach for Babies," "Secret Garden" by White Stones
Examples of different types of greeting cards

*Activity 1—Introduction/Warm-Up:* **Nonverbal warm-up.** S standing in personal space.

- *Arts Concept:* Dance is a form of communication.
- *Literacy Concept*: Creative problem solving used to "read" (interpret meaning from the actions of) the TA.

*Activity:* TA will nonverbally direct a series of movements to warm up students' bodies.

*Example:* Signal "my turn" to demo and then signal for them to echo the movement. S will have to "read" nonverbal cues to follow the directions.

*Activity 2—Content Activity:* **What is dance?** S will sit personal space.

- *Arts Concept:* Dance elements of BEST: body, energy, space, and time
- *Literacy Concept:* Abstract versus literal interpretation

*Activity:* Part discussion and part movement. S will be directed to explore literal gestures, pantomime, and sign language and then compare these to abstract movements with multiple interpretations for meaning.

*See clips from this lesson at MEL under Strategies for Teaching.

*Activity 3—Content Activity:* **Greeting card dance.** *S* standing in personal space.

- *Arts Concept:* To create a dance, we use the dance "alphabet": BEST
- *Literacy Concept:* Creative problem solving; literal and abstract thinking

*Activity:* Show and ask about aspects of different types of greeting cards. S and TA will collaborate to create an abstract dance using meaningful movement, communicating ideas parallel to paper greeting card messages.

*Activity 4—Closure and Reflection:* Working as class or in small groups.

- *Arts Concept:* Dance is a way of expressing thoughts and feelings.
- *Literacy Concept:* Meaningful movement can be created (like writing) and interpreted (like reading).

*Activity:* Ask S to reflect on connections between reading, writing, and dance as a form of communication. Ask the following:

1. What kinds of thinking did you do to create the dance? (probe for visualize, connect to past experiences, infer, experiment, etc.)
2. What are the similarities and differences between our movement greeting card and a written card?
3. How do we know what dancers are saying with their movements?
4. What movements seemed the most interesting and why?
5. Did you prefer watching the other group perform or performing for them? Why?

**Assessment:** Observation checklist or rubric for dance participation and dance rubric. Student writing and/or discussion about five questions.

**Unit Centers.** In Chapter 3, five different integrated unit cores were explained. The core or unit body can be extended using the nine academic and arts legs (Planning Page 3.8). For example, a teacher or team might plan integrated lessons and units using one or more of the traditional subject areas as a unit body, or a unit may be a study of a person, genre, or core work and the arts; math, science, social studies, and literacy become the legs that support and move the unit along. Dance and movement would be used as learning tools in such a unit, just as any other leg. Planning Page 10.9 shows an example of a dance/health unit organized around study of the skeleton.

Teachers are encouraged to think creatively and plan units that focus on a dancer or choreographer, a dance (jazz, ballet, tap), dance questions (e.g., Why do people dance? How do dances emerge?), or a core dance work (e.g., minuet and early American history) or even a dance-based children's book such

as *Sometimes I Dance Mountains* (Baylor et al.). Math, science, social studies, reading and language arts, and the other art forms would be the support legs. Involving students in research on dancers and dance genre enables them to connect literature, social studies, and other art forms as they search for the whys and hows that motivated the creation of dance throughout human history. Planning Page 6.14 shows planning for an author-artist study. Examine how dance is used.

Topics to be explored through dance can also be solicited from students (feelings, interests, questions, and concerns). These can develop into whole units or a single integrated lesson. To create the dance connection, students are asked to list movements that correspond to the topic. Movements can be explored in unison and then in small groups and can grow into full compositions with a three-part "frozen shape-moves-frozen shape" structure dance using BEST elements.

## Planning Page *10.9*

### Skeleton Dance Unit Overview (Wrenn Cook)

Designed for Dance, Grade 3, and can be taught solely within the dance curriculum or as a collaboration between the dance specialist and classroom teacher.

#### Unit Goals

1. To develop skillful use of the body by applying underlying principles regarding skeletal alignment and joint movement.
2. To use knowledge of the skeletal system for analytical and creative purposes in dance.

#### Dance Standards

The Roman numerals relate to the National Standards available at www.menc.org.

  I. A/B, H, I, J (extensions I, F, G, K)
 II. B, D, G (extensions A, E)
III. (extension)
 IV. A (extension E)
  V. A, B (extension C)
 VI. B (extension C)

#### Third-Grade Science Standards

Students will . . .

  I. A.2.b. Recognize bones, joints, and muscles in the arms and legs of the human body as structural adaptations responsible for movement.

#### Preassessment (Prior Knowledge)

Before introducing this unit, students should have . . .

- Participated in lessons based on dance elements
- Participated in enough improvisation activities to be comfortable with movement exploration
- Had prior experience working with partners or small groups to complete brief composition tasks

If the classroom teacher already has introduced the skeletal system in science, then components of this unit can be shortened or deleted, retaining those concepts and activities that are specifically related to dance.

#### Lesson Sequence

1. Our Bones Help Us Dance
2. Name the Bones
3. Getting Our Bones and Joints Ready to Dance
4. Create a Dance About Our Bones

#### Bibliography

Frank, M. S., et al. (2000). *Harcourt science.* Orlando, FL: Harcourt.
Meeks, L., & Heit, P. (1999). *Totally awesome health.* Blacklick, OH: Meeks Heit.

#### Children's Literature

Anderson, K. C., & Cumbaa, S. (1993). *The bones and skeleton gamebook: A challenging collection of puzzles & projects.* New York: Workman Publishing.
Balestrino, P., & Kelley, T. (1989). *The skeleton inside you.* New York: Harper Collins
Barner, B. (1996). *Dem bones.* San Francisco, CA: Chronicle.
Hvass, U., & Theinhardt, V. (1986). *How my body moves.* New York: Viking.
Simon, S. (1998). *Bones: Our skeletal system.* New York: Harper Collins.

---

Note: Stinson (1988, p. 51) recommends staying away from the topic of "superheroes" because of aggressive actions. Also, avoid stereotyped movements such as sitting "Indian style" or doing "war dances" during Native American studies.

## Two-Pronged Lesson Plans

*I now know that a reading experience involves more than just books and words. It involves the child's life and interest as a source, his mind for thinking, his voice for verbalization (stories, poems, songs), his hands for writing, and his whole body for a deeper understanding through creative movement and dance. A child must sense and respond for true learning and understanding."*
(Loretta Woolard, fourth-grade teacher, quoted in Fleming, 1990)

Planning lessons that integrate dance begins with deciding that important concepts and skills will be taught about both a subject and about dance. Planning makes meaning prominent when it focuses on selecting topics and problems and then deriving themes and questions to investigate. Dance-based lessons should be full of movement possibilities—actions and shapes should readily come to mind. A topic of "fruits and vegetables" may have more possibilities for sensory explorations, more visual artwork than movement. If a topic seems to mostly lend itself to pretending in role (drama/pantomime) it is harder to extend to dance. If a book lists specifics about getting dressed such as zipping, buttoning, and tying, then a teacher would need to stretch to open up movement possibilities: "such things as tying yourself into a knot or buttoning your hand to your knee" (Stinson, 1988, p. 51). The question is, What is the goal and does this kind of stretching lead to the goal or does this kind of work trivialize dance?

When dance is integrated, teachers need to be honest about using it in respectful ways. Both dance and the other subject to be integrated should be treated as areas of substance. For example, a circle-cycle dance created to a steady beat for a lesson on the circulatory system truly helps students feel the heart pumping and beating, the blood moving, and how the whole system operates on a cyclical basis. Planning Page 10.10 shows such a lesson.

**Dance-Based Field Units.** Figure skating is now the most popular Olympic event in terms of audience viewing. This is not surprising since it combines athleticism with artistry that engages

## ◆ Planning Page 10.10
## Dance and Health, Fifth Grade

*Two-Pronged Focus:* (1) circulatory system, (2) dance elements
*Dance Standards:* 1–4, 6–7 (Ready Reference 10.7)
*Student Objectives:* Students should be able to:

1. Show dance phrases that express differing heartbeats (rhythms).
2. Show movement qualities that express changes in the circulatory system (e.g., flow).
3. Use body shapes and personal space to show heart's shapes and movement.
4. Maintain focus.
5. Work cooperatively in groups.

*Teaching Procedure:* The teacher will: (S = students)

### Introduction

1. Signal for attention and tell S to sit in personal space.
2. Remind S about posted rules.
3. Use riddle routine (riddle about heart on board).
4. Ask what they remember about circulatory system. Use visual of circulatory system.
5. Show how to take pulse and move to beat. Use slit drum.
6. Ask "What if ____?" and "Show me ____" beats and rhythms during rest, anger, etc.

### Development

1. Read aloud fantasy journey and ask S to show with body shape and focus what is described (about heart changing rhythms).
2. Choral read and move to "Dr. Heart" chant to show heartbeat and blood flow. Repeat and increase rate.
3. Pause to ask about flow (sustained movement) and rhythm or beat (percussive).
4. Play "Tranquility" tape and ask S to create a sustained or percussive movement to go with it.
5. Group S to create a dance with a beginning-middle-end to show flow and beat. Challenge S to include creative use of the "circle."
6. Circulate and give descriptive feedback as S work.

### Conclusion

1. Divide class so half observes while others dance.
2. Audience gives feedback about concentration, percussive versus sustained beats, and shapes (e.g., circles to represent cycle).
3. Repeat chant.
4. Ask what they learned.

### Assessment and Evaluation

1. Observe S and use checklist with range of criteria from "clear" to "not present" based on objectives 1 to 5.

emotions like no other competitive event. This artistry happens to be a kind of dance. Unfortunately, most of us just watch on television, and miss the emotional impact of a live performance.

A fifth kind of dance-based unit focuses on an event, usually a field trip to see a live dance performance. "Arts-based field trips aren't isolated experiences, but part of what we've been learning," says Mary-Mac Jennings, first-grade teacher at Ashley River Creative Arts. "When we went to see 'Peter and the Wolf,' the children couldn't stop talking about how the dancers were doing what they had learned."

Dance concert attendance is an invaluable opportunity for children to see skilled amateurs and professionals perform dances from traditional ballet to the South Carolina shag. Concerts by local companies, including those at colleges, as well as national touring events such as "Riverdance," expand students' personal visions of career possibilities. They also offer the educational opportunity to disband negative cultural and gender stereotypes associated with dance. Nothing is more powerful than live performance to show children the athletic connections to dance and to help them see strong men and women with the skills, artistry, and confidence to use movement expressively.

Without school-sponsored trips, many children experience only in-house assemblies, few of which will be devoted to dance. As with other field trips, however, dance expeditions should be carefully selected and planned to align with curricular goals. Critical to maintaining the integrity of dance excursions is the three-part structure discussed in Chapter 3: (1) Prepare students for the trip, (2) help them become mentally focused during the trip, and (3) follow up with debriefing about what was learned. Live performances are different from video or television dramas

because the audience shares in the event. There is a feeling of spontaneity that causes the performers to respond to the energy of the audience. Following is a short checklist to help prepare.

**1.** *Make clear expectations.* Students need to know and use appropriate audience etiquette so that everyone enjoys the performance and the dancers are respected. A discussion of behavior consequences is important. This means the teacher must know the expected behaviors for the site being visited. It is useful to ask students to role-play how to act before, during, and after the concert.

**2.** *Set purpose.* Make sure students know how the trip is integral to the unit; ask them to generate questions they want answered during the trip. Cue sheets (i.e., worksheets listing things to notice during the performance) help students anticipate what is coming. Ask for materials to help prepare cue sheets for the class so they can experience a sense of discovery about the moves dancers make (e.g., "That was a triple lutz!"). Concept mini-lessons that focus on key terms such as *choreographer* or the use of music, sets, and costumes help students become mindful viewers.

**3.** *Give cues.* Do a preview about what students are expected to learn from the field trip and hold them accountable. If students know there is to be an assessment (not just a test, either), they are more focused on the trip's purpose and less on socializing. Review study sheets and general questions before the trip that are to be used when the class returns. For example: "What is one thing you could follow up on and find out more about? How did the experience make you feel? Why? What did the trip have to do with what we've been studying? Show the most important thing you learned about ____ using art materials, drama, music, or dance and movement. Write a poem about the trip. Write a letter convincing me that trips like these are important in school. Write a thank you note to _____."

4. *Rehearse signals.* Children will need reminders during performances. Nonverbal signals can be seen across a theatre and reinforce the concept that communication can be without words. It is particularly helpful to use sign language for "sit down," "line up," and "listen." See books of sign such as Riekehof's *The Joy of Signing* (1987).

5. *Participate.* It is important for teachers to participate as learners and viewers, as well as managers of their classes. Teachers should be models of good audience etiquette.

6. *Debrief.* Take time to debrief after the dance, even on the bus. Encourage discussions about a variety of points of view. Ask, "What did you notice? How did it make you feel? What in the dance made you feel that way? What was it really about? What was missing? What was the choreographer trying to say?"

Field trips to concerts are not unusual. What is unusual is the meaningful integration of these trips, which begins with planning. See detailed field trip guidelines in Appendix H.

**Observation and Discovery Trips.** Field trips do not have to mean a bus trip. Students often get so excited about trips that they cannot get serious about learning. We can take only a few field trips, but short, close-to-school trips can be practice for larger trips and are valuable. For example, a walk around the block to discover how people move as they do their work or play can give insight into the body, energy, space, and time dance elements used in everyday life. Observation walks to see how plants and animals move can be a rich foundation to refine students' use of verbs to describe movements.

# Building Block IV: Aesthetic Learning Environment

I remember a student who was in trouble for frequently getting up to sharpen his pencil. When asked why his pencil tip broke so often he replied, "It doesn't. I just need to move." Hopefully, the curtain has closed on rigid classroom procedures that require children to sit still on hard chairs for periods of time few teachers would endure.

Dance is "the cheapest and most available material to use for creative experiences" (Fleming, 1990, p. 5). But it does take space—physical and psychological room to move—what has been called a "third space" (Deasy, 2005). The latter has to do with the degree to which a teacher makes children feel comfortable using their bodies to express thoughts and feelings. That comfort level is created by the many verbal and nonverbal messages teachers send. Frequent exhortations to "sit still" and "quit wiggling" send the message that frozen bodies are better. Kids who routinely experience raised eyebrows and dismissive nods when they experiment with moving their bodies in novel ways can develop a confined view that inhibits the potential to use dance as a key learning tool.

Teachers show they value dance through their words and through how they manage their own bodies. Those who are comfortable in their own skins and readily use a range of movement during teaching show they value kinesthetic knowing.

Flexibility is key—a flexible attitude and flexible physical space promote dance frame of mind.

Dance requires some physical space, but only a little to get started. Psychological and physical safety can be established by beginning small. Students can be directed to stand and reach out to establish a personal space bubble near their desks. Work in that space can initially be highly directed by the teacher, with the goal of giving more space and less direction as students gain skills at controlling their bodies, minds, and voices. Explicit teaching about how to increase focus and concentration is necessary, and there are many enjoyable dance warm-ups that target the development of these abilities. Control is not about rigidity; it is about skilled management of the amazing capacities of our minds, bodies, and voices. Control should extend possibilities to communicate, not contract them.

Some schools now have designated areas for dance shared by teachers, but dance integration mostly happens in classrooms. Students can become very efficient at pushing back desks to create an open area. Teachers can also permanently rearrange the room in a U shape with desks in groups to leave an open area. When open space is a priority, teachers find their own CPS kicks in. There are many creative classroom design options. Larger spaces can actually increase anxiety and cause some students to become overstimulated. In any space, students need to know dance used to make meaning is not free play or recess. When you need more space, move the lessons outside, in the gym, or in the cafeteria.

What else makes a dance-uplifting environment? First, the space needs to be physically safe, as do the materials. Talk with the PE teacher and dance specialist, if possible. Teachers need to scan the space to find potential hazards. There should be no protruding objects and the floor needs to be responsive and not too slick. Concrete floors are unsafe. It is helpful to have the following available.

- Props such as scarves, streamers, elastic bands, beanbags, balloons, and rubber-backed carpet squares that can easily be moved around
- Musical instruments, especially drums and other rhythm instruments for accompaniment; ones that represent other cultures send important signals
- Music CDs and CD player
- DVD player to view dance-related videos
- Dance-based books to use as references as students plan
- Display areas that feature dance photos, dance elements
- An ongoing word wall of dance/movement-related words collected by students.

The *Opportunity to Learn Standards* were created to help schools plan for arts learning. One section is about facilities and materials. South Carolina educators have converted the standards into a useful checklist that can be downloaded for dance and the other arts at www.winthrop.edu/ABC/.

# Building Block V: Literature as a Core Art Form

There are dance-based books in every genre, from biography to folktales, including books about how to dance and dancers. A book like *I Feel Like Dancing: A Year with Jacques D'Amboise and the National Dance Institute* (Barboza) can be paired with the award-winning video by the same title to enlarge students' concept of possibilities of their own bodies and lives. Dance-based books can easily be linked with historical units, with the goal to increase understanding of the era and events by examining dances, dancers, and choreographers of the period. A list of dancers and dances appears in Ready References 10.4 and 10.5. Find picture books using references such as *A to Zoo* listed in Ready Reference 4.11.

Any literature that includes movement or movement imagery has potential for dance and creative movement as well. For example, *Sometimes I Dance Mountains* (Baylor et al., 1973) has a lovely poetic text that can stimulate many movement explorations before, during, or after the book is read, and rhythm instruments can be added. Isadora's (1976) *Max* relates to both dance and sports. Carl Sandburg's "Lines Written for Gene Kelly to Dance To" is a poem that asks the famous dancer to dance such ideas as the alphabet and the wind. The entire poem

offers wonderful possibilities. Try it with a musical background using, for example, Leroy Anderson's "Sandpaper Ballet." (Say a line, turn up the volume, fade down, say the next line, and so on.)

Make it a habit to coach students to tune in on dance in any book by asking about how characters move and encouraging students to visualize movement in texts. Questions such as "How might this character have moved?" and "What might have been his or her favorite dances?" can open windows to deeper understanding because they expand viewpoints.

A permanent display that highlights arts-based literature is an AI must. Dance-based literature should be a feature. Displays need not take up a lot of room. A clear plastic bag can be hung up and used to display a different book each week. Invite students to find books about dance or ones with movement and allow them to assume responsibility for displays. Ready Reference 10.11 lists examples of dance-based books; also see additional suggestions in Appendix J.

## **Ready Reference 10.11** Dance-Based Children's Literature

Ackerman, K. (2003). *Song and dance man.* Knof. (grandpa relives his vaudeville days)

Archambault, J., Martin, B., & Rand, T. (1986). *Barn dance.* Henry Holt. (farm animals gather with a little boy for a hoedown)

Barboza, S. (1992). *I feel like dancing: A year with Jacques D' Amboise and the National Dance Institute.* Crown. (three students spend a year at the Institute)

Bierhorts, J. (1997). *The dancing fox: Arctic folktales.* (18 Inuit folktales)

Bozylinsky, H. (1993). *Lala Salama.* SRA. (African lullaby in Swahili and English; boy says goodnight to all the animals)

Cleary, B. (2001). *Ellen Tibbets.* HarperCollins. (travails in dance class)

Garcia, R. (2006). *Blue tights.* Puffin. (Joyce confronts adolescent crises; black urban teenager is cut from ballet but joins African dance group)

Gauch, P., & Ichikawa, S. (1992). *Bravo, Tanya.* Philomel. (girl loves to dance in the meadow but cannot dance in ballet class)

Glassman, B. (2001). *Mikhail Baryshnikov: Dance genius.* Gale Group. (biography)

Glover, S., & Weber, B. (2000). *Savion!: My life in tap.* Morrow. (biography)

Gray, L. (1999). *My mama had a dancing heart.* Scholastic. (mother and daughter dance to welcome each season)

Hest, A. (2004). *Mr. George Baker.* Candlewick. (100-year-old African American can still dance)

Jonas, A. (1989). *Color dance.* Greenwillow. (three dancers show how colors combine using scarves)

Lasky, K. (2005). *Portraits: Dancing through fire.* Scholastic. (19th-century Paris, Sylvia is one of Degas's dancers)

Lobel, A. (1980). "The camel dances" in *Fables.* Scott Foresman. (camel loves to do ballet but performs for unappreciative friends)

Locker, T. (2002). *Water dance.* Voyager. (explains how water dances)

Malcolm, J. (2000). *Drat! We're rats!* Starcatcher. (girls who hate ballet get cast as rats in Nutcracker)

Marshall, J. (1977). *George and Martha Encore.* Sandpiper. (married hippos dance)

McKissack, P. (1988). *Mirandy and Brother Wind.* Knopf. (girl tries to capture the wind as her dance partner for a contest)

Patrick, D., & Ransome, J. (1993*). Red dancing shoes.* Tambourine Books. (girl is given shoes that allow her to dance)

Pavlova, A. (2001). *I dreamed I was a ballerina.* Simon & Schuster. (biography, illustrated by Edgar Degas)

Reich, S. (2005). *Jose ! Born to dance.* Simon and Schuster. (biography of great Mexican dancer)

Ryder, J. (1999). *Earthdance.* Henry Holt. (imaginative look at dancing with the earth)

Sotto, G. (2004). *Marisol.* American Girl. (Hispanic girl is "born to dance")

Sotto, G. (2006). *My little car.* Putman. (Teresa "dances" grandpa's lowrider car)

Staples, S. (2001). *Shiva's fire.* HarperCollins. (Indian girl pursues dance talent)

Stout, S. (2009). *Fiona Finkelstein, Big-time ballerina!!* Aladdin.

Van Laan, N. (1993). *Buffalo dance: A Blackfoot legend.* Little, Brown. (story of traditional ritual before buffalo hunts)

Wallace, I. (1984). *Chi Chiang and the dragon's dance.* Atheneum. (boy gains status when he performs the dragon's dance)

Waters, K., & Cooper, M. (1990). *Lion dancer: Ernie Wan's Chinese New Year.* Scholastic. (boy describes his first lion dance performance)

Wells, R. (1999). *Tallchief: America's prima ballerina.* Viking. (Osage Indian ballerina-biography)

Wilson, F. (1988). *What it feels like to be a building.* Preservation. (architectural features made with people)

## Dance-able Books

It is common for teachers to want to explore meanings in books using dance. Some books are more dance-able than others. Look for the following qualities when choosing books to dance.

**Compelling Artwork.**   Great art can inspire movement, such as that in books by Thomas Locker, Cynthia Rylant, Maurice Sendak, Eric Carle, and Ezra Jack Keats.

**Artful Language.**   Books that easily lend themselves to dancing have a few well-written sentences per page. The themes in wordier books and stories can and should be used, but starting with books with spare, but artistic, use of words is recommended. Examples are *Barndance!* (Martin), *The Snowy Day* (Keats), and *Rain Rain Rivers* (Shulevitz).

**Action-Based Plot.**   Almost any concept can be explored with movement, but it is easier to dance a book that has built in movement words and action. Examples are *Angelina at the Fair* (Holabird), *Tacky the Penguin* (Lester), and *Three Days on a River in a Red Canoe* (Williams). Remember dance is not the same as pantomime. Students should be stretched to do more than present literal representations of a plot.

## Guidelines for Dancing Books

Here are a few pointers once you have selected a book to dance.

1. Start small. Plan a 10- to 15-minute lesson focusing on a few movement possibilities. Expand as you become more comfortable and students gain increased body control and skill.
2. Comb the text and the art for movement ideas using the BEST dance elements. Seek possibilities for locomotor and nonlocomotor *body* movements, use of different kinds of *energy,* varying use of *space,* and exploring *time.* Check the *Dance Standards* for more ideas.
3. Choose one or two movement problems to explore at each age or choose vivid plot events.
4. Decide whether you will do "inserted dance" or full text exploration. With inserted dance you read a portion or page and then stop to explore movement possibilities. Whole text response involves completing a whole book and then planning dance activities to explore and significant character movements, plot events, themes/emotions (e.g., courage, dreams), or style (i.e., language or art style). It is possible to even explore the setting, if it is integral to the literary work. For example, the barn and barnyard in *Charlotte's Web* presents movement possibilities related to explorations of that space/setting.

# Building Block VI: Best Teaching Practices

*I just dance, I put my feet in the air and move them around.* (Fred Astaire)

## What You Teach Is Who You Are

Any teacher who values creativity and understands that kinesthetic learning is powerful can learn to integrate dance. Teachers who feel uncomfortable about dancing in front of students need to understand that modeling dance moves is not necessary to meaningful integration. The goal of integrating dance is not to get students to mimic. Students can be asked or directed to move in certain ways without any demonstration. Lack of a "model" can induce more creative problem solving than being shown steps; however, students need to be taught about the BEST dance options. Demonstrations of these elements and possible combinations are very helpful.

Most important is for teachers to show enthusiasm and interest in dance. Teachers need to work toward a level of personal dance literacy. That is a given in any area. But literacy is for naught if it is not used. AI relies on teachers who value the "imaginative rather than imitative uses of movement" (Fleming, 1990, p. 77). Dance knowledge doesn't go far without knowhow plus enthusiasm. As Martha Graham said, nobody cares how you look, just get up and dance.

Agree to try assuming the "what if" vantage point of an artist. Sensitize yourself to being on the lookout for how movement plays out in life. Think about BEST elements as you watch television and observe friends in different contexts. Next comes a bit of risk taking to investigate movement possibilities in lessons—not just how something moves, but how it might move under different circumstances—while maintaining a focus on curricular targets.

**Start Small.**   Rather than beginning with a whole unit infused with dance, teachers should try a lesson or two. For example, start with a health lesson on body parts or the shapes bodies can make using different muscles. Explore common daily life movements by stretching them with BEST categories: Sweep with different body parts at different levels and speeds. Freeze in a sweeping shape and then set it to a 1-2-3 rhythm. Look for teachable moments in language arts lessons that connect body language and verbal communication (e.g., verbs and adverbs). The key is to make sure first attempts are successful, for you and for students. Consult the energizers and warm-ups in Chapter 11 for quick dance ideas to introduce the day or individual lessons.

## Inside-Out Motivation

Dance is fun. It needs no outside reward. Even babies react negatively to attempts to confine or restrict movement exploration. In contrast they delight in movement. We need and want to dance.

Attaching dance to any lesson makes the lesson come alive. Best practice dictates we go further and clearly explain how dance contributes to understanding and extends expression possibilities, which brings us to the self-fulfilling prophecy.

**We Get What We Expect.**   Hundreds of studies have examined the influence of teacher expectation, or the self-fulfilling prophecy (SFP). The conclusion is that a demonstrated belief in students' creative potential makes it much more likely they will rise to the occasion (Tauber, 1997). Teachers can engage CPS with the SFP. For example, it is important to teach organizational structures like the common three-part sequence of (1) beginning frozen shape, (2) movements, and (3) a frozen ending shape. This is a solid structure, but to get students to innovate teachers need to show they expect stretching. These expectations are conveyed verbally and nonverbally through goal setting, coaching, the classroom environment, and nonverbal teacher responses (e.g., smiling, nodding, frowning).

There are many ways to write a sentence and many types of writing forms, so it is with dance. Alert students to new dances that are constantly being created and solicit "finds" during regular discussions about the role of the arts in life. Ready Reference 3.4 lists example discussion prompts. Most of all take and show genuine delight in original ideas that flow from the creative minds of children.

**Teachable Moments.** Once students are comfortable with the general purposes and some options to create meaningful dance, teachers can easily capitalize on "movement moments" that spontaneously arise. There are obvious occasions. When it starts to snow, BEST elements can be explored for blizzards, snowflakes, and sleet. Movements can be abstracted and explored from current events (e.g., storms on the sun that resulted in magnetic "belches"). Invite students to be on the lookout for ideas that can be danced in any unit under study.

**The Group Effect.** Students have an innate desire to exhibit progress. Dance performances can fulfill that need. In the opening Classroom Snapshot, Wrenn Cook's students begged to perform their skeleton dances for audiences beyond their peers. Audiences are a powerful motivator and AI has the potential to provide a broader group of students with performance experience (Korn-Bursztyn, 2003).

Consider inviting parents and grandparents for regular Friday performances that synthesize learning for the week. Some schools have combined this with kids lunching with parents in the cafeteria. Of course, there is always the split audience idea of dividing the class in half and taking turns performing. This puts students in both "do and view" roles. Remember to ask audiences to expect to give descriptive feedback after performances. This gives the audience a more active role and gives performers needed feedback. Students can learn good audience social skills and also gain ability to do higher order thinking such as analysis and evaluation called for in critiquing performances.

## Engagement and Active Learning

Dance engages head, hands, and heart in problem solving. Students are called upon to use their own ideas to transform important concepts through movement. This causes students to cognitively restructure information, and they are in turn personally transformed.

**Engagement.** When two people become engaged, they make a commitment. This is a choice. We cannot make students engage, but we can set up circumstances under which they will likely choose to do so. Physical energizers are excellent tools (see Chapter 11). They get students up and moving. Another effective engagement habit is to ask students to show, instead of tell.

**Show versus Tell.** Opportunities for dance expression can be woven throughout lessons. For example, many students would not be able to verbally define "cycle" but could use their hands, head, and body posture to do so. When students are asked to show, describe, and relate (e.g., connect to their lives), they begin to form more meaningful links. If this becomes just pantomime, coach students to use different body parts or change energy or time to convey the dimensions of the concept.

## Creative Problem Solving

*You are lost the instant you know what the result will be.* (Juan Gris)

Pilobolus ("sun-loving fungus") is a dance ensemble that appears on television commercials and was profiled on *60 Minutes*. Using grace, tension, strength, and endurance, the dancers demonstrate themes related to aquatics, animals (e.g., seahorses and spiders), and gravity using their bodies in surprising ways (www.pilobolus.com). These dancers remind us that the most creative ideas come from people who are not bound by conventions. Creative problem solving depends on flexibility, risk taking, and openness to possibilities. The greatest football coaches have used CPS with dance. For example, Notre Dame's famed coach Knute Rockne was inspired to pattern backfield formations for his "Four Horsemen" after watching a dance performance (Boston, 1996).

Every lesson can be a daily opportunity to engage students in creative thinking that results in products that give kids a sense of accomplishment. Such products are a core instructional pursuit in AI, not a diversion. Creating drama, visual art, music, and dance requires students to dig to represent their ideas (Rabkin & Redmond, 2005b). Dance integration puts the CPS process center stage as students learn to use dance thinking to connect and imagine ideas, conduct inquiry, and grow in new perspectives. Teachers need to show students how the CPS described in Chapter 2 (see Ready Reference 2.6) is used in both dance making and understanding dances they view. This begins with creating conditions for creative problem solving. By the way, Pilobolus has an incredible human alphabet book (Kane).

**Freedom with Structure.** Paradoxically, creativity loves limits. As we solve problems, the boundaries of time, materials, and structures (e.g., beginning, middle, and end) can give focus to exploring possibilities, which is essential to creative thinking. Creative dance is no exception. Freedom alone does not ensure creative thinking. Freedom with structure and focus does. Students need to know the restrictions on space, time, touching others, following directions, obeying signals, and using props that produce creative dance. When rules are clear and consistently applied, students learn self-discipline and are helped to think divergently about the specific context in which they are working. None of us can move "any way we want, any time we want" in our homes or at work. Purposeful movement done with concentration on a specific problem is the goal; even in free-time dance, guidelines about space and other issues are needed.

**Who's Dance?** To help students understand the importance of using CPS to make dance, instead of mimicking steps modeled by a leader, try this. Play a familiar piece (e.g., "Dance of the Flowers"). Model teacher-invented movements and give time for students to imitate. Repeat the dance until students can do it in unison. Next, play another piece of music and ask students to invent movements. Use music that *suggests* flowers or plants (e.g., Enya's "In Memory of Trees"). Ask students to practice. Then split the class in half to do performances. The audience should then give descriptive feedback. After both halves perform, ask about the thinking and feeling between the two ways to learn. Which induces more ownership?

**Questions.** Teachers pose questions such as "What if?" and "How could you ____?" to set CPS in motion. Just about any idea can be related to dance by asking questions involving the BEST elements and then connecting elements (locomotor moves in different shapes or levels). Ideas are also given depth by use of contrast: Ask students to do the opposite or show a nonexample. Sustained or continuous movements of the circulatory system can be contrasted with the bound movements of the digestive system such as food being swallowed (moving in clumps).

**Visual Imagining.** Most of how we think involves visual images; but imagery is limited to what is stored in the brain, so it, like pantomime, can restrict thinking through dance. One way to avoid the downside of imagery in dance is to use CPS to explore dance elements. For example, explore many ways to move body parts first, and then invite students to "become" through drama. This helps expand the initial imagery.

Similes, metaphors, and other image-based language can be powerful helpers to stretch imaginations for movement: "Show me you are as solid as igneous rock" or "Let me see you shrink as small as an atom." Ask for images that lead to movement, too: "Stretch your body as if it is being pulled by magnets on either side of you. Use as many body parts as you can." Comment on images that spring from movement: "You're in a round shape. What else do you know that is round in our environment?" This use of imagery enriches concept development through movement, rather than reinforce stereotyped behavior. Finally, images can be used as a basis for movement: "What kind of movements might a starfish do?" instead of "Pretend you are a starfish and move around." It is a subtle but significant difference in thinking.

**Experimenting with Elements.** Skill and artistry is gained as control grows. "Move any way you want to the music" assumes that students know many ways to move. But they may, in fact, have limited experiences, especially on a conscious level. The goal of integrating dance and movement is to help students expand communication choices. Once students know many possibilities for using their bodies to respond to music, or another stimulus, teachers can give time for free creative movement without students feeling awkward. Embarrassment stems from not knowing what to do or feeling you have done the "wrong thing." We can teach children many ways to move and that there really are no "wrong" moves—some just are not school appropriate! Sequence, balance, and matching movement to the context are the secrets here.

## Explicit Teaching

Effective dance integration rests on teachers developing student dance literacy and clearly explaining that what they learn in dance can be used in other subjects. Explicit teaching occurs in 5- to 10-minute mini-lessons that deal with the why-what-how-when-where of important dance concepts and skills. Demonstrations are followed by scaffolded practice in problem solving using controlled use of the body. See Chapter 3 for more information on explicit teaching.

By giving children clear dance language and a predictable lesson structure, they acquire the skills to succeed and feel safer about taking risks. Explicit instruction to teach basic elements of body, energy, space, and time (BEST) should be accompanied by visual aids such as charts. Lessons should target just one or two dance elements or ideas so that students can go into some depth and explore possibilities of each. Dancing about images such as happiness or sadness or inviting free dance before the BEST elements are grasped can be stumbling blocks to student success. Students may simply get silly (humor is used to cope) or even withdraw if they lack the necessary meaning-making tools.

**Mnemonics.** Dance memory aids are fun to create and should also be posted. Students enjoy co-writing songs and poems for class big books or posters. The following is an example of co-writing by a first grader, called the "BEST Dance Rap."

> Body, Energy, Space, Time
> Change Your Levels
> Change Your Lines
> Keep Your Focus
> Move and Freeze
> Make New Shapes
> Balance, but Watch Your Knees!

**Transfer.** If learning in dance is to transfer to other curricular areas, students must be shown the connections and have chances to practice them. Transfer should be explicitly addressed and is the responsibility of both teachers and arts specialists since it should work two ways. Promote transfer in these ways: Tell about, show it, question students for connections, and give many examples.

**Free Dancing?** Undirected versus directed or explicit lessons are debated throughout education today. The concern is how much is really needed and how direct instruction may inhibit creative and higher order thinking. Some even argue that direct instruction can cause students to get mired down in literal thinking, which leads to passivity and low or no motivation to learn.

In AI and in dance integration in particular there are concerns about using explicit teaching. But the problem is if dance integration is initiated by playing music and inviting students to do any dance they wish, many students will be embarrassed to do any moving. Others will engage in rigid, and sometimes vulgar, movements they have seen elsewhere, such as by Britney Spears or Michael Jackson. For this reason, it is recommended that free dance be made available after teaching dance elements. The time lag should be short. Information about movement options makes all the difference, as does warm-up time to explore ways to communicate through body language. This sequence assures student success and builds confidence. Students focus more on what their bodies can do and how it can be done. Cognitive and physical processes are thus engaged.

## Aesthetic Orienting

*Anyone who says sunshine brings happiness has never danced in the rain.* (Anonymous)

Aesthetic response develops over time and with experience (see Chapter 6). This special form of understanding is facilitated when teachers slow it down, teach students to observe carefully, and expect interpretations to be grounded in evidence. In dance this usually occurs after class performances during which students discuss what they observed—usually dance concepts. The focus is not on right or wrong movement. Students should be urged to talk about movements that are more pleasing or surprising and ones that work better than others to get across the dancers' intentions. In response to all performances, students learn that applause is a part of good audience etiquette.

**Questioning.** Open or fat questions are a mainstay in creating an aesthetic orientation to making and understanding dance: "How many ways? What's another way? What if? What is the shape of ____? How might ____ move? How does that affect the feel?" These types of questions direct students to think about how to create variety and interest through details. Alert students to these kinds of questions so that they can also begin to ask them of one another and to respond to teacher questions.

## Apply–Practice–Rehearse

It takes practice to learn the range of ways the body can be used to communicate. Dance integration cannot be meaningful without daily time for students to practice using dance elements, with feedback. This is where the line between teaching and assessing becomes blurred as teachers coach students using specific feedback. The result is quality student work.

## Process or Product

The dominant purpose for creative dance and movement is the doing of it—the process, not the product. This cannot be overemphasized. To show to students how important kinesthetic learning is, do a bit of action research. Give half the class a set of numbers to learn (8-3-9-6-11-23-87-92). Send them out of the room to study for 10 minutes. With the remaining group, tell them to study kinesthetically by creating dance movements to remember the number sequence—a movement to go with each number. Have them practice the number movements in order, saying the numbers with the movements for 10 minutes. Bring the whole class back together and give them a test to write the number sequence. Ask students to grade their own papers and then compare the scores of the two groups. Regardless of the scores, ask students to tell how they learned and how it felt. (Usually the dance group does better and enjoys the studying more.)

**Make/Do/View.** Using dance as a teaching tool involves planning for students to create, perform, and respond aesthetically to dances they see. The viewing gives ideas for the making and doing of dance, and doing dance makes students more astute viewers. For example, by learning to "read" peer dances and video dance performances, students can develop a discriminating awareness of movement as an artistic medium. Choreography is the creative composing of original dances, an additional way to express ideas and feelings using dance thinking.

**Products.** While there is a place for structured dances in the regular classroom (e.g., when studying Ireland, a guest might teach the Irish jig), it is not desirable or feasible daily or even weekly. If dance is to be used as an important learning tool, the emphasis needs to be on process strategies to help students make meaning kinesthetically, creatively, and artistically. This does not mean that dance products will not result from movement explorations. In fact, when students become adept at using dance to understand and express themselves, there will be many times when they will create full dances for science and social studies. The pride in these creations compels many students to want to perform—at least for classmate audiences.

## Management Tips

Dance integration proceeds more smoothly and enjoyably when expectations and limits are clear. Class control during creative movement comes from teaching students the discipline of dance—how to control their bodies as they move. There is no magic trick or perfect set of techniques to make a class behave. A lot of management has to do with a kind of presence the teacher exudes—a demeanor that conveys "I'm in charge but I want to work together to have you enjoy learning." Appendix E lists time-tested techniques and habits used by teachers to establish discipline and interventions for common problems. Following are a few basics, particularly for dance making.

**Noise.** Dance involves movement and some noise. Start with this expectation and make it clear to the principal and other teachers, who may not understand what you are doing. As students gain knowledge about the purpose and nature of dance, they will take it more seriously. As confidence and self-control increase, students will be less noisy.

**Enthusiasm.** The mood of the day is often set by how the teacher greets the class in the morning. Use sign language or other kinesthetic ways to say, "Hello, glad to see you." The book *The Joy of Signing* (Riekehof, 1987) is an excellent reference.

**Climate.** Invite participation to reduce resistance. Rather than order students, say "I'd like to invite all of you to try to make a shape on a low level that you think no one else will think of."

**Music.** Build a collection of CDs to rev up, cool down, set mood, and more.

**Visualizing Success.** Imagine on a step-by-step basis how you will involve students. Teach students to imagine movements before doing them. Ask students to demonstrate. Instead of you showing simple ideas, ask a student to show swaying, low level, slithering, and other movement.

**Attention Getters and Signals.** Signals are needed to get attention, start and stop action, and make transitions. Rehearse a "Listening Stance": Teach students to sit, stop, or stand with hands clasped or behind their backs.

A drum or tambourine is a good investment. Start the class with students echoing a rhythm so students feel different rhythms that can be used in dance exploration. Patterns can be clapped or drummed: 1–2–3, 1–2–3–4, or 1–2–3–4–5–6–7–8. Changing the stress causes students to feel and think about the effect of energy/emphasis. Use signals for silence (raised hand palm out) and for "noise" (two hand "taking"). Practice until they are automatic. Check references such as *The Joy of Signing* (Riekehof, 1987) for ideas.

Start and stop signals will also need to be used to structure dance performances (e.g., say "curtain," "show time," "close your eyes," "positions," and "lights" as cues). Options: Rhythm claps, countdown, drum beat, call and response, and chants work. Quickly follow with instructions for what is to be done next.

**Ground Rules.** Post and explain the four "must controls": body, mind, voice, and space. Use a game format to practice. First establish a freeze signal (drum or clap). Tell students to find personal space. On signal they can move around freely, but they are not to touch anyone, even accidentally. They are to make no sounds, including no whispering and giggling. On signal, they must freeze. If they violate the freeze they must sit out until the next freeze.

Another game format is "home base." Tell students the goal is not to be the last one to get in their personal spot when they hear "home base." Directions can be given in the form of a challenge to create interest: "Before I count to eight see if you can get into a perfect circle."

Rules can be taught using role playing and games. Take time to have students role-play each rule. Role-play nonexamples, or the opposite, so that there is no misunderstanding.

Another option to the four "musts" is the rules of thumb or High five rules. Write rules on the fingers of a large hand on poster board. Use a raised hand as a signal to think about the rules. Common ones include the following:

1. Follow directions: obey cues and signals.
2. Respect others (e.g., personal space).
3. Be responsible.
4. Participate actively (enthusiasm).
5. Concentrate (no talking during movement).

Note: If the students seem to lose interest, cut the lesson short. Wrap it up and return when everyone is fresh.

**Consequences.** Consequences for breaking rules need to be imposed quickly. Inconsistent teachers who fail to take care of business confuse students, who perceive the teachers as unfair. A hierarchy of consequences, appropriate to the transgressions, should be made clear to students, such as the following:

1. Warning (verbal or nonverbal)
2. 1-minute time-out
3. 5-minute time-out and conference with the teacher after the lesson
4. Loss of a chance to participate in the lesson that day and a phone call to parents

A teacher must be as good as his or her word: Follow through, immediately, when a problem occurs. *Students will not believe or respect the teacher who continually threatens and warns without taking the promised action.*

Adams (2002) recommends teachers ask the students who can control body, mind, voice, and space to stand. Those students are invited to the circle. Others are told to join the circle when they decide to control themselves. If a child loses control, ask first, "Have you lost control of _____?" to cause self-evaluation. A yes answer is followed by the direction to sit out until control is regained. The student decides when to rejoin.

Of course, hitting another child or disrespect for the teacher calls for a high-level consequence right away (number 4!) and probably would involve the principal. Post general consequences with the understanding that a teacher must do what is necessary to ensure the class is learning. Discuss consequences explicitly during the same time the rules are introduced, usually in the first week of school. Inform parents about rules and consequences at the start of school. Finally, there is no substitute for good judgment and common sense.

**Purpose Setting.** Tell the students the learning objectives such as work on using CPS and dance to learn about weather.

**Getting Started.** Start small and involve the whole group. Plan short lessons of about 10 minutes at first. Begin with students staying at their desks or help them learn about movement in a personal spot marked with a sticky colored dot or piece of masking tape on the floor. Personal dots or spots can serve as "home base," which can be signaled at any time to control or stop movement. Start with directed movement (e.g., energizer/warm-up) with everyone before doing small-group creative work. Explore everyday familiar movements so students will not feel foolish.

**Concentration and Focus.** Remove distractions and limit the space to increase focus. Masking tape or imaginary lines can be used for this purpose, too. Beyond that, concentration and focus are teachable. We cannot expect students to attend if they lack the know-how. A game structure works well. For example, "Frozen Shape" challenges students to make a shape in their personal space and hold it for so many counts. Students enjoy trying to increase the hold time each day and can graph their efforts. This is also a chance to compliment original shapes students create, especially stable ones that have a base and are balanced. Spotlight students who focus. Demonstrate concentration aspects when needed. See the energizers and warm-ups in the seed strategy chapters for more ideas to prepare the mind and body for dance problem solving.

**Grouping.** Use several ways to choose a partner and form groups. For random small groups, ask students to find others whose names begin with the same letter or who are wearing a particular pattern (stripes, circles). Readjust initial groups to even out numbers, if necessary. This causes students to think in categories and take time to examine details.

**Transitions.** Choreograph to make them dance alike, such as tiptoe very slowly to desks, using a high level.

**Interspersed Dance.** When you intersperse dancing with reading a book, bring students back to listening by using cues to pretzel sit, freeze, stop and stand, and so forth. Also ask students to find out what will happen next that can be danced.

**Scaffolding and Feedback.** Circulate and give feedback: Stay in the perimeter of the space. Coach students using descriptive feedback, and ask students to give each other feedback to create a positive community feeling. Many students initially feel uncomfortable about dance so it is important to create positive associations with early dance efforts.

**Cool Down.** Use activities such as mirroring and inhale-exhales and slow motion versions of energizers and warm-ups. Give direction in a low volume, talk more slowly, and direct students toward a sitting position.

# Building Block VII: Instructional Design: Routines and Structures

Dance offers ways to understand and express ideas that will remain locked inside our students if movement is not taught as a meaning-making option. Dance is made integral when it becomes a predictable part of lessons and the school schedule. Dance and movement can be used to start the day or period and in the introduction, development, and conclusion of lessons and units.

## IDC Lesson Framework

It helps to think of a lesson as a performance. It needs an introduction, development, and conclusion to be complete. The IDC orchestrates teaching strategies to reach the lesson objectives. That means the lesson begins with students understanding how dance will play a role in learning science, math, or social studies. Here are basic ideas for a dance-based IDC.

**Introduction.** Lessons need to begin with brief attention getters, warm-ups, and other focus strategies. Teachers may tell or ask students how the lesson goals and objectives relate to real-life uses and contexts. Early on it is effective to ask for examples, rather than telling, so that students do as much or more thinking than the teacher. Basic dance elements may be reviewed or explicitly taught directly at this time, telling the name of the element, using visuals, and repeatedly asking students about target dance concepts throughout the lesson.

**Development.** This is a time for students to experiment and explore: Ask how, what, and where questions about the dance elements. Ask students to move in place and then in space. Try the movement with different body parts and then with different locomotor movements. Change levels, directions, time and speed, and energy. Ask students to combine elements. For example, walk at a low level slowly or with energy. Teachers need only model a movement to help clarify thinking. The goal is not to get students to simply imitate, except in the case of teaching specific folk or ethnic dance step sequences.

**Conclusion.** The conclusion of the lesson involves students showing what they have learned. They may be asked to demonstrate movements, write, or tell one thing learned. A "memory minute" can be a time for everyone to close their eyes and review the lesson or a relaxation exercise to preserve the aesthetics of the lesson. At this point students should be able to put what they have learned to artistic use in a simple form.

If students are to create a dance for classmates to observe, structure is essential. A frozen shape–movements–frozen shape sequence is a basic structure students can use to create dances and involves creating a beginning, middle, and end. Encourage students to build in level changes that will make dances more interesting. Ask students to freeze the starting shape so that you and their peers can give descriptive positive feedback on what the shape says and how it feels. Students can be asked to give each other feedback on the element focus and what the dance communicated after a dance sharing. Finally, to achieve closure and gain important assessment information, ask students to explain what they learned about dance in general and the lesson focal points, including other subject matter content in the lesson.

## Lessons That Fall Flat

Many lesson failures occur because the teacher is not clear about the lesson objectives. In other words, what exactly should students know and be able to do by the end that they could not do or did not know at the start? Inadequate preparation or lack of structure can also doom a lesson. By using a lesson framework, a teacher can alleviate much of this problem. Following are additional suggestions.

1. *Structure lessons so that behavior expectations are crystal clear.* Chaos derives from loss of clarity about goals, and uncertainty about how to achieve them. This does not imply a classroom needs rigid structure, but a general organizational scheme. An enormous variety of strategies and activities can then be selected within any structure. For example, think of all the ways to introduce a lesson using pictures, questions, objects, songs, or a movement challenge. Keep in mind that too many directions confuse students and that dance is kinesthetic. Get students moving as soon as possible.

2. *Learning to integrate dance involves trial and error.* When something is not working, teachers should feel free to alter strategies in the lesson plan while maintaining the dance and other curricular focus. It is important to be flexible within the parameters of research-based concepts of (1) effective teaching, (2) learning theory, and (3) the philosophy and principles of arts integration. Chapters 1 through 3 provide an overview of these areas.

3. *Dance construction by the children should not be considered essential to every integrated lesson.* Teachers who do not feel well prepared in dance may initially confine teaching to movement exploration, such as more teacher-directed dance element experimentation. Eventually, students spontaneously begin to construct dance sequences, if they are given experiences that focus on problem solving through movement exploration, invention, and improvisation. Teachers should not rush into having students compose

dances. They should feel proud to see that students are enlarging their repertoire of movements and are gaining poise in use and confidence about their bodies.

4. *Consider preplanning by squeezing.* Preplanning is about squeezing the material for dance possibilities before creating an actual lesson plan. The BEST elements are used to create questions and directions for students. Once movement possibilities have been squeezed from the topic or theme, the lesson can be planned including an introduction, development, and conclusion. Squeezing also helps teachers decide whether to involve students in creating a full dance or focus just on using warm-ups or isolated dance strategies in the IDC or lesson. In any case, assessment should be planned to gauge learning in dance and the target curricular area. Planning Page 10.12 shows an example of preplanning a literature lesson and other dance-based plans.

## Planning Page 10.12
### Preplanning by Squeezing

Squeezing yields information needed *before* lesson planning begins. Squeezing begins in step 4 of this integrated dance/ literature example.

1. Choose standards for dance, literature, and student needs.
2. Choose one of five "bodies" for lessons/units: (1) problem/ topic, (2) person, (3) core work, (4) genre/ form, or (5) event. Decide the content focus for the dance exploration. Decision: core book, *Where the Wild Things Are*.
3. Determine themes possibilities. Example: No one likes to feel powerless. We all like to be in control.
4. SQUEEZE: Brainstorm BEST elements to find best fit. Decisions: (1) energy: flow (bound versus sustained) and using concentration on speed (fast and slow) to develop feel of control (inside self); (2) body: all parts, shapes doing nonlocomotor and locomotor with "powerless qualities" (e.g., floppy, jerky, uncertain).
5. Plan questions and directions to cause "exploration" of literary themes using dance. Example: How did Max feel when he had to stay in his room (out of control)? Use your hand to control your foot without touching it, like it is attached to an invisible string. Use a finger to control your knee, your elbow. Bend over and hang loose, dangle your fingers and arms. Explore loose and controlled with body parts. Take steps forward and backward as if pulled by an invisible force. Now, move with lots of control and flow. How does this feel differently? Start at head and move to feet doing controlled, sustained, and slow moves and then faster. Do same with controlled and bound, slow and then fast.
6. Plan composition criteria: In small groups, make a dance that compares powerlessness with self-control. Start with a frozen shape. Create up to 10 moves. End with a frozen shape. Include a different variety of levels and shapes in your dance.

See integrated lesson plan framework form in Ready Reference 3.10 to plan IDC.

## Routines and Rituals

Simple props, such as a tambourine or bell, are important tools for teachers to use as start and stop signals. Students enjoy using rhythm instruments to beat out rhythms for dance. Wooden spoons and oatmeal boxes work well for this. Whistles are not the best musical instrument for signaling because they tend to demand and alarm, like a scream, rather than create an aesthetic mood. The human voice is a perfect vehicle to accompany or signal. If it is comfortable, sing or hum a rhythm for students (left and right and left and right and stop) or use a special word or phrase to signal for attention or as a start-stop. For example, try famous dancers names as signals: "Isadora Duncan" rolls off the tongue and kids enjoy echoing it.

**Start and Wrap-Up.** Dance is a great way to start each day because it puts students in a positive frame of mind and body for learning. Begin with easy movement warm-ups such as the ones in Chapter 11. Play music as students enter, to invite clapping, tapping, or using the whole body. From there, children can be given more space. There are recommended books of dance strategies and activities in the bibliography. For example, Gilbert's (1992) *Creative Dance for All Ages* is full of activities useful to energize and warm up.

**Transitions.** Good instructional design includes strategies for transitions and ways to dismiss by groups. Music, a rhythm, or a sign may be used to signal time to move. To dismiss groups, use strategies such as Ticket Out, during which students tell or do something on their way out the door. A movement example is, "All those who _____ (e.g., know what *sway* or *sustain* mean) may 'slither' up for our reptiles lesson."

## Four Corners Stations

The four corners station is a unique adaptation of the learning station idea that can be a daily routine. Designate a specific movement problem for each of the four corners of the room. Small groups go to each corner and solve the problem. For example, Corner 1 = warm-ups to a music CD; 2 = stretch station, 3 = wiggle station, 4 = walk in place station. At a signal, students rotate to the next station.

## Clubs

*Our children see the arts as part of everyday life. We have girls and boys who sign up for Ballet Club or Clay Club. Our kids think everybody learns this way.* (Mary-Mac Jennings, Ashley River Creative Arts)

Many schools now offer time for interest-based clubs during the school day. For example, Columbus School in Berkeley, California, has a dance discovery club (Fleming, 1990). When choice club time is a part of the school structure, students benefit greatly. They try out many arts that can become lifelong pursuits. In the case of dance, that can range from tap, jazz, ballet, or pop dance groups to folk dances.

# Building Block VIII: Differentiating for Diverse Student Needs

*In the dance, even the weakest can do wonders.* (Karl Gross)

When creative inventor Thomas Edison finished an early proto-type of his light bulb, he called a boy to take it to the factory. The boy dropped it on the way. Edison had to start all over. When he had another light bulb, many days later, he sent for the same boy. He told him to take it to the factory. Edison would certainly have understood the importance of an education rich in promoting creative thinking. He also would have understood how the arts give second chances to so many by opening other avenues to learn.

Arts-based lessons allow teachers and learners to escape the confines of conventional instruction that focus on standardizing rather than individualizing, leaving no room for surprise or mystery (Rabkin & Redmond, 2005a). The arts are major ways we can differentiate to meet a large diversity of student needs.

Appendix A includes a general developmental continuum with guidelines that are important to use when planning appropriate lessons for primary and intermediate students. In general, physical development, like other development, proceeds from general to more specific.

Children ages 5 to 12 years are in transition but usually have increasing balance, strength, and endurance. Instruction and experiences are everything to development. They determine rate of growth and range. Children are more likely to get hurt or hurt others because of carelessness, not because their bodies and muscles are not ready to move. Diligent use of ground rules, signals, and other rituals helps prevent collisions with objects or other children. Consider the following general safety tips.

- Clear the space of dangerous objects—anything that could be slipped on or that protrudes.
- If the students take off their shoes, have them remove their socks, too, to prevent slipping.
- Begin slowly and watch for signs that a student may lack self-control. Students need time to work with different body parts in place and across space to see the results of physical actions. They also need time to release energy.
- Some students will need individual attention, but this needs to be provided in a way that does not embarrass.

## Differentiation for Special Needs

The PARTICULAR ways to differentiate introduced in Chapter 3 (Ready Reference 3.11) center around the following 10 areas to adapt.

- Place
- Amount
- Rate
- Target objectives
- Instruction
- Curriculum materials
- Utensils
- Levels of difficulty
- Assistance
- Response

Making changes in one or more of these categories can help match lessons to students' stages (e.g., older students may laugh a lot at first because they are unsure of themselves and are so conscious of changing bodies; laughing is a natural way to deal with problems). For example, amount and rate can be adjusted by starting with basic dance warm-ups and doing a thorough job of teaching the BEST elements one at a time so that students are comfortable. Target objectives, materials, and response may need to be adjusted for students with physical disabilities; for example, students in wheelchairs, with limited use of the body, might be given the role of beat keeper or be in charge of start and stop signaling. Appendix B has a chart of additional adaptations for students with special needs.

# Building Block IX: Assessment for Learning

*Increasingly, the artists and teachers began to see that the more powerful the art, the greater the evidence of learning.* (Baker and colleagues, 2004)

Arts integration emphasizes assessment *for* learning that focuses finding student strengths and needs, and is authentic, continuous, and multifactored (see Chapter 3). This is called *formative assessment*, and it mostly happens *during* the learning process to increase achievement.

The majority of assessment of dance-based lessons occurs as students problem solve through movement. Teachers observe students in process and use rubrics and checklists to make notes. Feedback is given immediately to increase the quality of work. It becomes routine for students to self-assess during and after lessons, and peer feedback is encouraged throughout work.

Assessment of dance-making performances/products does happen. There is a dual purpose. Performances are assessed for aesthetic qualities, and use of dance knowledge and performances are used to show learning in science, social studies, and math. Assessment criteria reflect both prongs: academics and arts. Dance skills and concepts must be united in the minds of the teachers (Baker et al., 2004). For example, at Ashley River Creative Arts, most units result in performances or exhibits called the "unit celebration."

## Assessment Criteria: Observing and Creating Dance

As with the language arts, dance is (1) receptive communication that allows us to understand by "reading" observations through seeing and other senses, and (2) expressive communication through which we show thoughts and feelings. Unlike the language arts, the art of dance uses the body instead of words to communicate or create meaning. With this in mind, The *Dance Standards* can be used to create criteria, at least in these two basic

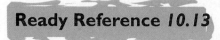

## Ready Reference 10.13 · Criteria to Create and Evaluate Dance-Based Lessons

Here are examples of criteria for creating rubrics and checklists. To what extent does the student do the following:

- Control body, mind, space, and voice, including concentration and focus
- Use specific aspects of CPS to create and refine dances (e.g., observation as data gathering, experimenting/improvising, revision based on feedback)
- Compose a meaningful movement sequence (e.g., uses beginning-middle-end; effective entrance-exit) that shows important curricular ideas
- Integrate whole body movement as opposed to relying on isolated body parts
- Use dance vocabulary to create and understand dance
- Show understanding of dance elements and dance composition (i.e., can the student make sense of what is observed?)

- Give and receive feedback on details observed to support conclusions
- Use and explain aesthetic principles to improve dance compositions, as follows:

     *Variety* in use of body parts, shapes, levels, energy, and space in compositions
     *Interesting* transitions
     *Repetition* to emphasize importance
     *Contrast* to explain and highlight
     *Unity* to bring together parts into a meaningful whole

- Work well with others to create a meaningful movement sequence
- Show respect by using good audience etiquette (active listening and appropriate responses)

---

areas that are also referred to as *responding* and *creating/performing*. Ready Reference 10.13 lists important criteria.

## Assessment *for* Learning

Checklists and rubrics have the power to change how students think as they learn in any area. They can motivate students to take movement seriously and scaffold their work toward excellence. This power relies on *how* they are used. The following are recommended.

**Collaborate.** Before giving students a list of what makes good dance, show videos of dance performances, especially of other students, and ask students to brainstorm what is communicated and how. Coach students to create a list and then connect their ideas to those in Ready Reference 10.13.

**Establish Purposes.** Tell students that dance criteria will be used for several purposes, especially helping them learn how to use movement more skillfully. Ask students for examples of skilled and artistic use of movement/dance in life. Coach them to think about how people carry themselves, their posture, walk, gestures, and what they demonstrate. Target familiar people at the school or in the news such as President Obama.

**Make It Visual.** Increase attention to criteria by using the force of visuals. Post criteria on charts or in some prominent place in the classroom so they can use it as a reference to make their work better. Consider adapting goals for placement in a student's personal portfolio that tracks growth.

## Feedback

Clear and focused descriptive feedback (not just vacuous praise) is needed throughout dance making. Wrenn Cook demonstrated this in her skeleton dance lesson as she pointed out what the students did. She also coached them to stretch their imaginations

by using "what if" type of questions. Her skeleton dance rubric appears in Planning Page 10.14.

## Anecdotal Records

Catterall (2003) explains that "paper and pencil tests on literacy and numeracy give us but a slim slice of the information pie. We need close and expert observations of learners" (p. 113). Teachers should rely on observation to see if students are progressing toward lesson targets. Jot down notes about specific student behaviors on cards or sticky notes that can be added to portfolios. Use a clipboard to make quick observation notes easier. This kind of assessment captures authentic evidence during the lesson process, as opposed to fabricated "virtual reality" assessments.

## Group Debriefing

An effective teaching habit is to take a few minutes at the end of lessons to discuss what students learned that was most important. Responses can be written on a chart to give them value and linked to lesson objectives. If dances have been videotaped, ask students "What worked?" Start an ongoing list of these ideas, including ways dancer create interest. Use the list to modify rubrics and checklists that focus on quality work criteria.

At the same time, words and ideas can be added to an ongoing arts word wall or other cumulative class charts.

## Self-Assessment

After lessons, students need time to write and discuss questions, such as those that follow:

How did you challenge yourself physically?
What did you try? What worked?
What choices did you make?
What did you learn about dance/choreography that you did not know before?

## Planning Page *10.14*

### Skeleton Dance Choreography Rubric (Wrenn Cook)

*Rating:*
Needs Improvement = 0–1, Good = 2–4, Excellent = 4–5

**Science Information Criteria**
1. Group really knows the skeletal system. Every command was obeyed with 100 percent accuracy.
2. More commands were accurate than not.
3. All or most commands were not accurate.

**Dance Elements (space, movement qualities/dynamics, time)**
1. Group found diverse ways to use dance elements to create an interesting dance.
2. Group used some dance elements to create interest.
3. No attempt or almost no attempt was made to create interest through the use of space, dynamics, and time elements.

**Originality**
1. Group came up with creative and unexpected ways to satisfy commands and to use dance elements.
2. Group found somewhat creative ways to satisfy the commands and use dance elements.
3. Group showed little or no attempt to find unique ways to satisfy the commands or use dance elements.

**Teamwork/Rehearsal**
1. Group had some trouble working together. They either did not complete the task or did not use their time well.
2. Group completed the task and had some time remaining for practice.
3. Group worked well together to choreograph and to rehearse their dance. "Practice makes perfect," and this dance was perfectly performed!

## Portfolio Entries

To document growth in dance literacy, the following items can be included in an arts folio (see Appendix D)

- Charts and personal checklists of dance elements
- Anecdotal observation notes from teacher and peers about BEST elements use
- Photos and videos of dance making along with critique (see Ready Reference 10.13)
- Journal entries or other reflective pieces based on assessment criteria

Students can pair up to share folios with focus on what they liked, what they would change, and what they had learned.

Explicitly tell students about their progress. Use charts and checklists to show them what they have learned. Add new dance information to large class webs about dance or use KWL charts.

Appendix D includes examples of informal assessment tools to use with integrated dance lessons. For program evaluation, check out the *Opportunity to Learn Standards* checklists (www.winthrop.edu/ABC/).

# Building Block X: Arts Partnerships

Consult Chapter 3 for a list of potential art partners and Appendix C for a checklist to set up dance artist residencies. Of course, an onsite dance teacher is the most likely partner, and more and more schools are hiring them. Although creative dance broke with physical education in the 1980s, many PE teachers have an interest and background in creative movement and make excellent partners. Local dance teaching artists may be contacted through local arts agencies.

## Initiating Collaboration

Teachers interested in partnering for dance integration should initiate conversations with the physical education teacher or, if the school is fortunate to have one, the dance teacher. Local college faculty members are other sources to ask for advice about dance and movement strategies that could be used in the regular classroom. It is a good idea to make an appointment to talk in more depth. A positive way to begin is to ask to observe dance and movement lessons. If a dance specialist is on staff, provide a list of units, concepts, and skills to be taught during the month. Specialists can be asked to provide the same information to the classroom teacher so that both can look for possible links. Once a working relationship begins to develop, specialists can be asked to do lessons with students that connect to classroom lessons. Classroom teachers need to expect to reciprocate or extend specialists' lessons.

**Planning.** How is collaboration with specialists made a reality? Teacher Mary-Mac Jennings explains that Ashley River Creative Arts starts with a daylong planning meeting each spring. The whole school plans together, focusing mainly on the science and social studies units for the next year. "This is incredibly valuable," she says. Teachers also meet with arts specialists once a month. As a planning/accountability device, one column from teachers' lesson plans is "on file" in the office. This column shows how the arts are used in each unit. Ms. Jennings likes this idea because it "keeps everyone focused and aware."

## Residencies

Artist residencies are an important part of the arts integration model in many schools. At ARCA each year, every grade looks forward to the 1 or 2 weeks when artists come into classrooms. This year Ms. Jennings is planning for a local musician/dancer to come for a week of mornings. "The residencies keep everyone excited. We love having artists come and we look forward to the student performances that the artists facilitate." Residencies are usually paid for by grants from South Carolina and the PTA raises matching funds. See the guidelines in Chapters 3 and 4 for residencies.

# Teacher Spotlight

## Mary-Mac's Minuet

Mary-Mac Jennings is currently teaching her kindergartners to do the minuet. "I just went on the Internet and got the directions and found a CD with music that fit. Of course, I adapted it for my children." Ms. Jennings teaches at Ashley River Creative Arts elementary school, where nearly all content and skills are taught through the arts. The academic connection to the minuet is math, and the focus is on patterns. "They are also learning to listen for changes in the music so listening skills are involved," she explains.

What does Ms. Jennings recommend for teachers just starting to integrate dance? "Just do it!" she exclaims. "Talk with teachers who are integrating the arts, visit if you can, plan with others. Don't feel like you have to have all the ideas and get it right. There is no right."

What other dance-based lessons are ahead? "This year the spring insect unit will culminate in insect dances based on the dance learning begun in the winter. One thing builds on another," she adds. 

Keep the beat!

## Conclusion

*When we teach a child to draw, we teach him how to see. When we teach a child to play a musical instrument, we teach her how to listen. When we teach a child how to dance, we teach him how to move through life with grace. When we teach a child to read or write, we teach her how to think. When we nurture imagination, we create a better world, one child at a time.* (Jane Alexander, chair for the National Endowment for the Arts)

Schools that integrate the arts show that "we learn what thrills us with risk, what warms us with applause, what beckons to us to learn just over the edge of the familiar, what comforts us with harmony and resolution" (Grumet, 2004, p. 61). This chapter introduced integrating dance throughout the curriculum so that more students can be thrilled, warmed, beckoned, and comforted. Meaningful integration was described with reference to the 10 AI building blocks, beginning with a justification for dance integration. Research and educational theories were reviewed and combined in a philosophy overview. Building Block II outlined the dance literacy needed by classroom teachers. The *how to integrate dance* question was addressed using essential building blocks of collaborative planning, aesthetic environment, use of literature as a core art, best practices, instructional design, differentiating instruction, assessment, and forming arts partnerships. In Chapter 11, seed strategies for teaching dance basics and integrating dance throughout the curriculum are described, including ideas for integrating dance with other art forms.

---

### Teachers as Leaders: AI Advocacy

Create a webquest to help teachers to learn the why-what-how of meaningful dance integration. Start with the resources in this chapter and use websites of dance organizations, as well as ArtsEdge and the Arts Education Partnership. For help with creating a webquest, go to www.webquest.sdsu.edu.

---

### myeducationlab

Go to the Activities and Applications section of the Topic *Strategies for Teaching* at the MyEducationLab for your course and complete the video activity entitled "Using Dance to Engage Creative Problem Solving and Develop Literacy."

Go to the Book Specific Resources section in the MyEducationLab for your course, select your book and Chapter 10 to view the Questions to Guide Reading, Response Options, and Bibliography of Dance Based Children's Literature.

## Resources

See the Appendix for more study materials, including websites in Appendix I. Chapter 11 has activity book recommendations.

### Professional Organizations

National Dance Association: www.aahperd.org/nda/
National Dance Education Organization: www.ndeo.org

### DVDs, Videos, CDs

Anne Green Gilbert's site: www.creativedance.org (click "Workshops," then resources for people, places, and props).

*BrainDance.* AGG Production. www.creativedance.org. *Teaching Creative Dance,* AGG Production (85 min.).

Cirque du Soleil (YouTube).

*Creative movement: A step towards intelligence.* (1993). West Long Branch, NJ: Kultur (80 min.).

Dana, A. (1991). *All-time favorite dances.* Long Branch, NJ: Kimbo Educational.

*Dance and grow.* (1994). Scotch Plains, NJ: Dance Horizons (60 min.).

*He makes me feel like dancin'.* National Dance Institute: www.nationaldance.org. (award-winning documentary; NDI offers a teacher/choreographer's handbook)

*Move 'n Groove Kids.* (2002). PBS: www.pbs.org (26 min.). (videos available about dance and dancers)

# Dance and Movement Seed Strategies

*When children create they are making sense of the world.*
(Robert Alexander)

## Overview

This chapter is a compendium of starter or "seed" ideas intended to jump start creative thinking for integration purposes. The sections focus on energizers and warm-ups, teaching dance elements and concepts, curricular areas, and integrating dance with other arts.

## Introduction

*Remember, Ginger Rogers did everything that Fred Astaire did, backward and on high heels.* (Anonymous)

In the opening Classroom Snapshot, Cyrus Longo takes several seed strategies and develops them for a science lesson. Notice the energizers and warm-ups, his focus on BEST dance elements, and how he causes students to create unique three-part dances that transform concepts about water. He uses many best practices, including CPS, open questions, EPR, and coaching with feedback.

## Classroom Snapshot

### States of Water through Dance

A small sign on Mr. Longo's desk says, "Who can turn a child's mouth into a smile? Who can turn a child's walk into a dance? A teacher."

The desks are pushed back, and 27 fourth graders are in "personal **space bubbles**." **Nature music** conveys the subtle rhythm of rushing water and crashing waves. Mr. Longo's voice is quiet but easily heard as he begins.

"Okay, **stretches.** Reach over your head. Now one arm higher and alternate back and forth. Let's do eight counts: 1-2-3-4-5-6-7-8. Both arms up and drop to your sides. Relax. Reach out with both arms, in front. Let your hips tilt so your back and arms are parallel to the floor. Now relax your back and curve it so you can dangle your head and hands. Let's slowly roll up with your head coming up last. **I'll count down from 8.**"

Students give a unison sigh and wait for the next activity, which is another warm-up for **specific body parts**, working from top to bottom: head, neck, torso/core (shoulders, hips, back, abdomen), arms and elbows, hands, fingers and wrists, legs and knees, and feet and ankles.

"Ready, **shake out!** Right arm. Left arm. Whole body. Take a deep breath and slowly let it out. Take another. Hold it. Very slowly release it without letting your body slump. I see straight bodies out there. Good concentration. Now, sit in your space without using your hands. Eyes on me."

The warm-ups take about 5 minutes. Mr. Longo begins his introduction to the science lesson.

"Put your **thumb up** if you can tell me something about the water cycle."

Almost everyone responds. They talk about where water is found on Earth, how much water there is, what causes pollution, and what makes water. One boy lists three forms of water (ice, liquid, and steam), and Mr. Longo asks what causes these states. The students seem uncertain.

"It's fine if you're not sure about what causes water to be in a solid, liquid, or gas because that's what our lesson is. Let's **start with what you do know**. Stand up. In your space, when I say "three," show me a body shape that feels like water in solid form. Ready, 1-2-3. Yes! I see stiff bodies and straight lines. Without losing your shape, try to look around. **What do you notice?**"

"Everyone is compact."

"I see angles."

"Sarah, what do you mean by angles?"

"Like James has his arms and legs bent straight. I think 45-degree angles, aren't they?"

"Good observation!"

"I'll count again. This time, every time **I say "three," change** your solid shape in some way. Try a different level or direction. Look at the **Dance Elements Chart.** Okay, ready? 1-2-3. 1-2-3. 1-2-3. Wow! You really thought of lots of hard shapes. How did you do it?" Lots of thumbs go up.

"I wanted to do what you said, but be different. I tried to feel really solid, but change to a high level and use new body parts," explains a tall girl.

"I thought about how it feels inside a piece of ice. I used more energy to hold my molecules together," says a boy.

"Hey, I'm getting cold. B-R-R-R," jokes Mr. Longo and the class laughs. "But why is ice cold?" he asks.

The class tells what they know about temperature and its effects on water. Mr. Longo then uses the comment about molecules and asks what they think the distance is among the molecules in ice. They concur that they "felt" close together.

Mr. Longo takes the students through **dance explorations** of liquid water and finally water vapor. He increasingly focuses his questions and **coaches** with descriptive comments related to the molecular structure of the three states and how each feels when they make their individual shapes. After about 10 minutes, he tells the students to get into small groups, previously assigned. They know where the group space is.

"**Your problem** is to create a dance using movements related to all three forms of water. Remember, you're not pretending to be water. Use dance to communicate about the states showing possible movements. Don't be literal. How will the dance be organized?"

"**Beginning, middle, and end**" they respond chorally.

"Frozen, moving, frozen shape" one girl elaborates.

"We need an entrance and exit and creative ideas" says another.

"Thanks for reminding us, Gloria! Yes, making a dance uses the scientific method. Creative ideas can be brainstormed about ways water gets from one form to another. Brainstorm movements to show these changes at different speeds and levels," Mr. Longo says as he flips up a chart that says **"Dance Checklist"** and quickly jots down the criteria just generated.

"I'll come around as you work" he says.

Students huddle in groups of four and five. Mr. Longo hangs back to let them get started. After a few minutes, he **circulates** to listen in. He uses a **clipboard** with yellow sticky notes all over it and jots notes as he listens.

"Ice melts when it gets warmer—above 32 degrees. We could show melting by starting high (a girl tiptoes and reaches up) and slowly get lower and spread out. Each person could use a different body part."

"We could get in the shape of a rigid ice sculpture with lots of angles. We need to be really close together." Everyone giggles.

"What about when we melt and spread out. We'd be liquid. Somehow we need to show getting hotter, so we can evaporate."

"We could show being cooked to boiling. Wow. You'd really have to move fast and jump around. Look at my fingers boiling!" Gloria demonstrates with wild finger movements. The others join in, and a boy declares, "Look, my foot is boiling!"

Mr. Longo smiles and moves to another group. They are discussing cloud movements and how to show water moving from a gas to precipitation (liquid). He **asks what the difference is** between precipitation and condensation, and they spend a few minutes differentiating the terms. A third group is working on water appearing as frost and is experimenting with "quick-freeze" movements and shapes.

After about 10 minutes, Mr. Longo announces they have **5 minutes** to decide a starting shape, how to use movements related to the three states, and an ending shape. He **coaches** them to think about how to use the space in the room. He tells them to sit in their groups when they are ready.

Each of the four groups **performs** their dances. The rest of the class acts as **audience**. Each dance takes 3 or 4 minutes. After each, Mr. Longo asks the audience to "tell what they saw" and points at the posted checklist. He compliments students who give **specific observations** about shapes, movements, and connections to the states of water.

The lesson ends with a **debriefing.** Mr. Longo asks students what they learned about states of water. Finally, students rearrange their desks and take out science **learning logs** to write for 5 minutes about states of matter. There is a reading assignment on the board about the water cycle in the science text.

Mr. Longo explains that there is little in the reading that hasn't already come up in the lesson. He tells me some students need the print reinforcement, and he claims he's too traditional to do away with the textbook completely. Students begin to read as they finish their logs.

Mr. Longo circulates and gives each student a yellow sticky **note, with an observation he made about their work.** I see them take out a special folder and stick it inside where there are several others.

I ask if I might read what one girl has written in her log. It says: "I'll never forget the three water states and where the molecules are. I like to learn this way because you just remember science better and it is fun."

# Organization

The seed strategies in this chapter are organized into sections, including a section on integrating dance with other art form. However, there is a great deal of possibilities for using any seed idea for many different purposes and curricular contexts.

All seed ideas need to be developed for integration purposes. They are just idea starters to get creative problem solving going. The energizers and the section on dance elements have ideas for preparing students for problem solving (e.g., concentration) and using dance basics. It is important for teachers to choose seeds that fit with curricular objectives and adapt them using the 10 PARTICULAR ways to differentiate (see Chapter 3). Students should be invited to adapt strategies and lead activities, as soon as possible. Also, Appendix B has more ideas for students with special needs.

# I. Energizers and Warm-Ups

Energizers and warm-ups are used to get attention, set mood, and warm up the body for movement and the brain for creative problem solving. If used regularly, many build focus, concentration, and self-control, so students are better able to understand and express thoughts and feelings.

Most of the following begin with students in personal spaces or in a circle formation and nearly all present a series of

**Dance and Movement**

movement problems for students to solve. The first set target concentration and focus along with body warm-up.

**Brain Dance.** Gilbert (2005) recommends a warm-up sequence for the whole body, which involves breathing deeply and touching and moving all body parts; head to toe and back to core; head–tail separate and together; upper/lower body parts; body sides isolated, cross-lateral midline and upper/lower body; and moving off balance. See the website www.creativedance.org.

**Inhale/Exhale/Stretch.** Direct students to do the following: "Slowly inhale, reach up and overhead and to floor with knees bent. Exhale. Repeat to each side. Roll head and shoulders forward and backward, bend arms, do socket rolls, touch head to shoulders, touch knees, touch toes, sit and twist and bend, do slow windmills, toe presses, heel to toe slowly, clasp hands behind and stretch shoulders, spine stretches, squat and press forward (exhale), bend one leg and repeat (exhale)." Slow, nonrhythmic mood music can be used. Nature sounds on CDs and tapes work well.

**Slow Breathing.** Tell students to do all these slowly: "Breathe in through your right nostril and out the left. Become as high and large as you can and then exhale and shrink as small as possible. Breathe in and exhale, making a single sound (e.g., short vowel sound). Suck in breath through clenched teeth and breathe out through your nose. Breathe to the rhythm of music. Place hands on abdomen and breathe in and exhale."

**Stretch It.** Form a circle. Narrate as follows: "Let's try different ways of 'stretching' with your whole body and body parts. Stretch up to the ceiling with both hands. Stretch across your desk leading with one hand. Stretch your neck, fingers, left foot, right foot. Look around to gather different ideas." *Variation:* Do with "rolling" movements.

**Watch My Hand.** Partner students. One is the "hand" and the other must visually follow the partner's hand. Leader should change levels and directions. At signal, partners reverse roles.

**Hang Loose.** Use an object to represent the concepts of "relaxed and tense" or "loose and tight" (e.g., piece of yarn versus pencil). Call out a body part and ask students to make it tight and hard, then loose and soft.

**Wiggle and Giggle.** Ask students to giggle with a foot, a knee, and on up the body to the head. Shaking and wiggling with controls (signals, numbers) develops focus.

**Foot to Foot (Weight Shift).** Ask students to "Move foot to foot (most basic locomotor step). Go smaller, larger, faster, slower." Expand to "leap with body curved forward."

**Shake It Out.** In circle, the leader invites everyone to shake the left foot out, counting down from 10. Next, do the same with the right foot, and then do right foot and arm. Ask, "What else could we shake out?" Then coach them about different ways to shake (e.g., fast, slow, low, high).

Note: Do head and neck moves to slow count for safety and variety.

**Hand Warm-Up.** Direct everyone to make a fist and then show one, then two, then three, then four, and then five fingers. Repeat. Do other hand and then both. Change tempo.

**Hug Yourself.** Call out a body part to hug (e.g., hand hugs, finger hugs). Encourage creative thinking. *Variation:* Do as partners.

**Who Started the Motion?** Stand or sit in a circle. One person leaves the room while another is selected to be IT. IT leads others through different motions, such as waving hands or tapping feet. Player 1 returns and watches to figure out who is starting the movements as the leader begins each new one. Give three guesses.

**Head, Shoulders, Knees, and Toes.** First practice singing this song. Repeat, stand in a circle, and touch body parts mentioned in the song. *Variation:* Use a rhythm or chant (e.g., "Touch your head, head, head . . . touch your toes, toes, toes"), as students do choice creative moves.

**Rubber Duckie.** Pass rubber duckie around a circle. As students receive it, they say, "Look what I can do," and demonstrate a dance movement with the duckie (e.g., jump, hop, skip, twist, turn).

**Freeze (Self-control).** Play music or use a tambourine. Tell students to move in a specific way until the sound stops and then freeze. When the music begins again, they move in their frozen shapes. For example, "When the drum begins, walk in place to the beat."

**Magic Shoes.** Students imagine they have on magic shoes that allow them to walk in special ways (e.g., on water, on air). *Variation:* Brainstorm ways to walk. Write on cards and draw from a hat. Call out with a creative change (e.g., speed, level, shape, energy).

**Body Directions.** Give a series of directions, such as "Show me 'up' with your body, now 'down.' How can you make your body go way up? Way down? How high can you get? Show me halfway down. Make yourself as small as you can. Now great big. Pretend your feet are glued to the floor. Now move your body up and down."

**Noodle-Freeze (Following Directions).** Direct students to move in loose and relaxed ways, first in one spot, varying the speed and levels. At a signal, students freeze in a shape. *Variation:* Students say a one-liner about their shape (e.g., "I feel like I'm melting.").

**Slow-Mo Concentration.** Students pick an everyday movement and do it slowly (e.g., sweeping, bending over, reaching). Groups perform by dividing class in half. Audience gives feedback on focus and concentration.

**Lightning.** Form circle and join hands. Leader squeezes a rhythm to both the right- and left-hand partners. The rhythm is passed around until it collides in one person. That person shouts "lightning" and becomes the leader.

**Paranoia.** Students spread out to fill up space. On signal (e.g., drum beat), they walk around the room filling up the space, leaving no holes. The leader then calls "one" and everyone finds someone to follow, not letting the person know he's being followed and still trying to fill up the space. Then call "two" and students follow a second person. Finally "three" is called. The leader then alternates numbers.

**Popcorn.** On signal, students walk around, filling up space. At the signal "one," each person picks a person to visually track. Whenever they come near that person, they jump. Next the leader says "two" and they track a second person, while still tracking the first. When they pass by the second person, students freeze for 1 second. Everyone now walks around jumping. Finally, the leader says "three," and they begin to track a third person. When they pass that person, students say "popcorn." Continue until "freeze" signal.

**Imagination Journey.** Narrate a series of movements, similar to the following example: "Put your feet into warm water and wiggle your toes. Now put your legs in and swish them around. Make circles in the water. Slip farther into the water and sway your hips back and forth. You are up to your waist. Slowly walk in place. Feel the weight of the water. Raise your hands up out of the water and stretch them over your head. Jump up and down. Feel the water. Sink down up to your neck. Let your arms float on top of the water. Press your hands down in the water to your sides and then raise them up. Put your hands on your hips and twist, twist, twist. Now rotate your head forward, to left and back, then right and around again. Oops, the water splashes up your nose. Wiggle your nose and blow the water from your lips. With your toes, pull the plug. The water slowly drains out. You shiver as it moves below your armpits. As it reaches your thighs, you raise your knees up and down, up and down. Finally the water drains out. You twirl around and sit down."

**Mood Setting.** Use music to relax before movement. Allow students to move or not move. Artists like Enya and George Winston work well. *Example:* Enya's "In Memory of Trees" CD.

**Sound to Motion.** Use sound effects tapes, rhythm instruments, bells, and environmental "found sounds." Ask students to show motions for a series of sounds (e.g., strong, high, low, direction changes).

**Circle Back Rub (Relaxation).** Students form a circle, facing sideways. Each student touches the shoulders of the person in front. Leader says "go" and each person rubs the back of the person in front. Leader says "switch," and all turn and repeat.

## Energizers and Warm-Ups for Cooperation

**Add On.** Form four or five lines with students standing, side to side. At one end a person starts a movement, and the next picks it up and adds to it. The movement travels down the line until the end. The starter person then moves to the end and a new starter begins.

Note: Each line will be doing its own thing.

**Movement Chain.** Stand in a line or U shape. On signal, people on the two ends start a movement or a rhythm and send it around until it reaches the end. End people then go to the center of the line, and new end people start movements or rhythms.

**Don't Cross the Line.** Pairs face each other and grasp shoulders. They imagine a line between them. Each starts pushing but cannot cross the line. The goal is to push hard, but not push each other over. Repeat back to back or side to side.

**Buddy Walk.** Pairs lean back to back against each other. First, they silently walk around. Then they try to sit on the floor and rise up again. The activity can also be done side by side.

**Back-to-Back.** Pairs slightly lean against each other and begin dancing with music. Use slow music at first. Each must try to sense what moves to make to stay together.

**Co-op Musical Chairs.** Remove chairs, as in the traditional version, but all find a place to sit when the music stops and must help everyone sit somewhere. No one is eliminated.

**Sheet Music.** Use an old sheet and tell children to hold on around the edge. Put several balloons in the center and put on a CD with slow tempo music. The goal is to keep balloons afloat, while keeping the beat of the music.

**Shrink and Stretch.** Group forms a circle stretching out so only fingertips touch. Move out as much as possible without losing touch. At the signal "shrink," the circle moves in to take up as small a space as possible. Then the leader says "stretch," and so forth.

**Balloon Balance or Bust.** Small groups join hands and form a circle. Each group receives a balloon, and the object is to keep it in the air without dropping each other's hands.

**Stuck Together.** Pairs hold a note card between two body parts (e.g., head to head with card in between). Another card is then added, and so on, until one card falls. Can be done in small groups with one person in the center and others joined to the one person with a card in between. At signal, the center person moves and the group must follow without dropping cards. *Variation:* Do without cards. Leader calls two body parts to touch.

**No Holes.** Group spreads out to fill up all space. On signal (e.g., drum beat), everyone walks around trying to keep the space completely filled. When leader signals "stop," all must freeze. If there is a hole, leader points to it and someone must fill it up.

**Body Count.** Everyone walks around filling up the space. Leader then calls out a combination (e.g., three heads and two hands). Students quickly find others to create this combination of touching body parts.

**Human Spider Web.** Everyone must be touching someone else in an appropriate spot. When the leader signals, everyone moves slowly around the room, always touching someone (e.g., with a foot, hand, shoulder). At the stop signal, everyone must be touching (i.e., connected by the human web).

## II. Dance Best Elements and Concepts

Ideas in this section are to teach basic dance concepts. BEST elements appear in Ready Reference 10.2.

**Dance and Movement**

Cheering and chanting vocabulary at Ashley River

**Personal Space.** Students find a personal spot. They explore their personal space, not moving from the spot, by making shapes at low, middle, and high levels. Combine with force, time, and leading with different body parts (e.g., bend slowly, leading with shoulder). *Variation:* Use carpet squares or hula hoops to define personal space.

**Spread Out.** Leader gives a 10 count for students to "loco-mote" from personal space to spread out in space and freeze. Next, do 10 count back to personal space. Repeat to a 10 count, but must go out on 5 and come back by 10. Repeat using 8 count, 4, and 2.

**Space Bubbles.** Use imaginary bubbles or hula hoops. Students imagine that the hoops are big bubbles around them. Ask them to explore the limits. Ask them to walk around and do moves and steps without touching other's bubbles. Use drum or count to change time, space, energy.

**No Words (Dance Communication).** Use only gestures and motions to give directions: "Come forward, turn, sit." Partners then create their own movement directions. Remind students not to show, but tell with movements. *Challenge:* Repeat without using hands. Afterward, discuss the role of gestures and movements in communication.

**Follow the Leader.** Students imitate actions or words of the leader. For example, wiggle hips at a low level or punch elbows at a high level. Use the BEST elements for ideas. Leader passes the lead to another who takes over.

**Simon Says.** Play "Simon Says" using BEST element (Ready Reference 10.2) and Laban combination (Ready Reference 10.3). For example, "Simon Says" use your body to show a circle. Relate to units (e.g., time lesson: move clockwise in a circle).

**Cumulative Name Game.** Form a circle and ask students to create a movement to match the syllables in their own name. The leader demonstrates using a unique level, body part, and move. *Example:* Su'-san: starting at low level and slither up to high level saying "Suuuu-san!" After each student demonstrates her or his name move, everyone mimics it. *Challenge:* To learn names, repeat everyone's move from the beginning each time.

**Step In.** Use this movement activity to review any content. Students form a circle. The teacher gives movement directions. *Example:* "Take two steps in if you know the capital of Ohio. Step back one if you know the state bird." *Variation:* Brainstorm ways to get into the circle. Use BEST dance elements for ideas. After modeling, students take over.

**Walk Different Ways.** Give directions to walk: in place—slow and fast, forward, backward, and sideways. Work on posture and alignment: Call out "tiny steps, giant steps, on heels, on tiptoe, in place, backward, forward, as lightly as possible (an element of force), or slowly (an element of time)." *Variations:* Add "as ifs" (e.g., you are tired, hungry, nervous, scared). Or, students throw scarves, balls, hoops, or ropes and try to catch with body parts. Can be done to music.

**Abstracting Movement Ideas.** Brainstorm movements that are implied or feel like each of the following suggestions. Coach students to respond to the quality and not be literal: sounds (use tape of everyday sounds), colors, shapes (e.g., cut out of paper), personal objects such as prints, photos, feathers, plants, and so on. Coach students to respond to colors, line, shapes, patterns, and textures.

**Quick Combinations.** With students in personal space, call out a series of movement problems for them to solve. *Examples:* walk/twist, hop/twist, twist at different levels, in different shapes and different directions, twist leading to different places, twist sharp/smooth, strong/light/ tense/loose, twist quick/slow/sustained/in a pattern (e.g., twist, twist, pause, twist).

**Movement Words Hunt.** Challenge students to find words that are either locomotor or nonlocomotor moves (Ready Reference 11.1). Examples for locomotor include: walk, leap, jump, drag, slide, scoot, skip, crawl, dash, float, pounce, prance, spin, swoop. Examples for nonlocomotor include: twist, swing, rock, sway, collapse, curl, dodge, explode, grab, lean, lift, point, poke, press, push, quiver, rise, shake, shiver, sink, squirm, turn, writhe.

**Card Draw and Move.** Students call out ways to move. Write them on cards. Groups sort cards into locomotor and non-locomotor. Next, students list adverbs that qualify each (e.g., walk slowly, fast, with force, in a "shape," using a lot of space, in a rhythm). Form a circle. Put cards in two piles and draw one from each and act on it.

**Movement Bingo.** Use the words from Ready Reference 11.1 to play bingo. When someone wins, everyone does the moves to check.

## Ready Reference 11.1   Locomotor and Nonlocomotor Moves

Make word cards for a pocket chart and use to play Movement Bingo, do warm-ups, and expand vocabulary.

*Walk:* shift weight from one foot to the other with one foot always on the ground.

*Run:* same as walk, but there are moments when neither foot touches the ground.

*Gallop:* a step leap with the same foot always leading in an uneven rhythm.

*Leap:* like a run but you are in the air longer with both feet off the ground.

*Skip:* combines step and hop in an uneven rhythm, and the lead foot alternates.

*Jump:* weight changes from both feet to both feet.

*Hop:* requires weight change from one foot to the same foot.

*Shake:* a wiggle done in place.

*Bend:* close up your joints.

*Stretch:* open up your joints.

*Push:* use your body to move against a resistance.

*Pull:* use your body away from a resistance.

*Twist:* rotate in a direction up to the body's limit.

*Turn:* spin around, whirl, and twirl.

*Rise:* come up to a higher level.

*Sink:* move down to a lower level.

Other action words include *zoom, slither, scatter, explode, crumple, melt,* and *tiptoe.*

---

**I'm Stuck.**   Narrate series of sticky situations using different body parts: You are clapping your hands when they suddenly will not come apart. You try to get them to separate. Finally, they pop apart. You reach up to scratch your face. Now your hand sticks to your face. You try different ways to pull your hand off, but it is hard. Blop! It comes off. You start to walk around when your left foot sticks to the floor. You try to make the best of it. You move around with your left foot glued down.

**Body Moves and Steps.**   Use the following activities to explore types of moves and steps.

*Leap:* Pretend to leap over real or imagined objects (e.g., a log or a rubber swimming pool).

*Hop:* Use a hoop. Hop in and out. Hop all the way around the hoop. Change tempo.

*Jump (in different ways):* with feet together, then apart, alternate these, land on one foot.

*Run:* Explore with imagery. Run on hot sand, to the finish line, to catch a bus, and so on.

*Slide:* Slide as if the floor was slick or warm. Slide like you are tired or in a hurry.

*Step hop:* Clap a one–two beat. Students step on beat 1 and hop on beat 2. Try it to music.

*Stretch ("as if"):* you are waking up, yawning. Challenge to stretch out long and then wide.

*Bend:* Do real-life bends (e.g., tie shoes or pet a dog).

*Sit:* Try to sit, kneel, and lie down without use of hands.

*Shake:* Ask for real-life shaking and practice these (e.g., a bowl of jelly or baby's rattle).

*Turn, twist, lift:* Practice turning with feet at different levels and speeds.

*Rock and sway:* Sway like the wind. Gradually increase the force so that it becomes rocking. Sway while walking, slowly, faster, larger, smaller, and so forth (Pica, 1991).

**Laban Effort Actions.**   Practice these eight actions changing body parts, amounts of energy, and/or the timing (sustained versus quick): punch, slash, wring, press, dab, flick, float, glide. Lead with different parts of body (e.g., glide with your shoulder, flick with a hand, punch with a shoulder). Finally, give three Laban actions and students create a dance with five moves. Use the three-part frozen shape–movements–shape sequence. Partner and have students teach each other their dances.

**Across the Floor.**   Divide into relay teams. Call a move (e.g., walk, run, leap, jump, skip) or a combination. When ITs touch a target, the next team member moves.

**Walks.**   Students walk to drum beats (e.g., half-time, double-time, walk time, march time). Next, students explore walking by talking them through a sequence: "Walk in place. Now walk around the room without bumping into people. Cover the whole room. Walk with toes first. Walk as if you just got a compliment, were embarrassed, have a stomach ache, are worried, have a heavy load." Vary walks in low, medium, and high levels using music (e.g., jazz).

**Imagination Walk.**   Students line up and take turns walking to a destination as others observe and describe. Each walks a different way across the room. Repeat and add energy, change time, use space and body differently, repeat phrases.

**Shape Shifters.**   The goal is to create, number, and remember five shapes. Leader then says "one" and students make the first shape. On "two," they make a second shape. This continues through "five." Then the leader calls numbers at random, and students make the shape for that number.

**Shake and Shape.**   On a signal, everyone shakes and wiggles a body part. Leader does a countdown and on "freeze," all must stop. Begin again. Ask students to give descriptive comments about frozen body shapes.

**Shape Flex Countdown.**   Leader does a slow eight count down while students create eight shapes from high to low level, then from low to high. Next do a four count, then a two count.

**Shapes Stretch.** Each person stands in elastic loop (use 1 yard of tied together elastic). Make movements while holding onto the elastic. Ask students to then move to music while creating a variety of shapes with the band.

**Shape Rope.** In personal space, students each hold up a rope high and drop it. Tell them to observe how the rope landed and make the same shape with your body. Continue dropping the rope in different ways.

**Shape Go Round (Adapted from Celeste Miller).** Form a circle. One child goes into the center and makes an emotion shape at a low, middle, or high level. The next comes in and connects to the shape. When the people sculpture is set, the first person leaves. A third comes in and so on. *Variation:* Do with two at a time or three. Challenge students to enter and exit consistent with the target emotion.

**Shape Relay.** Form circle. One person goes into the center and makes a shape (low, middle, or high) that they can hold. The next person connects to that shape in some way. When the sculpture is stable, the first person leaves. A third person goes in and so on. Repeat all around the circle. *Variation:* Increase the number of people in the center and coach students to use interesting entrances and exits.

**Contagious Shapes.** Form a circle. Narrate slowly: "In place, take four counts to go from standing to a low level shape. Hold." Give feedback on similarities, differences, etc. "Now, take four counts to go from this low level shape to a high level shape. Add an element of balance. Now, take four counts to go to a middle level shape." Repeat low, high, and middle levels exploring shapes and coaching to try unusual ones. Brainstorm new shapes? Coach with cues such as centered/off balance, narrow/wide, symmetrical/assymmetrical. Ask students to choose one shape, freeze, then look around the circle to choose someone else's shape. On signal, students are to echo that shape. Repeat several times at different levels. *Variations:* Use different transitions when moving from shape to shape, such as staccato. Try use different kinds of energy. Brainstorm other ways to transition.

**Movement Problems.** Start a movement such as arm swinging. Ask questions such as "How can you make it smaller? Show me. Now larger. Move the swinging to whole body and then back to just arms. What are the effects of these movements?" Ask half the class to do while others observe. Then reverse. Ask fat questions such as "What did you see? How did it feel?"

**Jump–Turn–Freeze.** Students walk around and keep an eye on one person. They should not follow the person. Next, add a second person and then, after a while, a third person to the list of others that each student is trying to watch. Students are to keep walking. Then say, "When you pass the first person, JUMP!" Continue for a while and then add TURN for the second person and finally FREEZE for the third.

**Three Levels.** Students create a shape and then freeze in low, middle, and high levels on a count or signal.

**Get Moving: Pathways.** Everyone spies a destination and moves there in a straight pathway and back home, then a curvy pathway and back home, using as little space as possible. Use start-stop signals.

**Balance Pantomime.** Brainstorm times when balance is important (e.g., walking on a wall, crossing a creek on stepping stones). Ask half to pantomime, while the other half observes and gives feedback. Reverse. Discuss differences between pantomime and dance and brainstorm how to "abstract" movements, that is, make them less literal by changing up BEST elements.

**Balancing Moves.** Ask students to stand in one spot and do particular moves (e.g., stand on one foot, on tiptoes, twist), while balancing a book on their heads.

**Ball Bounce.** Direct students to bounce an imaginary small ball (e.g., a tennis ball). Change to a beach ball, basketball, and so on. Tell them to show the size and hardness of the ball with their bodies. Change energy and speed.

**Adopt a Dance.** Each student chooses a move or step and gives it a "unique touch." Sustain until you make eye contact with someone and then adopt their dance.

**Dance Machine.** Each student chooses a move that can be repeated. One student goes to the center and begins his or her move. One by one all "add on" by touching on some plane and repeating his or her move until all are "one" machine with a variety of moving parts. Machine can be around an idea (e.g., a book or chapter in a book, a concept or feeling).

**Pass-It-On Moves.** One person in the circle starts a move and others imitate until the moves get all the way around to the starter. The next person to the right then starts a move, and so on. *Variation:* Each person must "abstract" from the original. Use music.

**Dance Freeze.** After learning dance elements, put on music without lyrics (new age or classical) for students to free dance. When the music stops, each freezes and gives a one-liner about a dance element he or she is using. *Example:* "I am at a high level because the music was fast and made me feel happy."

**Everyday Dance.** Brainstorm movements from everyday life using these prompts: "I use low level to _____, I stretch to _____, I twist to _____, I use force to _____, I run to _____, I walk to _____," and so forth. *Extension:* Combine into a three-part dance that begins in a frozen shape, then six to eight moves, and then frozen shape.

**Responding to Accent.** Clap a phrase accenting the first beat (e.g., think of "I love you" with accent on three different words). Clap the same phrase accenting the last beat. Children move to the phrase, showing the accent by a change of movement (use after time element is taught).

**Scarf Dancing.** In a large space, allow experimentation with dancing to music with scarves or ribbons. Tape 2 feet of ribbon to the end of a pencil to create a wand for each student.

**Energy Boost.** Ask for things that move slowly, strong, quick, weak, light. Combine ideas by asking, "What moves slowly and lightly?" Students try each combination.

**Statues.** Students assume a choice shape. On signal they change to another shape. Say "memorize your body." Do at different speeds. Do three shapes and put together as a shape or statue dance. *Variation:* Move freely around the room until "freeze" signal. Students stand still in a shape and do not move until "thaw" signal. Leader should give descriptive comments on shapes (e.g., levels, space).

**Movement Sentence Add-On.** Do in circle. First student creates a sentence (e.g., three moves or steps) and next person imitates, but adds on something. Do in small groups.

**Dance Echo.** Group students to create a dance phrase (set of movements) to perform using a 1-2-3-4 count. *Example:* see "Stretch It." Form a whole group circle. Group 1 performs their dance and on the counts 5-6-7-8 the rest of the classes echoes what they saw. Then Group 2 dances, and so on. Debrief by asking: "What was hard? What was easy? How did you solve the problems?" *Variation:* Combine the two groups. First dances to 4 count and second responds with their dance on 5-6-7-8. Reverse.

**Music Video Response.** Watch a video (e.g., Michael Jackson's "Thriller" or musical "Oklahoma") that ties into a lesson and has a dance connection. Direct students to watch for specific dance elements (BEST) and how they are used to communicate an idea or feeling. This can be a jigsaw cooperative learning activity. *Variation:* Show an animal film like *March of the Penguins* to analyze movements. Compare with a dance video like *Dying Swan* (Ann Shea, Chattanooga).

**Musicals with Dance.** Watch a musical (e.g., "Mary Poppins"). Discuss how dance is used. What does dance communicate about the story and characters that would be missing without the dance?

**Experts.** Students research a famous dance (e.g., minuet), dancer, or choreographer. Expert panels present their findings and take questions from the audience. *Variations:* Experts demonstrate dance aspects. Or, dancers appear in Ready Reference 10.4.

**Four Square Feedback.** Divide notebook paper into four sections labeled BEST. As groups present dances, the audience writes what they saw and felt in a square for each. Encourage specific ideas about each BEST element. Afterward, all share comments.

# III. Connecting Dance to Curricular Areas

This section describes seed strategies to prompt thinking about using dance to explore concepts and skills in science, social studies, math, and language arts. Look for content that has "movement possibilities." Ready Reference 11.2 offers ideas, largely related to science.

Solicit topics for dance exploration from students, too. Ask for movement ideas related to categories such as feelings, weather, celebrations, cooking, weddings, birthday parties, funerals, shopping, and work. Explore movements in unison and then in small groups. As a culminating activity, ask students to collaborate to create a dance based on a concept. Suggest the dance have a beginning, middle, and end. Use the *three-part freeze-move-freeze* structure to get started.

**Choreographing Criteria.** See Ready Reference 10.13. Post and discuss ways to create more artful dances, such as the following:

- Interesting transitions (variety)
- Different levels
- Different kinds of energy
- Different entrances/exits
- Positive/negative space
- Clear beginning/middle/end
- Best vantage point for the audience
- Unison and individual movement?
- Physically challenging movement
- How dance changed thinking about science, social studies, etc.

**Evaluate and Revise.** Groups perform for each other and then think of one thing that they would like to expand upon, improve, change, highlight. Groups are then given time to revise dances and re-perform. Audience talks about differences.

## Science Focus

**Science Standards.** All standards can be accessed at the National Science Teachers Association (NSTA) website (www.nsta.org).

**Dance Webbing.** Choose a science topic such as seasons (Ready Reference 11.2). Web associated movement using BEST dance elements of body, energy, space, and time. *Example:* Falling leaves twist, turn, and float at high levels down to the ground (low level). Break into groups, and each group chooses one idea to explore further. Reassemble to show top three dance moves.

Fourth position—arms en haute

## Ready Reference 11.2 Environmental Sources of Dance Making

*Directions: Use these categories to cause students to think about and generate movement.*

**Body systems:** respiratory, circulatory, digestive, nervous
**Body actions:** eat, walk, run, hug, hop, skip, sit
**Seasons and cycles:** life cycles (e.g., butterfly)
**Growing things:** small to large movements, slow, sustained
**Weather:** contrasts in nature (e.g., force of tornado versus gentleness of a breeze)
**Plants:** sizes, shapes, ways they grow
**Animals and insects:** cats creep, stretch, sneak, roll, slink, ball up, leap
**Places or environments:** movements at beach, mountains, desert
**Machines and mechanical actions:** pulleys and levers, tools

**Electricity and magnetic forces:** north and south poles, pull, repel
**Space and solar system:** rotate, use of space, size, shape, pathways
**Gravity:** force, pull, weight
**States of matter:** solid, liquid, gas
**Causes and effects:** temperature, wind
**Energy:** fire, steam, solar, nuclear
**Technology:** computer, elevator
**Inventions and objects:** crepe paper, cotton balls, rope scarves, elastic

---

**North Pole, South Pole (Magnetic Force).** Students walk as if the floor is a giant magnet. Then suggest that the ceiling is the magnet. Call out the pull on different body parts. Suggest they walk as if the body is an opposite pole of a magnet.

**Environmental Dance.** Choose a category from Ready Reference 11.2 to explore. *Example:* Pairs experiment with movements related to pollution and create a dance phrase or sentence to a count of eight that shows something about pollution. *Variation:* Students first write down a main point they have learned about the environment. Use these as captions to create dance sentences.

**Environmental Walk.** Brainstorm places in the environment. Leader calls out a place and students walk (in place) based on the conditions (e.g., hot sand on beach, thick forest, marsh, rocky path). *Variations:* (1) Do in small groups and each perform. Audience describes the conditions they observed. (2) Add an environmental problem that would change walking conditions (e.g., oil spill on beach, broken glass trash on a prairie). Explore showing conditions with different body parts.

**Think Like a Scientist.** Explain that a behavioral scientist is a person who studies by quietly observing and collecting data. Brainstorm movement characteristics of animals (slithery, stalkers, swimmers, etc). Pair students with one being an animal and the other a scientist. The animal uses one of the movement categories and the scientist records what is seen—not the name of the animal. Reverse. Spotlight some volunteers in the whole group. Debrief about what movements were most helpful.

**Introducing Science Vocabulary.** Choose movement words from an upcoming science passage. Group students and give each a word to show through movement. For example, sedimentary rock is layered so layering movements are suggested. Each group pronounces word, shows movement, and pronounces again. Audience tells what they observed about the meaning.

**Dancing Animals.** Brainstorm the movement of many different animals. Play various types of danceable music. Encourage students to use their bodies to explore animal movements, concentrating on trying different levels and using a variety of body parts (e.g., slither with arm only).

**Fossil Fuels and Energy Dance.** Discuss the conditions needed to create fossil fuels: heat, pressure, time, no air, no movement. In a circle, warm up, then turn backs to the circle and ask students to create gestures/movement for "heat." Turn around and share. Do the same for the other words. Choose one or two movements for each word. Put them together to create a dance phrase. Break up into groups of four to six to create an original "fuel dance." *Variation:* Add background music.

**Places to Sit.** Experiment to find the effect of sitting in different places such as a bicycle, horse, swing, airplane, step. Discuss the science/health behind designing places to sit and work (ergonomics). Students then decide on a frozen sitting position they can hold. Coach them to use a variety of shapes and levels. On signal, half the class freezes and the other half views and comments, as they would at a museum exhibit. Reverse roles. *Variation:* Combine with photos and art, such as Rodin's *Thinker*.

**Water Dance.** Students create movement sentences to represent the different phases of the water cycle. First, read aloud *Water Dance* by Thomas Locker. Next, explore movement options for the words. Divide the class into 13 groups and give each a slip of paper with a sentence from the book or use fewer groups and give each several sentences. Each group creates a set of movements for the sentence. Read the book, stopping for each group to dance their sentence. Repeat in order from 1 to 13 without background reading. *Variation:* Play background music, add colorful fabrics or scarves, and use sound instruments such as rain sticks and drums.

**Tool Dance.** Brainstorm tools used for eating, gardening, building, schoolwork, and others. List movements associated with tools. Try them at different speeds and levels. *Example:* Shovel-push in, dig, lift, throw, pat down. *Variation:* Pairs choose a tool and create a dance phrase. Do to a count.

**Sound Movement Collages.** Sounds of the body, city, nature, animals, machines, children's names, and names of states and cities can all suggest movement. Brainstorm a category and then stretch it for movement possibilities. Encourage students to think of the shape, size, rhythm, and energy of the words. Break into groups and ask each to make a collage (an assemblage of items glued together) of sounds and movement. Groups can then create a freeze–move–freeze dance and perform. This activity can be followed by an actual visual art collage around the topics danced.

**Mechanical Movements.** Brainstorm things that move in nonorganic ways (e.g., jerky moves of robot or computer). In pairs or small groups, explore moving different body parts at varying levels using mechanical movements.

**Machine Dances.** Create a whole or small group dance based on BEST elements of machines. *Examples:* elevator, escalator, or computer. (See description of "machine" earlier.)

**Insect Dances.** Each student or group chooses an insect to explore through movement. Each performs a freeze–move–freeze dance: Start frozen, do three to five moves, then freeze in a shape. Dances can include movements related to eating, life cycle, environmental changes, and their effects. Coach for variety in using BEST elements.

**Real-Life Sounds.** Brainstorm sounds in categories: body, city, nature, animals, machines, chants, rhymes ("Pease Porridge Hot"), songs ("Row Row Row Your Boat"), and nonsense phrases (e.g., "slip, slap, slop"). Student's names, names of states, cities, work chants ("heave heave ho, yo yo, heave heave ho") are also sources. Explore the rhythm, size, shape, and energy of sounds. Stress original moves that no one else does.

**Inventions Dance.** Use common items such as tissue, boxes, paper clips, ropes, and elastic bands to create a dance of inventions. Movement with the object should be explored, not pantomimed. *Example:* Experiment with ways to move with a tissue using BEST elements.

**States of Water.** Students dance molecular movement in a solid, liquid, or gas. Lead students through small-group explorations to move as if melting, condensing, and evaporating. Explore changing from a solid to a liquid and then to a gas. Use different parts of the body, energy, space, and time. Finally, ask each group to create a freeze–move–freeze dance that shows concepts about molecular movement and structure.

**Animal Movement Exploration.** Students show different animal movements (e.g., different ways to walk, stretch, and sleep). Coach them to show movement of breath, bones, and muscles. Do movements to a count of 10 to increase concentration and focus.

**Endangered Species.** Pick an endangered animal and explore ways it moves and under different circumstances (tired, hungry, scared). Use "what if" questions to explore possibilities. Use children's literature for ideas, such as *The Girl Who Loved Wild Horses* for horse actions.

**Heartbeat.** Ask students to feel their own heartbeats. Show them how to take a pulse. In the classroom space, direct students to move to their own heartbeats using a variety of shapes and moves. Ask "what if" questions: "You got really scared? Tired?"

**Chambers of the Heart.** Do after studying circulation. Break into small groups to create the pathway of the blood using movement. Have each person in the group share a movement related to respiration/circulation such as movement of the diaphragm or pulse of blood through arteries,. Remind students that respiration and circulation are continuous, but their dance needs a clear beginning, middle, and end. Pass out red scarves to represent oxygen and blue for carbon dioxide in the blood. Give the students time for practice and then have each group present.

**Body Painting.** Pretend each body part is a paintbrush and explore a variety of brushstrokes (e.g., broad and sweeping, quick and short, slow and thick). *Variation:* Explore movements associated with any career.

**Bird Flight.** Groups create a dance based on different types of bird flight. Include different formations (space and pathway) birds use, changes in speed and level, and changes in leaders. Think about different body parts. Dances should have a beginning, middle, and end.

**Weather Dance.** Students are frozen in a shape. Weather changes are announced by narrator, and students respond by changing levels and shapes for snow, light rain, and raging hailstorm. Begin by restricting movement to one spot and then move to locomotor. *Variation:* Convert to a relay dance in which all start frozen and then begin to move, one at a time, until all are moving. Then reverse the action. This works well if the weather event starts small and slow, escalates, then slows and stops.

**Art Alive.** Make action come to life from a painting by creating a freeze–move–freeze dance that explores concepts of gravity, balance, momentum, muscles, and use of light and shade. For example, use "fighting" art like *Dempsey and Firpo* or *Stag at Sharkey's* by artist George Bellows.

**Life Cycle.** Students dance each phase of the life cycle of an animal or plant separately by using BEST elements. After each phase, have them put it together in a dance. Stress that movements can convey feelings. Sounds can be added.

**Constellations.** Groups form frozen shapes of constellations. Small groups then move across night sky to night sounds. *Variation:* Small groups rotate in and out of the "stage" space or come in low, move to high formation, and back to low across the night sky.

**Horse Dancing (from Todd Lyon, Horse Trainer).** Invite a horse trainer to speak and demonstrate the commands and moves horses are taught (e.g., Tennessee Walkers). View a video, if possible, and discuss horse "dance" routines using BEST elements. Create a chart that lists special vocabulary (e.g., *trot, gallop, canter, pace*).

# Social Studies Focus

**Social Studies Standards.** All standards can be accessed at the National Council for the Social Studies (NCSS) website (www.socialstudies.org).

**Dance Possibilities.** Ready Reference 11.3 uses BEST elements to give ideas for dance possibilities in social studies.

**The Feel of Freedom.** Help students understand the concept of freedom by exploring free-flowing versus confined movements. Coach students to imagine a leaf swept up by the wind and use their bodies to show different movements that are light and airy. Explore movements abstracted from other images such as wind blowing through the hair. Next explore confined movements by using images such as being in a cage. Debrief by asking the different emotions for each. *Extension:* Students work individually or in groups to create contrast dances or freedom dances using criteria from Ready Reference 10.13. *Resource:* Show video of Isadora Duncan's style.

**Real-Life Rituals.** Brainstorm movement in life (e.g., greetings, farewells). Divide into pairs and portray each in various ways using different body parts, moves, steps, space, energy, and time.

**Get to Work.** Brainstorm ways people work: picking, washing, sweeping, raking, fixing. Each person or small group creates a work dance based on a real or imaginary prop associated with work (e.g., broom) and moves in creative ways. Music can be added. Dance should have a beginning, middle, and end.

**Trio Community Dances.** Trios form and each member develops a shape and moves using a community concept or problem (e.g., loneliness, sharing). Members teach their part to their group. The final dance consists of members doing the dances of all members in a sequence.

**Ceremonies.** Invent a ceremony related to daily life within the classroom. Create a dance to accompany it and use high, medium, and low levels in the dance, such as a start-the-day ceremony.

**Military Moves.** Research military moves used in different countries (e.g., pivot, straight-leg Nazi march). Learn terms and moves such as left flank, right, center, offense, and defense (Joyce, 1994).

**Magic Wand.** Display a full-length portrait such as a narrative scene from history with several figures in it. Students assume figures' positions. When touched by a magic wand, they move in ways the figure might move. Coach them to become conscious of how to bend and walk, the use of curved and straight lines, and positive and negative space. Leader can add emotions and motives: "Move as if you are in a hurry."

**Country or State.** Students show "terrain" using changes in levels as narrator describes a tour of a place. Students can also show the size of the state or country in relation to other countries or states as leader calls them, for example, Texas versus Rhode Island. *Variation:* Students show what they know about a place (products, industries, climate, or plant life) by interacting with them through movements and imagination.

**Create a Folk Dance.** Select a folk song, such as "Home on the Range," and ask groups to create movements for one line. Distinguish between pantomime and dance by focusing on BEST elements (Ready Reference 10.2) to explore possibilities. Sing the song and each group teaches its dance sentence.

**Historical Event.** Brainstorm movements that would have been part of a special event such as the signing of the Declaration of Independence. Do in slow motion, changing rhythm and space. Create the mood of the moment with your body.

**Holiday and Season Dances.** Brainstorm movement qualities of Halloween characters (stiff movements of a skeleton) or create a "giving" dance for Thanksgiving (focus on rituals and feasts), or "loving shapes" to rhythms for Valentine's Day. Spring dances can focus on rising and stretching and other growing movements.

**Current Events Dances.** Use teachable moments and brainstorm movement possibilities. For example, the Olympic Games or national elections can inspire sports dances or dances related to the opening or closing event.

**Foreign Language.** Dance terminology can be an entrée into a culture or country study. For example, ballet was born in Italy, but grew up in France so its "language" is French: *plie* means "to bend" (root for pliers) and *revele* means "to rise." *Pas de chat* means "step of the cat" (think of when ballerinas shake their toes).

**Folktale Dance.** Focus on an event in a folktale. For example, for Gag's *Millions of Cats*, consider dance shapes and sizes cats might have taken when the old man found them.

**Sports Dance.** Create dances using sports moves. Ask students to plan warm-ups and then move into motions of the actual game. Choose music to go with the movements and organize final explorations into a freeze–move–freeze dance.

**Folk and Ethnic Dances.** Discuss different ways dances have been used through history (ceremonies, prayers, celebrations)

---

## Ready Reference 11.3 Social Studies Movement Possibilities

- Brainstorm and then explore BEST dance elements related to economic development, citizenship, communities, cultures and diversity, customs, directions, global understanding, governments, holidays, land and water formations, legends, occupations, housing, population density, rituals, and transportation

- Everyday actions (cook, wash)
- Map skills and geography
- Social interactions (sharing, cooperation, respect, trust)
- Physical environment (e.g., use of natural resources)
- Thinking skills: cause and effect, sequencing, gathering data, discovering relationships, making judgments

and how forms of dance have evolved, using common movements for expressive purposes. View a whole dance or steps from another culture or time period. Discuss what is represented (rituals for marriage, weather, seasons).

Folk dances are usually appropriate for upper primary and intermediate students. Begin with short dances based on a step such as walk in time to music and walk in a circle. Horahs and kolas of the Middle East are basically a series of steps and variations on the steps performed without partners in a circle. Some demand challenging footwork. Common dances include the conga (Cuba), polka (Bohemia), bolero (Spain), tango (Argentina), merengue (Dominican Republic), cachucha (Spain), la raspa (Mexico), and mazurka (Poland) (see Ready Reference 10.5).

When teaching traditional dance steps, it helps to use a "I do, we do, you do" sequence: All face the same direction. Show the whole dance, then practice in unison until all have the basics. Involve children in identifying step components and then join steps to create a whole work or even a new step. Steps do need to be mastered before doing dance figures in which they are to be used. Mix up partners frequently so no one feels "stuck." (This process deviates from total teacher direction requiring only student imitation.)

*Variation:* Create original dances around the same topics. For example, an Irish jig. First play Irish folk tunes and/or show a video (e.g., *Riverdance*). Ask open questions about the BEST elements and the feel of the dance. Group students to choreograph their own jig with focus on feet and legs. Hands are held behind the back. Encourage them to kick to the beat, but create new steps, turns, and so forth.

## Colonial America.
Watch or invite a guest to teach one these dances popular during colonial times. Ask students about what each dance shows about the time period: Scottish reel, six-hand reel, Malbrouk cotillion, and London Bridge.

## Global Issues Dance.
Brainstorm current problems from around the world (e.g., poverty, racism, global warming, genocide). Groups research the issue and then show their understanding by creating a three-part dance (freeze, move, freeze) to show key points about the issue.

## Cultural Dance.
View videos of different dances available on the Internet, such as YouTube Look for folk dances (e.g., Andalusian Spanish flamenco and the Romanian hora). Ask students to notice specific BEST elements in each dance and hypothesize what is being communicated. Focus on the structure of the dance (beginning, middle, end), what is repeated, and more. Example video sources include www.youtube.com/watch?v=AwFipMozFeg and www.folkmootusa.org/.

# Literacy: Reading and Language Arts Focus

## Literacy/Literature Standards.
All standards can be accessed at the National Council of the Teachers of English (NCTE) and the International Reading Association (IRA) websites (www.ncte.org or www.ira.org).

## Phonics Shapes.
Ask students to make the following:

- Soft shapes for soft *c* and *g* words and hard shapes for hard *c* and *g* (e.g., *city, giraffe, cat, go, gone*).
- Sustained movements for vowels, which can be held continuously. *Example:* "Make your body long or short depending on the sound you hear in *hat, hate* and *cot, coat*. Vowel digraphs can be shown in pairs with one person becoming "silent."
- Bound moves for consonants that make "stop" sounds (*b, p, t,* hard *c, k, d,* hard *g, j, v*) and sustained for consonants such as *s, l, r, m,* and *n.* For consonant blends, partner to show blending.

## Letters of the Alphabet.
Pairs make letters using high, medium, and low levels. Stress original ideas and ask students to explain their interpretations. *Variation:* Students make a shape of an object that starts with the letter. Change levels and speeds.

## Rhyming Words.
Give a spelling pattern (*-ack, -ick, -ot, -eek, -op*). Read a poem that contains the pattern or read a list of words, some with the target. When students hear a word that rhymes with the pattern, they do a creative movement or make different shapes. *Suggestion:* Rehearse possibilities. Post chart of words, such as *bend, twist, reach,* and *push out,* to extend thinking.

## Syllables.
Ask students to change BEST dance elements according to number of syllables. Say words aloud. For example, "Hippopotamus has five syllables so make five shapes as I say each syllable." Vary the elements (e.g., time, energy) during word repetitions.

## Spelling.
Teacher gives a word and students spell it by moving in a floor pattern to "write it" using a chosen pathway to shape the letters. *Variation:* Pairs call words to each other.

## Antonyms.
Brainstorm movement words and opposites, such as smooth-jerky, tight-loose. Then (1) call a word and students do it at different levels and speeds, (2) call a word and students do its opposite, or (3) partner doing the word and the other its opposite. Use with different levels, qualities, and tempo.

## AB Antonym Dances.
Brainstorm movement antonyms (e.g., high-low, fast-slow, smooth-jagged, left-right). Next, guide exploration of meanings of word pairs using BEST elements. For example, "Show me fast with your foot, hand, and head." Small groups then choreograph an AB dance using one pair of antonyms: A = a movement phrase or sentence with the first word, and B = the second word (should show contrast with section A in as many ways as possible). Perform dances with audience/class giving "what worked" comments, afterwards.

## Word a Day.
Pick a movement word. Students squeeze the word for possible meanings by exploring it through movement and finding synonyms and related words (e.g., jump-bound, vault).

## Word Walls and Webs.
Develop vocabulary through movement by asking students to look for action and movement words in their reading. Put up a large sheet of paper. Ask students to add to the dance word wall web. At any point, these words can then be used for movement (e.g., slither, sneak, ambulate, dodge, dragged, plod, saunter, amble, trot). *Variation:* Make a dance word collage.

**Shapes Vocabulary.** Explain that in dance, the word *shape* is not limited to circle, square, or other. It refers to a physical design made with the body that can be held still—like a sculpture. Count to four and ask students to go from standing to a low level shape (close to the ground). Hold. Do split audience to observe and comment. Next, use a 4 count to go from the low level shape to a high level shape, but add an element of balance. Repeat at a middle level. *Variations:* Do dance echo. Or, instead of moving smoothly from shape to shape, try staccato movements or using different energy. Brainstorm other ways to move in and out of the shapes. Describe the shapes: narrow/wide? symmetrical/assymetrical? off-balance/centered?

**Compare and Contrast.** Contrast movements such as strong–light, tight–loose, explosive–smooth, up–down, and wide–narrow by asking students to jump all these ways. Compare ways to do the same move: walk, stride, pace, shuffle.

**Cause-Effect.** Pairs face each other. One is the cause and the other is the effect. Cause moves and the effect must respond appropriately (e.g., if cause steps forward, effect must move to keep from being stepped on). Encourage creative effect responses.

**Classification.** Call out a category to classify a movement. Students explore all they can do in that category (e.g., quick at low level, quick bending, quick twisting, quick reaching). *Variation:* Students take turns demonstrating three different moves or actions and the group must figure out what all have in common.

**Adverb Dance.** Explore adverbs by asking students to move different ways. For example, do locomotor/nonlocomotor moves/steps merrily, sadly). Web words from a story, put on cards, and explore different ways (e.g., run slowly, crawl sneakily). Combine into dances, with a beginning, middle, and end, about a chapter or event in a story.

**Parts of Speech Dance.** Brainstorm words in categories: verbs, adverbs, and prepositions. Explore the list with different body parts. *Example:* "Stretch strongly with your hand; twist foot slowly behind leg." Distribute cards to each student: one verb card, one adverb card, and one preposition card. Students form trios. Students discuss ways their nine cards might be combined to create a dance with a beginning, middle, and end. They may choose dance in unison, individually, or other. Coach as they rehearse, then groups perform for the class. Audience gives constructive feedback after each about the clarity and artistry.

**Gestures.** Brainstorm everyday nonverbal communication used to greet or respond (e.g., wave, beckon, stop). Explore how to do these different ways (e.g., fast, slow, different body parts, levels).

**Story Tableau.** Small groups use body shape and space to show a story concept (e.g., grief, celebration, loneliness). Freeze in the shape. On signal, each person unfreezes and does moves to a count (e.g., count of three).

**Talking Dance.** Students create a freeze–move–freeze dance, but actually talk aloud as they dance, changing voice to match movements. For example, "low level, low level, flick fingers, flick toes, jump jump, twirl, high level, punch, shrink, collapse."

**Dance a Story.** Stories abound with characters and situations with movement potential. To be dance, not drama, only the essence of the character or situation is used. A literal movement translation results in pantomime (drama), not dance. Stories can be danced or pantomimed; both call for targeting an event or image, rather than a whole story. This example combines dance and drama based on McCulley's *Mirette on a High Wire.* Put masking tape on the floor. Groups take turns balancing in different ways: one foot, tiptoes along the line, with dance movements exploration. Those waiting pantomime the audience members as they watch and react.

**Character Dance.** Any story character can be explored through movement by considering ways a character might move. For example, how would Wilbur in *Charlotte's Web* move if he was happy? Hungry? Afraid? Tired? How is his movement different from Charlotte's or Templeton's? How does body shape show something about a character? On signal, students dance in character. Divide the class in half so one group can observe and comment. Reverse. *Example:* Do three moves Charlotte might use in a spider dance.

**Character Walk.** Each student walks around the room as a famous person or character, varying normal level, posture, rhythm, gate, and so forth. When leader says "change," each person tries another walk variation.

**Words A–Z.** Start a list of interesting words that can be moved. Invite students to find words to add. Make this a daily movement routine. *Examples:* bubble, congeal, decay, evaporate, expand, flicker, melt, ooze, simmer, shrivel, swirl. *Extension:* Group to create short dances, for example, antonym dances (expand-shrink), that explore ways to show they understand the concepts using BEST elements.

**Character Traits.** Do in small groups. Choose a literary character and identify the personality traits (bright, cheerful, sad, depressed, ruthless, gentle, and so forth). Invent several movement phrases that express the traits. Then decide how the character changed by the end of the book. Choreograph several more phrases that express the changes. Students then connect the movement phrases to create a short dance that expresses the transformation.

**Poem Dances.** Write individual or collaborative movement poems and then dance them. *Example:* Cinquain = Title plus five lines about movement. Title = Working

Must Dos

Sweep, Lift, Dust
Getting more and more tired
Carry, Push, Pull
Collapse

**Theme Dance.** Any theme from a poem or book can be danced by first brainstorming ways to express the theme with body parts, movements, energy, and use of space and time. For example, the theme "Courage comes out of fear," can be danced in a frozen shape, movements, and frozen shape (three-part dance) planned and performed by small groups that each present a very different interpretation.

**Key Topic Dance.** Brainstorm important words or topics in a poem or book. Next, list web movements, shapes, levels, energy, and so forth that could be used to convey the topic. Give small groups the choice of a topic or word to plan a dance or a series of movements to show it.

**Dance Poetry.** Read a poem about dance and ask students to listen for movement possibilities. For example, encourage showing different ways to use the body and space to express the joy of dance in these poems: "Dancing Pants," "Dancin' in the Rain," and "Danny O'Dare," by Shel Silverstein. Make poem charts of dance poems for repeat dancing.

**Poetry in Motion.** Read aloud a poem first for enjoyment, then ask students to interpret movement as the poem is reread. Narrate movement or excerpt words and sentences for students to speak and dance. Music or percussion instruments can be used to highlight poem action. Example poems are "Push Button" by Shel Silverstein, "Jump or Jiggle" by Evelyn Beyer, "The Swing" by Robert Louis Stevenson, and "Jump-Jump-Jump" by Kate Greenaway. Jump rope rhymes are also wonderful ways to energize with rhythmic words. See collections such as *Miss Mary Mack and Other Children's Street Rhymes* (Cole) and Booth's *Doctor Knickerbocker and Other Rhymes*.

**Line by Line.** Read aloud a poem. Give each student or group a line to explore the movement possibilities within (e.g., rhythm of the words, emotions, images). Encourage more than pantomiming. The poetry can then be danced line by line as a narrator reads, or groups can plan to perform just one line.

**Write about a Dance.** After any dance or creative movement, students write about what they did and felt. The BEST elements give writing focus. The writing can be in the form of a story, informational piece, or a poem (Ready Reference 5.2) about the dance. Here is a diamante based on observed shapes.

Shapes
Round Angled
Changing Size and Levels
Dance Shapes Show Feelings
Frozen Moving Forms
Pointed Curvy
Shapes

**Story Tension.** Discuss tension in a story and how characters go about relieving it. Ask, "What point is the climax or most intense part?" Students then show with the body the tension.

**Characters Alive!** Use a painting or picture from a book with several characters in it. Groups become the characters by posing as a frozen picture. They then "come alive" and do three dance moves consistent with the characters. Coach students to do locomotor moves and use low, medium, and high levels. Finally, they return to original frozen positions.

## Math Focus

**Math Standards.** All standards can be accessed at the National Council of Teachers of Mathematics (NCTM) website (www.nctm.org).

**Math/Dance Connection.** Math is basically the study of quantitative relationships. Dance is also concerned with relationships among shape, time, and size. Through dance, students can come to understand basic math concepts such as add, subtract, divide, and duration (second or minute). Higher level math skills require sequential thinking, examining situations for important details and patterns. Dance also involves these types of thinking, so dance and math can reinforce one another. Planning Page 11.4 shows a dance-based math plan.

**Two Guys Dancing Math.** This dance duo does school performances and residencies (one "guy" is a college professor). Check out their 2001 book *Math Dance*, by Karl Schaffer and Erik Stern (www.mathdance.org; published by MoveSpeakSpin ).

**Math Movement Possibilities.** Brainstorm moves in math, including estimating, adding, multiplying, dividing, patterns, geometric shapes, fractions, lines, curves, and subtracting. Give each group one concept. Each decides at least three different ways to show their math concept through movement.

**Geometric Shapes.** Everyone walks around filling up the space. When a leader calls a shape, all freeze in that shape (circle, triangle, square). Leader gives feedback for unusual ideas (use of energy or space). *Variation:* Students partner to make the shape. Do also with letters of the alphabet.

**Body Architecture.** Explore geometric shapes and principles of physics by finding body postures that represent arches, columns, cantilevers, domes, posts and beams, vaults, and trusses used in buildings. Relate to school building, homes, and local buildings.

**Telling Time.** Use masking tape to make a large clock on the floor. Children move around in the 12 hour spaces by stretching arms to a person in the middle of the clock as the teacher calls a time. Explore different times: recess time and lunch time and ways to move around (fast, slow, hop, slide).

**Shape Dance.** Many folk dances are done in a circle, square, or line. Invite a guest to teach one and relate it to the math concept. Challenge students to find other math ideas in the dance (e.g., counting, parallel lines, sequencing—first, second, third).

**Body Composition.** Create groups of three to five. Explain that the goal is to create a group composition using their bodies to show these math concepts: triangles, planes, diagonals, circles, among others. Groups are to explore diverse positions and shapes and choose one in which to freeze. Each group presents and the audience members discuss what they see. *Extension:* Take digital photographs of each freeze and display with student captions about the math concept.

**Get the Facts!** Call out math problems to solve by jumping, hopping, or walking along a number line. Give a different way to move each time (fast, slow, low, halting, flowing). Sounds, chants, and instruments can be added.

**Angles and Degrees.** Tape a large rectangle on the floor so that every student can stand on the tape. Give a series of directions related to the rectangle: "Take three straight forward steps in.

◆ **Planning Page 11.4**

## Dance and Math (Third Grade)

*Two-Pronged Focus:* (1) fractions and problem solving;
(2) dance elements: body shapes, levels, and choreography
*Dance Standards:* See Ready Reference 10.7.
*Student Objectives:* Students will:

1. Use high, middle, and low levels and body shapes that are curved, straight, angular, and twisted to show (1) equivalent fractions, and (2) fractional parts of wholes and sets that have been divided into as many as 16 parts.
2. Maintain focus.
3. Work cooperatively in groups.

*Materials:* Two charts, fraction problem cards
*Teaching Procedure:* The teacher will: (S = students)

### Introduction

1. Signal for S to group into regularly assigned squads. Remind students about posted rules.
2. Tell objectives of lesson for fractions and dance.
3. Play inspirational music and do warm-up routine.

### Development

1. Show charts of four body shapes and three levels. With each S in personal space, call a shape and level in which to freeze (e.g., curved low or straight high).
2. Show fraction chart to review: whole, 1/2, 1/3, 1/4, 1/5, 1/8, 1/16. Ask S to show each (e.g., show 1/2 by dividing into two groups). Do for each, letting S figure out how to arrange themselves.
3. Ask about equivalent fractions (review from previous lesson). Give examples: 1/2 = 2/4. Group to work in squads to show a fraction problem through dance. Ask how they could create a three-part dance for 1/2 transforming to 2/4 starting with frozen shapes/levels, adding movements, and then ending with a frozen shape. Brainstorm and try their ideas.
4. Break into squads and give each a fraction problem card.
5. Circulate and give feedback as S work.

### Conclusion
*Performances*

1. Divide class so half observes while others dance.
2. Audience observes to figure out fraction problem.
3. Audience gives feedback on what worked.
4. Reverse groups and repeat.
5. Ask what they learned about dance and fractions.

### Assessment and Evaluation

1. Teachers/self/peer complete evaluation checklist with criteria (objectives).
2. Use from "clear" to "not present" based.
3. Photograph students to aid assessment.

*Source:* Mr. Crabb and Mrs. Peterson, Lady's Island Elementary School, Beaufort, South Carolina.

---

Now step back to the perimeter. Turn 45 degrees right. Stick out your left arm. What's that angle? (acute) Face forward on the perimeter. Turn 90 degrees left. Stick out your left arm. What is the angle from the tape? (right) Corner people, change positions. What does the line they are walking do to the rectangle? (makes two triangles) How could we show 180 degrees? 360 degrees?"

**Basic Math.** Form small groups to practice these concepts: addition, subtraction, multiplication, division, geometry, area, volume. Leader creates a phrase of three moves. Each small group then changes the phrase by adding on, subtracting from it, multiplying it, or dividing it. Rehearse and perform with audience feedback.

**Geometric Shapes.** In personal spaces each student shows the following as announced: circles, arcs, line segments, diamonds, parallel lines, right angles.

**Octet Dance.** Form groups of eight. Students number themselves: Student 1 creates a movement/shape and teaches it to the group; student 2 creates a movement and "adds" it to student 1's movement, then all perform. Student 3 adds on to students 2 and 1, and so forth. The group then choreographs a composition by choosing a beginning shape or entrance (one dancer enters, add another, add another). The middle consists of the performance of movements 1–8, or performance of 1, 1-2, 1-2-3, etc. The group will also create an ending.

**Math Exploration.** Students sit in personal space with legs in a diamond-shaped position (a symmetrical shape, body perpendicular to the floor, creating right angles, etc.). Using an upbeat 4\4 musical selection, "arc" the torso forward eight counts, sideward eight counts, backward eight counts, and then the other side eight counts. Divide the counts by 2 = 4 counts to each side; divide by 2 = 2 counts to each side; divide by 2 = 1 count to each direction. Change the legs to a parallel shape straight out in front of the body and repeat the directional and divisional combinations. Change the leg position to create a right angle with the legs on the floor and repeat the directions.

**Math Pathways.** Students create a movement phrase of 48 counts that travels along the pathway. Add other criteria as desired, such as phrase must include two changes in levels (low, middle, high), four different locomotor movements, two different shapes (not including beginning and ending shape), and 48 counts.

**Perimeter Dances.** Partner students to sequence movements that create to a rectangle (i.e., four slides to right, two zigzag jumps back, two slides left, two zigzag jumps forward). Next, figure out the perimeter of the dance space to be used. Rehearse and perform.

**Latin Perimeter Dance.** Using forward, back, and lateral dance steps, students create a Samba that results in a square or rectangle. They then calculate the perimeter and area of their dances. *Extension:* Draw and calculate the perimeter of their dance.

**Math Glue.** Everyone moves around in slow motion. Teacher says "glue 2" and students find others to stick to in that number (everyone must keep moving in slow motion). Teacher then calls "unstick" and continues with a new number.

**Twos and Threes.** Teach number groups by calling out a way to move and giving the pattern. For example, "Hop in twos with a pause after the two hops." Make into dances of moves grouped into twos and threes.

**Angle Dance.** Students create a dance that illustrates angles (right, oblique). Each dance should have a beginning, middle, and end and can be locomotor or nonlocomotor. Use freeze–move–freeze form.

**Math Dance.** Students choreograph a dance to teach to others by creating instructions in math terms. For example, to do the "math hop," take two steps forward, slide right, hold for four counts, and hop three times.

**Number Shapes.** Teacher signals and students make their bodies into shapes of numbers. They may need to work together. Challenge them to make these shapes combine with time, space, and force.

# IV. Multiarts Focus: Dance Integrated with Other Arts

This book focuses on integrating the arts with core curricular areas. Yet, this is not the only important integration plan. The arts have much in common with one another and should be used in concert to work toward both academic and arts standards. It is also important to integrate the arts with each other to magnify the unique impact the arts can have, as described in Chapter 1 (Ready Reference 1.4).

**Art Dance Connection.** Much of visual art involves movement (e.g., draw, paint) and art and dance possess parallel elements such as line and shape. Dance can awaken the kinesthetic sense and put feelings into motion. Students can dance a painting or paint the dances they create. The kinesthetic center of dance can motivate children to want to move. The need to express through movement can extend to scribbles, drawing, and painting. Relate dance elements to other art forms and the language arts to make connections and develop thinking structures. For example, explore shape in art and dance by painting to music on big paper. Find line, pattern, rhythm, and images expressed in art, music, and so forth. Movement possibilities include explorations of lines, shapes, and directions.

**Choreograph to Music.** Play a piece of music and ask students to listen closely to the tempo, mood, and rhythm. Discuss and repeat listening. Brainstorm ways to show the important parts of the music with dance. As a whole or in groups, create a dance to go with the music. Devise a symbol system to note how to perform the dance (e.g., circles, lines, and squares to show movements).

**Dynamics!** Use a drum, finger cymbals, and other percussion instruments. Ask students to change the size of body actions according to the sound (e.g., loud makes large movements). Use a variety of instruments to help students understand how timbre can change and still have a loud or soft sound.

**Body Melody Match.** Select a familiar song. Explain that the body may show melodic pattern. As children sing or listen, ask them to move up or down in a space to illustrate the shape of the melody.

**Sing with Your Hands.** Post and teach the Kodaly hand signs to add kinesthetics to hearing the scale. See Chapter 12 for the hand movements called Curwen signs that show the scale from "do" up.

**Sign Language.** Teach songs in sign language or add signs to any song. See Riekehof's (1978) *The Joy of Signing*.

**Art in Motion.** Show art with physical motion in it. Discuss how motion is shown and why a particular step is sometimes "frozen" by the artist (e.g., "Which part of a sneeze would you depict?"). Recreate the artwork as a dance. Freeze as shown, move to a count, and freeze again. *Variation:* Create dances that show what happened before and after the moment in the artwork.

**Sculpture or Architecture Dances.** Display pieces of sculpture or pictures of buildings or furniture. Ask about space, curves, and movements and how each might move if it came to life. Ask students to show the size, energy, and flow with their bodies.

**Artists that Move.** Set up a station with art books or assign students to locate art that includes movement (e.g., Matisse and Degas). Discuss or write journal entries about how artists show movement through line, shape of body, and use of space.

**Dance a Painting.** Display a print and ask students to brainstorm shapes, movements, and emotions (note the word *motion* in this word). Direct attention to the foreground, middle ground, and background in subjects such as landscape, seascape, and still life. Divide into groups. Each decides a way to dance the painting, using a beginning–middle–end structure. The goal is not to pantomime but stretch for ideas: "What movements came before this moment in the art, during, and after? What is just outside the subject matter (e.g., other people, movements)?" After students prepare, take turns presenting. Background or mood music can be added.

**Paint a Dance.** Use large paper to capture a dance after doing it. This can begin on a small scale with just painting or drawing certain movements (e.g., curved lines, circles, shaking, turning).

**Negative and Positive Space.** On signal, students make body shapes. Start with "fixed spot" shapes before locomotor. Stress the use of different levels. At freeze signal, all stop and look for "holes" in people's body shapes, made with arms, legs, or fingers. Ask students to squint to see hole shapes—the negative space. *Variation:* Partner with another student. Person A makes a shape with holes (negative space) in it, and person B then makes a shape that interacts with the negative space.

**Emotion or Color Dance.** Make cards with emotions (pictures or words) or colors. Groups choose three cards and put them in an order (beginning, middle, end) to create a dance. Encourage students to repeat actions and use variety. Dances can be accompanied with readings of color poems such as those in O'Neill's *Hailstones and Halibut Bones.* Appropriate "emotion" music can be used, too.

## Teacher Spotlight
### From Ballet to Fifth Grade

Libba Allen is an animated woman who has been teaching at Ashley River Creative Arts for more than 20 years. She has seen the dream of the school's first principal, Rose Maree Myers, grow into a reality.

Ms. Allen, who now teaches fifth grade, was initially hired because of her background in ballet. "Rose Maree thought ballet had given me discipline. She is a very detail-oriented person, and she convinced us we could do it."

The "it" that Ms. Allen refers to is arts integration. "This approach gives students an outlet to express themselves," she says. She describes examples such as using pictographs in math and writing based on student photographs or art stimuli. Her students keep science journals in which they draw their observations about things like the terrarium/aquarium in her room.

Ms. Allen is particularly proud of the photography lab at ARCA, constructed from a $50,000 grant. The grant also provided professional development for teachers to learn photographic skills.

Like other teachers at arts-based schools, Ms. Allen acknowledges that considerable time is involved in planning for arts integration. The students are "out" for 80 minutes a day, however, so teachers have a good block of planning time.

It is worth it? "All students can excel!" Ms. Allen exclaims passionately. "The arts give them the expressive tools to do so." And she had the discipline from ballet to make it happen. ✹

## Conclusion

*An ulcer is an unkissed imagination taking its revenge for having been jilted. It is an unwritten poem, it's an undanced dance, it's an unpainted watercolor. It is a declaration that a clear spring of joy has not been tapped and that it must break through muddling on its own.* (John Ciardi, poet)

This chapter is a compendium of starter ideas to use in dance integration. These seed strategies can be adapted and developed to create integrated lessons for science, social studies, math, and literacy lessons. Used in combination with the AI building blocks explained in Chapter 10, these strategies can get the curriculum *moving* in the right direction.

### Teachers as Leaders: AI Advocacy

Attend a school board meeting and sign up to speak under the "hearing of the public" agenda item. Plan to read a 5-minute statement about reasons why dance should be integrated throughout the curriculum. Try to get the audience to rethink what dance is and consider its many purposes. Emphasize connections to problem solving, thinking, real life, and literacy.

---

**PEARSON**
**myeducationlab**

Go to the Activities and Applications section for Topic *Strategies for Teaching* at MyEducationLab for your course and complete the video activities entitled "Using Dance Warm Up for Creative Problem Solving", "Using Visual Art, Drama, and Songs to Teach Science."

Go to the Book Specific Resources section in the MyEducationLab for your course, select your book and Chapter 11 to view the Questions to Guide Reading and Response Options for this chapter.

## Resources

See Appendix for further study, including more websites.

### Dance Activity Books

Alison, L. (1992). *A handbook of creative dance and drama.* Portsmouth, NH: Heinemann.

Bennett, J. P. (2006). *Rhythmic activities and dance.* Champaign, IL: Human Kinetics.

Berthoz, A. (2002). *The brain's sense of movement.* Cambridge, MA: Harvard University Press.

Brehm, M. (2007). *Creative dance for learning: The kinesthetic link.* New York: McGraw Hill.

Gilbert, A. (1992). *Creative dance for all ages.* Reston, VA: National Dance Association.

Gilbert, A. (2002). *Teaching the 3 R's: Through movement experiences.* Retson, VA: National Dance Association.

Hanna, J. (1999). *Partnering dance and education: Intelligent moves for changing times.* Champaign, IL Human Kinetics.

Joyce, M. (1994). *First steps in teaching creative dance to children* (3rd ed.). Mountain View, CA: Mayfield.

Landalf, H. (1997). *Moving the earth: Teaching earth science through movement for grades 3–6.* Lye, NH: Smith & Kraus.

Malam, J. (2002). *Song and dance.* New York: Franklin Watts.

McGreevy-Nichols, S. (2004). *Building dances: A guide to putting movements together.* Reston, VA: Human Kinetics.

Pica, R. (2006). *Moving and learning across the curriculum.* Albany, NY: Delmar Cengage Learning.

Rowen, B. (1994). *Dance and grow: Developmental dance activities for three-through eight-year-olds.* Pennington, NJ: Princeton Book.

Stinson, S. (1988). *Dance for young children: Finding the magic in movement.* Reston, VA: American Alliance for Health, Physical Education, Recreation and Dance.

**Dance and Movement**

# 12 Integrating Music Throughout the Curriculum

*I have a real heartburn for those who somehow believe that there is a disconnect between arts and education and, quote, "real education," because I would contend that arts education is Real Education, and it's a critical part of the other disciplines.* (Mike Huckabee, governor of Arkansas)

## Overview

This chapter outlines basics about the meaningful integration of music. The practices of several classroom teachers are profiled in light of the 10 AI building blocks. Block I explains reasons for integrating music, which are used to construct a philosophy. Block II describes the music literacy classroom teachers need to start integration, and Blocks III through X outline *how* to implement full integration with attention to planning, teaching, assessing, differentiation, setting up the classroom, establishing routines, and partnering with music specialists. Music-based children's literature is given special attention in Block V.

## Introduction: Our Insatiable Appetite for Music

*Where words leave off, music begins.* (Heinrich Heine)

At Indiana University, a mycology professor assigns song writing for students to summarize learning about fungus. A Stanford University biology instructor, Tom McFadden, teaches about genetics with raps like "Regulatin' Genes" (www.youtube.com/watch?v=9k_oKK4Teco). These educators are serious about their content. They've discovered that using music as a teaching tool can cause students to get deep into difficult subject matter. This is not new news, of course, artists, inventors, and scientists who have long used music to boost thinking—especially to jump-start creative problem solving.

Music fires up cognition, and conveys unforgettable messages through powerful patterns. Thinking is coupled with emotion as music kindles vivid feelings and images. We experience feelings of grandeur listening to Baroque music (e.g., Bach or Vivaldi) and dreamy images from Chopin and other Romantic composers.

Then there is the music that exudes a passion that nearly hurts, from Puccini's operas to Manilow's melodies. Not to be minimized are the physical effects of music. Sousa and Marsalis energize us to march, tap, sway, and smile. Music makes the drudgery of exercise palatable. Time flies by as the music plays on.

The human aesthetic appetite for music is insatiable and outside of school music is totally integrated into our lives. Joggers run with iPods, music is piped throughout airports, and CD players are basic car equipment. Lawyers sing in their offices while workers sing in farm fields. Nurses whistle in hospital halls, musicians play on street corners, and families gather to sing "Happy Birthday" and watch *American Idol*. Even greeting cards now come with a computer chip. Open the card and the music bursts forth.

Boosted by multiple intelligences theory and growing research that connects music and learning, classroom teachers have joined in. They now use all styles of music from Mozart to nature sounds to start the day, make transitions, and relax or rouse after lunch. Arts integration goes further to leverage the motivational capacity of music for learning purposes. For example, in the Sweetwater School District, 8 miles from the U.S.-Mexico border, teachers use mariachi music to engage Hispanic students (Brown, 2005). Interest in learning is up and so is attendance at Bugg Elementary (Raleigh, North Carolina) where test scores were once below average. What changed? Students now listen to Gustav Holst's symphonic suite "The Planets" in science and learn about fractions as they study musical notation. Rhythm and other music elements hook and hold students causing learning to soar.

Madeline Grumet (2004) credits such practices with rescuing the arts from "educational cul-de-sacs" where they have been reserved for the rich or talented. AI has made the arts integral to learning. The arts, in turn, have thrown a lifeline to traditional academic disciplines that have often become "dead ends in the flat, dull routines of school that leave students intellectually unchallenged and emotionally disengaged" (p. 50). No art form has more power to cognitively challenge and emotionally engage than music.

Music is being made integral to daily learning in the way it is integral to daily life: to engage, celebrate, unify, comfort, and make ideas memorable. Compelling evidence supports this full integration into the curriculum (see Research Updates that

Bowing away in the Ashley River garden

follow). Jensen (2001) concludes, "If this were a court case, the ruling would be that music is valuable beyond a reasonable doubt" (p. 14). Although the case may be closed on the value of using the arts as meaningful teaching and learning tools, AI is not intended to be the exclusive form in which the arts are experienced. AI acknowledges that students need sequential and comprehensive arts instruction taught by qualified specialists, including music teachers (Burnaford, 2007).

In the opening Classroom Snapshot, Bernadette Chilcote couples the teaching of reading with both a music listening and music creating experience. At Ashley River Creative Arts, students regularly experience this kind of music integration, along with weekly lessons from music teacher Ann Cheek, featured in Chapter 13. In Bernadette's lesson, she uses music strategically to expand vocabulary and reading fluency for the purpose of deepening comprehension. These children are doing the hard work of learning to read, willingly. Music plays a key role in making them want to learn.

# Classroom Snapshot
## Music-Based Literacy

"Criss-cross applesauce!" Ms. Chilcote is on the floor with her first graders. They sit up for a "close listening" to a CD based on *Follow the Drinking Gourd* (Winter, 1988), yesterday's picture book read-aloud. The **lyrics** of the song are today's reading material. Their teacher tells the children to **focus on the voices** to see what they **notice.**

"Listen for how these voices and the **musical instruments** make you feel," she says.

A male and female duet sing, "Follow the Drinking Gourd" (Harris). After the first verse, Ms. C pauses the CD and asks, "What instruments do you hear?" and "How did the music feel?" She waits until many hands are up before she calls on anyone.

"The man's voice is deeper," says a curly-haired boy.

"Her voice is beautiful. Like an angel," says a small girl.

"High-pitched," explains another boy.

"What else did you notice?" she coaches and students guess there is a guitar because of the "strumming" and "plucking."

"Those are great words, *strumming* and *plucking*," Ms. C responds. "**Let's say them** three times like they sound." Tongues vibrate on the /str/ and smack on the plucking. Next she asks them again about the feeling of the song.

"I think they are afraid they'll get caught," a redheaded girl whispers.

"Yes, it feels like it has to be a secret or they'll die," the boy next to her adds.

Ms. C nods to each responder. **She follows up** with "What makes you think that?" and "Why do you think so?" to hold the students accountable for evidence to support conclusions.

The class does a **close listening** to the entire song, and then Ms. C asks how the **song lyrics connect** to the picture book from yesterday. She holds up the cover.

"The book has pictures but no singing," notes a boy.

"The song is in it, though," points out another.

**Show us where,**" Ms. C hands another copy of the book to him, and he flips to a page and points.

"Here," he points to a line that has "follow the drinking gourd in it." "Here, too," he continues and turns the page.

"The song is in the whole book," a girl says emphatically.

Ms. C turns to the back of the book. "What is this?" she asks as she shows the music for the song. Three hands shoot up and she smiles broadly, "John, first, then Lynn and Morgan."

"It's how to play the notes!"

"It's the sheet music—what you read."

"Yeah, I can read these notes on the staff!"

"Wow . . . so we can read words and read notes to make music. Is music another kind of reading?" she asks, and 22 heads bob up and down. She then asks about other books from the social studies unit. Some talk about the "sadness" of the time. One child says that the "world is better without slaves and we all have freedom."

In a version of **repeated reading,** Ms. C distributes copies of the lyrics and the children use their fingers to **follow along** as they do two more **close listenings.** But now they sing along. It is a lot of reading for first graders, but most are on track, especially for the refrain, "Follow the drinking gourd! Follow the drinking gourd. For the old man is a waiting for to carry you to freedom, If you follow the drinking gourd" (Winter, 1988, p. 45).

The lesson ends with Ms. Chilcote explaining how they will be able to show their comprehension of the song using art materials. Students cut the lyrics into verses. She points to a chart on the wall that says, "How to Make Art."

"You'll have lots of **choices** for how you use the art elements to show what you think and feel about the verses," she says.

"I want to make mine blue for sadness," says a girl.

"I'm using brown and black with jaggedness, like for ripped pants and scaredness," explains the girl next to her.

"Everyone will have a different one," their teacher reminds them. "It's important to remember to **use our freedom.**" ⁜

# Arts Integration Building Blocks

In Chapter 3, the 10 AI building blocks were introduced as a scaffold to implement arts integration (see Ready Reference 3.3). The first has to do with *why* arts integration should be implemented (philosophical beliefs based on learning theories and research). Next comes *what* teachers should know (arts literacy) and *how* to plan lessons, create an aesthetic environment, use literature and best teaching practices, design instructional routines, differentiate for diverse learners, assess, and work cooperatively with arts specialists. The building blocks are applied to music in this chapter.

Groundbreaking brain research undergirds Building Block I. Let's review some of the findings before beginning Block I.

## Music and the Brain

There is growing interest in how the arts affect the brain. Music has been a particular focus with accumulating evidence to support "a tight correlation" with academic performance and desirable character traits thought to account for higher test scores (Mauk, 2009). It appears that a music-rich environment creates more complex brain structures. The lesson for teachers is that "every musical [arts] experience that we offer our students affects their brains, bodies and feelings. In short, it changes their minds permanently"(Reimer, 2004, p. 25). Here is why:

**Hardwired for Music.** "By any measure, our brain is a music box (Hotz, 2009, p. A9). The brain is predisposed to detect patterns and sounds. Every child begins life immersed in rhythm, the most basic music element. The steady beat of the mother's heart attunes the baby to patterned sound. Voices, with unique rhythms and timbre, enter the world of the womb. The unborn child physically responds, showing an innate desire to listen and a preference for consonant versus dissonant sounds. Early on, the tiny fetus reacts to phonemes (the smallest sound units in language) such as the percussive consonant sounds of /t/, /p/, and /f/. As the growing child eavesdrops, the brain grows, absorbs, and makes connections (Begley, 2004; Jensen, 2001; Wolfe, 2001). Phonemic awareness will later form spoken language that in turn is the foundation for reading.

**Overlapping Regions.** A review of studies on the Mozart effect (listening to music to increase learning) shows that areas of the brain used for spatial reasoning (mentally visualizing, moving, and relating objects) are also used to process music (Deasy, 2002). Some music brain circuits reside near or overlap somewhat with those used in disciplines such as math (Begley, 2004). Physicist Gordon Shaw, known for research on the Mozart effect, believes music uses many of the same higher brain functions as both science and math (2000). Language and music seem to share certain neural circuits as well. This suggests learning functions in the brain are more integrated than previously thought.

**Whole Brain.** Music is processed in both the left and right hemispheres and activates cognitive, affective, psychomotor, visual, and auditory systems depending on "whether you are reading music, playing an instrument, composing a song, beating out a rhythm or just listening to a melody" (Wolfe, 2001, p. 161). Brain scans show that virtually the entire cortex is active when musicians play. Different areas perform different functions, from directing movement to thinking to feeling to remembering (Weinberger, 1998). Multiple brain sites are synchronized by firing patterns that oscillate across the brain, enhancing efficiency and effectiveness (Jensen, 2000).

Music activates different areas of the brain in musicians and nonmusicians. Which areas are activated depends on what is listened to and for (e.g., melody in the right hemisphere, lyrics in Wernicke's areas, rhythm in Broca's area) (Jensen, 2000).

**Changing Minds.** There is evidence that the younger the child is when music lessons begin, the more brain cortex is developed. In musicians, the corpus callosum nerve bundle that connects hemispheres is enlarged as much as 15 percent (Hotz, 2009). Listening to music for as little as 1 hour per day can cause rewiring of the synapses in the cortex. Different types of music do different things. More complex music (e.g., Mozart's "Sonata for Two Pianos in D Major" may create greater brain "coherence" (Jensen, 2000; Malyarenko et al., 1996). Music also triggers different brain states: harp music for theta (half awake), Muzak and smooth jazz for alpha (relaxes alertness), and upbeat and pop for beta (alert) (Jensen, 2000). Rhythms enhance visualization (e.g., rain forest recording).

**Emotion and Memory.** Music changes emotions by activating areas of the brain that regulate chemicals such as epinephrine, endorphins, and cortisol, which causes the "flight or fight" reaction to an event (Wolfe, 2001). The brain also responds to musical patterns and rhythms, which early humans used to their advantage to store symbolic information (Hotz, 2009). We still use that capacity today to intentionally and unintentionally remember content that is embedded or coupled with music.

---

### Research Update *12.1*    Music Integration in U.S. Schools

- Brighton, Massachusetts. Standardized test scores have risen significantly at the Conservatory Lab Charter School (www.conservatorylab.org/), an average of 10 percentile points in reading and 20 in math by the third year. Substantially more third graders were highly proficient in reading than the district average of 79 percent versus 38 percent, even though students spend less time on reading and more time on music. The correlation between music and test scores increases over time. Literacy-challenged students usually receive tutoring in reading using music (Scripp, 2003; Weissman, 2004).
- Tucson, Arizona Classical music plays all day in hallways to calm and relax students at schools that participate in Opening Minds through the Arts. OMA targets at-risk students. OMA students score significantly higher than non-OMA students on measures of words, pictures, and listening (Kippelen, 2002).
- Chicago, Illinois. At Telpochcalli, a small school with a high proportion of Mexican American students, *corridos*

(story songs) are central to social studies and language arts. Students come to see themselves as musicians as they learn to play corridos on the violin, mandolin, guitar, marimba, and bass. Between 1997 and 2002, the number of students scoring at or above national averages on reading comprehension tripled. Defying trends, the longer students stay at the school the more they gain (Weissman, 2004).
- Lynn, Massachusetts. Ford Elementary now ranks number one in state standardized tests for third-grade reading. This change is attributed to the Learning through Music program for students with low reading and math scores who spend an hour a day reading music and doing computer-enhanced composition work (Scripp, 2003).
- Pawtucket, Rhode Island. First graders involved in a special music program performed significantly better in math and reading than a comparison group without the music (Chan, Ho, & Cheung, 1998).

---

**Website Recommendation.** To track ongoing brain research related to the arts, go to the Dana Foundation website at www.dana.org.

# Building Block I: Philosophy: Why Integrate Music?

*Music was my refuge. I could crawl into the space between the notes and curl my back to loneliness.* (Maya Angelou, in *Gather Together in My Name*)

Beliefs about music integration are justified by brain research, like that previously summarized, along with educational studies that link music and academic achievement. The latter are summarized in Research Updates 12.1 and 12.2. In addition, beliefs also grow out of theories, including multiple intelligences and creative problem solving, outlined in Chapter 2. Accumulated professional experience with music-based practices informs beliefs, as well. Together these sources yield the following reasons to integrate music.

## Music Is a Significant Part of Life

*Alas for those who never sing, but die with their music in them.* (Oliver Wendell Holmes)

Bone flutes 30,000 years old have been found in France and even older ones in German caves (Hotz, 2009; Jensen, 2001). Ancient drums have been unearthed at sites in Africa. These artifacts show that music has been with us from our

beginnings and, just as today, served many purposes: to amuse, comfort, and relax; to pass on history, information, and values; to inspire; and to celebrate achievements. Every culture has discovered music. Parents the world over instinctively sing and rhythmically rock fussy babies, and readily spice up brussel sprouts and broccoli with spontaneous ditties: "Here comes broccoli. It's so green. Yummy, yummy tree trunks. Open up to eat."

Imagine a day without music. Out would go the radio, I-tunes, and much of television. Life would be dull. Music elements are so embedded in language that it would be hard to even talk. A simple sentence, "Turn out the lights," can have many meanings, depending on changes in pitch, rhythm, dynamics (volume variations), and accent. The command, "Turn *out* the lights," can become a seductive whisper, "Turn out the li-i-i-ghts?" It's all in the music.

The economic impact of music on our lives is staggering. More than 130,000 persons list their livelihoods as musicians or composers; that figure does not include dozens of related careers, such as teachers and music storeowners. More than 1,500 orchestras generate employment for thousands more (U.S. census, 2000). We spend billions each year on concerts, CDs, downloads, and music DVDs. One Rolling Stones concert tour grossed more than $27 million. Cell phone ring tones are a $3 billion business.

Much of the motivation to learn inside school depends on connecting learning to life outside school. Music is out there. We need to bring it in and not just in isolated weekly music classes. Music is integrated in real life and it should be integrated at school. A myriad of music–life connections dovetail with every area of the curriculum and should be made explicit to students.

## Research Update *12.2*  Music's Effects on Learning

- A meta-analyses of studies from 1950 to 1999 about the causal effects of integrating the arts found two reliable links: (1) Listening to music showed a medium-sized causal relationship on spatial-temporal reasoning. (2) A large causal relationship was found between learning to make music and spatial-temporal reasoning; and the relationship worked equally well for both general and at-risk populations (Winner & Hetland, 2000a, 2000b).
- Several studies have concluded that music training can improve related cognitive functions. Regular music instruction and practice increases children's brain plasticity and improves cognitive functions related to music (Dana Foundation, 2008).
- Kids who read music well, read and do math well. The ability to process musical symbols and representations is a "leading predictor" of learning. Learning to notate music correlates with reading and math: Notating pitch was found to be more predictive of math and rhythm more predictive of reading. "This cannot be considered random or irrelevant" (Scripp, 2003, p. 122; Weissman, 2004). Also see the website: http://nec-musicined.org.
- A strong relationship was found between awareness of pitch and ability to sound out in reading (Weinberger, 1998).
- Kindergartners who listened to music and watched an educational video scored higher on the DIBELS test than those who just watched the video. Students also had less off-task behavior while listening to music (Register, 2004).
- First graders who received music listening instruction had significantly higher reading scores than a control (88th percentile versus 72nd) (Weinberger, 1998).
- Fourth-grade "emotionally disturbed" students improved their writing quality and quantity when they listened to music (with headphones) versus writing in silence (Deasy, 2002).

- Various approaches to music instruction were found to increase spatial-temporal reasoning; music notation led to the strongest results (Deasy, 2002). Preschoolers given 8 months of keyboarding and singing showed enhanced spatial-temporal (abstract) reasoning as compared to a control group. Spatial-temporal reasoning is important in subjects such as mathematics and science (Rauscher et al., 1997).
- In a sample of 25,000 kids from every region of the United States, 20 percent of the 12th-grade class could do high-level mathematics. However, among low-SES students involved in instrumental music, fully *one-third* performed at high levels of math (Catterall, 2003).

  Note: Low SES associates with low performance in nearly every published study.

- Fifty-seven studies showed arts experiences increased self-concept, language, cognitive development, critical thinking, and social skills. Of special note was the positive effect of music participation on self-concept (Trusty & Oliva, 1994).
- College students who listened to Mozart had temporary increase in spatial reasoning (Shaw, 2000). In another study, however, complex rhythms, even a rhythmic rain forest background, proved to be three times better than Mozart (Jensen, 2001, citing Parsons et al.).
- Math performance improved in a study in which one group studied math with a Mozart sonata and scored an eight-point increase over a control group (Campbell, 1997; www.musica.uci.edu).
- The College Board reports students with 4 years of music coursework scored an average of 49 points higher on the combined verbal and math portions of the SAT. The more years students spend in music, the higher the scores (MENC: www.menc.org/information/advocate/sat.html).

## Music Is a Vital Communication Vehicle

*Music is the "universal language of mankind."* (Henry Wadsworth Longfellow, *Outre-Mer*)

Villagers in remote areas of Cameroon are able to identify emotions expressed in music that they could not possibly have heard before and mothers the world over sing songs that bare close resemblance to western lullabies. From early childhood, music allows communication that is unavailable through words alone. Preschoolers ask questions beyond their vocabularies with songs such as Mozart's "Twinkle, Twinkle Little Star, How I wonder what you are" (Page, 1995). Musical listening and making experiences stimulate imaginative thinking and sharpen problem solving. Young children readily create their own songs and accompany themselves with hand clapping and "found" rhythm instruments such as spoons and keys. These sound experiments use creative problem solving to discover possibilities.

"Me" egocentrism eventually morphs into a world of "we" as children discover peers. The very emotional communication that music permits is reflected in adolescent song preferences. Music is used to grapple with powerful feelings and attempts to understand relationships with others. A vast range of music pieces and songs are available to reflect our deepest emotions from love to despair. As adults we are flooded with vivid autobiographical "you are there" emotions when we hear certain songs from our past, especially teen and young adult years.

In a pedestrian tunnel at Chicago's O'Hare Airport, neon art rhythmically pulses along the ceilings as synthesized music plays. Lyrics softly urge "keep walking, keep walking." The message is understood, often subconsciously, and everyone seems to comply—at least every time I'm there. Music is highly cognitive and is rightfully counted as one of the eight ways of knowing that Gardner (1999) classifies as a distinct human intelligence. Communication is about understanding and expressing ideas and feelings. Music does both, but in unique ways. Music involves thinking to produce it and thinking to understand it, which enhances cross-lateral brain activity and time in the "zone" or "flow"(Campbell, 1997).

## Music Provides a Learning Foundation

A new industry of private music schools, such as Kindermusik, International, and Music Together, has sprung up in response to research studies and child development theories that show how very young children can intuitively make music. These programs provide early music listening and music-making experiences that attune children to phonemes (sound units)—awareness necessary for speaking and reading. Research shows that poor phonemic awareness accounts for many reading problems; children need to hear sound nuances to decode. Babbling babies and singing toddlers can grow into children who learn to seek out music to sort out feelings, as well as to glean information.

**Attention and Memory.** Advertisers deftly use the attention-getting and mnemonic powers of music. Jingles compel us to buy products: "You deserve a break today, so get out and get away." Sometimes these ditties, with their "rent it—eat it—buy it" messages invade our thinking and we are powerless to quash them as our brains are compelled to find associations (Wolfe, 2001). Learning through music can seem effortless because we unconsciously *entrain* to patterns; for example, we adjust our gaits when we walk with someone. Heart rate, body cycles, and brain waves imitate or entrain to rhythms around us (Armstrong, 1993; Page, 1995).

Whereas inhabitants of New Guinea learn thousands of clan names using a musical chant (Armstrong, 1993), most Americans first experience musical mnemonics when learning the alphabet. Children repeatedly sing to Mozart's "Twinkle, Twinkle Little Star" melody (also used for "Ba Ba Black Sheep"), thus placing the letters into memory. Music creates winning combination to make practice enjoyable. Not every song works. Lyrics have to have "positive message and resonate emotionally with kids" (Jensen, 2000, p. 90). To enhance concentration, Jensen suggests using background music like jazz or Baroque with 65 to 80 beats per minute.

## Music Promotes Physical and Mental Health

Since drumbeats were first heard in ancient Africa, the soothing properties of music have been known. Music is now used across cultures to alter mental state by changing brain chemistry (Jensen, 2000). Therapists have used music for more than 50 years for illnesses ranging from anorexia to drug addiction. Music is tapped for its capacity to reduce stress hormones, boost the immune system, increase healing antibodies, and lower heart rate as blood pressure and respiration rates respond to the tempo of music. Songs can provoke cathartic effects such as sobbing. Musical sounds can trigger "chromothesia"—pleasant colors and images. Faster musical rhythms can induce smiling, even laughing as they stimulate the release of endorphins, the body's

natural opiates, and change brain waves. Parkinson's patients have even regained cadence rhythms for walking when music is used a scaffold.

Music is a medicine that "sustains people under the most degraded circumstances" (Booth, 2003, p. 20). Music is used to cope in the way slaves sang to endure and, in a manner to control, their suffering. Music gives solace during wrenching moments such as funerals, lost loves, and fear ("I whistle a happy tune"). We hum and rock to find physical and mental peace and we sing lullabies to calm cranky children. We sing to make unpleasant work more pleasant and to ease the passage of time.

Listening to music is also a "form of mental priming" that promotes multitasking by the brain (Scripp, 2003, p. 134). Business and industry use this power of music to increase workplace productivity. For example, music is intentionally used to create positive mood and energize employees, which increases attendance.

## Music Makes Us Happy

*Music is the shorthand of emotion.* (Leo Tolstoy)

Einstein claimed that he not only thought in music, but got the most joy from his violin. To be happy is an educational goal not to be dismissed (Noddings, 2005). Music can change the feel of learning and is one of the ways our "cognitive skills remind our emotional self that life is joyful" (Scripp, 2003, p. 31).

Music is a form of beauty that can transform any environment, charging us with aesthetic responses. Students and teachers immersed in music are uplifted and energized. Students who are guided to develop diverse musical tastes have more options for using music as a special way of knowing, expressing, and enjoying.

Music has great power, but that power can and has been abused. Music integration should include discussions about the downside to music euphoria. Hateful lyrics that provoke aggressive responses are harmful for the writers, listeners, and singers. In fact, any art form that demeans a person or group should be questioned.

Back to the main point: Music is fun, and fun is fundamental to motivation to learn. Said simply, happy children learn better. As the song says, "Hava Nagila," or "Let Us Be Happy" (written by a 12-year-old Jewish boy 100 years ago).

## Music Bonds

*Music cures a lot of loneliness.* (Anonymous)

Educators at the singing schools of Hungary believe music brings people together. Choirs are big. When individuals sing together an invisible web of community spirit weaves them together. Group musical experiences build sensitivity, harmony, and cooperation as individuals unite in common emotional responses. Patriotic songs, folksongs, and marches have this cementing effect, which is played out in our tradition of singing before sports events—which can surprise foreign visitors. We stand as individuals, but unite as Americans in the choral singing of "The Star-Spangled Banner."

Creating "harmony" is a social and personal skill as well as a musical achievement. Songs sung around campfires on chilly nights envelop people in communal sound. Then there are the young lovers who bind themselves together with "our song." Shared music is communication that can bridge generations and mend fences among disparate groups. For example, Union and Confederate soldiers, weary from fighting each other by day were known to join in songs across the night.

## Music Builds Desirable Character Traits

There is growing evidence for the positive influence of music on social-emotional development and behavior. Musical activities require self-discipline, respect, empathy, dealing with frustration, and collaboration (Scripp, 2003).

While music can be enjoyed without instruction, a person who learns to sing or play an instrument well has to commit to a regimen of practice to develop skill. Musical development requires the extension of self-discipline and a desire to improve (Hope, 2003). By learning to sing or play an instrument, children develop confidence, posture, and poise. Through musical achievements, children gain insight into important connections between sustained effort and satisfaction. Pride is a powerful fuel for the learning engine. When children see that significant adults share pride in their hard work, this self-discipline grows and can be transferred to other areas of life. From Bill Clinton's saxophone experiences to Arkansas Governor Mike Huckabee's guitar playing come testimonials to this effect.

## Music Expresses Cultural and Personal Identity

Study the music of a culture to find out what people value and fear. Music shows up in our most important ceremonies and traditions from birthdays to New Orleans–style funerals. Music is central to most religions. Music is such an important part of every culture that the act of music making is considered a gift. It is a high tribute to have a song written especially for you.

Throughout history, each tribe and group has crafted a unique musical identity. Today, diverse music represents our diverse human family. In the United States we embrace every genre and style from folk to classical, rock and roll to rap. Blues? Jazz? All are readily available at the local mall or online.

On a personal level, teenagers become passionate about "our music" as bodies and brains go through sweeping changes. During adolescence, music also becomes a means to carve out individual identity. For example, at age 16, Mozart wrote a great symphony to "grapple with the torment of being a teen" (Lockwood, 2005). Today rap and hip-hop styles are popular and influence youth. Some children go much further into this music world than their parents fathom, while researchers warn about the negative effects such as reported instances of heavy metal and gangsta rap, which stimulates the brain's seizure center.

## Music Records and Reflects History

History is replete with songs and music that tell tales of heroes, passions, and wars. Composers inspired by historical events have given us well-known songs, such as "God Bless America," written by Irving Berlin at the brink of World War II.

It is impossible to think of the civil rights movement without recalling songs of marchers or to not associate World War II with Glenn Miller's big-band sound. Songs and chants with attractive rhythms, satisfying repetition, and unforgettable melodies instill lessons from the past, celebrate victories, and lament disasters. Information and values are passed along in hymns, military chants, and folk and pop songs.

## Music Is a Vehicle for Learning

Alex Kajitani, a California math teacher, works in one of the poorest school districts in the state. He noticed that his students did not pay attention, do assigned work, or remember the simplest math formula, but they could recite every word of hip-hop songs. So Alex went home and wrote a song called "The Itty Bitty Dot" about adding and subtracting decimals. After 1 week, students' test scores dramatically improved, so he wrote more raps with lyrics such as the following:

- "Negative to the left positive to the right it's the number line dance I can dance all night."
- Improper fractions ("If it's bigger on the topper, it must be improper.")
- "Line up the dot and give it all you've got!" (adding and subtracting decimals)

He now has composed more than two dozen rap songs and expanded his topics to include teaching classroom routines. What's more, his students now write math raps. Mr. Kajitani credits music for making learning both relevant and fun. In 2007, he was selected as a California teacher of the year. Visit his website at www.mathraps.com.

The special term for using music as a learning tool is musicogeniceupadia, which, as the term implies, combines the motivational effect of music with its communication capacity to cause students to want to learn and to learn more. It isn't surprising that music raises interest in subject matter as it taps into the instinct to create and express.

Musical sounds charge the brain, stimulating whole brain involvement. Through songs and music, students increase general vocabulary, fluency, and understanding. Music develops listening skills, and listening is a main pillar of learning. Beyond the cause-effect "scientific" results that show music can increase test scores is strong evidence that music promotes intrinsic motivation, disciplined work habits, and collaboration—all of which are necessary for achievement.

Of course music attracts attention so it has the potential to increase time on task and qualitatively improve thinking while learning. These attributes account for music's ability to increase both learning efficiency and retention (Campbell, 1998). Jensen (2000) explains, "The more educators use music to assist in learning other material, the more quickly and accurately the material will become embedded" (pp. 74–75).

# Building Block II: Music Literacy: Content and Skills

*The woods would be very silent if no birds sang except those that sang best.* (Henry David Thoreau)

Classroom teachers who effectively use music as a learning vehicle throughout the curriculum have a basic level of music knowledge and skills. The necessary minimum music literacy level for teachers depends on the level expected of students. The *National Standards for the Arts* addressing music are listed later in the chapter, in Ready Reference 12.10. In general, students are expected to know (1) music's historical, social, and cultural role in life; (2) communicating through music by learning to read/understand music, creating original music, and performing; and (3) the aesthetic aspects of music.

The Interstate New Teacher Assessment and Support Consortium (INTASC) recently developed standards for what classroom teachers need to know about the arts. The music section can be downloaded at www.ccsso.org/projects/browse_by_name/index.cfm. In this section of the building blocks, music literacy needed by classroom teachers is outlined in the following areas.

- Definitions of music
- Purposes and roles
- Music elements and concepts
- Music processes or skills
- Musical instruments
- Genre, forms, and styles
- People
- Music materials
- Teaching approaches

## Defining Music

The world is full of sound. Even birds and whales seem to sing. Is that music? What about the whirring of a fan or the babbling of a brook? The question "What is music?" does not have one answer but should be part of an ongoing conversation about the arts (see Ready Reference 3.4). There is agreement that sound must be organized in time and space to make music. It would seem that understanding the nature of music would be highly dependent on a certain body part, the ears; however, Beethoven and others who acquired deafness continued to compose, and today most schools for the deaf include marching bands and choirs (Jensen, 2000). Indeed we perceive rhythm and beat with the entire body; producing and understanding music requires both cognitive and emotional perception.

There is a difference, though, between sound and music. Imagine an African drumbeat and compare it to the patter of a baby's feet. Both have rhythm. Both evoke emotional response. The difference is the drumbeat is an intentional organization of sounds for the sake of making sound. The sounds evoke feelings and emotions through the use of rhythm, tempo, melody, harmony, pitch, and repetition. These basic elements are used to create sound images and ideas in a musical form. So, music can be thought of as sound patterns over time intended to express moods, ideas, or feelings.

## Purposes and Roles

*It gives a soul to the universe, wings to the mind, flight to the imagination, a charm to sadness, gaiety and life to everything. It is the essence of order and leads to all that is good, just, and beautiful, of which it is the invisible, but nevertheless dazzling, passionate, and eternal form.* (Plato, on music)

Like all the arts, music is a form of communication. It is used to understand and express thoughts and feelings, just as in the language arts of reading, writing, speaking, and listening. However, music goes beyond words to intend to provoke aesthetic knowing and response. The goal is not limited to sending and receiving information but is expanded to giving a sense of beauty. Within music is wonder, yearning, curiosity, and new connections. Born of creative problem solving, musical inventing causes us to marvel at the capabilities of humans to stretch the possibilities of sound.

## Music Elements and Concepts

*I am music. I make the world weep, laugh, wonder and worship.* (Goethe)

Musical elements alone do not create music, but they are building blocks. These elements create a common language teachers can use to engage students in deeper listening and give students scaffolds to create music. In other words, these are tools to meaningfully integrate music. The following is one way to categorize musical elements.

**Rhythm.**   Rhythm is movement of sounds through time. In songs the words usually match the rhythm. Try saying and clapping the syllables in the words "happy birthday to you." Now do the same with "She'll be comin' round the mountain when she comes." Feel the different rhythm?

**Beat and Accent.**   Beat has to do with a steady underlying rhythmic pulse, such as a clock ticking. The accent is where the strongest emphasis is placed as in the waltz: *one* two three, *one*. Everything we sing or say has a rhythm that can be varied by changing the tempo, beat, and accent.

**Meter.**   Meter is the beat and accent groupings of rhythms (e.g., triple meter = 3/4 [waltz] or songs like "Happy Birthday").

**Syncopation.**   Uneven rhythms occur in syncopation, as in jazz, but with a steady beat. Try to say, "Charlie Parker Played Be Bop" by syncopating it to "Charrrr-lie Parrr-ker Played Be Bop." (Parker was a renowned jazz saxophone player.)

Rhythm, tempo, beat, and accent show the strong connections between math and music. There is a numerical pattern of beats over a length of time. Rhythm is represented by a series of notes ranging from whole (usually one beat per measure) to quarter notes (four beats per measure) to 8th, 16th, and even 32nd. In order to understand music, one must also understand math concepts of time and fractions and be able to count beats.

**Melody.**   Melody is the tune. It is a series (more than one) of musical tones or pitches falling into a recognizable pattern (e.g., in "I'm a Little Teapot," the motions show melodic direction). Melodies may be based on major or minor scales, but you do not need to know what a scale is to make a melody. When we sing words, they become melodies.

An octave is the distance between the first and last notes of our Western scales of eight notes (think of Do Re Mi Fa So La Ti Do) or between any pitched note and the next note with the same name (eight notes higher or lower). Most of our folk songs use the eight main notes of the Western scale. The five other notes that come between the scale notes are called *sharps* and *flats*; think of the black keys on a piano.

**Pitch.**    Pitch is the high or low tones in a sound pattern.

**Harmony.**    Harmony is the blending of tones or sounds (e.g., chords). When two or more pitches are blended simultaneously, harmony is made. Children often know about barbershop quartet harmony.

**Tempo.**    Tempo is the time or speed—how fast the music is. Tempo is usually labeled using Italian words. From slowest to fastest they are *largo, lento, adagio, andante, moderato, allegretto, allegro, vivace, presto,* and *prestissimo.* The term *ritardando* means to slacken the tempo, and *accelerando* means to quicken.

**Dynamics.**    Dynamics is the volume or relative loudness or softness of the sound. Dynamics give emotional intensity. The Italian words *forte, piano, pianissimo,* and *crescendo* appear in music to indicate dynamics or how loud the music should be played.

**Timbre.**    Timbre (pronounced "tambur") is the same as tone color and has to do with the unique qualities of a sound (e.g., voices or sounds made by plucking or blowing instruments). Each sound has a timbre that enables you to hear whether you've dropped your keys or a pencil. Children enjoy experimenting with timbres using body parts, sticks, and rulers.

**Form.**    Form is the structure, shape, or pattern of a piece of music or a song, such as AB (binary form, as in "Yankee Doodle"), ABA (ternary, as in "Happy Birthday"), and ABACA (rondo form). The As and Bs represent separate themes or ideas. The order of repetition is the key and largely determines the form of a piece of music. Musical styles and genre are closely related to form (e.g., jazz versus opera).

**Ostinato.**    Ostinato is simple rhythmic or melodic content repeated over and over to accompany a song. Ready Reference 12.3 summarizes music elements and concepts.

## Music Processes or Skills

All communication is basically either receptive (taking in information and feelings) or expressive (giving out). You can think about music using the following divisions.

1. Listening and reading music is receptive communication that seeks aesthetic understanding, also called "appreciation." Classroom teachers can learn to guide music listening, as Ms. Chilcote did in the opening Classroom Snapshot. Reading music involves learning to decode the agreed upon notation symbol system on sheet music.

2. Composing (creating or improvising to make original pieces or songs) and performing, that is, playing an instrument or singing, is expressive communication. Music is made more expressive by manipulating elements such as tempo and dynamics to create meaning, especially emotional meaning. By layering instruments and/or voices, a person creates a thin or full feeling, called *texture.* Melodies, rhythms, and timbres can be combined to create textures. We can create texture by combining voices, as in singing the round "Frère Jacques." Orchestral music is an example of a full texture.

**Reading Music.**    A non-Western perspective sees everyone as a music participant. This view helps us consider how music can become more integral to learning. Music is a natural extension of the human spirit, so it has a place in every discipline that examines people's courage, creativity, inventiveness, and resiliency. Reading music goes further to allow participation in a range of activities from using hymnals to playing music from a score. Teaching students to read musical notation can be a joint venture of the specialist and classroom teachers. With that said, Ready Reference 12.4 is for those with absolutely no experience but a desire to know some basics.

Both listening to music and making music involve cognitive, emotional, and aesthetic processes. You do not need to be a music specialist to involve children in purposeful listening and music making including singing, using simple instruments, and song writing. All of these musical experiences are invaluable.

## Musical Instruments

*Just about any animal skin can be stretched over a frame to make a pleasant sound once the animal is removed.* (A student's test answer)

The first musical instrument humans undoubtedly used was the voice, and it remains one of the most used today. The other instruments are broken into families: strings, brass, woodwinds, and percussion. Of course, today we have electronic instruments, including software like Garage Band to compose on the computer.

Instruments from different cultures are important additions to units and can be demonstrated, shown in pictures, and heard on recordings, as students study uniqueness among peoples. Check websites for pictures and sites where instruments can be heard. Teachers may not be able to stock many kinds of instruments, but sounds can be explored through "found," homemade, or inexpensive ones. Hopkins's *Making Simple Musical Instruments* lists easy ones made from everyday items. Examples include the following:

- Sound makers (sticks, stones, shakers)
- Percussion or rhythm: anything that can be struck, scraped, or rubbed (tambourines, triangles, wood blocks, bells, maracas)
- Melody instruments to make tunes (bells, xylophone, tone bars, glasses of water, bamboo flutes, rubber bands)
- Harmony instruments (autoharp, guitar, dulcimer)
- Orchestral and band (violins, trumpets, organs, accordions, harmonicas, Indian sitar)

## Ready Reference 12.3 Music Elements and Concepts

### Basic Elements of Music

**Rhythm:** movement of sounds through time (matches words, not beat); includes underlying beat
    **Beat:** Strong steady pulse
    **Accent:** Strongest emphasis
    **Meter:** Groupings of beats and accents
    **Syncopation:** Uneven rhythms as in jazz
**Melody (tune):** a series (more than one) of musical tones falling into a pattern; includes pitch
    **Pitch:** highness or lowness of a sound.
    **Tone:** a sound of well-defined pitch, represented by a note
    **Notation:** when symbols for tones are written on a staff
**Harmony:** the blending of sounds, such as chords; two or more pitches simultaneously
**Tempo (time):** Slow (adagio) or fast (allegro)

**Dynamics:** volume or relative loudness or softness of the sound; gives emotion: Forte = loud, Piano = soft, Crescendo = volume goes up, Decrescendo = volume goes down
**Timbre:** tone color or unique qualities of sound
**Form:** structure, shape, or distinct patterns; related to style and genre (e.g., call/response, verse/refrain, theme/variation, Cannon, AB, ABA, Rondo [ABACA])
    **Ostinato:** simple rhythmic or melodic content repeated over and over to accompany a song

### Music Processes or Skills

Listening to understand ideas and emotions
Singing, and/or performing with an instrument using expressive elements (e.g., dynamics, tempo)
Composing music using principles such as unity, variety, repetition/contrast, balance, tension/release

*Source:* Rozmajzl & Boyer-White, 2005.

## Ready Reference 12.4 Reading Music: Quick Reference

1. Each note is represented by these letters of the alphabet: ABCDEFG (no note letters above G).
2. Notes are written on a staff, which has five lines and four spaces. Each line represents a note, as does each space. The staff looks like this:

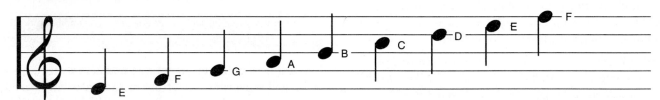

3. To remember the notes on the lines, the phrase "Every Good Boy Does Fine" can be used. For the notes in the spaces, use the acronym FACE (treble clef only).
4. Notes can go above or below the five-line staff by adding ledger lines. To figure a note on a ledger line, just keep using the A–G sequence; for example, the ledger line (one above) the top staff line would be A because the top staff line is F; the next space is G and, again, the next ledger line would be A.
5. If music has two staffs, one is for the higher notes and the other the lower notes. (It gets confusing to keep adding more and more ledger lines so this is easier.) The top staff is the treble or G clef and has this special sign: 𝄞 The bottom staff is the bass or F clef and has this sign 𝄢:
6. On a piano, middle C is in the center of the keyboard. To figure out the white notes on either side of it use the A–G sequence. The black keys are the sharps (#) and flats (b). A sharp raises a note a half-tone (makes it higher) and a flat lowers it a half-tone.
7. The staff is divided into measures or bars (vertical lines) and can have any combination of notes and rhythms. Special symbols convey notes worth different counts or number of beats. For example,

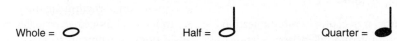

8. The time signature is two numbers (looks like a fraction) at the start of the staff that tells you the number of beats in a measure (bar) and what kind of note gets one beat (e.g., 3/4 means 3 beats to a measure and the quarter note gets one beat).

- Orff xylophone (wooden) and the metallophone (metal) with removable bars (Ask the music teacher about Orff instruments.)

## Genre and Music Styles

> *Jazz tickles your muscles, symphonies stretch your soul.* (Paul Whiteman)

The terms *genre* and *style* are sometimes used interchangeably in music, but style generally refers to the distinctive way in which musical elements are used. For example, periods of musical development (e.g., Baroque) have a unique style. Style can also refer to media to make music (e.g., keyboard style).

It would take more than one course in music history to become familiar with all music genres and styles. Teachers with a music history background start integration with a definite advantage, but most teachers actually know more than they think they do. For example, everyone is familiar with classical music from cartoons, such as Bugs Bunny, and advertisers frequently sneak in Bach or Beethoven to sell a product. Films such as *Platoon* and *Ordinary People* introduced millions to composers such as Vivaldi and Pachelbel.

Teachers new to music integration are encouraged to begin with genre and styles they know and enjoy so that they can transfer their enthusiasm to students. Once integration is under way, teachers can branch out and explore, along with students. Ready Reference 12.5 lists genres in alphabetical order.

Ready Reference 12.6 clarifies some of the eras or periods of music commonly used to classify Western classical music (music with lasting significance). "Classical" is also one of the periods. The example works listed are just that, examples. They are offered as a place to begin as teachers attempt to increase music background. Dates are included for those interested in plotting birthdays on a timeline to go along with social studies. Celebrating artist birthdays is also a routine to integrate the arts (see Appendix G).

Both 20th- and 21st-century American music have much to offer, for example, 1930s Latin, 1940s big band, 1950s rock and roll, 1980s punk rock and New Age, 1990s country music, and the evolution of rap and hip hop in the third millennium. To get up on rap and hip-hop, check out books like Stanley's *Rap, the Lyrics: The Words to Rap's Greatest Hits* and Toop's *Rap Attack 2: African Rap to Global Hip Hop.*

## People of Music

Music people take on many roles: composer, musician, singer, conductor, sound engineer, critic, and teacher. Students need to know the range of careers available and add a "real person" element to songs and musical works.

A number of book-based videos related to biographies of musicians are now available. One of the most well known is *Beethoven Lives Upstairs* (Nichol, 1994) and the picture book has the same title. Most biographies give students an opportunity to learn something of the struggles and inspiration behind success that propelled these people to such heights.

Studying real people who lived in a particular time and place also allows students to see how context influences artistic work. Students can identify with the troubles and triumphs of composers and other people who have made music an integral part of their lives. It can give hope and comfort to children to see they share life experiences with famous artists. Weaving in the lives and works of musicians from different backgrounds offers children a broader worldview and provides ideas for experimenting with forms as they create original music.

For ideas about genre, styles, composers, songs, and other potential questions about what to teach, you may want to consult *The Music Teacher's Book of Lists* (Ross & Stangl, 1994). Ready Reference 12.6 lists people in the music world to get started. Sadie's *New Grove Dictionary of Music and Musicians* (1988) is a reference for finding background on people, music, and songs, including "Happy Birthday." For folk songs try Sing Out Corporation, which publishes *Sing Out! The Folk Song Magazine,* started by Pete Seeger (www.singout.org/). Finally, consider making your own list of A–Z singers and musicians by enlisting students in the search and selection, including family and community members.

## Music Materials: Sources

The goal is to use music from a variety of periods, cultures, and genres as appropriate to units and students. Children's concept of what is "good" is malleable, so this is the time to stretch not narrow. Choose music that touches emotions, stimulates curiosity, is accessible, and has lasting value and enduring meaning. Use music you are drawn to over and over. The music specialist will usually be responsible for a sequential music curriculum, leaving the classroom teacher free to explore genres from gospel to opera according to preferences, student interests, and unit

---

## Ready Reference *12.5* Music Genre and Style

| | | | |
|---|---|---|---|
| Barbershop | Dixieland | March | Rap |
| Baroque | Environmental | Motown | Reggae |
| Big Band and Swing | Folk Songs | Movie Themes/Soundtracks | Rock and Roll |
| Bluegrass | Hip-Hop | Musicals | Romantic Era |
| Blues | Jazz | New Age | Soul |
| Choral | Latino | Opera | World Beat |
| Classical | Lullaby | Pop | Zidico or zydeco |
| Country | Madrigal | Ragtime | |

## Ready Reference 12.6 Music Eras and Composers

### Selected Periods, Composers, and Example Works

### Baroque

1650–1750: Ornate, flamboyant with predictable forms (*Note:* good for background)

Bach (1685–1750), German: *Brandenburg Concerti* and 22 preludes and fugues
Pachelbel (1653–1706), German: *Canon in D Major*
Vivaldi (1678–1741), Italian: *Four Seasons*
Handel (1685–1759), German: *Messiah, Water Music,* and *Royal Fireworks Music*

### Classical

1750–1820: Emotional restraint and simplicity

Haydn (1732–1809), Austrian: *Clock Symphony, Surprise Symphony, The Creation, The Seasons*
Mozart (1756–1791), Austrian: Operas (*Don Giovanni, Marriage of Figaro, The Magic Flute*), *Jupiter Symphony, Coronation Concerto for Piano, A Little Night Music*
Beethoven (1770–1827), German: nine symphonies

### Romantic

1820–1870: Dreamlike and emotional, may suggest a story or concept

Schubert (1792–1828), Austrian: *Unfinished Symphony, The Great Symphony*
Schumann (1810–1856), German: *Spring Symphony, Papillons* (butterflies)
Mendelssohn (1809–1847), German: *Scottish Symphony* (No. 3) and *Italian Symphony* (No. 4), *Songs without Words*
Chopin (1810–1849), Polish: all his piano works
Strauss (1804–1849), Austrian: waltzes
Liszt (1811–1886), Hungarian: *Hungarian Rhapsodies*

Rossini (1792–1868), Italian: operas (*The Barber of Seville, William Tell, Cinderella*)
Verdi (1813–1901), Italian: operas (*La Traviata, Rigoletto, Falstaff, Aida, Otello*)
Puccini (1858–1924), Italian: operas (*La Boheme, Tosca, Madame Butterfly*)
Berlioz (1803–1869), French: *Symphony Fantastique, Romeo et Juliette*
Tchaikovsky (1840–1893), Russian: *Symphonies 4–6, Swan Lake, The Sleeping Beauty, The Nutcracker, 1812 Overture*
Brahms (1833–1897), German: *Symphonies 1–4*
Wagner (1813–1883), German: operas (*Tristan and Isolde, The Flying Dutchman, The Valkyries*)

### Post-Romantic/Twentieth Century

1890–1930: Focuses more on mood and experimentation with music "without melody"

Mahler (1860–1911), Bohemian: *Songs of the Wayfarer, The Song of the Earth, Symphony of a Thousand* (No. 8)
Debussy (1862–1918), French: *The Sea (La Mer), Prelude to the Afternoon of a Faun*
Prokofiev (1891–1953), Russian: *Peter and the Wolf, Romeo and Juliet*
Sousa (1854–1932): all his marches
Strauss (1864–1949), German: *Don Quixote, Macbeth,* operas (*Salome, Elektra*)
Stravinsky (1882–1971), Russian: *The Rite of Spring, The Firebird, Petrushka, The Soldier's Tale*

### Others to Know

Bernstein (1918–1990): *West Side Story*
Bizet (1838–1875): *Carmen, Symphony in C Major*
Copeland (1900–1990): *Fanfare for the Common Man, Appalachian Spring*
Rimisky-Korsacov (1844–1908): *Sheherazade, The Snow Queen*
Williams (1932–): *Jaws, E.T., Raiders of the Lost Ark, Superman*

---

connections. Start small by collecting background music, music to introduce units, and songs to sing.

**Materials Collection.** To begin music integration, teachers need the following basic materials.

*Books:* Song collections, biographies of musicians, finger plays, chants and rhymes, how to make instruments, and other music-based children's literature (see Appendix J).
*Poems, quotes, cartoons:* See Livingston's *Call Down the Moon, Poems of Music.*
*Pictures:* Musicians and instruments, including art prints
*CDs, tapes, and videos:* Start a discography of music to use in units (see Ready Reference 12.7 for music ideas) (Be sure to consult with the music teacher, who will have references by curricular topics, dates, and holidays.)
*Construction materials (to make instruments):* tubes, boxes, beans, sticks, tubs (see Chapter 7 for papier mâché)

## Music and Songs to Know

*This song will live forever.* (Kate Smith, 1938)

The great singer, Kate Smith, made the previous statement right before she sang Irving Berlin's "God Bless America." It was the first time anyone performed the song in public. It is always touchy to start listing books or topics everyone should know, but music "that will live forever" is a good criterion to get started.

Music Educators National Conference (MENC) is on a campaign to "Get America Singing . . . Again" and has compiled a list of songs music teachers believe all Americans should know and treasure as part of our national common culture (see Ready Reference 12.8). It includes folk songs, Negro spirituals, patriotic songs, a Jewish celebration song, a Japanese folk melody, and many old favorites. In addition, you may want to survey your own community and involve students in compiling a "favorites

## Ready Reference *12.7* Music Resources

Music Educators National Conference is the main professional organization: www.menc.org. Also, see Activity Books at the end of Chapter 13.

### Websites

American Symphony Orchestra League:
**www.playmusic.org**

Children's Music Web:
**www.childrensmusic.org/** (public domain music, monthly recommendations/artist webs, custom CDs)

Classical Archives:
**www.prs.net/**

Creating Music:
**www.creatingmusic.com/**
(compose and perform music)

**Composer of the Day:**
free app from ITunes Internet store

Education Planet:
**www.educationplanet.com**
(books, music, and lesson plans)

Instrument Encyclopedia:
**www.music.umich.edu/research/stearns_collection**

Kiddles:
**www.kiddles.com/mouseum/index.html**
(songs by subject area)

Kids Space:
**www.kids-space.org** (create your own music, stories, and art)

MIDI information:
**www.midi.org/**

Music Maker:
**www.iknowthat.com/com/L3?Area=Music&Cook=**

Music Education Online:
**www.geocities.com/Athens/2405/index.html** (many links)

Music Notes:
**http://library.thinkquest.org/15413/**

Music Sites:
**www.educationworld.com/a_tech/sites/sites034.shtml**
(composers, conductors, and instruments)

Songs for Teaching:
**www.songsforteaching.com** (lyrics, clips, songs for every subject, including "Dirt Made My Lunch," "Action Preposition Blues," and "From Your Seat" for children with physical challenges)

Songs of the Century:
**http://en.wikipedia.org/wiki/Songs_of_the_Century**
(365 classic songs selected from the 20th century)

### Multicultural Websites

American Folklore Society (Journal of Folklore):
**http://afsnet.org/**

Center for Southern Folklore:
**www.southernfolklore.com**

Country Music Association, Inc.:
**www.cmaworld.com**

Digital Tradition Folk Song Database:
**www.mudcat.org/**

Smithsonian Institution:
**www.smithsonianglobalsound.org/**

The World Music Institute:
**www.worldmusicinstitute.org**

---

list." Ready Reference 12.9 includes favorites from teachers and children nationwide. Ross and Stangl's *The Music Teacher's Book of Lists* is another useful source of music.

## Music Approaches

*The human voice is the most readily available and most important musical instrument for children to explore . . . accompaniment can distract the children's attention from the musical elements of pitch, volume, and timbre, produced by the voice alone.* (Zoltan Kodaly)

In real life, music is everywhere, all day, every day—on our iPods, on the radio, in the mall, and in the hums and whistles of people around us. Music is more than a pleasant background. It is a powerful tool. Classroom teachers are now tapping that power by providing significant experiences that used to be reserved for music class. Music has become as integral to inside school as it is to outside life.

Knowledge of specific approaches to music teaching helps classroom teachers communicate with specialists and expands their own strategy repertoire. The following summaries give background on what specialists know and do and put integration into perspective as classroom teachers start using music as a teaching tool. A common thread in most is the active involvement of students in making and responding to music using movement. All these approaches connect music to a wide array of curricular areas, from language arts to social studies. Generalists can investigate each further by talking with specialists in their schools and visiting music-based websites.

**Eurythmics.** In the 1890s, Swiss educator Émile Jacques Dalcroze proposed a theory called *eurythmics*. He believed control of balance and body movements, along with the use of the senses, prepared children to attend and concentrate—skills necessary for school success. He observed that sensory-based learning relaxed muscles, while maintaining alertness, and helped to open learning channels for concentration. In eurythmics, music and movement are inseparable; the body is used as a natural instrument for the study of rhythm. Dalcroze showed how any musical idea could be transformed into movement, and any movement could be translated into a musical idea.

## Ready Reference 12.8 Top 40 Songs to Know

Recommended by Music Educators National Conference (www.menc.org)

Amazing Grace
America (My Country 'Tis of Thee)
America the Beautiful
Battle Hymn of the Republic
Blue Skies
Danny Boy
De Colores
Dona Nobis Pacem
Do-Re-Mi
Down by the Riverside
Frère Jacques
Give My Regards to Broadway
God Bless America
Green, Green Grass of Home
Hava Nagila
He's Got the Whole World in His Hands
Home on the Range
If I Had a Hammer
I've Been Working on the Railroad
Let There Be Peace on Earth

Lift Ev'ry Voice and Sing
Michael (Row Your Boat Ashore)
Music Alone Shall Live
Oh! Susanna
Oh, What a Beautiful Mornin'
Over My Head
Puff the Magic Dragon
Rock-a My Soul
Sakura
Shalom Chaverim
She'll Be Comin' Round the Mountain
Shenandoah
Simple Gifts
Sometimes I Feel Like a Motherless Child
Star-Spangled Banner
Swing Low, Sweet Chariot
This Land Is Your Land
This Little Light of Mine
Yesterday
Zip-a-Dee-Doo-Dah

To start off, students "become" the music as they listen and move to it. Later they study musical symbols and instruments. Unfortunately, Dalcroze was dismissed from the Geneva Conservatory for encouraging students to remove their shoes. We have him to thank for helping to advance the idea of body-kinesthetic learning widely accepted today. Eurythmics has a strong presence in arts-based Waldorf schools across the United States.

**Orff.** Dalcroze was joined by Carl Orff in Germany, who also linked music and movement. (Music and dance were not connected until the 20th century, because music was considered high art, while dance was thought common.) Orff developed a music education program that worked off the idea that feeling comes before understanding. He stressed the thrill of music making through chants, rhythms, and language. The Orff method employs rhymes and proverbs as a basis for teaching rhythm, phrasing, and musical expression. Orff's instruments, created for children with no technical facility, are widely used in American schools to experiment with musical sounds.

**Kodaly.** Zoltan Kodaly was a Hungarian composer and early childhood expert who believed singing should be the basis of a music program. His work provided impetus for the singing schools in Budapest, Hungary. These schools are still highly regarded as some of the best in the world. Kodaly thought children should learn many simple songs, sing in tune, and do listening activities to develop aural skills. He contended that children can learn complex musical ideas in games, and all can become musically literate (read and write music) by developing concepts in experiential ways rather than through rote teaching. Kodaly believed quality musical listening enhanced concentration, focus, and

thinking. He reasoned that language, reading ability, and coordination are developed as students discern musical sound patterns.

Kodaly's methods are based primarily on singing nursery songs and doing traditional circle games that include movement. Eventually, children learn musical terms, and they read music using folk songs. Skills are developed through a sequential curriculum for sight reading and singing. The Kodaly system of hand signs (solfege) are often used by music teachers to help children sing and gesture the notes of the scale: *do* is a fist in knocking position; *re* is a palm outstretched down and tilted up; *mi* is palm down; *fa* is thumb down; *so* is a handshake; *la* is with the first two fingers and thumb making a downward U; *ti* is pointing the index finger up (Choksy, 1974). For more information on Kodaly, visit www.oake.org/.

# Building Block III: Collaborative Planning

Music integration uses the models and theories for thinking about curriculum and instruction in Chapters 1 through 3. Ideally, integration is planned collaboratively using the different co-planning/co-teaching options discussed in Chapter 3. Most models rely on unit teaching and are planned with attention to the following:

- Academic and arts standards, along with other goals
- Mutual connections (shared concepts/processes) between academic and arts areas

## Ready Reference 12.9  Favorite Songs (Not in Top 40)

Alphabet Song
The Ants Go Marching
Baby Bumble Bee
Be Kind to Your Web-footed Friends
Bear Song
A Bear Went over the Mountain
Bingo
Boom Boom Ain't It Great to Be Crazy
Camptown Races
Chicka Boom
Clementine
Do Your Ears Hang Low?
Down by the Bay
Down in the Valley
Found a Peanut
Go In and Out the Window
Good Night, Ladies
Greasy Grimy Gopher Guts
Green Grass All Around
Hambone
Have You Ever Seen a Lassie?
Head, Shoulders, Knees, and Toes
Hokey Pokey
I Know an Old Lady
I Wish I Were
If You're Happy
I'm a Nut
In the Good Old Summer Time
It Ain't Gonna Rain
It's a Small World
John Brown's Body
Kum-Ba-Ya
Little Skunk's Hole

Loop de Loo
Make New Friends
Miss Mary Mack
My Aunt Came Back
My Bonnie Lies over the Ocean
Ninety-Nine Miles from Home
Noble Duke of York
Oh, Chester
Old Hogan's Goat
Old MacDonald
On Top of Old Smoky (Spaghetti/Pizza)
One Bottle of Pop
Over the River
Peanut Butter Song
Polly Wolly Doodle
Pop! Goes the Weasel
Popeye, the Sailor Man
Rise and Shine
Singing Bee
Six Little Ducks
Skip to My Lou
Take Me Out to the Ball Game
Ten Little Indians
There's a Hole in the Bottom of the Sea
There's a Hole in the Bucket
This Old Man
Turkey in the Straw
Twinkle, Twinkle
Up in the Air, Junior Bird Man
Waltzing Matilda
When the Saints Go Marching In
Yankee Doodle
You're a Grand Old Flag

---

- Five unit centers
- Aligning authentic assessment and arts-based instruction with standards
- Student interests and questions
- Culminating performances and/or exhibits
- Sequencing lessons and writing two-pronged plans

## Nine National Standards for Music K–8

Ready Reference 12.10 summarizes the music standards for elementary and middle school students. These are a part of the *National Standards for the Arts* discussed in Chapters 1 and 3. Both the music standards and academic standards are needed to plan meaningful integrated lessons that teach *about*, *in*, and *through* music.

Standards and other curriculum frameworks help teachers to know what to teach, but they do not explain teaching methodology or specific integration strategies. Nor do they give

ideas about materials. These are discussed throughout Building Block III. In addition, Chapter 13 is a compendium of music seed strategies.

All the strategies and activities in this chapter relate to one or more of the music standards. Consult your local and state courses of study for ideas tailored to the specific needs of your community. For examples of arts standards developed at the state level, visit your state department of education or websites in states such as Connecticut, Kentucky, Ohio, North and South Carolina, Virginia, and Wisconsin.

## Respected, Not Trivialized

Meaningful arts integration targets teaching for two-way transfer. This means finding ways music can assist in learning traditional subjects and the reverse; music knowledge and skill is increased by studying social studies, math, and so on. Collaborative planning among classroom teachers and music specialists seeks connections that are mutually beneficial for academic areas and, in this case, music.

## Ready Reference 12.10  Nine National Standards for Music

1. *Singing, alone and with others, a varied repertoire of music.* Example activities: Learn songs from different cultures, traditional American songs, songs from different genres (lullabies, gospels, rounds, work songs). Observe conductor's cues during singing (change dynamics, sing expressively, use appropriate posture and rhythm).

2. *Performing on instruments, alone and with others, a varied repertoire of music.* Example activities: Echo short rhythms (clap, stamp, etc.). Play rhythm instruments while others sing.

3. *Improvising melodies, variations, and accompaniments.* Example activities: Use "sounds" to create songs with a beginning, middle, and end. Improvise rhythm and ostinato accompaniments.

4. *Composing and arranging music within specific guidelines.* Example activities: Make and use instruments with songs. Find background music to go with poetry or literature readings.

5. *Reading and notating music.* Example activities: Recognize 2/4, 3/4, and 4/4 meter signatures. Read pitch (do re mi . . .) with hand signals.

6. *Listening to, analyzing, and describing music.* Example activities: Do close critical listening to identify music elements and characteristics of styles and genre.

7. *Evaluating music and music performances.* Example activity: Explain personal preferences and why using musical terms.

8. *Understanding relationships between music, the other arts, and disciplines outside the arts.* Example activities: Compare and contrast concepts across art forms (texture, line, rhythm). Connect ways music intersects with reading and language arts, science, social studies, and math.

9. *Understanding music in relation to history and culture.* *Example activities:* Explain how music expresses culture and history. Investigate musical careers. Use appropriate audience behavior.

*Source:* Content Standards (material printed in bold type) excerpted from the National Standards for Arts Education, published by Music Educators National Conference (MENC). Copyright © 1994 by MENC. Reprinted with permission. The complete National Standards and additional materials are available from MENC; The National Association for Music Education: www.menc.org.

The question to ask is, can music play a meaningful role in the unit? Perhaps another arts communication form (e.g., drama or writing) may be a better fit. The goal is to find shared concepts and processes, while acknowledging that CPS thinking is always shared. When shared clusters are found, there has to be a commitment to more than music exposure. To teach *through* music involves teaching *about* music and involving students *in* using music knowledge to problem solve to create meaning. Opportunities to sing or listen to music, without instruction, do injustice to music as a discipline and limit children's enjoyment, understanding, and expressive skill development.

An important integration question is, "What did my students learn *about* each discipline being integrated?" not just "What subjects were used?" Although classroom teachers are not required to sing or play an instrument *well*, all need basic knowledge and skills to use music language and present examples of music possibilities. Students also need time to sing or listen to music for the sake of enjoyment. Students are regularly given free reading time, but they are also taught *how* to read. Students need to be taught *how* to read music and express themselves through the language of music, as well.

## Complementary Connections: Shared Processes and Concepts

Analyses of many studies leave little doubt that there are strong associations between music and other subject areas (Scripp, 2003). To begin with there are songs and pieces of music *about* each area, including songs specifically written to teach math facts, states and capitals, and bones of the body.

Finding shared structures, processes, and concepts is essential to planning and implementing integration. Teachers and music specialists will find many connections. Music, mathematics, and science share structures, concepts, and processes. Shared structures include hierarchies, periodicity, units, ratio–proportion, symmetry, patterns, and constants–variables. Shared processes include counting and measuring, parts/wholes, similar/different, parsing/chunking, classifying, and naming (Bamberger, 2000, p. 32).

Music, language, and math are symbol systems with the potential to be mutually reinforcing. Both stories and songs have a beginning, middle, and end and ballads have all the literary elements, along with music elements.

**Literacy and Music.**   Good readers and writers read in a special way, with an artistic eye and ear toward the way everything is put together, how it looks, sounds, feels, and moves, not just what the text says. Without this "arts sense," early literacy learning stagnates.

Reading aloud is similar to singing lyrics. Both require use of music elements to create a fluent performance. There is a special association between rhythm and reading, including meaningful phrasing and even the rhythmic (beats and accent) nature of syllables in words (Scripp, 2003). Musical messages are "read" or received by listening, just as we listen to a story versus reading one. The listening process is similar with music being a different language.

Drilling down to a more specific level, reading music involves the same kinds of decoding skills needed to read print—turning abstract symbols into sound. In reading printed words the most important symbols are the letters that represent the 44 phonemes (sounds) in English. In music, written symbols have also been created to record sounds (e.g., the pitch of notes). Pitch matching relates to hearing phonemes, which is needed for phonics.

**Composition.** We compose our thoughts and express them verbally through speaking and writing. Music composition happens when people spontaneously sing original songs, hum melodies, or use an instrument to try out musical ideas. Some composers actually try out the music in their heads and go right to writing it down using musical notation. Children who compose songs, collect favorite songs, and respond to music in journals are writing—another language arts area. The patterned nature of music makes it useful in spelling as well. Students can be taught to tap out word rhythms (e.g., "en-cy-clo ped-i-a") or sing the spelling of words (Disney tune). This draws on the mnemonic power of music. Students can also create original word melodies using patterns as basic as the universal combination of the notes G, E, and A or adapt any melody (tune). Small groups can each be given a word to spell using different rhythms, tempos, and varied dynamics to create new word melodies.

**Vocabulary.** Hundreds of words specific to music overlap with many areas of life. Consider just two: *line* and *score*. Then there are the millions of words in song lyrics—every part of speech and every possible spelling pattern studied in phonics.

**Comprehension.** To understand a written or spoken message, it is necessary to problem solve, using all levels of thinking to create meaning. Meaning increases enjoyment. Music is understood and appreciated in the same way as any other text—using CPS.

**Literature.** Music and song share many structures with literature. For example, themes, songs, plots, and characters are most evident in forms like opera and ballads. Poetry, in particular, shares the following with music and song: rhyme, rhythm, beat, pitch, volume, speed, stress. All literature is more or less a written conveyance of the author's images of how words, phrases, and sentences would sound (i.e., music elements of language, like dialect, are imagined and represented).

**Math.** Math and music share concepts such as order, sequence, patterns, counting, hierarchies, and proportion. Through the strategic use of music, teachers can improve skills in measuring, counting, graphing, fractions, problem solving, time, and spatial reasoning. Examples follow:

- Graziano, Peterson, and Shaw (1999) documented how music training can enhance understanding of proportional math, because the concept of fractions relates to whole, half notes, and distances of notes within scales.
- Number awareness can be taught through music combining many mathematical concepts: "Seven is larger than three, seven is higher than three (on the scale), and a note on the seventh beat comes in later than a note on the third" (Scripp, 2003, p. 137).
- The five-line musical staff is basically a mathematical graph that shows pitches. Keyboard training has been shown to have a "significant effect on children's ability to classify and recognize similarities and relationships between objects" (Rauscher et al., 1997). In particular, there seems to be a strong connection between pitch skills and math (Scripp, 2003).
- In particular, mastering a musical instrument develops mathematical understanding, and vice versa (Hope, 2003).

- For a three-way connection, study the math basis of cultural music. For example, German songs are often grouped into threes, whereas Australian songs frequently have grouped beats into twos and fours and are organized using eighth notes. Japanese music is often based on a scale of five notes, rather than the eight-note scale used in Western cultures.

Math songs, especially counting songs, have long been a part of early childhood, and for good reason. See the music-based bibliography in Appendix J for collections of math songs such as Baker's (1991) *Raps and Rhymes in Maths* (probability and time).

**Science.** Music shares many processes with sciences such as measurement, inquiry, observation, experimentation, discovery, and classification. The science of sound (acoustics) is a fit. Of course there are hundreds of pieces of music about science, ranging from Debussy's "La Mere" to John Denver's "Rocky Mountain High."

**Social Studies.** Music and social studies fit well together because of the historical and cultural basis of music. Traditional songs and folk music, passed from generation to generation, help teach the rules and values of cultures. Each culture puts its own signature on its music; Indian ragas cannot be mistaken for American country. In many cultures work songs are still an integral part of life. In some, music and dance are still believed to have power to coax plants to grow (Page, 1995). Hundreds of high-quality multicultural materials are now available, including CDs and videos. See Page's (1995) *Sing and Shine On! A Teacher's Guide to Multicultural Song Leading*, and check out *www.songsforteaching.com* (click on "Social Studies").

Songs can provide an interesting and informative introduction to an era. For example, "America" was first written as a poem in 1892. The poet, Katherine Bates, was inspired by a trip out west where was touched by the beauty of the country. People loved the poem and began to sing it using some 75 different melodies, including polkas and marches. Eventually a church hymn called "Our Mother Dear Jerusalem" was coupled with the poem, and it is this melody we know today.

Songs also record poignant moments in history and are responsible for saving lives. For example, American slaves sang, "Follow the Drinking Gourd," which maps the stars in the night sky and the path to freedom.

**Arts with Arts.** Music shares many concepts and processes with the other arts, including timing, coordination, gesture, composition, pattern, shapes, line, and color. These concepts are inseparable in areas such as musical theatre and ballroom dance.

## Unit Centers

Planning Page 3.8 shows common integrated unit structures that center on five different bodies and are supported by nine legs (four traditional subjects plus the five arts). Ideally teacher teams co-plan with music specialists around the unit bodies: (1) topic or problem, (2) genre or form, (3) single work (poem, book, song), (4) person, and/or (5) event. For example, they might collaborate on a study of a musician, such as Charlie Parker, using the picture book *Charlie Parker Played Be Bop* (Raschka) as a key resource. All the arts, as well as math, science, social studies, and literacy, could be legs to support the body. Students might read and write about Mr. Parker, study the conditions of the early 20th century that influenced his music, learn the math of syncopated rhythms, and so on. Music would be used as a learning tool, just as any other leg, as students do critical listening to his works.

Alternatively, teachers may choose a particular music genre, such as gospel, as a body. Units may be planned around problem solving initiated by questions that arise during other learning, for example, "What causes all these kinds of music to be created?" A core work unit is another option with book, poem, or song as the unit center. Again, music may be the body (e.g., song) or a support leg. For example, a sixth-grade class did a core study of Hesse's *Out of the Dust* (1998 Newbery Award). Not only did they vicariously experience the life of a teenager during the 1930s Dust Bowl, but they also found and constructed significant themes about music from the main character's life. Songs her family might have sung were brought into the unit, including work and wedding songs and funeral music. Planning Page 6.14 shows a planning web for an integrated unit with some music ideas in it. For other arts-with-arts unit ideas, see Burz and Marshall's *Performance-Based Curriculum for Music and the Visual Arts* (1999).

**Music Event Units.** Music performances may be brought to the school or music-related field trips may be planned. These are important unit adjuncts or can be the centerpiece of a study, using the event as the starter or culmination. Opportunities to hear the local symphony or a special concert can be pivotal in children's musical development and their lives. Many communities now have arts coordinators who contact schools to schedule trips and provide pre- and post-performance lesson ideas. Appendix H provides a checklist for planning arts-based field trips. In addition, Chapters 8 and 10 include ideas that apply to music events. See the sections on preparing students for live performances and using simulated mind trips to take students to places they cannot go physically.

Check the websites of the local and state arts council and use the phone book to find other music resources in the community. Take meaningful field trips to music stores and local colleges. For example, combine a lesson on running a business with a trip to a music store. Easy field trips can be a part of many units, including listening walks to collect sounds in the cafeteria or on the playground. Planning Page 12.11 suggests a literature unit incorporating music.

## Planning Page *12.11*

### Ann Cheek's Literature Through Music Lesson (Grades 1–2)

*Two-Pronged Focus:* (1) music making and (2) literature interpretation (rhythm of words/alphabet)
*Music Standards: 1, 2, 3, 7, 8* (Ready Reference 12.10)
*Literature Standards: 1, 3, 4* (Ready Reference 4.6)
*Student Objectives:* Students should be able to:
1. Echo rhythms and pitches of words
2. Perform on cue
3. Suggest ways to show meaning with instruments
4. Tell one way to improve

*Materials: Chicka Chicka Boom Boom* by Bill Martin/John Archambault, Alphabet, Musical instruments: piano, Orff percussion instruments
*Teaching Procedure:* (S = students)

**Introduction**
1. Play "Twinkle Twinkle" on the piano and ask S to name the tune. Explain that the alphabet song melody was written by Mozart. Show picture. Display alphabet and play again with all singing the alphabet.
2. Do Echo Me (expressively): (1) Chicka chicka boom boom (clap), (2) Skit skat skoodle doot (pat on lap), (3) Flip flop flea (use low middle and high pitches and pat lap, clap hands, and snap fingers, (4) Coconut tree (say and put rhythm in shoulders). Repeat 3 times.
3. Read book and invite practiced responses.
4. Tell S they will bring the book to life with music and a theme song. Ask what you would hear if CCBB was a movie if you closed your eyes (moods: happy, sad music).

**Development**
1. Sing theme song using sol-feg syllables.
2. Ask three S to play a steady beat on xylophone, metallophone, and contra bass bars and all sing together with

accompaniment. Repeat to find silent beats (holes) in melody. Add snaps for these and S to do glockenspiels (for rests).
3. All sing and keep the steady beat. Ask about silent beats (rests) and teach to snap on whole rests.
4. Ask what the alphabet does. Teach glissando (sliding sound) to show going up the alphabet tree (xylophone).
5. Perform first verse with new instruments. Ask for changes to make it better. Ask about how to show crash at end. Ask about adding a middle section.
6. Divide into four groups: (1) Chicka chicka with hand drums/tambours (say and play); (2) skit skat with tambourines; (3) flip flop flea with Chinese temple blocks or wood blocks with three different sounds; (4) coconut tree using congos or unpitched drums. Add Wheeee with a vibraslap.

**Conclusion**
1. Full performance rehearsal. Direct and read book with inserted song. Ask for other places to add instruments and actions.
2. Final performance. Ask what worked.

**Assessment**
1. Students match up the four chanted sounds with their rhythmic notation.
2. Observation and record keeping on individual computer checklist.

*Source:* Ann Cheek, Ashley River Creative Arts Elementary.

**Lesson Sequence.** Lessons must be ordered in a unit—what will be taught first, second, third, and so on. The flow of lessons is established by thinking about how one will lead into another. For this reason, it is important to think about which lesson will be the introduction and which will wrap up the unit. The culminating lesson generally involves students presenting projects that synthesize learning from the entire unit. For example, students might write and perform original "scat" songs to show they understand jazz concepts such as syncopation, but also overlapping language concepts such as onomatopoeia, rhyme, and repetition.

## Two-Pronged Integrated Plans

Once the overall unit design has been planned and an order of lessons determined, teachers get down to nitty-gritty daily lesson planning. Integrated plans need a minimum of two prongs—one focus on an academic area and another on an art form. Lessons can have more than two, and the two can both be arts prongs. The prongs are not just what will be used, but what will be taught and assessed, so two is plenty. You may incorporate many art forms into instruction, but you cannot teach in depth and assess everything in one lesson.

See the lesson format using a two-pronged focus and student objectives in Chapter 3. Refer to the detailed discussion about dividing teaching strategies into introduction, development, and conclusion. Keep in mind that if students are expected to create a song, structure is important. At first, students are often shown how to create new lyrics for a familiar tune or, in the case of the Charlie Parker book, they might write new words to replace *be bop, fisk fisk,* and other "scat" words. Plans need to include strategies for transition, use of space, materials, and even ways to dismiss groups: "Your ticket out today is _____" or "All those who can/know _____ may _____." Planning Page 12.11 shows a two-pronged plan created by music specialist Ann Cheek.

**Start Small and Grow.** Rather than plan a whole unit on music or even one with significant use of music, novice teachers are encouraged to try single lessons (e.g., teach the history of a song, such as "Row, Row, Row Your Boat" and use the lyrics for reading material). The key is to make sure first attempts are successful, for you and for your students. Begin by integrating energizing music warm-ups to introduce the day. For example, teach a new song every Monday. Explore the language arts connections by using a song chart and the "I Spy" strategy in which students tell types of words and language structures they see in the song. Ease toward more meaningful integration by using a music elements chart to discuss songs and accustom the class to discovering music connections with other subjects.

# Building Block IV: Aesthetic Learning Environment

*South Carolina:* Baroque music plays in the background during regular independent reading time. Examples are Bach's *Brandenburg Concertos,* Handel's *Water Music,* and Vivaldi's *Four Seasons.*

*California:* The relaxing sounds of New Age music waft through the halls and cafeteria of an arts-based elementary school. A teacher boasts about the bus drivers who also play music to set mood and control behavior. Drivers and students negotiate radio stations and CDs, contingent on students using desired "bus etiquette."

*Illinois:* An elementary principal, who is a John Phillip Sousa fan, plays marches over the intercom every Monday as students and teachers arrive. All report they cannot help but walk to the beat.

Although the goal of music integration is not to create more Mozarts, it is a fact that he and other musical geniuses grew up in rich music environments. From the South, to the Midwest, to the West, educators are now creating more music-rich environments in the name of learning enhancement.

We are all formed by the sounds around us. As evidence, consider how babies the world over babble in the phonemes of the language they hear. Children grow to like and value the sounds that surround them. Arts integration takes advantage of this fact by providing diverse musical experiences. Such variety broadens interest and builds respect for people's diverse musical expressions.

Immersing students in a musically rich environment is an important path to increasing aesthetic knowing, too. Aesthetic thinking takes us into a different state of awareness; we experience full sensory perception, concentration, imagination, reflection, consideration, questioning, even confusion as we perceive sounds or images that are pleasing or displeasing (Goldberg, 1997). Teachers attune their students to the sound patterns created as people and machines go about their work. Nature is a limitless source to develop musical sensitivity.

Creating a music-rich environment is also about teaching students that music can have both positive and negative influences. For example, in a study of felons, males cited rap as their top musical preference. Other studies show that immersion in heavy metal and rap correlated with lower grades, behavioral problems, early sex, arrest, and drug use (Took & Weiss, 1994).

## Background Music: Research

*Music gets me thinking about sounds. I like the way there are patterns and every note is important. It makes me calmer like I'm in a different zone.* (Andrew, age 8)

A critical factor in creating an aesthetic environment is music immersion. *Immerse* means to totally cover or involve. Background music plays a major role.

Music has been used to enhance mood in a number of studies and even cause a change of mind (e.g., influence whether a painting is liked or not). The type of music is important; sad music caused subjects to rate art as more depressing (Jensen, 2000). Certain kinds of background music are used to boost mood and survival rates in Alzheimer's patients and those with mental illness (Wigram & Backer, 1999). On the downside, loud music in public places can repel customers.

**Purposes.** In general, background music is used to promote good feelings about school, to motivate and energize. It is

## Ready Reference 12.12 Background Music

Music affects people differently so try different pieces to find a fit. (bpm = beats per minute)

### General

Baroque Music (Mozart, Bach, Handel, Vivaldi, and Pachelbel),
    which is 60 bpm (resting heart rate)
*Also try:* Beethoven, Berlioz, Debussy, Chopin, Liszt
Jazz: George Benson, Kenny G., Duke Ellington, Issac Hayes
Environmental: ocean, waterfall, rain forest, Indian ragas

### Beginning of the Year

The King and I (Getting to Know You)

### Start the Day

Handel's Hallelujah Chorus
Beatles, especially Good Morning
Bobby McFerrin's Be Happy
Disney's Hakuna Matata
Richie Valens' La Bamba
Movie themes: Superman, Chariots of Fire, Rocky
Village People's YMCA

### Calm/Relax

Piano, harp, or classical guitar, jazz
Yo Yo Ma (cellist)
Pachelbel's Canon
Bach's Concertos
Disney's Fantasia
Brian Eno (e.g., Music for Airports)
Artists: David Kobialka, Georgia Kelly, Michael Jones

### Memory

Lozanov "Superlearning" (research on 4/4 time)
Mozart, Beethoven, Bach, Vivaldi, Pachelbel, Handel, and Haydn

### Imagination and Creative Thinking

Jazz (Miles Davis, David Sanborn)
    New Age (Windham Hill, Ken Davis, Tony O'Conner)
    Beethoven, Tchaikovsky, Liszt
    Hungarian Rhapsodies

Fantasia (Disney)
Debussy's Claire de Lune
Indian ragas
Mozart (e.g., Musical Joke)
Prokofiev (e.g., Peter and the Wolf)

### Transitions

Vince Guaraldi's Peanuts theme
Mozart
Hadyn

### Celebration

Tina Turner's Simply the Best
Three Dog Night's Celebrate
Chili Pepper's Hot, Hot, Hot
Queen's We Are the Champions
Kool and the Gang's Celebration
Handel's Hallelujah Chorus
Otis Day and the Knights's Shout

### Energizing (75 bpm + in major key, rhythmic)

Mother Goose Suites
Flamenco from Spain (e.g., Fire and Grace)
Cossack from Russia
Polynesian drums
Isley Bros' Shout
Little Richard
Jerry Lee Lewis' Great Balls of Fire
Beach Boys' Fun, Fun, Fun
Jive Bunny and the Mixmasters
Pete Seeger

### Wrap Up

Sound of Music (So Long, Farewell)
William Tell Overture
Louis Armstrong's Wonderful World
I've Been Working on the Railroad

---

also used to heighten awareness and increase concentration and focus. Background music is used to relax before tests and to create mood and give background for reading, writing, and making art. Ready Reference 12.12 lists music for different classroom purposes.

**Relaxed Alertness.**    Appropriate background music played for 20 minutes at a time can induce an alpha state of relaxation (Jensen, 2000). The research and work of A. A. Tomatis in France and Georgi Lozanov (1978) in Bulgaria provides specifics on how to enhance learning through music. They found that relaxation caused by specific music leaves the mind

alert and able to concentrate. For example, concertos by Bach and Pachelbel's *Canon* have been played as information about a topic is presented verbally. The most conducive music is Baroque music, such as that of Mozart, Bach, Handel, Vivaldi, and Pachelbel, which matches the average resting heart beat of 60 beats to the minute. This creates a relaxed alertness that can enhance test performance (Cockerton, Moore, & Norman, 1997; Giles, 1991).

**Imagination and Creativity.**    Artists, scientists, and writers routinely use music to stimulate divergent thinking. See Ready Reference 12.12 for recommendations such as "Crystal

Meditations" (Don Campbell). Music with dolphin, whale, and bird calls and sounds of nature blended with woodwinds and piano and strings are good for stimulating imaginative thinking.

**Guidelines.** Background music should be played daily. Music should greet students as they come in and can accompany art making, silent reading, and writing times. Students learn to adapt. At the Conservatory Lab Charter School in Boston, high-quality background music is important to the mission. "Students have learned to subdue their voices and be respectful of others, and yet they still remember the music. They have increased their social-emotional skills, too, by altering their behavior in order to get choice music played" (Scripp, 2003, p. 134). Repeated exposure to excellent music develops listening skills measured by comprehension tests. For example, several variations on Mozart's "Twinkle, Twinkle Little Star" were played, and students learned to listen and analyze at the same time—counting the variations. Discussions about what causes the differences in the variations increased comprehension.

Rhythms of the brain tend to echo the rhythms of music. In general, Jensen (2000) recommends music with the following qualities.

- Purposefully selected (e.g., to calm or excite or to relax)
- Predictable and repetitive; use major key (for productivity)
- Instrumental, especially single instruments (less distracting)
- Low volume
- Simply structured (e.g., Baroque and jazz; movements are adagio or andante; orchestras can overwhelm)

## Besides Background Music

Additional ideas from schools throughout the United States help to increase aesthetic knowing through music.

**Music Lending Library.** Sets of CDs and tapes, similar to a class library of books, can be made available for checkout. Parents and PTAs often will contribute to this project. CDs are sometimes paired with a song-based book and placed in a zip-lock bag for take-home purposes. Simple directions are included about what to listen for or to do repeated reading/singing of lyrics. This is an excellent fluency development tool because singing adds music to words, and music increases the emotional effect of words.

**Music Journals.** Journaling includes prompts to write about how music is a part of life. Specific pages are designated for an ongoing listing of favorite songs, musical pieces, musicians, or even music jokes (What do you get if you divide a tuba in half? Answer: A one ba).

**Quotes and Poems.** Music poems and quotes are collected and posted. Livington's *Call Down the Moon* is a lovely collection of poetry about music. Teachers who use routines such as "poem a day" or "a quote a day" include music-related ones. Repeated poetry readings allow for students to focus on the musical qualities of poems (e.g., rhythm, beat, dynamics).

# Building Block V: Literature as a Core Art Form

Is Wynton Marsalis's *Jazz ABZ: A Collection of Jazz Portraits* (2005) an alphabet book for kids or an informational book for jazz lovers? Since he uses poetry patterns from tanka to haiku, maybe it is poetry. As discussed in Chapter 4, humans resist classification. What is for sure is that this is a music-based picture book (photography) so it has many connections and uses throughout the curriculum. His book joins a growing list of arts-based literature.

Never has more high-quality literature been available to teachers. A plethora of books is specifically devoted to music (e.g., multicultural song collections) and a variety of genre of music-based children's books (e.g., picture book fiction). When literature is viewed from the lens of music, it seems more books than not are linked. Seeking the connections increases the awareness of music's importance and adds another avenue to find quality material for units.

Music-based literature is now center stage in arts integration (Cornett, 2006). *Charlie Parker Played Be Bop* is a striking picture book appropriate for any age. If it is read while playing a tape or CD of "Night in Tunisia," it becomes a magical lesson with messages about history as well as genre and styles. (Thanks to Duxberry Elementary teachers for this idea.)

Biographies are particularly important for in-depth accounts and introduce students to people with whom they might identify. Biographies also add the human element to both science and social studies. For example, Krull's *The Lives of Musicians* gives short bios with interesting facts and a perspective on the time in which each musician lived. Planning Pages 12.13 and 12.14 offer titles focused on music and curricular topics. Ready Reference 12.15 lists artists who record for children. More examples appear in Appendix J.

# Building Block VI: Best Teaching Practices

*Before teaching anyone else, I must teach myself. (Sylvia Ashton Warner)*

## What You Teach Is Who You Are

"She loves music more than anybody," according to students of Mrs. Engle. It all started because she played big band records to get in a positive mood for teaching. One morning she was in a rush and left a record on when her fifth graders came in. They were shocked, but begged to hear more. Mrs. Engle was

## Planning Page 12.13
## Music-Based Literature by Topic

### Abilities and Disabilities
Keats, E. J. (2005). *Whistle for Willie*. Live Oak Media.
McCloskey, R. (1978). *Lentil*. Puffin.
Walter, M. (1987). *Ty's one-man band*. Four Winds. (child meets a one-legged man who brings music to a community)
White, E. B. (2001). *The trumpet of the swan*. HarperCollins.

### Animals
Brothers Grimm. (2007). *The Bremen-town musicians*. Bell-Pond Books.
Hurd, T. (1987). *Mama don't allow: Starring Miles and the Swamp Band*. Harpercrest.
Karas, G. (1994). *I know an old lady who swallowed a fly*. Scholastic.
Kraus, R. (1990). *Musical Max*. Simon and Schuster. (musical hippo drives everyone crazy with his practices)
Prokofiev, S. (1961). *Peter and the wolf*. Franklin Watts.
Steig, W. (1997). *Zeke Pippin*. HarperCollins.

### Creativity and Imagination
Clement, C. (1990) *Musician from darkness*, Little, Brown. (outsider from a primitive society discovers the power of music)
Isadora, R. (1998). *Ben's trumpet*. Live Oak. (jazz)
Pinkney, B. (1997). *Max found two sticks*. Aladdin. (Max discovers the joy of percussion)
Rylant, C. (1988). *All I see*. Orchard Books.

### Cumulative and Repetitive Stories
Dodd, M. (1988). *This old man*. Houghton Mifflin.
Emberley, B. (1967). *Drummer Hoff*. Simon & Schuster.
Karas, G. (1994). *I know an old lady who swallowed a fly*. Scholastic.
Martin, B. (2006). *Chicka chicka boom boom*. Simon & Schuster.
Raffi. (1987). *Down by the bay*. Crown.

### Dance and Movement
Gray, M. (1972). *Song and dance man*. Dutton.
Isadora, R. (1984). *Max*. Macmillan.
Martin, B. (1986). *Barn dance!* Henry Holt.

### Fairy and Folk Tales
Lewis, R. (1995). *All of you was singing*. Atheneum.
Whitehead, P. (1989). *The nutcracker*. Stoneway Books.

### Families and Friends
Griffin, H. (1986). *Georgia music*. Greenwillow.
Pinkwater, D. (1991). *Doodle flute*. Macmillan.
Williams, V. B. (1988). *Music, music for everyone*. Greenwillow.

### Language Arts
Marsalis, W. (2005). *Jazz ABZ*. Candlewick.
McMillan, B. (1977). *The alphabet symphony: An ABC book*. Greenwillow.

### Nursery Rhymes and Lullabies
Beall, P. (1996). *Wee sing sing-alongs* (with tape or CD). Price Stern Sloan.
dePaola, T. (1984). *Mary had a little lamb*. Holiday House. (rounds)

### Science, Nature, Health
Jenkins, E. (1989). *Rhythms of childhood* (with tape or CD). Smithsonian/Folkways.
Papp, C. (1988). *Follow the sunset: A beginning geography record with nine songs from around the world* (with tape or CD). Entomography Publications.

### Social Studies
Cutler, J. (1999). *The cello of Mr. O*. Dutton. (music sustains hope in time of war)
Johnston, T. (2004). *The harmonica*. Charlesbridge. (harmonica sustains boy during Nazi brutality)
Morpurgo, M. (2008). *The Mozart question*. Scholastic. (teenage journalist interviews survivor and violinist Palo Levi about his music)
Ryan, P. (2002). Scholastic. *When Marian sang: The true recital of Marian Anderson, the voice of the century*. (biography of first African American to sing at the Metropolitan Opera)
Spier, P. (1973). *The star-spangled banner*. Doubleday.
Stotts, S. (2010). *We shall overcome: A song that changed the world*. Clarion. (impact the song had on civil rights movement)
Winter, J. (1988). *Follow the drinking gourd*. Knopf. (slavery)

### Sports
Isadora, R. (1976). *Max*. Macmillan.

---

surprised the kids liked the "old stuff," but it became a routine to start the day with music. It lasted 42 years. This spunky lady credits much of her career longevity to using music.

Classroom teachers do not need to sing *well*, play an instrument, or read music to start music integration. Being a Mozart fan is not required. What is needed is a commitment to the philosophy of arts integration and a willingness to learn. Put music into perspective. It is a way of knowing—an intelligence every person possesses.

Arts integration begins with where teachers are as people—starting with whatever music experience and interest each has. Continuing to grow one's musical intelligence is essential to moving on to more meaningful music integration. The choices

are many: attend concerts, sing in a choir, take music lessons, or just become a more dedicated music collector.

**"I Can't Carry a Tune in a Bucket!"** To start off, it's more important that classroom teachers sing with enthusiasm than to worry about singing quality. Music teachers claim that most everyone can learn to sing in tune, with practice. Teachers who take the risk to sing with and for students add a strong dimension to integration. If a teacher plays an instrument, playing for the students provides an influential model. Teacher performance allows students to broaden their view of "teacher" in the way Bill Clinton's sax playing on *Saturday Night Live* portrayed him in a different light.

## Planning Page 12.14

### Books by Music Categories

Aliki. (2005). *Ah music!* HarperTrophy. (informational book)

**Picture Books Based on Songs**

Fox, D. (1987). *Go in and out the window.* Metropolitan Museum of Art. (various styles)

Hurd, T. (1987). *Mama don't allow: Starring Miles and the Swamp Band.* Harpercrest.

Karas, B. (1994). *I know an old lady who swallowed a fly.* Scholastic.

Mattox, C. (1990). *Shake it to the one that you love the best.* JTG.

**Orchestras and Bands**

Johnston, T. (1988). *Pages of music.* Putnam.

Koscielniak, B. (2003). *The story of the incredible orchestra: An introduction to musical instruments and the symphony orchestra.* Houghton Mifflin.

Kuskin, K. (1986). *The Philharmonic gets dressed.* Harper & Row.

Martin, B. (1994). *The maestro plays.* Holt.

Moss, L. (1995). *Zin! zin! zin!: A violin.* School & Library Binding.

Moss, L. (2002). *Music is.* School & Library Binding.

Williams, V. (1984). *Music, music for everyone.* Greenwillow.

**Musical Genre and Styles**

Bryan, A. (2003). *All night, all day: A child's first book of African-American spirituals.* Atheneum.

Collier, J. (1994). *The jazz kid.* Holt.

Fleischman, P. (1988). *Rondo in C.* Harper & Row. (classical)

Gray, M. (1972). *Song and dance man.* Dutton. (vaudeville)

Hart, J. (1989). *Singing bee! A collection of favorite children's songs.* Lothrop, Lee & Shepard.

Isadora, R. (2002). *Bring on that beast.* Putnam. (jazz)

Mack, J. (2009). *Hip hop.* Raintree.

Raschka, C. (2001). *Charlie Parker played be bop.* Live Oak.

**Musical Instruments**

Czernecki, C. (1993) *The singing snake.* Hyperion. (Australian folktale about the didgeridoo)

Turner, J., & Schiff, R. (1995). *Let's make music!* Hal Leonard (with CD). (recycled items; multicultural)

Wiseman, A. (2003). *Making music: How to make and use 70 homemade musical instruments.* Storey Books.

**Collections of Songs/Singing Games** (Also see Chapter 13 bibliography)

Barkman, A. (1987). *Rise and shine* (with tape or CD). Moody.

Cote, P. (1995). *Do your ears hang low? Fifty more musical fingerplays.* Scholastic.

Fox, D. (1987). *Go in and out the window.* Metropolitan Museum of Modern Art.

Glazer, T. (1992). *Eye winker, Tom Tinker, chin chopper: Fifty musical fingerplays.* Doubleday.

Hart, J. (1989). *Singing bee! A collection of favorite children's songs.* Lothrop, Lee & Shepard.

Jenkins, E. (1989). *You'll sing a song and I'll sing a song* (tape or CD). Smithsonian.

Raffi. (1990). *Baby Beluga* (with tape or CD). Crown.

Seeger, M. (1987). *American folk songs for children* (with tape or CD). Cambridge Rounder.

**Careers: Musicians, Singers, and Composers**

Celenza, A. (2004). *The heroic symphony.* Charlesbridge. (Beethoven struggles to write a symphony while going deaf)

Celenza, A. (2005).*Bach's Goldberg variations* (with CD). Charlesbridge. (Bach helps young musician)

Fleischman, P. (1988). *Rondo in C.* Harper & Row.

Freedman, R. (2004). *The voice that challenged a nation: Marian Anderson and the struggle for equal rights.* Clarion.

Isadora, R. (1998). *Ben's trumpet.* Live Oak. (jazz)

Johnston, T. (1988). *Pages of music.* Putnam.

Krull, K. (1993). *Lives of musicians.* Harcourt Brace Jovanovich.

Mitchell, B., & Smith, J. (1988). *America, I hear you: A story about George Gershwin.* Carolrhoda.

Parker, R. (2009). *Piano starts here: The young Art Tatum.* Random House/Schwartz & Wade. (biography)

Rappaport, D. (2004). *John's secret dreams: The John Lennon story.* Hyperion.

**Humor**

Keller, C. (compiled). (1985). *Swine lake: Music and dance riddles.* Prentice Hall.

## Inside-Out Motivation

Anyone reading this sentence has experienced the aesthetic motivation music provides. It is saying the obvious to point out that music is self-motivating. Children innately want and need to create, explore, and imitate sounds. They enjoy activities involving sound discrimination, classifying, sequencing, improvising, and organizing sounds into songs and music.

Teachers capitalize on the intrinsic motivational power of music whenever they pair meaningful music experiences with other curricular areas. A further way to establish meaningfulness (essential to inside-out motivation) is to connect music to life. Teachers do this by showing how music is used in daily rituals from waking up to the radio to jogging with an MP3 player. Students can also log or web music in their lives for one day or imagine a single day without music. Class music surveys can uncover places music happens and the many types of music classmates know.

An excellent teacher habit is to routinely ask how songs and music are linked to topics in math, science, and social studies. Musical intelligence can be activated by posing questions, such as "What kind of music would show how it felt when they signed the Declaration of Independence?" or "What pop songs do you think Benjamin Franklin would have liked?" Ask students how the use of music changes the classroom and learning (e.g., motivation and concentration) to help them own their learning.

## Ready Reference 12.15 Musical Artists Who Record for Children

| | | |
|---|---|---|
| Peter Alsop | Gemini | Sarah Pirtle |
| Linda Arnold | Red Grammer | David Polansky |
| Fran Avni | Greg and Steve | Barry Louis Polisar |
| Pamela Ballingham | Bill Harley | Raffi |
| Joanie Bartels | Chris Holder | Rosenshontz |
| Steve Bergman | Janet and Judy | Phil Rosenthal |
| Marcia Berman | Ella Jenkins | Kevin Roth |
| Heather Bishop | Kathi and Milenko | Nancy Rumel and Friends |
| Kim and Jerry Brodey | Kids on the Block | Pete Seeger |
| Rachel Buchman | The Kids of Widney High | Sharon, Lois, and Bram |
| Janice Buckner | Lois LaFond | Paul Strausman |
| Frank Cappelli | Francine Lancaster | Marlo Thomas and Friends |
| Tom Chapin | John McCutcheon | Tickle Toon Typhoon |
| Rick Charette | Marcia Merman | Uncle Ruthie |
| The Children of Selma | Mary Miche | Bill Usher |
| Jon Crosse | Eric Nagler | Jim Valley |
| Charlotte Diamond | Hap Palmer | The Weavers |
| Jonathan Edwards | Tom Paxton | Weird Al Yankovic |
| Terrence Farrell | Peter, Paul, and Mary | Patty Zeitli |

**Expectation.** The motivational force of teacher expectation has been documented in hundreds of studies. The self-fulfilling prophecy has been confirmed for music, too. When participants were told that music would enhance learning, it did. In contrast, when a group was told the music would detract, it did (Dibben, 2004).

**Audience Effect.** The motivational power of an audience enhances the already powerful effects of music involvement, as was demonstrated in a study of juvenile delinquent males. One group received both guitar lessons and performance opportunities while the other only received lessons. The performance group improved in self-confidence while the other did not (Deasy, 2002).

As Ashley River music teacher Ann Cheek puts it, "It is just awesome. Regardless of how small their part is, everybody gets to be on stage. It is a validation that they are an important piece of the puzzle. They know we need everybody involved." She explains that a musical production involves all of the arts, so it compounds the motivational force of many art forms.

**Negative Effects.** Music also can have certain negative effects. For example, Scheel and Westefeld (1999) detail connections between heavy metal music and adolescent suicide. Motivation comes from a focus on understanding; students need to know that the typical teenager has 40 percent hearing loss caused by music played at more than 90 decibels over a sustained time.

## Engagement and Active Learning

Musicogeniceupadia works because music making, music reading, and listening engage the mind, emotions, and body. The bulk of music-based instruction has to do with providing curriculum-based singing and listening experiences. Music is used to introduce units (e.g., listen/sing "The Star Spangled Banner" and teach its history at the start of a study of the War of 1812) or as a lesson response (e.g., teach song writing about curricular topics).

**Singing with Students.** Students will not mind if the teacher does not have a fine singing voice if genuine enthusiasm is expressed. Making the effort to sing with students builds relationships and community—staples for discipline. Since classroom teachers are not perceived as specialists, students accept amateur efforts as natural and normal, especially if teachers sing throughout the grades at the school. With experience and commitment to music integration, all teachers can learn to sing without embarrassment, without being limited by the Western notion that only the talented should sing out. Remember Thoreau's point that the forest would be a very quiet place if only the talented birds sang.

**Language Arts.** Singing naturally integrates the language arts of listening, speaking, and reading (Douglas & Willatts, 1994; Kantrowitz & Leslie, 1997; Lamb & Gregory, 1993). To sing, we must hear in our heads, in the same way we hear musical elements of words when reading silently: Which words are to be stressed? What rate? What volume? Singing also emphasizes diction, or clear enunciation of words. Because we usually sing words, vocabulary is built through singing. By pointing out lyrics on a large chart or the overhead, students make the speech-to-print match essential for reading success.

Children enjoy singing the same songs repeatedly, which builds competence and confidence. Teachers usually begin with songs they know (see Ready References 12.8 and 12.9) and then continue to learn new songs (e.g., ones with limited voice

range and notes), often suggested by a music specialist. A repertoire of a dozen action songs (e.g., "Little Bunny Foo Foo") is a good goal. These serve many purposes, including acting as sponge activities when there are schedule delays. Use the Ready References to start a class songbook with lyrics to use as reading material. Consider taping singing at different points in the year and giving a tape to each child as an end-of-year gift.

**Teaching Songs.** Classroom teachers must be able to teach songs. I recommend the film *The Chorus* about a classroom teacher who transforms the lives of juvenile delinquents by spending the time it takes to teach them to sing. It is a superb French film for adults, especially teachers. To learn a song, students need to be motivated to learn and do close listening to hear specific pitches, grasp the tempo and underlying beat, and identify the rhythmic patterns. Teachers can help them do this and put it all together in a whole, using the following guidelines (also see Ready Reference 12.16).

1. Consider developmental levels. Keep songs for younger students simple—easy lyrics, limited melody (not too high or too low), and a catchy beat. See, for example, Jarnow's (1991) *All Ears: How to Use and Choose Recorded Music for Children*.

2. Combine singing with movement. Teachers who move when they sing demonstrate the increased enjoyment from combining the two. Singing accompanied by appropriate facial expressions is more engaging. Sign language can also be used to add movement. Riekehof's *Joy of Signing* is a reference, or you may improvise hand signs and motions. Clap, tap, or use rhythm instruments to keep a steady beat. Use the beat to invite movement. In collaboration with the music specialist, move up to singing rounds and creating harmony.

3. Stay on a specific key. The ideal range for children is usually from about middle C up to G. If songs are pitched too high or low, they have trouble matching the pitch. Usually, students who sing out of tune are not hearing the notes

clearly and may need to have a note or phrase isolated for practice. Use the amount of repetitions needed for success. Almost all children can learn to sing well if they are taught to take time to listen closely. Even middle school students who have not done much singing can succeed if the teacher coaches them to listen so that intonation is accurate. Suggest they try to hear the notes in their heads before singing. If students are not perfect singers immediately, remind them that singing in tune, like all skills, comes with practice.

4. Start with favorite songs. See recommended lists in the Ready References or the *Music Teachers' Book of Lists* (Ross & Stangl, 1994). Consult the music basal in the school district and check with specialists for ideas, especially for folk and patriotic songs.

5. In general, it is recommended that students learn to sing without accompaniment so they listen to themselves and develop their voices—no karaoke at first. One easy way to begin is with "call and response" songs in which students simply echo. Keep a steady beat and clap or snap rhythms to echo. Students can also become leaders. Here is a favorite chant for call and response:

**T:** Acka lacka ching (Students echo).
**T:** Acka lacka chow (S echo).
**T:** Acka lacka ching ching chow chow (S echo).
**T:** Booma lacka booma alack sis boom bah (S echo).
**T:** Reading Reading-Rah Rah Rah (substitute any phrase) (S echo).

6. Teach new songs slowly. Use many repetitions. Nonsense syllables such as "la," "ti," and "tah" can also be used to explore the singing voice. Give frequent encouragement and be supportive of efforts; singing requires risk taking. Explain that everyone can sing well in their own range if they listen carefully and do their best. To teach a round, make sure students master the whole song first, or the song will fall apart

---

## Ready Reference 12.16  Teaching Songs

### Rote Method

1. Motivate by stimulating interest. For example, give background on the song.
2. Sing the whole song or play a recording. Sing in your normal voice, not too high pitched. The range should be appropriate for the students. Enthusiasm is critical at this step, so show it.
3. Ask students to describe what they heard using music terms (e.g., rhyme, repetition, rhythm).
4. Echo sing. Sing a line or phrase and students echo. Continue to build up by repeating previous phrases and adding on. Go through the whole song. If the song is difficult, slow down, but keep a steady beat. If there are unusual words, try echoing the whole song in a speaking voice the first time. Repeat this step as much as necessary.

5. Display the lyrics on a chart, overhead, or pocket chart.
6. Sing through many times. Ask students for ideas on how they can improve by targeting elements (e.g., dynamics, enunciation).

### Rounds

1. Use the rote method to teach the whole song. When it is mastered, go to previous step 5.
2. Instruct students to sing softly so that they can hear each other. Establish start and stop hand signals to direct each group. Keep a steady beat.
3. Start with two parts to keep it simple, with each group singing through twice.

during the round. Music is a skill learned through the three Ps: practice, practice, and practice. Neural pathways and muscle tone develop with multiple repetitions.

7. Use explicit teaching. Model, imitate, and repeat is the most typical sequence for songs. Students should hear the whole song first, before seeing the lyrics, which puts the focus on an enjoyable aesthetic experience. Give direct instruction line by line or phrase by phrase. Finally, sing the whole song several times to increase fluency and enjoyment.

   Note: Some music educators recommend starting with the parts and building up to the whole song, rather than having students hear the whole to begin with. Both whole-to-part and part-to-whole methods involve listening to a part of a song and then echoing the teacher for the bulk of the lesson. As parts are mastered, the song builds up until students can sing the entire song well. Ready Reference 12.16 summarizes steps.

8. Sing daily. Post lyrics *after* students hear a new song so they initially do close listening. Write words large enough to see. Pocket charts enable one line to be put up at a time. Sing songs to start the day and to clean up (e.g., "Kum Ba Yah" works). Instead of giving directions, sing or chant; use the universal melody of "na na na NA na"—think of the childhood taunt—and sing, "Line up and go home."

9. Teach songs from diverse cultures for holidays, traditional songs, and others that go with units. See Appendix J and the Ready References in this chapter and the next for recommendations. Students and their families are also sources of songs and music. Involving them can build more feelings of comfort and ownership about learning. Help students learn songs that make up a cultural bank, including songs from their own culture.

**Song Writing.** Teachers harness the mnemonic power of music by teaching students how to put curricular information into songs, raps, and chants. When students write original songs about content areas, they transform information, which entails elaborate thinking. Warren's (1991) *Piggyback Songs for School* is one collection of songs about science, math, and social studies concepts. Use these as *examples* for students to write their own, which is better for learning than memorizing somebody else's song. Memorizing is low-level thinking. Song writing proceeds like any writing. Check the poetic devices in Chapter 4 for help and be sure to discuss how song lyrics aid memory (*why* they work). Co-writing lyrics to familiar melodies can ease students into seeing how music can be used to transform curricular concepts and skills. Simple rhythm instruments can be made or found to perform songs.

**Music Listening.** Children are inundated with music. We need to ensure that music chosen for school gives exposure to music they would not otherwise hear. Of course, worthy music is a subjective concept, but it is important to develop criteria for quality. For example, if music lyrics are to be examined, then the words should be audible and clear. Some orchestral music can overwhelm students and elicit exaggerated responses. Consult music specialists and use the bibliographies in this chapter and in Appendix J to help find quality music.

Listening goes beyond hearing. Listening is understanding and can be taught. When it comes to music, there is a great deal for students to understand. Within music, with and without lyrics, there are messages in the form of images, stories, and emotions. Directed music listening helps move students beyond hearing. For example, two versions of any song can be played with listening for specifics that cause the variation. Deeper listening is developed through discussions that focus on important details.

**Teach for Transfer.** Arts integration seeks to maximize learning by bringing the motivational and communication power of the arts to bear on other curricular areas. This purpose needs to be explicitly addressed with students by showing connections. For example, demonstrate how reading comprehension involves adding musical elements to printed words by experimenting with the music of reading and talking. Read aloud this sentence, "George Washington was the very first president of the United States of America." Now, try again and change the dynamics (volume). Try again and change tempo (speed). Once more and change pitch and tone. Finally, try changing the rhythm (group phrases differently and add a regular beat, e.g., 1-2-3-4).

Students enjoy manipulating musical elements using words and discover how words really convey very little without the added music. Take time to ask how different versions of the same sentence mean different things based on how the person interprets them by adapting music elements. Discuss how different words, phrases, and sentences feel different based on how they are said and read. The habit of playing with musical elements of language will increase comprehension and help students speak in more interesting ways and more effectively communicate what they want to say.

**Musical Instruments.** Classroom teachers combine art and music when they show how to make and play simple instruments. Instruments extend expression of ideas and feelings with everything from songs to poems. Any story or writing form can be performed with Orff instruments or simple shakers, bells, or drums. For example, parts of speech can be emphasized using particular instruments. See previous instrument examples.

## Creative Problem Solving

Just as in the other arts and in language arts, creative problem solving is used when students write original songs and music, play and perform music, and listen to music. The process needs to be explicitly taught (Ready Reference 2.6), which is exactly what they do at the Conservatory Lab School in Massachusetts (www.conservatorylab.org/); only they call them "shared processes." To make the process kid-friendly, teachers post and teach "Five Shared Processes" for learning with, about, in, and through music (Scripp, 2003).

1. *Listen:* observe, discriminate, decipher, perceive, describe
2. *Create:* invent, transform, improvise, produce, compose
3. *Perform:* demonstrate, interpret, follow through, work with deadlines, memorize, achieve fluency and mastery of skills

4. *Inquire:* question, investigate, analyze, discover
5. *Reflect:* make connections, self-assess, establish goals, revise work

**Arts with Arts.**   Integrating the arts is about helping students discover interrelationships that exist in our world and using CPS to make meaning through all art forms. To achieve this goal, students need to be shown how the arts share common aspects. Basic elements cut across art forms (rhythm, line, shape), and all art forms are created through the creative problem-solving process. We can ease students into the risk taking necessary to do higher order thinking to create, perform, and respond in the arts by setting the stage with expectations. For example, begin to collect and share anecdotes about the struggles and failures most famous artists endure before achieving any measure of success. Share stories about the reactions to highly innovative ideas; Igor Stravinsky's "Rites of Spring" caused a riot when it was first played because it did not conform to what people thought was good music. When students learn how people are often uncomfortable with the unfamiliar, they can learn to be more open to difference and thus grow in flexibility and tolerance.

## Explicit Teaching

While the Mozart effect got a lot of press related to the potential of background music to increase learning, we now know the effects are temporary. Scripp (2003) explains that there are many more studies that support "making music and becoming literate in music—being able to read, interpret, and write music—[these] make a greater and more sustainable difference in enhancing learning in other subjects" (p. 122). Students will not become literate in music without explicit teaching.

Classroom teachers usually cooperate with the music specialist to teach music elements and concepts as needed for lessons and units. The music teacher often takes the lead in certain areas (e.g., teaching the reading of music notation). Classroom teachers can both lead and follow in other areas (e.g., song writing and teaching basic music elements to do close listening to music).

Explicit teaching of musical elements is particularly important and proceeds using the guidelines laid out in Chapter 3: Teach *why* to know the elements, *what* they are, and *how* to use them to listen and make music. This is done in an I do–we do–you do sequence with the teacher first demonstrating, followed by group practice and individual practice. During practice, the teacher coaches students to increase success.

**Whole to Part.**   Music elements and other specific concepts and skills are best taught as needed in a context. For example, a favorite song might be sung, and then the teacher would explicitly teach an element or two to better understand the music. The lesson would conclude with singing the song again. This whole–part–whole sequence is recommended for introducing all arts: (1) Experience the art form as a whole, (2) work on the skills or individual parts, and (3) put it all back together again.

Knowledge of basic musical elements enables students to understand music better and can assist them in music making. During integrated activities, basic elements are needed to talk about the music of cultures under study or music elements in songs and poems. Elements are labels for words, and words contribute to general vocabulary development; so by teaching elements, students develop language and conceptual anchors to explore ways music can be thought about and created. There is a sampling of strategies to develop concepts about elements in Chapter 13 under "Basic Elements and Musical Concepts."

**Visual Displays.**   Music element charts offer students a permanent reference to make, think about, and discuss music. Chapter 3 has other ideas for word walls, charts, and banners. Common mnemonics should also be posted. For example, "Every good boy does fine" is a time-tested mnemonic for musical notes on the staff lines for the treble clef. The mnemonic STAB (soprano, tenor, alto, bass) helps us remember the voices in a quartet. Arts content, just like any other content, can be learned through arts strategies. Students enjoy co-writing songs and poems for class big books or posters about music concepts.

**Reading Music.**   The special skills of reading and notating music notation (symbol system that represents elements of rhythm and pitch—the fundamental building blocks of music) may be beyond the classroom teacher's capabilities to start off. It is worth trying to learn to read some music, and a few basics are listed in Ready Reference 12.4. Research shows the importance of students gaining skill in "reading notes, letters, and numbers at the same time" (Scripp, 2003, pp. 137–138). He calls these "complementary multiple representations" that allow students to solve problems that result in improved test scores in math and reading.

## Aesthetic Orienting

> *To read Schiller's poem "Ode to Joy" is to know one kind of beauty, yet to hear it sung by a great chorus as the majestic conclusion to Beethoven's Ninth Symphony is to experience beauty of an entirely different kind.* (Bruce Boston, 1996)

One goal of music integration is to learn how to get more personal enjoyment from music. Aesthetic-oriented teaching gives students tools to further understand sensory experiences; with understanding comes the possibility for more pleasure. This begins with discussion about how music is an expression of our humanity and culture and a way of expressing and understanding ourselves.

**Stretching.**   We have a tendency to disdain the strange. If we are serious about teaching tolerance, flexibility, and respect for diversity, music is a powerful tool to stretch the concept of the familiar. Here are some suggestions. First, never give students the chance to say they do not like unfamiliar music. Start right in and have them listen with a purpose—to identify instruments they hear, voices, the beat, and so on. Next, ask them to *describe* what they heard as best as they can, but not to evaluate it for preferences yet. Then, give students many opportunities to hear a piece over and over (at least three times, with different purposes) so that they become familiar with it. This simple strategy is effective in expanding musical taste. Make the strange familiar.

**Close Listening.**    There are many reasons to provide critical and creative music listening experiences. Listening to music stimulates the right and left brain hemispheres, triggers cognitive and emotional processes, and enlarges us as whole persons. Music is primarily an art form created for enjoyment, so students need to experience it for the pleasure it brings. This implies we should give time to just listen and just sing. Even when students are to do critical thinking (analysis and evaluation) of a piece of music, it is helpful to let them experience the music as a whole, as an enjoyable art form, before breaking it down for study.

To increase critical listening, give students a "listen for" or purpose (element, instrument, style, or genre) and do repeated listening to selections to develop abilities. Try this: Distribute cards with pictures of instruments, and ask children to hold up the card that corresponds with the instrument when they hear its timbre. Take in-room trips to the windows to stop and listen closely to the sounds outside or stop and listen to school and body sounds and rhythms. Ask students to label sounds they hear as fast or slow, high or low. Describe and model sounds made with instruments, and ask students to describe them. Develop the concept of how sounds express emotions. Ask students to make sounds that are tired, happy, or fearful. In general, develop sensitivities to the role that sound plays in how they feel about a place.

**Live Music.**    Nothing substitutes for the real thing when it comes to developing aesthetic understanding. If you do not play an instrument, invite friends to do so. Children need to see cellos and violins played up close. They benefit from chances to talk with drummers and trumpeters after performances.

**Preferences.**    It is natural to develop music preferences. Teachers should share the music they love and invite students to do the same. Students can come to understand that aesthetic preferences are legitimate reasons for making decisions and are worth discussing. Aesthetic discussions are not intended to change preferences, but to broaden understanding. Just as we can never have too many friends, we should never confine ourselves or our students to what we and they already know. Aesthetic orienting is about continually trying out new music that may become another one of our favorites.

## Management

Chapters 3, 8, and 10 described specific ways teachers manage time, materials, and student behavior that are apropos to music integration. Music is often used as a signal to start and stop

activities. A drum and a tambourine are recommended tools. Rhythmic words can be chanted as attention getters: "Mozart, Beethoven, Manilow, Bach. Get cleaned up and beat the clock." Even a name or word that has musical powers can be used as the attention getter of the day: "Rimsky-Korsakov." Basic rhythms are routinely clapped or snapped to get attention and to signal transitions. See Ready Reference 8.7 for more ideas.

## Practice and Independence

Even music geniuses devote long hours to practice, because they are self-motivated to develop both skill and artistry. Arts integration is not about developing prodigies, but it is about developing skill and self-discipline that set the stage for artistry. One specialized example of how practice leads to independence comes from the Suzuki program at Ashley River Creative Arts. Although every school would not choose to offer Suzuki, all educators should know why it is highly successful.

**Practice—Suzuki Style.**    Shinichi Suzuki applied observations about how German children gained early language fluency to teaching music. The hallmarks of the Suzuki process are daily close listening to music, repeated imitation of sounds, and encouragement through feedback and praise. Practice sessions are short, only 3 to 5 minutes to start, but they must be daily. Suzuki teacher Debby Mennick insists that a nurturing environment and following the Suzuki protocol ensure every child can learn to play the violin. The goal is to develop musical ability by growing skills in concentration, memory, analytical thinking, problem solving, physical coordination, confidence, and self-esteem. A trained ear and love for beautiful music is the result—as well as ability to play the violin.

At Ashley River, students have two 40-minute Suzuki classes per week. One is a master class that must be attended by a parent or "home teacher." This class has no more than three students who each receive an individual lesson observed by the other students and parents. The group learns by observing and serves to encourage and motivate individuals to play pieces. The home teacher/parent learns how and what to teach and, if absent, must send a cassette tape to record the class. A child who comes without a parent can observe, but will not have a lesson. More than three absences can result in discontinuing the child from the program; such is the importance placed on consistency and daily practice.

# Building Block VII: Instructional Design: Routines and Structures

Arts routines are institutionalized into the daily schedule of Mary-Mac Jennings, a kindergarten teacher at Ashley River Creative Arts. Every morning begins with music and movement. "All of our phonemic awareness is done with songs like 'Willoughby Wallaby' where children's names are substituted." She uses lots of Mozart and particularly likes "Beethoven's Wig," which includes lyrics written to classics such as "The Fifth Symphony." Mary-Mac also recommends old favorites such as "Shake the Sillies Out" for morning music and movement.

Putting predictable routines and rituals in place early in the school year makes a substantial contribution to music integration and enables students to assume increasing responsibility. Once students understand how music will happen weekly, daily, and within lessons, they can predict, conduct, adapt, and suggest new routines, much like Mrs. Lucas's class did in the Classroom Snapshot in Chapter 3.

## Lesson Introductions

Music is used to introduce specific lessons by selecting songs and pieces that relate. For example, the lesson may begin with listening to Japanese flute music to set the mood for a reading of *Crow Boy* (Yashima). Students can be asked to discuss how the music feels and what it shows about the composer's background. After reading, the same music can be replayed and connected to the story. Do a repeated listening several times so students develop skills for close listening. Teachers also use music as a background *during* lessons. See "Read to Music" seed strategy in Chapter 13 under "Literacy."

## Daily and Weekly Routines

Teachers use a variety of daily or weekly routines that are music based. Here are examples.

**Start the Day.** Background music and singing familiar songs are common day starters. Songs can be sung with or without posting lyrics and the routine should be varied. If visuals are used, song charts should be easy to read. Some teachers and students create a collaborative collection of favorite songs, and each student ends up with a personal collection. Singing can be followed with a study of language patterns. Teachers often use the lyrics as the primary material for explicit phonics and spelling lessons (e.g., use personal copies for students to find patterns). Students should be invited to bring in tapes and CDs to begin the day, during recess, or during silent reading and writing times. Any opening music listening or singing can be given more depth by focusing on music elements and/or information about the music (composer, genre, etc.). See Ready Reference 12.16 and the Appendix J for more on teaching songs and songbook titles.

**Disc Jockey of the Day.** A student is in charge of the CD player and/or music instruments used for background at the start of the day, transitions, and wrap-up.

Suzuki master class lesson at Ashley River Creative Arts

**Music Critic.** Students listen to a piece of music or song and give their opinions (backed up by evidence). TV shows like *American Idol,* which captivate millions, are discussed in light of the pros and cons of judges, winners, and losers.

**Circle Discussions.** Teachers often begin the day with a circle meeting. Music can be part of this kind of sharing and discussion. Music-related newspaper articles, TV shows, and radio programs can be connected to units under study. Songs and music used in advertisements can be discussed to develop the concept of using music to focus, set mood, and make ideas memorable. See Ready Reference 3.4 for conversation starters.

**Composer of the Day.** A few facts about the composer and a musical piece or song are shared in this routine. There is a free app for this available at the iTunes Internet store. This is more effective if the composer is connected to a current unit, but musicians' birthdays can be celebrated as they come up by playing music examples. Some schools do this schoolwide on the morning TV show (source: www.classical.net/music/composer/dates/comp4.html).

**Wrap-Up.** The pairing of music with other tasks creates an opportunity to respond to common work in uncommon ways. For example, music and songs can be used as a part of cleanup rituals. Here's a song used by a fourth-grade teacher for that purpose (to the tune of "I've Been Working on the Railroad"): "We've been working in this classroom, all the live long day. We've been working in this classroom—it's a mess now, wouldn't you say? Can't you see the clock a ticking? Soon the bell will ring. Let's get this place in order. Clean up as we sing." This teacher also plays fast tempo music, such as the "William Tell Overture," to get chores done before dismissal.

Note: Marching to a cadence is used similarly in the military for tedious drills. In this way the day also ends on a positive note.

## Energizers and Warm-Ups

Numerous music energizers and warm-ups can be used to prepare students for risk taking and creative thinking. They activate or relax and tap into interests. Since performing music is also a physical activity, the body often needs to be prepared as well. Energizers and warm-ups cause students to use both body and mind. Chapter 13 suggests energizers and starter ideas for teaching musical concepts and elements. Many of these can also be used as warm-ups, as can seed strategies from other arts chapters. For example, drama verbal strategies and dance rhythm strategies link with music. In general, think about doing song sharing, poems, chants, and rhythms that take a few minutes and cause both mental and physical engagement. One example follows.

**Name Rhythms.** Call a child's name and beat out the rhythm using syllable patterns and accent. Ask students to echo. The teacher can also beat out the rhythm of a name and the owner echoes and becomes the leader. For example, "Virginia" would be four claps with the second accented. Relate this to poetry meter patterns. See the discussion about word rhythms in Chapter 13.

## Centers, Stations, Displays

**Music Displays.** Students can become more aware of music in everyday life if there is a special table to display ordinary objects with music potential (keys, pencils, boxes, and bottles filled with beans). Displays can include any music-related items, each tagged with a plaque prepared by students to show title, use, and other information.

**Music-Based Book Displays.** Teachers now include a special crate of music-based books or a labeled space in book nooks and other free reading areas. Heightened awareness about music-based books can be coupled with the book ad routine (see Chapter 4). Students may be in charge of supplying a special section of the chalk tray with books they find about music. Once a spot is established, students can display personal books or library books. A question can be posted above each book to entice readers: "How *does* an orchestra get dressed?"

**Instruments Center.** Inexpensive instruments can be found at tag sales or made from common materials (see Arts Literacy section, which is building block II. ). Ask parents to donate old guitars, drums, flutes, and so on. This is a popular center, especially during inside recess.

**Listening Centers.** Stations with headphones are particularly useful in integrating music because students can independently listen to CDs connected to units (e.g., environmental sounds that can be classified or identified). Students can also choose listening centers during free time. There they can help select music for start of the day or other routines. Alternatively they can just choose relaxing music. Musical selections should be available along with information about the composers or styles. Children can also match musical selections with composers as a follow-up to "close listening" done as a group to discern genre and traits. This kind of activity has the potential to spur a lifelong interest and further expand musical tastes.

## Schoolwide Structures

Schools sometimes choose yearly themes that almost always include music. Every country or culture has specific music that may become a monthly schoolwide focus for singing and listening. This may include broadcasts on the morning TV show.

At many arts-based schools, children may choose to join a diversity of music groups. For example, at Ashley River Creative Arts, the last 40 minutes of every day is reserved for clubs and groups, including a chorus and the Piped Pipers percussion group.

# Building Block VIII: Differentiation for Diverse Needs

*If you can talk, you can sing. If you can walk, you can dance.* (Zimbabwe aphorism)

## Nature and Nurture

We are born with music in us. The natural inclination for music is there, but the brain is plastic. Environment and instruction make all the difference, but even children from impoverished environments usually start school with some musical background. Many have well-established preferences since music is often associated with powerful social contexts. This result is sometimes a passionate attachment to specific artists, styles, or genres. Personal musical tastes develop through the process of acculturation: If parents sing and play many kinds of music, children are more likely to sing well and develop diverse tastes. Atypical of American culture, some cultures expect everyone to sing or play an instrument. For example in Polynesian culture, harmony is highly valued, and most children sing well. In other cultures each child's first rattles and bangs are celebrated and converted into musical rhythms (similar to how American parents expand babblings of "ma-ma" into "Mother, yes, I am your mother") (Page, 1995).

## Musical Development

Children progress through stages of musical development that parallel other development. See Appendix A for general stage characteristics. Primary teachers need to know that children come with natural musical background that can be tapped in lessons throughout the curriculum.

**Preschool.** Even toddlers bounce and rock to music and love to play with sounds. Preschoolers can learn simple songs, and by age 3 the brain has developed so rhythm improves. Kids cannot get enough of marching, clapping, tapping, and swaying. They are ready for simple keyboard practice, kazoos, and recorders. By age 4, children understand rhythm, tempo, volume, and pitch and can create their own songs with improvised lyrics. They love songs that suggest actions, such as "Head, Shoulders, Knees, and Toes," and enjoy fingerplays, rhythm instruments, and creative movement. Folk songs, marches, and easy pop songs work well.

**Primary Grades.** The following are guidelines for 5- to 8-year-olds.

- Able to sing and echo rhythms and melodies during call and response songs
- Out of tune is normal; pitch awareness develops with modeling
- Some music preferences, like silly songs and lots of rhythm (Sousa marches)
- Open to diverse musical genres from classical to hip-hop
- Ready for music lessons on recorder, keyboard, or violin between the ages of 3 and 8, but the sooner the better
- Able to compose music, so give opportunities to both sing and compose (e.g., on a keyboard) (Habemeyer, 1999; Upitis & Smithrim, 2003)
- Recommended musical artists for this age group include Hap Palmer, The Kids of Widney High, Rosenshontz, Pete Seeger, Steve and Greg, Marlo Thomas and Friends, Tickle Tune Typhoon, Peter Alsop, Heather Bishop, Tom Chapin, Ella Jenkins, Kids on the Block, and Disney tunes

**Intermediate Grades.** There is increasing variation in children because of experiences and instruction. Preferences are more pronounced. Considerations for the intermediate grades (ages 9 through 12) include the following:

- Promote music lessons; competence on an instrument is still possible (Jensen, 2001, p. 19). Vocal training can begin around age 12.
- Plan singing in groups, such as musicals, choirs, and quartets.
- Emphasize nonmusical benefits: memory, creativity, relaxation, enjoyment, self-discipline, and satisfaction.
- Provide positive musical role models.
- Recommended musical artists include Bill Harley, Janet and Judy, Mary Miche, The Weavers, and Weird Al Yankovic.

Classroom teachers have a lot to build on as they integrate music. Begin with what children already know. Use an interest inventory to identify favorite music and musicians. Start with their strengths and interests and use ideas for differentiating instruction (see Ready Reference 3.11). Literacy instruction, in particular, can be coupled with music and songs children enjoy. For example, ask children to dictate lyrics to a favorite song and use the chart for reading and singing to build fluency. Songs are naturally motivating and provide rich material to teach high-frequency words and phonic and spelling patterns. After singing, play "I Spy" using any language concept from letters to parts of speech. With more mature students, use school-appropriate songs to teach sentence structure (grammar), usage, alliteration, and so forth.

# Building Block IX: Assessment for Learning

Arts integration has blossomed at an interesting time in the evolution of assessment. On the one hand, assessment traditions in the arts have informed cutting-edge thinking in assessment; the use of portfolios, exhibits, and performances are arts tools that are being incorporated into assessment plans in non-arts-based as well as arts-based schools. The increased effort to balance the use of formative (during learning) with summative assessment (final work) is another assessment pattern that has long been used in the arts; critiques and coaching are time-honored ways to increase quality of work. It isn't surprising that integrated arts schools have embraced assessment *for* learning, as opposed to overemphasis on assessment *of* learning. (For a discussion of the difference, see Chapter 3.)

What is surprising is the slowness with which the arts themselves have been included in assessment. Perhaps this is attached to the lingering misconception that assessment may somehow limit creative development. Indeed, the opposite is true. Progressive teachers and schools are finding ways to give feedback to students as they engage in music and the other arts to increase the quality of learning. That includes boosting engagement in creative problem solving, which usually increases happiness with the learning process.

## Two-Pronged Assessment Planning

In the case of arts integration, assessment must be at least two pronged. We need to support learning in traditional academic areas and in the arts. This is planned from the outset using a lesson plan format in which curricular objectives and arts objectives are specified with assessment planned for both, during and at the end of work.

## Feedback

The most important formative assessment is observation (using criteria) that is shared in the form of feedback. Students benefit from feedback from the teacher and peers to increase use of music concepts and skills. For example, a teacher can say, "You have great volume. You are breathing from your diaphragm!" This reinforces a singing skill that can be carried forward.

Both students and teachers need evidence that all the work put into music integration is paying off. Classroom teachers can cooperate with music specialists to provide such evidence. For example, Ashley River music specialist Ann Cheek records each child's status on music objectives according to "beginning, developing, or applying levels." Progress is tracked on concepts such as melody, rhythm, timbre, and creative expression. She does individual reports by using print merge on her computer.

There have been discussions in previous chapters of performances and cumulative portfolios. Both of these are relevant to music growth. Portfolios can include original songs, video and audio recordings, checklists of progress, journal entries, and other writing about music. Tests and quizzes can be included as well, as appropriate to the goals and standards (see music standards in Ready Reference 12.10). Appendix D includes 10 assessment examples and an explanation of how to set up and manage arts folios.

## Interest Inventories

Assessing music interests and preferences gives valuable diagnostic information for teachers to adapt lessons. Much can be learned about music background through conversations, observation, and talks with parents. A sample interest inventory is included in Appendix D.

## Program Evaluation

For specific checklists to examine the quality of music education, go to the South Carolina ABC Schools' website (www.winthrop.edu/ABC/). The *Opportunity to Learn Standards* are downloadable.

# Building Block X: Music Partnerships

In Brooklyn, New York, PS 314 used to be on the state's list of worst schools, but not any more. The school partnered with the Metropolitan Opera for arts-based units. Students attend dress rehearsals, use the plots and settings to learn history (e.g., *Aida*) and literature (e.g., *Faust*), and write their own operas.

When classroom teachers partner with music specialists, there is incredible potential to change students' learning. Even a small encounter can make a difference. I recently met a teacher in Chattanooga, Tennessee, who has been teaching for 31 years. In the conversation, Arlene Sneed explained:

> I was an at-risk child. When I was in the sixth grade, Norman Woodall, the Hixson High School band director, came to show musical instruments. If I had been absent, I would not be who I am today. That one day literally changed my life. Learning to play a musical instrument gave me the confidence, discipline, and determination to pursue the education I needed to get here.

Partnering doesn't have to mean a residency, even though this arrangement is desirable. Teachers should seek out community partnerships using the resources in Chapter 3, especially the local arts council. Musical guests can be sought out in the form of local singers and musicians who may be able to perform music connected to units in science, social studies, and the like.

Often students find potential candidates in their families. Appendix C is a checklist of planning for an artist's residency or visit. Arlene Sneed's experience reminds us it is worth the effort to try to find musicians for even one-shot visits.

## Music Teachers

Of course the music teacher is the specialist most likely to partner with classroom teachers. Ashley River music teacher Ann Cheek has a sizable lending library of music-based children's literature available to teachers. She also burns CDs for them and is part of the planning teams for units.

## Technology

Ten years ago, teachers rarely looked to technology for help in music integration. Today, the Internet is a first stop. There is now music software to learn to read music and understand music history. Music-computer specialists can show teachers how to involve students in creating original musical compositions with software, which often requires a musical instrument digital interface (MIDI). This is an electric musical keyboard that plugs into a computer. Other software does not require a MIDI nor any amplification. Books, such as *The Musical PC,* review software.

CD-ROMs can now be purchased that allow students to see and hear orchestras playing and get background information on composers or instruments. Social studies, math, reading, and language arts experiences are automatically integrated in this type of software experience. Consult sources in your own locale.

# Classroom Snapshot
## African American Music and History

Teacher Sylvia Horres brings this chapter back to where it started: a regular classroom teacher using music in an integral way.

Ms. Horres is seated in a canvas director's chair. Students sit pretzel style on the carpet.

"Remember, there is no one right answer!" she tells the class as she shows a page from a picture book about Booker T. Washington. The book is *More Than Anything Else* (Bradby), and Sylvia is doing an introduction for her daily read-aloud. This month it is connected to a social studies unit on African American history.

"Look closely at what is in his hands," Ms. Horres coaches them.

"Maybe they are pictures of his family and he misses them," says one boy.

"What makes you say that, Sam?"

"Well, because he looks so sad. His head is way down."

"So, what might this book be about—just from our close look at the pictures?"

A girl responds, "Maybe it is about getting freedom." The teacher again **asks for evidence** from the picture. There are more student observations and requests for evidence to support their hypotheses.

"Reading a book for the first time is like watching a movie," she tells them. "I want you to just view and listen. Think about our predictions and find details you want to discuss. Especially, enjoy!"

The class is focused as she reads this moving story about a boy's desire to learn to read. Of course, it isn't exactly like watching a movie because Ms. Horres is skilled at using **inserted questions** to actively engage students in making meaning from the pictures and the story. She asks about the theme with questions, such as "Why is it important for him to learn to read?" She also focuses on idioms and metaphors, such as "he jumped into another world," by asking what this means, how it feels, and why the author didn't just "say it straight."

Ms. Horres reads expressively. She is a model of **fluency.** She "makes music" with her voice, varying the volume, tempo, pitch, and rate to cause the words to seem like song lyrics. It is obvious that she believes reading aloud is an art; this is no unrehearsed performance.

At one poignant moment in the story she stops and asks, "What does 'taking the sounds of my name and draw them on the ground' mean?" The room is quiet. It is as if a sacred act has been described. In a whisper, one boy says, "He is writing his letters." There is a respectful **wait time** and then Ms. Horres asks,

"What do you think this boy might have done with his life?"

"He got to be free?" asks another hopefully.

"He did. But, how could reading make him free?"

"Maybe he became an author and writing let his ideas be free," thinks a boy.

"What a **beautiful** way to say it, Germaine. Now I have to tell you that this is not a fiction book. It is *nonfiction*. It is about a real person and his name was Booker."

Sylvia turns to the computer behind her that is hooked to a TV monitor. She clicks to display a picture from the **Internet** and tells the rest of the story of Booker's life, including setting a context for "blues music in troubled times."

At the end of the storytelling, she asks the students to **connect** books they've read that had to do with slave songs and secret messages. In particular, they remember *The Drinking Gourd* and how the song gave directions for escaping slaves.

"Today we're going to learn more songs, not just ones with secret codes, but music about how black people felt after they were free. This is sad music about their troubles. What colors are sad?"

"Blue!" say two boys at once.

"You got it. This is 'blues' music. Let's listen to some."

"Yeah!" shout the students.

"**Listen for** two things: How people use their voices and the instruments they are using now that they are free. Who remembers our **movement rules**?"

"Body controlled," says one girl.

"No talking," says another girl.

"What else?"

"Just feeling the music and moving for yourself," a boy adds.

"Yes. Find your place in the room and freeze." Ms. Horres starts the CD. Students sway to mellow blues sounds. She also moves and coaches students to use their arms, legs, feet, head, and hips. After a few minutes she counts to three, and the students freeze.

"How did you feel when you were dancing?" she asks.

Students say they felt tired, sad, drowsy, sleepy, worn out, and hungry. Ms. Horres starts a **vocabulary web** of words and asks students to "spell for me" as she writes.

She asks how the music **caused** the feelings and students say it was slow. Sylvia tells them this is the **tempo**. She asks what they noticed about the voices and instruments. Students think they heard horns "stretched out," and the voices were "flowing," some deep and some high pitched.

Walk to Read is almost over. Ms. Horres tells the students to move like the blues to line up. As they exit, she asks them to each tell one thing they learned. Quickly 17 students offer 17 different ideas from "blues is sad music" to "Booker liked books."

## Text Set for African American Unit

*When Marion Sang* (CD of Boy's Choir of Harlem)
*God Bless the Child* (CD/Billy Holiday lyrics)
*Ella Fitzgerald*
*If I Only Had a Horn*
*Perfect Harmony*
*No Mirrors in My Mama's House*
*Ben's Trumpet*
*I See the Rhythm*
*More than Anything Else*
*Barefoot*
*Back Home*
*A Lesson for MLK, Jr.*
*Five Bold Freedom Fighters*
*Amazing Grace*
*The Sounds that Make Jazz*
*Little Stevie Wonder* (with CD)
*A Blue So Blue* ✳

## Conclusion

*What's more, the teachers are positive about it and the parents are happy.*
(Larry Scripp)

Scripp (2003) is talking about music-based learning. Every child deserves to grow up with music woven into the fabric of learning, not as an isolated event that happens every other Tuesday. This chapter explains *why*, as well as *what*, classroom teachers need to know to make this a reality using AI Building Blocks I and II. *How* music may be integrated was presented in AI Building Blocks II through X. In the next chapter, more specific ideas are given to teach music elements so that students can use music as a way of learning. There are also energizers and seed strategies for integrating music throughout curricular areas.

## Teachers as Leaders: AI Advocacy

Be inspired by teachers like those described in this chapter, who write and perform songs that teach about their fields. Write songs with a group about the unique contributions of music to life and learning. Post on YouTube or ask to perform in a public forum such as a faculty meeting or local radio station.

**PEARSON**
**myeducationlab**

Go to the Activities and Applications section for Topic *Strategies for Teaching* at MyEducationLab for your course and complete the video activities entitled "Teaching Fractions through Music" and "Using Arts-Based Read Aloud to Engage Students."

Go to the Book Specific Resources section in the MyEducationLab for your course, select your book and Chapter 12 to view the Questions to Guide Reading, Response Options, and Bibliography of Music Based Children's Literature.

## Resources

See the Appendix for study materials, including websites. Chapter 13 lists music activity books.

### Videos

*Let's Sing!* (1998). Berkeley, CA: Langstaff Video Project. (teaching children songs with their own accompanying percussion)

*Making music in the classroom.* (1995). Berkeley, CA: Langstaff Video Project. (cultural songs)

*Stomp out loud!* (1998). HBO studios. www.stomponline.com. (amazing percussion group makes music using found objects)

# 13

# Music Seed Strategies

*For hundreds of years it has been known that teaching arts, along with history, math and biology, helps create the "well-rounded mind" that western civilization and America are grounded upon. We need that well-rounded mind now, for it is from creativity and imagination that the solutions to our political and social problems will come.* (Richard Dreyfuss, music teacher in Mr. Holland's Opus)

## Overview

This chapter starts with a Classroom Snapshot of a music teacher integrating literature. The bulk of the chapter is a compendium of seed strategies to prompt creative lesson planning using music.

## Introduction

Most of my arts integration courses culminate in Show Time! Preservice and practicing teachers show their knowledge about AI through drama, dance, visual art, poetry, and music—especially song. It is fitting for the last chapter of this book to start with an example of how teachers use CPS to show they know about CPS.

*Group One:* Chants
Think left, Think right, Think low, Think high
Oh, the thinks you can think up if you only try. (adapted from Dr. Seuss)
*Group Two:* Sings
Bub-bub-bub-bubblin'
Bub-bub-bub-bubblin'
Bub-bub-bub-bubblin'
Bub-bub-bub-bubblin'
*Group Three:* Sings
Arts ideas are a bubblin' over
Arts ideas bubble in my soul (3X)
*Group Two:* Joins in on 2-3X.
*Group Four:* Raps "The CPS Rap"(in four parts)
Problem Find/Motivate/Hypothesize/to Create
*Refrain (Whole Group):* Cogitate to create
**Question Question Question Question**
Data gather/Visualize/SCAMPER it/Empathize
REFRAIN
Zoom in/Zoom out/Incubate/Insight comes/If you wait
REFRAIN

Summarize/Synthesize/Connect/Transform before your eyes
REFRAIN
Reflect/Revise/Evaluate/Make it public/Celebrate!
ALL:
Cogitate to create
Unique is what we celebrate!

This particular group aced the final. Anyone who doubts the power of music to make learning unforgettable just should have been there. In the opening Snapshot a music teacher shows how she uses performances to showcase learning.

## Teacher Spotlight
### Literature through Music

Ann Cheek, the music teacher at Ashley River Creative Arts, is famous for her mini-musicals. Each year her students turn books such as *Chicka Chicka Boom Boom, Zomo the Rabbit,* and *The Very Hungry Caterpillar* into performance pieces. They use musical instruments, often bought through a box top program. "Last year we raised $3,000 to buy two glockenspiels and a computer," Ms. Cheek reports. (See www.boxtops4education.com.) She especially focuses on Orff instruments, noting that "Orff pedagogy has taught me how to work with poetry and speech to teach music."

Ms. Cheek is passionate about integration. "Without the arts, you are missing a whole important part of life and history." She challenges anyone to try to understand the Great Depression without Woody Guthrie's songs. "This Land Is Your Land" cheered up a nation. "In life things aren't separated," she insists. "The arts should be integral to life inside school, too." Ms. Cheek explains that music is another dimension to express yourself and shows the evolution of a culture. "Americans play the harmonica, banjos, and other folk instruments, and we also enjoy music at the 'high end' of culture—orchestras and operas," she says.

### Literacy

"We need to model a love of reading," Ms. Cheek says as she gestures to her large music-based classroom library for free reading. She especially enjoys integrating children's

Ann Cheek, music teacher, using Solfege

adapted and fleshed out for them to become examples of the meaningful music integration described in Chapter 12. Many seed strategies fit in more than one section, and some use multiple arts, not just music.

Seed strategies are organized into three categories: energizers and warm-ups, music elements and concepts, and curricular areas (ideas for science, social studies, literacy, and math).

# I. Energizers and Warm-ups

Energizers are used to get attention, increase focus and concentration, start creative problem solving, and warm up the voice and body. Also see the energizers and warm-ups in chapters on dance, drama, art, and literature.

literature into music lessons, and the room is filled with children's books for units of study. Ann explains that music involves learning specific content and skills, just like any other form of literacy. "Classroom teachers can integrate aspects of the arts, but specialists are needed to go into the kind of depth that eventually creates music literacy," she recommends. Ms. Cheek brings in every area of the curriculum to music and is ready to be a resource for classroom teachers. Teachers sing her praises for everything from burning CDs for them to helping them understand music concepts.

## Math and Music

On the bulletin board is the Pizza Rondo. It shows whole, half, quarter, eighth, and sixteenth notes used to teach fractions to all grade levels. "They learn the relative value of notes," Ms. Cheek explains. She shows how each represents a fraction of a pizza. When she teaches the Pizza Rondo, she uses manipulatives with layers so she can show how whole notes relate to the other notes. Students sing as they pull felt pizza pieces off of the big pizza, singing "Make me a pizza if you can. . ." ✳

# Organization

*At my age, I'm not going to be playing tackle football, but I'm still making music. And the great thing about music, our theater, our dance is that it's not something you outgrow once you get past 17.* (Arkansas Governor (and guitarist) Mike Huckabee)

Seed strategies are kernel ideas to help teachers think creatively about integrating music. All of the seeds need to be

**Morning TV Show.** Use a schoolwide broadcast to spotlight/play different genres of music each morning, followed by 30-second music genre reports by students. Lots can be learned about jazz on the 2-minute-a-day plan.

**Mood Music.** When students enter the room, have music playing that creates the mood for upcoming work. *Example:* Play nature sounds related to a science lesson. Stop the CD and ask students to listen again to notice sounds, instruments, patterns, and the like. Ready Reference 12.12 gives more pointers about background music.

**Clap Rhythm.** List suggestions of favorite poems or songs. Then, instead of singing, clap the rhythm by syllables. Do as a call and response or echo. *Variation:* Clap the beat instead of the rhythm.

**Echo Me.** A leader claps, slaps, snaps, or clicks a series of rhythms that are echoed by the class. Use children's names: Divide them into syllables and accent (e.g., Clau' di a). Adapt for phrases or topics such as days of the week, months of the year, animal names, or plants. Challenge by turning rhythm patterns into a round: Divide the class in half with a leader for each half to start the pattern at varying times.

**Name Echo.** Stand in a circle. Leader says her name and class echoes using the exact volume, pitch, dynamics, tempo, and so forth. Student to right then does the same. Class echoes. *Variation:* Do as a cumulative name echo, repeating from the first name. Add movement if desired.

**Name Songs.** Sing songs that call for use of student names. *Examples:* "Willoughby Wallaby Woo" or "Name Game." *Variation:* Adapt songs like "My Aunt Came Back" to student names.

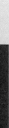
Music

**Name Polyrhythms.** Sit in circle and leader says his or her name on one beat. Group echoes. Continue around circle. Next, leader says his or her name on one beat and keeps saying it. Person to left comes in with her or his name and so on until everyone is chanting on one beat.

**Sing the Scales.** Warm up voices by singing major and minor scales, with or without words or instruments. Major and minor scale music can be purchased at music supply stores. *Variation:* Sing using short or long vowel sounds.

**Tongue Twisters.** Warm up students' voices for singing with tongue twisters. See more examples in Chapter 9. Here is one for singing: "Tip of the tongue, the teeth, and the lips." Say it three to five times. *Variation:* Sing the scale using one vowel sound, such as short a.

**Theme Song.** Select or do a collaborative writing of a class song. Sing together as a daily routine. *Example:* Sing "High Hopes," about an ant moving a rubber plant. *Variation:* Change songs for each social studies or science unit.

**Say It Different Ways.** Form a circle. IT says a sentence, which is passed around with each person changing the volume, rate, pitch, accent, and rhythm patterns. *Example:* "The rain in Spain falls mainly on the plain."

**Question and Answer Songs.** Many songs involve asking and answering questions, such as "Baa Baa Black Sheep" and "Are You Sleeping?" Divide the class in half and direct one-half to sing questions and other half the answers.

**Poem One Liners.** Explain that words are made meaningful by adding "music" to words: changing the volume/dynamics, accent, pitch, rhythm, and so forth. Choose a poem (e.g., see O'Neil's *Hailstones & Halibut Bones*). Give each student one line to memorize. Give time to experiment with saying lines in various ways. Stand in a circle and distribute three beanie bags randomly. On the count of three, they toss the beanies to other students. Receivers speak their lines, expressively and loudly. (Beanies will be caught simultaneously, so three students will be speaking at the same time.) After everyone has had a go, choose one poem line. Pass that one line around the circle with each student changing it using music elements. Debrief with questions, such as "How did the meaning change? What was hardest to vary: pitch, dynamics, tempo, and accent? What did you discover from observing other students?"

**Join In.** Form small groups to listen to a musical selection. Challenge each group to create a movement pattern involving clapping hands and tapping feet as the music is replayed. Then stop the music. Have the first group do its movements when the music starts. Keep adding more groups until all groups are doing their movements.

**Musical Memories.** Students close their eyes and imagine different sounds as they are described (e.g., crickets chirping, wind chimes, jingle bells, song on keyboard). Give time to create the sound images. After each, ask the student to describe the images.

**Celebrate.** Use a rhythmic chant or cheer to celebrate class and individual efforts. *Example:* Pat pat pat / on the back back back / for a job well done (3X). Add patting movement.

**Tempo Change.** Students get into personal spaces. Music is played with varying speeds. They move in response to music (in place or locomotor). Use slow, fast, staccato (choppy), or legato (smooth) or music that has accelerando. For "Beep Beep" (the Little Nash Rambler song), divide into groups according to vehicles (six in a van, four in a car, two on a motorcycle, etc.). Vehicles "drive" around as this 1950s song accelerates.

**Rag Doll.** Stand in a circle with feet apart and balanced. Tell students: "Stretch up tall. Then bend over collapsing quickly from the waist. Relax your arms and let your hands dangle. Keep your arms, hands, and neck loose like a rag doll. Slowly raise body up, staying relaxed. Repeat. While your neck is still relaxed slowly roll your head to the left, then back, right, and down in front. Reverse the rotation. Be sure to keep your neck relaxed. Immediately after the head roll with arms still relaxed, swing them in large circles one at a time. Slowly yawn, sounding an 'ahhhhhh' on exhalation from the yawn. Open your throat. Then in an exaggerated fashion say, 'A, E, I, O, U.'"

**Rhythm Mirror.** Form a circle with IT in the middle, who begins a rhythm or movement. Others must mirror. IT passes the rhythm on by staring at one person, who slowly takes over and changes places with IT. The class observes and begins to mirror the new rhythms and actions when they feel the exchange is complete.

**Rhythm Sync.** Group forms a circle. When leader says "begin," everyone makes an original rhythm using hands, feet, or voice. Slowly, by listening to each other, the group becomes one rhythm. Then individuals slowly begin new rhythms, and a new group rhythm emerges.

**Exchange.** Two lines form on opposite sides of the room. The first pair at one end starts. Each person in the pair begins a unique rhythm and walks toward her partner. As they pass, the two exchange rhythms. Then the next pair goes and on down the line. Focus on unusual rhythms.

**Rhythm Pass.** Do in groups of four to six. Pass a rhythm around a circle. *Example:* With a 1-2 rhythm all slap knees, palms down on downbeat, and then palms up. IT slaps hand of right neighbor on 2, and neighbor passes and so on until the pass is complete and the group is back to each slapping own knees on 1. The last person to receive the pass becomes IT.

**"Head, Shoulders, Knees, and Toes."** First, sing the song through. Then add motions. Practice at a slow tempo. Finally, ask students to stand in a circle and do movements as they sing, gradually substituting body parts with hums, but continuing the actions: Touch head, touch shoulders, touch knees, touch toes, and so forth. Sing at different volumes and tempos.

**Shoe Beat.** Everyone sits in a circle and removes one shoe. Agree on a song or rhythm pattern to do together during which shoes are passed, left to right, and held. For example, "Mary had a little lamb" could be "pass–pass–hold." If you don't keep the rhythm, the shoes pile up on you!

Music

Making music at Ashley River Creative Arts

**Be Glad It's Monday (BGIM).** Start each Monday with a celebration song. *Example:* Using the tune "You Are My Sunshine" or "This Land Is Your Land," sing "Be glad it's Monday. Day after Sunday. Be glad it's Monday, all day today. Be glad it's Monday. It's such a fun day. Be glad that Monday's here to stay."

**Music Jokes and Riddles.** Boost interest in music and use of CPS by starting the day with a joke or riddle. Involve students in finding, creating, and sharing. *Example:* "Which composer did the chickens say they liked best?" (Answer: B _____ch, B _____ch, B _____ch).

**Balloon Movement.** Put on classical music (e.g., Haydn pastoral) and give small groups a balloon to waft to the beat. Be sure to discuss behavior expectations and explain how the activity is about concentrating to stay on beat.

**Knock and Respond.** When someone knocks on a door to the rhythm "da-da da-da-DA," we know to reply "da-da." Create original rhythms by having partners make up ones to demonstrate. Challenge the group to learn new knock and respond patterns.

**Rhythm Circle.** Stand in a circle with IT, who creates a rhythmic phrase that is passed around the circle to the right until it returns to IT. The person to right is then IT.

**Add-On Songs.** Collect songs that invite improvised verses such as "If You're Happy and You Know It" and "The More We Are Together." "Down by the Bay" requires adding original rhyming words. A funny example of a copycat song is "On Legs You'll Find Two Legs Behind" to the Scottish tune "Auld Lang Syne."

**Music Bingo.** Brainstorm and write down musical categories and examples, such as musical genre and styles, composers, singers, instruments, elements, and particular songs. Fold blank paper four times to create 16 bingo squares. At a signal, students search for peers who know about each concept. The goal is to write names under each music word until bingo happens—across, down, or diagonally.

**Hum Groups.** Type four song titles on slips of paper. Repeat the titles until you have enough for everyone. Students draw a slip and on a signal sing or hum the melody while trying to find others singing the same melody. Fellow hummers remain together until everyone is grouped. *Example:* "Row, Row, Row Your Boat."

## II. Music Elements and Concepts

The seed strategies in this section are examples of ideas to develop a music knowledge and skill base needed to use music as a learning tool.

**Rhythm Symphony.** The leader creates a rhythm and the group echoes it. Keep going, getting increasingly complicated, with whistles, clicks, claps, and slaps, slower and faster. At any point the leader can "pass it on," and another person becomes leader.

**Hum Melodies.** Choose a song students know. Hum the first line. Keep humming until someone guesses. Everyone sings the words as soon as the song is named. Then have a student take a turn humming a song. *Examples:* "I've Been Working on the Railroad" and "Row, Row, Row Your Boat."

**Listening Phones.** Use PVC pipe to make "phones" for students to hear their own voices. Use two curved pieces to make the earpiece and voice piece. Cut a 3-inch straight piece for the handle. Use phones to rehearse and self-evaluate.

**Name Harmonies.** Pair children with long and short names. Pairs take turns beating out their names in rotation and together. Rhythm instruments or body parts can be used. *Variation:* Student pairs sing their names in harmony.

**Name Duet.** Pairs explore combinations using just their names (e.g., Dan-Amber, Dan-Dan-Dan, Amber-Dan-Amber-Dan-Amber-Dan). Vary by changing the tempo of one name, the other, or both. Change the combination of tempo and volume in different ways. Explore harmonies created by beating out both names or varying volume and tempo.

Music

**Name Melody.** Students work in pairs or small groups to create a melody for each person's name or put all the names together to a tune.

**Cumulative Counterpoint Melodies.** Make a list of songs everyone knows, such as "Row, Row, Row Your Boat." Form small groups. Each student chooses one song to hum using a syllable, such as "la la" or "ti ti." IT starts humming. Then the student to the right starts humming on top of IT's song during the second time around, the third person adds on, and so on. Humming overlapping melodies at the same time, without words, teaches counterpoint.

**Kazoo Melodies.** Make kazoos from combs by folding paper over them or use empty candy boxes (e.g., small Milk Dud boxes). A leader plays a melody on a kazoo. Others echo on kazoos.

**Environment Sounds (Pitch).** Record common sounds. Ask students to signal if the sounds are high or low or in between high and low. Examples are a doorbell, mixer, and computer hum.

**Guess Who (Timbre).** A panel of five students comes to the front. All students close their eyes. Leader taps one panel member on the shoulder. Tapped person says, "Who did that?" Students open their eyes and guess who spoke. Each time a name is guessed ask, "How did you know?" Coach for answers to describe the uniqueness of voices. Repeat but have students sing, "Who did that?" Stress that each speaking and singing voice is unique.

**Old MacMajor.** Use the tune of "Old MacDonald" to learn the key signatures (idea from music teacher Aurelia Cornett):

> Old Macmajor had some keys e-i-e-i-o. And in these keys there were some sharps e-i-e-i-o. With a one sharp G and two sharps D and the key of A has one, two, three. Old Macmajor had some keys e-i-e-i-o. Old Macmajor had some keys e-i-e-i-o. See how easy it can be e-i-e-i-o. Four sharps give up the key of E and A has three and two in D and there's just one in the key of G. Old Macmajor had some keys e-i-e-i-o.

**Name that Instrument (Timbre).** First students experiment with rhythm instruments to become familiar with their sound qualities. Label each instrument (e.g., tambourine, shaker). Then tell them to close their eyes as IT plays one. Stress that each instrument has a unique sound, even though some sound similar. Take guesses along with reasons. *Variation:* Use a tape or CD of orchestral instruments or other music instruments (guitar, banjo).

**Dynamics Dial.** Dynamics has to do with volume. Make a volume dial out of cardboard or use an old clock. Label "soft" to "loud" on the dial with the musical symbols *pp* (very soft), *p* (soft), *mp* (medium soft), *mf* (medium loud), *f* (loud), *ff* (very loud), and *mfz* (loudest). Invite students to sing a familiar song as someone turns the dial or volume button. The children should sing accordingly. For example, if the dial said "pp," children sing very, very softly. *Variation:* Teach hand signals to show dynamics. Make them up or use ones from books such as *Joy of Signing* (Riekehof, 1987).

**Conduct Dynamics.** Use with any musical instruments (Orff, homemade, or found sounds). Ask students to play very soft, soft, loud, and very loud. Challenge to start softly and gradually play louder (crescendo) and vice versa (decrescendo). Invite students to conduct. Students play louder as the conductor raises the hands and softer as the hands go lower. Have the conductor try quick raises to practice sudden dynamic changes.

**Pretend to Conduct.** Let students pretend to conduct using conducting patterns. Teach start and stop signals, and then practice actual patterns, learning "downbeat" and "upbeat." Orchestra members can use different sounds as their instruments (e.g., click, hum, pop, hiss, whistle). Basic conducting patterns are as follows:

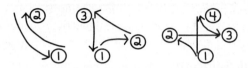

**Musical Elements in Art.** After teaching the elements of music, use a piece of art and ask students to find the same elements. For example, folk art and folk music can be compared. Find rhythm in art, texture, tempo, style aspects, and dynamics (areas that are louder or softer).

**Sound Textured Story.** Read a story that has repeated language. Cumulative stories work, as do sound stories (see Chapter 4). Next, assign repetitive words and ask students to think of different ways to say words or add sound effects. For example, every time the word *hen* is heard, students say "cluck cluck cluck" or strike triangles. Involve everyone using unison, duos, trios, or individual sounds. Discuss how textured layers are created as sounds enter and reenter. Ask students to compare sound textures to fabric textures (e.g., rough, soft).

**Thick and Thin Voices (Texture).** Use poems or stories and assign different numbers of students to participate in solo and choral readings of parts. Ask how it sounds when more people are reading compared to fewer. Label as "thick" and "thin" sounds. Repeat using singing voices. Relate to using individual versus multiple instruments by playing recordings of the same song or music done by an orchestra versus a single instrument.

**Barbershop Quartet (Harmony).** One person sings the main melody while others harmonize or echo the tune to make a barbershop quartet. Some good songs for quartets are "By the Light of the Silvery Moon," "Sweet Adeline," "Down by the Old Mill Stream," and "Down by the Bay." (This is a good time to introduce the terms *soprano*, *alto*, *tenor*, and *bass* and the acronym STAB to remember them.)

**Rounds or Canon (Harmony).** Start by speaking in rounds. Students can also sing with a CD that features rounds. "Row, Row, Row Your Boat" is a popular round. Once they can sing along, they are ready to sing on their own. Movements can be created for each line and performed while singing, which helps students keep track of where they are. After each group practices and knows its lines, all groups can also sing simultaneously.

**Picturing Form.** Play a variety of musical pieces. Discuss repetitive patterns and similar and contrasting sections. Target one piece. Ask students to raise a hand when the first line or phrase is heard. Label this A and draw a picture of an object that begins with A. Have students raise the same hand if the next line is similar and draw another A object on the board. If the line is different, have them raise the other hand and draw an item that begins with B. Continue until there is a complete picture to represent all the phrases. Sing again and have students raise appropriate hands as symbols are designated. For example, "Mary Had a Little Lamb" would be "ABAC."

**Instrument Pantomime.** After reading a book such as Isadora's *Ben's Trumpet* or Raschka's *Charlie Parker Played Be Bop* (saxophone), brainstorm types of instruments. In small groups, one student pantomimes playing different instruments, when the leader signals. Group members write down their guesses. Change players in the groups at the end of 1 minute and start again.

**Musical Rainbow.** Add food coloring to each of eight glasses filled with different amounts of water. (Each should have about 1 inch more than the previous glass.) The eight notes will make a beautiful rainbow when put in order. 1 is clear; 2 is red; 3 is orange; 4 is yellow; 5 is green; 6 is blue; 7 is purple; 8 is clear. *Note:* Red plus yellow makes orange. Blue plus yellow makes green. Red plus blue makes purple. Under each glass, put a paper with the number of the tone that the glass plays.

**Form Books.** Read a book based on a song (e.g., Raffi's "Shake My Sillies Out"). Sing the song. Ask students how form (pattern) is illustrated in the story or song. Give children phrases of a favorite song to illustrate to create a class book. Children draw a picture for each line of the song. If a line repeats, they should draw the same picture. The final book will show the song's form.

**Repeat a Beat (Ostinato).** Make a sound and repeat it a number of times: tap the window, click your tongue, or repeat a syllable (dum dum dum). Tell students to listen carefully and to count how many times they hear the sound. Then they repeat the sound exactly. Let students take turns making a sound while others count and echo the pattern.

**Poem Ostinati.** First students memorize a poem. Explain the concept of ostinato (something repeated over and over). Then ask one group to recite the poem, while another group recites an ostinato (a line or word that repeats). The ostinato may be a line they have created, the title of the poem, or a selected line from the poem. After students have practiced the last two activities, break the class into three groups. Two groups perform the poem as a spoken round, while the third group performs the ostinato. An example poem is Silverstein's "Listen to the Mustn'ts" (repeat "mustn'ts"). *Variation:* Use rhythm instruments to create ostinati.

**Staff Walk (Notation).** Make a large musical staff on the floor (masking tape). Students walk horizontally across a certain space of the staff without touching a line, or do this with the lines on the staff. Everyone says or sings notes touched as they walk. *Variation:* Throw bean bags on lines or spaces of the staff and name the notes.

**Syllable Sing (Critical Listening).** This helps hear note tones, phrasing, and rhythm. Choose a jingle from a commercial or a familiar melody. Sit in a circle and ask each student to sing only one syllable. Go around until it is blended. *Variation:* Use whole words or phrases to help hear ostinati (repetition).

**Instruments Notation.** Find everyday items, or "found sounds," that make music. See Ready Reference 13.1. Even body parts can be used. The goal is to write music for each sound. First, pairs choose two found sound instruments and decide ways to notate (make symbols for) timbre, pitch, and volume. For example, jingle bells might be small dots to show the high, light sound. Next, pairs write the numbers 1 to 8 across the top of the paper and the names of two instruments at the top of the left margin. Next, put symbols for each instrument under the numbers to show when each should be played. When both are to be played, place them under the same number. Loudness can be shown by drawing a symbol larger or smaller. Pairs then perform.

**Music Concentration (Notation).** Draw music symbols and different kinds of notes on the chalkboard. Students take turns naming each symbol to remember it. Students then close their eyes while a symbol is erased. They open their eyes and try to guess what symbol was erased. As more are erased, students are to name the most recent deletions, as well as the previous ones. Correct answers are reinforced by writing the answer back on the board. *Variation:* Ask for examples or an explanation of each concept.

**Musical Notation.** Use a favorite song. First, speak the lyrics while clapping the rhythm (e.g., "Happy Birthday"). Decide where long, short, and silent sounds occur (not vowels). Invent symbols to record musical sounds (e.g., circles, squares, or lines for notes). The symbols should show if the melody goes up or down and if the notes are long or short in time; for example, use small circles for short notes and large circles for long notes. Chant the lyrics again while pointing to symbols. Ask students again how to represent high and low sounds in the melody, as well as symbols for rhythm. Repeat and then ask children to create symbols to address tempo and dynamics. Sing the complete song while pointing to the symbols.

**Body Sound Compositions (Notation and Composition).** Ask students to demonstrate sounds that can be made with their hands, fingers, feet, tongue, lips, cheeks, and other body parts. Pairs create a composition using various combinations. *Variation:* Put sounds and actions to any favorite musical recording.

**Jives (Rhythm).** Hand and body jives allow exploration of rhythm. Examples include "Shimmy, Shimmy Cocoa Puff" and "Hambone." Basically, you slap and brush your hands to a rhythm. See Mattox's *Shake It to the One That You Love Best*.

**Two-Part Rhythm.** One group chants and claps a steady beat to the nursery rhyme "Hot Cross Buns," while another group chants "One a Penny, Two a Penny" over and over.

**Rhythm Box Beats.** Each student needs an empty milk carton or shoe box and a wooden spoon or big pencil. The inside

# Ready Reference 13.1  Using Found Sounds as Musical Instruments

**Blow**

- Cover plastic comb with paper and blow.
- Use small candy boxes and blow through them.
- Blow into a conch shell.

**Shake and Rattle**

- Fill empty plastic, wood, or cardboard containers with rice, beans, stones, or seeds.
- Use a gourd with dried seeds inside as a shaker.
- Rattle keys on a string.
- Use embroidery hoops and bottle caps to make tambourines.
- Make clappers from seashells, buttons, and flattened bottle caps.

**Strike**

- Hit together large wooden knitting needles or large metal or wooden spoons, PVC pipe sections.
- Hang kitchen utensils, or tools such as wrenches, from a string and tap with a pencil.
- Hang a metal cookie sheet and strike to make a gong.
- Ping the prongs of a plastic fork.
- Use pot lids for cymbals or tap with fingernails or thimble fingers.

- Tap glasses with different amounts of water with a spoon.
- Make tapping fingers with thimbles, acorns, or sew/glue buttons on tips of glove fingers. Strum a washboard.
- Tap spoons together or make finger castanets from buttons with glued on loops for thumb and index finger.
- Make drums from empty coffee can or large plastic tubs (from ice cream or slaw). Stretch fabric, leather, or rubber over opening.

**Strum, Scrape, or Rub**

- Strum a slitted metal spatula.
- Scrape a cheese grater with a stick.
- Stretch rubber bands around a box and strum.
- Rub rims of stemmed glasses with different amounts of water.
- Glue sandpaper around old cassette tape covers for sand blocks.

**Other**

- Wind an eggbeater and hear it whir.
- Make sounds with zippers and pulling apart Velcro fasteners.
- Fill stainless bowls with ½ cup water. Swirl water and strike bottom.

---

of the box or carton is struck, one side at a time, in the same order to create a 1-2-3-4 beat (common in music). Try at different tempos and put to music by playing along with four-beat songs (see the time signature on sheet music). Next, strike the box using other music beats: 1-2 or 1-2-3 (waltz time).

**Follow the Leader.**  Use rhythm instruments, homemade or purchased (sticks, tambourines, drums, cymbals). Leader plays different rhythms. Everyone echoes the rhythm on his or her instrument (e.g., "ta-tum ta-tum ta-tum tum tum").

**Make It Italian.**  Use Italian tempo words to expand vocabulary and spice up class activities, especially when giving directions such as walking to lunch or cleaning up at the end of the day. *Variation:* Teach the effect of speed on singing or on any task. Use a metronome and sing a familiar song at each tempo, such as "Happy Birthday." Discuss changes in pitch, enunciation, and the like. Following are examples from Ross and Stangl's *Music Teacher's Book of List.*

Lento = slow (60–66 bpm)
Moderato = moderate (108–120 bpm)
Allegro = quick/happy (120–168 bpm)
Presto = very fast (168–200 bpm)
Prestissimo = fast as possible (200–208 bpm)

**Singing Speeds.**  Play examples of accelerando (e.g., Strauss's "Acceleration Waltz," the 1950s song "Beep Beep," and Brahms's "Hungarian Dances"—they get faster and faster). Try singing any song using accelerando. Add dynamic changes such

as crescendo and decrescendo (get louder and get softer) or use staccato (choppy) and legato (very smooth). *Variation:* Students create three different shapes and remember them. Repeat the shapes to the different tempos marked by the metronome. Discuss how tempo changes movements (e.g., sustained versus bound).

**Instrument Categories.**  Collect pictures of orchestral instruments. Ask students about people (family members) who have similar, but unique voice sounds. Explain this is also true for instruments. Show pictures grouped in families (percussion, strings, woodwind, and brass). Shuffle cards and have students regroup them by similar sound. Reinforce efforts based on sound groupings (some may group by size, material, etc.). Explain how instruments are grouped by (1) sound similarity, (2) the way they are played, and (3) the material from which they are made.

**Instrument Rummy.**  Make a deck of 52 cards, with pictures of instruments (percussion, strings, woodwind, and brass replace the four groups of face cards). Each player gets five cards. Place remaining cards on the table. The object is to acquire sets of four common instruments (string, brass, woodwind, and percussion). The first player draws from the pile and chooses to keep the card or discard it face up. The player with the most instrument sets at the end is the winner.

**Homemade Jam.**  Have a jam session with student-made instruments. Put on music and play along. *Variation:* Create a parade using all the instruments. (Titles of instrument-making books can be found in Appendix J.)

**Musical-Style Party.** Have a party during which students come dressed as country, jazz, rock, opera, or other type of musicians. Students may choose a specific musician, such as Louis Armstrong. *Variation:* Invite students to imitate a favorite musical artist by lipsyncing Clay Aiken, Alvin and the Chipmunks, Garth Brooks, or The Beatles (combine with the "style party").

Note: Be sure to discuss school-appropriate costumes and artist imitation.

**Music Response Options.** Students can use their musical intelligences to respond to a book or unit of study using a variety of activities. Nineteen ideas are given in Ready Reference 13.2.

# III. Connecting Music to Curricular Areas

There is nothing more integrated than real life, and more specifically in this example, the life-saving power of music. In Colorado Springs, 5-year-old Jasmine saved her mother's life because she knew a song. Her mother started having a seizure. Jasmine knew how to call 911 because of a CD the Colorado Symphony Orchestra distributes to children. The "Safety Hop" CD has hits like "Buckle Up," "Under the Smoke," and, yes, "Call 911" (to the tune of "My Boyfriend's Back"). Jasmine said she remembered the lyrics and just did what the song said. So far, more than 25,000 CDs have been distributed (*Early Show* on CBS, Interview, April 6, 2005).

You don't have to be in a symphony to write songs that have important information in them. The seed strategies in this section include a composition process and several examples of songs written by students in collaboration with their teachers.

**Webbing.** There are many ways to meaningfully integrate music. Webbing is an all-purpose brainstorming strategy that helps locate connections between music and other areas. Choose any topic and web all the kinds of music associated with it. Web to plan lessons or as a starter for student research. In the latter, break students into groups with each selecting one or several kinds of music to explore in depth. Culminate with group sharing.

The following are starter ideas for integrating music with science, social studies, literacy, and math.

---

**Ready Reference 13.2** Music Response Options

Use these ideas to respond to a book or area of study.

1. **Songwriting.** Write a song about the characters or people, plot, theme, or setting (place or time period). Use a familiar melody.
2. **Sing it, rap it.** Choose an important part of the story or event to put to music (sing it, rap it, or write a poem; Ready Reference 5.2 lists poem patterns).
3. **Background music read-aloud.** Choose a part and add rhythm instruments or music that suits the mood.
4. **Scavenger hunt.** Find music and songs that relate to story emotions, topics, themes, time period, or culture.
5. **Song list.** Make a list of songs the main character would like to listen to or sing. Use these to plan an operetta.
6. **Match instruments.** List musical instruments associated with characters, parts of the plot, setting, or a topic (e.g., a plant or animal). *Example:* "What instrument would the wolf sound like in *Three Little Pigs?*"
7. **Diagram the story plot.** Choose musical elements to recreate the action. For example, show rising action with faster rhythm and climax with loud music.
8. **Rhythm plus.** Make a list of special words and phrases. Put them to a rhythm or even create a melody. Think about which words or phrases could be repeated over and over (ostinato). *Example:* Cats here, cats there, cats and kittens everywhere (*Millions of Cats*)!
9. **Word choir.** List words or feelings for characters, plot, or theme. Groups line up and a category is given (e.g., a character). The "director" then points to each student, who must make a sound or say a word about the character and continue as long as the director indicates. The director indicates dynamics, tempo, and so forth. All can be cued to respond solo or in unison.
10. **Opera.** Sing the story. Make the story into an opera. Rewrite words so they can be sung (libretto).
11. **Musical instruments.** Make musical instruments (kazoo, drum, shaker, etc.) that characters might play or that represent characters. Reread story and when each character enters, students play a short rhythm or melody.
12. **Make a mix.** Create a tape or CD mix of songs and music for a favorite character.
13. **Musical mobile.** Use items that relate to the book or topic that will make sounds as they move.
14. **Music fans.** List musicians characters would prefer.
15. **Rock band?** If the characters in the book formed a band, what would it be called? What kind of music would they play?
16. **Jingle writing.** Write an advertising jingle to sell the book.
17. **Sound collage.** List all the sounds in the book. Make a sound collage by recreating the sounds and organizing them on a tape.
18. **Singing words.** Practice reading a section, sentence, or phrase aloud, adding music elements to make the print sing (e.g., change dynamics, tempo, or pitch).
19. **Lip sync.** Find a song that a character would sing (e.g., What might Jacob sing to Sarah in *Sarah, Plain and Tall?*)

Music

# Science Focus

**Science Standards.** A complete listing of standards can be accessed at the National Science Teachers Association (NSTA) website (www.nsta.org).

**Music Month.** March is the official music month, so plan a musical focus for each day: a composer, song, genre, or fact.

**Vegetable Orchestra.** Check out a Vienna-based orchestra who makes all its instruments from vegetables, such as a carrot flute. They play all music genres and then cook them into a soup for the audience. Website: www.gemueseorchester.org.

**Science Summary Songs.** Students summarize important science concepts by writing lyrics using familiar or original melodies. See songwriting steps under "Literacy: Reading and Language Arts" in this chapter. Invite groups to create additional verses. Examples include the following:

1. "Four Oceans" (Tune: "Bingo")
   There is a planet with four oceans, and this is what we call them:
   Atlantic, Pacific, Indian, Arctic (3X)
   And that is what we call them.
2. "North, South, East, and West" (Tune: "Oscar Meyer Weiner")
   *North, south, east, west* are directions
   Go north to find lots of ice and snow. BRRRR
   Go south and the temperature changes
   This is where the warm breezes blow. WHEW
   Go east to find the Atlantic Ocean
   And there you see great big towns
   Go west and cross the Rocky Mountains
   Keep going 'cause you're Pacific bound.
3. "Metamorphosis" (caterpillar) (Tune: "Farmer in the Dell")
   The butterfly lays eggs. The butterfly lays eggs.
   REFRAIN: Changes o' changes, Metamorphosis.
   Caterpillars hatch from eggs, caterpillars hatch from eggs.
   REFRAIN
   Caterpillars eat leaves. Caterpillars eat leaves. REFRAIN
   and so on.
4. "Two Hundred Bones" Rap (tap each bone to the rhythm):
   Skull head bone, head bone, head bone.
   Skull head bone, head bone, YEAH!
   Ribs, vertebrae, pelvis, pelvis. Ribs, vertebrae, pelvis,
   BONES!
   Clavicle-collar bone, scapula-shoulder bone.
   Bones Bones. Two hundred bones REPEAT (in decrescendo).
   Humerus, radius-ulna arm bones. Humerus, radius ulna, Yeah!
   Femur, tibia-fibula leg bones. Femur, tibia-fibula, Yeah!
   Two hundred bones in the body, body. Two hundred bones in the body, Yeah!
   *Variation:* Students find additional bones to add. (Thanks to teachers at Duxberry Elementary for this idea!)

**Musical Season Stories.** Play seasonal music without words, and pantomime events from the season. For a spring story, students may mime a flower blossoming. Students may also practice writing about the process of a flower growing from a tiny seed sprout afterward. Vivaldi's *The Four Seasons* works.

**Science Symphonies.** Many pieces of music celebrate or describe aspects of our world or universe. Collect examples to listen to and discuss what they depict through tempo and timbre of instruments. *Examples:* "La Mer" (The Sea), "Grand Canyon Suite," "Flight of the Bumble Bee," "Water Music," "Theme to 2001." *Variation:* Discuss how science is shown in songs such as John Denver's "Rocky Mountain High" or "Country Roads." Gustav Holst's "The Planets" can be used with an invitation for students to write an "Earth" one since Holst did not include it.

**Vibration Study.** Vibrations pass through the eardrum, hammer, stirrups, and the water of the cochlea and are sent as an electrical nerve signal to the brain. We also hear sounds because sound is conducted through our bones. Ask students to cover their ears and hum to hear the sound coming through the bones. Students can try as many different timbres as possible with a pencil, hands, and the like.

**Musical Weather Reports.** What would a rainy day sound like? Towering cumulus clouds? Thunder and lightning? Hurricane? Help students create and present weather reports in which the meteorologist makes the sounds as the type of weather is mentioned. *Variation:* Write or find songs about the weather to introduce or conclude weather reports (e.g., "April Showers" from Disney's *Bambi*). Poetry can also be used (e.g., "Rain, Rain Go Away"). Try creating a full operetta based on a weather report and songs.

**Bird Songs.** Use instruments, such as a recorder, for students to learn to play bird songs such as the bobwhite, phoebe, and red-winged blackbird.

**Bird Song Survey.** In the spring, go on a listening walk for bird songs. Tape each song and match with bird pictures. Discuss differences in melody, pitch, rhythm, and timbre of each bird. *Variation:* Use musical notation to write down songs or ask a music teacher to help do so. Students can also write lyrics to bird songs, similar to the "bob white" we use to make the quail song. Ask, "What does it sound like the bird is saying?"

**Sound Sorts.** Students sort musical instruments by different attributes, including materials used to make them, sounds they make, construction to produce sounds, or orchestra groups. Students should be encouraged to find a variety of ways to categorize.

**Science and Sound.** Explore acoustics by inviting a speaker from a sound system company, or a conductor who can show and explain a score (a graph of frequencies, intensities, and volume).

**Rainstorm Simulation.** This is a rhythm activity. Sit in a circle with eyes closed. A leader begins by rubbing palms together. Person to right picks it up until the whole class is participating. Then the leader switches to finger snaps that move around the circle. Next is thigh slaps, then foot stomps, with periodical "claps" of lightning. Reverse the order to show the storm dying out.

**Nature Sounds Orchestra.** Students imitate or tape sounds in nature, such as a bird whistling, dog barking, water splashing, and the wind. Combine sounds to create a nature orchestra.

Note: Try the Word Choir Seed Strategy. *Variation:* Compose environmental rhythms song; rap or chant by using these sounds—live or taped: door shutting, stirring with a metal spoon, clock ticking, typing, and fan whirring.

**Sound Mobiles.** Study the reasons behind how sound is created. Make mobiles from silverware or other objects that will create music as they move. Use string or wire to tie objects to a stick, pipe, or hanger.

**Sound Collage.** During a study on sound (how it travels) students can choose magazine pictures that show items that produce sounds (animals, machines, people, etc.). Arrange on a large piece of paper, overlapping to make a collage. As collages are shared, students can point at a picture while the class makes the appropriate sound.

# Social Studies Focus

*Music and the other arts are primary carriers and extenders of this history.* (Hope, 2003)

**Social Studies Standards.** A complete list of standards are available from the National Council for the Social Studies (NCSS) website (www.socialstudies.org).

**Music and Culture.** Explore a culture by listening to its music and songs. Discuss what the music shows about the culture (values, ideas). Possible questions are as follows:

- How does the music feel? What does it sound like?
- Who makes the music?
- How is music made?
- What instruments are used?
- Why would a culture create this kind of music?
- When was the music made?
- What kind of music is this? How is it like other music?
- How has music in the culture changed over time?

*Variation:* Challenge students to create an imaginary culture and answer questions about its music.

**Summary Songs.** Song writing is a valuable way to synthesize information and it is most effective when students write their own compositions, as opposed to memorizing songs of others. Why? "The person doing the work is the one growing the dendrites" (Wolfe, 2001, p. 187). Here are verses from a song written after a field trip to the Hunley Submarine (Lisa Trott, Ashley River Creative Arts, Charleston, South Carolina). (Tune: "Yellow Submarine")

> In the town where I was born
> There sat a sub beneath the sea
> And its tale is really hip
> It fired and sank a Yankee ship.
> The first time the sub went down

> Eight men from Erin, they did drown
> Then the next stop in the drink
> Horace Hunley, he did sink
> But this third and famous trip
> Took Captain Dixon and a ship
> *REFRAIN: We all lived in the Hunley submarine*
> *The Hunley submarine, the Hunley submarine*
> *We all drowned in the Hunley submarine*
> *The Hunley submarine, the Hunley submarine*

**How Instruments Began.** Use this idea with a unit on early human history. Explain how our ancestors did not have the kind of musical instruments we have today. Music was made about their feelings and experiences using available materials. They plucked, blew through, and struck using bones, rocks, wood, and shells. Invite students to design an instrument using plucking, blowing, or striking of a familiar item in their environment. *Variation:* Each student researches an instrument played in the manner of the one made and presents findings.

**Musical Classifieds (Newspaper Unit).** Students create ads about instruments, musicians, or musical needs. *Example:* "Lost—large musical instrument, percussion type. Black and white in color on main part. Last seen standing on three legs." Students read aloud and guess instrument. *Suggestion:* Make at least three clues for classifieds, with the first clue general and the last one the most specific.

**Music Current Events.** Start a "Music in the News" weekly routine. Invite students to find music-related stories and/or write songs based on news events using familiar tunes. *Note:* Many folk songs are old tunes with new lyrics (e.g., civil rights songs were based on spirituals).

**Multicultural Song Book.** Students collect songs from different cultures and countries by making notebooks of lyrics and sheet music and mixes using CDs and tapes. *Variation:* Each student or group selects one culture for which to find songs or music. Each student's contribution is put into a class collection.

**Multicultural Music and Dances.** Analyze songs as historical records of how people felt, thought, and acted. Research the significance of songs—how music has influenced history (e.g., France's "La Marseillaise" or the Mexican American workers' "De Colores"). Other possibilities include Native American music, Irish jigs, civil rights music, tribal mountain music, Western cowboy tunes, patriotic songs, and African tribal music. Guide students to understand that music helps create identity and expresses a people's values and passions. For example, the Apache song "I Walk with Beauty" (based on a Navajo poem) expresses a concept of beauty with all things living in harmony. (See Burton's *Moving within the Circle: Contemporary Native American Music and Dance*.)

**Song Sources.** Review purposes of songs and various types (lullabies, work songs, sea chanteys, patriotic songs, etc.). Ask for examples of social and historical events that use certain types of songs, such as birthdays and weddings. Read about an event and brainstorm types of songs that people or characters might sing, play, or compose. Ask students to explain their reasons. This is also a good time to share picture books that are based on songs (e.g., "The Star-Spangled Banner" or "Follow the Drinking Gourd"). Discuss how some songs were once work songs ("I've Been Working on the Railroad" and "Erie Canal") that we now sing for enjoyment and to remember history.

**Song Box.** Students create a piece of artwork based on lyrics from a historically relevant song. For example, a cereal box could be collaged or painted with images related to geography concepts in "America the Beautiful," with information about the composer, maps, facts, and photos inside.

**States and Capitals Rap.** Use drums or sticks to develop a basic beat and compose a mnemonic for chanting cities and states (e.g., Columbus, Ohio; Philadelphia, Pennsylvania; Atlanta, Georgia; Sacramento, California).

**Continents Song.** Use familiar tunes to summarize factual information (e.g., the names of the seven continents). *Example:* Use the tune "She'll Be Comin' Round the Mountain" with these words: "There are seven continents on the earth (2X). We have seven great big land forms, seven great big land forms. There are seven continents on the earth. There are North and South America. Australia, Africa and Europe. Then there is Asia and Antarctica. Asia and Antarctica. Asia and Antarctica make it seven."

**Song Experts.** Invite students to become experts on the history of important songs. Have a group sing interspersed with short reports or start a daily "song a day" routine. Here's an important one to know: Before March 3, 1931, "America the Beautiful" was the national anthem. In 1916, President Wilson ordered all Army and Navy bands to cease playing it and play "The Star-Spangled Banner," a song that was considered almost unsingable. So, why did Wilson make the change? It had to do with his wife.

On September 14, 1814, Francis Scott Key was on a British warship that was bombarding Fort McHenry. Key was on a diplomatic mission, which deprived him of liquor, when he wrote song lyrics to the tune of a British drinking song, called "Anacreon in Heaven" (Anacreon is the Greek god of wine). He supposedly said that no sober person could actually carry the melody. When Wilson knew the United States would have to enter the Great War, his wife declared that "America the Beautiful" was too peaceable for a country about to declare war.

**Music Time Line.** Read about composers of different time periods and place contributions on a time line. Add other significant events (composers' birthdays, song or music events). *Variation:* Make a time line of periods (Middle Ages, Renaissance, Baroque, Classical, Romantic, and 20th century) and find example music pieces/songs for each. Combine pictures of artwork, clothing, architecture, dances, or theatrical productions from the time. Discuss how all art reflects societal changes and investigate the materials and technology available at the time or in the area.

**Community Sing.** Start the day or week with a "community sing." Singing together is a way to bond a group and is used in most cultures. Write or sing patriotic, camp, folk, or appropriate contemporary songs. A collaborative class anthem can be written to share student beliefs about school and learning, and special songs can be found or written to celebrate people, seasons, or special events, such as Secretary's Day. *Variation:* Ask the music teacher for examples from different cultures or use the 42 songs recommended by Music Educators National Conference.

**History Through Music.** Find songs and music that reflect the environment and times, for example, music or songs about specific historical events and values ("Battle Hymn of the Republic"). Examine a period song to discover its origins and how it expressed the attitudes, worries, and values of the time. *Example:* "Dixie" had to do with a currency issued by a southern bank. Dix is the French word for 10.

**Introduce a Time Period.** Play music to introduce a social studies unit. Ask, "What do you hear? What does it tell you about this time? How does this music sound different from contemporary music? Why?"

**Cultural Contrasts.** Use a Venn diagram (two overlapping circles) to compare music from countries, cultures, and ethnic groups with music that is familiar to students. Use music elements to categorize likenesses and differences. *Variation:* Contrast two songs about the same topic (e.g., war).

**Song Source.** Ross and Stangl's *The Music Teacher's Book of List* is a good starter source for lists of songs about wars, immigration, westward expansion, cowboys, slavery, Negro spirituals, work songs, civil rights/protest songs, patriotic and holiday/seasonal songs and the national anthems of various counties.

## Literacy: Reading and Language Arts Focus

**Literacy/Literature Standards.** A complete listing of standards is available from the National Council of the Teachers of English (NCTE) and the International Reading Association (IRA) websites (*www.ncte.org* or *www.ira.org*).

**Integral Connections.** Music and the language arts have a lot in common: Music involves decoding symbols, fluency, comprehension (understanding), and composition (writing). Song lyrics include every type of vocabulary and are structured in manners that make them ideal for teaching reading. For example, ballads are stories with all the features of the narrative genre. Songs are also available at every "reading level"—many have simple vocabulary, repeated lines, and a predictable structure; other songs are complex and present comprehension challenges for even sophisticated readers. In particular, music and poetry share many traits such as rhythm and repetition that appeal to student's somatic (body) perception. Most important is the inherent interest songs and music possess; they compel us to attend and to participate—to sing along. No sound 21st-century literacy program is without a body of music and songs that are integral to teaching key literacy concepts and skills.

**Literacy Through Songs.** Ready Reference 13.3 lists ways to use songs to teach reading, writing, speaking, and listening skills.

**Song Dance/Mime.** Cut up the lyrics to a song that suggests movement (e.g. "Make New Friends") without being literal like the Hokey Pokey is. Break students into groups to interpret the meaning using dance movements. Regroup to perform. *Variation:* Choose a song that tells a story for students to mime as it is sung. *Example:* "My Aunt Came Back" allows students to invent new verses through mime.

**Guided Music and Literacy Lesson.** Music and listening, speaking, reading, and writing are integrated in this special guided lesson. This is a variation on the two-pronged plan format, but it still includes an introduction, development, and conclusion. The instructional steps are to listen closely and think, predict, read, share, write, music response, publish. These can be posted so that students can eventually guide small- or whole-group lessons. The guided music and language arts lesson teaching steps are outlined in Planning Page 13.4.

**Word Choirs.** Ask for volunteers to form a choir line. Give a topic such as happiness. When a leader points to each choir member, she or he must say or sing a word or make a sound related to the topic. For example, students say "play, laugh, or love" for happiness. Create directing signals for students to say or sing their words or sounds and hold or sing at different pitches. Teach students how to conduct word choirs. Word choirs can relate to any unit, such as growing things or other cultures. See previous conducting signals.

**Dynamic Word Singing.** The teacher leads students in singing, chanting, cheering, clapping, and snapping letters and syllables in spelling or vocabulary words. Use forte (loud), piano (soft), crescendo (getting louder), and other musical terms to change the volume. See "Make It Italian" for tempo words. *Variation:* Do body spelling to background music with a beat. (Idea from Fannie Petros, Ashley River Creative Arts)

**Word Rhythms.** Students find examples of phrase patterns in names of classmates, song lyrics, place names, and so forth. Each of the patterns can also be played with rhythm instruments.

1. Iamb: dah DAH: Do what? (Iambic pentameter is 5 iambs "I like to eat my peas without a fork.")
2. Trochaic: DAH dah: Rudy, Eileen
3. Anapestic: dah dah DAH: Virginia
4. Dactylic: DAH dah dah: Claudia (Double dactyl: Gloria Zittercoff)
5. Spondaic: DAH DAH: Go there.

**Echo Me.** Explore oral interpretation using the musical concepts of dynamics, pitch, tempo, beat, accent, and rhythm. Recite the alphabet or a nursery rhyme in a normal manner. Repeat and talk fast or slow, use a high-pitched voice or deep, bass voice. Break everything into distinct separate syllables or put the accent on every third word. Challenge students to echo you exactly. For example, "Mary Had a Little Lamb" could become a mystery or a proclamation by varying the delivery. Also try dialects and foreign accents.

**Sound Substitution.** Phonological and phonemic awareness are developed through singing songs and changing the sounds of letters. For example, "I Like to Eat, Eat, Eat Apples and Bananas." The song is sung over and over changing the vowels to short and long sounds like "I like to oat oat oat, opples and bononos."

---

## Ready Reference 13.3  Songs for Literacy

*Directions: Make song lyrics visible for student using by printing on chart paper, using a Smart Board or overhead transparencies.*

- **Echoic Reading:** Use lyrics (my turn–your turn) to develop fluency elements (EAR = expression, accuracy, rate); expression includes changes in volume/dynamics, pitch, pause, and stress.
- **Repeated Reading:** Rehearse lyrics to build EAR fluency.
- **Speech-to-Lyrics Match:** Point at lyrics and lines as they are sung. Use creative pointers (e.g., conductor's wand).
- **Song Sentence Strips:** Cut apart lines and students put them in order to make sense.
- **Sing a Word:** Stretch sounds for phonemic awareness.
- **Dictation:** Students sing as scribe writes or they write down lyrics known by heart to practice phonics/spelling, and handwriting. Bind into individual or class books for reading.
- **Big Song Books:** Each student or a group illustrates a line or a book page.
- **Song Cut-Ups:** Students sort words, phrases, and lines into categories (parts of speech, syllables, alphabetical).
- **Comprehension Cloze:** Use sticky notes on a song chart to block out words or use white out on individual song copies.

Students "sing" and make sense by figure out what's missing.

- **Ballads (songs that tell stories):** Map according to literary elements (characters, plot, theme, style) and discuss using Ready Reference 6.12.
- **Song Adaptations:** Collaboratively write new verses (e.g., "Down by the Bay," "My Aunt Came Back" give practice with rhyming words).
- **Songbooks:** Students make a favorite song into an individual book by illustrating each line of the song. See bookmaking options in Chapter 7.
- **Song Anthologies:** Collect students' favorite songs (lyrics/sheet music) in a notebook or file. These can be bound and given as gifts.
- **Word Wall:** Students find interesting words in songs to post. Can also use categories such as high-frequency words or spelling patterns (silent *e*, r-controlled, phonograms, etc.) from lyrics.

Music

# Planning Page *13.4*
## Guided Music and Literacy Lesson

*Two-Pronged Focus:* Choose from (1) music elements and concepts, and (2) reading and language arts skills and concepts.

*Standards:* 6, 8, 9 (Ready Reference 12.10)

*Student Objectives:* Students should be able to . . . (list specific music and literacy outcomes here)

*Teaching Procedure:* The teacher will ask students to . . .

### Introduction
1. *Listen closely:* Play a piece of music/song for a few minutes so students can hear and feel everything it seeks to convey. No talking at this stage.
2. *Predict:* Students write predictions about what the composer is trying to convey. Teachers can scribe for younger children.

### Development
1. *Gather data:* Read about the musician and/or the work. Teachers may read to the students.
2. *Present evidence:* Students give evidence to confirm or reject their predictions about the work. Emphasize that the goal is to find the truth, not to be right. Can be done in pairs, small groups, or whole group.

### Conclusion
1. *Write:* Students write a response. Focus on important ideas learned about the music or composer. Provide examples of writing forms students may use (Ready Reference 5.1).
2. *Music response:* Give musical response options lesson, such as replay music and free write, move, or paint (Ready Reference 13.2).
3. *Publish:* Student responses are "made public" through displays, oral sharing, and singing.

---

**Sing to Spell.** Add the mnemonic power of music to spelling by using recognizable tunes. Any five-letter word can be spelled to "You Are My Sunshine." Use "Happy Birthday" to spell six-letter words and "Twinkle, Twinkle Little Star" for seven-letter words.

**Sing Letter Sounds.** To develop particular letter and sound skills in reading, have students hum melodies using only the target sound. For example, hum "Happy Birthday" just using the /s/ or /b/. This also can be done to teach short vowels. For example, sing "Happy Birthday" with just the short *a* sound.

**Sing the Vowels.** Professional singers warm up by singing vowels because vowels are made with the throat loose and open, allowing more sounds to come out. Consonants stop sounds. For example, in a speaking voice: "Happy birthday to you." In a singing voice: "Haa py Birrrthday to youououo." Children can learn the differences between the sounds of vowels and consonants by singing. This is particularly helpful with students who

have trouble hearing individual phonemes since this stretches sounds and increases phonemic awareness.

**Finger Plays and Songs.** Finger plays and songs can be used to develop vocabulary, reading skills, sequencing, rhyming, and, of course, musical form (e.g., "Five Little Squirrels" and "Five Green and Speckled Frogs"). Suggested sequence: (1) Students listen to the song, without accompaniment. (2) Repeat listening with a focus (e.g., listen for words that start with /f/). (3) Sing together using printed lyrics. (4) Repeat several times, and (5) cut song apart for sorting and ordering (e.g., sequence lines, sort vocabulary by syllables, rhymes). (6) End with repeat singing.

Note: If using finger plays, model possible movements during step 1 and invite new ideas from students. In step 2, everyone does the finger movements.

**Emotion Symphony.** Divide into groups, and ask each to choose a character emotion (fear, sadness, frustration, grumpiness, etc). Groups create ways to make sounds that evoke the emotion. Explain that the groups will be combined to form a symphony and they will need to vary the pitch, tempo, and dynamics according to directions (create conducting signals). Start by bringing in one group (the instruments) and have them start, stop, speed up, slow down, get louder, get softer, or use another directive, according to your signals. Bring in a second group, third, and so forth, until all are "playing." Variation: Add musical instruments, scarves, and movement.

**Emotion Art.** Use oil pastels for students to create abstract art using colors, lines, and shapes to convey how they think the music feels.

**Character Interviews.** Students listen to a song with several characters. Students each choose one character and listen again to find out about the character from the music and lyrics. For example, "Three Blind Mice" has mice, the farmer's wife, and other characters that could be inferred (e.g., farmer, neighbors, representative of the humane society). The teacher takes the role of an interviewer and uses a prop microphone to ask the characters questions (e.g., "Who are you? What do you want? What are your problems? What will you do about your problems?"). This can be done in pairs, with students taking turns interviewing one another.

**Haiku Duets.** Students find or write haiku (nature poems with 5-7-5 syllable pattern). In pairs they plan how to use rhythm instruments and/or vocal musical elements to present the haiku. Consider the following example.

> Snakey limbs stretch high (whisper and use sand blocks, then hiss)
> Scaley skins with broken bark (increase volume and emphasize /sk/ sound)
> Bear the rustling leaves (sand blocks and then tambourine)

**Read-Arounds** (Adapted from Tompkins & McGee, 1993). After reading a story, each student chooses one sentence and rehearses to read it aloud. Each student then reads aloud the line, varying the expression elements of dynamics, tempo, pitch, pause, and accent to interpret meaning. Afterward, students discuss why they chose their lines (e.g., the special sound or sense in the passage). *Variation:* Use each line to make a class big book with each page having one line and student art.

**Song Writing.** Use the steps in Ready Reference 13.5. Following is the final version of a song created to remember the most common prepositions.

> 78 Prepositions (Tune = "Yankee Doodle")
> Out from under in between over of into through
> About above across against along at after but by
> Next of out outside till to
> Round since than unlike
> Up upon within without
> Toward to till since throughout
> Among around as by before behind below besides
> Beyond except down for from in onto like near next off on
> Plus regarding opposite
> Past down underneath
> Unto considering than despite
> During inside concerning

(Source of prepositions, *The Bedford Handbook for Writers,* 4th ed.) For additional resources on songwriting, try Wiggins's (1991) *Composition in the Classroom: A Tool for Teaching.* Also see Appendix J.

**Interviews.** Small groups list questions to ask musicians, songwriters, conductors, and so forth. Guests are invited to visit and students interview using planned questions.

**Singing Commercials.** Divide into teams and give each a magazine with picture advertisements. Teams create a song to promote the product in the picture. They may select from familiar tunes or write lyrics to an original melody. Teams then present their commercial jingles.

**Musician Expert (Research Skills).** See Ready Reference 13.6 for this long-term project.

**Hootenanny.** Have weekly sing-alongs using student-made song collections. Add songs to a class list as they find new favorites. Put lyrics on posters or transparencies and invite

students to create personal song anthologies. Use song posters and songbooks as resources for teaching or reinforcing reading skills and concepts. For example, ask students to find words (play I Spy) that fit a specific phonic pattern (vowel digraphs, rhymes, phonograms, or rimes). In addition, fluency is increased by singing lyrics, if students are looking at the lyrics to do repeated reading.

**Music and Emotions.** Play a piece such as Vivaldi's *The Four Seasons.* Ask students to use their faces to show the feelings of the music. *Variations:* (1) Use art materials to show the feelings of the music (e.g., colors, lines, shapes). (2) List or write about the feelings.

**Music Response Journals (Listening).** Students write about thoughts and feelings triggered by music. They can write while listening to a selection or after listening. Examples: (1) Write song title (real or created). (2) Sketch or list instruments heard. (3) List adjectives to describe sounds or emotions. (4) Write a story or poem that suits the music. (5) Write a description or write about visual images stimulated by the music (latter is called *chromesthesia*).

**Cloze Telegrams (Spelling and Musical Notation).** Students complete telegrams or secret messages by writing the correct musical note on the staff using music paper (request from music teacher) or a staff on the board. Individual wipe-off boards also work, and everyone can show their note at a signal. For example, "Moz__rt pl__ys concert__t Town H__ll" (*a* is missing). "Sousa promot__d to Marin__ band dir__ctor" (*e* is missing). *Variation:* If instruments are available, students can play the missing notes.

**Operettas.** An opera is a story told with music. Introduce opera using books such as Englander's *Opera! What's All the Screaming About,* Price's *Aida: A Picture Book for All Ages,* or Rosenberg's *Sing Me a Song: Metropolitan Opera's Book of Opera Stories for Children.* Listen to examples. Next, choose a familiar story and list key scenes. Students compose (new or familiar melodies) or find songs for scenes. Songs can be sung without accompaniment, or instruments or recorded music can be added. Lead characters can sing their dialogue and some parts may be spoken. If actual words from the story are sung, they are called a *libretto. Example:* The

---

## Ready Reference 13.5 Song Writing

Use these basic steps to show students how to write original songs. This is an adaptation of a strategy for teaching reading and writing, called the *language experience approach*, in which students work under the guidance of a teacher and then work independently.

1. Choose a topic (e.g., prepositions).
2. Brainstorm words and feelings related to the topic. The teacher can serve as a recorder using a chart or the overhead projector. Ideas can be webbed. Use dictionaries and other resources for more ideas.
3. Students organize ideas. Phrases can be dictated to the teacher as he or she scribes or students can work in small groups.
4. Look at other songs for structure. Lyrics are put in an order. Students decide the form, rhythm, melody, and tempo

(e.g., "Will there be a background beat? Rhythm instruments? Which lines or words are to be repeated? How fast, slow? What melody?"). If students just use the universal melody—the three notes G, E, A—they can make many songs. (They all know this because it is the taunt used worldwide: Na na na na na.) Let students know that composers often repeat melodies (listen to pieces to discover this).

5. Make final revisions.
6. Perform: Tape, do live sharing. Use visuals to accompany.

## Ready Reference 13.6  Music Experts

Students work individually or in groups to research a song, composer, musician, or musical style. Panels present and audience members (other students) ask questions. *Variation:* (1) Groups work on the same composer and everyone is the same person on the panel (i.e., simultaneous casting). (2) Panel members become a person or people who may have lived during the time. To become experts, students can do the following:

- **Collection:** Find works by the person (e.g., tapes, CDs, sheet music). Include pictures.
- **Mini-biography:** Students write one-page bios on a musician. *Variation:* Obituary or tribute writing.
- **Song tribute:** Write a song about the musician.
- **Ape the greats:** Use the mood, style/genre, and techniques of the music as a frame to create adaptations (e.g., add verses, write new lyrics, or original work in the style of the artist).
- **Update:** Make or find a modern-day version of the work (e.g., *Hooked on Classics* versions of the classics).
- **Guests and experts:** Invite a local musician, singer, college professor, or conductor to speak about a musician. Prepare questions to interview the guest speaker.
- **Concert:** Attend a live performance or find a DVD.
- **Musician's studio:** Visit the place where a musician works (e.g., a concert hall). Ask to shadow a musician for a day.

- **Video/DVD:** Watch a video of the musician's life (e.g., *Beethoven Lives Upstairs*) and take notes.
- **Music show:** Have an event to display the musician's work. Set up classroom stations to listen to tapes or CDs.
- **Mini-display:** Set up a display in the hall, classroom, or special place in the school. Include works by famous musicians and students' works (e.g., compositions, pictures, information about the musician).
- **Vary it:** Do another version of a piece of music (e.g., use just a part of a song or piece of music to play or sing; write different lyrics to a song).

*Culmination:* A class performance with each student choosing 1 minute of his or her expertise to share in any form.

---

"Three Pigs Opera" would have songs about leaving home, fear, strong foundations, evil, and bad judgments. When a pig is afraid, sing "Whenever I Feel Afraid" (from "The King and I"). Teach students to write cues in dramatic opera form (e.g., Enter Big Bad Wolf, shifting eyes from side to side, or Trees [chorus] sing).

Note: *Into the Woods* is a musical based on fairy tales. Disney created several, such as *Beauty and the Beast* and there is a Broadway musical based on a spelling bee.

**Sing Literature.**   Read aloud books that are based on music or a song. Invite students to "sing" lines from the story. *Example: Charlie Parker Played Be Bop* has many possibilities.

**Read to Music.**   Find music that can be played in the background as a story is read or told. *Example:* "Claire de Lune" works for the beginning of Yashima's *Crow Boy*, while Ma Mere (Debussy) gives emotion to the end of the story. Ask students how reading to music changes the read-aloud. *Variation:* Invite students to find background music for scenes in books.

**Song Story.**   Students select a song and brainstorm who might have written it and why. Work in groups to write a story that explains how the song came to be. *Variation:* Students research song origins using references such as the *New Grove Dictionary of Music and Musicians* available in libraries. Website: *www.oxfordmusiconline.com/public/book/omo_gmo*

**Read and Write All About It.**   Students choose to research the life of a musician, composer, or singer to find biographical information such as birth, death, marriage, children, friends. Guidelines are as follows:

- Who and what most influenced the artist?
- What was the time period in which the artist lived? How did it influence the artist?

- What country or countries did the artist live in? Why?
- What musical style did the artist work in?
- What is the artist most known for, including particular works?
- What did others think of the artist's work (criticism or reviews)?
- What other artists worked at the same time?

**Write All About It.**   Students choose to write one of the following:

- Letter to the musician
- Letter to the music publishing company to request information about a song, piece, or the musician
- Biographical sketch of the musician
- Story in a modern setting that includes the music (e.g., background)
- Description of the music or song
- Menu during the time the music was created
- Report on the customs of the time of the artist
- Report on the clothing styles of the time
- Story about how a particular piece of music came to be composed
- Report about the time period and its influences
- A paragraph about what the musician would think/do if alive today
- Poem about the musician's life or music
- Comparison between the work of two musicians
- Time line of the musician's work
- Children's book about the musician, style, or genre of music

**Music Dictionary.**   Students make personal dictionaries of musical elements, concepts, song titles, and composers. Use wallpaper for covers and encourage students to illustrate entries.

Note: Many music words overlap with other vocabulary (e.g., consider the many meanings of the word *line*).

**Song Charts.** Write lyrics on poster board or large newsprint. Use sticky notes on the charts to cover certain words or word parts. Practice figuring out concealed parts. *Variations:* (1) Cut apart charts and put song line strips in a pocket chart or make big songbooks from the charts. (2) Give each student or group a line from a song to illustrate for a class big book.

**Class Song Books.** Create class anthologies of favorite songs, composer fact sheets, song fact sheets, poems, or riddles about music. For example, brainstorm ideas and make a chart of favorite songs. Have each student sign up to write the lyrics and research the song. Sing or read from the book each week.

Pizza Rondo: math and music

Have students make individual songbooks, song collections, or tape collections to go with their interests and needs (e.g., moods, study music).

**Musical Poetry.** Use chants, street rhymes, and jump rope rhymes for language arts. Ask students to describe musical elements in poetry. Encourage students to make up movements and add homemade or found sound rhythm instruments (see collections such as Cole and Calmenson's [1990] *Miss Mary Mack*).

**Song Scavenger Hunts.** Use songs as content to find language patterns, or conduct a weeklong hunt to find songs in certain categories (e.g., ones with lots of B words, with rhyme or alliteration, about books).

**Musical Chair Story.** Put on music. Everyone starts writing a story and writes until the music stops. Each person then passes his or her story to another and music begins again. The goal is to write a complete story in a designated number of passes.

**Instrument Experts.** Students choose to do research on a musical instrument or music in a particular culture. They then make a presentation to the class on their findings, including a demonstration.

**Read to Music.** First read aloud a poem or story without a music background. Next, read with music. Ask students to tell how the two were different and relate this to music in films or television shows. Invite students to find appropriate music to go with a story or poem. *Example:* Play "Claire de Lune" to read the beginning of Yashima's *Crow Boy*.

**Compare and Contrast.** Compare versions of the same song, for example, "Peter and the Wolf" or Mozart's "Twinkle, Twinkle Little Star." Use a Venn diagram to note differences in musical elements and instruments.

**Language Mentors.** Music is a language with a special symbol system. Encourage students who wish to learn to read and speak (sing and play) this language by pairing them with a mentor. Invite students to share their prowess with the class.

**Culture and Language through Song.** Teach students to sing a familiar song in the language of the country under study (e.g., "Frère Jacques" or "Allouette" from France).

## Math Focus

**Math Standards.** A complete listing of standards are available from the National Council of Teachers of Mathematics (NCTM) website (*www.nctm.org*).

**Math Music Connections.** Music and math have a lot in common. Music is constructed using patterns and is organized sequentially. Notes have different fractional values, and every piece of music has a time signature. Math and music even share similar vocabulary (e.g., measure, count). Music concepts such as crescendo and decrescendo rely on the ability to think about math concepts such as "less than" and "greater than." Just as in math, the relationships of the parts to the whole in music is critical.

**Musical Graphs.** Have students listen to a melody and look at the notes on the staff. Count and tally the number of times each note occurs. Create a bar graph that shows how many times a pitch shows up in the melody. *Variation:* List and tally instruments heard on a graph. Compare which were used the most and the least.

**Instrument Categories.** Label and then sort instruments using categories such as size, materials, and how played (blown, struck, plucked or bowed).

Music

**Pattern Echo.** Play or show a melody or pattern on a keyboard. The class listens and echoes the rhythmic pattern. *Extension:* Students create new patterns to play with classmates echoing.

**Scale Numbering.** Number the notes on the musical scale from 1 through 8 with do = 1, re = 2, mi = 3, fa = 4, so = 5, la = 6, ti = 7, and do = 8. Sing the scale with numbers instead of syllables. Invite students to construct math problems by singing them. *Example:* Sing "ti minus re = sol." *Variation:* Give students a series of numbers to sing according to the scale match (e.g., 1155665 would come out "Twinkle, Twinkle Little Star"). Challenge students to sing backwards and present their own number song phrases for the class to decode by singing.

**Data Graph.** Students listen to music and record names of instruments and tally the times each is heard. Students then are shown how to create bar graphs of results. *Suggestion:* Discuss the effects of the instrument quantities.

**Patterns.** Teach a song, such as "Are You Sleeping?" Ask students to listen for the repeated pattern. Show ways to represent the pattern through shapes and numbers. For example, the different pitches of the lyrics can be represented with the numbers 12311231 to show the sound goes up up up down, up up up down, and so forth. Ask students for other ways to represent the pattern (e.g., letters, shapes, hand signals). *Transformation:* Ask students to change the sound pattern in some way and sing the results.

**Fraction Pies or Pizza.** Because music is based on subdivisions of time into fractions, students can cut pies into fractions and use musical notation to label the pieces. For example, divide pies in half with a picture of a half-note on each slice.

**Song Graphs.** Students graph the notes of two or three songs by color coding the songs. Put the scale (do-re-mi-fa-so-la-ti-do) along the x-axis and a number of notes along the y-axis (e.g., graph the first 10 notes). Students then color in the boxes.

Note: Some boxes will have more than one color. *Example:* Graph the first 10 notes of "Row, Row, Row Your Boat," "Twinkle, Twinkle Little Star," and "Happy Birthday."

**Musical Math.** Give math problems for students to apply music knowledge (adapted from Athey & Hotchkiss, 1995), as follows:

Take the number of keys on a piano: 88
Add the number in a quartet: 4
Add the number in a trio: 3
TOTAL = 95

Use the following musical concepts to construct problems.

1. Solo/quarter note/quarter rest
2. Duet/half note/half rest
3. Trio/dotted half note/number of valves on a trumpet/legs on a grand piano
4. Quartet/whole note/whole rest/number of strings on a violin

5. Quintet
6. Number of strings on a guitar/sextet
7. Septet
8. Octave/octet

**Note Math.** After students have learned the symbols for whole, half, quarter, eighth, and sixteenth notes, they can solve and create note math problems. *Example:* "A whole note minus a quarter note = _____?"

**Word Problems.** Students listen to a piece of music, list instruments heard and number of times each was heard. Next, students write a word problem. *Example for addition:* "I heard (musical instrument) beats. I heard (music instrument) beats. How many beats were heard altogether?"

**Number Lyrics.** Students sing familiar songs replacing lyrics with numbers. This can be as simple as singing "Twinkle, Twinkle Little Star" and starting with "One, two, three, four . . ." or as challenging as singing odd numbers, even numbers, or by 10s or 5s. *Variation:* Use the tune to "San Fermin" to sing numbers or months in Spanish.

**Mnemonic Songs.** Use the memory power of music to help learn basic mathematical processes. *Example:* Here is a "Long Division Rap" written by sixth graders in Hayes, Kansas, to help them remember the process.

> I'm Dr. D, and I'm on the scene
> With my division rap that's oh so mean
> It goes divide, multiply, subtract, and bring down (repeat)
> Now you can do it wrong or you can do it right
> But if you do it wrong you'll be here all night
> I say, divide, multiply, subtract, and bring down (repeat)

**Rhythm and Sound Math.** Students use rhythm instruments or body sounds to present addition and subtraction problems. For example, student pairs (A and B) present, with student A doing two beats and student B ringing bells four times. Class responds with six claps or snaps.

**Numerals and Counting.** Prepare flashcards from 1 to 10 to use with "Ten Little Indians" (change to pumpkins, if desired). Play steady beat for four measures, then two measures—ending with fast sixteenth notes. Ask students about the difference between slow and fast sounds (rhythm, division of beats, steady beat). Repeat for students to signal for fast sounds.

Next, sit in a circle and review numerals 1 through 10 with flashcards. Teacher plays slow steady beat again, and students pass cards around the circle clockwise. When children hear fast beats they hold up cards, instead of passing. Practice. Next, everyone sings the song and students hold up the right card when the number is sung. Practice. Sing numbers going down from 10 as teacher plays beat and cards are passed around. Everyone holds cards high when the sixteenth notes are heard. Then the song begins again and cards are passed. Each child holds up a new card when the song is sung again. *Variation:* Sing in another language to reinforce counting (uno, dos, tres inditos, quatro, cinco, seis inditos . . .). Or, use number words instead of numerals (idea from Amy Golden, New York City music teacher).

**Water Music (Measurement).** Use 10 clear glasses. Students measure the side of each glass and subtract 1 inch from the top. Divide this measurement by 10. Use a crayon to mark 10 sections on each glass. Fill glasses with water to the lines. Label the first glass 1, the second glass 2, and so on, through 10. With a teaspoon, gently tap the first glass near the rim. Listen for the sound. As the numbers get higher and water increases, the tones get lower. Have students tap out phone numbers to listen for pitches, and create other addition and subtraction problems to play.

**Add On.** Use songs such as "Down in the Valley" and start singing with two children. Then those two each select a partner and there are four, those four select, and so forth. The song "Wishy Washy" starts with two sailors and one boat, then four sailors and two boats, and so forth. Ask children to figure out how many will come next (idea from Debbie Fahmie, Florida music teacher).

**Counting Songs and Chants.** Teach counting songs and chants to help students learn this skill (e.g., "One potato, two potato," "The Ants Go Marching"). Some of these songs are also good for marching to a 1-2 beat. See Appendix J under "Music" for book titles.

**Musical Quilt.** Read about how quilts are made. Examine patterns and geometric shapes. Discuss how quilts portray feelings or events. Tell students they will be composing a song quilt. Decide on an experience, event, or emotion. Divide into small groups. Each group contributes a line to a song. Select a traditional folk tune to accompany the lyrics that children create. Next, children write lyrics on a fabric square or colored paper (e.g., origami paper) using permanent markers. Assemble quilt and sing the squares as a leader points to each.

**Shape Composition.** Students need 15 to 20 pieces of paper in geometric shapes (multiple numbers of three to five different shapes cut ahead, or they can cut triangles, squares, circles, and diamonds). Review shape names. In groups, students lay out a pattern they like and then decide on a sound for each shape. Homemade rhythm instruments may be used. Groups rehearse and then perform their composition (e.g., square for drum, circle for shaker). Think of how the following pattern would sound.

**Rhythm Instruments.** Many resource books show ways to make rhythm instruments that can be painted and decorated. Also see Ready Reference 13.1. Make rain sticks by inserting toothpicks up and down a wrapping paper tube (it helps to make the holes ahead with a small drill). Fill tubes with rice or small beans and plug the ends. Sticks can then be painted or covered with collage materials.

- Body percussion: rub palms, snap fingers, clap hands, slap knees, tap fingers, tap toes, stamp, click tongue
- Vocals/ostinati: doo wop/shu-wop; dum diddy diddy; shuboom shu-boom; chicka chicka boom boom; bu-bu-bu-bubblin'; a do run run run a do run run

# Artist Spotlight
## A Master Creative Problem Solver

Classroom teachers sometimes think music integration is particularly difficult. One problem is having the right music materials. This closing Artist Spotlight is on a real-life artist who had the same problem. It is about the great violinist Itzhak Perlman, and it happened in 1995 during a performance at the Lincoln Center in New York City.

Mr. Perlman had polio as a child and now wears braces on both legs. He uses crutches to walk. When he was introduced for this performance, he slowly made his way across the stage, one step at a time. When he reached his chair, he carefully sat down and laid down his crutches. Then he undid one leg clasp and then the other. He tucked one foot back, and stretched the other forward. Finally, he bent down, picked up his violin, put it beneath his chin, nodded to the conductor, and began.

After he had played only a few bars, there was a loud bang. One of the violin strings had broken. The whole audience knew what Mr. Perlman had to do—go through the whole struggle with clasps and crutches to get another violin or replace the string.

But he didn't. After a moment he took a deep breath and closed his eyes. When he opened them, he signaled and the orchestra began again.

The audience was stunned. They knew it is impossible to play a symphonic piece with just three strings. On that night Itzhak Perlman refused to know this. He recomposed in his head and coaxed sounds from the remaining strings that seemed unbelievable.

When he finished, the audience was absolutely silent. Then, as if on cue, everyone stood up and applauded wildly. People cheered and whistled. It went on and on. Mr. Perlman mopped his brow and smiled. Finally, he raised his bow. The applause stopped and the audience waited for him to speak. When he did his voice was soft.

"You know, sometimes it is the artist's task to find out how much music you can still make with what you have left" (Author Unknown).

## Conclusion

*Many of us go to our grave with the music still inside of us.* (Anonymous)

This chapter is a compendium of dozens of ways to get the music out. Used in conjunction with the AI building blocks described in Chapter 12, teachers should be more prepared to approach teaching like Itzak Perlman did—to take risks and to make music with what they have.

## Teachers as Leaders: AI Advocacy

Choose one from the following: (1) Work with a group to create a directory of musical talent for a group like a college class, or better yet, a school or school district. First make a list of possible talents (e.g., sing, play instrument) and develop a short survey to circulate. (2) Work with a librarian to organize a music-based book display at a school to "make public" what is available. See bibliographies in Chapter 13 and in the Appendix. (3) Post inspirational quotes about music in public places such as the cafeteria, hall, or classroom or offer to insert them in a school's monthly newsletter. (4) Write a letter to the editor of a newspaper about the importance of music education and music integration. In particular, respond to articles about schools that are considering cutting music programs.

## myeducationlab

Go to the Activities and Applications section for Topic *Strategies for Teaching* at MyEducationLab for your course and complete the video activities entitled "Using Energizers and Warm-Ups to Prepare for Creative Problem Solving" and "Using Keyboarding to Teach Mathematics."

Go to the Activities and Applications section for Topic *Attaining Arts Literacy* and complete the video activity entitled "A Music Specialist Talks about Using Music as a Teaching Tool."

Go to the Book Specific Resources section in the MyEducationLab for your course, select your book and Chapter 13 to view the Questions to Guide Reading and Response Options for this chapter.

## Resources

See the Appendix for additional materials, including websites in Appendix I.

### Websites

Musical Mouseum: www.kididdles.com/mouseum/index.html (listen to children's song lyrics)

Mudcat Café: www.mudcat.org (folk song database, 8,000+ songs, large section on children's music plus more)

### Music Resource Books

Barrett, J., Veblen, K., & McCoy, C. (1997). *Sound ways of knowing*. Thomson Learning. (excellent resources)

Beall, P. (2005). *Wee sing sing-alongs*. Price Stern Sloan. (American folk; CD)

Birkenshaw-Fleming, L. (2002). *Come on everybody let's sing*. Alfred.

Choksy, L., & Brummitt, D. (1987). *120 singing games and dances for elementary schools*. Prentice Hall. (games and dances)

Cohn, A. (Ed.). (1993). *From sea to shining sea: A treasury of American folklore and songs*. Scholastic.

Davidson, L., & Norton, A. (1999). *The learning through music handbook*. New England Conservatory.

Durell, A. (1997). *The Diane Goode book of American folk tales and songs*. Scholastic.

Eddleman, D. (Ed.). (1999). *Great children's songbook: A treasure chest of music & activities*. Carl Fischer Music Publisher.

Eston, R., & Economopoulos, K. (2006). *Pattern trains and hopscotch paths: Exploring pattern*. Scott Foresman.

Flohr, J. (2005). *The musical lives of young children*. Prentice Hall.

Fosterm J. (2001). *Ready set rap*. Oxford Press.

Hackett, P. (1998). *The melody book* (3rd ed.). Prentice Hall. (300 songs with easy accompaniments)

Krull, K. (1992). *Gonna sing my head off!* Knopf. (folk songs)

Metropolitan Museum of Art Staff. (1987). *Go in and out the window: An illustrated songbook for young people*. Henry Holt.

Miche, M. (2002). *Weaving music into young minds*. Delmar/Thomson Learning. (practical ideas and resources, websites, connections to top names in children's music; CD)

Mitchell, L. (1993). *One, two, three-echo me! Ready-to-use songs, games, and activities to help children sing in tune*. Heritage Music Press.

Schiller, P., & Moore, T. (1993). *Where is Thumbkin?* Gryphon House. (activities based on songs)

Sporborg, J. (1998). *Music in every child's classroom: A resource guide for integrating music across the curriculum K–8*. Libraries Unlimited.

Wright, T., Neminovsky, R., & Tierney, C. (2006). *Timelines and rhythm patterns: Representing time*. Scott Foresman.

Yelton, G. (Ed.). (1991). *The musical PC*. MIDI America.

### Multicultural Books/Music

Barchas, S. (1999). *Bridges across the world* (with CD). High Haven Music.

Bryan, A. (2003). *All night, all day: A child's first book of African-American spirituals*. Atheneum.

Campbell, P. (1994). *Roots and branches* (with CD). World Music Press. (background information and songs from more than 25 countries)

Floyd, M. (Arr.). (2001). *Folksongs from Africa*. Faber Music.

Gritton, P. (1991). *Folksongs from the Far East*. Faber Music.

Gritton, P. (1993). *Folksongs from India*. Faber Music.

Lewis, R. (1995). *All of you was singing* (African American). Macmillan.

Lipman, D. (1993). *We all go together: Creative activities for children to use with multicultural folksongs*. Oryx Press.

Mattox, C. (1990). *Shake it to the one that you love best: Play songs and lullabies from black musical tradition*. Warren Mattox.

National Gallery of Art. (1994). *An illustrated treasury of songs*. Rizzoli International. (songs, ballads, folk songs)

Page, N., & Clark, K. (2001). *Sing and shine on!* World Music.

Seeger, P. (2004). *Rise up singing! Singout*. (folk songs including the round "Hava Nagila")

Toop, D. (1991). *Rap attack 2: African rap to global hip hop*. Serpent's Tail.

### Book Sellers and Sources: Recordings and Media

Canyon Records: www.store.canyonrecords.com/ (Native American music)

www.Amazon.com/ (large collection across many areas of interest)

Cellar Book Shop, 18090 Wyoming, Detroit, MI 48221 (Philippines, Asia, the Pacific, Australia, and New Zealand)

Children's Book and Music Center: www.santamonicamusic.com/ (folk and world music, offers preview service)

Best Children's Music: www.bestchildrensmusic.com/

Floyd's Record Shop: www.floydsrecordshop.com/ (Cajun and Creole music)

G.P.N. Media: www.shopgpn.com/ (videos and instruments from Africa, South America, and Japan)

Homespun Tapes: www.homespuntapes.com/ (folk, jazz, yodeling)

Ladyslipper: www.ladyslipper.org/ (music by women artists)

Music for Little People: www.musicforlittlepeople.com/ (audio/video recordings/instruments)

Sing Out: www.singout.org/ (publishes *Sing Out! The Folksong Magazine on North American Music* and *Rise Up Singing!* —an excellent collection; song reprints)

Tower Records: www.tower.com/ (recordings in print)

World Music Press: www.worldmusicpress.com/ (multicultural books, recordings, videos)

## Instrument Sources

Carroll Sound: www.carollmusic.com/ (drums, percussion, ethnic instruments)

House of Musical Traditions: www.hmtrad.com/

John's Music Center: www.johnsmusiccenter.com/ (ethnic and Orff instruments)

Lark in the Morning: www.larkinmorning.com/ (American and European folk)

Rhythm Band, Inc.: www.rhythmband.com/ (ethnic instruments and materials)

# Epilogue

Dr. Seuss could have been referring to using creative problem solving to reform American education. Many educators and arts advocates have concluded schooling is out of whack with real life. Their solution is arts integration.

Educators across the country feel intense pressure to raise test scores. Some say they cannot afford to divert attention from literacy and math to integrate the arts. Increasingly, however, "the conclusion is schools cannot afford NOT to embrace the arts" (Corbett, Wilson, & Morse, 2005, p. 43). Mounting research connects the arts to academic achievement. Meaningful integration is strongly linked to cognitive and motivational growth that underlies both school success and, more importantly, life success. When "insinuated seriously and systematically" into instruction, the arts extend every teacher's reach to children who will not thrive in the regimen of traditional schooling (p. 43). What's more arts integration provides those already doing well with opportunities to develop creative thinking abilities essential to life success.

No child's education should depend on the luck of the draw. Each and every one deserves a teacher who is committed to serious arts integration—not adding the arts on but making the arts a full curricular partner, a "Fourth R" (Broudy, 1979). Students become active meaning *creators* as lessons are laced with rich arts strategies that engage "head, heart, and hands." As unique communication vehicles, the arts expand messages—they permit understanding and expression of ideas and feelings beyond the limits of words alone.

While arts integration demands genuine collaboration with arts specialists, classroom teachers are center stage. Drawing upon the artist within, they invent, stretch, and twist ideas to solve learning problems. They move out of a zone of comfort to the edge of teaching possibilities. Teachers involved in arts integration say it's worth the risk and work. They believe they can change the future—one child at a time. The passion they feel about their roles is expressed poetically by Hiam Ginott (1985):

I am the decisive element in the classroom. It is my personal approach that creates the climate. It is my daily mood that makes the weather. As a teacher, I possess tremendous power to make a child's life miserable or joyous. I can be a tool of torture or an instrument of inspiration. I can humiliate, humor, hurt or heal. In all situations, it is my response that decides whether a crisis will be escalated or deescalated and a child humanized or dehumanized.

*Best wishes,*
*Claudia E. Cornett*

A+ Schools Program. (2001). North Carolina A+ Schools Program. In *The arts and education reform*. Greensboro, NC: University of North Carolina.

Adams, J. (2002). *The arts teachers handbook: Dance*. North Carolina Department of Public Instruction. www.ncpublicschools.org/curriculum/artsed/resources

Adomat, D. (2009). Actively engaging with stories through drama: Portraits of two young readers. *The Reading Teacher, 62*(8), 628–636.

Alexander, K., & Michael, D. (Eds.). (1991). *Discipline-based art education: A curriculum sample*. Santa Monica, CA: Getty Center for Education in the Arts.

Allen, J., Michalove, B., & Shockley, B. (1991, March). I'm really worried about Joseph: Reducing the risks of literacy learning. *Reading Teacher, 44*, 458–472.

Allen, M. (1999). *What are little girls made of? A guide to female role models in children's books*. New York: Facts on File.

Allen, R. (2004, Spring). *The arts give students a ticket to learning*. www.ascd.org

Allington, R. (1983). The reading instruction provided readers of differing reading abilities. *Elementary School Journal, 83*, 548–559.

Allington, R. (2002). What I've learned about effective reading instruction. *Kappan, 83*(10), 740–747.

Allington, R. (2005, February). *What really matters for struggling readers*. Keynote, South Carolina Reading Association, Myrtle Beach, SC.

Allington, R., & McGill-Franzen, A. (1989). School response to reading failure: Instruction for chapter 1 and special education students in grades 2, 4 & 8. *The Elementary School Journal, 89*, 529–542.

Amabile, T. (1996). *Creativity in context*, Boulder, CO: Westview Press.

Anderson, R. C., Hiebert, E., Scott, J., & Wilkinson, I. (1985). *Becoming a nation of readers: The report of the Commission on Reading*. Washington, DC: National Institute of Education.

Anderson, R. C., et al. (1986). Interestingness of children's reading materials. In R. Snow & M. Farr (Eds.), *Aptitude, learning and instruction*. Hillsdale, NJ: Erlbaum.

Andrzejczak, N., Trainin, F., & Poldberg, M. (2005). From image to text: Using images in the writing process. *International Journal of Education and the Arts, 6*(12), 1–17.

Annenberg Institute for School Reform at Brown University. (1998). How the arts transform schools: A challenge for all to share. *Challenge Journal, 3*(1). www.annenberginstitute.org/Challenge

Annenberg Institute for School Reform. (2002). *Opportunity and accountability: Arts environment as models of equity*. www.annenberginstitute.org

Annenberg Institute for School Reform. (2003). *The arts and school reform: Lessons and possibilities from the Annenberg Challenge Arts Projects*. Providence, RI: Author.

Armstrong, K. (2004). *History of God: The 4000 year quest of Judaism, Christianity and Islam*. New York: Gramercy Books.

Armstrong, T. (1993). *7 kinds of smart*. New York: Penguin.

Armstrong, T. (2000; 1994). *Multiple intelligences in the classroom*. Alexandria, VA: Association for Supervision and Curriculum Development.

Arnheim, R. (1989). *Thoughts on art education*. Los Angeles: Getty Center for Education in the Arts.

Arts Skill Map. (2010). Available from the Partnership for 21st Century Skills (www.21stcenturyskills.org/), Music Educator's National Conference (www.menc.org), or Arts Education Partnership (www.aep-arts-org).

ArtsSmart Institute for Learning. (2006). *Summary: Program evaluation of ArtsSmart Institute for Learning*. Texarkana, TX: Texarkana Regional Arts and Humanities Council. www.trahc.org

*Artistic employment in 2000*. (2000, May). Research Division Note 78. Washington, DC: National Endowment for the Arts. *The arts in every classroom*. (2005). Video series from Annenberg/CPB channel. www.learner.org

Arts Education Partnership. (1998). *Young children and the arts: Making the creative connection*. Washington, DC: Author.

Arts Education Partnership. (1999). *Learning partnerships: Improving learning in schools with arts partners in the community*. Washington, DC: Author.

Arts environments as models of equity (proposal). (Undated). Providence, RI: Brown University. www.annenberginstitute.org

Arts Project and The Grove/Tanglewood Model Arts Project. (2005, May). Summary report (Unpublished document). Greenville SC: Greenville County Schools.

Aschbacher, P., & Herman, J. (1995). The humanities program evaluation. In *The arts and education: Partners in achieving our national education goals*. Washington, DC: National Endowment for the Arts.

Athey, M., & Hotchkiss, G. (1995). *A galaxy of games for the music class*. West Nyack, NY: Parker.

Au, K. (2002). Multicultural factors and the effective instruction of students of diverse backgrounds. In A. Farstrup & S. J. Samuels, *What research has to say about reading instruction*. Newark, DE: International Reading Association.

Baker, R., Boughton, D., Freedman, K., Horowitz, R., & Ingram, D. (2004, April). *Artistic production as evidence of learning in interdisciplinary contexts*. San Diego, CA: American Educational Research Association.

Balick, D. (1999). Learning from artists: Working with teachers from other disciplines. In D. P. Wolf & D. Balick (Eds.), *Arts works! Interdisciplinary learning powered by the arts* (pp. 153–166). Portsmouth, NH: Heinemann.

Bamberger, J. (2000). Music, math and science: Towards an integrated curriculum. Journal for Learning through Music, 1(Summer), 32–35.

Barboza, S. (1992). *I feel like dancing: A year with Jacques d'Amboise and the National Dance Institute*. New York: Crown.

Barker, A. (2005, April 11). W.Va. Health study tried video dance game as weight loss for kids. *Beaufort Gazette*, 3C.

Barlow, J. (2002, August 7). Complex physical learning may compensate for prenatal alcohol exposure, study shows. *Innovations Report*. Urbana, IL: University of Illinois. www.innovationsreport.com

Baron, R. (1997, February). *Scientific thought in motion*. Presentation at The Kennedy Center, Washington, DC.

Barr, R., Kamil, M., & Mosenthal, P. (Eds.). (1996). *Handbook of reading research* (vol. 2). Mahwah, NJ: Erlbaum.

Barron, F. (1969). *Creative person and creative thinking*. New York: Holt, Rinehart, & Winston.

Barton, P. (2005, July 23). Huckabee builds a case for arts in school. *Arkansas Democrat-Gazette* (Little Rock), A1.

Baumann, J. F., & Ivey, G. (1997). Delicate balances: Striving for curricular and instructional equilibrium in a second grade, literature/strategy-based classroom. *Reading Research Quarterly, 32*, 244–275.

Beck, I., & McKeown, M. (2002). Comprehension: The sine qua non of reading. In S. Patton & M. Holmes (Eds.), *The keys to literacy* (p. 54). Washington, DC: Council for Basic Education.

Begley, S. (1996). Your child's brain. *Newsweek, 127*(8), 55–61.

Begley, S. (2000, July 24). Music and the mind. *Newsweek*. www.keepmedia.com/pubs/Newsweek/2000/07/24

Begley, S. (2004, June 18). Math whizzes do excel at music, but is link merely a coincidence? *The Wall Street Journal*, B1.

Berthoff, A. E. (1981). *The making of meaning*. Montclair, NJ: Boynton/Cook.

Bettleheim, B. (1989). *The uses of enchantment*. New York: Vintage.

Bierhorst, J. (1976). *The red swan: Myths & tales of the American Indian*. New York: Farrar, Straus & Giroux.

Bill, B. (1988). *Many manys: A life of Frank Lloyd Wright*. London: Heinemann.

Bishop, R. (1992). Multicultural literature for children. In V. Harris (Ed.), *Teaching multicultural literature in grades K–8*. Norwood, MA: Christopher-Gordon.

Bizar, M. (2005). *Teaching the best practices way*. Alexandria, VA: Association for Supervision and Curriculum Development.

Bloom, A., & Hanny, J. (2006). Integrating art from around the world into the classroom. *Phi Delta Kappan, 87*(8).

Blythe, T., & Gardner, H. (1990, April). A school for all intelligences. *Educational Leadership,* 33–36.

Block, C., & Pressley, M. (2007). Best practices in teaching comprehension. In Gambrell, L., Morrow, L., & Pressley, M. (Eds.), *Best practices in literacy instruction* (3rd ed., pp. 220–242). New York/London: Guilford Press.

Block, C. (2004). *Teaching comprehension: The comprehension process approach.* New York: Pearson/Allyn Bacon.

Bloom, A. (2004, July 30). Now even lads face the music and dance. *Times Educational Supplement,* 5. The bookfinder: A guide to children's literature (vol. 1). (1994). Circle Pines, MN: American Guidance.

Bloom, B. (1956). *Taxonomy of educational objectives.* New York: Longman.

Bolak, K., Bialach, D., & Dunphy, M. (2005, May). Standards-based, thematic units integrate the arts and energize students and teachers. *Middle School Journal, 36,* 9–19.

Booth, E. (2003, Summer). Arts for art's sake and art as a learning tool: Achieving a balance. *Journal for Learning Through Music, 2,* 19–22.

Booth, E. (2005, Winter). The teaching artist. *The Teaching Artist, 1*(2).

Bopegedera, A. (2005). The art and science of light: An interdisciplinary teaching and learning experience. *Journal of Chemical Education, 82*(1), 55–59.

Boston, B. (1996). Educating for the workplace through the arts. Reprinted from *BusinessWeek,* October 28, 1996. Columbus, OH: McGraw-Hill.

Bransford, J., Brown, A., Cocking, R., Donovan, M., & Pellegrino, J. (Eds.). (2000). *How people learn: Brain, mind, experience and school.* Washington, DC: National Academy Press.

Brookes, M. (1996). *Drawing with children.* New York: Putnam.

Broudy, H. S. (1979). How basic is aesthetic education? Or is it the fourth R? *Language Arts, 54,* 631–637.

Boyer, E. (1993). Keynote speech for the Association for Supervision and Curriculum Development.

Brown, P. (2005, April 24). Sousa? Many students march to mariachi instead. *New York Times,* final section, 1.

Brownlee, S. (1997, February 17). What science says about those tender feelings. *U.S. News and World Report,* 58–60.

Brozo, W. (1998). *Readers, teachers and learners: Expanding literacy across the content areas.* Upper Saddle River, NJ: Merrill/Prentice Hall.

Bruer, J. T. (1999). In search of brain based education. *Kappan, 80*(9), 648–654.

Bryon, E. (2005, July 27). To master the art of solving crimes, cops study Vermeer. *Wall Street Journal,* 1.

Burchers, S. (1996). *Vocabutoons.* Punta Gorda, FL: New Monic.

Burgard, R. (1997). *Schools as communities: Public education and social cohesion.* Washington, DC: National Endowment for the Arts.

Burger, K., & Winner, E. (2000). Instruction in visual art: Can it help children learn to read? *Journal of Aesthetic Education, 34*(3/4), 277–293.

Burmark, L. (2002). *Learn to see, see to learn.* Alexandria, VA: Association for Supervision Curriculum Development.

Burnaford, B., April, A., & Weiss, C. (Eds.). (2001). *Arts integration and learning: Chicago arts partnerships in education.* Mahwah, NJ: Lawrence Erlbaum.

Burnaford, G., April, A., & Weiss, C. (2002). *Renaissance in the classroom: Arts integration and meaningful learning.* Mahwah, NJ: Lawrence Erlbaum.

Burnaford, B. (2007). *Arts integration frameworks, research & practice: A literature review.* Washington, DC: Arts Education Partnership.

Burner, J. (1960). *The process of education.* Cambridge, MA: Harvard University Press.

Burton, J., Horowitz, R., & Abeles, H. (1999). *Learning in and through the arts: Curriculum implications.* New York: Teachers College Press, Columbia University.

Burton, J. M., Horowitz, R., & Abeles, H. (2000). Learning in and through the arts: The question of transfer. *Studies in Art Education, 41*(3), 228–257.

Burz, H., & Marshall, K. (1999). *Performance-based curriculum for music and the visual arts.* Thousand Oaks, CA: Corwin.

Caine, R., & Caine, G. (2005). *12 brain/mind learning principles in action.* Thousand Oaks, CA: Corwin Press.

Cambourne, B. (2002). Holistic, integrated approaches to reading and language arts instruction: The constructivist framework of an instructional theory. In A. Farstrup & S. J. Samuels (Eds.), *What research has to say about reading instruction.* Newark, DE: International Reading Association.

Cambourne, B. (2009, March 30). The sound and the fury about making sense of written words. *The Sydney Morning Herald.* www.smh.com.au/national/the-sound-and-the-fury-about-making-sense-of-written-words-20090329-9fm8.html?page=-1

Campbell, D. (1997). *The Mozart effect.* New York: Avon.

Campbell, J. (2008). *Hero with a thousand faces.* New York: MJF.

Campbell, P., Brabson, E., & Tucker, J. (1994). *Roots and branches: A legacy of multicultural music for children.* Danbury, CT: WorldMusic.

Cantrell, S. (1999). The effects of literacy instruction on primary students' reading and writing achievement. *Reading Research and Instruction, 39,* 3–26.

Carlo, M. (2007). Best practices for literacy instruction for English-language learners. In L. Gambrell, L. Morrow, & M. Pressley, (Eds.). *Best practices in literacy instruction* (3rd ed.,). New York/London: Guilford.

Carlo, M. (2007). Best practices for literacy instruction for English-language learners. In L. Gambrell, L. Morrow, & M. Pressley (Eds.), *Best practices in literacy instruction* (3rd ed.). New York/London: Guilford Press.

Carter, D., & Diaz, J. (1999). *The elements of pop-up.* New York: Simon and Schuster.

Catterall, J. (1995). *Different ways of knowing: 1991–1994 National Longitudinal Study final report.* Los Angeles: The Galef Institute.

Catterall, J. (1998). *Involvement in the arts and success in secondary school.* Washington, DC: Americans for the Arts.

Catterall, J. (2002). Research on drama and theatre in education. In R. Deasy (Ed.), *Critical links: Learning in the arts and student academic and social development.* Washington, DC: Arts Education Partnership.

Catterall, J. (2003, Summer). Education policy implications of recent research on the arts and academic and social development. *Journal of Learning Through Music, 2,* 103–109.

Catterall, J. (2005). Conversation and silence: Transfer of learning through the arts. *Journal for Learning through the Arts: A Research Journal on Arts Integration in Schools and Communities, 1*(1), 1–12.

Catterall, J., Chapleau, R., & Iwanaga, J. (1999). The imagination project at UCLA. In E. Fiske (Ed.), *Champions of change.* Washington, DC: Arts Education Partnership.

Catterall, J., Chapleau, R., & Iwanaga, J. (1999). Involvement in the arts and human development: General involvement and intensive involvement in music and theater arts. In E. Fiske (Ed.), *Champions of change: Impact of the arts on learning.* Washington, DC: Arts Education Partnership.

Catterall, J., & Waldorf, J. (1999). Chicago arts partnerships in education: Summary evaluation. In E. Fiske (Ed.), *Champions of change: The impact of the arts on learning.* Washington, DC: The Arts Education Partnership.

Cecil, N., & Lauritzen, P. (1994). *Literature and the arts for the integrated classroom.* White Plains, NY: Longman.

Chan, A. S., Ho, Y. C., & Cheung, M. C. (1998). Music training improves verbal memory. *Nature, 396*(607), 128.

Chauvet, J., Deschamps, E., & Hilliare, C. (1996). *Dawn of art: The Chauvet Cave: The oldest known paintings in the world.* New York: Abrams.

Chessin, D., & Zander, M. J. (2006). The nature of science and art. *Science Scope, 29*(8), 42–46.

Chilman, K. (2004). An integrated mural project. *School Arts, 103*(8), 50–51.

Choksy, L. (1974). *The Kodaly method.* Upper Saddle River, NJ: Prentice Hall.

Chomsky, C. (1972). Stages in language development and reading exposure. *Harvard Educational Review, 42,* 1–33.

Clements, R., & Wachowiak, F. (2010). *Emphasis art: A qualitative art program for elementary and middle schools* (9th ed.). Boston, MA: Allyn & Bacon/Pearson.

Cockerton, T., Moore, S., & Norman, D. (1997). Cognitive test performance and background music. *Perceptual and Motor Skills, 85,* 1435–1438.

Coufal, K. L., & Coufal, D. (2002). Colorful wishes: The fusion of drawing, narratives, and social studies. *Communication Disorders Quarterly, 23*(2), 109–121.

Cohen, D. (1968). The effect of literature on vocabulary and reading achievement. *Elementary English, 45,* 209–213, 217.

Coleman, L. (1997). *Serendipity encyclopedia.* Grand Rapids, MI: Serendipity.

Collins, R. (1994). Story told at Storyfest, Jackson, MI.

Collins, R. (1997). Storytelling: Water from another time. *Drama Theatre Teacher, 5*(2), 6.

Collins, R., & Cooper, P. (1996). *The power of story.* Upper Saddle River, NJ: Prentice Hall.

Connor, S. (2003, December 8). Glaxo Chief: Our drugs do not work on most patients. *Independent, 1.*

Consortium of National Arts Education Associations. (1994). *National standards for arts education: What every young person should know and be able to do in the arts.* Reston, VA: Music Educators National Conference.

Cooper, R. (1998). *Socio-cultural and within-school factors that affect the quality of implementation of school-wide programs* (Report No. 28). Baltimore, MD: Center for Research on the Education of Students Placed at Risk (ERIC ED426173).

Corbett, D., McKenney, M., Noblit, G., & Wilson, B. (2001). *The arts, school identity, and comprehensive education reform: A final report from the evaluation of the A+ Schools Program.* Winston-Salem, NC: Kenan Institute for the Arts.

Corbett, D., Wilson, B., & Morse, D. (2005). *The arts are an "R" too: Integrating the arts and improving student literacy (and more) in the Mississippi Arts Commission's whole schools initiative.* Jackson, MI: Mississippi Arts Commission. www.mswholeschools.org

Cornett, C. (1997, March). Beyond plot retelling. *Reading Teacher,* 527–528.

Cornett, C. (2001). *Learning through laughter, again.* Bloomington, IN: Phi Delta Kappa.

Cornett, C. (2006). Center stage: Arts-based read alouds. *Reading Teacher, 60*(3).

Cornett, C. (2010). *Comprehension: Inquiry into big ideas using important questions.* Scottsdale, AZ: Holcomb Hathaway.

Cornett, C., & Cornett, C. (1980). *Bibliotherapy: The right book at the right time.* Bloomington, IN: Phi Delta Kappa.

Cortines, R. (1999). Introduction. In L. Longley (Ed.), *Gaining the arts advantage: Lessons from school districts that value arts education.* Washington, DC: President's Committee on the Arts and the Humanities.

Cowan, K., & Albers, P. (2006). Semiotic representations: Building complex literacy practices through the arts. *The Reading Teacher, 60*(2), 124–137.

Csikszentmihalyi, M. (1990). The domain of creativity. In M. A. Runco & R. S. Albert (Eds.), *Theories of creativity* (pp. 190–212). Newbury Park, CA: Sage.

Cullinan, B. (1989). *Literature and the child* (2nd ed.). New York: Harcourt Brace Jovanovich.

Cunningham, A., & Shagoury, R. (2005, October). The sweet work of reading. *Educational Leadership,* 53–57.

Dacey, J. S. (1989). *Fundamentals of creative thinking.* Lexington, MA: Lexington Books.

Dana Foundation. (2008, March). *Conference Proceedings from the Arts and Cognition Consortium.* www.dana.org

Daniels, H., & Bizar, M. (2005). *Teaching the best practices way.* Alexandria, VA: Association for Supervision Curriculum Development.

Daniels, H., Darby, J. T., & Catterall, J. S. (1994). The fourth R: The arts and learning. *Teachers College Record, 96,* 299–328.

Darby, J., & Catterall, J. (1994). The fourth R: The arts and learning. *Teachers College Record,* 299–328.

Darigan, D., Tunnell, M., & Jacobs, J. (2002). *Children's literature: Engaging teachers and children in good books.* Upper Saddle River, NJ: Pearson.

Davidson, L., Claar, C., & Stampf, M. (2003, Summer). Strategies for school change through music and the arts. *Journal of Learning Through Music, 2,* 64–76.

Deasy, R. (2008, March). Why the arts deserve center stage: Committing to creative learning for students that will restore America's role as a leader in nurturing innovation. *School Administrator.*

Deasy, R. (Ed.). (2002). *Critical links: Learning in the arts and student academic and social development.* Washington, DC: Arts Education Partnership.

Deasy, R., & Fulbright, H. (2001, November 24). The arts' impact on learning. *Education Week, 34,* 38.

Deasy, R., & Stevenson, L. (2005). *Third space: When learning matters.* Washington, DC: Arts Education Partnership.

deBono, E. (1991). *Six thinking hats for schools: 3–5 resource book.* Logan, IA: Perfection Learning.

DeMoss, K., & Morris, T. (2002). *How arts integration supports student learning: Students shed light on the connections.* www.capeweb.org/rcape.html

Dewey, J. (1899). *The school and society / The child and the curriculum.* Chicago: University of Chicago Press.

Dewey, J. (1997). *How we think.* Mineola, NY: Dover Press.

Dibben, N. (2004). The role of peripheral feedback in emotional experience. *Music Perception, 22*(1), 79–115.

Donohue, K. (1997). *Imagine! Introducing your child to the arts.* Washington, DC: National Endowment for the Arts.

Doughty, R. (2002). *Arts education in South Carolina: A brief retrospective.* Greenwood, SC: South Carolina Alliance for Arts Education.

Douglas, S., & Willatts, P. (1994). Musical ability enhances reading skills. *Journal of Research in Reading, 17,* 99–107.

Drake, S., & Burns, R. (2004). *Meeting standards through integrated curriculum.* Alexandria, VA: Association for Supervision and Curriculum Development.

Dreeszen, C., April, A., & Deasy, R. (1999). *Learning partnerships: Improving learning in schools with arts partners in the community.* Washington, DC: Arts Education Partnership.

Dressel, J. H. (1990). The effects of listening to and discussing different qualities of children's literature on the narrative writing of fifth graders. *Research in the Teaching of English, 24,* 397–414.

Duke, N. K. (2000). For the rich it's richer: Print environments and experiences offered to first grade students in very low and very high-SES school districts. *American Educational Research Journal, 37,* 456–457.

Duncan, A. (2009). Press release on results of NAEP 2008 arts assessment. Washington, DC: U.S. Department of Education.

Duma, A. (2005, April). Phone interview with director of Teacher and School Programs, The Kennedy Center, Washington, DC.

Dupont, S. (1992). The effectiveness of creative drama as an instructional strategy to enhance reading comprehension skill. *Reading Research and Instruction, 31*(3), 41–52.

Eberle, R. (1971). *SCAMPER: Games for imagination development.* Buffalo, NY: Development of Knowledge.

Edelsky, C., Altwerger, A. B., & Flores, B. (1991). *Whole language: What's the difference?* Portsmouth, NH: Heinemann.

Edwards, K. L. (1994). *North American Indian music instruction: Influences upon attitudes, cultural perceptions and achievement.* D.M.A. dissertation, Tempe, AZ: Arizona State.

Eeds, M., & Wells, D. (1989). Grand conversations: An exploration of meaning construction in literature study groups. *Research in the Teaching of English, 23,* 4–29.

Efland, A. D. (2002). *Art and cognition: Integrating the visual arts in the curriculum.* New York: Teachers College.

Eger, J. (2004). Nurturing a creative community. *Cosmos.*

Eisenkraft, A., Heltzel, C., Johnson, D., & Radcliffe, B. (2006). Artist as chemist. *The Science Teacher, 73*(8), 33–37.

Eisner, E. (1983). *Beyond creating.* Los Angeles: Getty Center for Education in Art.

Eisner, E. (1992, April). The misunderstood role of the arts in human development. *Kappan,* 591–595.

Eisner, E. (1997, November). *The arts and imagination.* Keynote delivered at the Imagination Celebration Conference, Columbia University, New York.

Eisner, E. (1998a). *The kind of schools we need.* Portsmouth, NH: Heinemann.

Eisner, E. (1998b). *The enlightened eye.* Upper Saddle River, NJ: Merrill Prentice Hall.

Eisner, E. (2000). Ten lessons the arts teach. In *Learning and the arts: Crossing boundaries.* www.giarts.org/pdf/Learning.pdf

Eisner, E. (2002a). *The arts and the creation of mind.* New Haven, CT: Yale University Press.

Eisner, E. (2002b). What can education learn from the arts about the practice of education? *Journal of Curriculum and Supervision, 18,* 4–16.

Eisner, E. (2005). An introduction to a special section on the arts and the intellect. *Kappan, 87*(1), 8–10.

Eldredge, J. L., & Butterfield, D. (1986). Alternatives to traditional reading instruction. *Reading Teacher, 40,* 33–37.

Ellis, R. D. (1999). The dance form of the eyes: What cognitive science can learn from art. *Journal of Consciousness, 6,* 6–7.

Ellison, L. (1992, October). Using multiple intelligence to set goals. *Educational Leadership,* 69–72.

Erikson, E. (1950). *Childhood and society.* New York: Norton.

Esq Esquith R. (2008, July). Keynote for the Value Plus Summer Teacher Institute, Renaissance Center, Dickson, TN.

Evans, J., & Moore, J. E. (1985). *How to make books with children.* Monterey, CA: Evan Moore.

Fader, D., & McNeil, E. (1976). *The new hooked on books.* New York: Berkeley.

Faltis, C., Hudelson, S., & Hudelson, S. (1997). *Bilingual education in elementary and secondary school communities: Toward understanding and caring.* New York: Allyn & Bacon.

Farstrup, A., & Samuels, S. J. (2002). *What research has to say about reading instruction.* Newark, DE: International Reading Association.

Fauth, B. (1990). Linking the visual arts with drama, movement, and dance for the young child. In J. Stinson (Ed.), *Moving and learning for the young child*. Reston, VA: American Alliance for Health, Physical Education, and Dance.

Feeney, S., & Moravcik, E. (1987). A thing of beauty: Aesthetic development in young children. *Young Children, 42*(6), 7–15.

Ferrero, D. (2005). Pathways to reform: Start with values. *The Best of Educational Leadership,* 21–26.

Fineberg, C. (2002). Integrating the arts into the wider curriculum. In *Planning an arts-centered school: A handbook*. New York: The Dana Foundation.

Fineberg, C. (2003). *Planning an arts-centered school.* New York: Dana Press.

Fineberg, C. (2004). *Creating islands of excellence: Arts education as a partner in school reform.* Portsmouth, NH: Heinemann.

Fiske, E. (Ed.). (1999). *Champions of change: The impact of the arts on learning.* Washington, DC: The Arts Education Partnership and The President's Committee on the Arts.

Fitzgerald, J., & Graves, M. (2004). *Scaffolding reading experiences for English language learners.* Norwood, MA: Christopher-Gordon.

Five, C. (1986). Fifth graders respond to a changed reading program. *Harvard Educational Review, 56,* 395–405.

Fleming, G. A. (Ed.). (1990). *Children's dance.* Reston, VA: American Alliance for Health, Physical Education, and Dance.

Florida, R. (2004). *The rise of the creative class.* New York: Basic Books.

Fogarty, R. (1991). *The mindful school: How to integrate the curricula.* Palatine, IL: Skylight Publishing.

Fogg, T., & Smith, M. (2001). The artists in the classroom project: A closer look. *Educational Forum, 66,* 60 70.

Ford Foundation. (2005, Winter). *Deep in the heart of Texas.* www.fordfound.org

Freeman, C., Seashore, K. R., & Werner, L. (2003). *Methods of implementing arts for academic achievement: Challenging contemporary classroom practice.* Minneapolis: University of Minnesota, Center for Applied Research and Educational Improvement.

Friedmann, S. (2004, April 4). How colors affect feelings. *Beaufort Gazette,* 2.

Friedman, T. (2009, May 6). Interview. www.aasa.org/publications/saarticledetail.cfm?Item Number=9736&snItemNumber=950&tnItem Number

Frye, N. (1957). Theory of symbol. In *Anatomy of criticism.* Princeton, NJ: Princeton University Press.

Gallagher, K., & Booth, D. (Eds.). (2003). *How theatre educates.* Toronto, ON: University of Toronto Press.

Gambrell, L., & Koskinen, P. S. (2002). Imagery: A strategy for enhancing comprehension. In C. B. Block & M. Pressley (Eds.), *Comprehension instruction: Research-based best practices.* New York: Guilford Publications.

Gambrell, L., Morrow, L., & Pressley, M. (Eds.). (2007). *Best practices in literacy instruction* (3rd ed.)., New York/London: Guilford Press.

García, G. E. (1991). Factors influencing the English reading test performance of Spanish-speaking Hispanic children. *Reading Research Quarterly, 26*(4), 371–392.

Gardner, H. (1993). *Multiple intelligences: The theory in practice.* New York: Basic Books.

Gardiner, M. (1996). Learning improved by arts training. *Scientific Correspondence in Nature, 381*(580), 284.

Gardner, H. (1973). *The arts and human development.* New York: Wiley.

Gardner, H. (1983; 1993). *Frames of mind: The theory of multiple intelligences.* New York: Basic Books.

Gardner, H. (1989, Winter). Zero-based arts education: An introduction to ARTS PROPEL. *Studies in Art Education,* 71–83.

Gardner, H. (1990). *Art education and human development.* Los Angeles: Getty Center for Education in the Arts.

Gardner, H. (1993a). *Creating minds.* New York: Basic Books.

Gardner, H. (1993b). *Multiple intelligences: The theory in practice.* New York: Basic Books.

Gardner, H. (1999). *The disciplined mind.* New York: Simon & Schuster.

Gaskins, I. (2003). Taking charge of reader, text, activity, and content variables. In A. Sweet & C. Snow (Eds.), *Rethinking reading comprehension* (pp. 141–165). New York: Guilford.

Gazzaniga, M. (2005). *Arts and cognition.* Washington, DC: Dana Foundation.

Gazzaniga, M. (2008). Learning, arts and the brain: Findings hint at relationships. In M. Gazzaniga (Ed.), *Dana Consortium Report on Arts and Cognition.* New York/Washington, DC: Dana Press.

Gelman, R. (1979). Preschool thought. *American Psychologist, 34,* 900–905.

Gersten, R., & Baker, S. (2000). What we know about effective instructional practices for English-language learners. *Exceptional Children, 66,* 454–470.

Getzels, J. W., & Jackson, P. W. (1962). *Creativity and intelligence.* New York: Wiley.

Gilbert-Greene, A. (1977). *Teaching the 3 Rs through movement experiences.* New York: Macmillan.

Gilbert-Greene, A. (1992). *Creative dance for all ages.* Reston, VA: National Dance Association.

Gilbert, A. (2005). *Brain-compatible dance education.* www.creativedance.org

Giles, M. (1991). A little background music please. *Principal, 71,* 141–167.

Ginott, H. (1985). *Between teacher and child.* New York: Avon.

Given, B. (2002). *Teaching to the brain's natural learning systems.* Alexandria, VA: Association for Supervision and Curriculum Development.

Ginsberg, H., & Opper, S. (1969). *Piaget's theory of intellectual development.* Upper Saddle River, NJ: Prentice Hall.

Glazer, J. (1997). *Introduction to children's literature* (2nd ed.). Upper Saddle River, NJ: Prentice Hall.

Goldberg, M. (1997). *Arts and learning.* White Plains, NY: Longman.

Goldberg, M., Bennett, T., & Jacobs, V. (1999, April). Artists in the classroom: A role in the professional development of classroom teachers. Montreal, Quebec, Canada: American Educational Research Association.

Goldberg, M. (2004). *Teaching English language learners through the arts—A SUAVE experience.* Boston: Pearson.

Goldberg, M. R., & Phillips, A. (2000). *Arts as education.* Cambridge, MA: Harvard Educational Review.

Goleman, D. (2005). *Emotional intelligence: Why it can matter more than IQ.* New York: Bantam.

Gopnik, A., Kuhl, P., & Meltzoff, A. (1999). *The scientist in the crib: Minds, brains and how children learn.* New York: William Morrow.

Gourgey, A., Bousseau, J., & Delgado, J. (1985). The impact of an improvisational dramatics program on student attitudes and achievement. *Children's Theater Review, 34*(3), 9–14.

Graziano, A., Peterson, M., & Shaw, G. (1999, March). Enhanced learning of proportional math through music training and spatial-temporal training. *Neurological Research, 21*(2), 139–152.

Greene, M. (1997, February). Why ignore forms of art? *Education Week,* 4–5.

Greene, M. (2001). *Variations on a blue guitar: The Lincoln Center lectures on aesthetic education.* New York: Teachers College Press.

Gregorian, V. (1997, March 13). 10 things you can do to make our schools better. *Parade Magazine.*

Griss, S. (1998). *Minds in motion.* Portsmouth, NH: Heinemann.

Grossman, P., Wineburg, S., & Beers, S. (2000). Introduction: When theory meets practice in the world of school. In S. Wineburg & P. Grossman (Eds.), *Interdisciplinary curriculum: Challenges to implementation* (pp. 1–16). New York: Teachers College.

Grumet, M. (2004). No one learns alone. In N. Rabkin & R. Redmond (Eds.), *Putting the arts in the picture: Reframing education in the 21st century.* Chicago: Center for Arts Policy at Columbia College.

Güngör, A. (2009). Effects of drama on the use of reading comprehension strategies and on attitudes toward reading. *Journal for Learning through the Arts: A Research Journal on Arts Integration in Schools and Communities, 4*(1), art. 5. http://repositories.cdlib.org/clta/lta/vol4/iss1/art5

Gunzenhauser, M. G., & Gerstl-Pepin, C. I. (2002). Guest editors' introduction: The shifting context of accountability in North Carolina and the implications for arts-based reform. *Educational Foundations, 16,* 3–14.

Guskey, T. (2000). *Evaluating professional development.* Thousand Oaks, CA: Corwin Press.

Guthrie, J. (2000). Contexts for engagement and motivation in reading. In M. Kamil, P. Mosenthal, P. Pearson, & R. Barr (Eds.), *Handbook of reading research* (vol. 3). New York: Erlbaum.

Guthrie, J. (2004). Motivating students to read. In P. McCardle & U. Chhabra (Eds.), *The voice of evidence in reading research.* Baltimore, MD: Brookes.

Habemeyer, S. (1999). *Good music, brighter children.* Rocklin, CA: Prince.

Hall, G. E., & Hord, S. M. (1987). *Change in schools: Facilitating the process.* Albany, NY: State University of New York.

Hall, G. E., Loucks, S. F., Rutherford, W. L., & Newlove, B. W. (1975). Levels of use of the innovation: A framework for analyzing innovation adoption. *Journal of Teacher Education, 26*(1), 52–56.

Hall, J. (2005). Neuroscience and education. *Education Journal, 84,* 27–29.

Hallet, M. (1999, May). *Gray matters: Sports, fitness and the brain.* Interview on National Public Radio.

Hallet, V. (2005, July 25). The power of Potter. *U.S. News and World Report,* 45–49.

Hanna, J. (1992, April). Connections: Arts, academics and productive citizens. *Kappan,* 601–607.

Hanna, J. (1999). *Partnering dance and education.* Champaign, IL: Human Kinetics.

Hansen, L., & Monk, M. (2002). Brain development and structure of learning. *International Journal of Science Education, 24*(4), 343–356.

Hansen-Krening, N. (1992). Authors of color: A multicultural perspective. *Journal of Reading, 26*(2), 124–129.

Harris, L. (1992). *Americans and the arts VI/Nationwide survey of public opinion.* Washington, DC: Americans for the Arts.

Harste, J., Short, K., & Burke, C. (1988). *Creating classrooms for authors.* Portsmouth, NH: Heinemann.

Hart, A., & Mantell, P. (1993). *Kids make music!* Charlotte, VT: Williamson.

Hart, B., & Risley, T. (2003, Spring). The early catastrophe: The 30-million word gap. *American Educator.* www.aft.org/American_Educator/spring2003/catastrophe.html

Hartzler, D. (2000). A meta-analysis of studies conducted on integrated curriculum programs and their effects on student achievement. Unpublished dissertation, Indiana University, Bloomington.

Harvard Project Zero. (2000). *Project SUMIT: Schools using multiple intelligence theory* (Outcomes section, para. 1-9). www.pz.harvard.edu/SUMIT/OUTCOMES.HTM

Heath, S. B., with Roach, A. (1999). Imaginative actuality: Learning in the arts during the nonschool hours. In E. Fiske (Ed.), *Champions of change: Impact of the arts on learning.* Washington, DC: The Arts Education Partnership and the President's Committee on the Arts and Humanities.

Heathcote, D., & Bolton, G. (1995). *Drama for learning.* Portsmouth, NH: Heinemann.

Hebert, D. (2005). *Getting to the top: Arts essential academic learning requirements.* Seattle, WA: New Horizons for Learning.

Hedblad, A. (1998). *Something about the author.* Detroit: Gale.

Hefferen, J. (2005). Professional development: Building a faculty of reflective practitioners. In B. Rich (Ed.), *Partnering arts education: A working model from ArtsConnection* (pp. 22–26). New York: Dana Press.

Heinig, R. B. (1993). *Creative drama for the classroom teacher.* Upper Saddle River, NJ: Prentice Hall.

Henderson, L. C., & Shanker, L. C. (1978). The use of interpretive dramatics versus basal reader workbooks. *Reading World, 17,* 239–243.

Hepler, S. (1982). Patterns of response to literature: A one year study of a fifth and sixth grade classroom. Unpublished doctoral dissertation, The Ohio State University, Columbus.

Herman, J., & Baker, E. (2005, November). Making benchmark testing work. *Educational Leadership, 63*(3), 48–54.

Hetland, L. "Basically, Arts are Basic." American Association of School Administrators. March 6, 2008. Available at http://www.aasa.org/publications/content.cfm?ItemNumber=10130

Hetland, L., & Winner, E. (Eds.). (2000, Fall/Winter). The arts and academic achievement: What the evidence shows. *The Journal of Aesthetic Education, 34.* Champaign, IL: University of Illinois Press.

Hetland, L., Winner, E., Veenema, S., & Sheridan, K. (2007). *Studio thinking: The real benefits of visual arts education.* New York: Teacher's College Press.

Hillman, C., & Castelli, D. (2009, April 1). Physical activity may strengthen children's ability to pay attention. *Science Daily. http://www.sciencedaily.com/releases/2009/03/090331183800.htm*

Hochman, D. (2005, February 25). Their fingers do the talking. *Life Magazine,* 8–11.

Holdaway, D. (1982). Shared book experience: Teaching reading using favorite books. *Theory into Practice, 21,* 293–300.

Hope, S. (2003, Summer). Questions and challenges concerning music's role in education. *Journal for Learning Through Music, 2.*

Hopkins, L. (1969). *Books are by people.* New York: Citation.

Hopkins, L. B. (1987). *Pass the poetry please.* New York: Harper & Row.

Horowitz, R. (2004). *Summary of large-scale arts partnership evaluations.* Washington, DC: Arts Education Partnership.

Hotz, R. (2009, July 3–5). Magic flute: Primal find sings of music's mystery. *Wall Street Journal,* A9.

Housen, A., & Yenwine, P. (2000). *Visual thinking strategies, basic manual K–2.* New York: Visual Understanding.

Hubel, D. (1988). *Eye, brain, and vision.* New York: Freeman.

Huck, C., Hepler, S., & Hickman, J. (2001). *Children's literature in the elementary school* (4th ed.). Dubuque, IA: McGraw-Hill.

Huckabee, M. (2005, October 2). Why we need arts education. Presentation at Arts Education Partnership Forum, Charleston, SC. Available at www.aep-arts.org.

Huckabee, M. (2005). *Initiative on the arts in education 2005–2006.* Education Commission of the States. www.ecs.org

Hudson, R., Lane, H., & Pullen, P. (2005, May). Reading fluency assessment and instruction: What, why, and how? *Reading Teacher, 58*(8), 702–713.

Hutchens, J., & Pankratz, D. B. (2000). Change in arts education: Transforming education through the arts challenge (tetAc). *Arts Education Policy Review, 101*(4), 5–10. (2002). National Governor's Association. Retrieved from http://www.nga.org/.

Hume, H. (2005). *The art teacher's book of lists.* Hoboken, NJ: Jossey-Bass.

Ingram, D., & Riedel, E. (2003). *Arts for academic achievement: What does arts integration do for students?* Minneapolis: University of Minnesota, Center for Applied Research and Educational Improvement.

Ingram, D., & Seashore, K. R. (2003). *Arts for academic achievement: Summative evaluation report.* Minneapolis: University of Minnesota, Center for Applied Research and Educational Improvement.

International Association of Visual and Performing Arts High Schools. (2000, February). Annual meeting, Mobile, AL.

Interstate New Teacher Assessment and Support Consortium (INTASC). (2002, June). *Model standards for licensing classroom teachers and specialists in the arts.* Washington, DC: Council of Chief State School Officers. www.ccsso.org/projects

Intrator, S. (2004–2005). The engaged classroom. *The Best of Educational Leadership,* 2–5.

Isaksen, S. G., & Treffinger, D. J. (1985). *Creative problem solving: The basic course.* Buffalo, NY: Bearly Limited.

J. Paul Getty Trust. (1993). *The power of arts to transform education.* Los Angeles, CA.

Jack, C. (2005, July 18). *Arts in school can have lifelong impact. Plain Dealer* (Cleveland, OH), D1.

Jacobs, H. (Ed.). (1989). *Interdisciplinary curriculum: Design and implementation.* Alexandria, VA: Association for Supervision and Curriculum Development.

Jacobs, H. (1997). *Mapping the big picture: Integrating curriculum and assessment, K–12.* Alexandria, VA: Association for Supervision and Curriculum Development.

Jacobs, J. (2002). *Children's literature.* Columbus, OH: Merrill/Prentice Hall.

Jakes, D. (2006). *Coloring the curriculum through the arts.* Alabama Alliance for Arts Education. www.alaae.org/manual_06.pdf

Jarnow, J. (1991). *All ears: How to use and choose recorded music for children.* New York: Viking.

Jay, D. (1991). Effect of a dance program on the creativity of preschool handicapped children. *Adapted Physical Activity Quarterly, 8,* 305–316.

Jenkins, P. (1986). *Art for the fun of it.* New York: Simon & Schuster.

Jennings, C. (1998). *Jenning's theatre for young audiences: Twenty great plays for children.* New York: St. Martin's Press.

Jensen, E. (2000). *Music with the brain in mind.* San Diego, CA: Brain Store.

Jensen, E. (2001). *Arts with the brain in mind.* Alexandria, VA: Association for Supervision and Curriculum Development.

Jewitt, C., Kress, G., & Ogborn, J. (2001). Exploring learning through visual, actional, and linguistic communication: The multimodal environment of a science classroom. *Educational Review, 53*(1), 5–19.

Johnson, T., & Louis, D. (1987). *Literacy through literature.* Portsmouth, NH: Heinemann.

Jorm, A. F. (1977). Effect of word imagery on reading performance as a function of reader ability. *Journal of Educational Psychology, 69,* 46–64.

Joyce, M. (1994). *First steps in teaching creative dance to children* (3rd ed.). Mountain View, CA: Mayfield.

Kamil, M. (2004). Reading comprehension. In P. McCardle & U. Chhabra (Eds.), *The voice of evidence in reading research.* Baltimore, MD: Brookes.

Kantrowitz, B., & Leslie, C. (1997, April 14). Readin', writin', rhythm. *Newsweek,* 71.

*Kappan.* (2005). Themed issue on art and the intellect, *87*(1).

Kardash, C., & Wright, L. (1987, Winter). Does creative drama benefit elementary school students? A meta-analysis. *Youth Theater Journal*, 11–18.

Karioth, E. (1967). Creative dramatics as an aid to developing creative thinking abilities. Unpublished doctoral dissertation, University of Minnesota.

Keefner, G. (2005). Personal conversation with the principal of Hilton Head Creative Arts Elementary, Hilton Head, South Carolina.

Keirstead, C., & Graham, W. (2004). *VSA arts research study: Using the arts to help special education students meet their learning goals.* Portsmouth, NH: RMC Research Corporation.

Kellogg, R. (1969). *Analyzing children's art.* Palo Alto, CA: Mayfield.

Keppel, P. (2003, Summer). Teaching musicians the art of possibility: Observations on a master class by Ben Zander. *Journal for Learning Through Music, 2*, 28–30.

Kiefer, B. (1994). *The potential of picture books: From visual literacy to aesthetic understanding.* Upper Saddle River, NJ: Prentice Hall.

Kinney, D., & Forsythe, J. (2005, Spring). The effects of the Arts IMPACT curriculum upon student performance on the Ohio Fourth-Grade Proficiency Test. *Bulletin of the Council for Research in Music Education, 164*, 35–48.

Kippelen, V. (2002, March). *The halls are alive.* http://connectforkids.org.

Koster, J. (1997). *Growing artists.* Albany, NY: Delmar.

Krashen, S. (2005, February). Is in-school free reading good for children? Why the National Reading Panel (NRP) is still wrong. *Kappan, 86*(6), 444–447.

Kutiper, K., & Wilson, P. (1993). Updating poetry preferences: A look at the poetry children really like. *Reading Teacher, 47*(1), 28–35.

LaFosse, M. (2003). *Origami activities: Asian arts and crafts for creative kids.* North Clarendon, VT: Tuttle.

Lakshmanan, I. (2005, June 22). For Venezuela's poor, music opens doors. www.boston.com/news/world/latinamerica

Lamb, S. J., & Gregory, A. H. (1993). The relationship between music and reading in beginning readers. *Educational Psychology, 13*, 19–26.

Langer, E. (1989). *Mindfulness.* New York: Addison-Wesley.

Langer, E. (1997). *The power of mindful learning.* New York: Addison-Wesley.

Larson, G. (1997). *American canvas.* Washington, DC: National Endowment for the Arts.

Leahy, S., Lyon, C., Thompson, M., & William, D. (2005). Classroom assessment: Minute by minute, day by day. *Educational Leadership*, 18–26.

Learning and the Arts: Crossing boundaries. (2000, January). *Proceedings from an Invitational Meeting for Education, Arts and Youth Funders,* Los Angeles. www.giarts.org/Learning.pdf

Lehr, S. S. (1991). *The child's developing sense of theme: Responses to literature.* New York: Teachers College Press.

Leigh, S., & Heid, K. (2008). First graders constructing meaning through drawing and writing. *Journal for Learning through the Arts: A Research Journal on Arts Integration in Schools and Communities,*

4(1), art. 3. http://repositories.cdlib.org/clta/lta/vol4/iss1/art3

Levine, M. (2002). *A mind at a time.* New York: Simon and Schuster.

Levi-Straus, C. (1967). *Scope of anthropology.* London: Cape.

Levstik, L. (1986). The relationship between historical response and narrative in a sixth-grade classroom. *Theory and Research in Social Education, 14*, 1–15.

Lewis, C. S. (1980). On three ways of writing for children. In S. Egoff et al. (Eds.), *Only connect readings on children's literature.* New York: Oxford University Press.

Lewis, R. (2002, September). I made it by myself. *New Horizons for Learning.* www.newhorizons.org The Lexile Framework. (1995). Durham, NC: Metametrics.

Lima, C. (2005). *A to zoo: Subject access to children's picture books.* New York: Simon and Schuster.

Lindsey, G. (1998–99, Winter). Brain research and implications for early childhood education. *Childhood Education, 75*(2), 97–100.

Lindstrom, R. (1999, April 19). Being visual: The emerging visual enterprise. *Business Week:* Special Section.

Lockwood, S. (2005, March). *The window: Saving creativity in Teens.* Seattle, WA: New Horizons Learning. www.newhorizons.org

Longley, L. (Ed.). (1999). *Gaining the arts advantage: Lessons from school districts that value arts education.* Washington, DC: President's Committee on the Arts and the Humanities.

Longo, P. (1999, November 8). *Distributed knowledge in the brain: Using visual thinking networking to improve students' learning.* Boston: Learning and the Brain Conference.

Lowenfeld, V., & Brittain, W. L. (1975). *Creative and mental growth.* New York: Macmillan.

Lozanov, G. (1978). *Suggestology and outlines of suggestopedy.* New York: Gordon & Breach.

Luftig, R. (1994). *The schooled mind: Do the arts make a difference? An empirical evaluation of the Hamilton Fairfield SPECTRA1 Program 1992–93.* Oxford, OH: Miami University, Center for Human Development.

Lushington, K. (2003, December). *Lighting the fire of imagination through theatre and drama in Ontario schools.* www.code.on/Pages/dramaarticle.html

MacKinnon, D. W. (1978). *In search of human effectiveness.* Buffalo, NY: Creative Education Foundation.

MacMahon, S., Roe, D., & Parks, M. (2003). Basic reading through dance program: The impact on first-grade students' basic reading skills. *Evaluation Review, 27*, 104–125.

Macon, J. (1991). *Responses to literature.* Newark, DE: International Reading Association.

Malyarenko, T. N., Kuraev, G. S., Malyarenko, Y. E., Khvatova, M. V., Romanova, N. G., & Gurina, V. I. (1996). The development of brain's electric activity in 4 yr. old children by long-term sensory stimulation with music. *Human Physiology, 23*, 76–81.

Mantione, R., & Smead, S. (2003). *Weaving through words: Using the arts to teach reading comprehension strategies.* Newark, DE: International Reading Association.

Marantz, S. (1992). *Picture books for looking and learning: Awakening visual perceptions through the art of children's books.* Westport, CT: Greenwood.

Mardirosian, G. H., & Fox, L. (2003). Literacy learning intervention for at-risk students through arts-based instruction: A case study of the imagination quest model. Presentation at the Learning Conference 2003: What Learning Means, Institute of Education, University of London.

Marron, V. (2003, Summer). The A+ schools program: Establishing and integrating the arts as four languages of learning. *Journal for Learning Through Music, 2*, 91–97.

Marzano, R., Pickering, D., & Pollock, J. (2001). *Classroom instruction that works: Research-based strategies for increasing student achievement.* Alexandria, VA: Association for Supervision and Curriculum Development.

Mauk, M. (2009, June). Brain scientists identify close links between arts, learning. *Dana Foundation's Arts in the News, 7*(2).

Maslow, A. (1968). *Toward a psychology of being.* Princeton, NJ: Van Nostrand.

Maslow, A. (1970). *Motivation and personality.* New York: Harper & Row.

Mason, C., & Steedly, K. (2006). Rubrics and an arts integration community of practice. *Teaching Exceptional Children, 39*(1), 36–43

Mason, C., Thormann, M., & Steedly, K. (2004). *VSA arts affiliate research project: How students with disabilities learn in and through the arts.* Washington, DC: Very Special Arts.

Maxim, G. (2010). *Dynamic social studies for constructivist classrooms* (9th ed.). Boston: Allyn & Bacon.

McCardle, P., & Chhabra, U. (Ed.). (2004). *The voice of evidence in reading research.* Baltimore, MD: Brookes.

McCaslin, N. (1990). *Creative drama in the classroom* (5th ed.). New York: Longman.

McDermott, P. (2004). Using the visual arts for learning: The case of one urban charter school. *Second Annual Ethnography in Education Research Forum*, 27–28.

McDermott, R., & Varenne, H. (1995). Culture as disability. *Anthropology & Education Quarterly, 26*, 324–348.

McElmeel, S. (1994). *ABCs of an author/illustrator visit.* Worthington, OH: Lippincott.

McGill-Franzen, A. (1989). See Allington. R., (1989)

McKinsey and Company. (2009). *The economic impact of the achievement Gap in America's schools.* www.mckinsey.com/clientservice/socialsector/achievement_gap_report.pdf

McTighe, J., & O'Connor, K. (2005, November). Seven practices for effective learning. *Educational Leadership*, 10–18.

McTighe, J., & Wiggins, G. (2004). *Understanding by design: Professional workbook.* Alexandria, VA: Association for Supervision and Curriculum Development.

McWinnie, H. J. (1992). Art in early childhood education. In C. Seefeldt (Ed.), *The early childhood curriculum.* New York: Teachers College Press.

Mello, R. (2004, March). When pedagogy meets practice: Combining arts integration and teacher education in the college classroom. *The Journal of the Arts and Learning, 20*(1), 135–164.

Meyrink, G. (1994). The curse of the toad. In *The opal and other stories.* Riverside, CA: Ariadne.

Miles, M. B., & Huberman, A. M. (1994). *Qualitative data analysis* (2nd ed.). Newbury Park, CA: Sage.

Miller, H., Rynders, J., & Schleien, S. (1993). Drama: A medium to enhance social interaction between students with and without mental retardation. *Mental Retardation, 31*(4), 228–233.

Mitchell, C., & Weber, S. (1998). Picture this! Class line-ups, vernacular portraits, and lasting impressions of school. In J. Prosser (Ed.), *Image-based research: A sourcebook for qualitative researchers* (pp. 197–213). London: Falmer.

Moats, L. (2004). Science language and imagination in the professional development of reading teachers. In P. McCardle & U. Chhabra (Eds.), *The voice of evidence in reading research*. Baltimore, MD: Brookes.

Moore, B., & Caldwell, H. (1993). Drama and drawing for narrative writing in primary grades. *Journal of Educational Research, 8*(2), 100–110.

Moore, T. (1998). *Care of the soul: How to add depth and meaning to your everyday life*. New York: HarperCollins.

Morrison, C. (2003, February 24). Arts-in-education efforts. *The Asheville Citizen-Times*, B1.

Morrow, L. (2001). Literacy development and young children: Research to practice. In S. L. Golbeck (Ed.), *Psychological perspectives on early childhood education* (pp. 253–279). International Reading Association Journal.

Morrow, L. (2003). *Handbook of research on teaching the English language arts*. Mahwah, NJ: Lawrence Erlbaum.

Morrow, L. (1992). The impact of a literature-based program on literacy achievement, use of literature, and attitudes of children from minority backgrounds. *Reading Research Quarterly, 27,* 250–275.

Morrow, L., Pressley, M., Smith, J., & Smith, M. (1997). The effect of a literature-based program integrated into literacy and science instruction with children from diverse backgrounds. *Reading Research Quarterly, 32*(1), 54–76.

Murfee, E. (1995). *Eloquent evidence: Arts at the core of learning*. Washington, DC: The President's Committee on the Arts and the Humanities.

Murray, R. L. (1975). *Dance in elementary education: A program for boys and girls* (3rd ed.). New York: Harper & Row.

Music therapy at Case Western Medical School. (1997, June 7). *Springfield New Sun,* 1.

Myers, D., & Scripp, L. (2007). Evolving forms of music-in-education practices and research in the context of arts-in-education reform: Implications for schools that choose music as a measure of excellence and as a strategy for change. *Journal for Music-in-Education: Advancing Music for Changing Times, 1*(2), 381–396.

Nash, J. M. (1997, February 3). Fertile minds. *Time,* 48–49.

National Art Education Association. (2002). *Authentic connections: Interdisciplinary work in the arts*. Reston, VA: Author.

National Center for Education Statistics. (2000). http://nces.ed.gov

National Center for Education Statistics. (1997). *Highlights of the NAEP 1997 arts assessment report card*. Washington, DC: U.S. Department of Education. http://nces.ed.gov/nationsreportcard/pdf/main1997/1999486.pdf

National Reading Panel. (2000). *Teaching children to read: An evidence-based assessment of the scientific reading literature and its implications for reading instruction*. Washington, DC: National Institute Child Health.

National Assessment of Educational Progress. (2003–2008). http://nces.ed.gov/nationsreportcard/

Neeld, E. C. (1986). *Writing* (2nd ed.). Glenview, IL: Scott, Foresman.

Nelson, C. (2001). *The arts and education reform: Lessons from a four-year evaluation of the A+ Schools Program* (Executive Summary). Winston-Salem, NC: Kenan Institute for the Arts.

Nelson, K. (1998). *Developing students multiple intelligences*. New York: Scholastic.

New American Schools. (2003). The Leonard Bernstein center for learning. http://naschools.org

New York City Board of Education. (1992–1993). *Chapter I developer/demonstration program: Learning to read through the arts*. New York: Office of Educational Research.

No Child Left Behind Act of 2001, Pub. L. No. 107-110. (2001). www.ed.gov/nclb/landing.jhtml

Noddings, N. (2005, September). What does it mean to educate the whole child? *Educational Leadership, 63*(1), 8–13.

Nordlund, C. (2006). *Art experiences in Waldorf Education: Graduates' meaning making reflections,* Dissertation, University of Missouri–Columbia.

Norton, D. (2003). *Through the eyes of a child: An introduction to children's literature* (6th ed.). Upper Saddle River, NJ: Merrill/Prentice Hall.

Norton, D., & Norton, S. (2005). *Multicultural children's literature*. Upper Saddle River, NJ: Merrill/Prentice Hall.

Ogle, D. (1989). The know, want to know, learn strategy. In K. Muth (Ed.), *Children's comprehension of text: Research into practice*. Newark, DE: International Reading Association.

Ohler, J. (2006). *Digital stories in the classroom: A telling experience*. Thousand Oaks, CA: Corwin Press.

Ohio Department of Education. (1996). *Ohio's model competency-based program: Comprehensive arts education*. Columbus, Ohio: Author.

Olhansky, B. (2006, Summer). Helping all students succeed. Teaching the art of writing. *Educational Leadership, 63*. www.ascd.org

Olshansky, B. (2008). *The power of pictures*. San Francisco: Jossey-Bass.

Ohlhausen, M. M., & Jepsen, M. (1992). Lessons from Goldilocks: Somebody's been choosing my books but I can make my own choices now! *New Advocate, 5,* 31–46.

O'Neill, C. (1995). *Drama worlds: A framework for process drama*. Portsmouth, NH: Heinemann.

O'Neill, C., & Johnson, L. (1984). *Dorothy Heathcote: Collected writings on education and drama*. Cheltenham, UK: L Stanley Thomas (Publishers) Ltd.

Oppenheimer, T. (1999, September). Schooling the imagination. *Atlantic Monthly, 284*(3), 71–83.

Oreck, B., Baum, S., & McCartney, H. (1999). Artistic talent development for urban youth: The promise and the challenge. In E. Fiske (Ed.), *Champions of change*. Washington, DC: Arts Education Partnership.

Osborne, A. (1963). *Applied imagination* (3rd ed.). New York: Scribner's.

Page, N. (1995). *Sing and shine on! A teacher's guide to multicultural song leading*. Portsmouth, NH: Heinemann.

Paige, R., & Huckabee, M. (2005). Putting arts education front and center. *Education Week, 24*(20), 40, 52.

Palmarini, J. (2001, Summer). The REAP report. *Teaching Theatre,* 12–20.

Palmarini, J. (2005, Winter). The teaching artist. *Teaching Theatre, 16*(2), 1–6.

Parrish, M. (2007). Speak out: Dancing into problem-based learning. *Journal for Learning through the Arts: A Research Journal on Arts Integration in Schools and Communities, 3*(1), art. 2. http://repositories.cdlib.org/clta/lta/vol3/iss1/art2

Parsons, M. J. (1987). *How we understand art: A cognitive developmental account of aesthetic experience*. Cambridge, NY: Cambridge University Press.

Partnership for 21st Century Skills. (2009). www.21stcenturyskills.org/

Patchen, J. (1996, September). Overview of discipline-based music education. *Music Educator's Journal,* 19–25.

Pate, G. (1988). Research on reducing prejudice. *Social Education, 52*(4), 287–291.

Peck, R. (1988). *Secrets of successful fiction*. Seattle: Romar.

PEN. (2004, March 4). *Public Education News Weekly NewsBlast*.

Perkins, D. (1998). *The intelligent eye: Learning to think by looking at art*. Santa Monica, CA: Getty Center.

Perkins, D. N. (1987–1988, December/January). Art as an occasion of intelligence. *Educational Leadership,* 36–42.

Perrin, S. (1994, February). Education in the arts is an education for life. *Kappan,* 452–453.

Piaget, J. (1950). *The psychology of intelligence*. New York: Harcourt Brace.

Piaget, J. (1977). The role of action in the development of thinking. In W. F. Overton & J. M. Gallagher (Eds.), *Advances in research and theory*. New York: Plenum Press.

Piaget, J. (1980). *To understand is to invent*. New York: Penguin.

Piazza, C. (1999). *Multiple forms of literacy*. Upper Saddle River, NJ: Merrill/Prentice Hall.

Pica, R. (1991). *Moving and learning*. Champaign, IL: Human Kinetics.

Pink, D. (2006). *A whole new mind: Why right brainers will rule the future*. New York: River Head Trade.

Pinnell, G. (1986). *Reading recovery in Ohio, 1985–86: Final report*. Columbus, Ohio: The Ohio State University.

Pinnell, G., & Fountas, I. (2005). *Leveled books, K–8: Matching texts to readers for effective teaching*. Portsmouth, NH: Heinemann.

Posner, M., & Rothbart, M. (2005). Influencing brain networks. *Trends in cognitive science, 9*(3), 99–103.

Podlozny, A. (2000). Strengthening verbal skills through the use of classroom drama: A clear link. *Journal of Aesthetic Education, 34*(3/4), 239–275. *The power of the arts to transform education*. (1993). Los Angeles: J. Paul Getty Trust.

Preble, W., & Knowles, K. (2005). *Integrated Learning Project Research Consultant's Final Report,* New Hampshire Department of Education. www.ed.state.nh.us/education/doe/organization/Curriculum/Arts/Integrated%20Learning%20Project%20Research%20Report.pdf

President's Commission on National Goals. (1960). *Goals for Americans.* New York: The American Assembly, Columbia University.

Pressley, M. (2002). Metacognition and self-regulated comprehension. In A. Farstrup & S. J. Samuels, *What research has to say about reading instruction.* Newark, DE: International Reading Association.

Project Zero. (2000). *Reviewing education and the arts project (REAP), Executive summary.* Cambridge, MA: Harvard University. www.pz.harvard.edu/Research?REap/REAP

Psilos, P. (2002). *The impact of arts education on workforce preparation: Issue brief.* Washington, DC: National Governors' Association, Center for Best Practices. www.nga.org/

Purcell-Gates, V. (1988). Lexical and syntactic knowledge of written narrative held by well-read-to kindergartners and second graders. *Research in the Teaching of English, 22,* 128–160.

Rabkin, N., & Redmond, R. (2005, January 8). The art of education. *Washington Post,* A19.

Rabkin, N., & Redmond, R. (2005, April 13). Arts education: Not all is created equal. *Education Week, 24*(31), 46–47.

Rabkin, N., & Redmond, R. (Eds.). (2004). *Putting the arts in the picture: Reframing education in the 21st century.* Chicago: Center for Arts Policy at Columbia College.

Rabkin, N., & Redmond, R. (2006). The arts make a difference. *Educational Leadership, 63*(5).

RAND Reading Study Group. (2002). *Reading for understanding: Toward an R & D program in reading comprehension.* Santa Monica, CA: RAND Corporation. www.rand.org/publications/MR/MR1465/

Rauscher, F., Shaw, G., & Ky, K. (1995). Listening to Mozart enhances spatial-temporal reasoning: Towards a neurophysiological basis. *Neuroscience Letters, 185,* 44–47.

Rauscher, F., Shaw, G., Levine, L., Wright, E., Dennis, W., & Newcomb, R. (1997). Music training causes long-term enhancement of preschool children's spatial-temporal reasoning. *Neurological Research, 19,* 2–8.

Rauscher, F. H., & Shaw, G. L. (1993). Music and spatial task performance. *Nature.* Cited in *Why to Learn Music.* www.uwgb.breznayp/music.htm

REAP (Reviewing Education and the Arts Project). (2000). Project Zero at Harvard University. *Journal of Aesthetic Education, 34*(3).

Register, D. (2004, Spring). The effects of live music groups versus an educational children's television program on the emergent literacy of young children. *Journal of Music Therapy, 41*(1), 2–27.

Reimer, B. (2004). New brain research on emotion and feelings, dramatic implications for music education. *Arts Education Policy Review, 106*(2), 21–28.

Remer, J. (1996). *Beyond enrichment.* New York: American Council for the Arts.

Reutzel, D., & Cooter, R. (1992). *Teaching children to read: From basals to books.* Upper Saddle River, NJ: Prentice Hall.

Riccio, L., Rollins, J., & Morton, K. (2003). *The sail effect: Development of a model for measuring the effectiveness of the arts as an instrumental element in overall academic and social development for students in an arts-infused elementary school.* Washington, DC: WVSA Arts Connection.

Richards, J. C., Gipe, J. P., & Moore, R. C. (2000). *The challenge of integrating literacy learning and the visual and communicative arts: A Portal School focus* (ERIC ED 442784).

Richmond-Cullen, C. (2005, April 28). Congressional testimony on behalf of Pennsylvania Department of Education and Americans for the Arts.

Riekehof, L. (1987). *Joy of signing.* Springfield, MO: Gospel.

Ritter, N. (1999). *Teaching interdisciplinary thematic units in language arts.* Bloomington, IN: ERIC Clearinghouse on Reading, English, and Communication.

Roberts, T. (2004, September 29). The discipline of wonder (Editorial). *Education Week,* 31.

Robinson, K. (2000). *Learning and the arts: Crossing boundaries.* www.giarts.org/pdf/Learning.pdf

Robinson, K. (Ed.). (1990). *Exploring theater and education.* London: Heinemann.

Rooney, R. (2004). *Arts-based teaching and learning: Review of the literature.* Rockville, MD: Westat. www.vsarts.org/x954.xml

Root-Bernstein, R., & Root-Bernstein, M. (1999). *Sparks of genius: The 13 thinking tools of the world's most creative people.* New York: Houghton Mifflin.

Rose, L., & Gallup, A. (2005, September). The 37th annual Phi Delta Kappa/Gallup Poll of the public's attitudes toward the public schools. *Kappan,* 41–54.

Rosenberg, H. (1987). *Creative drama and imagination: Transforming ideas into action.* New York: Holt, Rinehart & Winston.

Rosenblatt, L. (1985). Viewpoints: Transaction versus interaction—a terminological rescue operation. *Research in the Teaching of English, 19,* 98–107.

Roser, N. L., Hofman, J. V., & Farest, C. (1990). Language, literature, and at-risk children. *Reading Teacher, 43,* 554–559.

Rozmajzl, M., & Boyer-White, R. (2005). *Music fundamental, methods, and materials,* White Plains, NY: Longman.

Ross, C., & Stangl, K. (1994). *The music teacher's book of lists.* West Nyack, NY: Parker.

Ruppert, S. (2006). *Critical evidence: How the arts benefit student achievement.* Washington, DC: National Assembly of State Arts Agencies and Arts Education Partnership.

Russell, D. (1994). *Literature for children: A short introduction* (2nd ed.). New York: Longman.

Sabine, G., & Sabine, P. (1983). *Books that made the difference.* Hamden, CT: Libraries Professional.

Sadie, S. (Ed.). (2001). *New Grove dictionary of music and musicians.* New York: Grove.

Sadoski, M., & Paivio, A. (2001). *Imagery and text: A dual coding theory of reading and writing.* Mahwah, NJ: Lawrence Erlbaum Associates.

Sadoski, M., & Paivio, A. (2004). A dual coding theoretical model of reading. In R. B. Ruddell & N. J. Unrau (Eds.), *Theoretical models and processes of reading* (5th ed., pp. 1329–1362). Newark, DE: International Reading Association.

Sadoski, M., & Quast, Z. (1990). Reader response and long term recall for journalistic text: The roles of imagery, affect, and importance. *Reading Research Quarterly, 25,* 256–272.

Safire, W. (1991, April 29). On language. *New York Times Magazine,* 16.

Samuels, J. (2002). Reading fluency. In A. Farstrup & S. J. Samuels, *What research has to say about reading instruction.* Newark, DE: International Reading Association.

Sanders Bustle, L. (2004). The role of visual representation in the assessment of learning. *Journal of Adolescent and Adult Literacy, 47*(5), 416–423.

Saunders, S. (1999). *The author visit handbook.* Portsmouth, NH: Heinemann.

Schacter, D. (2002). *Searching for memory: The brain the mind and the past.* New York: Basic Books.

Scheel, K. R., & Westefeld, J. S. (1999, Summer). Heavy metal music and adolescent suicidality: An empirical investigation. *Adolescent, 34*(134), 253–273.

Schmidt, B. (1991). Story map. In J. Macon (Ed.), *Responses to literature.* Newark, DE: International Reading Association.

Scripp, L. (2003, Summer). Critical links, next steps: An evolving conception of music and learning in public school education. *Journal of Learning Through Music, 2,* 119–140.

Scripp, L., & Subotnik, R. F. (2003). Directions for innovation in music education: Integrating conceptions of musical giftedness into general educational practice and enhancing innovation on the part of musically gifted students. In L. Shavina (Ed.), *International handbook on innovation.* Oxford, England: Pergamon.

Schwen, M. R. (1995). Theatre as liberal arts pedagogy. *Liberal Education, 81*(2), 32–38.

Seaman, M. A. (1999). *The arts in basic curriculum project: A ten year evaluation. Looking at the past and preparing for the future.* Columbia: University of South Carolina.

Seashore, F. (2001). *Arts survive: A study of sustainability in arts education partnerships.* Cambridge, MA: Project Zero, Harvard Graduate School of Education.

Seashore, F., Werner, K., & Werner, L. (2003). *Methods of implementing arts for academic achievement: Challenging contemporary classroom practice* (pp. ii–iii). Minneapolis, MN: Center for Applied Research and Educational Improvement.

Seidel, S. (1999). Stand and unfold yourself. A monograph on the Shakespeare and Company research study. In E. Fiske (Ed.), *Champions of change.* Washington, DC: Arts Education Partnership and the President's Committee on the Arts.

Shanahan, T. (2004). Critique of NRP Panel Report. In P. McCardle & U. Chhabra (Eds.), *The voice of evidence in reading research.* Baltimore, MD: Brookes.

Shaw, G. (2000). *Keeping Mozart in mind.* San Diego: Academic.

Shaywitz, S. (2004). Neurological basis for reading disability. In P. McCardle & U. Chhabra (Eds.), *The voice of evidence in reading research.* Baltimore, MD: Brookes.

Shephard, A. (2005). *Stories on stage.* Olympia, WA: Shepard.

Short, G. (2001). Arts-based school reform: A whole school studies one painting. *Art Education, 54,* 4–11.

Short, K., Schroeder, J., Laird, J., Kauffman, F., Ferguson, M., & Crawford, K. (1996). *Learning together through inquiry.* Portland, ME: Stenhouse.

Siegel, D. J. (1999). *The developing mind: Toward a neurobiology of interpersonal experience.* New York: Guilford Press.

Siks, G. (1983). *Drama with children.* New York: Harper.

Simmons, T., & Sheehan, R. (1997, February 16). Brain research manifests importance of first years. *The News & Observer.* www.nando.net/nao/2little2late/stories/dayl-main

Smith, S. (2003, April 2). Why not dance? *Chicago Tribune,* 2.

Smutny, J. (2002). *Integrating the arts into the curriculum for gifted students* (ERIC ED470524).

Snyder, S. (2001). Connection, correlation, and integration. *Music Educators Journal, 87*(5), 32–39, 70.

Soep, E. (2005, September). Critique: Where art meets assessment. *Kappan, 7*(1), 36–63.

Sostarich, J. (1974). A study of the reading behavior of sixth graders: Comparisons of active and other readers. Unpublished doctoral dissertation, The Ohio State University, Columbus.

South Carolina Arts Commission. (2002, April). *The economic impact of the arts in South Carolina.* Columbia, SC: Author.

Speer, N., Reynolds, J., Swallow, K., & Zacks, J. (2009). Reading stories activates neural representations of perceptual and motor experiences. *Psychological Science, 20,* 989–999.

Spilka, R. (2002). Approximately "real world" learning with the hybrid model. *Teaching with Technology Today, 8*(6). www.uwsa.edu/ttt/articles/spilka.htm

Spolin, V. (1999). *Improvisation for the theater: A handbook of teaching and directing techniques.* Evanston, IL: Northwestern University Press.

Spolin, V. (2001). *Theater games for the lone actor.* Evanston, IL: Northwestern University Press.

Stack, Y. (2007). *ArtsSmarts at Caslan School: A longitudinal case study.* Kelowna, British Columbia, Canada: Society for the Advancement of Excellence in Education.

Standing, L. (1973). 10,000 pictures. *Quarterly Journal of Experimental Psychology, 25,* 207–222.

Starko, A. (1995). *Creativity in the classroom: Schools of curious delight.* White Plains, NY: Longman.

Starnes, D., & Siegesmund, R. (2004). *Literacy: An integrated visual arts student learning delivery system.* Atlanta: EMSTAR Research.

Stauffer, R. (1969). *Directing reading maturity as a cognitive process.* New York: Harper & Row.

Steiner, D. (2003, Summer). Making music work for education. *Journal for Learning Through Music, 2,* 9.

Sternberg, R. J. (Ed.). (1988). *The nature of creativity* (pp. 429–440). New York: Cambridge University Press.

Sternberg, R. J., & Lubar, T. I. (1991). Creating creative minds. *Kappan, 72,* 608–614.

Stewig, J. (1988). *Reading pictures.* New Berlin, WI: Jenson.

Stewig, J., & McKee, J. (1980). Drama and language growth: A replication study. *Children's Theater Review, 29*(3), 1.

Stiggins, R. (2002, June). Assessment crisis: The absence of assessment for learning. *Kappan, 83*(10), 758–765.

Stinson, S. (1988). *Dance for young children: Finding the magic in movement.* Reston, VA: American Alliance for Health, Physical Education, Recreation and Dance.

Strauss, A., & Corbin, J. (Eds.). (1997). *Grounded theory in practice.* Thousand Oaks, CA: Sage.

Stronge, J. H. (2002). *Qualities of effective teachers.* Alexandria, VA: Association for Supervision and Curriculum Development.

Subramaniam, K. (2006). Six rules for integrating the arts. *Science Scope, 29*(8), 61–62.

Taboh, J. (2009, March 23). Can right-brain thinking change the world? *Voice of America News.*

Tardif, T. Z., & Sternberg, R. J. (1988). What do we know about creativity? In R. J. Sternberg (Ed.) (1997), *Successful intelligence: How practical and creative intelligence determine success in life.* New York: Dutton/Plume.

Tauber, R. (1997). *Self-fulfilling prophecy: A practical guide to its use in education.* Westport, CT: Greenwood.

Temple, C. (1991). Seven readings of a folktale: Literary theory in the classroom. *New Advocate, 4,* 29.

Thaut, M. H., Moore, D. M., & Peterson, D. A. (2003). Correlates of cortical plasticity in musical template learning. *Journal of Cognitive Neuroscience.* In *Gray matters: The arts and the brain.* www.dana.org/books/

Thiessen, D., Matthias, M., & Smith, J. (Eds.). (1998). *The wonderful world of mathematics: A critically annotated list of children's books in mathematics.* Reston, VA: National Council of Teachers of Mathematics.

Thomas, K. (2009, June). Best practices forum. Texarkana, TX: Texarkana Regional Arts and Humanities Council. Contact Kay Thomas at artsinfo@trahc.org

Thompson, M., & Barniskis, B. (2005). *Artful teaching and learning handbook: Student achievement through the arts.* Minneapolis, MN: Minneapolis Public Schools and the Perpich Center for Arts Education.

3M Corporation. (2001). Polishing your presentation. *3M Meeting Network Articles.* http://3m.com/meetingnetwork/readingroom/meetingguide_pres.html

Tierney, R., Soter, A., & O'Flahavan, J. (1989). The effects of reading and writing upon thinking critically. *Reading Research Quarterly, 24,* 134–173.

Tishman, S. (2003). *MoMA's visual thinking curriculum: Project Zero investigated the educational impact and potential of the Museum of Modern Art's Visual Thinking Curriculum.* Cambridge, MA: Harvard Graduate School of Education, Project Zero. www.pz.harvard.edu/Research/MoMA.htm

Tomlinson, C., & Brown, C. (1996). *Essentials of children's literature* (2nd ed.). Boston: Allyn & Bacon.

Tomlinson, C. (2002, September). Reconcilable differences: Standards-based teaching and differentiation. *Educational Leadership, 58*(1), 6–11.

Tomlinson, C., Brimijoin, K., & Narvaez, L. (2008). *The differentiated school: Making revolutionary changes in teaching and learning.* Alexandria, VA: Association for Supervision and Curriculum Development.

Tompkins, G. (1990). *Teaching writing: Balancing process and product.* Upper Saddle River, NJ: Merrill/Prentice Hall.

Tompkins, G. (1997). *Literacy for the 21st century.* Upper Saddle River, NJ: Prentice Hall.

Tompkins, G. (2003). *Literacy for the 21st century.* Upper Saddle River, NJ: Merrill/Prentice Hall.

Tompkins, G., & McGee, L. (1993). *Teaching reading with literature: Case studies to action plans.* New York: Merrill.

Took, K. S., & Weiss, D. S. (1994). The relationship between heavy metal and rap music and adolescent turmoil: Real or artifact? *Adolescence, 29,* 613–621.

Torrance, E. P. (1962). *Guiding creative talent.* Upper Saddle River, NJ: Prentice Hall.

Torrance, E. P. (1973). *Is creativity teachable?* Bloomington, IN: Phi Delta Kappa.

Tortello, R. (2004, October). Tableaux vivants in the literature classroom. *Reading Teacher, 58*(2), 206–208.

Trelease, J. (1995). *The read-aloud handbook.* New York: Penguin.

Trudeau, M. (2005, April 26). Inner city teacher takes no shortcuts to success. *All Things Considered,* National Public Radio.

Trusty, J., & Oliva, G. (1994). The effects of arts and music education on students' self-concept. *Update: Applications of Research in Music Education, 13*(1), 23–28.

Tunnell, M. O., & Jacobs, J. S. (1989). Using "real" books: Research findings on literature-based reading instruction. *Reading Teacher, 42,* 470–477.

Upitis, R., & Smithrim, K. (2003, April). *Learning through the arts:* Kingston, Ontario: Royal Conservatory of Music.

U.S. Department of Education. (2005, March). *Arts education: Improving students' academic performance.* (Televised series viewed at www.connectlive.com/events/ednews/)

Valliant, G. E., & Valliant, C. O. (1981). Natural history of male psychological health, X: Work as a predictor of positive mental health. *American Journal of Psychiatry, 138,* 1433–1440.

VanSledright, B., & Kelley, C. (1998). Reading American history: The influence of using multiple sources on six fifth graders. *The Elementary School Journal, 98*(3), 239–265.

VanValkenburg, R. (August, 2005). Personal interview with the director of Arts Education for Allied Arts of Greater Chattanooga, TN.

Venturelli, S. (2001). *From the information economy to the creative economy: Moving culture to the center of international public policy.* Centre for Arts and Culture. www.culturalpolicy.org

Villegas, A., & Lucas, T. (2007, March). The culturally responsive teacher. *Educational Leadership,* 28–33.

Vitz, K. (1983). A review of empirical research in drama and language. *Children's Theater Review, 32*(4), 17–25.

Vreeland, S. (1999). *Girl in hyacinth blue.* Denver: McMurry & Beck.

Vygotsky, L. S. (1978). *Mind in society.* Cambridge, MA: Harvard University Press.

Vygotsky, L. S. (1986). *Thought and language.* Cambridge, MA: MIT Press.

Wagner, B. J. (1988). A review of empirical research in drama and language. *Language Arts, 65*(1), 46–55.

Wagner, B. J. (1998). *Educational drama and language arts.* Portsmouth, NH: Heinemann.

Wagner, B. J. (1999). *Drama as a learning medium.* Portsmouth, NH: Heinemann.

Waldorf, L. A. (2002). *The professional artist as public school educator: A research report of the Chicago Arts Partnerships in Education, 2000–2001.* Los Angeles: UCLA Graduate School of Education & Information Studies.

Wallace, G. (1926). *The art of thought.* New York: Harcourt Brace.

Wallin, N., Merker, B., & Brown, S. (1999). *The origins of music. A Bradford book.* Cambridge, MA: MIT Press.

Walling, D. (2001, April). Rethinking visual arts education: A convergence of influences. *Phi Delta Kappan,* 626–631.

Warren, J. (1991). *Piggyback songs for school.* Torrance, CA: Frank Shaffer.

Weinberger, N. (1998, November). The music in our minds. *Educational Leadership,* 36–40.

Weinberger, N. M. (2003). The nucleus basalis and memory codes: Auditory cortical plasticity and the induction of specific, associative behavioral memory. *Neurobiology of Learning and Memory, 80*(3), 268–284. In *Gray matters: The arts and the brain.* www.dana.org/books/radiotv/gm_0902.cfm

Weinstein, M., & Goodman, J. (1980). *Play fair: Everybody's guide to noncompetitive play.* San Luis Obispo, CA: Impact Publishers.

Weiss, C., & Lichtenstein, A. (2008). *AIM print: New relationships in the arts and learning.* Chicago: Columbia College.

Weissman, D. (2004). You can't get much better than that. In N. Rabkin & R. Redmond (Eds.), *Putting the arts in the picture.* Chicago: Center for Arts Policy at Columbia College.

Welch, N. (1995). *Schools, communities, and the arts: A research compendium.* Washington, DC: National Endowment for the Arts.

Whitehurst, R. (2008, December). *Education Update, 50*(12), 3.

Wiggins, G. (2007, June 23). Four things art education can teach other educators. www.authenticeducation.org/bigideas/article.lasso?artId=48

Wiggins, G., & McTighe, J. (1998). *Understanding by design.* Alexandria, VA: Association for Supervision and Curriculum Development.

Wiggins, J. (1991). *Composition in the classroom: A tool for teaching.* Reston, VA: Music Educators National Conference.

Wiggins, J., & McTighe, J. (2005). *Understanding by design.* Alexandria, VA: Association for Supervision and Curriculum Development.

Wigram, T., & Backer, J. (1999). *Clinical applications of music therapy in psychiatry.* London: Jessica Kingsley.

Williams, J. (2002). Reading comprehension strategies and teacher preparation. In A. Farstrup & S. J. Samuels (Eds.), *What research has to say about reading instruction.* Newark, DE: International Reading Association.

Wilson, Egan, K. (1999). *Children's minds: Talking rabbits and clockwork oranges.* New York: Teachers College Press.

Wilson, G. P., Martens, P., Arya, P., & Altwerger, B. (2004). Readers, instruction, and the NRP. *Phi Delta Kappan, 86*(3), 242.

Wingert, P., & Brant, M. (2005, August 15). Reading your baby's mind. *Newsweek.* http:newsweek.com

Winner, E. (1983). Children's sensitivity to aesthetic properties in line drawings. In D. R. Rogers & J. A. Sloboda (Eds.), *The acquisition of symbolic skills.* London: Plenum.

Winner, E., & Cooper, M. (2000). Mute those claims: No evidence (yet) for a causal link between arts study and academic achievement. *Journal of Aesthetic Education, 34*(3/4), 11–75.

Winner, E., & Hetland, L. (2000a.). The arts and academic improvement: What the evidence shows. *The Journal of Aesthetic Education.* www.pz.harvard.edu/REAP.htm

Winner, E., & Hetland, L. (2000b, November 1.). Does studying the arts enhance academic achievement? *Education Week, 64,* 46.

Wiske, M. (1997). *Teaching for understanding: Linking research with practice.* San Francisco: Jossey-Bass.

Wolfe, P. (2001). *Brain matters: Translating research into classroom practice.* Alexandria: VA: Association for Supervision and Curriculum Development.

Wolfman, J. (2004). *Stories for reader's theatre.* Portsmouth, NH: Libraries Unlimited.

Wood, K. (1988). Guiding students through informational text. *Reading Teacher, 41,* 912–920.

Wright, M., & Kowalczyk, S. (2000). Peace by piece: The freeing power of language and literacy through the arts. *English Journal, 89*(5), 55–63.

Yenawine, P. (2005). Thoughts on visual literacy. In J. Flood, S. B. Heath, & D. Lapp (Eds.), *Handbook of research on teaching literacy through the communicative and visual arts* (pp. 485–546). Mahwah, NJ: Lawrence Erlbaum.

Yen, W., & Ferrara, S. (1997). The Maryland School Performance Assessment Program: Performance assessment with psychometric quality suitable for high stages usage. *Journal of Educational and Psychological Measurement, 57,* 60–84.

Young, P. (2003, January–February). Don't leave your students playing the blues. *Principal, 83*(3), 220–225.

Zemelman, S., Daniels, H., & Hyde, A. (1998). *Best practice: New standards for teaching and learning in America's schools.* Portsmouth, NH: Heinemann.

Zuk, B., & Dalton, R. (Eds.). (2001). *Student art exhibitions: New ideas and approaches.* Reston, VA: National Art Education Association.

Zull, J. (2005). Arts, neuroscience, and learning. *New Horizons for Learning.* www.newhorizons.org

# Bibliography:
# Children's Literature References

Adoff, A. (1977). *Tornado.* New York: Delacorte.

Ahlberg, J. (1986). *The jolly postman's or other people's letters.* Boston: Little, Brown.

Ai-Lang, L. (1982). *Yen Sen: A Chinese Cinderella story.* New York: Philomel.

Aliki. (1986). *How a book is made.* New York: Harper & Row.

Aliki. (2003). *Ah, music!* New York: HarperCollins.

Ambrus, V. (1970). *Seven skinny goats.* New York: Harcourt, Brace & World.

Ancona, G. (2003). *Murals: Walls that sing.* Singapore: Marshall Cavendish.

Anderson, P. (1993). *Three hearts and three lions.* Garden City, New York: Doubleday.

Anno, M. (1977). *Anno's counting book.* New York: Crowell.

Anno, M. *Anno series of books.* New York: Philomel.

Auch, M., & Auch, H. (2005). *Chickarella.* New York: Holiday House.

Avi. (1994). *Night journeys.* New York: Beech Tree.

Babbitt, N. (1975). *Tuck everlasting.* New York: Farrar, Straus & Giroux.

Baker, A., & Baker, J. (1991). *Raps & rhymes in math.* Portsmouth, NH: Heinemann.

Banks, L. (1980). *The Indian in the cupboard.* Garden City, NJ: Doubleday.

Barboza, S. (1992). *I feel like dancing: A year with Jacques D'Amboise and the National Dance Institute.* New York: Crown.

Barrett, J. (1989). *Animals should definitely not wear clothing.* New York: Aladdin.

Bates, K. (2004). *America the beautiful.* New York: Little Simon.

Bauer, J. (1992). *What's your story? A young person's guide to writing fiction.* New York: Clarion.

Baylor, B. (1974). *Everybody needs a rock.* New York: Scribner.

Baylor, B. (1987). *When clay sings.* New York: Macmillan.

Baylor, B. (1992). *Guess who my favorite person is?* New York: Atheneum.

Baylor, B., Sears, B., & Longtemps, K. (1973). *Sometimes I dance mountains.* New York: Atheneum.

Berger, B. (1984). *Grandfather twilight.* New York: Putnam.

Bishop, C. (1996). *Five Chinese brothers.* New York: Putnam.

Bjork, C. (1987). *Linnea in Monet's garden.* New York: R&S Books.

Booth, D. (1993). *Dr. Knickerbocker and other rhymes.* New York: Ticknor and Fields.

Bradby, M. (1995). *More than anything else.* New York: Orchard.

Brett, J. (1989). *The Mitten: A Ukrainian folktale.* New York: Putnam.

Brown, A. (1990). *The piggybook.* New York: Knopf.

Brown, L. K., & Brown, M. (1992). *Visiting the art museum.* New York: Dutton.

Bruchac, J., & London, J. (1992). *Thirteen moons on a turtle's back.* New York: Philomel.

Bryan, A. (1987). *Beat the story drum, pum-pum.* New York: Aladdin.

Bunting, E. (1994). *Smoky night.* San Diego, CA: Harcourt Brace.

Burnie, D. (2004). *Endangered planet.* Boston: Kingfisher.

Burton, B. (1993). *Moving within the circle: Contemporary Native American music and dance.* Danbury, CT: World Music.

Cameron, P. (1961). *I can't said the ant.* New York: Putnam.

Camp, C. A. (2004). *American women inventors.* Berkeley Heights, NJ: Enslow.

Carle, E. (1984). *The very hungry caterpillar.* New York: Putnam.

Carter, D., & Diaz, J. (1999). *The elements of pop-up.* New York: Simon & Schuster.

Chaconas, D. (1970). *The way the tiger walked.* New York: Simon & Schuster.

Charlip, R. (1984). *Fortunately.* New York: Simon & Schuster.

Christelow, E. (2004). *Vote!* New York: Clarion.

Christopher, J. (1967). *The white mountains.* New York: Simon & Schuster.

Cleary, B. (1992). *Ramona Quimby, age 8.* New York: HarperCollins.

Cleary, B. (1996). *Dear Mr. Henshaw.* New York: Avon.

Coerr, E. (1977). *Sadako and the thousand paper cranes.* New York: Putnam.

Cole, J. (1993). *Six sick sheep: 101 tongue twists.* Long Beach, CA: Beech Tree.

Cole, J., & Calmenson, S. (1990). *Miss Mary Mack and other children's street rhymes.* Long Beach, CA: Beech Tree.

Conger, D. (1987). *Many lands, many stories: Asian folktales for children.* Rutland, VT: Charles E. Tuttle.

Corbett, S. (1984). *Jokes to tell your worst enemy.* New York: Dutton.

Crane, S. (2002). *The red badge of courage.* New York: Atheneum.

Creech, S. (1994). *Walk two moons.* New York: HarperCollins.

Cummings, P. (1992). *Talking with artists.* New York: Bradbury.

Dahl, R. (1983). *James and the giant peach.* New York: Puffin.

Day, A. (1985). *Good dog, Carl.* San Diego, CA: Green Tiger.

dePaola, T. (1986). *The clown of God.* New York: Harcourt Brace.

dePaola, T. (1989). *Strega Nona.* New York: Harcourt Brace.

dePaola, T. (2002). *Adelita: A Mexican Cinderella story.* New York: G. P. Putnam's Sons.

DeRegniers, B. S. (1978). *The Abraham Lincoln joke book.* New York: Random Library.

DiCamillo, K. (2000). *Because of Winn-Dixie.* Cambridge, MA: Candlewick.

Dyson, J. (1991). *Westward with Columbus.* New York: Scholastic.

Edwards, P. (1997). *Barefoot.* New York: Harper Trophy.

Elting, M. (1980). *Q is for duck.* New York: Houghton Mifflin.

Englander, R. (1983). *Opera! What's all the screaming about?* New York: Walker.

Estes, E. (1994). *The hundred dresses.* New York: Harcourt Brace Jovanovich.

Felix, M. (1993). *The colors.* Mankato, MN: Creative Education.

Fitch, S. (2002). *The other author Arthur.* East Lawrencetown, Nova Scotia: Pottersfield.

Fleischman, P. (1988). *Joyful noise: Poems for two voices.* New York: Harper & Row.

Footman-Smothers, E. (2003). *The hard-times jar.* New York: Farrar, Straus & Giroux.

Forest, H. (1990). *The woman who flummoxed the fairies.* San Diego, CA: Harcourt Brace Jovanovich.

Fox, M. (1987). *Women astronauts: Aboard the shuttle.* New York: Julian Messner.

Fox, M. (1989). *Night noises.* San Diego, CA: Harcourt Brace Jovanovich.

Freedman, R. (1987). *Lincoln: A photobiography.* New York: Clarion.

Froman, R. (1987). *Seeing things: A book of poems.* New York: HarperCollins.

Gag, W. (1928). *Millions of cats.* New York: Coward-McCann.

Gibbons, G. (1989). *Monarch butterfly.* New York: Holiday House.

Gilman, P. (1992). *Something from nothing.* New York: Scholastic.

Goble, P. (1978). *The girl who loved wild horses.* Scarsdale, NY: Bradbury.

Goodman, J. (1981). *Magic and the educated rabbit.* Paoli, PA: Instructo/McGraw-Hill.

Greenfield, H. (1991). *Marc Chagall.* New York: Abrams.

Griffith, H. (1992). *Granddaddy's place.* New York: Morrow.

Gwynne, F. (1970). *The king who rained.* New York: Trumpet.

Hampton, W. (2003). *September 11, 2001: Attack on New York City.* Cambridge, MA: Candlewick.

Hansen, J., & McGowan, G. (2003). *Freedom roads: Searching for the underground railroad.* Peterborough, NH: Cricket.

Harris, J. (2005). *The least of these: Wild baby bird rescue stories.* Portland OR: West Winds Press.

Heller, R. (1995). *Color! Color! Color!* New York: Grosset & Dunlap.

Hesse, K. (1998). *Out of the dust.* New York: Classic Press.

Highwater, J. (1977). *Anpao: An American Indian odyssey.* New York: Lippincott.

Highwater, J., & Scholder, F. (1992). *Anpao: An American Indian odyssey.* New York: HarperCollins.

Hill, S. (1990). *Raps and rhymes.* New York: Penguin.

Hoban, T. (1971). *Look again.* New York: Macmillan.

Hoban, T. (1998). *So many circles, so many squares.* New York: Greenwillow.

Hoff, S. (1999). *Sammy the seal.* New York: HarperCollins.

Hopkins, B. (1995). *Making simple musical instruments.* Asheville, NC: Lark.

Hopkinson, D. (1993). *Sweet Clara and the freedom quilt.* New York: Knopf.

Hopkinson, D. (2002). *Under the quilt of the night.* New York: Atheneum.

Hopping, L. (2005). *Bone detective: The story of forensic anthropologist Diane France.* New York: Franklin Watts/Scholastic.

Howe, D., & Howe, J. (1999). *Bunnicula.* New York: Atheneum.

Hughes, S. (2004). *Ella's big chance: A jazz-age Cinderella.* New York: Simon & Schuster.

Hunt, I. (1994). *Across five Aprils.* New York: Silver Burdett.

Hutchins, P. (1978). *Don't forget the bacon.* New York: Puffin.

Inkpen, M. (2006). *The blue balloon.* London: Hodder.

Isadora, R. (1976). *Max.* New York: Simon & Schuster.

Isadora, R. (1991). *Ben's trumpet.* New York: Harpertrophy.

Jacobs, J. (1890). *English fairy tales.* London, England: David Nutt.

James, S. (1991). *Dear Mr. Blueberry.* New York: M. K. McElderry.

Jay, W. (1990). *Laughing time.* New York: Farrar, Straus & Giroux.

Jukes, M. (1987). *Like Jake and me.* New York: Knopf.

Kane, J. (2005). *The human alphabet.* New York: Roaring Brook Press.

Keats, E. J. (1962). *A snowy day.* New York: Viking.

Keller, C. (1985). *Swine lake: Music and dance riddles.* Upper Saddle River, NJ: Prentice Hall.

Kraus, R. (1971). *The tail who wagged the dog.* New York: Windmill.

Krull, K. (1995). *Lives of the artists.* San Diego, CA: Harcourt Brace.

Krull, K. (1995). *Lives of the musicians: Good times, bad times, and what the neighbors thought.* San Diego, CA: Harcourt Brace.

Lamorisse, A. (1967). *The red balloon.* New York: Doubleday.

Lasky, K. (2003). *The man who made time travel.* New York: Farrar, Straus & Giroux.

Lemaosolai-Leukton, J. (2003). *Facing the lion: Growing up Maasai on the African savanna.* Washington, DC: National Geographic.

Lester, J. (1972). *Long journey home.* Scholastic.

Le Tord, B. (1999). *A bird or two: A story about Henri Matisse.* Grand Rapids, MI: William B. Eerdmans.

Lindbergh, R. (1996). *View from the air: Charles Lindbergh's earth and sky.* New York: Puffin.

Lionni, L. (1963). *Swimmy.* New York: Pantheon.

Lionni, L. (1987). *Frederick.* New York: Knopf.

Lionni, L. (1995). *Matthew's dream.* New York: Knopf.

Little, I. (1990). *The blue balloon.* Boston: Little Brown Young Readers.

Livingston, M. (1995). *Call down the moon, poems of music.* New York: Margaret McElderry.

Lobel, A. (2004). *Frog and Toad.* New York: HarperCollins.

Locker, T. (2002). *Water dance.* New York: Harcourt.

Locker, T. (2003). *Cloud dance.* New York: Harcourt.

Louie, A. (1982). *Yeh-shen: A Cinderella story from China.* New York: Philomel.

Lowe, S. (1992). *The log of Christopher Columbus.* New York: Philomel.

Lowry, L. (1993). *The giver.* New York: Bantam Doubleday Dell.

Maclachlan, P. (1985). *Sarah, plain and tall.* Santa Barbara, CA: ABC-Clio.

Marsalis, W. (2005). *Jazz ABZ: A to z collections of jazz portraits.* New York: Candlewick.

Marshall, J. (1973). *George and Martha: Encore.* Boston: Houghton Mifflin.

Martin, B. (1992). *Brown bear, brown bear, what do you see?* New York: Henry Holt.

Marzollo, J. (1998). *I spy.* New York: Scholastic: Cartweel.

Mattox, C. (1990). *Shake it to the one you love best: Play songs and lullabies from the black musical tradition.* El Sobrante, CA: Warren Mattox.

McCloskey, R. (1978). *Lentil.* New York: Viking.

McCully, E. A. (1992). *Mirette on the high wire.* New York: Putnam.

McGovern, A. (1966). *Too much noise.* Boston: Houghton Mifflin.

McKissack, P. (1988). *Mirandy and brother wind.* New York: Knopf.

McLerran, A. (1992). *Roxaboxen.* New York: Puffin.

McMillan, B., and McMillan, B. (1982) *Puniddles.* Boston: Houghton Mifflin.

McMillan, B. (1986). *Counting wildflowers.* New York: William Morrow.

Miles, M. (1971). *Annie and the old one.* Boston: Little, Brown.

Mille, R. (1997). *Put your mother on the ceiling.* Highland, NY: Gestalt Journal Press.

Montgomery, S. (2004). *Search for the golden moon bear: Science and adventure in the Asian tropics.* Boston: Houghton Mifflin.

Morin, A. (1995). *The ghost dance.* Clarion.

Morrison, G. (2004). *Nature in the neighborhood.* Boston: Houghton Mifflin.

Munsch, R. (1980). *The paper bag princess.* Toronto: Annick.

Munsch, R. (1988). *Thomas' snowsuit.* Toronto, Ontario: Annick.

Murphy, J. (1992). *Peace at last.* New York: Dial.

Ness, E. (1971). *Sam, bangs & moonshine.* New York: Henry Holt.

Nichol, B. (1994). *Beethoven lives upstairs.* New York: Orchard.

Nixon, J. (1998). *If you were a writer.* New York: Aladdin.

Nixon, J., & Degen, B. (1995). *If you were a writer.* New York: Simon and Schuster.

Nolte, D. (April, 1959). Children learn what they live. *Torrance Schools Board of Education Newsletter.* Torrance, CA.

Norris, J. (1999). *Read a book, make a book.* Monterey, CA: Evan-Moor.

Norton, A. (1961). *Cat's eye.* Orlando: Harcourt.

Norton, M. (1953/1991). *The borrowers.* New York: Harcourt Brace.

Novak, M. (1994). *Mouse TV.* New York: Orchard Books.

Numeroff, L. J. (1985). *If you give a mouse a cookie.* New York: HarperCollins.

O'Neill, M. (1989). *Hailstones and halibut bones: Adventures in color.* New York: Doubleday.

Orbach, R. (1981). *Apple pigs.* New York: Putnam.

Park, B. (1992). *Junie B. Jones and the stupid smelly bus.* New York: Random Library.

Pasachoff, N. (2004). *Linus Pauling: Advancing science, advocating peace.* Berkeley Heights, NJ: Enslow.

Paterson, K. (1973). *Sign of the chrysanthemum.* New York: Crowell.

Paterson, K. (1977). *Bridge to Terabithia.* New York: Crowell.

Paterson, K. (1980). *Jacob have I loved.* New York: Crowell.

Paulsen, G. (1999). *Hatchet.* New York: Aladdin.

Peck, R. (1976). *Hamilton.* Boston: Little, Brown.

Pinkwater, D. (1993). *The big orange splot.* New York: Scholastic.

Pinkwater, D. (1998). *Author's day.* Madison, WI: Demco Media.

Pinkwater, D., & dePaola, T. (1988). *The Wuggie Norple story.* Palmer, AK: Aladdin.

Polacco, P. (1994). *Pink and say.* New York: Philomel.

Price, L. (1990). *Aida: A picture book for all ages.* San Diego, CA: Harcourt Brace Jovanovich.

Randi, J. (1989). *The magic world of the Amazing Randi.* Holbrook, MA: Adams.

Raschka, C. (1992). *Charlie Parker plays be bop.* New York: Orchard.

Rathman, P. (1995). *Officer Buckles and Gloria.* New York: Putnam.

Ringgold, F. (1991). *Tar Beach.* New York: Crown.

Ringgold, F., Freeman, L., & Roucher, N. (1996). *Talking with Faith Ringgold.* New York: Crown.

Rockwell, T. (1973). *How to eat fried worms.* New York: Franklin Watts.

Rosenberg, J. (1989). *Sing me a song: Metropolitan Opera's book of opera stories for children.* New York: Thames & Hudson.

Ryan, P. (2000). *Esperanza rising.* New York: Scholastic.

Rylant, C. (1992). *When I was young in the mountains.* New York: Dutton.

Rylant, C. (1994). *All I see.* New York: Scholastic.

Schaefer, L. (2004). *Arrowhawk.* New York: Henry Holt.

Schwartz, A. (1972). *A twister of twists, a tangler of tongues.* New York: Harper & Row.

Schwartz, A. (1992). *Scarey stories boxed set.* New York: Harper Trophy.

Scieszka, J. (1991). *The true story of the 3 little pigs.* New York: Viking.

Sendak, M. (1962). *Chicken soup with rice.* New York: Harpercrest.

Sendak, M. (1962). *Pierre: A cautionary tale.* New York: Harpercrest.

Sendak, M. (1963). *Where the wild things are.* New York: Harper & Row.

Seuss, Dr. (1937). *And to think I saw it on Mulberry Street.* New York: Vanguard.

Shehata, K. (2006). *Seabiscuit.* Cincinnati, OH: Angelbee.

Skurzynski, G. (2004). *Are we alone? Scientists search for life in space.* New York: National Geographic Society.

Stanley, L. (Ed.). (1992). *Rap, the lyrics: The words to rap's greatest hits.* New York: Penguin.

Steig, W. (1986). *Caleb and Kate.* New York: Farrar, Straus & Giroux.

Steig, W. (2007). *Abel's island.* New York: Farrar, Straus & Giroux.

Steptoe, J. (1987). *Mufaro's beautiful daughter: An African tale.* New York: Lothrop, Lee and Shepard.

Stevens, J. (1995). *From pictures to words.* New York: Holiday.

Stevenson, J. (1987). *It could be worse.* New York: Morrow.

Taback, S. (2002). *This is the house that Jack built.* New York: Putman.

Tang, G. (2001). *Grapes of math.* New York: Scholastic.

Tang, G. (2003). *Math-terpieces.* New York: Scholastic.

Terban, M. (1985). *Too hot to hoot.* New York: Clarion.

Tolstoy, A. (2002). *The enormous turnip.* San Diego, CA: Harcourt.

Toop, D. (1991). *Rap attack 2: African rap to global hip hop.* London: Serpent's Tail.

Uhlberg, M. (2003). *The printer.* Berkeley, CA: Peachtree.

Van Allsburg, C. (1987). *The z was zapped.* Boston: Houghton Mifflin.

Van Allsburg, C. (1991). *The wretched stone.* Boston: Houghton Mifflin.

Van Laan, N. (1992). *Possum come a-knockin'.* New York: Knopf.

Verne, J. (1997). *20,000 leagues under the sea.* New York: Random House.

Viorst, J. (1972). *Alexander and the terrible, horrible, no good, very bad day.* New York: Atheneum.

Waldman, N. (1999). *The starry night.* Honesdale, PA: Boyds Mills.

Wallace, R. (1993). *Smart-rope jingles: Jump rope rhymes, raps, and chants for active learning.* Tucson, AZ: Zephyr.

Walsh, E. (1989). *Mouse paint.* San Diego, CA: Harcourt.

Ward, L. (1973). *The silver pony.* Boston: Houghton Mifflin.

Wenzel, G. C. (2004). *Feathered dinosaurs of China.* Watertown, MA: Charlesbridge.

White, E. B. (1952). *Charlotte's web.* New York: Harper & Row.

Wilder, L. E. (1971). *Little house in the big woods.* New York: Harper Trophy.

Willard, N. (1981). *A visit to William Blake's inn: Poems for innocent and experienced travelers.* San Diego, CA: Harcourt.

Williams, B., & Chorao, K. (1991). *Kevin's grandma.* New York: Dutton.

Winter, J. (1997). *Follow the drinking gourd.* New York: Knopf.

Wisniewski, D. (1997). *Golem.* New York: Clarion.

Wolf, A. (1993). *It's show time!: Poetry from the page to the stage.* Asheville, NC: Poetry Alive!

Wood, A. (1984). *The napping house.* New York: Harcourt Brace.

Yashima, T. (1965). *Crow boy.* New York: Scholastic.

Yep, L. (1992). *The rainbow people.* New York: HarperCollins.

Yolen, J. (1987). *Owl moon.* New York: Philomel.

Yolen, J. (1990). *Sky dogs.* San Diego, CA: Harcourt.

Yolen, J. (1992). *Encounter.* San Diego, CA: Harcourt.

Yolen, J. (1997). *Sleeping ugly.* New York: Coward, McCann & Geoghegan.

Zolotow, C. (1989). *Someday.* New York: Harper Trophy.

# Appendix A

# Developmental Stages and the Arts

Use these general guidelines to observe for cues to developmental needs. Forcing children to "move ahead" does not work and can harm. Consult a pediatrician if a child does not seem to be developing appropriately.

## Important Points

- Children develop at different rates depending on genetic inheritance and experiences.
- Developmental benchmarks are flexible. They *describe* and should not *prescribe* what a child can do. Any child may be atypical of a description.
- Children learn in an integrated way. It is vital that lessons address multiple areas of development (e.g., cognitive, emotional, social, and physical).
- Development is more spiral than sequential. There is a gradual building during which children may skip or reverse stages depending on their familiarity with activities. It is natural to regress to "messing around" when a new tool is introduced.
- Patterns of development are more obvious in early years before culture and education do major sculpting of children's minds.
- Interest plays a forceful role in individuating development.
- Developmental stages become muddied as diversity increases. Predicting becomes more difficult.
- Instruction alters the ability to see and to do. Use of more detail and variety show the child is keenly observing.
- Without good teaching, a student's interest and development can stall.
- Finding a personal medium is one of life's mysteries. Imagine Disney without film or McCartney without the guitar. It is hard to predict how a child will respond to media/tools. Diverse experiences are vital.

## General Patterns

Artistic development parallels cognitive, physical, and socioemotional growth outlined by theorists such as Piaget, Maslow, and Gardner (see Chapter 2). In general, it proceeds as follows:

*General to specific.* Gross motor to fine motor, wholes to parts, with increasing attention to detail. Physically, children grow increasingly stronger and more coordinated and have more endurance and balance.

*Uncontrolled to controlled.* From exploration of media/body, tools, and skills children move to increasing control.

*Known to seen.* Concentration causes children to notice/see more. What they see changes what they know.

*Me to others.* Children become increasingly group/peer oriented, with steady growth in interest in the community and world.

*Single to multiple perspectives,* with increasing use of evidence to draw conclusions. As children become more logical and more systematic, they gain ability to self-evaluate.

*"Abstract" to realistic (for art),* as they first draw images that represent the "known" and show feelings. These evolve into realistic images, which peaks about age 11.

*Gender awareness.* Children increasingly are aware of boy-girl differences and tend to conform to cultural expectations.

# Primary: Ages 5–7

Young children are egocentric and perceive things as happening to, for, or because of them. They see one point of view or one aspect at a time. Attention span is short, and short-term memory is limited. They are concrete and learn best through physical and multisensory activities.

## Characteristics

- Respond to/through the arts, with feelings and emotion
- Motivated by curiosity
- Little concept of age, time, distance, or culture
- Have concern for others and want to comfort
- Assume events are causally related because they occur together
- Give life to inanimate objects (animism—e.g., thinks moon is smiling because of a curved shape); think objects move for a purpose (e.g., trees move to get air)
- Begin spelling, writing, and enjoy telling stories
- Become increasingly independent; try new activities
- Can compare and contrast sounds, pictures, and movements
- Can create original art, songs, stories, and dance
- Can dramatize and dance familiar actions and events
- Can explore, experiment, play, and pretend using art materials, props, music, and movement
- Need encouragement to experiment
- Need an inviting environment, rich in sensory stimulation
- Work with repetition and patterns (e.g., 3s, word play)
- Need frequent rest periods

## Potential Problems

- Working in groups
- Understanding why, how, and when questions
- Distinguishing fact from fantasy
- Understanding relationships of parts to whole
- Sorting or grouping by function or dimension
- Making comparisons to achieve understanding
- One-to-one correspondence

## Suggestions

- Frequently call children by name and give feedback.
- Use concrete examples and activities. Show rather than tell.
- Ask children to show (arts), not just tell.
- Limit focus of discussions (e.g., target arts elements).
- Use humor. Play with words, terms, and labels. Sing and chant.
- Limit lessons to 20 minutes and use variety.
- Ask children to get a "personal space."
- Make connections to children's lives: "Raise your hand if . . ."
- Refrain from discussing time periods and using the passive voice.
- Ask children to pretend or "be" (drama/role-play).
- Ask about sizes of objects and nearness and farness.
- Allow movement choices and ask the reasons for choices.
- Write and recite poetry and paint pictures that depict themes such as nature, school, and family. Encourage discussion.
- Exhibit children's artwork so it is easily seen.
- Make portfolios to keep favorite stories, photos, and artwork.
- Encourage children to select favorite musical recordings.
- Encourage improvisations and storytelling using imaginary props.

# Intermediate: Approximate Ages 7–9

Children want to learn to control techniques, skills, and language/vocabulary. Direct them to "fill up the space" and "use variety to create interest." Children improve quickly when taught such basics. Amenability to instruction contrasts with the previous stage. When given examples of how to use dance or poetic elements, students catch on quickly but need time to practice. Teachers need to be knowledgeable about arts content and skill, and be thorough and systematic in their presentations, encouraging, and disciplined, to create time on task.

## Characteristics

- Understand past and present; can sequence/order
- Egocentric (until about age 9) but can now see other viewpoints
- Understand relationship between parts and whole
- See a sharp line between good and evil and want justice
- Can sort by function and dimension
- Longer short-term memory, but still limited attention span
- Beginning to perceive differences between the sexes
- Need activity alternated with rest
- Want to be independent; get annoyed at conformity
- Accept defeat poorly; need encouragement and feedback
- Want to excel and love to be challenged
- Learning to abide by rules and play fair
- Place high priority on friends
- Interested in the artist's role in the creative process
- Like to "show they know" (e.g., point out differences between themselves and representations in paintings)
- Interested in textures, colors, characters, sports, humor, and trivia (e.g., Guinness World Records)
- Like to find out why and how things work and collect things
- Like to be physically active
- Make believe and use imagination (e.g., what if)
- Want attention, and all want a turn
- Work in small groups

# Middle Graders: Ages 11–13

Children are trying to find out who they are. They begin to strive to be like friends. The peer group is increasingly important. Cliques form. Girls and boys begin to differ greatly. This is a period of rapid growth during which girls grow quicker. There is more interest in the opposite sex.

## Characteristics

- Can make hypotheses without direct experiences; can do some abstract thinking (e.g., "What does this mean?")
- Conservation and reversibility learned
- Like to discuss more complex ideas (e.g., mood, perspective)
- Want to know how and why
- Interested in hearing others' ideas
- Anxious to explore different lifestyles
- Increasingly independent and begin to test rules and limits
- Will choose peers over adults
- Adopt social values; look to adult behavior rather than words
- Link good morals to rewards
- Industrious, like to make things and accomplish goals
- Competitive urge is strong; enjoy team and group activity
- Develop special interests and hobbies

## Suggestions

- Partner and use small groups; separate boys and girls at times.
- Ask for evidence to support conclusions (why-how questions after what-where-when questions).
- Limit historical information and connect to daily life.
- Use humor (e.g., riddles and tongue twisters).
- Focus on art and music about animals, children, and friends.
- Ask students to "make believe" and tell or show.
- Ask students to find paintings or other art that fits into categories (e.g., landscapes) or ask for categories.
- Give challenges (e.g., "Who can find the most . . .").
- Ask to pretend they are in artwork, be a character, and say something or create a tableau.
- Give generous feedback. Use student names.
- Ask students to compare and contrast (e.g., music).
- Tell interesting facts about artists and process/media.
- Give responsibility (e.g., group leader) and allow some competition.
- Invite focus on one work to become "experts."
- Ask for alternate ways to express or understand.
- Use a mini-lesson and then ask for application.
- Make clear criteria for quality work.
- Survey interests and connect to students' lives.
- Study careers related to the arts (e.g., museum curator).

# Teens: Approximate Ages 12+

Youth begin to develop "individual style" and personal interpretation in artistic interests and expressions. They should have basic arts literacy so they can move on to experimenting and applying ideas in unique ways. Copying and imitating are not considered "creative." From here on, further artistic development is contingent upon increasing involvement with specialists who can challenge young people. Students become frustrated when their efforts do not produce the quality they envision and need help learning to self-evaluate, seek alternative solutions, and set goals.

# Appendix B

# Differentiating for Students with Diverse Needs

Use the following guidelines to increase appropriateness.

- Increase concreteness. Add pictures, props, labels, charts, nametags, and more. Example: Post charts of arts concepts with symbols for *line*, *shape*, and *color*.
- Move from easy to more difficult, shorter to longer. Example: Teach pantomime before verbal improvisation.
- Repeat activities and plan time for exploration. Experiment more with a new material such as clay.
- Teach key points explicitly, especially abstract concepts. Increase amount of labeling, modeling, examples, and practice.
- Use more hands-on activities for those lacking verbal skills. Examples: art making, pantomime, use of rhythm instruments (e.g., home-made shakers and found sounds).
- Design challenge so students feel successful. The arts liberate so children can surprise teachers with insights and show more concentration.
- Instead of praising work, use "I see . . ." statements.
- Provide mixed group work in the arts to use "peer power."

## Students with Physical Disabilities

- Limit space to make it easier for them to manage.
- Use more verbal activities for those with limited movements.
- Match students with a "buddy" who can quietly explain to those with hearing impairments, help move a wheelchair, or clear an area for those with limited mobility.
- Find ways to involve those in wheelchairs. Expect participation and use touch to calm, direct, and assist.
- Adapt dance and pantomime for a student's most mobile part (e.g., emphasize gestures if hands and arms are mobile).
- Paint mental pictures and give clear details. Describe art materials, tools, pictures, and props. Allow students with visual impairments to explore with touch.
- Place students with hearing impairments close to music to feel the vibrations. Seat students to easily see your face, especially if they can lip-read. A window behind you will cast a shadow on your face.
- Don't exaggerate speech. This distorts sounds students are taught to notice.
- Repeat other students' comments for those with hearing loss.
- Use more visuals: pictures, props, gestures, directions.

## Students with Emotional Disabilities

- Some have difficulty with self-control; others are withdrawn.
- A consistent and supportive environment is important. Students need extra feedback and small successes. Start with energizers and warm-ups, to increase comfort.
- Students with short attention spans need to change tasks more often. Be ready to cut an activity short.
- Move in slow increments to increase concentration. Select energizers that increase focus.
- Movement using large muscles is often successful (e.g., dance and drama—especially pantomime—and mural making).

## Students from Diverse Language and Cultural Backgrounds

Success for students from varied cultural and linguistic backgrounds depends on teachers who have a whole child focus and celebrate diversity, and use assessment data to adjust best teaching practices. A whole child focus includes believing that all children can participate in dance, art, and drama because the arts are universal languages.

Students from diverse cultures benefit from cultural connections with holidays, customs, and people that foster respect for diversity. Multiethnic music, visual art, and dance activities are valuable. Students and guest artists and students should be regularly tapped for cultural arts study. Since folk literature is universal, it is a good source of multicultural arts enjoyment and learning. Student storytelling related to their backgrounds is wonderful for all students, as is offering diverse response options including drama, dance, art, and music responses.

### English Language Learners

The following conclusions should guide work with students whose first language is not English (Au, 2002 Fitzgerald & Graves, 2004; Gersten & Baker, 2000). All students need and deserve excellent instruction. English language learners (ELLs) need time to engage in extended reading of diverse texts, just as any other student does and benefit from choices to respond to texts, including arts-based, written, and computer options. They need to learn how to use technology and multimedia to support learning, as well. English language learners have the following special needs.

- Teachers who believe "being bilingual is not detrimental" to learning (Carlo, 2007, p. 106)
- Respect for their native languages (i.e., teachers who view language as an asset)
- Comfortable and psychologically supportive and stimulating learning environments
- Teachers who understand how learning to read and write builds on oral language. Students need to hear lots of English (e.g., read-alouds, storytelling, discussion). The arts provide many opportunities for informal and formal oral language (e.g., through drama)
- Teachers who realize a person need only learn to read and write once. If students are literate in one language, instruction should build on this ability and not overemphasize accurate word pronunciation (Au, 2002, p. 40)
- Freedom to use their native language to explain difficult concepts, including translating test directions; validate the worth of that language; and form relationships (e.g., friendships)
- Familiar content (i.e., background for lessons, even if English words for concepts may not be known)
- Scaffolded instruction that includes modeling and coaching students for success
- Arts-based lessons that allow participation (e.g., use of visual art, dance, and pantomime that are nonverbal communication tools)
- Simplified definitions of relevant vocabulary and key concepts in English. Charts and other visuals (e.g., labels) are important, as they aid in vocabulary development and concept understanding. *Example:* Post key words (e.g., directions, high-frequency environmental words such as *exit* and *entrance* with pictures)
- English language correction, when appropriate (e.g., grammar and usage) and in a context and manner that minimizes embarrassment and humiliation (e.g., private conference)
- Rich diverse texts including bilingual dictionaries to use as references and native language texts to validate and confirm
- Dual language children's literature and texts with strong visual supports (e.g., pictures), assistive technology (e.g., CD-ROMs that allow students to click on words for pronunciation or meaning and speech synthesizer software for spelling support). English vocabulary can be taught through children's literature (e.g., wordless picture books) and cultural songs translated into English. Use dual language nametags or hats for characters during drama (e.g., stepsister, mother)
- Texts, such as arts-based children's literature about universal problems, such as being a newcomer that can prompt arts-based responses
- Vocabulary development and word-solving strategies to anchor comprehension. *Example:* Teach cognates that are shared among languages and point out similar words
- Arts-based teaching that allows nonverbal responses

# Children with Speech Difficulties

- Provide a relaxed atmosphere so students have fun and forget about speech problems. Engage with dance, art, and pantomime (nonverbal communication).
- Use oral activities that have a "play" feel, such as energizers and warm-ups.
- Allow students to use a puppet speak or use pictures and other props.
- Give opportunities to sing, speak, and hear others use creative and conversational language (e.g., drama activities).
- To lessen stuttering, use rhythmic activities, singing, unison choral speaking, and dramatic role playing.

# Students with Academic Gifts and Talents

- Allow students to bypass some basics, but keep in mind that many will not have knowledge of arts elements and skills. Use short assessments to determine when adjustment is needed.
- Academically gifted children are usually ahead of peers in language. They may excel in dialogue, improvisation, and writing, but benefit from learning how the arts can expand their capabilities to communicate.
- Allow students to lead arts activities (e.g., narrate a pantomime or direct poetry performances), but teach how to lead by drawing others out.
- Offer more long-term projects (e.g., playwriting and puppet shows).
- Locate mentors for more in-depth work (e.g., artists, musicians, composers, dancers, writers, actors).
- Encourage group work even if students want to work independently. Group work in the arts gives chances to learn social skills such as cooperation and active listening.

# Appendix C

## Checklist for Planning with Artists

Also see Block X in Chapter 4 for more information about author/artist visits.

Teachers need to plan with artists before they come to a school or class. The following are important topics to address.

- Beliefs that undergird arts integrated learning and the definition for AI at your school
- Learning goals, purposes, and standards/courses of study that can be used as resources in the search for shared concepts and processes (Search for connections between the unit and the artist's art form. If there is not a good fit, stop here.)
- A focus on important learning: big ideas/themes and questions that will direct unit study
- Specific unit/lesson objectives to address as the artist works
- Assessment plan to determine what students are to learn
- CPS process: How can the artist can teach "artistic thinking" along with use of artistic tools, techniques, and materials? (Give a copy of the CPS process and ask for those terms to be used in lessons.)
- Sequence of lessons and materials

- Roles of teacher and artist, especially ways the teacher can actively participate throughout the artist's work
- Composition of the class (economic, social, and developmental levels) and special needs of students
- Best teaching practices (see Ready Reference 3.9)
- Preparing students for the artist's work and how to introduce the artist
- Management of small and whole groups
- Classroom discipline, especially how to prevent problems and resolve conflicts (see "Discipline" in Appendix E)
- Follow-up ideas for the teacher to extend learning

A written agreement should be signed and include the following:

- Description of specific expectations related to goals
- Schedule: exact dates and times
- Location: room arrangement
- Materials needed
- Emergency planning: fire drills, snow days, illness (include e-mail, cell phone, home phone, and school phone)
- Assessment of student learning (what and how)

# Appendix D

# Assessment Tools and Resources

## Example 1: Assessing Artistic Thinking and Working

*Directions:* Show students how to self-assess their progress in developing artistic thinking and working. Use the following categories and questions as starters.

## I. Develop Craft

Artists work with tools (e.g., brushes, musical instruments) and materials (e.g., canvas, props) using different techniques (e.g., mixing colors). They get better with practice and by experimenting. Assess your use of craft by asking the following questions.

1. What did I learn about use of tools, materials, and techniques?
2. How is my new learning reflected in my product?

## II. Collaborate with Others

Artists work with other artists and are influenced by them.

1. What ideas did I get from another artist (includes another student or teacher)?
2. How did working with others influence your work?
3. How did I help another person or contribute to the work of the group?

## III. Use CPS to Make Meaning

### Before

**Use Interests to Get Motivated**   Artists start and stick with projects because they choose problems that interest them. Interest motivates them to persist when they encounter difficulties.

1. What interest started my creative problem solving?

**Brainstorm Possible Solutions**   Artists think about what they already know to create predictions of possible ways of working.

1. What hypotheses did you start with?
2. How did brainstorming help your work?

**Ask Questions**   Artists ask themselves questions, such as "What am I trying to say? What resources might help me?"

1. What questions did you start with?

### During

**Gather Information**   Artists notice details and patterns others may not see or hear.

1. What were the most useful sources of information?
2. What were the most important details and patterns that you observed or found?

3. How did you use your different senses to observe?
4. What did you notice or find that was new to you?

**Experiment**   Artists push themselves to take risks to try new ways to think and work.

1. How did you play with or explore ideas, materials, and techniques?
2. How did you turn mistakes into opportunities?
3. What did you try that was new for you?
4. What happened that was unexpected?

**Imagine**   Artists make mental pictures to solve their problems.

1. What pictures did you imagine to solve your problem?

**Empathize**   Artists try to look at things from different viewpoints.

1. How did you take different perspectives?
2. How did new perspectives change your work?

**Monitor Progress and Persist**   Artists continually ask themselves questions about their progress.

1. What questions did you use to check your progress?
2. What were some of your difficulties and how did you deal with them? Why did you keep going?

**Incubate**   Artists take time out to get distance on their work.

1. How did you use incubation time?

**Connect and Transform Ideas in Unique Ways**

1. What are the most important ideas and feelings that you found and created?
2. How did you organize your ideas in a unique way?

### After

**Evaluate and Revise**   Artists take time to think about the quality of their work.

1. How does my work measure up against criteria for good work (e.g., rubric or checklist)?
2. What in your work are you most proud of?
3. What didn't work?
4. What could you change to make it better?
5. What did you learn that you will use in future work?

**Publish**   Artists share their work with others.

1. How would you like to make your work "public"?.

## Example 2: Arts-Based Interest Inventory

**Name** _____    **Nickname** _____

**Birthday** _____    **Favorite Color** _____

What are your favorites?
- Foods
- Sports
- TV shows or movies
- Books
- Songs and music
- Hobbies/collections
- Things about school

1. Do you have any pets?
2. What do you enjoy doing with your family?
3. What do you do well?
4. How do you like to spend your free time?
5. Where have you traveled?
6. Do you belong to any clubs or organizations?
7. Do you play or would you like to play a musical instrument?

8. What dances do you know?
9. What museums have you visited?
10. Have you ever been in or seen a live play?
11. What have you written? Any poetry or songs?
12. What types of art do you like, make, or look at?
13. Who do you admire? Why?
14. Do you like to act or pretend?
15. Do you like to tell stories? Listen to stories?
16. What makes you laugh? How do you make other people laugh?
17. What artist would you like to meet (musician, dancer, actor, etc.)? What three questions would you ask this person?
18. What type of literature do you enjoy reading?
19. If you could write a book, what would it be about?
20. What would you like to know more about or be able to do in the arts?

## Example 3: Teacher Self-Evaluation of Integrated Arts Lessons

See Example 1 about using artistic thinking.

Reflect on your teaching using the following questions. Think of evidence for each. Rate yourself from 1 to 4, with 4 being very evident (use with a videotape and peer observation).

1. How satisfied were you with the overall lesson? Why?
2. To what extent did students learn important concepts and skills in both an arts area and another curricular area?
3. What evidence do you have for what students learned in the art form?
4. How did you focus on lesson objectives/criteria for assessment from the start?
5. How was mood set in the lesson? How did you develop interest?
6. How did you engage head-heart-hands during the lesson?
7. What adaptations were made for student needs?
8. How did you show enthusiasm for the art form? How did students respond?

9. How did you cause students to be involved in creative and artistic ways (CPS modeling, open questions, coaching, etc.)?
10. How did the lesson feel? How comfortable were you and the students during the lesson?
11. How were audiences used to increase quality work?
12. What discipline prevention/intervention and management strategies were used and to what effect?
13. What risks did you take?
14. How did you use the 10 AI building blocks?

## Example 4: Student Checklist of Artistic and Creative Skills

Observe students during arts listening, viewing, and doing. Rate each student behavior on a scale of 1 to 4, with 4 = very evident and 1 = not evident. Next to the rating, date when evident (3+).

**Student Name** _____

_____ 1. Uses the arts to communicate ideas and feelings.
_____ 2. Intentionally uses CPS strategies such as SCAMPER and brainstorming.
_____ 3. Uses arts vocabulary to describe what is seen, heard, and felt.
_____ 4. Uses a variety of arts tools, media, and techniques.
_____ 5. Seeks alternative ways to understand and express through the arts.
_____ 6. Takes risks to offer personal interpretations.
_____ 7. Gives supporting evidence for opinions.

_____ 8. Compares and contrasts using prior arts experiences.
_____ 9. Builds on previous arts experiences.
_____ 10. Notices details and patterns.
_____ 11. Is open to and respectful of alternative perspectives.
_____ 12. Shows interest in arts reflections and discussions.
_____ 13. Offers both first impressions and revisions of impressions.
_____ 14. Works collaboratively.
_____ 15. Works independently.
_____ 16. Is aware of special strengths in arts areas.

## Example 5: Class Checklist/Drama Rubric

Discuss the rubric at the start of the school year. Encourage self-evaluation throughout the year. Create a class list to regularly rate the degree to which each student shows evidence of these drama skills. Level 1 = low evidence; Level 2 = moderate evidence; Level 3 = the highest level. Level 3 is described below.

## Level 3

*Body:* Very able to coordinate and control body. Uses appropriate energy. Displays sensory awareness and expression. Uses gestures and facial expressions skillfully to communicate through pantomime and to accompany verbal work. Responds appropriately to non-verbal communication of others.

*Verbal expression:* Speaks clearly. Uses appropriate variety in volume, rate, tone and pitch, pause, stress, emphasis, and inflection. Is fluent and can improvise dialogue.

*Focus:* Can concentrate and stay involved. Makes others believe in the realness of the character. Follows directions.

*Imagination:* Uses flexible creative thinking to solve drama problems. Contributes unique ideas and elaborates on others' ideas. Shows spontaneity.

*Evaluation:* Gives constructive feedback and uses suggestions of others. Can self-evaluate and adapt own behavior.

*Social skills:* Works cooperatively with groups: listens and responds to others.

*Audience etiquette:* Attends, listens, and responds appropriately to others' performances.

## Example 6: Art Project Self/Peer Evaluation Rubric

Art projects will be graded using these criteria. Your "Reflections" paper will be used, along with your project and any drafts as evidence. Self-evaluate before turning in your work. N = no evidence, 1 = little evidence, 2 = satisfactory evidence, 3 = strong evidence.

| Criteria | Rating |
|---|---|
| Directions followed | —— |
| Information gathered from several sources | —— |
| Risk taking and experimentation (tools, techniques, and media) | —— |
| Original (new to you) ideas used | —— |
| Project completeness | —— |
| Organized reflections with examples | —— |
| Met deadline | —— |

1. What did you learn most from this project?
2. How did you feel about your product?
3. What obstacles did you have to overcome while creating your product?
4. Would you like to publicly exhibit your art?

## Example 7: Dance: Student Reflection

**Student Name** _____ **Date** _____

1. How did you feel about the dance making and sharing?
2. What did you contribute to the group work on dance making?
3. What was the most interesting thing about the process of creating the dance or the dance itself?
4. What problems or obstacles came up during the dance creation? How were they solved?
5. How do you take risks and experiment with BEST dance elements?
6. How did you encourage other students?
7. How did you show involvement and concentration?
8. What did you learn that you can now use in the future?

## Example 8: Teacher Anecdotal Records for Integrated Dance Lessons

*Directions:* Place a sticky note for each student on a clipboard. During group planning and sharing, note observations about individuals. Place sticky notes in student portfolios. Comment on the following:

- Collaboration skills
- Risk taking and experimentation
- Positive attitude
- Use of various body parts and moves
- Use of energy
- Use of space
- Use of time
- Concentration
- Dance form: beginning–middle–end
- Creativity (ideas used in new ways)

## Example 9: Music Student Self-Evaluation

Student Name _____ Date _____

1. How have you used music to express ideas and feelings in other subjects?
2. What have you learned about making music that has helped you?
3. What have you learned about listening to music?

4. What were your favorite integrated music lessons/projects? Why?
5. What would you like to learn more about in music?
6. How do you feel about singing together in class?
7. How is music related to real life?

## Example 10: Literary Arts Checklist

Name _____ Date Observed _____

1. Chooses to read in free time
2. Has favorite authors
3. Has favorite genre
4. Uses literary elements to discuss and evaluate books
5. Uses books and authors as "models" for own writing

6. Uses art elements to comment on illustrations
7. Connects personal experiences to books
8. Shares feelings and insights about books
9. Responds to books through a variety of art forms
10. Participates in book discussions by preparing and by leading

## Example 11: Haiku/Watercolor Rubric

*Directions:* Use for self, peer, and teacher evaluation. Rate on a scale of 1 to 3, with 3 = highest evidence and 1 = low evidence. N = no evidence.

| Criteria | Rating |
|---|---|
| 1. Used 5-7-5 syllable pattern | ____ |
| 2. Nature ideas | ____ |
| 3. Original variations | ____ |
| 4. Experimentation (words and watercolor techniques) | ____ |
| 5. Explained choices | ____ |
| 6. Connected to Japanese culture | ____ |

## Arts Folios

Each student needs a container to keep evidence of growth toward benchmarks in music, art, drama, and dance/movement. This evidence serves as a motivator for students to move toward more independent learning. Students need access to folios to check their own progress and should be able to add dated evidence to document progress.

*Note:* Keep a range of work samples, not just "good" work.

## Organization

1. Student decorated front cover.
2. Goals (benchmarks) inside cover. Include a separate checklist for each arts area (music, visual art, drama, dance). By the end of the year each student should be able to do the following:

**EXAMPLES:**

- Use art elements (vocabulary/key concepts) to talk/write about each art area.
- Use techniques/skills to create each art form.
- Look at and/or listen to each art form and show understanding (what it means/feels).
- Explain how each art form contributes to culture and history.
- Explain or show how each art form is a unique way to communicate: express, receive, or respond to thoughts or feelings.
- Show growth in using CPS thinking skills.

3. Dated work examples that show progress towards benchmarks.

(*Note:* Only items that relate to the previously listed goals are included.)

**EXAMPLES:**

**Arts Vocabulary Evidence (Goal 1)**

- Word rings, webs, and charts (targeted arts vocabulary)
- Word wall folder/dictionary (e.g., mini word wall on tag board)

**Performances/Exhibitions (Goal/benchmark 3)**

- Checklist of audience etiquette used (self, peer, teacher)
- Written or art responses that show specific benchmarks (also video and audio recordings)
- Logs of attendance at nonschool sponsored concerts, etc.

# Suggestions: Maintaining and Using Arts Folios

1. Start a class arts word wall from which students can choose words to learn.
2. Number folios so students can easily keep them in alphabetical order.
3. Glue generic goals to the inside of everyone's folder, but have each child set some individual targets (e.g., self-chosen arts words to learn each week). Include a CPS chart checklist.
4. Explain the goals and folio items to monitor student learning. Encourage students to focus on the goals and look for evidence to put in folios.
5. Discuss each goal individually at the start of the year. Refer to goals throughout the day; for example, when you read aloud connect fluency (EAR = expression, accuracy, rate) with drama skills.
6. Use the folios to motivate learning. *Example:* "I'll be looking for people who are concentrating during the performance. I have my clipboard with stickies to make notes. I'll give you my notes to put in your arts folio."
7. Target four or five students per day/week for observation (e.g., check for focus during drama/dance). Use class observation checklists or individual checklists.

8. Do 1- to 3-minute individual conferences to review folios. Use an egg timer. Try "doing lunch" with students for conferences.
9. Schedule folio time each week for students to look at work and note progress (e.g., with a partner). Bring the class together for students to share one thing added.
10. Monthly, ask students to look at goals and think about what to do to keep growing. Do in small groups or as a whole class. Direct by giving examples of goals and ways to meet goals. *Example:* "Everyone has a goal to pronounce, spell, and tell/show the meanings of words in drama. I am putting a check on each word on your word ring for each of the three things. You need three checks to show you know the word. How can you learn more words?"
11. Portfolio Presentations: Partner students to share folders once a month. Come together as a whole to share what was learned from partners.
12. Make the folios the focus of parent conferences. Ask students to show their folders and share with parents their evidence of progress toward goals.
13. Tie grades to folio evidence by creating a rubric of what needs to be documented to get an A, B, and so on. Do this by grading period or as an end-of-the-year rubric with progress reports during the year, as long as students and parents are clear about progress in meeting the year-end grade goals.
14. Let students keep their folders at the end of the year.

# Assessment Internet Resources

*Glossary of assessment terms:* www.hbem.com/library/glossary.htm.
*Example standards-based tools:* www.exemplars.com/
*American Association for Supervision and Curriculum Development (ASCD):* www.ascd.org (books, videos, journal)

# Discipline Prevention and Intervention

## Prevention

____ Think of the classroom as a living room. Bring in rugs, art, plants, and music.

____ Be the teacher you would want for yourself. Model expectations for attitude, courtesy, respect, and enthusiasm for learning. Use active listening techniques with students.

____ Enjoy the students. Laugh with them and share their humor. Do not use sarcasm.

____ Post the few rules and consequences that are necessary. Start out firm and allow students to "earn" more and more freedom.

____ Involve students in making rules. Role play: "Show me how you'll look when you are listening," and "Show me a scene of showing respect."

____ Write down specific positive behaviors on stickies and give to students to keep in a "Positive Post-Its" folder.

____ Teach with variety and connect to real life. Change methods. Integrate the arts!

____ Give choices within limits (e.g., "When you finish ___ you can either ___ or ___.").

____ Capitalize on students' interests to boost success as much as 25 times.

____ Get attention before starting by using signals (e.g., a rhythm, chant, sign language). Stop if you don't have attention and state your expectation in a businesslike way (e.g., "I need ___" and follow with an every pupil response signal).

____ Set up predictable routines: Open and end the day with a poem, song, or riddle. Assign jobs and responsibilities. Post a daily agenda. Tell the lesson focus and goals.

____ No one wants to be around blah know-nothing teachers. Let students know you read books and like to dance, sing, and draw. Vary your voice (no monotone lectures).

____ Ask open questions to get more thought and participation (e.g., "What did you learn about ___?" versus "Who was the main character?").

____ Foster intrinsic motivation. Focus on learning for its own worth and its relation to the world. Extrinsic rewards can harm interest. Use stickers and stamps rarely and only as "symbols" of hard work: Make them intermittent and phase out as soon as possible, focused on privileges versus "things," and show students they are making progress toward goals. Vague certificates at the end of the week are ineffective.

____ Let students choose where to sit until they show they cannot learn in that spot. Show them how to establish personal space.

____ Expect that students will have bad days. Give a coupon to turn in homework late one time a grading period. Allow use of the "pass" option, occasionally, during questioning.

____ Send silent signals. Use sign language to communicate, nod your head, and make eye contact.

____ Remember to start fresh each day. Greet children and make them feel welcome.

## Discipline Interventions

____ Use proximity. Stand close and circulate as you teach. Vary the pattern so everyone has a chance to be close. Walk about three steps toward a nonlistener and he or she will usually attend, or stand between inattentive students. Use the two-finger touch technique or touch a student's paper or desk to focus attention.

____ Ignore behavior unless it interferes with learning. Follow up with a private conference with students who perpetually cause problems. Some teachers keep a camera handy.

____ Encourage shy or hesitant speakers. Nod and smile as they speak.

____ Never threaten, but if you promise, carry it out. Be consistent.

____ Do not publicly humiliate. Talk to repeat offenders privately. Focus on what you observed, what you expect, and why. Ask, "What can you do to solve your problem?" Set behavior goals.

____ Lower volume or slow rate or pause to get attention.

____ Elevate with descriptive feedback. Say, "John, you put three different colors on your quilt piece so far" (praise controls and may seem empty).

____ Never gossip about student problems with other teachers. This is unprofessional. Never talk about kids in front of other kids as if they aren't listening.

____ Ensure that time-outs include a chance to return when the student agrees to follow the rules. Ask what rule was broken and discuss how to behave the next time a similar situation arises.

____ Use hierarchical and appropriate consequences. A warning is a courtesy we all appreciate. Take away 1 or 2 minutes of recess, instead of a whole recess. Never assign sentence writing as a consequence because writing should not be a punishment. Loss of a privilege is often an appropriate measure.

____ On-the-spot assistance: Make eye contact, move toward the student, and state your expectation (e.g., "Joe, I want you to sit in your chair and start writing"). Give *the eye*. Attack the problem, not the person. Mention names (e.g., "This morning Pat was saying she thought ___"). Say a name before asking a question to help a student "tune in."

____ State what you want children *to do* versus *not to do*. Instead of "Don't talk," say "Listen." Address the group as a first step: "There are people who are talking who need to listen."

____ Negative remarks do not solve problems. "Don't talk" (negative) versus "Susan, what do you need to do, and how can I help you do it?" (positive).

# Appendix F

# Arts-Based Book Response Options

*Directions:* Use these suggestions to give students choices to show understanding of a book and further investigate interests.

## Poetry

*Poem match:* Find or write a poem that goes with the book.

*Poem patterns:* Write a cinquain, diamante, or clerihew about the story, a main point, or a character (see Ready Reference 5.2).

*Poetry alive:* Share a poem using a poetry performance strategy (Ready Reference 5.4): choral, antiphonal, cumulative.

## Writing and Speaking

*Adjective blitz:* List 10 adjectives that describe a character.

*Book dedications:* Dedicate a book to a character.

*Call an author:* Plan the questions for a conference call.

*Connecting:* Write about how the book connects to your life.

*Copycat story:* Write a story using the same title, theme, or pattern of the book.

*Current events:* Tell how a character would react to an event.

*Decision making:* Take a familiar story. Brainstorm what would have happened if a character made a different decision.

*Demonstration:* Show something you learned from the book.

*Diary:* Write several diary entries as if you were a character.

*Dictionary:* Make a dictionary of special words in the book.

*Episode cards:* Put plot events on cards to tell the story.

*Episode or sequel:* What happened after the story ended?

*Friendship:* Explain why you would like a character as a friend.

*Grocery list or menu:* Create a menu for the characters.

*Heinz 57:* Describe the book in 57 words.

*Humorous event:* Write or tell about the funniest part.

*Important or interesting:* Write or tell about the most important or interesting part.

*Interview:* Interview someone about a topic in the book, or write an interview between a character and the author or between you and the author.

*Library recommendation:* List reasons to buy the book.

*Lifeline:* Make a timeline of the events in a character's life.

*Movie:* Explain why a book could (or could not) become a movie.

*Newspaper:* Write stories or ads based on characters and episodes.

*Next-door neighbor:* Name a character you'd like as a neighbor.

*Object talk:* Use objects or props to tell the story.

*Past to present:* Bring a book character from past to present.

*Principal recommendation:* Tell the principal about the book.

*Puzzling or exciting:* Write or tell about a puzzling or exciting event.

*Scrapbook.* Collect and label items related to the book.

*Sentence list:* List the five most interesting sentences.

*Simplify:* Rewrite the book for a younger reader.

*Summarization:* Get the plot down to one paragraph.

*Telegram:* Summarize the book in 15 to 50 words.

*Venn diagram:* Compare to another book (literary/art elements).

*Word hunt:* List 10 words to describe the book or 10 unusual words in the book.

*Write:* Write to a favorite character (Ready Reference 5.1).

## Music and Dance

*Dance moves:* Show movements in the story with different body parts.

*Dancing characters:* List dances a character might do.

*Favorites list:* List songs or music the main character would like.

*Make a mix:* Collect music that goes with the book.

*Music mesh:* List ways music connects to the book, such as songs, music, rhythm, melody, and instruments.

*Slow motion:* Show a character in slow motion at three moments.

*Songwriting:* Write a song or rap using literary elements in the book.

*Tape record:* Tape part of the story using background music.

*Three-part dance:* Choreograph a frozen shape–moves–frozen shape dance about a feeling or main idea in the story.

## Visual Art

*Book jacket:* Create a book jacket to advertise the book.

*Bookmarks:* Make a bookmark with book quotes and a blurb.

*Bulletin board:* Display literary elements in the book.

*Can do:* Fill a can with quotes and objects about the book.

*Cartoons:* Draw cartoons of important scenes.

*Clay model:* Create a character or special object in the book.

*Clothesline props:* Pin up props/pictures to retell the story.

*Collage:* Make a collage about the book's theme.

*Cooking:* Prepare and serve food related to the book.

*Diorama:* Create a diorama that illustrates the setting.

*Flannel board pieces:* Use to retell the story.

*Greeting card:* Create a greeting card about the theme, characters, or setting.

*Lost and found:* Create a lost or found advertisement.

*Map:* Make a map of the country or imaginary land in the book.

*Media and style:* Experiment with the techniques in the book.

*Mobile:* Make a mobile with characters or objects in the book.

*Mural:* Create a mural about the book.

*Paper dolls:* Cut and dress paper dolls of the main characters.

*Photography:* Take pictures that relate to the story.

*Postcard:* Create a postcard that describes your book.

*Poster ad:* Create a poster that sells the book.

*Relief map:* Create a map of the setting using a dough recipe.

*Scroll:* Create a scroll to unroll and show important ideas.

*Sketch:* Draw an action sequence. Make into a flip book.

*Stage:* Use a box to design a miniature stage setting.

*Travelog:* Create a travelog using pictures, postcards, and magazine clips to show the settings.

*Wordless book:* Make a book about the story and use no words. Use any media or techniques.

# Drama

*Author:* Become the author and tell why you wrote this story.

*Author's prerogative:* Tell how you would change the story if you wrote it.

*Be the book:* Pretend to be a book and advertise yourself.

*Be a character:* Tell what you think of the author.

*Book review:* Be a book critic. Evaluate the text and the art.

*Chalk talk:* Draw on the board as you tell the main story events.

*Character interview:* Write an interview between two characters.

*Charades:* Play charades based on book characters.

*Commercial:* Do a 1-minute ad for a book.

*Dinner date:* Invite a character to dinner. Create a menu.

*Doll clothes:* Dress a doll as one of the book's characters.

*Dress up:* Create a costume for a character.

*Flannel board:* Make felt characters and tell the story.

*Minor character:* Become a minor character and tell the story.

*Movie producer:* Evaluate the book as a possible film.

*Movie version:* Compare the movie or TV version with the book.

*Panel discussion:* Organize a pro and con panel to debate an issue. One person can be the author.

*Pantomime:* Do a slow-motion pantomime of a character or scene.

*Pretend and write:* Be a character and write to another character or keep a journal.

*Puppets:* Make a character puppet. Set up dialogue for the story.

*Reader's theatre:* Write a script and present the book.

*Reporter:* Be a TV reporter and report on the book. Choose an exciting part for "Live on the scene? . . ."

*Sales talk:* Pretend your audience consists of bookstore owners.

*Skit:* Mime or use dialogue in a skit about an event.

*Stump the expert:* Have classmates try to stump you with questions about the book.

*Television show:* Create a game show or news show about the book.

*Unpopular position:* Choose a character and defend why his or her role in a story should be changed.

# Literature

*Biography imagination:* Pretend you visited the person. Tell or write about your visit.

*Character web:* Web what the main character looks like, acts like, feels like, and says.

*Critical reading:* Evaluate the book using literary elements.

*Experiment:* Do a scientific experiment associated with an informational book about science.

*Fairy tales:* Read several fairy tales and create your own tale using the common elements.

*Folktales:* Mix characters from folktales to write a new one.

*Genre change:* Write the book in another genre.

*Historical fiction:* Find music that was popular in the period.

*Mystery:* Put a story object inside a box. Give clues to guess the book.

*Plot diagram:* Draw the plot organization (linear, episodic, cumulative).

*Plot graph:* List the events and then graph them on a scale of good news to bad news events.

*Point of view:* Rewrite from the point of view of another character.

*Read another book:* Choose another by the same author, illustrator, theme, or genre or with the same character.

# Appendix G

## Artistic Birthday Buddies Project

Birthday Buddies is a yearlong integrated project that connects students with artists, musicians, dancers, actors, writers, singers, and composers. First help students find an artist, author, or musician born on their birthdays. Suggested references, in addition to the internet, are *Something about the Author, Krull's Lives of Musicians* (Krull), *The Music Teacher's Book of Lists* (Ross & Stangl), and *The Art Teacher's Book of Lists* (Hume). Students choose from the following activities.

1. Gather information: biographical facts, unique artistic style, time period when the person lived and worked, geographic area(s), and birth country.

   Note: Videos are now available on many artists, authors, musicians, actors, and dancers.

2. Collect quotes from the birthday buddy, fascinating or funny facts, pictures, and other information (use websites, including publishers' websites for authors).

3. Make a time line of the artist's life and most important works. Include visual images (e.g., pictures, drawings) along the line.

4. Use a map to display the artist's birthplace, cities where the artist worked, and the person's burial site, if deceased. Use a class map for students to pin small flags with artist information.

5. Write: (1) a newspaper story with headlines about the artist; (2) a letter to the artist; (3) a news article in the role of a critic; (4) a description of the artistic, literary, or musical work including a discussion of a favorite work; (5) a tribute to your birth mate; (6) a poem (e.g., couplet, diamante, haiku) about the person; (7) a dialogue between the artist and you, if you were to meet; (8) a scene about your birth mate visiting your school; or (9) a list of questions to ask the person.

6. Create a birthday card with a poem or riddles about the artist. Make a birthday present (e.g., a piece of art, song, or poem) or a time capsule of items your buddy would want saved for the future.

7. Create an exhibit of the artist, author, or musician's work.

8. Announce birthdays as they come up during the year (e.g., on school's morning show). For summer birthdays, pick a day during the school year. For example, select a special date in the life of the birthday buddy such as a first publication, exhibit, or concert date.

9. Plan a class birthday party. Students come in role and use props and simple costumes (e.g., design a hat the artist might wear). Each student plans a short first-person presentation. This may be done panel style or designate a special chair. The audience should prepare questions.

# Appendix H

# Arts-Based Field Trip Guidelines

## Initial Planning

- Get information from the arts organization about the nature of the visit. Some museums, orchestras, and arts centers provide activity packets to "frontload" students for the visit.
- Visit the site prior to the trip. Check about coat racks, restrooms, seating, and so forth. Ask about food and water availability and regulations about eating packed lunches.
- At the site, take time to generate questions or points for pretrip lessons. For example, list concepts or questions related to special exhibits at a museum. Pick up printed information and take pictures at the site to share.
- Meet with arts specialists and professionals and plan together. This includes informing museum professionals about standards/goals and the unit to which the field experience connects. Determine what materials students will need if they are to work at the site, such as clipboards, paper, and pencils.

## Pretrip Activities

At integrated schools in the Dallas, Texas, ArtsPartners program, students do a series of activities before each arts/cultural event. If they are attending a concert, teachers may have students examine pictures of orchestra instruments and listen to recordings of each. Students may then mime instruments by choosing a body shape and making instrument sounds (idea from program director Donna Farrell). Other pretrip student preparation activities include the following:

- Instruct students to generate questions they want answered during the trip.
- Conduct mini-lessons on concepts that build background and put field learning into context. For example, key concepts for an art museum visit include museum, sculpture, and abstract (see Ready Reference 6.11). A trip to a concert needs to be preceded with a mini-lesson on orchestra setup and composition, the role of the conductor, and the difference between a song and a musical piece.
- Make behavior expectations and consequences clear. This means the teacher must know expectations of the site being visited. For example, art museums do not allow people to touch artwork or run in the galleries. Teachers need to make these rules explicit to students. It is worthwhile to role-play how to behave, especially how to use appropriate audience etiquette.
- Discuss guidelines about what students are expected to learn *during* the trip and how they will show that learning *after* the trip. When students know how they will be held accountable (e.g., there will be an assessment after the trip) they will be more focused on the trip's purpose. Create and use study sheets or at least give general questions to be discussed after the trip. Questions

include: "What was the most important thing you learned? What is one thing you could find out more about? How did the experience make you feel? Why? What did the trip have to do with what we've been studying?" Extension/assessment activities might include: "Write about the trip and what you learned. Show what you learned with art materials, drama, music, or dance and movement. Write a poem about the trip. Write a letter convincing the teacher that field trips like these are important in school. Write a thank-you note citing specific things you saw or felt." Also see guidelines in all arts chapters, including Ready Reference 6.15 about doing scavenger hunts in art museums.

## During the Trip

It is important for teachers to participate as learners and as managers of their classes during all trips. Many times I've conducted student tours at museums only to have teachers distract from learning. For example, they stand with parents at the back and talk. Teachers should be models of active learning. This includes scaffolding the whole experience by asking questions of docents and coaching students to stay focused on pretrip expectations.

## Concluding the Trip

It is a good idea to debrief students before leaving the site. This also lets hosts know some of what students gained. Students should be told, in advance, about this expectation and reminded a couple of times during the visit. For example, tell students you'll be asking each one to tell one thing learned or ask one question. Without advance notice, students will embarrass themselves and their teachers with poor responses.

## Responses and Extensions

Field trips can be used to initiate a unit, take place at a special time during the unit, or be a culminating event. Whatever the timing, students should know they will be expected to "make meaning" from the experience by responding. Responses can take many forms and usually involve students in transforming and extending ideas through the arts. Students should be given choices, including letters, journal entries, songwriting, skits, and art making. See some of many choices in Appendix F. At Dallas ArtsPartners schools, trip responses and extensions often tie into academic subjects such as connecting time signatures or making instruments for math or science. Go to their website for more examples. Whatever form activities take, they should be selected to reveal the quantity and quality of creating meaning that students did as a result of the visit.

# Appendix I

## Website Resources for Arts Integration

See the ends of all chapters for additional website recommendations.

### Organizations

*American Alliance for Theatre and Education:* www.aate.com
*Americans for the Arts:* www.artsusa.org
*Arts Education Partnership:* http://aep-arts.org
*ArtsEdge:* http://artsedge.kennedy-center.org
*Dana Foundation:* www.dana.org
*J. Paul Getty Museum:* www.getty.edu/
*International Reading Association:* www.reading.org/
*The Kennedy Center's Partners in Education:* http://artsedge
    .kennedy-center.org
*Leonard Bernstein Center:* www.artfullearning.com/about_thelbc/history.dot
*Lincoln Center Institute:* www.lcinstitute.org/
*National Art Education Association:* www.arts.arizona.edu/arted/
*National Assembly of State Arts Agencies (NASAA):* www.nasaa-arts.org/
*National Association for Music Education:* http://menc.org
*National Council for the Teachers of English:* www.ncte.org
*National Dance Educators Organization:* www.ndeo.org
*National Dance Association:* www.aahperd.org/nda/
*National Endowment for the Arts:* www.nea.gov/
*Public Broadcasting:* www.pbs.org
*Very Special Arts:* www.vsarts.org/

### Miscellaneous Arts Sites

*Arts for Learning:* www.arts4learning.org
*Arts Wire:* www.artswire.org
*Crayola Arts Education:* www.crayola.com
*Virtual Museums:* www.icom.org/vlmp
*South Carolina's ETV sponsored site:* http://knowitall.org/artopia/
*World Wide Arts Resources:* www.wwar.org

### Locating Schools

See website in Chapter 1 (Ready Reference 1.6).
*Arts School Network:* http://artsschoolnetwork.org/
*Magnet Schools of America (includes 500 arts-based schools):* www.magnet.edu/
*Great Schools:* www.greatschools.net or http://schoolmatch.com
*See dissemination sites at the National Endowment for the Arts:* www.nea.gov

### Education Clearinghouse Sites

*What Works Clearinghouse:* www.whatworks.ed.gov
*Kathy Schrock's Guide for Educators:* http://school.discovery.com/
    schrockguide/

### Children's Literature (see end of Chapter 4)

#### Copyright Information

*U.S. Copyright Office:* http://loc.gov/copyright/

### Museums and Exhibits (see end of Chapter 6)

#### Censorship Policies and Perspectives

*American Library Association:* www.ala.org
*National Art Education Association:* www.naea-reston.org/
*National Association for Music Education:* www.menc.org

### Funding Information

www.arts.gov/
www.artsschoolsnetwork.org
www.ed.gov/fund/grant
www.grantsalert.com
www.nea.gov/grants
www.fdncenter.org/funders/
www.publiceducation.org
www.eschoolnews.com/resources/
www.foundations.org/grantmakers.html

# Appendix J

# Arts-Based Children's Literature

Arts-based books are ones that are about the art form (e.g., history), are about making or creating in the art form, are about artists (people), have the arts as part of the theme, or are artworks, themselves, such as picture books or scripts.

The following books are samples from the vast treasury of arts-based children' literature. These are additions to books cited in previous chapters. Go to MyEducationLab for a bibliography of more books. Also check children's literature websites listed at the end of Chapter 4.

For more books with artistic protagonists, go to the following children's literature websites: www.ucalgary.ca/~dkbrown/ or www.carolhurst.com.

## Visual Art

Angelou, M. (1994). *My painted house, my friendly chicken*. Clarkson-Potter.

Anholt, L. (2007). *Picasso and the girl with a ponytail*. Barron's.

Carroll, C. (1996–2004). *How artists see* (series). Abbeville.

Desnoettes, C. (2006). *Look closer: Art masterpieces through the ages*. Walker. (how to appreciate art in a whole new way)

Elliott, Z. (2009). *Bird*. Lee & Low. (young African American artist discovers art can inspire, comfort, and elevate)

Goldman, S. (2006). *Andy Warhol; Pop art painter*. Abrams. (traces his rise from poverty to fame)

Governar, A. (2006). *Extraordinary ordinary people: Five American masters of traditional arts*. Candlewick. (masters demonstrate art of American Widow life)

Greenberg, J., & Greenberg, S. (2009). *Christo and Jeanne-Claude: Through the gates and beyond*. Roaring Brook/Neal Porter. (outdoor artists decorate New York's Central Park; great photographs)

Johnson, C. (2003). *Harold and the purple crayon: Harold takes a trip*. Piggy Toes Press.

Lionni, L. (2006). *A color of his own*. Knopf.

Mark, T., & Watson, E. (2006). *Whacha mean, what's a zine?: The art of making zines and mini-comics*. Graphia. (how-to guide)

Markel, M. (2005). *Dreamer from the village: The story of Marc Chagall*. Henry Holt.

Raczka, B. (2006). *Here's looking at me: How artists see themselves*. Harcourt. (artists' self-portraits)

Ray, D. (2009). *Wanda Gág: The girl who lived to draw*. Viking/Penguin. (biography of children's book artist and writer)

Reynolds, P. (2003). *The dot*. Candlewick. (aspiring young artist "can't draw")

Roalf, P. (1992). *Looking at painting series: Dancers, cats, families, seascapes, self-portraits*. New York: Hyperion.

Siebert, D. (2006). *Tour America through poems and art*. Chronicle.

Tang, G. (2003). *MATH-terpieces: The art of problem-solving*. New York: Scholastic.

Winter, J. (2003). *My name is Georgia*. Voyager.

## Drama

Almond, D. (2005). *Two plays*. Delacourte. (highly acclaimed plays for older students)

Cooper, S. (1999). *King of shadows*. Simon & Schuster. (a child actor travels back in time to act with Shakespeare)

Davis, O. (1982). *Langston: A play*. Delacorte. (Hughes helps young actors do a play)

Forward, T. (2006). *Shakespeare's globe: An interactive pop up theater*. Candlewick. (a tour plus a chance to perform some plays)

Georges, C., & Cornett, C. (1986). *Reader's theatre*. Aurora, NY: Developers of Knowledge.

Giblin, J. (2005). *Good brother, bad brother: The story of Edwin and John Wilkes Booth*. Clarion.

Haskins, J. (1982). *Black theater in America*. Crowell. (informational book)

Koscielniak, X. (2004). *Hear, hear, Mr. Shakespeare: Story, illustrations, and selections*. Houghton Mifflin.

Manning, M. (2009). *Drama school*. Francis Lincoln. (ideas for putting on a show)

Schafer, L., & Spann, M. (Ed.). (1994). *Plays around the year: More than 20 thematic plays for the classroom*. New York: Scholastic Professional Books.

Sheldon, D. (1999). *Confessions of a teenage drama queen*. Candlewick. (student sets her sites on the lead in a play)

Underwood, D. (2009). *Staging a play*. Raintree. (informational)

Wolf, A. (1993). *It's show time! Poetry from the page to the stage*. Asheville, NC: Poetry Alive!

Yashima, T. (1976). *Crow boy*. New York: Puffin.

## Dance

dePaolo, T. (1979). *Oliver button is a sissy*. Harcourt Brace Jovanovich. (boy loves to dance)

Freedman, R. (1998). *Martha Graham: A dancers life*. Clarion. (biography)

Gauch, P. (1989). *Dance, Tanya*. New York: Philomel.

Govenar, A. (2006). *Stomping at the Savoy: The story of Norma Miller*. Candlewick. (autobiography of a Lindy Hopper during Harlem renaissance)

Hest, A. (2004). *Mr. George Baker*. Candlewick. (100-year-old African American can still dance)

Holabird, K. (1998). *Angelina ballerina*. New York: Crown.

Lasky, K. (2005). *Portraits: Dancing through fire*. Scholastic. (in 19th-century Paris, Sylvia is one of Degas's dancers)

Levine, E. (1995). *Anna Paulova: Genius of the dance*. Scholastic. (biography)

Littlesugar, A. (1996). *Marie in fourth position*. Philomel. (fictional story about Degas's "The Little Dancer" sculpture)

Michelson, R. (2005). *Happy feet: The Savoy Ballroom lindy hoppers and me*. New York: Gulliver's Books.

Reich, S. (2005). *Jose! Born to dance*. Simon and Schuster. (biography of great Mexican dancer)

Sotto, G. (2004). *Marisol.* American Girl. (Hispanic girl is "born to dance")

Sotto, G. (2006). *My little car.* Putman. (Teresa "dances" grandpa's lowrider car)

Spinelli, E. (1993). *Boy, can he dance!* New York: Four Winds.

Stout, S. (2009). *Fiona Finkelstein, Big-time ballerina!!* Aladdin.

Underwood, D. (2009). *Ballroom dancing.* Raintree. (informational book)

VaLaan, N. (1993). *Buffalo dance: A Blackfoot legend.* Little Brown. (the story of the Blackfoot ritual dance)

Wells, R. (1999). *Tallchief: America's prima ballerina/Maria Tallchief.* New York: Viking Penguin.

## Music

Bierhorst, J. (1979). *A cry from the earth: Music of the North American Indians.* New York: Four Winds.

Celenza, A. (2004). *The heroic symphony.* Charlesbridge. (Beethoven struggles to write a symphony while going deaf)

Freedman, R. (2004). *The voice that challenged a nation: Marian Anderson and the struggle for equal rights.* Clarion. (great singer and civil rights)

Giovanni, N. (1971). *Spin a soft black song: Poems for children.* New York: Hill.

Guthrie, W. (1998). *This land is your land.* Waltham, MA: Little, Brown.

Hesse, K. (1997). *Out of the dust.* New York: Scholastic.

Krull, K. (2003). *M is for music.* Orlando, FL: Harcourt.

Levine, G. (1999). *Dave at night.* Scholastic. (Jewish boy encounters Harlem renaissance)

Livingston, M. (1995). *Call down the moon: Poems of music.* New York: Margaret McElderry.

Mack, J. (2009). *Hip hop.* Raintree.

Morpurgo, M. (2008). *The Mozart question.* Scholastic. (teenage journalist interviews Holocaust survivor and violinist Palo Levi about his music)

National Gallery of Art. (1991). *An illustrated treasury of songs: Traditional American songs, ballads, folk songs, nursery rhymes.* New York: Rizzoli International.

Panahi, H. (2005). *Bebop express.* Amistad. (unique U.S. music)

Parker, R. (2009). *Piano starts here: The young Art Tatum.* Random House/Schwartz & Wade.

Paterson, K. (1985). *Come sing, Jimmy Jo.* New York: Dutton.

Philip, N. (1995). *Singing America: Poems that define a nation.* New York: Viking Press.

Pinkney, B. (2005). *Max found two sticks.* Aladdin. (youth expresses himself through drumming)

Rappaport, D. (2004). *John's secret dreams: The John Lennon story.* Hyperion.

Smith, N. S. (1996). *Songs for survival: Songs and chants from tribal people around the world.* New York: Dutton.

Stevens, B. (1983). *Ben Franklin's glass harmonica.* Minneapolis, MN: Carolrhoda.

Stotts, S. (2010). *We shall overcome: A song that changed the world.* Clarion. (impact the song had on civil rights movement)

Urban, L. (2009). *A crooked kind of perfect.* Harcourt. (Zoe longs to be a famous pianist)

van Kampen, V., & Eugen, I. C. (1989). *Orchestranimals.* New York: Scholastic.

Wong, I. (2002). *Bring on that beast.* Putnam. (jazz)

Yolen, J. (1992). *Jane Yolen's Mother Goose songbook.* Honesdale, PA: Caroline House/Boyds Mills.

# Seed Strategy Index

## Drama and Storytelling, 229–254

# Subject Index

In the Index LADDM is an abbreviation for "Literary Arts, Visual Art, Drama, Dance and Music". A separate *Seed Strategy Index* appears after the Subject Index.